NINTH EDITION

OPERATIONS MANAGEMENT

Processes and Supply Chains

Global Edition

LEE J. KRAJEWSKI

Professor Emeritus at
The Ohio State University
and the University of Notre Dame

LARRY P. RITZMAN

Professor Emeritus at
The Ohio State University
and Boston College

MANOJ K. MALHOTRA

University of South Carolina

PEARSON

Upper Saddle River Boston Columbus San Francisco New York
Indianapolis London Toronto Sydney Singapore Tokyo Montreal
Dubai Madrid Hong Kong Mexico City Munich Paris Amsterdam Cape Town

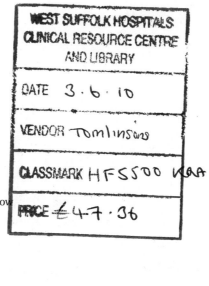
AVP/ Executive Editor: Mark Pfaltzgraff
Acquisitions Editor, Global Edition: Steven Jackson
Editorial Director: Sally Yagan
AVP/Editor in Chief: Eric Svendsen
Product Development Manager: Ashley Santora
Editorial Assistant: Valerie Patruno
Editorial Project Manager: Susie Abraham
Marketing Manager: Anne Fahlgren
Executive Marketing Manager, International: Patrick Leow
Marketing Assistant: Susan Osterlitz
Permissions Project Manager: Charles Morris
Permissions Researcher: Marcy Lunetta
Senior Managing Editor: Judy Leale
Production Project Manager: Kerri Tomasso
Senior Operations Specialist: Arnold Vila
Operations Specialist: Benjamin Smith
Art Director: Jonathan Boylan
Interior Designer: Suzanne Behnke
Cover Designer: Jodi Notowitz
Cover Illustration/Photo: © istock.com/Mariana Alija
Director, Image Resource Center: Melinda Patelli
Manager, Rights and Permissions: Zina Arabia
Manager, Visual Research: Beth Brenzel
Image Permission Coordinator: Debbie Latronica
Image Researcher: Sheila Norman
Manager, Cover Visual Research & Permissions: Karen Sanatar
Composition/Full-Service Project Management: GEX Publishing Services
Printer/Binder: Courier/Kendallville
Typeface: 9/11 Utopia

If you purchased this book within the United States or Canada you should be aware that it has been wrongfully imported without the approval of the Publisher or the Author.

Credits and acknowledgments borrowed from other sources and reproduced, with permission, in this textbook appear on appropriate page within text (or on page 651).

Microsoft® and Windows® are registered trademarks of the Microsoft Corporation in the U.S.A. and other countries. Screen shots and icons reprinted with permission from the Microsoft Corporation. This book is not sponsored or endorsed by or affiliated with the Microsoft Corporation.

10 9 8 7 6 5 4 3 2 1

ISBN-13: 978-0-13-245891-7
ISBN-10: 0-13-245891-8

Dedicated with love to our families.

■

Judie Krajewski
Gary and Christine
Lori and Dan; Aubrey, Madeline, Amelia, and Marianna
Carrie and Jon; Jordanne, Alaina, and Bradley
Selena and Jeff; Alex
Virginia and Jerry
Virginia and Larry

■

Barbara Ritzman
Karen and Matt; Kristin and Alayna
Lisa and Todd; Cody, Cole, Taylor, and Clayton
Kathryn and Paul
Mildred and Ray

■

Maya Malhotra
Vivek, Pooja, and Neha
Santosh and Ramesh Malhotra
Indra and Prem Malhotra; Neeti and Neil Ardeshna, and Deeksha
Sadhana Malhotra
Leela and Mukund Dabholkar
Aruna and Harsha Dabholkar; Aditee
Mangala and Pradeep Gandhi; Priya and Medha

ABOUT THE AUTHORS

Lee J. Krajewski is Professor Emeritus at The Ohio State University and Professor Emeritus at the University of Notre Dame. While at The Ohio State University, he received the University Alumni Distinguished Teaching Award and the College of Business Outstanding Faculty Research Award. He initiated the Center for Excellence in Manufacturing Management and served as its director for 4 years. In addition, he received the National President's Award and the National Award of Merit of the American Production and Inventory Control Society. He served as president of the Decision Sciences Institute and was elected a fellow of the institute in 1988. He received the Distinguished Service Award in 2003.

Lee received his PhD from the University of Wisconsin. Over the years, he has designed and taught courses at both graduate and undergraduate levels on topics such as operations strategy, introduction to operations management, operations design, project management, and manufacturing planning and control systems.

Lee served as the editor of *Decision Sciences*, was the founding editor of the *Journal of Operations Management*, and has served on several editorial boards. Widely published himself, Lee has contributed numerous articles to such journals as *Decision Sciences, Journal of Operations Management, Management Science, Production and Operations Management, International Journal of Production Research, Harvard Business Review*, and *Interfaces*, to name just a few. He has received five best-paper awards. Lee's areas of specialization include operations strategy, manufacturing planning and control systems, supply chain management, and master production scheduling.

Larry P. Ritzman is Professor Emeritus at The Ohio State University and Professor Emeritus at Boston College. While at The Ohio State University, he served as department chairman and received several awards for both teaching and research, including the Pace Setters' Club Award for Outstanding Research. While at Boston College, he held the Thomas J. Galligan, Jr. chair and received the Distinguished Service Award from the School of Management. He received his doctorate at Michigan State University, having had prior industrial experience at the Babcock and Wilcox Company. Over the years, he has been privileged to teach and learn more about operations management with numerous students at all levels—undergraduate, MBA, executive MBA, and doctorate.

Particularly active in the Decision Sciences Institute, Larry has served as council coordinator, publications committee chair, track chair, vice president, board member, executive committee member, doctoral consortium coordinator, and president. He was elected a fellow of the institute in 1987 and earned the Distinguished Service Award in 1996. He has received three best-paper awards. He has been a frequent reviewer, discussant, and session chair for several other professional organizations.

Larry's areas of particular expertise are service processes, operations strategy, production and inventory systems, forecasting, multistage manufacturing, and layout. An active researcher, Larry's publications have appeared in such journals as *Decision Sciences, Journal of Operations Management, Production and Operations Management, Harvard Business Review*, and *Management Science*. He has served in various editorial capacities for several journals.

Manoj K. Malhotra is the Jeff B. Bates Professor in the Moore School of Business, and has served as the chairman of the Management Science Department at the University of South Carolina (USC), Columbia, since 2000. He is the founding director of the Center for Global Supply Chain and Process Management (GSCPM), which has been in operation since 2005. He earned an engineering undergraduate degree from the Indian Institute of Technology (IIT), Kanpur, India, in 1983, and a PhD in operations management from The Ohio State University in 1990. He is a fellow of the Decision Sciences Institute and is certified as a fellow of the American Production and Inventory Management Society (CFPIM). Manoj has conducted seminars and consulted with firms such as John Deere, Metso Paper, Phelps Dodge, Sonoco, UCB Chemicals, Verizon, and Westinghouse Nuclear Fuels Division, among others.

Apart from teaching operations management, supply chain management, and global business issues at USC, Manoj has also taught at the Terry School of Business, University of Georgia; Wirtschaftsuniversität Wien in Austria; and the Graduate School of Management at Macquarie University, Australia. His research has thematically focused on the deployment of flexible resources in manufacturing and service firms, and on the interface between operations and supply chain management and other functional areas of business. His work on these and related issues has been published in refereed journals such as *Decision Sciences, European Journal of Operational Research, IIE Transactions, International Journal of Production Research, Journal of Operations Management, OMEGA,* and *Production and Operations Management Journal.* He is a recipient of the Decision Sciences Institute's Outstanding Achievement Award for the best application paper in 1990, and the Stan Hardy Award in 2002 and 2006 for the best paper published in the field of operations management. In 2007, his co-authored study on the evolution of manufacturing planning systems was a finalist for the best paper award in the *Journal of Operations Management.* In 2007, Manoj won the University of South Carolina Educational Foundation Award for Professional Schools, which is the university's most prestigious annual prize for innovative research, scholarship, and creative achievement.

Manoj has won several teaching awards, including the Michael J. Mungo Outstanding Graduate Teaching Award in 2006 from the University of South Carolina and the Alfred G. Smith Jr. Excellence in Teaching Award in 1995 from the Moore School of Business. He was voted by the students as an outstanding professor in the international MBA program by the classes of 1997, 1998, 1999, 2000, 2005, and 2008; and as the outstanding professor in the IMBA-Vienna program by the classes of 1998 and 2004. He was designated as one of the first "Master Teachers" in the Moore School of Business in 1998, and has been listed in "Who's Who among America's Teachers" in 1996 and 2000.

Manoj is an associate editor of *Decision Sciences* and *Journal of Operations Management,* past area editor of *POMS Journal* (2000–2003), and an editorial review board member of *Journal of Managerial Decision-Making.* He is an active referee for several other journals in the field, and has served as the co-editor for special focus issues of *Decision Sciences* (1999) and *Journal of Operations Management* (2002). He was the program chair for the 36th International Meeting of the Decision Sciences Institute (DSI) in San Francisco in 2005, and has also served as an associate program chair for the POMS national meeting. He has been involved in the Mid-Carolina chapter of APICS as its past president, executive board member, and as an instructor of professional level CPIM certification courses. He is a founding board member of Shingo Prize for Lean Excellence in South Carolina.

BRIEF CONTENTS

CONTENTS

PREFACE

CREATING VALUE THROUGH OPERATIONS MANAGEMENT

Operations management is a vital topic that every business student needs to understand because it is at the heart of the creation of wealth for businesses and the improvement in the living standard of citizens of all countries. Operations managers are responsible for the production of services and products in an ethical and environmentally responsible way while being responsive to the market. Sound like a challenge? Add to it the need to manage supply chains of materials, information, and funds reaching to all areas of the world. While challenging, there are concepts, tools and methods that managers use to deal with operating problems in a global environment. The mission of this text is to provide you with a comprehensive framework for addressing operational and supply chain issues. We accomplish this mission by using a systemized approach while focusing on issues of current interest to you. It is important to be efficient and capable with respect to internal processes; however, it is critical for organizations to be able to link those processes to those of their customers and their suppliers to provide a competitive supply chain. This text is unique in that it builds the concept of a supply chain from the ground up. Starting with the analysis of business processes and how they relate to the overall operational goals of a firm, our text proceeds to show how these processes are integrated to form supply chains and how they can be managed to obtain efficient flows of materials, information, and funds. This approach reinforces the concept that supply chains are only as good as the processes within and across each firm in the supply chain.

This text has been thoroughly revised to meet your needs regardless of your major. Any manager needs to know the global implications of supply chains and how to make decisions in a dynamic environment. We address these contemporary issues of interest through opening vignettes and managerial practices in each chapter. We show you the essential tools you will need to improve process performance. Irrespective of the industry in which you are seeking a career, processes and supply chains are analyzed from the perspective of service as well as manufacturing firms. Our philosophy is that you will learn by doing; consequently, the text has ample opportunities for you to experience the role of a manager with challenging problems, cases, a library of videos customized to the individual chapters, simulations, experiential exercises, and tightly integrated online computer resources. With this text, you will develop the capability to analyze problems and support managerial decisions.

WHAT'S NEW IN THE NINTH EDITION?

Since the introduction of the successful *eighth* edition, we have been hard at work to make the *ninth* edition even better. We have more figures, photos, company examples, cases, videos, and problems to test your understanding of the material. Here are some of the highlights of the many changes:

NEW! Supply Chain Management Orientation: Beginning in Chapter 1 and continuing throughout the text, we demonstrate the role that operations managers play in the design and execution of effective supply chains for service firms as well as manufacturing firms. As pointed out earlier, our philosophy is that the best supply chains begin with effective internal processes, which are then linked to processes in other firms. The flow of the material in this edition supports that philosophy. To punctuate the new focus on supply chains, we have added a second chapter on how to integrate supply chains that contains added tools for decision making and shows how firms are changing their supply chains to be environmentally responsible.

NEW! Video Cases: We have added five new video cases, which consist of case material supported by video footage, to show how operations management can be used to solve real-world problems. Two cases show how Southwest Airlines copes with gate turnaround operations and the passenger boarding process. We also showcase Autoliv for lean systems, Clif Bar & Company for supply chain design and sustainability, and Deckers Outdoor Corporation for forecasting and related supply chain issues. These cases are added to our growing video library of Starwood Hotels and other leading companies. Adding these videos means that the video library offers 23 videos, with at least one available for each chapter.

NEW! Streamlined Presentation: The *ninth* edition has fewer chapters, fewer pages, and enhanced clarity so that you can engage each topic as efficiently and effectively as possible. We have added figures and photos to improve the presentation of key concepts and techniques. Chapters have been trimmed to "bite-sized" modules to improve retention. All of these changes have been accomplished without sacrificing the content you need to be an effective manager in a dynamic global environment. Substantive changes have been made in almost every chapter and supplement, without losing the main themes that have been valued in past editions. For example:

- **Chapter Count:** Relative to the *eighth* edition, we have cut 3 chapters and incorporated the essential information in other chapters, and added 2 new chapters, for a total of only 15 chapters. A central figure in the margin of each chapter shows how each chapter fits into our general theme of processes to supply chains.

- **Part 1: Competing with Operations** – The first part of the text lays the foundation for why operations management is a strategic weapon. Chapter 1, "Using Operations to Compete," defines operations management and supply chain management. In the *ninth* edition, it now includes material on operations strategy and shows how operations decisions must be consistent with a firm's market strategy. Chapter 2, "Managing Effective Projects," opens with the product development story of Xbox 360 and shows how you can manage the projects needed to achieve efficient processes and supply chains.

- **Part 2: Designing and Managing Processes** – The second part of the text shows how you can design and manage the internal processes of a firm. Chapter 3, "Developing a Process Strategy," after being reorganized and trimmed for clarity, focuses on the major process strategy decisions managers make to achieve a firm's strategy. Chapter 4, "Analyzing Processes," now with a section on work measurement, shows how to assess and improve the performance of processes. Chapter 5, "Managing Quality," with additional material on ethics, Six Sigma, and acceptance sampling, provides the essential statistical tools for identifying the onset of process performance problems. Chapter 6, "Planning Capacity," is new to the *ninth* edition and focuses on the long-term capacity decisions that define the process capacities of the firm to do business in the future. Chapter 7, "Managing Process Constraints," now with material on line balancing, shows how you can get the best output rates within the process capacities you have to work with. Chapter 8, "Designing Lean Systems," which reveals the methods you can use to improve the system performance, now introduces the concept of "House of Toyota," and has many more photos and additional material on eight types of waste, lean system characteristics, and hybrid layouts.

- **Part 3: Designing and Managing Supply Chains** – The third part of the text provides the tools and perspectives you will need to manage the flow of materials, information, and funds between your suppliers, your firm, and your customers. Chapter 9, "Designing Effective Supply Chains," has been completely revised to focus on the importance of supply chains and their connection to major financial measures, the role of inventory in supply chains, and how to decide whether or not to outsource. Chapter 10, "Integrating the Supply Chain," is a new chapter that focuses on the importance of integrating processes along the supply chain, how to choose a supplier, how to determine the capacity of a logistics system, and how to design supply chains that are environmentally responsible. Chapter 11, "Locating Facilities," now greatly streamlined and simplified, provides guidelines and tools for finding the

COMPETING WITH OPERATIONS

Using Operations to Compete
Managing Effective Projects

DESIGNING AND MANAGING PROCESSES

Developing a Process Strategy
Analyzing Processes
Managing Quality
Planning Capacity
Managing Process Constraints
Designing Lean Systems

DESIGNING AND MANAGING SUPPLY CHAINS

Designing Effective Supply Chains
Integrating the Supply Chain
Locating Facilities
Managing Inventories
Forecasting Demand
Planning and Scheduling Operations
Planning Sufficient Resources

best location for single or multiple facilities in a supply chain. Chapter 12, "Managing Inventories," revised for simplicity and clarity, focuses on the design of inventory systems that firms use up and down the supply chain. Chapter 13, "Forecasting Demand," has been streamlined and includes a new experiential exercise to test your skills in forecasting. Chapter 14, "Planning and Scheduling Operations," offers new material on operations scheduling and an added emphasis on revenue management. It has been significantly revised to show how operations planning and scheduling provides a link between a firm, its suppliers, and its customers to create a capability that lies at the core of supply chain integration. Chapter 15, "Planning Sufficient Resources," focuses on translating the demands for services and products to requirements for the resources to produce them. The book also offers five supplements that dig deeper on technical topics, and another five online supplements.

HELPING YOU LEARN

Key Features

Several new additions and changes have been made to the book to retain and enhance its theme of processes and supply chains and to expand these themes through new content, Managerial Practices, Examples, and End-of-Chapter Problems and Cases. Several key features designed to help aid in the learning process are highlighted next:

Chapter Opening Vignettes engage and stimulate student interest by profiling how real companies apply specific operational issues addressed in each chapter.

PART 1   USING OPERATIONS TO COMPETE

1 COMPETING WITH OPERATIONS

The seventh novel in Harry Potter Series was released on July 21, 2007 and became an instant best seller around the globe. Because the book had to be delivered in a tight time window to the customers, Scholastic coordinated its publishing and distribution processes in USA months in advance of the release date.

SCHOLASTIC AND HARRY POTTER

Scholastic is the world's largest publisher and distributor of children's books and educational materials. Founded in 1920, it has over $2 billion in revenues with offices in 16 countries including North America, Europe, Southeast Asia, Latin America, the Middle East, Australia, New Zealand, and Africa. Scholastic started planning in early 2007 for the worldwide release of the eagerly awaited seventh book "Harry Potter and the Deathly Hallows" in the acclaimed series by J.K. Rowling on the boy wizard. When the author finished the book in Spring 2007, Scholastic's printers R.R. Donnelly & Sons and Quebecor World worked around the clock to make sure that the book would be ready by the release date. To save time in loading and unloading, Scholastic bypassed its own warehouses and required its truckers, Yellow Transportation and JB Hunt Transport Services, to use the same size trailers and pallets to ship books directly from six printing sites to big retailers like Barnes & Noble and Amazon.com. The fleet of trucks, if lined up bumper-to-bumper, would stretch for 15 miles. GPS transponders were used to alert Scholastic by e-mail if the driver or the trailer veered off the designated routes. The timing was particularly tricky for e-tailers, who had to directly ship books in advance for individual orders to arrive simultaneously around the country to minimize the risk of someone leaking the book's ending.

Since close to 90 percent of sales of such special books occur in the first week, they get special treatment to save time, money, space, and work. Scholastic had to customize, coordinate, and synchronize its operations and supply chain processes across multiple

Managerial Practices provide current examples of how companies deal—either successfully or unsuccessfully—with process and supply chain issues facing them as they run their operations.

Examples demonstrate how to apply what students have learned and walk them through the solution process modeling good problem-solving techniques. These examples always close with a unique feature called **Decision Point**, which focuses students on the decision implications for managers.

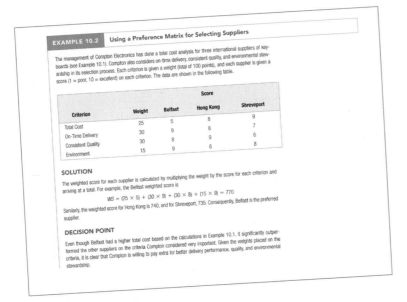

End of Chapter Resources

- **Key Equations** for review purposes.

- **Key Terms** for review highlight where the concept was first discussed.

- **Solved Problems** reinforce and help students prepare their homework assignments by detailing how to solve model problems with the appropriate techniques presented in the chapter.

- **Discussion Questions** test student comprehension of the concepts through the use of short scenarios.

- **Problems** sharpen students' quantitative skills by providing a bridge between chapter materials with a wide selection of homework material. Advanced problems are also included to increase the level of difficulty. Most of the homework problems can be done manually, or students can utilize a variety of software tools through my**om**lab, which is discussed in a later section.

- **Active Model Exercises** enable students to use pre-created spreadsheets to do "what-if" analysis of examples presented in the text to see what would happen if certain parameters were changed.

- **Video Cases** provide a summary of content covered in a series of on-location video profiles of real-world service and manufacturing companies and challenges they face in their operations. Questions are included for classroom discussion or assignment purposes.

- **Cases** challenge students to grapple with a capstone problem that can be used as an in-class exercise or a homework assignment or team project.

- A **Video Library** of 23 cases (including 3 tutorials) offers at least one video customized for each chapter, which make for excellent class discussion and learning.

TEACHING AND LEARNING SUPPORT

myomlab   A key capability of my**om**lab is as an online homework and assessment tool designed to help students practice operations management problems and improve their understanding of course concepts, and to give their instructors feedback on their performance. This online product lets professors assign homework that is automatically graded, but also serves as a tutorial experience for students.

my**om**lab lets you teach your course your way. Use my**om**lab as an out-of-the-box resource for students who need extra help, or take full advantage of its advanced customization options.

For Instructors

Instructor's Resource Center

These password-protected resources are accessible from **www.pearsonglobaleditions.com/ krajewski** for Krajewski/Ritzman/Malhotra, *Operations Management, 9th edition.* Downloadable resources include the following:

- Instructor's Solutions Manual

- Instructor's Resource Manual

- Image Library—Access most of the images and illustrations featured in the text

- PowerPoint lecture slides by Jeff Heyl in chapter-by-chapter files for classroom presentation purposes

- TestGen EQ—A computerized test item file

Instructor's Solutions Manual—Prepared by Lee Krajewski, Larry Ritzman, and Manoj Malhotra, this resource provides solutions and answers to end-of-chapter questions, problems, and cases.

Instructor's Resource Manual—Prepared by Pedro Reyes of Baylor University, this resource offers a course outline, chapter outlines, teaching notes, sample course syllabi, and video case notes.

Test Item File—Prepared by Larry Zimmer and Paul Yazel of the University of South Carolina, this resource offers an array of questions and problems ranging from easy to difficult. This resource includes true/false, multiple choice, short answer, and essay questions.

For Students

Besides having access to study plans and tutorial resources in my**om**lab, students can utilize the following additional course resources within my**om**lab:

OM Explorer – a text-specific software tool consisting of Excel worksheets and including tutors, additional exercises, and solvers.

- **Tutors** provide coaching for more than 60 analytical techniques presented in the text. The tutors also provide additional examples for learning and practice.

- **Additional Exercises** pose questions and can be answered with one or more of the tutor applications.

- **Solvers** provide general purpose routines often encountered in practice. These are great for experiential exercises and homework problems.

POM for Windows an easy-to-use software program that covers over 25 common OM techniques.

Active Models include 29 spreadsheets requiring students to evaluate different situations based on problem scenarios.

Companion Web site offers access to additional student resources such as data files and virtual tours.

ACKNOWLEDGEMENTS

No book is just the work of the authors. We greatly appreciate the assistance and valuable contributions by several people who made this edition possible. Thanks to Beverly Amer of Aspenleaf Productions for her efforts in filming and putting together the new video segments for this edition; appreciation to Pedro Reyes, of Baylor University, for his work on the Instructor's Resource Manual; thanks to Jeff Heyl, of Lincoln University, for his PowerPoint slide contributions; to Larry Zimmer and Paul Yazel of the University of South Carolina for their efforts on the Test Item File; and Annie Puciloski for her diligent work of accuracy checking the book and ancillary materials. Special thanks are due to Howard Weiss, of Temple University, whose expertise in upgrading the software for this edition was greatly appreciated.

Many colleagues at other colleges and universities provided valuable comments and suggestions for this and previous editions. Three different groups participated in focus groups that guided the direction of this revision:

POMS, 2008 Focus Group Participants:

Karen Chinander Dye
Florida Atlantic University

Vaidy Jayaraman
University of Miami

Pedro Reyes
Baylor University

Neil Geismar
Texas A&M University

Frank Montabon
Iowa State University

November 2007 Focus Group Participants:

Stephen Allen
Truman State University

John Grandzol
Bloomsburg University

Marie Matta
George Washington University

Michael Dutch
Greensboro College

Morgan Henrie
University of Alaska

Fariborz Partovi
Drexel University

Bruce Fischer
Elmhurst College

Wil Huang
Alfred University

Don Schreiber
Baylor University

December 2007 Focus Group Participants:

Leslie Arney
IUPUI

Marilyn Helms
Dalton State College

Richard Vail
Mesa State College

Khurrum Bhutta
Nicholls State University

Leonard Presby
William Paterson University

Dursun Delen
Oklahoma State University

William Roach
Washburn University

We would also like to thank the following faculty members who gave extensive written feedback and commentary to us:

Frank Barnes
UNC-Charlotte

Marilyn Helms
Dalton State University

Vijay Kannan
Utah State University

Kathryn Marley
Duquesne University

Ruth Seiple
University of Cincinnati

Eddie Davila
Arizona State University

Faizul Huq
Ohio University

Peter Kelle
Louisiana State University

Tim McClurg
University of Wisconsin

Daniel Wright
Villanova University

A.A. Elimam
San Francisco State University

Ziaul Huq
University of Nebraska at Omaha

David Levy
Bellevue University

Dee Piziak
Cardinal Stritch University

We would like to thank the people at Pearson Prentice Hall, including Eric Svendsen, Mark Pfaltzgraff, Susie Abraham, Valerie Patruno, Anne Fahlgren, Kerri Tomasso, Judy Leale, Jon Boylan, Arnold Villa, Carol O'Rourke, Allison Longley, Denise Vaughn, and Kelly Morrison at GEX Publishing Services. Without their hard work, dedication, and guidance this book would not have been possible.

At the University of Notre Dame Mendoza College of Business, we want to thank Jerry Wei, Sarv Devaraj, Dave Hartvigsen, Carrie Queenan, Xuying Zhao and Daewon Sun for their constant encouragement and for their willingness to share their teaching secrets. At the University of South Carolina, we thank Sanjay Ahire, Michael Galbreth, Alan Mackelprang, Patrick Philipoom, and Dan Steele for contributing their thoughts and insights on classroom pedagogical issues to this text. Thanks go to colleagues at The Ohio State University for their encouragement, and particularly to Peg Pennington for her insights on lean systems and the Autoliv video case.

Finally, we thank our families for supporting us during this long project. They even allowed us to sequester ourselves for a week at Eagle River where the soul of this edition was formed. Our wives, Judie, Barb, and Maya, have provided the love, stability, and encouragement that sustained us while we transformed the eight edition into the ninth.

Pearson gratefully acknowledges the following people for their work on the Global Edition:

Dr. Peter Bollen, Department of Organization and Strategy, Maastricht University, The Netherlands.

Dr. Ananda Jeeva, Senior Lecturer, Procurement & Supply Chain Management, Faculty of Business & Informatics, CQUniversity, Rockhampton, Australia.

Janny M.Y. Leung, Systems Engineering and Engineering Management Department, The Chinese University of Hong Kong, Hong Kong.

Balkrishnan Natarajan, Adjunct Associate Professor, NUS Business School, National University of Singapore, Singapore.

Dr. David Parker, Senior Lecturer, Business School, The University of Queensland, Brisbane, Australia.

Dr. Ramakrishnan Ramanathan, Associate Professor in Operations Management, Nottingham University Business School, Jubilee Campus, Wollaton Road, Nottingham, United Kingdom.

Dr. Jeff Yeung, Professional Consultant, Faculty of Business Administration, The Chinese University of Hong Kong, Hong Kong.

Dr. Hassan Younies, Assistant Professor, College of Business and Economics, United Arab Emirate University, United Arab Emirates.

Max Zornada, Adjunct Lecturer, University of Adelaide Business School, 10 Pultney Street, Adelaide, Australia.

1 USING OPERATIONS TO COMPETE

The seventh novel in Harry Potter Series was released on July 21, 2007 and became an instant best seller around the globe. Because the book had to be delivered in a tight time window to the customers, Scholastic coordinated its publishing and distribution processes in USA months in advance of the release date.

SCHOLASTIC AND HARRY POTTER

Scholastic is the world's largest publisher and distributor of children's books and educational materials. Founded in 1920, it has over $2 billion in revenues with offices in 16 countries including North America, Europe, Southeast Asia, Latin America, the Middle East, Australia, New Zealand, and Africa. Scholastic started planning in early 2007 for the worldwide release of the eagerly awaited seventh book "Harry Potter and the Deathly Hallows" in the acclaimed series by J.K. Rowling on the boy wizard. When the author finished the book in Spring 2007, Scholastic's printers R.R. Donnelly & Sons and Quebecor World worked around the clock to make sure that the book would be ready by the release date. To save time in loading and unloading, Scholastic bypassed its own warehouses and required its truckers, Yellow Transportation and JB Hunt Transport Services, to use the same size trailers and pallets to ship books directly from six printing sites to big retailers like Barnes & Noble and Amazon.com. The fleet of trucks, if lined up bumper-to-bumper, would stretch for nearly 25 kilometers. GPS transponders were used to alert Scholastic by e-mail if the driver or the trailer veered off the designated routes. The timing was particularly tricky for e-tailers, who had to directly ship books in advance for individual orders to arrive simultaneously around the globe to minimize the risk of someone leaking the book's ending.

Since close to 90 percent of sales of such special books occur in the first week, they get special treatment to save time, money, space, and work. Scholastic had to customize, coordinate, and synchronize its operations and supply chain processes across multiple

LEARNING GOALS

After reading this chapter, you should be able to:

1. Describe operations and supply chains in terms of inputs, processes, outputs, information flows, suppliers, and customers.

2. Define an operations strategy and its role as a source of competitive advantage in a global marketplace

3. Identify nine competitive priorities used in operations strategy, and their linkage to marketing strategy.

4. Explain how a pattern of decisions about processes and supply chains helps develop the capabilities to achieve competitive priorities.

5. Identify the global trends and challenges facing operations management.

6. Explain how operations can be used as a competitive weapon.

partners at the printing, warehousing, distribution, and retailing locations to ensure that the last book in the Harry Potter series reached the final customers no more than a few hours before the scheduled July 21, 12:01 A.M. release deadline. Not bad for a bunch of Muggles who transported 12 million copies in a short time window without the magical floo powder, portkeys, and broomsticks.

Source: Dean Foust, "Harry Potter and the Logistical Nightmare," *Business Week* (August 6, 2007), p. 9; Michelle Regenold, "Shipping Harry Potter: How Do They Do That?" www.go-explore-trans.org/2007/mar-apr/shipping_HP.cfm; www.scholastic.com, 2008.

my**om**lab and the Companion Website at **www.pearsonglobaleditions.com/krajewski** contain many tools, activities, and resources designed for this chapter.

operations management

The systematic design, direction, and control of processes that transform inputs into services and products for internal, as well as external, customers.

process

Any activity or group of activities that takes one or more inputs, transforms them, and provides one or more outputs for its customers.

operation

A group of resources performing all or part of one or more processes.

supply chain

An interrelated series of processes within and across firms that produces a service or product to the satisfaction of customers.

supply chain management

The synchronization of a firm's processes with those of its suppliers and customers to match the flow of materials, services, and information with customer demand.

Operations management refers to the systematic design, direction, and control of processes that transform inputs into services and products for internal, as well as external, customers. This book deals with managing those fundamental activities and processes that organizations use to produce goods and services that people use every day. A **process** is any activity or group of activities that takes one or more inputs, transforms them, and provides one or more outputs for its customers. For organizational purposes, processes tend to be clustered together into operations. An **operation** is a group of resources performing all or part of one or more processes. Processes can be linked together to form a **supply chain**, which is the interrelated series of processes within a firm and across different firms that produce a service or product to the satisfaction of customers.[1] A firm can have multiple supply chains, which vary by the product or service provided. **Supply chain management** is the synchronization of a firm's processes with those of its suppliers and customers to match the flow of materials, services, and information with customer demand. For example, Scholastic must schedule the printing of a very large quantity of books in a timely fashion, receive orders from its largest customers, directly load and dispatch a fleet of trucks by specific destination while bypassing regular warehouses, keep track of their progress using technology, and finally bill their customers and collect payment. The operational planning at Scholastic, along with internal and external coordination within its supply chain, provides one example of designing customized processes for competitive operations.

OPERATIONS AND SUPPLY CHAIN MANAGEMENT ACROSS THE ORGANIZATION

Broadly speaking, operations and supply chain management underlie all departments and functions in a business. Whether you aspire to manage a department or a particular process within it, or if you just want to understand how the process you are a part of fits into the overall fabric of the business, you need to understand the principles of operations and supply chain management.

Operations serve as an excellent career path to upper management positions in many organizations. The reason is that operations managers are responsible for key decisions that affect the success of the organization. In manufacturing firms, the head of operations usually holds the title chief operations officer (COO) or vice president of manufacturing (or production or operations). The corresponding title in a service organization might be COO or vice president (or director) of operations. Reporting to the head of operations are the managers of departments, such as customer service, production and inventory control, and quality assurance.

Figure 1.1 shows operations as one of the key functions within an organization. The circular relationships in Figure 1.1 highlight the importance of the coordination among the three mainline functions of any business; namely, operations, marketing, and finance. Each function is unique and has its own knowledge and skill areas, primary responsibilities, processes, and decision domains. From an external perspective, finance generates resources, capital, and funds from investors and sales of its goods and services in the marketplace. Based on business strategy, the finance and operations functions then decide how to invest these resources and convert them into physical assets and material inputs. Operations subsequently transforms these material and service inputs into product and service outputs. These outputs must match the characteristics that can be sold in the selected markets by marketing. Marketing is responsible for producing sales revenue of the outputs, which become returns to investors and capital for supporting operations. Functions such as accounting, information systems, human resources, and engineering make the firm complete by providing essential information, services, and other managerial support.

These relationships provide direction for the business as a whole, and are aligned to the same strategic intent. It is important to understand the entire circle, and not just the individual functional areas. How well these functions work together determines the effectiveness of the organization. Functions should be integrated and should pursue a common strategy. Success depends on how well they are able to do so.

FIGURE 1.1 ▼
Integration between Different Functional Areas of a Business

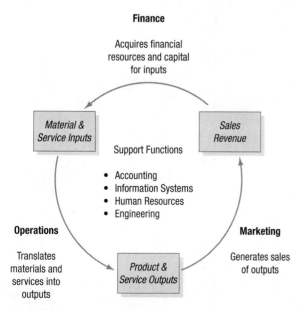

[1] The terms *supply chain* and *value chain* are sometimes used interchangeably.

No part of this circle can be dismissed or minimized without loss of effectiveness, and regardless of how departments and functions are individually managed, they are always linked together through processes. Thus, a firm competes not only by offering new services and products, creative marketing, and skillful finance, but also through its unique competencies in operations and sound management of core processes.

A PROCESS VIEW

You might wonder why we begin by looking at processes, rather than at departments or even the firm. The reason is that a process view of the firm provides a much more relevant picture of the way firms actually work. Departments typically have their own set of objectives, set of resources with capabilities to achieve those objectives, and managers and employees responsible for performance. Some processes, such as billing, may be so specific that they are contained wholly within a single department, such as accounting.

The concept of a process, however, can be much broader. A process can have its own set of objectives, involve a work flow that cuts across departmental boundaries, and require resources from several departments. You will see examples throughout this text of companies that discovered how to use their processes to gain a competitive advantage. You will notice that the key to success in many organizations is a keen understanding of how their processes work, since an organization is only as effective as its processes. Therefore, operations management is relevant and important for all students, regardless of major, because all departments have processes that must be managed effectively to gain a competitive advantage.

How Processes Work

Figure 1.2 shows how processes work in an organization. Any process has inputs and outputs. Inputs can include a combination of human resources (workers and managers), capital (equipment and facilities), purchased materials and services, land, and energy. The numbered circles in Figure 1.2 represent operations through which services, products, or customers pass and where processes are performed. The arrows represent flows, and can cross because one job or customer can have different requirements (and thus a different flow pattern) than the next job or customer.

Processes provide outputs to customers. These outputs may often be services (that can take the form of information) or tangible products. Every process and every person in an organization has customers. Some are **external customers**, who may be end users or intermediaries (e.g., manufacturers, financial institutions, or retailers) buying the firm's finished services or products. Others are **internal customers**, who may be employees in the firm whose process inputs are actually the outputs of earlier processes managed within the firm. Either way, processes must be managed with the customer in mind.

In a similar fashion, every process and every person in an organization relies on suppliers. **External suppliers** may be other businesses or individuals who provide the resources, services, products, and materials for the firm's short-term and long-term needs. Processes also have **internal suppliers**, who may be employees or processes that supply important information or materials.

Inputs and outputs vary, depending on the service or product provided. For example, inputs at a jewelry store include merchandise, the store building, registers, the jeweler, and customers; outputs to external customers are services and sold merchandise. Inputs to a factory manufacturing blue jeans include denim, machines, the plant, workers, managers, and services provided by outside consultants; outputs are clothing and supporting services. The fundamental role of inputs, processes, and customer outputs holds true for processes at all organizations.

Figure 1.2 can represent a whole firm, a department, a small group, or even a single individual. Each one has inputs and uses processes at various operations to provide outputs. The dashed lines represent two special types of input: participation by customers and information on performance from both internal and external sources. Participation by customers occurs not only when they receive outputs, but also when they take an active part in the processes, such as when students participate in a class discussion. Information on performance

external customers

A customer who is either an end user or an intermediary (e.g., manufacturers, financial institutions, or retailers) buying the firm's finished services or products.

internal customers

One or more employees or processes that rely on inputs from other employees or processes in order to perform their work.

external suppliers

The businesses or individuals who provide the resources, services, products, and materials for the firm's short-term and long-term needs.

internal suppliers

The employees or processes that supply important information or materials to a firm's processes.

▼ FIGURE 1.2
Processes and Operations

includes internal reports on customer service or inventory levels and external information from market research, government reports, or telephone calls from suppliers. Managers need all types of information to manage processes most effectively.

Nested Processes

nested process

The concept of a process within a process.

Processes can be broken down into subprocesses, which in turn can be broken down further into still more subprocesses. We refer to this concept of a process within a process as a **nested process**. It may be helpful to separate one part of a process from another for several reasons. One person or one department may be unable to perform all parts of the process, or different parts of the process may require different skills. Some parts of the process may be designed for routine work while other parts may be geared for customized work. The concept of nested processes is illustrated in greater detail in Chapter 4, "Analyzing Processes," where we reinforce the need to understand and improve activities within a business and each process's inputs and outputs.

Service and Manufacturing Processes

Two major types of processes are service and manufacturing. Service processes pervade the business world and have a prominent place in our discussion of operations management. Manufacturing processes are also important; without them the products we enjoy as part of our daily lives would not exist. In addition, manufacturing gives rise to service opportunities.

Differences   Why do we distinguish between service and manufacturing processes? The answer lies at the heart of the design of competitive processes. While Figure 1.3 shows several distinctions between service and manufacturing processes along a continuum, the two key differences that we discuss in detail are (1) the nature of their output and (2) the degree of customer contact. In general, manufacturing processes also have longer response times, are more capital intensive, and their quality can be measured more easily than those of service processes.

Manufacturing processes convert materials into goods that have a physical form we call products. For example, an assembly line produces a 350 Z sports car, and a tailor produces an outfit for the rack of an upscale clothing store. The transformation processes change the materials on one or more of the following dimensions:

1. Physical properties
2. Shape
3. Size (e.g., length, breadth, and height of a rectangular block of wood)
4. Surface finish
5. Joining parts and materials

The outputs from manufacturing processes can be produced, stored, and transported in anticipation of future demand.

If a process does not change the properties of materials on at least one of these five dimensions, it is considered a service (or nonmanufacturing) process. Service processes tend to produce intangible, perishable outputs. For example, the output from the auto loan process of a bank would be a car loan, and an output of the order fulfillment process of the U.S. Postal Service is the delivery of your letter. The outputs of service processes typically cannot be held in a finished goods inventory to insulate the process from erratic customer demands.

A second key difference between service processes and manufacturing processes is degree of customer contact. Service processes tend to have a higher degree of customer contact. Customers may take an active role in the process itself, as in the case of shopping in a supermarket, or they may be in close contact with the service provider to communicate specific needs, as in the case of a medical clinic. Manufacturing processes tend to have less customer contact. For example, washing machines are ultimately produced to meet retail forecasts. The process requires little information from the ultimate consumers (you and me), except indirectly through market surveys and market focus groups. Even though the distinction between service and

FIGURE 1.3 ▼
Continuum of Characteristics of Manufacturing and Service Processes

- Physical, durable output
- Output can be inventoried
- Low customer contact
- Long response time
- Capital intensive
- Quality easily measured

- Intangible, perishable output
- Output cannot be inventoried
- High customer contact
- Short response time
- Labor intensive
- Quality not easily measured

manufacturing processes on the basis of customer contact is not perfect, the important point is that managers must recognize the degree of customer contact required when designing processes.

Similarities   At the level of the firm, service providers do not just offer services and manufacturers do not just offer products. Patrons of a restaurant expect good service and good food. A customer purchasing a new computer expects a good product as well as a good warranty, maintenance, replacement, and financial services.

Further, even though service processes do not keep finished goods inventories, they do inventory their inputs. For example, hospitals keep inventories of medical supplies and materials needed for day-to-day operations. Some manufacturing processes, on the other hand, do not inventory their outputs because they are too costly. Such would be the case with low-volume customized products (e.g., tailored suits) or products with short shelf lives (e.g., daily newspapers).

When you look at what is being done at the process level, it is much easier to see whether the *process* is providing a service or manufacturing a product. However, this clarity is lost when the whole company is classified as either a manufacturer or a service provider because it often performs both types of processes. For example, the process of cooking a meat at a McDonald's is a manufacturing process because it changes the material's physical properties (dimension 1), as is the process of assembling the hamburger with the bun (dimension 5). However, most of the other processes visible or invisible to McDonald's customers are service processes. You can debate whether to call the whole McDonald's organization a service provider or a manufacturer, whereas classifications at the process level are much less ambiguous.

THE SUPPLY CHAIN VIEW

Most services or products are produced through a series of interrelated business activities. Each activity in a process should add value to the preceding activities; waste and unnecessary cost should be eliminated. Our process view of a firm is helpful for understanding how services or products are produced and why cross-functional coordination is important, but it does not shed any light on the strategic benefits of the processes. The missing strategic insight is that processes must add value for customers throughout the supply chain. The concept of supply chains reinforces the link between processes and performance, which includes a firm's internal processes as well as those of its external customers and suppliers. It also focuses attention on the two main types of processes in the supply chain, namely core processes and support processes. Figure 1.4 shows the links between the core and support processes in a firm and a firm's external customers and suppliers within its supply chain.

▲ FIGURE 1.4
Supply Chain Linkages Showing Work and Information Flows

Core Processes

core process

A set of activities that delivers value to external customers.

A **core process** is a set of activities that delivers value to external customers. Managers of these processes and their employees interact with external customers and build relationships with them, develop new services and products, interact with external suppliers, and produce the service or product for the external customer. Examples include a hotel's reservation handling, a new car design for an auto manufacturer, or Web-based purchasing for an online retailer like Amazon.com. Of course, each of the core processes has nested processes within it.

In this text we focus on four core processes:

supplier relationship process

A process that selects the suppliers of services, materials, and information and facilitates the timely and efficient flow of these items into the firm.

1. *Supplier Relationship Process.* Employees in the **supplier relationship process** select the suppliers of services, materials, and information and facilitate the timely and efficient flow of these items into the firm. Working effectively with suppliers can add significant value to the services or products of the firm. For example, negotiating fair prices, scheduling on-time deliveries, and gaining ideas and insights from critical suppliers are just a few of the ways to create value.

new service/product development process

A process that designs and develops new services or products from inputs received from external customer specifications or from the market in general through the customer relationship process.

2. *New Service/Product Development Process.* Employees in the **new service/product development process** design and develop new services or products. The services or products may be developed to external customer specifications or conceived from inputs received from the market in general.

order fulfillment process

A process that includes the activities required to produce and deliver the service or product to the external customer.

3. *Order Fulfillment Process.* The **order fulfillment process** includes the activities required to produce and deliver the service or product to the external customer.

customer relationship process

A process that identifies, attracts, and builds relationships with external customers, and facilitates the placement of orders by customers, sometimes referred to as *customer relationship management*.

4. *Customer Relationship Process*, sometimes referred to as *customer relationship management*. Employees involved in the **customer relationship process** identify, attract, and build relationships with external customers, and facilitate the placement of orders by customers. Traditional functions, such as marketing and sales, may be a part of this process.

Support Processes

support process

A process that provides vital resources and inputs to the core processes and therefore is essential to the management of the business.

A **support process** provides vital resources and inputs to the core processes and is essential to the management of the business. Firms have many support processes. Examples include budgeting, recruiting, and scheduling. Support processes provide key resources, capabilities, or other inputs that allow the core processes to function. Table 1.1 provides some examples of support processes.

Adding Value with Process Innovation in Supply Chains

Managerial Practice 1.1 shows how process innovation can make a big difference even in a low-growth industry. Examining processes from the perspective of the value they add is an important part of a successful manager's agenda, as is gaining an understanding of how core

TABLE 1.1	**EXAMPLES OF SUPPORT PROCESSES**
Capital acquisition	The provision of financial resources for the organization to do its work and to execute its strategy
Budgeting	The process of deciding how funds will be allocated over a period of time
Recruitment and hiring	The acquisition of people to do the work of the organization
Evaluation and compensation	The assessment and payment of people for the work and value they provide to the company
Human resource support and development	The preparation of people for their current jobs and future skill and knowledge needs
Regulatory compliance	The processes that ensure that the company is meeting all laws and legal obligations
Information systems	The movement and processing of data and information to expedite business operations and decisions
Enterprise and functional management	The systems and activities that provide strategic direction and ensure effective execution of the work of the business

Source: Peter S. Pande, R. P. Neuman, and R. R. Cavanagh, *The Six Sigma Way* (New York: McGraw-Hill, 2000), p. 161.

MANAGERIAL PRACTICE 1.1	Operational Innovation is a Competitive Weapon at Progressive Insurance

Progressive Insurance, an automobile insurer that started business in 1937, had approximately $1.3 billion in sales in 1991. By 2004 it had more than $11 billion in sales, and by 2007 was ranked 159 in the Fortune 500 list with $14 billion in sales covering 10 million policies in force. How did it accomplish this amazing growth rate in a 100-year-old industry that traditionally does not experience that sort of growth? You might think that Progressive diversified into new businesses, or that it sought sales in global markets through aggressive marketing campaigns or low prices that undercut profit margins. None of these tactics is the secret. In fact, profit margins are quite healthy. So, how did Progressive do it?

The answer is simple but the implementation was challenging: offer low prices and better service through operational innovation. That is, provide more value to customers by dramatically changing the way work is done. *Operational innovation* means designing entirely new processes to do the work. For example, Progressive reinvented claims processing to lower costs and increase customer satisfaction and retention. Progressive's agency-dedicated Web site, ForAgentsOnly.com (FAO), lets agents quickly, easily, and securely access payments; view policy, billing, and claims information; and send quote information directly to customers via e-mail. Customers are encouraged to go online to perform routine tasks such as address changes or simple billing inquiries. In addition, Immediate Response Claims Handling allows a claimant to now reach a Progressive representative by phone 24 hours a day. The representative immediately sends a claims adjuster to inspect the damaged vehicle. The adjuster drives to the vehicle accident site in a mobile claims van, examines the vehicle, prepares an onsite estimate of damage, and if possible, writes a check on the spot. It now takes only 9 hours to complete the cycle, compared with 7–10 days before the changes were made.

The operational innovations to the processes in the customer relationship–order fulfillment supply chain for claims processing produced several benefits. First, claimants received faster service with less hassle,

Via operational innovations that add value to its services, Progressive Insurance has been able to achieve amazing growth in a low-growth industry. Under the company's Immediate Response Claims Handling program, for example, claims adjusters are quickly dispatched to the scene of an accident to examine the vehicle and process claims.

which helped retain them as customers. Second, the shortened cycle time significantly reduced costs. The costs of storing a damaged vehicle and providing a rental car can often wipe out the expected underwriting profit for a six-month policy. This cost becomes significant when you realize that the company processes more than 10,000 claims a day. Third, the new supply chain design requires fewer people for handling the claim, which reduces operational costs. Finally, the operational innovations improved Progressive's ability to detect fraud by arriving on the accident scene quickly and helped to reduce payouts because claimants often accept less money if the payout is quick and hassle free. Progressive Insurance found a way to differentiate itself in a low-growth industry without compromising profitability, and it accomplished that feat with operational innovation.

Source: Michael Hammer, "Deep Change: How Operational Innovation Can Transform Your Company," *Harvard Business Review* (April 2004), pp. 85–93; http://www.progressive.com/progressive-insurance/about-progressive-insurance.aspx, 2008.

processes and related supply chains are linked to their competitive priorities, markets, and the operations strategy of a firm.

Operations Strategy

Operations strategy specifies the means by which operations implements corporate strategy and helps to build a customer-driven firm. It links long-term and short-term operations decisions to corporate strategy and develops the capabilities the firm needs to be competitive. It is at the heart of managing processes and supply chains. A firm's internal processes are only building blocks: They need to be organized to ultimately be effective in a competitive environment. Operations strategy is the linchpin that brings these processes together to form supply chains that extend beyond the walls of the firm, encompassing suppliers as well as customers. Since customers constantly desire change, the firm's operations strategy must be driven by the needs of its customers.

Developing a customer-driven operations strategy begins with *corporate strategy,* which as shown in Figure 1.5, coordinates the firm's overall goals with its core processes. It determines the markets the firm will serve and the responses the firm will make to changes in the environment. It provides the resources to develop the firm's core competencies and core processes, and it identifies the strategy the firm will employ in international markets. Based on corporate strategy, a *market analysis* categorizes the firm's customers, identifies their needs, and assesses competitors' strengths. This information is used to develop *competitive priorities*. These priorities help managers develop the services or products and the processes

operations strategy

The means by which operations implements the firm's corporate strategy and helps to build a customer-driven firm.

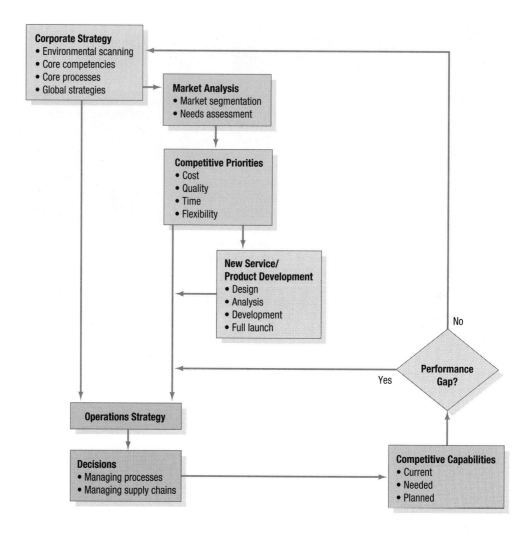

needed to be competitive in the marketplace. Competitive priorities are important to the design of new services or products, the processes that will deliver them, and the operations strategy that will develop the firm's capabilities to fulfill them. Developing a firm's operations strategy is a continuous process because the firm's capabilities to meet the competitive priorities must be periodically checked and any gaps in performance must be addressed in the operations strategy.

Corporate Strategy

Corporate strategy provides an overall direction that serves as the framework for carrying out all the organization's functions. It specifies the business or businesses the company will pursue, isolates new opportunities and threats in the environment, and identifies growth objectives.

Developing a corporate strategy involves four considerations: (1) monitoring and adjusting to changes in the business environment, (2) identifying and developing the firm's core competencies, (3) developing the firm's core processes, and (4) developing the firm's global strategies.

Environmental Scanning The external business environment in which a firm competes changes continually and an organization needs to adapt to those changes. Adaptation begins with *environmental scanning*, the process by which managers monitor trends in the environment (e.g., the industry, the marketplace, and society) for potential opportunities or threats. A crucial reason for environmental scanning is to stay ahead of the competition. Competitors may be gaining an edge by broadening service or product lines, improving quality, or lowering costs. New entrants into the market or competitors that offer substitutes for a firm's service or product may threaten continued profitability. Other important environmental concerns include economic trends, technological changes, political conditions, social changes (i.e., attitudes toward work), and the availability of vital resources. For example, car manufacturers recognize that dwindling oil reserves will eventually require alternative fuels for their cars. Consequently, they have designed prototype cars that use hydrogen or electric power as supplements to gasoline as a fuel.

Developing Core Competencies   Good managerial skill alone cannot overcome environmental changes. Firms succeed by taking advantage of what they do particularly well—that is, the organization's unique strengths. **Core competencies** are the unique resources and strengths that an organization's management considers when formulating strategy. They reflect the collective learning of the organization, especially in how to coordinate processes and integrate technologies. These competencies include the following:

core competencies
The unique resources and strengths that an organization's management considers when formulating strategy.

1. *Workforce.* A well-trained and flexible workforce allows organizations to respond to market needs in a timely fashion. This competency is particularly important in service organizations, where customers come in direct contact with employees.

2. *Facilities.* Having well-located facilities (offices, stores, and plants) is a primary advantage because of the long **lead time** needed to build new ones. In addition, flexible facilities that can handle a variety of services or products at different levels of volume provide a competitive advantage.

lead time
The elapsed time between the receipt of a customer order and filling it.

3. *Market and Financial Know-How.* An organization that can easily attract capital from stock sales, market and distribute its services or products, or differentiate them from similar services or products on the market has a competitive edge.

4. *Systems and Technology.* Organizations with expertise in information systems have an edge in industries that are data intensive, such as banking. Particularly advantageous is expertise in Internet technologies and applications, such as business-to-consumer and business-to-business systems. Having the patents on a new technology is also a big advantage.

Developing Core Processes   A firm's core competencies should drive its core processes: customer relationship, new service/product development, order fulfillment, and supplier relationship. Many companies have all four processes, while others focus on a subset of them to better match their core competencies, since they find it difficult to be good at all four processes and still be competitive. For instance, in the credit card business within the banking industry, some companies primarily specialize in finding customers and maintaining relationships with them. American Airlines's credit card program reaches out and achieves a special affinity to customers through its marketing database. On the other hand, specialized credit card companies, such as CapitalOne, focus on service innovation by creating new features and pricing programs. Finally, many companies are taking over the order fulfillment process by managing the processing of credit card transactions and call centers. The important point is that every firm must evaluate its core competencies and choose to focus on those processes that provide it the greatest competitive strength.

Global Strategies   Identifying opportunities and threats today requires a global perspective. A global strategy may include buying foreign services or parts, combating threats from foreign competitors, or planning ways to enter markets beyond traditional national boundaries. Although warding off threats from global competitors is necessary, firms should also actively seek to penetrate foreign markets. Two effective global strategies are strategic alliances and locating abroad.

One way for a firm to open foreign markets is to create a *strategic alliance*. A strategic alliance is an agreement with another firm that may take one of three forms. One form of strategic alliance is the *collaborative effort*, which often arises when one firm has core competencies that another needs but is unwilling (or unable) to duplicate. Such arrangements commonly arise out of buyer–supplier relationships. Another form of strategic alliance is the *joint venture*, in which two firms agree to produce a service or product jointly. This approach is often used by firms to gain access to foreign markets. For example, to get access to the large Chinese market, General Motors (GM) and Volkswagen (VW) each developed joint ventures with Shanghai Automotive Industry Corporation or SAIC.[2] The Chinese partner is a large manufacturer of automobiles, producing more than 600,000 cars with GM and VW. Finally, *technology licensing* is a form of strategic alliance in which one company licenses its service or production methods to another. Licenses may be used to gain access to foreign markets.

---

[2] Alex Taylor, "Shanghai Auto Wants to Be the World's Next Great Car Company," *Fortune* (October 4, 2004), pp. 103–110.

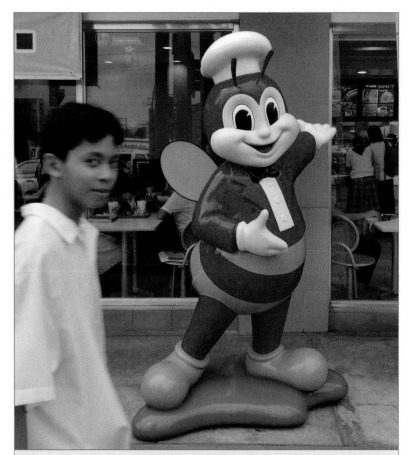

The popular smiling red bee, the mascot of Jollibee, welcomes customers at an outlet in Manila. What began from a two ice cream parlors in Manila in 1975, Jollibee has grown into the biggest Philippines fast-food company employing over 26,000 people in over 1,000 stores in seven countries. By catering to local tastes and preferences, Jollibee took 65 percent of the fiercely competitive Philippine fast-food market, pushing the world giant McDonald into second place.

Another way to enter global markets is to locate operations in a foreign country. However, managers must recognize that what works well in their home country might not work well elsewhere. The economic and political environment or customers' needs may be significantly different. For example, McDonald's is known for the consistency of its products—a Big Mac tastes the same anywhere in the world. By contrast, the family-owned chain Jollibee Foods Corporation has become the dominant fast-food chain in the Philippines by catering to a local preference for sweet and spicy flavors, which it incorporates into its fried chicken, spaghetti, and burgers. Jollibee's strength is its creative marketing programs and an understanding of local tastes and claims that its burger is similar to the one a Filipino would cook at home. McDonald's responded by introducing its own Filipino-style spicy burger, but competition is stiff. McDonald's experience demonstrates that, to be successful, corporate strategies must recognize customs, preferences, and economic conditions in other countries.

Locating abroad is a key decision in the design of supply chains because it affects the flow of materials, information, and employees in support of the firm's core processes. Chapter 9, "Designing Effective Supply Chains," and Chapter 11, "Locating Facilities," offer more in-depth discussion of these other implications.

Market Analysis

One key to successfully formulating a customer-driven operations strategy for both service and manufacturing firms is to understand what the customer wants and how to provide it. *A market analysis* first divides the firm's customers into market segments and then identifies the needs of each segment. In this section, we examine the process of market analysis and we define and discuss the concepts of market segmentation and needs assessment.

Market Segmentation   *Market segmentation* is the process of identifying groups of customers with enough in common to warrant the design and provision of services or products that the group wants and needs. To identify market segments, the analyst must determine the characteristics that clearly differentiate each segment. The company can then develop a sound marketing program and an effective operating strategy to support it. For instance, The Gap, Inc., a major provider of casual clothes, targets teenagers and young adults while the parents or guardians of infants through 12-year-olds are the primary targets for its GapKids stores. At one time, managers thought of customers as a homogeneous mass market, but now realize that two customers may use the same product for different reasons. Identifying the key factors in each market segment is the starting point in devising a customer-driven operations strategy.

Needs Assessment   The second step in market analysis is to make a *needs assessment*, which identifies the needs of each segment and assesses how well competitors are addressing those needs. Each market segment's needs can be related to the service or product and its value chain. Market needs should include both the tangible and intangible attributes and features of products and services that a customer desires. Market needs may be grouped as follows:

- *Service or Product Needs.* Attributes of the service or product, such as price, quality, and degree of customization.
- *Delivery System Needs.* Attributes of the processes and the supporting systems, and resources needed to deliver the service or product, such as availability, convenience, courtesy, safety, accuracy, reliability, delivery speed, and delivery dependability.

- *Volume Needs.* Attributes of the demand for the service or product, such as high or low volume, degree of variability in volume, and degree of predictability in volume.
- *Other Needs.* Other attributes, such as reputation and number of years in business, after-sale technical support, ability to invest in international financial markets, and competent legal services.

Once it makes this assessment, the firm can incorporate the needs of customers into the design of the service or product and the supply chain that must deliver it. We further discuss these new service and product development-related issues in Chapter 10, "Integrating the Supply Chain."

COMPETITIVE PRIORITIES AND CAPABILITIES

A customer-driven operations strategy requires a cross-functional effort by all areas of the firm to understand the needs of the firm's external customers and to specify the operating capabilities the firm requires to outperform its competitors. Such a strategy also addresses the needs of internal customers because the overall performance of the firm depends upon the performance of its core and supporting processes, which must be coordinated to provide the overall desirable outcome for the external customer.

Competitive priorities are the critical operational dimensions a process or supply chain must possess to satisfy internal or external customers, both now and in the future. Competitive priorities are planned for processes and the supply chain created from them. They must be present to maintain or build market share or to allow other internal processes to be successful. Not all competitive priorities are critical for a given process; management selects those that are most important. **Competitive capabilities** are the cost, quality, time, and flexibility dimensions that a process or supply chain actually possesses and is able to deliver. When the capability falls short of the priority attached to it, management must find ways to close the gap or else revise the priority.

We focus on nine broad competitive priorities that fall into the four capability groups of cost, quality, time, and flexibility. Table 1.2 provides definitions and examples of these competitive priorities, as well as how firms achieve them at the process level.

At times, management may emphasize a cluster of competitive priorities together. For example, many companies focus on the competitive priorities of delivery speed and development speed for their processes, a strategy called **time-based competition**. To implement the strategy, managers carefully define the steps and time needed to deliver a service or produce a product and then critically analyze each step to determine whether they can save time without hurting quality.

To link to corporate strategy, management assigns selected competitive priorities to each process (and the supply chains created from them) that are consistent with the needs of external as well as internal customers. Competitive priorities may change over time. For example, consider a high-volume standardized product, such as color ink-jet desktop printers. In the early stages of the ramp-up period when the printers had just entered the mass market, the manufacturing processes required consistent quality, delivery speed, and volume flexibility. In the later stages of the ramp-up when demand was high, the competitive priorities became low-cost operations, consistent quality, and on-time delivery. As Managerial Practice 1.2 illustrates further, for FedEx, competitive priorities must change and evolve over time along with changing business conditions and customer preferences.

Order Winners and Qualifiers

Competitive priorities focus on what operations can do to help a firm be more competitive, and are in response to what the market wants. Another useful way to examine a firm's ability to

competitive priorities

The critical dimensions that a process or supply chain must possess to satisfy its internal or external customers, both now and in the future.

competitive capabilities

The cost, quality, time, and flexibility dimensions that a process or supply chain actually possesses and is able to deliver.

time-based competition

A strategy that focuses on the competitive priorities of delivery speed and development speed.

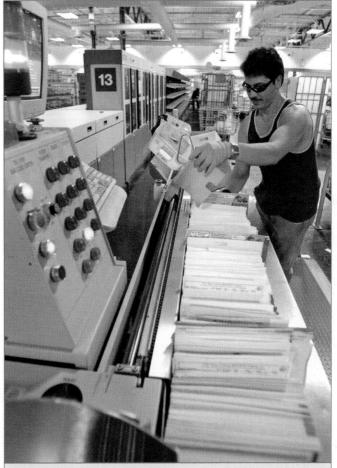

US Postal Service mail processing clerk Alberto Fonseca feeds mail into an automated letter sorter Monday, Dec. 17, 2007, at the USPS San Francisco processing and distribution center in San Francisco. Due to the Christmas holiday season, this week is traditionally the busiest of the year for the U.S. Postal Service.

TABLE 1.2	DEFINITIONS, PROCESS CONSIDERATIONS, AND EXAMPLES OF COMPETITIVE PRIORITIES		
COST	**Definition**	**Processes Considerations**	**Example**
1. **Low-cost operations**	Delivering a service or a product at the lowest possible cost to the satisfaction of external or internal customers of the process or supply chain	To reduce costs, processes must be designed and operated to make them efficient using rigorous process analysis that addresses workforce, methods, scrap or rework, overhead, and other factors, such as investments in new automated facilities or technologies to lower the cost per unit of the service or product.	**Costco** achieves low costs by designing all processes for efficiency, stacking products on pallets in warehouse-type stores, and negotiating aggressively with their suppliers. Costco can provide low prices to its customers because they have designed operations for low cost.
QUALITY			
2. **Top quality**	Delivering an outstanding service or product	To deliver top quality, a service process may require a high level of customer contact, and high levels of helpfulness, courtesy, and availability of servers. It may require superior product features, close tolerances, and greater durability from a manufacturing process.	**Ferrari's** processes deal with providing superior product features and more demanding performance requirements.
3. **Consistent quality**	Producing services or products that meet design specifications on a consistent basis	Processes must be designed and monitored to reduce errors, prevent defects, and achieve similar outcomes over time, regardless of the "level" of quality.	**McDonald's** standardizes work methods, staff training processes, and procurement of raw materials to achieve the same consistent product and process quality from one store to the next.
TIME			
4. **Delivery speed**	Quickly filling a customer's order	Design processes to reduce **lead time** (elapsed time between the receipt of a customer order and filling it) through keeping backup capacity cushions, storing inventory, and using premier transportation options.	**Dell** engineered its customer relationship, order fulfillment, and supplier relationship processes to create an integrated and an agile supply chain that delivers reliable and inexpensive computers to its customers with short lead times.
5. **On-time delivery**	Meeting delivery-time promises	Along with processes that reduce lead time, planning processes (forecasting, appointments, order promising, scheduling, and capacity planning) are used to increase percent of customer orders shipped when promised (95% is often a typical goal).	**United Parcel Services (UPS)** uses its expertise in logistics and warehousing processes to deliver a very large volume of shipments on-time across the globe.
6. **Development speed**	Quickly introducing a new service or a product	Processes aim to achieve cross-functional integration and involvement of critical external suppliers in the service or product development process.	**Li & Fung** can get a new product idea for a sweater or other lines of clothing from its customer, design the sweater, transmit the design to Hong Kong and Southeast Asia where it is produced, ship the sweater back to the United States, and put the sweater on the store shelves of the customer within a few weeks.
FLEXIBILITY			
7. **Customization**	Satisfying the unique needs of each customer by changing service or product designs	Processes with a customization strategy typically have low volume, close customer contact, and an ability to reconfigure processes to meet diverse types of customer needs.	**Ritz Carlton** customizes services to individual guest preferences.
8. **Variety**	Handling a wide assortment of services or products efficiently	Processes supporting variety must be capable of larger volumes than processes supporting customization. Services or products are not necessarily unique to specific customers and may have repetitive demands.	**Amazon.com** uses information technology and streamlined customer relationship and order fulfillment processes to reliably deliver a vast variety of items to its customers.
9. **Volume flexibility**	Accelerating or decelerating the rate of production of services or products quickly to handle large fluctuations in demand	Processes must be designed for excess capacity and excess inventory to handle demand fluctuations that can vary in cycles from days to months. This priority could also be met with a strategy that adjusts capacity without accumulation of inventory or excess capacity.	**The United States Post Office (USPS)** can have severe demand peak fluctuations at large postal facilities where processes are flexibly designed for receiving, sorting, and dispatching mail to numerous branch locations.

MANAGERIAL PRACTICE 1.2	Changing Competitive Priorities at FedEx

FedEx is a $38-billion-a-year delivery service company that thrives on delivery speed and reliability. FedEx delivers 7.5 million packages each day. Because 60 percent of the packages go by plane, FedEx charges premium prices for the service. For years, companies traditionally chose FedEx because of its on-time delivery and technological superiority in tracking packages. The Internet, however, changed things drastically. Many businesses use complex Web-based processes designed to eliminate much of the unpredictability in their operations by communicating directly with customers and suppliers. E-mail delivers documents instantaneously, and low-cost truck lines, discount air carriers, and even ocean vessels can now track shipments via the Internet.

These technological advances cut into the demand for FedEx's traditional services. The growth potential now lies in ground transportation, presently dominated by United Parcel Service. This demand is fueled by Internet companies, such as Amazon.com, which relies on ground transportation services to deliver packages directly to the customer's door, and by the vast business-to-business supply networks created by Web-based purchasing systems. To remain competitive, FedEx created two new services: FedEx Ground and FedEx Home Delivery. FedEx Ground focuses on business-to-business deliveries via a recently procured trucking company. FedEx Home Delivery specializes in deliveries to residences. In addition, FedEx invested $100 million in processes to coordinate the flow of goods. The goals are now low-cost operations and dependable delivery—a change from past operations goals that stressed speed.

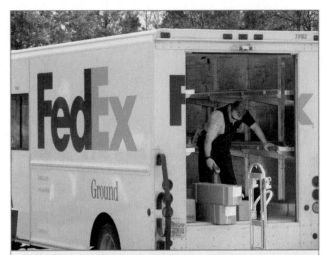

A FedEx employee scans a package for ground delivery. Because the Internet makes it easy for people to send documents to one another instantly, FedEx is now focusing more on its ground service.

Source: Brian O'Reilly, "They've Got Mail!" *Fortune* (February 7, 2000), pp. 101–112; www.fedex.com, 2008.

---

be successful in the marketplace is to identify the order winners and order qualifiers. An **order winner** is a criterion that customers use to differentiate the services or products of one firm from those of another.[3] Order winners can include price (which is supported by low-cost operations) and other dimensions of quality, time, and flexibility. However, order winners also include criteria not directly related to the firm's operations, such as after-sale support (Are maintenance service contracts available? Is there a return policy?); technical support (What help do I get if something goes wrong? How knowledgeable are the technicians?); and reputation (How long has this company been in business? Have other customers been satisfied with the service or product?). It may take good performance on a subset of the order-winner criteria, cutting across operational as well as nonoperational criteria, to make a sale.

Order winners are derived from the considerations customers use when deciding which firm to purchase a service or product from in a given market segment. Sometimes customers demand a certain level of demonstrated performance before even contemplating a service or product. In these cases an order winner becomes an **order qualifier**, which is a minimal requirement for doing business in a particular market segment. Fulfilling the order qualifier will not ensure competitive success; it will only position the firm to compete in the market. From an operations perspective, understanding which competitive priorities are order qualifiers and which ones are order winners is important for the investments made in the design and management of processes and supply chains.

Figure 1.6 shows how order winners and qualifiers are related to achieving the competitive priorities of a firm. If a minimum threshold level is not met for an order-qualifying dimension (consistent quality, for example) by a firm, then it would get disqualified from even being considered further by its customers. For example, there is a level of quality consistency that is minimally tolerable by customers in the auto industry. When

order winner

A criterion customers use to differentiate the services or products of one firm from those of another.

order qualifier

A demonstrated level of performance of an order winner that is required for a firm to do business in a particular market segment.

---

[3] Terry Hill, *Manufacturing Strategy: Text and Cases*, 3rd ed. (Burr Ridge, IL: Irwin/McGraw-Hill, 2000).

FIGURE 1.6 ▲
Relationship of Order Winners and Order Qualifiers to Competitive Priorities

the subcompact car Yugo built by Zastava Corporation could not sustain the minimal level of quality, consistency, and reliability expected by customers, it had to exit the U.S. car market in 1991 despite offering very low prices (order winner) of under $4,000. However, once the firm qualifies by attaining consistent quality beyond the threshold, it may only gain additional sales at a very low rate by investing further in improving that order-qualifying dimension. In contrast, for an order-winning dimension (i.e., low price driven by low cost operations), a firm can reasonably expect to gain appreciably greater sales and market share by continuously lowering its prices as long as the order qualifier (i.e., consistent quality) is being adequately met. Toyota Corolla and Honda Civic have successfully followed this route in the marketplace to become leaders in their target market segment.

Order winners and qualifiers are often used in competitive bidding. For example, before a buyer considers a bid, suppliers may be required to document their ability to provide consistent quality as measured by adherence to the design specifications for the service or component they are supplying (order qualifier). Once qualified, the supplier may eventually be selected by the buyer on the basis of low prices (order winner) and the reputation of the supplier (order winner).

Using Competitive Priorities: an Airline Example

To get a better understanding of how companies use competitive priorities, let us look at a major airline. We will consider two market segments: first-class passengers and coach passengers. Core services for both market segments are ticketing and seat selection, baggage handling, and transportation to the customer's destination. The peripheral services are quite different across the two market segments. First-class passengers require separate airport lounges; preferred treatment during check-in, boarding, and deplaning; more comfortable seats; better meals and beverages; more personal attention (cabin attendants who refer to customers by name); more frequent service from attendants; high levels of courtesy; and low volumes of passengers (adding to the feeling of being special). Coach passengers are satisfied with standardized services (no surprises), courteous flight attendants, and low prices. Both market segments expect the airline to hold to its schedule. Consequently, we can say that the competitive priorities for the first-class segment are *top quality* and *on-time delivery*, whereas the competitive priorities for the coach segment are *low-cost operations, consistent quality*, and *on-time delivery*.

The airline knows what its collective capabilities must be as a firm, but how does that get communicated to each of its core processes? Let us focus on the four core processes: customer relationship, new service/product development, order fulfillment, and supplier relationship. Competitive priorities are assigned to each core process to achieve the service required to provide complete customer satisfaction. Here are some possible assignments, just to give you an idea of how this works.

Customer Relationship   This process involves high levels of customer contact through ticketing (both electronic and telephone), elite lounge service, and boarding. It also has marketing and sales functions. Possible competitive priorities include the following:

- *Top Quality*. High levels of customer contact and lounge service for the first-class passengers.
- *Consistent Quality*. The information and service must be error free.
- *Delivery Speed*. Customers want immediate information regarding flight schedules and other ticketing information.
- *Variety*. The process must be capable of handling the service needs of all market segments and promotional programs, such as frequent-flier services.

New Service Development New services must continually be developed to stay ahead of the competition. Such services include tours to the world's vacation paradises, new routes, or new dinner service. Competitive priorities might include the following:

- *Development Speed.* It is important to get to market fast to preempt the competition.
- *Customization.* The process must be able to create unique services.
- *Top Quality.* New services must be carefully designed because the future of the airline depends on them.

Order Fulfillment This process is responsible for delivering the service to the customer's satisfaction. It is a huge process in an airline, involving scheduling, gate operations, maintenance, cabin service, pilot operations, and baggage handling. It has many nested processes, and many competitive priorities, which might include the following:

One of the competitive priorities of airline companies is on-time delivery of their services. Being able to repair and maintain planes rapidly to avoid delays is a crucial aspect of this.

- *Low-Cost Operations.* Airlines compete on price and must keep costs in check.
- *Top Quality.* The service provided to first-class passengers must be top notch. To a large extent, this service aspect involves well-trained and experienced cabin attendants and a high-quality meal and beverage service.
- *Consistent Quality.* Once the quality level is set, it is important to achieve it every time.
- *On-Time Delivery.* The airline strives to arrive at destinations on schedule, otherwise the passengers might miss connections to other flights.
- *Variety.* Maintenance operations are required for a variety of aircraft models.

Supplier Relationship This process is responsible for acquiring all of the inputs the airline requires to do business, which range from human resources to capital goods. Competitive priorities might include the following:

- *Low-Cost Operations.* The cost of acquiring inputs must be kept to a minimum to allow for competitive pricing.
- *Consistent Quality.* The quality of the inputs must adhere to the required specifications. In addition, the information provided to the suppliers must be accurate.
- *On-Time Delivery.* Inputs must be delivered to tight schedules, particularly meal services.
- *Variety.* Many different inputs must be acquired, including maintenance items, meals and beverages, and even aircraft.
- *Volume Flexibility.* The process must be able to handle variations in supply quantities efficiently.

OPERATIONS STRATEGY AS A PATTERN OF DECISIONS

Operations strategy translates service or product plans and competitive priorities for each market segment into decisions affecting the supply chains that support those market segments. Even if it is not formally stated, the current operations strategy for any firm is really the pattern of decisions that have been made for its processes and supply chains. As we have previously seen in Figure 1.5, corporate strategy provides the umbrella for key operations management decisions that contribute to the development of the firm's ability to compete successfully in the marketplace. Once managers determine the competitive priorities for a process, it is necessary to assess the *competitive capabilities* of the process. Any gap between a competitive priority and the capability to achieve that competitive priority must be closed by an effective operations strategy.

Developing capabilities and closing gaps is the thrust of operations strategy. To demonstrate how this works, suppose the management of a bank's credit card division decides to embark on a marketing campaign to significantly increase its business, while keeping costs low. A key process in this division is billing and payments. The division receives credit transactions from the merchants, pays the merchants, assembles and sends the bills to the credit card holders, and processes payments. The new marketing effort is expected to significantly increase the volume of bills and payments. In assessing the capabilities the process must have to serve the bank's customers and to meet the challenges of the new market campaign, management assigns the following competitive priorities for the billing and payments process:

- *Low-Cost Operations*. It is important to maintain low costs in the processing of the bills because profit margins are tight.
- *Consistent Quality*. The process must consistently produce bills, make payments to the merchants, and record payments from the credit card holders accurately.
- *Delivery Speed*. Merchants want to be paid for the credit purchases quickly.
- *Volume Flexibility*. The marketing campaign is expected to generate many more transactions in a shorter period of time.

Management assumed that customers would avoid doing business with a bank that could not produce accurate bills or payments. Consequently, consistent quality is an order qualifier for this process.

Is the billing and payment process up to the competitive challenge? Table 1.3 shows how to match capabilities to priorities and uncover any gaps in the credit card division's operations strategy. The procedure for assessing an operations strategy begins with identifying good measures for each priority. The more quantitative the measures are, the better. Data are gathered for each measure to determine the current capabilities of the process. Gaps are identified by comparing each capability to management's target values for the measures, and unacceptable gaps are closed by appropriate actions.

The credit card division shows significant gaps in the process's capability for low-cost operations. Management's remedy is to redesign the process in ways that reduce costs but will not impair the other competitive priorities. Likewise, for volume flexibility, management realized that a high level of utilization is not conducive for processing quick surges in volumes while maintaining delivery speed. The recommended actions will help build a capability for meeting more volatile demands.

TRENDS IN OPERATIONS MANAGEMENT

Several trends are currently having a great impact on operations management: productivity improvement; global competition; and ethical, workforce diversity, and environmental issues. Accelerating change in the form of information technology, e-commerce, robotics,

TABLE 1.3	OPERATIONS STRATEGY ASSESSMENT OF THE BILLING AND PAYMENT PROCESS			
Competitive Priority	**Measure**	**Capability**	**Gap**	**Action**
Low-cost operations	■ Cost per billing statement	■ $0.0813	■ Target is $0.06	■ Eliminate microfilming and storage of billing statements
	■ Weekly postage	■ $17,000	■ Target is $14,000	■ Develop Web-based process for posting bills
Consistent quality	■ Percent errors in bill information	■ 0.90%	■ Acceptable	■ No action
	■ Percent errors in posting payments	■ 0.74%	■ Acceptable	■ No action
Delivery speed	■ Lead time to process merchant payments	■ 48 hours	■ Acceptable	■ No action
Volume flexibility	■ Utilization	■ 98%	■ Too high to support rapid increase in volumes	■ Acquire temporary employees
				■ Improve work methods

and the Internet is dramatically affecting the design of new services and products as well as a firm's sales, order fulfillment, and purchasing processes. In this section, we look at these trends and their challenges for operations managers.

Productivity Improvement

Productivity is a basic measure of performance for economies, industries, firms, and processes. Improving productivity is a major trend in operations management because all firms face pressures to improve their processes and supply chains so as to compete with their domestic and foreign competitors. **Productivity** is the value of outputs (services and products) produced divided by the values of input resources (wages, cost of equipment, and so on) used:

$$\text{Productivity} = \frac{\text{Output}}{\text{Input}}$$

productivity

The value of outputs (services and products) produced divided by the values of input resources (wages, costs of equipment, etc.).

It is interesting and even surprising to compare productivity improvements in the service and manufacturing sectors. In the United States, employment in the service sector has grown rapidly, outstripping the manufacturing sector, but service-sector productivity gains have been much lower. If productivity growth in the service sector stagnates, so does the overall standard of living regardless of which part of the world you live in. Other major industrial countries, such as Japan and Germany, are experiencing the same problem. Yet, signs of improvement are appearing. The surge of investment across national boundaries can stimulate productivity gains by exposing firms to greater competition. Increased investment in information technology by service providers also increases productivity.

Measuring Productivity   As a manager, how do you measure the productivity of your processes? Many measures are available. For example, value of output can be measured by what the customer pays or simply by the number of units produced or customers served. The value of inputs can be judged by their cost or simply by the number of hours worked.

Managers usually pick several reasonable measures and monitor trends to spot areas needing improvement. For example, a manager at an insurance firm might measure office productivity as the number of insurance policies processed per employee per week. A manager at a carpet company might measure the productivity of installers as the number of square yards of carpet installed per hour. Both measures reflect *labor productivity*, which is an index of the output per person or per hour worked. Similar measures may be used for *machine productivity*, where the denominator is the number of machines. Accounting for several inputs simultaneously is also possible. *Multifactor productivity* is an index of the output provided by more than one of the resources used in production; it may be the value of the output divided by the sum of labor, materials, and overhead costs. Here is an example:

EXAMPLE 1.1	**Productivity Calculations**

Calculate the productivity for the following operations:

a.   Three employees process 600 insurance policies a week. They work 8 hours per day, 5 days per week.

b.   A team of workers makes 400 units of a product, which is valued by its standard cost of $10 (before markups for other expenses and profits.) The accounting department reports that for this job the actual costs are $400 for labor, $1000 for materials, and $300 for overhead.

Tutor 1.1 in my**omlab** provides a new example for calculating productivity.

SOLUTION

a.   Labor productivity $= \dfrac{\text{Policies processed}}{\text{Employee hours}}$

$$= \frac{600 \text{ policies}}{(3 \text{ employees})(40 \text{ hours/employee})} = \text{almost 5 policies/hour}$$

b.   Multifactor productivity $= \dfrac{\text{Value of output}}{\text{Labor cost} + \text{Materials cost} + \text{Overhead cost}}$

$$= \frac{(400 \text{ units})(\$10/\text{unit})}{\$400 + \$1,000 + \$300} = \frac{\$4,000}{\$1,700} = 2.35$$

DECISION POINT

We want multifactor productivity to be as high as possible. These measures must be compared with performance levels in prior periods and with future goals. If they do not live up to expectations, the process should be investigated for improvement opportunities.

The Role of Management   The way processes are managed plays a key role in productivity improvement. Managers must examine productivity from the level of the supply chain because it is the collective performance of individual processes that makes the difference. The challenge is to increase the value of output relative to the cost of input. If processes can generate more output or output of better quality using the same amount of input, productivity increases. If they can maintain the same level of output while reducing the use of resources, productivity also increases.

Global Competition

Most businesses realize that, to prosper, they must view customers, suppliers, facility locations, and competitors in global terms. Firms have found that they can increase their market penetration by locating their production facilities in foreign countries because it gives them a local presence that reduces customer aversion to buying imports. For example, Elasticos Selectos, a Mexico City–based elastics company, built a plant in the United States primarily to gain customers who demand a "made-in-the-USA" label on their goods. As illustrated in Managerial Practice 1.3, globalization also allows firms to balance cash flows from other regions of the world when economic conditions are less robust in the home country.

MANAGERIAL PRACTICE 1.3 — Impact of Globalization on Sonoco

Finding viable locations for operations throughout the world can stabilize financial performance in a changing global economy. Such is the case with **Sonoco**, a $4-billion-a-year industrial and consumer packaging company in Hartsville, South Carolina, with 335 locations worldwide in Australia, China, Europe, Mexico, New Zealand, and Russia. Its 18,600 employees provide innovative packaging solutions to a variety of customers in 85 nations. In Europe alone, where Sonoco has operated since 1923, it has 41 industrial product manufacturing facilities and 6 paper mills. These global operations resulted in international sales and income growth in 2007 while domestic sales were stumbling. Sonoco's fourth quarter income increased 37 percent to $54 million, with an overall income growth of 10 percent in 2007. How did Sonoco do it? Locating operations in countries with favorable tax laws is one reason. Lower tax rates in Italy and Canada helped in padding the earnings margin. Another reason is a weak dollar, whereby a $46 million boost came from turning foreign currencies into dollars as Sonoco exported such items as snack bag packaging, and tubes and cores used to hold tape and textiles, to operations it owned in foreign countries. The exchange rate difference was more than enough to counter the added expense of increased raw materials, shipping, and energy costs in the United States.

With over $400 million cash on hand expected in 2008, Sonoco is looking to grow the business with large capital expenditures during the year. Even though lower sales volumes and higher costs are troubling in the short run, the future is bright because the overseas business is helping the company weather the current financial storm. Instead of catching a cold when the U.S. economy sneezes, firms with diversified global operations like Sonoco now consider foreign currency as chicken noodle soup for the bottom line!

Sonoco is a leading global manufacturer of industrial and consumer packaging goods with more than 300 locations in 35 countries serving 85 nations.

Source: Ben Werner, "Sonoco Holding Its Own," *The State* (February 7, 2008); www.sonoco.com, 2008.

Most products today are composites of materials and services from all over the world. Your Gap polo shirt is sewn in Honduras from cloth cut in the United States. Sitting in a Cineplex theater (Canadian), you munch a Nestle's Crunch bar (Swiss) while watching a Columbia Pictures movie (Japanese). Five developments spurred the need for sound global strategies: (1) improved transportation and communications technologies, (2) loosened regulations on financial institutions, (3) increased demand for imported services and goods, (4) reduced import quotas and other international trade barriers due to the formation of regional trading blocks, such as the European Union (EU) and the North American Free Trade Agreement (NAFTA), and (5) comparative cost advantages.

Comparative Cost Advantages   China and India have recently become the sources for low-cost, but skilled, labor.[4] In the late 1990s, companies manufactured products in China to grab a foothold in a huge market, or to get cheap labor to produce low-tech products despite doubts about the quality of the workforce and poor roads and rail

Foreign companies have opened tens of thousands of new facilities in China over the past decade, with as many as 60,000 new factories between 2000 and 2003 alone.

systems. Today, however, China's new factories, such as those in the Pudong industrial zone in Shanghai, produce a wide variety of products that are sold overseas in other regions of the world.

Foreign companies have opened tens of thousands of new facilities in China over the past decade, with as many as 60,000 new factories between 2000 and 2003 alone. Over 55 percent of the goods the United States imports from China now come from foreign-owned companies with operations there. These companies include telephone makers, such as Nokia and Motorola, and nearly all of the big footwear and clothing brands. Many more major manufacturers are there as well. The implications for competition are enormous. Companies that don't have operations in China are finding it difficult to compete on the basis of low prices with companies that do. Instead, they must focus on speed and small production runs.

What China is to manufacturing, India is to service. As with the manufacturing companies, the cost of labor is a key factor. A programmer in India may get one-sixth the wages of a programmer in the United Kingdom with comparable skills and experience. Indian software companies have grown sophisticated in their applications and offer a big advantage in cost. The computer services industry is also affected. To remain competitive, Electronic Data Systems increased its staff in India almost tenfold in three years. Back-office operations are affected for the same reason. Many firms are using Indian companies for accounting and bookkeeping, preparing tax returns, and processing insurance claims. Many tech companies, such as Intel and Microsoft, are opening significant research and development (R&D) operations in India.

Disadvantages of Globalization   Of course, operations in other countries can have disadvantages. A firm may have to relinquish proprietary technology if it turns over some of its component manufacturing to offshore suppliers or if suppliers need the firm's technology to achieve desired quality and cost goals. Political risks may also be involved. Each nation can exercise its sovereignty over the people and property within its borders. The extreme case is nationalization, in which a government may take over a firm's assets without paying compensation. Exxon and other large multinational oil firms are scaling back operations in Venezuela due to nationalization concerns. Further, a firm may actually alienate customers back home if jobs are lost to offshore operations.

Employee skills may be lower in foreign countries, requiring additional training time. South Korean firms moved much of their sports shoe production to low-wage Indonesia and China, but they still manufacture hiking shoes and in-line roller skates in South Korea because of the greater skills required. In addition, when a firm's operations are scattered

---

[4] For additional information on global issues involving India and China, see Neil King Jr., "A Whole New World," *Wall Street Journal* (September 27, 2004); and Bill Powell, "It's All Made in China Now," *Fortune* (March 4, 2002), pp. 121–128.

Shortage of components from suppliers and capacity shortfalls prevented Nintendo from meeting the customer demand for its popular Wii game system.

globally, customer response times can be longer. We discuss these issues in more depth in Chapter 9, "Designing Effective Supply Chains," because they should be considered when making decisions about outsourcing. Coordinating components from a wide array of suppliers can be challenging, as Nintendo found out in the production and world-wide distribution of its Wii game systems.[5] Despite twice increasing capacity since April 2007 to 1.8 million Wii's a month, Nintendo could only ship the completed units to retailers like Best Buy, Costco, and Circuit City in limited quantities that did not meet the large demand through the 2007 holiday season and beyond.

Strong global competition affects industries everywhere. For example, U.S. manufacturers of steel, appliances, household durable goods, machinery, and chemicals have seen their market share decline in both domestic and international markets. With the value of world trade in services now at more than $1.5 trillion per year, banking, data processing, airlines, and consulting services are beginning to face many of the same international pressures. Regional trading blocs, such as EU and NAFTA, further change the competitive landscape in both services and manufacturing. Regardless of which area of the world you live in, the challenge is to produce services or products that can compete in a global market, and to design the processes that can make it happen.

Ethical, Workforce Diversity, and Environmental Issues

Businesses face more ethical quandaries than ever before, intensified by an increasing global presence and rapid technological change. As companies locate new operations and acquire more suppliers and customers in other countries, potential ethical dilemmas arise when business is conducted by different rules. Some countries are more sensitive than others about conflicts of interest, bribery, discrimination against minorities and women, minimum-wage levels, and unsafe workplaces. Managers must decide whether to design and operate processes that do more than just meet local standards. In addition, technological change brings debates about data protection and customer privacy. In an electronic world, businesses are geographically far from their customers, so a reputation of trust is paramount.

In the past, many people viewed environmental problems, such as toxic waste, poisoned drinking water, poor air quality, and climate change, as quality-of-life issues; now, many people and businesses see them as survival issues. The automobile industry has seen innovation in electric and hybrid cars in response to environmental concerns and economic benefits arising from using less expensive fuels. Industrial nations face a particular burden because their combined populations, representing only 25 percent of the total global population, consume 70 percent of all resources. Just seven nations, including the United States and Japan, produce almost half of all greenhouse gases. The United States and some European nations now spend 2 percent of their gross domestic products on environmental protection.

The challenge is clear: Issues of ethics, workforce diversity, and the environment are becoming part of every manager's job. When designing and operating processes, managers should consider integrity, respect for the individual, and customer satisfaction along with more conventional performance measures such as productivity, quality, cost, and profit.

OPERATIONS MANAGEMENT AS A SET OF DECISIONS

In this text we cover the major decisions operations managers make in practice. At the strategic level, operations managers are involved in the development of new capabilities and the maintenance of existing capabilities to best serve the firm's external customers. Operations

---

[5] Peter Svensson, "GameStop to Sell Rain Checks for Wii," *The State* (December 18, 2007).

managers design new processes that have strategic implications, and they are deeply involved in the development and organization of supply chains that link external suppliers and external customers to the firm's internal processes. Operations managers are often responsible for key performance measures such as cost and quality. These decisions have strategic impact because they affect the processes the firm uses to gain a competitive edge.

The operations manager's decisions should reflect corporate strategy. Plans, policies, and actions should be linked to those in other functional areas to support the firm's overall goals and objectives. These links are facilitated by taking a process view of a firm. Regardless of whether you aspire to be an operations manager, or you just want to use the principles of operations management to become a more effective manager, remember that effective management of people, capital, information, and materials is critical to the success of any process and any supply chain.

As you study operations management, keep two principles in mind:

1. Each part of an organization, not just the operations function, must design and operate processes that are part of a supply chain and deal with quality, technology, and staffing issues.

2. Each function of an organization has its own identity and yet is connected with operations through shared processes.

Great strategic decisions lead nowhere if the tactical decisions that support them are wrong. Operations managers are also involved in tactical decisions, including process improvement and performance measurement, managing and planning projects, generating production and staffing plans, managing inventories, and scheduling resources. You will find numerous examples of these decisions, and the implications of making them, throughout this text. You will also learn about the decision-making tools practicing managers use to recognize and define the problem and then choose the best solution.

Computerized Decision-Making Tools

my**om**lab contains a unique set of decision tools we call OM Explorer. This package contains powerful Excel-based computer routines to solve problems often encountered in practice. OM Explorer also has several tutors that provide coaching for all of the difficult analytical techniques in this text, and can be accessed from the drop-down menu.

my**om**lab also contains POMS for Windows, which is an extensive set of useful decision-making tools to complete your arsenal for solving operations problems, many Active Models (spreadsheets designed to help you learn more about important decision-making techniques), and a spreadsheet-based simulation package called SimQuick.

ADDRESSING THE CHALLENGES IN OPERATIONS MANAGEMENT

How can firms meet challenges today and in the future? One way is to recognize challenges as opportunities to improve existing processes and supply chains or to create new, innovative ones. The management of processes and supply chains goes beyond designing them; it requires the ability to ensure they achieve their goals. Firms should manage their processes and supply chains to maximize their competitiveness in the markets they serve. We share this philosophy of operations management, as illustrated in Figure 1.7. We use this figure at the start of each chapter to show how the topic of the chapter fits into our philosophy of operations management. In addition, this text also contains several chapter supplements that are not explicitly shown in Figure 1.7.

The figure shows that all effective operations decisions follow from a sound operations strategy. Consequently, our text has three major parts: "Competing with Operations," "Designing and Managing Processes," and "Designing and Managing Supply Chains." The flow of topics reflects our approach of first understanding how a firm's operations can help provide a solid foundation for competitiveness before tackling the essential process design decisions that will support its strategies. Each part begins with a strategy discussion to support the decisions in that part. Once it is clear how firms design and improve processes, and how they implement those designs, we examine the design and operation of supply chains that link processes, whether they are internal or external to the firm. The performance of the supply chains determines the firm's outcomes, which include the services or products the firm produces, the financial results, and feedback from the firm's customers. These outcomes, which are considered in the firm's strategic plan, are discussed throughout this text.

COMPETING WITH OPERATIONS

↓

Using Operations to Compete
Managing Effective Projects

DESIGNING AND MANAGING PROCESSES

↓

Developing a Process Strategy
Analyzing Processes
Managing Quality
Planning Capacity
Managing Process Constraints
Designing Lean Systems

DESIGNING AND MANAGING SUPPLY CHAINS

↓

Designing Effective Supply Chains
Integrating the Supply Chain
Locating Facilities
Managing Inventories
Forecasting Demand
Planning and Scheduling Operations
Planning Sufficient Resources

▲ FIGURE 1.7
Managing Processes and
Supply Chains

Part 1: Competing with Operations

The concluding chapter of this part is a discussion of the methods and tools of project management. Project management is an effective approach to implementing operations strategy through the introduction of new services or products as well as any changes to a firm's processes or supply chains. Supplement A, "Decision Making Models," follows this chapter and covers some decision techniques that apply to multiple chapters.

Part 2: Designing and Managing Processes

In this part we focus on analyzing processes and how they can be improved to meet the goals of the operations strategy. We begin by addressing the strategic aspects of process design and then present a six-step systematic approach to process analysis: (1) identify the opportunity, (2) define the scope, (3) document the process, (4) evaluate performance, (5) redesign the process, and (6) implement the changes. Each chapter in this part deals with some aspect of that approach. We discuss the tools that help managers analyze processes, and we reveal the methods firms use to measure process performance and quality. These methods provide the foundation for programs such as Six Sigma and total quality management.

Determining the best process capacity with effective constraint management and making processes "lean" by eliminating activities that do not add value while improving those that do are also key decisions in the redesign of processes. The activities involved in managing processes are essential for providing significant benefits to the firm. Take, for example, HIP Health Plan of New York, which completely reengineered its claims processing system to allow its 1.1 million members to view claims and refill prescriptions online. Doctors can use the system to authorize CAT scans and visits to specialists. Effective management of its processes provides HIP Health Plan of New York with annual savings of $10 million in claims processing.

Part 3: Designing and Managing Supply Chains

The management of supply chains is based upon process management and operations strategy. In Part 2 we focus on individual processes. The focus of Part 3, however, is on supply chains involving processes both internal and external to the firm and the tools that enhance their execution. We begin this part with a look at the design of supply chains and how major strategic decisions, such as outsourcing and inventory placement, affect performance. We also look at contemporary issues surrounding supply chain integration. We follow that with chapters focused on five key planning activities that are useful for the effective operation of supply chains: (1) location, (2) inventory management, (3) forecasting, (4) operations planning and scheduling, and (5) resource planning.

It is important to note that the effective operation of a supply chain is as important as its design. Yellow Transportation, Inc., found out its importance when it completely redesigned its operations planning and scheduling processes to cut costs in its supply chain. Every day the $2.6 billion company receives 60,000 orders over the Internet or at its call centers. The new planning process determines down to the person how many drivers the company will need during the four shifts at each of its terminals the next day. Drivers who are not needed are told to take the day off—without pay—which is quite a feat, considering that the process includes 19,300 unionized truckers, 8,250 trucks, and 335 facilities across the United States. Orders vary 15 to 20 percent from Monday to Friday; having the capability to match resources to requirements shaves $100 million a year in operating costs. Who says operations management does not make a difference?

The topics in this text will help you meet operations challenges regardless of your chosen career path.

INTERNET RESOURCES

my**om**lab and the Companion Website at **www.pearsonglobaleditions.com/krajewski** contain many tools, activities, and resources designed for this chapter.

KEY EQUATION

Productivity is the ratio of output to input:

$$\text{Productivity} = \frac{\text{Output}}{\text{Input}}$$

KEY TERMS

competitive capabilities 33
competitive priorities 33
consistent quality 34
core competencies 31
core process 28
customer relationship process 28
customization 34
delivery speed 34
development speed 34
external customers 25
external suppliers 25
internal customers 25

internal suppliers 25
lead time 34
low-cost operations 34
nested process 26
new service/product development
   process 28
on-time delivery 34
operation 24
operations management 24
operations strategy 29
order fulfillment process 28
order qualifier 35

order winner 35
process 24
productivity 39
supplier relationship process 28
supply chain 24
supply chain management 24
support process 28
time-based competition 33
top quality 34
variety 34
volume flexibility 34

SOLVED PROBLEM 1

A manufacturer of machine-made rugs in Turkey wants to measure the productivity of his workers. He employs 10 workers. Over a week, his workers produce 120 rugs, each 3 feet by 5 feet. Labor costs are $60 a week per worker, making for a total of $600. Material costs are $200 per carpet, making for a total of $24,000. The overhead costs are $400. Each rug is valued at $600 before markups for other expenses and profit.

a. What is the productivity of the workers measured by day?

b. What is the *multifactor* productivity ratio for the factory?

SOLUTION

a. Labor productivity is the ratio of the value of output to labor hours.

$$\text{Labor productivity} = \frac{\text{Rugs produced}}{\text{Employee hours}}$$

$$= \frac{120 \text{ rugs}}{(10 \text{ employees}) (6 \text{ days/employee})} = 2 \text{ rugs/day}$$

b. Multifactor productivity is the ratio of the value of output to the value of input resources.

$$\text{Multifactor productivity} = \frac{\text{Quality at standard cost}}{\text{Labor cost } + \text{ Materials cost } + \text{ Overhead cost}}$$

$$= \frac{(120 \text{ units}) (\$600/\text{units})}{\$600 + \$24{,}000 + \$400} = \frac{\$72{,}000}{\$25{,}000} = 2.88$$

Solved Problem 2

Natalie Attire makes fashionable garments. During a particular week employees worked 360 hours to produce a batch of 132 garments, of which 52 were "seconds" (meaning that they were flawed). Seconds are sold for $90 each at Attire's Factory Outlet Store. The remaining 80 garments are sold to retail distribution at $200 each. What is the *labor* productivity ratio of this manufacturing process?

SOLUTION

$$\text{Value of output} = (52 \text{ defective} \times 90/\text{defective}) + (80 \text{ garments} \times 200/\text{garment})$$

$$= \$20,680$$

$$\text{Labor hours of input} = 360 \text{ hours}$$

$$\text{Labor productivity} = \frac{\text{Output}}{\text{Input}} = \frac{\$20,680}{360 \text{ hours}/}$$

$$= \$57.44 \text{ in sales per hour}$$

Discussion Questions

1. Although all nine of the competitive priorities discussed in this chapter are relevant to a company's success in the marketplace, explain why a company should not necessarily try to excel in all of them. What determines the choice of the competitive priorities that a company should emphasize for its key processes?

2. Consider your last (or current) job.

   a. What activities did you perform?

   b. Who were your customers (internal and external), and how did you interact with them?

   c. How could you measure the customer value you were adding by performing your activities?

   d. Was your position in accounting, finance, human resources, management information systems, marketing, operations, or other? Explain.

3. Choosing which processes are core to a firm's competitive position is a key strategic decision. For example, Nike, a popular sports shoe company, focuses on the customer relationship, new product development, and supplier relationship processes and leaves the order fulfillment process to others. Edmonds, a top-quality shoe company, considers all four processes to be core processes. What considerations would you make in determining which processes should be core to your manufacturing company?

4. Suppose that you were conducting a market analysis for a new textbook about technology management. What would you need to know to identify a market segment? How would you make a needs assessment? What should be the collection of services and products?

5. Consider Amazon.com, whose Web site enjoys millions of "hits" each day and puts customers in touch with millions of services and products. What are Amazon.com's competitive priorities and what should its operations strategy focus on?

6. FedEx built its business on quick, dependable delivery of items being shipped by air from one business to another (see Managerial Practice 1.2). Its early advantages included global tracking of shipments using Web technology. The advancement of Internet technology enabled competitors to become much more sophisticated in order tracking. In addition, the advent of Web-based businesses put pressure on increased ground transportation deliveries. Explain how this change in the environment has affected FedEx's operations strategy, especially relative to UPS, which has a strong hold on the business-to-consumer ground delivery business.

7. A local hospital declares that it is committed to provide *care* to patients arriving at the emergency unit in less than 15 minutes and that it will never turn away patients who need to be hospitalized for further medical care. What implications does this commitment have for strategic operations management decisions (i.e., decisions relating to capacity and workforce)?

8. Wild West, Inc., is a regional telephone company that inherited nearly 100,000 employees and 50,000 retirees from AT&T. Wild West has a new mission: to diversify. It calls for a 10-year effort to enter the financial services, real estate, cable TV, home shopping, entertainment, and cellular communication services markets—and to compete with other telephone companies. Wild West plans to provide cellular and fiber-optic communications services in markets with established competitors, such as the United Kingdom, and in markets with essentially no competition, such as Russia and former Eastern Bloc countries.

a. What types of strategic plans must Wild West make? Is the "do-nothing" option viable? If Wild West's mission appears too broad, which businesses would you trim first?

b. What environmental forces could be at work that Wild West should consider?

c. What are the possible core competencies of Wild West? What weaknesses should it avoid or mitigate?

9. You are designing a grocery delivery business. Via the Internet, your company will offer staples and frozen foods in a large metropolitan area and then deliver them within a customer-defined window of time. You plan to partner with two major food stores in the area. What should be your competitive priorities and what capabilities do you want to develop in your core and support processes?

10. Kathryn Shoemaker established Grandmother's Chicken Restaurant in Middlesburg five years ago. It features a unique recipe for chicken, "just like grandmother used to make." The facility is homey, with relaxed and friendly service. Business has been good during the past two years, for both lunch and dinner. Customers normally

wait about 15 minutes to be served, although complaints about service delays have increased recently. Shoemaker is currently considering whether to expand the current facility or open a similar restaurant in neighboring Uniontown, which has been growing rapidly.

a. What types of strategic plans must Shoemaker make?

b. What environmental forces could be at work in Middlesburg and Uniontown that Shoemaker should consider?

c. What are the possible distinctive competencies of Grandmother's?

11. A local fast-food restaurant processes several customer orders at once. Service clerks cross paths, sometimes nearly colliding, while they trace different paths to fill customer orders. If customers order a special combination of toppings on their hamburgers, they must wait quite some time while the special order is cooked. How would you modify the restaurant's operations to achieve competitive advantage? Because demand surges at lunchtime, volume flexibility is a competitive priority in the fast-food business. How would you achieve volume flexibility?

Problems

Software, such as OM Explorer, Active Models, and POM for Windows, is available in my**om**lab. Check with your instructor on how best to use it. In many cases, the instructor wants you to understand how to do the calculations by hand. At most, the software provides a check on your calculations. When calculations are particularly complex and the goal is interpreting the results in making decisions, the software replaces entirely the manual calculations.

1. The output of a process is valued at $100 per unit. The cost of labor is $50 per hour including benefits. The accounting department provided the following information about the process for the past four weeks:

	Week 1	Week 2	Week 3	Week 4
Units Produced	1,124	1,310	1,092	981
Labor ($)	12,735	14,842	10,603	9,526
Material ($)	21,041	24,523	20,442	18,364
Overhead ($)	8,992	10,480	8,736	7,848

a. Use the multifactor productivity ratio to see whether recent process improvements had any effect and, if so, when the effect was noticeable.

b. Has labor productivity changed? Use the labor productivity ratio to support your answer.

2. Alyssa's Custom Cakes currently sells 5 birthday, 2 wedding, and 3 specialty cakes each month for $50, $150, and $100 each, respectively. The cost of labor is $50 per hour including benefits. It takes 90 minutes to produce a birthday cake, 240 minutes to produce a wedding cake, and 60 minutes to produce a specialty cake. Alyssa's current multifactor productivity ratio is 1.25.

a. Assuming each cake costs the same to make, what is the average cost to produce a cake?

b. Calculate Alyssa's labor productivity ratio in dollars per hour for each type of cake.

c. Based solely on the labor productivity ratio, which cake should Alyssa try to sell the most?

d. Based on your answer in part (a), is there a type of cake Alyssa should stop selling?

3. Coach Bjourn Toulouse led the Big Red Herrings to several disappointing football seasons. Only better recruiting will return the Big Red Herrings to winning form. Because of the current state of the program, Boehring University fans are unlikely to support increases in the $192 season ticket price. Improved recruitment will increase overhead costs to $30,000 per class section from the current $25,000 per class section. The university's budget plan is to cover recruitment costs by increasing the average class size to 75 students. Labor costs will

increase to $6,500 per 3-credit course. Material costs will be about $25 per student for each 3-credit course. Tuition will be $200 per semester credit, which is supplemented by state support of $100 per semester credit.

a. What is the multifactor productivity ratio?

b. If instructors work an average of 20 hours per week for 16 weeks for each 3-credit class of 75 students, what is the *labor* productivity ratio?

4. Suds and Duds Laundry washed and pressed the following numbers of dress shirts per week.

Week	Work Crew	Total Hours	Shirts
1	Sud and Dud	24	68
2	Sud and Jud	46	130
3	Sud, Dud, and Jud	62	152
4	Sud, Dud, and Jud	51	125
5	Dud and Jud	45	131

a. Calculate the *labor* productivity ratio for each week.

b. Explain the labor productivity pattern exhibited by the data.

5. CD players are produced on an automated assembly line process. The standard cost of CD players is $150 per unit (labor, $30; materials, $70; and overhead, $50). The sales price is $300 per unit.

a. To achieve a 10 percent multifactor productivity improvement by reducing materials costs only, by what percentage must these costs be reduced?

b. To achieve a 10 percent multifactor productivity improvement by reducing labor costs only, by what percentage must these costs be reduced?

c. To achieve a 10 percent multifactor productivity improvement by reducing overhead costs only, by what percentage must these costs be reduced?

Advanced Problems

6. The Big Black Bird Company (BBBC) has a large order for special plastic-lined military uniforms to be used in an urgent military operation. Working the normal two shifts of 40 hours each per week, the BBBC production process usually produces 2,500 uniforms per week at a standard cost of $120 each. Seventy employees work the first shift and 30 the second. The contract price is $200 per uniform. Because of the urgent need, BBBC is authorized to use around-the-clock production, six days per week. When each of the two shifts works 72 hours per week, production increases to 4,000 uniforms per week but at a cost of $144 each.

a. Did the multifactor productivity ratio increase, decrease, or remain the same? If it changed, by what percentage did it change?

b. Did the labor productivity ratio increase, decrease, or remain the same? If it changed, by what percentage did it change?

c. Did weekly profits increase, decrease, or remain the same?

7. Mack's guitar fabrication shop produces low cost, highly durable guitars for beginners. Typically, out of the 100 guitars that begin production each month, only 80 percent are considered good enough to sell. The other 20 percent are scrapped due to quality problems that are identified after they have completed the production process. Each guitar sells for $250. Because some of the production process is automated, each guitar only requires 10 labor hours. Each employee works an average 160 hours per month. Labor is paid at $10/hour, materials cost is $40/guitar, and overhead is $4,000.

a. Calculate the labor and multifactor productivity ratios.

b. After some study, the operations manager Darren Funk recommends 3 options to improve the company's multifactor productivity: (1) increase the sales price by 10 percent, (2) improve quality so that only 10 percent are defective, or (3) reduce labor, material, and overhead costs by 10 percent. Which option has the greatest impact on the multifactor productivity measure?

ACTIVE MODEL EXERCISE

This Active Model appears in my**om**lab. It allows you to evaluate the important elements of labor productivity.

QUESTIONS

1. Suppose that, during the summer, the company works for only four days per week. What will be the weekly number of policies processed if the productivity of five policies per hour is maintained?

2. If an employee is hired, what will be the weekly number of policies processed if the productivity of five policies per hour is maintained?

3. Suppose the 8-hour day includes a 45-minute lunch. What is the revised productivity measure, excluding lunch?

4. If the insurance company can process 60 (10 percent) more policies per week, by what percentage will the productivity measure rise?

ACTIVE MODEL 1.1 ▶
Labor Productivity Using Data from Example 1.1

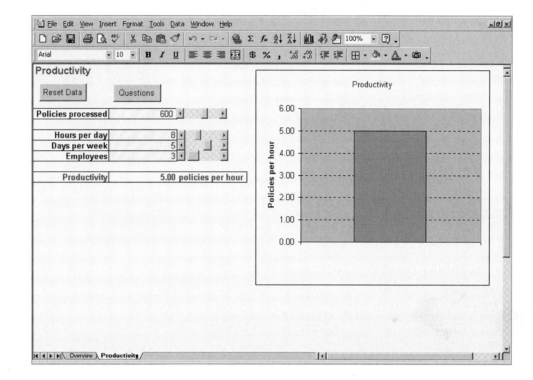

VIDEO CASE   Operations as a Competitive Weapon at Starwood

Starwood is one of the world's largest hotel companies, with more than 750 owned, managed, and franchised properties in more than 80 countries. The company's lodging brands include The Luxury Collection, St. Regis, Sheraton, Westin, Four Points, and W Hotels. Its hotels regularly appear on lists of top hotels around the world. On any given night, guests in the hotels may be individual leisure travelers, independent business guests, or part of a meeting or convention.

When guests stay at a Starwood property as part of a meeting or convention, arrangements are typically made by a meeting planner. The meeting planner works with a location to arrange meeting facilities, banquet rooms, lodging, and events for participants. Prior to 2002, the company's individual properties had their own approaches to convention planning, yet no consistent, coordinated program within or across brands made it easy for meeting planners to do business with Starwood. For example, paperwork for confirming program details, rooms, and food and beverage requirements differed between properties and brands. Some hotels had diagrams of meeting space, while others did not. Technology available for meeting rooms varied widely, and a hotel liaison was not always immediately available during the event in case a need arose.

Recognizing that Starwood's future growth and success relied heavily on its relationships with meeting planners, the company held focus groups to gather information about their needs and expectations. One clear priority emerged: consistency in the meeting planning process, whether that meeting was held at the Sheraton in New York, the Westin Kierland in Phoenix, or the W Hotel in Lakeshore, Chicago. Such a program could create consistency across all brands, and generate loyalty and increased revenues from those meeting planners who drive large volumes of business to Starwood properties annually.

As a result of the meetings, Starwood created the Starwood Preferred Planner program. Every hotel property now has the same paperwork for the meeting planning process, and shares that paperwork electronically across properties and brands. Contracts were standardized and new standards created to recognize and reward frequent VIP meeting planners. Each meeting is assigned a "Star Meeting Concierge" whose sole responsibility is to anticipate and fulfill any needs of the meeting planner during the event. Handheld Nextel radio phones are now issued at check-in to the meeting planners at no extra charge so that they have 24-hour access to the concierge.

To measure the performance of the new process, Starwood set high internal targets for scores on the surveys given to meeting planners after their events concluded. For instance, at the Luxury Collection and St. Regis brands, individual meeting scores must be 4.55 on a 5-point scale. At the Westin and W Hotels, scores must be above 4.35 on the 5-point scale. Scores from Sheraton properties must exceed 4.30, and Four Points hotels have a target of

4.25 on the 5-point scale. Because the expectations for an airport location one-day meeting (not held at the St. Regis or Luxury Collection) differ from a multiday resort experience, the targets reflect those expectations.

In 2002, Starwood standardized its operating processes so that it could measure, improve, and ultimately grow its convention business. Each meeting is assigned a Star Meeting Concierge who works closely with meeting planners.

QUESTIONS

1. What are the key inputs and outputs associated with Starwood's new meeting planning process?
2. How does the meeting planning process at Starwood interact with the following core processes in their hotels?
   a. Customer relationship (internal and external)
   b. New service or product development
   c. Order fulfillment
   d. Supplier relationship

CASE   Theorganicgrocer.com

Theorganicgrocer.com is an online supplier of organically produced fruit and vegetables. Clients within a 50 km radius of Bangor in Wales are promised next-day delivery at a time and place selected by the customer. Maria Heales, a joint owner says, "Our business has been based on market research. We've done a great deal of background work to ensure our business model works. All the early signs suggested that people would order online if the quality was good, payment was secure, the price was right and delivery could be trusted.... 'Dependability, reliability, timeliness, quality and price' were the words that sung out," she says. The service offering includes delivery, 9 a.m.

to 9 p.m., six days a week; organic produce; and customer-specified date and time of delivery. All produce is direct from the market on the day of delivery from a chilled vehicle. The Web site is updated daily to reflect current price and in-season produce. "The key to our success," Maria says, "is the simplicity of use of our Web site."

Vehicle route planning ensures deliveries are optimized, and aggregated stock ordering means only produce previously ordered by customers is purchased. Customers' payments are made online using a secure, encrypted facility administered by a national bank. "But our business has grown, so we need to expand capacity and capability. We are no longer a fruit and 'veg' stall online!" Maria's husband and business partner, Marcus, says. Their goal now is to expand their business to include regional franchising, product range expansion and, for example, birthday gifts, filled baskets, and ready-to-eat gourmet selections. Operating from a small "lock-up" unit on the fringe of town, expansion of the business would require considerable capital investment. Moreover, the operations of the future business will be more complex.

Currently, 95 percent of the customers are households, with the remainder being local restaurants. Approximately 20 percent of their customer base generates 80 percent of the profit. Theorganicgrocer.com has a financial system—a computer application that Marcus modified to meet its needs. A separate computer package generates advertising material and mail-outs. This tends to be done by Maria when time permits. However, there is little market information to support strategic operations planning. Much of Maria and Marcus's aspiration is based on the success of their current operations and the hope that the trend continues. Whilst there are several competitors supplying online vegetables, they do not offer organic products and they have limited products. They are, however, some 20 percent cheaper than Theorganicgrocer.com.

As business has grown, there have been complaints of damaged products, and growth in customers has caused the average on-time deliveries

(plus or minus 20 minutes) to fall from 95 percent to 75 percent. All this, Maria and Marcus argue, is more reason for expanding the business.

Marcus enjoys the technical aspects of the online business, and spends much of his time modifying and improving the Web site. When necessary, he helps to consolidate customers' orders. "I think my time is better spent on Web site development," Marcus says; "It's critical for the business… if it goes down or it isn't showing current product information, then sales are jeopardized." Presently, Maria takes responsibility for placing orders to their thirty suppliers. Maria and the delivery drivers pack customer orders into salvaged cardboard boxes that are of various sizes and often damaged. "But at least they are free!" she laughs.

QUESTIONS

1. What are the comparative operational differences of a conventional "bricks and mortar" grocery to an online operation? What are the comparative value chains for each system?

2. What are the key processes in the online operation?

3. Where are the possible operational problem areas of their online business, now and in the future?

4. What operational improvements need to be taken now to improve competitiveness?

Source: This fictional case was prepared by Dr. David Parker, The University of Queensland, Business School, as a basis of classroom discussion.

SELECTED REFERENCES

Berry, W. L., C. Bozarth, T. Hill, and J. E. Klompmaker. "Factory Focus: Segmenting Markets from an Operations Perspective." *Journal of Operations Management*, vol. 10, no. 3 (1991), pp. 363–387.

Blackburn, Joseph. *Time-Based Competition: The Next Battle-Ground in American Manufacturing.* Homewood, IL: Business One-Irwin, 1991.

Chase, R. B., and U. M. Apte. "A History of Research in Service Operations: What's the Big Idea?" *Journal of Operations Management*, vol. 25, no. 2 (2007), pp. 375–386.

Chatterjee, S. "Delivering Desired Outcomes Efficiently: The Creative Key to Competitive Strategy." *California Management Review*, vol. 40, no. 2 (1998), pp. 78–95.

Dewan, Sanjeev, and Haim Mendelson. "Information Technology and Time-Based Competition in Financial Markets." *Management Science*, vol. 44, no. 5 (1998), pp. 595–609.

Fitzsimmons, James A., and Mona Fitzsimmons. *Service Management.* New York: McGraw-Hill, 2005.

Gilmore, James H., and B. Joseph Pine II. "The Four Faces of Mass Customization." *Harvard Business Review*, vol. 75, no. 1 (1997), pp. 91–101.

Goldstein, Susan Meyer, Robert Johnson, JoAnn Duffy, and Jay Rao. "The Service Concept: The Missing Link in Service Design Research?" *Journal of Operations Management*, vol. 20 (2002), pp. 121–134.

Green, Heather. "The Web Smart 50." *Business Week* (November 24, 2003), pp. 82–106.

Hammer, Michael. "Deep Change: How Operational Innovation Can Transform Your Company." *Harvard Business Review* (April 2004), pp. 85–93.

Hayes, Robert H., and Gary P. Pisano. "Beyond World-Class: The New Manufacturing Strategy." *Harvard Business Review* (January–February 1994), pp. 77–86.

Hayes, Robert H., and G. P. Pisano. "Manufacturing Strategy: At the Intersection of Two Paradigm Shifts." *Production and Operations Management*, vol. 5, no. 1 (1996), pp. 25–41.

Heineke, Janelle, and Mark Davis. "The Emergence of Service Operations as an Academic Discipline." *Journal of Operations Management*, vol. 25, no. 2 (2007), pp. 364–374.

Heskett, James L., and Leonard A. Schlesenger. "The Service-Driven Service Company." *Harvard Business Review* (September–October 1991), pp. 71–81.

Hill, Terry. *Manufacturing Strategy: Text and Cases*, 3d ed. Homewood, IL: Irwin/McGraw-Hill, 2000.

"The Horizontal Corporation." *Business Week* (December 20, 1993), pp. 76–81.

Jack, Eric P., and Thomas L. Powers. "Volume Flexible Strategies in Health Services: A Research Framework." *Production and Operations Management*, vol. 13, no. 3 (2004), pp. 230–244.

Kaplan, Robert S., and David P. Norton. Balanced Scoreboard. Boston, MA: Harvard Business School Press, 1997.

King Jr., Neil. "A Whole New World." *Wall Street Journal* (September 27, 2004).

Menor, Larry J., Mohan V. Tatikonda, and Scott E. Sampson. "New Service Development: Areas for Exploitation and Exploration." *Journal of Operations Management*, vol. 20 (2002), pp. 135–157.

O'Reilly, Brian. "They've Got Mail!" *Fortune* (February 7, 2000), pp. 101–112.

Pande, Peter S., Robert P. Neuman, and Roland R. Cavanagh. *The Six Sigma Way.* New York: McGraw-Hill, 2000.

Porter, Michael. *Competitive Advantage.* New York: The Free Press, 1987.

Porter, Michael. E., and Mark. R. Kramer. "Strategy and Society: The Link Between Competitive Advantage and Corporate Social Responsibility." *Harvard Business Review*, vol. 84, no. 12 (2006), pp.78–92.

Powell, Bill. "It's All Made in China Now." *Fortune* (March 4, 2002), pp. 121–128.

Prahalad, C. K., and Venkatram Ramaswamy. "Co-Opting Customer Competence." *Harvard Business Review* (January– February 2000), pp. 79–87.

Rayport, Jeffrey F., and Bernard J. Jaworski. "Best Face Forward." *Harvard Business Review*, vol. 82, no. 12 (2003), pp. 47–58.

Roth, Aleda V., and Marjolijn van der Velde. "Operations as Marketing: A Competitive Service Strategy." *Journal of Operations Management*, vol. 10, no. 3 (1993), pp. 303–328.

Rudberg, Martin, and Jan Olhager. "Manufacturing Networks and Supply Chains: An Operations Strategy Perspective." *Omega*, vol. 31, no. 1 (2003), pp. 29–39.

Safizadeh, M. H., L. P. Ritzman, D. Sharma, and C. Wood. "An Empirical Analysis of the Product–Process Matrix." *Management Science*, vol. 42, no. 11 (1996), pp. 1576–1591.

Skinner, Wickham. "Manufacturing—Missing Link in Corporate Strategy." *Harvard Business Review* (May–June 1969), pp. 136–145.

Skinner, Wickham. "Manufacturing Strategy on the 'S' Curve." *Production and Operations Management*, vol. 5, no. 1 (1996), pp. 3–14.

Svensson, Peter. "GameStop to Sell Rain Checks for Wii." *The State* (December 18, 2007).

"Time for a Reality Check in Asia." *Business Week* (December 2, 1996), pp. 58–66.

van Biema, Michael, and Bruce Greenwald. "Managing Our Way to Higher Service-Sector Productivity." *Harvard Business Review* (July–August 1997), pp. 87–95.

Ward, Peter T., Deborah J. Bickford, and G. Keong Leong. "Configurations of Manufacturing Strategy, Business Strategy, Environment and Structure." *Journal of Management*, vol. 22, no. 4 (1996), pp. 597–626

Ward, Peter T., and Rebecca Duray. "Manufacturing Strategy in Context: Environment, Competitive Strategy and Manufacturing Strategy." *Journal of Operations Management*, vol. 18 (2000), pp. 123–138.

Wheelwright, Steven C., and H. Kent Bowen. "The Challenge of Manufacturing Advantage." *Production and Operations Management*, vol. 5, no. 1 (1996), pp. 59–77.

Womack, James P., Daniel T. Jones, and Daniel Roos. *The Machine That Changed the World.* New York: HarperPerennial, 1991.

A DECISION MAKING MODELS

LEARNING GOALS

After reading this supplement, you should be able to:

1. Explain break-even analysis, using both the graphic and algebraic approaches.

2. Define a preference matrix.

3. Identify the maximin, maximax, Laplace, minimax regret, and expected value decision rules.

4. Explain how to construct a payoff table.

5. Describe how to draw and analyze a decision tree.

Operations managers make many decisions as they manage processes and supply chains. Although the specifics of each situation vary, decision making generally involves the same basic steps: (1) recognize and clearly define the problem, (2) collect the information needed to analyze possible alternatives, and (3) choose and implement the most feasible alternative.

Sometimes, hard thinking in a quiet room is sufficient. At other times, reliance on more formal procedures is needed. Here, we present four such formal procedures: break-even analysis, the preference matrix, decision theory, and the decision tree.

- Break-even analysis helps the manager identify how much change in volume or demand is necessary before a second alternative becomes better than the first alternative.

- The preference matrix helps a manager deal with multiple criteria that cannot be evaluated with a single measure of merit, such as total profit or cost.

- Decision theory helps the manager choose the best alternative when outcomes are uncertain.

- A decision tree helps the manager when decisions are made sequentially—when today's best decision depends on tomorrow's decisions and events.

my**om**lab and the Companion Website at **www.pearsonglobaleditions.com/krajewski** contain many tools, activities, and resources designed for this supplement.

BREAK-EVEN ANALYSIS

To evaluate an idea for a new service or product, or to assess the performance of an existing one, determining the volume of sales at which the service or product breaks even is useful. The **break-even quantity** is the volume at which total revenues equal total costs. Use of this technique is known as **break-even analysis**. Break-even analysis can also be used to compare processes by finding the volume at which two different processes have equal total costs.

Evaluating Services or Products

We begin with the first purpose: to evaluate the profit potential of a new or existing service or product. This technique helps the manager answer questions, such as the following:

- Is the predicted sales volume of the service or product sufficient to break even (neither earning a profit nor sustaining a loss)?
- How low must the variable cost per unit be to break even, based on current prices and sales forecasts?
- How low must the fixed cost be to break even?
- How do price levels affect the break-even volume?

Break-even analysis is based on the assumption that all costs related to the production of a specific service or product can be divided into two categories: variable costs and fixed costs. The **variable cost**, c, is the portion of the total cost that varies directly with volume of output: costs per unit for materials, labor, and usually some fraction of overhead. If we let Q equal the number of customers served or units produced per year, total variable cost = cQ. The **fixed cost**, F, is the portion of the total cost that remains constant regardless of changes in levels of output: the annual cost of renting or buying new equipment and facilities (including depreciation, interest, taxes, and insurance); salaries; utilities; and portions of the sales or advertising budget. Thus, the total cost of producing a service or good equals fixed costs plus variable costs times volume, or

$$\text{Total cost} = F + cQ$$

The variable cost per unit is assumed to be the same no matter how small or large Q is, and thus, total cost is linear. If we assume that all units produced are sold, total annual revenues equal revenue per unit sold, p, times the quantity sold, or

$$\text{Total revenue} = pQ$$

If we set total revenue equal to total cost, we get the break-even quantity point as

$$pQ = F + cQ$$
$$(p - c)Q = F$$
$$Q = \frac{F}{p - c}$$

We can also find this break-even quantity graphically. Because both costs and revenues are linear relationships, the break-even quantity is where the total revenue line crosses the total cost line.

Sidebar definitions

break-even quantity
The volume at which total revenues equal total costs.

break-even analysis
The use of the break-even quantity; it can be used to compare processes by finding the volume at which two different processes have equal total costs.

variable cost
The portion of the total cost that varies directly with volume of output.

fixed cost
The portion of the total cost that remains constant regardless of changes in levels of output.

EXAMPLE A.1	**Finding the Break-Even Quantity**

Active Model A.1 in my**om**lab provides additional insight on this break-even example and its extensions.

A hospital is considering a new procedure to be offered at $200 per patient. The fixed cost per year would be $100,000, with total variable costs of $100 per patient. What is the break-even quantity for this service? Use both algebraic and graphic approaches to get the answer.

SOLUTION

The formula for the break-even quantity yields

$$Q = \frac{F}{p - c} = \frac{100,000}{200 - 100} = 1,000 \text{ patients}$$

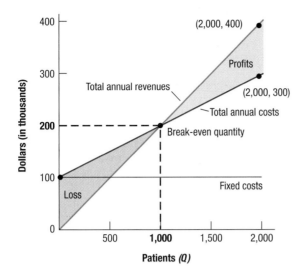

◀ **FIGURE A.1**
Graphic Approach to Break-Even
Analysis

To solve graphically we plot two lines: one for costs and one for revenues. Two points determine a line, so we begin by calculating costs and revenues for two different output levels. The following table shows the results for $Q = 0$ and $Q = 2,000$. We selected zero as the first point because of the ease of plotting total revenue (0) and total cost (F). However, we could have used any two reasonably spaced output levels.

Tutor A.1 in my**om**lab provides a new
example to practice break-even
analysis.

Quantity (patients) (Q)	Total Annual Cost ($) (100,000 + 100$Q$)	Total Annual Revenue ($) (200$Q$)
0	100,000	0
2,000	300,000	400,000

We can now draw the cost line through points (0, 100,000) and (2,000, 300,000). The revenue line goes between (0, 0) and (2,000, 400,000). As Figure A.1 indicates, these two lines intersect at 1,000 patients, the break-even quantity.

DECISION POINT

Management expects the number of patients needing the new procedure will exceed the 1,000-patient break-even quantity but first wants to learn how sensitive the decision is to demand levels before making a final choice.

Break-even analysis cannot tell a manager whether to pursue a new service or product idea or drop an existing line. The technique can only show what is likely to happen for various forecasts of costs and sales volumes. To evaluate a variety of "what-if" questions, we use an approach called **sensitivity analysis**, a technique for systematically changing parameters in a model to determine the effects of such changes. The concept can be applied later to other techniques, such as linear programming. Here we assess the sensitivity of total profit to different pricing strategies, sales volume forecasts, or cost estimates.

sensitivity analysis

A technique for systematically changing
parameters in a model to determine the
effects of such changes.

EXAMPLE A.2	Sensitivity Analysis of Sales Forecasts

The same hospital featured in Example A.1 performs a sensitivity analysis of its new procedure. What will happen if 1,200 patients have this new procedure? Will the hospital make a profit? If so, how much? Consult Figure A.1.

SOLUTION

Figure A.1 shows that a sales figure of 1,200 new procedures surpasses the break-even volume of 1,000. This means the hospital will earn a profit. The product's total contribution, found by subtracting total costs from total revenues, is

$$pQ - (F + cQ) = 200(1,200) - [100,000 + 100(1,200)]$$
$$= 240,000 - 220,000$$
$$= \$20,000$$

DECISION POINT

The new procedure is forecast to contribute $20,000 in profit per year. Management should evaluate the proposal according to the present value method and then add the new procedure to the hospital's services.

Evaluating Processes

Often, choices must be made between two processes or between an internal process and buying services or materials on the outside. In such cases, we assume that the decision does not affect revenues. The manager must study all the costs and advantages of each approach. Rather than find the quantity at which total costs equal total revenues, the analyst finds the quantity for which the total costs for two alternatives are equal. For the make-or-buy decision, it is the quantity for which the total "buy" cost equals the total "make" cost. Let F_b equal the fixed cost (per year) of the buy option, F_m equal the fixed cost of the make option, c_b equal the variable cost (per unit) of the buy option, and c_m equal the variable cost of the make option. Thus, the total cost to buy is $F_b + c_b Q$ and the total cost to make is $F_m + c_m Q$. To find the make-or-buy quantity, we set the two cost functions equal and solve for Q:

$$F_b + c_b Q = F_m + c_m Q$$

$$Q = \frac{F_m - F_b}{c_b - c_m}$$

The make option should be considered, ignoring qualitative factors, only if its variable costs are lower than those of the buy option. The reason is that the fixed costs for making the service or product are typically higher than the fixed costs for buying. Under these circumstances, the buy option is best if production volumes are less than the break-even quantity. Beyond that quantity, the make option becomes best.

EXAMPLE A.3	Break-Even Analysis for Make-or-Buy Decisions

Active Model A.2 in my**om**lab provides additional insight on this make-or-buy example and its extensions.

The manager of a fast-food restaurant featuring hamburgers is adding salads to the menu. For each of the two new options, the price to the customer will be the same. The make option is to install a salad bar stocked with vegetables, fruits, and toppings and let the customer assemble the salad. The salad bar would have to be leased and a part-time employee hired. The manager estimates the fixed costs at $12,000 and variable costs totaling $1.50 per salad. The buy option is to have preassembled salads available for sale. They would be purchased from a local supplier at $2.00 per salad. Offering preassembled salads would require installation and operation of additional refrigeration, with an annual fixed cost of $2,400. The manager expects to sell 25,000 salads per year.

What is the make-or-buy quantity?

SOLUTION

The formula for the break-even quantity yields the following:

$$Q = \frac{F_m - F_b}{c_b - c_m}$$
$$= \frac{12,000 - 2,400}{2.0 - 1.5} = 19,200 \text{ salads}$$

Tutor A.2 in my**om**lab provides a new example to practice break-even analysis on make-or-buy decisions.

Figure A.2 shows the solution from OM Explorer's *Break-Even Analysis* Solver. The break-even quantity is 19,200 salads. As the 25,000-salad sales forecast exceeds this amount, the make option is preferred. Only if the restaurant expected to sell fewer than 19,200 salads would the buy option be better.

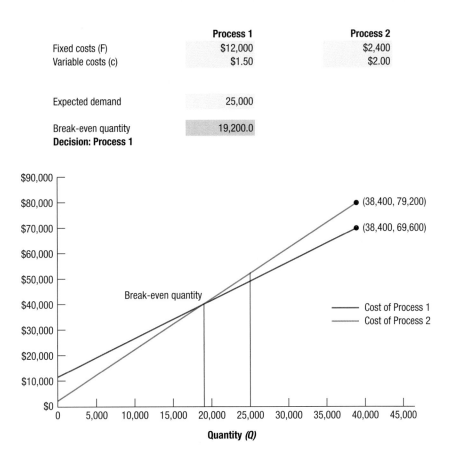

	Process 1	Process 2
Fixed costs (F)	$12,000	$2,400
Variable costs (c)	$1.50	$2.00
Expected demand	25,000	
Break-even quantity	19,200.0	

Decision: Process 1

DECISION POINT

Management chose the make option after considering other qualitative factors, such as customer preferences and demand uncertainty. A deciding factor was that the 25,000-salad sales forecast is well above the 19,200-salad break-even quantity.

PREFERENCE MATRIX

Decisions often must be made in situations where multiple criteria cannot be naturally merged into a single measure (such as dollars). For example, a manager deciding in which of two cities to locate a new plant would have to consider such unquantifiable factors as quality of life, worker attitudes toward work, and community reception in the two cities. These important factors cannot be ignored. A **preference matrix** is a table that allows the manager to rate an alternative according to several performance criteria. The criteria can be scored on any scale, such as from 1 (worst possible) to 10 (best possible) or from 0 to 1, as long as the same scale is applied to all the alternatives being compared. Each score is weighted according to its perceived importance, with the total of these weights typically equaling 100. The total score is the sum of the weighted scores (weight × score) for all the criteria. The manager can compare the scores for alternatives against one another or against a predetermined threshold.

preference matrix

A table that allows the manager to rate an alternative according to several performance criteria.

EXAMPLE A.4	Evaluating an Alternative with a Preference Matrix

The following table shows the performance criteria, weights, and scores (1 = worst, 10 = best) for a new product: a thermal storage air conditioner. If management wants to introduce just one new product and the highest total score of any of the other product ideas is 800, should the firm pursue making the air conditioner?

Tutor A.3 in my**om**lab provides a new example to practice with preference matrixes.

Performance Criterion	Weight *(A)*	Score *(B)*	Weighted Score *(A × B)*
Market potential	30	8	240
Unit profit margin	20	10	200
Operations compatibility	20	6	120
Competitive advantage	15	10	150
Investment requirement	10	2	20
Project risk	5	4	20
			Weighted score = 750

SOLUTION

Because the sum of the weighted scores is 750, it falls short of the score of 800 for another product. This result is confirmed by the output from OM Explorer's *Preference Matrix* Solver in Figure A.3.

FIGURE A.3 ▶
Preference Matrix Solver for
Example A.4

	Weight (A)	Score (B)	Weighted Score (A x B)
Market potential	30	8	240
Unit profit margin	20	10	200
Operations compatability	20	6	120
Competitive advantage	15	10	150
Investment requirement	10	2	20
Project risk	5	4	20
	Final Weighted Score		750

Buttons: Insert a Criterion | Add a Criterion | Remove a Criterion

DECISION POINT

Management should drop the thermal storage air-conditioner idea. Another new product idea is better, considering the multiple criteria, and management only wanted to introduce one new product at the time.

Not all managers are comfortable with the preference matrix technique. It requires the manager to state criteria weights before examining the alternatives, although the proper weights may not be readily apparent. Perhaps only after seeing the scores for several alternatives can the manager decide what is important and what is not. Because a low score on one criterion can be compensated for or overridden by high scores on others, the preference matrix method also may cause managers to ignore important signals. In Example A.4, the investment required for the thermal storage air conditioner might exceed the firm's financial capability. In that case, the manager should not even be considering the alternative, no matter how high its score.

DECISION THEORY

decision theory

A general approach to decision making when the outcomes associated with alternatives are often in doubt.

Decision theory is a general approach to decision making when the outcomes associated with alternatives are often in doubt. It helps operations managers with decisions on process, capacity, location, and inventory because such decisions are about an uncertain future. Decision theory can also be used by managers in other functional areas. With decision theory, a manager makes choices using the following process:

1. List the feasible *alternatives*. One alternative that should always be considered as a basis for reference is to do nothing. A basic assumption is that the number of alternatives is finite. For example, in deciding where to locate a new retail store in a certain part of the city, a manager could theoretically consider every grid coordinate on the city's map. Realistically, however, the manager must narrow the number of choices to a reasonable number.

2. List the *events* (sometimes called *chance events* or *states of nature*) that have an impact on the outcome of the choice but are not under the manager's control. For example, the

demand experienced by the new facility could be low or high, depending not only on whether the location is convenient to many customers, but also on what the competition does and general retail trends. Then group events into reasonable categories. For example, suppose that the average number of sales per day could be anywhere from 1 to 500. Rather than have 500 events, the manager could represent demand with just 3 events: 100 sales/day, 300 sales/day, or 500 sales/day. The events must be mutually exclusive and exhaustive, meaning that they do not overlap and that they cover all eventualities.

3. Calculate the *payoff* for each alternative in each event. Typically, the payoff is total profit or total cost. These payoffs can be entered into a **payoff table**, which shows the amount for each alternative if each possible event occurs. For 3 alternatives and 4 events, the table would have 12 payoffs (3 × 4). If significant distortions will occur if the time value of money is not recognized, the payoffs should be expressed as present values or internal rates of return. For multiple criteria with important qualitative factors, use the weighted scores of a preference matrix approach as the payoffs.

payoff table

A table that shows the amount for each alternative if each possible event occurs.

4. Estimate the likelihood of each event, using past data, executive opinion, or other forecasting methods. Express it as a *probability*, making sure that the probabilities sum to 1.0. Develop probability estimates from past data if the past is considered a good indicator of the future.

5. Select a *decision rule* to evaluate the alternatives, such as choosing the alternative with the lowest expected cost. The rule chosen depends on the amount of information the manager has on the event probabilities and the manager's attitudes toward risk.

Using this process, we examine decisions under three different situations: certainty, uncertainty, and risk.

Decision Making Under Certainty

The simplest situation is when the manager knows which event will occur. Here the decision rule is to pick the alternative with the best payoff for the known event. The best alternative is the highest payoff if the payoffs are expressed as profits. If the payoffs are expressed as costs, the best alternative is the lowest payoff.

EXAMPLE A.5	Decisions Under Certainty

A manager is deciding whether to build a small or a large facility. Much depends on the future demand that the facility must serve, and demand may be small or large. The manager knows with certainty the payoffs that will result under each alternative, shown in the following payoff table. The payoffs (in $000) are the present values of future revenues minus costs for each alternative in each event.

	Possible Future Demand	
Alternative	**Low**	**High**
Small facility	200	270
Large facility	160	800
Do nothing	0	0

What is the best choice if future demand will be low?

SOLUTION

In this example, the best choice is the one with the highest payoff. If the manager knows that future demand will be low, the company should build a small facility and enjoy a payoff of $200,000. The larger facility has a payoff of only $160,000. The "do nothing" alternative is dominated by the other alternatives; that is, the outcome of one alternative is no better than the outcome of another alternative for each event. Because the "do nothing" alternative is dominated, the manager does not consider it further.

DECISION POINT

If management really knows future demand, it would build the small facility if demand will be low and the large facility if demand will be high. If demand is uncertain, it should consider other decision rules.

Decision Making Under Uncertainty

Here, we assume that the manager can list the possible events but cannot estimate their probabilities. Perhaps a lack of prior experience makes it difficult for the firm to estimate probabilities. In such a situation, the manager can use one of four decision rules:

1. *Maximin.* Choose the alternative that is the "best of the worst." This rule is for the *pessimist,* who anticipates the "worst case" for each alternative.

2. *Maximax.* Choose the alternative that is the "best of the best." This rule is for the *optimist* who has high expectations and prefers to "go for broke."

3. *Laplace.* Choose the alternative with the best *weighted payoff.* To find the weighted payoff, give equal importance (or, alternatively, equal probability) to each event. If there are n events, the importance (or probability) of each is $1/n$, so they add up to 1.0. This rule is for the *realist.*

4. *Minimax Regret.* Choose the alternative with the best "worst regret." Calculate a table of regrets (or opportunity losses), in which the rows represent the alternatives and the columns represent the events. A regret is the difference between a given payoff and the best payoff in the same column. For an event, it shows how much is lost by picking an alternative to the one that is best for this event. The regret can be lost profit or increased cost, depending on the situation.

EXAMPLE A.6	Decisions Under Uncertainty

Tutor A.4 in my**om**lab provides a new example to make decisions under uncertainty.

Reconsider the payoff matrix in Example A.5. What is the best alternative for each decision rule?

SOLUTION

a. *Maximin.* An alternative's worst payoff is the *lowest* number in its row of the payoff matrix, because the payoffs are profits. The worst payoffs ($000) are

Alternative	Worst Payoff
Small facility	200
Large facility	160

The best of these worst numbers is $200,000, so the pessimist would build a small facility.

b. *Maximax.* An alternative's best payoff ($000) is the *highest* number in its row of the payoff matrix, or

Alternative	Best Payoff
Small facility	270
Large facility	800

The best of these best numbers is $800,000, so the optimist would build a large facility.

c. *Laplace.* With two events, we assign each a probability of 0.5. Thus, the weighted payoffs ($000) are

Alternative	Weighted Payoff
Small facility	0.5(200) + 0.5(270) = **235**
Large facility	0.5(160) + 0.5(800) = **480**

The best of these weighted payoffs is $480,000, so the realist would build a large facility.

d. *Minimax Regret.* If demand turns out to be low, the best alternative is a small facility and its regret is 0 (or 200 – 200). If a large facility is built when demand turns out to be low, the regret is 40 (or 200 – 160).

| Alternative | Regret | | Maximum Regret |
	Low Demand	High Demand	
Small facility	200 – 200 = **0**	800 – 270 = **530**	530
Large facility	200 – 160 = **40**	800 – 800 = **0**	40

The column on the right shows the worst regret for each alternative. To minimize the maximum regret, pick a large facility. The biggest regret is associated with having only a small facility and high demand.

DECISION POINT

The pessimist would choose the small facility. The realist, optimist, and manager choosing to minimize the maximum regret would build the large facility.

Decision Making Under Risk

Here we assume that the manager can list the events and estimate their probabilities. The manager has less information than with decision making under certainty, but more information than with decision making under uncertainty. For this intermediate situation, the *expected value* decision rule is widely used. The expected value for an alternative is found by weighting each payoff with its associated probability and then adding the weighted payoff scores. The alternative with the best expected value (highest for profits and lowest for costs) is chosen.

This rule is much like the Laplace decision rule, except that the events are no longer assumed to be equally likely (or equally important). The expected value is what the *average* payoff would be if the decision could be repeated time after time. Of course, the expected value decision rule can result in a bad outcome if the wrong event occurs. However, it gives the best results if applied consistently over a long period of time. The rule should not be used if the manager is inclined to avoid risk.

EXAMPLE A.7   Decisions Under Risk

Reconsider the payoff matrix in Example A.5. For the expected value decision rule, which is the best alternative if the probability of small demand is estimated to be 0.4 and the probability of large demand is estimated to be 0.6?

SOLUTION

The expected value for each alternative is as follows:

Alternative	Expected Value
Small facility	0.4(200) + 0.6(270) = **242**
Large facility	0.4(160) + 0.6(800) = **544**

DECISION POINT

Management would choose a large facility if it used this expected value decision rule, because it provides the best long-term results if consistently applied over time.

DECISION TREES

The decision tree method is a general approach to a wide range of operations and supply chain decisions, such as product planning, process analysis, process capacity, and location. It is particularly valuable for evaluating different capacity expansion alternatives when demand is uncertain and sequential decisions are involved. For example, a company may expand a facility in 2007 only to discover in 2010 that demand is much higher than forecasted. In that case, a second decision may be necessary to determine whether to expand again or build a second facility.

A **decision tree** is a schematic model of alternatives available to the decision maker, along with their possible consequences. The name derives from the tree-like appearance of the model. It consists of a number of square *nodes*, representing decision points, that are left by *branches* (which should be read from left to right), representing the alternatives. Branches leaving circular, or chance, nodes represent the events. The probability of each chance event, *P(E)*, is shown above each branch. The probabilities for all branches leaving a chance node must sum to 1.0. The conditional payoff, which is the payoff for each possible alternative-event combination, is shown at the end of each combination. Payoffs are given only at the outset, before the analysis begins, for the end points of each alternative-event combination. In Figure A.4, for example, payoff 1 is the financial outcome the manager expects if alternative 1 is chosen and then chance event 1 occurs. No payoff can be associated yet with any branches farther to the left, such as alternative 1 as a whole, because it is followed by a chance event and is not an end point. Payoffs often are expressed as the present value of net profits. If revenues are not affected by the decision, the payoff is expressed as net costs.

decision tree

A schematic model of alternatives available to the decision maker, along with their possible consequences.

FIGURE A.4 ▶
A Decision Tree Model

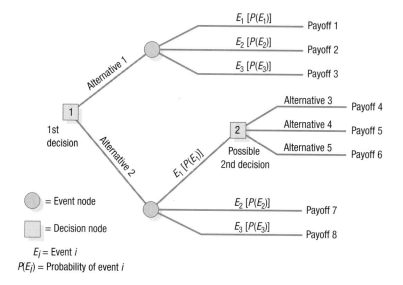

After drawing a decision tree, we solve it by working from right to left, calculating the *expected payoff* for each node as follows:

1. For an event node, we multiply the payoff of each event branch by the event's probability. We add these products to get the event node's expected payoff.

2. For a decision node, we pick the alternative that has the best expected payoff. If an alternative leads to an event node, its payoff is equal to that node's expected payoff (already calculated). We "saw off," or "prune," the other branches not chosen by marking two short lines through them. The decision node's expected payoff is the one associated with the single remaining unpruned branch. We continue this process until the leftmost decision node is reached. The unpruned branch extending from it is the best alternative to pursue. If multistage decisions are involved, we must await subsequent events before deciding what to do next. If new probability or payoff estimates are obtained, we repeat the process.

Various software is available for drawing decision trees. PowerPoint can be used to draw decision trees, although it does not have the capability to analyze the decision tree. More extensive capabilities, in addition to OM Explorer, are found with SmartDraw (www.smartdraw.com), PrecisionTree decision analysis from Palisade Corporation (www.palisade.com), and TreePlan (www.treeplan.com/treeplan.htm).

EXAMPLE A.8	Analyzing a Decision Tree

A retailer must decide whether to build a small or a large facility at a new location. Demand at the location can be either low or high, with probabilities estimated to be 0.4 and 0.6, respectively. If a small facility is built and demand proves to be high, the manager may choose not to expand (payoff = $223,000) or to expand (payoff = $270,000). If a small facility is built and demand is low, there is no reason to expand and the payoff is $200,000. If a large facility is built and demand proves to be low, the choice is to do nothing ($40,000) or to stimulate demand through local advertising. The response to advertising may be either modest or sizable, with their probabilities estimated to be 0.3 and 0.7, respectively. If it is modest, the payoff is estimated to be only $20,000; the payoff grows to $220,000 if the response is sizable. Finally, if a large facility is built and demand turns out to be high, the payoff is $800,000.

Draw a decision tree. Then analyze it to determine the expected payoff for each decision and event node. Which alternative—building a small facility or building a large facility—has the higher expected payoff?

Active Model A.3 in my**om**lab provides additional insight on this decision tree example and its extensions.

SOLUTION

The decision tree in Figure A.5 shows the event probability and the payoff for each of the seven alternative-event combinations. The first decision is whether to build a small or a large facility. Its node is shown first, to the left, because it is the decision the retailer must make now. The second decision node—whether to expand at a later date—is reached only if a small facility is built and demand turns out to be high. Finally, the third decision point—whether to advertise—is reached only if the retailer builds a large facility and demand turns out to be low.

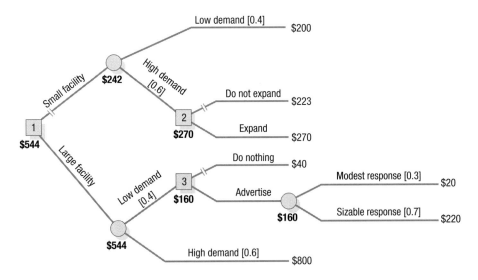

◄ **FIGURE A.5**
Decision Tree for Retailer (in $000)

Analysis of the decision tree begins with calculation of the expected payoffs from right to left, shown on Figure A.5 beneath the appropriate event and decision nodes.

1. For the event node dealing with advertising, the expected payoff is 160, or the sum of each event's payoff weighted by its probability [0.3(20) + 0.7(220)].

2. The expected payoff for decision node 3 is 160 because *Advertise* (160) is better than *Do nothing* (40). Prune the *Do nothing* alternative.

3. The payoff for decision node 2 is 270 because *Expand* (270) is better than *Do not expand* (223). Prune *Do not expand*.

4. The expected payoff for the event node dealing with demand, assuming that a small facility is built, is 242 [or 0.4(200) + 0.6(270)].

5. The expected payoff for the event node dealing with demand, assuming that a large facility is built, is 544 [or 0.4(160) + 0.6(800)].

6. The expected payoff for decision node 1 is 544 because the large facility's expected payoff is largest. Prune *Small facility*.

DECISION POINT

The retailer should build the large facility. This initial decision is the only one made now. Subsequent decisions are made after learning whether demand actually is low or high.

INTERNET RESOURCES

my**om**lab and the Companion Website at **www.pearsonglobaleditions.com/krajewski** contain many tools, activities, and resources designed for this supplement.

KEY EQUATIONS

1. Break-even quantity:

$$Q = \frac{F}{p - c}$$

2. Evaluating processes, make-or-buy indifference quantity:

$$Q = \frac{F_m - F_b}{c_b - c_m}$$

SOLVED PROBLEM 1

The owner of a small manufacturing business has patented a new device for washing dishes and cleaning dirty kitchen sinks. Before trying to commercialize the device and add it to his or her existing product line, the owner wants reasonable assurance of success. Variable costs are estimated at $7 per unit produced and sold. Fixed costs are about $56,000 per year.

a. If the selling price is set at $25, how many units must be produced and sold to break even? Use both algebraic and graphic approaches.

b. Forecasted sales for the first year are 10,000 units if the price is reduced to $15. With this pricing strategy, what would be the product's total contribution to profits in the first year?

FIGURE A.6 ▶

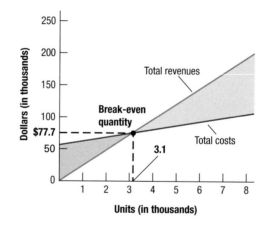

SOLUTION

a. Beginning with the algebraic approach, we get

$$Q = \frac{F}{p - c} = \frac{56,000}{25 - 7}$$
$$= 3,111 \text{ units}$$

Using the graphic approach, shown in Figure A.6, we first draw two lines:

$$\text{Total revenue} = 25Q$$

$$\text{Total cost} = 56,000 + 7Q$$

The two lines intersect at $Q = 3,111$ units, the break-even quantity.

b. Total profit contribution = Total revenue − Total cost

$$= pQ - (F + cQ)$$
$$= 15(10,000) - [56,000 + 7(10,000)]$$
$$= \$24,000$$

SOLVED PROBLEM 2

White Valley Ski Resort is planning the ski lift operation for its new ski resort. Management is trying to determine whether one or two lifts will be necessary; each lift can accommodate 250 people per day. Skiing normally occurs in the 14-week period from December to April, during which the lift will operate 7 days per week. The first lift will operate at 90 percent capacity if economic conditions are bad, the probability of which is believed to be about a 0.3. During normal times the first lift will be utilized at 100 percent capacity, and the excess crowd will provide 50 percent utilization of the second lift. The probability of normal times is 0.5. Finally, if times are really good, the probability of which is 0.2, the utilization of the second lift will increase to 90 percent. The equivalent annual cost of installing a new lift, recognizing the time value of money and the lift's economic life, is $50,000. The annual cost of installing two lifts is only $90,000 if both are purchased at the same time. If used at all, each lift costs $200,000 to operate, no matter how low or high its utilization rate. Lift tickets cost $20 per customer per day.

Should the resort purchase one lift or two?

SOLUTION

The decision tree is shown in Figure A.7. The payoff ($000) for each alternative-event branch is shown in the following table. The total revenues from one lift operating at 100 percent

Alternative	Economic Condition	Payoff Calculation (Revenue – Cost)
One lift	Bad times	0.9(490) – (50 + 200) = 191
	Normal times	1.0(490) – (50 + 200) = 240
	Good times	1.0(490) – (50 + 200) = 240
Two lifts	Bad times	0.9(490) – (90 + 200) = 151
	Normal times	1.5(490) – (90 + 400) = 245
	Good times	1.9(490) – (90 + 400) = 441

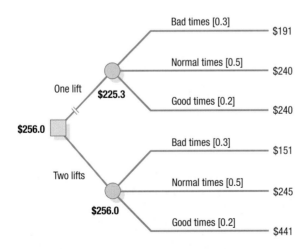

◀ FIGURE A.7

SOLVED PROBLEM 3

A textile factory in Turkey is screening three new textile ideas, A, B, and C. Resource constraints allow the factory to produce only one of them. The table below shows the performance criteria and rating, on a scale of 1 (worst) to 10 (best). The factory managers give equal weights to the performance criteria. Which is the best alternative, as indicated by the preference matrix method?

	Rating		
Performance Criterion	**Product A**	**Product B**	**Product C**
1. Project risk	5	7	7
2. Similarity to present products	6	8	4
3. Expected return on investment (ROI)	4	7	8
4. Market potential	7	7	5
5. Compatibility with current manufacturing process	5	2	8

SOLUTION

Each of the five criteria receives a weight of 1/5 or 0.20.

Product	Calculation	Total Score
A	$(0.20 \times 5) + (0.20 \times 6) + (0.20 \times 4) + (0.20 \times 7) + (0.20 \times 5)$	$= 5.4$
B	$(0.20 \times 7) + (0.20 \times 8) + (0.20 \times 7) + (0.20 \times 7) + (0.20 \times 2)$	$= 6.2$
C	$(0.20 \times 7) + (0.20 \times 4) + (0.20 \times 8) + (0.20 \times 5) + (0.20 \times 8)$	$= 6.4$

The best choice is Product C. Product B scored almost as well, but Product C is well ahead in terms of total weighted score.

SOLVED PROBLEM 4

Tutor A.6 in my**om**lab examines decisions under uncertainty for a location example.

Adele Weiss manages the campus flower shop. Flowers must be ordered three days in advance from her supplier in Mexico. Although Valentine's Day is fast approaching, sales are almost entirely last-minute, impulse purchases. Advance sales are so small that Weiss has no way to estimate the probability of low (25 dozen), medium (60 dozen), or high (130 dozen) demand for red roses on the big day. She buys roses for $15 per dozen and sells them for $40 per dozen. Construct a payoff table. Which decision is indicated by each of the following decision criteria?

  a. Maximin

  b. Maximax

  c. Laplace

  d. Minimax regret

SOLUTION

The payoff table for this problem is

	Demand for Red Roses		
Alternative	**Low (25 dozen)**	**Medium (60 dozen)**	**High (130 dozen)**
Order 25 dozen	$625	$625	$625
Order 60 dozen	$100	$1,500	$1,500
Order 130 dozen	($950)	$450	$3,250
Do nothing	$0	$0	$0

a. Under the maximin criteria, Weiss should order 25 dozen, because if demand is low, Weiss's profits are $625, the best of the worst payoffs.

b. Under the maximax criteria, Weiss should order 130 dozen. The greatest possible payoff, $3,250, is associated with the largest order.

c. Under the Laplace criteria, Weiss should order 60 dozen. Equally weighted payoffs for ordering 25, 60, and 130 dozen are about $625, $1,033, and $917, respectively.

d. Under the minimax regret criteria, Weiss should order 130 dozen. The maximum regret of ordering 25 dozen occurs if demand is high: $3,250 – $625 = $2,625. The maximum regret of ordering 60 dozen occurs if demand is high: $3,250 – $1,500 = $1,750. The maximum regret of ordering 130 dozen occurs if demand is low: $625 – (–$950) = $1,575.

PROBLEMS

Software, such as OM Explorer, Active Models, and POM for Windows, is available in my**om**lab. Check with your instructor on how best to use it. In many cases, the instructor wants you to understand how to do the calculations by hand. At most, the software provides a check on your calculations. When calculations are particularly complex and the goal is interpreting the results in making decisions, the software replaces entirely the manual calculations.

BREAK-EVEN ANALYSIS

1. Tri-County G&T sells 150,000 MWh per year of electrical power to Boulder at $75 per MWh, has fixed costs of $82.5 million per year, and has variable costs of $25 per MWh. If Tri-County has 1,000,000 MWh of demand from its customers (other than Boulder) what will Tri-County have to charge to break even?

2. Earthquake, drought, fire, economic famine, flood, and a pestilence of TV court reporters have caused an exodus from the City of Angels to Boulder, Colorado. The sudden increase in demand is straining the capacity of Boulder's electrical system. Boulder's alternatives have been reduced to buying 150,000 MWh of electric power from Tri-County G&T at a price of $75 per MWh, or refurbishing and recommissioning the abandoned Pearl Street Power Station in downtown Boulder. Fixed costs of that project are $10 million per year, and variable costs would be $35 per MWh. Should Boulder build or buy?

3. The Tri-County Generation and Transmission Association is a nonprofit cooperative organization that provides electrical service to rural customers. Based on a faulty long-range demand forecast, Tri-County overbuilt its generation and distribution system. Tri-County now has much more capacity than it needs to serve its customers. Fixed costs, mostly debt service on investment in plant and equipment, are $82.5 million per year. Variable costs, mostly fossil fuel costs, are $25 per megawatt-hour (MWh, or million watts of power used for one hour). The new person in charge of demand forecasting prepared a short-range forecast for use in next year's budgeting process. That forecast calls for Tri-County customers to consume 1 million MWh of energy next year.

   a. How much will Tri-County need to charge its customers per MWh to break even next year?

   b. The Tri-County customers balk at that price and conserve electrical energy. Only 95 percent of forecasted demand materializes. What is the resulting surplus or loss for this nonprofit organization?

4. Techno Corporation is currently manufacturing an item at variable costs of $5 per unit. Annual fixed costs of manufacturing this item are $140,000. The current selling price of the item is $10 per unit, and the annual sales volume is 30,000 units.

   a. Techno can substantially improve the item's quality by installing new equipment at additional annual fixed costs of $60,000. Variable costs per unit would increase by $1, but, as more of the better-quality product could be sold, the annual volume would increase to 50,000 units. Should Techno buy the new equipment and maintain the current price of the item? Why or why not?

   b. Alternatively, Techno could increase the selling price to $11 per unit. However, the annual sales volume would be limited to 45,000 units. Should Techno buy the new equipment and raise the price of the item? Why or why not?

5. Hahn Manufacturing purchases a key component of one of its products from a local supplier. The current purchase price is $1,500 per unit. Efforts to standardize parts succeeded to the point that this same component can now be used in five different products. Annual component usage should increase from 150 to 750 units. Management wonders whether it is time to make the component in-house, rather than to continue buying it from the supplier. Fixed costs would increase by about $40,000 per year for the new equipment and tooling needed. The cost of raw materials and variable overhead would be about $1,100 per unit, and labor costs would be $300 per unit produced.

   a. Should Hahn make rather than buy?

   b. What is the break-even quantity?

   c. What other considerations might be important?

6. A news clipping service is considering modernization. Rather than manually clipping and photocopying articles of interest and mailing them to its clients, employees electronically input stories from most widely circulated publications into a database. Each new issue is searched for key words, such as a client's company name, competitors' names, type of business, and the company's products, services, and officers. When matches occur, affected clients are instantly notified via an online network. If the story is of interest, it is electronically transmitted, so the client often has the story and can prepare comments for follow-up interviews before the publication hits the street. The manual process has

fixed costs of $400,000 per year and variable costs of $6.20 per clipping mailed. The price charged the client is $8.00 per clipping. The computerized process has fixed costs of $1,300,000 per year and variable costs of $2.25 per story electronically transmitted to the client.

a. If the same price is charged for either process, what is the annual volume beyond which the automated process is more attractive?

b. The present volume of business is 225,000 clippings per year. Many of the clippings sent with the current process are not of interest to the client or are multiple copies of the same story appearing in several publications. The news clipping service believes that by improving service and by lowering the price to $4.00 per story, modernization will increase volume to 900,000 stories transmitted per year. Should the clipping service modernize?

c. If the forecasted increase in business is too optimistic, at what volume will the new process break even?

7. Gabriel Manufacturing must implement a manufacturing process that reduces the amount of toxic by-products. Two processes have been identified that provide the same level of toxic by-product reduction. The first process would incur $300,000 of fixed costs and $600 per unit of variable costs. The second process has fixed costs of $120,000 and variable costs of $900 per unit.

a. What is the break-even quantity beyond which the first process is more attractive?

b. What is the difference in total cost if the quantity produced is 800 units?

8. A restaurant is considering adding fresh brook trout to its menu. Customers would have the choice of catching their own trout from a simulated mountain stream or simply asking the waiter to net the trout for them. Operating the stream would require $10,600 in fixed costs per year. Variable costs are estimated to be $6.70 per trout. The firm wants to break even if 800 trout dinners are sold per year. What should be the price of the new item?

9. An interactive television service that costs $10 per month to provide can be sold on the information highway for $15 per client per month. If a service area includes a potential of 15,000 customers, what is the most a company could spend on annual fixed costs to acquire and maintain the equipment?

10. A product at the Jennings Company enjoyed reasonable sales volumes, but its contributions to profits were disappointing. Last year, 17,500 units were produced and sold. The selling price is $22 per unit, c is $18, and F is $80,000.

a. What is the break-even quantity for this product? Use both graphic and algebraic approaches to get your answer.

b. Jennings is considering ways to either stimulate sales volumes or decrease variable costs. Management believes that sales can be increased by 30 percent or that c can be reduced to 85 percent of its current level. Which alternative leads to higher contributions to profits, assuming that each is equally costly to implement? (*Hint:* Calculate profits for both alternatives and identify the one having the greatest profits.)

c. What is the percent change in the per-unit profit contribution generated by each alternative in part (b)?

11. Mary Williams, owner of Williams Products, is evaluating whether to introduce a new product line. After thinking through the production process and the costs of raw materials and new equipment, Williams estimates the variable costs of each unit produced and sold at $6 and the fixed costs per year at $60,000.

a. If the selling price is set at $18 each, how many units must be produced and sold for Williams to break even? Use both graphic and algebraic approaches to get your answer.

b. Williams forecasts sales of 10,000 units for the first year if the selling price is set at $14.00 each. What would be the total contribution to profits from this new product during the first year?

c. If the selling price is set at $12.50, Williams forecasts that first-year sales would increase to 15,000 units. Which pricing strategy ($14.00 or $12.50) would result in the greater total contribution to profits?

d. What other considerations would be crucial to the final decision about making and marketing the new product?

PREFERENCE MATRIX

12. You are in charge of analyzing five new product ideas and have been given the information shown in Table A.1 (1 = worst, 10 = best). Management has decided that criteria 2 and 3 are equally important and that criteria 1 and 4 are each four times as important as criterion 2. Only two new products can be introduced, and a product can be introduced only if its score exceeds 70 percent of the maximum possible total points. Which product ideas do you recommend?

TABLE A.1	ANALYSIS OF NEW PRODUCT IDEAS				
	Rating				
Performance Criterion	**Product A**	**Product B**	**Product C**	**Product D**	**Product E**
Compatibility with current manufacturing	8	7	3	6	9
Expected return on investment (ROI)	3	8	4	7	7
Compatibility with current workforce skills	9	5	7	6	5
Unit profit margin	7	6	9	2	7

13. Accel Express, Inc., collected the following information on where to locate a warehouse (1 = poor, 10 = excellent):

Location Factor	Factor Weight	Location Score A	Location Score B
Construction costs	10	8	5
Utilities available	10	7	7
Business services	10	4	7
Real estate cost	20	7	4
Quality of life	20	4	8
Transportation	30	7	6

a. Which location, A or B, should be chosen on the basis of the total weighted score?

b. If the factors were weighted equally, would the choice change?

14. The Forsite Company is screening three ideas for new services. Resource constraints allow only one idea to be commercialized at the present time. The following estimates have been made for the five performance criteria that management believes to be most important:

Performance Criterion	Rating Service A	Rating Service B	Rating Service C
Capital equipment investment required	0.6	0.8	0.3
Expected return on investment (ROI)	0.7	0.3	0.9
Compatibility with current workforce skills	0.4	0.7	0.5
Competitive advantage	1.0	0.4	0.6
Compatibility with EPA requirements	0.2	1.0	0.5

a. Calculate a total weighted score for each alternative. Use a preference matrix and assume equal weights for each performance criterion. Which alternative is best? Worst?

b. Suppose that the expected ROI is given twice the weight assigned to each of the remaining criteria. (Sum of weights should remain the same as in part (a).) Does this modification affect the ranking of the three potential services?

DECISION THEORY AND DECISION TREE

15. Benjamin Moses, chief engineer of Offshore Chemicals, Inc., must decide whether to build a new processing facility based on an experimental technology. If the new facility works, the company will realize a net profit of $20 million. If the new facility fails, the company will lose $10 million. Benjamin's best guess is that there is a 40 percent chance that the new facility will work.

What decision should Benjamin Moses make?

16. A manufacturing plant has reached full capacity. The company must build a second plant—either small or large—at a nearby location. The demand is likely to be high or low. The probability of low demand is 0.3. If demand is low, the large plant has a present value of $5 million and the small plant, $8 million. If demand is high, the large plant pays off with a present value of $18 million and the small plant with a present value of only $10 million. However, the small plant can be expanded later if demand proves to be high, for a present value of $14 million.

a. Draw a decision tree for this problem.

b. What should management do to achieve the highest expected payoff?

17. A manager is trying to decide whether to build a small, medium, or large facility. Demand can be low, average, or high, with the estimated probabilities being 0.25, 0.40, and 0.35, respectively.

A small facility is expected to earn an after-tax net present value of just $18,000 if demand is low. If demand is average, the small facility is expected to earn $75,000; it can be increased to average size to earn a net present value of $60,000. If demand is high, the small facility is expected to earn $75,000 and can be expanded to average size to earn $60,000 or to large size to earn $125,000.

A medium-sized facility is expected to lose an estimated $25,000 if demand is low and earn $140,000 if demand is average. If demand is high, the medium-sized facility is expected to earn a net present value of $150,000; it can be expanded to a large size for a net payoff of $145,000.

If a large facility is built and demand is high, earnings are expected to be $220,000. If demand is average for the large facility, the present value is expected to be $125,000; if demand is low, the facility is expected to lose $60,000.

a. Draw a decision tree for this problem.

b. What should management do to achieve the highest expected payoff?

18. A manager is trying to decide whether to buy one machine or two. If only one is purchased and demand proves to be excessive, the second machine can be purchased later. Some sales will be lost, however, because the lead time for producing this type of machine is six months. In addition, the cost per machine will be lower if both are purchased at the same time. The probability of low demand is estimated to be 0.20. The after-tax net present value of the benefits from purchasing the two machines together is $90,000 if demand is low and $180,000 if demand is high.

If one machine is purchased and demand is low, the net present value is $120,000. If demand is high, the manager has three options. Doing nothing has a net present value of $120,000; subcontracting, $160,000; and buying the second machine, $140,000.

a. Draw a decision tree for this problem.

b. How many machines should the company buy initially? What is the expected payoff for this alternative?

19. Analyze the decision tree in Figure A.8. What is the expected payoff for the best alternative? First, be sure to infer the missing probabilities.

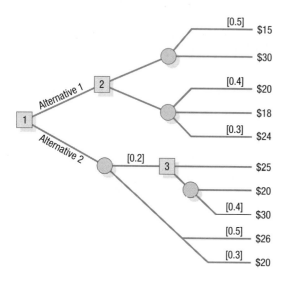

FIGURE A.8 ▲

20. Build-Rite Construction has received favorable publicity from guest appearances on a public TV home improvement program. Public TV programming decisions seem to be unpredictable, so Build-Rite cannot estimate the probability of continued benefits from its relationship with the show. Demand for home improvements next

	Demand for Home Improvements		
Alternative	**Low**	**Moderate**	**High**
Hire	($250,000)	$100,000	$625,000
Subcontract	$100,000	$150,000	$415,000
Do nothing	$50,000	$80,000	$300,000

year may be either low or high. But Build-Rite must decide now whether to hire more employees, do nothing, or develop subcontracts with other home improvement contractors. Build-Rite has developed the following payoff table:

Which alternative is best, according to each of the following decision criteria?

a. Maximin

b. Maximax

c. Laplace

d. Minimax regret

SELECTED REFERENCES

Bonini, Charles P., Warren H. Hausman, and Harold Bierman, Jr. *Quantitative Analysis for Management.* Burr Ridge Parkway, IL: Irwin/McGraw-Hill, 1996.

Clemen, Robert T. *Making Hard Decisions: An Introduction to Decision Analysis.* Boston: PWS-Kent, 1991.

2 MANAGING EFFECTIVE PROJECTS

Visitors play the Xbox 360 game "Lost Planet Extreme Conditions" at the 2006 Electronic Entertainment Expo (E3) at the Los Angeles Convention Center.

XBOX 360

In 2005, Sony dominated the $27 billion market for video games. PlayStation 2, a second generation console that used a 128-bit processor, had a commanding 67 percent share of the second-generation market. Microsoft's first attempt in the video game market, Xbox, came in a distant second with 17 percent, barely ahead of Nintendo's GameCube at 16 percent. Two of the factors contributing to Sony's success were that it was the first to market, beating Microsoft by 12 months, and that it could build on the prior success of its PlayStation 1. Four years after the introduction of Xbox, Microsoft needed to design, develop, and produce a new product quickly. Developing such a product is a project of massive proportions. The project consisted of four phases: design, analysis, development, and launch. The result was Xbox 360.

Design

The design of the Xbox 360 was a collaborative effort between Microsoft and many other firms, including Astro Studios in San Francisco, which designed the overall console and controller, IBM, which designed the processor chip, ATI, which designed the graphics chip, and a host of game design firms, to develop games for the new product. A key element of the new product was the built-in Internet access that allowed

LEARNING GOALS

After reading this chapter, you should be able to:

1. Define the major activities associated with defining, organizing, planning, monitoring, and controlling projects.

2. Identify the sequence of critical activities that determines the duration of a project.

3. Define the options available to project managers to alleviate resource problems.

4. Diagram the network of interrelated activities in a project.

5. Describe the considerations managers make in assessing the risks in a project and calculate the probability of completing a project on time.

6. Explain how to determine a minimum-cost project schedule.

gamers to access online games, buy game add-ons, and access multiplayer games developed exclusively for Xbox 360. Microsoft also included its primary manufacturers, Flextronics and Wistron, in the design process to optimize the production and assembly of the more than 1,000 parts contained in an Xbox 360.

Analysis

Getting an estimate of future sales for a new product is always difficult; however, in this case the historic patterns for PlayStation 1, PlayStation 2, and Xbox were useful. Analysts found that the peak year for a PlayStation product was 4 years after its introduction and that the life cycle for those products is about 11 years. This information provided a basis for estimating the sales potential of Xbox 360, although actual sales may be limited due to supply constraints. Nonetheless, Microsoft realized that the potential was there to open a new generation of game consoles well ahead of the market.

Development

Microsoft worked closely with Flextronics, Wistron, and the various design firms to iron out manufacturing problems in the early phases of Xbox 360 production. Once initial production was underway, Microsoft brought on Celestica to add production capacity. The decision was made to focus manufacturing operations in China. All told, 10,000 workers in China would be involved in Xbox 360 production.

Launch

The promotional campaign for Xbox 360 began on March 14, 2005, and the new gaming system was released on November 22, 2005, in the United States and Canada, closely followed by Europe and Japan. All told, the product was released in 36 countries in the first year of production, a Herculean effort requiring extensive coordination and a high level of project management skill. Sales of the Xbox 360 exceeded expectations with more than 10 million units sold in the first year alone. Nonetheless, Microsoft experienced difficulties in getting the supply chain to meet customer demands in a timely fashion. The lesson to be learned is that projects can be planned and executed properly, however, the underlying infrastructure that delivers the product is equally important in the ultimate success of the venture.

Source: David Holt, Charles Holloway, and Hau Lee, "Evolution of the Xbox Supply Chain," Stanford Graduate School of Business, Case:GS-49, (April 14, 2006); "Xbox 360," Wikipedia, the free encyclopedia, http://en.wikipedia.org/wiki/Xbox_360.

myomlab and the Companion Website at **www.pearsonglobaleditions.com/krajewski** contain many tools, activities, and resources designed for this chapter.

project

An interrelated set of activities with a definite starting and ending point, which results in a unique outcome for a specific allocation of resources.

project management

A systemized, phased approach to defining, organizing, planning, monitoring, and controlling projects.

program

An interdependent set of projects that have a common strategic purpose.

C ompanies such as Microsoft are experts at managing projects such as Xbox 360. They master the ability to schedule activities and monitor progress within strict time, cost, and performance guidelines. A **project** is an interrelated set of activities with a definite starting and ending point, which results in a unique outcome for a specific allocation of resources.

Projects are common in everyday life as well as in business. Planning weddings, remodeling bathrooms, writing term papers, and organizing surprise parties are examples of small projects in everyday life. Conducting company audits, planning mergers, creating advertising campaigns, reengineering processes, developing new services or products, and establishing a strategic alliance are examples of large projects in business.

The three main goals of any project are (1) complete the project on time or earlier, (2) do not exceed the budget, and (3) meet the specifications to the satisfaction of the customer. When we must undertake projects with some uncertainty involved, it does not hurt to have flexibility with respect to resource availability, deadlines, and budgets. Consequently, projects can be complex and challenging to manage. **Project management**, which is a systemized, phased approach to defining, organizing, planning, monitoring, and controlling projects, is one way to overcome that challenge.

Projects often cut across organizational lines because they need the skills of multiple professions and organizations. Furthermore, each project is unique, even if it is routine, requiring new combinations of skills and resources in the project process. For example, projects for adding a new branch office, installing new computers in a department, or developing a sales promotion may be initiated several times a year. Each project may have been done many times before; however, differences arise with each replication. Uncertainties, such as the advent of new technologies or the activities of competitors, can change the character of projects and require responsive countermeasures. Finally, projects are temporary because personnel, materials, and facilities are organized to complete them within a specified time frame and then are disbanded.

Projects, and the application of project management, facilitate the implementation of strategy. However, the power of this approach goes beyond the focus on one project. Operations strategy initiatives often require the coordination of many interdependent projects. Such a collection of projects is called a **program**, which is an interdependent set of projects with a common strategic purpose. As new project proposals come forward, management must assess their fit to the current operations strategy and ongoing initiatives and have a means to prioritize them because funds for projects are often limited.[1] Projects can be also used to implement changes to processes and value chains. For example, projects involving the implementation of major information technologies may affect all of a firm's core processes and supporting processes as well as some of their suppliers' and customers' processes. As such, projects are a useful tool for improving processes and supply chains.

PROJECT MANAGEMENT ACROSS THE ORGANIZATION

Even though a project may be under the overall purview of a single department, other departments likely should be involved in the project. For example, consider an information systems project to develop a corporate customer database at a bank. Many of the bank's customers are large corporations that require services spanning several departments at the bank. Because no department at the bank knows exactly what services a corporate customer is receiving from other departments, the project would consolidate information about corporate customers from many areas of the bank into one database. From this information, corporate banking services could be designed not only to better serve the corporate customers, but also to provide a basis for evaluating the prices that the bank charges. Marketing is interested in knowing all the services a customer is receiving so that it can package and sell other services that the customer may not be aware of. Finance is interested in how profitable a customer is to the bank and whether the provided services are appropriately priced. The project team, led by the information systems department, should consist of representatives from the marketing and finance

---

[1] This approach is referred to as the *project portfolio process*. See Samuel J. Mantel, Jr., Jack R. Meredith, Scott M. Shafer, and Margaret M. Sutton, *Project Management in Practice*, 2nd ed. (New York: John Wiley & Sons, 2005), pp. 26–30.

departments who have a direct interest in corporate clients. All departments in a firm benefit from sound project management practices, even if the projects remain within the purview of a single department.

DEFINING AND ORGANIZING PROJECTS

A clear understanding of a project's organization and how personnel are going to work together to complete the project are keys to success. In this section, we will address (1) defining the scope and objectives, (2) selecting the project manager and team, and (3) selecting the organizational structure.

Defining the Scope and Objectives of a Project

A thorough statement of a project's scope, time frame, and allocated resources is essential to managing the project. This statement is often referred to as the *project objective statement*. The scope provides a succinct statement of project objectives and captures the essence of the desired project outcomes in the form of major deliverables, which are concrete outcomes of the project. Changes to the scope of a project inevitably increase costs and delay completion. Collectively, changes to scope are called *scope creep* and, in sufficient quantity, are primary causes of failed projects. The time frame for a project should be as specific as possible, as in "the project should be completed by January 1, 2012." Finally, although specifying an allocation of resources to a project may be difficult during the early stages of planning, it is important for managing the project. The allocation should be expressed as a monetary figure or as full-time equivalents of personnel time. A specific statement of allocated resources makes it possible to make adjustments to the scope of the project as it proceeds.

Selecting the Project Manager and Team

Once the project is selected, a project manager must be chosen. The qualities of a good project manager should be well aligned with the roles a project manager must play.

- *Facilitator.* The project manager often must resolve conflicts between individuals or departments to ensure that the project has the appropriate resources for the job to be completed. Successful project managers have good leadership skills and a *systems view*, which encompasses the interaction of the project, its resources, and its deliverables with the firm as a whole.

- *Communicator.* Project progress and requests for additional resources must be clearly communicated to senior management and other stakeholders in a project. The project manager must also frequently communicate with the project team to get the best performance.

- *Decision Maker.* Good project managers will be sensitive to the way the team performs best and be ready to make tough decisions if necessary. The project manger must organize the team meetings, specify how the team will make decisions, and determine the nature and timing of reports to senior management.

Selecting the project team is just as important as the selection of the project manager. Several characteristics should be considered.

- *Technical Competence.* Team members should have the technical competence required for the tasks to which they will be assigned.

- *Sensitivity.* All team members should be sensitive to interpersonal conflicts that may arise. Senior team members should be politically sensitive to help mitigate problems with upper-level management.

- *Dedication.* Team members should feel comfortable solving project problems that may spill over into areas outside their immediate expertise. They should also be dedicated to getting the project done, as opposed to maintaining a comfortable work schedule.

Organizational Structure

The relationship of the project manager to the project team is determined by the firm's organizational structure. Each of the three types of organizational structure described below has its own implications for project management.

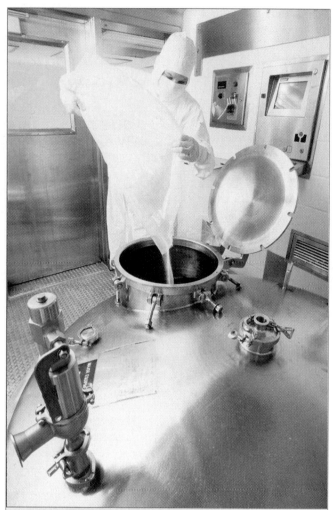

Baxter International produces products for the healthcare industry worldwide. The company uses global communication technologies to manage projects involving team members located in different parts of the world.

- *Functional.* The project is housed in a specific department or functional area, presumably the one with the most interest in the project. Assistance from personnel in other functional areas must be negotiated by the project manager. In such cases, the project manager has less control over project timing than if the entire scope of the project fell within the purview of the department.

- *Pure Project.* The team members work exclusively for the project manager on a particular project. This structure simplifies the lines of authority and is particularly effective for large projects that consist of enough work for each team member to work full time. For small projects it could result in significant duplication of resources across functional areas.

- *Matrix.* The matrix structure is a compromise between the functional and pure project structures. The project managers of the firm's projects all report to a "program manager" who coordinates resource and technological needs across the functional boundaries. The matrix structure allows each functional area to maintain control over who works on a project and the technology that is used. However, team members, in effect, have two bosses: the project manager and the department manager. Resolving these "line of authority" conflicts requires a strong project manager.

PLANNING PROJECTS

After the project is defined and organized, the team must formulate a plan that identifies the specific tasks to be accomplished and a schedule for their completion. Planning projects involves five steps: (1) defining the work breakdown structure, (2) diagramming the network, (3) developing the schedule, (4) analyzing cost–time trade-offs, and (5) assessing risks.

Defining the Work Breakdown Structure

The **work breakdown structure (WBS)** is a statement of all work that has to be completed. Perhaps the single most important contributor to delay is the omission of work that is germane to the successful completion of the project. The project manager must work closely with the team to identify all work tasks. Typically, in the process of accumulating work tasks, the team generates a hierarchy to the work breakdown. Major work components are broken down to smaller tasks by the project team. Figure 2.1 shows a WBS for a major project involving the relocation of a hospital. In the interest of better serving the surrounding community, the board of St. John's Hospital has decided to move to a new location. The project involves constructing a new hospital and making it operational. The activities at level 1 in the WBS are major work components that can be broken down into smaller tasks. For example, "Organizing and Site Preparation" can be divided into six tasks at level 2, and "Prepare Final Construction Plans" can be further divided into tasks at level 3 (not shown in Figure 2.1). It is easy to conclude that the total WBS for the hospital relocation project may include many more than 100 tasks. Regardless of the project, care must be taken to include all important tasks in the WBS to avoid project delays. Often overlooked are the tasks required to plan the project, get management approval at various stages, run pilot tests of new services or products, and prepare final reports.

An **activity** is the smallest unit of work effort consuming both time and resources that the project manager can schedule and control. Each activity in the WBS must have an "owner" who is responsible for doing the work. *Task ownership* avoids confusion in the execution of activities and assigns responsibility for timely completion. The team should have a defined procedure for assigning tasks to team members, which can be democratic (consensus of the team) or autocratic (assigned by the project manager).

work breakdown structure (WBS)

A statement of all work that has to be completed.

activity

The smallest unit of work effort consuming both time and resources that the project manager can schedule and control.

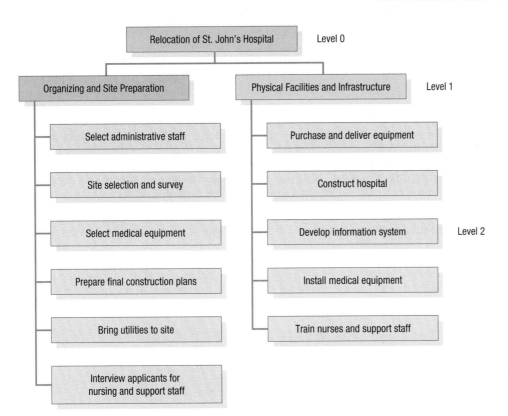

◀ **FIGURE 2.1**
Work Breakdown Structure for the
St. John's Project

Diagramming the Network

Network planning methods can help managers monitor and control projects. These methods treat a project as a set of interrelated activities that can be visually displayed in a **network diagram**, which consists of nodes (circles) and arcs (arrows) that depict the relationships between activities. Two network planning methods were developed in the 1950s. The **program evaluation and review technique (PERT)** was created for the U.S. Navy's Polaris missile project, which involved 3,000 separate contractors and suppliers. The **critical path method (CPM)** was developed as a means of scheduling maintenance shutdowns at chemical-processing plants. Although early versions of PERT and CPM differed in their treatment of activity time estimates, today the differences are minor. For purposes of our discussion, we refer to them collectively as PERT/CPM. These methods offer several benefits to project managers, including the following:

network diagram

A network planning method, designed to depict the relationships between activities, that consists of nodes (circles) and arcs (arrows).

program evaluation and review technique (PERT)

A network planning method created for the U.S. Navy's Polaris missile project in the 1950s, which involved 3,000 separate contractors and suppliers.

1. Considering projects as networks forces project teams to identify and organize the data required and to identify the interrelationships between activities. This process also provides a forum for managers of different functional areas to discuss the nature of the various activities and their resource requirements.

2. Networks enable project managers to estimate the completion time of projects, an advantage that can be useful in planning other events and in conducting contractual negotiations with customers and suppliers.

3. Reports highlight the activities that are crucial to completing projects on schedule. They also highlight the activities that may be delayed without affecting completion dates, thereby freeing up resources for other, more critical activities.

4. Network methods enable project managers to analyze the time and cost implications of resource trade-offs.

critical path method (CPM)

A network planning method developed in the 1950s as a means of scheduling maintenance shutdowns at chemical-processing plants.

Diagramming the project network involves establishing precedence relationships and estimating activity times.

Establishing Precedence Relationships A **precedence relationship** determines a sequence for undertaking activities; it specifies that one activity cannot start until a preceding activity has been completed. For example, brochures announcing a conference for executives must first be designed by the program committee (activity A) before they can be printed (activity B). In other words, activity A must *precede* activity B. For large projects, this task is essential because incorrect or omitted precedence relationships will result in costly delays. The precedence relationships are represented by a network diagram.

precedence relationship

A relationship that determines a sequence for undertaking activities; it specifies that one activity cannot start until a preceding activity has been completed.

Estimating Activity Times When the same type of activity has been done many times before, time estimates will have a relatively high degree of certainty. Several ways can be used to get time estimates in such an environment. First, statistical methods can be used if the project team has access to data on actual activity times experienced in the past (see Supplement H, "Measuring Output Rates," in my**om**lab). Second, if activity times improve with the number of replications, the times can be estimated using learning curve models (see Supplement I, "Learning Curve Analysis," in my**om**lab). Finally, the times for first-time activities are often estimated using managerial opinions based on similar prior experiences (see Chapter 13, "Forecasting Demand"). If the estimates involve a high degree of uncertainty, probability distributions for activity times can be used. We discuss how to incorporate uncertainty in project networks when we address risk assessment later in this chapter. For now, we assume that the activity times are known with certainty.

Using the Activity-On-Node Approach The diagramming approach we use in this text is referred to as the **activity-on-node (AON) network**, in which nodes represent activities and arcs represent the precedence relationships between them. Some diagramming conventions must be used for AON networks. In cases of multiple activities with no predecessors, it is usual to show them emanating from a common node called *start*. For multiple activities with no successors, it is usual to show them connected to a node called *finish*. Figure 2.2 shows how to diagram several commonly encountered activity relationships.

activity-on-node (AON) network

An approach used to create a network diagram, in which nodes represent activities and arcs represent the precedence relationships between them.

FIGURE 2.2 ▶

Diagramming Activity Relationships

AON	Activity Relationships
S → T → U	S precedes T, which precedes U.
S, T → U	S and T must be completed before U can be started.
S → T, S → U	T and U cannot begin until S has been completed.
S, T → U, V	U and V cannot begin until both S and T have been completed.
S → U, T → V	U cannot begin until both S and T have been completed; V cannot begin until T has been completed.
S → T → V, U	T and U cannot begin until S has been completed and V cannot begin until both T and U have been completed.

EXAMPLE 2.1	Diagramming the St. John's Hospital Project

Judy Kramer, the project manager for the St. John's Hospital project, divided the project into two major modules. She assigned John Stewart overall responsibility for the Organizing and Site Preparation module and Sarah Walker the responsibility for the Physical Facilities and Infrastructure module. Using the WBS shown in Figure 2.1, the project team developed the precedence relationships, activity time estimates, and activity responsibilities shown in the following table:

Activity	Immediate Predecessors	Activity Times (wks)	Responsibility
ST. JOHN'S HOSPITAL PROJECT			Kramer
START		0	
ORGANIZING and SITE PREPARATION			Stewart
A. Select administrative staff	START	12	Johnson
B. Site selection and survey	START	9	Taylor
C. Select medical equipment	A	10	Adams
D. Prepare final construction plans	B	10	Taylor
E. Bring utilities to site	B	24	Burton
F. Interview applicants for nursing and support staff	A	10	Johnson
PHYSICAL FACILITIES and INFRASTRUCTURE			Walker
G. Purchase and deliver equipment	C	35	Sampson
H. Construct hospital	D	40	Casey
I. Develop information system	A	15	Murphy
J. Install medical equipment	E, G, H	4	Pike
K. Train nurses and support staff	F, I, J	6	Ashton
FINISH	K	0	

Draw the network diagram for the hospital project.

SOLUTION

The network diagram, activities, and activity times for the hospital project are shown in Figure 2.3. The diagram depicts activities as circles, with arrows indicating the sequence in which they are to be performed. Activities A and B emanate from a *start* node because they have no immediate predecessors. The arrows connecting activity A to activities C, F, and I indicate that all three require completion of activity A before they can begin. Similarly, activity B must be completed before activities D and E can begin, and so on. Activity K connects to a *finish* node because no activities follow it. The start and finish nodes do not actually represent activities. They merely provide beginning and ending points for the network.

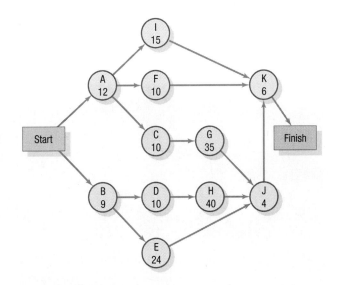

▲ FIGURE 2.3
Network Showing Activity Times for the St. John's Hospital Project

Developing the Schedule

A key advantage of network planning methods is the creation of a schedule of project activities that will help managers achieve the objectives of the project. Managers can (1) estimate the completion time of a project by finding the critical path, (2) identify the start and finish times for each activity for a project schedule, and (3) calculate the amount of slack time for each activity.

Critical Path   A crucial aspect of project management is estimating the time of completion of a project. If each activity in relocating the hospital were done in sequence, with work proceeding on only one activity at a time, the time of completion would equal the sum of the times for all the activities, or 175 weeks. However, Figure 2.3 indicates that some activities can be carried on simultaneously given adequate resources. We call each sequence of activities between the project's start and finish a **path**. The network describing the hospital relocation project has five paths: (1) A–I–K, (2) A–F–K, (3) A–C–G–J–K, (4) B–D–H–J–K, and (5) B–E–J–K. The **critical path** is the sequence of activities between a project's start and finish that takes the longest time to complete. Thus, the activities along the critical path determine the completion time of the project; that is, if one of the activities on the critical path is delayed, the entire project will be delayed. The estimated times for the paths in the hospital project network are

path

The sequence of activities between a project's start and finish.

critical path

The sequence of activities between a project's start and finish that takes the longest time to complete.

Path	Estimated Time (weeks)
A–I–K	33
A–F–K	28
A–C–G–J–K	67
B–D–H–J–K	69
B–E–J–K	43

The activity string B–D–H–J–K is estimated to take 69 weeks to complete. As the longest, it constitutes the critical path. Because the critical path defines the completion time of the project, Judy Kramer and the project team should focus on these activities and any other path that is close in length to the critical path.

Project Schedule   The typical objective is to finish the project as early as possible as determined by the critical path. The project schedule is specified by the start and finish times for each activity. For any activity, managers can use the earliest start and finish times, the latest start and finish times (and still finish the project on time), or times in between these extremes.

earliest finish time (EF)

An activity's earliest start time plus its estimated duration, t, or $EF = ES + t$.

latest finish time (LF)

The latest start time of the activity that immediately follows.

earliest start time (ES)

The earliest finish time of the immediately preceding activity.

latest start time (LS)

The latest finish time minus its estimated duration, t, or $LS = LF - t$.

- **Earliest Start and Earliest Finish Times** The earliest start and earliest finish times are obtained as follows:

    1. The **earliest finish time (EF)** of an activity equals its earliest start time plus its estimated duration, t, or $EF = ES + t$.

        The **earliest start time (ES)** for an activity is the earliest finish time of the immediately preceding activity. For activities with more than one preceding activity, ES is the latest of the earliest finish times of the preceding activities.

        To calculate the duration of the entire project, we determine the EF for the last activity on the critical path.

- **Latest Start and Latest Finish Times** To obtain the latest start and latest finish times, we must work backward from the finish node. We start by setting the latest finish time of the project equal to the earliest finish time of the last activity on the critical path.

    1. The **latest finish time (LF)** for an activity is the latest start time of the activity that immediately follows. For activities with more than one activity that immediately follow, LF is the earliest of the latest start times of those activities.

    2. The **latest start time (LS)** for an activity equals its latest finish time minus its estimated duration, t, or $LS = LF - t$.

Chinese workers labor near the Beijing Institute of Technology Gymnasium, venue for the volleyball event during the 2008 Beijing Olympic Games, in Beijing, China. The construction of more than 30 sites had to be coordinated as one large project, which was largely problem-free and ahead of schedule.

EXAMPLE 2.2   **Calculating Start and Finish Times for the Activities**

Calculate the ES, EF, LS, and LF times for each activity in the hospital project. Which activity should Kramer start immediately? Figure 2.3 contains the activity times.

SOLUTION

To compute the early start and early finish times, we begin at the start node at time zero. Because activities A and B have no predecessors, the earliest start times for these activities are also zero. The earliest finish times for these activities are

$$EF_A = 0 + 12 = 12 \text{ and } EF_B = 0 + 9 = 9$$

Because the earliest start time for activities I, F, and C is the earliest finish time of activity A,

$$ES_I = 12, ES_F = 12, \text{ and } ES_C = 12$$

Similarly,

$$ES_D = 9 \text{ and } ES_E = 9$$

After placing these ES values on the network diagram (see Figure 2.4), we determine the EF times for activities I, F, C, D, and E:

$$EF_I = 12 + 15 = 27, EF_F = 12 + 10 = 22, EF_C = 12 + 10 = 22,$$
$$EF_D = 9 + 10 = 19, \text{ and } EF_E = 9 + 24 = 33$$

The earliest start time for activity G is the latest EF time of all immediately preceding activities. Thus,

$$ES_G = EF_C = 22, ES_H = EF_D = 19$$
$$EF_G = ES_G + t = 22 + 35 = 57, EF_H = ES_H + t = 19 + 40 = 59$$

◀ FIGURE 2.4
Network Diagram Showing Start and Finish Times and Activity Slack

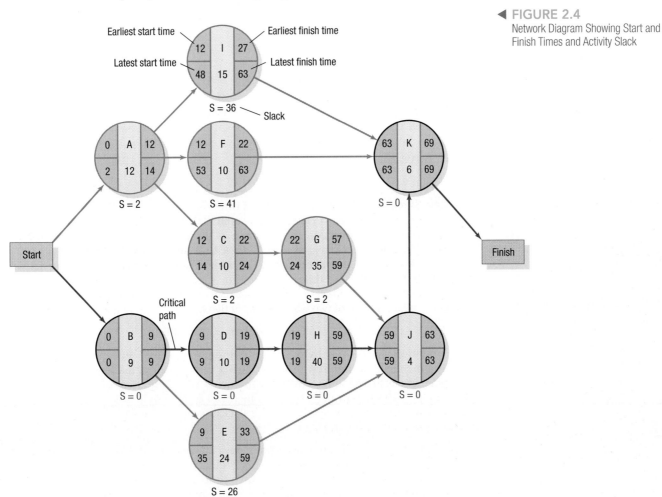

The project team can now determine the earliest time any activity can be started. Because activity J has several predecessors, the earliest time that activity J can begin is the latest of the EF times of any of its preceding activities: EF_G, EF_H, or EF_E. Thus, $EF_J = 59 + 4 = 63$. Similarly, $ES_K = 63$ and $EF_K = 63 + 6 = 69$. Because activity K is the last activity on the critical path, the earliest the project can be completed is week 69. The earliest start and finish times for all activities are shown in Figure 2.4.

To compute the latest start and latest finish times, we begin by setting the latest finish activity time of activity K at week 69, which is its earliest finish time as determined in Figure 2.4. Thus, the latest start time for activity K is

$$LS_K = LF_K - t = 69 - 6 = 63$$

If activity K is to start no later than week 63, all its predecessors must finish no later than that time. Consequently,

$$LF_I = 63, LF_F = 63, \text{ and } LF_J = 63$$

The latest start times for these activities are shown in Figure 2.4 as

$$LS_I = 63 - 15 = 48, LS_F = 63 - 10 = 53, \text{ and } LS_J = 63 - 4 = 59$$

After obtaining LS_J, we can calculate the latest start times for the immediate predecessors of activity J:

$$LS_G = 59 - 35 = 24, LS_H = 59 - 40 = 19, \text{ and } LS_E = 59 - 24 = 35$$

Similarly, we can now calculate the latest start times for activities C and D:

$$LS_C = 24 - 10 = 14 \text{ and } LS_D = 19 - 10 = 9$$

Activity A has more than one immediately following activity: I, F, and C. The earliest of the latest start times is 14 for activity C. Thus,

$$LS_A = 14 - 12 = 2$$

Similarly, activity B has two immediate followers: D and E. Because the earliest of the latest start times of these activities is 9,

$$LS_B = 9 - 9 = 0$$

DECISION POINT

The earliest or latest start times can be used for developing a project schedule. For example, Kramer should start activity B immediately because the latest start time is 0; otherwise, the project will not be completed by week 69. When the LS is greater than the ES for an activity, that activity could be scheduled for any date between ES and LS. Such is the case for activity E, which could be scheduled to start anytime between week 9 and week 35, depending on the availability of resources. The earliest start and earliest finish times and the latest start and latest finish times for all activities are shown in Figure 2.4.

activity slack

The maximum length of time that an activity can be delayed without delaying the entire project, calculated as $S = LS - ES$ or $S = LF - EF$.

Active Model 2.1 in my**omlab** provides additional insight on Gantt charts and their uses for the St. John's Hospital project.

Gantt chart

A project schedule, usually created by the project manager using computer software, that superimposes project activities, with their precedence relationships and estimated duration times, on a time line.

Activity Slack   The maximum length of time that an activity can be delayed without delaying the entire project is called **activity slack**. Consequently, *activities on the critical path have zero slack*. Information on slack can be useful because it highlights activities that need close attention. In this regard, activity slack is the amount of schedule slippage that can be tolerated for an activity before the entire project will be delayed. Slack at an activity is reduced when the estimated time duration of an activity is exceeded or when the scheduled start time for the activity must be delayed because of resource considerations. Activity slack can be calculated in one of two ways for any activity:

$$S = LS - ES \quad \text{or} \quad S = LF - EF$$

Computers calculate activity slack and prepare periodic reports for large projects, enabling managers to monitor progress. Using these reports, managers can sometimes manipulate slack to overcome scheduling problems. When resources can be used on several different activities in a project, they can be taken from activities with slack and given to activities that are behind schedule until the slack is used up. The slack for each activity in the hospital project is shown in Figure 2.4.

Gantt Chart   The project manager, often with the assistance of computer software, creates the project schedule by superimposing project activities, with their precedence relationships and estimated duration times, on a time line. The resulting diagram is called a **Gantt chart**. Figure 2.5 shows a Gantt chart for the hospital project created with Microsoft

	Task Name	Duration	Start	Finish	Predecessors
1	⊟ St John's Hospital Project	69 wks	9/14/09	1/7/11	
2	Start	0 wks	9/14/09	9/14/09	
3	⊟ Organizing and Site Prep	33 wks	9/14/09	4/30/10	
4	A. Select Staff	12 wks	9/14/09	12/4/09	2
5	B. Select Site	9 wks	9/14/09	11/13/09	2
6	C. Select Equipment	10 wks	12/7/09	2/12/10	4
7	D. Construction Plans	10 wks	11/16/09	1/22/10	5
8	E. Utilities	24 wks	11/16/09	4/30/10	5
9	F. Interviews	10 wks	12/7/09	2/12/10	4
10	⊟ Facilities and Infrastructure	57 wks	12/7/09	1/7/11	
11	G. Purchase Equipment	35 wks	2/15/10	10/15/10	6
12	H. Construct Hospital	40 wks	1/25/10	10/29/10	7
13	I. Information System	15 wks	12/7/09	3/19/10	4
14	J. Install Equipment	4 wks	11/1/10	11/26/10	8,11,12
15	K. Train Staff	6 wks	11/29/10	1/7/11	9,13,14
16	Finish	0 wks	1/7/11	1/7/11	15

▲ FIGURE 2.5
MS Project Gantt Chart for the St. John's Hospital Project Schedule

Project, a popular software package for project management. The critical path is shown in red. The chart clearly shows which activities can be undertaken simultaneously and when they should be started. You perhaps noticed that the number of calendar days between the start and finish dates for an activity is greater than the expected duration in weeks. The reason is that Microsoft Project's default setting is to schedule Saturdays and Sundays as off days. Also, Figure 2.5 shows the earliest start schedule for the project. Both the calendar and the schedule priority can be changed as needed. Gantt charts are popular because they are intuitive and easy to construct.

Analyzing Cost–Time Trade-Offs

Keeping costs at acceptable levels is almost always as important as meeting schedule dates. In this section, we discuss the use of PERT/CPM methods to obtain minimum-cost schedules.

The reality of project management is that there are always cost–time trade-offs. For example, a project can often be completed earlier than scheduled by hiring more workers or running extra shifts. Such actions could be advantageous if savings or additional revenues accrue from completing the project early. *Total project costs* are the sum of direct costs, indirect costs, and penalty costs. These costs are dependent either on activity times or on project completion time. *Direct costs* include labor, materials, and any other costs directly related to project activities. *Indirect costs* include administration, depreciation, financial, and other variable overhead costs that can be avoided by reducing total project time: The shorter the duration of the project, the lower the indirect costs will be. Finally, a project may incur penalty costs if it extends beyond some specific date, whereas a bonus may be provided for early completion. Managers can shorten individual activity times by using additional direct resources, such as overtime, personnel, or equipment. Thus, a project manager may consider *crashing*, or expediting, some activities to reduce overall project completion time and total project costs.

Cost to Crash To assess the benefit of crashing certain activities—from either a cost or a schedule perspective—the project manager needs to know the following times and costs:

1. The **normal time (NT)** is the time necessary to complete an activity under normal conditions.
2. The **normal cost (NC)** is the activity cost associated with the normal time.
3. The **crash time (CT)** is the shortest possible time to complete an activity.
4. The **crash cost (CC)** is the activity cost associated with the crash time.

normal time (NT)
The time necessary to complete an activity under normal conditions.

normal cost (NC)
The activity cost associated with the normal time.

crash time (CT)
The shortest possible time to complete an activity.

crash cost (CC)
The activity cost associated with the crash time.

FIGURE 2.6 ▲

Cost-Time Relationships in Cost Analysis

Our cost analysis is based on the assumption that direct costs increase linearly as activity time is reduced from its normal time. This assumption implies that for every week the activity time is reduced, direct costs increase by a proportional amount. For example, suppose that the normal time for activity C in the hospital project is 10 weeks and is associated with a direct cost of $4,000. We can crash its time to only 5 weeks at a total cost of $7,000; the net time reduction is 5 weeks at a net cost increase of $3,000. We assume that crashing activity C costs $3,000/5 = $600 per week—an assumption of linear marginal costs that is illustrated in Figure 2.6. Thus, if activity C were expedited by 2 weeks (i.e., its time reduced from 10 weeks to 8 weeks), the estimated direct costs would be $4,000 + 2($600) = $5,200. For any activity, the cost to crash an activity by one week is

$$\text{Cost to crash per period} \; = \; \frac{\text{CC} - \text{NC}}{\text{NT} - \text{CT}}$$

Table 2.1 contains direct cost and time data, as well as the costs of crashing per week for the activities in the hospital project.

Minimizing Costs   The objective of cost analysis is to determine the project schedule that minimizes total project costs. Suppose that project indirect costs are $8,000 per week. Suppose also that, after week 65, the Regional Hospital Board imposes on St. John's a penalty cost of $20,000 per week if the hospital is not fully operational. With a critical path completion time of 69 weeks, the hospital faces potentially large penalty costs unless the schedule is changed. For every week that the project is shortened—to week 65—the hospital saves one week of penalty *and* indirect costs, or $28,000. For reductions beyond week 65, the savings are only the weekly indirect costs of $8,000.

TABLE 2.1	DIRECT COST AND TIME DATA FOR THE ST. JOHN'S HOSPITAL PROJECT					
Activity	Normal Time (NT) (weeks)	Normal Cost (NC) ($)	Crash Time (CT) (weeks)	Crash Cost (CC) ($)	Maximum Time Reduction (week)	Cost of Crashing per Week ($)
A	12	$12,000	11	13,000	1	1,000
B	9	50,000	7	64,000	2	7,000
C	10	4,000	5	7,000	5	600
D	10	16,000	8	20,000	2	2,000
E	24	120,000	14	200,000	10	8,000
F	10	10,000	6	16,000	4	1,500
G	35	500,000	25	530,000	10	3,000
H	40	1,200,000	35	1,260,000	5	12,000
I	15	40,000	10	52,500	5	2,500
J	4	10,000	1	13,000	3	1,000
K	6	30,000	5	34,000	1	4,000
	Totals	$1,992,000		$2,209,500		

The minimum possible project duration can be found by using the crash times of each activity for scheduling purposes. However, the cost of that schedule could be prohibitive. Project managers are most interested in minimizing the costs of their projects so that budgets are not exceeded. In determining the **minimum-cost schedule**, we start with the normal time schedule and crash activities along the critical path, whose length equals the length of the project. We want to determine how much we can add in crash costs without exceeding the savings in indirect and penalty costs. The procedure involves the following steps:

minimum-cost schedule

A schedule determined by starting with the normal time schedule and crashing activities along the critical path, in such a way that the costs of crashing do not exceed the savings in indirect and penalty costs.

Step 1. Determine the project's critical path(s).

Step 2. Find the activity or activities on the critical path(s) with the lowest cost of crashing per week.

Step 3. Reduce the time for this activity until (a) it cannot be further reduced, (b) another path becomes critical, or (c) the increase in direct costs exceeds the savings that result from shortening the project. If more than one path is critical, the time for an activity on each path may have to be reduced simultaneously.

Step 4. Repeat this procedure until the increase in direct costs is larger than the savings generated by shortening the project.

EXAMPLE 2.3	Find a Minimum-Cost Schedule

Determine the minimum-cost schedule for the St. John's Hospital project. Use the information provided in Table 2.1 and Figure 2.4.

PEARSON
myomlab

Active Model 2.2 in my**om**lab provides additional insight on cost analysis for the St. John's Hospital project.

SOLUTION

The projected completion time of the project is 69 weeks. The project costs for that schedule are $1,992,000 in direct costs, 69($8,000) = $552,000 in indirect costs, and (69 − 65) ($20,000) = $80,000 in penalty costs, for total project costs of $2,624,000. The five paths in the network have the following normal times:

A–I–K:	33 weeks
A–F–K:	28 weeks
A–C–G–J–K:	67 weeks
B–D–H–J–K:	69 weeks
B–E–J–K:	43 weeks

It will simplify our analysis if we can eliminate some paths from further consideration. If all activities on A–C–G–J–K were crashed, the path duration would be 47 weeks. Crashing all activities on B–D–H–J–K results in a project duration of 56 weeks. Because the *normal* times of A–I–K, A–F–K, and B–E–J–K are less than the minimum times of the other two paths, we can disregard those three paths; they will never become critical regardless of the crashing we may do.

STAGE 1

Step 1. The critical path is B–D–H–J–K.

Step 2. The cheapest activity to crash per week is J at $1,000, which is much less than the savings in indirect and penalty costs of $28,000 per week.

Step 3. Crash activity J by its limit of three weeks because the critical path remains unchanged. The new expected path times are

A–C–G–J–K: 64 weeks and B–D–H–J–K: 66 weeks

The net savings are 3($28,000) − 3($1,000) = $81,000. The total project costs are now $2,624,000 − $81,000 = $2,543,000.

STAGE 2

Step 1. The critical path is still B–D–H–J–K.

Step 2. The cheapest activity to crash per week is now D at $2,000.

Step 3. Crash D by two weeks. The first week of reduction in activity D saves $28,000 because it eliminates a week of penalty costs, as well as indirect costs. Crashing D by a second week saves only $8,000 in indirect costs because, after week 65, no more penalty costs are incurred. These savings still exceed the cost of crashing D by two weeks. Updated path times are

A–C–G–J–K: 64 weeks and B–D–H–J–K: 64 weeks

The net savings are $28,000 + $8,000 − 2($2,000) = $32,000. Total project costs are now $2,543,000 − $32,000 = $2,511,000.

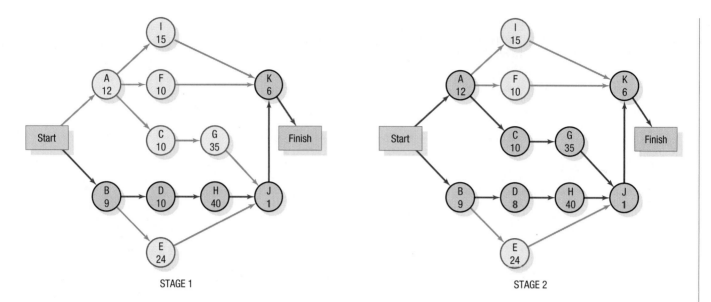

STAGE 1

STAGE 2

STAGE 3

Step 1. After crashing D, we now have two critical paths. *Both* critical paths must now be shortened to realize any savings in indirect project costs. If one is shortened and the other is not, the length of the project remains unchanged.

Step 2. Our alternatives are to crash one of the following combinations of activities—(A, B); (A, H); (C, B); (C, H); (G, B); (G, H)—or to crash activity K, which is on both critical paths (J has already been crashed). We consider only those alternatives for which the cost of crashing is less than the potential savings of $8,000 per week. The only viable alternatives are (C, B) at a cost of $7,600 per week and K at $4,000 per week. We choose activity K to crash.

Step 3. We crash activity K to the greatest extent possible—a reduction of one week—because it is on both critical paths. Updated path times are

A–C–G–J–K: 63 weeks and B–D–H–J–K: 63 weeks

The net savings are $8,000 − $4,000 = $4,000. Total project costs are $2,511,000 − $4,000 = $2,507,000.

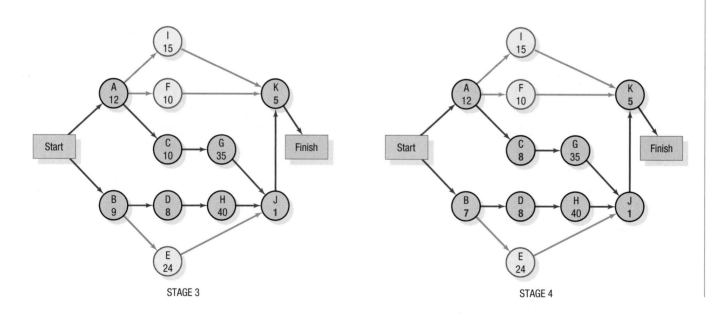

STAGE 3

STAGE 4

STAGE 4

Step 1. The critical paths are B–D–H–J–K and A–C–G–J–K.

Step 2. The only viable alternative at this stage is to crash activities B and C simultaneously at a cost of $7,600 per week. This amount is still less than the savings of $8,000 per week.

Step 3. Crash activities B and C by two weeks, the limit for activity B. Updated path times are

A–C–G–J–K: 61 weeks and B–D–H–J–K: 61 weeks

Net savings are 2($8,000) − 2($7,600) = $800. Total project costs are $2,507,000 − $800 = $2,506,200.
    The following table summarizes the analysis:

Stage	Crash Activity	Time Reduction (weeks)	Resulting Critical Path(s)	Project Duration (weeks)	Project Direct Costs, Last Trial ($000)	Crash Cost Added ($000)	Total Indirect Costs ($000)	Total Penalty Costs ($000)	Total Project Costs ($000)
0	—	—	B–D–H–J–K	69	1,992.0	—	552.0	80.0	2,624.0
1	J	3	B–D–H–J–K	66	1,992.0	3.0	528.0	20.0	2,543.0
2	D	2	B–D–H–J–K	64	1,995.0	4.0	512.0	0.0	2,511.0
			A–C–G–J–K						
3	K	1	B–D–H–J–K	63	1,999.0	4.0	504.0	0.0	2,507.0
			A–C–G–J–K						
4	B,C	2	B–D–H–J–K	61	2,003.0	15.2	488.0	0.0	2,506.2
			A–C–G–J–K						

DECISION POINT

Because the crash costs exceed weekly indirect costs, any other combination of activities will result in a net increase in total project costs. The minimum-cost schedule is 61 weeks, with a total cost of $2,506,200. To obtain this schedule, the project team must crash activities B, D, J, and K to their limits and activity C to eight weeks. The other activities remain at their normal times. This schedule costs $117,800 less than the normal-time schedule.

Assessing Risks

Risk is a measure of the probability and consequence of not reaching a defined project goal. Risk involves the notion of uncertainty as it relates to project timing and costs. Often, project teams must deal with uncertainty caused by labor shortages, weather, supply delays, or the outcomes of critical tests. In this section we discuss risk management plans and the tools managers can use to analyze the risks, such as simulation and statistical analysis, which enable managers to estimate the probability of completing a project on time and the potential for near-critical paths to affect the project completion time.

Risk-Management Plans   A major responsibility of the project manager at the start of a project is to develop a **risk-management plan**, which identifies the key risks to a project's success and prescribes ways to circumvent them. A good risk-management plan will quantify the risks, predict their impact on the project, and provide contingency plans. Project risk can be assessed by examining four categories:

risk-management plan

A plan that identifies the key risks to a project's success and prescribes ways to circumvent them.

- **Strategic Fit** The project may not be a good strategic fit in that it may not be clearly linked to the strategic goals of the firm.
- **Service/Product Attributes** If the project involves the development of a new service or product, there may be market, technological, or legal risks. There is a chance that competitors may offer a superior product, or a technological discovery may render the service or product obsolete before it even hits the market. There may also be a legal risk of potential lawsuits or liability that could force a design change after product development has begun.
- **Project Team Capability** The project team may not have the capability to complete the project successfully because of the size and complexity of the project or the technology involved.
- **Operations** There may be an operations risk because of poor information accuracy, lack of communication, missing precedence relationships, or bad estimates for activity times.

These risks should be identified and the significant ones should have contingency plans in case something goes wrong. The riskier a project is, the more likely the project will experience difficulties as Managerial Practice 2.1 shows.

Simulation PERT/CPM networks can be used to quantify risks associated with project timing. Often, the uncertainty associated with an activity can be reflected in the activity's time duration. For example, an activity in a new product development project might be developing the enabling technology to manufacture it, an activity that may take from eight months to a year. To incorporate uncertainty into the network model, probability distributions of activity times can be calculated using two approaches: computer simulation and statistical analysis. With simulation, the time for each activity is randomly chosen from its probability distribution (see Supplement B, "Simulation Models"). The critical path of the network is determined and the completion date of the project computed. The procedure is repeated many times, which results in a probability distribution for the completion date. We will have more to say about simulation when we discuss near critical paths later in this chapter.

MANAGERIAL PRACTICE 2.1 — Deadline 2004

When the city of Athens, Greece, was chosen in 1997 as the site for the 2004 Olympic Games, it was a proud moment for the Greek people. Preparing Athens for the Games would be a huge task that requires a great deal of planning, manpower, and money. Planners in Athens had a lot of work to do, starting with the building of 22 facilities. On top of that, more than 10,000 athletes would need a place to stay while competing in the Games. A total of about 75 miles of new roads, a tram system, a suburban railway, and a metro system all had to be built to allow the expected spectators, journalists, and athletes to easily move around the congested city. Existing roads and hotels also needed to be renovated. Another major and costly concern was security. The Athens Games were taking place in a post-9/11 world, so security was a high priority. The security budget for the 2004 Games was $1.2 billion, four times what it was for the Sydney Olympics just four years earlier.

Officials in Athens saw the awarding of the hosting duties as a sign that the International Olympic Committee (IOC) had confidence that the city could stage a successful Olympics. But by early 2000, the IOC was close to taking the Olympics away from Athens. What went wrong? And could anything have been done to prevent the delays, skyrocketing costs, and other issues that plagued the Athens Olympic Games?

One of the biggest problems encountered by the organizers was time. Construction of the Olympic venues started slowly, which is what led to the rebuke by the IOC. Once the construction process was finally accelerated, there was little room in the schedule for further delays. But ancient relics were found during the construction of the equestrian center, an occurrence that is common when doing any kind of excavation in history-rich Greece. Construction had to be halted at this venue while archaeologists catalogued and protected the artifacts. Labor issues and unforeseen terrain problems also delayed construction. Organizers had expected to be able to perform test runs in the venues, but many of the facilities weren't completed until just weeks before the Games began. The installation of the security system and the construction of the new transportation components also faced delays. Workers were laboring day and night to complete everything that had to be done. With no time to spare and many doubts lingering in the air, Athens made itself ready in time for the opening ceremonies.

The construction of the Olympic Games site at Athens was so far behind schedule that the International Olympic Committee seriously considered removing their license to stage the event. The facilities were completed just weeks before the start of the games.

The city of Athens did not start planning what to do with the facilities after the Games were over until after the closing ceremonies. Four years after the Games, almost all of the facilities were standing empty and unused, as the organizers discovered that they had no use for the sports facilities after the Games were over. Attempts to sell the facilities had been unsuccessful, and the government was considering tearing down some of them because of the high costs associated with maintaining the facilities.

Although the 2004 Olympics are an example of meeting major deadlines under pressure, they are also a reminder that good planning and project management are essential, especially when dealing with a large, complex project. Although planners and project managers cannot predict every possible challenge that may arise, they need to build in ways to deal with these problems so that the project can stay on budget and on time. Costly missteps in the process almost lost Athens the hosting duties for the Olympic Games.

Sources: Coral Davenport, "Athens' Olympic Preparations Come Down to the Wire," *USA Today*, August 10, 2004, http://www.usatoday.com/travel/destinations/2004-07-07-olympics-athens-preparations_x.htm; George Savvaides, "The Athens 2004 Olympic Games a Challenge and an Opportunity for Greece," March 6, 2004, http://www.greekembassy.org/embassy/content/en/Article.aspx?office=2&folder=168&article=13065; Lisa Orkin, "Athens 2004 Plans Fall Further Behind Schedule," *Independent*, March 30, 2002, http://www.independent.co.uk/sport/general/athens-2004-plans-fall-further-behind-schedule-655912.html; Canadian Press, "Montrealers Identify with Athens' Challenges.

Statistical Analysis   The statistical analysis approach requires that activity times be stated in terms of three reasonable time estimates:

1. The **optimistic time (*a*)** is the shortest time in which an activity can be completed, if all goes exceptionally well.
2. The **most likely time (*m*)** is the probable time required to perform an activity.
3. The **pessimistic time (*b*)** is the longest estimated time required to perform an activity.

With three time estimates—the optimistic, the most likely, and the pessimistic—the project manager has enough information to estimate the probability that an activity will be completed on schedule. To do so, the project manager must first calculate the mean and variance of a probability distribution for each activity. In PERT/CPM, each activity time is treated as though it were a random variable derived from a beta probability distribution. This distribution can have various shapes, allowing the most likely time estimate (*m*) to fall anywhere between the pessimistic (*b*) and optimistic (*a*) time estimates. The most likely time estimate is the *mode* of the beta distribution, or the time with the highest probability of occurrence. This condition is not possible with the normal distribution, which is symmetrical, because the normal distribution requires the mode to be equidistant from the end points of the distribution. Figure 2.7 shows the difference between the two distributions.

optimistic time (*a*)

The shortest time in which an activity can be completed, if all goes exceptionally well.

most likely time (*m*)

The probable time required to perform an activity.

pessimistic time (*b*)

The longest estimated time required to perform an activity.

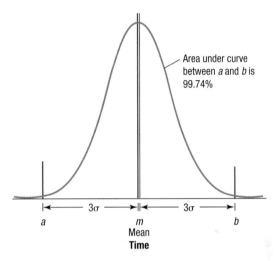

(a) **Beta distribution:** The most likely time (*m*) has the highest probability and can be placed anywhere between the optimistic (*a*) and pessimistic (*b*) times.

(b) **Normal distribution:** The mean and most likely times must be the same. If *a* and *b* are chosen to be 6σ apart, there is a 99.74% chance that the actual activity time will fall between them.

▲ FIGURE 2.7
Differences Between Beta and Normal Distributions for Project Analysis

Analysis

Two key assumptions are required. First, we assume that *a*, *m*, and *b* can be estimated accurately. The estimates might best be considered values that define a reasonable time range for the activity duration negotiated between the project manager and the team members responsible for the activities. Second, we assume that the standard deviation, σ, of the activity time is one-sixth the range *b* – *a*. Thus, the chance that actual activity times will fall between *a* and *b* is high. Why does this assumption make sense? If the activity time followed the normal distribution, six standard deviations would span approximately 99.74 percent of the distribution.

Even with these assumptions, derivation of the mean and variance of each activity's probability distribution is complex. These derivations show that the mean of the beta distribution can be estimated by using the following weighted average of the three time estimates:

$$t_e = \frac{a + 4m + b}{6}$$

Note that the most likely time has four times the weight of the pessimistic and optimistic estimates.

The variance of the beta distribution for each activity is

$$\sigma^2 = \left(\frac{b - a}{6} \right)^2$$

The variance, which is the standard deviation squared, increases as the difference between b and a increases. This result implies that the less certain a person is in estimating the actual time for an activity, the greater will be the variance.

EXAMPLE 2.4	**Calculating Means and Variances**

Suppose that the project team has arrived at the following time estimates for activity B (site selection and survey) of the St. John's Hospital project:

$$a = 7 \text{ weeks}, \ m = 8 \text{ weeks, and } b = 15 \text{ weeks}$$

a. Calculate the expected time and variance for activity B.

b. Calculate the expected time and variance for the other activities in the project.

SOLUTION

a. The expected time for activity B is

$$t_e = \frac{7 + 4(8) + 15}{6} = \frac{54}{6} = 9 \text{ weeks}$$

Note that the expected time (nine weeks) does not equal the most likely time (eight weeks) for this activity. These times will be the same only when the most likely time is equidistant from the optimistic and pessimistic times. We calculate the variance for activity B as

$$\sigma^2 = \left(\frac{15 - 7}{6} \right)^2 = \left(\frac{8}{6} \right)^2 = 1.78$$

b. The following table shows expected activity times and variances for the activities listed in the project description.

	Time Estimates (week)			**Activity Statistics**	
Activity	**Optimistic (a)**	**Most Likely (m)**	**Pessimistic (b)**	**Expected Time (t_e)**	**Variance (σ^2)**
A	11	12	13	12	0.11
B	7	8	15	9	1.78
C	5	10	15	10	2.78
D	8	9	16	10	1.78
E	14	25	30	24	7.11
F	6	9	18	10	4.00
G	25	36	41	35	7.11
H	35	40	45	40	2.78
I	10	13	28	15	9.00
J	1	2	15	4	5.44
K	5	6	7	6	0.11

DECISION POINT

The project team should notice that the greatest uncertainty lies in the time estimate for activity I, followed by the estimates for activities E and G. These activities should be analyzed for the source of the uncertainties and actions should be taken to reduce the variance in the time estimates.

Analyzing Probabilities   Because time estimates for activities involve uncertainty, project managers are interested in determining the probability of meeting project completion deadlines. To develop the probability distribution for project completion time, we assume that the duration time of one activity does not depend on that of any other activity. This assumption enables us to estimate the mean and variance of the probability distribution of the time duration of the entire project by summing the duration times and variances of the activities along the critical path. However, if one work crew is assigned two activities that can be done at the same time, the activity times will be interdependent and the assumption is not valid. In addition, if other paths in the network have small amounts of slack, one of them might become the critical path before the project is completed; we should calculate a probability distribution for those paths as well.

Because of the assumption that the activity duration times are independent random variables, we can make use of the central limit theorem, which states that the sum of a group of independent, identically distributed random variables approaches a normal distribution as the number of random variables increases. The mean of the normal distribution is the sum of the expected activity times on the path. In the case of the critical path, it is the earliest expected finish time for the project:

$T_E = \Sigma$ (Expected activity times on the critical path) = Mean of normal distribution

Similarly, because of the assumption of activity time independence, we use the sum of the variances of the activities along the path as the variance of the time distribution for that path. That is, for the critical path,

$\sigma^2 = \Sigma$ (Variances of activities on the critical path)

To analyze probabilities of completing a project by a certain date using the normal distribution, we use the z-transformation formula:

$$z = \frac{T - T_E}{\sqrt{\sigma^2}}$$

where

T = due date for the project

Given the value of z, we use the Normal Distribution appendix to find the probability that the project will be completed by time T, or sooner. An implicit assumption in this approach is that no other path will become critical during the time span of the project.

The procedure for assessing the probability of completing any activity in a project by a specific date is similar to the one just discussed. However, instead of the critical path, we would use the longest time path of activities from the start node to the activity node in question.

Near-Critical Paths   A project's duration is a function of its critical path. However, paths that are close to the same duration as the critical path may ultimately become the critical path over the life of the project. In practice, at the start of the project managers typically do not know the activity times with certainty and may never know which path was the critical path until the actual activity times are known at the end of the project. Nonetheless, this uncertainty does not reduce the usefulness of identifying the probability of one path or another causing a project to exceed its target completion time; it helps to identify the activities that need close management attention. To assess the chances of near-critical paths delaying the project completion, we can focus on the longest paths in the project network keeping in mind that both duration and variance along the path must be considered. Shorter paths with high variances could have just as much a chance to delay the project as longer paths with smaller variances. We can then estimate the probability that each path will exceed the project target completion time. We demonstrate that approach using statistical analysis in Example 2.5. Alternatively, simulation can be used to estimate the probabilities. The advantage of simulation is that you are not restricted to the use of the beta distribution for activity times. Also, activity or path dependencies, such as decision points that could involve different groups of activities to be undertaken, can be incorporated in a simulation model much more easily than with the statistical analysis approach. Fortunately, regardless of the approach used, it is rarely necessary to evaluate every path in the network. In large networks, many paths will have both short durations and low variances, making them unlikely to affect the project duration.

EXAMPLE 2.5	Calculating the Probability of Completing a Project by a Given Date

Active Model 2.3 in myomlab provides additional insight on probability analysis for the St. John's Hospital project.

Calculate the probability that St. John's Hospital will become operational in 72 weeks, using (a) the critical path and (b) path A–C–G–J–K.

SOLUTION

a. The critical path B–D–H–J–K has a length of 69 weeks. From the table in Example 2.4, we obtain the variance of path B–D–H–J–K: $\sigma^2 = 1.78 + 1.78 + 2.78 + 5.44 + 0.11 = 11.89$. Next, we calculate the z-value:

$$z = \frac{72 - 69}{\sqrt{11.89}} = \frac{3}{3.45} = 0.87$$

Length of critical path

Normal distribution: Mean = 69 weeks; σ = 3.45 weeks

Probability of meeting the schedule is 0.8078

Probability of exceeding 72 weeks is 0.1922

69 72

Project duration (weeks)

FIGURE 2.8 ▲

Probability of Completing the St. John's Hospital Project on Schedule

Using the Normal Distribution appendix, we go down the left-hand column until we arrive at the value 0.8, and then across until we arrive at the 0.07 column, which shows a tabular value of 0.8078. Consequently, we find that the probability is about 0.81 that the length of path B–D–H–J–K will be no greater than 72 weeks. Because this path is the critical path, there is a 19 percent probability that the project will take longer than 72 weeks. This probability is shown graphically in Figure 2.8.

b. From the table In Example 2.4, we determine that the sum of the expected activity times on path A–C–G–J–K is 67 weeks and that $\sigma^2 = 0.11 + 2.78 + 7.11 + 5.44 + 0.11 = 15.55$. The z-value is

$$z = \frac{72 - 67}{\sqrt{15.55}} = \frac{5}{3.94} = 1.27$$

The probability is about 0.90 that the length of path A–C–G–J–K will be no greater than 72 weeks.

DECISION POINT

The project team should be aware of the 10 percent chance that path A–C–G–J–K will cause a delay in the project. Although the probability is not high for that path, activities A, C, and G bear watching during the first 57 weeks of the project to make sure no more than 2 weeks of slippage occurs in their schedules. This attention is especially important for activity G, which has a high time variance.

MONITORING AND CONTROLLING PROJECTS

Once project planning is over, the challenge becomes keeping the project on schedule within the budget of allocated resources. In this section, we discuss how to monitor project status and resource usage. In addition, we identify the features of project management software useful for monitoring and controlling projects.

Monitoring Project Status

A good tracking system will help the project team accomplish its project goals. Effective tracking systems collect information on three topics: open issues, risks, and schedule status.

Open Issues and Risks   One of the duties of the project manager is to make sure that issues that have been raised during the project actually get resolved in a timely fashion. The tracking system should remind the project manager of due dates for open issues and who was responsible for seeing that they are resolved. Likewise, it should provide the status of each risk to project delays specified in the risk management plan so that the team can review them at each meeting. To be effective, the tracking system requires team members to update information periodically regarding their respective responsibilities.

Schedule Status   Even the best laid project plans can go awry. A tracking system that provides periodic monitoring of slack time in the project schedule can help the project manager control activities along the critical path. Periodic updating of the status of ongoing activities in the project allows the tracking system to recalculate activity slacks and indicate those activities that are behind schedule or are in danger of using up all of their slack. Management can then focus on those activities and reallocate resources as needed.

Monitoring Project Resources

Experience has shown that the resources allocated to a project are consumed at an uneven rate that is a function of the timing of the schedules for the project's activities. Projects have a *life cycle* that consists of four major phases: (1) definition and organization, (2) planning, (3) execution, and (4) close out. Figure 2.9 shows that each of the four phases requires different resource commitments.

We have already discussed the activities associated with the project definition and organization and project planning phases. The phase that takes the most resources is the *execution phase*, during which managers focus on activities pertaining to deliverables. The project schedule becomes very important because it shows when each resource devoted to a given activity will be required. Monitoring the progress of activities throughout the project is important to avoid potential overloading of resources. Problems arise when a specific resource, such as a construction crew or staff specialist, is required on several activities with overlapping schedules. Project managers have several options to alleviate resource problems, including the following:

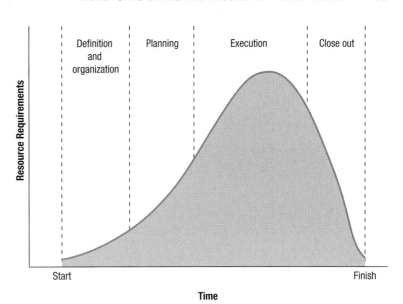

- *Resource Leveling.* The attempt to reduce the peaks and valleys in resource needs by shifting the schedules of conflicting activities within their earliest and latest start dates. Software packages such as MS Project have algorithms that move activities to avoid violating resource constraints.

▲ FIGURE 2.9
Project Life Cycle

- *Resource Allocation.* The assignment of resources to the most important activities. Most popular project management software packages have a few priority rules that can be used to decide which activity a critical resource should be scheduled to perform when conflicts arise. For example, for all the activities requiring a given resource, assign the resource to the one with the earliest start time. An activity slack report identifies potential candidates for resource shifting–shift resources from high slack activities to those behind schedule.

- *Resource Acquisition.* The addition of more of an overloaded resource to maintain the schedule of an activity. Obviously, this tactic is constrained by the project budget.

Controlling Projects

Project managers have the responsibilities of accounting for the effective use of the firm's resources as well as managing the activities to achieve the time and quality goals of the project. The firm's assets include the physical assets, human resources, and financial resources. Physical assets are controlled by the timely maintenance of machines and equipment so that their failure does not delay the project. Inventories must be received, stored for future use, and replenished. Project managers are also responsible for human resource development. Projects provide a rich environment to develop future leaders; project managers can take advantage of the situation by assigning team members important tasks to aid in their managerial development. Last, but not least, project managers must control the expenditures of the firm's financial resources. Most project management software packages contain accounting reports, budget reports, capital investment controls, and cash flow reports. Deviations from the project plan, often referred to as variances, must be periodically reported and analyzed for their causes.

Monitoring and controlling projects are ongoing activities throughout the execution phase of the project life cycle. The project **close out**, however, is an activity that many project managers forget to include in their consideration of resource usage. The purpose of this final phase in the project life cycle is to write final reports and complete remaining deliverables. An important aspect of this phase, however, is compiling the team's recommendations for improving the project process of which they were a part. Many team members will be assigned to other projects where they can apply what they learned.

close out An activity that includes writing final reports, completing remaining deliverables, and compiling the team's recommendations for improving the project process.

In this chapter we have underscored the importance of project management to any firm or organization. It affects every function and can be used to implement changes to processes and supply chains that are required for a competitive operations strategy. Effective project management begins with consideration for the scope and objectives of the project and selecting the project leader, the supporting team, and the organizational structure for the project. Beyond these important start-up issues, there are critical aspects of planning projects that must be undertaken, including defining the work breakdown structure, diagramming the network, developing the schedule, analyzing cost-time tradeoffs, and assessing the project risks. At some point in your career, you will either be part of a project team or leading it for a major project. Project management is a useful approach for implementing change in any organization.

Internet Resources

my**om**lab and the Companion Website at **www.pearsonglobaleditions.com/krajewski** contain many tools, activities, and resources designed for this chapter.

Key Equations

1. Start and finish times:

    ES = latest of the (EF times of all activities immediately preceding activity)

    EF = ES + t

    LS = LF − t

    LF = earliest of the (LS times of all activities immediately following activity)

2. Activity slack:

    S = LS − ES or S = LF − EF

3. Project costs:

    $$\text{Crash cost per period} = \frac{\text{Crash cost} - \text{Normal cost}}{\text{Normal time} - \text{Crash time}}$$

    $$= \frac{\text{CC} - \text{NC}}{\text{NT} - \text{CT}}$$

4. Activity time statistics:

    $$t_e = \frac{a + 4m + b}{6} \text{ (Expected activity time)}$$

    $$\sigma^2 = \left(\frac{b - a}{6}\right)^2 \text{ (Variance)}$$

5. z-transformation formula:

    $$z = \frac{T - T_E}{\sqrt{\sigma^2}}$$

    where

    T = due date for the project

    T_E = Σ (expected activity times on the critical path)

    = mean of normal distributions

    σ^2 = Σ (variances of activities on the critical path)

Key Terms

activity 76
activity-on-node (AON) network 78
activity slack 82
close out 93
crash cost (CC) 83
crash time (CT) 83
critical path 80
critical path method (CPM) 77
earliest finish time (EF) 80
earliest start time (ES) 80

Gantt chart 82
latest finish time (LF) 80
latest start time (LS) 80
minimum-cost schedule 84
most likely time (m) 89
network diagram 77
normal cost (NC) 83
normal time (NT) 83
optimistic time (a) 89
path 80

pessimistic time (b) 89
precedence relationship 77
program 74
program evaluation and review
    technique (PERT) 77
project 74
project management 74
risk-management plan 87
work breakdown structure (WBS) 76

Solved Problem 1

Your company has just received an order from a good customer for a specially designed electric motor. The contract states that, starting on the thirteenth day from now, your firm will experience a penalty of $100 per day until the job is completed. Indirect project costs amount to $200 per day. The data on direct costs and activity precedence relationships are given in Table 2.2.

TABLE 2.2 | ELECTRIC MOTOR PROJECT DATA

Activity	Normal Time (days)	Normal Cost ($)	Crash Time (days)	Crash Cost ($)	Immediate Predecessor(s)
A	4	1,000	3	1,300	None
B	7	1,400	4	2,000	None
C	5	2,000	4	2,700	None
D	6	1,200	5	1,400	A
E	3	900	2	1,100	B
F	11	2,500	6	3,750	C
G	4	800	3	1,450	D, E
H	3	300	1	500	F, G

a. Draw the project network diagram.

b. What completion date would you recommend?

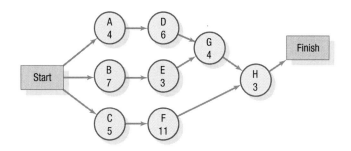

SOLUTION

a. The network diagram, including normal activity times, for this procedure is shown in Figure 2.10. Keep the following points in mind while constructing a network diagram.

1. Always have start and finish nodes.
2. Try to avoid crossing paths to keep the diagram simple.
3. Use only one arrow to directly connect any two nodes.
4. Put the activities with no predecessors at the left and point the arrows from left to right.
5. Be prepared to revise the diagram several times before you come up with a correct and uncluttered diagram.

▲ FIGURE 2.10
Network Diagram for the Electric Motor Project

b. With these activity durations, the project will be completed in 19 days and incur a $700 penalty. Determining a good completion date requires the use of the minimum-cost schedule procedure. Using the data provided in Table 2.2, you can determine the maximum crash-time reduction and crash cost per day for each activity. For example, for activity A

$$\text{Maximum crash time} = \text{Normal time} - \text{Crash time} =$$
$$4 \text{ days} - 3 \text{ days} = 1 \text{ day}$$

$$\frac{\text{Crash cost}}{\text{per day}} = \frac{\text{Crash cost} - \text{Normal cost}}{\text{Normal time} - \text{Crash time}} = \frac{\text{CC} - \text{NC}}{\text{NT} - \text{CT}} =$$

$$\frac{\$1,300 - \$1,000}{4 \text{ days} - 3 \text{ days}} = \$300$$

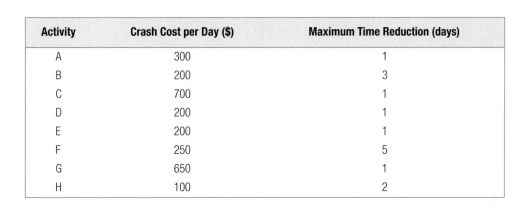

Activity	Crash Cost per Day ($)	Maximum Time Reduction (days)
A	300	1
B	200	3
C	700	1
D	200	1
E	200	1
F	250	5
G	650	1
H	100	2

Table 2.3 summarizes the analysis and the resultant project duration and total cost. The critical path is C–F–H at 19 days, which is the longest path in the network. The cheapest of these activities to crash is H, which costs only an extra $100 per day to crash. Doing so saves $200 + $100 = $300 per day in indirect and penalty costs. If you crash this activity for two days (the maximum), the lengths of the paths are now

A–D–G–H: 15 days, B–E–G–H: 15 days, and C–F–H: 17 days

The critical path is still C–F–H. The next cheapest critical activity to crash is F at $250 per day. You can crash F only two days because at that point you will have three critical paths. Further reductions in project duration will require simultaneous crashing of more than one activity (D, E, and F). The cost to do so, $650, exceeds the savings, $300. Consequently, you should stop. Note that every activity is critical. The project costs are minimized when the completion date is day 15. However, some goodwill costs may be associated with disappointing a customer who wants delivery in 12 days.

TABLE 2.3	PROJECT COST ANALYSIS								
Stage	Crash Activity	Time Reduction (days)	Resulting Critical Path(s)	Project Duration (days)	Project Direct Costs, Last Trial ($)	Crash Cost Added ($)	Total Indirect Costs ($)	Total Penalty Costs ($)	Total Project Costs ($)
0	—	—	C–F–H	19	10,100	—	3,800	700	14,600
1	H	2	C–F–H	17	10,100	200	3,400	500	14,200
2	F	2	A–D–G–H	15	10,300	500	3,000	300	14,100
			B–E–G–H						
			C–F–H						

SOLVED PROBLEM 2

An advertising project manager developed the network diagram shown in Figure 2.11 for a new advertising campaign. In addition, the manager gathered the time information for each activity, as shown in the accompanying table.

	Time Estimates (weeks)			
Activity	Optimistic	Most Likely	Pessimistic	Immediate Predecessor(s)
A	1	4	7	—
B	2	6	7	—
C	3	3	6	B
D	6	13	14	A
E	3	6	12	A, C
F	6	8	16	B
G	1	5	6	E, F

a. Calculate the expected time and variance for each activity.

b. Calculate the activity slacks and determine the critical path, using the expected activity times.

c. What is the probability of completing the project within 23 weeks?

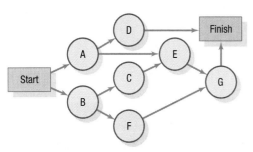

FIGURE 2.11 ▲
Network Diagram for the Advertising Project

SOLUTION

a. The expected time and variance for each activity are calculated as follows:

$$t_e = \frac{a + 4m + b}{6}$$

Activity	Expected Time (weeks)	Variance
A	4.0	1.00
B	5.5	0.69
C	3.5	0.25
D	12.0	1.78
E	6.5	2.25
F	9.0	2.78
G	4.5	0.69

b. We need to calculate the earliest start, latest start, earliest finish, and latest finish times for each activity. Starting with activities A and B, we proceed from the beginning of the network and move to the end, calculating the earliest start and finish times:

Activity	Earliest Start (weeks)	Earliest Finish (weeks)
A	0	0 + 4.0 = 4.0
B	0	0 + 5.5 = 5.5
C	5.5	5.5 + 3.5 = 9.0
D	4.0	4.0 + 12.0 = 16.0
E	9.0	9.0 + 6.5 = 15.5
F	5.5	5.5 + 9.0 = 14.5
G	15.5	15.5 + 4.5 = 20.0

Based on expected times, the earliest finish for the project is week 20, when activity G has been completed. Using that as a target date, we can work backward through the network, calculating the latest start and finish times (shown graphically in Figure 2.12):

Activity	Latest Start (weeks)	Latest Finish (weeks)
G	15.5	20.0
F	6.5	15.5
E	9.0	15.5
D	8.0	20.0
C	5.5	9.0
B	0.0	5.5
A	4.0	8.0

FIGURE 2.12 ▶

Network Diagram with All Time Estimates
Needed to Compute Slack

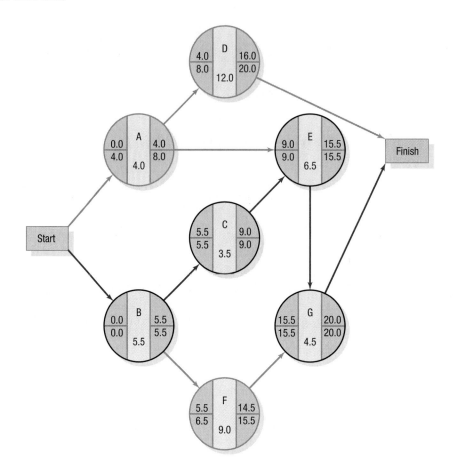

We now calculate the activity slacks and determine which activities are on the critical path:

Activity	Start (weeks) Earliest	Latest	Finish (weeks) Earliest	Latest	Slack	Critical Path
A	0.0	4.0	4.0	8.0	4.0	No
B	0.0	0.0	5.5	5.5	0.0	Yes
C	5.5	5.5	9.0	9.0	0.0	Yes
D	4.0	8.0	16.0	20.0	4.0	No
E	9.0	9.0	15.5	15.5	0.0	Yes
F	5.5	6.5	14.5	15.5	1.0	No
G	15.5	15.5	20.0	20.0	0.0	Yes

The paths, and their total expected times and variances, are

Path	Total Expected Time (weeks)	Total Variance
A–D	4 + 12 = 16	1.00 + 1.78 = 2.78
A–E–G	4 + 6.5 + 4.5 = 15	1.00 + 2.25 + 0.69 = 3.94
B–C–E–G	5.5 + 3.5 + 6.5 + 4.5 = 20	0.69 + 0.25 + 2.25 + 0.69 = 3.88
B–F–G	5.5 + 9 + 4.5 = 19	0.69 + 2.78 + 0.69 = 4.16

The critical path is B–C–E–G, with a total expected time of 20 weeks. However path B–F–G is 19 weeks and has a large variance.

c. We first calculate the z-value:

$$z = \frac{T - T_E}{\sqrt{\sigma^2}} = \frac{23 - 20}{\sqrt{3.88}} = 1.52$$

Using the Normal Distribution appendix, we find that the probability of completing the project in 23 weeks or fewer is 0.9357. Because the length of path B–F–G is close to that of the critical path and has a large variance, it might well become the critical path during the project.

DISCUSSION QUESTIONS

1. When a large project is mismanaged, it makes news. Form a discussion group and identify penalties associated with a mismanaged project in your experience or in recent headlines. Identify the cause of the problem, such as inaccurate time estimates, changed scope, unplanned or improperly sequenced activities, inadequate resources, or poor management–labor relations.

2. Describe a project in which you participated. What activities were involved and how were they interrelated? How would you rate the project manager? What is the basis of your evaluation?

3. One of your colleagues comments that software is the ultimate key to project management success. How would you respond?

PROBLEMS

Software, such as OM Explorer, Active Models, and POM for Windows is available in my**om**lab. Check with your instructor on how best to use it. In many cases, the instructor wants you to understand how to do the calculations by hand. At most, the software provides a check on your calculations. When calculations are particularly complex and the goal is interpreting the results in making decisions, the software replaces entirely the manual calculations.

1. The following information is known about a project.

Activity	Activity Time (days)	Immediate Predecessor(s)
A	7	—
B	2	A
C	4	A
D	4	B, C
E	4	D
F	3	E
G	5	E

   a. Draw the network diagram for this project.

   b. Determine the critical path and project duration.

   c. Calculate the slack for each activity.

2. A project has the following precedence relationships and activity times:

Activity	Activity Time (weeks)	Immediate Predecessor(s)
A	4	—
B	10	—
C	5	A
D	15	B, C
E	12	B
F	4	D
G	8	E
H	7	F, G

   a. Draw the network diagram.

   b. Calculate the slack for each activity. Which activities are on the critical path?

3. Consider the following data for a project:

Activity	Activity Time (days)	Immediate Predecessor(s)
A	2	—
B	4	A
C	5	A
D	2	B
E	1	B
F	8	B, C
G	3	D, E
H	5	F
I	4	F
J	7	G, H, I

a. Draw the network diagram.

b. Calculate the critical path for this project.

c. How much slack is in activities G, H, and I?

4. Barbara Gordon, the project manager for Web Ventures, Inc., compiled a table showing time estimates for each of the company's manufacturing activities of a project, including optimistic, most likely, and pessimistic.

a. Calculate the expected time, t_e, for each activity.

b. Calculate the variance, σ^2, for each activity.

Activity	Optimistic (days)	Most Likely (days)	Pessimistic (days)
A	3	8	19
B	12	15	18
C	2	6	16
D	4	9	20
E	1	4	7

5. Recently, you were assigned to manage a project for your company. You have constructed a network diagram depicting the various activities in the project (Figure 2.13). In addition, you have asked your team to estimate the amount of time that they would expect each of the activities to take.

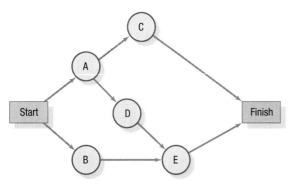

FIGURE 2.13 ▲

Network Diagram for Your Project

Their responses are shown in the following table:

Activity	Time Estimates (days)		
	Optimistic	Most Likely	Pessimistic
A	5	8	11
B	4	8	11
C	5	6	7
D	2	4	6
E	4	7	10

a. What is the expected completion time of the project?

b. What is the probability of completing the project in 21 days?

c. What is the probability of completing the project in 17 days?

6. Consider the following data for a project never before attempted by your company:

Activity	Expected Time t_e (weeks)	Immediate Predecessor(s)
A	5	—
B	3	—
C	2	A
D	5	B
E	4	C, D
F	7	D

a. Draw the network diagram for this project.

b. Identify the critical path and estimate the project's duration.

c. Calculate the slack for each activity.

7. The following information is available about a project:

Activity	Activity Time (days)	Immediate Predecessor(s)
A	3	—
B	4	—
C	5	—
D	4	—
E	7	A
F	2	B, C, D
G	4	E, F
H	6	F
I	4	G
J	3	G
K	3	H

a. Draw the network diagram.

b. Find the critical path.

8. The following information has been gathered for a project:

Activity	Activity Time (weeks)	Immediate Predecessor(s)
A	4	—
B	7	A
C	9	B
D	3	B
E	14	D
F	10	C, D
G	11	F, E

a. Draw the network diagram.

b. Calculate the slack for each activity and determine the critical path. How long will the project take?

9. Consider the following project information.

Activity	Activity Time (weeks)	Immediate Predecessor(s)
A	4	—
B	3	—
C	5	—
D	3	A, B
E	6	B
F	4	D, C
G	8	E, C
H	12	F, G

a. Draw the network diagram for this project.

b. Specify the critical path.

c. Calculate the slack for activities A and D.

d. What happens to the slack for activity D if A takes five weeks?

10. The director of continuing education at Bluebird University just approved the planning for a sales training seminar. Her administrative assistant identified the various activities that must be done and their relationships to each other, as shown in Table 2.4.

Because of the uncertainty in planning the new course, the assistant also has supplied the following time estimates for each activity:

	Time Estimates (days)		
Activity	Optimistic	Most Likely	Pessimistic
A	5	7	8
B	6	8	12
C	3	4	5
D	11	17	25
E	8	10	12
F	3	4	5
G	4	8	9
H	5	7	9
I	8	11	17
J	4	4	4

The director wants to conduct the seminar 47 working days from now. What is the probability that everything will be ready in time?

11. Table 2.5 contains information about an environmental clean-up project. Shorten the project three weeks by finding the minimum-cost schedule. Assume that project indirect costs and penalty costs are negligible. Identify activities to crash while minimizing the additional crash costs.

TABLE 2.4	ACTIVITIES FOR THE SALES TRAINING SEMINAR	
Activity	**Description**	**Immediate Predecessor(s)**
A	Design brochure and course announcement	—
B	Identify prospective teachers	—
C	Prepare detailed outline of course	—
D	Send brochure and student applications	A
E	Send teacher applications	B
F	Select teacher for course	C, E
G	Accept students	D
H	Select text for course	F
I	Order and receive texts	G, H
J	Prepare room for class	G

TABLE 2.5	ENVIRONMENTAL PROJECT DATA			
Activity	Normal Time (weeks)	Crash Time (weeks)	Cost to Crash ($ per week)	Immediate Predecessor(s)
A	7	6	200	None
B	12	9	250	None
C	7	6	250	A
D	6	5	300	A
E	1	1	—	B
F	1	1	—	C, D
G	3	1	200	D, E
H	3	2	350	F
I	2	2	—	G

12. In Solved Problem 2, estimate the probability that the noncritical path B–F–G will take more than 20 weeks. *Hint:* Subtract from 1.0 the probability that B–F–G will take 20 weeks or less.

13. You are the manager of a project to improve a billing process at your firm. Table 2.6 contains the data you will need to conduct a cost analysis of the project. Indirect costs are $1,600 per week, and penalty costs are $1,200 per week after week 12.

   a. What is the minimum-cost schedule for this project?

   b. What is the difference in total project costs between the earliest completion time of the project using "normal" times and the minimum-cost schedule you derived in part (a)?

14. Information concerning a product design project is given in Table 2.7. Indirect project costs amount to $250 per day. The company will incur a $100 per day penalty for each day the project lasts beyond day 14.

   a. What is the project's duration if only normal times are used?

   b. What is the minimum-cost schedule?

   c. What is the critical path for the minimum-cost schedule?

TABLE 2.6	DATA FOR THE BILLING PROCESS PROJECT					
Activity	Immediate Predecessor(s)	Normal Time (weeks)	Crash Time (weeks)	Normal Cost ($)	Crash Cost ($)
A	—	4	1	5,000	8,000
B	—	5	3	8,000	10,000
C	A	1	1	4,000	4,000
D	B	6	3	6,000	12,000
E	B, C	7	6	4,000	7,000
F	D	7	6	4,000	7,000

TABLE 2.7	PRODUCT DESIGN PROJECT DATA				
Activity	Normal Time (days)	Normal Cost ($)	Crash Time (days)	Crash Cost ($)	Immediate Predecessor(s)
A	5	1,000	4	1,200	—
B	5	800	3	2,000	—
C	2	600	1	900	A, B
D	3	1,500	2	2,000	B
E	5	900	3	1,200	C, D
F	2	1,300	1	1,400	E
G	3	900	3	900	E
H	5	500	3	900	G

15. Jason Ritz, district manager for Gumfull Foods, Inc., is in charge of opening a new fast-food outlet in the college town of Clarity. His major concern is the hiring of a manager and a cadre of hamburger cooks, assemblers, and dispensers. He also has to coordinate the renovation of a building that was previously owned by a pet supplies retailer. Ritz has gathered the data shown in Table 2.8.

Top management told Ritz that the new outlet is to be opened as soon as possible. Every week that the project can be shortened will save the firm $1,200 in lease costs. Ritz thought about how to save time during the project and came up with two possibilities. One was to employ Arctic, Inc., a local employment agency, to locate some good prospects for the manager's job. This approach would save three weeks in activity A and cost Gumfull

c. What additional expenditures should be made to reduce the project's duration? Use the expected time for each activity as though it were certain.

16. Table 2.9 contains data for the installation of new equipment in a manufacturing process at your customer's plant. Your company is responsible for the project. Indirect costs are $10,000 per week, and a penalty cost of $10,000 per week will be incurred for every week the project is delayed beyond week 9.

a. What is the shortest time duration for this project regardless of cost?

b. What is the minimum total cost associated with completing the project in 12 weeks?

c. What is the total time of the minimum-cost schedule?

TABLE 2.8 | DATA FOR THE FAST-FOOD OUTLET PROJECT

Activity	Description	Immediate Predecessor(s)	Time (weeks) a	m	b
A	Interview at college for new manager	—	2	4	6
B	Renovate building	—	5	8	11
C	Place ad for employees and interview applicants	—	7	9	17
D	Have new manager prospects visit	A	1	2	3
E	Purchase equipment for new outlet and install	B	2	4	12
F	Check employee applicant references and make final selection	C	4	4	4
G	Check references for new manager and make final selection	D	1	1	1
H	Hold orientation meetings and do payroll paperwork	E, F, G	2	2	2

Foods $2,500. The other was to add a few workers to shorten the time for activity B by two weeks at an additional cost of $2,700.

Help Jason Ritz by answering the following questions:

a. How long is the project expected to take?

b. Suppose that Ritz has a personal goal of completing the project in 14 weeks. What is the probability that it will happen this quickly?

17. The diagram in Figure 2.14 was developed for a project that you are managing. Suppose that you are interested in finding ways to speed up the project at minimal additional cost. Determine the schedule for completing the project in 25 days at minimum cost. Penalty and project-overhead costs are negligible. Time and cost data for each activity are shown in Table 2.10.

TABLE 2.9 | DATA FOR THE EQUIPMENT INSTALLATION PROJECT

Activity	Immediate Predecessor(s)	Normal Time (weeks)	Crash Time (weeks)	Normal Cost ($)	Crash Cost ($)
A	—	3	2	7,000	10,000
B	—	1	1	3,000	3,000
C	A	4	2	12,000	40,000
D	B	2	1	12,000	28,000
E	C	1	1	8,000	8,000
F	D, E	4	2	5,000	15,000
G	E	2	1	9,000	18,000

TABLE 2.10 | **PROJECT ACTIVITY AND COST DATA**

Activity	Normal		Crash	
	Time (days)	Cost ($)	Time (days)	Cost ($)
A	12	1,300	11	1,900
B	13	1,050	9	1,500
C	18	3,000	16	4,500
D	9	2,000	5	3,000
E	12	650	10	1,100
F	8	700	7	1,050
G	8	1,550	6	1,950
H	2	600	1	800
I	4	2,200	2	4,000

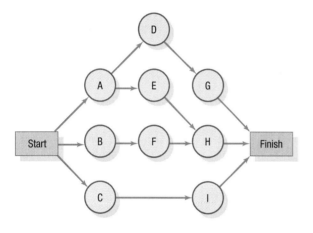

FIGURE 2.14 ▲
Network Diagram for Problem 17

18. Reliable Garage is completing production of the J2000 kit car. The following data are available for the project:

Activity	Activity Time (days)	Immediate Predecessor(s)
A	2	—
B	6	A
C	4	B
D	5	C
E	7	C
F	5	C
G	5	F
H	3	D, E, G

a. Draw the network diagram for the project.

b. Determine the project's critical path and duration.

c. What is the slack for each activity?

19. The following information concerns a new project your company is undertaking:

Activity	Activity Time (days)	Immediate Predecessor(s)
A	10	—
B	11	—
C	9	A, B
D	5	A, B
E	8	A, B
F	13	C, E
G	5	C, D
H	10	G
I	6	F, G
J	9	E, H
K	11	I, J

a. Draw the network diagram for this project.

b. Determine the critical path and project completion time.

20. Paul Silver, owner of Sculptures International, just initiated a new art project. The following data are available for the project:

Activity	Activity Time (days)	Immediate Predecessor(s)
A	4	—
B	1	—
C	3	A
D	2	B
E	3	C, D

a. Draw the network diagram for the project.

b. Determine the project's critical path and duration.

c. What is the slack for each activity?

ADVANCED PROBLEMS

21. Consider the office renovation project data in Table 2.11. A "zero" time estimate means that the activity could take a very small amount of time and should be treated as a numeric zero in the analysis.

    a. Based on the critical path, find the probability of completing the office renovation project by 39 days.

    b. Find the date by which you would be 90 percent sure of completing the project.

22. The project manager of Good Public Relations gathered the data shown in Table 2.12 for a new advertising campaign.

    a. How long is the project likely to take?

    b. What is the probability that the project will take more than 38 weeks?

    c. Consider the path A–E–G–H–J. What is the probability that this path will exceed the expected project duration?

TABLE 2.11   DATA FOR THE OFFICE RENOVATION PROJECT

Activity	Time Estimates (days)			Immediate Predecessor(s)
	Optimistic	Most Likely	Pessimistic	
START	0	0	0	—
A	6	10	14	START
B	0	1	2	A
C	16	20	30	A
D	3	5	7	B
E	2	3	4	D
F	7	10	13	C
G	1	2	3	D
H	0	2	4	G
I	2	2	2	C, G
J	2	3	4	I
K	0	1	2	H
L	1	2	3	J, K
FINISH	0	0	0	E, F, L

TABLE 2.12   ACTIVITY DATA FOR ADVERTISING PROJECT

Activity	Time Estimates (weeks)			Immediate Predecessor(s)
	Optimistic	Most Likely	Pessimistic	
A	8	10	12	START
B	5	8	17	START
C	7	8	9	START
D	1	2	3	B
E	8	10	12	A, C
F	5	6	7	D, E
G	1	3	5	D, E
H	2	5	8	F, G
I	2	4	6	G
J	4	5	8	H
K	2	2	2	H

23. The information in Table 2.13 is available for a large fund-raising project.

a. Determine the critical path and the expected completion time of the project.

b. Plot the total project cost, starting from day 1 to the expected completion date of the project, assuming the earliest start times for each activity. Compare that result to a similar plot for the latest start times. What implication does the time differential have for cash flows and project scheduling?

24. You are in charge of a project at the local community center. The center needs to remodel one of the rooms in time for the start of a new program. Delays in the project mean that the center must rent other space at a nearby church at additional cost. Time and cost data for your project are contained in Table 2.14. Your interest is in minimizing the cost of the project to the community center.

a. Using the **normal** times for each activity, what is the earliest date you can complete the project?

b. Suppose the variable overhead costs are $50 per day for your project. Also, suppose that the center must pay $40 per day for a temporary room on day 15 or beyond. Find the minimum-cost project schedule.

TABLE 2.13	FUND-RAISING PROJECT DATA		
Activity	**Activity Time (days)**	**Activity Cost ($)**	**Immediate Predecessor(s)**
A	3	100	—
B	4	150	—
C	2	125	A
D	5	175	B
E	3	150	B
F	4	200	C, D
G	6	75	C
H	2	50	C, D, E
I	1	100	E
J	4	75	D, E
K	3	150	F, G
L	3	150	G, H, I
M	2	100	I, J
N	4	175	K, M
O	1	200	H, M
P	5	150	N, L, O

TABLE 2.14	DATA FOR THE COMMUNITY CENTER PROJECT				
Activity	**Normal Time (days)**	**Normal Cost ($)**	**Crash Time (days)**	**Crash Cost ($)**	**Immediate Predecessor(s)**
START	0	0	0	0	—
A	10	50	8	150	START
B	4	40	2	200	START
C	7	70	6	160	B
D	2	20	1	50	A, C
E	3	30	NONE	NONE	A, C
F	8	80	5	290	B
G	5	50	4	180	D
H	6	60	3	180	E, F
FINISH	0	0	0	0	G, H

25. Consider the project described in Table 2.15.

   a. If you start the project immediately, when will it be finished?

   b. You are interested in completing your project as soon as possible. You have only one option. Suppose you could assign Employee A, currently assigned to Activity G, to help Employee B, currently assigned to Activity F. Each week that Employee A helps Employee B will result in Activity G increasing its time by one week and Activity F reducing its time by one week. How many weeks should Employee A work on Activity F?

26. You are the project manager of the software installation project in Table 2.16. You would like to find the minimum-cost schedule for your project. There is a $1,000-per-week penalty for each week the project is delayed beyond week 25. In addition, your project team determined that indirect project costs are $2,500 per week.

   a. What would be your target completion week?

   b. How much would you save in total project costs with your schedule?

TABLE 2.15	PROJECT DATA FOR PROBLEM 25	
Activity	**Activity Time (weeks)**	**Immediate Predecessor(s)**
START	0	—
A	3	START
B	4	START
C	4	B
D	4	A
E	5	A, B
F	6	D, E
G	2	C, E
FINISH	0	F, G

TABLE 2.16	DATA FOR SOFTWARE INSTALLATION PROJECT				
Activity	**Immediate Predecessors**	**Normal Time (weeks)**	**Normal Cost ($)**	**Crash Time (weeks)**	**Crash Cost ($)**
A	—	5	2,000	3	4,000
B	—	8	5,000	7	8,000
C	A	10	10,000	8	12,000
D	A, B	4	3,000	3	7,000
E	B	3	4,000	2	5,000
F	D	9	8,000	6	14,000
G	E, F	2	2,000	2	2,000
H	G	8	6,000	5	9,000
I	C, F	9	7,000	7	15,000

ACTIVE MODEL EXERCISE

This Active Model appears in my**om**lab. It allows you to evaluate the sensitivity of the project time to changes in activity times and activity predecessors.

QUESTIONS

1. Suppose that building codes may change and, as a result, activity C would have to be completed before activity D could be started. How would this affect the project?

2. Activity A is not critical. How many weeks can you increase activity A until it becomes critical? What happens when activity A becomes critical?

3. What happens when you increase activity A by one week after it becomes critical?

4. Activity F is not critical. Use the scroll bar to determine how many weeks you can increase activity F until it becomes critical.

5. Activity B and activity K are critical activities. Describe the difference that occurs on the graph when you increase activity B versus when you increase activity K.

Gantt Chart

Reset Data   Questions

Activity	Time				Pred 1	Pred 2	Pred 3
A	12	◄	▌	►			
B	9	◄	▌	►			
C	10	◄	▌	►	a		
D	10	◄	▌	►	b		
E	24	◄	▌	►	b		
F	10	◄	▌	►	a		
G	35	◄	▌	►	c		
H	40	◄	▌	►	d		
I	15	◄	▌	►	a		
J	4	◄	▌	►	e	g	h
K	6	◄	▌	►	f	l	j

Project Time	69 weeks

Gantt Chart Using Data from Example 2.2

The Phoenician in Phoenix, Arizona, is part of Starwood's Luxury Collection and its only AAA Five Diamond Award resort in the Southwestern United States. Sophistication, elegance, and excellence only begin to describe the guest experience at the hotel. Guests can dine in one of nine restaurants, relax poolside, play tennis, take in 27 holes of golf on three 9-hole courses, or relax with a variety of soothing spa treatments at the 22,000-square-foot Centre for Well-Being.

The Phoenician recently embarked on an ambitious $38 million spa and golf renovation program. The resort's golf and spa programs historically earned high marks from surveys in their industries over the years, but the environment was changing. Evidence of this change was seen in the explosive growth of new golf courses and spas in the Southwest region. Phoenix alone has over 275 golf courses, and the Southwest boasts the largest concentration of new luxury spas anywhere. The Phoenician's facilities, while world-class and highly rated, were more than 15 years old. The hotel's recently awarded Five Diamond status renewed emphasis on bringing every process and service at the property up to Five Diamond level.

The decision to renovate the golf course and existing spa became not a question of *whether* to undertake the projects, but *to what degree* they needed to be pursued. Key considerations centered on (1) whether to build basic facilities or commit to the grandiose luxury level, (2) having a domestic versus international reputation, and (3) developing creative packaging of the new facilities to attract loyal guests, such as through a spa and golf

When the Phonoecian, a luxury hotel in Phoenix, Arizona, sought to redesign its spa facilities, its management team created a work breakdown structure in order to compare different project options and choose the best one.

"country club-like" membership program. Such a program would be limited to about 600 spa/golf memberships, with a one-time fee of $65,000 each.

The company's senior management considered three options for the Centre for Well-Being spa. First, the existing space in the heart of the resort could be renovated. This option would require relocating the spa to another part of the resort and offering limited treatments during this time, thereby reducing spa revenues significantly. With option 2, hilly terrain directly behind the resort could be carved out to create a new mountainside facility with sweeping vistas. This option meant the closure of one of the hotel's buildings housing 60 guest rooms and suites during the construction period. The existing spa could remain open, however. Under option 3, a parking structure on existing hotel property could be used, having the least impact on revenues. The first option was seen as a short-term fix, while the remaining two were viewed as having longer-term potential.

Additional discussion centered on the type of spa to be built. Recent acquisition of the Bliss spa brand for Starwood's W Hotels was an option, offering day spa amenities and an indulgence atmosphere. The second option was to remain a holistic resort spa with an emphasis on health and restoration. The third option was to become a destination spa with dedicated guest stays and week-long programs. Day spas are the fastest-growing category, with few destination spas.

The Phoenician management team, with assistance from Starwood Field Operations and Corporate offices, prepared an extensive analysis of strengths, weaknesses, opportunities, and threats to better understand the environment. The result of this analysis was used by the team to identify the set of activities necessary for each option. The Corporate Design and Construction group developed architectural and engineering plans, as well as the work breakdown structure and diagrams showing the critical path for the possible project options. The work breakdown structure, activity times, and activity precedence relationships are shown in the following table:

Work Breakdown Structure	Activity Time (days)	Activity Precedence Relationships
Project Conception		
A. Kick-off meeting	2	
B. Creation of spa specifications	30	A
Geotechnical Investigation		
C. Preliminary site characterizations	10	B
D. Subsurface investigation	10	C
E. Laboratory testing	5	D
F. Geologic hazard assessments	10	E
Design Development		
G. Initial designs	70	B
H. Preliminary zoning compliance plan	15	C, G
I. Final designs	18	H
J. Owner approval of designs	5	I
Documentation and Cost Estimation		
K. Construction documentation and landscape package	80	F, I
L. Acquisition of contractor estimates and bids	90	J, K
Decision		
M. Owner approval of one of the three projects	60	L

QUESTIONS

1. Coordinating departments in a major project is always a challenge. Which departments within the Starwood organization likely played a role in each of the following project related activities?
   a. Defining and organizing the project
   b. Planning the project
   c. Monitoring and controlling the project

2. Many times, project decision makers do not rely solely on financial hurdles, such as return on investment or internal rates of return, but put a lot of weight on intangible factors. Which are the salient intangible factors associated with selecting one of the three options for the spa?

3. Timing is always a challenge in managing projects. Construct a network diagram for the spa selection process. How soon can The Phoenician management make a decision on the spa?

CASE   The Pert Mustang

Roberts Auto Sales and Service (RASAS) consists of three car dealerships that sell and service several makes of American and Japanese cars, two auto parts stores, a large body shop and car painting business, and an auto salvage yard. Vikky Roberts, owner of RASAS, went into the car business when she inherited a Ford dealership from her father. She was able to capitalize on her knowledge and experience to build her business into the diversified and successful mini-empire it is today. Her motto, "Sell 'em today, repair 'em tomorrow!" reflects a strategy that she refers to in private as "Get 'em coming and going."

Roberts has always retained a soft spot in her heart for high-performance Mustangs and just acquired a 1965 Shelby Mustang GT 350 that needs a lot of restoration. She also notes the public's growing interest in the restoration of vintage automobiles.

Roberts is thinking of expanding into the vintage car restoration business and needs help in assessing the feasibility of such a move. She wants to restore her 1965 Shelby Mustang to mint condition, or as close to mint condition as possible. If she decides to go into the car restoring business, she can use the Mustang as an exhibit in sales and advertising and take it to auto shows to attract business for the new shop.

Roberts believes that many people want the thrill of restoring an old car themselves but they do not have the time to run down all the old parts. Still, others just want to own a vintage auto because it is different and many of them have plenty of money to pay someone to restore an auto for them.

Roberts wants the new business to appeal to both types of people. For the first group, she envisions serving as a parts broker for NOS ("new old stock"), new parts that were manufactured many years ago and are still packaged in their original cartons. It can be a time-consuming process to find the right part. RASAS could also machine new parts to replicate those that are hard to find or that no longer exist.

In addition, RASAS could assemble a library of parts and body manuals for old cars to serve as an information resource for do-it-yourself restorers. The do-it-yourselfers could come to RASAS for help in compiling parts lists, and RASAS could acquire the parts for them. For others, RASAS would take charge of the entire restoration.

Roberts asked the director of service operations to take a good look at her Mustang and determine what needs to be done to restore it to the condition it was in when it came from the factory more than 40 years ago. She wants to restore it in time to exhibit it at the Detroit Auto Show. If the car gets a lot of press, it will be a real public relations coup for RASAS—especially if Roberts decides to enter this new venture. Even if she does not, the car will be a showpiece for the rest of the business.

Roberts asked the director of service operations to prepare a report about what is involved in restoring the car and whether it can be done in time for the Detroit show in 45 working days using PERT/CPM. The parts manager, the body shop manager, and the chief mechanic have provided the following estimates of times and tasks that need to be done, as well as cost estimates:

a. Order all needed material and parts (upholstery, windshield, carburetor, and oil pump). Time: 2 days. Cost (phone calls and labor): $100.

b. Receive upholstery material for seat covers. Cannot be done until order is placed. Time: 30 days. Cost: $2,100.

c. Receive windshield. Cannot be done until order is placed. Time: 10 days. Cost: $800.

d. Receive carburetor and oil pump. Cannot be done until order is placed. Time: 7 days. Cost: $1,750.

e. Remove chrome from body. Can be done immediately. Time: 1 day. Cost: $200.

f. Remove body (doors, hood, trunk, and fenders) from frame. Cannot be done until chrome is removed. Time: 1 day. Cost: $300.

g. Have fenders repaired by body shop. Cannot be done until body is removed from frame. Time: 4 days. Cost: $1,000.

h. Repair doors, trunk, and hood. Cannot be done until body is removed from frame. Time: 6 days. Cost: $1,500.

i. Pull engine from chassis. Do after body is removed from frame. Time: 1 day. Cost: $200.

j. Remove rust from frame. Do after the engine has been pulled from the chassis. Time: 3 days. Cost $900.

k. Regrind engine valves. Do after the engine has been pulled from the chassis. Time: 5 days. Cost: $1,000.

l. Replace carburetor and oil pump. Do after engine has been pulled from chassis and after carburetor and oil pump have been received. Time: 1 day. Cost: $200.

m. Rechrome the chrome parts. Chrome must have been removed from the body first. Time: 3 days. Cost: $210.

n. Reinstall engine. Do after valves are reground and carburetor and oil pump have been installed. Time: 1 day. Cost: $200.

o. Put doors, hood, and trunk back on frame. The doors, hood, and trunk must have been repaired first. The frame must have had its rust removed first. Time: 1 day. Cost: $240.

p. Rebuild transmission and replace brakes. Do so after the engine has been reinstalled and the doors, hood, and trunk are back on the frame. Time: 4 days. Cost: $2,000.

q. Replace windshield. Windshield must have been received. Time: 1 day. Cost: $100.

r. Put fenders back on. The fenders must have been repaired first, the transmission rebuilt, and the brakes replaced. Time: 1 day. Cost: $100.

s. Paint car. Cannot be done until the fenders are back on and windshield replaced. Time: 4 days. Cost: $1,700.

t. Reupholster interior of car. Must have received upholstery material first. Car must have been painted first. Time: 7 days. Cost: $2,400.

u. Put chrome parts back on. Car must have been painted and chrome parts rechromed first. Time: 1 day. Cost: $100.

v. Pull car to the Detroit Auto Show. Must have completed reupholstery of interior and have put the chrome parts back on. Time: 2 days. Cost: $1,000.

Roberts wants to limit expenditures on this project to what could be recovered by selling the restored car. She has already spent $50,000 to acquire the car.

In addition, she wants a brief report on some of the aspects of the proposed business, such as how it fits in with RASAS's other businesses and what RASAS's operations task should be with regard to cost, quality, customer service, and flexibility.

In the restoration business there are various categories of restoration. A basic restoration gets the car looking great and running, but a mint condition restoration puts the car back in original condition—as it was "when it rolled off the line." When restored cars are resold, a car in mint condition commands a much higher price than one that is just a basic restoration. As cars are restored, they can also be customized. That is, something is put on the car that could not have been on the original. Roberts wants a mint condition restoration for her Mustang, without customization. (The proposed new business would accept any kind of restoration a customer wanted.)

The total budget cannot exceed $70,000 including the $50,000 Roberts has already spent. In addition, Roberts cannot spend more than $3,600 in any week given her present financial position. Even though much of the work will be done by Roberts's own employees, labor and materials costs must be considered. All relevant costs have been included in the cost estimates.

QUESTIONS

1. Using the information provided, prepare the report that Roberts requested, assuming that the project will begin immediately. Assume 45 working days are available to complete the project, including transporting the car to Detroit before the auto show begins. Your report should briefly discuss the aspects of the proposed new business, such as the competitive priorities that Roberts asked about.

2. Construct a table containing the project activities using the letter assigned to each activity, the time estimates, and the precedence relationships from which you will assemble the network diagram.

3. Draw a network diagram of the project similar to Figure 2.4. Determine the activities on the critical path and the estimated slack for each activity.

4. Prepare a project budget showing the cost of each activity and the total for the project. Can the project be completed within the budget? Will the project require more than $3,600 in any week? To answer this question, assume that activities B, C, and D must be paid for when the item is received (the earliest finish time for the activity). Assume that the costs of all other activities that span more than one week can be prorated. Each week contains five work days. If problems exist, how might Roberts overcome them?

Source: This case was prepared by and is used by courtesy of Professor Sue Perrott Siferd, Arizona State University (Updated September, 2007).

SELECTED REFERENCES

Bloom, R. "Software for Project Management." *Transportation & Distribution*, vol. 34 (1993), pp. 33–34.

Branston, Lisa. "Construction Firms View the Web As a Way to Get Out from Under a Mountain of Paper." *The Wall Street Journal* (November 15, 1999).

Caland, D. I. *Project Management: Strategic Design and Implementation*. New York: McGraw-Hill, 1994.

Day, P. J. *Microsoft Project 4.0 for Windows and the Macintosh: Setting Project Management Standards*. New York: Van Nostrand Reinhold, 1995.

Goldratt, E. M. *Critical Chain*. Great Banington, MA: North River, 1997.

Hartvigsen, David. *SimQuick: Process Simulation with Excel*. 2nd ed. Upper Saddle River, NJ: Prentice Hall, 2004.

IPS Associates. *Project Management Manual*. Boston: Harvard Business School Publishing, 1996.

Kerzner, Harold. *Advanced Project Management: Best Practices on Implementation*, 2nd ed. New York: John Wiley & Sons, 2004.

Kerzner, Harold. *Project Management: A Systems Approach to Planning, Scheduling, and Controlling*, 6th ed. New York: John Wiley & Sons, 1998.

Leach, Larry P. "Critical Chain Project Management Improves Project Performance." *Project Management Journal* (June 1999), pp. 39–51.

Lewis, J. P. *Mastering Project Management*. New York: McGraw-Hill, 1998.

Littlefield, T. K., and P. H. Randolph. "PEAT Duration Times: Mathematical or MBO." *Interfaces*, vol. 21, no. 6 (1991), pp. 92–95.

Mantel Jr., Samuel J., Jack R. Meredith, Scott M. Shafer, and Margaret M. Sutton. *Project Management in Practice*, 2nd ed. New York: John Wiley & Sons, 2005.

Meredith, Jack R., and Samuel J. Mantel, *Project Management: A Managerial Approach*, 5th ed. New York: John Wiley & Sons, 2003.

Nichols, John M. *Managing Business and Engineering Projects*. Englewood Cliffs, NJ: Prentice Hall, 1990.

Pellegrinelli, Sergio, and Cliff Bowman. "Implementing Strategy Through Projects." *Long Range Planning*, vol. 27, no. 4 (1994), pp. 125–132.

"Project Management Body of Knowledge." Available from the Project Management Institute at www.pmi.org.

"Project Management Software Buyer's Guide." *Industrial Engineering* (March 1995), pp. 36–37.

Srinivasan, Mandyam, Darren Jones, and Alex Miller. "CORPS Capabilities." *APICS Magazine* (March 2005), pp. 46–50. For additional chapter resources check the Companion Website at **www.pearsonglobaleditions.com/krajewski**

3 DEVELOPING A PROCESS STRATEGY

At any given time eBay has approximately 113 million listings worldwide, and yet its workforce consists of just 15,000 employees. The explanation? Customers do most of the work in eBay's buying and selling processes. Here a customer prepares items for shipping from sales on his ebay account.

EBAY

Most manufacturers do not have to contend with customers waltzing around their shop floors, showing up intermittently and unannounced. Such customer contact can introduce considerable variability, disrupting carefully designed production processes. Costs and quality can be adversely affected. While customer contact is an issue even with manufacturers, (each process does have at least one customer), extensive customer contact and involvement are business as usual for many processes of service providers. Customers at restaurants or rental car agencies are directly involved in performing the processes. The area where the sales person interacts with the customer *is* the shop floor.

How much should customers be involved in a process, so as to provide timely delivery and consistent quality, and at sustainable cost? Various ways are available—some accommodate customer-introduced variability and some reduce it. eBay illustrates one way to accommodate variability. An online auction house, eBay has high volume and request variability. Its customers do not want service at the same time or at times necessarily convenient to the company. They have request variability, seeking to buy and sell an endless number of items. They also have variability in customer capability, some with considerable Internet experience and some needing more handholding. Such variability would greatly complicate workforce scheduling if eBay required its employees to conduct all of its processes. It connects hundreds of millions of people around the world every day. It

LEARNING GOALS

After reading this chapter, you should be able to:

1. Discuss the four major process decisions.
2. Position a process on the customer-contact matrix or product-process matrix.
3. Configure operations into layouts.
4. Define customer involvement, automation, capital intensity, economies of scope, and focus.
5. Discuss how process decisions should fit together.
6. Define process reengineering and process improvement.

has a global presence in 39 markets, with gross merchandise volume of $17.2 billion in more than 50,000 categories—and only with 15,000 employees. This relatively small workforce is possible in the face of customer-induced variability because its customers perform virtually all of the selling and buying processes through the eBay Web site. When the customer is responsible for much of the work, the right labor is provided at the right moment.

Sources: Frances X. Frei, "Breaking the Trade-Off Between Efficiency and Service," *Harvard Business Review* (November 2006), pp. 93–101; http://news.ebay.com/about.cfm (April 19, 2008).

myomlab and the Companion Website at **www.pearsonglobaleditions.com/krajewski** contain many tools, activities, and resources designed for this chapter.

process strategy

The pattern of decisions made in managing processes so that they will achieve their competitive priorities.

Process decisions, such as the amount of customer involvement allowed at eBay, are strategic in nature: As we saw in Chapter 1, they should further a company's long-term competitive goals. In making process decisions, managers focus on controlling such competitive priorities as quality, flexibility, time, and cost. Process management is an ongoing activity, with the same principles applying to both first-time and redesign choices.

In this chapter we focus on **process strategy**, which specifies the pattern of decisions made in managing processes so that the processes will achieve their competitive priorities. Process strategy guides a variety of process decisions, and in turn is guided by operations strategy and the organization's ability to obtain the resources necessary to support them. We begin by defining four basic process decisions: (1) process structure (including layout), (2) customer involvement, (3) resource flexibility, and (4) capital intensity. We discuss these decisions for both service and manufacturing processes, and also methods for focusing operations. We pay particular attention to ways in which these decisions fit together, depending on factors such as competitive priorities, customer contact, and volume. We conclude with two basic change strategies for analyzing and modifying processes: (1) process reengineering and (2) process improvement.

Three principles concerning process strategy are particularly important:

1. The key to successful process decisions is to make choices that fit the situation and that make sense together. They should not work at cross-purposes, with one process optimized at the expense of other processes. A more effective process is one that matches key process characteristics and has a close *strategic fit*.

2. Although this section of the text focuses on individual processes, they are the building blocks that eventually create the firm's whole supply chain. The cumulative effect on customer satisfaction and competitive advantage is huge.

3. Whether processes in the supply chain are performed internally or by outside suppliers and customers, management must pay particular attention to the interfaces between processes. Having to deal with these interfaces underscores the need for cross-functional coordination.

PROCESS STRATEGY ACROSS THE ORGANIZATION

As we explained in Chapter 1, processes are everywhere and are the basic unit of work. They are found in accounting, finance, human resources, management information systems, marketing, and operations. Managers in all departments must make sure that their processes are adding as much customer value as possible. They must understand that many processes cut across organizational lines, regardless of whether the firm is organized along functional, product, regional, or process lines.

Processes also cut across organizations, linking the firm with its external suppliers and external customers. A coherent process strategy is a key to managing supply chains effectively (Part 3). Each process in the chain, from suppliers to customers, must be designed to achieve its competitive priorities and add value to the work performed.

PROCESS STRATEGY DECISIONS

A process involves the use of an organization's resources to provide something of value. No service can be provided and no product can be made without a process, and no process can exist without at least one service or product. One recurring question in managing processes is deciding *how* to provide services or make products. Many different choices are available in selecting human resources, equipment, outsourced services, materials, work flows, and methods that transform inputs into outputs. Another choice is which processes are to be done in-house, and which processes are to be outsourced—that is, done outside the firm and purchased as materials and services. This decision helps to define the supply chain, and is covered more fully in subsequent chapters. Supplement A, "Decision Making Models," also introduces make-or-buy break-even.

Process decisions directly affect the process itself and indirectly the services and the products that it provides. Whether dealing with processes for offices, service providers, or manufacturers, operations managers must consider four common process decisions. Figure 3.1 shows that they are all important steps toward an effective process design. These four decisions are best understood at the process or subprocess level, rather than at the firm level.

- **Process structure** determines the process type relative to the kinds of resources needed, how resources are partitioned between them, and their key characteristics. A **layout**, which is the physical arrangement of operations created from the various processes, puts these decisions into tangible form.

- **Customer involvement** reflects the ways in which customers become part of the process and the extent of their participation.

- **Resource flexibility** is the ease with which employees and equipment can handle a wide variety of products, output levels, duties, and functions.

- **Capital intensity** is the mix of equipment and human skills in a process. The greater the relative cost of equipment, the greater is the capital intensity.

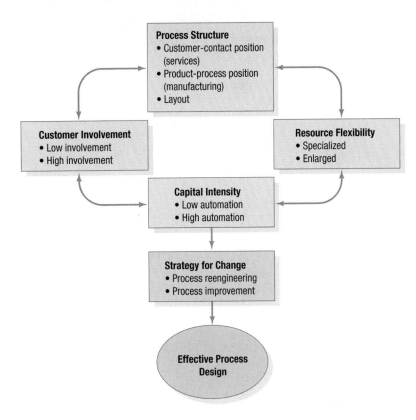

▲ FIGURE 3.1
Major Decisions for Effective Processes

PROCESS STRUCTURE IN SERVICES

One of the first decisions a manager makes in designing a well-functioning process is to choose a process type that best achieves the relative importance of quality, time, flexibility, and cost for that process. Strategies for designing processes can be quite different, depending on whether a service is being provided or a product is being manufactured. We begin with service processes, given their huge share of the workforce in industrialized countries.

Nature of Service Processes: Customer Contact

An effective service process strategy in one situation can be a poor choice in another. A process strategy that gets customers in and out of a fast-food restaurant quickly would not be the right process strategy for a five-star restaurant, where customers seek a leisurely dining experience. Further, a good strategy for the servers at a restaurant might be totally inappropriate for a process back in the restaurant's business office. To get insights, we must start at the process level and recognize key contextual variables associated with the process. Only by doing so can we recognize appropriate patterns and see how decisions should be grouped together.

A good process strategy for a service process depends first and foremost on the type and amount of customer contact. **Customer contact** is the extent to which the customer is present, is actively involved, and receives personal attention during the service process. Face-to-face interaction, sometimes called a *moment of truth* or *service encounter*, brings the customer and service providers together. At that time, customer attitudes about the quality of the service provided are shaped. Table 3.1 shows several dimensions of customer contact. Many levels are possible on each of the five dimensions. Only when they are taken together can you truly measure the kind and extent of customer contact. The nested-process concept applies to customer contact, because some parts of a process can have low contact and other parts of a process can have high contact. Further, even a subprocess can be high on some dimensions and low on others.

Customer-Contact Matrix

The customer-contact matrix, shown in Figure 3.2, brings together three elements: (1) the degree of customer contact, (2) customization, and (3) process characteristics. It synchronizes the service to be provided with the delivery process. The matrix is the starting point for evaluating and improving a process.

Customer Contact and Customization   The horizontal dimension of the matrix represents the service provided to the customer in terms of customer contact and competitive priorities. A key competitive priority is how much customization is needed. Positions on the left side of the matrix represent high customer contact and highly customized services. The

process structure

A process decision that determines the process type relative to the kinds of resources needed, how resources are partitioned between them, and their key characteristics.

layout

The physical arrangement of operations created by the various processes.

customer involvement

The ways in which customers become part of the process and the extent of their participation.

resource flexibility

The ease with which employees and equipment can handle a wide variety of products, output levels, duties, and functions.

capital intensity

The mix of equipment and human skills in a process.

customer contact

The extent to which the customer is present, is actively involved, and receives personal attention during the service process.

TABLE 3.1	DIMENSIONS OF CUSTOMER CONTACT IN SERVICE PROCESSES	
Dimension	**High Contact**	**Low Contact**
Physical presence	Present	Absent
What is processed	People	Possessions or information
Contact intensity	Active, visible	Passive, out of sight
Personal attention	Personal	Impersonal
Method of delivery	Face-to-face	Regular mail or e-mail

customer is more likely to be present and active. The process is more likely to be visible to the customer, who receives more personal attention. The right side of the matrix represents low customer contact, passive involvement, less personalized attention, and a process out of the customer's sight.

Process Divergence and Flow The vertical dimension of the customer-contact matrix deals with two characteristics of the process itself: (1) process divergence and (2) flow. Each process can be analyzed on these two dimensions.

process divergence

The extent to which the process is highly customized with considerable latitude as to how its tasks are performed.

Process divergence is the extent to which the process is highly customized with considerable latitude as to how its tasks are performed. If the process changes with each customer, virtually every performance of the service is unique. Examples of highly divergent service processes where many steps in them change with each customer are found in consulting, law, and architecture. For an architect's nested processes, completing the home design can take on a different character for each customer, even if many activities are common to all designs. They involve much judgment and discretion, depending on what the situation and customer dictate. Services that involve interpretative skills, as with creating art works, also are highly divergent because the execution of the process is individualized. A service with low divergence, on the other hand, is repetitive and standardized. The work is performed exactly the same with all customers, and tends to be less complex. Certain hotel services and telephone services are highly standardized to assure uniformity. At many hotels, every step from room cleaning to checkout is standardized with documentation and rules governing how the process is performed.

flexible flow

The customers, materials, or information move in diverse ways, with the path of one customer or job often crisscrossing the path that the next one takes.

Closely related to divergence is how the customer, object, or information being processed flows through the service facility. Work progresses through the sequence of steps in a process, which could range from highly diverse to linear. When divergence is considerable, the work flow tends to be more flexible. A **flexible flow** means that the customers, materials, or information move in diverse ways, with the path of one customer or job often crisscrossing the path that the next one takes. Each one can follow a carefully preplanned path, even though the first impression is one of disorganized, jumbled flows. Such an appearance goes naturally with high process divergence. A **line flow** means that the customers, materials, or information move linearly from one operation to the next, according to a fixed sequence. When diversity is low and the process standardized, line flows are a natural consequence. With line flows, the work invariably goes from one workstation to the next in the same sequence for every customer or job.

line flow

The customers, materials, or information move linearly from one operation to the next, according to a fixed sequence.

Service Process Structuring

Figure 3.2 shows several desirable positions in the matrix that effectively connect the service product with the process. The manager has three process structures, which form a continuum, to choose from: (1) front office, (2) hybrid office, and (3) back office. It is unlikely that a process can be a top performer if a process lies too far from one of these diagonal positions, occupying instead one of the extreme positions represented by the light blue triangles in the matrix (refer to Figure 3.2). Such positions represent too much of a disconnect between the service provided and process characteristics. A much more likely position is somewhere within the light-colored area, or band, that stretches down from the front-office position to the back-office position. Some deviation from the diagonal is expected and even desirable, allowing for special niches. However, the extreme positions are to be avoided.

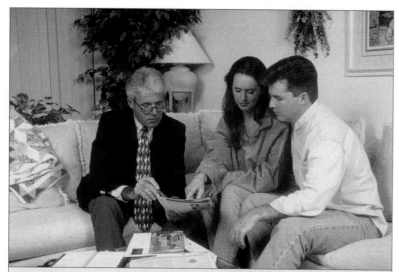

A financial consultant discusses options with a young couple at their home. This process scores high on customer contact, because the customers are present, take an active part in creating the service, receive personal attention, and have face-to-face contact.

▲ FIGURE 3.2
Customer-Contact Matrix for Service Processes

Front Office   A **front-office** process has high customer contact where the service provider interacts directly with the internal or external customer. Because of the customization of the service and variety of service options, many of the steps in it have considerable divergence. Work flows are flexible, and they vary from one customer to the next. More freedom is allowed or inherent in the steps and sequence of the process. The work involves many exceptions to the usual work pattern. The high-contact service process tends to be adapted or tailored to each customer. The customer has more choice in how each step of the service process is carried out and sometimes even where the service encounter occurs.

Hybrid Office   A hybrid office tends to be in the middle of the five dimensions in Table 3.1, or perhaps high on some contact measures and low on others. A **hybrid-office** process has moderate levels of customer contact and standard services, with some options available from which the customer chooses. The work flow progresses from one workstation to the next, with some dominant paths apparent. The work is reasonably divergent, and some customization exists in how the process is performed.

Back Office   A **back-office** process has low customer contact and little service customization. The work is standardized and routine, with line flows from one service provider to the next until the service is completed. Preparing the monthly client fund balance reports in the financial services industry is a good example. The process is almost completely standardized and repeated frequently. It has low customer contact, low divergence, and a line flow.

PROCESS STRUCTURE IN MANUFACTURING

Many processes at a manufacturing firm are actually services to internal or external customers, and so the previous discussion on services applies to them. Here we focus instead on the manufacturing

The Ritz-Carlton Hotel Company targets the top 1 to 3 percent of luxury travelers, and so gives a huge emphasis on customization and top quality. Its sophisticated processes allow it to manage details like few other hotels do, regardless of customer special requests. These associates at the front desk epitomize a front office, because the customers are present, take an active part in creating the service, receive personal attention, and have face-to-face contact.

front office

A process with high customer contact where the service provider interacts directly with the internal or external customer.

hybrid office

A process with moderate levels of customer contact and standard services with some options available.

back office

A process with low customer contact and little service customization.

process choice

A way of structuring the process by organizing resources around the process or organizing them around the products.

FIGURE 3.3 ▼

Product-Process Matrix for Manufacturing Processes

processes themselves. Because of the differences between service and manufacturing processes, we need a different view on process structure.

Product-Process Matrix

The product-process matrix, shown in Figure 3.3, brings together three elements: (1) volume, (2) product customization, and (3) process characteristics. It synchronizes the product to be manufactured with the manufacturing process itself.

A good strategy for a manufacturing process depends first and foremost on volume. Customer contact, a primary feature of the customer-contact matrix for services, normally is not a consideration for manufacturing processes (although it *is* a factor for the many service processes throughout manufacturing firms). For many manufacturing processes, high product customization means lower volumes for many of the steps in the process. If customization, top quality, and product variety are strongly emphasized, the likely result is lower volume for any particular step in the manufacturing process.

The vertical dimension of the product-process matrix deals with the same two characteristics in the customer-contact matrix: process divergence and flow. Each manufacturing process should be analyzed on these two dimensions, just as was done for a service process.

Manufacturing Process Structuring

Figure 3.3 shows several desirable positions (often called *process choices*) in the product-process matrix that effectively connect the manufactured product with the process. **Process choice** is the way of structuring the process by organizing resources around the process or organizing them around the products. Organizing around the process means, for example, that all milling machines are grouped together and process all products or parts needing that kind of transformation. Organizing around the product means bringing together all the different human resources and equipment needed for a specific product and dedicating them to producing just that product. The manager has four process choices, which form a continuum, to choose from: (1) job process, (2) batch process, (3) line process, and (4) continuous-flow process. As with the customer-contact matrix, it

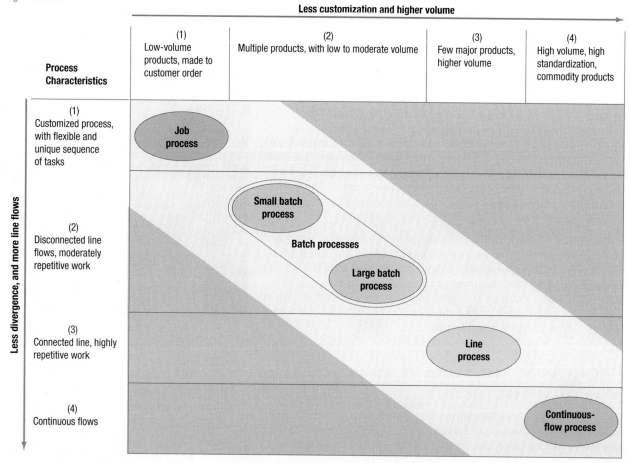

is unlikely that a manufacturing process can be a top performer if its position is too far from the diagonal. The fundamental message in Figure 3.3 is that the best choice for a manufacturing process depends on the volume and degree of customization required of the process. The process choice might apply to an entire manufacturing process or just one subprocess nested within it. For example, one step of the process might be a job process where a specific part is machined (along with parts for many different products), whereas another step might be a line process where the part is assembled with other parts and materials to create the final product. We now concentrate on the differences among the four choices for manufacturing processes.

Job Process   Examples are machining a metal casting for a customized order or producing customized cabinets. A **job process** creates the flexibility needed to produce a wide variety of products in significant quantities, with considerable divergence in the steps performed. Customization is high and volume for any one product is low. The workforce and equipment are flexible to handle considerable task divergence. Companies choosing job processes often bid for work. Typically, they make products to order and do not produce them ahead of time. The specific needs of the next customer are unknown, and the timing of repeat orders from the same customer is unpredictable. Each new order is handled as a single unit—as a job.

A job process primarily organizes all like resources around itself (rather than allocating them out to specific products); equipment and workers capable of certain types of work are located together. These resources process all jobs requiring that type of work. Because customization is high and most jobs have a different sequence of steps, this process choice creates flexible flows through the operations rather than a line flow. Even though considerable variability may exist in the flows through a job process, some line flows may occur within it as well, due to identical nested processes and repeat orders from customers.

Batch Process   The batch process is by far the most common process choice found in practice, leading to terms such as *small batch* or *large batch* to further distinguish one process choice from another. Examples of a batch process are making standard components that feed an assembly line or some processes that manufacture capital equipment. A **batch process** differs from the job process with respect to volume, variety, and quantity. The primary difference is that volumes are higher because the same or similar products or parts going into them are produced repeatedly. Some of the components going into the final product may be processed in advance. Another difference is that a narrower range of products is provided. A third difference is that production lots are handled in larger quantities (or *batches*) than they are with job processes. A batch of one product (or component part going into it or perhaps other products) is processed, and then production is switched to the next one. Eventually the first product is produced again. A batch process has average or moderate volumes, but process divergence is still too great to warrant dedicating a separate process for each product. The process flow is flexible, with no standard sequence of steps throughout the facility. However, more dominant paths emerge than at a job process, and some segments of the process have a line flow.

Line Process   Products created by a line process include the assembly of computers, automobiles, appliances, and toys. A **line process** lies between the batch and continuous processes on the continuum; volumes are high and products are standardized, which allows resources to be organized around particular products. Divergence is minimal in the process or line flows, and little inventory is held between the processing steps. Each step performs the same process over and over, with little variability in the products manufactured. Production and material handling equipment is specialized.

Production orders are not directly linked to customer orders, as is the case with job processes. Standard products are produced in advance of their need and held in inventory so that they are ready when a customer places an order. Product variety is possible by careful control of the addition of standard options to the main product.

Continuous Flow Process   Examples of a continuous flow process are petroleum refining; chemical processes; and processes making steel, soft drinks, and food (such as Borden's huge pasta-making plant). A **continuous flow process** is the extreme end of high-volume standardized production, with rigid line flows. Process divergence is negligible. Its name derives from the way materials move through the process. Usually, one primary material (such as a liquid, a gas, or a powder) moves without stopping through the process. The process seems more like a separate entity by itself. The process is often capital-intensive and operates around the clock

job process

A process with the flexibility needed to produce a wide variety of products in significant quantities, with considerable complexity and divergence in the steps performed.

batch process

A process that differs from the job process with respect to volume, variety, and quantity.

line process

A process that lies between the batch and continuous processes on the continuum; volumes are high and products are standardized, which allows resources to be organized around particular products.

continuous-flow process

The extreme end of high-volume standardized production and rigid line flows, with production not starting and stopping for long time intervals.

A batch of apple fritters roll off one of the pastry lines at the King Soopers's Bakery in Denver to be packaged for transportation. The pastry line is a batch process, and a different kind of pastry will be made next.

to maximize utilization and to avoid expensive shutdowns and start-ups. A continuous-flow process differs from a line process in one important respect: Materials (be they undifferentiated or discrete) flow through the process without stopping until the whole batch is finished. The time span can be several shifts or even several months. Line processes, on the other hand, can be started and stopped with each shift or day, even if the batch is not finished.

Production and Inventory Strategies

Strategies for manufacturing processes differ from those in services, not only because of low customer contact and involvement, but also because of the ability to use inventories. Make-to-order, assemble-to-order, and make-to-stock strategies are three approaches to inventory that should be coordinated with process choice.

make-to-order strategy

A strategy used by manufacturers that make products to customer specifications in low volumes.

Make-to-Order Strategy   Manufacturers that make products to customer specifications in low volumes tend to use the **make-to-order strategy**, coupling it with job or small batch processes. It is a more complex process than assembling a final product from standard components, such as assembling a Dell computer to customer order. Many different types of manufacturing processes might be used, other than primarily "assembly or joining parts and materials." The process is viewed with a make-to-order strategy as a set of subprocesses that can be used in many different ways to satisfy the unique needs of customers. This strategy provides a high degree of customization and typically uses job or small batch processes. The processes have high divergence. Because most products, components, and assemblies are custom-made, the manufacturing process must be flexible to accommodate the variety. Specialized medical equipment, castings, and expensive homes are suited to the make-to-order strategy. The assemble-to-order strategy is another possibility.

assemble-to-order strategy

A strategy for producing a wide variety of products from relatively few subassemblies and components after the customer orders are received.

Assemble-to-Order Strategy   The **assemble-to-order strategy** is an approach to producing a wide variety of products from relatively few subassemblies and components after the customer orders are received. Typical competitive priorities are variety and fast delivery times. The assemble-to-order strategy often involves a line process for assembly and a batch process for fabrication. Because they are devoted to manufacturing standardized components and subassemblies in high volumes, the fabrication processes focus on creating appropriate amounts of component inventories for the assembly processes. Once the specific order from the customer is received, the assembly processes create the product from standardized components and subassemblies produced by the fabrication processes.

postponement

The strategy of delaying final activities in the provision of a product until the orders are received.

mass customization

The strategy that uses highly divergent processes to generate a wide variety of customized products at reasonably low costs.

Stocking finished products would be economically prohibitive because the numerous possible options make forecasting relatively inaccurate. Thus, the principle of **postponement** is applied, whereby the final activities in the provision of a product are delayed until the orders are received. For example, a manufacturer of upscale upholstered furniture can produce hundreds of a particular style of sofa, with no two alike, to meet customers' selections of fabric and wood. The assemble-to-order strategy is also linked to **mass customization**, where highly divergent processes generate a wide variety of customized products at reasonably low costs. Both postponement and mass customization are covered more fully in Chapter 9, "Designing Effective Supply Chains."

make-to-stock strategy

A strategy that involves holding items in stock for immediate delivery, thereby minimizing customer delivery times.

mass production

A term sometimes used in the popular press for a line process that uses the make-to-stock strategy.

Make-to-Stock Strategy   Manufacturing firms that hold items in stock for immediate delivery, thereby minimizing customer delivery times, use a **make-to-stock strategy**. This strategy is feasible for standardized products with high volumes and reasonably accurate forecasts. It is the inventory strategy of choice for line or continuous-flow processes. For example, a company producing a sensor for the transmission of a Toyota Camry would have enough volume to operate a production line specifically for that sensor and would carry a stock of the finished product for the scheduled shipments to the factory. Other examples of products produced with a make-to-stock strategy include garden tools, electronic components, soft drinks, and chemicals.

Combining a line process with the make-to-stock strategy is sometimes called **mass production**. It is what the popular press commonly envisions as the classical manufacturing process, because the environment is stable and predictable, with workers repeating narrowly defined tasks with low divergence. However, a line process is only one of four manufacturing process choices.

Layout

Human and capital resources used by processes must be arranged physically within their facilities, which gives the process structure a physical form. For organizational purposes, processes tend to be clustered together into operations. An *operation* is a group of resources performing all or part of one or more processes. For example, an operation could be a group of people preparing campaign posters; several customer service representatives in a customer reception area; bank associates staffing teller window stations; a group of machines and workers producing cell phones; or a marketing department. The processes within an operation that provide services to others could have the characteristics of a front office, back office, or a mixture of all office types. Similarly, the processes at a manufacturing operation can encompass a mixture of several process choices. Regardless of how processes are grouped together organizationally, many of them cut across departmental boundaries. The flows across departmental lines could be informational, services, or products.

Here we demonstrate an approach to layout design that seeks to give form to process structure. The objective is to position those departments close together that have strong interactions between them. It involves three basic steps, whether the design is for a new layout or for revising an existing layout: (1) gather information, (2) develop a block plan, and (3) design a detailed layout. We illustrate these steps with the Office of Budget Management (OBM), which is a major division in a large provincial government.

Gather Information   OBM consists of 120 employees assigned to six different departments. Workloads have expanded to the extent that 30 new employees must be hired and somehow housed in the space allocated to OBM. The goal is to improve communication among people who must interact with each other effectively, creating a good work environment.

Three types of information are needed to begin designing the revised layout for OBM: (1) space requirements by center, (2) available space, and (3) closeness factors. OBM has grouped its processes into six different departments: (1) administration, (2) social services, (3) institutions, (4) accounting, (5) education, and (6) internal audit. The exact space requirements of each department, in square feet, are as follows:

Department	Area Needed (ft²)
1. Administration	3,500
2. Social services	2,600
3. Institutions	2,400
4. Accounting	1,600
5. Education	1,500
6. Internal audit	3,400
Total	15,000

Management must tie space requirements to capacity and staffing plans; calculate the specific equipment and space needs for each center; and allow circulation space, such as aisles and the like. At OBM, a way must be found to include all 150 employees in its assigned area. Consulting with the managers and employees involved can help avoid excessive resistance to change and make the transition smoother.

A **block plan** allocates space and indicates placement of each operation. To describe a new facility layout, the plan need only provide the facility's dimensions and space allocations. When an existing facility layout is being modified, the current block plan is also needed. OBM's available space is 150 feet by 100 feet, or 15,000 square feet. The designer could begin the design by dividing the total amount of space into six equal blocks (2,500 square feet each). The equal-space approximation shown in Figure 3.4 is sufficient until the detailed layout stage, when larger departments (such as administration) are assigned more space than smaller departments.

The layout designer must also know which operations need to be located close to one another. The table on the next page shows OBM's **closeness matrix**, which gives a measure of the relative importance of each pair of operations being located close together. The metric used depends on the type of processes involved and the organizational setting. It can be a qualitative judgment on a scale from 0 to 10 that the manager uses to account for multiple performance criteria, as in the OBM's case. Only the right-hand portion of the matrix is used. The closeness factors are indicators of the need for proximity based on an analysis of information flows and the need for face-to-face meetings. They give clues as to which departments should be located close together. For example, the most important interaction is between the administration and internal audit departments for OBM, with a score of 10.

block plan

A plan that allocates space and indicates placement of each operation.

closeness matrix

A table that gives a measure of the relative importance of each pair of operations being located close together.

▲ **FIGURE 3.4**
Current Block Plan for the Office of Budget Management

	Closeness Factors					
Department	1	2	3	4	5	6
1. Administration	—	3	6	5	6	10
2. Social services		—	8	1	1	
3. Institutions			—	3	9	
4. Accounting				—	2	
5. Education					—	1
6. Internal audit						—

This closeness factor is given in the first row and last column. Thus, the designer should locate departments 1 and 6 close together, which is not the arrangement in the current layout. Entries in both the columns and rows result in five factor scores for each department.

At a manufacturing plant, the closeness factor could be the number of trips (or some other measure of materials movement) between each pair of operations per day. This information can be gleaned by conducting a statistical sampling, polling supervisors and materials handlers, or using the routings and ordering frequencies for typical items made at the plant.

Finally, the information gathered for OBM includes performance criteria that depend not on the relative location of department pairs, but the *absolute* location of a single department. OBM has two such criteria.

1. Education (department 5) should remain where it is because it is next to the office library.
2. Administration (department 1) should remain where it is because that location has the largest conference room, which administration uses often. Relocating the conference room would be costly.

Develop a Block Plan Having gathered the needed information, the next step is to develop a block plan that best satisfies performance criteria and area requirements. The most elementary way to do so is by trial and error. Because success depends on the designer's ability to spot patterns in the data, this approach does not guarantee the selection of the best or even a nearly best solution. When supplemented by the use of a computer to evaluate solutions, however, research shows that such an approach compares quite favorably with more sophisticated computerized techniques.

EXAMPLE 3.1	Developing a Block Plan

Develop an acceptable block plan for the Office of Budget Management, using trial and error. The goal is to locate the departments that have the greatest interaction between them (largest closeness factor) as close to each other as possible.

SOLUTION

A good place to start is with the largest closeness ratings (say, 8 and above). Beginning with the largest factor scores and working down the list, you might plan to locate departments as follows:

a. Departments 1 and 6 close together,

b. Departments 3 and 5 close together,

c. Departments 2 and 3 close together.

Departments 1 and 5 should remain at their current locations because of absolute location criteria.

If after several attempts you cannot meet all three requirements, drop one or more and try again. If you can meet all three easily, add more (such as for interactions below 8).

The block plan in Figure 3.5 shows a trial-and-error solution that satisfies all three requirements. We started by keeping departments 1 and 5 in their original locations. As the first requirement is to locate departments 1 and 6 close to each other, we put 6 in the upper-left corner of the layout. The second requirement is to have departments 3 and 5 close to each other, so we placed 3 in the space just above 5, and so on.

FIGURE 3.5 ▲
Proposed Block Plan

DECISION POINT

This solution fell into place easily for this particular problem, but it might not be the best layout. Management wants to consider several alternative layouts before making a final choice and needs some measure of effectiveness with which to compare the alternative layouts.

Applying the Weighted-Distance Method   When *relative* locations are a primary concern, such as for effective information flow, communication, material handling, and stockpicking, the weighted-distance method can be used to compare alternative block plans. The **weighted-distance method** is a mathematical model used to evaluate layouts based on proximity factors. A similar approach, sometimes called the *load-distance method,* can be used to evaluate facility locations. The objective is to select a layout (or facility location) that minimizes the total weighted distances. The distance between two points is expressed by assigning the points to grid coordinates on a block diagram or map. An alternative approach is to use time rather than distance.

For a rough calculation, which is all that is needed for the weighted-distance method, either a Euclidean or rectilinear distance measure may be used. **Euclidean distance** is the straight-line distance, or shortest possible path, between two points. To calculate this distance, we create a graph. The distance between two points, say, points A and B, is

$$d_{AB} = \sqrt{(x_A - x_B)^2 + (y_A - y_B)^2}$$

where

$$d_{AB} = \text{distance between points } A \text{ and } B$$
$$x_A = x\text{-coordinate of point } A$$
$$y_A = y\text{-coordinate of point } A$$
$$x_B = x\text{-coordinate of point } B$$
$$y_B = y\text{-coordinate of point } B$$

Rectilinear distance measures the distance between two points with a series of 90-degree turns, as along city blocks. The distance traveled in the x-direction is the absolute value of the difference between the x-coordinates. Adding this result to the absolute value of the difference between the y-coordinates gives

$$d_{AB} = |x_A - x_B| + |y_A - y_B|$$

For assistance in calculating distances using either measure, see Tutor 3.1 in OM Explorer.

The layout designer seeks to minimize the weighted-distance (wd) score by locating centers that have high-closeness ratings close together. To calculate a layout's wd score, we use either of the distance measures and simply multiply the proximity scores by the distances between centers. The sum of those products becomes the layout's final wd score—the lower the better. The location of a center is defined by its x-coordinate and y-coordinate.

weighted-distance method

A mathematical model used to evaluate flexible-flow layouts (of facility locations) based on proximity factors.

Euclidean distance

The straight-line distance, or shortest possible path, between two points.

rectilinear distance

The distance between two points with a series of 90-degree turns, as along city blocks.

Tutor 3.1 in my**om**lab provides an example to calculate both Euclidean and rectilinear distance measures.

EXAMPLE 3.2	Calculating the Weighted-Distance Score

How much better, in terms of the *wd* score, is the proposed block plan that was shown in Figure 3.5 than the current plan that was shown in Figure 3.4? Use the rectilinear distance measure.

SOLUTION

The accompanying table lists each pair of departments that has a nonzero closeness factor in the closeness matrix. For the third column, calculate the rectilinear distances between the departments in the current layout. For example, departments 3 and 5 in the current plan are in the upper-left corner and bottom-right corner of the building, respectively. The distance between the centers of these blocks is three units (two horizontally and one vertically). For the fourth column, we multiply the weights (closeness factors) by the distances, and then add the results for a total *wd* score of 112 for the current plan. Similar calculations for the proposed plan produce a *wd* score of only 82. For example, between departments 3 and 5 is just one unit of distance (one vertically and zero horizontally).

Active Model 3.1 in my**om**lab allows evaluation of the impact of swapping OBM departmental positions.

Current Plan

3	6	4
1	2	5

Proposed Plan

6	2	3
1	4	5

Department Pair	Closeness Factor (w)	Current Plan Distance (d)	Current Plan Weighted-Distance Score (wd)	Proposed Plan Distance (d)	Proposed Plan Weighted-Distance Score (wd)
1, 2	3	1	3	2	6
1, 3	6	1	6	3	18
1, 4	5	3	15	1	5
1, 5	6	2	12	2	12
1, 6	10	2	20	1	10
2, 3	8	2	16	1	8
2, 4	1	2	2	1	1
2, 5	1	1	1	2	2
3, 4	3	2	6	2	6
3, 5	9	3	27	1	9
4, 5	2	1	2	1	2
5, 6	1	2	2	3	3
			Total 112		Total 82

To be exact, we could multiply the two *wd* total scores by 50 because each unit of distance represents 50 feet. However, the relative difference between the two totals remains unchanged.

DECISION POINT

The *wd* score for the proposed layout makes a sizeable drop from 112 to 82, but management is not sure the improvement outweighs the cost of relocating four of the six departments (i.e., all departments but 1 and 5).

Although the *wd* score for the proposed layout in Example 3.2 represents an almost 27 percent improvement, the designer may be able to improve on this solution. Furthermore, the manager must determine whether the revised layout is worth the cost of relocating four of the six departments. If relocation costs are too high, a less-expensive proposal must be found.

OM Explorer and POM for Windows can help identify some even more attractive proposals. For example, one option is to modify the proposed plan by switching the locations of departments 3 and 4. OM Explorer's output in Figure 3.6 shows that the *wd* score for this second revision not only drops to 80, but requires that only three departments be relocated compared with the original layout in Figure 3.4. Perhaps this second proposed plan is the best solution.

FIGURE 3.6 ▼
Second Proposed Block Plan (Analyzed with *Layout* Solver)

◉ Rectilinear Distances   ○ Euclidean Distances

6	2	4
1	3	5

Department Pair	Closeness Factor	Distance	Score
1, 6	10	1	10
3, 5	9	1	9
2, 3	8	1	8
1, 3	6	1	6
1, 5	6	2	12
1, 4	5	3	15
1, 2	3	2	6
3, 4	3	2	6
4, 5	2	1	2
2, 4	1	1	1
2, 5	1	2	2
5, 6	1	3	3
Total			80

Design a Detailed Layout After finding a satisfactory block plan, the final step translates it into a detailed representation, showing the exact size and shape of each center; the arrangement of elements (e.g., desks, machines, and storage areas); and the location of aisles, stairways, and other service space. These visual representations can be two-dimensional drawings, three-dimensional models, or computer-aided graphics. This step helps decision makers discuss the proposal and problems that might otherwise be overlooked. Such visual representations can be particularly important when evaluating high customer-contact processes.

CUSTOMER INVOLVEMENT

Having covered process structure decisions, we now turn to a second major decision—customer involvement—shown in Figure 3.1. Customer involvement reflects the ways in which customers become part of the process and the extent of their participation. It is especially important for many service processes, particularly if customer contact is (or should be) high.

While eBay devised one way to accommodate the variability created by customer involvement, Starbucks faces a different kind of customer variability. The coffee shop chain allows customers to choose among many permutations of sizes, flavors, and preparation techniques in its beverages. In order to fill orders accurately and efficiently, Starbucks trains its counter clerks to call out orders to beverage makers in a particular sequence. It is even better when customers themselves can do so. Starbucks attempts to teach customers its ordering protocol. First, it provides a "guide-to-ordering pamphlet" for customers to look over. Second, it trains clerks to repeat the order in the correct sequence for the beverage makers, which may not be how the customer presented it. This process not only makes it easier for the beverage makers, but also indirectly "trains" the customers in how to place their orders.

The detailed layout becomes a reality. Shown here is part of the office in one of the ABB facilities, a global leader in power and automation technologies. Here the workstations are small and semiprivate, but "outposts" are available. This common area has easy chairs fitted with arms that provide a surface for writing or laptops. People meet comfortably for face-to-face talks, rather than communicating by e-mail.

Possible Disadvantages

Customer involvement is not always a good idea. In some cases giving the customer more active contact in a service process will just be disruptive, making the process less efficient and too divergent. Managing the timing and volume of customer demands becomes more challenging if the customer is physically present and expects prompt delivery. Quality measurement also becomes more difficult and exposing the facilities and employees to the customer can have important quality implications (favorable or unfavorable). Such changes make interpersonal skills a prerequisite to the service provider's job, but higher skill levels come at a cost. Revising the facility layout might be a necessary investment, now that managing customer perceptions becomes an important part of the process. It also might mean having many smaller decentralized facilities closer to the various customer concentration areas if the customer comes to the service providers.

Possible Advantages

Despite these possible disadvantages, the advantages of a more customer-focused process might increase the net value to the customer. Some customers seek active participation in and control over the service process, particularly if they will enjoy savings in both price and time. The manager must assess whether advantages outweigh disadvantages, judging them in terms of the competitive priorities and customer satisfaction. More customer involvement can mean better quality, faster delivery, greater flexibility, and even lower cost. Self-service is the choice of many retailers, such as gasoline stations, supermarkets, and bank services. Manufacturers of products (such as toys, bicycles, and furniture) may also prefer to let the customer perform the final assembly because product, shipping, and inventory costs frequently are lower, as are losses from damage.

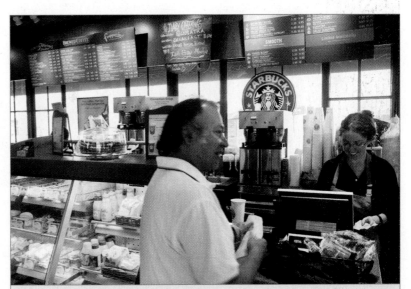

A customer at Starbucks, a large coffee shop chain, places his order in the correct way. By structuring the ordering process for counter clerks and customers, Starbucks can deal efficiently with the variety in products offered, and with no hit on the service experience.

Customer involvement can also help coordinate across the supply chain (see Chapter 10, "Integrating the Supply Chain"). Emerging technologies allow companies to engage in an active dialogue with customers and make them partners in creating value and forecasting future demand. Companies can also revise some of their traditional processes, such as pricing and billing systems, to account for their customers' new role. For example, in business-to-business relationships, the Internet changes the roles that companies play with other businesses. Suppliers to automobile companies can be close collaborators in the process of developing new vehicles and no longer are passive providers of materials and services. The same is true for distributors. Wal-Mart does more than just distribute Procter & Gamble's products: It shares daily sales information and works with Procter & Gamble in managing inventories and warehousing operations.

RESOURCE FLEXIBILITY

Just as managers must account for customer contact when making customer involvement decisions, so must they account for process divergence and diverse process flows when making resource flexibility decisions in Figure 3.1. High task divergence and flexible process flows require more flexibility of the process's resources—its employees, facilities, and equipment. Employees need to perform a broad range of duties, and equipment must be general purpose. Otherwise, resource utilization will be too low for economical operations.

Workforce

flexible workforce

A workforce whose members are capable of doing many tasks, either at their own workstations or as they move from one workstation to another.

Operations managers must decide whether to have a **flexible workforce**. Members of a flexible workforce are capable of doing many tasks, either at their own workstations or as they move from one workstation to another. However, such flexibility often comes at a cost, requiring greater skills and thus more training and education. Nevertheless, benefits can be large: Worker flexibility can be one of the best ways to achieve reliable customer service and alleviate capacity bottlenecks. Resource flexibility helps to absorb the feast-or-famine workloads in individual operations that are caused by low-volume production, divergent tasks, flexible flows, and fluid scheduling.

The type of workforce required also depends on the need for volume flexibility. When conditions allow for a smooth, steady rate of output, the likely choice is a permanent workforce that expects regular full-time employment. If the process is subject to hourly, daily, or seasonal peaks and valleys in demand, the use of part-time or temporary employees to supplement a smaller core of full-time employees may be the best solution. However, this approach may not be practical if knowledge and skill requirements are too high for a temporary worker to grasp quickly. Controversy is growing over the practice of replacing full-time workers with temporary or part-time workers.

Equipment

Low volumes mean that process designers should select flexible, general-purpose equipment. Figure 3.7 illustrates this relationship by showing the total cost lines for two different types of equipment that can be chosen for a process. Each line represents the total annual cost of the process at

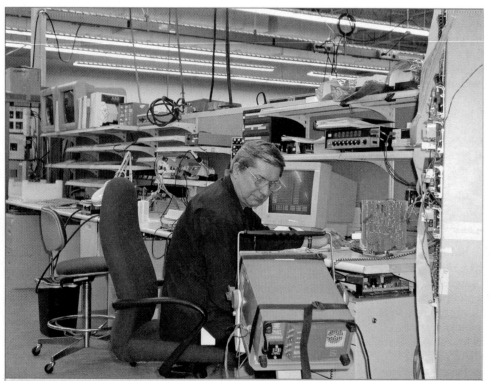

Technicians in the parts repair department of this ABB facility must be flexible enough to repair many different parts for automation equipment installed at customer locations in the field. This operation has 30 different workstations configured to perform different types of processes. Workers are cross-trained to move from one station to another, depending on what needs to be done.

different volume levels. It is the sum of fixed costs and variable costs (see Supplement A, "Decision Making Models"). When volumes are low (because customization is high), process 1 is the best choice. It calls for inexpensive general-purpose equipment, which keeps investment in equipment low and makes fixed costs (F_1) small. Its variable unit cost is high, which gives its total cost line a relatively steep slope. Process 1 does the job, but not at peak efficiency. However, volumes are not high enough for total variable costs to overcome the benefit of low fixed costs.

Conversely, process 2 is the best choice when volumes are high and customization is low. Its advantage is low variable unit cost, as reflected in the flatter total cost line. This efficiency is possible when customization is low because the equipment can be designed for a narrow range of products or tasks. Its disadvantage is high equipment investment and, thus, high fixed costs (F_2). When annual volume produced is high enough, spreading these fixed costs over more units produced, the advantage of low variable costs more than compensates for the high fixed costs.

The break-even quantity in Figure 3.7 is the quantity at which the total costs for the two alternatives are equal. At quantities beyond this point, the cost of process 1 exceeds that of process 2. Unless the firm expects to sell more than the break-even amount, which is unlikely with high customization and low volume, the capital investment of process 2 is not warranted.

▲ FIGURE 3.7
Relationship Between Process Costs and Product Volume

Tutor 3.2 in my**om**lab demonstrates how to do break-even analysis for equipment selection.

CAPITAL INTENSITY

Capital intensity is the mix of equipment and human skills in the process; the greater the relative cost of equipment, the greater is the capital intensity. As the capabilities of technology increase and its costs decrease, managers face an ever-widening range of choices, from operations utilizing very little automation to those requiring task-specific equipment and little human intervention. **Automation** is a system, process, or piece of equipment that is self-acting and self-regulating. Although automation is often thought to be necessary to gain competitive advantage, it has both advantages and disadvantages. Thus, the automation decision requires careful examination.

automation

A system, process, or piece of equipment that is self-acting and self-regulating.

Automating Manufacturing Processes

Substituting labor-saving capital equipment and technology for labor has been a classic way of improving productivity and quality consistency in manufacturing processes. If investment costs are large, automation works best when volume is high, because more customization typically means reduced volume. Gillette, for example, spent $750 million on the production lines and robotics that gave it a capacity to make 1.2 billion razor cartridges a year. The equipment is complicated and expensive. Only with such high volumes could this line process produce the product at a price low enough that consumers could afford to buy it.

One big disadvantage of capital intensity can be the prohibitive investment cost for low-volume operations (see Figure 3.7). Generally, capital-intensive operations must have high utilization to be justifiable. Also, automation does not always align with a company's competitive priorities. If a firm offers a unique product or high-quality service, competitive priorities may indicate the need for skilled servers, hand labor, and individual attention rather than new technology. A case in point is the downstream processes in Gillette's supply chain that package and store the razor cartridges. It customizes the packaging for different regions of the world, so that volumes for any one type of package are much lower. As a result of the low volumes, Gillette does not use expensive automation for these processes. In fact, it outsources them. Producing razor cartridges to stock using highly automated processes, and then packaging them in customized fashion at remote locations on demand, is also a good example of the principle of postponement.

Fixed Automation   Manufacturers use two types of automation: fixed and flexible (or programmable). Particularly appropriate for line and continuous-flow process choices, **fixed automation** produces one type of part or product in a fixed sequence of simple operations. Operations managers favor fixed automation when demand volumes are high, product designs are stable, and product life cycles are long. These conditions compensate for the process's two primary drawbacks: large initial investment cost and relative inflexibility. However, fixed automation maximizes efficiency and yields the lowest variable cost per unit if volumes are high.

fixed automation

A manufacturing process that produces one type of part or product in a fixed sequence of simple operations.

flexible (or programmable) automation

A manufacturing process that can be changed easily to handle various products.

industrial robot

Versatile, computer-controlled machine programmed to perform various tasks.

Flexible Automation **Flexible (or programmable) automation** can be changed easily to handle various products. The ability to reprogram machines is useful for both low-customization and high-customization processes. In the case of high customization, a machine that makes a variety of products in small batches can be programmed to alternate between products. When a machine has been dedicated to a particular product or family of products, as in the case of low customization and a line flow, and the product is at the end of its life cycle, the machine can simply be reprogrammed with a new sequence of operations for a new product. An **industrial robot**, which is a versatile, computer-controlled machine programmed to perform various tasks, is a classic example of flexible automation. These "steel-collar" workers operate independently of human control. A robot's arm has up to six standard movements. The robot's "hand" actually does the work. The hand can be changed to perform different tasks, such as materials handling, assembly, and testing.

Managerial Practice 3.1 describes how the focus on operations efficiency at DP World have earned the company worldwide acclaim.

Automating Service Processes

Using capital inputs as a labor-saving device is also possible for service processes. In educational services, for example, long-distance learning technology now can supplement or even replace the traditional classroom experience by using books, computers, Web sites, and videos as facilitating goods that go with the service. Justifying technology need not be limited to cost reduction. Sometimes it can actually allow more task divergence by making available a wide menu of choices to the customer. Technology in the future will surely make possible even a greater degree of customization and variety in services that currently only human providers can now deliver. Beyond cost and variety considerations, management must understand the customer and how much close contact is valued. If the customers seek a visible presence and personal attention, technologies reduced to sorting through a variety of options on the Internet or over the telephone might be a poor choice.

The need for volume to justify expensive automation is just as valid for service processes as for manufacturing processes. Increasing the volume lowers the cost per dollar of sales. Volume is essential for many capital-intensive processes in the transportation,

Flexible Automation at JustBorn, a candy company in Pennsylvania (www.justborn.com).

On the left, a robot picks up yellow bunnies with great speed in groups of four and places them into preformed trays, which then move to automatic shrink-wrapping machines. The trays are then boxed into cases for shipment. Upstream in this line process, the bunnies were extruded in shape on a belt with about 1/2 inch of sugar on it and then cooled as the conveyor moves along. The robot is regularly reprogrammed based on the marshmallow configuration being produced.

On the right, robot using vacuum cups on the "hand" of its arm picks up boxes of five-pound Hot Tamale bags that are packaged with five bags in a box. The robot reads the bar code, knows the pallet configuration, picks up and places the pallet and a thin cardboard liner on the conveyor, and stacks the boxes until complete. The pallet then comes toward the camera to be picked off the line by a fork truck, and then shrink-wrapped (automatically) and loaded into a 54-foot trailer.

| MANAGERIAL PRACTICE 3.1 | DP World Steps Up International Shipping |

Originating in Dubai in 1999, the port management company Dubai Ports International (DPI) was initially formed to improve the efficiency of operations in Middle Eastern ports. After successfully transforming the Jeddah Islamic Port into the most successful in Saudi Arabia, other countries realized that DPI could improve their ports as well. In 2005, DPI combined with the Dubai Ports Authority and formed Dubai Ports World (DP World), which is now a world leader in international port management.

DP World's first major business move was the acquisition of CSX World Terminals in January 2005. This purchase gave the company a major presence in several Asian countries, Australia, Germany, Dominican Republic, and Venezuela. In addition to these already functioning ports, DP World also took over the contracts that CSX had for several major projects that were under construction. Since these mergers and acquisitions, DP World has continued to expand and currently holds contracts all over the world.

The business approach of DP World is customer centered, as they cater to the needs of individual ports. Their primary focus is to improve the efficiency of operations and, in doing so, to improve the profit margin of the port. These effective managerial practices have earned the company worldwide acclaim. A flat management structure is employed, with a focus on entrepreneurial drive rather than bureaucracy. These management practices have proved successful in turning around struggling ports and terminals time and time again.

With the purchase of six ports in the United States in 2006, DP World encountered a small scandal. The executive branch of the United States government approved the deal, but there were U.S. security concerns about a company based in the United Arab Emirates. U.S. authorities urged that the deal be completed, but legislation was introduced in Congress to delay the sale. The House of Representatives was vehemently opposed to the deal, and DP World ended up turning over management of the ports to a United States-based company. Despite this blip, DP World has continued to grow at an exponential rate.

Saudi Arabia recruited the help of Dubai Port International to regenerate the Jeddah Islamic port, which is now one of the most successful and thriving port in the Middle East.

Dubai Ports World has attained international success through applying a simple managerial model to all of its business ventures. The company holds a number of major contracts for future ports and shows no signs of slowing down in the future. International trade is more prevalent than it has ever been in history, and DP World is a major force in improving port efficiency to aid the process of worldwide trade.

Sources: "DP World Official Website," www.dpworld.com, Accessed September 29, 2008; "Congress Declares War on Ports Deal," Cnn.com, March 8, 2006, http://www.cnn.com/2006/POLITICS/03/08/port.security/index.html.

communications, and utilities industries. A jetliner idled because of low demand is very expensive, a reality reflected in recent income statements of airline companies.

It is often correctly assumed that volumes are higher in back-office processes, where customer contact is low. Physical contact, personalized treatment, and face-to-face communication often create divergent tasks and low volume, but not always. A recent study of financial services shows that high volumes are just as likely in front offices as in back offices. As a result, automation is not concentrated in the back office, but is just as likely found in front-office processes. Automation of financial services comes primarily from information technology, which can flexibly handle a wide array of processes at multiple locations.

Economies of Scope

If capital intensity is high, resource flexibility usually is low. In certain types of manufacturing operations, such as machining and assembly, programmable automation breaks this inverse relationship between resource flexibility and capital intensity. It makes possible both high capital intensity and high resource flexibility, creating economies of scope. **Economies of scope** reflect the ability to produce multiple products more cheaply in combination than separately. In such situations, two conflicting competitive priorities—customization and low price—become more compatible. However, taking advantage of economies of scope requires that a family of parts or products have enough collective volume to utilize equipment fully.

Economies of scope also apply to service processes. Consider, for example, Disney's approach to the Internet. When the company's managers entered the volatile Internet world, their businesses were only weakly tied together. Disney's Infoseek business, in fact, was not even fully owned. However, once its Internet markets became more crystallized, managers at Disney moved to reap the benefits of economies of scope. They aggressively linked their

economies of scope

Economies that reflect the ability to produce multiple products more cheaply in combination than separately.

Internet processes with one another and with other parts of Disney. A flexible technology that handles many services together can be less expensive than handling each one separately, particularly when the markets are not too volatile.

STRATEGIC FIT

The manager should understand how the four major process decisions tie together, so as to spot ways of improving poorly designed processes. The choices should fit the situation and each other. When the fit is more *strategic*, the process will be more effective. We examine services and manufacturing processes, looking for ways to test for strategic fit.

Decision Patterns for Service Processes

After analyzing a process and determining its position on the customer-contact matrix in Figure 3.2, it may be apparent that it is improperly positioned, either too far to the left or right, or too far to the top or bottom. Opportunities for improvement become apparent. Maybe more customization and customer contact is needed than the process currently provides. Perhaps, instead, the process is too divergent, with unnecessarily flexible flows. Reducing divergence might reduce costs and improve productivity.

The process should reflect its desired competitive priorities. Front offices generally emphasize top quality and customization, whereas back offices are more likely to emphasize low-cost operation, consistent quality, and on-time delivery. But many exceptions to this pattern do and should exist. Processes at the same service facility can have different competitive priorities. Processes for McDonald's walk-in customers must be more personal than for its drive-through customers, and need more personal attention at the counter. By contrast drive-through customers, who want even faster delivery speed and an efficient transaction, are likely to be less concerned about getting personal attention.

The process structure selected then points the way to appropriate choices on customer involvement, resource flexibility, and capital intensity. Figure 3.8 shows how these key process decisions are tied to customer contact. High customer contact at a front-office service process means:

1. *Process Structure.* The customer (internal or external) is present, actively involved, and receives personal attention. These conditions create processes with high divergence and flexible process flows.

2. *Customer Involvement.* When customer contact is high, customers are more likely to become part of the process. The service created for each customer is unique.

3. *Resource Flexibility.* High process divergence and flexible process flows fit with more flexibility from the process's resources—its workforce, facilities, and equipment.

FIGURE 3.8 ▼
Decision Patterns for Service Processes

4. *Capital Intensity.*   When volume is higher, automation and capital intensity are more likely. Even though higher volume is usually assumed to be found in the back office, it is just as likely to be in the front office for financial services. Information technology is a major type of automation at many service processes, which brings together both resource flexibility and automation.

Of course, this list provides general tendencies rather than rigid prescriptions. Exceptions can be found, but these relationships provide a way of understanding how service process decisions can be linked coherently.

Decision Patterns for Manufacturing Processes

Just as a service process can be repositioned in the customer-contact matrix, so can a manufacturing process be moved in the product-process matrix. Changes can be made either in the horizontal direction of Figure 3.3 by changing the degree of customization and volume, or they can be moved in the vertical direction by changing process divergence. Process flows can be made more linear by dedicating human and capital resources to a specific product or perhaps a group of similar products. In that way, the sequence of tasks becomes the same. Little divergence is present because, essentially, the same product is made repetitively with no deviations. The production and inventory strategy can also be changed.

Competitive priorities must be considered when translating strategy into specific manufacturing processes. Figure 3.9 shows some usual tendencies found in practice. Job and small batch processes are usual choices if top quality, on-time delivery, and flexibility (customization, variety, and volume flexibility) are given primary emphasis. Large batch, line, and continuous-flow processes match up with an emphasis on low-cost operations, consistent quality, and delivery speed.

For production and inventory strategies, the make-to-order strategy matches up with flexibility (particularly customization) and top quality. Because delivery speed is more difficult, meeting due dates and on-time delivery get the emphasis on the time dimension. The assemble-to-order strategy allows delivery speed and flexibility (particularly variety) to be achieved, whereas the make-to-stock strategy is the usual choice if delivery speed and low-cost operations are emphasized. Keeping an item in stock assures quick delivery because it is generally available when needed, without delays in producing it. High volumes open up opportunities to reduce costs.

The process structure selected once again points the way to appropriate choices on customer involvement, resource flexibility, and capital intensity. Figure 3.10 summarizes the relationships between volume and the four key process decisions. High volumes per part type at a manufacturing process typically mean:

▼ **FIGURE 3.9**
Links of Competitive Priorities with Manufacturing Strategy

(a) Links with Process Choice

(b) Links with Production and Inventory Strategy

1. *Process Structure.*   High volumes, combined with a standard product, make a line flow possible. It is just the opposite where a job process produces to specific customer orders.

2. *Customer Involvement.*   Customer involvement is not a factor in most manufacturing processes, except for choices made on product variety and customization. Less discretion is allowed with line or continuous-flow processes in order to avoid the unpredictable demands required by customized orders.

3. *Resource Flexibility.*   When volumes are high and process divergence is low, flexibility is not needed to utilize resources effectively, and specialization can lead to more efficient processes.

4. *Capital Intensity.*   High volumes justify the large fixed costs of an efficient operation. The King Soopers's bread line is capital-intensive. It is automated from dough mixing to placement of the product on shipping racks. Expanding this process would be expensive. By way of contrast, the King Soopers's custom cake process is labor-intensive and requires little investment to equip the workers.

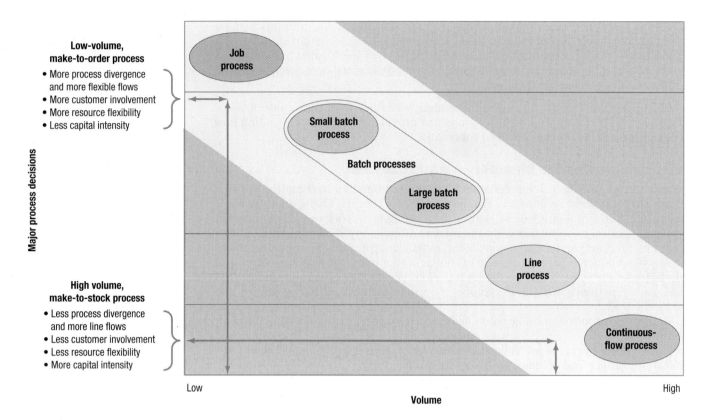

FIGURE 3.10 ▲
Decision Patterns for Manufacturing
Processes

Gaining Focus

In the past, new services or products often were added to a facility in the name of better utilizing fixed costs and keeping everything under the same roof. The result was a jumble of competitive priorities, process structures, and technologies. In the effort to do everything, nothing was done well.

Focus by Process Segments   A facility's operations often can neither be characterized nor actually designed for one set of competitive priorities and one process choice. King Soopers had three processes under one roof, but management segmented them into three separate operations that were relatively autonomous. At a services facility, some parts of the process might seem like a front office and other parts like a back office. Such arrangements can be effective, provided that sufficient focus is given to each process.

plants within plants (PWPs)

Different operations within a facility with individualized competitive priorities, processes, and workforces under the same roof.

   Plants within plants (PWPs) are different operations within a facility with individualized competitive priorities, processes, and workforces under the same roof. Boundaries for PWPs may be established by physically separating subunits or simply by revising organizational relationships. At each PWP, customization, capital intensity volume, and other relationships are crucial and must be complementary. The advantages of PWPs are fewer layers of management, greater ability to rely on team problem solving, and shorter lines of communication between departments.

Focused Service Operations   Service industries also implement the concepts of focus and PWPs. Specialty retailers opened stores with smaller, more accessible spaces. These focused facilities generally chipped away at the business of large department stores. Using the same philosophy, some department stores now focus on specific customers or products. Remodeled stores create the effect of many small boutiques under one roof.

focused factories

The result of a firm's splitting large plants that produced all the company's products into several specialized smaller plants.

Focused Factories   Hewlett-Packard, S.C. Johnson and Sons, Japan's Ricoh and Mitsubishi, and Britain's Imperial Chemical Industries PLC are some of the firms that created **focused factories**, splitting large plants that produced all the company's products into several specialized smaller plants. The theory is that narrowing the range of demands on a facility will lead to better performance because management can concentrate on fewer tasks and lead a workforce toward a single goal. In some situations, a plant that used to produce all the components of a product and assemble them may split into one that produces the components and another that assembles them, so that each can focus on its own individual process technology.

STRATEGIES FOR CHANGE

The four major process decisions represent broad, strategic issues. Decisions that are made must be translated into actual process designs or redesigns. We conclude with two different but complementary philosophies for process design: (1) process reengineering and (2) process improvement.

Process Reengineering

Reengineering is the fundamental rethinking and radical redesign of processes to improve performance dramatically in terms of cost, quality, service, and speed. Process reengineering is about reinvention, rather than incremental improvement. It is strong medicine and not always needed or successful. Pain, in the form of layoffs and large cash outflows for investments in information technology, almost always accompanies massive change. However, reengineering processes can have big payoffs. Table 3.2 lists the key elements of the overall approach.

Reengineering has led to many successes and will continue to do so. However, it is not simple or easily done, nor is it appropriate for all processes or all organizations. The best understanding of a process, and how to improve it, often lies with the people who perform the work each day, not cross-functional teams or top management.

reengineering

The fundamental rethinking and radical redesign of processes to improve performance dramatically in terms of cost, quality, service, and speed.

TABLE 3.2	KEY ELEMENTS OF REENGINEERING
Element	**Description**
Critical processes	The emphasis of reengineering should be on core business processes. Normal process-improvement activities can be continued with the other processes.
Strong leadership	Senior executives must provide strong leadership for reengineering to be successful. Otherwise, cynicism, resistance ("we tried that before"), and boundaries between departments can block radical changes.
Cross-functional teams	A team, consisting of members from each functional area affected by the process change, is charged with carrying out a reengineering project. Self-managing teams and employee empowerment are the rule rather than the exception.
Information technology	Information technology is a primary enabler of process engineering. Most reengineering projects design processes around information flows, such as customer order fulfillment.
Clean-slate philosophy	Reengineering requires a "clean-slate" philosophy—that is, starting with the way the customer wants to deal with the company. To ensure a customer orientation, teams begin with internal and external customer objectives for the process.
Process analysis	Despite the clean-slate philosophy, a reengineering team must understand things about the current process: what it does, how well it performs, and what factors affect it. The team must look at every procedure involved in the process throughout the organization.

Process Improvement

Process improvement is the systematic study of the activities and flows of each process to improve it. Its purpose is to "learn the numbers," understand the process, and dig out the details. Once a process is really understood, it can be improved. The relentless pressure to provide better quality at a lower price means that companies must continually review all aspects of their operations. Process improvement goes on, whether or not a process is reengineered.

An individual or a whole team examines the process, using the tools described in the next chapter. One must look for ways to streamline tasks, eliminate whole processes entirely, cut expensive materials or services, improve the environment, or make jobs safer. One must find the ways to trim costs and delays and to improve customer satisfaction.

process improvement

The systematic study of the activities and flows of each process to improve it.

INTERNET RESOURCES

my**om**lab and the Companion Website at **www.pearsonglobaleditions.com/krajewski** contain many tools, activities, and resources designed for this chapter.

KEY EQUATIONS

1. Euclidean distance: $d_{AB} = \sqrt{(x_A - x_B)^2 + (y_A - y_B)^2}$

2. Rectilinear distance: $d_{AB} = |x_A - x_B| + |y_A - y_B|$

KEY TERMS

assemble-to-order strategy 120
automation 127
back office 118
batch process 119
block plan 121
capital intensity 115
closeness matrix 121
continuous-flow process 119
customer contact 115
customer involvement 115
economies of scope 129
Euclidean distance 123
fixed automation 127

flexible (or programmable)
    automation 128
flexible flow 116
flexible workforce 126
focused factories 132
front office 118
hybrid office 118
industrial robot 128
job process 119
layout 115
line flow 116
line process 119
make-to-order strategy 120

make-to-stock strategy 120
mass customization 120
mass production 120
plants within plants (PWPs) 132
postponement 120
process choice 118
process divergence 116
process improvement 133
process strategy 114
process structure 115
rectilinear distance 123
reengineering 133
resource flexibility 115
weighted-distance method 123

SOLVED PROBLEM 1

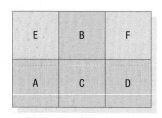

FIGURE 3.11 ▲
Current Layout

A defense contractor is evaluating its machine shop's current layout. Figure 3.11 shows the current layout, and the table shows the closeness matrix for the facility measured as the number of trips per day between department pairs. Safety and health regulations require departments E and F to remain at their current locations.

	Trips Between Departments					
Department	**A**	**B**	**C**	**D**	**E**	**F**
A	—	8	3		9	5
B		—		3		
C			—		8	9
D				—		3
E					—	3
F						—

a. Use trial and error to find a better layout.

b. How much better is your layout than the current layout in terms of the *wd* score? Use rectilinear distance.

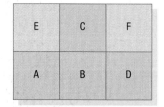

FIGURE 3.12 ▲
Proposed Layout

SOLUTION

a. In addition to keeping departments E and F at their current locations, a good plan would locate the following department pairs close to each other: A and E, C and F, A and B, and C and E. Figure 3.12 was worked out by trial and error and satisfies all these requirements. Start by placing E and F at their current locations. Then, because C must be as close as possible to both E and F, put C between them. Place A below E, and B next to A. All of the heavy traffic concerns have now been accommodated. Department D, located in the remaining space, does not need to be relocated.

Department Pair	Number of Trips (1)	Current Plan Distance (2)	Current Plan *wd* Score (1) × (2)	Proposed Plan Distance (3)	Proposed Plan *wd* Score (1) × (3)
A, B	8	2	16	1	8
A, C	3	1	3	2	6
A, E	9	1	9	1	9
A, F	5	3	15	3	15
B, D	3	2	6	1	3
C, E	8	2	16	1	8
C, F	9	2	18	1	9
D, F	3	1	3	1	3
E, F	3	2	6	2	6
			wd = 92		*wd* = 67

b. The table reveals that the *wd* score drops from 92 for the current plan to 67 for the revised plan, a 27 percent reduction.

DISCUSSION QUESTIONS

1. Select one of the three processes shown in the video for King Soopers (bread, pastry, or custom cakes). What kind of transformation process, process choice, and inventory strategy are involved? Is the process properly aligned? Explain.

2. Rate a service process with which you are familiar on each of the five dimensions of customer contact in Table 3.1. Use a seven-point scale, where 1 = very low and 7 = very high. Explain your ratings, and then calculate a combined score for the overall customer contact. Did you use equal weights in calculating the combined score? Why or why not? Where is your process positioned on the customer-contact matrix? Is it properly aligned? Why or why not?

3. Performance criteria important in creating a layout can go well beyond communication and materials handling. Identify the types of layout performance criteria that might be most important in the following settings.
   a. Airport
   b. Bank
   c. Classroom
   d. Product designers' office
   e. Law firm

4. Consider the range of processes in the financial services industry. What position on the customer-contact matrix would the process of selling financial services to municipalities occupy? The process of preparing monthly fund balance reports? Explain why they would differ.

5. Medical technology can outfit a patient with an artificial heart, or cure vision defects with the touch of a laser. However, hospitals still struggle with their back-office processes, such as getting X-ray files from radiology on the fourth floor to the first-floor view boxes in the emergency room without having to send a runner. More than 90 percent of the estimated 30 billion health transactions each year are conducted by phone, fax, or mail. To what extent, and how, can information technology improve productivity and quality for such processes? Remember that some doctors are not ready to give up their pads and pencils, and many hospitals have strong lines drawn around its departments, such as pharmacy, cardiology, radiology, and pediatrics.

6. How do the process strategies of eBay and McDonald's differ, and how do their choices relate to customer-introduced variability?

7. Consider this sign seen in a local restaurant: "To-go orders do NOT include complimentary chips and salsa. If you have any questions, see our management, NOT our employees." What impact does this message have on its employees, their service processes, and customer satisfaction? Contrast this approach with the one taken by The Ritz-Carlton Hotels (see pg 97). Are the differences primarily due to different competitive priorities?

8. What processes at manufacturing firms are really service processes that involve considerable customer contact? Can customer contact be high, even if the process only has internal customers?

PROBLEMS

Software, such as OM Explorer, Active Models, and POM for Windows, is available in my**om**lab. Check with your instructor on how best to use it. In many cases, the instructor wants you to understand how to do the calculations by hand. At most, the software provides a check on your calculations. When calculations are particularly complex and the goal is interpreting the results in making decisions, the software replaces entirely the manual calculations. Problems 4 and 5 apply break-even analysis (discussed in Supplement A, "Decision Making Models") to process decisions.

1. Baker Machine Company is a job shop that specializes in precision parts for firms in the aerospace industry. Figure 3.13 shows the current block plan for the key manufacturing centers of the 75,000-square-foot facility. Refer to the following closeness matrix and use rectilinear distance (the current distance from inspection to shipping and receiving is three units) to calculate the change in the weighted distance, *wd*, score if Baker exchanges the locations of the tool crib and inspection.

Closeness Matrix						
	Trips Between Departments					
Department	**1**	**2**	**3**	**4**	**5**	**6**
1. Burr and grind	—	8	3		9	5
2. Numericaly controlled (NC) equipment		—	3			
3. Shipping and receiving			—		8	9
4. Lathes and drills				—		3
5. Tool crib					—	3
6. Inspection						—

▲ FIGURE 3.13
Current Layout

2. Use trial and error to find a particularly good block plan for Baker Machine (see Problem 1). Because of excessive relocation costs, shipping and receiving (department 3) must remain at its current location. Compare *wd* scores to evaluate your new layout, again assuming rectilinear distance.

3. The head of the information systems group at Conway Consulting must assign six new analysts to offices. The following closeness matrix shows the expected frequency of contact between analysts. The block plan in Figure 3.14 shows the available office locations (1–6) for the six analysts (A–F). Assume equal-sized offices and rectilinear distance. Owing to their tasks, Analyst A must be assigned to location 4 and Analyst D to location 3. What are the best locations for the other four analysts? What is the *wd* score for your layout?

Closeness Matrix						
	Contacts Between Analysts					
Analyst	**A**	**B**	**C**	**D**	**E**	**F**
Analyst A	—		6			
Analyst B		—		12		
Analyst C			—		2	7
Analyst D				—		4
Analyst E					—	
Analyst F						—

▲ FIGURE 3.14
Conway Consulting's Block Plan

4. Dr. Gulakowicz is an orthodontist. She estimates that adding two new chairs will increase fixed costs by $150,000, including the annual equivalent cost of the capital investment and the salary of one more technician. Each new patient is expected to bring in $3,000 per year in additional revenue, with variable costs estimated at $1,000 per patient. The two new chairs will allow Dr. Gulakowicz to expand her practice by as many as 200 patients annually. How many patients would have to be added for the new process to break even?

5. Two different manufacturing processes are being considered for making a new product. The first process is less capital-intensive, with fixed costs of only $50,000 per year and variable costs of $700 per unit. The second process has fixed costs of $400,000 but variable costs of only $200 per unit.

   a. What is the break-even quantity, beyond which the second process becomes more attractive than the first?

   b. If the expected annual sales for the product is 800 units, which process would you choose?

6. Richard Garber is the head designer for Matthews and Novak Design Company. Garber has been called in to design the layout for a newly constructed office building.

From statistical samplings over the past three months, Garber developed the following closeness matrix for daily trips between the department's offices.

Closeness Matrix

Trips Between Departments

Department	A	B	C	D	E	F
A	—	25	90			185
B		—			105	
C			—		125	125
D				—	25	
E					—	105
F						—

a. If other factors are equal, which two offices should be located closest together?

b. Figure 3.15 shows an alternative layout for the department. What is the total weighted-distance score for this plan based on rectilinear distance and assuming that offices A and B are three units of distance apart?

c. Swapping which two departments will most improve the total weighted-distance score?

▲ **FIGURE 3.15**
Alternative Block Plan

7. A firm with four departments has the following closeness matrix and the current block plan shown in Figure 3.16.

   a. What is the weighted-distance score for the current layout (assuming rectilinear distance)?

Closeness Matrix

Trips Between Departments

Department	A	B	C	D
A	—	12	10	8
B		—	20	6
C			—	0
D				—

▲ **FIGURE 3.16**
Current Block Plan

b. Develop a better layout. What is its total weighted-distance score?

8. The department of engineering at a university in New Jersey must assign six faculty members to their new offices. The following closeness matrix indicates the expected number of contacts per day between professors. The available office spaces (1–6) for the six faculty members are shown in Figure 3.17. Assume equal-sized offices. The distance between offices 1 and 2 (and between offices 1 and 3) is 1 unit, whereas the distance between offices 1 and 4 is 2 units.

Closeness Matrix

Contacts Between Professors

Professor	A	B	C	D	E	F
A	—		4			
B		—	12		10	
C			—	2	7	
D				—		4
E					—	
F						—

a. Because of their academic positions, Professor A must be assigned to office 1, Professor C must be assigned to office 2, and Professor D must be assigned to office 6. Which faculty members should be assigned to offices 3, 4, and 5, respectively, to minimize the total weighted-distance score (assuming rectilinear distance)?

b. What is the weighted-distance score of your solution?

▲ **FIGURE 3.17**
Available Space

ACTIVE MODEL EXERCISE

This Active Model for Example 3.1 appears in my**om**lab. It allows you to see the effects of performing paired swaps of departments.

QUESTIONS

1. What is the current total weighted-distance score?

2. Use the swap button one swap at a time. If the swap helps, move to the next pair. If the swap does not help, hit the swap button once again to put the departments back. What is the minimum weighted-distance score after all swaps have been tried?

3. Look at the two data tables, and use the yellow-shaded column to put departments in spaces. What space assignments lead to the minimum cost? What is this cost?

Layout Using Data from Example 3.1

CASE	Custom Molds, Inc.

Custom Molds, Inc., manufactures custom-designed molds for plastic parts and produces custom-made plastic connectors for the electronics industry. Located in Tucson, Arizona, Custom Molds was founded by the father and son team of Tom and Mason Miller in 1987. Tom Miller, a mechanical engineer, had more than 20 years of experience in the connector industry with AMP, Inc., a large multinational producer of electronic connectors. Mason Miller graduated from the Arizona State University in 1986 with joint degrees in chemistry and chemical engineering.

The company was originally formed to provide manufacturers of electronic connectors with a source of high-quality, custom-designed molds for producing plastic parts. The market consisted mainly of the product design and development divisions of those manufacturers. Custom Molds worked closely with each customer to design and develop molds to be used in the customer's product development processes. Thus, virtually every mold had to meet exacting standards and was somewhat unique. Orders for multiple molds would arrive when customers moved from the design and pilot-run stage of development to large-scale production of newly designed parts.

As the years went by, Custom Molds's reputation grew as a designer and fabricator of precision molds. Building on this reputation, the Millers decided to expand into the limited manufacture of plastic parts. Ingredient-mixing facilities and injection-molding equipment were added, and by the mid-1990s Custom Molds developed its reputation to include being a supplier of high-quality plastic parts. Because of limited capacity, the company concentrated its sales efforts on supplying parts that were used in limited quantities for research and development efforts and in preproduction pilot runs.

Production Processes

By 2000, operations at Custom Molds involved two distinct processes: one for fabricating molds and one for producing plastic parts. Although different, in many instances these two processes were linked, as when a customer would have Custom Molds both fabricate a mold and produce the necessary parts to support the customer's research and design efforts. All fabrication and production operations were housed in a single facility. The layout was characteristic of a typical job shop, with like processes and similar equipment grouped in various places in the plant. Figure 3.18 shows a layout of the plant floor. Multiple pieces of various types of high-precision machinery,

▲ **FIGURE 3.18**
Plant Layout

including milling, turning, cutting, and drilling equipment, were located in the mold-fabrication area.

Fabricating molds is a skill-oriented, craftsman-driven process. When an order is received, a design team, comprising a design engineer and one of 13 master machinists, reviews the design specifications. Working closely with the customer, the team establishes the final specifications for the mold and gives them to the master machinist for fabrication. It is always the same machinist who was assigned to the design team. At the same time, the purchasing department is given a copy of the design specifications, from which it orders the appropriate raw materials and special tooling. The time needed to receive the ordered materials is usually three to four weeks. When the materials are received for a particular mold, the plant master scheduler reviews the workload of the assigned master machinist and schedules the mold for fabrication.

Fabricating a mold takes from two to four weeks, depending on the amount of work the machinist already has scheduled. The fabrication process itself takes only three to five days. Upon completion, the mold is sent to the testing and inspection area, where it is used to produce a small number of parts on one of the injection molding machines. If the parts meet the design specifications established by the design team, the mold is passed on to be cleaned and polished. It is then packed and shipped to the customer. One day is spent inspecting and testing the mold and a second day cleaning, polishing, packing, and shipping it to the customer. If the parts made by the mold do not meet design specifications, the mold is returned to the master machinist for retooling and the process starts over. Currently, Custom Molds has a published lead time of nine weeks for delivery of custom-fabricated molds.

The manufacturing process for plastic parts is somewhat different from that for mold fabrication. An order for parts may be received in conjunction with an order for a mold to be fabricated. In instances where Custom Molds has previously fabricated the mold and maintains it in inventory, an order may be just for parts. If the mold is already available, the order is reviewed by a design engineer, who verifies the part and raw material specifications. If the design engineer has any questions concerning the specifications, the customer is contacted and any revisions to specifications are mutually worked out and agreed upon.

Upon acceptance of the part and raw material specifications, raw material orders are placed and production is scheduled for the order. Chemicals and compounds that support plastic-parts manufacturing are typically ordered and received within one week. Upon receipt, the compounds are first dry-mixed and blended to achieve the correct composition. Then the mixture is wet-mixed to the desired consistency (called *slurry*) for injection into molding machines. When ready, the slurry is transferred to the injection molding area by an overhead pipeline and deposited in holding tanks adjacent to the injection machines. The entire mixing process takes only one day.

When the slurry is staged and ready, the proper molds are secured—from inventory or from the clean and polish operation if new molds were fabricated for the order—and the parts are manufactured. Although different parts require different temperature and pressure settings, the time to produce a part is relatively constant. Custom Molds has the capacity to produce 5,000 parts per day in the injection-molding department; historically, however, the lead time for handling orders in this department has averaged one week. Upon completion of molding, the parts are taken to the cut and trim operation, where they are disconnected and leftover flashing is removed. After being inspected, the parts may be taken to assembly or transferred to the packing and shipping area for shipment to the customer. If assembly of the final parts is not required, the parts can be on their way to the customer two days after being molded.

Sometimes the final product requires some assembly. Typically, this entails attaching metal leads to plastic connectors. If assembly is necessary, an additional three days are needed before the order can be shipped. Custom Molds is currently quoting a three-week lead time for parts not requiring fabricated molds.

The Changing Environment

In early 2009, Tom and Mason Miller began to realize that the electronics industry they supplied, along with their own business, was changing. Electronics manufacturers had traditionally manufactured their own component parts to reduce costs and ensure a timely supply of parts. By the 1990s, this trend had changed. Manufacturers were developing strategic partnerships with parts suppliers to ensure the timely delivery of high-quality, cost-effective parts. This approach allowed funds to be diverted to other uses that could provide a larger return on investment.

The impact on Custom Molds could be seen in sales figures over the past three years. The sales mix was changing. Although the number of orders per year for mold fabrication remained virtually constant, orders for multiple molds were declining, as shown in the following table:

	Number of Orders		
Order Size	**Molds 2006**	**Molds 2007**	**Molds 2008**
1	80	74	72
2	60	70	75
3	40	51	55
4	5	6	5
5	3	5	4
6	4	8	5
7	2	0	1
8	10	6	4
9	11	8	5
10	15	10	5
Total orders	230	238	231

The reverse was true for plastic parts, for which the number of orders per year had declined, but for which the order sizes were becoming larger, as illustrated in the following table:

	Number of Orders		
Order Size	**Parts 2006**	**Parts 2007**	**Parts 2008**
50	100	93	70
100	70	72	65
150	40	30	35
200	36	34	38
250	25	27	25
500	10	12	14
750	1	3	5
1,000	2	2	8
3,000	1	4	9
5,000	1	3	8
Total orders	286	280	277

During this same period, Custom Molds began having delivery problems. Customers were complaining that parts orders were taking four to five weeks instead of the stated three weeks and that the delays were disrupting production schedules. When asked about the situation, the master scheduler said that determining when a particular order could be promised for delivery was difficult. Bottlenecks were occurring during the production process, but where or when they would occur could not be predicted. The bottlenecks always seemed to be moving from one operation to another.

Tom Miller thought that he had excess labor capacity in the mold-fabrication area. So, to help push through those orders that were behind schedule, he assigned one of the master machinists the job of identifying and expediting those late orders. However, that tactic did not seem to help much. Complaints about late deliveries were still being received. To add to the problems, two orders had been returned recently because of the number of defective parts. The Millers knew that something had to be done. The question was "What?"

QUESTIONS

1. What are the major issues facing Tom and Mason Miller?
2. What are the competitive priorities for Custom Molds's processes and the changing nature of the industry?
3. What alternatives might the Millers pursue? What key factors should they consider as they evaluate these alternatives?

Source: This case was prepared by Dr. Brooke Saladin, Wake Forest University, as a basis for classroom discussion.

Selected References

Bitner, Mary Jo. "Servicescapes: The Impact of Physical Surroundings on Customers and Employees." *Journal of Marketing*, vol. 56 (April 1992), pp. 57–71.

Bowen, John, and Robert C. Ford. "Managing Service Organizations: Does Having a 'Thing' Make a Difference?" *Journal of Management*, vol. 28, no. 3 (2002), pp. 447–469.

Collier, D. A., and Meyer, S. "An Empirical Comparison of Service Matrices." *International Journal of Operations and Production Management*, vol. 20, no. 5–6 (2000), pp. 705–729.

Collins, Jim. *Good to Great: Why Some Companies Make the Leap...and Others Don't*. New York: HarperCollins, 2001.

Cook, David P., Chon-Huat Goh, and Chen H. Chung. "Service Typologies: A State of the Art Survey." *Production and Operations Management*, vol. 8, no. 3 (1999), pp. 318–338.

Dixon, J. Robb, Peter Arnold, Janelle Heineke, Jay S. Kim, and Paul Mulligan. "Business Process Reengineering: Improving in New Strategic Directions." *California Management Review* (Summer 1994), pp. 1–17.

Goldhar, J. D., and Mariann Jelinek. "Plan for Economies of Scope." *Harvard Business Review* (November–December 1983), pp. 141–148.

Grover, Varun, and Manoj K. Malhotra. "Business Process Reengineering: A Tutorial on the Concept, Evolution, Method, Technology and Application." *Journal of Operations Management*, vol. 15, no. 3 (1997), pp. 194–213.

Hall, Gene, Jim Rosenthal, and Judy Wade. "How to Make Reengineering Really Work." *Harvard Business Review* (November–December 1993), pp. 119–131.

Hammer, Michael. *Beyond Reengineering*. New York: Harper Business, 1996.

Hammer, Michael. "Deep Change: How Operational Innovation Can Transform Your Company." *Harvard Business Review*, vol. 82, no. 4 (April 2004), pp. 85–93.

Hammer, Michael, and James Champy. *Reengineering the Corporation: A Manifesto for Business Revolution*. New York: HarperBusiness, 1993.

Hill, Terry. *Manufacturing Strategy: Text and Cases*, 3d ed. Homewood, IL: Irwin/McGraw-Hill, 2000.

Hill, Terry. *The Strategy Quest*. Coventry, Great Britain: AMD Publishing (UK), 1998.

Jack, Eric, and John Collis. "Strengthen and Tone: A Flexible Approach to Operations Can Build Some Serious Muscle." *APICS Magazine* (June 2006), pp. 35–38.

Kelliher, Clare, and Michael Riley. "Beyond Efficiency: Some By-Products of Functional Flexibility." *Service Industries Journal*, vol. 23, no. 4 (2003), pp. 98–114.

Kellogg, Deborah L., and Winter Nie. "A Framework for Strategic Service Management." *Journal of Operations Management*, vol. 13, no. 4 (1995), pp. 323–337.

Lovelock, Christopher H., and George S. Yip. "Developing Global Strategies for Service Businesses." *California Management Review*, vol. 38, no. 2 (1996), pp. 64–86.

Makowe, J. *Beyond the Bottom Line*. New York: Simon & Schuster, 1994.

Malhotra, Manoj K., and Larry P. Ritzman. "Resource Flexibility Issues in Multistage Manufacturing." *Decision Sciences*, vol. 21, no. 4 (1990), pp. 673–690.

Mersha, Tigineh. "Enhancing the Customer Contact Model." *Journal of Operations Management*, vol. 9, no. 3 (1990), pp. 391–405.

Metters, Richard, Kathryn King-Metters, and Madeleine Pullman. *Successful Service Operations Management*. Mason, OH: South-Western, 2003.

Narasimhan, Ram, and Jayanth Jayaram. "Reengineering Service Operations: A Longitudinal Case Study." *Journal of Operations Management*, vol. 17, no. 1 (1998), pp. 7–22.

Port, Otis. "The Responsive Factory." *Business Week*, Enterprise 1993, pp. 48–51.

"Process, Process, Process." *Planning Review* (special issue), vol. 22, no. 3 (1993), pp. 1–56.

Quinn, J. B. "The Productivity Paradox Is False: Information Technology Improves Services Performance." *Advances in Services Marketing and Management*, vol. 5 (1996), pp. 71–84.

Rayport, Jeffrey F., and Bernard J. Jaworski. "Best Face Forward." *Harvard Business Review*, vol. 82, no. 12 (2003), pp. 47–58.

Safizadeh, M. Hossein, Joy M. Field, and Larry P. Ritzman. "An Empirical Analysis of Financial Services Processes with a Front-Office or Back-Office Orientation." *Journal of Operations Management*, vol. 21, no. 5 (2003), pp. 557–576.

Safizadeh, M. Hossein, Larry P. Ritzman, and Debasish Mallick. "Revisiting Alternative Theoretical Paradigms in Manufacturing." *Production and Operations Management*, vol. 9, no. 2 (2000), pp. 111–127.

Schlosser, Julie. "The Great Escape." *Fortune* (March 20, 2006), pp. 107–110.

Schmenner, Roger W. *Service Operations Management*. Englewood Cliffs, NJ: Prentice Hall, 1998.

Shostack, G. Lynn. "Service Positioning Through Structural Change." *Journal of Marketing*, vol. 51, no. 1 (1987), pp. 34–43.

Skinner, Wickham. "Operations Technology: Blind Spot in Strategic Management." *Interfaces*, vol. 14 (January–February 1984), pp. 116–125.

Wemmerlöv, U. "A Taxonomy for Service Processes and Its Implications for System Design." *International Journal of Service Industry Management*, vol. 1, no. 1 (1990), pp. 20–40.

Wheelwright, Steven C., and Robert H. Hayes. "Competing Through Manufacturing." *Harvard Business Review* (January–February 1985), pp. 99–109.

4 ANALYZING PROCESSES

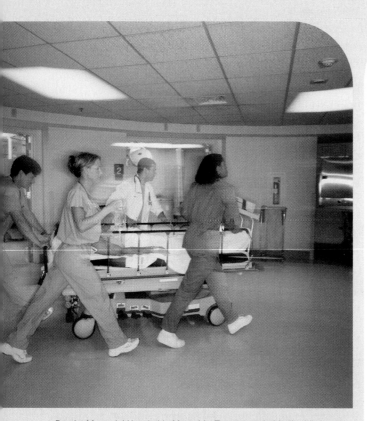

Baptist Memorial Hospital in Memphis, Tennessee, holds "huddle meetings" at least three times a day seeking out process improvements. The meetings bring together the hospital's house supervisor, housekeeping supervisor, and key nurses. Improvements have been dramatic.

BAPTIST MEMORIAL HOSPITAL

Baptist Memorial Hospital–Memphis is a 706-bed tertiary care hospital. It had a capacity problem, or so it seemed, with occupancy routinely exceeding 90 percent. However, it solved the problem with process improvement, rather than adding staff or bed capacity. Administration, nurses, and physicians centralized bed assignments and added a new bed-tracking system to provide bed information in real time. They then focused on improving processes at the emergency department (ED). An express admission unit (EAU), a 21-bed dedicated area that processes direct and emergency department admissions, was opened to remove responsibility for a particularly time-intensive activity from busy unit nurses. The new processes were less divergent and had more of a line flow. They then began testing process improvement ideas for change on a small scale, altering processes to improve them, and spreading the processes to other areas when they are successful. They began to fax reports from the ED to the receiving unit, shifted more nurses to work during peak periods, began lab and X-ray diagnostic procedures at triage when the EU was at capacity, took patients directly to a room when one became available with bedside registration, and segmented the urgent care population within the ED.

Redesigned processes reduced patient delays. Turnaround time for the overall ED was reduced by 9 percent, even while the ED volume was increasing. Length of stay was reduced by 2 days, the equivalent of building 12 Intensive care unit (ICU) beds. The mortality rate decreased, volume increased by

LEARNING GOALS

After reading this chapter, you should be able to:

1. Explain a systematic way to analyze processes.
2. Define flowcharts, service blueprints, and process charts.
3. Describe the various work measurement techniques.
4. Identify metrics for process evaluation.
5. Describe Pareto charts, cause-and-effect diagrams, and process simulation.
6. Create better processes using benchmarking.
7. Identify keys for effective process management.

20 percent, and patient satisfaction improved significantly. What first appeared to be a capacity problem was resolved without adding staff or the number of beds—it was solved with redesigned processes.

Sources: Suzanne S. Horton, "Increasing Capacity While Improving the Bottom Line," *Frontiers of Health Services Management*, vol. 20, no. 4 (Summer 2004), pp. 17–23; Richard S. Zimmerman, "Hospital Capacity, Productivity, and Patient Safety—It All Flows Together," *Frontiers of Health Services Management*, vol. 20, no. 4 (Summer 2004), pp. 33–38.

myomlab and the Companion Website at **www.pearsonglobaleditions.com/krajewski** contain many tools, activities, and resources designed for this chapter.

process analysis

The documentation and detailed understanding of how work is performed and how it can be redesigned.

FIGURE 4.1 ▼
Blueprint for Process Analysis

Processes are perhaps the least understood and managed aspect of a business. No matter how talented and motivated people are, a firm cannot gain competitive advantage with faulty processes. Just as Mark Twain said of the Mississippi River, a process just keeps rolling on—with one big difference. Most processes can be improved if someone thinks of a way and implements it effectively. Indeed, companies will either adapt processes to the changing needs of customers or cease to exist. Long-term success comes from managers and employees who really understand their businesses. But all too often, highly publicized efforts that seem to offer quick-fix solutions fail to live up to expectations over the long haul, be they programs for conceptualizing a business vision, conducting culture transformation campaigns, or providing leadership training.

Within the field of operations management, many important innovations over the past several decades include work-simplification or better-methods programs, statistical process control, optimization techniques, statistical forecasting techniques, material requirements planning, flexible automation, lean manufacturing, total quality management, reengineering, Six Sigma programs, enterprise resource planning, and e-commerce. We cover these important approaches in the following chapters because they can add significant customer value to a process. However, they are best viewed as just part of a total system for the effective management of work processes, rather than cure-alls.

Of course, process analysis is needed for both reengineering and process improvement, but it is also part of monitoring performance over time. In this chapter, we begin with a systematic approach for analyzing a process that identifies opportunities for improvement, documents the current process, evaluates the process to spot performance gaps, redesigns the process to eliminate the gaps, and implements the desired changes. The goal is continual improvement.

Three supporting techniques—flowcharts, service blueprints, and process charts—can give good insights into the current process and the proposed changes. Work measurement techniques provide the all-important estimates on how long different tasks will take. Data analysis tools, such as checklists, bar charts, Pareto charts, and cause-and-effect diagrams, allow the analyst to go from problem symptoms to root causes. Simulation is a more advanced technique to evaluate process performance. We conclude with some of the keys to managing processes effectively, to ensuring that changes are implemented and an infrastructure is set up for making continuous improvements. Process analysis, however, extends beyond the analysis of individual processes. It is also a tool for improving the operation of supply chains.

PROCESS ANALYSIS ACROSS THE ORGANIZATION

All parts of an organization need to be concerned about process analysis simply because they are doing work, and process analysis focuses on how work is actually done. Are they providing the most value to their customers (internal or external), or can they be improved? Operations and sales departments are often the first areas that come to mind because they are so closely connected with the core processes. However, support processes in accounting, finance, and human resources are crucial to an organization's success as well. Top management also gets involved, as do other departments. During these handoffs of the "baton," disconnects are often the worst and opportunities for improvement the greatest.

A SYSTEMATIC APPROACH

Figure 4.1 shows a six-step blueprint for process analysis. **Process analysis** is the documentation and detailed understanding of how work is performed and how it can be redesigned. Process analysis begins with identifying a new opportunity for improvement and ends with implementing a revised process. The last step goes back to the first step, thus creating a cycle of continual improvement. Of course, many approaches can be used for systematically analyzing processes. See reengineering in Chapter 3,

"Developing a Process Strategy," the Six Sigma Improvement Model in Chapter 5, "Managing Quality," and the value stream mapping and other techniques used in Chapter 8, "Designing Lean Systems." A shared goal is: better processes.

Step 1: Identify Opportunities

In order to identify opportunities, managers must pay particular attention to the four core processes: (1) supplier relationship, (2) new service/product development, (3) order fulfillment, and (4) the customer relationship. Each of these processes, and the subprocesses nested within them, are involved in delivering value to external customers. Are customers currently satisfied with the services or products they receive, or is there room for improvement? How about internal customers? Customer satisfaction must be monitored periodically, either with a formal measurement system or with informal checks or studies. Managers sometimes develop an inventory of their core and support processes that provide a guide for what processes need scrutiny.

Another way to identify opportunities is by looking at the strategic issues. Do gaps exist between a process's competitive priorities and its current competitive capabilities, as was found for the assessment of operations strategy at a credit card division in Chapter 1, "Using Operations to Compete"? Do multiple measures of cost, top quality, quality consistency, delivery speed, and on-time delivery meet or exceed expectations? Is there a good *strategic fit* in the process? If the process provides a service, does its position on the customer-contact matrix (see Figure 3.2) seem appropriate? How does the degree of customer contact match up with process structure, customer involvement, resource flexibility, and capital intensity (see Figure 3.8)? Similar questions should be asked about manufacturing processes regarding the strategic fit between process choice, volume, and product customization (see Figure 3.10).

Employees who actually perform the process or internal suppliers or customers should be encouraged to bring their ideas to managers and staff specialists (such as industrial engineers), or perhaps pass on their ideas through a formal suggestion system. A **suggestion system** is a voluntary system by which employees submit their ideas on process improvements. Usually, a specialist evaluates the proposals, makes sure worthy suggestions are implemented, and provides feedback to those who make the suggestions. Sometimes the person or team making a good suggestion is rewarded with money or special recognition.

suggestion system

A voluntary system by which employees submit their ideas on process improvements.

Step 2: Define the Scope

Step 2 establishes the boundaries of the process to be analyzed. Is it a broad process that stretches across the whole organization, involving many steps and many employees, or a more narrowly bracketed nested subprocess that is just part of one person's job? A process's scope can be too narrow or too broad. For example, a broadly defined process that outstrips the resources available, sometimes called "trying to boil the ocean," is doomed because it will increase employee frustration without producing any results.

The resources that management assigns to improving or reengineering a process should match the scope of the process. For a small nested process involving only one employee, perhaps he or she is asked to redesign the process. For a project that deals with a major core process, managers typically establish one or more teams. A **design team** consists of knowledgeable, team-oriented individuals who work at one or more steps in the process, do the process analysis, and make the necessary changes. Other resources may be full-time specialists called internal or external *facilitators*. Facilitators know process analysis methodology, and they can guide and train the design team. If the process cuts across several departmental lines, it may benefit from a *steering team* of several managers from various departments, headed by a project manager who oversees the process analysis.

design team

A group of knowledgeable, team-oriented individuals who work at one or more steps in the process, do the process analysis, and make the necessary changes.

Step 3: Document the Process

Once scope is established, the analyst should document the process. Documentation includes making a list of the process's inputs, suppliers (internal or external), outputs, and customers (internal or external). This information then can be shown as a diagram, with a more detailed breakdown given in a table.

The next part of documentation is understanding the different steps performed in the process, using one or more of the diagrams, tables, and charts described later in this chapter. When breaking down the process into steps, the analyst notes the degrees and types of customer contact and process divergence along the various steps in the process. The analyst also notes what steps are visible to the customer and where in the process work is handed off from one department to the next.

Step 4: Evaluate Performance

It is important to have good performance measures to evaluate a process for clues on how to improve it. **Metrics** are performance measures for the process and the steps within it. A good place to start is with competitive priorities, but they need to be specific. The analyst creates multiple measures of quality, customer satisfaction, time to perform each step or the whole process, cost, errors, safety, environmental measures, on-time delivery, flexibility, and the like.

Once the metrics are identified, it is time to collect information on how the process is currently performing on each one. Measurement can be rough-cut estimates or quite extensive. Techniques for analyzing wait times and delays can provide important information (see Supplement B, "Simulation Models" and Supplement C, "Waiting Line Models"). Work measurement techniques are also more extensive and are previewed in a later section of this chapter.

Step 5: Redesign the Process

A careful analysis of the process and its performance on the selected metrics should uncover *disconnects*, or gaps, between actual and desired performance. Performance gaps can be caused by illogical, missing, or extraneous steps. They can be caused by metrics that reinforce the silo mentality of individual departments when the process spans across several departments. The analyst or design team should dig deep to find the root causes of performance gaps.

Using analytical and creative thinking, the design team generates a long list of ideas for improvements. These ideas are then sifted and analyzed. Ideas that are justifiable, where benefits outweigh costs, are reflected in a new process design. The new design should be documented "as proposed." Combining the new process design with the documentation of the current process gives the analysts clear before and after pictures. The new documentation should make clear how the revised process will work and the performance expected for the various metrics used.

Step 6: Implement Changes

Implementation is more than developing a plan and carrying it out. Many processes have been redesigned effectively, but never get implemented. People resist change: "We have always done it that way" or "we tried that before." Widespread participation in process analysis is essential, not only because of the work involved but also because it builds commitment. It is much easier to implement something that is partly your own idea. In addition, special expertise may be needed, such as for developing software. New jobs and skills may be needed, involving training and investments in new technology. Implementation brings to life the steps needed to bring the redesigned process online. Management or the steering committee must make sure that the implementation project goes according to schedule.

In the remainder of this chapter, we examine steps in process analysis in detail. Managerial Practice 4.1 describes how McDonald's analyzed its processes to spot ways to improve them and restore customer satisfaction.

DOCUMENTING THE PROCESS

Three techniques are effective for documenting and evaluating processes: (1) flowcharts, (2) service blueprints, and (3) process charts. They allow you to lift the lid and peer inside to see how an organization does its work. You can see how a process operates, at any level of detail, and how well it is performing. Trying to create one of these charts might even reveal a lack of any established process. It may not be a pretty picture, but it is how work actually gets done. Techniques for documenting the process lend themselves to finding performance gaps, generating ideas for process improvements, and documenting the look of a redesigned process.

Flowcharts

A **flowchart** traces the flow of information, customers, equipment, or materials through the various steps of a process. Flowcharts are also known as flow diagrams, process maps, relationship maps, or blueprints. Flowcharts have no precise format and typically are drawn with boxes (with a brief description of the step inside), and with lines and arrows to show sequencing. The rectangle ($\square$) shape is the usual choice for a box, although other shapes ($\bigcirc$, $\bigcirc$, $\bigtriangledown$, or $\square$) can differentiate between different types of steps (e.g., operation, delay,

MANAGERIAL PRACTICE 4.1	Process Improvement at McDonald's

System sales (including franchised and affiliated sales) at McDonald's reached $69.7 billion in 2007, up from $44.5 billion in 2002 and there are more than 31,000 restaurants around the world. Things were not so good in 2002, when customer complaints were growing more frequent and bitter. McDonald's is now listening to the customers again, and changing its processes to reflect it. The board brought on a new CEO who had spent 20 years on the operational side of the business. With a zeal for measuring customer satisfaction and sharing the data freely with operators, he pulled off a turnaround that stunned everyone in the business with its speed and scope. A million more diners flocked daily to the arches in 2003 than in 2002. The stock price is also up, from $16.08 at the end of 2002 to $58.91 at the end of 2007.

Initiatives were launched to collect performance measures and revamp McDonald's processes to meet customer expectations. McDonald's sends mystery shoppers to restaurants to conduct anonymous reviews using a hard-number scoring system. Mystery diners from outside survey firms jot down on a paper checklist their grades for speed of service; food temperature; presentation and taste; cleanliness of the counter, tables and condiment islands; even whether the counter crewperson smiles at diners. Trailing six-month and year-to-date results are posted on an internal McDonald's Web site so owners can compare their scores with regional averages. Operators could now pinpoint lingering problems, and performance measures focus operators' attention on needed process changes. Customers now are encouraged to report their experience at a particular U.S. restaurant by e-mail, regular mail, or toll-free telephone call.

Another initiative was to send 900 operations missionaries into the field, each visiting stores multiple times to fine-tune processes while also conducting day-long seminars where store managers could share tips from corporate kitchen gurus—such as where to place staff—that would shave precious seconds off average service times. The process was changed back to toasting buns rather than microwaving them, giving them an even sweeter caramelized flavor. Other initiatives were taken on McDonald's fast lane. Every six seconds shaved off the wait time adds a percentage point to sales growth. Outdoor menu boards now have more pictures and fewer words. An LED display confirms what customers say, reducing confusion later on. Premium sandwiches are put in boxes rather than paper wrappers,

saving a few seconds, and boxes are color coded by sandwich to improve speed and accuracy.

McDonald's uses mystery shoppers to evaluate its stores. It also sends operations "emissaries" to its stores to help managers fine-tune their processes, while revising processes and its supply chain to be more environmentally friendly.

Processes are also being changed to be environment friendly, reaching back from the counters of its restaurants into its supply chain. The U.S. menu involves 330 unique consumer package designs, with 83 percent now made from paper or some other wood-fiber material. Its bulk cooking oil delivery system uses reusable containers, eliminating more than 1,500 pounds of packaging waste per restaurant per year. It is working with its suppliers to improve coatings on its food packaging. It has shifted more than 18,000 metric tons of fish away from unsustainable sources over the past 5 years. It emphasizes reuse and recycling, managing electrical energy, and effective water management.

All in all, performance measurement and process analysis are increasing customer value and paying off on the bottom line.

Sources: Daniel Kruger, "You Want Data with That?" *Forbes*, vol. 173, no. 6 (March 2004), pp. 58–60; http://www.mcdonalds.com, May 18, 2008.

storage, inspection, and so on). Colors and shading can also call attention to different types of steps, such as those particularly high on process divergence. Divergence is also communicated when an outgoing arrow from a step splits into two or more arrows that lead to different boxes. Although many representations are acceptable, there must be agreement on the conventions used. They can be given as a key somewhere in the flowchart, or described in accompanying text. It is also important to communicate *what* (e.g., information, customer order, customer, materials, and so on) is being tracked.

You can create flowcharts with several programs. Microsoft PowerPoint offers many different formatting choices for flowcharts (see the Flowchart submenu under AutoShapes). The "Flowcharting Tutor in Excel" in my**om**lab offers another option. Other powerful software packages for flowcharting and drawing diagrams (such as organization charts and decision trees) are SmartDraw (www.smartdraw.com), Microsoft Visio (www.microsoft.com/office/vision), and Micrografx (www.micrografx.com). Often, free downloads are available at such sites on a trial basis.

Flowcharts can be created for several levels in the organization. For example, at the strategic level, they could show the core processes and their linkages, as in Figure 1.4. At this

A consultant discusses the proposal for a new organizational development program with clients during a follow-up meeting. The use of flowcharts can help in understanding this step as just one part of the overall sales process for a consulting company.

level, the flowcharts would not have much detail; however, they would give a bird's eye view of the overall business. Just identifying a core process is often helpful. Let us now turn to the process level, where we get into the details of the process being analyzed. Figure 4.2 shows such a process, which consists of many steps that have subprocesses nested within them. Rather than representing everything in one flowchart, Figure 4.2 presents an overview of the whole process. It describes the sales process for a consulting firm that specializes in organizational development and corporate education programs. Four different departments (accounting, consulting, marketing, and sales) interact with the external customer (client). The process goes through three main phases: (1) generating business leads, (2) client agreement and service delivery, and (3) billing and collection.

Figure 4.2 illustrates one other feature. The diamond shape ($\diamond$) represents a yes/no decision or outcome, such as the results of an inspection or a recognition of different kinds of customer requirements. In Figure 4.2, the diamond represents three yes/no decision points: (1) whether the proposal is complete, (2) whether consulting approves the invoice, and (3) whether payment is received. These yes/no decision points are more likely to appear when a process is high in divergence.

Nested processes can then be created for steps that were more aggregated. For example, Figure 4.3 flowcharts

FIGURE 4.2 ▼
Flowchart of the Sales Process for a Consulting Company

a nested process within the client agreement and service delivery step in Figure 4.2. Figure 4.3 brings out more details, such as invoicing the customer for 50 percent of the total estimated cost of the service before the service is delivered, and then putting together a final invoice after the service is finished. This nesting approach often becomes a practical necessity because only so much detail can be shown in any single flowchart.

Figure 4.4 shows still another format that is most appropriate when the process spans several department boundaries. This flowchart illustrates the order-filling process of a manufacturing company. The process starts when an order is generated by a customer and ends when payment is received by the company. All functions contributing to this process are included in the flowchart. The rows represent different departments or functional areas, and the steps appear in the department row where they are performed. This approach shows the *handoffs* from one department to another when the outgoing arrow from a step goes to another row. Special arrows are another way to show handoffs. Handoffs are points where cross-functional coordination is at particular risk due to the silo mentality. Misunderstandings, backlogs, and errors are more likely at these points. Such a

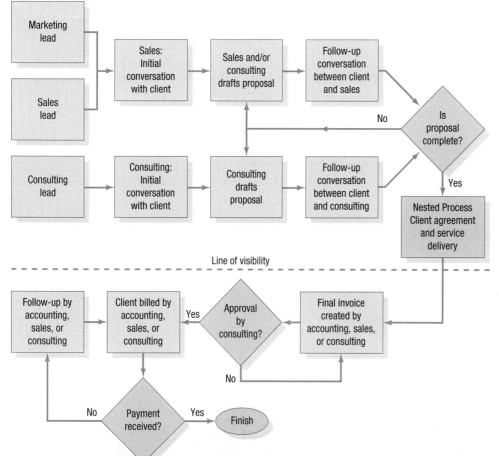

process flowchart is also known as a *swim lane* diagram because visual representation of different departments is similar to swimming lanes in a pool.

Flowcharts allow the process analyst and managers to look at the horizontal organization, rather than the vertical organization and departmental boundaries implied by a typical organizational chart. Flowcharts show how organizations produce their outputs through cross-functional work processes, and allow the design team to see all the critical interfaces between functions and departments.

Service Blueprints

A good design for service processes depends first and foremost on the type and amount of customer contact. A **service blueprint** is a special flowchart of a service process that shows which steps have high customer contact. Consider Figure 4.2 once again. It actually qualifies as a service blueprint because it shows a line of visibility. This special feature identifies which steps are visible to the customer (and thus more of a front-office process) and those that are not (back office process).

Of course, visibility is just one aspect of customer contact, and it may not adequately capture how actively the customer is involved or how much personal attention is required. A service blueprint can use colors, shading, or box shapes, instead of the line of visibility, to show the extent and type of customer contact. Another approach to service blueprinting is to tag each step with a number, and then have an accompanying table that describes in detail the customer contact for each numbered step.

▲ **FIGURE 4.3**
Flowchart of the Nested Subprocess of Client Agreement and Service Delivery

service blueprint

A special flowchart of a service process that shows which steps have high customer contact.

▼ **FIGURE 4.4**
Flowchart of the Order-Filling Process Showing Handoffs Between Departments

Source: Geary A. Rummler and Alan P. Brache, *Improving Performance*, 2nd ed. (San Francisco: Jossey-Bass, 1995).

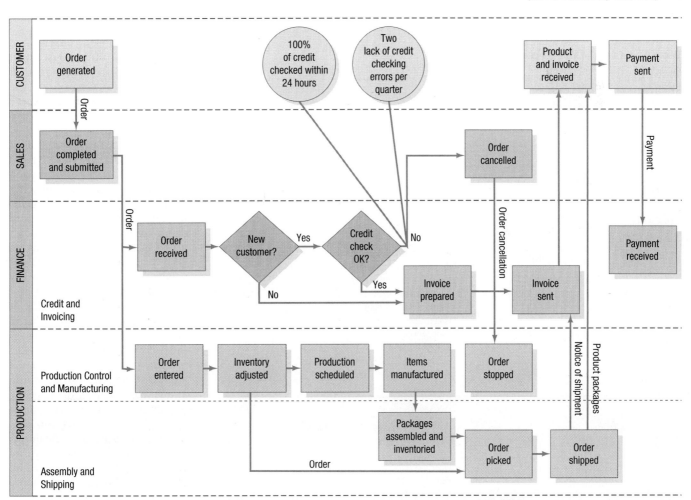

Process Charts

A **process chart** is an organized way of documenting all the activities performed by a person or group of people at a workstation, with a customer, or working with certain materials. It analyzes a process using a table, and provides information about each step in the process. Often it is used to drill down to the job level for an individual person, a team, or a focused nested process. It can have many formats. Here we group the type of activities for a typical process into five categories:

- *Operation.* Changes, creates, or adds something. Drilling a hole or serving a customer are examples of operations.

- *Transportation.* Moves the study's subject from one place to another (sometimes called *materials handling*). The subject can be a person, a material, a tool, or a piece of equipment. A customer walking from one end of a counter to the other, a crane hoisting a steel beam to a location, and a conveyor carrying a partially completed product from one workstation to the next are examples of transportation.

- *Inspection.* Checks or verifies something but does not change it. Getting customer feedback, checking for blemishes on a surface, weighing a product, and taking a temperature reading are examples of inspections.

- *Delay.* Occurs when the subject is held up awaiting further action. Time spent waiting for a server; time spent waiting for materials or equipment; cleanup time; and time that workers, machines, or workstations are idle because they have no work to complete are examples of delays.

- *Storage.* Occurs when something is put away until a later time. Supplies unloaded and placed in a storeroom as inventory, equipment put away after use, and papers put in a file cabinet are examples of storage.

Depending on the situation, other categories can be used. For example, subcontracting for outside services might be a category, temporary storage and permanent storage, or environmental waste might be three separate categories. Choosing the right category for each activity requires taking the perspective of the subject charted. A delay for the equipment could be inspection or transportation for the operator.

FIGURE 4.5 ▼
Process Chart for Emergency Room Admission

To complete a chart for a new process, the analyst must identify each step performed. If the process is an existing one, the analyst can actually observe the steps and categorize each step according to the subject being studied. The analyst then records the distance traveled and the time taken to perform each step. After recording all the activities and steps, the analyst summarizes the steps, times, and distances data. Figure 4.5 shows a process chart prepared using OM Explorer's *Process Chart* solver. It is for a patient with a twisted ankle being treated at a hospital. The process begins at the entrance and ends with the patient exiting after picking up the prescription.

After a process is charted, the analyst sometimes estimates the annual cost of the entire process. It becomes a benchmark against which other methods for performing the process can be evaluated. Annual labor cost can be estimated by finding the product of (1) time in hours to perform the

Process:	Emergency room admission
Subject:	Ankle injury patient
Beginning:	Enter emergency room
Ending:	Leave hospital

Insert Step
Append Step
Remove Step

	Summary		
Activity	Number of Steps	Time (min)	Distance (ft)
Operation ●	5	23.00	
Transport ➡	9	11.00	815
Inspect ■	2	8.00	
Delay ❱	3	8.00	
Store ▼	—	—	

Step No.	Time (min)	Distance (ft)	●	➡	■	❱	▼	Step Description
1	0.50	15.0			X			Enter emergency room, approach patient window
2	10.00		X					Sit down and fill out patient history
3	0.75	40.0		X				Nurse escorts patient to ER triage room
4	3.00				X			Nurse inspects injury
5	0.75	40.0		X				Return to waiting room
6	1.00					X		Wait for available bed
7	1.00	60.0		X				Go to ER bed
8	4.00					X		Wait for doctor
9	5.00				X			Doctor inspects injury and questions patient
10	2.00	200.0		X				Nurse takes patient to radiology
11	3.00		X					Technician x-rays patient
12	2.00	200.0		X				Return to bed in ER
13	3.00					X		Wait for doctor to return
14	2.00		X					Doctor provides diagnosis and advice
15	1.00	60.0		X				Return to emergency entrance area
16	4.00		X					Check out
17	2.00	180.0		X				Walk to pharmacy
18	4.00		X					Pick up prescription
19	1.00	20.0		X				Leave the building

process each time, (2) variable costs per hour, and (3) number of times the process is performed each year, or

$$\text{Annual labor cost} = \left(\begin{array}{c}\text{Time to perform}\\\text{the process in hours}\end{array}\right)\left(\begin{array}{c}\text{Variable costs}\\\text{per hour}\end{array}\right)\left(\begin{array}{c}\text{Number of times process}\\\text{performed per year}\end{array}\right)$$

For example, if the average time to serve a customer is 4 hours, the variable cost is $25 per hour, and 40 customers are served per year, then the labor cost is $4,000 per year (or 4 hrs/customer × $25/hr × 40 customers/yr).

In the case of the patient in Figure 4.5, this conversion would not be necessary, with total patient time being sufficient. What is being tracked is the patient's time, not the time and costs of the service providers.

You can design your own process chart spreadsheets to bring out issues that are particularly important for the process you are analyzing, such as categories for customer contact, process divergence, and the like. You can also track performance measures other than time and distance traveled, such as error rates. In addition, you can also create a different version of the process chart spreadsheet that examines processes much as done with flowcharts, except now in the form of a table. The columns that categorize the activity type could be replaced by one or more columns reporting different metrics of interest, rather than trying to fit them into a flowchart. Although it might not look as elegant, it could be just as informative—and easier to create.

WORK MEASUREMENT TECHNIQUES

Process documentation would not be complete without estimates of the average time each step in the process would take. Time estimates are needed not just for process improvement efforts, but for capacity planning, constraint management, performance appraisal, and scheduling. Estimating task times can be as simple as making a reasoned guess, asking a knowledgeable person, or taking notes while observing the process. More extensive studies involve collecting data for several weeks, consulting cost accounting data, or checking data recorded in information systems.

Formal techniques are also available that rely on the judgment of skilled observers: (1) the time study method, (2) elemental standard data approach, (3) predetermined data approach, and (4) work sampling method. A fifth method, learning curve analysis, is particularly appropriate when a new product or process is introduced and the time per unit produced has not yet stabilized. The method chosen depends on the purpose of the data, process type (job or line), and degree of product customization. A more comprehensive treatment of these techniques is provided in Supplement H, "Measuring Output Rates" and Supplement I, "Learning Curve Analysis" in my**om**lab.

Time Study Method

Time study uses a trained analyst to perform four basic steps in setting a time standard for a job or process: (1) selecting the work elements (steps in a flowchart or process chart) within the process to be studied, (2) timing the elements, (3) determining the sample size, and (4) setting the final standard. It is essentially the average time observed, adjusted for normal effort and making an allowance for breaks, unavoidable delays, and the like. The analyst records time spent on each element of the process being studied using a stopwatch, and records the time spent on each element for several repetitions. The analyst assigns a performance rating for each element to adjust for normal effort. Some elements may be performed faster or slower than normal, in the analyst's judgment. The allowance is expressed as a proportion or percent of the total normal time.

time study

A work measurement method using a trained analyst to perform four basic steps in setting a time standard for a job or process: selecting the work elements (or nested processes) within the process to be studied, timing the elements, determining the sample size, and setting the final standard.

Elemental Standard Data Approach

Another approach is needed when products or services are highly customized, job processes prevail, and process divergence is great. **Elemental standard data** is a database of standards compiled by a firm's analysts for basic elements that they can draw on later to estimate the time required for a particular job. This approach works well when work elements within certain jobs are similar to those in other jobs. Sometimes the time required for a work element depends on variable characteristics of the jobs, such as the amount of metal to be deposited for a welding process. In such cases, an equation that relates these characteristics to the time required is also stored in the database. Another method, such as time study or past records, still must be used to compile the normal times (before the allowance is added) stored in the database.

elemental standard data

A database of standards compiled by a firm's analysts for basic elements that they can draw on later to estimate the time required for a particular job, which is most appropriate when products or services are highly customized, job processes prevail, and process divergence is great.

EXAMPLE 4.1	Time Study of Revised Process

A process at a watch assembly plant has been changed. The process is divided into three work elements. A time study has been performed with the following results. The time standard for process previously was 14.5 minutes. Based on the new time study, should the time standard be revised?

SOLUTION

The new time study had an initial sample of four observations, with the results shown in the following table. The performance rating factor (RF) is shown for each element, and the allowance for the whole process is 18 percent of the total normal time.

	Obs 1	Obs 2	Obs 3	Obs 4	Average (min)	RF	Normal Time
Element 1	2.60	2.34	3.12	2.86	2.730	1.0	2.730
Element 2	4.94	4.78	5.10	4.68	4.875	1.1	5.363
Element 3	2.18	1.98	2.13	2.25	2.135	0.9	1.922
						Total Normal Time =	**10.015 minutes**

The normal time for an element in the table is its average time, multiplied by the RF. The total normal time for the whole process is the sum of the normal times for the three elements, or 10.015 minutes. To get the standard time (ST) for the process, just add in the allowance, or

$$ST = 10.015 \, (1 + 0.18) = \textbf{11.82} \text{ minutes/watch}$$

DECISION POINT

The time to assemble a watch appears to have decreased considerably. However, based on the precision that management wants, and the sample standard deviations in the last column of the table, the analyst decided to increase the sample size before setting a new standard. Supplement H, "Measuring Output Rates," gives more information on determining the number of additional observations needed.

Predetermined Data Approach

predetermined data approach

A database approach that divides each work element into a series of micromotions that make up the element. The analyst then consults a published database that contains the normal times for the full array of possible micromotions.

The **predetermined data approach** divides each work element even more, into a series of micromotions that make up the element. The analyst then consults a published database that contains the normal times for the full array of possible micromotions. A process's normal time can then be calculated as the sum of the times given in the database for the elements performed in the process. This approach makes most sense for highly repetitive processes with little process divergence and line flows. The micromotions (such as reach, move, or apply pressure) are very detailed.

Work Sampling Method

work sampling method

A process that estimates the proportion of time spent by people or machines on different activities, based on observations randomized over time.

Work sampling estimates the proportion of time spent by people or machines on different activities, based on observations randomized over time. Examples of these activities include working on a service or product, doing paperwork, waiting for instructions, waiting for maintenance, or being idle. Such data can then be used to assess a process's productivity, estimate the allowances needed to set standards for other work measurement methods, and spot areas for process improvement. It is best used when the processes are highly divergent with flexible flows. Figure 4.6(a) shows the input data and numerical results for one week of observations. Figure 4.6(b) shows an idle time of 23.81 percent for the week. It also reports that 237 more observations are needed to achieve the confidence and precision levels required with the input data. How these conclusions are reached is explained in Supplement H, "Measuring Output Rates" in my**om**lab.

Learning Curve Analysis   The time estimation techniques just covered assume that the process is stable. If the process is revised, then just repeat the method for the revised process after it stabilizes. Learning curve analysis, on the other hand, takes into account that learning takes place on an ongoing basis, such as when new products or services are introduced frequently. With instruction and repetition, workers learn to perform jobs more efficiently,

(a) Input Data and Numerical Results

Increase Observations		Remove An Observation	

Confidence z		1.96	Precision p		0.05

Observation Period	Times Busy	Times Idle	Observations
Monday	6	1	7
Tuesday	5	2	7
Wednesday	7	0	7
Thursday	9	2	11
Friday	5	5	10
Total	32	10	42

(b) Idle Time and Observations Required

Portion of idle times	0.2381
Total observations required	279
Additional observations required	237

▲ **FIGURE 4.6**
Work Sampling Study of Admission Clerk at Health Clinic Using *OM Explorer*

process improvements are identified, and better administration methods are created. These learning effects can be anticipated with a **learning curve**, a line that displays the relationship between processing time and the cumulative quantity of a product or service produced. The time required to produce a unit or create a service decreases as more units or customers are processed. The learning curve for a process depends on the rate of learning and the actual or estimated time for the first unit processed. Figure 4.7 demonstrates the learning curve assuming an 80 percent learning rate, with the first unit taking 120,000 hours and the cumulative average time for the first 10 units produced. The learning rate deals with each *doubling* of the output total. The time for the second unit is 80 percent of the first (or 120,000 × .80 = 96,000 hours), the time for the fourth unit is 80 percent of the second unit (or 96,000 × .80 = 76,800 hours), and so on. Finding the time estimate for a unit that is not an exact doubling (such as the fifth unit), and also the cumulative average time for the first 10 units, is explained in Supplement I, "Learning Curve Analysis" in my**om**lab.

learning curve

A line that displays the relationship between processing time and the cumulative quantity of a product or service produced.

Time for first unit	120,000
Unit number	10
Time for unit 10	57,172
Cumulative average time per unit	75,784

EVALUATING PERFORMANCE

Metrics and performance information complete the documentation of a process (see step 4 in Figure 4.1). Metrics can be displayed in various ways. Sometimes they can be added directly on the flowchart or process chart. Figure 4.4 shows metrics with circled entries. They establish the goals for the credit check: (1) all credit checks completed within 24 hours and (2) no more than two instances of continuing the process without a credit check. When the number of metrics gets unwieldy, another approach is to create a supporting table for the chart. Its rows are the steps in the flowchart, service blueprint, or process charts. The columns are the current performance, goals, and performance gaps for various metrics.

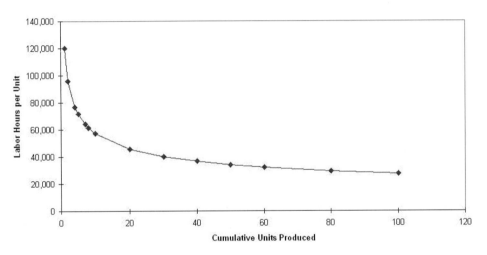

▲ **FIGURE 4.7**
(a) and (b) Learning Curve with 80% Learning Rate Using *OM Explorer*

The specific metrics analysts choose depends on the process being analyzed and on the competitive priorities. Good starting points are the per-unit processing time and cost at each step, and the time elapsed from beginning to end of the process. Capacity utilization and customer (or job) waiting times reveal where in the process delays are most likely to occur. Customer satisfaction measures, error rates, and scrap rates identify possible quality problems. We introduce many such metrics in subsequent chapters. Figure 4.8 shows the chapter and/or supplement that relates to some basic metrics. Only when these subsequent chapters are understood do we really complete our discussion of process analysis.

Data Analysis Tools

Metrics may reveal a performance gap. Various tools are available to help you understand the causes of the problem. Here we present six tools: (1) checklists, (2) histograms and bar charts, (3) Pareto charts, (4) scatter diagrams, (5) cause-and-effect diagrams, and (6) graphs. Many of them were developed initially to analyze quality issues, but they apply equally well

checklist

A form used to record the frequency of occurrence of certain process failures.

Chapter 5, Managing Quality

- Customer satisfaction measures
- Error rate
- Rework or scrap rate
- Internal failure cost

Chapter 6, Planning Capacity; Supplement C, Waiting Line Models; Supplement H, Measuring Output Rates; Supplement I, Learning Curve Analysis

- Processing time
- Setup time
- Capacity utilization
- Average waiting time
- Average number of customers or jobs waiting in line

Chapter 7, Managing Process Constraints

- Total time from start to finish (throughput time)
- Setup time
- Cycle time
- Idle time
- Operating expenses

Chapter 8, Designing Lean Systems

- Setup time
- Takt time
- Average waiting time
- Waste

FIGURE 4.8 ▲

Metrics for Flowcharts, Process Charts, and Accompanying Tables

process failure

Any performance shortfall, such as error, delay, environmental waste, rework, and the like.

histogram

A summarization of data measured on a continuous scale, showing the frequency distribution of some quality characteristic (in statistical terms, the central tendency and dispersion of the data).

bar chart

A series of bars representing the frequency of occurrence of data characteristics measured on a yes-or-no basis.

Pareto chart

A bar chart on which factors are plotted in decreasing order of frequency along the horizontal axis.

to the full range of performance measures.

Checklists Data collection through the use of a checklist is often the first step in the analysis of a metric. A **checklist** is a form used to record the frequency of occurrence of certain process failures. A **process failure** is any performance shortfall, such as error, delay, environmental waste, rework, and the like. The characteristics may be measurable on a continuous scale (e.g., weight, customer satisfaction on a 1-to-7 scale, unit cost, scrap loss percentage, time, or length) or on a yes-or-no basis (e.g., customer complaint, posting error, paint discoloration, or inattentive servers).

Histograms and Bar Charts The data from a checklist often can be presented succinctly and clearly with histograms or bar charts. A **histogram** summarizes data measured on a continuous scale, showing the frequency distribution of some process failure (in statistical terms, the central tendency and dispersion of the data). Often the mean of the data is indicated on the histogram. A **bar chart** (see Figure 4.9) is a series of bars representing the frequency of occurrence of data characteristics measured on a yes-or-no basis. The bar height indicates the number of times a particular process failure was observed.

Pareto Charts When managers discover several process problems that need to be addressed, they have to decide which should be attacked first. Vilfredo Pareto, a nineteenth-century Italian scientist whose statistical work focused on inequalities in data, proposed that most of an "activity" is caused by relatively few of its factors. In a restaurant quality problem, the activity could be customer complaints and the factor could be "discourteous server." For a manufacturer, the activity could be product defects and the factor could be "missing part." Pareto's concept, called the 80–20 rule, is that 80 percent of the activity is caused by 20 percent of the factors. By concentrating on the 20 percent of the factors (the "vital few"), managers can attack 80 percent of the process failure problems. Of course, the exact percentages vary with each situation, but inevitably relatively few factors cause most of the performance shortfalls.

The few vital factors can be identified with a **Pareto chart**, a bar chart on which the factors are plotted in decreasing order of frequency along the horizontal axis (see Figure 4.10). The chart has two vertical axes, the one on the left showing frequency (as in a histogram) and the one on the right showing the cumulative percentage of frequency. The cumulative frequency curve identifies the few vital factors that warrant immediate managerial attention.

EXAMPLE 4.2	**Pareto Chart for a Restaurant**

Active Model 4.1 in my**om**lab provides additional insights on this Pareto chart example and its extensions.

The manager of a neighborhood restaurant is concerned about the smaller numbers of customers patronizing his eatery. Complaints have been rising, and he would like to find out what issues to address and present the findings in a way his employees can understand.

SOLUTION

The manager surveyed his customers over several weeks and collected the following data:

Complaint	Frequency
Discourteous server	12
Slow service	42
Cold dinner	5
Cramped tables	20
Atmosphere	10

Figure 4.9 is a bar chart and Figure 4.10 is a Pareto chart, both created with OM Explorer's *Bar, Pareto, and Line Charts* solver. They present the data in a way that shows which complaints are more prevalent (the vital few). You can reformat these charts for any "yes-or-no" metrics. Just click on "unprotect sheet" under the spreadsheet's Tools menu, and then make your revisions. Another approach is to create your own spreadsheets from scratch. More advanced software with point-and-click interfaces include Minitab (www.minitab.com/index.htm), SAS (www.sas.com/rnd/app/qc.html), and Microsoft Visio (www.microsoft.com/office/visio).

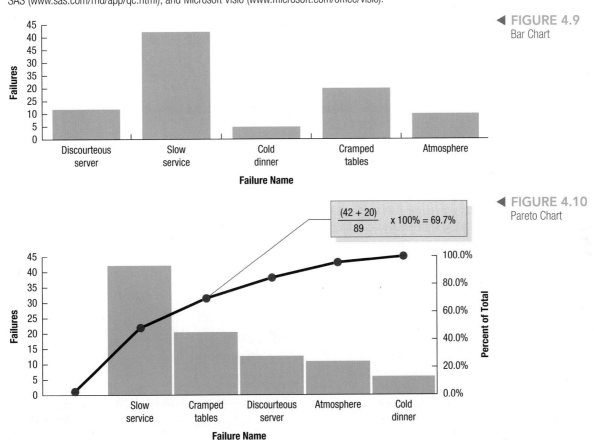

◄ **FIGURE 4.9**
Bar Chart

◄ **FIGURE 4.10**
Pareto Chart

DECISION POINT

It was clear to the manager (and all employees) which complaints, if rectified, would cover most of the process failure problems in the restaurant. First, slow service will be addressed by training the existing staff, adding another server, and improving the food preparation process. Removing some decorative furniture from the dining area and spacing the tables better will solve the problem with cramped tables. The Pareto chart shows that these two problems, if rectified, will account for almost 70 percent of the complaints.

Scatter Diagrams   Sometimes managers suspect that a certain factor is causing a particular process failure. A **scatter diagram**, which is a plot of two variables showing whether they are related, can be used to verify or negate the suspicion. Each point on the scatter diagram represents one data observation. For example, the manager of a castings shop

scatter diagram

A plot of two variables showing whether they are related.

may suspect that casting defects are a function of the diameter of the casting. A scatter diagram could be constructed by plotting the number of defective castings found for each diameter of casting produced. After the diagram is completed, any relationship between diameter and number of process failures will be clear.

Cause-and-Effect Diagrams   An important aspect of process analysis is linking each metric to the inputs, methods, and process steps that build a particular attribute into the service or product. One way to identify a design problem is to develop a **cause-and-effect diagram** that relates a key performance problem to its potential causes. First developed by Kaoru Ishikawa, the diagram helps management trace disconnects directly to the operations involved. Processes that have no bearing on a particular problem are not shown on the diagram.

The cause-and-effect diagram sometimes is called a *fishbone diagram*. The main performance gap is labeled as the fish's "head," the major categories of potential causes as structural "bones," and the likely specific causes as "ribs." When constructing and using a cause-and-effect diagram, an analyst identifies all the major categories of potential causes for the problem. These might be personnel, machines, materials, and processes. For each major category, the analyst lists all the likely causes of the performance gap. Under personnel might be listed "lack of training," "poor communication," and "absenteeism." Creative thinking helps the analyst identify and properly classify all suspected causes. The analyst then systematically investigates the causes listed on the diagram for each major category, updating the chart as new causes become apparent. The process of constructing a cause-and-effect diagram calls management and worker attention to the primary factors affecting process failures. Example 4.3 demonstrates the use of a cause-and-effect diagram by an airline.

cause-and-effect diagram

A diagram that relates a key performance problem to its potential causes.

EXAMPLE 4.3   **Analysis of Flight Departure Delays**

The operations manager for Checker Board Airlines at Port Columbus International Airport noticed an increase in the number of delayed flight departures.

SOLUTION

To analyze all the possible causes of that problem, the manager constructed a cause-and-effect diagram, shown in Figure 4.11. The main problem, delayed flight departures, is the "head" of the diagram. He brainstormed all possible causes with his staff, and together they identified several major categories: equipment, personnel, materials, procedures, and "other factors" that are beyond managerial control. Several suspected causes were identified for each major category.

FIGURE 4.11 ▼
Cause-and Effect Diagram for Flight Departure Delays

Source: Adopted from D. Daryl Wyckoff, "New Tools for Achieving Service Quality," *The Cornell H.R.A. Quarterly.* Used by permission. All rights reserved.

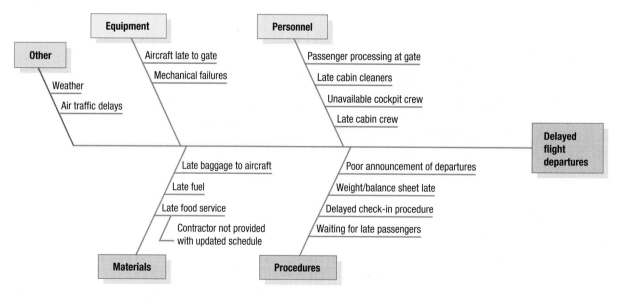

DECISION POINT

The operations manager, having a good understanding of the process, suspected that most of the flight delays were caused by problems with materials. Consequently, he had food service, fueling, and baggage-handling operations examined. He learned that the number of tow trucks for the baggage-transfer operations was insufficient and that planes were delayed waiting for baggage from connecting flights.

Graphs   **Graphs** represent data in a variety of pictorial formats, such as line charts and pie charts. *Line charts* represent data sequentially with data points connected by line segments to highlight trends in the data. Line charts are used in control charts (see Chapter 5, "Managing Quality") and forecasting (see Chapter 13, "Forecasting Demand"). Pie charts represent process factors as slices of a pie; the size of each slice is in proportion to the number of occurrences of the factor. Pie charts are useful for showing data from *a group of factors* that can be represented as percentages totaling 100 percent.

graphs

Representations of data in a variety of pictorial forms, such as line charts and pie charts.

Data Snooping

Each of the tools for improving quality may be used independently, but their power is greatest when they are used together. In solving a process-related problem, managers often must act as detectives, sifting data to clarify the issues involved and deducing the causes. We call this process *data snooping*. Example 4.4 demonstrates how the tools for improving quality can be used for data snooping.

Simulation

A simulation model goes one step further than data analysis tools, because it can show how the process dynamically changes over time. **Process simulation** is the act of reproducing the behavior of a process, using a model that describes each step. Once the process is modeled, the analyst can make changes in the model to measure the impact on certain metrics, such as response time, waiting lines, resource utilization, and the like. To learn more about how simulation works, see Supplement B, "Simulation Models," which follows this chapter. More advanced capabilities are possible using software packages such as SimQuick, found in my**om**lab. (www.nd.edu/~dhartvig/simquick/top.htm), Extend (www.imaginethatinc.com), SIMPROCESS (www.caciasl.com), ProModel (www.promodel.com), and Witness (www.lanner.com).

process simulation

The act of reproducing the behavior of a process, using a model that describes each step.

REDESIGNING THE PROCESS

A doctor pinpoints an illness after a thorough examination of the patient, and then the doctor recommends treatments based on the diagnosis; so it is with processes. After a process is documented, metrics data collected, and disconnects identified, the process analyst or design team puts together a set of changes that will make the process better. At this step, people directly involved in the process are brought in to get their ideas and inputs. This chapter's opener describes how various people at Baptist Memorial Hospital came together to improve their processes, avoiding the need to add expensive capacity.

Generating Ideas: Questioning and Brainstorming

Sometimes ideas for reengineering or improving a process become apparent after documenting the process and carefully examining the areas of substandard performance, handoffs between departments, and steps where customer contact is high. Example 4.4 illustrates how such documentation pointed to a better way of handling the fiber boards through better training. In other cases, the better solution is less evident. Ideas can be uncovered (because there is always a better way) by asking six questions about each step in the process, and about the process as a whole:

1. *What* is being done?
2. *When* is it being done?
3. *Who* is doing it?
4. *Where* is it being done?
5. *How* is it being done?
6. *How well* does it do on the various metrics of importance?

Answers to these questions are challenged by asking still another series of questions. *Why* is the process even being done? *Why* is it being done where it is being done? *Why* is it being done when it is being done?

Creativity can also be stimulated by **brainstorming**, letting a group of people knowledgeable about the process propose ideas for change by saying whatever comes to mind. A facilitator records the ideas on a flipchart, so that all can see. Participants are discouraged from evaluating any of the ideas generated during the session. The purpose is to encourage creativity and to get as many ideas as possible, no matter how far-fetched the ideas may seem.

brainstorming

Letting a group of people, knowledgeable about the process, propose ideas for change by saying whatever comes to mind.

EXAMPLE 4.4	Identifying Causes of Poor Headliner Process Failures

The Wellington Fiber Board Company produces headliners, the fiberglass components that form the inner roof of passenger cars. Management wanted to identify which process failures were most prevalent and to find the cause.

FIGURE 4.12 ▼
Application of the Tools for Improving Quality

SOLUTION

Figure 4.12 shows the sequential application of several tools for improving quality.

Step 1. Checklist

Headliner failures

Process failure	Tally	Total
A. Tears in fabric	IIII	4
B. Discolored fabric	III	3
C. Broken fiber board	ЖЖ ЖЖ ЖЖ ЖЖ ЖЖ ЖЖ ЖЖ I	36
D. Ragged edges	ЖЖ II	7
		Total 50

Step 2. Pareto Chart

Step 3. Cause-and-Effect Diagram

Step 4. Bar Chart

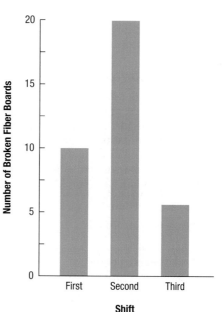

Step 1:   A checklist of different types of process failures was constructed from last month's production records.

Step 2:   A Pareto chart prepared from the checklist data indicated that broken fiber board accounted for 72 percent of the quality defects.

Step 3:   A cause-and-effect diagram for broken fiber board identified several potential causes for the problem. The one strongly suspected by the manager was employee training.

Step 4: The manager reorganized the production reports into a bar chart according to shift because the personnel on the three shifts had varied amounts of experience.

DECISION POINT

The bar chart indicated that the second shift, with the least experienced workforce, had most of the process failures. Further investigation revealed that workers were not using proper procedures for stacking the fiber boards after the press operation, which caused cracking and chipping. The manager set up additional training sessions focused on board handling. Although the second shift was not responsible for all the process failures, finding the source of many of the failures enabled the manager to improve the performance of her operations.

The participants of a brainstorming session need not be limited to the design team as long as they have seen or heard the process documentation. A growing number of big companies, such as Sun Life Financial and Georgia-Pacific, are taking advantage of the Internet and specially designed software to run brainstorming sessions that allow people at far-flung locations to "meet" online and hash out solutions to particular problems. The technology lets employees see, and build on, one another's ideas, so that one person's seed of a notion can grow into a practical plan.

After the brainstorming session is over, the design team moves into the "get real" phase: They evaluate the different ideas. The team identifies the changes that give the best payoffs for process redesign. The redesign could involve issues of capacity, layout, technology, or even location, all of which are discussed in more detail in the following chapters.

The redesigned process is documented once again, this time as the "after" view of the process. Expected payoffs are carefully estimated, along with risks. For changes involving investments, the time value of money must be considered (see Supplement F, "Financial Analysis," in my**om**lab). The impact on people (skills, degree of change, training requirements, and resistance to change) must also be factored into the evaluation of the new design.

Benchmarking

Benchmarking can be another valuable source for process redesign. **Benchmarking** is a systematic procedure that measures a firm's processes, services, and products against those of industry leaders. Companies use benchmarking to better understand how outstanding companies do things so that they can improve their own processes.

Benchmarking focuses on setting quantitative goals for improvement. *Competitive* benchmarking is based on comparisons with a direct industry competitor. *Functional* benchmarking compares areas such as administration, customer service, and sales operations with those of outstanding firms in any industry. For instance, Xerox benchmarked its distribution function against L.L. Bean's because L.L. Bean is renowned as a leading retailer in distribution efficiency and customer service.

Internal benchmarking involves using an organizational unit with superior performance as the benchmark for other units. This form of benchmarking can be advantageous for firms that have several business units or divisions. All forms of benchmarking are best applied in situations where you are looking for a long-term program of continuous improvement.

Typical measures used in benchmarking include cost per unit, service upsets (breakdowns) per customer, processing time per unit, customer retention rates, revenue per unit, return on investment, and customer satisfaction levels.

Benchmarking consists of four basic steps:

Step 1. Planning. Identify the process, service, or product to be benchmarked and the firm(s) to be used for comparison; determine the performance metrics for analysis; collect the data.

benchmarking

A systematic procedure that measures a firm's processes, services, and products against those of industry leaders.

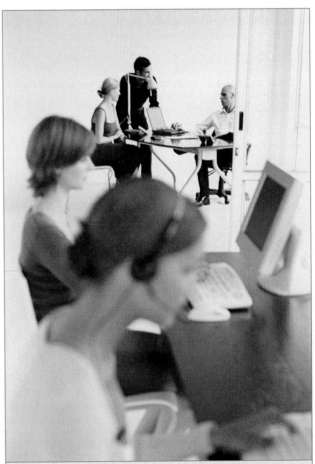

Omgeo is a behind-the-scenes company that settles trades between financial services firms. The process used to involve dozens of scribbled faxes, telexes, and phone calls made for the typical trade costs from $10 to $12. Now the process costs only 20 cents to $1 per trade—and investment managers essentially got the service free. A key change was using the Internet and new information technology solutions. Information goes into a central database that the broker, investment manager, and custodian banks all have access to in real time. The details of the trades are automatically compared to eliminate errors.

Customer Relationship Process

- Total cost of "enter, process, and track orders" per $1,000 revenue
- System costs of process per $100,000 revenue
- Value of sales order line item not fulfilled due to stockouts, as percentage of revenue
- Percentage of finished goods sales value that is returned
- Average time from sales order receipt until manufacturing or logistics is notified
- Average time in direct contact with customer per sales order line item

Order Fulfillment Process

- Value of plant shipments per employee
- Finished goods inventory turnover
- Reject rate as percentage of total orders processed
- Percentage of orders returned by customers due to quality problems
- Standard customer lead time from order entry to shipment
- Percentage of orders shipped on time

New Service/Product Development Process

- Percentage of sales due to services/products launched last year
- Cost of "generate new services/products" process per $1,000 revenue
- Ratio of projects entering the process to projects completing the process
- Time to market for existing service/product improvement project
- Time to market for new service/product project
- Time to profitability for existing service/product improvement project

Supplier Relationship Process

- Cost of "select suppliers and develop/maintain contracts" process per $1,000 revenue
- Number of employees per $1,000 of purchases
- Percentage of purchase orders approved electronically
- Average time to place a purchase order
- Total number of active vendors per $1,000 of purchases
- Percentage of value of purchased material that is supplier certified

Support Process

- Systems cost of finance function per $1,000 revenue
- Percentage of finance staff devoted to internal audit
- Total cost of payroll processes per $1,000 revenue
- Number of accepted jobs as percentage of job offers
- Total cost of "source, recruit, and select" process per $1,000 revenue
- Average employee turnover rate

FIGURE 4.13 ▲
Illustrative Benchmarking Metrics by Type of Process

Step 2. Analysis. Determine the gap between the firm's current performance and that of the benchmark firm(s); identify the causes of significant performance gaps.

Step 3. Integration. Establish goals and obtain the support of managers who must provide the resources for accomplishing the goals.

Step 4. Action. Develop cross-functional teams of those most affected by the changes; develop action plans and team assignments; implement the plans; monitor progress; recalibrate benchmarks as improvements are made.

Collecting benchmarking data can sometimes be a challenge. Internal benchmarking data is surely the most accessible. One way of benchmarking is always available—tracking the performance of a process over time. Functional benchmarking data are often collected by professional associations or consulting firms. Several corporations and government organizations have agreed to share and standardize performance benchmarks. The American Productivity and Quality Center, a nonprofit organization, created thousands of measures, as Figure 4.13 illustrates. The full range of metrics can be explored at www.apqc.org. Another source is the Supply-Chain Council, which has defined key metrics in its Supply-Chain Operations Reference (SCOR) model (see Chapter 10, "Integrating the Supply Chain").

MANAGING PROCESSES

Failure to manage processes is failure to manage the business. Implementing a beautifully redesigned process is only the beginning to continually monitoring and improving processes. Metrics goals must be continually evaluated and reset to fit changing requirements. Avoid the following seven mistakes when managing processes:[1]

1. *Not Connecting with Strategic Issues.* Is particular attention being paid to core processes, competitive priorities, impact of customer contact and volume, and strategic fit during process analysis?

2. *Not Involving the Right People in the Right Way.* Does process analysis closely involve the people performing the process, or those closely connected to it as internal customers and suppliers?

3. *Not Giving the Design Teams and Process Analysts a Clear Charter, and then Holding Them Accountable.* Does management set expectations for change and maintain pressure for results? Does it allow paralysis in process improvement efforts by requiring excessive analysis?

---

[1] Geary A. Rummler and Alan P. Brache, *Improving Performance*, 2nd ed. (San Francisco: Jossey-Bass, 1995), pp. 126–133.

4. *Not Being Satisfied Unless Fundamental "Reengineering" Changes are Made.* Is the radical change from process reengineering the expectation? If so, the cumulative effect of many small improvements that could be made incrementally could be lost. Process management efforts should not be limited to downsizing or to reorganization only, even though jobs may be eliminated or the structure changed. It should not be limited to big technological innovation projects, even though technological change occurs often.

5. *Not Considering the Impact on People.* Are the changes aligned with the attitudes and skills of the people who must implement the redesigned process? It is crucial to understand and deal with the *people side* of process changes.

6. *Not Giving Attention to Implementation.* Are processes redesigned, but never implemented? A great job of flowcharting and benchmarking is of only academic interest if the proposed changes are not implemented. Sound project management practices are required.

7. *Not Creating an Infrastructure for Continuous Process Improvement.* Is a measurement system in place to monitor key metrics over time? Is anyone checking to see whether anticipated benefits of a redesigned process are actually being realized?

Managers must make sure that their organization spots new performance gaps in the continual search for process improvements. Process redesign efforts need to be part of periodic reviews and even annual plans. Measurement is the particular focus of the next chapter. It covers how a performance tracking system is the basis for feedback and improvement efforts. The essence of a learning organization is the intelligent use of such feedback.

INTERNET RESOURCES

my**om**lab and the Companion Website at **www.pearsonglobaleditions.com/krajewski** contain many tools, activities, and resources designed for this chapter.

KEY TERMS

bar chart 154
benchmarking 159
brainstorming 157
cause-and-effect diagram 156
checklist 153
design team 145
elemental standard data 151
flowchart 146

graphs 157
histogram 154
learning curve 153
metrics 146
Pareto chart 154
predetermined data approach 152
process analysis 144
process chart 150

process failure 154
process simulation 157
scatter diagram 155
service blueprint 149
suggestion system 145
time study 151
work sampling method 152

SOLVED PROBLEM 1

GPM is the name of a company that manufactures pharmaceuticals. Their packaging process has four steps: mixing ingredients, filling capsules, sealing capsules, and labelling capsules. They have had the reported defects analyzed, which is shown in the table below.

Defect		Frequency
Incorrect mixture of ingredients (mix)		5
Capsules over- or underfilled (fill)		7
Capsules did not seal (seal)		16
Labels smudged (label)		20
	Total	48

SOLUTION

Defective labels account for 41.67 percent of the total number of defects:

$$\frac{20}{48} \times 100\% = 41.67\%$$

Improperly sealed capsules account for 33.3 percent of the total number of defects:

$$\frac{16}{48} \times 100\% = 33.33\%$$

The cumulative percent for the two most frequent defects is:

$$41.67\% + 33.33\% = 75\%$$

Capsules over- and underfilled represent $\frac{7}{48} \times 100\% = 14.58\%$ of defects; the cumulative percentage is:

$$75 + 14.58 = 89.58\%$$

Improperly mixed ingredients represent $\frac{5}{48} \times 100\% = 10.42\%$ of defects; the cumulative percentage is

$$10.42 + 89.58 = 100.00\%$$

The Pareto chart is shown in Figure 4.14.

FIGURE 4.14 ▶
Pareto Chart

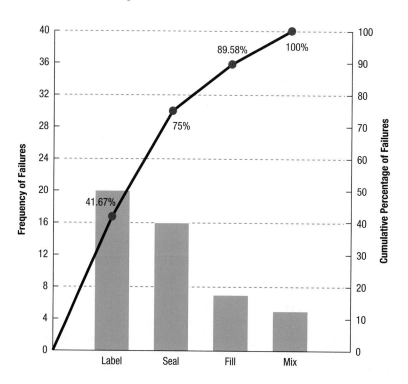

SOLVED PROBLEM 2

Create a flowchart for the following telephone-ordering process at a retail chain that specializes in selling books and music CDs. It provides an ordering system via the telephone to its time-sensitive customers besides its regular store sales.

First, the automated system greets customers and identifies whether they have a tone or pulse phone. Customers choose 1 if they have a tone phone; otherwise, they wait for the first available service representative to process their request. If customers have a tone phone, they complete their request by choosing options on the phone. First, the system checks to see whether customers have an existing account. Customers choose 1 if they have an existing account or choose 2 if they want to open a new account. Customers wait for the service representative to open a new account if they choose 2.

Next, customers choose between the options of making an order, canceling an order, or talking to a customer representative for questions and/or complaints. If customers choose to make an order, then they specify the order type as a book or a music CD, and a specialized customer representative for books or music CDs picks up the phone to get the order details. If customers choose to cancel an order, then they wait for the automated response. By entering the order code via phone, customers can cancel the order. The automated system says the name of the ordered item and asks for the confirmation of the customer. If the customer validates the cancellation of the order, then the system cancels the order; otherwise, the system asks the customer to input the order code again. After responding to the request, the system asks whether the customer has additional requests; if not, the process terminates.

SOLUTION

Figure 4.15 shows the flowchart.

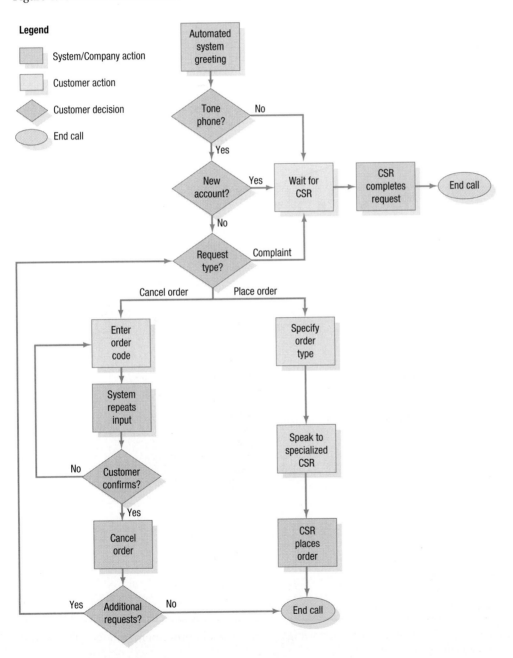

◀ **FIGURE 4.15**
Flowchart of Telephone Ordering Process

SOLVED PROBLEM 3

An automobile service is having difficulty providing oil changes in the 29 minutes or less mentioned in its advertising. You are to analyze the process of changing automobile engine oil. The subject of the study is the service mechanic. The process begins when the mechanic directs the customer's arrival and ends when the customer pays for the services.

SOLUTION

Figure 4.16 shows the completed process chart. The process is broken into 21 steps. A summary of the times and distances traveled is shown in the upper right-hand corner of the process chart.

The times add up to 28 minutes, which does not allow much room for error if the 29-minute guarantee is to be met and the mechanic travels a total of 420 feet.

FIGURE 4.16 ▶
Process Chart for Changing Engine Oil

Process:	Changing engine oil
Subject:	Mechanic
Beginning:	Direct customer arrival
Ending:	Total charges, receive payment

Insert Step

Append Step

Remove Step

Summary

Activity		Number of Steps	Time (min)	Distance (ft)
Operation	●	7	16.50	
Transport	➡	8	5.50	420
Inspect	■	4	5.00	
Delay	▶	1	0.70	
Store	▼	1	0.30	

Step No.	Time (min)	Distance (ft)	●	➡	■	▶	▼	Step Description
1	0.80	50.0		X				Direct customer into service bay
2	1.80		X					Record name and desired service
3	2.30				X			Open hood, verify engine type, inspect hoses, check fluids
4	0.80	30.0		X				Walk to customer in waiting area
5	0.60		X					Recommend additional services
6	0.70					X		Wait for customer decision
7	0.90	70.0		X				Walk to storeroom
8	1.90		X					Look up filter number(s), find filter(s)
9	0.40				X			Check filter number(s)
10	0.60	50.0		X				Carry filter(s) to service pit
11	4.20		X					Perform under-car services
12	0.70	40.0		X				Climb from pit, walk to automobile
13	2.70		X					Fill engine with oil, start engine
14	1.30				X			Inspect for leaks
15	0.50	40.0		X				Walk to pit
16	1.00				X			Inspect for leaks
17	3.00		X					Clean and organize work area
18	0.70	80.0		X				Return to auto, drive from bay
19	0.30						X	Park the car
20	0.50	60.0		X				Walk to customer waiting area
21	2.30		X					Total charges, receive payment

SOLVED PROBLEM 4

What improvement can you make in the process shown in Figure 4.15?

SOLUTION

Your analysis should verify the following three ideas for improvement. You may also be able to come up with others.

a. **Move Step 17 to Step 21.** Customers should not have to wait while the mechanic cleans the work area.

b. **Store Small Inventories of Frequently Used Filters in the Pit.**   Steps 7 and 10 involve travel to and from the storeroom. If the filters are moved to the pit, a copy of the reference material must also be placed in the pit. The pit will have to be organized and well lighted.

c. **Use Two Mechanics.**   Steps 10, 12, 15, and 17 involve running up and down the steps to the pit. Much of this travel could be eliminated. The service time could be shortened by having one mechanic in the pit working simultaneously with another working under the hood.

DISCUSSION QUESTIONS

1. Paul O'Neill, former U.S. Treasury Secretary, estimates that arguably half of the $2 trillion a year that Americans spend on health care is needlessly wasted. Brainstorm up to 10 blue-sky ideas to solve the following problems:

   a. A typical retail pharmacy spends 20 percent of its time playing telephone tag with doctors trying to find out what the intent was for a given prescription.

   b. After the person responsible for filling the prescription determines what they think they are supposed to do, errors can be made even in filling the prescription. For example, administering an adult dose (rather than the dose for a premature baby) of Heparin in a preemie ICU is fatal.

   c. Drugs get distributed at a hospital on a batch basis. For example, carts can be filled on Monday, Wednesday, and Friday. A huge volume of drugs can come back on Monday because they are not consumed on the wards between Friday and Monday, patient conditions changed, or the doctor decided on a different intervention. A technician spends the rest of the day restocking the shelves with the returns and 40 percent of the intravenous materials prepared on Friday morning are poured down the drain.

   d. Sometimes the administration of the drug was not done on the agreed schedule, because the nurses were busy doing something else.

   e. For every bed in an acute care hospital system, someone falls during the year. Most falls occur after 11 P.M. and before 6 A.M. Sometimes a bone is fractured, leading to immobilization and then pneumonia.

   f. One in every 14 people who goes to a U.S. medical care system gets an infection they did not bring with them.

2. Continuous improvement recognizes that many small improvements add up to sizable benefits. Will continuous improvement take a company at the bottom of an industry to the top? Explain.

3. The Hydro-Electric Company (HEC) has three sources of power. A small amount of hydroelectric power is generated by damming wild and scenic rivers; a second source of power comes from burning coal, with emissions that create acid rain and contribute to global warming; the third source of power comes from nuclear fission. HEC's coal-fired plants use obsolete pollution-control technology, and an investment of several hundred million dollars would be required to update it. Environmentalists urge HEC to promote conservation and purchase power from suppliers that use the cleanest fuels and technology.

   However, HEC is already suffering from declining sales, which have resulted in billions of dollars invested in idle equipment. Its large customers are taking advantage of laws that permit them to buy power from low-cost suppliers. HEC must cover the fixed costs of idle capacity by raising rates charged to its remaining customers or face defaulting on bonds (bankruptcy). The increased rates motivate even more customers to seek low-cost suppliers, the start of a death spiral for HEC. To prevent additional rate increases, HEC implements a cost-cutting program and puts its plans to update pollution controls on hold.

   Form sides and discuss the ethical, environmental, and political issues and trade-offs associated with HEC's strategy.

PROBLEMS

Software, such as OM Explorer, Active Models, and POM for Windows, is available in my**om**lab. Check with your instructor on how best to use it. In many cases, the instructor wants you to understand how to do the calculations by hand. At most, the software provides a check on your calculations. When calculations are particularly complex and the goal is interpreting the results in making decisions, the software replaces entirely the manual calculations..

1. Consider the Custom Molds, Inc. case at the end of Chapter 3, "Developing a Process Strategy." Prepare a flowchart of the mold fabrication process and the parts manufacturing process, showing how they are linked. For a good tutorial on how to create flowcharts, see http://www.hci.com.au/hcisite5/library/materials/

Flowcharting.htm. Also check out the Flowcharting Tutor in Excel in my**om**lab.

2. Founded in 1970, ABC is one of the world's largest insurance companies with locations in 28 countries. Given the following description, flowchart the new policy setup process as it existed in 1970:

   Individual customers who wanted to set up a new policy would visit one of ABC's 70 branch offices or make contact with an agent. They would then fill out an application and sometimes attach a check. The branch office then sent the application package through company mail to the XYZ division in London. In addition, a customer might also fill out the application at home and send it directly to any number of ABC locations, which would then transfer it to the London operation. Once received, XYZ separated the various parts of the application, then scanned and digitized it. The electronic image was then retrieved from a server and delivered to an associate's desktop client computer. The associate was responsible for entering the information on the form into the appropriate database. If the information supplied on the application was complete, a confirmation notice was automatically printed and sent to the customer. If the information was incomplete, then another associate, trained to deal with customers on the phone, would call the customer to obtain the additional information. If the customer noticed something wrong on the confirmation notice received, she or he would either call a toll-free number or send in a letter describing the problem. The Customer Problem Resolution division dealt with problems arising at this point. An updated confirmation notice was sent to the customer. If the information was correct, the application transaction was complete.

3. Do Problem 1 using a process chart spreadsheet of your own design, one that differs from the *Process Chart* Solver in OM Explorer. It should have one or more columns to record information or metrics that you think are relevant, be it external customer contact, time delays, completion times, percent rework, costs, capacity, and/or demand rates. Your entries should show what information you would collect, even though only part of it is available in the case.

4. After viewing the *Process Choice at the King Soopers Bakery* video on my**om**lab, prepare a flowchart for the three processes at King Soopers. For additional information on the processes, see the *Big Picture* for Chapter 3 that is also in my**om**lab.

5. Prepare a flowchart of the field service division process at DEF, as described here. Start from the point where a call is received and end when a technician finishes the job.

DEF was a multibillion dollar company that manufactured and distributed a wide variety of electronic, photographic, and reprographic equipment used in many engineering and medical system applications. The Field Service Division employed 475 field service technicians, who performed maintenance and warranty repairs on the equipment sold by DEF. Customers would call DEF's National Service Center (NSC), which received about 3,000 calls per day. The NSC staffed its call center with about 40 call-takers. A typical incoming service call was received at the NSC and routed to one of the call-takers, who entered information about the machine, caller's name, and type of problem into DEF's mainframe computer. In some cases, the call-taker attempted to help the customer fix the problem. However, call-takers were currently only able to avoid about 10 percent of the incoming emergency maintenance service calls. If the service call could not be avoided, the call-taker usually stated the following script: "Depending upon the availability of our technicians, you should expect to see a technician sometime between now and (now + X)." ("X" was the target response time based on the model number and the zone.) This information was given to the customer because many customers wanted to know when a tech would arrive on site.

Call-takers entered service call information on DEF's computer system, which then sent the information electronically to the regional dispatch center assigned to that customer location. (DEF had four regional dispatch centers with a total of about 20 dispatchers.) Service call information was printed on a small card at the dispatch center. About every hour, cards were ripped off the printer and given to the dispatcher assigned to that customer location. The dispatcher placed each card on a magnetic board under the name of a tech that the dispatcher believed would be the most likely candidate for the service call, given the location of the machine, the current location of the tech, and the tech's training profile. After completing a service call, techs called the dispatcher in the regional dispatch center, cleared the call, and received a new call assigned by the dispatcher. After getting the service call from a dispatcher, a tech called the customer to give an expected time of arrival, drove to the customer site, diagnosed the problem, repaired the machine if parts were available in the van, and then phoned the dispatcher for the next call. If the tech did not have the right parts for a repair, the tech informed the NSC and the part was express mailed to the customer; the repair was done the next morning.

6. Your class has volunteered to work for Referendum 13 on the November ballot, which calls for free tuition and books for all college courses except operations management. Support for the referendum includes assembling 10,000 yard signs (preprinted water-resistant paper signs to be glued and stapled to a wooden stake) on a fall Saturday. Construct a flowchart and a process chart for yard sign assembly. What inputs in terms of materials, human effort, and equipment are involved? Estimate the amount of volunteers, staples, glue, equipment, lawn and garage space, and pizza required.

7. Do Problem 2 using a process chart spreadsheet of your own design, one that differs from the *Process Chart* Solver in OM Explorer. It should have one or more columns to record information or metrics that you think should be collected to analyze the process (see Problem 3).

8. Suppose that you are in charge of a large mailing to the alumni of your college, inviting them to contribute to a scholarship fund. The letters and envelopes have been individually addressed (mailing labels were not used). The letters are to be folded and stuffed into the correct envelopes, the envelopes are to be sealed, and a large commemorative stamp is to be placed in the upper right-hand corner of each envelope. Make a process chart for this activity, assuming that it is a one-person operation. Estimate how long it will take to stuff, seal, and stamp 2,000 envelopes. Assume that the person doing this work is paid $8 per hour. How much will it cost to process 2,000 letters, based on your time estimate? Consider how each of the following changes would affect the process:

- Each letter has the greeting "Dear Alumnus or Alumna," instead of the person's name.

- Mailing labels are used and have to be put on the envelopes.

- Prestamped envelopes are used.

- Envelopes are stamped by a postage meter.

- Window envelopes are used.

- A preaddressed envelope is included with each letter for contributions.

   a. Given your time estimates, which of these changes would reduce the time and cost of the process?

   b. Would any of these changes be likely to reduce the effectiveness of the mailing? If so, which ones? Why?

   c. Would the changes that increase time and cost be likely to increase the effectiveness of the mailing? Why or why not?

   d. What other factors need to be considered for this project?

9. Do Problem 5 using a process chart spreadsheet of your own design, one that differs from the *Process Chart* Solver in OM Explorer. It should have one or more columns to record information or metrics that you think should be collected to analyze the process (see Problem 3).

10. Diagrams of two self-service gasoline stations, both located on corners, are shown in Figure 4.17(a) and (b). Both have two rows of four pumps and a booth at which an attendant receives payment for the gasoline. At neither station is it necessary for the customer to pay in advance. The exits and entrances are marked on the diagrams. Analyze the flows of cars and people through each station.

   a. Which station has the more efficient flows from the standpoint of the customer?

   b. Which station is likely to lose more potential customers who cannot gain access to the pumps because another car is headed in the other direction?

   c. At which station can a customer pay without getting out of the car?

11. As a graduate assistant, your duties include grading and keeping records for operations management course homework assignments. Five sections for 40 students each are offered each semester. A few graduate students attend sections 3 and 4. Graduate students must complete some extra work to higher standards for each assignment. Every student delivers (or is supposed to deliver) directly to (under) the door of your office one homework assignment every Tuesday. Your job is to correct the homework, record grades, sort the papers by class section, sort by student last name in alphabetical order, and return the homework papers to the appropriate instructors (not necessarily in that order). There are some complications. A fair majority of the students sign their names legibly, others identify work with their correct ID number, and a few do neither. Rarely do students identify their section number or graduate status. Prepare a list of process chart steps and place them in an efficient sequence.

12. At the Department of Motor Vehicles (DMV), the process of getting license plates for your car begins when you enter the facility and take a number. You walk 50 feet to the waiting area. During your wait, you count about 30 customers waiting for service. You notice that many customers become discouraged and leave. When a number is called, if a customer stands, the ticket is checked by a uniformed person, and the customer is directed to the available clerk. If no one stands, several minutes are lost while the same number is called repeatedly. Eventually, the next number is called, and more often than not, that customer has left too. The DMV clerk has now been idle for several minutes but does not seem to mind.

    After 4 hours, your number is called and checked by the uniformed person. You walk 60 feet to the clerk, and the process of paying city sales taxes is completed in 4 minutes. The clerk then directs you to the waiting area for paying personal property tax, 80 feet away. You take a different number and sit down with some different customers who are just renewing licenses. A 1-hour, 40-minute wait this time, and after a walk of 25 feet you pay property taxes in a process that takes 2 minutes. Now that you have paid taxes you are eligible to pay registration and license fees. That department is 50 feet away, beyond the employees' cafeteria.

    The registration and license customers are called in the same order in which personal property taxes were paid. There is only a 10-minute wait and a 3-minute process. You receive your license plates, take a minute to abuse the license clerk, and leave exactly 6 hours after arriving.

▲ **FIGURE 4.17**
Two Self-Service Gasoline Stations

Make a process chart to depict this process, and suggest improvements.

13. The management of the Just Like Home restaurant has asked you to analyze some of its processes. One of these processes is making a single-scoop ice cream cone. Cones can be ordered by a server (for table service) or by a customer (for takeout).

Figure 4.18 illustrates the process chart for this operation.

- The ice cream counter server earns $10 per hour (including variable fringe benefits).

- The process is performed 10 times per hour (on average).

- The restaurant is open 363 days a year, 10 hours a day.

a. Complete the Summary (top-right) portion of the chart.

b. What is the total labor cost associated with the process?

c. How can this operation be made more efficient? Make a process chart of the improved process. What are the annual labor savings if this new process is implemented?

14. A time study of an employee assembling peanut valves resulted in the following set of observations. What is the standard time, given a performance rating of 95 percent and an allowance of 20 percent of the total normal time?

Average Time (seconds)	Observations
15	14
20	12
25	15

15. Refer to the process chart for the automobile oil change in Solved Problem 3. Calculate the annual labor cost if:

- The mechanic earns $40 per hour (including variable fringe benefits).

- The process is performed twice per hour (on average).

- The shop is open 300 days a year, 10 hours a day.

a. What is the total labor cost associated with the process?

b. If steps 7, 10, 12, and 15 were eliminated, estimate the annual labor savings associated with implementing this new process.

16. A work sampling study was conducted to determine the proportion of the time a worker is idle. The following information was gathered on a random basis:

Day	Number of Times Worker Idle	Total Number of Observations
Monday	17	44
Tuesday	18	56
Wednesday	14	48
Thursday	16	60

FIGURE 4.18 ▶
Process Chart for Making Ice Cream Cones

Process: Making one ice cream cone
Subject: Server at counter
Beginning: Walk to cone storage area
Ending: Give it to server or customer

Insert Step
Append Step
Remove Step

Summary

Activity	Number of Steps	Time (min)	Distance (ft)
Operation ●			
Transport ➡			
Inspect ■			
Delay ❱			
Store ▼			

Step No.	Time (min)	Distance (ft)	●	➡	■	❱	▼	Step Description
1	0.20	5.0		X				Walk to cone storage area
2	0.05		X					Remove empty cone
3	0.10	5.0		X				Walk to counter
4	0.05		X					Place cone in holder
5	0.20	8.0		X				Walk to sink area
6	0.50					X		Ask dishwasher to wash scoop
7	0.15	8.0		X				Walk to counter with clean scoop
8	0.05		X					Pick up empty cone
9	0.10	2.5		X				Walk to flavor ordered
10	0.75		X					Scoop ice cream from container
11	0.75		X					Place ice cream in cone
12	0.25				X			Check for stability
13	0.05	2.5		X				Walk to order placement area
14	0.05		X					Give server or customer the cone

a. Based on these preliminary results, what percent of the time is the worker working?

b. If idle time is judged to be excessive, what additional categories might you add to a follow-up work sampling study to identify the root causes?

17. An initial time study was done on a process with the following results (in minutes). Based on the data obtained so far, assuming an allowance of 20 percent of the normal time, what do you estimate for the time per unit customer served, based on this preliminary sample?

Element	Performance Rating	Obs 1	Obs 2	Obs 3	Obs 4	Obs 5
Element 1	70	4	3	5	4	3
Element 2	110	8	10	9	11	10
Element 3	90	6	8	7	7	6

18. Return to Problem 16. Using *OM Explorer*, how long do you estimate the time required to install the fifth pool? What is your estimate of the total time for all five pools?

19. Smith, Schroeder, and Torn (SST) is a short-haul household furniture moving company. SST's labor force, selected from the local community college football team, is temporary and part-time. SST is concerned with recent complaints, as tabulated on the following tally sheet:

Complaint	Tally
Broken glass	HHT HHT III
Delivered to wrong address	HHT IIII
Furniture rubbed together while on truck	HHT HHT HHT HHT
Late delivery	HHT
Late arrival for pickup	HHT HHT HHT III
Missing items	HHT HHT HHT HHT HHT I
Nicks and scratches from rough handling	HHT HHT
Soiled upholstery	HHT III

a. Draw a bar chart and a Pareto chart to identify the most serious moving problems.

b. Use a cause-and-effect diagram to identify potential causes of complaints.

20. A contractor is preparing a bid to install swimming pools at a new housing addition. The estimated time to build the first pool is 35 hours. The contractor estimates an 85 percent learning rate. Without using the computer:

a. How long do you estimate the time required to install the second pool?

b. How long do you estimate the time required to install the fourth pool?

21. Rick DeNeefe, manager of the Golden Valley Bank credit authorization department, recently noticed that a major competitor was advertising that applications for equity loans could be approved within two working days. Because fast credit approval was a competitive priority, DeNeefe wanted to see how well his department was doing relative to the competitor's. Golden Valley stamps each application with the date and time it is received and again when a decision is made. A total of 104 applications were received in March. The time required for each decision, rounded to the nearest hour, is shown in the following table. Golden Valley's employees work 8 hours per day.

Decision Process Time (hours)	Frequency
7–9	8
10–12	19
13–15	28
16–18	10
19–21	25
22–24	4
25–27	10
Total	104

a. Draw a bar chart for these data.

b. Analyze the data. How is Golden Valley Bank doing with regard to this competitive priority?

22. Last year, the manager of the service department at East Woods Ford instituted a customer opinion program to find out how to improve service.

One week after service on a vehicle was performed, an assistant would call the customer to find out whether the work had been done satisfactorily and how service could be improved. After a year of gathering data, the assistant discovered that the complaints could be grouped into the following five categories:

Complaint	Frequency
Unfriendly atmosphere	5
Long wait for service	17
Price too high	20
Incorrect bill	8
Needed to return to correct problem	50
Total	100

a. Draw a bar chart and a Pareto chart to identify the significant service problems.

b. Use a cause-and-effect diagram to identify potential causes of complaints.

23. The manager of Perrotti's Pizza collects data concerning customer complaints about delivery. Pizza arrives late, or the wrong pizza is delivered.

Problem	Frequency
Topping stuck to box lid	17
Pizza arrives late	35
Wrong topping or combination	9
Wrong style of crust	6
Wrong size	4
Pizza is partially eaten	3
Pizza never arrives	6

a. Use a Pareto chart to identify the "vital few" delivery problems.

b. Use a cause-and-effect diagram to identify potential causes of late pizza delivery.

24. Management of a shampoo bottling company introduced a new 13.5-ounce pack and used an existing machine, with some modifications, to fill it. To measure filling consistency by the modified machine (set to fill 13.85 ounces), an analyst collected the following data (volume in ounces) for a random sample of 100 bottles:

a. Draw a histogram for these data.

b. Bottles with less than 12.85 ounces or more than 14.85 ounces are considered to be out of specification. Based on the sample data, what percentage of the bottles filled by the machine will be out of specification?

Bottle Volume (ounces)									
13.0	13.3	13.6	13.2	14.0	12.9	14.2	12.9	14.5	13.5
14.1	14.0	13.7	13.4	14.4	14.3	14.8	13.9	13.5	14.3
14.2	14.1	14.0	13.9	13.9	14.0	14.5	13.6	13.3	12.9
12.8	13.1	13.6	14.5	14.6	12.9	13.1	14.4	14.0	14.4
13.1	14.1	14.2	12.9	13.3	14.0	14.1	13.1	13.6	13.7
14.0	13.6	13.2	13.4	13.9	14.5	14.0	14.4	13.9	14.6
12.9	14.3	14.0	12.9	14.2	14.8	14.5	13.1	12.7	13.9
13.6	14.4	13.1	14.5	13.5	13.3	14.0	13.6	13.5	14.3
13.2	13.8	13.7	12.8	13.4	13.8	13.3	13.7	14.1	13.7
13.7	13.8	13.4	13.7	14.1	12.8	13.7	13.8	14.1	14.3

25. Plastomer, Inc. specializes in the manufacture of high-grade plastic film used to wrap food products. Film is rejected and scrapped for a variety of reasons (e.g., opacity, high carbon content, incorrect thickness or gauge, scratches, and so on). During the past month, management collected data on the types of rejects and the amount of scrap generated by each type. The following table presents the results:

Type of Failure	Amount of Scrap (lbs.)
Air bubbles	500
Bubble breaks	19,650
Carbon content	150
Unevenness	3,810
Thickness or gauge	27,600
Opacity	450
Scratches	3,840
Trim	500
Wrinkles	10,650

Draw a Pareto chart to identify which type of failure management should attempt to eliminate first.

26. The operations manager for Superfast Airlines at Chicago's O'Hare Airport noticed an increase in the number of delayed flight departures. She brainstormed possible causes with her staff:

- Aircraft late to gate
- Acceptance of late passengers
- Passengers arrive late at gate
- Passengers processing delays at gate
- Late baggage to aircraft
- Other late personnel or unavailable items
- Mechanical failures

Draw a cause-and-effect diagram to organize the possible causes of delayed flight departures into the following major categories: equipment, personnel, material, procedures, and "other factors" beyond managerial control. Provide a detailed set of causes for each major cause identified by the operations manager, and incorporate them in your cause-and-effect diagram.

27. Grindwell, Inc., a manufacturer of grinding tools, is concerned about the durability of its products, which depends on the permeability of the sinter mixtures used in production. Suspecting that the carbon content might be the source of the problem, the plant manager collected the following data:

Carbon Content (%)	Permeability Index
5.5	16
3.0	31
4.5	21
4.8	19
4.2	16
4.7	23
5.1	20
4.4	11
3.6	20

   a. Draw a scatter diagram for these data.

   b. Is there a relationship between permeability and carbon content?

   c. If low permeability is desirable, what does the scatter diagram suggest with regard to the carbon content?

28. Oregon Fiber Board makes roof liners for the automotive industry. The manufacturing manager is concerned about product quality. She suspects that one particular failure, tears in the fabric, is related to production-run size. An assistant gathers the following data from production records:

Run	Size	Failures (%)	Run	Size	Defects (%)
1	1,000	3.5	11	6,500	1.5
2	4,100	3.8	12	1,000	5.5
3	2,000	5.5	13	7,000	1.0
4	6,000	1.9	14	3,000	4.5
5	6,800	2.0	15	2,200	4.2
6	3,000	3.2	16	1,800	6.0
7	2,000	3.8	17	5,400	2.0
8	1,200	4.2	18	5,800	2.0
9	5,000	3.8	19	1,000	6.2
10	3,800	3.0	20	1,500	7.0

   a. Draw a scatter diagram for these data.

   b. Does there appear to be a relationship between run size and percent failures? What implications does this data have for Oregon Fiber Board's business?

ADVANCED PROBLEMS

29. At Conner Company, a custom manufacturer of printed circuit boards, the finished boards are subjected to a final inspection prior to shipment to its customers. As Conner's quality assurance manager, you are responsible for making a presentation to management on quality problems at the beginning of each month. Your assistant has analyzed the reject memos for all the circuit boards that were rejected during the past month. He has given you a summary statement listing the reference number of the circuit board and the reason for rejection from one of the following categories:

   A = Poor electrolyte coverage
   B = Improper lamination
   C = Low copper plating
   D = Plating separation
   E = Improper etching

   For 50 circuit boards that had been rejected last month, the summary statement showed the following:

   C B C C D E C C B A D A C C C B C A C D C A C C B

   A C A C B C C A C A A C C D A C C C E C C A B A C

   a. Prepare a tally sheet (or checklist) of the different reasons for rejection.

   b. Develop a Pareto chart to identify the more significant types of rejection.

   c. Examine the causes of the most significant type of defect, using a cause-and-effect diagram.

30. This problem should be solved as a team exercise:

   Shaving is a process that most men perform each morning. Assume that the process begins at the bathroom sink with the shaver walking (say, 5 feet) to the cabinet (where his shaving supplies are stored) to pick up bowl, soap, brush, and razor. He walks back to the sink, runs the water until it gets warm, lathers his face, shaves, and inspects the results. Then, he rinses the razor, dries his face, walks over to the cabinet to return the bowl, soap, brush, and razor, and comes back to the sink to clean it up and complete the process.

   a. Develop a process chart for shaving. (Assume suitable values for the time required for the various activities involved in the process.)

   b. Brainstorm to generate ideas for improving the shaving process. (Do not try to evaluate the ideas until the group has compiled as complete a list as possible. Otherwise, judgment will block creativity.)

ACTIVE MODEL EXERCISE

This Active Model appears in my**om**lab. It allows you to evaluate the structure of a Pareto chart.

QUESTIONS

1. What percentage of overall complaints do the three most common complaints account for?

2. How does it affect the chart if we eliminate discourteous service?

3. What percentage of overall complaints does discourteous service account for?

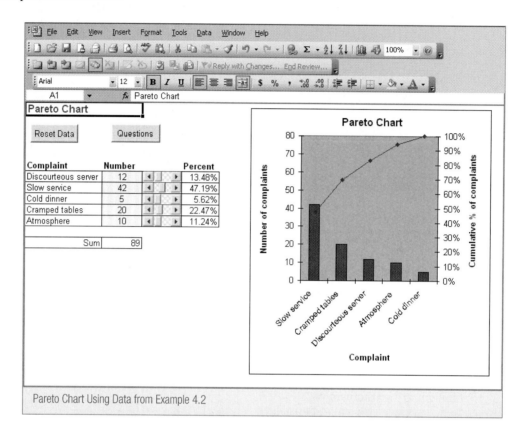

Pareto Chart Using Data from Example 4.2

VIDEO CASE	Process Analysis at Starwood

The features and layout of The Phoenician property of Starwood Hotels and Resorts at Scottsdale, Arizona, are shown in the following figure. Starwood Hotels and Resorts is no stranger to process improvement. In fact, the president's letter in a recent annual report stated that through "...benchmarking, Six Sigma, and recognition of excellence, [Starwood is] driving results in a virtual cycle of self-improvement at all levels of the Company." Recognizing that improved processes in one department of a single hotel, if rolled out across the organization, could lead to significant improvements, the company recently created a program called the "Power of Innovation," or POI.

The Power of Innovation program in Starwood seeks to capture best practices that exist throughout hotels across all brands in North America. An internal team with expertise in kitchen preparation and production, laundry, stewarding, front office, and housekeeping works with individual properties to build upon and maximize the existing knowledge of local property management teams. The team usually spends about a week on property entrenched in operations to really see day-to-day activity over an extended period. Of particular interest is scheduling the workforce to meet the demand of each hotel's individual operations while streamlining operations processes.

At the Westin Galleria-Oaks in Houston, Texas, for example, the POI team helped management achieve a 6 percent productivity improvement in the kitchen preparation and production job, with a reduction of 2,404 hours used and $23,320 in annual payroll savings alone. At the same time, other POI projects at the hotel generated an additional $14,400 in annual payroll savings.

The Phoenician in Scottsdale also had a visit from the POI team. One area the team focused on was stewarding. The typical stewarding process includes the following duties: dishwashing, kitchen trash removal, polishing silver, and assisting with banquet meal food prep lines. Stewards support eight kitchens and two bakeries, and work with housekeeping in keeping public areas, such as restrooms and pool cabanas, clean.

A flowchart that diagrams the existing stewarding process that the team documented is shown in the figure. In any given day, a particular steward may provide support to more than one kitchen, and be called upon to do a variety of tasks.

Before the POI team arrived, stewards were dedicated to a particular kitchen or area during their shift. Each kitchen required stewarding coverage as outlined by the executive chef, so more than one steward may be assigned

```
┌──────────┐   ┌──────────┐   ╱Dishes,╲      ┌──────────┐
│ Steward  │──▶│ Report to│──▶╱silver or╲ No │ Remain in│
│  shift   │   │ assigned │   ╲ trash   ╱────▶│ kitchen  │
│  begins  │   │ kitchen  │   ╲ready for╱     │ until work│
└──────────┘   └──────────┘    ╲handling?╱    │ is ready │
                                   │          └──────────┘
                                   │ Yes
                                   ▼
                             ┌──────────┐
                             │ Complete │
                             │  task    │
                             │ (dishes, │
                             │  trash,  │
                             │  silver  │
                             │ handling)│
                             └──────────┘
                                   │
            No        ╱End of╲ Yes      ╱────────╲
       ┌─────────────╱ shift? ╲───────▶( Finish  )
                     ╲        ╱          ╲────────╱
```

to an area. A certain amount of stewarding work could be forecast by the food and beverage manager, based on scheduled banquets, afternoon teas, conference buffets, and restaurant reservations. Considerable uncertainty also arose from traffic generated by leisure travelers and local clientele, meaning that stewards assigned to designated areas periodically did not have a steady flow of work.

On a weekly basis, activity levels for the dedicated stewarding staff were determined, based on executive chef input. Other factors considered in the weekly planning included prior year activity, special events and holidays, and number of children. With this information, the executive steward created a summary of all meals, called covers, by location, date, and time of day. Then, an Excel spreadsheet template was used to create the schedule for deployment of stewarding staff throughout the resort's kitchens and restaurants.

In performing its analysis, the POI team examined staff availability, banquet events, restaurants, occupied room counts, and other drivers of business to areas supported by stewards. Time studies were done to determine how far stewards were traveling throughout the property, and how long it took to perform each stewarding task. Some restaurants and kitchens did not require full-time coverage by a steward, so the steward would be assigned multiple kitchens to fill a work shift. In the case of coverage between the 19th Hole restaurant on one side of the resort, and the Canyon Building on the other side, that steward would walk one-half kilometer, one way, to take care of duties in both locations because they lacked enough work for a dedicated steward in each location.

Often, stewards had downtime as they waited for banquet dishes to be cleared, or kitchen pots and utensils to be brought in for cleaning. Some restaurants had china with special cleaning requirements, meaning those dishes had to be handwashed instead of being placed in an automated sanitizing dishwasher. This situation required a dedicated steward to perform that task.

Time studies revealed how long it took stewards to move from one kitchen to the next. The studies also helped the POI team understand how long it took to wash dishes in the five-star restaurant versus the casual poolside dining area's kitchen. Additionally, the studies uncovered building design and landscaping limitations that prevented staff from moving between kitchens quickly. In some cases, a maze of corridors added kilometers to the distances covered each day, and thick privacy hedges barred entry to sidewalk shortcuts.

QUESTIONS

1. How can the management specifically improve the stewarding process at The Phoenician? Using the information provided, create a flowchart illustrating the new process.

2. What are the benefits that the POI program can bring to Starwood? Can these benefits be extended to other processes and properties within the Starwood system?

3. Of the seven mistakes organizations can make when managing processes (see last section of this chapter), which ones might Starwood be most at risk of making? Why?

CASE Process Analysis in Carrefour Group

Commencing in 2003 and continuing to this day, Carrefour is undertaking systematic process analysis of its purchasing and supply operations to gain detailed understanding of how work is performed and to identifying areas for improvement. The key steps it is taking include the following:

- Identify opportunities
- Define the scope
- Document the process
- Evaluate performance
- Redesign the process
- Implement the changes

This has meant that the company has reviewed its four core processes of supplier relationships, new service/product development, order fulfillment, and customer relationships, while recognizing strategic issues, including gaps between competitive priorities and competitive capabilities, and lack of strategic fit.

Over the past 40 years, the Carrefour group has grown to become one of the world's leading distribution groups. It is the world's second-largest retailer and the biggest in Europe. The group currently operates four main grocery store formats: hypermarkets, supermarkets, discount, and convenience stores. The Carrefour group currently has over 15,000 stores, either company-operated or franchises, with over 490,000 employees and annual sales in 2007 of $128.8 billion. The group currently operates in three major markets: Europe, Latin America, and Asia. With a presence in 30 countries, over 54 percent of group turnover derives from outside its home country of France. Typically, the Carrefour group will be one of the leading private employers in any country where it operates. Naturally, this is the case for France, where the group was originally founded, but it is also true of such countries as Brazil, Argentina, Colombia, Italy, and Greece. The group also seeks to support local suppliers, with some 90-95 percent of the products on its shelves sourced locally.

However, now the foundation of Carrefour's empire is looking shaky. More and more French consumers are spurning its hypermarkets in favor of discount chains such as Germany's ALDI and Lidl. That is squeezing Carrefour's bottom line, just as the group is facing tougher competition abroad.

The Need for Undertaking Process Analysis

Chief Executive Jose Luis Duran has taken personal control of the process analysis and improvement exercise due to the importance attributed the undertaking. To-date, billions of euros associated with the processes in delivering products from factories to the supermarkets have been saved. In the process, Duran transformed the company from one that was complacent with its position at the head of a cozy duopoly and whose offerings were stable, to one that is highly efficient and competitive, resulting in sharp increases in its market share and profitability. Carrefour receives deliveries from suppliers on a daily and weekly basis. The company sells to customers and restocks every day with popular products being restocked more than once a day. Duran questioned why the company had a 50+ days of stock in the pipelines, a 4–6 percent out of stock level and an average service level of 90 percent. Currently, the world-best practice for average inventory-turnover rate is 20 days, so why was Carrefour's performance so poor? Further complicating the problem was the fact that customer satisfaction rates were not good. A key cause of this was the high levels of out-of-stock incidences. These were occurring with suppliers and retailers, and it was difficult to pinpoint exactly where and how they were occurring. There were times when there would be no stock of items on the retailers' shelves, but

plenty in the warehouses. The fault was with in-store processes and systems communications up and down the supply chains. Moreover, Duran stated that large overseas companies such as Wal-Mart and Tesco had identified Carrefour's poor operations and were considering moving into the Continental market. Duran realized that action was urgently needed; otherwise, there was a strong possibility that Carrefour would not survive for long.

Based on process improvement practices of Wal-Mart, Tesco, and other successful international retailers, Carrefour is now completely overhauling its organizational structure, supply chains, and logistics systems. A five-year exercise will cost more than a billion euros to implement. The key elements of this plan, most of which are now in place, are the following:

- Centralization of the buying function for Continental Europe, as Carrefour previously had a country-based structure in which each country had different pallet load sizes, order cycles, IT interfaces with suppliers, etc. Moving to a central buying structure means that decision-making processes are streamlined, suppliers deal with a single point of contact, opportunities for national marketing have been created, and duplication of efforts is removed.

With centralization of the key buying function, it made sense to create and operate a shared services functional structure to take care of backroom processes.

- Redesign of distribution network. This involved consolidation of 31 distribution centers to 9 regional distribution centers (RDCs) and the introduction of 4 national distribution centers (NDCs) where goods are received directly from suppliers and distributed to regional distribution centers.

- Redesign of transportation system. The company implemented a transport management system (TMS) to reduce the volume of direct store deliveries and take control of inbound freight volumes to the distribution centers. This, as opposed to the previous practice where suppliers supplied goods directly to the regional distribution centers.

- Development and implementation of IT-based inventory replenishment systems. Specifically, forecast-based replenishment systems for distribution centers and stores have been installed in all the NDCs and stores. In addition, point-of-sale data signaling systems have been integrated into the store and NDC communication systems.

- Establishing electronic data interchange (EDI) connection with top suppliers. Carrefour has established full two-way, live, electronic inter-connection with most of its 3,000 suppliers.

Early Results of Process Analysis

To date the project has been an overwhelming success. Consider the following:

- Cost savings of 5.2 percent of sales. This represents 8.6 billion euros in savings over five years.

- The average inventory-holding period has decreased dramatically. This was close to 50 days in 1999, was down to 34.1 days by 2003, and is now tracking in the 20s. Considering that reducing inventory holdings by two days represents about 100 million euros a year in free cash flow, this dramatic and significant improvement in inventory turnover rate has generated at least a billion euros of free cash flow.

- Carrefour has put most of the savings to good use—reducing prices and improving in-store amenities.

QUESTIONS

1. How did Carrefour connect its process analysis with strategic issues, such as those tactics to combat market competition?

2. How did the company identify and implement the six steps in applying the systematic approach to process analysis?

3. How did the company's improvement initiative identify market opportunities and business expansion?

Source: This case was prepared by Dr. David Parker, The University of Queensland, Business School, as a basis for classroom discussion.

SELECTED REFERENCES

Anderson, Merrill C. "Transforming Human Resources: Maximizing Value While Increasing Productivity." *National Productivity Review*, vol. 17, no. 3 (Autumn 2000), pp. 75–80.

Anupindi, Ravi, Sunil Chopra, Sudhakar D. Deshmukj, Jan A. Van Mieghem, and Eitan Zemel. *Managing Business Process Flows.* Upper Saddle River, NJ: Prentice Hall, 1999.

Banker, R. D., J. M. Field, R. G. Schroeder, and K. K. Sinha. "Impact of Work Teams on Manufacturing Performance: A Longitudinal Field Study." *Academy of Management Journal*, vol. 39, no. 4 (1996), pp. 867–890.

Carey, Susan. "Case of the Vanishing Airport Lines." *Wall Street Journal* (August 9, 2007).

Collier, D. A. *The Service/Quality Solution.* Burr Ridge, IL: Irwin Professional Publishing, 1993.

Davenport, Thomas H. "The Coming Commoditization of Processes." *Harvard Business Review*, (June 2005), pp. 101–108.

Drucker, Peter F. "The Discipline of Innovation." *Harvard Business Review*, vol. 80, no. 8 (August 2002), pp. 95–101.

Ellis, Christian M., and Lea A. P. Tonkin. "Mature Team Rewards and the High-Performance Workplace: Change and Opportunity." *Target*, vol. 11, no. 6 (1995).

Fisher, Anne. "Get Employees to Brainstorm Online." *Fortune*, vol. 150, no. 11 (November 2004), p. 72.

Fitzsimmons, James A., and Mona J. Fitzsimmons. *Service Management: Operations, Strategy, and Information Technology.* New York: McGraw-Hill, 1998.

Fleming, John H., Curt Coffman, and James K. Harter. "Manage Your Human Sigma." *Harvard Business Review*, (July–August 2005), pp. 101–108.

Hartvigsen, David. *SimQuick: Process Simulation with Excel*, 2d ed. Upper Saddle River, NJ: Prentice Hall, 2004.

Healy, Beth. "One Day, Not Three: A Push to Trade Faster." *The Boston Globe* (July 19, 2000).

Iakovou, Eleftherios T., and Olga L. Oritz. "Reengineering of the Laundry Service at a University Campus: A Continuous-Improvement Quality-Management Methodology." *Quality Engineering*, vol. 16, no. 2 (2004), pp. 245–255.

Karmarkar, Uday. "Will You Survive the Services Revolution?" *Harvard Business Review*, vol. 82, no. 6 (June 2004), pp. 100–107.

Katzenbach, Jon R., and Douglas K. Smith. "The Discipline of Teams." *Harvard Business Review* (March–April 1993), pp. 111–120.

La Ferla, Beverly. "Mapping the Way to Process Improvement." *IEE Engineering Management* (December 2004–January 2005), pp. 16–17.

Lee, Hau L. "The Triple-A Supply Chain." *Harvard Business Review* (October 2004), pp. 102–112.

Liebs, Scott. "A Little Help from Their Friends." *Industry Week* (February 2, 1998).

Melnyk, Steven A., Douglas M. Stewart, and Morgan Swink. "Metrics and Performance Measurement in Operations Management: Dealing with the Metrics Maze." *Journal of Operations Management*, vol. 22, no. 3 (June 2004), pp. 209–217.

Metters, Richard, Kathryn King-Metters, and Madeleine Pullman. *Successful Service Operations Management.* Mason, OH: South-Western, 2003.

Pande, Peter S., Robert P. Neuman, and Roland R. Cavanagh. *The Six Sigma Way.* New York: McGraw-Hill, 2000.

"Process, Process, Process." *Planning Review* (special issue), vol. 22, no. 3 (1993), pp. 1–56.

Pullman, Madeleine E., and William L. Moore. "Optimal Service Design: Integrating Marketing and Operations Perspectives." *International Journal of Service Industry Management*, vol. 10, no. 2 (1999), pp. 239–260.

Rampersad, Hubert K. *Total Performance Scorecard.* New York: Butterworth-Heinemann, 2003.

Rummler, Geary A., and Alan P. Brache. *Improving Performance*, 2nd ed. San Francisco: Jossey-Bass Inc., 1995.

Senge, P. *The Fifth Discipline: The Art and Practice of the Learning Organization.* New York: Doubleday, 1990.

Shapiro, Benson R., V. Kasturi Rangan, and John J. Sviokla. "Staple Yourself to an Order." *Harvard Business Review*, vol. 82, no. 7/8 (July–August 1992), pp. 113–122.

B SIMULATION MODELS

LEARNING GOALS

After reading this supplement, you should be able to:

1. Identify problems best suited for simulation models.

2. Describe the Monte Carlo simulation process.

3. Explain how to create a simulation model and use it to help make a decision.

4. Create a simple simulation model with an Excel spreadsheet.

5. Describe the advanced capabilities of SimQuick.

The act of reproducing the behavior of a system using a model that describes the processes of the system is called **simulation**. Once the model has been developed, the analyst can manipulate certain variables to measure the effects of changes on the operating characteristics of interest. A simulation model cannot prescribe what should be done about a problem. Instead, it can be used to study alternative solutions to the problem. The alternatives are systematically used in the model, and the relevant operating characteristics are recorded. After all the alternatives have been tried, the best one is selected.

Simulation can be used in managing processes as well as supply chains. Various simulation models can help in understanding how a process performs dynamically over time and how well revised processes will work. Some of the changes that simulation can be used to assess include quality improvement ideas, capacity changes aimed at relieving bottlenecks, the layout of the process, or even changes that come from implementing lean systems ideas—in effect, all of the decision areas covered in Part 2. Simulation can also be used for many of the decisions related to managing supply chains (Part 3), such as where to position inventory and in what quantities, or how different scheduling procedures work.

Waiting-line models (see Supplement C, "Waiting Line Models") are not simulation models because they describe the operating characteristics with known

myomlab and the Companion Website at **www.pearsonglobaleditions.com/krajewski** contain many tools, activities, and resources designed for this supplement.

equations. With simulation, the equations describing the operation characteristics are unknown. Using a simulation model, the analyst actually generates customer arrivals, puts customers into waiting lines, selects the next customer to be served by using some priority discipline, serves that customer, and so on. The model keeps track of the number in line, waiting time, and the like during the simulation and calculates the averages and variances at the end.

simulation

The act of reproducing the behavior of a system using a model that describes the processes of the system.

REASONS FOR USING SIMULATION

Simulation is useful when waiting-line models become too complex. Using simulation for analyzing processes may be based on other reasons as well. First, when the relationship between the variables is nonlinear or when the situation involves too many variables or constraints to handle with optimizing approaches, simulation models can be used to estimate operating characteristics or objective function values and analyze a problem.

Second, simulation models can be used to conduct experiments without disrupting real systems. Experimenting with a real system can be costly. For example, a simulation model can be used to estimate the benefits of purchasing and installing an automated processing system without first installing such a system. Also, the model could be used to evaluate different configurations or processing decision rules without disrupting production schedules.

Third, simulation models can be used to obtain operating characteristic estimates in much less time than is required to gather the same operating data from a real system. This feature of simulation is called **time compression**. For example, a simulation model of airport operations can generate statistics on airplane arrivals, landing delays, and terminal delays for a year in a matter of minutes on a computer. Alternative airport designs can be analyzed and decisions made quickly.

time compression

The feature of simulation models that allows them to obtain operating characteristic estimates in much less time than is required to gather the same operating data from a real system.

Finally, simulation is useful in sharpening managerial decision-making skills through gaming. A descriptive model that relates managerial decisions to important operating characteristics (e.g., profits, market share, and the like) can be developed. From a set of starting conditions, the participants make periodic decisions with the intention of improving one or more operating characteristics. In such an exercise, a few hours' "play" can simulate a year's time. Gaming also enables managers to experiment with new ideas without disrupting normal operations.

THE SIMULATION PROCESS

The simulation process includes data collection, random-number assignment, model formulation, and analysis. This process is known as **Monte Carlo simulation**, after the European gambling capital, because of the random numbers used to generate the simulation events.

Monte Carlo simulation

A simulation process that uses random numbers to generate simulation events.

Data Collection

Simulation requires extensive data gathering on costs, productivities, capacities, and probability distributions. Typically, one of two approaches to data collection is used. Statistical sampling procedures are used when the data are not readily available from published sources or when the cost of searching for and collecting the data is high. Historical search is used when the data are available in company records, governmental and industry reports, professional and scientific journals, or newspapers. Example B.1 provides the data that Specialty Steel collected.

EXAMPLE B.1	**Data Collection for a Simulation**

The Specialty Steel Products Company produces items, such as machine tools, gears, automobile parts, and other specialty items, in small quantities to customer order. Because the products are so diverse, demand is measured in machine-hours. Orders for products are translated into required machine-hours, based on time standards for each operation. Management is concerned about capacity in the lathe department. Assemble the data necessary to analyze the addition of one more lathe machine and operator.

SOLUTION

Historical records indicate that lathe department demand varies from week to week as follows:

Weekly Production Requirements (hr)	Relative Frequency
200	0.05
250	0.06
300	0.17
350	0.05
400	0.30
450	0.15
500	0.06
550	0.14
600	0.02
	Total 1.00

To gather these data, all weeks with requirements of 175.00–224.99 hours were grouped in the 200-hour category, all weeks with 225.00–274.99 hours were grouped in the 250-hour category, and so on. The average weekly production requirements for the lathe department are

$$200(0.05) + 250(0.06) + 300(0.17) + \ldots + 600(0.02) = 400 \text{ hours}$$

Employees in the lathe department work 40 hours per week on 10 machines. However, the number of machines actually operating during any week may be less than 10. Machines may need repair, or a worker may not show up for work. Historical records indicate that actual machine-hours were distributed as follows:

Regular Capacity (hr)	Relative Frequency
320 (8 machines)	0.30
360 (9 machines)	0.40
400 (10 machines)	0.30

The average number of operating machine-hours in a week is

$$320(0.30) + 360(0.40) + 400(0.30) = 360 \text{ hours}$$

The company has a policy of completing each week's workload on schedule, using overtime and subcontracting if necessary. The maximum amount of overtime authorized in any week is 100 hours, and requirements in excess of 100 hours are subcontracted to a small machine shop in town. Lathe operators receive $10 per hour for regular time. However, management estimates that the cost for overtime work is $25 per hour per employee, which includes premium-wage, variable-overhead, and supervision costs. Subcontracting costs $35 per hour, exclusive of materials costs.

To justify adding another machine and worker to the lathe department, weekly savings in overtime and subcontracting costs should be at least $650. These savings would cover the cost of the additional worker and provide for a reasonable return on machine investment. Management estimates from prior experience that with 11 machines the distribution of weekly capacity machine-hours would be

Regular Capacity (hr)	Relative Frequency
360 (9 machines)	0.30
400 (10 machines)	0.40
440 (11 machines)	0.30

Random-Number Assignment

Before we can begin to analyze this problem with simulation, we must specify a way to generate demand and capacity each week. Suppose that we want to simulate 100 weeks of lathe operations with 10 machines. We would expect that 5 percent of the time (5 weeks of the 100) we would have a demand for 200 hours. Similarly, we would expect that 30 percent of the time (30 weeks of the 100) we would have 320 hours of existing capacity with the 10 machines. However, we cannot use these averages of demand in our simulation because a real system does not operate that way. Demand may be 200 hours one week but 550 hours the next.

We can obtain the effect we want by using a random-number table to determine the amount of demand and capacity each week. A **random number** is a number that has the same probability of being selected as any other number (see the Table of Random Numbers in Appendix 2 for five-digit random numbers).

The events in a simulation can be generated in an unbiased way if random numbers are assigned to the events in the same proportion as their probability of occurrence. We expect a demand of 200 hours 5 percent of the time. If we have 100 random numbers (00–99), we can assign 5 numbers (or 5 percent of them) to the event "200 hours demanded." Thus, we can assign the numbers 00–04 to that event. If we randomly choose numbers in the range of 00–99 enough times, 5 percent of the time they will fall in the range of 00–04. Similarly, we can assign the numbers 05–10, or 6 percent of the numbers, to the event "250 hours demanded." In Table B.1 we show the allocation of the 100 random numbers to the demand events in the same proportion as their probability of occurrence. We similarly assigned random numbers to the *capacity* events for 10 machines. The capacity events for the 11-machine simulation would have the same random-number assignments, except that the events would be 360, 400, and 440 hours, respectively.

random number

A number that has the same probability of being selected as any other number.

TABLE B.1 | RANDOM-NUMBER ASSIGNMENTS TO SIMULATION EVENTS

Event					
Weekly Demand (hr)	Probability	Random Number	Existing Weekly Capacity (hr)	Probability	Random Numbers
200	0.05	00–04	320	0.30	00–29
250	0.06	05–10	360	0.40	30–69
300	0.17	11–27	400	0.30	70–99
350	0.05	28–32			
400	0.30	33–62			
450	0.15	63–77			
500	0.06	78–83			
550	0.14	84–97			
600	0.02	98–99			

Model Formulation

Formulating a simulation model entails specifying the relationships among the variables. Simulation models consist of decision variables, uncontrollable variables, and dependent variables. **Decision variables** are controlled by the decision maker and will change from one run to the next as different events are simulated. For example, the number of lathe machines is the decision variable in the Specialty Steel Products problem in Example B.1. **Uncontrollable variables**, however, are random events that the decision maker cannot control. At Specialty Steel Products, the weekly production requirements and the *actual* number of machine-hours available are uncontrollable variables for the simulation analysis. Dependent variables reflect the values of the decision variables and the uncontrollable variables. At Specialty Steel Products, operating characteristics such as idle time, overtime, and subcontracting hours are dependent variables.

The relationships among the variables are expressed in mathematical terms so that the dependent variables can be computed for any values of the decision variables and uncontrollable variables. For example, in the simulation model for Specialty Steel Products, the

decision variables

Variables that are controlled by the decision maker and will change from one run to the next as different events are simulated.

uncontrollable variables

Random events that the decision maker cannot control.

methods of determining weekly production requirements and actual capacity availability must be specified first. Then the methods of computing idle-time hours, overtime hours, and subcontracting hours for the values of production requirements and capacity hours can be specified.

EXAMPLE B.2	Formulating a Simulation Model

Formulate a simulation model for Specialty Steel Products that will estimate idle-time hours, overtime hours, and subcontracting hours for a specified number of lathes. Design the simulation model to terminate after 20 weeks of simulated lathe department operations.

SOLUTION

Let us use the first two rows of random numbers in the random number table for the demand events and the third and fourth rows for the capacity events (see the Table of Random Numbers in Appendix 2). Because they are five-digit numbers, we use only the first two digits of each number for our random numbers. The choice of the rows in the random-number table was arbitrary. The important point is that we must be consistent in drawing random numbers and should not repeat the use of numbers in any one simulation.

To simulate a particular capacity level, we proceed as follows:

Step 1: Draw a random number from the first two rows of the table. Start with the first number in the first row, then go to the second number in the first row, and so on.

Step 2: Find the random-number interval for production requirements associated with the random number.

Step 3: Record the production hours (PROD) required for the current week.

Step 4: Draw another random number from row 3 or 4 of the table. Start with the first number in row 3, then go to the second number in row 3, and so on.

Step 5: Find the random-number interval for capacity (CAP) associated with the random number.

Step 6: Record the capacity hours available for the current week.

Step 7: If CAP ≥ PROD, then IDLE HR = CAP − PROD.

Step 8: If CAP < PROD, then SHORT = PROD − CAP.

If SHORT ≤ 100, then OVER TIME HR = SHORT and SUBCONTRACT HR = 0.

If SHORT > 100, then OVERTIME HR = 100 and SUBCONTRACT HR = SHORT − 100.

Step 9: Repeat steps 1–8 until you have simulated 20 weeks.

Analysis

Table B.2 contains the simulations for the two capacity alternatives at Specialty Steel Products. We used a unique random-number sequence for weekly production requirements for each capacity alternative and another sequence for the existing weekly capacity to make a direct comparison between the capacity alternatives.

Based on the 20-week simulations, we would expect average weekly overtime hours (highlighted in orange) to be reduced by 41.5 − 29.5 = 12 hours and subcontracting hours (highlighted in gray) to be reduced by 18 − 10 = 8 hours per week. The average weekly savings would be

$$\text{Overtime:} \quad (12 \text{ hours})(\$25/\text{hours}) = \$300$$

$$\text{Subcontracting:} \quad (8 \text{ hours})(\$35/\text{hour}) = \underline{\quad 280}$$

$$\text{Total savings per week} = \$580$$

This amount falls short of the minimum required savings of $650 per week. Does this outcome mean that we should not add the machine and worker? Before answering, let us look at Table B.3, which shows the results of a *1,000-week* simulation for each alternative. The costs (highlighted in lavender) are quite different from those of the 20-week simulations. Now the savings are estimated to be $1,851.50 − $1,159.50 = $692 and exceed the minimum required savings for the additional investment. This result emphasizes the importance of selecting the proper run length for a simulation analysis. We can use statistical tests to check for the proper run length.

TABLE B.2	20-WEEK SIMULATIONS OF ALTERNATIVES

| | | | | 10 Machines | | | | 11 Machines | | | |
Week	Demand Random Number	Weekly Production (hr)	Capacity Random Number	Existing Weekly Capacity (hr)	Idle Hours	Overtime Hours	Subcontract Hours	Existing Weekly Capacity (hr)	Idle Hours	Overtime Hours	Subcontract Hours
1	71	450	50	360		90		400		50	
2	68	450	54	360		90		400		50	
3	48	400	11	320		80		360		40	
4	99	600	36	360		100	140	400		100	100
5	64	450	82	400		50		440		10	
6	13	300	87	400	100			440	140		
7	36	400	41	360		40		400			
8	58	400	71	400				440	40		
9	13	300	00	320	20			360	60		
10	93	550	60	360		100	90	400		100	50
11	21	300	47	360	60			400	100		
12	30	350	76	400	50			440	90		
13	23	300	09	320	20			360	60		
14	89	550	54	360		100	90	400		100	50
15	58	400	87	400				440	40		
16	46	400	82	400				440	40		
17	00	200	17	320	120			360	160		
18	82	500	52	360		100	40	400		100	
19	02	200	17	320	120			360	160		
20	37	400	19	320	___	80	___	360	___	40	___
				Total	490	830	360		890	590	200
				Weekly average	24.5	41.5	18.0		44.5	29.5	10.0

TABLE B.3	COMPARISON OF 1,000-WEEK SIMULATIONS

	10 Machines	11 Machines
Idle hours	26.0	42.2
Overtime hours	48.3	34.2
Subcontract hours	18.4	8.7
Cost	**$1,851.50**	**$1,159.50**

Simulation analysis can be viewed as a form of hypothesis testing, whereby the results of a simulation run provide sample data that can be analyzed statistically. Data can be recorded and compared with the results from other simulation runs. Statistical tests also can be made to determine whether differences in the alternative operating characteristics are statistically significant.

Even though a difference between simulation experiments may be statistically significant, it may not be *managerially* significant. For example, suppose that we developed a simulation model of a car wash operation. We may find by changing the speed of the car wash from 3 to 2.75 minutes per car that we can reduce the average waiting time per customer by 0.20 minute. Even though this may be a statistically significant difference in the average waiting time, the difference is so small that customers may not even notice it. What is managerially significant often is a judgment decision.

Computer Simulation

The manual simulation of the lathe process in Examples B.1 and B.2 demonstrates the basics of simulation. However, the simulation involves only one step in the process, two uncontrollable variables (weekly production requirements and the actual number of machine-hours available), and 20 time periods. It is important to simulate a process long enough to achieve **steady state**, so that the simulation is repeated over enough time that the average results for performance measures remain constant. Manual simulations can be excessively time-consuming, particularly if they include many subprocesses, many services or products with unique flow patterns, many uncontrollable variables, complex logic for releasing new jobs and assigning work, and the like.

Simulating these real-world situations manually can become too time-consuming and therefore requires a computer instead. Simple simulation models, say with one or two uncontrollable variables, can be developed using Excel. Its ability to generate random numbers—coupled with adding formulas elsewhere in the worksheet to specify relations between demand, customer served, inventory, and output—allow the Monte Carlo simulation approach to be implemented. Even more computer power comes from commercial, prewritten simulation software.

Simulation with Excel Spreadsheets

The starting point in creating an Excel simulation is generating random numbers, the computer equivalent of using Appendix 2 for manual simulations. Equally important is random-number assignment, which translates a random number into a value for an uncontrollable variable.

Generating Random Numbers   Random numbers can be created from 0 to 1 by entering the formula = RAND() into a cell of the Excel spreadsheet. This formula then can be copied to other cells in the spreadsheet as needed. Figure B.1 shows a table of 100 random numbers generated with the RAND() function in the range A3:J12. They were formatted to show four-digit numbers, although the format can be changed as desired. These random numbers are fractions from 0 to 1, rather than the two-digit integer numbers from 0 through 99 in Table B.1. If you attempt to replicate Figure B.1, or reopen an Excel file that was created earlier and saved, you will see a different set of random numbers. To use the same exact set or *stream* of random numbers, such as for experiments that compare the effectiveness of different policies, you should *freeze* the random numbers. First, select with your mouse the cells holding the random numbers that you wish to freeze. For example, cover A3:J12 in Figure B.1. Next, click Edit/Copy in the menu at the top of your spreadsheet. Then click Edit/Paste Special and choose the Values option. When you click OK, a copy of the numbers in these cells is pasted over the same cells with the = RAND() formulas in them. The result is that they are fixed in place and will not change from one use of the spreadsheet to the next. Each simulation is conducted with the same stream of random numbers. In fact, the numbers in Figure B.1 were frozen using this procedure.

steady state

The state that occurs when the simulation is repeated over enough time that the average results for performance measures remain constant.

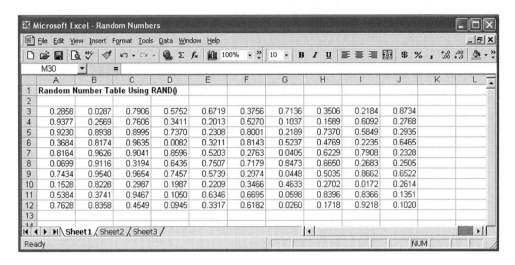

▲ FIGURE B.1
A Spreadsheet with 100 Random
Numbers Generated with RAND( )

Random-Number Assignment   A second capability that is needed for Excel simulations is to translate random numbers into values for the uncontrollable variables. It is equivalent to identifying the random-number interval in which a random number falls and then selecting the value of the uncontrollable variable assigned to that interval (see Table B.1 for the demand or capacity variables). In an Excel spreadsheet, the Lookup feature serves this purpose. Read about the VLOOKUP() function under Excel's Help Topics and check out the function by selecting Insert/Function/Lookup & Reference/VLOOKUP. Example B.3 demonstrates the use of both the VLOOKUP() and RAND() functions.

EXAMPLE B.3	Excel Simulation Model for BestCar Auto Dealer

The BestCar automobile dealership sells new automobiles. The BestCar store manager believes that the number of cars sold weekly has the following probability distribution:

Weekly Sales (cars)	Relative Frequency (probability)
0	0.05
1	0.15
2	0.20
3	0.30
4	0.20
5	0.10
	Total 1.00

The selling price per car is $20,000. Design a simulation model that determines the probability distribution and mean of the weekly sales.

FIGURE B.2 ▲
BestCar Simulation Model

SOLUTION

Figure B.2 simulates 50 weeks of sales at BestCar. A longer run length, say 500 or 1,000 weeks, would be prudent, but here we keep it small for demonstration purposes. The bottom right of the spreadsheet shows that the average weekly sales is 2.88 cars, for $57,600 per week. The distribution of the simulated weekly demand is shown in cells B17:E22. For example, 13 of the 50 weeks experienced a demand for 3 cars, which translates into 26 percent of the weeks (see cell D20). The chance that sales are not more than 3 cars is 60 percent (see cell E20).

The first step in creating this spreadsheet is to input the probability distribution, including the cumulative probabilities associated with it. These input values are highlighted in yellow in cells B6:B11 of the spreadsheet, with corresponding demands in D6:D11. The lower range of cumulative probabilities is calculated in cells C6:C11 by entering 0 in C6 and then entering the formula "=C6+B6" into cell C7 and copying it to cells C8:C11. The cumulative values provide a basis to associate random numbers to the corresponding demand, using the VLOOKUP() function. For example, the first random number for week 1 has the value 0.5176 and will result in a demand of 3 cars, because 0.5176 is greater than the lower range for a demand of 3 cars, but smaller than the lower range for demand of 4 cars. In a similar way, any random number with a value greater than 0.70 but smaller than 0.90 will correspond to a demand of 4 cars.

The next step is to create a table with four columns. Column G identifies each of the 50 weeks to be simulated in cells G6:G55. Column H generates the random numbers, one for each of the 50 weeks. To create the random numbers, we enter the formula "=RAND()" into cell H6 of our spreadsheet and then copy it to the cells H7:H55. After generating the random numbers, we need to match these numbers with the corresponding demand values. We can do this by using the VLOOKUP function. We enter the formula "=VLOOKUP(H6,$C$6:$D$11,2)" into cell 16 and copy it through I7:I55. With this use of the VLOOKUP function, Excel's logic identifies (or "looks up") for each week's random number (in column H) which demand it corresponds to in the lookup array defined by $C$6:$D$11. Once it finds the probability range (defined by column C) in which the random number fits, it posts the car demand (in column D) for this range back into the week's sales (in column I). When searching the lookup array, it moves down through column C until it finds a cell that has a value greater than the random number. It goes back to the previous cell, gets the corresponding demand value from column D, and returns it to the cell in column I. The weekly revenue column is the fourth column in the simulation table, created in cells J6:J55 by multiplying the weekly demand values (column I) by average selling price ($20,000). The average car sales is calculated in cell I56 using the =AVERAGE(I6:I55) function, and the average revenue in cell J56 using the = AVERAGE(J6:J55) function. Note that Figure B.2 only shows the first 19 weeks and the last 3 weeks. This compression is possible using the Window/Freeze Panes option. Here, the window is frozen through week 19 (at start of row 25). You can scroll down or up to show just a few of the last weeks or most of them, depending on how much you want to display.

Finally, the results table is created at the lower left portion of the spreadsheet to summarize the simulation output. By entering the FREQUENCY function into cells C17:C22, we calculate the number of observations in each demand category out of a total of 50 observations. The function looks through the simulated demand values in cells I6:I55 and compares them to the demand categories in cells B17:B22, which are defined as the bin array of the FREQUENCY function. Percentage and cumulative columns next to the frequency column show the frequencies in percentage and cumulative percentage terms.

Simulation with More Advanced Software

Simulation programming can be done in a variety of computer languages, including general-purpose programming languages such as VISUAL BASIC, FORTRAN, or C++. The advantage of general-purpose programming languages is that they are available on most computer systems. Special simulation languages, such as GPSS, SIMSCRIPT, and SLAM, are also available. These languages simplify programming because they have macroinstructions for the commonly used elements of simulation models. These macroinstructions automatically contain the computer instructions needed to generate arrivals, keep track of waiting lines, and calculate the statistics on the operating characteristics of a system.

Simulation is also possible with powerful PC-based packages, such as SimQuick (www.nd.edu/~dhartvig/simquick/top.htm), Extend (www.imaginethatinc.com), SIM-PROCESS (www.caciasl.com), ProModel (www.promodel.com), and Witness (www.lan-ner.com/corporate). Here we illustrate process simulation with the SimQuick software (provided on my**om**lab).

SimQuick   SimQuick is an easy-to-use package that is simply an Excel spreadsheet with some macros. Models can be created for a variety of simple processes, such as waiting lines, inventory control, and projects. Here we consider the passenger security process at one terminal of a medium-sized airport between the hours of 8 A.M. and 10 A.M. The process works as follows. Passengers arriving at the security area immediately enter a single line. After waiting in line, each passenger goes through one of two inspection stations, which involves walking through a metal detector and running any carry-on baggage through a scanner. After completing this inspection, 10 percent of the passengers are randomly selected for an additional inspection, which typically involves a more thorough search of each person's carry-on baggage. Two stations handle this additional inspection, and selected passengers go through only one of them. Management is interested in examining the effect of increasing the percentage of passengers who undergo the second inspection. In particular, they want to compare the waiting times for the second inspection when 10 percent, then 15 percent, and then 20 percent of the passengers are randomly selected for this inspection. Management also wants to know how opening a third station for the second inspection would affect these waiting times.

A first step in simulating this process with SimQuick is to draw a flowchart of the process using SimQuick's building blocks. SimQuick has five building blocks that can be combined in a wide variety of ways. Four of these types are used to model this process. An *entrance* is used to model the arrival of passengers at the security process. A *buffer* is used to model each of the two waiting lines, one before each type of inspection, as well as the passengers that have finished the process. Each of the four inspection stations is modeled with a *workstation*. Finally, the random selection of passengers for the second inspection is modeled with a *decision point*. Figure B.3 shows the flowchart.

Information describing each building block is entered into SimQuick tables. In this model, three key types of information are entered: (1) when people arrive at the entrance, (2) how long inspections take at the four stations, and (3) what percentage of passengers are randomly selected for the additional inspection. All of this information must be entered into SimQuick in the form of statistical distributions. The first two types of information are determined by observing the real process from 8 A.M. and 10 A.M. The third type of information is a policy decision (10 percent, 15 percent, or 20 percent).

The original model is run 30 times, simulating the hours from 8 A.M. to 10 A.M. Statistics are collected by SimQuick and summarized. Figure B.4 provides some key results for the model of the current process as output by SimQuick (many other statistics are collected, but not displayed here).

The numbers shown are averages across the 30 simulations. The number 237.23 is the average number of passengers that enter line 1 during the simulated two hours. The two mean inventory statistics tell us that, on average, 5.97 simulated passengers were standing in line 1 and 0.10 standing in line 2. The two mean cycle time statistics tell us that the simulated passengers in line 1 waited an average of 3.12 minutes, while those in line 2 waited 0.53 minutes. The final inventory statistic tells us that, on average, 224.57 simulated passengers passed through the security process in the simulated two hours. The next step is to change the percentage of simulated passengers

▼ **FIGURE B.3**
Flowchart of Passenger Security Process

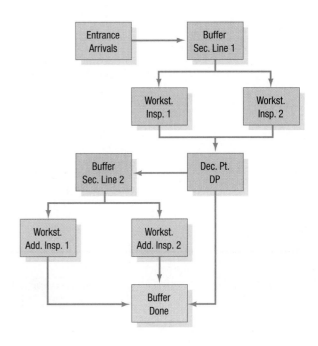

FIGURE B.4 ▶
Simulation Results of Passenger Security
Process

Element Types	Element Names	Statistics	Overall Means
Entrance(s)	Door	Objects entering process	237.23
Buffer(s)	Line 1	Mean inventory	5.97
		Mean cycle time	3.12
	Line 2	Mean inventory	0.10
		Mean cycle time	0.53
	Done	Final inventory	224.57

selected for the second inspection to 15 percent, and then to 20 percent, and rerun the model. Of course, these process changes will increase the average waiting time for the second inspection, but by how much? The final step is to rerun these simulations with one more workstation and see its effect on the waiting time for the second inspection. All the details for this model (as well as many others) appear in the book *SimQuick: Process Simulation with Excel*, which is included, along with the SimQuick software, in my**om**lab.

INTERNET RESOURCES

my**om**lab and the Companion Website at **www.pearsonglobaleditions.com/krajewski** contain many tools, activities, and resources designed for this supplement.

SOLVED PROBLEM 1

Customers enter a small bank, get into a single line, are served by a teller, and finally leave the bank. Currently, this bank has one teller working from 9 A.M. to 11 A.M. Management is concerned that the wait in line seems to be too long. Therefore, it is considering two process improvement ideas: adding an additional teller during these hours or installing a new automated check-reading machine that can help the single teller serve customers more quickly. Use SimQuick to model these two processes. All the details for this model (as well as many others) appear in the book *SimQuick: Process Simulation with Excel*, which is included, along with the SimQuick software, in my**om**lab.

SOLUTION

A first step in using SimQuick is to draw a flowchart of the process using SimQuick's building blocks. Figure B.5(a) shows that the one-teller bank (both the original and the variation with a check-reading machine) can be modeled with four building blocks: an entrance (modeling the arrival of customers at the bank), a buffer (modeling the waiting line), a workstation (modeling the teller), and a final buffer (modeling served customers). The two-teller variation can be modeled with five building blocks, as shown in Figure B.5(b).

FIGURE B.5A ▶
Flowchart of Bank Flowchart for a One-Teller Bank

FIGURE B.5B ▶
Flowchart for a two-teller bank

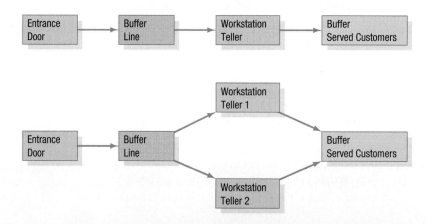

Information describing each building block is entered into SimQuick tables. Three key pieces of information need to be entered: when people arrive at the door, how long the teller takes to serve a customer, and the maximum length of the line. The first two pieces of information are described by statistical distributions. Each of the three models is run 30 times, simulating the hours from 9 A.M. to 11 A.M. Statistics are collected by SimQuick and summarized. Figure B.6 shows the key results for the model of the original one-teller process as output by SimQuick (many other statistics are collected, but they are not displayed here).

The numbers shown in Figure B.6 are averages across the 30 simulations. The service level for Door tells us that 90 percent of the simulated customers who arrived at the bank were able to get into Line (hence 10 percent found Line full and immediately left). The mean inventory for Line tells us that, on average, 4.47 simulated customers were standing in line. The mean cycle time tells us that simulated customers waited an average of 11.04 minutes in line.

Element Types	Element Names	Statistics	Overall Means
Entrance(s)	Door	Service level	0.90
Buffer(s)	Line	Mean inventory	4.47
		Mean cycle time	11.04

◀ FIGURE B.6
Simulation Results of Bank

When we run the model with two tellers, we find that the service level increases to 100 percent, the mean inventory in Line decreases to 0.37 customers, and the mean cycle time drops to 0.71 minutes. These are all dramatic improvements. When we run the one-teller model with the faster check-reading machine we find that the service level is 97 percent, the mean inventory in Line is 2.89 customers, and the mean cycle time is 6.21 minutes. These statistics, together with cost information, should help management select the best process.

SOLVED PROBLEM 2

A manager of an assembly line in an Eastern European factory is considering reorganization to avoid a common bottleneck in production and thereby improve productivity. He needs to present a simulation to the manager of the plant to justify the reorganization. The manager will present a simulation showing the productivity of two workers according to his new organizational plan. The simulation will show the output of two workers, Rudolf and Stefan, using automated equipment on the assembly line. Every batch of work will contain 10 units. A waiting line of several batches will be maintained in front of Rudolf. When Rudolf completes his portion of the work, the batch will then be transferred directly to Stefan.

$$\boxed{\text{Waiting line}} \rightarrow \text{Rudolf} \rightarrow \text{Stefan}$$

Each worker incurs a setup before he can begin processing a batch. Each unit in the batch has equal run times. The distribution of the setup times and run times for Rudolf and Stefan are identical. But because Rudolf and Stefan will perform different operations, simulation of each batch requires four random numbers from the table. The first random number determines Rudolf's setup time, the second determines Rudolf's run time per unit, and the third and fourth random numbers determine Stefan's setup and run times, respectively.

Setup Time (min)	Probability	Run Time per Unit (sec)	Probability
1	0.10	5	0.10
2	0.20	6	0.20
3	0.40	7	0.30
4	0.20	8	0.25
5	0.10	9	0.15

Estimate how many units will be produced in an hour. Then simulate 60 minutes of operation for Rudolf and Stefan. The random numbers have already been selected in Table B.4 for each of the four uncontrolled variables. For example, the third column provides the random numbers for determining Rudolf's setup time for each batch, and the fifth column provides the random numbers for determining Stefan's processing times.

SOLUTION

Except for the time required for Rudolf to set up and run the first batch, we assume that the two workers run simultaneously. The expected average setup time per batch is

$$[(0.1 \times 1 \text{ min}) + (0.2 \times 2 \text{ min}) + (0.4 \times 3 \text{ min}) + (0.2 \times 4 \text{ min}) + (0.1 \times 5 \text{ min})]$$

$$= 3 \text{ minutes,} \quad \text{or} \quad 180 \text{ seconds per batch}$$

The expected average run time per batch (of 10 units) is

$$[(0.1 \times 5 \text{ sec}) + (0.2 \times 6 \text{ sec}) + (0.3 \times 7 \text{ sec}) + (0.25 \times 8 \text{ sec}) + (0.15 \times 9 \text{ sec})]$$

$$= 7.15 \text{ seconds/unit} \times 10 \text{units/batch} = 71.5 \text{ seconds per batch}$$

Thus, the total of average setup and run times per batch is 251.5 seconds. In an hour's time we might expect to complete about 14 batches (3,600/251.5 seconds = 14.3). However, this estimate is probably too high.

Keep in mind that Rudolf and Stefan operate in sequence and that Stefan cannot begin to do work until Rudolf is finished (see batch 2 of Table B.4). Nor can Rudolf start a new batch until Stefan is ready to accept the previous one. Refer to batch 6, where Rudolf completes this batch at 25:50 but cannot begin the seventh batch until Stefan is ready to accept the sixth batch at time 28:00.

| TABLE B.4 | SIMULATION RESULTS FOR RUDOLF AND STEFAN |

| Batch No. | Rudolf | | | | | | Stefan | | | | | |
	Start Time	Random No.	Setup	Random No.	Process	Cumulative Time	Start Time	Random No.	Setup	Random No.	Process	Cumulative Time
1	0:00	71	4 min	50	7 sec	5 min 10 sec	5:10	21	2 min	94	9 sec	8 min 40 sec
2	5:10	50	3 min	63	8 sec	9 min 30 sec	9:30	47	3 min	83	8 sec	13 min 50 sec
3	9:30	31	3 min	73	8 sec	13 min 50 sec	13:50	04	1 min	17	6 sec	15 min 50 sec
4	13:50	96	5 min	98	9 sec	20 min 20 sec	20:20	21	2 min	82	8 sec	23 min 40 sec
5	20:20	25	2 min	92	9 sec	23 min 50 sec	23:50	32	3 min	53	7 sec	28 min 00 sec
6	23:50	00	1 min	15	6 sec	25 min 50 sec	28:00	66	3 min	57	7 sec	32 min 10 sec
7	28:00	00	1 min	99	9 sec	30 min 30 sec	32:10	55	3 min	11	6 sec	36 min 10 sec
8	32:10	10	2 min	61	8 sec	35 min 30 sec	36:10	31	3 min	35	7 sec	40 min 20 sec
9	36:10	09	1 min	73	8 sec	38 min 30 sec	40:20	24	2 min	70	8 sec	43 min 40 sec
10	40:20	79	4 min	95	9 sec	45 min 50 sec	45:50	66	3 min	61	8 sec	50 min 10 sec
11	45:50	01	1 min	41	7 sec	48 min 00 sec	50:10	88	4 min	23	6 sec	55 min 10 sec
12	50:10	57	3 min	45	7 sec	54 min 20 sec	55:10	21	2 min	61	8 sec	58 min 30 sec
13	55:10	26	2 min	46	7 sec	58 min 20 sec	58:30	97	5 min	31	7 sec	64 min 40 sec

Rudolf and Stefan completed only 12 batches in one hour. Even though they used the same probability distributions and therefore have perfectly balanced production capacities, Rudolf and Stefan did not produce the expected capacity of 14 batches because Stefan was sometimes idle while waiting for Rudolf (see batch 2) and Rudolf was sometimes idle while waiting for Stefan (see batch 6). This loss-of-throughput phenomenon occurs whenever variable processes are closely linked, whether those processes are mechanical or functional, such as production and marketing. The simulation shows the need to place between the workers sufficient space to store several batches to absorb the variations in process times. Subsequent simulations could be run to show how many batches are needed.

PROBLEMS

The SimQuick simulation software is on my**om**lab, along with its user's manual. Exercises also are provided on how to use SimQuick to simulate various problems encountered in managing processes and supply chains.

1. The Precision Manufacturing Company is considering the purchase of an NC machine and has narrowed the possible choices to two models. The company produces several products, and batches of work arrive at the NC machine every six minutes. The number of units in the batch has the following discrete distribution:

Number of Units in Batch	Probability
3	0.1
6	0.2
8	0.3
14	0.2
18	0.2

The distributions of the setup times and processing times for the two NC models follow. Assume that the work in a batch shares a single setup and that each unit in the batch has equal processing time. Simulate two hours (or 10 batch arrivals) of operation for the two NC machines. Use the following random numbers—the first one for the number of units in a batch, the second one for setup times, and the third one for run times:

(71, 21, 50), (50, 94, 63), (96, 93, 95), (83, 09, 49), (10, 20, 68),

(48, 23, 11), (21, 28, 40), (39, 78, 93), (99, 95, 61), (28, 14, 48)

Which one would you recommend if both machines cost the same to purchase, operate, and maintain?

NC Machine 1

Setup Time (min)	Probability	Run Time per Unit (sec)	Probability
1	0.10	5	0.10
2	0.20	6	0.20
3	0.40	7	0.30
4	0.20	8	0.25
5	0.10	9	0.15

NC Machine 2

Setup Time (min)	Probability	Run Time per Unit (sec)	Probability
1	0.05	3	0.20
2	0.15	4	0.25
3	0.25	5	0.30
4	0.45	6	0.15
5	0.10	7	0.10

2. In Problem 1, what factors would you consider if the initial cost of NC Machine 1 was $4,000 less than that of NC Machine 2?

3. Comet Dry Cleaners specializes in same-day dry cleaning. Customers drop off their garments early in the morning and expect them to be ready for pickup on their way home from work. The risk is, however, that the work needed on a garment cannot be done that day, depending on the type of cleaning required. Historically, an average of 20 garments have had to be held over to the next day. The outlet's manager is contemplating expanding to reduce or eliminate that backlog. A simulation model was developed with the following distribution for garments per day:

Number	Probability	Random Numbers
50	0.10	00–09
60	0.25	10–34
70	0.30	35–64
80	0.25	65–89
90	0.10	90–99

With expansion, the maximum number of garments that could be dry-cleaned per day is

Number	Probability	Random Numbers
60	0.30	00–29
70	0.40	30–69
80	0.30	70–99

In the simulation for a specific day, the number of garments needing cleaning (NGNC) is determined first. Next, the maximum number of garments that could be dry-cleaned (MNGD) is determined. If MNGD ≥ NGNC, all garments are dry-cleaned for that day. If MNGD < NGNC, then (NGNC – MNGD) garments must be added to the number of garments arriving the next day to obtain the NGNC for the next day. The simulation continues in this manner.

a. Assuming that the store is empty at the start, simulate 15 days of operation. Use the following random numbers, the first determining the number of arrivals and the second setting the capacity:

(49, 77), (27, 53), (65, 08), (83, 12), (04, 82),

(58, 44), (53, 83), (57, 72), (32, 53), (60, 79),

(79, 30), (41, 48), (97, 86), (30, 25), (80, 73)

Determine the average daily number of garments held overnight, based on your simulation.

b. If the cost associated with garments being held over is $25 per garment per day and the added cost of expansion is $200 per day, is expansion a good idea?

4. The 30 management professors at Omega University find out that telephone calls made to their offices are not being picked up. A call-forwarding system redirects calls to the management office after the fourth ring. A department office assistant answers the telephone and takes messages. An average of 90 telephone calls per hour are placed to the management faculty, and each telephone call consumes about 1 minute of the assistant's time. The calls arrive to a Poisson distribution, as shown in Figure B.7(a), with an average of 1.5 calls per minute. Because the professors spend much of their time in class and in conferences, there is only a 40 percent chance that they will pick up a call themselves, as shown in Figure B.7(b). If two or more telephone calls are forwarded to the office during the same minute, only the first call will be answered.

a. Without using simulation, make a preliminary guess of what proportion of the time the assistant will be on the telephone and what proportion of the telephone calls will not be answered.

b. Now use random numbers to simulate the situation for one hour starting at 10:00 A.M. Table B.5 will get you started.

c. What proportion of the time is the office assistant on the telephone? What proportion of the telephone calls are not answered? Are these proportions close to what you expected?

5. The management chair at is considering installing a voice-mail system. Monthly operating costs are $25 per voice-mailbox, but the system will reduce the amount of time the office assistant spends answering the telephone by 60 percent. The department has 32 telephones. Use the results of your simulation in Problem 4 to estimate the proportion of the assistant's time currently spent answering the telephone. The office assistant's salary (and overhead) is $3,000 per month. Should the management chair order the voice-mail system?

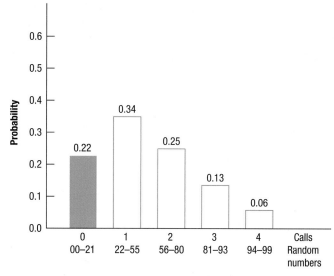

(a) Probabilities of numbers of telephone calls placed per minute

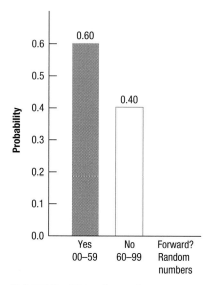

(b) Probability of forwarding a call

▲ FIGURE B.7
Probability Distributions for Omega University

6. The Brakes-Only Service Shop promises its customers same-day service by working overtime if necessary. The shop's two mechanics can handle a total of 12 brake jobs a day during regular hours. Over the past 100 days, the number of brake jobs at the shop varied between 10 and 14, as shown in the following table:

Demand (jobs)	Number of Days
10	10
11	30
12	30
13	20
14	10
	Total 100

TABLE B.5 | OFFICE ASSISTANT SIMULATION

Time	RN	Number of Calls Made	RN	1st Call Forwarded? (Yes/No)	RN	2d Call Forwarded? (Yes/No)	RN	3d Call Forwarded? (Yes/No)	RN	4th Call Forwarded? (Yes/No)	Number of Calls Not Answered	Assistant Idle (✓)
10:00	68	2	30	Yes	54	Yes					1	
10:01	76	2	36	Yes	32	Yes					1	
10:02	68	2	04	Yes	07	Yes					1	
10:03	98	4	08	Yes	21	Yes	28	Yes	79	No	2	
10:04	25	1	77	No							0	✓
10:05	51	1	23	Yes							0	
10:06	67	2	22	Yes	27	Yes					1	
10:07	80	2	87	No	06	Yes					0	
10:08	03	0									0	✓
10:09	03	0									0	✓
10:10	33	1	78	No							0	✓

a. Assign random numbers between 00 and 99 to simulate the demand probability distribution for brake jobs.

b. Simulate the demand for the next 10 days, using the random numbers 28, 83, 73, 7, 4, 63, 37, 38, 50, and 92.

c. On how many days will overtime work be necessary? On how many days will the mechanics be underutilized?

d. What percent of days, on average, will overtime work be necessary?

7. Weekly demand at a local E-Z Mart convenience store for 1-gallon jugs of low-fat milk for the past 50 weeks varied between 60 and 65 jugs, as shown in the following table. Demand in excess of stock cannot be backordered.

a. Assign random numbers between 00 and 99 to simulate the demand probability distribution.

b. E-Z Mart orders 62 jugs every week. Simulate the demand for this item for 10 weeks, using the random

Demand (jugs)	Number of Weeks
60	5
61	7
62	17
63	11
64	6
65	4
	Total 50

numbers 97, 2, 80, 66, 99, 56, 54, 28, 64, and 47. Determine the shortage or excess stock for each week.

c. What is the average shortage and the average excess stock for the 10 weeks?

8. Keep the same weekly sales distribution for BestCar as in Example B.3, but assume that the price of cars is distributed as follows:

Sales Price (price/car)	Relative Frequency (probability)
$18,000	0.15
$20,000	0.35
$22,000	0.35
$24,000	0.10
$26,000	0.05
	Total 1.00

Create an Excel model that simulates 500 weeks at BestCar. It should calculate from the simulated experience the average number of cars and revenue per week and also a frequency table on car sales.

9. The sales activity at BestCar (see Example B.3) has changed. Weekly sales are now estimated to be distributed as follows:

Weekly Sales (cars)	Relative Frequency (probability)
0	0.02
1	0.03
2	0.05
3	0.10
4	0.15
5	0.30
6	0.20
7	0.10
8	0.05
	Total 1.00

Create an Excel model that simulates 500 weeks at BestCar. It should calculate from the simulated experience the average number of cars and revenue per week and also a frequency table on car sales.

10. A machine center handles four types of clients: A, B, C, and D. The manager wants to assess the number of machines required to produce goods for these clients. Setup times for changeover from one client to another are negligible. Annual demand and processing times are uncertain; demand may be low, normal, or high. The probabilities for these three events are shown in the following tables:

Client A			
Demand (units/yr)	Probability	Processing Time (hr/unit)	Probability
3,000	0.10	10	0.35
3,500	0.60	20	0.45
4,200	0.30	30	0.20

Client B			
Demand (units/yr)	Probability	Processing Time (hr/unit)	Probability
500	0.30	60	0.25
800	0.50	90	0.50
900	0.20	100	0.25

Client C			
Demand (units/yr)	Probability	Processing Time (hr/unit)	Probability
1,500	0.10	12	0.25
3,000	0.50	15	0.60
4,500	0.40	20	0.15

Client D			
Demand (units/yr)	Probability	Processing Time (hr/unit)	Probability
600	0.40	60	0.30
650	0.50	70	0.65
700	0.10	80	0.05

a. Explain how simulation could be used to generate a probability distribution for the total number of machine-hours required per year to serve the clients.

b. Simulate one year, using the following random numbers. Use random number 88 for client A's demand, 24 for client A's processing time, and so forth.

88, 24, 33, 29, 52, 84, 37, 92

MANAGING QUALITY

...n is one of the engineers who inspired Verizon Wireless' ...an You Hear Me Now?" advertising campaign. She is ...th her test vehicle and the campaign's popular "Test ...regional network facility in Branchburg, N.J.

VERIZON WIRELESS

Anyone who owns a cell phone knows the agony of a dropped call. Did you know that the reason for the dropped call may be the phone itself, and not the strength of the signal? Verizon Wireless serves more than 62 million customers in the United States and, along with the other major carriers, it knows that if the phone conks out, the company, and not the manufacturer, will likely take the blame from the customer. Verizon touts the reliability of its services and can ill afford the failure of cell phones due to the quality of manufacture. Verizon expects manufacturers such as Motorola, Samsung, and LG Electronics to provide defect-free phones; however, experience has indicated that extensive testing by Verizon employees is also needed.

In addition to a tear-down analysis that looks for weaknesses in a phone's hardware and components, the device is tested for its ability to withstand temperature extremes, vibration, and stress. Beyond these physical tests, Verizon uses two approaches to assess a phone's capability to receive cellular signals and clearly communicate to the caller. First, Verizon hires 98 test personnel who drive $300,000 specially-equipped vans more than 1 million miles a year to measure network performance using prospective new cell phones. They make more than 3 million voice call attempts and 16 million data tests annually. The tests check the coverage of the network as well as the capability of the cell phones to pick up the signals and clearly communicate to the caller. Second, Verizon uses Mr. Head, a robotic mannequin,

SELECTED REFERENCES

Abdou, G., and S. P. Dutta. "A Systematic Simulation Approach for the Design of JIT Manufacturing Systems." *Journal of Operations Management*, vol. 11, no. 3 (1993), pp. 25–38.

Brennan, J. E., B. L. Golden, and H. K. Rappoport. "Go with the Flow: Improving Red Cross Bloodmobiles Using Simulation Analysis." *Interfaces*, vol. 22, no. 5 (1992), p. 1.

Christy, D. P., and H. J. Watson. "The Application of Simulation: A Survey of Industry Practice." *Interfaces*, vol. 13, no. 5 (October 1983), pp. 47–52.

Conway, R., W. L. Maxwell, J. D. McClain, and S. L. Worona. *XCELL & Factory Modeling System Release 4.0.* San Francisco: Scientific Press, 1990.

Hartvigsen, David. *SimQuick: Process Simulation with Excel*, 2d ed. Upper Saddle River, NJ: Prentice Hall, 2004.

Imagine That! (www.imaginethatinc.com). *Extend Simulation Package.* San Jose, CA.

Law, A. M., and W. D.
Analysis, 2d ed. New Y

MicroAnalysis and
Overcrowding Soluti
Industrial Engineering

Pritsker, A. A. B., C. E. Si
Network Models for D
NJ: Prentice Hall, 1989

Swedish, Julian. "Simula
ments to the Social S
Engineering (May 199;

Winston, Wayne L. *Si*
Belmont, CA: Wadswo

5

Kriston Desjac
long-running "
pictured here
Man" outside

LEARNING GOALS

After reading this chapter, you should be able to:

1. Define the four major costs of quality.

2. Identify *quality* from the customer's perspective.

3. Explain the differences between common causes and assignable causes of variation in process performance and why the distinction is important.

4. Describe how to construct control charts and use them to determine whether a process is out of statistical control.

5. Describe how to determine whether a process is capable of producing a service or product to specifications.

6. Explain the basic principles of TQM and Six Sigma programs.

who has a recorded voice and is electronically equipped with a rubber ear that evaluates how well the phones mouthpiece transmits certain phonetics. Mr. Head utters what sounds like gibberish; however, it actually covers the range of sounds in normal speech patterns. Other systems monitor the tests and summarize results.

Some phones spend so much time in the test phase that ultimately they never make it to the market. Clearly, in those cases, the cost of poor quality to the manufacturer is very high.

Source: Amol Sharma, "Testing, Testing," *Wall Street Journal* (October 23, 2007); Janet Hefler, "Verizon Tester Checks Vineyard Networks," *The Martha's Vineyard Times* (August 30, 2007); Jon Gales, "Ride Along With a Verizon Wireless Test Man," *Mobile Tracker* (April 4, 2005) http://investor.verizon.com (2007).

my**om**lab and the Companion Website at **www.pearsonglobaleditions.com/krajewski** contain many tools, activities, and resources designed for this chapter.

The challenge for businesses today is to satisfy their customers through the exceptional performance of their processes. Verizon Wireless is one example of a company that met the challenge by designing and managing processes that provide customers with total satisfaction. Evaluating process performance is important if this is to happen.

Evaluating process performance is also necessary for managing supply chains. For example, at Verizon Wireless, the process of delivering cell phone communications to the customer might be measured on the consistency of service and the sound quality of the voice transmissions. The procurement process, which involves selecting the suppliers for the cell phones and evaluating how they deliver their products, might be measured in terms of the quality of the cell phones delivered to Verizon, the on-time delivery performance of the suppliers, and the cost of the cell phones. Ultimately, the evaluation of the supply chain consisting of these two processes and many others will depend on how well it satisfies the customers of Verizon, who consider the value of the service to be how well it meets or exceeds expectations. The performance of these individual processes must be consistent with the performance measures for the supply chain.

Quality and Performance across the Organization

Quality and performance should be everybody's concern. Take for example QVC, a $7 billion televised shopping service. QVC airs 24 hours a day, all year round except on Christmas. QVC sells some 60,000 items ranging from jewelry, tools, cookware, clothing, and gourmet food to computers and annually ships more than 165 million packages worldwide.

QVC's processes, which span all the functional areas, spring into action with a customer order: Order taking and delivery date promising, billing, and order delivery all ensue once an order is placed. QVC operates four call centers that handle 179 million calls annually from customers who want to order something, complain about a problem, or just get product information. The call center representative's demeanor and skill are critical to achieving a successful customer encounter. QVC management keeps track of productivity, quality, and customer satisfaction measures for all processes. When the measures slip, problems are addressed aggressively. Knowing how to assess whether the process is performing well and when to take action are key skills QVC managers must have. In this chapter we first address the costs of quality and then focus on Total Quality Management and Six Sigma, two philosophies and supporting tools that many companies embrace to evaluate and improve quality and performance.

Costs of Quality

defect

Any instance when a process fails to satisfy its customer.

When a process fails to satisfy a customer, the failure is considered a **defect**. For example, according to the California Academy of Family Physicians, defects for the processes in a doctor's practice are defined as "anything that happened in my office that should not have happened, and that I absolutely do not want to happen again." Obviously, this definition covers process failures that the patient sees, such as poor communication and errors in prescription dosages. It also includes failures the patient does not see, such as incorrect charting.

Many companies spend significant time, effort, and expense on systems, training, and organizational changes to improve the quality and performance of their processes. They believe that it is important to be able to gauge current levels of performance so that any process gaps can be determined. Gaps reflect potential dissatisfied customers and additional costs for the firm. Most experts estimate that the costs of quality range from 20 to 30 percent of gross sales. These costs can be broken down into four major categories: prevention, appraisal, internal failure, and external failure.

Prevention Costs

prevention costs

Costs associated with preventing defects before they happen.

Prevention costs are associated with preventing defects before they happen. They include the costs of redesigning the process to remove the causes of poor performance, redesigning the service or product to make it simpler to produce, training employees in the methods of continuous improvement, and working with suppliers to increase the quality of purchased items or contracted services. In order to prevent problems from happening, firms must invest additional time, effort, and money.

Appraisal Costs

Appraisal costs are incurred when the firm assesses the level of performance of its processes. As the costs of prevention increase and performance improves, appraisal costs decrease because fewer resources are needed for quality inspections and the subsequent search for causes of any problems that are detected.

appraisal costs

Costs incurred when the firm assess the performance level of its processes.

Internal Failure Costs

Internal failure costs result from defects that are discovered during the production of a service or product. Defects fall into two main categories: *rework*, which is incurred if some aspect of a service must be performed again or if a defective item must be rerouted to some previous operation(s) to correct the defect; and *scrap*, which is incurred if a defective item is unfit for further processing. For example, an analysis of the viability of acquiring a company might be sent back to the mergers and acquisitions department if an assessment of the company's history of environmental compliance is missing. The proposal for the purchase of the company may be delayed, which may result in the loss of the purchase opportunity.

internal failure costs

Costs resulting from defects that are discovered during the production of a service or product.

External Failure Costs

External failure costs arise when a defect is discovered after the customer receives the service or product. For instance, suppose that you have the oil changed in your car and that the oil filter is improperly installed, causing the oil to drain onto your garage floor. You might insist that the company pay for the car to be towed and restore the oil and filter immediately. External failure costs to the company in this case include the towing and additional oil and filter costs, as well as the loss of future revenue because you decide never to take your car back there for service.

Dissatisfied customers talk about bad service or products to their friends, who in turn tell others. If the problem is bad enough, consumer protection groups may even alert the media. The potential impact on future profits is difficult to assess, but without doubt external failure costs erode market share and profits. Encountering defects and correcting them after the product is in the customer's hands is costly.

External failure costs also include warranty service and litigation costs. A **warranty** is a written guarantee that the producer will replace or repair defective parts or perform the service to the customer's satisfaction. Usually, a warranty is given for some specified period. For example, television repairs are usually guaranteed for 90 days and new automobiles for 5 years or 50,000 miles, whichever comes first. Warranty costs must be considered in the design of new services or products.

external failure costs

Costs that arise when a defect is discovered after the customer receives the service or product.

warranty

A written guarantee that the producer will replace or repair defective parts or perform the service to the customer's satisfaction.

Ethics and Quality

External failure costs go beyond the out-of-pocket costs associated with warranties, litigation, or the lost sales from dissatisfied customers. There is a greater societal effect that must be factored into decision making involving the production of services or products,[1] which often requires balancing the traditional measures of quality performance and the overall benefits to society. For example, in the health care industry, aiming for zero complications in cardiac surgery might sound good; however, if it comes at the cost of turning down high-risk patients, is society being served in the best way? Or, how much time, energy, and money should go into delivering vaccines or preventing complications? These are questions that often do not have clear answers. Ethical behavior falls on the shoulders of all employees of an organization. It is not ethical to knowingly pass defective services or products to internal or external customers. The well-being of all stakeholders, such as stockholders, customers, employees, partners, and creditors, should be considered.

The quality costs of prevention, assessment, internal failure, and external failure must be balanced with ethical considerations to arrive at the appropriate processes and approaches to manage them. Nonetheless, developing the cultural environment for ethical

---

[1] Additional discussion of the interface between ethics and quality can be found at the following two sources: Matthew Wynia, "Performance Measures for Ethics Quality," *American College of Physicians*, www.acponline.org/journals/ecp/novdec99/wynia.htm,; Yannick Julliard, "Ethics Quality Management," *Techne' Journal*, Vol. 8, No. 1 (Fall 2004), pp. 117–135.

behavior is not cost-free. Employees must be educated in how ethics interfaces with their jobs. The firm may organize an ethics task force or an ethics public relations group to provide an interface between the firm and society. Documentation may be required. We now turn to a discussion of Total Quality Management and Six Sigma, two philosophies companies use to evaluate and improve quality and process performance along technical, service, and ethical dimensions.

TOTAL QUALITY MANAGEMENT

total quality management (TQM)

A philosophy that stresses three principles for achieving high levels of process performance and quality: customer satisfaction, employee involvement, and continuous improvement in performance.

Total quality management (TQM) is a philosophy that stresses three principles for achieving high levels of process performance and quality. These principles are related to customer satisfaction, employee involvement, and continuous improvement in performance. As Figure 5.1 indicates, TQM also involves a number of other important elements. We have covered tools and process analysis techniques useful for process problem solving, redesign, and improvement in Chapter 4. Service/product design and purchasing are covered later in this text. Here we just focus on the three main principles of TQM.

Customer Satisfaction

quality

A term used by customers to describe their general satisfaction with a service or product.

Customers, internal or external, are satisfied when their expectations regarding a service or product have been met or exceeded. Often, customers use the general term **quality** to describe their level of satisfaction with a service or product. Quality has multiple dimensions in the mind of the customer, which cut across the nine competitive priorities we introduced in Chapter 1, "Using Operations to Compete." One or more of the following five definitions apply at any one time.

Conformance to Specifications   Although customers evaluate the service or product they receive, it is the processes that produced the service or product that are really being judged. In this case, a process failure would be the process's inability to meet certain advertised or implied performance standards. Conformance to specifications may relate to consistent quality, on-time delivery, or delivery speed.

Bell Canada measures the performance of its call center process by the length of time it takes to process a call (called "handle time"). If the average time exceeds the standard of 23 seconds, managers work with the employees to reduce the time. Customers become agitated if they cannot get access to an operator quickly. Conformance to specifications at the call center is important because customers rate Bell Canada in part by the performance of the call center.

Value   Another way customers define quality is through value, or how well the service or product serves its intended purpose at a price customers are willing to pay. The service/product development process plays a role here, as do the firm's competitive priorities relating to top quality versus low-cost operations. The two factors must be balanced to produce value for the customer. How much value a service or product has in the mind of the customer depends on the customer's expectations before purchasing it.

Fitness for Use   When assessing how well a service or product performs its intended purpose, the customer may consider the convenience of a service, the mechanical features of a product, or other aspects such as appearance, style, durability, reliability, craftsmanship, and serviceability. For example, you may define the quality of the entertainment center you purchased on the basis of how easy it was to assemble and its appearance and styling.

FIGURE 5.1 ▲
TQM Wheel

Support   Often the service or product support provided by the company is as important to customers as the quality of the service or product itself. Customers get upset with a company if its financial statements are incorrect, responses to its warranty claims are delayed, its advertising is misleading, or its employees are not helpful when problems are incurred. Good support once the sale has been made can reduce the consequences of quality failures.

Psychological Impressions   People often evaluate the quality of a service or product on the basis of psychological impressions: atmosphere, image, or aesthetics. In the provision of services where the customer is in close contact with the provider, the appearance and actions of the provider are especially important. Nicely dressed, courteous, friendly, and sympathetic employees can affect the customer's perception of service quality. For example, rumpled, discourteous, or grumpy waiters can undermine a restaurant's best efforts to provide high-quality service. In manufacturing, product quality often is judged on the basis of the knowledge and personality of salespeople, as well as the product image presented in advertisements.

Attaining quality in all areas of a business is a difficult task. To make things even more difficult, consumers change their perceptions of quality. In general, a business's success depends on the accuracy of its perceptions of consumer expectations and its ability to bridge the gap between those expectations and operating capabilities. Good quality pays off in higher profits. High-quality services and products can be priced higher and yield a greater return. Poor quality erodes the firm's ability to compete in the marketplace and increases the costs of producing its service or product. For example, by improving its conformance to specifications, a firm often can increase its market share *and* reduce the cost of its services or products, which in turn increase profits. Management is better able to compete on both the basis of price and quality. Managerial Practice 5.1 shows how Omega took on timekeeping responsibilities at the Olympics and has updated its processes over the years to meet those expectations.

MANAGERIAL PRACTICE 5.1   Quality and Performance at Omega

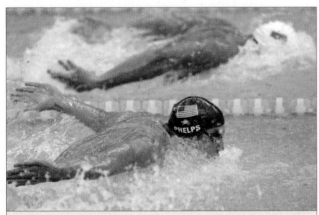

Michael Phelps captures the gold medal in the 100-meter butterfly at the Beijing Olympics 2008. The high-tech touch pad system from Omega recorded a one-hundreth of a second victory for Phelps.

During the last moments of the 100-meter butterfly in the 2008 Beijing Olympics, it appeared that Serbia's Milorad Cavic would capture the gold medal. However, suddenly, with only seconds remaining, U.S. swimmer Michael Phelps made a rush for the wall. When the race ended, spectators in the arena and people at home could not tell who won the race. Even with the use of slow-motion replay, it was still difficult to determine a winner. Fortunately, the Olympic committee used high-tech timekeeping devices by Omega. Through use of Omega's touch pad system it was determined that Phelps won the race by one 1/100th of a second. As this historic moment proves, timekeeping in the Olympics is a colossal responsibility. So why was Omega chosen to assume this responsibility? The more than 150-year-old Swiss time company has a reputation for high-quality timepieces and precise timekeeping technology. Omega was the first company to be entrusted with the official timekeeping for all events at the 1932 Los Angeles Games. Omega used chronographs, timepieces with both timekeeping and stopwatch capabilities, to record the start and finish times of athletes in multiple disciplines. Over the years, Omega has maintained its reputation for accuracy and developed new technologies to improve the timekeeping process. The 1968 Mexico City Games marked the first time that electronic

timekeeping was used in all Olympic disciplines, including the touch pad system for swimming. By the 1996 Summer Olympic Games in Atlanta, Omega, and its subsidiary Swatch, developed and implemented 20 new forms of timekeeping technology, including the use of the global positioning system (GPS), to record the results of 10,318 athletes, a record unto itself. One hundred ninety-six engineers and technicians came from Switzerland with over 100 tons of equipment to support this high-tech effort. By the 2008 Beijing Olympic Games, Omega enlisted the help of 450 engineers and technicians and 420 tons of equipment. Although this support may seem excessive, it is a vital part of maintaining the integrity of Omega products and services.

Omega applies the same level of dedication to its line of personal timepieces. The Quality Assurance Department puts every aspect of each timepiece through extensive tests to ensure that it reaches specific standards of quality.

Four quality tests for Omega timepieces include:

- **The Movement** The movement of the internal mechanisms of the timepieces is put through rigorous tests to examine the precision of the piece. The Technical Development Department also conducts lab tests to make certain each watch maintains an appropriate level of temperature resistance, vibration resistance, and shock resistance.

- **The Case** The outer casing of each piece must be approved in the prototype stage before it can ever reach the manufacturing stage. A series of tests, such as its ability to resist water, must be passed before it moves to the next stage.

- **Dial and Hands** Omega guarantees that all aspects of its timepieces can stand up to the strongest elements in the environment, so each dial and hand are put through an ultraviolet test to ensure that the timepiece will remain unchanged after exposure to extreme sunlight or heat.

- **The Bracelet** Although it may not be the most technical aspect of an Omega timepiece, the bracelet of each piece must also maintain certain quality standards. Each one is put through strict mechanical tests to demonstrate its durability.

Omega's dedication to quality is what makes the company so respected. Whether its timepieces are used to help a person be on time to a business dinner or to determine the results of Olympic performances, Omega aims to deliver a quality product that has withstood many test of time.

Sources: AP, "Phenomenal Phelps wins 7th gold by 0.01 seconds to tie Spitz," AP News, August 16, 2008, http://sports.espn.go.com/oly/summer08/swimming/news/story?id=3537831; "Olympic Timekeeping History," Omega Web site, http://www.omegawatches.com/index.php?id=394&L=, accessed October 16, 2008.

Employee Involvement

One of the important elements of TQM is employee involvement, as shown in Figure 5.1. A program in employee involvement includes changing organizational culture and encouraging teamwork.

Cultural Change   One of the main challenges in developing the proper culture for TQM is to define *customer* for each employee. In general, customers are internal or external. External customers are the people or firms who buy the service or product. Some employees, especially those having little contact with external customers, may have difficulty seeing how their jobs contribute to the whole effort.

It is helpful to point out to employees that each employee also has one or more internal customers—employees in the firm who rely on the output of other employees. All employees must do a good job of serving their internal customers if external customers ultimately are to be satisfied. They will be satisfied only if each internal customer demands value be added that the external customer will recognize and pay for. The notion of internal customers applies to all parts of a firm and enhances cross-functional coordination. For example, accounting must prepare accurate and timely reports for management, and purchasing must provide high-quality materials on time for operations.

In TQM, everyone in the organization must share the view that quality control is an end in itself. Errors or defects should be caught and corrected at the source, not passed along to an internal or external customer. For example, a consulting team should make sure its billable hours are correct before submitting them to the accounting department. This philosophy is called **quality at the source**. In addition, firms should avoid trying to "inspect quality into the product" by using inspectors to weed out unsatisfactory services or defective products after all operations have been performed. By contrast, in some manufacturing firms, workers have the authority to stop a production line if they spot quality problems.

Teams   Employee involvement is a key tactic for improving processes and quality. One way to achieve employee involvement is by the use of **teams**, which are small groups of people who have a common purpose, set their own performance goals and approaches, and hold themselves accountable for success.

The three approaches to teamwork most often used are problem-solving teams, special-purpose teams, and self-managed teams. All three use some amount of **employee empowerment**, which moves responsibility for decisions further down the organizational chart—to the level of the employee actually doing the job.

First introduced in the 1920s, *problem-solving teams*, also called **quality circles**, became popular in the late 1970s after the Japanese used them successfully. Problem-solving teams are small groups of supervisors and employees who meet to identify, analyze, and solve process and quality problems. Employees take more pride and interest in their work if they are allowed to help shape it. Although problem-solving teams can successfully reduce costs and improve quality, they die if management fails to implement many of the suggestions they generate.

An outgrowth of the problem-solving teams, **special-purpose teams** address issues of paramount concern to management, labor, or both. For example, management may form a special-purpose team to design and introduce new work policies or new technologies or to address customer service problems. Essentially, this approach gives workers a voice in high-level decisions. Special-purpose teams first appeared in the United States in the early 1980s.

The **self-managed team** approach takes worker participation to its highest level: A small group of employees work together to produce a major portion, or sometimes all, of a service or product. Members learn all the tasks involved in the operation, rotate from job to job, and take over managerial duties such as work and vacation scheduling, ordering supplies, and hiring. In some cases, team members design the process and have a high degree of latitude as to how it takes shape. Self-managed teams essentially change the way work is organized because employees have control over their jobs. Some self-managed teams have increased productivity by 30 percent or more in their firms.

Continuous Improvement

Continuous improvement, based on a Japanese concept called *kaizen*, is the philosophy of continually seeking ways to improve processes. Continuous improvement involves identifying benchmarks of excellent practice and instilling a sense of employee ownership in the process. The focus of continuous improvement projects is to reduce waste, such as reducing the length of time required to process requests for loans at a bank, the amount of scrap generated at a milling machine, or the number of employee injuries at a construction site. The bases of the continuous improvement philosophy are the beliefs that virtually any aspect of a process can be improved

---

quality at the source

A philosophy whereby defects are caught and corrected where they were created.

teams

Small groups of people who have a common purpose, set their own performance goals and approaches, and hold themselves accountable for success.

employee empowerment

An approach to teamwork that moves responsibility for decisions further down the organizational chart—to the level of the employee actually doing the job.

quality circles

Another name for problem-solving teams; small groups of supervisors and employees who meet to identify, analyze, and solve process and quality problems.

special-purpose teams

Groups that address issues of paramount concern to management, labor, or both.

self-managed team

A small group of employees who work together to produce a major portion, or sometimes all, of a service or product.

continuous improvement

The philosophy of continually seeking ways to improve processes based on a Japanese concept called *kaizen*.

and that the people most closely associated with a process are in the best position to identify the changes that should be made. The idea is not to wait until a massive problem occurs before acting.

Employees should be given problem-solving tools, such as the statistical process control (SPC) methods we discuss later in this chapter, and a sense of ownership of the process to be improved. A sense of operator ownership emerges when employees feel a responsibility for the processes and methods they use and take pride in the quality of the service or product they produce. It comes from participation on work teams and in problem-solving activities, which instill in employees a feeling that they have some control over their workplace and tasks.

Most firms actively engaged in continuous improvement train their work teams to use the **plan-do-study-act cycle** for problem solving. Another name for this approach is the Deming Wheel, named after the renowned statistician W. Edwards Deming who taught quality improvement techniques to the Japanese after World War II. Figure 5.2 shows this cycle, which lies at the heart of the continuous improvement philosophy. The cycle comprises the following steps:

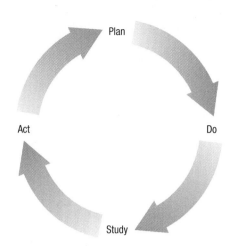

▲ FIGURE 5.2
Plan-Do-Study-Act Cycle

plan-do-study-act cycle

A cycle, also called the Deming Wheel, used by firms actively engaged in continuous improvement to train their work teams in problem solving.

1. *Plan.* The team selects a process (an activity, method, machine, or policy) that needs improvement. The team then documents the selected process, usually by analyzing related data; sets qualitative goals for improvement; and discusses various ways to achieve the goals. After assessing the benefits and costs of the alternatives, the team develops a plan with quantifiable measures for improvement.

2. *Do.* The team implements the plan and monitors progress. Data are collected continuously to measure the improvements in the process. Any changes in the process are documented, and further revisions are made as needed.

3. *Study.* The team analyzes the data collected during the *do* step to find out how closely the results correspond to the goals set in the *plan* step. If major shortcomings exist, the team reevaluates the plan or stops the project.

4. *Act.* If the results are successful, the team documents the revised process so that it becomes the standard procedure for all who may use it. The team may then instruct other employees in the use of the revised process.

Problem-solving projects often focus on those aspects of processes that do not add value to the service or product. Value is added in processes such as machining a part or serving a customer through a Web page. No value is added in activities such as inspecting parts for quality defects or routing requests for loan approvals to several different departments. The idea of continuous improvement is to reduce or eliminate activities that do not add value and, thus, are wasteful.

Six Sigma

A comprehensive and flexible system for achieving, sustaining, and maximizing business success by minimizing defects and variability in processes.

Six Sigma

Six Sigma, which relies heavily on the principles of TQM, is a comprehensive and flexible system for achieving, sustaining, and maximizing business success by minimizing defects and variability in processes. Six Sigma has a different focus than TQM: It is driven by a close understanding of customer needs; the disciplined use of facts, data, and statistical analysis; and diligent attention to managing, improving, and reinventing business processes. Figure 5.3 shows how Six Sigma focuses on reducing variation in processes as well as centering processes on their target measures of performance. Either flaw—too much variation or an off-target process—degrades performance of the process. For example, a mortgage loan department of a bank might advertise loan approval decisions in two days. If the actual performance ranges from one day to five days, with an average of two days, those customers who had to wait longer than two days would be upset. Process variability causes customer dissatisfaction. Similarly, if actual performance consistently produced loan decisions in three days, all customers would dissatisfied. In this case, the process is consistent, but off the target. Six Sigma is a rigorous approach to align processes with their target performance measures with low variability.

▲ FIGURE 5.3
Six-Sigma Approach Focuses on Reducing Spread and Centering the Process

Hospital personnel at a trauma center rush a patient to the emergency room. Six Sigma can be used to improve service processes such as those in a trauma center.

Motorola is credited with developing Six Sigma more than 20 years ago to improve its manufacturing capability in a world marketplace that was becoming increasingly competitive. Management noticed that some customers were complaining about the quality of Motorola's products and that competitor products were outperforming its products. Motorola began by soliciting new ideas from its employees and benchmarking its competitors. What followed were extensive changes to employee compensation and reward programs, training programs, and critical processes. The procedures were documented and refined and became known as Six Sigma. Its name relates to the goal of achieving low rates of defective output by developing processes whose mean output for a performance measure is six standard deviations (sigma) from the design specifications for the service or product. We will discuss variability and its implications on the capability of a process to perform at acceptable levels when we present the tools of statistical process control.

Although Six Sigma was rooted in an effort to improve manufacturing processes, credit General Electric with popularizing the application of the approach to non-manufacturing processes such as sales, human resources, customer service, and financial services. The concept of eliminating defects is the same, although the definition of "defect" depends on the process involved. For example, a human resource department's failure to meet a hiring target counts as a defect. Six Sigma has been successfully applied to a host of service processes, including financial services, human resource processes, marketing processes, and health care administrative processes.

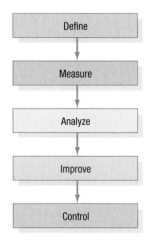

FIGURE 5.4 ▲
Six Sigma Improvement Model

Six Sigma Improvement Model

Figure 5.4 shows the Six Sigma Improvement Model, a five-step procedure that leads to improvements in process performance. The model can be applied to projects involving incremental improvements to processes or to projects requiring major changes, including a redesign of an existing process or the development of a new process. The following steps comprise the model:

- *Define.* Determine the characteristics of the process's output that are critical to customer satisfaction and identify any gaps between these characteristics and the process's capabilities. Get a picture of the current process by documenting it using *flowcharts* and *process charts.*

- *Measure.* Quantify the work the process does that affects the gap. Select what to measure, identify data sources, and prepare a data collection plan.

- *Analyze.* Use the data on measures to perform process analysis, applying tools such as Pareto charts, scatter diagrams, and cause-and-effect diagrams and the statistical process control (SPC) tools in this chapter to determine where improvements are necessary. Whether or not major redesign is necessary, establish procedures to make the desired outcome routine.

- *Improve.* Modify or redesign existing methods to meet the new performance objectives. Implement the changes.

- *Control.* Monitor the process to make sure that high performance levels are maintained. Once again, data analysis tools such as Pareto charts, bar charts, scatter diagrams, as well as the statistical process control tools can be used to control the process.

Successful users of Six Sigma have found that it is essential to rigorously follow the steps in the Six Sigma Improvement Model, which is sometimes referred to as the *DMAIC process* (whose name comes from using the first letter of each step in the model). To accomplish the goals of Six Sigma, employees must be trained in the "whys" and the "how-tos" of quality and what it means to customers, both internal and external. Successful firms using Six Sigma develop a cadre of internal teachers who then are responsible for teaching and assisting teams involved in a process improvement project. These teachers have different titles depending on their experience and level of achievement. **Green Belts** devote part of his or her time to teaching and helping teams with their projects and the rest of his or her time to their normally assigned duties. **Black Belts** are full-time teachers and leaders of teams involved in Six Sigma projects. Finally, **Master Black Belts** are full-time teachers who review and mentor Black Belts.

ACCEPTANCE SAMPLING

Before any internal process can be evaluated for performance, the inputs to that process must be of good quality. **Acceptance sampling**, which is the application of statistical techniques to determine if a quantity of material from a supplier should be accepted or rejected based on the inspection or test of one or more samples, limits the buyer's risk of rejecting good-quality materials (and unnecessarily delaying the production of goods or services) or accepting bad-quality materials (and incurring downtime due to defective materials or passing bad products to customers). Relative to the specifications for the material the buyer is purchasing, the buyer specifies an *acceptable quality level* (AQL), which is a statement of the proportion of defective items (outside of specifications) that the buyer will accept in a shipment. These days, that proportion is getting very small, often measured in parts per ten-thousand. The idea of acceptance sampling is to take a sample, rather than testing the entire quantity of material, because that is often less expensive. Therein lies the risk—the sample may not be representative of the entire lot of goods from the supplier. The basic procedure is straightforward.

1. A random sample is taken from a large quantity of items and tested or measured relative to the specifications or quality measures of interest.

2. If the sample passes the test (low number of defects), the entire quantity of items is accepted.

3. If the sample fails the test, either (a) the entire quantity of items is subjected to 100 percent inspection and all defective items repaired or replaced or (b) the entire quantity is returned to the supplier.

In a supply chain, any company can be both a producer of goods purchased by another company and a consumer of goods or raw materials supplied by another company. Figure 5.5 shows a flowchart of how acceptance sampling and internal process performance (TQM or Six Sigma) interface in a supply chain. From the perspective of the supply chain, the buyer's specifications for various dimensions of quality become the targets the supplier shoots for in a supply contract. The supplier's internal processes must be up to the task; TQM or Six Sigma can

Green Belt

An employee who achieved the first level of training in a Six Sigma program and spends part of his or her time teaching and helping teams with their projects.

Black Belt

An employee who reached the highest level of training in a Six Sigma program and spends all of his or her time teaching and leading teams involved in Six Sigma projects.

Master Black Belt

Full-time teachers and mentors to several Black Belts.

acceptance sampling

The application of statistical techniques to determine whether a quantity of material should be accepted or rejected based on the inspection or test of a sample.

▲ **FIGURE 5.5**
Interface of Acceptance Sampling and Process Performance Approaches in a Supply Chain

help achieve the desired performance. The buyer's sampling plan will provide a high probability of accepting AQL (or better). Supplement G, "Acceptance Sampling Plans," in my**om**Lab, shows how to design an acceptance sampling plan that meets the level of risk desired.

STATISTICAL PROCESS CONTROL

Regardless of whether a firm is producing a service or a product, it is important to ensure that the firm's processes are providing the quality that customers want. A key element of TQM or Six Sigma is building the capability to monitor the performance of processes so that corrective action can be initiated in a timely fashion. Evaluating the performance of processes requires a variety of data gathering approaches. We already discussed checklists, histograms and bar charts, Pareto charts, scatter diagrams, cause-and-effect diagrams, and graphs (see Chapter 4, "Analyzing Processes").

statistical process control (SPC) is the application of statistical techniques to determine whether a process is delivering what customers want. In SPC, tools called control charts are used primarily to detect defective services or products or to indicate that the process has changed and that services or products will deviate from their design specifications unless something is done to correct the situation. SPC can also be used to inform management of improved process changes. Examples of process changes that can be detected by SPC include the following:

statistical process control (SPC)

The application of statistical techniques to determine whether a process is delivering what the customer wants.

- A decrease in the average number of complaints per day at a hotel
- A sudden increase in the proportion of defective gear boxes
- An increase in the time to process a mortgage application
- A decline in the number of scrapped units at a milling machine
- An increase in the number of claimants receiving late payment from an insurance company

Let us consider the last situation. Suppose that the manager of the accounts payable department of an insurance company notices that the proportion of claimants receiving late payments rose from an average of 0.01 to 0.03. The first question is whether the rise is a cause for alarm or just a random occurrence. Statistical process control can help the manager decide whether further action should be taken. If the rise in the proportion is large, the manager should not conclude that it was just a random occurrence and should seek explanations of the poor performance. Perhaps the number of claims significantly increased, causing an overload on the employees in the department. The decision might be to hire more personnel. Or perhaps the procedures being used are ineffective or the training of employees is inadequate. SPC is an integral part of TQM and Six Sigma.

Variation of Outputs

No two services or products are exactly alike because the processes used to produce them contain many sources of variation, even if the processes are working as intended. Nonetheless, it is important to minimize the variation in outputs because frequently variation is what the customer sees and feels. Suppose a physicians' clinic submits claims on behalf of its patients to a particular insurance company. In this situation, the physicians' clinic is the customer of the insurance company's bill payment process. In some cases the clinic receives payment in 4 weeks, and in other cases 20 weeks. The time to process a request for payment varies because of the load on the insurance company's processes, the medical history of the patient, and the skills and attitudes of the employees. Meanwhile, the clinic must cover its expenses while it waits for payment. Regardless of whether the process is producing services or products, nothing can be done to eliminate variation in output completely; however, management should investigate the *causes* of the variation in order to minimize it.

Performance Measurements   Performance can be evaluated in two ways. One way is to measure **variables**—that is, service or product characteristics, such as weight, length, volume, or time, that can be *measured*. For example, United Parcel Service (UPS) managers monitor the length of time drivers spend delivering packages. Similarly, inspectors at Harley-Davidson measure the diameter of a piston to determine whether the product adheres to the specifications (within the allowable tolerance) and they identify differences in the diameter over time. The advantage of using performance variables is that if a service or product misses its performance specifications, the inspector knows by how much. The disadvantage is that such measurements typically involve special equipment, employee skills, exacting procedures, and time and effort. Another way to evaluate performance is to measure **attributes**, or service or product characteristics that can be quickly *counted* for acceptable performance. This method allows inspectors to make a simple yes/no decision about whether a service or product meets the specifications.

variables

Service or product characteristics, such as weight, length, volume, or time, that can be measured.

attributes

Service or product characteristics that can be quickly counted for acceptable performance.

Attributes often are used when performance specifications are complex and measurement of variables is difficult or costly. Some examples of attributes that can be counted are the number of insurance forms containing errors that cause underpayments or overpayments, the proportion of radios inoperative at the final test, the proportion of airline flights arriving within 15 minutes of scheduled times, and the number of stove-top assemblies with spotted paint.

The advantage of counting attributes is that less effort and fewer resources are needed than for measuring variables. The disadvantage is that, even though attribute counts can reveal that process performance has changed, they do not indicate by how much. For example, a count may determine that the proportion of airline flights arriving within 15 minutes of their scheduled times declined, but the result does not show how much beyond the 15-minute allowance the flights are arriving. For that, the actual deviation from the scheduled arrival, a variable, would have to be measured.

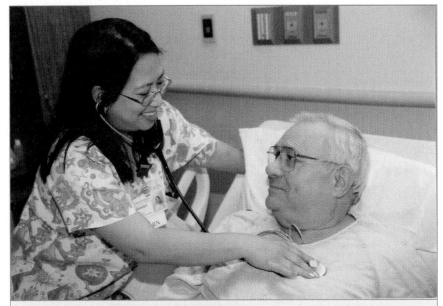

A nurse at Robert Wood Johnson University in Hamilton, New Jersey, monitors the heart rate of a patient. The hospital uses a performance measurement system to track how well it accomplishes its daily operations—including customer satisfaction. The hospital's managers examine the data monthly, and employees, quarterly.

Sampling The most thorough approach to inspection is to inspect each service or product at each stage of the process for quality. This method, called *complete inspection*, is used when the costs of passing defects to an internal or external customer outweigh the inspection costs. Firms often use automated inspection equipment that can record, summarize, and display data. Many companies find that automated inspection equipment can pay for itself in a reasonably short time.

A well-conceived **sampling plan** can approach the same degree of protection as complete inspection. A sampling plan specifies a **sample size**, which is a quantity of randomly selected observations of process outputs, the time between successive samples, and decision rules that determine when action should be taken. Sampling is appropriate when inspection costs are high because of the special knowledge, skills, procedures, and expensive equipment that are required to perform the inspections, or because the tests are destructive.

sampling plan

A plan that specifies a sample size, the time between successive samples, and decision rules that determine when action should be taken.

sample size

A quantity of randomly selected observations of process outputs.

Sampling Distributions Relative to a performance measure, a process will produce output that can be described by a *process distribution*, with a mean and variance that will be known only with a complete inspection with 100 percent accuracy. The purpose of sampling, however, is to estimate a variable or attribute measure for the output of the process without doing a complete inspection. That measure is then used to assess the performance of the process itself. For example, the time required to process specimens at an intensive care unit lab in a hospital (a variable measure) will vary. If you measured the time to complete an analysis of a large number of patients and plotted the results, the data would tend to form a pattern that can be described as a process distribution. With sampling, we try to estimate the parameters of the process distribution using statistics such as the sample mean and the sample range or standard deviation.

1. The *sample mean* is the sum of the observations divided by the total number of observations:

$$\bar{x} = \frac{\sum_{i=1}^{n} x_i}{n}$$

where

$x_i =$ observation of a quality characteristic (such as time)

$n =$ total number of observations

$\bar{x} =$ mean

2. The *range* is the difference between the largest observation in a sample and the smallest. The *standard deviation* is the square root of the variance of a distribution. An estimate of the process standard deviation based on a sample is given by

$$\sigma = \sqrt{\frac{\Sigma(x_i - \bar{x})^2}{n - 1}} \text{ or } \sigma = \sqrt{\frac{\Sigma x_i^2 - \frac{(\Sigma x_i)^2}{n}}{n - 1}}$$

where

σ = standard deviation of a sample

n = total number of observations in the sample

$\bar{x}$ = mean

x_i = observation of a quality characteristic

Relatively small values for the range or the standard deviation imply that the observations are clustered near the mean.

These sample statistics have their own distribution, which we call a *sampling distribution*. For example, in the lab analysis process, an important performance variable is the time it takes to get results to the critical care unit. Suppose that management wants results available in an average of 25 minutes. That is, it wants the process distribution to have a mean of 25 minutes. An inspector periodically taking a sample of five analyses and calculating the sample mean could use it to determine how well the process is doing. Suppose that the process is actually producing the analyses with a mean of 25 minutes. Plotting a large number of these sample means would show that they have their own sampling distribution with a mean centered on 25 minutes, as does the process distribution mean, but with much less variability. The reason is that the sample means offset the highs and lows of the individual times in each sample. Figure 5.6 shows the relationship between the sampling distribution of sample means and the process distribution for the analysis times.

Some sampling distributions (e.g., for means with sample sizes of 4 or more and proportions with sample sizes of 20 or more) can be approximated by the normal distribution, allowing the use of the normal tables (see Appendix 1, "Normal Distribution"). For example, suppose you wanted to determine the probability that a sample mean will be more than 2.0 standard deviations greater than the process mean. Go to Appendix 1 and note that the entry in the table for $z = 2.0$ standard deviations is 0.9772. Consequently, the probability is $1.0000 - 0.9772 = 0.0228$, or 2.28 percent. The probability that the sample mean will be more than 2.0 standard deviations lower than the process mean is also 2.28 percent because the normal distribution is symmetric to the mean. The ability to assign probabilities to sample results is important for the construction and use of control charts.

Common Causes   The two basic categories of variation in output include common causes and assignable causes. **Common causes of variation** are the purely random, unidentifiable sources of variation that are unavoidable with the current process. A process distribution can be characterized by its *location*, *spread*, and *shape*. Location is measured by the *mean* of the distribution, while spread is measured by the *range* or *standard deviation*. The shape of process distributions can be characterized as either symmetric or skewed. A *symmetric* distribution has the same number of observations above and below the mean. A *skewed* distribution has a greater number of observations either above or below the mean. If process variability results solely from common causes of variation, a typical assumption is that the distribution is symmetric, with most observations near the center.

common causes of variation

The purely random, unidentifiable sources of variation that are unavoidable with the current process.

assignable causes of variation

Any variation-causing factors that can be identified and eliminated.

Assignable Causes   The second category of variation, **assignable causes of variation**, also known as *special causes*, includes any variation-causing factors that can be identified and eliminated. Assignable causes of variation include an employee needing training or a machine needing repair. Let us return to the example of the lab analysis process. Figure 5.7 shows how assignable causes can change the distribution of output for

FIGURE 5.6 ▶

Relationship Between the Distribution of Sample Means and the Process Distribution

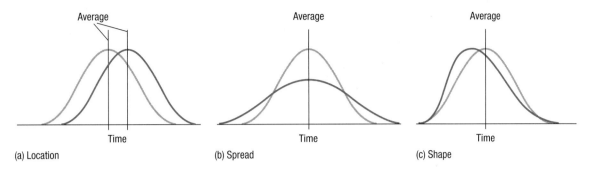

▲ **FIGURE 5.7**
Effects of Assignable Causes on the Process Distribution for the Lab Analysis Process

the analysis process. The green curve is the process distribution when only common causes of variation are present. The **purple** curves depict a change in the distribution because of assignable causes. In Figure 5.7(a), the **purple** curve indicates that the process took more time than planned in many of the cases, thereby increasing the average time of each analysis. In Figure 5.7(b), an increase in the variability of the time for each case affected the spread of the distribution. Finally, in Figure 5.7(c), the **purple** curve indicates that the process produced a preponderance of the tests in less than average time. Such a distribution is skewed, or no longer symmetric to the average value. A process is said to be in statistical control when the location, spread, or shape of its distribution does not change over time. After the process is in statistical control, managers use SPC procedures to detect the onset of assignable causes so that they can be addressed.

Control Charts

To determine whether observed variations are abnormal, we can measure and plot the performance measure taken from the sample on a time-ordered diagram called a **control chart**. A control chart has a nominal value, or central line, which can be the process's historic average or a target that managers would like the process to achieve, and two control limits based on the sampling distribution of the quality measure. The control limits are used to judge whether action is required. The larger value represents the *upper control limit* (UCL), and the smaller value represents the *lower control limit* (LCL). Figure 5.8 shows how the control limits relate to the sampling distribution. A sample statistic that falls between the UCL and the LCL indicates that the process is exhibiting common causes of variation. A statistic that falls outside the control limits indicates that the process is exhibiting assignable causes of variation.

> **control chart**
> A time-ordered diagram that is used to determine whether observed variations are abnormal.

Observations falling outside the control limits do not always mean poor quality. For example, in Figure 5.8 the assignable cause may be a new billing process introduced to reduce the number of incorrect bills sent to customers. If the proportion of incorrect bills, that is, the performance measure from a sample of bills, falls *below* the LCL of the control chart, the new procedure likely changed the billing process for the better, and a new control chart should be constructed.

Managers or employees responsible for evaluating a process can use control charts in the following way:

1. Take a random sample from the process and calculate a variable or attribute performance measure.

2. If the statistic falls outside the chart's control limits or exhibits unusual behavior, look for an assignable cause.

3. Eliminate the cause if it degrades performance; incorporate the cause if it improves performance. Reconstruct the control chart with new data.

4. Repeat the procedure periodically.

Sometimes problems with a process can be detected even though the control limits have not been exceeded. Figure 5.9 contains four examples of control

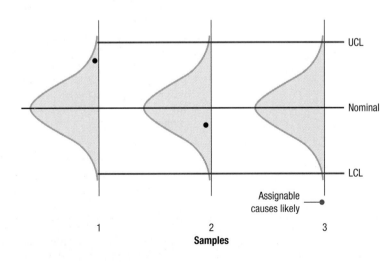

▲ **FIGURE 5.8**
How Control Limits Relate to the Sampling Distribution: Observations from Three Samples

(a) Normal—No action

(b) Run—Take action

(c) Sudden change—Monitor

(d) Exceeds control limits—Take action

FIGURE 5.9 ▲
Control Chart Examples

type I error

An error that occurs when the employee concludes that the process is out of control based on a sample result that falls outside the control limits, when in fact it was due to pure randomness.

type II error

An error that occurs when the employee concludes that the process is in control and only randomness is present, when actually the process is out of statistical control.

charts. Chart (a) shows a process that is in statistical control. No action is needed. However, chart (b) shows a pattern called a *run*, or a sequence of observations with a certain characteristic. A typical rule is to take remedial action when five or more observations show a downward or upward trend, even if the points have not yet exceeded the control limits. Here, nine sequential observations are below the mean and show a downward trend. The probability is low that such a result could take place by chance.

Chart (c) shows that the process takes a sudden change from its normal pattern. The last four observations are unusual: The first drops close to the LCL the next two rise toward the UCL, and the fourth remains above the nominal value. Managers or employees should monitor processes with such sudden changes even though the control limits have not been exceeded. Finally, chart (d) indicates that the process went out of control twice because two sample results fell outside the control limits. The probability that the process distribution has changed is high. We discuss more implications of being out of statistical control when we discuss process capability later in this chapter.

Control charts are not perfect tools for detecting shifts in the process distribution because they are based on sampling distributions. Two types of error are possible with the use of control charts. A **type I error** occurs when the conclusion is made that the process is out of control based on a sample result that falls outside the control limits, when in fact it was due to pure randomness. A **type II error** occurs when the conclusion is that the process is in control and only randomness is present, when actually the process is out of statistical control.

These errors can be controlled by the choice of control limits. The choice would depend on the costs of looking for assignable causes when none exist versus the cost of not detecting a shift in the process. For example, setting control limits at three standard deviations from the mean reduces the type I error because chances are only 0.26 percent that a sample result will fall outside of the control limits unless the process is out of statistical control. However, the type II error may be significant; more subtle shifts in the nature of the process distribution will go undetected because of the wide spread in the control limits. Alternatively, the spread in the control limits can be reduced to two standard deviations, thereby increasing the likelihood of sample results from a non-faulty process falling outside of the control limits to 4.56 percent. Now the type II error is smaller, but the type I error is larger because employees are likely to search for assignable causes when the sample result occurred solely by chance. As a general rule, use wider limits when the cost for searching for assignable causes is large relative to the cost of not detecting a shift in the process distribution.

STATISTICAL PROCESS CONTROL METHODS

Statistical process control (SPC) methods are useful for both measuring the current process performance and detecting whether the process has changed in a way that will affect future performance. In this section, we first discuss mean and range charts for variable measures of performance and then consider control charts for attributes measures.

Control Charts for Variables

Control charts for variables are used to monitor the mean and the variability of the process distribution.

R-chart

A chart used to monitor process variability.

***R*-Chart** A range chart, or ***R*-chart**, is used to monitor process variability. To calculate the range of a set of sample data, the analyst subtracts the smallest from the largest measurement in each sample. If any of the ranges fall outside the control limits, the process variability is not in control.

The control limits for the *R*-chart are

$$\text{UCL}_R = D_4\overline{R} \text{ and } \text{LCL}_R = D_3\overline{R}$$

where

$\bar{R} = $ average of several past R values and the central line of the control chart

$D_3, D_4 = $ constants that provide three standard deviation (three-sigma) limits for a given sample size

Notice that the values for D_3 and D_4 shown in Table 5.1 change as a function of the sample size. Notice, too, that the spread between the control limits narrows as the sample size increases. This change is a consequence of having more information on which to base an estimate for the process range.

| TABLE 5.1 | FACTORS FOR CALCULATING THREE-SIGMA LIMITS FOR THE $\bar{x}$-CHART AND R-CHART |

Size of Sample (n)	Factor for UCL and LCL for $\bar{x}$-Chart (A_2)	Factor for LCL for R-Chart (D_3)	Factor for UCL for R-Chart (D_4)
2	1.880	0	3.267
3	1.023	0	2.575
4	0.729	0	2.282
5	0.577	0	2.115
6	0.483	0	2.004
7	0.419	0.076	1.924
8	0.373	0.136	1.864
9	0.337	0.184	1.816
10	0.308	0.223	1.777

Source: 1950 *ASTM Manual on Quality Control of Materials*, copyright © American Society for Testing Materials. Reprinted with permission.

$\bar{x}$-Chart An $\bar{x}$-**Chart** (read "x-bar chart") is used to see whether the process is generating output, on average, consistent with a target value set by management for the process or whether its current performance, with respect to the average of the performance measure, is consistent with its past performance. A target value is useful when a process is completely redesigned and past performance is no longer relevant. When the assignable causes of process variability have been identified and the process variability is in statistical control, the analyst can then construct an $\bar{x}$-chart. The control limits for the $\bar{x}$-chart are

$$\text{UCL}_{\bar{x}} = \bar{\bar{x}} + A_2\bar{R} \text{ and } \text{LCL}_{\bar{x}} = \bar{\bar{x}} - A_2\bar{R}$$

where

$\bar{\bar{x}} = $ central line of the chart, which can be either the average of past sample means or a target value set for the process

$A_2 = $ constant to provide three-sigma limits for the sample mean

The values for A_2 are contained in Table 5.1. Note that the control limits use the value of $\bar{R}$; therefore, the $\bar{x}$-chart must be constructed *after* the process variability is in control.

To develop and use $\bar{x}$- and R-charts do the following:

Step 1. Collect data on the variable quality measurement (such as time, weight, or diameter) and organize the data by sample number. Preferably, at least 20 samples should be taken for use in constructing a control chart.

Step 2. Compute the range for each sample and the average range, $\bar{R}$, for the set of samples.

Step 3. Use Table 5.1 to determine the upper and lower control limits of the R-chart.

Step 4. Plot the sample ranges. If all are in control, proceed to step 5. Otherwise, find the assignable causes, correct them, and return to step 1.

$\bar{x}$-chart

A chart used to see whether the process is generating output, on average, consistent with a target value set by management for the process or whether its current performance, with respect to the average of the performance measure, is consistent with past performance.

At ADM Cocao, heated chocolate is poured from a holding tank into this depositing machine that forms chocolate drops. Every hour, a random sample of 100 drops is taken and the average number of drops per pound is calculated and monitored to see if any process changes are taking place.

Step 5. Calculate $\bar{x}$ for each sample and determine the central line of the chart, $\bar{\bar{x}}$.

Step 6. Use Table 5.1 to determine the parameters for $\text{UCL}_{\bar{x}}$ and $\text{LCL}_{\bar{x}}$ and construct the $\bar{x}$-chart.

Step 7. Plot the sample means. If all are in control, the process is in statistical control in terms of the process average and process variability. Continue to take samples and monitor the process. If any are out of control, find the assignable causes, correct them, and return to step 1. If no assignable causes are found after a diligent search, assume that the out-of-control points represent common causes of variation and continue to monitor the process.

EXAMPLE 5.1 | Using $\bar{x}$- and R-Charts to Monitor a Process

Active Model 5.1 in my**om**lab provides additional insight on the x-bar and R-charts and their uses for the metal screw problem.

Tutor 5.1 in my**om**lab provides a new example to practice the use of x-bar and R-charts.

The management of West Allis Industries is concerned about the production of a special metal screw used by several of the company's largest customers. The diameter of the screw is critical to the customers. Data from five samples appear in the accompanying table. The sample size is 4. Is the process in statistical control?

SOLUTION

Step 1: For simplicity, we use only 5 samples. In practice, more than 20 samples would be desirable. The data are shown in the following table.

Data for the $\bar{x}$- and R-Charts: Observations of Screw Diameter (in.)						
	Observation					
Sample Number	**1**	**2**	**3**	**4**	**R**	**$\bar{x}$**
1	0.5014	0.5022	0.5009	0.5027	0.0018	0.5018
2	0.5021	0.5041	0.5024	0.5020	0.0021	0.5027
3	0.5018	0.5026	0.5035	0.5023	0.0017	0.5026
4	0.5008	0.5034	0.5024	0.5015	0.0026	0.5020
5	0.5041	0.5056	0.5034	0.5047	0.0022	0.5045
				Average	0.0021	0.5027

Step 2: Compute the range for each sample by subtracting the lowest value from the highest value. For example, in sample 1 the range is $0.5027 - 0.5009 = 0.0018$ in. Similarly, the ranges for samples 2, 3, 4, and 5 are 0.0021, 0.0017, 0.0026, and 0.0022 in., respectively. As shown in the table, $\bar{R} = 0.0021$.

Step 3: To construct the R-chart, select the appropriate constants from Table 5.1 for a sample size of 4. The control limits are

$$UCL_R = D_4\overline{R} = 2.282(0.0021) = 0.00479 \text{ in.}$$

$$LCL_R = D_3\overline{R} = 0(0.0021) = 0 \text{ in.}$$

Step 4: Plot the ranges on the R-chart, as shown in Figure 5.10. None of the sample ranges falls outside the control limits. Consequently, the process variability is in statistical control. If any of the sample ranges fall outside of the limits, or an unusual pattern appears (see Figure 5.9), we would search for the causes of the excessive variability, correct them, and repeat step 1.

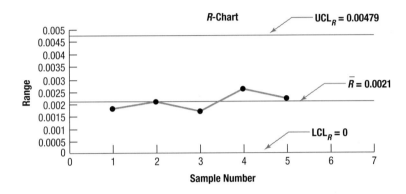

◀ FIGURE 5.10
Range Chart from the *OM Explorer* $\overline{x}$- and *R-Chart* Solver for the Metal Screw, Showing That the Process Variability Is in Control

Step 5: Compute the mean for each sample. For example, the mean for sample 1 is

$$\frac{0.5014 + 0.5022 + 0.5009 + 0.5027}{4} = 0.5018 \text{ in.}$$

Similarly, the means of samples 2, 3, 4, and 5 are 0.5027, 0.5026, 0.5020, and 0.5045 in., respectively. As shown in the table, $\overline{\overline{x}} = 0.5027$.

Step 6: Now construct the $\overline{x}$-chart for the process average. The average screw diameter is 0.5027 in., and the average range is 0.0021 in., so use $\overline{\overline{x}} = 0.5027$, $\overline{R} = 0.0021$, and A_2 from Table 5.1 for a sample size of 4 to construct the control limits:

$$UCL_{\overline{x}} = \overline{\overline{x}} + A_2\overline{R} = 0.5027 + 0.729(0.0021) = 0.5042 \text{ in.}$$

$$LCL_{\overline{x}} = \overline{\overline{x}} - A_2\overline{R} = 0.5027 - 0.729(0.0021) = 0.5012 \text{ in.}$$

Step 7: Plot the sample means on the control chart, as shown in Figure 5.11.

The mean of sample 5 falls above the UCL, indicating that the process average is out of statistical control and that assignable causes must be explored, perhaps using a cause-and-effect diagram.

◀ FIGURE 5.11
The x-bar Chart from the *OM Explorer* $\overline{x}$- and *R-Chart* Solver for the Metal Screw, Showing That Sample 5 Is out of Control

DECISION POINT

A new employee operated the lathe machine that makes the screw on the day sample 5 was taken. To solve the problem, management initiated a training session for the employee. Subsequent samples showed that the process was back in statistical control.

If the standard deviation of the process distribution is known, another form of the $\bar{x}$-chart may be used:

$$\text{UCL}_{\bar{x}} = \bar{\bar{x}} + z\sigma_{\bar{x}} \text{ and } \text{LCL}_{\bar{x}} = \bar{\bar{x}} - z\sigma_{\bar{x}}$$

where

$\sigma_{\bar{x}} = \sigma/\sqrt{n}$ = standard deviation of sample means

σ = standard deviation of the process distribution

n = sample size

$\bar{\bar{x}}$ = central line of the chart, which can be either the average of past sample means or a target value set for the process

z = normal deviate (number of standard deviations from the average)

The analyst can use an R-chart to be sure that the process variability is in control before constructing the $\bar{x}$-chart. The advantage of using this form of the $\bar{x}$-chart is that the analyst can adjust the spread of the control limits by changing the value of z. This approach can be useful for balancing the effects of type I and type II errors.

EXAMPLE 5.2   **Designing an $\bar{x}$-Chart Using the Process Standard Deviation**

The Sunny Dale Bank monitors the time required to serve customers at the drive-by window because it is an important quality factor in competing with other banks in the city. After analyzing the data gathered in an extensive study of the window operation, bank management determined that the mean time to process a customer at the peak demand period is 5 minutes, with a standard deviation of 1.5 minutes. Management wants to monitor the mean time to process a customer by periodically using a sample size of six customers. Assume that the process variability is in statistical control. Design an $\bar{x}$-chart that has a type I error of 5 percent. That is, set the control limits so that there is a 2.5 percent chance a sample result will fall below the LCL and a 2.5 percent chance that a sample result will fall above the UCL. After several weeks of sampling, two successive samples came in at 3.70 and 3.68 minutes, respectively. Is the customer service process in statistical control?

SOLUTION

$$\bar{\bar{x}} = 5.0 \text{ minutes}$$
$$\sigma = 1.5 \text{ minutes}$$
$$n = 6 \text{ customers}$$
$$z = 1.96$$

The process variability is in statistical control, so we proceed directly to the $\bar{x}$-chart. The control limits are

$$\text{UCL}_{\bar{x}} = \bar{\bar{x}} + z\sigma/\sqrt{n} = 5.0 + 1.96(1.5)/\sqrt{6} = 6.20 \text{ minutes}$$

$$\text{LCL}_{\bar{x}} = \bar{\bar{x}} - z\sigma/\sqrt{n} = 5.0 - 1.96(1.5)/\sqrt{6} = 3.80 \text{ minutes}$$

The value for z can be obtained in the following way. The normal distribution table (see Appendix 1) gives the proportion of the total area under the normal curve from $-\infty$ to z. We want a type I error of 5 percent, or 2.5 percent of the curve above the UCL and 2.5 percent below the LCL. Consequently, we need to find the z value in the table that leaves only 2.5 percent in the upper portion of the normal curve (or 0.9750 in the table). The value is 1.96. The two new samples are below the LCL of the chart, implying that the average time to serve a customer has dropped. Assignable causes should be explored to see what caused the improvement.

DECISION POINT

Management studied the time period over which the samples were taken and found that the supervisor of the process was experimenting with some new procedures. Management decided to make the new procedures a permanent part of the customer service process. After all employees were trained in the new procedures, new samples were taken and the control chart reconstructed.

Control Charts for Attributes

Two charts commonly used for performance measures based on attributes measures are the p- and c-chart. The p-chart is used for controlling the proportion of defects generated by the process. The c-chart is used for controlling the number of defects when more than one defect can be present in a service or product.

p-Charts The **p-chart** is a commonly used control chart for attributes. The performance characteristic is counted rather than measured, and the entire service or item can be declared good or defective. For example, in the banking industry, the attributes counted might be the number of nonendorsed deposits or the number of incorrect financial statements sent to customers. The method involves selecting a random sample, inspecting each item in it, and calculating the sample proportion defective, p, which is the number of defective units divided by the sample size.

Sampling for a p-chart involves a yes/no decision: The process output either is or is not defective. The underlying statistical distribution is based on the binomial distribution. However, for large sample sizes, the normal distribution provides a good approximation to it. The standard deviation of the distribution of proportion defectives, σ_p, is

$$\sigma_p = \sqrt{\bar{p}(1 - \bar{p})/n}$$

where

n = sample size
$\bar{p}$ = central line on the chart, which can be either the historical average population proportion defective or a target value

We can use σ_p to arrive at the upper and lower control limits for a p-chart:

$$\text{UCL}_p = \bar{p} + z\sigma_p \text{ and } \text{LCL}_p = \bar{p} - z\sigma_p$$

where

z = normal deviate (number of standard deviations from the average)

The chart is used in the following way. Periodically, a random sample of size n is taken, and the number of defective services or products is counted. The number of defectives is divided by the sample size to get a sample proportion defective, p, which is plotted on the chart. When a sample proportion defective falls outside the control limits, the analyst assumes that the proportion defective generated by the process has changed and searches for the assignable cause. Observations falling below the LCL_p indicate that the process may actually have improved. The analyst may find no assignable cause because it is always possible that an out-of-control proportion occurred randomly. However, if the analyst discovers assignable causes, those sample data should not be used to calculate the control limits for the chart.

p-chart

A chart used for controlling the proportion of defective services or products generated by the process.

| EXAMPLE 5.3 | Using a p-Chart to Monitor a Process |

The operations manager of the booking services department of Hometown Bank is concerned about the number of wrong customer account numbers recorded by Hometown personnel. Each week a random sample of 2,500 deposits is taken, and the number of incorrect account numbers is recorded. The results for the past 12 weeks are shown in the following table. Is the booking process out of statistical control? Use three-sigma control limits, which will provide a Type I error of 0.26 percent.

Sample Number	Wrong Account Numbers	Sample Number	Wrong Account Numbers
1	15	7	24
2	12	8	7
3	19	9	10
4	2	10	17
5	19	11	15
6	4	12	3
			Total 147

Active Model 5.2 in my**om**lab provides additional insight on the p-chart and its uses for the booking services department.

Tutor 5.2 in my**om**lab provides a new example to practice the use of the p-chart.

SOLUTION

Step 1: Using this sample data to calculate p-bar

$$\bar{p} = \frac{\text{Total defectives}}{\text{Total number of observations}} = \frac{147}{12(2,500)} = 0.0049$$

$$\sigma_p = \sqrt{\bar{p}(1 - \bar{p})/n} = \sqrt{0.0049(1 - 0.0049)/2,500} = 0.0014$$

$$\text{UCL}_p = \bar{p} + z\sigma_p = 0.0049 + 3(0.0014) = 0.0091$$

$$\text{LCL}_p = \bar{p} - z\sigma_p = 0.0049 - 3(0.0014) = 0.0007$$

Step 2: Calculate the sample proportion defective. For sample 1, the proportion of defectives is 15/2,500 = 0.0060.

Step 3: Plot each sample proportion defective on the chart, as shown in Figure 5.12.

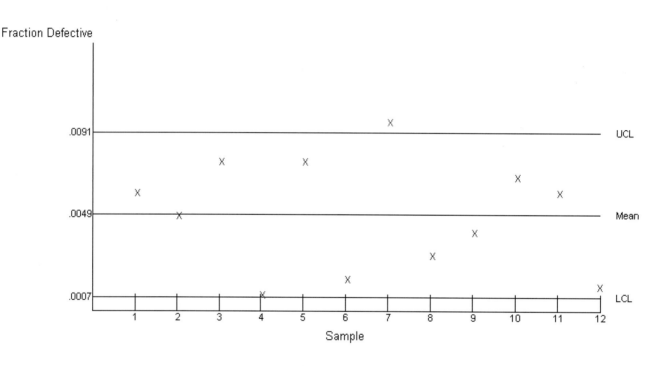

FIGURE 5.12 ▲
The p-Chart from POM for Windows for Wrong Account Numbers, Showing That Sample 7 is Out of Control

Sample 7 exceeds the UCL; thus, the process is out of control and the reasons for the poor performance that week should be determined.

DECISION POINT

Management explored the circumstances when sample 7 was taken. The encoding machine used to print the account numbers on the checks was defective that week. The following week the machine was repaired; however, the recommended preventive maintenance on the machine was not performed for months prior to the failure. Management reviewed the performance of the maintenance department and instituted changes to the maintenance procedures for the encoding machine. After the problem was corrected, an analyst recalculated the control limits using the data without sample 7. Subsequent weeks were sampled, and the booking process was determined to be in statistical control. Consequently, the p-chart provides a tool to indicate when a process needs adjustment.

c-Charts Sometimes services or products have more than one defect. For example, a roll of carpeting may have several defects, such as tufted or discolored fibers or stains from the production process. Other situations in which more than one defect may occur include accidents at a particular intersection, bubbles in a television picture face panel, and complaints from a patron at a hotel. When management is interested in reducing the number of defects per unit or service encounter, another type of control chart, the **c-chart**, is useful.

c-chart

A chart used for controlling the number of defects when more than one defect can be present in a service or product.

The underlying sampling distribution for a *c*-chart is the Poisson distribution. The Poisson distribution is based on the assumption that defects occur over a continuous region on the surface of a product or a continuous time interval during the provision of a service. It further assumes that the probability of two or more defects at any one location on the surface or at any instant of time is negligible. The mean of the distribution is $\bar{c}$, and the standard deviation is $\sqrt{\bar{c}}$. A useful tactic is to use the normal approximation to the Poisson so that the central line of the chart is $\bar{c}$ and the control limits are

$$\text{UCL}_c = \bar{c} + z\sqrt{\bar{c}} \text{ and } \text{LCL}_c = \bar{c} - z\sqrt{\bar{c}}$$

EXAMPLE 5.4	Using a *c*-Chart to Monitor Defects per Unit

The Woodland Paper Company produces paper for the newspaper industry. As a final step in the process, the paper passes through a machine that measures various product quality characteristics. When the paper production process is in control, it averages 20 defects per roll.

Tutor 5.3 in myomlab provides a new example to practice the use of the *c*-chart.

a. Set up a control chart for the number of defects per roll. For this example, use two-sigma control limits.

b. Five rolls had the following number of defects: 16, 21, 17, 22, and 24, respectively. The sixth roll, using pulp from a different supplier, had 5 defects. Is the paper production process in control?

SOLUTION

a. The average number of defects per roll is 20. Therefore

$$\text{UCL}_c = \bar{c} + z\sqrt{\bar{c}} = 20 + 2(\sqrt{20}) = 28.94$$

$$\text{LCL}_c = \bar{c} - z\sqrt{\bar{c}} = 20 - 2(\sqrt{20}) = 11.06$$

The control chart is shown in Figure 5.13.

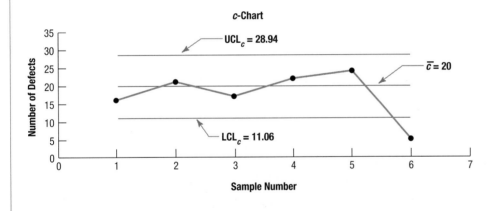

◀ **FIGURE 5.13**
The *c*-Chart from the *OM Explorer* *c*-Chart Solver for Defects per Roll of Paper

b. Because the first five rolls had defects that fell within the control limits, the process is still in control. Five defects, however, is less than the LCL, and therefore, the process is technically "out of control." The control chart indicates that something good has happened.

DECISION POINT

The supplier for the first five samples has been used by Woodland Paper for many years. The supplier for the sixth sample is new to the company. Management decided to continue using the new supplier for a while, monitoring the number of defects to see whether it stays low. If the number remains below the LCL for 20 consecutive samples, management will make the switch permanent and recalculate the control chart parameters.

PROCESS CAPABILITY

Statistical process control techniques help managers achieve and maintain a process distribution that does not change in terms of its mean and variance. The control limits on the control charts signal when the mean or variability of the process changes. However, a process that is in statistical control may not be producing services or products according to

process capability

The ability of the process to meet the design specifications for a service or product.

nominal value

A target for design specifications.

tolerance

An allowance above or below the nominal value.

their design specifications because the control limits are based on the mean and variability of the *sampling distribution*, not the design specifications. **Process capability** refers to the ability of the process to meet the design specifications for a service or product. Design specifications often are expressed as a **nominal value**, or target, and a **tolerance**, or allowance above or below the nominal value.

For example, the administrator of an intensive care unit lab might have a nominal value for the turnaround time of results to the attending physicians of 25 minutes and a tolerance of ±5 minutes because of the need for speed under life-threatening conditions. The tolerance gives an *upper specification* of 30 minutes and a *lower specification* of 20 minutes. The lab process must be capable of providing the results of analyses within these specifications; otherwise, it will produce a certain proportion of "defects." The administrator is also interested in detecting occurrences of turnaround times of less than 20 minutes because something might be learned that can be built into the lab process in the future. For the present, the physicians are pleased with results that arrive within 20 to 30 minutes.

Defining Process Capability

Figure 5.14 shows the relationship between a process distribution and the upper and lower specifications for the lab process turnaround time under two conditions. In Figure 5.14(a), the process is capable because the extremes of the process distribution fall within the upper and lower specifications. In Figure 5.14(b) the process is not capable because the lab process produces too many reports with long turnaround times.

FIGURE 5.14 ▶
The Relationship Between a Process Distribution and Upper and Lower Specifications

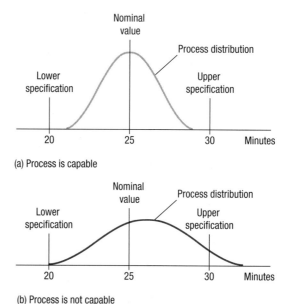

(a) Process is capable

(b) Process is not capable

Figure 5.14 shows clearly why managers are so concerned with reducing process variability. The less variability—represented by lower standard deviations—the less frequently bad output is produced. Figure 5.15 shows what reducing variability means for a process distribution that is a normal probability distribution. The firm with two-sigma quality (the specification limits equal the process distribution mean ±2 standard deviations) produces 4.56 percent defects, or 45,600 defects per million. The firm with four-sigma quality produces only 0.0063 percent defects, or 63 defects per million. Finally, the firm with six-sigma quality produces only 0.0000002 percent defects, or 0.002 defects per million.[2]

How can a manager determine quantitatively whether a process is capable? Two measures commonly are used in practice to assess the capability of a process: the process capability index and the process capability ratio.

---

[2] Our discussion assumes that the process distribution has no assignable causes. Six Sigma programs, however, define defect performance with the assumption that the process average has moved 1.5 standard deviations. In such a case, there would be 3.4 defects per million. See www.isixsigma.com for the rationale behind that assumption.

Process Capability Index The **process capability index**, C_{pk} is defined as

$$C_{pk} = \text{Minimum of} \left[\frac{\overline{\overline{x}} - \text{Lower specification}}{3\sigma}, \frac{\text{Upper specification} - \overline{\overline{x}}}{3\sigma} \right]$$

where

σ = standard deviation of the process distribution

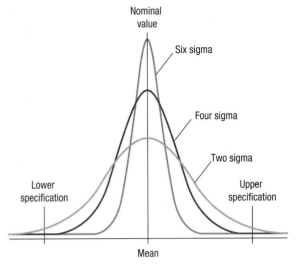

▲ FIGURE 5.15
Effects of Reducing Variability on Process Capability

The process capability index measures how well the process is centered as well as whether the variability is acceptable. As a general rule, most values of any process distribution fall within ±3 standard deviations of the mean. Consequently, ± 3 standard deviations is used as the benchmark. Because the process capability index is concerned with how well the process distribution is centered relative to the specifications, it checks to see if the process average is at least three standard deviations from the upper and lower specifications. We take the minimum of the two ratios because it gives the *worst-case* situation.

The process capability index must be compared to a critical value to judge whether a process is capable. Firms striving to achieve three-sigma quality use a critical value for the ratio of 1.0. A firm targeting four-sigma quality will use 1.33 (or 4/3), a firm targeting five-sigma quality will use 1.67 (or 5/3), and a firm striving for six-sigma quality will use 2.00 (or 6/3). Processes producing services or products with less than three-sigma quality will have C_p values less than 1.0.

If a process passes the process capability index test, we can declare the process is capable. Suppose a firm desires its processes to produce at the level of four-sigma quality. If C_{pk} is greater than or equal to the critical value of 1.33 we can say the process is capable. If C_{pk} is less than the critical value, either the process average is too close to one of the tolerance limits and is generating defective output, or the process variability is too large. To find out whether the variability is the culprit, we need another test.

process capability index, C_{pk}

An index that measures the potential for a process to generate defective outputs relative to either upper or lower specifications.

Process Capability Ratio If a process fails the process capability *index* test, we need a quick test to see if the process variability is causing the problem. If a process is *capable* it has a process distribution whose extreme values fall within the upper and lower specifications for a service or product. For example, if the process distribution is normal, 99.74 percent of the values fall within ±3 standard deviations. In other words, the range of values of the quality measure generated by a process is approximately 6 standard deviations of the process distribution. Hence, if a process is capable at the three-sigma level, the difference between the upper and lower specification, called the *tolerance width*, must be greater than 6 standard deviations. The **process capability ratio**, C_p, is defined as

$$C_p = \frac{\text{Upper specification} - \text{Lower specification}}{6\sigma}$$

process capability ratio, C_p

The tolerance width divided by 6 standard deviations.

Suppose management wants four-sigma capability in their processes, and a process just failed the process capability index test at that level. A C_p value of 1.33, say, implies that the variability of the process is at the level of four-sigma quality and that the process is capable of consistently producing outputs within specifications, assuming that the process is centered. Because C_p passed the test, but C_{pk} did not, we can assume that the problem is that the process is not centered adequately.

Using Continuous Improvement to Determine the Capability of a Process

To determine the capability of a process to produce outputs within the tolerances, use the following steps.

Step 1. Collect data on the process output, and calculate the mean and the standard deviation of the process output distribution.

Step 2. Use the data from the process distribution to compute process control charts, such as an $\overline{x}$- and an R-chart.

Step 3. Take a series of at least 20 consecutive random samples from the process and plot the results on the control charts. If the sample statistics are within the control limits of the charts, the process is in statistical control. If the process is not in statistical control, look for assignable causes and eliminate them. Recalculate the mean and standard deviation of the process distribution and the control limits for the charts. Continue until the process is in statistical control.

Step 4. Calculate the process capability *index*. If the results are acceptable, the process is capable and document any changes made to the process; continue to monitor the output by using the control charts. If the results are unacceptable, calculate the process capability *ratio*. If the results are acceptable, the process variability is fine and management should focus on centering the process. If the results of the process capability ratio are unacceptable, management should focus on reducing the variability in the process until it passes the test. As changes are made, recalculate the mean and standard deviation of the process distribution and the control limits for the charts and return to step 3.

EXAMPLE 5.5	Assessing the Process Capability of the Intensive Care Unit Lab

Active Model 5.3 in my**om**lab provides additional insight on the process capability problem at the intensive care unit lab.

Tutor 5.4 in my**om**lab provides a new example to practice the process capability measures.

The intensive care unit lab process has an average turnaround time of 26.2 minutes and a standard deviation of 1.35 minutes. The nominal value for this service is 25 minutes with an upper specification limit of 30 minutes and a lower specification limit of 20 minutes. The administrator of the lab wants to have four-sigma performance for her lab. Is the lab process capable of this level of performance?

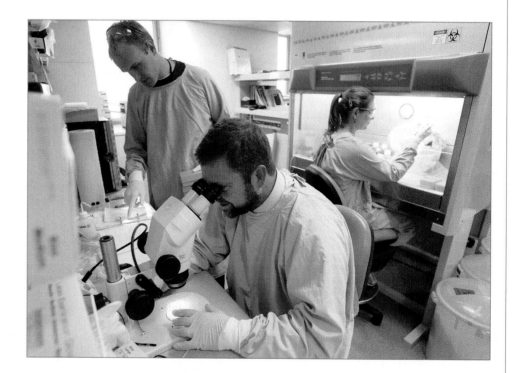

SOLUTION

The administrator began by taking a quick check to see if the process is capable by applying the process capability index:

$$\text{Lower specification calculation} = \frac{26.2 - 20.0}{3(1.35)} = 1.53$$

$$\text{Upper specification calculation} = \frac{30.0 - 26.2}{3(1.35)} = 0.94$$

$$C_{pk} = \text{Minimum of}[1.53, 0.94] = 0.94$$

Since the target value for four-sigma performance is 1.33, the process capability index told her that the process was not capable. However, she did not know whether the problem was the variability of the process, the centering of the process, or both. The options available to improve the process depended on what is wrong.

She next checked the process variability with the process capability ratio:

$$C_p = \frac{30.0 - 20.0}{6(1.35)} = 1.23$$

The process variability did not meet the four-sigma target of 1.33. Consequently, she initiated a study to see where variability was introduced into the process. Two activities, report preparation and specimen slide preparation, were identified as having inconsistent procedures. These procedures were modified to provide consistent performance. New data were collected and the average turnaround was now 26.1 minutes with a standard deviation of 1.20 minutes. She now had the process variability at the four-sigma level of performance, as indicated by the process capability ratio:

$$C_p = \frac{30.0 - 20.0}{6(1.20)} = 1.39$$

However, the process capability index indicated additional problems to resolve:

$$C_{pk} = \text{Minimum of} \left[\frac{(26.1 - 20.0)}{3(1.20)}, \frac{(30.0 - 26.1)}{3(1.20)} \right] = 1.08$$

DECISION POINT

The lab process was still not at the level of four-sigma performance on turnaround time. The lab administrator searched for the causes of the off-center turnaround time distribution. She discovered periodic backlogs at a key piece of testing equipment. Acquiring a second machine provided the capacity to reduce the turnaround times to four-sigma capability.

Quality Engineering

Successful quality performance is often more than process improvement; it also involves service/product design. Originated by Genichi Taguchi, **quality engineering** is an approach that involves combining engineering and statistical methods to reduce costs and improve quality by optimizing product design and manufacturing processes. Taguchi believes that unwelcome costs are associated with *any* deviation from a quality characteristic's target value. Taguchi's view is that the **quality loss function** is zero when the quality characteristic of the service or product is exactly on the target value, and that the quality loss function value rises exponentially as the quality characteristic gets closer to the specification limits. The rationale is that a service or product that barely conforms to the specifications is more like a defective service or product than a perfect one. Figure 5.16 shows Taguchi's quality loss function schematically. Taguchi concluded that managers should continually search for ways to reduce *all* variability from the target value in the production process and not be content with merely adhering to specification limits.[3]

INTERNATIONAL QUALITY DOCUMENTATION STANDARDS

Once a company has gone through the effort of making its processes capable, it must document its level of quality so as to better market its services or products. This documentation of quality is especially important in international trade. However, if each country had its own set of standards, companies selling in international markets would have difficulty complying with quality documentation standards in each country where they did business. To overcome this problem, the International Organization for Standardization devised a set of standards called ISO 9000 for companies doing business in the European Union. Subsequently, a new set of documentation standards, ISO 14000, was devised for environmental management systems.

quality engineering

An approach originated by Genichi Taguchi that involves combining engineering and statistical methods to reduce costs and improve quality by optimizing product design and manufacturing processes.

quality loss function

The rationale that a service or product that barely conforms to the specifications is more like a defective service or product than a perfect one.

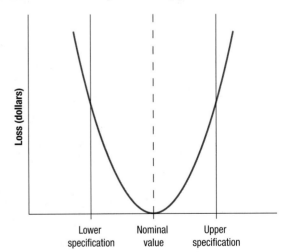

▲ FIGURE 5.16
Taguchi's Quality Loss Function

---

[3] For a more detailed discussion and animation of the Taguchi Loss Function, see http://elsmar.com/Taguchi.html.

The ISO 9000:2000 Documentation Standards

ISO 9000:2000 is a set of standards governing documentation of a quality program. According to the International Organization for Standardization, "the ISO 9000:2000 family addresses *quality management* by specifying what the firm does to fulfill the customer's quality requirements and applicable regulatory requirements, while aiming to enhance customer satisfaction and achieve continual improvement of its performance in pursuit of these objectives." Companies become certified by proving to a qualified external examiner that they comply with all the requirements. Once certified, companies are listed in a directory so that potential customers can see which companies are certified and to what level. Compliance with ISO 9000:2000 standards says *nothing* about the actual quality of a product. Rather, it indicates to customers that companies can provide documentation to support whatever claims they make about quality.

ISO 9000:2000 covers a wide variety of levels of certification for which a firm may apply. For example, there is a standard that focuses on 20 aspects of a quality program for companies that design, produce, install, and service products. These aspects include management responsibility, quality system documentation, purchasing, product design, inspection, training, and corrective action. It is the most comprehensive and difficult standard to attain. There is another standard for companies that produce to the customer's designs or have their design and service activities at another location. Another standard addresses only the production process. Becoming certified is typically not a trivial endeavor, often taking many months to achieve.

ISO 14000:2004 Environmental Management System

The **ISO 14000:2004** standards require documentation of a firm's environmental program. According to the International Organization for Standardization, "the ISO 14000:2004 family *addresses environmental management* by specifying what the firm does to minimize harmful effects on the environment caused by its activities, and to achieve continual improvement of its environmental performance." The documentation standards require participating companies to keep track of their raw materials use and their generation, treatment, and disposal of hazardous wastes. Although not specifying what each company is allowed to emit, the standards require companies to prepare a plan for ongoing improvement in their environmental performance. ISO 14000:2004 covers a number of areas, including the following:

- *Environmental Management System.* Requires a plan to improve performance in resource use and pollutant output.
- *Environmental Performance Evaluation.* Specifies guidelines for the certification of companies.
- *Environmental Labeling.* Defines terms such as *recyclable, energy efficient,* and *safe for the ozone layer.*
- *Life-Cycle Assessment.* Evaluates the lifetime environmental impact from the manufacture, use, and disposal of a product.

To maintain their certification, companies must be inspected by outside, private auditors on a regular basis.

Benefits of ISO Certification

Completing the certification process can take as long as 18 months and involve many hours of management and employee time. The cost of certification can exceed $1 million for large companies. Despite the expense and commitment involved in ISO certification, it bestows significant external and internal benefits. The external benefits come from the potential sales advantage that companies in compliance have. Companies looking for a supplier will more likely select a company that has demonstrated compliance with ISO documentation standards, all other factors being equal. Consequently, more and more firms are seeking certification to gain a competitive advantage. Over 800,000 companies worldwide have implemented ISO 9000:2000 and ISO 14000 (1994 and 2004 versions).

Internal benefits can be substantial. Registered companies report an average of 48 percent increased profitability and 76 percent improvement in marketing. The British Standards Institute, a leading third-party auditor, estimates that most ISO 9000-registered companies experience a 10 percent reduction in the cost of producing a product because of the quality improvements they make while striving to meet the documentation requirements. Certification in ISO 9000:2000 requires a company to analyze and document its procedures, which is necessary in any event for implementing continuous improvement, employee involvement, and similar programs. The guidelines and requirements of the ISO documentation standards provide companies with a jump-start in pursuing TQM programs.

MALCOLM BALDRIGE NATIONAL QUALITY AWARD

Regardless of where a company does business, it is clear that all organizations have to produce high-quality products and services if they are to be competitive. To emphasize that point, in August 1987 the United States Congress signed into law the Malcolm Baldrige National Quality Improvement Act, creating the **Malcolm Baldrige National Quality Award** (www.quality.nist.gov). Named for the late secretary of commerce, who was a strong proponent of enhancing quality as a means of reducing the trade deficit, the award promotes, recognizes, and publicizes quality strategies and achievements.

The application and review process for the Baldrige award is rigorous. However, the act of preparing the application itself is often a major benefit to organizations because it helps firms define what *quality* means for them. According to the U.S. Commerce Department's National Institute of Standards and Technology (NIST), investing in quality principles and performance excellence pays off in increased productivity, satisfied employees and customers, and improved profitability, both for customers and investors. The seven major criteria for the award are the following:[4]

1. *Leadership.* Examines how senior executives guide the organization and how the organization addresses its responsibilities to the public and practices good citizenship.

2. *Strategic Planning.* Examines how the organization sets strategic directions and how it determines key action plans.

3. *Customer and Market Focus.* Examines how the organization determines requirements and expectations of customers and markets; builds relationships with customers; and acquires, satisfies, and retains customers.

4. *Measurement, Analysis, and Knowledge Management.* Examines the management, effective use, analysis, and improvement of data and information to support key organizational processes and the organization's performance management system.

5. *Workforce Focus.* Examines how the organization enables its workforce to develop its full potential and how the workforce is aligned with the organization's objectives.

6. *Process Management.* Examines aspects of how key production/delivery and support processes are designed, managed, and improved.

7. *Results.* Examines the organization's performance and improvement in its key business goals, including customer satisfaction, financial and marketplace performance, human resources, supplier and partner performance, operational performance, and governance and social responsibility. The category also examines how the organization performs relative to competitors.

Customer satisfaction underpins these seven criteria. Criterion 7, business results, is given the most weight in selecting winners.

High levels of quality performance are essential for successful operations. In this chapter we have identified the important characteristics of quality and how they can be measured. Attaining good quality performance requires a framework to work within. Firms have used Total Quality Management or Six Sigma to motivate employees to reach difficult quality goals. Regardless of the framework, a core element is statistical process control because it provides a quantitative approach to assess quality performance. We have discussed the statistical tools for variable measures and attributes measures and showed how to assess the capability of a process. These tools help management improve quality; however, to convince customers that their quality has improved, firms may have to also invest in documentation processes that meet ISO standards. In addition to opening the doors to business worldwide, a potential side benefit of ISO documentation is winning national quality recognitions, such as the Malcolm Baldrige National Quality Award. Quality is an important concern for any organization.

Malcolm Baldrige National Quality Award

An award named for the late secretary of commerce, who was a strong proponent of enhancing quality as a means of reducing the trade deficit; the award promotes, recognizes, and publicizes quality strategies and achievements.

---

[4] Details on the Malcolm Baldrige National Quality program can be found at www.quality.nist.gov.

INTERNET RESOURCES

my**om**lab and the Companion Website at **www.pearsonglobaleditions.com/krajewski** contain many tools, activities, and resources designed for this chapter.

KEY EQUATIONS

1. Mean: $\bar{x} = \dfrac{\sum\limits_{i=1}^{n} x_i}{n}$

2. Standard deviation of a sample:

$$\sigma = \sqrt{\frac{\Sigma(x_i - \bar{x})^2}{n-1}} \text{ or } \sigma = \sqrt{\frac{\Sigma x_i^2 - \dfrac{(\Sigma x_i)^2}{n}}{n-1}}$$

3. Control limits for variable process control charts

   a. R-chart, range of sample:

   $$\text{Upper control limit} = \text{UCL}_R = D_4\bar{R}$$
   $$\text{Lower control limit} = \text{LCL}_R = D_3\bar{R}$$

   b. $\bar{x}$-chart, sample mean:

   $$\text{Upper control limit} = \text{UCL}_{\bar{x}} = \bar{\bar{x}} + A_2\bar{R}$$
   $$\text{Lower control limit} = \text{LCL}_{\bar{x}} = \bar{\bar{x}} - A_2\bar{R}$$

   c. When the standard deviation of the process distribution, σ, is known:

   $$\text{Upper control limit} = \text{UCL}_{\bar{x}} = \bar{\bar{x}} + z\sigma_{\bar{x}}$$
   $$\text{Lower control limit} = \text{LCL}_{\bar{x}} = \bar{\bar{x}} - z\sigma_{\bar{x}}$$

   where

   $$\sigma_{\bar{x}} = \frac{\sigma}{\sqrt{n}}$$

4. Control limits for attribute process control charts

   a. p-chart, proportion defective:

   $$\text{Upper control limit} = \text{UCL}_p = \bar{p} + z\sigma_p$$
   $$\text{Lower control limit} = \text{LCL}_p = \bar{p} - z\sigma_p$$

   where

   $$\sigma_p = \sqrt{\bar{p}(1-\bar{p})/n}$$

   b. c-chart, number of defects:

   $$\text{Upper control limit} = \text{UCL}_c = \bar{c} + z\sqrt{\bar{c}}$$
   $$\text{Lower control limit} = \text{LCL}_c = \bar{c} - z\sqrt{\bar{c}}$$

5. Process capability index:

$$C_{pk} = \text{Minimum of} \left[\frac{\bar{\bar{x}} - \text{Lower specification}}{3\sigma}, \frac{\text{Upper specification} - \bar{\bar{x}}}{3\sigma} \right]$$

6. Process capability ratio:

$$C_p = \frac{\text{Upper specification} - \text{Lower specification}}{6\sigma}$$

KEY TERMS

SOLVED PROBLEM 1

The data processing department of the Arizona Bank has five data entry clerks. Each working day their supervisor verifies the accuracy of a random sample of 250 records. A record containing one or more errors is considered defective and must be redone. The results of the last 30 samples are shown in the table. All were checked to make sure that none was out of control.

Sample	Number of Defective Records	Sample	Number of Defective Records	Sample	Number of Defective Records	Sample	Number of Defective Records
1	7	9	6	17	12	24	7
2	5	10	13	18	4	25	13
3	19	11	18	19	6	26	10
4	10	12	5	20	11	27	14
5	11	13	16	21	17	28	6
6	8	14	4	22	12	29	11
7	12	15	11	23	6	30	9
8	9	16	8				
						Total	300

a. Based on these historical data, set up a p-chart using $z = 3$.

b. Samples for the next four days showed the following:

Sample	Number of Defective Records
Tues	17
Wed	15
Thurs	22
Fri	21

What is the supervisor's assessment of the data-entry process likely to be?

SOLUTION

a. From the table, the supervisor knows that the total number of defective records is 300 out of a total sample of 7,500 [or 30(250)]. Therefore, the central line of the chart is

$$\bar{p} = \frac{300}{7,500} = 0.04$$

The control limits are

$$UCL_p = \bar{p} + z\sqrt{\frac{\bar{p}(1-\bar{p})}{n}} = 0.04 + 3\sqrt{\frac{0.04(0.96)}{250}} = 0.077$$

$$LCL_p = \bar{p} - z\sqrt{\frac{\bar{p}(1-\bar{p})}{n}} = 0.04 - 3\sqrt{\frac{0.04(0.96)}{250}} = 0.003$$

b. Samples for the next four days showed the following:

Sample	Number of Defective Records	Proportion
Tues	17	0.068
Wed	15	0.060
Thurs	22	0.088
Fri	21	0.084

Samples for Thursday and Friday are out of control. The supervisor should look for the problem and, upon identifying it, take corrective action.

SOLVED PROBLEM 2

Pioneer Chicken advertises "lite" chicken with 30 percent fewer calories. (The pieces are 33 percent smaller.) The process average distribution for "lite" chicken breasts is 420 calories, with a standard deviation of the population of 25 calories. Pioneer randomly takes samples of six chicken breasts to measure calorie content.

a. Design an $\bar{x}$-chart using the process standard deviation.
b. The product design calls for the average chicken breast to contain 400 ± 100 calories. Calculate the process capability index (target = 1.33) and the process capability ratio. Interpret the results.

SOLUTION

a. For the process standard deviation of 25 calories, the standard deviation of the sample mean is

$$\sigma_{\bar{x}} = \frac{\sigma}{\sqrt{n}} = \frac{25}{\sqrt{6}} = 10.2 \text{ calories}$$

$$UCL_{\bar{x}} = \bar{\bar{x}} + z\sigma_{\bar{x}} = 420 + 3(10.2) = 450.6 \text{ calories}$$

$$LCL_{\bar{x}} = \bar{\bar{x}} - z\sigma_{\bar{x}} = 420 - 3(10.2) = 389.4 \text{ calories}$$

b. The process capability index is

$$C_{pk} = \text{Minimum of} \left[\frac{\bar{\bar{x}} - \text{Lower specification}}{3\sigma}, \frac{\text{Upper specification} - \bar{\bar{x}}}{3\sigma} \right]$$

$$= \text{Minimum of} \left[\frac{420 - 300}{3(25)} = 1.60, \frac{500 - 420}{3(25)} = 1.07 \right] = 1.07$$

The process capability ratio is

$$C_p = \frac{\text{Upper specification} - \text{Lower specification}}{6\sigma} = \frac{500 \text{ calories} - 300 \text{ calories}}{6(25)} = 1.33$$

Because the process capability ratio is 1.33, the process should be able to produce the product reliably within specifications. However, the process capability index is 1.07, so the current process is not centered properly for four-sigma performance. The mean of the process distribution is too close to the upper specification.

SOLVED PROBLEM 3

A committee is organized to evaluate safety at a large food-processing factory in Kuala Lumpur, Malaysia. The committee will review all accidents that occurred in the factory over the last five years. On average, the factory has three accidents per year.

a. Which type of control chart should be used? Construct a control chart with three-sigma control limits.

b. Last year, six accidents occurred in the factory. Is this sufficient evidence to justify a claim that the factory is becoming increasingly unsafe?

SOLUTION

a. The safety committee cannot determine the number of accidents that did not occur, so it has no way to compute a proportion defective for the factory. Therefore, the committee must use a c-chart for which

$$\text{UCL}_c = \bar{c} + z\sqrt{\bar{c}} = 3 + 3\sqrt{3} = 8.20$$

$$\text{LCL}_c = \bar{c} - z\sqrt{\bar{c}} = 3 - 3\sqrt{3} = -2.196, \text{ adjusted to } 0$$

There cannot be a negative number of accidents, so the LCL in this case is adjusted to zero.

b. The number of accidents last month falls within the UCL and LCL of the chart. We conclude that no assignable causes are present and that the increase in accidents was due to chance.

SOLVED PROBLEM 4

The Watson Electric Company produces incandescent lightbulbs. The following data on the number of lumens for 40-watt lightbulbs were collected when the process was in control.

Sample	Observation			
	1	2	3	4
1	604	612	588	600
2	597	601	607	603
3	581	570	585	592
4	620	605	595	588
5	590	614	608	604

a. Calculate control limits for an R-chart and an $\bar{x}$-chart.

b. Since these data were collected, some new employees were hired. A new sample obtained the following readings: 570, 603, 623, and 583. Is the process still in control?

SOLUTION

a. To calculate $\bar{x}$, compute the mean for each sample. To calculate R, subtract the lowest value in the sample from the highest value in the sample. For example, for sample 1,

$$\bar{x} = \frac{604 + 612 + 588 + 600}{4} = 601$$

$$R = 612 - 588 = 24$$

Sample	$\bar{x}$	R
1	601	24
2	602	10
3	582	22
4	602	32
5	604	24
Total	2,991	112
Average	$\bar{\bar{x}} = 598.2$	$\bar{R} = 22.4$

The R-chart control limits are

$$\text{UCL}_R = D_4\bar{R} = 2.282(22.4) = 51.12$$

$$\text{LCL}_R = D_3\bar{R} = 0(22.4) = 0$$

The $\bar{x}$-chart control limits are

$$\text{UCL}_{\bar{x}} = \bar{\bar{x}} + A_2\bar{R} = 598.2 + 0.729(22.4) = 614.53$$

$$\text{LCL}_{\bar{x}} = \bar{\bar{x}} - A_2\bar{R} = 598.2 - 0.729(22.4) = 581.87$$

b. First check to see whether the variability is still in control based on the new data. The range is 53 (or 623 – 570), which is outside the UCL for the R-chart. Since the process variability is out of control, it is meaningless to test for the process average using the current estimate for $\bar{R}$. A search for assignable causes inducing excessive variability must be conducted.

Discussion Questions

1. Consider Managerial Practice 5.1 and the discussion of Omega's approach to achieving top quality. To get a better idea of the detail-oriented quality control process, visit www.omegawatches.com. Omega only sells its watches through authorized retailers in order to help customers avoid replica watches. Considering the importance Omega places on quality control, why would replicated products be a problem for the company? How do replicated products affect Omega's customers?

2. Recently, the Polish General Corporation, well-known for manufacturing appliances and automobile parts, initiated a $13 billion project to produce automobiles. A great deal of learning on the part of management and employees was required. Even though pressure was mounting to get a new product to market in early 2009, the production manager of the newly formed automobile division insisted on almost a year of trial runs before sales started because workers have to do their jobs 60 to 100 times before they can memorize the right sequence. The launch date was set for early 2010. What are the consequences of using this approach to enter the market with a new product?

3. Form a group and choose a service provider or manufacturer and a functional area, such as accounting, finance, or marketing. Define a process important to that functional area and then identify a key performance measure for that process. How can SPC be used to manage that process?

Problems

Software, such as OM Explorer, Active Models, and POM for Windows, is available in my**om**lab. Check with your instructor on how best to use it. In many cases, the instructor wants you to understand how to do the calculations by hand. At most, the software provides a check on your calculations. When calculations are particularly complex and the goal is interpreting the results in making decisions, the software replaces entirely the manual calculations. The software also can be a valuable resource well after your course is completed.

1. At Isogen Pharmaceuticals, the filling process for its asthma inhaler is set to dispense 150 milliliters (ml) of steroid solution per container. The average range for a sample of 4 containers is 3 ml. Use Table 5.1 to establish control limits for sample means and ranges for the filling process.

2. Garcia's Garage desires to create some colorful charts and graphs to illustrate how reliably its mechanics "get under the hood and fix the problem." The historic average for the proportion of customers that return for the same repair within the 30-day warranty period is 0.10. Each month, Garcia tracks 100 customers to see whether they return for warranty repairs. The results are plotted as a proportion to report progress toward the goal. If the control limits are to be set at two standard deviations on either side of the goal, determine the control limits for this chart. In March, 8 of the 100 customers in the sample group returned for warranty repairs. Is the repair process in control?

3. At Quickie Car Wash, the wash process is advertised to take less than 7 minutes. Consequently, management has set a target average of 390 seconds for the wash process. Suppose the average range for a sample of 9 cars is 10 seconds. Use Table 5.1 to establish control limits for sample means and ranges for the car wash process.

4. The Marlin Company produces plastic bottles to customer order. The quality inspector randomly selects four bottles from the bottle machine and measures the outside diameter of the bottle neck, a critical quality dimension that determines whether the bottle cap will fit properly. The dimensions (in.) from the last six samples are

	Bottle			
Sample	1	2	3	4
1	0.604	0.612	0.588	0.600
2	0.597	0.601	0.607	0.603
3	0.581	0.570	0.585	0.592
4	0.620	0.605	0.595	0.588
5	0.590	0.614	0.608	0.604
6	0.585	0.583	0.617	0.579

a. Assume that only these six samples are sufficient, and use the data to determine control limits for an R- and an $\bar{x}$-chart.

b. Suppose that the specification for the bottle neck diameter is 0.600 ± 0.050 in. If the population standard deviation is 0.013 in., and the firm is seeking four-sigma quality, is the process capable of producing the bottle?

5. The Canine Gourmet Company produces delicious dog treats for canines with discriminating tastes. Management wants the box-filling line to be set so that the process average weight per packet is 45 grams. To make sure that the process is in control, an inspector at the end of the filling line periodically selects a random box of 10 packets and weighs each packet. When the process is in control, the range in the weight of each sample has averaged 6 grams.

a. Design an R- and an $\bar{x}$-chart for this process.

TABLE 5.2	TEST SCORES ON EXIT EXAM

					Student						
Year	1	2	3	4	5	6	7	8	9	10	Average
1	63	57	92	87	70	61	75	58	63	71	69.7
2	90	77	59	88	48	83	63	94	72	70	74.4
3	67	81	93	55	71	71	86	98	60	90	77.2
4	62	67	78	61	89	93	71	59	93	84	75.7
5	85	88	77	69	58	90	97	72	64	60	76.0
6	60	57	79	83	64	94	86	64	92	74	75.3
7	94	85	56	77	89	72	71	61	92	97	79.4
8	97	86	83	88	65	87	76	84	81	71	81.8
9	94	90	76	88	65	93	86	87	94	63	83.6
10	88	91	71	89	97	79	93	87	69	85	84.9

b. The results from the last 5 samples of 10 packets are

Sample	$\bar{x}$	R
1	44	9
2	40	2
3	46	5
4	39	8
5	48	3

Is the process in control? Explain.

6. As a hospital administrator of a large hospital, you are concerned with the absenteeism among nurses' aides. The issue has been raised by registered nurses, who feel they often have to perform work normally done by their aides. To get the facts, absenteeism data were gathered for the last three weeks, which is considered a representative period for future conditions. After taking random samples of 64 personnel files each day, the following data were produced:

Day	Aides Absent	Day	Aides Absent
1	4	9	7
2	3	10	2
3	2	11	3
4	4	12	2
5	2	13	1
6	5	14	3
7	3	15	4
8	4		

Because your assessment of absenteeism is likely to come under careful scrutiny, you would like a type I error of only 1 percent. You want to be sure to identify any instances of unusual absences. If some are present, you will have to explore them on behalf of the registered nurses.

a. Design a p-chart.

b. Based on your p-chart and the data from the last 3 weeks, what can you conclude about the absenteeism of nurses' aides?

7. In an attempt to judge and monitor the quality of instruction, the administration of Mega-Byte Academy devised an examination to test students on the basic concepts that all should have learned. Each year, a random sample of 10 graduating students is selected for the test. The average score is used to track the quality of the educational process. Test results for the past 10 years are shown in Table 5.2.

Use these data to estimate the center and standard deviation for this distribution. Then calculate the two-sigma control limits for the process average. What comments would you make to the administration of the Mega-Byte Academy?

8. The Big Black Bird Company produces fiberglass camper tops. The process for producing the tops must be controlled so as to keep the number of dimples low. When the process

was in control, the following defects were found in 10 randomly selected camper tops over an extended period of time:

Top	Dimples
1	7
2	9
3	14
4	11
5	3
6	12
7	8
8	4
9	7
10	6

a. Assuming 10 observations are adequate for this purpose, determine the three-sigma control limits for dimples per camper top.

b. Suppose that the next camper top has 15 dimples. What can you say about the process now?

9. Jim's Outfitters, Inc., makes custom fancy shirts for cowboys. The shirts could be flawed in various ways, including flaws in the weave or color of the fabric, loose buttons or decorations, wrong dimensions, and uneven stitches. Jim randomly examined 10 shirts, with the following results:

Shirt	Defects
1	8
2	0
3	7
4	12
5	5
6	10
7	2
8	4
9	6
10	6

a. Assuming that 10 observations are adequate for these purposes, determine the three-sigma control limits for defects per shirt.

b. Suppose that the next shirt has 13 flaws. What can you say about the process now?

10. A travel agency is concerned with the accuracy and appearance of itineraries prepared for its clients. Defects can include errors in times, airlines, flight numbers, prices, car rental information, lodging, charge card numbers, and reservation numbers, as well as typographical errors. As the possible number of errors is nearly infinite, the agency measures the number of errors that do occur. The current process results in an average of three errors per itinerary.

a. What are the two-sigma control limits for these defects?

b. A client scheduled a trip to Dallas. Her itinerary contained six errors. Interpret this information.

11. The U.S. Internal Revenue Service (IRS) is concerned with improving the accuracy of tax information given by its representatives over the telephone. Previous studies involved asking a set of 25 questions of a large number of IRS telephone representatives to determine the proportion of correct responses. Historically, the average proportion of correct responses has been 70 percent. Recently, IRS representatives have been receiving more training. On April 1, the set of 25 tax questions were again asked of 20 randomly selected IRS telephone representatives. The proportions of correct answers were 0.88, 0.76, 0.64, 1.00, 0.76, 0.76, 0.72, 0.88, 0.50, 0.50, 0.40, 1.00, 0.88, 1.00, 0.64, 0.76, 0.76, 0.88, 0.40, and 0.76. Interpret the results of that study.

12. A textile manufacturer wants to set up a control chart for irregularities (e.g., oil stains, shop soil, loose threads, and tears) per 100 square yards of carpet. The following data were collected from a sample of twenty 100-square-yard pieces of carpet:

Sample	1	2	3	4	5	6	7	8	9	10
Irregularities	11	8	9	12	4	16	5	8	17	10
Sample	11	12	13	14	15	16	17	18	19	20
Irregularities	11	5	7	12	13	8	19	11	9	10

a. Using these data, set up a c-chart with $z = 3$.

b. Suppose that the next five samples had 15, 18, 12, 22, and 21 irregularities. What do you conclude?

13. The Money Pit Mortgage Company is interested in monitoring the performance of the mortgage process. Fifteen samples of five completed mortgage transactions each were taken during a period when the process was believed to be in control. The times to complete the transactions were measured. The means and ranges of the mortgage process transaction times, measured in days, are as follows:

Sample	1	2	3	4	5	6	7	8	9	10	11	12	13	14	15
Mean	17	14	8	17	12	13	15	16	13	14	16	9	11	9	12
Range	6	11	4	8	9	14	12	15	10	10	11	6	9	11	13

Subsequently, samples of size 5 were taken from the process every week for the next 10 weeks. The times were measured and the following results obtained:

Sample	16	17	18	19	20	21	22	23	24	25
Mean	11	14	9	15	17	19	13	22	20	18
Range	7	11	6	4	12	14	11	10	8	6

a. Construct the control charts for the mean and the range, using the original 15 samples.

b. On the control charts developed in part (a), plot the values from samples 16 through 25 and comment on whether the process is in control.

c. In part (b), if you concluded that the process was out of control, would you attribute it to a drift in the mean, or an increase in the variability, or both? Explain your answer.

14. The Money Pit Mortgage Company of Problem 13 made some changes to the process and undertook a process capability study. The following data were obtained for 15 samples of size 5. Based on the individual observations, management estimated the process standard deviation to be 4.21 (days) for use in the process capability analysis. The lower and upper specification limits (in days) for the mortgage process times were 5 and 25.

Sample	1	2	3	4	5	6	7	8	9	10	11	12	13	14	15
Mean	11	12	8	16	13	12	17	16	13	14	17	9	15	14	9
Range	9	13	4	11	10	9	8	15	14	11	6	6	12	10	11

a. Calculate the process capability index and the process capability ratio values.

b. Suppose management would be happy with three-sigma performance. What conclusions is management likely to draw from the capability analysis? Can valid conclusions about the process be drawn from the analysis?

c. What remedial actions, if any, do you suggest that management take?

15. Webster Chemical Company produces mastics and caulking for the construction industry. The product is blended in large mixers and then pumped into tubes and capped. Management is concerned about whether the filling process for tubes of caulking is in statistical control. The process should be centered on eight ounces per tube. Several samples of eight tubes were taken, each tube was weighed, and the weights in Table 5.3 were obtained.

TABLE 5.3		OUNCES OF CAULKING PER TUBE					
			Tube Number				
Sample	**1**	**2**	**3**	**4**	**5**	**6**	**7**	**8**
1	7.98	8.34	8.02	7.94	8.44	7.68	7.81	8.11
2	8.33	8.22	8.08	8.51	8.41	8.28	8.09	8.16
3	7.89	7.77	7.91	8.04	8.00	7.89	7.93	8.09
4	8.24	8.18	7.83	8.05	7.90	8.16	7.97	8.07
5	7.87	8.13	7.92	7.99	8.10	7.81	8.14	7.88
6	8.13	8.14	8.11	8.13	8.14	8.12	8.13	8.14

a. Assume that only six samples are sufficient and develop the control charts for the mean and the range.

b. Plot the observations on the control chart and comment on your findings.

16. Management at Webster, in Problem 15, is now concerned as to whether caulking tubes are being properly capped. If a significant proportion of the tubes are not being sealed, Webster is placing its customers in a messy situation. Tubes are packaged in large boxes of 144. Several boxes are inspected, and the following numbers of leaking tubes are found:

Sample	Tubes	Sample	Tubes	Sample	Tubes
1	3	8	6	15	5
2	5	9	4	16	0
3	3	10	9	17	2
4	4	11	2	18	6
5	2	12	6	19	2
6	4	13	5	20	1
7	2	14	1	Total	72

Calculate p-chart three-sigma control limits to assess whether the capping process is in statistical control.

17. At Webster Chemical Company, lumps in the caulking compound could cause difficulties in dispensing a smooth bead from the tube. Even when the process is in control, an average of four lumps per tube of caulk will remain. Testing for the presence of lumps destroys the product, so an analyst takes random samples. The following results are obtained:

Tube No.	Lumps	Tube No.	Lumps	Tube No.	Lumps
1	6	5	6	9	5
2	5	6	4	10	0
3	0	7	1	11	9
4	4	8	6	12	2

Determine the c-chart two-sigma upper and lower control limits for this process. Is the process in statistical control?

18. The production manager at Sunny Soda, Inc., is interested in tracking the quality of the company's 12-ounce bottle filling line. The bottles must be filled within the tolerances set for this product because the dietary information on the label shows 12 ounces as the serving size. The design standard for the product calls for a fill level of 12.00 ± 0.10 ounces. The manager collected the following sample data (in fluid ounces per bottle) on the production process:

Sample	Observation 1	2	3	4
1	12.00	11.97	12.10	12.08
2	11.91	11.94	12.10	11.96
3	11.89	12.02	11.97	11.99
4	12.10	12.09	12.05	11.95
5	12.08	11.92	12.12	12.05
6	11.94	11.98	12.06	12.08
7	12.09	12.00	12.00	12.03
8	12.01	12.04	11.99	11.95
9	12.00	11.96	11.97	12.03
10	11.92	11.94	12.09	12.00
11	11.91	11.99	12.05	12.10
12	12.01	12.00	12.06	11.97
13	11.98	11.99	12.06	12.03
14	12.02	12.00	12.05	11.95
15	12.00	12.05	12.01	11.97

a. Are the process average and range in statistical control?

b. Is the process capable of meeting the design standard at four-sigma quality? Explain.

19. Representatives of the Franklin Insurance Company take medical information over the phone from prospective policy applicants prior to a visit to the applicant's place of residence by a registered nurse who takes vital sign measurements. When the phone interview has incorrect or incomplete information, the entire process of approving the application is unnecessarily delayed and has the potential of causing loss of business. The following data were collected to see how many applications contain errors. Each sample has 300 randomly selected applications.

Sample	Defects	Sample	Defects
1	18	16	13
2	15	17	17
3	18	18	17
4	6	19	21
5	20	20	18
6	16	21	16
7	16	22	14
8	19	23	33
9	20	24	46
10	16	25	10
11	10	26	12
12	14	27	13
13	21	28	18
14	13	29	19
15	13	30	14

a. Construct a *p*-chart for the number of defective applications.

b. Is the process in statistical control? Explain.

20. Janice Sanders, CEO of Pine Crest Medical Clinic, is concerned over the number of times patients must wait more than 30 minutes beyond their scheduled appointments. She asked her assistant to take random samples of 64 patients to see how many in each sample had to wait more than 30 minutes. Each instance is considered a defect in the clinic process. The table below contains the data for 15 samples.

Sample	Number of Defects
1	5
2	2
3	1
4	3
5	1
6	5
7	2
8	3
9	6
10	3
11	9
12	9
13	5
14	2
15	3

a. Assuming Janice Sanders is willing to use three-sigma control limits, construct a *p*-chart.

b. Based on your *p*-chart and the data in the table, what can you conclude about the waiting time of the patients?

21. An automatic lathe produces rollers for roller bearings, and the process is monitored by statistical process control charts. The central line of the chart for the sample means is set at 8.50 and for the mean range at 0.31 mm. The process is in control, as established by samples of size 5. The upper and lower specifications for the diameter of the rollers are (8.50 + 0.25) and (8.50 − 0.25) mm, respectively.

a. Calculate the control limits for the mean and range charts.

b. If the standard deviation of the process distribution is estimated to be 0.13 mm, is the process capable of meeting specifications? Assume four-sigma quality.

c. If the process is not capable, what percent of the output will fall outside the specification limits? (*Hint:* Use the normal distribution.)

22. A critical dimension of the service quality of a call center is the wait time of a caller to get to a sales representative. Periodically, random samples of three customer calls are measured for time. The results of the last four samples are in the following table:

Sample	Time (sec)		
1	495	501	498
2	512	508	504
3	505	497	501
4	496	503	492

a. Assuming that management is willing to use three-sigma control limits, and using only the historical information contained in the four samples, show that the call center access time is in statistical control.

b. Suppose that the standard deviation of the process distribution is 5.77. If the specifications for the access time are 500 ± 18 sec., is the process capable? Why or why not? Assume three-sigma quality.

23. The Farley Manufacturing Company prides itself on the quality of its products. The company is engaged in competition for a very important project. A key element is a part that ultimately goes into precision testing equipment. The specifications are 8.000 ± 3.000 millimeters. Management is concerned about the capability of the process to produce that part. The following data (shown below) were randomly collected during test runs of the process:

Sample	1	2	3	4	5	6	7	8
				Observation (millimeters)				
1	9.100	8.900	8.800	9.200	8.100	6.900	9.300	9.100
2	7.600	8.000	9.000	10.100	7.900	9.000	8.000	8.800
3	8.200	9.100	8.200	8.700	9.000	7.000	8.800	10.800
4	8.200	8.300	7.900	7.500	8.900	7.800	10.100	7.700
5	10.000	8.100	8.900	9.000	9.300	9.000	8.700	10.000

Assume that the process is in statistical control. Is the process capable of producing the part at the three-sigma level? Explain.

24. The Digi-Secure Company issues policies that protect clients from downtime costs due to computer system failures. It is very important to process the policies quickly because long cycle times not only put the client at risk, they could also lose business for Digi-Secure. Management is concerned that customer service is degrading because of long cycle times. The following table contains the data from five samples, each sample consisting of eight observations.

Observation								
Sample	1	2	3	4	5	6	7	8
1	11	7	6	10	6	13	10	8
2	9	13	10	8	12	12	12	13
3	10	9	6	9	10	10	11	13
4	10	9	10	11	9	10	10	10
5	10	10	8	10	9	7	10	10

a. What is your estimate of the process average?

b. What is your estimate of the average range?

c. Are assignable causes present in this process? Explain.

ADVANCED PROBLEMS

25. The manager of the customer service department of Omega Credit Card Service Company is concerned about the number of defects produced by the billing process. Every day a random sample of 250 statements was inspected for errors regarding incorrect entries involving account numbers, transactions on the customer's account, interest charges, and penalty charges. Any statement with one or more of these errors was considered a defect. The study lasted 30 days and yielded the data in Table 5.5. Based on the data, what can you tell the manager about the performance of the billing process? Do you see any nonrandom behavior in the billing process? If so, what might cause this behavior?

26. The Precision Machining Company makes hand-held tools on an assembly line that produces one product every minute. On one of the products, the critical quality dimension is the diameter (measured in thousandths of an inch) of a hole bored in one of the assemblies. Management wants to detect any shift in the process average diameter from 0.015 in. Management considers the variance in the process to be in control. Historically, the average range has been 0.002 in., regardless of the process average. Design an $\bar{x}$-chart to control this process, with a center line at 0.015 in. and the control limits set at three sigmas from the center line.

Management provided the results of 80 minutes of output from the production line, as shown in Table 5.4. During these 80 minutes, the process average changed once. All measurements are in thousandths of an inch.

a. Set up an $\bar{x}$-chart with $n = 4$. The frequency should be sample four and then skip four. Thus, your first sample would be for minutes 1–4, the second would be for minutes 9–12, and so on. When would you stop the process to check for a change in the process average?

b. Set up an $\bar{x}$-chart with $n = 8$. The frequency should be sample eight and then skip four. When would you stop the process now? What can you say about the desirability of large samples on a frequent sampling interval?

27. Using the data from Problem 26, continue your analysis of sample size and frequency by trying the following plans.

a. Using the $\bar{x}$-chart for $n = 4$, try the frequency sample four, then skip eight. When would you stop the process in this case?

b. Using the $\bar{x}$-chart for $n = 8$, try the frequency sample eight, then skip eight. When would you consider the process to be out of control?

c. Using your results from parts (a) and (b), determine what trade-offs you would consider in choosing between them.

28. Canine Gourmet Super Breath dog treats are sold in boxes labeled with a net weight of 12 ounces (340 grams) per box. Each box contains 8 individual 1.5-ounce packets. To reduce the chances of shorting the customer, product design specifications call for the packet-filling process average to be set at 43.5 grams so that the average net weight per box of 8 packets will be 348 grams. Tolerances are set for the box to weigh 348 ± 12 grams. The standard deviation for the *packet-filling* process is 1.01 grams. The target process capability ratio is 1.33.

TABLE 5.4	SAMPLE DATA FOR PRECISION MACHINING COMPANY

Minutes	Diameter (thousandths of an inch)											
1–12	15	16	18	14	16	17	15	14	14	13	16	17
13–24	15	16	17	16	14	14	13	14	15	16	15	17
25–36	14	13	15	17	18	15	16	15	14	15	16	17
37–48	18	16	15	16	16	14	17	18	19	15	16	15
49–60	12	17	16	14	15	17	14	16	15	17	18	14
61–72	15	16	17	18	13	15	14	14	16	15	17	18
73–80	16	16	17	18	16	15	14	17				

TABLE 5.5 | SAMPLE DATA FOR OMEGA CREDIT CARD SERVICE

Samples	Number of Errors in Sample of 250									
1–10	4	9	6	12	8	2	13	10	1	9
11–20	4	6	8	10	12	4	3	10	14	5
21–30	13	11	7	3	2	8	11	6	9	5

One day, the packet-filling process average weight drifts down to 43.0 grams. Is the packaging process capable? Is an adjustment needed?

29. Beaver Brothers, Inc., is conducting a study to assess the capability of its 150-gram bar soap production line. A critical quality measure is the weight of the soap bars after stamping. The upper and lower specification limits are 162 and 170 grams, respectively. As a part of an initial capability study, 25 samples of size 5 were collected by the quality assurance group and the observations in Table 5.6 were recorded.

After analyzing the data by using statistical control charts, the quality assurance group calculated the process capability ratio, C_p, and the process capability index, C_{pk}. It then decided to improve the stamping process, especially the feeder mechanism. After making

TABLE 5.6 | SAMPLE DATA FOR BEAVER BROTHERS, INC.

Sample	OBS.1	OBS.2	OBS.3	OBS.4	OBS.5
1	167.0	159.6	161.6	164.0	165.3
2	156.2	159.5	161.7	164.0	165.3
3	167.0	162.9	162.9	164.0	165.4
4	167.0	159.6	163.7	164.1	165.4
5	156.3	160.0	162.9	164.1	165.5
6	164.0	164.2	163.0	164.2	163.9
7	161.3	163.0	164.2	157.0	160.6
8	163.1	164.2	156.9	160.1	163.1
9	164.3	157.0	161.2	163.2	164.4
10	156.9	161.0	163.2	164.3	157.3
11	161.0	163.3	164.4	157.6	160.6
12	163.3	164.5	158.4	160.1	163.3
13	158.2	161.3	163.5	164.6	158.7
14	161.5	163.5	164.7	158.6	162.5
15	163.6	164.8	158.0	162.4	163.6
16	164.5	158.5	160.3	163.4	164.6
17	164.9	157.9	162.3	163.7	165.1
18	155.0	162.2	163.7	164.8	159.6
19	162.1	163.9	165.1	159.3	162.0
20	165.2	159.1	161.6	163.9	165.2
21	164.9	165.1	159.9	162.0	163.7
22	167.6	165.6	165.6	156.7	165.7
23	167.7	165.8	165.9	156.9	165.9
24	166.0	166.0	165.6	165.6	165.5
25	163.7	163.7	165.6	165.6	166.2

all the changes that were deemed necessary, 18 additional samples were collected. The summary data for these samples are

$$\bar{\bar{x}} = 163 \text{ grams}$$

$$\bar{R} = 2.326 \text{ grams}$$

$$\sigma = 1 \text{ gram}$$

All sample observations were within the control chart limits. With the new data, the quality assurance group recalculated the process capability measures. It was pleased with the improved C_p but felt that the process should be centered at 166 grams to ensure that everything was in order. Its decision concluded the study.

a. Draw the control charts for the data obtained in the initial study and verify that the process was in statistical control.

b. What were the values obtained by the group for C_p and C_{pk} for the initial capability study? Comment on your findings and explain why further improvements were necessary.

c. What are the C_p and C_{pk} after the improvements? Comment on your findings, indicating why the group decided to change the centering of the process.

d. What are the C_p and C_{pk} if the process were centered at 166? Comment on your findings.

30. Red Baron Airlines serves hundreds of cities each day, but competition is increasing from smaller companies affiliated with major carriers. One of the key competitive priorities is on-time arrivals and departures. Red Baron defines *on time* as any arrival or departure that takes place within 15 minutes of the scheduled time. To stay on top of the market, management set the high standard of 98 percent on-time performance. The operations department was put in charge of monitoring the performance of the airline. Each week, a random sample of 300 flight arrivals and departures was checked for schedule performance. Table 5.7 contains the numbers of arrivals and departures over the last 30 weeks that did not meet Red Baron's definition of on-time service. What can you tell management about the quality of service? Can you identify any nonrandom behavior in the process? If so, what might cause the behavior?

TABLE 5.7	SAMPLE DATA FOR RED BARON AIRLINES								
Samples	**Number of Late Planes in Sample of 300 Arrivals and Departures**								
1–10	3	8	5	11	7	2	12	9	1	8
11–20	3	5	7	9	12	5	4	9	13	4
21–30	12	10	6	2	1	8	4	5	8	2

ACTIVE MODEL EXERCISE

This Active Model appears in my**om**Lab. It allows you to see the effects of sample size and z-values on control charts.

QUESTIONS

1. Has the booking process been in statistical control?

2. Suppose we use a 95 percent p-chart. How do the upper and lower control limits change? What are your conclusions about the booking process?

3. Suppose that the sample size is reduced to 2,000 instead of 2,500. How does this affect the chart?

4. What happens to the chart as we reduce the z-value?

5. What happens to the chart as we reduce the confidence level?

p-Chart

Reset Data	Questions

Number of samples	12
Sample size	2500 ◄ ▯ ►
z value	3.0000 ◄ ▯ ►
Confidence	99.73% ◄ ▯ ►

Total Sample Size	30000	Upper Control Limit	0.0091
Total Defects	147	Center Line	0.0049
Percentage defects	0.0049	Lower Control Limit	0.0007
Std dev of *p*-bar	0.0014		

	# Defects	Fraction Defective
Sample 1	15	0.0060
Sample 2	12	0.0048
Sample 3	19	0.0076
Sample 4	2	0.0008
Sample 5	19	0.0076
Sample 6	4	0.0016
Sample 7	24	0.0096 Above UCL
Sample 8	7	0.0028
Sample 9	10	0.0040
Sample 10	17	0.0068
Sample 11	15	0.0060
Sample 12	3	0.0012

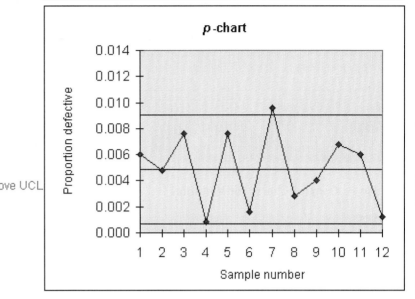

p-Chart Using Data from Example 5.3

VIDEO CASE	Process Performance and Quality at Starwood Hotels & Resorts

Starwood Hotels & Resorts is no stranger to quality measurement. In the most recent year, Starwood properties around the globe held 51 of approximately 700 spots on Condé Nast's Gold List of the world's best places to stay. Its spa and golf programs have consistently been ranked among the best in the world.

At Starwood, processes and programs are driven by the work of its team of Six Sigma experts, called Black Belts. Developed by Motorola more than 20 years ago, Six Sigma is a comprehensive and flexible system for achieving, sustaining, and maximizing business success by driving out defects and variability in a process. Starwood uses the five-step DMAIC process: define, measure, analyze, improve, and control.

Clearly, understanding customer needs is paramount. To this end, Starwood collects data from customers on its Guest Satisfaction Index survey, called the "Voice of the Customer." The survey covers every department guests may have encountered during their stay, from the front desk and hotel room, to restaurants and concierge. Past surveys indicated that how well problems were resolved during the guest stay was a key driver in high guest satisfaction scores. To increase its scores for problem resolution, the Sheraton brand of Starwood launched the Sheraton Service Promise program in the United States and Canada. The program was designed to give guests a single point of contact for reporting any problems. It was intended to focus associate (employee) attention on taking care of service issues during the guest's stay within 15 minutes of first receiving notice.

However, although scores did increase, they did not increase by enough. Consequently, Sheraton brought in its Six Sigma team to see what it could do. The team employed the basic Six Sigma model of define-measure-analyze-improve-control to guide its work. To define the problem, the Six Sigma team worked with data collected and analyzed by an independent survey organization, National Family Opinion. The study indicated that three key factors are needed in problem resolution: speed, empathy, and efficiency. All three must be met in order for the guests to be satisfied and the Sheraton Service Promise fulfilled. Then the team looked at the specific processes that affected performance: telephone operators' handling of requests, procedures for determining who to call, engineering workloads, and so on. The work identified in each area was measured. For example, call logs were established to track speed, empathy of associate handling the call, and efficiency of the staff charged with fixing the problem. The data collected were analyzed to determine why guests' problems were not resolved within the 15-minute standard. Pareto charts and other techniques were used for the analysis.

The final step involved control and monitoring to be sure that the improved processes developed by the Six Sigma team became part of the property's culture, and that they were not abandoned after the team's work was finished. Tracking continues for 12 to 18 months, with monthly feedback to the manager or department head responsible for the improvement of the Sheraton Service Promise program. The improvement effort also receives visibility through the company's intranet so the rest of the organization sees the benefits—including service levels and financial performance—and can use the experience to improve their own operations.

QUESTIONS

1. Implementing Six Sigma programs takes considerable time and commitment from an organization. In terms of top-down commitment, measurement systems to track progress, tough goal setting, education, communication, and customer priorities, evaluate the degree to which Starwood successfully addressed each with the redesign of the Sheraton Service Promise program.

2. How might the new Sheraton Service Promise process help Starwood avoid the four costs of poor process performance and quality (prevention, appraisal, internal failure, and external failure)?

3. Starwood is the first major hotel brand to commit to a dedicated Six Sigma program for improving quality. Why might an organization be reluctant to follow this type of formalized methodology? What other approaches could Starwood or its competitors use?

EXPERIENTIAL LEARNING   Statistical Process Control with a Coin Catapult

Exercise A: Control Charts for Variables

Materials

1 ruler
1 pen or pencil
1 coin (a quarter will do nicely)
1 yardstick
An exercise worksheet
Access to a calculator

Tasks

Divide into teams of two to four. If four people are on a team,

one person holds the yardstick and observes the action,

one person adjusts the catapult and launches the coin,

one person observes the maximum height for each trial, and

one person records the results.

If teams of fewer than four are formed, provide a support for the yardstick and combine the other tasks as appropriate.

Practice

To catapult the coin, put a pen or pencil under the 6-in. mark of the ruler. Put the coin over the 11-in. mark. Press both ends of the ruler down as far as they will go. Let the end that holds the coin snap up, catapulting the coin into the air. The person holding the yardstick should place the stick so that it is adjacent to, but does not interfere with, the trajectory of the coin. To observe the maximum height reached by the coin, the observer should stand back with his or her eye at about the same level as the top of the coin's trajectory. Practice until each person is comfortable with his or her role. The person operating the catapult should be sure that the pen or pencil fulcrum has not moved between shots and that the launch is done as consistently as possible.

Step 1: *Gather data.* Take four samples of five observations (launches) each. Record the maximum height reached by the coin in the first data table on the worksheet. When you have finished, determine the mean and range for each sample, and compute the mean of the means $\bar{\bar{x}}$ and the mean of the ranges $\bar{R}$.

Step 2: *Develop an R-chart.* Using the data gathered and the appropriate D_3 and D_4 values, compute the upper and lower three-sigma control limits for the range. Enter these values and plot the range for each of the four samples on the range chart on the worksheet. Be sure to indicate an appropriate scale for range on the y-axis.

Step 3: *Develop an $\bar{x}$-chart.* Now, using the data gathered and the appropriate value for A_2, compute the upper and lower three-sigma control limits for the sample means. Enter these values and plot the mean for each of the four samples on the $\bar{x}$-chart on the worksheet. Again, indicate an appropriate scale for the y-axis.

Step 4: *Observe the process.* Once a control chart has been established for a process, it is used to monitor the process and to identify when it is not running "normally." Collect two more samples of five trials each, as you did to collect the first set of data. Plot the range and the sample mean on the charts you constructed on the worksheet each time you collect a sample. What have you observed that affects the process? Does the chart indicate that the process is operating the way it did when you first collected data?

Step 5: *Observe a changed process.* Now change something (for instance, move the pencil out to the 8-in. mark). Collect data for samples 7 and 8. Plot the range and the sample mean on the charts you constructed on the worksheet as you complete each sample. Can you detect a change in the process from your control chart? If the process has changed, how sure are you that this change is real and not just due to the particular sample you chose?

Exercise B: Control Charts for Attributes

Materials

1 ruler
1 pen or pencil
1 coin (a quarter will do nicely)
1 paper or plastic cup (with a 4-in. mouth)
An exercise worksheet
Access to a calculator

Tasks

Divide into teams of two or three. If three people are on a team,

one person adjusts the catapult and launches the coin,

one person observes the results and fetches the coin, and

one person records the results.

If teams of two are formed, combine the tasks as appropriate.

Practice

The object is to flip a coin into a cup using a ruler. To catapult the coin, put a pen or pencil under the 6-in. mark of the ruler.

Put a coin over the 11-in. mark and let its weight hold that end of the ruler on the tabletop. Strike the raised end of the ruler with your hand to flip the coin into the air. Position a cup at the place where the coin lands so that on the next flip, the coin will land inside. You will have to practice several times until you find out how hard to hit the ruler and the best position for the cup. Be sure that the pen or pencil fulcrum has not moved between shots and that the launch is done as consistently as possible.

Step 1: *Gather data.* Try to catapult the coin into the cup 10 times for each sample. Record each trial in the data table on the worksheet as a hit (H) when the coin lands inside or a miss (M) when it does not. The proportion of misses will be the number of misses divided by the sample size, *n*, in this case 10. A miss is a "defect," so the proportion of misses is the proportion defective, *p*.

Step 2: *Develop a p-chart.* Compute the upper and lower three-sigma control limits for the average fraction defective. Plot these values and the mean for each of the four samples on the *p*-chart on the worksheet.

Step 3: *Observe the process.* Once a chart has been established for a process, it is used to monitor the process and to identify abnormal behavior. Exchange tasks so that someone else is catapulting the coin. After several practice launches, take four more samples of 10. Plot the proportion defective for this person's output. Is the process still in control? If it is not, how sure are you that it is out of control? Can you determine the control limits for a 95 percent confidence level? With these limits, was your revised process still in control?

Source: The basis for Exercise A was written by J. Christopher Sandvig, Western Washington University, as a variation of the "Catapulting Coins" exercise from *Games and Exercises for Operations Management* by Janelle Heinke and Larry Meile (Prentice Hall, 1995). Given these foundations, Larry Meile of Boston College wrote Exercise A. He also wrote Exercise B as a new extension.

SELECTED REFERENCES

Besterfield, Dale. *Quality Control*, 6th ed. Upper Saddle River, NJ: Prentice Hall, 2001.

Brady, Diane. "Will Jeff Immelt's New Push Pay Off for GE?" *Business Week* (October 13, 2003), pp. 94–98.

Brown, Ed. "The Best Business Hotels." *Fortune* (March 17, 1997), pp. 204–205.

Collier, David A. *The Service Quality Solution*. New York: Irwin Professional Publishing; Milwaukee: ASQC Quality Press, 1994.

Crosby, Philip B. *Quality Is Free: The Art of Making Quality Certain*. New York: McGraw-Hill, 1979.

Deming, W. Edwards. *Out of the Crisis*. Cambridge, MA: Massachusetts Institute of Technology Center for Advanced Engineering Study, 1986.

Denton, D. Keith. "Lessons on Competitiveness: Motorola's Approach." *Production and Inventory Management Journal* (Third Quarter 1991), pp. 22–25.

Duncan, Acheson J. *Quality Control and Industrial Statistics*, 5th ed. Homewood, IL: Irwin, 1986.

Feigenbaum, A.V. *Total Quality Control: Engineering and Management*, 3d ed. New York: McGraw-Hill, 1983.

Hartvigsen, David. *SimQuick: Process Simulation with Excel*, 2d ed. Upper Saddle River, NJ: Prentice Hall, 2004.

Juran, J. M., and Frank Gryna, Jr. *Quality Planning and Analysis*, 2d ed. New York: McGraw-Hill, 1980.

Kalinosky, Ian S. "The Total Quality System—Going Beyond ISO 9000." *Quality Progress* (June 1990), pp. 50–53.

Katzenbach, Jon R., and Douglas K. Smith. "The Discipline of Teams." *Harvard Business Review* (March–April 1993), pp. 111–120.

Kerwin, Kathleen. "When Flawless Isn't Enough." *Business Week* (December 8, 2003), pp. 80–82.

Lazarus, Ian R., and Keith Butler. "The Promise of Six Sigma." *Managed Healthcare Executive* (October 2001), pp. 22–26.

Lucier, Gregory T., and Sridhar Seshadri. "GE Takes Six Sigma Beyond the Bottom Line." *Strategic Finance* (May 2001), pp. 41–46.

Miller, Bill. "ISO 9000 and the Small Company: Can I Afford It?" *APICS—The Performance Advantage* (September 1994), pp. 45–46.

Mitra, Amitava. *Fundamentals of Quality Control and Improvement*, 2d ed. Upper Saddle River, NJ: Prentice Hall, 1998.

Nakhai, Benham, and Joao S. Neves. "The Deming, Baldrige, and European Quality Awards." *Quality Progress* (April 1994), pp. 33–37.

Neves, Joao S., and Benham Nakhai. "The Evolution of the Baldrige Award." *Quality Progress* (June 1994), pp. 65–70.

Pande, Peter S., Robert P. Neuman, and Roland R. Cavanagh. *The Six Sigma Way*. New York: McGraw-Hill, 2000.

Rabbitt, John T., and Peter A. Bergh. *The ISO 9000 Book*. White Plains, NY: Quality Resources, 1993.

Roth, Daniel. "Motorola Lives!" *Fortune* (September 27, 1999), pp. 305–306.

Rust, Roland T., Timothy Keiningham, Stephen Clemens, and Anthony Zahorik. "Return on Quality at Chase Manhattan Bank." *Interfaces*, vol. 29, no. 2 (March–April 1999), pp. 62–72.

Sanders, Lisa. "Going Green with Less Red Tape." *Business Week* (September 23, 1996), pp. 75–76.

Schwarz, Anne. "Listening to the Voice of the Customer Is the Key to QVC's Success." *Journal of Organizational Excellence* (Winter 2004), pp. 3–11.

Sester, Dennis. "Motorola: A Tradition of Quality." *Quality* (October 2001), pp. 30–34.

Sullivan, Lawrence P. "The Power of Taguchi Methods." *Quality Progress*, vol. 20, no. 6 (1987), pp. 76–79.

6 PLANNING CAPACITY

A model displays the new Sharp Corp.'s Aquos liquid-crystal display TVs during a news conference in Tokyo. The new flat-panel TVs, available with 20, 26, 32 and 37-inch screens, are called "Kameyama models," made at a newly built 150 billion yen (US$1.3 billion; euro1 billion) plant in Kameyama, Mie Prefecture, central Japan, which makes top-notch panels for flat-panel TVs called "eighth-generation" to meet surging demand in bigger but slimmer TVs.

SHARP CORPORATION

Sharp Corporation, founded in 1912 in Japan, is a global manufacturer and distributor of consumer and information products such as LCD TVs and projectors, DVD recorders, mobile communication handsets, point-of-sale systems, home appliances such as refrigerators and microwave ovens, and electronic components such as flash memories, LCD panels, and optical sensors, among others. It has manufacturing, sales, and R&D presence in 25 different countries and regions of the world. For production of its large size LCDs needed in television sets, Sharp increased the capacity of its Kameyama No. 2 plant in Japan from 15,000 LCD sheets per month in August 2006 to 30,000 LCD sheets per month during the second phase in January 2007. Capacity enhancements in the third phase (July 2007) were 60,000 LCD sheets per month, which were planned to be increased by 150 percent to 90,000 LCD sheets per month by July 2008.

Is such a rapid expansion of over 600 percent in long-term capacity in less than two years a good idea? Opinions vary. Even though Sharp had thrived in recent years due to its LCD business, the decision to expand was made because production capacity had reached its limit and Sharp was unable to meet its market demand. As a result, Sharp had been overtaken in global LCD television sales, and its share in the second quarter of 2006 was only 10.8 percent, fourth behind Sony, Samsung, and Philips Electronics. However, the competition did not stay idle even as Sharp quickly expanded its capacity for LCD sheets. A joint company of Sony and Samsung planned for opening a new plant in autumn

LEARNING GOALS

After reading this chapter, you should be able to:

1. Define capacity and utilization.
2. Describe economies and diseconomies of scale.
3. Identify a systematic approach to capacity planning.
4. Identify capacity gaps.
5. Describe how waiting-line models, simulation, and decision trees assist capacity decisions.

of 2007 that would have same capacity as Sharp's Kameyama plant. Critics fear that if all three major players continue to add capacity faster than the rate at which the market can grow, it will lead to a mature industry with too much capacity and too little profitability.

Sharp is meanwhile betting that costs for flat panel LCDs will decline rapidly due to mass production, a strategy that it is also using to increase the capacity of thin-film type solar cells at the Katsuragi plant that can support electricity generation output from 15 MW per year to 160 MW per year. Sharp is also hoping that large capacity investments in LCD sheets will help enhance its leadership position in the LCD industry well into the future, even though it may come at the expense of lowered profitability for the entire industry.

Source: William Trent, "LCD Producers Continue To Add Too Much Capacity As They Battle for Market Share," http://seekingalpha.com/article/19038-lcd-producers-continue-to-add-too-much-capacity-as-they-battle-for-market-share, October 2006; http://www.sharp-world.com/corporate/info/ci/g_organization/index.html, and http://www.sharp-world.com/corporate/ir/event/policy_meeting/pdf/shar080108e_1.pdf, July 2008.

myomlab and the Companion Website at **www.pearsonglobaleditions.com/krajewski** contain many tools, activities, and resources designed for this chapter.

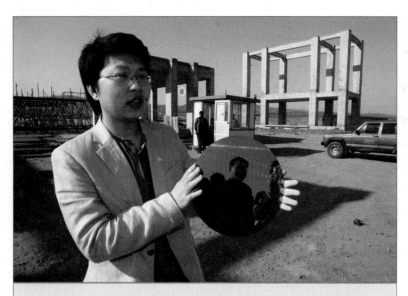

An Intel staff member shows a 12-inch (300-millimetre)wafer at the earmarked land for Intel Corp.'s new plant in Dalian in northeast China's Liaoning province on Tuesday March 27, 2007. Intel plans to invest $2.5 billion on the new wafer fabrication plant in China, which would have a monthly capacity of 52,000 chips.

capacity

The maximum rate of output of a process or a system.

COMPETING WITH OPERATIONS

Using Operations to Compete
Managing Effective Projects

DESIGNING AND
MANAGING PROCESSES

Developing a Process Strategy
Analyzing Processes
Managing Quality
Planning Capacity
Managing Process Constraints
Designing Lean Systems

DESIGNING AND
MANAGING SUPPLY CHAINS

Designing Effective Supply Chains
Integrating the Supply Chain
Locating Facilities
Managing Inventories
Forecasting Demand
Planning and Scheduling Operations
Planning Sufficient Resources

Capacity is the maximum rate of output of a process or a system. Managers are responsible for ensuring that the firm has the capacity to meet current and future demand. Otherwise, the organization will miss out on opportunities for growth and profits. Making adjustments to decrease capacity, or to overcome capacity shortfalls as Sharp Corporation did when trailing its nearest competitors for LCD TVs, is therefore an important part of the job. Acquisition of new capacity requires extensive planning, and often involves significant expenditure of resources and time. Bringing new capacity online can take several years, for instance in the semiconductor industry or in the construction of new nuclear power plants.

Capacity decisions related to a process need to be made in light of the role the process plays within the organization and the supply chain as a whole, because changing the capacity of a process will have an impact on other processes in the chain. Increasing or decreasing capacity by itself is not as important as ensuring that the entire supply chain, from order entry to delivery, is designed for effectiveness. Capacity decisions must be made in light of several long-term issues such as the firm's economies and diseconomies of scale, capacity cushions, timing and sizing strategies, and trade-offs between customer service and capacity utilization.

This chapter focuses on how managers can best revise capacity levels and best determine when to add or reduce capacity for the long term. The type of capacity decisions differ for different time horizons. Both long-term as well as short-term issues associated with planning capacity and managing constraints are important, and must be understood in conjunction with one another. While we deal here with the long-term decisions shown below in the capacity management framework, short-term decisions centered on making the most of existing capacity by managing constraints are more fully explored in Chapter 7, "Managing Process Constraints."

PLANNING CAPACITY ACROSS THE ORGANIZATION

Capacity decisions have implications for different functional areas throughout the organization. Accounting needs to provide the cost information needed to evaluate capacity expansion decisions. Finance performs the financial analysis of proposed capacity expansion investments and raises funds to support them. Marketing provides demand forecasts needed to identify capacity gaps. Management information systems designs the electronic infrastructure that is needed to make data such as cost information, financial performance measures, demand forecasts, and work standards available to those needing it to analyze capacity options. Operations is involved in the selection of capacity strategies that can be implemented to effectively meet future demand. Purchasing facilitates acquisition of outside capacity from suppliers. Finally, human resources focuses on hiring and training employees needed to support internal capacity plans. So all departments in a firm get involved with and are affected by long-term capacity planning decisions.

PLANNING LONG-TERM CAPACITY

Long-term capacity plans deal with investments in new facilities and equipment at the organizational level, and require top management participation and approval because they are not easily reversed. These plans cover at least two years into the future, but construction lead times can sometimes be longer and result in longer planning time horizons.

As already seen in our opening vignette, long-term capacity planning is central to the success of an organization. Too much capacity can be as agonizing as too little. Often entire industries can fluctuate over time between too much and too little capacity, as evidenced in the airline and cruise ship industry over the past 20 years. When choosing a capacity strategy, managers must consider questions such as the following: How much of a cushion is needed to handle variable, or uncertain, demand? Should we expand capacity ahead of demand, or wait until demand is more certain? Even before these questions can be answered, a manager needs to be able to measure a process's capacity. So a systematic approach is needed to answer these and similar questions and to develop a capacity strategy appropriate for each situation.

Measures of Capacity and Utilization

No single capacity measure is best for all situations. A retailer measures capacity as annual sales dollars generated per square foot, whereas an airline measures capacity as available seat-miles (ASMs) per month. A theater measures capacity as number of seats, while a job shop measures capacity as number of machine hours. In general, capacity can be expressed in one of two ways: in terms of output measures or input measures.

Output Measures of Capacity *Output measures* of capacity are best utilized when applied to individual processes within the firm, or when the firm provides a relatively small number of standardized services and products. High-volume processes, such as those in a car manufacturing plant, are a good example. In this case, capacity would be measured in terms of the number of cars produced per day. However, many processes produce more than one service or product. As the amount of customization and variety in the product mix increases, output-based capacity measures become less useful. Then input measures of capacity become the usual choice for measuring capacity.

Input Measures of Capacity *Input measures* are generally used for low-volume, flexible processes, such as those associated with a custom furniture maker. In this case, the furniture maker might measure capacity in terms of inputs such as number of workstations or number of workers. The problem with input measures is that demand is invariably expressed as an output rate. If the furniture maker wants to keep up with demand, he or she must convert the business's annual demand for furniture into labor hours and number of employees required to fulfill those hours. We will explain precisely how this input–output conversion is done later in the chapter.

Utilization   **Utilization** is the degree to which a resource such as equipment, space, or the workforce is currently being used, and is measured as the ratio of average output rate to maximum capacity (expressed as a percent). The average output rate and the capacity must be measured in the same terms—that is, time, customers, units, or dollars. The utilization rate indicates the need for adding extra capacity or eliminating unneeded capacity.

$$\text{Utilization} = \frac{\text{Average output rate}}{\text{Maximum capacity}} \times 100\%$$

utilization

The degree to which equipment, space, or the workforce is currently being used, and is measured as the ratio of average output rate to maximum capacity (expressed as a percent).

Here we refer to maximum capacity as the greatest level of output that a process can reasonably sustain for a longer period, using realistic employee work schedules and the equipment currently in place. In some processes, this capacity level implies a one-shift operation; in others, it implies a three-shift operation. A process can be operated above its capacity level using marginal methods of production, such as overtime, extra shifts, temporarily reduced maintenance activities, overstaffing, and subcontracting. Although they help with temporary peaks, these options cannot be sustained for long. For instance, being able to handle 40 customers for a one-week peak is quite different from sustaining it for six months. Employees do not want to work excessive overtime for extended periods, so quality drops. In addition, the costs associated with overtime drive up the firm's costs. So operating processes close to (or even temporarily above) their maximum capacity can result in low customer satisfaction, minimal profits, and even losing money despite high sales levels. Such was the case with U.S. aircraft manufacturers in the late 1980s, which culminated in Boeing acquiring McDonnell Douglas in 1997 in order to shore up skyrocketing costs and plummeting profits.

Economies of Scale

Deciding on the best level of capacity involves consideration for the efficiency of the operations. A concept known as **economies of scale** states that the average unit cost of a service or good can be reduced by increasing its output rate. Four principal reasons explain why economies of scale can drive costs down when output increases: (1) Fixed costs are spread over more units; (2) construction costs are reduced; (3) costs of purchased materials are cut; and (4) process advantages are found.

economies of scale

A concept that states that the average unit cost of a service or good can be reduced by increasing its output rate.

A China Southern Airlines (CSA) jetliner taking off at the Guangzhou Baiyun International Airport, China. The Boeing 777-2000 plane, along with the others waiting to take off, are part of an expanding CSA fleet. The capacity expansion helped CSA gain economies of scale as well as garner a greater share of China's domestic market.

Spreading Fixed Costs   In the short term, certain costs do not vary with changes in the output rate. These fixed costs include heating costs, debt service, and managers' salaries. The depreciation of plant and equipment already owned is also a fixed cost in the accounting sense. When the average output rate—and, therefore, the facility's utilization rate—increases, the average unit cost drops because fixed costs are spread over more units.

Reducing Construction Costs   Certain activities and expenses are required to build small and large facilities alike: building permits, architects' fees, and rental of building equipment. Doubling the size of the facility usually does not double construction costs.

Cutting Costs of Purchased Materials   Higher volumes can reduce the costs of purchased materials and services. They give the purchaser a better bargaining position and the opportunity to take advantage of quantity discounts. Retailers such as Wal-Mart and Toys "R" Us reap significant economies of scale because their national and international stores buy and sell huge volumes of each item.

Finding Process Advantages   High-volume production provides many opportunities for cost reduction. At a higher output rate, the process shifts toward a line process, with resources dedicated to individual products. Firms may be able to justify the expense of more efficient technology or more specialized equipment. The benefits from dedicating resources to individual services or products may include speeding up the learning effect, lowering inventory, improving process and job designs, and reducing the number of changeovers.

Diseconomies of Scale

diseconomies of scale

Occurs when the average cost per unit increases as the facility's size increases.

Bigger is not always better, however. At some point, a facility can become so large that **diseconomies of scale** set in; that is, the average cost per unit increases as the facility's size increases. The reason is that excessive size can bring complexity, loss of focus, and inefficiencies that raise the average unit cost of a service or product. Too many layers of employees and bureaucracy can cause management to lose touch with employees and customers. A less agile organization loses the flexibility needed to respond to changing demand. Many large companies become so involved in analysis and planning that they innovate less and avoid risks. The result is that small companies outperform corporate giants in numerous industries.

Figure 6.1 illustrates the transition from economies of scale to diseconomies of scale. The 500-bed hospital shows economies of scale because the average unit cost at its *best operating level*, represented by the blue dot, is less than that of the 250-bed hospital. However, assuming that sufficient demand exists, further expansion to a 750-bed hospital leads to higher average unit costs and diseconomies of scale. One reason the 500-bed hospital enjoys greater economies of scale than the 250-bed hospital is that the cost of building and equipping it is less than twice the cost for the smaller hospital. The 750-bed facility would enjoy similar savings. Its higher average unit costs can be explained only by diseconomies of scale, which outweigh the savings realized in construction costs.

Figure 6.1 does not mean that the optimal size for all hospitals is 500 beds. Optimal size depends on the number of patients per week to be served. On the one hand, a hospital serving a small community could have lower costs by choosing a 250-bed capacity rather than the 500-bed capacity. On the other hand, a large community might be served more efficiently by two 500-bed hospitals than by one 1,000-bed facility if diseconomies of scale exist at the bigger size.

FIGURE 6.1 ▼
Economies and Diseconomies of Scale

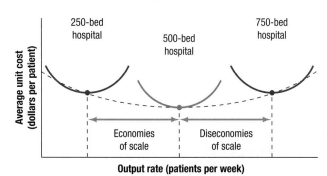

CAPACITY TIMING AND SIZING STRATEGIES

Operations managers must examine three dimensions of capacity strategy before making capacity decisions: (1) sizing capacity cushions, (2) timing and sizing expansion, and (3) linking process capacity and other operating decisions.

Sizing Capacity Cushions

Average utilization rates for any resource should not get too close to 100 percent over the long term, though it may occur for some processes from time to time in the short run. If the demand keeps increasing over time, then long-term capacity must be increased as well to provide some buffer against uncertainties. When average utilization rates approach 100 percent, it is usually a signal to increase capacity or decrease order acceptance to avoid declining productivity. The **capacity cushion** is the amount of reserve capacity a process uses to handle sudden increases in demand or temporary losses of production capacity; it measures the amount by which the average utilization (in terms of total capacity) falls below 100 percent. Specifically,

$$\text{Capacity cushion} = 100\% - \text{Average Utilization rate } (\%)$$

The appropriate size of the cushion varies by industry. In the capital-intensive paper industry, where machines can cost hundreds of millions of dollars each, cushions well under 10 percent are preferred. The less capital-intensive hotel industry breaks even with a 60 to 70 percent utilization (40 to 30 percent cushion), and begins to suffer customer-service problems when the cushion drops to 20 percent. The more capital-intensive cruise ship industry prefers cushions as small as 5 percent. Large cushions are particularly vital for front-office processes where customers expect fast service times.

Businesses find large cushions appropriate when demand varies. In certain service industries (the grocery industry, for example), demand on some days of the week is predictably higher than on other days, and even hour-to-hour changes are typical. Long customer waiting times are not acceptable because customers grow impatient if they have to wait in a supermarket checkout line for more than a few minutes. Prompt customer service requires supermarkets to maintain a capacity cushion large enough to handle peak demand. Large cushions also are necessary when future demand is uncertain, particularly if resource flexibility is low. Simulation and waiting-line analysis (see Supplement B, "Simulation Models," and Supplement C, "Waiting Line Models") can help managers better anticipate the relationship between capacity cushion and customer service.

Another type of demand uncertainty occurs with a changing product mix. Though total demand measured in monetary terms might remain stable, the load can shift unpredictably from one workstation to another as the product mix changes. Supply uncertainty tied to delivery of purchased materials also makes large capacity cushions helpful. Capacity often comes in large increments because a complete machine has to be purchased even if only a fraction of its available capacity is needed, which in turn creates a large cushion. Firms also need to build in excess capacity to allow for employee absenteeism, vacations, holidays, and any other delays. If a firm is experiencing high overtime costs and frequently needs to rely on subcontractors, it perhaps needs to increase its capacity cushions.

The argument in favor of small cushions is simple: Unused capacity costs money. For capital-intensive firms, minimizing the capacity cushion is vital. Studies indicate that businesses with high capital intensity achieve a low return on investment when the capacity cushion is high. This strong correlation does not exist for labor-intensive firms, however. Their return on investment is about the same because the lower investment in equipment makes high utilization less critical. Small cushions have other advantages. By implementing a small cushion, a company can sometimes uncover inefficiencies that were difficult to detect when cushions were larger. These inefficiencies might include employee absenteeism or unreliable suppliers. Once managers and workers identify such problems, they often can find ways to correct them.

Timing and Sizing Expansion

The second issue of capacity strategy concerns when to adjust capacity levels and by how much. While we deal with this issue from the perspective of capacity expansion in greater detail here, it must be noted that firms may not always be looking to expand capacity, but at times may be forced to retrench as evidenced by the situation in the airlines industry described in Managerial Practice 6.1.

Figure 6.2 illustrates two extreme strategies for expanding capacity: the *expansionist strategy*, which involves large, infrequent jumps in capacity, and the *wait-and-see strategy*, which involves smaller, more frequent jumps.

The timing and sizing of expansion are related; that is, if demand is increasing and the time between increments increases, the size of the increments must also increase. The expansionist strategy, which stays ahead of demand, minimizes the chance of sales lost to insufficient capacity. The wait-and-see strategy lags behind demand. To meet any shortfalls, it relies on short-term options, such as use of overtime, temporary workers, subcontractors, stockouts, and the postponement of preventive maintenance on equipment.

Several factors favor the expansionist strategy. Expansion can result in economies of scale and a faster rate of learning, thus helping a firm reduce its costs and compete on price.

MANAGERIAL PRACTICE 6.1 — Downsizing Capacity in the Airline Industry

In recent years, partly due to escalating costs caused by a surge in oil prices, and partly due to over-capacity on many routes, many air carriers find themselves in major trouble. The airline industry is reeling under the impact of these changes, and planning huge cuts even as travelers have been saddled with poor customer service and added costs in the form of extra baggage fees, fewer onboard meals, and the like. Passengers who fly out from smaller regional airports have limited flight options, and even popular vacation destinations such as Las Vegas and Honolulu are not immune from flight cuts since those routes are less profitable in spite of strong demand. United Airlines announced plans in June 2008 to cut domestic capacity by 18 percent and take 70 more jets out of service, including its entire fleet of single aisle 737s. Another 11 percent reduction in capacity is planned for 2009. Similarly, American Airlines planned to slash its domestic capacity by 12 percent after the busy travel season, retiring 45 to 50 gas guzzling MD-80 planes and 30 to 35 jets from its American Eagle sister

carrier. Northwest said it would cut mainline capacity in the fourth quarter by 8.5 percent to 9.5 percent, including removing fourteen 757's Airbus narrow body aircraft from its fleet and reducing its DC-9 fleet from 94 at the start of 2008 to 61 by the end of the year. Delta, which will acquire Northwest later on in 2008, Continental Airlines, and US Airways have all made announcements to slash jobs and flights.

So what went wrong? Most projections and planning for long-term capacity were done with the price of oil at $50 a barrel, while prices in June 2008 crossed $140 a barrel. Airlines with more capacity slack on certain routes could not absorb the increases in operating costs, and were left with few options other than seeking strategic alliances and undertaking large-scale capacity cuts. How well airlines match long-term capacity to demand will determine which ones survive and which ones go bankrupt and cease operating in a weakening economy.

Sources: Dave Carpenter, "United Airlines Plans Huge Cuts," *The Columbus Dispatch* (June 5, 2008); Andrew Shain, "As Costs Mount, Airlines Plan to Make Cutbacks," *The State* (June 6, 2008);

FIGURE 6.2 ▶
Two Capacity Strategies

(a) Expansionist strategy

(b) Wait-and-see strategy

This strategy might increase the firm's market share or act as a form of preemptive marketing. By making a large capacity expansion or announcing that one is imminent, the firm can preempt the expansion of other firms. These other firms must sacrifice some of their market share or risk burdening the industry with overcapacity. To be successful, however, the preempting firm must have the credibility to convince the competition that it will carry out its plans—and must signal its plans before the competition can act. Managerial Practice 6.2 illustrates the use of expansionist strategy in the ethanol industry.

The conservative wait-and-see strategy is to expand in smaller increments, such as by renovating existing facilities rather than building new ones. Because the wait-and-see strategy follows demand, it reduces the risks of overexpansion based on overly optimistic demand forecasts, obsolete technology, or inaccurate assumptions regarding the competition.

However, this strategy has its own risks, such as being preempted by a competitor or being unable to respond if demand is unexpectedly high. Critics claim the wait-and-see strategy is a short-term strategy typical of some U.S. management styles. Managers on the fast track to corporate advancement tend to take fewer risks. They earn promotions by avoiding the big mistakes and maximizing short-term profits and return on investment. The wait-and-see strategy fits this short-term outlook but can erode market share over the long run.

Management may choose one of these two strategies or one of the many between these extremes. With strategies in the more moderate middle, firms can expand more frequently (on a smaller scale) than they can with the expansionist strategy without lagging behind demand as with the wait-and-see strategy. An intermediate strategy could be to *follow the leader*, expanding when others do. If others are right, so are you, and nobody gains a competitive advantage. If others make a mistake and over expand, so do you, but everyone shares in the agony of overcapacity. Such a situation was noted for the airlines industry in Managerial

MANAGERIAL PRACTICE 6.2	Expansionist Capacity Strategy in the Ethanol Industry

A search for renewable energy and alternative sources of fuel has made ethanol production a big growth industry in the United States. The U.S. state of Nebraska alone has capital investments of more than $1.4 billion in 24 ethanol production plants, which together produce more than 1.7 billion gallons of ethanol each year. While Nebraska serves the ethanol markets in western United States, midwestern states like Iowa have the largest invested capacity. Many of these plants have gone into operation since 2007, and several others are scheduled for completion by the end of 2008.

But troubling signs may be on the horizon. Companies and farm cooperatives have built so many distilleries so quickly that the ethanol market is suddenly plagued by a glut and oversupply is putting downward pressure on price. At the same time, scarcity and price of raw materials needed to feed ethanol plants is becoming an issue. One bushel of corn produces approximately 2.6 gallons of ethanol, and the ethanol plants in the state of Nebraska alone require over 600 million bushels of grain in the process every year. As a result, the price of corn has risen steadily from under $2 per bushel in 2006 to $5 per bushel in 2008, further eroding profitability. Despite the steep increase in prices of crude oil, demand for ethanol has not increased proportionately because it is less efficient and constitutes 10 percent or less in most gasoline blends.

Capacity was also expanded without taking into consideration the transportation needs of ethanol. Unlike gasoline, traditional pipelines cannot be used due to the fact that ethanol is corrosive and contains traces of water. So it must be transported by specialized ethanol rail cars, trucks, and barges. Capacity of such a transportation network has not kept up with the surge in surplus ethanol production. Consequently, demand for ethanol along coastal regions of the country cannot be met quickly and efficiently from the heartland locations of Corn Belt ethanol plants.

While the government subsidies may keep the output of ethanol growing, experts believe that the expansion of the industry has been poorly managed. Some companies are modifying future plans and canceling new plant construction in fear of consolidation and going out of business.

The Lincolnway Energy plant, a midsize distillery in Nevada, Iowa converts corn into ethanol in a largely automated process. Lincolnway Energy was once virtually alone in the region. Today, though, competing distilleries are operating and pouring even more ethanol onto the market.

Sources: Clifford Krauss, "Ethanol's Boom Stalling as Glut Depresses Price," *New York Times* (September 30, 2007); Nebraska Ethanol Board, "Ethanol Plants in Nebraska," http://www.ne-ethanol.org/industry/ethplants.htm (October 16, 2008).

Practice 6.1, and may yet occur in the LCD industry due to large capacity expansions by Sharp Corporation, Sony, and Samsung as described in the opening vignette.

Linking Capacity and Other Decisions

Capacity decisions should be closely linked to processes and supply chains throughout the organization. When managers make decisions about designing processes, determining degree of resource flexibility and inventory, and locating facilities, they must consider its impact on capacity cushions. Capacity cushions in the long run buffer the organization against uncertainty, as do resource flexibility, inventory, and longer customer lead times. If a change is made in any one decision area, the capacity cushion may also need to be changed to compensate. For example, capacity cushions for a process can be lowered if less emphasis is placed on fast deliveries (*competitive priorities*), yield losses (*quality*) drop, or if investment in capital-intensive equipment increases or worker flexibility increases (*process design*). Capacity cushions can also be lowered if the company is willing to smooth the output rate by raising prices when inventory is low and decreasing prices when it is high.

Lines of meat cutters process beef at a Kansas meat packing plant. Tyson Foods cut 1,500 jobs at their beef processing plant in Emporia, Kansas in 2008 due to a dwindling supply of beef cattle.

A SYSTEMATIC APPROACH TO LONG-TERM CAPACITY DECISIONS

Long-term decisions for capacity would typically include whether to add a new plant or warehouse or to reduce the number of existing ones, how many workstations a given department should have, or how many workers are needed to staff a given process. Some of these decisions can take years to become operational. Hence a systematic approach is needed to plan for long-term capacity decisions.

Although each situation is somewhat different, a four-step procedure generally can help managers make sound capacity decisions. (In describing this procedure, we assume that management already performed the preliminary steps of determining the process's existing capacity and assessing whether its current capacity cushion is appropriate.)

1. Estimate future capacity requirements.
2. Identify gaps by comparing requirements with available capacity.
3. Develop alternative plans for reducing the gaps.
4. Evaluate each alternative, both qualitatively and quantitatively, and make a final choice.

Step 1: Estimate Capacity Requirements

capacity requirement

What a process's capacity should be for some future time period to meet the demand of customers (external or internal), given the firm's desired capacity cushion.

A process's **capacity requirement** is what its capacity should be for some future time period to meet the demand of the firm's customers (external or internal), given the firm's desired capacity cushion. Larger requirements are practical for processes or workstations that could potentially be bottlenecks in the future, and management may even plan for larger cushions than normal.

Capacity requirements can be expressed in one of two ways: with an output measure or with an input measure. Either way, the foundation for the estimate is forecasts of demand, productivity, competition, and technological change. These forecasts normally need to be made for several time periods in a **planning horizon**, which is the set of consecutive time periods considered for planning purposes. Long-term capacity plans need to consider more of the future (perhaps a whole decade) than do short-term plans. Unfortunately, the further ahead you look, the more chance you have of making an inaccurate forecast.

planning horizon

The set of consecutive time periods considered for planning purposes.

Using Output Measures The simplest way to express capacity requirements is as an output rate. As discussed earlier, output measures are appropriate for high-volume processes with little product variety or process divergence. Here, demand forecasts for future years are used as a basis for extrapolating capacity requirements into the future. If demand is expected to double in the next five years, then the capacity requirements also double. For example, if a process's current demand is 50 customers per day, then the demand in five years would be 100 customers per day. If the desired capacity cushion is 20 percent, management should plan for enough capacity to serve [100/(1 –0.2)] =125 customers in five years.

Using Input Measures Output measures may be insufficient in the following situations:

- Product variety and process divergence is high.
- The product or service mix is changing.
- Productivity rates are expected to change.
- Significant learning effects are expected.

In such cases, it is more appropriate to calculate capacity requirements using an input measure, such as the number of employees, machines, computers, or trucks. Using an input measure for the capacity requirement brings together demand forecasts, process time estimates, and the desired capacity cushion. When just one service or product is processed at an operation and the time period is a particular year, the capacity requirement, M, is

$$\text{Capacity requirement} = \frac{\text{Processing hours required for year's demand}}{\text{Hours available from a single capacity unit (such as an employee or machine) per year, after deducting desired cushion}}$$

$$M = \frac{Dp}{N[1-(C/100)]}$$

where

D = demand forecast for the year (number of customers serviced or units of product)

p = processing time (in hours per customer served or unit produced)

N = total number of hours per year during which the process operates

C = desired capacity cushion (expressed as a percent)

M is the number of input units required and should be calculated for each year in the time horizon. The processing time, p, depends on the process and methods selected to do the work. The denominator is the total number of hours, N, available for the year from one unit of capacity (an employee or machine), multiplied by a proportion that accounts for the desired capacity cushion, C. The proportion is simply $1.0 - C/100$, where C is converted from a percent to a proportion by dividing by 100. For example, a 20 percent capacity cushion means that $1.0 - C/100$ equals 0.80.

Setups may be involved if multiple products are being manufactured. **Setup time** is the time required to change a process or an operation from making one service or product to making another. The total setup time is found by dividing the number of units forecast per year, D, by the number of units made in each lot, Q, (number of units processed between setups), which gives the number of setups per year, and then multiplying by the time per setup, s. For example, if the annual demand is 1,200 units and the average lot size is 100, there are $1,200/100 = 12$ setups per year. Accounting for both processing and setup times for multiple services (products), we get

setup time

The time required to change a process or an operation from making one service or product to making another.

$$\text{Capacity requirement} = \frac{\begin{array}{c}\text{Processing and setup hours required for}\\\text{year's demand, summed over all services or products}\end{array}}{\begin{array}{c}\text{Hours available from a single capacity unit per year,}\\\text{after deducting desired cushion}\end{array}}$$

$$M = \frac{[Dp + (D/Q)s]_{\text{product 1}} + [Dp + (D/Q)s]_{\text{product 2}} + \cdots + [Dp + (D/Q)s]_{\text{product }n}}{N[1 - (C/100)]}$$

where

Q = number of units in each lot

s = setup time (in hours) per lot

What to do when M is not an integer depends on the situation. For example, it is impossible to buy a fractional machine. In this case, round up the fractional part, unless it is cost efficient to use short-term options, such as overtime or stockouts, to cover any shortfalls. If, instead, the capacity unit is the number of employees at a process, a value of 23.6 may be achieved using just 23 employees and a modest use of overtime (equivalent to having 60 percent of another full-time person). Here, the fractional value should be retained as useful information.

EXAMPLE 6.1	**Estimating Capacity Requirements When Using Input Measures**

A copy center in an office building prepares bound reports for two clients. The center makes multiple copies (the lot size) of each report. The processing time to run, collate, and bind each copy depends on, among other factors, the number of pages. The center operates 250 days per year, with one 8-hour shift. Management believes that a capacity cushion of 15 percent (beyond the allowance built into time standards) is best. It currently has three copy machines. Based on the following table of information, determine how many machines are needed at the copy center.

Item	Client X	Client Y
Annual demand forecast (copies)	2,000	6,000
Standard processing time (hour/copy)	0.5	0.7
Average lot size (copies per report)	20	30
Standard setup time (hours)	0.25	0.40

SOLUTION

$$M = \frac{[Dp + (D/Q)s]_{\text{product 1}} + [Dp + (D/Q)s]_{\text{product 2}} + \cdots + [Dp + (D/Q)s]_{\text{product } n}}{M[1 - (C/100)]}$$

$$= \frac{[2{,}000(0.5) + (2{,}000/20)(0.25)]_{\text{client X}} + [6{,}000(0.7) + (6{,}000/30)(0.40)]_{\text{client Y}}}{[(250 \text{ day/year})(1 \text{ shift/day})(8 \text{ hours/shift})][1.0 - (15/100)]}$$

$$= \frac{5{,}305}{1{,}700} = 3.12$$

Rounding up to the next integer gives a requirement of four machines.

Tutor 6.1 in my**om**lab provides a new example to practice calculating capacity requirements when using input measures.

DECISION POINT

The copy center's capacity is being stretched and no longer has the desired 15 percent capacity cushion with the existing three machines. Not wanting customer service to suffer, management decided to use overtime as a short-term solution to handle past-due orders. If demand continues at the current level or grows, it will acquire a fourth machine.

Step 2: Identify Gaps

capacity gap

Positive or negative difference between projected demand and current capacity.

A **capacity gap** is any difference (positive or negative) between projected capacity requirements (*M*) and current capacity. Complications arise when multiple operations and several resource inputs are involved. Expanding the capacity of some operations may increase overall capacity. However, as we will learn later in Chapter 7, "Managing Process Constraints," if one operation is more constrained than others, total process capacity can be expanded only if the capacity of the constrained operation is expanded.

Step 3: Develop Alternatives

base case

The act of doing nothing and losing orders from any demand that exceeds current capacity, or incur costs because capacity is too large.

The next step is to develop alternative plans to cope with projected gaps. One alternative, called the **base case**, is to do nothing and simply lose orders from any demand that exceeds current capacity or incur costs because capacity is too large. Other alternatives if expected demand exceeds current capacity are various timing and sizing options for adding new capacity, including the expansionist and wait-and-see strategies illustrated in Figure 6.2. Additional possibilities include expanding at a different location and using short-term options, such as overtime, temporary workers, and subcontracting. Alternatives for reducing capacity include the closing of plants or warehouses, laying off employees, or reducing the days or hours of operation.

Step 4: Evaluate the Alternatives

In this final step, the manager evaluates each alternative, both qualitatively and quantitatively.

Qualitative Concerns   Qualitatively, the manager looks at how each alternative fits the overall capacity strategy and other aspects of the business not covered by the financial analysis. Of particular concern might be uncertainties about demand, competitive reaction, technological change, and cost estimates. Some of these factors cannot be quantified and must be assessed on the basis of judgment and experience. Others can be quantified, and the manager can analyze each alternative by using different assumptions about the future. One set of assumptions could represent a worst case, in which demand is less, competition is greater, and construction costs are higher than expected. Another set of assumptions could represent the most optimistic view of the future. This type of "what-if" analysis allows the manager to get an idea of each alternative's implications before making a final choice.

cash flow

The difference between the flows of funds into and out of an organization over a period of time, including revenues, costs, and changes in assets and liabilities.

Quantitative Concerns   Quantitatively, the manager estimates the change in cash flows for each alternative over the forecast time horizon compared to the base case. **Cash flow** is the difference between the flows of funds into and out of an organization over a period of time, including revenues, costs, and changes in assets and liabilities. The manager is concerned here only with calculating the cash flows attributable to the project.

EXAMPLE 6.2	Evaluating the Alternatives

Grandmother's Chicken Restaurant is experiencing a boom in business. The owner expects to serve 80,000 meals this year. Although the kitchen is operating at 100 percent capacity, the dining room can handle 105,000 diners per year. Forecasted demand for the next five years is 90,000 meals for next year, followed by a 10,000-meal increase in each of the succeeding years. One alternative is to expand both the kitchen and the dining room now, bringing their capacities up to 130,000 meals per year. The initial investment would be $200,000, made at the end of this year (year 0). The average meal is priced at $10, and the before-tax profit margin is 20 percent. The 20 percent figure was arrived at by determining that, for each $10 meal, $8 covers variable costs and the remaining $2 goes to pretax profit.

> What are the pretax cash flows from this project for the next five years compared to those of the base case of doing nothing?

PEARSON
myomlab

Tutor 6.2 in my**om**lab provides a new example to practice projecting cash flows for capacity decisions.

SOLUTION

Recall that the base case of doing nothing results in losing all potential sales beyond 80,000 meals. With the new capacity, the cash flow would equal the extra meals served by having a 130,000-meal capacity, multiplied by a profit of $2 per meal. In year 0, the only cash flow is −$200,000 for the initial investment. In year 1, the 90,000-meal demand will be completely satisfied by the expanded capacity, so the incremental cash flow is (90,000−80,000)($2)=$20,000. For subsequent years, the figures are as follows:

Year 2: Demand = 100,000; Cash flow = (100,000 − 80,000)$2 = $40,000

Year 3: Demand = 110,000; Cash flow = (110,000 − 80,000)$2 = $60,000

Year 4: Demand = 120,000; Cash flow = (120,000 − 80,000)$2 = $80,000

Year 5: Demand = 130,000; Cash flow = (130,000 − 80,000)$2 = $100,000

If the new capacity were smaller than the expected demand in any year, we would subtract the base case capacity from the new capacity (rather than the demand). The owner should account for the time value of money, applying such techniques as the net present value or internal rate of return methods (see Supplement F, "Financial Analysis," in my**om**lab). For instance, the net present value (NPV) of this project at a discount rate of 10 percent is calculated here, and equals $13,051.76.

$$\text{NPV} = -200{,}000 + [(20{,}000/1.1)] + [40{,}000/(1.1)^2] + [60{,}000/(1.1)^3] + [80{,}000/(1.1)^4] + [100{,}000/(1.1)^5]$$

$$= -\$200{,}000 + \$18{,}181.82 + \$33{,}057.85 + \$45{,}078.89 + \$54{,}641.07 + \$62{,}092.13 = \$13{,}051.76$$

DECISION POINT

Before deciding on this capacity alternative, the owner should also examine the qualitative concerns, such as future location of competitors. In addition, the homey atmosphere of the restaurant may be lost with expansion. Furthermore, other alternatives should be considered (see Solved Problem 2).

TOOLS FOR CAPACITY PLANNING

Capacity planning requires demand forecasts for an extended period of time. Unfortunately, forecast accuracy declines as the forecasting horizon lengthens. In addition, anticipating what competitors will do increases the uncertainty of demand forecasts. Demand during any period of time may not be evenly distributed; peaks and valleys of demand may (and often do) occur within the time period. These realities necessitate the use of capacity cushions. In this section, we introduce three tools that deal more formally with demand uncertainty and variability: (1) waiting-line models, (2) simulation, and (3) decision trees. Waiting-line models and simulation account for the random, independent behavior of many customers, in terms of both their time of arrival and their processing needs. Decision trees allow anticipation of events, such as competitors' actions, which requires a sequence of decisions regarding capacities.

Waiting-Line Models

Waiting-line models often are useful in capacity planning, such as selecting an appropriate capacity cushion for a high customer-contact process. Waiting lines tend to develop in front of a work center, such as an airport ticket counter, a machine center, or a central computer.

The reason is that the arrival time between jobs or customers varies, and the processing time may vary from one customer to the next. Waiting-line models use probability distributions to provide estimates of average customer wait time, average length of waiting lines, and utilization of the work center. Managers can use this information to choose the most cost-effective capacity, balancing customer service and the cost of adding capacity.

Supplement C, "Waiting Line Models," follows this chapter and provides a fuller treatment of these models. It introduces formulas for estimating important characteristics of a waiting line, such as average customer waiting time and average facility utilization for different facility designs. For example, a facility might be designed to have one or multiple lines at each operation and to route customers through one or multiple operations. Given the estimating capability of these formulas and cost estimates for waiting and idle time, managers can select cost-effective designs and capacity levels that also provide the desired level of customer service.

Figure 6.3 shows output from POMS for Windows for waiting lines. A professor meeting students during office hours has an arrival rate of three students per hour and a service rate of six students per hour. The output shows that the capacity cushion is 50 percent (1 – average server utilization of 0.50). This result is expected because the processing rate is double the arrival rate. What might not be expected is that a typical student spends 20 minutes either in line or talking with the professor, and the probability of having two or more students at the office is 0.125. These numbers might be surprisingly high, given such a large capacity cushion.

Simulation

More complex waiting-line problems must be analyzed with simulation (see Supplement B, "Simulation Models"). It can identify the process's bottlenecks and appropriate capacity cushions, even for complex processes with random demand patterns and predictable surges in demand during a typical day. The SimQuick simulation package, provided in my**om**lab, allows you to build dynamic models and systems. Other simulation packages can be found with Extend, Simprocess, ProModel, and Witness.

Decision Trees

A decision tree can be particularly valuable for evaluating different capacity expansion alternatives when demand is uncertain and sequential decisions are involved (see Supplement A, "Decision Making Models"). For example, the owner of Grandmother's Chicken Restaurant (see Example 6.2) may expand the restaurant now, only to discover in year 4 that demand growth is much higher than forecasted. In that case, she needs to decide whether to expand further. In terms of construction costs and downtime, expanding twice is likely to

FIGURE 6.3 ▼
POMS for Windows Output for Waiting Lines during Office Hours

Waiting Lines Results

Example Solution					
Parameter	Value	Parameter	Value	Minutes	Seconds
Single-Server Model		Average server utilization	.5		
Arrival rate(lambda)	3	Average number in the line(Lq)	.5		
Service rate(mu)	6	Average number in the system(L)	1		
Number of servers	1	Average time in the line(Wq)	.17	10	600
		Average time in the system(W)	.33	20	1200

Table of Probabilities

k	Prob (num in sys = k)	Prob (num in sys <= k)	Prob (num in sys >k)
0	.5	.5	.5
1	.25	.75	.25
2	.13	.88	.13
3	.06	.94	.06
4	.03	.97	.03
5	.02	.98	.02
6	.01	1	.01
7	.0	1	.0

be much more expensive than building a larger facility from the outset. However, making a large expansion now, when demand growth is low, means poor facility utilization. Much depends on the demand.

Figure 6.4 shows a decision tree for this view of the problem, with new information provided. Demand growth can be either low or high, with probabilities of 0.40 and 0.60, respectively. The initial expansion in year 1 (square node 1) can either be small or large. The second decision node (square node 2), whether to expand at a later date, is reached only if the initial expansion is small and demand turns out to be high. If demand is high and if the initial expansion was small, a decision must be made about a second expansion in year 4. Payoffs for each branch of the tree are estimated. For example, if the initial expansion is large, the financial benefit is either $40,000 or $220,000, depending on whether demand is low or high. Weighting these payoffs by the probabilities yields an expected value of $148,000. This expected payoff is higher than the $109,000 payoff for the small initial expansion, so the better choice is to make a large expansion in year 1.

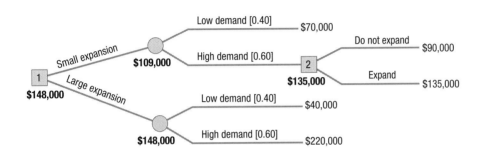

◀ FIGURE 6.4
A Decision Tree for Capacity Expansion

INTERNET RESOURCES

my**om**lab and the Companion Website at **www.pearsonglobaleditions.com/krajewski** contain many tools, activities, and resources designed for this chapter.

KEY EQUATIONS

1. Utilization, expressed as a percent:

$$\text{Utilization} = \frac{\text{Average output rate}}{\text{Maximum capacity}} \times 100\%$$

2. Capacity cushion, C, expressed as a percent:

$$C = 100\% - \text{Average Utilization rate}(\%)$$

3. **a.** Capacity requirement for one service or product:

$$M = \frac{Dp}{N[1 - (C/100)]}$$

b. Capacity requirement for multiple services or products:

$$M = \frac{[Dp + (D/Q)s]_{\text{product 1}} + [Dp + (D/Q)s]_{\text{product 2}} + \cdots + [Dp + (D/Q)s]_{\text{product } n}}{N[1 - (C/100)]}$$

KEY TERMS

base case 248
capacity 240
capacity cushion 243

capacity gap 248
capacity requirement 246
cash flow 248
diseconomies of scale 242

economies of scale 241
setup time 247
planning horizon 246
utilization 241

SOLVED PROBLEM 1

You have been asked to put together a capacity plan for a critical operation at the Ainsworth Pottery Company. Your capacity measure is the number of kilns. The company manufactures three different sizes of ceramic pots: 13 cm, 20 cm, and 27 cm. The time standards (processing and setup), lot sizes, and demand forecasts are given in the following table. The company operates two 7-hour shifts, 5 days per week, 48 weeks per year. Experience shows that a capacity cushion of 5 percent is sufficient.

| Product | Time Standards | | | |
	Processing (hr/pots)	Setup (hr/pots)	Lot Size (pots/lot)	Demand Forecast (pots/yr)
13-cm ceramic pot	0.05	0.5	240	80,000
20-cm ceramic pot	0.10	2.2	180	60,000
27-cm ceramic pot	0.02	3.8	360	120,000

a. How many kilns are needed?

b. If the operation currently has two kilns, what is the capacity gap?

SOLUTION

a. The number of hours of operation per year, N, is N, is $N = $ (2 shifts/day)(7 hours/shifts) (240 days/kiln-year) = 3,360 hours/kiln-year

The number of kilns required, K, is the sum of kiln-hour requirements for all three products divided by the number of productive hours available for one kiln.

$$K = \frac{[Dp + (D/Q)s]_{13\,cm} + [Dp + (D/Q)s]_{20\,cm} + [Dp + (D/Q)s]_{27\,cm}}{N[1 - (C/100)]}$$

$$= \frac{\begin{array}{c}[80,000(0.05) + (80,000/240)0.5] + [60,000(0.10) + (60,000/180)2.2] \\ + [120,000(0.02) + (120,000/360)3.8]\end{array}}{3,360[1 - (5/100)]}$$

$$= \frac{14,567 \text{ hours/year}}{3,192 \text{ hours/machine-year}} = 4.56 \text{ or 5 machines}$$

b. The capacity gap is 2.56 kilns (4.56 – 2). Three more kilns should be purchased, unless management decides to use short-term options to fill the gap.

The *Capacity Requirements* Solver in OM Explorer confirms these calculations, as Figure 6.5 shows, using only the "Expected" scenario for the demand forecasts.

Shifts/Day	2
Hours/Shift	7
Days/Week	5
Weeks/Year	48
Cushion (as %)	5%
Current capacity	2

Components [3]

▲ More Components
▼ Fewer Components

◀ FIGURE 6.5
Using the *Capacity Requirements*
Solver for Solved Problem 1

Components	Processing (hr/unit)	Setup (hr/lot)	Lot Size (units/lot)	Demand Forecasts Pessimistic	Demand Forecasts Expected	Demand Forecasts Optimistic
13-cm ceramic pot	0.05	0.5	240		80,000	
20-cm ceramic pot	0.10	2.2	180		60,000	
27-cm ceramic pot	0.02	3.8	360		120,000	

Productive hours from
one capacity unit for a year   3,192

	Pessimistic Process	Pessimistic Setup	Expected Process	Expected Setup	Optimistic Process	Optimistic Setup
13-cm ceramic pot	0	0.0	4,000	166.7	0	0.0
20-cm ceramic pot	0	0.0	6,000	733.3	0	0.0
27-cm ceramic pot	0	0.0	2,400	1,266.7	0	0.0
	0	0.0	12,400	2,166.7	0	0.0
Total hours required		0.0		14,566.7		0.0

Total capacity requirements (K)	0.00	4.56	0.00
Rounded	0	5	0
Scenarios that can be met with current system/capacity:		Pessimistic, Optimistic	

If capacity increased by	0%
Expanded current capacity	3,192

Total capacity requirements (K)	0.00	4.56	0.00
Rounded	0	5	0
Scenarios that can be met with expanded current capacity:		Pessimistic, Optimistic	

SOLVED PROBLEM 2

The base case for Grandmother's Chicken Restaurant (see Example 6.2) is to do nothing. The capacity of the kitchen in the base case is 80,000 meals per year. A capacity alternative for Grandmother's Chicken Restaurant is a two-stage expansion. This alternative expands the kitchen at the end of year 0, raising its capacity from 80,000 meals per year to that of the dining area (105,000 meals per year). If sales in year 1 and 2 live up to expectations, the capacities of both the kitchen and the dining room will be expanded at the *end* of year 3 to 130,000 meals per year. This upgraded capacity level should suffice up through year 5. The initial investment would be $80,000 at the end of year 0 and an additional investment of $170,000 at the end of year 3. The pretax profit is $2 per meal. What are the pretax cash flows for this alternative through year 5, compared with the base case?

SOLUTION

Table 6.1 shows the cash inflows and outflows. The year 3 cash flow is unusual in two respects. First, the cash inflow from sales is $50,000 rather than $60,000. The increase in sales over the base is 25,000 meals (105,000 − 10,000) instead of 30,000 meals (110,000 − 80,000) because the restaurant's capacity falls somewhat short of demand. Second, a cash outflow of $170,000 occurs at the end of year 3, when the second-stage expansion occurs. The net cash flow for year 3 is $50,000 − $170,000 = −$120,000.

For comparison purposes, the NPV of this project at a discount rate of 10 percent is calculated as follows, and equals negative $2,184.90.

$$\text{NPV} = -80,000 + (20,000/1.1) + [40,000/(1.1)^2] - [120,000/(1.1)^3] + [80,000/(1.1)^4] + [100,000/(1.1)^5]$$

$$= -\$80,000 + \$18,181.82 + \$33,057.85 - \$90,157.77 + \$54,641.07 + \$62,092.13$$

$$= -\$2,184.90$$

On a purely monetary basis, a single-stage expansion seems to be a better alternative than this two-stage expansion. However, other qualitative factors as mentioned earlier must be considered as well.

TABLE 6.1		CASH FLOWS FOR TWO-STAGE EXPANSION AT GRANDMOTHER'S CHICKEN RESTAURANT	
Year	Projected Demand (meals/yr)	Projected Capacity (meals/yr)	Calculation of Incremental Cash Flow Compared to Base Case (80,000 meals/yr)	Cash Inflow (outflow)
0	80,000	80,000	Increase kitchen capacity to 105,000 meals =	($80,000)
1	90,000	105,000	90,000 − 80,000 = (10,000 meals)($2/meal) =	$20,000
2	100,000	105,000	100,000 − 80,000 = (20,000 meals)($2/meal) =	$40,000
3	110,000	105,000	105,000 − 80,000 = (25,000 meals)($2/meal) =	$50,000
			Increase total capacity to 130,000 meals =	($170,000)
				($120,000)
4	120,000	130,000	120,000 − 80,000 = (40,000 meals)($2/meal) =	$80,000
5	130,000	130,000	130,000 − 80,000 = (50,000 meals)($2/meal) =	$100,000

DISCUSSION QUESTIONS

1. A young boy sets up a lemonade stand on the corner of College Street and Air Park Boulevard. Temperatures in the area climb to 100° during the summer. The intersection is near a major university and a large construction site. Explain to this young entrepreneur how his business might benefit from economies of scale. Explain also some conditions that might lead to diseconomies of scale.

2. What are the economies of scale in college class size? As class size increases, what symptoms of diseconomies of scale appear? How are these symptoms related to customer contact?

PROBLEMS

Software, such as OM Explorer, Active Models, and POM for Windows, is available in my**om**lab. Check with your instructor on how best to use it. In many cases, the instructor wants you to understand how to do the calculations by hand. At most, the software provides a check on your calculations. When calculations are particularly complex and the goal is interpreting the results in making decisions, the software replaces entirely the manual calculations.

Problems 9, 15, 17, 18, and 19 require reading of Supplement A, "Decision Making Models." Problems 10, 14, 17, and 18 require reading of Supplement F, "Financial Analysis," in my**om**lab.

1. A process currently services an average of 50 customers per day. Observations in recent weeks show that its utilization is about 90 percent, allowing for just a 10 percent capacity cushion. If demand is expected to be 75 percent of the current level in five years and management wants to have a capacity cushion of just 5 percent, what capacity requirement should be planned?

2. An airline company must plan its fleet capacity and its long-term schedule of aircraft usage. For one flight segment, the average number of customers per day is 70, which represents a 65 percent utilization rate of the equipment assigned to the flight segment. If demand is expected to increase to 84 customers for this flight segment in three years, what capacity requirement should

be planned? Assume that management deems that a capacity cushion of 25 percent is appropriate.

3. The Dahlia Medical Center has 30 labor rooms, 15 combination labor and delivery rooms, 3 delivery rooms, and 1 special delivery room reserved for complicated births. All of these facilities operate around the clock. Time spent in labor rooms varies from hours to days, with an average of about a day. The average uncomplicated delivery requires about one hour in a delivery room.

During an exceptionally busy three-day period, 109 healthy babies were born at Dahlia Medical Center. Sixty babies were born in separate labor and delivery rooms, 45 were born in combined labor and delivery rooms, and only 4 babies required a labor room and the complicated-delivery room. Which of the facilities (labor rooms, combination labor and delivery rooms, or delivery rooms) had the greatest utilization rate?

4. An automobile brake supplier operates on two 8-hour shifts, 5 days per week, 52 weeks per year. Table 6.2 shows the time standards, lot sizes, and demand forecasts for three components. Because of demand uncertainties, the operations manager obtained three demand forecasts (pessimistic, expected, and optimistic). The manager believes that a 20 percent capacity cushion is best.

TABLE 6.2	CAPACITY INFORMATION FOR AUTOMOTIVE BRAKE SUPPLIER

| | Time Standard | | | Demand Forecast | | |
Component	Processing (hr/unit)	Setup (hr/lot)	Lot Size (units/lot)	Pessimistic	Expected	Optimistic
A	0.05	1.0	60	15,000	18,000	25,000
B	0.20	4.5	80	10,000	13,000	17,000
C	0.05	8.2	120	17,000	25,000	40,000

a. What is the minimum number of machines needed? The expected number? The maximum number?

b. If the operation currently has three machines and the manager is willing to expand capacity by 20 percent through short-term options in the event that the optimistic demand occurs, what is the capacity gap?

5. The Astro World amusement park has the opportunity to expand its size now (the end of year 0) by purchasing adjacent property for $250,000 and adding attractions at a cost of $550,000. This expansion is expected to increase attendance by 30 percent over projected attendance without expansion. The price of admission is $30, with a $5 increase planned for the beginning of year 3. Additional operating costs are expected to be $100,000 per year. Estimated attendance for the next five years, *without expansion*, is as follows:

Year	1	2	3	4	5
Attendance	30,000	34,000	36,250	38,500	41,000

a. What are the pretax combined cash flows for years 0 through 5 that are attributable to the park's expansion?

b. Ignoring tax, depreciation, and the time value of money, determine how long it will take to recover (pay back) the investment.

6. Arabelle is considering expanding the floor area of her high-fashion import clothing store, The French Prints of Arabelle, by increasing her leased space in the upscale Cherry Creek Mall from 2,000 square feet to 3,000 square feet. The Cherry Creek Mall boasts one of the highest ratios of sales value per square foot. Rents (including utilities, security, and similar costs) are $110 per square foot per year. Salary increases related to French Prints' expansion are shown in the following table, along with projections of sales per square foot. The purchase cost of goods sold averages 70 percent of the sales price. Sales are seasonal, with an important peak during the year-end holiday season.

a. If Arabelle expands French Prints at the end of year 0, what will her quarterly pretax cash flows be through year 2?

b. Project the quarterly pretax cash flows assuming that the sales pattern (10 percent annually compounded increase) continues through year 3.

Year	Quarter	Sales (per sq ft)	Incremental Salaries
1	1	$ 90	$12,000
	2	60	8,000
	3	110	12,000
	4	240	24,000
2	1	99	12,000
	2	66	8,000
	3	121	12,000
	4	264	24,000

7. Tuff-Rider, Inc., manufactures touring bikes and mountain bikes in a variety of frame sizes, colors, and component combinations. Identical bicycles are produced in lots of 100. The projected demand, lot size, and time standards are shown in the following table:

Item	Touring	Mountain
Demand forecast	5,000 units/year	10,000 units/year
Lot size	100 units	100 units
Standard processing time	.25 hour/unit	.50 hour/unit
Standard setup time	2 hours/lot	3 hours/lot

The shop currently works 8 hours a day, 5 days a week, 50 weeks a year. It operates five workstations, each producing one bicycle in the time shown in the table. The shop maintains a 15 percent capacity cushion. How many workstations will be required next year to meet expected demand without using overtime and without decreasing the firm's current capacity cushion?

8. Up, Up, and Away is a producer of kites and wind socks. Relevant data on a bottleneck operation in the shop for the upcoming fiscal year are given in the following table:

Item	Kites	Wind Socks
Demand forecast	30,000 units/year	12,000 units/year
Lot size	20 units	70 units
Standard processing time	0.3 hour/unit	1.0 hour/unit
Standard setup time	3.0 hours/lot	4.0 hours/lot

The shop works two shifts per day, 8 hours per shift, 200 days per year. Currently, the company operates four machines, and desires a 25 percent capacity cushion. How many machines should be purchased to meet the upcoming year's demand without resorting to any short-term capacity solutions?

9. Dawson Electronics is a manufacturer of high-tech control modules for lawn sprinkler systems. Denise, the CEO, is trying to decide if the company should develop one of the two potential new products, the Water Saver 1000 or the Greener Grass 5000. With each product, Dawson can capture a bigger market share if it chooses to expand capacity by buying additional machines. Given different demand scenarios, their probabilities of occurrence, and capacity expansion versus no change in capacity, the potential sales of each product are summarized in Table 6.3.

TABLE 6.3	DEMAND AND SALES INFORMATION FOR DAWSON ELECTRONICS

	Water Saver 1000 Dollar Sales ($1000)	Greener Grass 5000 Dollar Sales ($1000)	Probability of Occurrence
With Capacity Expansion			
Low Demand	1000	2500	0.25
Medium Demand	2000	3000	0.50
High Demand	3000	5000	0.25
Without Capacity Expansion			
Low Demand	700	1000	0.25
Medium Demand	1000	2000	0.50
High Demand	2000	3000	0.25

a. What is the expected payoff for Water Saver 1000 and the Greener Grass 5000, with and without capacity expansion?

b. Which product should Denise choose to produce, and with which capacity expansion option?

10. MKM International is seeking to purchase a new CNC machine in order to reduce costs. Two alternative machines are in consideration. Machine 1 costs $500,000, but yields a 15 percent savings over the current machine used. Machine 2 costs $900,000, but yields a 25 percent savings over the current machine used. In order to meet demand, the following forecasted cost information for the current machine is also provided.

a. Based on the NPV of the cash flows for these 5 years, which machine should MKM International Purchase? Assume a discount rate of 12 percent.

Year	Projected Cost
1	1,000,000
2	1,350,000
3	1,400,000
4	1,450,000
5	2,550,000

b. If MKM International lowered its required discount rate to 8 percent, what machine would it purchase?

11. Roche Brothers is considering a capacity expansion of its supermarket. The landowner will build the addition to suit in return for $200,000 upon completion and a five-year lease. The increase in rent for the addition is $10,000 per month. The annual sales projected through year 5 follow. The current effective capacity is equivalent to 500,000 customers per year. Assume a 2 percent pretax profit on sales.

Year	1	2	3	4	5
Customers	560,000	600,000	685,000	700,000	715,000
Average Sales per Customer	$50.00	$53.00	$56.00	$60.00	$64.00

a. If Roche expands its capacity to serve 700,000 customers per year now (end of year 0), what are the projected annual incremental pretax cash flows attributable to this expansion?

b. If Roche expands its capacity to serve 700,000 customers per year at the end of year 2, the landowner will build the same addition for $240,000 and a 3-year lease at $12,000 per month. What are the projected annual incremental pretax cash flows attributable to this expansion alternative?

12. Kim Epson operates a full-service car wash, which operates from 8 A.M. to 8 P.M. seven days a week. The car wash has two stations: an automatic washing and drying station and a manual interior cleaning station. The automatic washing and drying station can handle 30 cars per hour. The interior cleaning station can handle 200 cars per day. Based on a recent year-end review of operations, Kim estimates that future demand for the interior cleaning station for the seven days of the week, expressed in average number of cars per day, would be as follows:

Day	Mon.	Tues.	Wed.	Thurs.	Fri.	Sat.	Sun.
Cars	160	180	150	140	280	300	250

By installing additional equipment (at a cost of $50,000) Kim can increase the capacity of the interior cleaning station to 300 cars per day. Each car wash generates a pretax contribution of $4.00. Should Kim install the additional equipment if she expects a pretax payback period of three years or less?

Advanced Problems

13. Two new alternatives have come up for expanding Grandmother's Chicken Restaurant (see Solved Problem 2). They involve more automation in the kitchen and feature a special cooking process that retains the original-recipe taste of the chicken. Although the process is more capital-intensive, it would drive down labor costs, so the pretax profit for *all* sales (not just the sales from the capacity added) would go up from 20 to 22 percent. This gain would increase the pretax profit by 2 percent of each sales dollar through $800,000 (80,000 meals × $10) and by 22 percent of each sales dollar between $800,000 and the new capacity limit. Otherwise, the new alternatives are much the same as those in Example 6.2 and Solved Problem 2.

   ■ *Alternative 1:* Expand both the kitchen and the dining area now (at the end of year 0), raising the capacity to 130,000 meals per year. The cost of construction, including the new automation, would be $336,000 (rather than the earlier $200,000).

   ■ *Alternative 2:* Expand only the kitchen now, raising its capacity to 105,000 meals per year. At the end of year 3, expand both the kitchen and the dining area to the 130,000 meals-per-year volume. Construction and equipment costs would be $424,000, with $220,000 at the end of year 0 and the remainder at the end of year 3. As with alternative 1, the contribution margin would go up to 22 percent.

   With both new alternatives, the salvage value would be negligible. Compare the cash flows of all alternatives. Should Grandmother's Chicken Restaurant expand with the new or the old technology? Should it expand now or later?

14. Several years ago, River City built a water purification plant to remove toxins and filter the city's drinking water. Because of population growth, the demand for water next year will be more than the plant's capacity of 120 million gallons per year. Therefore, the city must expand the facility. The estimated demand over the next 20 years is given in Table 6.4.

   The city planning commission is considering three alternatives.

   ■ *Alternative 1:* Expand enough at the end of year 0 to last 20 years, which means an 80 million gallon increase (200 – 120).

   ■ *Alternative 2:* Expand at the end of year 0 and at the end of year 10.

   ■ *Alternative 3:* Expand at the end of years 0, 5, 10, and 15.

   Each alternative would provide the needed 200 million gallons per year at the end of 20 years, when the value of the plant would be the same regardless of the alternative chosen. Significant economies of scale can be achieved in construction costs: A 20 million gallon expansion would cost $18 million; a 40 million gallon expansion, $30 million; and an 80 million gallon expansion, only $50 million. The level of future interest rates is uncertain, leading to uncertainty about the hurdle rate. The city believes that it could be as low as 12 percent and as high as 16 percent (see Supplement A, "Decision Making Models").

   a. Compute the cash flows for each alternative, compared to a base case of doing nothing. (*Note*: As a municipal utility, the operation pays no taxes.)

   b. Which alternative minimizes the present value of construction costs over the next 20 years if the discount rate is 12 percent? Sixteen percent?

   c. Because the decision involves public policy and compromise, what political considerations does the planning commission face?

TABLE 6.4		WATER DEMAND			
Year	Demand	Year	Demand	Year	Demand
0	120	7	148	14	176
1	124	8	152	15	180
2	128	9	156	16	184
3	132	10	160	17	188
4	136	11	164	18	192
5	140	12	168	19	196
6	144	13	172	20	200

15. A manager is trying to decide whether to buy one machine or two. If only one machine is purchased and demand proves to be excessive, the second machine can be purchased later. Some sales would be lost, however, because the lead time for delivery of this type of machine is six months. In addition, the cost per machine will be lower if both machines are purchased at the same time. The probability of low demand is estimated to be 0.30 and that of high demand to be 0.70. The after-tax NPV of the benefits from purchasing two machines together is $90,000 if demand is low and $170,000 if demand is high.

   If one machine is purchased and demand is low, the NPV is $120,000. If demand is high, the manager has three options: (1) doing nothing, which has an NPV of $120,000; (2) subcontracting, with an NPV of $140,000; and (3) buying the second machine, with an NPV of $130,000.

   a. Draw a decision tree for this problem.

   b. What is the best decision and what is its expected payoff?

16. Knott's Industries manufactures standard and super premium backyard swing sets. Currently it has four identical swing-set-making machines, which are operated

250 days per year and 8 hours each day. A capacity cushion of 20 percent is desired. The following information is also known:

	Standard Model	Super Premium Model
Annual Demand	20,000	10,000
Standard Processing Time	7 min	20 min
Average Lot Size	50	30
Standard Setup Time per Lot	30 min	45 min

a. Does Knott's have sufficient capacity to meet annual demand?

b. If Knott's was able to reduce the setup time for the Super Premium Model from 45 minutes to 30 minutes, would there be enough current capacity to produce 20,000 units of each type of swing set?

17. Darren Mack owns the "Gas n' Go" convenience store and gas station. After hearing a marketing lecture, he realizes that it might be possible to draw more customers to his high-margin convenience store by selling his gasoline at a lower price. However, the "Gas n' Go" is unable to qualify for volume discounts on its gasoline purchases, and therefore cannot sell gasoline for profit if the price is lowered. Each new pump will cost $95,000 to install, but will increase customer traffic in the store by 1,000 customers per year. Also, because the "Gas n' Go" would be selling its gasoline at no profit, Darren plans on increasing the profit margin on convenience store items incrementally over the next five years. Assume a discount rate of 8 percent. The projected convenience store sales per customer and the projected profit margin for the next five years are as follows:

Year	Projected Convenience Store Sales Per Customer	Projected Profit Margin
1	$5	20%
2	$6.50	25%
3	$8	30%
4	$10	35%
5	$11	40%

a. What is the NPV of the next five years of cash flows if Darren had four new pumps installed?

b. If Darren required a payback period of four years, should he go ahead with the installation of the new pumps?

18. Acme Steel Fabricators experienced booming business for the past five years. The company fabricates a wide range of steel products, such as railings, ladders, and light structural steel framing. The current manual method of materials handling is causing excessive inventories and congestion. Acme is considering the purchase of an overhead rail-mounted hoist system or a forklift truck to increase capacity and improve manufacturing efficiency.

The annual pretax payoff from the system depends on future demand. If demand stays at the current level, the probability of which is 0.50, annual savings from the overhead hoist will be $10,000. If demand rises, the hoist will save $25,000 annually because of operating efficiencies in addition to new sales. Finally, if demand falls, the hoist will result in an estimated annual loss of $65,000. The probability is estimated to be 0.30 for higher demand and 0.20 for lower demand.

If the forklift is purchased, annual payoffs will be $5,000 if demand is unchanged, $10,000 if demand rises, and −$25,000 if demand falls.

a. Draw a decision tree for this problem and compute the expected value of the payoff for each alternative.

b. Which is the best alternative, based on the expected values?

19. The vice president of operations at Dintell Corporation, a major supplier of passenger-side automotive air bags, is considering a $50 million expansion at the firm's Fort Worth, Texas, production complex. The most recent economic projections indicate a 0.60 probability that the overall market will be $400 million per year over the next 5 years and a 0.40 probability that the market will be only $200 million per year during the same period. The marketing department estimates that Dintell has a 0.50 probability of capturing 40 percent of the market and an equal probability of obtaining only 30 percent of the market. The cost of goods sold is estimated to be 70 percent of sales. For planning purposes, the company currently uses a 12 percent discount rate, a 40 percent tax rate, and the MACRS depreciation schedule. The criteria for investment decisions at Dintell are (1) the net expected present value must be greater than zero; (2) there must be at least a 70 percent chance that the net present value will be positive; and (3) there must be no more than a 10 percent chance that the firm will lose more than 20 percent of the initial value.

a. Based on the stated criteria, determine whether Dintell should fund the project.

b. What effect will a probability of 0.70 of capturing 40 percent of the market have on the decision?

c. What effect will an increase in the discount rate to 15 percent have on the decision? A decrease to 10 percent?

d. What effect will the need for another $10 million in the third year have on the decision?

20. Mackelprang, Inc., is in the initial stages of building the premier planned community in the greater Phoenix, Arizona, metropolitan area. The main selling point will be the community's lush golf courses. Homes with golf course views will generate premiums far larger than homes with no golf course views, but building golf courses is expensive and takes up valuable space that non-view homes could be built upon. Mackelprang, Inc., has limited land capacity. In order to maximize its profits, it is faced with a decision as to how many golf courses it should build, which in turn will impact how

many homes with and without golf course views it will be able to construct. Mackelprang, Inc., realizes that this decision is directly related to the premium buyers will be willing to spend to buy homes with golf course views. Mackelprang, Inc., is required to build at least one golf course, but has enough space to build up to three golf courses. The following table indicates the costs and potential revenues for each course:

a. Which golf course or courses should Mackelprang, Inc., build?

b. What is the expected payoff for this project?

	Indian River	The Cactus	Wildwood
Cost	$2.6M	$1.25M	$2.5M
Highest Possible Revenue	$4M	$2M	$2M
Probability of High Revenue	0.3	0.2	0.3
Likely Revenue	$2.5M	$1.5M	$4M
Probability of Likely Revenue	0.4	0.5	0.5
Lowest Possible Revenue	$1M	$1M	$1M
Probability of Low Revenue	0.3	0.3	0.2

VIDEO CASE   Gate Turnaround at Southwest Airlines

Rollin King and Herb Kelleher started Southwest Airlines in 1971 with this idea: if they could take airline passengers where they want to go, on time, at the lowest possible price, and have a good time while doing it, people would love to fly their airline. The result? No other airline in the industry's history has enjoyed the customer loyalty and extended profitability for which Southwest is now famous. The company now flies more than 3,400 times each day to over 64 destinations across the United States.

There's more to the story, however, than making promises and hoping to fulfill them. A large part of Southwest Airlines' success lies in its ability to plan long term capacity to better match demand, as also improving the utilization of its fleet by turning around an aircraft at the gate faster than its competitors. Capacity at Southwest is measured in seat-miles, and even a single minute reduction in aircraft turnaround time system wide means additional seat-miles being added to the available capacity of Southwest Airlines.

As soon as an aircraft calls "in range" at one of Southwest's airport locations, called a station, the local operations manager notifies the ground operations team so that they can start mobilizing all the parties involved in servicing the aircraft in preparation for its next departure. The grounds operations team consists of a baggage transfer driver who has responsibility for getting connecting flight bags to their proper planes, a local baggage driver who moves bags to baggage claim for passenger pick-up, a lavatory truck driver who handles restroom receptacle drainage, a lead gate agent to handle baggage carts and track incoming and outgoing bag counts, and a bin agent to manage baggage and cargo inside the plane. The ground operations team knows it must turn the plane around in 25 minutes or less. The clock starts when the pilot sets the wheel brakes.

Inbound and outbound flights are coordinated by the supervisors between Southwest's 64 airport stations through the company's Operations Terminal Information System (OTIS). Each local supervisor is able to keep track of their flights and manage any delays or problems that may have crept into the system by keeping in touch with headquarters in Dallas for system-wide issues that may impact a local station, along with using the OTIS information coming from stations sending flights their way.

Just what, exactly, does it take to turn around an aircraft? In-bound flight 3155 from Phoenix to Dallas' Love Field is a good example. In Phoenix, the

Baggage transfer starts less than forty seconds after engine shutdown at Southwest Airlines.

operations coordinators and ground operations team push back the plane as scheduled at 9:50 am. The flight is scheduled to arrive at 3:35 pm in Dallas. The Phoenix team enters into OTIS the information the ground operations team will need in Dallas, such as wheelchairs, gate-checked baggage, cargo bin locator data, and other data needed to close out the flight on their end. This action lets the Dallas station know what to expect when the plane lands.

In Dallas, the local ground operations coordinators have been monitoring all 110 inbound flights and now see Phoenix flight 3155 in the system, scheduled for an on-time arrival. When the pilot calls "in-range" as it nears Dallas, the ground crew prepares for action.

As the plane is guided to its "stop mark" at the gate, the lead agent waits for the captain's signal that the engines have been turned off and brakes set. Within just ten seconds, the provisioning truck pulls up to open the back door for restocking supplies such as drinks and snacks. The waiting fuel truck extends its hose to the underwing connection, and in less than two minutes, picks up refueling instructions and starts to load fuel. As soon as the aircraft is in position, the operations team steers the jetway into position and locks it against the aircraft. The door is opened, the in-flight crew is greeted, and passengers start to deplane.

Outside, less than forty seconds after engine shutdown, baggage is rolling off the plane and gets placed onto the first cart. Any transfer bags get sent to their next destination, and gate-checked bags are delivered to the top of the jetway stairs for passenger pick-up.

While passengers make their way out of the plane, the in-flight crew helps clean up and prepare the cabin for the next flight. If all goes well, the last passenger will leave the plane after only eight minutes. By this time, passengers waiting to board have already lined up in their designated positions for boarding. The gate agent confirms that the plane is ready for passenger boarding, and calls for the first group to turn in their boarding passes and file down the jetway.

At the completion of boarding, the operations agent checks the fuel invoice, cargo bin loading schedule with actual bag counts in their bins from the baggage agents, and a lavatory service record confirming that cleaning has taken place. Final paperwork is given to the captain. The door to the aircraft is closed, and the jetway is retracted. Thirty seconds later, the plane is pushed back and the operations agent gives a traditional salute to the captain to send the flight on its way. Total elapsed time: less than 25 minutes.

Managing Southwest's capacity has been somewhat simplified by strategic decisions made early on in the company's life. First, the company's fleet of aircraft is all Boeing 737's. This single decision impacts all areas of operations – from crew training to aircraft maintenance. The single-plane configuration also provides Southwest with crew scheduling flexibility. Since pilots and flight crews can be deployed across the entire fleet, there are no constraints with regard to training and certification pegged to specific aircraft types.

The way Southwest has streamlined its operations for tight turnarounds means it must maintain a high capacity cushion to accommodate variability in its daily operations. Anything from weather delays to unexpected maintenance issues at the gate can slow down the flow of operations to a crawl. To handle these unplanned but anticipated challenges, Southwest builds into its schedules enough cushion to manage these delays yet not so much that employees and planes are idle. Additionally, the company encourages discussion to keep on top of what's working and where improvements can be made. If a problem is noted at a downstream station, say bags weren't properly loaded, this information quickly travels back up to the originating station for correction so that it doesn't happen again.

Even with the tightly managed operations Southwest Airlines enjoys, company executives know that continued improvement is necessary if the company is to remain profitable into the future. Company executives know when they have achieved their goals when internal and external metrics are reached. For example, the Department of Transportation (DOT) tracks on-time departures, customer complaints, and mishandled baggage for all airlines. The company sets targets for achievement on these dimensions and lets employees know on a monthly basis how the company is doing against those metrics and the rest of the industry. Regular communication with all employees is delivered via meetings, posters, and newsletters. Rewards such as prizes and profit sharing are given for successful achievement.

As for the future, Bob Jordan, Southwest's Executive Vice President for Strategy and Planning, puts it this way: "We make money when our planes are in the air, not on the ground. If we can save one minute off every turn system-wide, that's like putting five additional planes in the air. If a single plane generates annual revenue of $25 million, there's $125 million in profit potential from those time savings."

QUESTIONS

1. How can capacity and utilization be measured at an airline such as SWA?
2. Which factors can adversely impact turn-around times at SWA?
3. How does Southwest Airlines know they are achieving their goals?
4. What are the important long-term issues relevant for managing capacity, revenue, and customer satisfaction for SWA?

CASE   Fitness Plus, Part A

Fitness Plus, Part B, explores alternatives to expanding a new downtown facility and is included in the Instructor's Resource Manual. If you are interested in this topic, ask your instructor for a preview.

Fitness Plus is a full-service health and sports club in Greensboro, North Carolina. The club provides a range of facilities and services to support three primary activities: fitness, recreation, and relaxation. Fitness activities generally take place in four areas of the club: the aerobics room, which can accommodate 35 people per class; a room equipped with free weights; a workout room with 24 pieces of Nautilus equipment; and a large workout room containing 29 pieces of cardiovascular equipment. This equipment includes nine stairsteppers, six treadmills, six life-cycle bikes, three airdyne bikes, two cross-aerobics machines, two rowing machines, and one climber. Recreational facilities comprise eight racquetball courts, six tennis courts, and

a large outdoor pool. Fitness Plus also sponsors softball, volleyball, and swim teams in city recreation leagues. Relaxation is accomplished through yoga classes held twice a week in the aerobics room, whirlpool tubs located in each locker room, and a trained massage therapist.

Situated in a large suburban office park, Fitness Plus opened its doors in 1995. During the first two years, membership was small and use of the facilities was light. By 1997, membership had grown as fitness began to play a large role in more and more people's lives. Along with this growth came increased use of club facilities. Records indicate that in 2000, an average of 15 members per hour checked into the club during a typical day. Of course, the actual number of members per hour varied by both day and time. On some days during a slow period, only six to eight members would check in per hour. At a peak time, such as Mondays from 4:00 P.M. to 7:00 P.M., the number would be as high as 40 per hour.

The club was open from 6:30 A.M. to 11:00 P.M. Monday through Thursday. On Friday and Saturday, the club closed at 8:00 P.M., and on Sunday the hours were 12:00 P.M. to 8:00 P.M.

As the popularity of health and fitness continued to grow, so did Fitness Plus. By May 2005, the average number of members arriving per hour during a typical day had increased to 25. The lowest period had a rate of 10 members per hour; during peak periods, 80 members per hour checked in to use the facilities. This growth brought complaints from members about overcrowding and unavailability of equipment. Most of these complaints centered on the Nautilus, cardiovascular, and aerobics fitness areas. The owners began to wonder whether the club was indeed too small for its membership. Past research indicated that individuals work out an average of 60 minutes per visit. Data collected from member surveys showed the following facilities usage pattern: 30 percent of the members do aerobics, 40 percent use the cardiovascular equipment, 25 percent use the Nautilus machines, 20 percent use the free weights, 15 percent use the racquetball courts, and 10 percent use the tennis courts. The owners wondered whether they could use this information to estimate how well existing capacity was being utilized.

If capacity levels were being stretched, now was the time to decide what to do. It was already May, and any expansion of the existing facility would take at least four months. The owners knew that January was always a peak membership enrollment month and that any new capacity needed to be ready by then. However, other factors had to be considered. The area was growing both in terms of population and geographically. The downtown area just received a major facelift, and many new offices and businesses were moving back to it, causing a resurgence in activity.

With this growth came increased competition. A new YMCA was offering a full range of services at a low cost. Two new health and fitness facilities had opened within the past year in locations 10 to 15 minutes from Fitness Plus. The first, called the Oasis, catered to the young adult crowd and restricted the access of children under 16 years old. The other facility, Gold's Gym, provided excellent weight and cardiovascular training only.

As the owners thought about the situation, they had many questions: Were the capacities of the existing facilities constrained, and if so, where? If capacity expansion was necessary, should the existing facility be expanded? Because of the limited amount of land at the current site, expansion of some services might require reducing the capacity of others. Finally, owing to increased competition and growth downtown, was now the time to open a facility to serve that market? A new facility would take six months to renovate, and the financial resources were not available to do both.

QUESTIONS

1. What method would you use to measure the capacity of Fitness Plus? Has Fitness Plus reached its capacity?

2. Which capacity strategy would be appropriate for Fitness Plus? Justify your answer.

3. How would you link the capacity decision being made by Fitness Plus to other types of operating decisions?

SELECTED REFERENCES

Bakke, Nils Arne, and Ronald Hellberg. "The Challenges of Capacity Planning." *International Journal of Production Economics*, vols. 31–30 (1993), pp. 243–264.

Bowman, Edward H. "Scale of Operations—An Empirical Study." *Operations Research* (June 1958), pp. 320–328.

Hammesfahr, R., D. Jack, James A. Pope, and Alireza Ardalan. "Strategic Planning for Production Capacity." *International Journal of Operations and Production Management*, vol. 13, no. 5 (1993), pp. 41–53.

Hartvigsen, David. *SimQuick: Process Simulation with Excel*, 2d ed. Upper Saddle River, NJ: Prentice Hall, 2004.

"Intel's $10 Billion Gamble." *Fortune* (November 11, 2002), pp. 90–102.

Klassen, Kenneth J., and Thomas R. Rohleder. "Combining Operations and Marketing to Manage Capacity and Demand in Services." *The Service Industries Journal*, vol. 21, no. 2 (2001), pp. 1–30.

Klassen, Robert D., and Larry J. Menor. "The process management triangle: An empirical investigation of process trade-offs." *Journal of Operations Management*, vol. 25 (2007), pp. 1015–1034.

Ritzman, Larry P., and M. Hossein Safizadeh. "Linking Process Choice with Plant-Level Decisions About Capital and Human Resources." *Production and Operations Management*, vol. 8, no. 4 (1999), pp. 374–392.

C WAITING LINE MODELS

LEARNING GOALS

After reading this supplement, you should be able to:

1. Identify the elements of a waiting-line problem in a real situation.

2. Describe the single-server, multiple-server, and finite-source models.

3. Explain how to use waiting-line models to estimate the operating characteristics of a process.

4. Explain how waiting lines can be used to make managerial decisions.

Anyone who has ever waited at a stoplight, at McDonald's, or at the registrar's office has experienced the dynamics of waiting lines. Perhaps one of the best examples of effective management of waiting lines is that of Walt Disney World. One day the park may have only 25,000 customers, but on another day the numbers may top 90,000. Careful analysis of process flows, technology for people-mover (materials handling) equipment, capacity, and layout keeps the waiting times for attractions to acceptable levels.

The analysis of waiting lines is of concern to managers because it affects process design, capacity planning, process performance, and ultimately, supply chain performance. In this supplement we discuss why waiting lines form, the uses of waiting-line models in operations management, and the structure of waiting-line models. We also discuss the decisions managers address with the models. Waiting lines can also be analyzed using computer simulation. Software such as SimQuick, a simulation package included in my**om**lab, or Excel spreadsheets can be used to analyze the problems in this supplement.

my**om**lab and the Companion Website at **www.pearsonglobaleditions.com/krajewski** contain many tools, activities, and resources designed for this supplement.

Why Waiting Lines Form

A **waiting line** is one or more "customers" waiting for service. The customers can be people or inanimate objects, such as machines requiring maintenance, sales orders waiting for shipping, or inventory items waiting to be used. A waiting line forms because of a temporary imbalance between the demand for service and the capacity of the system to provide the service. In most real-life waiting-line problems, the demand rate varies; that is, customers arrive at unpredictable intervals. Most often, the rate of producing the service also varies, depending on customer needs. Suppose that bank customers arrive at an average rate of 15 per hour throughout the day and that the bank can process an average of 20 customers per hour. Why would a waiting line ever develop? The answers are that the customer arrival rate varies throughout the day and the time required to process a customer can vary. During the noon hour, 30 customers may arrive at the bank. Some of them may have complicated transactions requiring above-average process times. The waiting line may grow to 15 customers for a period of time before it eventually disappears. Even though the bank manager provided for more than enough capacity on average, waiting lines can still develop.

Waiting lines can develop even if the time to process a customer is constant. For example, a subway train is computer controlled to arrive at stations along its route. Each train is programmed to arrive at a station, say, every 15 minutes. Even with the constant service time, waiting lines develop while riders wait for the next train or cannot get on a train because of the size of the crowd at a busy time of the day. Consequently, variability in the rate of demand determines the sizes of the waiting lines in this case. In general, if no variability in the demand occurs or service rates and enough capacity are provided, no waiting lines form.

Uses of Waiting-Line Theory

Waiting-line theory applies to service as well as manufacturing firms, relating customer arrival and service-system processing characteristics to service-system output characteristics. In our discussion, we use the term *service* broadly—the act of doing work for a customer. The service system might be hair cutting at a hair salon, satisfying customer complaints, or processing a production order of parts on a certain machine. Other examples of customers and services include lines of theatergoers waiting to purchase tickets, trucks waiting to be unloaded at a warehouse, machines waiting to be repaired by a maintenance crew, and patients waiting to be examined by a physician. Regardless of the situation, waiting-line problems have several common elements.

Structure of Waiting-Line Problems

Analyzing waiting-line problems begins with a description of the situation's basic elements. Each specific situation will have different characteristics, but four elements are common to all situations:

1. An input, or **customer population**, that generates potential customers
2. A waiting line of customers
3. The **service facility**, consisting of a person (or crew), a machine (or group of machines), or both necessary to perform the service for the customer
4. A **priority rule**, which selects the next customer to be served by the service facility

Figure C.1 shows these basic elements. The triangles, circles, and squares are intended to show a diversity of customers with different needs. The **service system** describes the number of lines and the arrangement of the facilities. After the service has been performed, the served customers leave the system.

Customer Population

A customer population is the source of input to the service system. If the potential number of new customers for the service system is appreciably affected by the number of customers already in the system, the input source is said to be *finite*. For example, suppose that a maintenance crew is assigned responsibility for the repair of 10 machines. The customer population for the maintenance crew is 10 machines in working order. The population generates customers for the maintenance crew as a function of the failure rates for the machines. As

FIGURE C.1 ▶
Basic Elements of Waiting-Line
Models

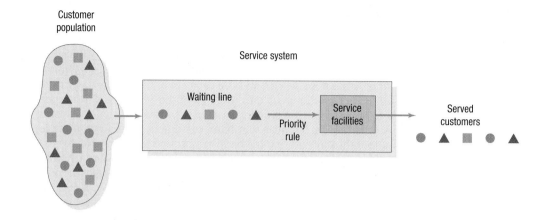

more machines fail and enter the service system, either waiting for service or being repaired, the customer population becomes smaller and the rate at which it can generate another customer falls. Consequently, the customer population is said to be finite.

Alternatively, an *infinite* customer population is one in which the number of customers in the system does not affect the rate at which the population generates new customers. For example, consider a mail-order operation for which the customer population consists of shoppers who have received a catalog of products sold by the company. Because the customer population is so large and only a small fraction of the shoppers place orders at any one time, the number of new orders it generates is not appreciably affected by the number of orders waiting for service or being processed by the service system. In this case, the customer population is said to be infinite.

Customers in waiting lines may be *patient* or *impatient*, which has nothing to do with the colorful language a customer may use while waiting in line for a long time on a hot day. In the context of waiting-line problems, a patient customer is one who enters the system and remains there until being served; an impatient customer is one who either decides not to enter the system (balks) or leaves the system before being served (reneges). For the methods used in this supplement, we make the simplifying assumption that all customers are patient.

The Service System

The service system may be described by the number of lines and the arrangement of facilities.

Number of Lines   Waiting lines may be designed to be a *single line* or *multiple lines*. Figure C.2 shows an example of each arrangement. Generally, single lines are utilized at airline counters, inside banks, and at some fast-food restaurants; whereas multiple lines are utilized in grocery stores, at drive-in bank operations, and in discount stores. When multiple servers are available and each one can handle general transactions, the single-line arrangement keeps servers uniformly busy and gives customers a sense of fairness. Customers believe that they are being served on the basis of when they arrived, and not on how well they guessed their waiting time when selecting a particular line. The multiple-line design

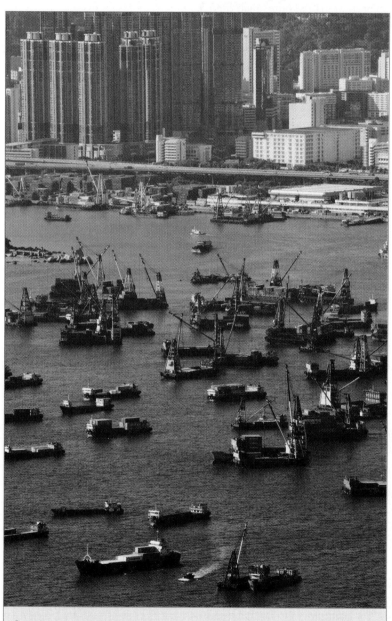

Sometimes customers are not organized neatly into lines. Here ships wait to use the port facilities in Victoria Harbor, West Kowloon, Hong Kong.

is best when some of the servers provide a limited set of services. In this arrangement, customers select the services they need and wait in the line where that service is provided, such as at a grocery store that provides special lines for customers paying with cash or having fewer than 10 items.

Sometimes customers are not organized neatly into "lines." Machines that need repair on the production floor of a factory may be left in place, and the maintenance crew comes to them. Nonetheless, we can think of such machines as forming a single line or multiple lines, depending on the number of repair crews and their specialties. Likewise, passengers who telephone for a taxi also form a line even though they may wait at different locations.

Arrangement of Service Facilities Service facilities consist of the personnel and equipment necessary to perform the service for the customer. Service facility arrangement is described by the number of channels and phases. A **channel** is one or more facilities required to perform a given service. A **phase** is a single step in providing the service. Some services require a single phase, while others require a sequence of phases. Consequently, a service facility uses some combination of channels and phases. Managers should choose an arrangement based on customer volume and the nature of services provided. Figure C.3 shows examples of the five basic types of service facility arrangements.

In the *single-channel, single-phase* system, all services demanded by a customer can be performed by a single-server facility. Customers form a single line and go through the service facility one at a time. Examples are a drive-through car wash and a machine that must process several batches of parts.

The *single-channel, multiple-phase* arrangement is used when the services are best performed in sequence by more than one facility, yet customer volume or other constraints limit the design to one channel. Customers form a single line and proceed sequentially from one service facility to the next. An example of this arrangement is a McDonald's drive-through, where the first facility takes the order, the second takes the money, and the third provides the food.

(a) Single line

(b) Multiple lines

▲ **FIGURE C.2**
Waiting-Line Arrangements

channel
One or more facilities required to perform a given service.

phase
A single step in providing a service.

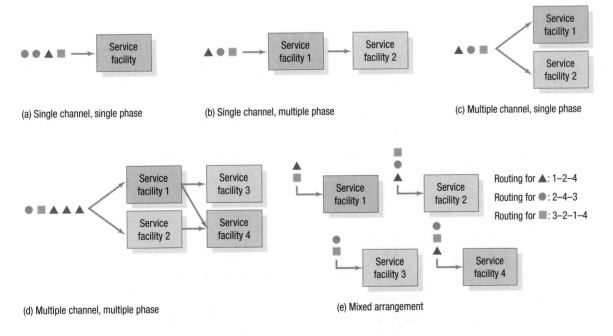

(a) Single channel, single phase

(b) Single channel, multiple phase

(c) Multiple channel, single phase

(d) Multiple channel, multiple phase

(e) Mixed arrangement

Routing for ▲: 1–2–4
Routing for ●: 2–4–3
Routing for ■: 3–2–1–4

▲ **FIGURE C.3**
Examples of Service Facility Arrangements

Commuters wait in line to purchase tickets at Grand Central Station in New York City. This is an example of a multiple-channel, single-phase service design.

The *multiple-channel, single-phase* arrangement is used when demand is large enough to warrant providing the same service at more than one facility or when the services offered by the facilities are different. Customers form one or more lines, depending on the design. In the single-line design, customers are served by the first available server, as in the lobby of a bank. If each channel has its own waiting line, customers wait until the server for their line can serve them, as at a bank's drive-through facilities.

The *multiple-channel, multiple-phase* arrangement occurs when customers can be served by one of the first-phase facilities but then require service from a second-phase facility, and so on. In some cases, customers cannot switch channels after service has begun; in others they can. An example of this arrangement is a laundromat. Washing machines are the first-phase facilities, and dryers are the second-phase facilities. Some of the washing machines and dryers may be designed for extra-large loads, thereby providing the customer a choice of channels.

The most complex waiting-line problem involves customers who have unique sequences of required services; consequently, service cannot be described neatly in phases. A *mixed* arrangement is used in such a case. In the mixed arrangement, waiting lines can develop in front of each facility, as in a medical center, where a patient goes to an exam room for a nurse to take his or her blood pressure and weight, goes back to the waiting room until the doctor can see him or her, and after consultation proceeds to the laboratory to give a blood sample, radiology to have an X–ray taken, or the pharmacy for prescribed drugs, depending on specific needs.

Priority Rule

The priority rule determines which customer to serve next. Most service systems that you encounter use the first-come, first-served (FCFS) rule. The customer at the head of the waiting line has the highest priority, and the customer who arrived last has the lowest priority. Other priority disciplines might take the customer with the earliest promised due date (EDD) or the customer with the shortest expected processing time (SPT).[1]

A **preemptive discipline** is a rule that allows a customer of higher priority to interrupt the service of another customer. For example, in a hospital emergency room, patients with the most life-threatening injuries receive treatment first, regardless of their order of arrival. Modeling of systems having complex priority disciplines is usually done using computer simulation.

preemptive discipline

A rule that allows a customer of higher priority to interrupt the service of another customer.

PROBABILITY DISTRIBUTIONS

The sources of variation in waiting-line problems come from the random arrivals of customers and the variations in service times. Each of these sources can be described with a probability distribution.

Arrival Distribution

Customers arrive at service facilities randomly. The variability of customer arrivals often can be described by a Poisson distribution, which specifies the probability that n customers will arrive in T time periods:

$$P_n = \frac{(\lambda T)^n}{n!} e^{-\lambda T} \text{ for } n = 0, 1, 2, \ldots$$

---

[1] We focus on FCFS in this supplement. See Chapter 14, "Planning and Scheduling Operations," for additional discussion of FCFS and EDD. See also Supplement J, "Operations Scheduling," for SPT and additional rules.

where

P_n = probability of n arrivals in T time periods

λ = average number of customer arrivals per period

e = 2.7183

The mean of the Poisson distribution is λT, and the variance also is λT. The Poisson distribution is a discrete distribution; that is, the probabilities are for a specific number of arrivals per unit of time.

EXAMPLE C.1	Calculating the Probability of Customer Arrivals

Management is redesigning the customer service process in a large department store. Accommodating four customers is important. Customers arrive at the desk at the rate of two customers per hour. What is the probability that four customers will arrive during any hour?

SOLUTION

In this case λ = 2 customers per hour, T = 1 hour, and n = 4 customers. The probability that four customers will arrive in any hour is

$$P_4 = \frac{[2(1)]^4}{4!}\, e^{-2(1)} = \frac{16}{24} e^{-2} = 0.090$$

DECISION POINT

The manager of the customer service desk can use this information to determine the space requirements for the desk and waiting area. There is a relatively small probability that four customers will arrive in any hour. Consequently, seating capacity for two or three customers should be more than adequate unless the time to service each customer is lengthy. Further analysis on service times is warranted.

Another way to specify the arrival distribution is to do it in terms of customer **interarrival times**—that is, the time between customer arrivals. If the customer population generates customers according to a Poisson distribution, the *exponential distribution* describes the probability that the next customer will arrive in the next T time periods. As the exponential distribution also describes service times, we discuss the details of this distribution in the next section.

interarrival times

The time between customer arrivals.

Service Time Distribution

The exponential distribution describes the probability that the service time of the customer at a particular facility will be no more than T time periods. The probability can be calculated by using the formula

$$P(t \le T) = 1 - e^{-\mu T}$$

where

μ = average number of customers completing service per period

t = service time of the customer

T = target service time

The mean of the service time distribution is $1/\mu$, and the variance is $(1/\mu)^2$. As T increases, the probability that the customer's service time will be less than T approaches 1.0.

For simplicity, let us look at a single-channel, single-phase arrangement.

EXAMPLE C.2	Calculating the Service Time Probability

The management of the large department store in Example C.1 must determine whether more training is needed for the customer service clerk. The clerk at the customer service desk can serve an average of three customers per hour. What is the probability that a customer will require less than 10 minutes of service?

SOLUTION

We must have all the data in the same time units. Because $\mu = 3$ customers per hour, we convert minutes of time to hours, or $T = 10$ minutes $= 10/60$ hour $= 0.167$ hour. Then

$$P(t \leq T) = 1 - e^{-\mu T}$$
$$P(t \leq 0.167 \text{ hour}) = 1 - e^{-3(0.167)} = 1 - 0.61 = 0.39$$

DECISION POINT

The probability that the customer will require only 10 minutes or fewer is not high, which leaves the possibility that customers may experience lengthy delays. Management should consider additional training for the clerk so as to reduce the time it takes to process a customer request.

Some characteristics of the exponential distribution do not always conform to an actual situation. The exponential distribution model is based on the assumption that each service time is independent of those that preceded it. In real life, however, productivity may improve as human servers learn about the work. Another assumption underlying the model is that very small, as well as very large, service times are possible. However, real-life situations often require a fixed-length start-up time, some cutoff on total service time, or nearly constant service time.

USING WAITING-LINE MODELS TO ANALYZE OPERATIONS

Operations managers can use waiting-line models to balance the gains that might be made by increasing the efficiency of the service system against the costs of doing so. In addition, managers should consider the costs of *not* making improvements to the system: Long waiting lines or long waiting times may cause customers to balk or renege. Managers should therefore be concerned about the following operating characteristics of the system.

1. *Line Length.* The number of customers in the waiting line reflects one of two conditions. Short lines could mean either good customer service or too much capacity. Similarly, long lines could indicate either low server efficiency or the need to increase capacity.

2. *Number of Customers in System.* The number of customers in line and being served also relates to service efficiency and capacity. A large number of customers in the system causes congestion and may result in customer dissatisfaction, unless more capacity is added.

3. *Waiting Time in Line.* Long lines do not always mean long waiting times. If the service rate is fast, a long line can be served efficiently. However, when waiting time seems long, customers perceive the quality of service to be poor. Managers may try to change the arrival rate of customers or design the system to make long wait times seem shorter than they really are. For example, at Walt Disney World, customers in line for an attraction are entertained by videos and also are informed about expected waiting times, which seems to help them endure the wait.

4. *Total Time in System.* The total elapsed time from entry into the system until exit from the system may indicate problems with customers, server efficiency, or capacity. If some customers are spending too much time in the service system, it may be necessary to change the priority discipline, increase productivity, or adjust capacity in some way.

5. *Service Facility Utilization.* The collective utilization of service facilities reflects the percentage of time that they are busy. Management's goal is to maintain high utilization and profitability without adversely affecting the other operating characteristics.

The best method for analyzing a waiting-line problem is to relate the five operating characteristics and their alternatives to dollars. However, placing a dollar figure on certain characteristics (such as the waiting time of a shopper in a grocery store) is difficult. In such cases, an analyst must weigh the cost of implementing the alternative under consideration against a subjective assessment of the cost of *not* making the change.

We now present three models and some examples showing how waiting-line models can help operations managers make decisions. We analyze problems requiring the single-server, multiple-server, and finite-source models, all of which are single phase. References to more advanced models are cited at the end of this supplement.

Single-Server Model

The simplest waiting-line model involves a single server and a single line of customers. To further specify the model, we make the following assumptions:

1. The customer population is infinite and all customers are patient.
2. The customers arrive according to a Poisson distribution, with a mean arrival rate of λ.
3. The service distribution is exponential, with a mean service rate of μ.
4. The mean service rate exceeds the mean arrival rate.
5. Customers are served on a first-come, first-served basis.
6. The length of the waiting line is unlimited.

With these assumptions, we can apply various formulas to describe the operating characteristics of the system:

$$\rho = \text{Average utilization of the system}$$
$$= \frac{\lambda}{\mu}$$
$$P_n = \text{Probability that } n \text{ customers are in the system}$$
$$= (1 - \rho)\rho^n$$
$$L = \text{Average number of customers in the service system}$$
$$= \frac{\lambda}{\mu - \lambda}$$
$$L_q = \text{Average number of customers in the waiting line}$$
$$= \rho L$$
$$W = \text{Average time spent in the system, including service}$$
$$= \frac{1}{\mu - \lambda}$$
$$W_q = \text{Average waiting time in line}$$
$$= \rho W$$

EXAMPLE C.3	Calculating the Operating Characteristics of a Single-Channel, Single-Phase System

The manager of a grocery store in the retirement community of Sunnyville is interested in providing good service to the senior citizens who shop in her store. Currently, the store has a separate checkout counter for senior citizens. On average, 30 senior citizens per hour arrive at the counter, according to a Poisson distribution, and are served at an average rate of 35 customers per hour, with exponential service times. Find the following operating characteristics:

a. Probability of zero customers in the system

b. Average utilization of the checkout clerk

c. Average number of customers in the system

d. Average number of customers in line

e. Average time spent in the system

f. Average waiting time in line

PEARSON
myomlab

Active Model C.1 in my**om**lab provides additional insight on the single-server model and its uses for this problem.

SOLUTION

The checkout counter can be modeled as a single-channel, single-phase system. Figure C.4 shows the results from the *Waiting-Lines* Solver from OM Explorer. Manual calculations of the equations for the *single-server model* are demonstrated in Solved Problem 1 at the end of the supplement.

FIGURE C.4 ▶

Waiting-Lines Solver for Single-Channel, Single-Phase System

Servers		(Number of servers *s* assumed to be 1 in single-serve model)
Arrival Rate (λ)	30	
Service Rate (μ)	35	

Probability of zero customers in the system (P_0)	0.1429
Probability of exactly ▼ 0 customers in the system	0.1429
Average utilization of the server (ρ)	0.8571
Average number of customers in the system (L)	6.0000
Average number of customers in line (L_q)	5.1429
Average waiting/service time in the system (W)	0.2000
Average waiting time in line (W_q)	0.1714

Both the average waiting time in the system (W) and the average time spent waiting in line (W_q) are expressed in hours. To convert the results to minutes, simply multiply by 60 minutes/ hour. For example, $W = 0.20(60) = 12.00$ minutes, and $W_q = 0.1714(60) = 10.28$ minutes.

EXAMPLE C.4   **Analyzing Service Rates with the Single-Server Model**

Tutor C.1 in my**om**lab provides a new example to practice the single-server model.

The manager of the Sunnyville grocery in Example C.3 wants answers to the following questions:

a.   What service rate would be required so that customers averaged only 8 minutes in the system?

b.   For that service rate, what is the probability of having more than four customers in the system?

c.   What service rate would be required to have only a 10 percent chance of exceeding four customers in the system?

SOLUTION

The *Waiting-Lines* Solver from OM Explorer could be used iteratively to answer the questions. Here we show how to solve the problem manually.

a.   We use the equation for the average time in the system and solve for μ.

$$W = \frac{1}{\mu - \lambda}$$

$$8 \text{ minutes} = 0.133 \text{ hour} = \frac{1}{\mu - 30}$$

$$0.133\mu - 0.133(30) = 1$$

$$\mu = 37.52 \text{ customers/hour}$$

b.   The probability of more than four customers in the system equals 1 minus the probability of four or fewer customers in the system.

$$P = 1 - \sum_{n=0}^{4} P_n$$

$$= 1 - \sum_{n=0}^{4} (1 - \rho)\rho^n$$

and

$$\rho = \frac{30}{37.52} = 0.80$$

Then,

$$P = 1 - 0.2(1 + 0.8 + 0.8^2 + 0.8^3 + 0.8^4)$$

$$= 1 - 0.672 = 0.328$$

Therefore, there is a nearly 33 percent chance that more than four customers will be in the system.

c.   We use the same logic as in part (b), except that μ is now a decision variable. The easiest way to proceed is to find the correct average utilization first, and then solve for the service rate.

$$P = 1 - (1 - \rho)(1 + \rho + \rho^2 + \rho^3 + \rho^4)$$

$$= 1 - (1 + \rho + \rho^2 + \rho^3 + \rho^4) + \rho(1 + \rho + \rho^2 + \rho^3 + \rho^4)$$

$$= 1 - 1 - \rho - \rho^2 - \rho^3 - \rho^4 + \rho + \rho^2 + \rho^3 + \rho^4 + \rho^5$$

$$= \rho^5$$

or

$$\rho = P^{1/5}$$

If $P = 0.10$,

$$\rho = (0.10)^{1/5} = 0.63$$

Therefore, for a utilization rate of 63 percent, the probability of more than four customers in the system is 10 percent. For $\lambda = 30$, the mean service rate must be

$$\frac{30}{\mu} = 0.63$$

$$\mu = 47.62 \text{ customers/hour}$$

DECISION POINT

The service rate would only have to increase modestly to achieve the 8-minute target. However, the probability of having more than four customers in the system is too high. The manager must now find a way to increase the service rate from 35 per hour to approximately 48 per hour. She can increase the service rate in several different ways, ranging from employing a high school student to help bag the groceries to installing self checkout stations.

Multiple-Server Model

With the multiple-server model, customers form a single line and choose one of s servers when one is available. The service system has only one phase. We make the following assumptions in addition to those for the single-server model: There are s identical servers, and the service distribution for each server is exponential, with a mean service time of $1/\mu$. It should always be the case that $s\mu$ exceeds λ.

With these assumptions, we can apply several formulas to describe the operating characteristics of the service system:

ρ = Average utilization of the system

$$= \frac{\lambda}{s\mu}$$

P_0 = Probability that zero customers are in the system

$$= \left[\sum_{n=0}^{s-1} \frac{(\lambda/\mu)^n}{n!} + \frac{(\lambda/\mu)^s}{s!}\left(\frac{1}{1-\rho}\right) \right]^{-1}$$

P_n = Probability that n customers are in the system

$$= \begin{cases} \dfrac{(\lambda/\mu)^n}{n!}P_0 & 0 < n < s \\ \dfrac{(\lambda/\mu)^n}{s!s^{n-s}}P_0 & n \geq s \end{cases}$$

L_q = Average number of customers in the waiting line

$$= \frac{P_0(\lambda/\mu)^s \rho}{s!(1-\rho)^2}$$

W_q = Average waiting time of customers in line

$$= \frac{L_q}{\lambda}$$

W = Average time spent in the system, including service

$$= W_q + \frac{1}{\mu}$$

L = Average number of customers in the service system

$$= \lambda W$$

EXAMPLE C.5 | **Estimating Idle Time and Hourly Operating Costs with the Multiple-Server Model**

Tutor C.2 in my**om**lab provides a new example to practice the multiple-server model.

Active Model C.2 in my**om**lab provides additional insight on the multiple-server model and its uses for this problem.

The management of the American Parcel Service terminal in Verona, Wisconsin, is concerned about the amount of time the company's trucks are idle (not delivering on the road), which the company defines as waiting to be unloaded and being unloaded at the terminal. The terminal operates with four unloading bays. Each bay requires a crew of two employees, and each crew costs $30 per hour. The estimated cost of an idle truck is $50 per hour. Trucks arrive at an average rate of three per hour, according to a Poisson distribution. On average, a crew can unload a semitrailer rig in one hour, with exponential service times. What is the total hourly cost of operating the system?

SOLUTION

The *multiple-server model* is appropriate. To find the total cost of labor and idle trucks, we must calculate the average number of trucks in the system.

Figure C.5 shows the results for the American Parcel Service problem using the *Waiting-Lines* Solver from OM Explorer. Manual calculations using the equations for the *multiple-server model* are demonstrated in Solved Problem 3 at the end of this supplement. The results show that the four-bay design will be utilized 75 percent of the time and that the average number of trucks either being serviced or waiting in line is 4.53 trucks. That is, on average at any point in time, we have 4.53 idle trucks. We can now calculate the hourly costs of labor and idle trucks:

Labor cost:	$30(s) = $30(4)	= $120.00
Idle truck cost:	$50(L) = $50(4.53) =	226.50
	Total hourly cost	= $346.50

FIGURE C.5 ▶
Waiting-Lines Solver for Multiple-Server Model

Servers	4
Arrival Rate (λ)	3
Service Rate (μ)	1

Probability of zero customers in the system (P_0)	0.0377
Probability of exactly ▼ 0 customers in the system	0.0377
Average utilization of the servers (p)	0.7500
Average number of customers in the system (L)	4.5283
Average number of customers in line (L_q)	1.5283
Average waiting/service time in the system (W)	1.5094
Average waiting time in line (W_q)	0.5094

DECISION POINT

Management must now assess whether $346.50 per day for this operation is acceptable. Attempting to reduce costs by eliminating crews will only increase the waiting time of the trucks, which is more expensive per hour than the crews. However, the service rate can be increased through better work methods; for example, L can be reduced and daily operating costs will be less.

Little's Law

Little's law

A fundamental law that relates the number of customers in a waiting-line system to the arrival rate and waiting time of customers.

One of the most practical and fundamental laws in waiting-line theory is **Little's law**, which relates the number of customers in a waiting-line system to the arrival rate and the waiting time of customers. Using the same notation we used for the single-server and multiple-server models, Little's law can be expressed as $L = \lambda W$ or $L_q = \lambda W_q$. This relationship holds for a wide variety of arrival processes, service-time distributions, and numbers of servers. The practical advantage of Little's law is that you only need to know two of the parameters to estimate the third. For example, consider the manager of a motor vehicle licensing facility who receives many complaints about the time people must spend either having their licenses renewed or getting new license plates. It would be difficult to obtain data on the times individual customers spend at the facility. However, the manager can have an assistant monitor

Customers of the motor vehicle administration in Beltsville, Maryland, wait for their numbers to be called. Little's law can be used to estimate the average time each customer spends in the facility.

the number of people who arrive at the facility each hour and compute the average (λ). The manager also could periodically count the number of people in the sitting area and at the stations being served and compute the average (L). Using Little's law, the manager can then estimate W, the average time each customer spent in the facility. For example, if 40 customers arrive per hour and the average number of customers being served or waiting is 30, the average time each customer spends in the facility can be computed as

$$\text{Average time in the facility} = W = \frac{L \text{ customers}}{\lambda \text{ customers/hour}} = \frac{30}{40} = 0.75 \text{ hours, or 45 minutes}$$

If the time a customer spends at the facility is unreasonable, the manager can focus on either adding capacity or improving the work methods to reduce the time spent serving the customers.

Likewise, Little's law can be used for manufacturing processes. Suppose that a production manager knows the average time a unit of product spends at a manufacturing process (W) and the average number of units per hour that arrive at the process (λ). The production manager can then estimate the average work-in-process (L) using Little's law. *Work-in-process* (WIP) consists of items, such as components or assemblies, needed to produce a final product in manufacturing. For example, if the average time a gear case used for an outboard marine motor spends at a machine center is 3 hours, and an average of five gear cases arrive at the machine center per hour, the average number of gear cases waiting and being processed (or work-in-process) at the machine center can be calculated as

$$\text{Work-in-process} = L = \lambda W = 5 \text{ gear cases/hour (3 hours)} = 15 \text{ gear cases}$$

Knowing the relationship between the arrival rate, the lead time, and the work-in-process, the manager has a basis for measuring the effects of process improvements on the work-in-process at the facility. For example, adding some capacity to a bottleneck in the process can reduce the average lead time of the product at the process, thereby reducing the work-in-process inventory.

Even though Little's law is applicable in many situations in both service and manufacturing environments, it is not applicable in situations where the customer population is finite, which we address next.

Finite-Source Model

We now consider a situation in which all but one of the assumptions of the single-server model are appropriate. In this case, the customer population is finite, having only N potential customers. If N is greater than 30 customers, the single-server model with the assumption of an infinite customer population is adequate. Otherwise, the finite-source model is the one to use. The formulas used to calculate the operating characteristics of this service system include the following:

$$P_0 = \text{Probability that zero customers are in the system}$$

$$= \left[\sum_{n=0}^{N} \frac{N!}{(N-n)!} \left(\frac{\lambda}{\mu} \right)^n \right]^{-1}$$

$$\rho = \text{Average utilization of the server}$$

$$= 1 - P_0$$

$$L_q = \text{Average number of customers in the waiting line}$$

$$= N - \frac{\lambda + \mu}{\lambda} (1 - P_0)$$

$$L = \text{Average number of customers in the service system}$$

$$= N - \frac{\mu}{\lambda} (1 - P_0)$$

$$W_q = \text{Average waiting time in line}$$

$$= L_q[(N - L)\lambda]^{-1}$$

$$W = \text{Average time spent in the system, including service}$$

$$= L[(N - L)\lambda]^{-1}$$

EXAMPLE C.6	Analyzing Maintenance Costs with the Finite-Source Model

Tutor C.3 in myomlab provides a new example to practice the finite-source model.

Active Model C.3 in myomlab provides additional insight on the finite-source model and its uses for this problem.

The Worthington Gear Company installed a bank of 10 robots about 3 years ago. The robots greatly increased the firm's labor productivity, but recently attention has focused on maintenance. The firm does no preventive maintenance on the robots because of the variability in the breakdown distribution. Each machine has an exponential breakdown (or interarrival) distribution with an average time between failures of 200 hours. Each machine hour lost to downtime costs $30, which means that the firm has to react quickly to machine failure. The firm employs one maintenance person, who needs 10 hours on average to fix a robot. Actual maintenance times are exponentially distributed. The wage rate is $10 per hour for the maintenance person, who can be put to work productively elsewhere when not fixing robots. Determine the daily cost of labor and robot downtime.

SOLUTION

The *finite-source model* is appropriate for this analysis because the customer population consists of only 10 machines and the other assumptions are satisfied. Here, $\lambda = 1/200$, or 0.005 break-down per hour, and $\mu = 1/10 = 0.10$ robot per hour. To calculate the cost of labor and robot downtime, we need to estimate the average utilization of the maintenance person and L, the average number of robots in the maintenance system at any time. Figure C.6 shows the results for the Worthington Gear Problem using the *Waiting-Lines* Solver from OM Explorer. Manual computations using the equations for the *finite-source model* are demonstrated in Solved Problem 2 at the end of this supplement. The results show that the maintenance person is utilized only 46.2 percent of the time, and the average number of robots waiting in line or being repaired is 0.76 robot. However, a failed robot will spend an average of 16.43 hours in the repair system, of which 6.43 hours of that time is spent waiting for service. While an individual robot may spend more than two days with the maintenance person, the maintenance person has a lot of idle time with a utilization rate of only 42.6 percent. That is why there is only an average of 0.76 robot being maintained at any point of time.

FIGURE C.6 ▶
Waiting-Lines Solver for Finite-Source Model

Customers	10
Arrival Rate (λ)	0.005
Service Rate (μ)	0.1

Probability of zero customers in the system (P_0)	0.5380
Probability of fewer than ▼ 0 customers in the system	#N/A
Average utilization of the server (ρ)	0.4620
Average number of customers in the system (L)	0.7593
Average number of customers in line (L_q)	0.2972
Average waiting/service time in the system (W)	16.4330
Average waiting time in line (W_q)	6.4330

The daily cost of labor and robot downtime is

Labor cost:	($10/hour)(8 hours/day)(0.462 utilization)	= $ 36.96
Idle robot cost:	(0.76 robot)($30/robot hour)(8 hours/day)	= 182.40
	Total daily cost	= $219.36

DECISION POINT

The labor cost for robot repair is only 20 percent of the idle cost of the robots. Management might consider having a second repair person on call in the event two or more robots are waiting for repair at the same time.

DECISION AREAS FOR MANAGEMENT

After analyzing a waiting-line problem, management can improve the service system by making changes in one or more of the following areas.

1. *Arrival Rates.*   Management often can affect the rate of customer arrivals, λ, through advertising, special promotions, or differential pricing. For example, hotels in the Caribbean will reduce their room rates during the hot, rainy season to attract more customers and increase their utilization.

2. *Number of Service Facilities.*   By increasing the number of service facilities, such as tool cribs, toll booths, or bank tellers, or by dedicating some facilities in a phase to a unique set of services, management can increase system capacity.

3. *Number of Phases.*   Managers can decide to allocate service tasks to sequential phases if they determine that two sequential service facilities may be more efficient than one. For instance, in assembly lines a decision concerns the number of phases or workers needed along the assembly line. Determining the number of workers needed on the line also involves assigning a certain set of work elements to each one. Changing the facility arrangement can increase the service rate, μ, of each facility and the capacity of the system.

4. *Number of Servers per Facility.*   Managers can influence the service rate by assigning more than one person to a service facility.

5. *Server Efficiency.*   By adjusting the capital-to-labor ratio, devising improved work methods, or instituting incentive programs, management can increase the efficiency of servers assigned to a service facility. Such changes are reflected in μ.

6. *Priority Rule.*   Managers set the priority rule to be used, decide whether to have a different priority rule for each service facility, and decide whether to allow preemption (and, if so, under what conditions). Such decisions affect the waiting times of the customers and the utilization of the servers.

7. *Line Arrangement.*   Managers can influence customer waiting times and server utilization by deciding whether to have a single line or a line for each facility in a given phase of service.

Obviously, these factors are interrelated. An adjustment in the customer arrival rate, might have to be accompanied by an increase in the service rate, λ, in some way. Decisions about the number of facilities, the number of phases, and waiting-line arrangements also are related.

For each of the problems we analyzed with the waiting-line models, the arrivals had a Poisson distribution (or exponential interarrival times), the service times had an exponential distribution, the service facilities had a simple arrangement, and the priority discipline was first-come, first-served. Waiting-line theory has been used to develop other models in which these criteria are not met, but these models are complex. Many times, the nature of the customer population, the constraints on the line, the priority rule, the service-time distribution, and the arrangement of the facilities are such that waiting-line theory is no longer useful. In these cases, simulation often is used.

INTERNET RESOURCES

my**om**lab and the Companion Website at **www.pearsonglobaleditions.com/krajewski** contain many tools, activities, and resources designed for this supplement.

KEY EQUATIONS

1. Customer arrival Poisson distribution:

$$P_n = \frac{(\lambda T)^n}{n!} e^{-\lambda T}$$

2. Service time exponential distribution:

$$P(t \le T) = 1 - e^{-\mu T}$$

	Single-Server Model	Multiple-Server Model	Finite-Source Model
Average utilization of the system	$\rho = \dfrac{\lambda}{\mu}$	$\rho = \dfrac{\lambda}{s\mu}$	$\rho = 1 - P_0$
Probability that n customers are in the system	$P_n = (1 - \rho)\rho^n$	$P_n = \begin{cases} \dfrac{(\lambda/\mu)^n}{n!} P_0 & 0 < n < s \\[2mm] \dfrac{(\lambda/\mu)^n}{s! s^{n-s}} P_0 & n \ge s \end{cases}$	
Probability that zero customers are in the system	$P_0 = 1 - \rho$	$P_0 = \left[\displaystyle\sum_{n=0}^{s-1} \frac{(\lambda/\mu)^n}{n!} + \frac{(\lambda/\mu)^s}{s!} \left(\frac{1}{1-\rho} \right) \right]^{-1}$	$P_0 = \left[\displaystyle\sum_{n=0}^{N} \frac{N!}{(N-n)!} \left(\frac{\lambda}{\mu} \right)^n \right]^{-1}$
Average number of customers in the service system	$L = \dfrac{\lambda}{\mu - \lambda}$	$L = \lambda W$	$L = N - \dfrac{\mu}{\lambda}(1 - P_0)$
Average number of customers in the waiting line	$L_q = \rho L$	$L_q = \dfrac{P_0(\lambda/\mu)^s \rho}{s!(1-\rho)^2}$	$L_q = N - \dfrac{\lambda + \mu}{\lambda}(1 - P_0)$
Average time spent in the system, including service	$W = \dfrac{1}{\mu - \lambda}$	$W = W_q + \dfrac{1}{\mu}$	$W = L[(N - L)\lambda]^{-1}$
Average waiting time in line	$W_q = \rho W$	$W_q = \dfrac{L_q}{\lambda}$	$W_q = L_q[(N - L)\lambda]^{-1}$

SOLVED PROBLEM 1

The head librarian of a small library in Egypt is evaluating checkout times. The library only has one checkout desk. The librarian at this desk has the capacity to check out an average of 32 patrons per hour. The checkout librarian must wait for patrons to arrive in line, so the time it takes to check out a patron is exponentially distributed. Patrons arrive at a Poisson-distributed average rate of 20 per hour.

a. What is the utilization of each checkout librarian?

b. How much time will the average patron spend at the checkout desk?

SOLUTION

a. The assumptions in the problem statement are consistent with a single-server model. Utilization is

$$\rho = \frac{\lambda}{\mu} = \frac{20}{32} = 0.63$$

b. The average time a patron spends at the checkout desk is

$$W = \frac{1}{\mu - \lambda} = \frac{1}{32 - 20} = 0.083 \text{ hour} = 5 \text{ minutes}$$

SOLVED PROBLEM 2

The Severance Coal Mine serves six trains having exponentially distributed interarrival times averaging 30 hours. The time required to fill a train with coal varies with the number of cars, weather-related delays, and equipment breakdowns. The time to fill a train can be approximated by an exponential distribution with a mean of 6 hours 40 minutes. The railroad requires the coal mine to pay large demurrage charges in the event that a train spends more than 24 hours at the mine. What is the average time a train will spend at the mine?

SOLUTION

The problem statement describes a finite-source model, with $N = 6$. The average time spent at the mine is $W = L[(N - L)\lambda]^{-1}$, with $1/\lambda = 30$ hours/train, $\lambda = 0.8$ train/day, and $\mu = 3.6$ trains/day. In this case,

$$P_0 = \left[\sum_{n=0}^{N} \frac{N!}{(N - n)!} \left(\frac{\lambda}{\mu} \right)^{n} \right]^{-1} = \frac{1}{\displaystyle\sum_{n=0}^{6} \frac{6!}{(6 - n)!} \left(\frac{0.8}{3.6} \right)^{n}}$$

$$= \frac{1}{\left[\frac{6!}{6!}\left(\frac{0.8}{3.6} \right)^{0} \right] + \left[\frac{6!}{5!}\left(\frac{0.8}{3.6} \right)^{1} \right] + \left[\frac{6!}{4!}\left(\frac{0.8}{3.6} \right)^{2} \right] + \left[\frac{6!}{3!}\left(\frac{0.8}{3.6} \right)^{3} \right] + \left[\frac{6!}{2!}\left(\frac{0.8}{3.6} \right)^{4} \right] + \left[\frac{6!}{1!}\left(\frac{0.8}{3.6} \right)^{5} \right] + \left[\frac{6!}{0!}\left(\frac{0.8}{3.6} \right)^{6} \right]}$$

$$= \frac{1}{1 + 1.33 + 1.48 + 1.32 + 0.88 + 0.39 + 0.09} = \frac{1}{6.49} = 0.1541$$

$$L = N - \frac{\mu}{\lambda}(1 - P_0) = 6 - \frac{3.6}{0.8}(1 - 0.1541) = 2.193 \text{ trains}$$

$$W = L\left[(N - L)\lambda \right]^{-1} = \frac{2.193}{(3.807)0.8} = 0.72 \text{ day}$$

Arriving trains will spend an average of 0.72 day at the coal mine.

SOLVED PROBLEM 3

The Mega Multiplex Movie Theater has three concession clerks serving customers on a first-come, first-served basis. The service time per customer is exponentially distributed with an average of 2 minutes per customer. Concession customers wait in a single line in a large lobby, and arrivals are Poisson distributed with an average of 81 customers per hour. Previews run for 10 minutes before the start of each show. If the average time in the concession area exceeds 10 minutes, customers become dissatisfied.

a. What is the average utilization of the concession clerks?

b. What is the average time spent in the concession area?

SOLUTION

a. The problem statement is consistent with the multiple-server model, and the average utilization rate is

$$\rho = \frac{\lambda}{s\mu} = \frac{81 \text{ customers/hour}}{(3 \text{ servers})\left(\dfrac{60 \text{ minutes/server hour}}{2 \text{ minutes/customer}}\right)} = 0.90$$

The concession clerks are busy 90 percent of the time.

b. The average time spent in the system, W, is

$$W = W_q + \frac{1}{\mu}$$

Here,

$$W_q = \frac{L_q}{\lambda} \quad L_q = \frac{P_0(\lambda/\mu)^s \rho}{s!(1-\rho)^2} \quad \text{and} \quad P_0 = \left[\sum_{n=0}^{s-1} \frac{(\lambda/\mu)^n}{n!} + \frac{(\lambda/\mu)^s}{s!}\left(\frac{1}{1-\rho}\right)\right]^{-1}$$

We must solve for P_0, L_q, and W_q, in that order, before we can solve for W:

$$P_0 = \left[\sum_{n=0}^{s-1} \frac{(\lambda/\mu)^n}{n!} + \frac{(\lambda/\mu)^s}{s!}\left(\frac{1}{1-\rho}\right)\right]^{-1}$$

$$= \frac{1}{1 + \dfrac{(81/30)}{1} + \dfrac{(2.7)^2}{2} + \left[\dfrac{(2.7)^3}{6}\left(\dfrac{1}{1-0.9}\right)\right]}$$

$$= \frac{1}{1 + 2.7 + 3.645 + 32.805} = \frac{1}{40.15} = 0.0249$$

$$L_q = \frac{P_0(\lambda/\mu)^s \rho}{s!(1-\rho)^2} = \frac{0.0249(81/30)^3\,(0.9)}{3!(1-0.9)^2} = \frac{0.4411}{6(0.01)} = 7.352 \text{ customers}$$

$$W_q = \frac{L_q}{\lambda} = \frac{7.352 \text{ customers}}{81 \text{ customers/hour}} = 0.0908 \text{ hour}$$

$$W = W_q + \frac{1}{\mu} = 0.0908 \text{ hours} + \frac{1}{30} \text{ hour} = (0.1241 \text{ hour})\left(\frac{60 \text{ minutes}}{\text{hour}}\right)$$

$$= 7.45 \text{ minutes}$$

With three concession clerks, customers will spend an average of 7.45 minutes in the concession area.

PROBLEMS

Software, such as OM Explorer, Active Models, and POM for Windows, is available in my**om**lab. Check with your instructor on how best to use it. In many cases, the instructor wants you to understand how to do the calculations by hand. At most, the software provides a check on your calculations. When calculations are particularly complex and the goal is interpreting the results in making decisions, the software replaces entirely the manual calculations.

1. Paula Caplin is manager of a major electronics repair facility owned by Fisher Electronics. Recently, top management expressed concern over the growth in the number of repair jobs in process at the facility. The average arrival rate is 120 jobs per day. The average job spends 4 days at the facility.

   a. What is the current work-in-process level at the facility?

   b. Suppose that top management has put a limit of one-half the current level of work-in-process. What goal must Paula establish and how might she accomplish it?

2. The manager of a branch office of Banco Mexicali observed that during peak hours an average of 20 customers arrives per hour and that there is an average of 4 customers in the branch office at any time. How long does the average customer spend waiting in line and being serviced?

3. The daughter of the owner of a local hamburger restaurant is preparing to open a new fast-food restaurant called Hasty Burgers. Based on the arrival rates at her father's outlets, she expects customers to arrive at the drive-up window according to a Poison distribution, with a mean of 20 customers per hour. The service rate is flexible; however, the service times are expected to follow an exponential distribution. The drive-in window is a single-server operation.

   a. What service rate is needed to keep the average number of customers in the service system (waiting line and being served) to four?

   b. For the service rate in part (a), what is the probability that more than four customers are in line and being served?

   c. For the service rate in part (a), what is the average waiting time in line for each customer? Does this average seem satisfactory for a fast-food business?

4. The supervisor at the Precision Machine Shop wants to determine the staffing policy that minimizes total operating costs. The average arrival rate at the tool crib, where tools are dispensed to the workers, is eight machinists per hour. Each machinist's pay is $20 per hour. The supervisor can staff the crib either with a junior attendant who is paid $5 per hour and can process 10 arrivals per hour or with a senior attendant who is paid $12 per hour and can process 16 arrivals per hour. Which attendant should be selected, and what would be the total estimated hourly cost?

5. Jake Tweet hosts a psychology talk show on KRAN radio. Jake's advice averages 10 minutes per caller but varies according to an exponential distribution. The average time between calls is 25 minutes, exponentially distributed. Generating calls in this local market is difficult, so Jake does not want to lose any calls to busy signals. The radio station has only three telephone lines. What is the probability that a caller receives a busy signal?

6. You are the manager of a local bank where three tellers provide services to customers. On average, each teller takes three minutes to serve a customer. Customers arrive, on average, at a rate of 50 per hour. Having recently received complaints from some customers that they waited a long time before being served, your boss asks you to evaluate the service system. Specifically, you must provide answers to the following questions:

   a. What is the average utilization of the three-teller service system?

   b. What is the probability that no customers are being served by a teller or are waiting in line?

   c. What is the average number of customers waiting in line?

   d. On average, how long does a customer wait in line before being served?

   e. On average, how many customers would be at a teller's station and in line?

7. Fantastic Styling Salon is run by two stylists, Jenny Perez and Jill Sloan, each capable of serving five customers per hour, on average. Eight customers, on average, arrive at the salon each hour.

   a. If all arriving customers wait in a common line for the next available stylist, how long would a customer wait in line, on average, before being served?

   b. Suppose that 50 percent of the arriving customers want to be served only by Perez and that the other 50 percent want only Sloan. How long would a customer wait in line, on average, before being served by Perez? By Sloan? What is the average customer waiting time in the line?

   c. Do you observe a difference in the answers to parts (a) and (b)? If so, why? Explain.

8. Moore, Aiken, and Payne is a dental clinic serving the needs of the general public on a first-come, first-served basis. The clinic has three dental chairs, each staffed by a dentist. Patients arrive at the rate of five per hour, according to a Poisson distribution, and do not balk or renege. The average time required for a dental checkup is 30 minutes, according to an exponential distribution.

   a. What is the probability that no patients are in the clinic?

   b. What is the probability that six or more patients are in the clinic?

   c. What is the average number of patients waiting in the lobby?

   d. What is the average total time that a patient spends in the clinic?

9. Benny's Arcade has six video game machines. The average time between machine failures is 50 hours. Jimmy, the maintenance engineer, can repair a machine in 15 hours on average. The machines have an exponential failure distribution, and Jimmy has an exponential service-time distribution.

   a. What is Jimmy's utilization?

   b. What is the average number of machines out of service, that is, waiting to be repaired or being repaired?

   c. What is the average time a machine is out of service?

10. The Solomon, Smith, and Samson law firm produces many legal documents that must be word processed for clients and the firm. Requests average eight pages of documents per hour, and they arrive according to a Poisson distribution. The secretary can word process 10 pages per hour on average according to an exponential distribution.

   a. What is the average utilization rate of the secretary?

   b. What is the probability that more than four pages are waiting or being word processed?

   c. What is the average number of pages waiting to be word processed?

ADVANCED PROBLEMS

11. You are in charge of a quarry that supplies sand and stone aggregates to your company's construction sites. Empty trucks from construction sites arrive at the quarry's huge piles of sand and stone aggregates and wait in line to enter the station, which can load either sand or aggregate. At the station, they are filled with material, weighed, checked out, and proceed to a construction site. Currently, nine empty trucks arrive per hour, on average. Once a truck has entered a loading station, it takes 6 minutes for it to be filled, weighed, and checked out. Concerned that trucks are spending too much time waiting and being filled, you are evaluating two alternatives to reduce the average time the trucks spend in the system. The first alternative is to add side boards to the trucks (so that more material could be loaded) and to add a helper at the loading station (so that filling time could be reduced) at a total cost of $50,000. The arrival rate of trucks would change to six per hour, and the filling time would be reduced to 4 minutes. The second alternative is to add another loading station at a cost of $80,000. The trucks would wait in a common line and the truck at the front of the line would move to the next available station.

    Which alternative would you recommend if you want to reduce the current average time the trucks spend in the system, including service?

12. The College of Business and Public Administration at Benton University has a copy machine on each floor for faculty use. Heavy use of the five copy machines causes frequent failures. Maintenance records show that a machine fails every 2.5 days (or $\lambda = 0.40$ failure/day). The college has a maintenance contract with the authorized dealer of the copy machines. Because the copy machines fail so frequently, the dealer has assigned one person to the college to repair them. The person can repair an average of 2.5 machines per day. Using the finite-source model, answer the following questions:

    a. What is the average utilization of the maintenance person?

    b. On average, how many copy machines are being repaired or waiting to be repaired?

    c. What is the average time spent by a copy machine in the repair system (waiting and being repaired)?

13. Three employees in the maintenance department are responsible for repairing the video games at Pinball Wizard, a video arcade. A maintenance worker can fix one video game machine every 8 hours on average, with an exponential distribution. An average of one video game machine fails every 3 hours, according to a Poisson distribution. Each down machine costs the Wizard $10 per hour in lost income. A new maintenance worker would cost $8 per hour.

    Should the manager hire any new personnel? If so, how many people? What would you recommend to the manager, based on your analysis?

SELECTED REFERENCES

Cooper, Robert B. *Introduction to Queuing Theory*, 2d ed. New York: Elsevier-North Holland, 1980.

Hartvigsen, David. *SimQuick: Process Simulation with Excel*, 2d ed. Upper Saddle River, NJ: Prentice Hall, 2004.

Hillier, F. S., and G. S. Lieberman. *Introduction to Operations Research*, 2d ed. San Francisco: Holden-Day, 1975.

Little, J. D. C. "A Proof for the Queuing Formula: $L = \lambda W$." *Operations Research*, vol. 9, (1961), pp. 383–387.

Moore, P. M. *Queues, Inventories and Maintenance*. New York: John Wiley & Sons, 1958.

Saaty, T. L. *Elements of Queuing Theory with Applications*. New York: McGraw-Hill, 1961.

7 Managing Process Constraints

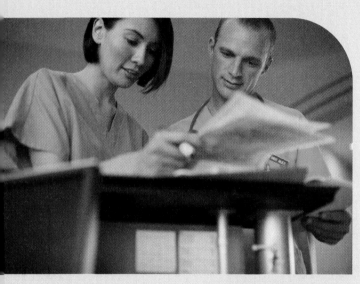

A staff member takes bookings for hospital beds. The Radcliffe Infirmary brought about a complete reduction in the number of surgeries that were being routinely cancelled, simply by limiting the number of bookings and appointing a manager to oversee the bookings process.

THE RADCLIFFE INFIRMARY

The Radcliffe Infirmary, part of the Oxford Radcliffe Hospital Trust, in Oxford, England, is one of the largest teaching hospitals in the United Kingdom. It provides high-quality health care services to the majority of the population in Oxfordshire County, as well as neighboring communities. Several years ago, the hospital was having difficulty keeping up with the demand of this large patient base. Hospital administrators often found their departments to be understaffed and were frequently forced to cancel elective surgeries. The staff that was available was overworked, causing employee sickness rates to rise and accelerating the problem. Hospital administrators knew this dilemma was caused by inefficiencies in hospital's operations; however, no department wanted to admit to causing a bottleneck. To correct the problem, director of operations Jan Elliott decided to initiate a theory of constraints (TOC) workshop. A similar workshop was used at a hospital in Cambridge and generated successful results.

During the workshop, Elliott realized that the problem stemmed from the organization's inconsistent method of booking beds. At the time, standard protocol called for the ward staff to handle the cumbersome task of bed management along with their other responsibilities. It was clear that in order to keep the approach to booking beds consistent, a bed manager needed to be appointed, and new protocol needed to be initiated. Previous protocol allowed up to 11 patients a day to be booked into the unit and to have a bed and surgery time reserved for each. Mondays and Tuesdays were frequently booked to capacity, as most surgeons scheduled

LEARNING GOALS

After reading this chapter, you should be able to:

1. Explain the theory of constraints.
2. Understand linkage of capacity constraints to financial performance measures.
3. Identify bottlenecks.
4. Apply theory of constraints to product mix decisions.
5. Describe how to manage constraints in an assembly line.

surgeries in the beginning of the week to ensure that their procedures would be performed before the week's end. Because the unit could not work adequately in this capacity, many of these surgeries were performed during off hours or cancelled.

To fix this problem, the new bed management protocol called for the bed manager to book a maximum of six patients a day. Cutting the number almost in half may have seemed counterproductive, but with a smaller number of patients to focus on, staff members were able to carry out their roles more effectively. During a three-month period after implementing this new protocol, not one elective surgery was cancelled. During a three-month period in the previous year, before the new protocol was implemented, nearly 64 surgeries were cancelled.

The new protocol not only improved the hospital's cancellation issues, it also improved the staff's morale. No longer overworked, hospital staff became visibly happier at their jobs.

Although it seemed obvious that initiating the theory of constraints greatly improved, the operations of the Radcliffe Infirmary, conclusive evidence was not formed until nine months later when the position of bed manager became vacant. Without someone to regulate the bed booking for the unit, the situation reverted. Once the position was filled, the improvements returned.

Source: "Our Hospitals," Oxford Radcliffe Hospitals, NHS Trust, at http://www.oxfordradcliffe.nhs.uk/aboutus/hospitals/hospitals.aspx, Accessed September 25, 2008; Belinda Phipps, "Hitting the Bottleneck," Health Management, February 1999, at http://www.goldratt.com/hlthmgmtmn.htm.

myomlab and the Companion Website at **www.pearsonglobaleditions.com/krajewski** contain many tools, activities, and resources designed for this chapter.

constraint

Any factor that limits the performance of a system and restricts its output.

bottleneck

A capacity constraint resource (CCR) whose available capacity limits the organization's ability to meet the product volume, product mix, or demand fluctuation required by the marketplace.

Suppose one of a firm's processes was recently reengineered, and yet results were disappointing. Costs were still high or customer satisfaction still low. What could be wrong? The answer might be constraints that remain in one or more steps in the firm's processes. A **constraint** is any factor that limits the performance of a system and restricts its output, while *capacity* is the maximum rate of output of a process or a system. When constraints exist at any step, as they did at Eastern Financial Florida Credit Union, capacity can become imbalanced—too high in some departments and too low in others. As a result, the overall performance of the system suffers.

Constraints can occur up or down the supply chain, with either the firm's suppliers or customers, or within one of the firm's processes like service/product development or order fulfillment. Three kinds of constraints can generally be identified: physical (usually machine, labor, or workstation capacity or material shortages, but could be space or quality), market (demand is less than capacity), or managerial (policy, metrics, or mind-sets that create constraints that impede work flow). A **bottleneck**[1] is a special type of a constraint that relates to the capacity shortage of a process, and is defined as any resource whose available capacity limits the organization's ability to meet the service or product volume, product mix, or fluctuating requirements demanded by the marketplace. A business system or a process would have at least one constraint or a bottleneck; otherwise, its output would be limited only by market demand. The experience of Eastern Financial Florida Credit Union and other firms in the health care, banking, and manufacturing industries demonstrates how important managing constraints can be to an organization's future.

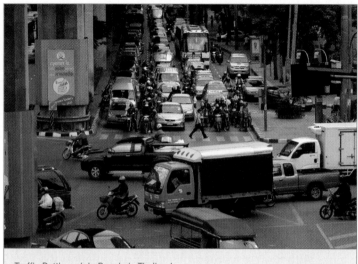

Traffic Bottleneck in Bangkok, Thailand

MANAGING CONSTRAINTS ACROSS THE ORGANIZATION

Firms must manage their constraints and make appropriate capacity choices at the individual-process level, as well as at the organization level. Hence this process involves inter-functional cooperation. Detailed decisions and choices made within each of these levels affect where resource constraints or bottlenecks show up, both within and across departmental lines. Relieving a bottleneck in one part of an organization might not have the desired effect unless a bottleneck in another part of the organization is also addressed. A bottleneck could be the sales department not getting enough sales or the loan department not processing loans fast enough as at EFFCU. The constraint could be a lack of capital or equipment, or it could be planning and scheduling.

Managers throughout the organization must understand how to identify and manage bottlenecks in all types of processes, how to relate the capacity and performance measures of one process to another, and how to use that information to determine the firm's best service or product mix. This chapter explains how managers can best make these decisions.

THE THEORY OF CONSTRAINTS

The **theory of constraints (TOC)** is a systematic management approach that focuses on actively managing those constraints that impede a firm's progress toward its goal of maximizing profits and effectively using its resources. The theory was developed nearly three decades ago by Eli Goldratt, a well-known business systems analyst. It outlines a deliberate process for identifying and overcoming constraints. The process focuses not just on the efficiency of individual processes, but also on the bottlenecks that constrain the system as a whole. EFFCU in the opening vignette followed this theory to improve its operations.

TOC methods increase the firm's profits more effectively by focusing on making materials flow rapidly through the entire system. They help firms look at the big picture—how

---

[1] Under certain conditions, a bottleneck is also called a *capacity constrained resource* (CCR). The process with the least capacity is called a bottleneck if its output is less than the market demand, or called a CCR if it is the least capable resource in the system but still has higher capacity than the market demand.

processes can be improved to increase overall work flows, and how inventory and workforce levels can be reduced while still effectively utilizing critical resources. To do this, it is important to understand the relevant performance and capacity measures at the operational level, as well as their relationship to the more broadly understood financial measures at the firm level. These measures and relationships, so critical in successfully applying the principles of the TOC, are defined in Table 7.1.

According to the TOC view, every capital investment in the system, including machines and work-in-process materials, represents inventory because they could all potentially be sold to make money. Producing a product or a service that does not lead to a sale will not increase a firm's throughput, but will increase its inventory and operating expenses. It is always best to manage the system so that utilization at the bottleneck resource is maximized in order to maximize throughput.

theory of constraints (TOC)

A systematic management approach that focuses on actively managing those constraints that impede a firm's progress toward its goal.

Key Principles of the TOC

The chief concept behind the TOC is that the bottlenecks should be scheduled to maximize their throughput of services or products while adhering to promised completion dates. The underlying assumption is that demand is greater or equal to the capacity of the process that produces the service or product. For example, manufacturing a garden rake involves attaching a bow to the rake's head. Rake heads must be processed on the blanking press, welded to the bow, cleaned, and attached to the handle to make the rake, which is packaged and finally shipped to Sears, Home Depot, or Wal-Mart, according to a specific delivery schedule. Suppose that the delivery commitments for all styles of rakes for the next month indicate that the welding station is loaded at 105 percent of its capacity but that the other processes will be used at only 75 percent of their capacities. According to the TOC, the welding station is the bottleneck resource, whereas the blanking, cleaning, handle attaching, packaging, and shipping processes are nonbottleneck resources. Any idle time at the welding station must be eliminated to maximize throughput. Managers should therefore focus on the welding schedule.

Seven key principles of the TOC that revolve around the efficient use and scheduling of bottlenecks and improving flow and throughput are summarized in Table 7.2.

Practical application of the TOC involves the implementation of following steps.

1. *Identify the System Bottleneck(s).* For the rake example, the bottleneck is the welding station because it is restricting the firm's ability to meet the shipping schedule and, hence, total value-added funds. Other ways of identifying the bottleneck will be looked at in more detail a little later in this chapter.

2. *Exploit the Bottleneck(s).* Create schedules that maximize the throughput of the bottleneck(s). For the rake example, schedule the welding station to maximize its utilization while meeting the shipping commitments to the extent possible. Also make sure that only good quality parts are passed on to the bottleneck.

3. *Subordinate All Other Decisions to Step 2.* Nonbottleneck resources should be scheduled to support the schedule of the bottleneck and not produce more than it can handle. That is, the blanking press should not produce more than the welding station can handle, and the activities of the cleaning and subsequent operations should be based on the output rate of the welding station.

TABLE 7.1	HOW THE FIRM'S OPERATIONAL MEASURES RELATE TO ITS FINANCIAL MEASURES	
Operational Measures	**TOC View**	**Relationship to Financial Measures**
Inventory (I)	All the money invested in a system in purchasing things that it intends to sell	A decrease in I leads to an increase in net profit, ROI, and cash flow.
Throughput (T)	Rate at which a system generates money through sales	An increase in T leads to an increase in net profit, ROI, and cash flows.
Operating Expense (OE)	All the money a system spends to turn inventory into throughput	A decrease in OE leads to an increase in net profit, ROI, and cash flows.
Utilization (U)	The degree to which equipment, space, or workforce is currently being used, and is measured as the ratio of average output rate to maximum capacity, expressed as a percentage	An increase in U at the bottleneck leads to an increase in net profit, ROI, and cash flows.

TABLE 7.2	SEVEN KEY PRINCIPLES OF THE THEORY OF CONSTRAINTS

1. The focus should be on balancing flow, not on balancing capacity.

2. Maximizing the output and efficiency of every resource may not maximize the throughput of the entire system.

3. An hour lost at a bottleneck or a constrained resource is an hour lost for the whole system. In contrast, an hour saved at a nonbottleneck resource is a mirage because it does not make the whole system more productive.

4. Inventory is needed only in front of the bottlenecks in order to prevent them from sitting idle, and in front of assembly and shipping points in order to protect customer schedules. Building inventories elsewhere should be avoided.

5. Work, which can be materials, information to be processed, documents, or customers, should be released into the system only as frequently as the bottlenecks need it. Bottleneck flows should be equal to the market demand. Pacing everything to the slowest resource minimizes inventory and operating expenses.

6. Activating a nonbottleneck resource (using it for improved efficiency that does not increase throughput) is not the same as utilizing a bottleneck resource (that does lead to increased throughput). Activation of nonbottleneck resources cannot increase throughput, nor promote better performance on financial measures outlined in Table 7.1.

7. Every capital investment must be viewed from the perspective of its global impact on overall throughput (T), inventory (I), and operating expense (OE).

Bal Seal Engineering is a designer and manufacturer of custom seals and canted-coil (tm) springs for aerospace, automotive, transportation, medical and other industries. By applying many modern management principles including the theory of constraints (TOC), the company has been able to grow and improve customer satisfaction.

4. *Elevate the Bottleneck(s).* After the scheduling improvements in steps 1–3 have been exhausted and the bottleneck is still a constraint to throughput, management should consider increasing the capacity of the bottleneck. For example, if the welding station is still a constraint after exhausting schedule improvements, consider increasing its capacity by adding another shift or another welding machine. Other mechanisms are also available for increasing bottleneck capacity, and we address them a little later.

5. *Do Not Let Inertia Set In.* Actions taken in steps 3 and 4 will improve the welder throughput and may alter the loads on other processes. Consequently, the system constraint(s) may shift. Then the practical application of Steps 1–4 must be repeated in order to identify and manage the new set of constraints.

Because of its potential for improving performance dramatically, many manufacturers have applied the principles of the theory of constraints, including National Semiconductor, Dresser Industries, Allied-Signal, Bethlehem Steel, Johnson Controls, and Rockwell Automotive. All manufacturers implementing TOC principles can also dramatically change the mind-set of employees and managers. Instead of focusing solely on their own functions, they can see the "big picture" and where other improvements in the system might lie.

IDENTIFICATION AND MANAGEMENT OF BOTTLENECKS

Bottlenecks can both be internal or external to the firm, and typically represent a process, a step, or a workstation with the lowest capacity. **Throughput time** is the total elapsed time from the start to the finish of a job or a customer being processed at one or more workcenters. Where a bottleneck lies in a given service or manufacturing process can be identified in any one of several different ways. A workstation in a process is a bottleneck if (1) it has the highest total time per unit processed, (2) it has the highest average utilization and total workload, or (3) a reduction of even a single minute in its processing time would reduce the average throughput time for the entire process.

throughput time

Total elapsed time from the start to the finish of a job or a customer being processed at one or more workcenters.

Managing Bottlenecks in Service Processes

Example 7.1 illustrates how a bottleneck step or activity can be identified for a loan approval process at a bank.

EXAMPLE 7.1	**Identifying the Bottleneck in a Service Process**

Managers at the First Community Bank are attempting to shorten the time it takes customers with approved loan applications to get their paperwork processed. The flowchart for this process, consisting of several different activities, each performed by a different bank employee, is shown in Figure 7.1. Approved loan applications first arrive at activity or step 1, where they are checked for completeness and put in order. At step 2, the loans are categorized into different classes according to the loan amount and whether they are being requested for personal or commercial reasons. While credit checking commences at step 3, loan application data are entered in parallel into the information system for record-keeping purposes at step 4. Finally, all paperwork for setting up the new loan is finished at step 5. The time taken in minutes is given in parentheses.

Which single step is the bottleneck? The management is also interested in knowing the maximum number of approved loans this system can process in a 5-hour work day.

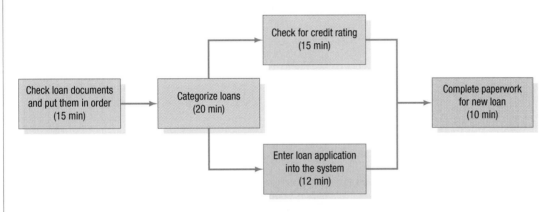

▲ FIGURE 7.1
Processing Credit Loan Applications at First Community Bank

SOLUTION

We define the bottleneck as step 2, where a single-minute reduction in its time reduces the average throughput time of the entire loan approval process. The throughput time to complete an approved loan application is $15 + 20 + \max(15, 12) + 10 = \mathbf{60}$ minutes. Although we assume no waiting time in front of any step, in practice such a smooth process flow is not always the case. So the actual time taken for completing an approved loan will be longer than 60 minutes due to nonuniform arrival of applications, variations in actual processing times, and the related factors.

The capacity for loan completions is derived by translating the "minutes per customer" at the bottleneck step to "customer per hour." At First Community Bank, it is 3 customers per hour because the bottleneck step 2 can process only 1 customer every 20 minutes (60/3).

DECISION POINT

Step 2 is the bottleneck constraint. The bank will be able to complete a maximum of only 3 loan accounts per hour, or 15 new loan accounts in a 5-hour day. Management can increase the flow of loan applications by increasing the capacity of step 2 up to the point where another step becomes the bottleneck.

A front-office process with high customer contact and divergence does not enjoy the simple line flows shown in Example 7.1. Its operations may serve many different customer types, and the demands on any one operation could vary considerably from one day to the next. However, bottlenecks can still be identified by computing the average utilization of each operation. However, the variability in workload also creates *floating bottlenecks*. One week the mix of work may make operation 1 a bottleneck, and the next week it may make operation 3 the bottleneck. This type of variability increases the complexity of day-to-day scheduling. In this situation, management prefers lower utilization rates, which allow greater slack to absorb unexpected surges in demand.

TOC principles outlined here are fairly broad-based and widely applicable. They can be useful for evaluating individual processes as well as large systems for both manufacturers as well as service providers. TOC principles are fairly broad based and widely applicable. They can be useful in evaluating individual, multiple, and concurrent processes in large systems, such as manufacturing, and health care service providers, such as hospitals. Managerial Practice 7.1 shows how TOC principles can improve the quality management program in the Australian health care system.

MANAGERIAL PRACTICE 7.1	Constraint Management in Health Care

Australia, similar to most Western nations, has a growing population and aging baby boomers. Quality medical care is becoming more prominent. There have been many studies and research into the Australian health care system. Improving the quality of heath care has been one of the main outcomes of these studies. Although government health policies promote quality health care, these studies indicate that the failure of quality health care has been generally due to poor systems management in clinical practice.

These policies promote evidence-based health care, which is complex and requires clinicians to modify their modes of practice for compliance. However, these policies do not support the collaboration of diverse interdisciplinary components, integrate multidisciplinary elements of health care, support geographical remoteness, and are temporally dispersed.

During the implementation of quality management demonstration programs in cancer health care, it was reported that managing and improving the quality of care is a core organizational activity requiring multiple strategies. A series of projects were implemented over a 5-year period.

Although there were several improvements in delivering quality heath care, a mid-term evaluation of this project revealed several constraints. The inhibiting factors against the quality improvement were insufficient guidance in policy documentation, contradictions between policy and practice, misaligned organizational objectives, lack of performance framework, and apathy to change.

Operating theatre staff prepare for surgery on a patient. Post-surgery care is complex and requires multiple processes.

Sources: R. Wilson, W. Runciman, R. Gibberd, B. Harrison, L. Newby, and J. Hamilton, "The Quality in Australian Health Care Study," *Medical Journal of Australia*, vol. 163 (1995), pp. 458–471; R. Wilson, B. Harrison, R. Gibberd, and J. Hamilton, "An Analysis of the Causes of Adverse Events from the Quality in Australian Health Care Study," *Medical Journal of Australia*, vol. 170 (1999), pp. 411–415.

Managing Bottlenecks in Manufacturing Processes

Bottlenecks can exist in all types of manufacturing processes, including the job process, batch process, line process, and continuous process. Since these processes differ in their design, strategic intent, and allocation of resources (see Chapter 3, "Developing a Process Strategy," for additional details), identification and management of bottlenecks will also differ accordingly with process type. We first discuss in this section issues surrounding management of bottlenecks in job and batch processes, while relegating constraint management in line processes for a later section.

Identifying Bottlenecks   Manufacturing processes often pose some complexities when identifying bottlenecks. If multiple services or products are involved, extra setup time at a workstation is usually needed to change over from one service or product to the next, which in turn increases the overload at the workstation being changed over. *Setup times* and their associated costs affect the size of the lots traveling through the job or batch processes. Management tries to reduce setup times because they represent unproductive time for workers or machines and thereby allow for smaller, more economic, batches. Nonetheless, whether setup times are significant or not, one way to identify a bottleneck operation is by its utilization. Example 7.2 illustrates how a bottleneck can be identified in a manufacturing setting.

| **EXAMPLE 7.2** | **Identifying the Bottleneck in a Batch Process** |

Diablo Electronics manufactures four unique products (A, B, C, and D) that are fabricated and assembled in five different workstations (V, W, X, Y, and Z) using a small batch process. Each workstation is staffed by a worker who is dedicated to work a single shift per day at an assigned workstation. Batch setup times have been reduced to such an extent that they can be considered negligible. A flowchart denotes the path each product follows through the manufacturing process as shown in Figure 7.2, where each product's price, demand per week, and processing times per unit are indicated as well. Inverted triangles represent purchased parts and raw materials consumed per unit at different workstations. Diablo can make and sell up to the limit of its demand per week, and no penalties are incurred for not being able to meet all the demand.

Which of the five workstations (V, W, X, Y, or Z) has the highest utilization, and thus serves as the bottleneck for Diablo Electronics?

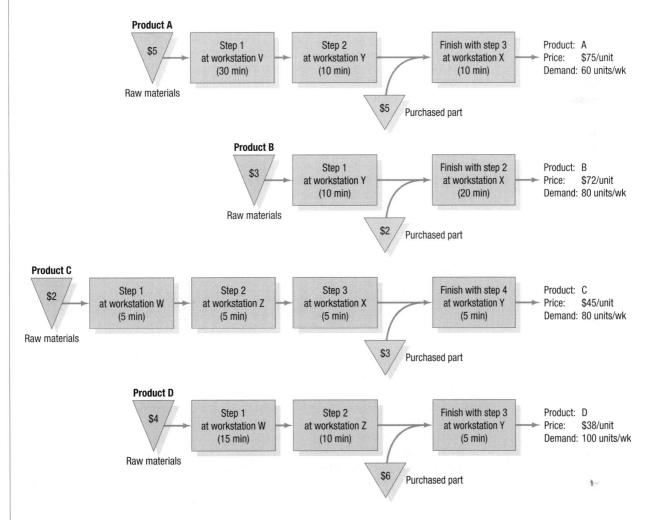

▲ FIGURE 7.2
Flowchart for Products A,B,C, and D

SOLUTION

Because the denominator in the utilization ratio is the same for every workstation, with one worker per machine at each step in the process, we can simply identify the bottleneck by computing aggregate workloads at each workstation.

The firm wants to satisfy as much of the product demand in a week as it can. Each week consists of 2,400 minutes of available production time. Multiplying the processing time at each station for a given product with the number of units demanded per week yields the workload represented by that product. These loads are summed across all products going through a workstation to arrive at the total load for the workstation, which is then compared with the others and the existing capacity of 2,400 minutes.

Workstation	Load from Product A	Load from Product B	Load from Product C	Load from Product D	Total Load (min)
V	60 × 30 = 1800	0	0	0	1,800
W	0	0	80 × 5 = 400	100 × 15 = 1,500	1,900
X	60 × 10 = 600	80 × 20 = 1,600	80 × 5 = 400	0	2,600
Y	60 × 10 = 600	80 × 10 = 800	80 × 5 = 400	100 × 5 = 500	2,300
Z	0	0	80 × 5 = 400	100 × 10 = 1,000	1,400

DECISION POINT

Workstation X is the bottleneck for Diablo Electronics because the aggregate workload at X is larger than the aggregate workloads of workstations V, W, Y, and Z and the maximum available capacity of 2,400 minutes per week.

Identifying the bottlenecks becomes considerably harder when setup times are lengthy and the degree of divergence in the process is greater than that shown in Example 7.2. Variability in the workloads will again likely create floating bottlenecks, especially if most processes involve multiple operations, and often their capacities are not identical. In practice, these bottlenecks can also be determined by asking workers and supervisors in the plant where the bottlenecks might lie and looking for piled up material in front of different workstations.

Relieving Bottlenecks   The key to preserving bottleneck capacity is to carefully monitor short-term schedules and keep bottleneck resource as busy as is practical. Managers should minimize idle time at the bottlenecks, caused by delays elsewhere in the system and make sure that the bottleneck has all the resources it needs to stay busy. When a changeover or setup is made at a bottleneck, the number of units or customers processed before the next changeover should be large compared to the number processed at less critical operations. Maximizing the number of units processed per setup means fewer setups per year and, thus, less total time lost to setups. The number of setups also depends on the required product variety; more variety necessitates more frequent changeovers.

The long-term capacity of bottleneck operations can be expanded in various ways. Investments can be made in new equipment and in brick-and-mortar facility expansions. The bottleneck's capacity also can be expanded by operating it more hours per week, such as by hiring more employees and going from a one-shift operation to multiple shifts, or by hiring more employees and operating the plant six or seven days per week versus five days per week. Managers also might relieve the bottleneck by redesigning the process, either through *process reengineering* or *process improvement*, or by purchasing additional machines or machines that can handle more capacity.

Product Mix Decisions   Managers might be tempted to produce the products with the highest contribution margins or unit sales. *Contribution margin* is the amount each product contributes to profits and overhead; no fixed costs are considered when making the product mix decision. We call this approach the *traditional method*. The problem with this approach is that the firm's actual throughput and overall profitability depend more upon the contribution margin generated at the bottleneck than by the contribution margin of each individual product produced. We call this latter approach the *bottleneck method*. Example 7.3 illustrates both of these methods.

EXAMPLE 7.3   **Determining the Product Mix Using Contribution Margin**

The senior management at Diablo Electronics (see Exercise 7.2) wants to improve profitability by accepting the right set of orders, and so collected some additional financial data. Variable overhead costs are $8,500 per week. Each worker is paid $18 per hour and is paid for an entire week, regardless of how much the worker is used. Consequently, labor costs are fixed expenses. The plant operates one 8-hour shift per day, or 40 hours each week. Currently, decisions are made using the traditional method, which is to accept as much of the highest contribution margin product as possible (up to the limit of its demand), followed by the next highest contribution margin product, and so on until no more capacity is available. Pedro Rodriguez, the newly hired production supervisor, is knowledgeable about the theory of constraints and bottleneck-based scheduling. He believes that profitability can indeed be improved if bottleneck resources were exploited to determine the product mix. What is the change in profits if, instead of the traditional method used by Diablo Electronics, the bottleneck method advocated by Pedro is used to select the product mix?

SOLUTION

Decision Rule 1: Traditional Method

Select the best product mix according to the highest overall contribution margin of each product.

Step 1:   Calculate the contribution margin per unit of each product as shown here.

	A	B	C	D
Price	$75.00	$72.00	$45.00	$38.00
Raw material and purchased parts	−10.00	−5.00	−5.00	−10.00
= Contribution margin	$65.00	$67.00	$40.00	$28.00

When ordered from highest to lowest, the contribution margin per unit sequence of these products is B, A, C, D.

Step 2:   Allocate resources V, W, X, Y, and Z to the products in the order decided in step 1. Satisfy each demand until the bottleneck resource (workstation X) is encountered. Subtract minutes away from 2,400 minutes available for each week at each stage.

Work Center	Minutes at the Start	Minutes Left After Making 80 B	Minutes Left After Making 60 A	Can Only Make 40 C	Can Still Make 100 D
V	2,400	2,400	600	600	600
W	2,400	2,400	2,400	2,200	700
X	2,400	800	200	0	0
Y	2,400	1,600	1,000	800	300
Z	2,400	2,400	2,400	2,200	1,200

The best product mix according to this traditional approach is then 60 A, 80 B, 40 C, and 100 D.

Step 3:   Compute profitability for the selected product mix.

Profits		
Revenue	(60 × $75) + (80 × $72) + (40 × $45) + (100 × $38)	= $15, 860
Materials	(60 × $10) + (80 × $5) + (40 × $5) + (100 × $10))	= −$2,200
Labor	(5 workers) × (8 hours/day) × (5 days/week) × ($18/hour))	= −$3,600
Overhead		= −$8,500
Profit		= $1,560

Manufacturing the product mix of 60 A, 80 B, 40 C, and 100 D will yield a profit of $1,560 per week.

Decision Rule 2: Bottleneck Method

Select the best product mix according to the dollar contribution margin per minute of processing time at the bottleneck workstation X. This method would take advantage of the principles outlined in the theory of constraints and get the most dollar benefit from the bottleneck.

Step 1:   Calculate the contribution margin/minute of processing time at bottleneck workstation X:

	Product A	Product B	Product C	Product D
Contribution margin	$65.00	$67.00	$40.00	$28.00
Time at bottleneck	10 minutes	20 minutes	5 minutes	0 minutes
Contribution margin per minute	$6.50	$3.35	$8.00	Not defined

When ordered from highest to lowest contribution margin/minute at the bottleneck, the manufacturing sequence of these products is D, C, A, B, which is reverse of the earlier order. Product D is scheduled first because it does not consume any resources at the bottleneck.

Step 2:   Allocate resources V, W, X, Y, and Z to the products in the order decided in step 1. Satisfy each demand until the bottleneck resource (workstation X) is encountered. Subtract minutes away from 2,400 minutes available for each week at each stage.

Work Center	Minutes at the Start	Minutes Left After Making 100 D	Minutes Left After Making 80 C	Minutes Left After Making 60 A	Can Only Make 70 B
V	2,400	2,400	2,400	600	600
W	2,400	900	500	500	500
X	2,400	2,400	2,000	1,400	0
Y	2,400	1,900	1,500	900	200
Z	2,400	1,400	1,000	1,000	1,000

The best product mix according to this bottleneck-based approach is then 60 A, 70 B, 80 C, and 100 D.

Step 3:   Compute profitability for the selected product mix.

Profits		
Revenue	$(60 \times \$75) + (70 \times \$72) + (80 \times \$45) + (100 \times \$38)$	= $16,940
Materials	$(60 \times \$10) + (70 \times \$5) + (80 \times \$5) + (100 \times \$10))$	= −$2,350
Labor	(5 workers) × (8 hours/day) × (5 days/week) × ($18 hour)	= −$3,600
Overhead		= −$8,500
Profit		$2,490

Manufacturing the product mix of 60 A, 70 B, 80 C, and 100 D will yield a profit of $2,490 per week.

DECISION POINT

By focusing on the bottleneck resources in accepting customer orders and determining the product mix, the sequence in which products are selected for production is reversed from **B, A, C, D** to **D, C, A, B**. Consequently, the product mix is changed from 60 A, 80 B, 40 C, and 100 D to 60 A, 70 B, 80 C, and 100 D. The increase in profits by using the bottleneck method is $930, ($2,490 − $1,560), or almost 60 percent over the traditional approach.

Linear programming models (see Supplement E) could also be used to find the best product mix in Example 7.3. It must be noted however that the problem in Example 7.3 did not involve significant setup times. Otherwise, they must be taken into consideration for not only identifying the bottleneck, but also in determining the product mix. The experiential learning exercise of Min-Yo Garment Company at the end of this chapter provides an interesting illustration of how the product mix can be determined when setup times are significant. In this way, the principles behind the theory of constraints can be exploited for making better decisions about a firm's most profitable product mix.

Drum-Buffer-Rope Systems   **Drum-Buffer-Rope (DBR)** is a planning and control system based on the theory of constraints that is often used in manufacturing firms to plan and schedule production. It works by regulating the flow of work-in-process materials at the bottleneck or the capacity constrained resource (CCR). The bottleneck schedule is the *drum* because it sets the beat or the production rate for the entire plant and is linked to the market demand. The *buffer* is a time buffer that plans early flows to the bottleneck and thus protects it from disruption. It also ensures that the bottleneck is never starved for work. A finished-goods inventory buffer can also be placed in front of the shipping point in order to protect customer shipping schedules. Finally, the *rope* represents the tying of material release to the drum beat, which is the rate at which the bottleneck controls the throughput of the entire plant. It is thus a communication device to ensure that raw material is not introduced into the system at a rate faster than what the bottleneck can handle. Completing the loop, *buffer management* constantly monitors the execution of incoming bottleneck work. Working together, the drum, the buffer, and the rope can help managers create a production schedule that reduces lead times and inventories while simultaneously increasing throughput and on-time delivery.

To better understand the drum-buffer-rope system, consider the schematic layout shown in Figure 7.3. Process B, with a capacity of only 500 units per week, is the bottleneck because the upstream Process A and downstream Process C have capacities of 800 units per week and 700 units per week, respectively, and the market demand is 650 units per week, on average. In this case, because the capacity at process B is less than the market demand, it is the bottleneck. A constraint time buffer, which can be in the form of materials arriving earlier than needed, is placed right in front of the bottleneck (Process B). A shipping buffer, in the form of finished goods inventory, can also be placed prior to the shipping schedule in order to protect customer orders that are firm. Finally, a rope ties the material release schedule to match the schedule, or drum beat, at the bottleneck. The material flow is pulled forward by the drum beat prior to the bottleneck, while it is pushed downstream toward the customer subsequent to the bottleneck.

drum-buffer-rope (DBR)

A planning and control system that regulates the flow of work-in-process materials at the bottleneck or the capacity constrained resource (CCR) in a productive system.

▼ FIGURE 7.3
Drum-Buffer-Rope System

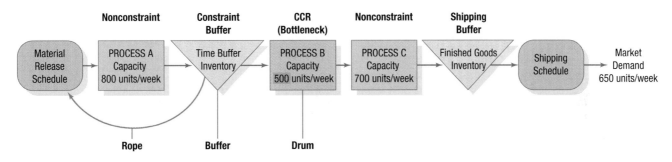

Unlike the other planning and control system discussed in greater detail in Chapter 15, "Planning Sufficient Resources," DBR specifically strives to improve throughput by better utilizing the bottleneck resource and protecting it from disruption through the time buffer and protective buffer capacity elsewhere. So while the process batch in the DBR is any size that minimizes setups and improves utilization at the bottleneck, at nonconstrained resources the process batches are equal to what is needed for production at that time. The material can consequently be released in small batches known as transfer batches at the release point, which then combine at the constraint buffer to make a full process batch at the bottleneck. Transfer batches can be as small as one unit each, to allow a downstream workstation to start work on a batch before it is completely finished at the prior process. Using transfer batches typically facilitates a reduction in overall lead time.

DBR can be an effective system to use when the product the firm produces is relatively simple and the production process has more line flows. Planning is greatly simplified in this case and primarily revolves around scheduling the constrained resource and triggering other points to meet that bottleneck's schedule. Effectively implementing a DBR system requires an understanding of the TOC principles. However such a system can be utilized in many different kinds of manufacturing and service organizations, either by itself or in conjunction with other planning and control systems. Managerial Practice 7.2 illustrates how the use of a DBR system improved the performance of the Marine Corps Maintenance Center in Albany, Georgia.

MANAGERIAL PRACTICE 7.2	The Drum-Buffer-Rope System at a U.S. Marine Corps Maintenance Center

The U.S. Marine Corps Maintenance Center in Albany, Georgia, overhauls and repairs vehicles used by the corps, such as fuel tankers, trucks, earth-moving equipment, amphibious vehicles, and light armored vehicles. The overhaul process starts with the disassembly of each vehicle to determine the amount and nature of work that needs to be performed. The type and duration of the repair work can vary tremendously for even the same type of vehicle. Faced with such uncertainty, the center was struggling until four years ago to complete its equipment repairs on time, and it had an increasing backlog to boot. For instance, the center was able to repair only about 5 MK-48s (heavy-duty haulers) per month, when twice as many MK-48s— 10 per month—typically needed repair. Different units of the corps were threatening to divert their orders to the private-sector repair companies.

TOC principles were used to identify the bottlenecks on the shop floor. After the center's operations were studied in depth, however, contrary to everyone's expectations, it was discovered that more than enough capacity was available to repair and overhaul 10 MK-48s per month. The problem was not capacity; it was the center's scheduling system. Products were being pushed onto the shop floor without regard for the status of the resources on the floor. Thus, what the center had was a policy constraint related to the scheduling process, not an actual physical resource constraint.

In order to improve the center's performance, its managers implemented a simplified form of a drum-buffer-rope system as shown in Figure 7.3. Since the Marine Corp Maintenance Center was not constrained by any internal resource, the drum in such a simplified system was based on firm orders. As orders came in, a quick check was done to measure the total load the center's least-capable resource was handling. If the resource was not too heavily loaded, the order was accepted and released onto the shop floor for processing. The rope tied the shipping schedule directly to the material release schedule instead of the bottleneck schedule, and the only buffer maintained was the shipping buffer. Such a simplified DBR system did not require any specialized software. It focused simply on the market demand for repairs.

The center's results following the change were impressive. Repair cycle times were reduced from an average of 167 days to 58 days, work-in-process levels were reduced from 550 percent of demand to 140 percent, and the cost to repair products went down by 25 to 30 percent due to an increased throughput. The center's ability to repair MK-48s became much more flexible, too. In fact, it can now repair as many as 23 MK-48s per month. The Center is on schedule for 99 percent of the production lines where the TOC principles have been implemented, and the repair costs have decreased by 25%. Carrying out these simple improvements made the Albany Maintenance Center a world-class overhaul and repair operation.

Repairs to equipment like this amphibious assault vehicle can vary tremendously at the U.S. Marine Corps Maintenance Center in Albany, Georgia. The center struggled to keep up with its repairs until managers implemented the simplified form of a drum-buffer-rope system. The result? Repair times fell from 167 days to just 58 days, on average.

Source: Mandyam Srinivasan, Darren Jones, and Alex Miller, "Applying Theory of Constraints Principles and Lean Thinking at the Marine Corps Maintenance Center," Defense Acquisition Review Journal, August-November 2004; M. Srinivasan, Darren Jones, and Alex Miller, "Corps Capabilities," APICS Magazine (March 2005), pp. 46–50.

Jeane Taiza Silva works on a Ford EcoSport SUV as it passes by the paint station on the assembly line at Ford's highly automated state-of-the-art Camaçari plant near Salvador da Bahia, Brazil.

line balancing

The assignment of work to stations in a line so as to achieve the desired output rate with the smallest number of workstations.

MANAGING CONSTRAINTS IN A LINE PROCESS

As noted in Chapter 3, "Developing a Process Strategy," products created by a line process include the assembly of computers, automobiles, appliances, and toys. Such assembly lines can exist in providing services as well. For instance, putting together a standardized hamburger with a fixed sequence of steps is akin to operating an assembly line. While the product mix or demand volumes do not change as rapidly for line processes as for job or batch processes, the load can shift between work centers in a line as the end product being assembled is changed or the total output rate of the line is altered. Constraints arising out of such actions can be managed by balancing the workload between different stations in a line, which we explain next in greater detail.

Line Balancing

Line balancing is the assignment of work to stations in a line process so as to achieve the desired output rate with the smallest number of workstations. Normally, one worker is assigned to a station. Thus, the line that produces at the desired pace with the fewest workers is the most efficient one. Achieving this goal is much like the theory of constraints, because both approaches are concerned about bottlenecks. Line balancing differs in how it addresses bottlenecks. Rather than (1) taking on new customer orders to best use bottleneck capacity or (2) scheduling so that bottleneck resources are conserved, line balancing takes a third approach. It creates workstations with workloads as evenly balanced as possible. It seeks to create workstations so that the capacity utilization for the bottleneck is not much higher than for the other workstations in the line. Another difference is that line balancing applies only to line processes that do assembly work, or to work that can be bundled in many ways to create the jobs for each workstation in the line. The latter situation can be found both in manufacturing and service settings.

Line balancing must be performed when a line is set up initially, when a line is rebalanced to change its hourly output rate, or when a product or process changes. The goal is to obtain workstations with well-balanced workloads (e.g., every station takes roughly 3 minutes per customer in a cafeteria line with different food stations).

The analyst begins by separating the work into **work elements**, which are the smallest units of work that can be performed independently. The analyst then obtains the time standard for each element and identifies the work elements, called **immediate predecessors**, which must be done before the next element can begin.

Precedence Diagram   Most lines must satisfy some technological precedence requirements; that is, certain work elements must be done before the next can begin. However, most lines also allow for some latitude and more than one sequence of operations. To help you visualize immediate predecessors better, let us run through the construction of a **precedence diagram**.[2] We denote the work elements by circles, with the time required to perform the work shown below each circle. Arrows lead from immediate predecessors to the next work element. Example 7.4 illustrates a manufacturing process, but a back office line-flow process in a service setting can be approached similarly.

work elements

The smallest units of work that can be performed independently.

immediate predecessors

Work elements that must be done before the next element can begin.

precedence diagram

A diagram that allows one to visualize immediate predecessors better; work elements are denoted by circles, with the time required to perform the work shown below each circle.

EXAMPLE 7.4	Constructing a Precedence Diagram

Green Grass, Inc., a manufacturer of lawn and garden equipment, is designing an assembly line to produce a new fertilizer spreader, the Big Broadcaster. Using the following information on the production process, construct a precedence diagram for the Big Broadcaster.

Work Element	Description	Time (sec)	Immediate Predecessor(s)
A	Bolt leg frame to hopper	40	None
B	Insert impeller shaft	30	A
C	Attach axle	50	A
D	Attach agitator	40	B
E	Attach drive wheel	6	B
F	Attach free wheel	25	C
G	Mount lower post	15	C
H	Attach controls	20	D, E
I	Mount nameplate	18	F, G
		Total 244	

SOLUTION

Figure 7.4 shows the complete diagram. We begin with work element A, which has no immediate predecessors. Next, we add elements B and C, for which element A is the only immediate predecessor. After entering time standards and arrows showing precedence, we add elements D and E, and so on. The diagram simplifies interpretation. Work element F, for example, can be done anywhere on the line after element C is completed. However, element I must await completion of elements F and G.

DECISION POINT

Management now has enough information to develop a line-flow layout that clusters work elements to form workstations, with a goal being to balance the workloads and, in the process, minimize the number of workstations required.

▲ FIGURE 7.4
Precedence Diagram for Assembling the Big Broadcaster

---

[2] Precedence relationships and precedence diagrams are also important in the entirely different context of project management.

Desired Output Rate The goal of line balancing is to match the output rate to the staffing or production plan. For example, if the plan calls for 4,800 units or customers per week and the line operates 80 hours per week, the desired output rate ideally would be 60 units or customers (4,800/80) per hour. Matching output to the plan ensures on-time delivery and prevents buildup of unwanted inventory or customer delays. However, managers should avoid rebalancing a line too frequently because each time a line is rebalanced many workers' jobs on the line must be redesigned, temporarily hurting productivity and sometimes even requiring a new detailed layout for some stations.

Cycle Time After determining the desired output rate for a line, the analyst can calculate the line's cycle time. A line's **cycle time** is the maximum time allowed for work on a unit at each station.[3] If the time required for work elements at a station exceeds the line's cycle time, the station will be a bottleneck, preventing the line from reaching its desired output rate. The target cycle time is the reciprocal of the desired hourly output rate:

$$c = \frac{1}{r}$$

where

$$c = \text{cycle time in hours per unit}$$

$$r = \text{desired output rate in units per hour}$$

For example, if the line's desired output rate is 60 units per hour, the cycle time is $c = 1/60$ hour per unit, or 1 minute.

Theoretical Minimum To achieve the desired output rate, managers use line balancing to assign every work element to a station, making sure to satisfy all precedence requirements and to minimize the number of stations, n, formed. If each station is operated by a different worker, minimizing n also maximizes worker productivity. Perfect balance is achieved when the sum of the work-element times at each station equals the cycle time, c, and no station has any idle time. For example, if the sum of each station's work-element times is 1 minute, which is also the cycle time, the line achieves perfect balance. Although perfect balance usually is unachievable in practice, owing to the unevenness of work-element times and the inflexibility of precedence requirements, it sets a benchmark, or goal, for the smallest number of stations possible. The **theoretical minimum (TM)** for the number of stations is

$$\text{TM} = \frac{\Sigma t}{c}$$

Where

Σt = total time required to assemble each unit (the sum of all work-element standard times)

c = cycle time

For example, if the sum of the work-element times is 15 minutes and the cycle time is 1 minute, TM = 15/1, or 15 stations. Any fractional values obtained for TM are rounded up because fractional stations are impossible.

Idle Time, Efficiency, and Balance Delay Minimizing n automatically ensures (1) minimal idle time, (2) maximal efficiency, and (3) minimal balance delay. Idle time is the total unproductive time for all stations in the assembly of each unit:

$$\text{Idle time} = nc - \Sigma t$$

where

$$n = \text{number of stations}$$

$$c = \text{cycle time}$$

$$\Sigma t = \text{total standard time required to assemble each unit}$$

---

[3] Except in the context of line balancing, *cycle time* has a different meaning. It is the elapsed time between starting and completing a job. Some researchers and practitioners prefer the term *lead time*.

Efficiency is the ratio of productive time to total time, expressed as a percent:

$$\text{Efficiency (\%)} = \frac{\Sigma t}{nc}(100)$$

Balance delay is the amount by which efficiency falls short of 100 percent:

$$\text{Balance delay (\%)} = 100 - \text{Efficiency}$$

As long as c is fixed, we can optimize all three goals by minimizing n.

balance delay

The amount by which efficiency falls short of 100 percent.

EXAMPLE 7.5	Calculating the Cycle Time, Theoretical Minimum, and Efficiency

Green Grass's plant manager just received marketing's latest forecasts of Big Broadcaster sales for the next year. She wants its production line to be designed to make 2,400 spreaders per week for at least the next 3 months. The plant will operate 40 hours per week.

a. What should be the line's cycle time?

b. What is the smallest number of workstations that she could hope for in designing the line for this cycle time?

c. Suppose that she finds a solution that requires only five stations. What would be the line's efficiency?

Tutor 7.1 in my**om**lab provides another example to calculate these line-balancing measures.

SOLUTION

a. First convert the desired output rate (2,400 units per week) to an hourly rate by dividing the weekly output rate by 40 hours per week to get $r = 60$ units per hour. Then the cycle time is

$$c = 1/r = 1/60 \text{ (hour/unit)} = 1 \text{ minute/unit} = 60 \text{ seconds/unit}$$

b. Now calculate the theoretical minimum for the number of stations by dividing the total time, Σt, by the cycle time, $c = 60$ seconds. Assuming perfect balance, we have

$$\text{TM} = \frac{\Sigma t}{c} = \frac{244 \text{ seconds}}{60 \text{ seconds}} = 4.067 \text{ or 5 stations}$$

c. Now calculate the efficiency of a five-station solution, assuming for now that one can be found:

$$\text{Efficiency (\%)} = \frac{\Sigma t}{nc}(100) = \frac{244}{5(60)}(100) = 81.3\%$$

DECISION POINT

If the manager finds a solution with five stations that satisfies all precedence constraints, then that is the optimal solution; it has the minimum number of stations possible. However, the efficiency (sometimes called the *theoretical maximum efficiency*) will be only 81.3 percent. Perhaps the line should be operated less than 40 hours per week (thereby adjusting the cycle time) and the employees transferred to other kinds of work when the line does not operate.

Finding a Solution   Often, many assembly-line solutions are possible, even for such simple problems as Green Grass's. The goal is to cluster the work elements into workstations so that (1) the number of workstations required is minimized, and (2) the precedence and cycle-time requirements are not violated. The idea is to assign work elements to workstations subject to the precedence requirements so that the work content for the station is equal (or nearly so, but less than) the cycle time for the line. In this way, the number of workstations will be minimized.

Here we use the trial-and-error method to find a solution, although commercial software packages are also available. Most of these packages use different decision rules in picking which work element to assign next to a workstation being created. The ones used by POM for Windows are described in Table 7.3. The solutions can be examined for improvement, because there is no guarantee that they are optimal or even feasible. Some work elements cannot be assigned to the same station, some changes can be made to reduce the number of stations, or some shifts can provide better balance between stations.

TABLE 7.3	HEURISTIC DECISION RULES IN ASSIGNING THE NEXT WORK ELEMENT TO A WORKSTATION BEING CREATED

Create one station at a time. For the station now being created, identify the unassigned work elements that qualify for assignment: They are candidates if

1.   All of their predecessors have been assigned to this station or stations already created.
2.   Adding them to the workstation being created will not create a workload that exceeds the cycle time.

Decision Rule	Logic
Longest work element	Picking the candidate with the longest time to complete is an effort to fit in the most difficult elements first, leaving the ones with short times to "fill out" the station.
Shortest work element	This rule is the opposite of the longest work element rule because it gives preference in workstation assignments to those work elements that are quicker. It can be tried because no single rule guarantees the best solution. It might provide another solution for the planner to consider.
Most followers	When picking the next work element to assign to a station being created, choose the element that has the most *followers* (due to precedence requirements). In Figure 7.4, item C has three followers (F, G, and I) whereas item D has only one follower (H). This rule seeks to maintain flexibility so that good choices remain for creating the last few workstations at the end of the line.
Fewest followers	Picking the candidate with the fewest followers is the opposite of the most followers rule.

Figure 7.5 shows a solution that creates just five workstations. We know that five is the minimum possible, because five is the theoretical minimum found in Example 7.5. All of the precedence and cycle-time requirements are also satisfied. Consequently, the solution is optimal for this problem. Each worker at each station must perform the work elements in the proper sequence. For example, workstation S5 consists of one worker who will perform work elements E, H, and I on each unit that comes along the assembly line. The processing time per unit is 44 seconds (6 + 20 + 18), which does not exceed the cycle time of 60 seconds (see Example 7.5). Furthermore, the immediate predecessors of these three work elements are assigned to this workstation or upstream workstations, so their precedence requirements are satisfied. The worker at workstation S5 can do element I at any time but will not start element H until element E is finished.

FIGURE 7.5 ▶
Big Broadcaster Precedence Diagram Solution

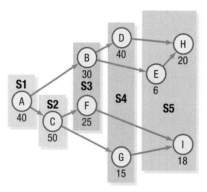

Managerial Considerations

In addition to balancing a line for a given cycle time, managers have four other considerations: (1) pacing, (2) behavioral factors, (3) number of models produced, and (4) different cycle times.

Pacing   The movement of product from one station to the next as soon as the cycle time has elapsed is called **pacing**. Pacing manufacturing processes allows materials handling to be automated and requires less inventory storage area. However, it is less flexible in handling unexpected delays that require either slowing down the entire line or pulling the unfinished work off the line to be completed later.

Behavioral Factors   The most controversial aspect of line-flow layouts is behavioral response. Studies show that installing production lines increases absenteeism, turnover, and grievances. Paced production and high specialization (say, cycle times of less than 2 minutes) lower job satisfaction. Workers generally favor inventory buffers as a means of avoiding mechanical pacing. One study even showed that productivity increased on unpaced lines.

Number of Models Produced   A line that produces several items belonging to the same family is called a **mixed-model line**. In contrast, a single-model line produces one model with no variations. Mixed-model production enables a plant to achieve both high-volume production *and* product variety. However, it complicates scheduling and increases the need for good communication about the specific parts to be produced at each station.

pacing

The movement of product from one station to the next as soon as the cycle time has elapsed.

mixed-model line

A production line that produces several items belonging to the same family.

Cycle Times   A line's cycle time depends on the desired output rate (or sometimes on the maximum number of workstations allowed). In turn, the maximum line efficiency varies considerably with the cycle time selected. Thus, exploring a range of cycle times makes sense. A manager might go with a particularly efficient solution even if it does not match the desired output rate. The manager can compensate for the mismatch by varying the number of hours the line operates through overtime, extending shifts, or adding shifts. Multiple lines might even be the answer.

In this chapter, we learned that constraints or bottlenecks can exist in the form of internal resources or market demand in both manufacturing and service organizations, and in turn play an important role in determining system performance. The TOC provides guidelines on how to identify and manage these constraints, as well as determine the best product mix that would maximize the contribution margin for the firm. Assembly line balancing, as a special form of a constraint in managing a line process within both manufacturing and services, can also be an effective mechanism for matching output to a plan and running such processes more efficiently.

INTERNET RESOURCES

my**om**lab and the Companion Website at **www.pearsonglobaleditions.com/krajewski** contain many tools, activities, and resources designed for this chapter.

KEY EQUATIONS

1. Cycle time: $c = \dfrac{1}{r}$

2. Theoretical minimum number of workstations: $TM = \dfrac{\Sigma t}{c}$

3. Idle time: $nc - \Sigma t$

4. Efficiency (%): $\dfrac{\Sigma t}{nc}(100)$

5. Balance delay (%): $100 - \text{Efficiency}$

KEY TERMS

balance delay 297
bottleneck 284
constraint 284
cycle time 296
drum-buffer-rope (DBR) 293

immediate predecessors 295
line balancing 294
mixed-model line 298
pacing 298
precedence diagram 295

theoretical minimum (TM) 296
theory of constraints (TOC) 285
throughput time 286
work elements 295

SOLVED PROBLEM 1

Ari's Falafel Stand offers two different types of falafel dishes: a regular falafel on pita with chickpea patties and tahini sauce or a falafel platter that has all of the ingredients of a regular falafel along with hummus and a salad of diced tomatoes, cucumbers, onions, and green peppers tossed with lemon juice and olive oil. The regular falafel is wrapped in foil, and the falafel platter comes on a plate with triangles of pita bread. Each goes through an assembly line-like process. The process flow for both types of dishes is shown in the following chart. Both regular falafels and falafel platters go through steps A1 and A2. The regular falafel then goes through steps A3 and A4, and the falafel platter goes through steps A5, A6, and A7. Both dishes finish at the cashier (step A8). The number in parentheses indicates how long that step usually takes in seconds.

a. Which step is the bottleneck for the preparation of a regular falafel? Which step is the bottleneck for the falafel platter?

b. What is the capacity—measured as customers served per hour—of Ari's Falafel Stand to serve regular falafels and the falafel platters to customers? Assume that no customers are waiting at steps A1, A2, and A8.

c. If 75 percent of the customers order regular falafels and 25 percent order a falafel platter, what is the average capacity of the falafel stand in customers served per hour?

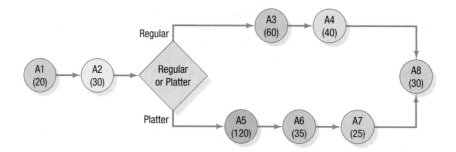

d. Where would you expect the preparation of regular falafels to experience a delay, assuming that new customers are always entering the shop and that none of them wants a falafel platter? Where would you expect the preparation of a falafel platter to experience a delay, again assuming that new customers are always entering the shop and that none of them want a regular falafel?

SOLUTION

a. Step A3 is the bottleneck for a regular falafel, and step A5 is the bottleneck for the falafel platter. These steps take the longest time in the flow.

b. The capacity for regular falafel is 60 customers per hour because the bottleneck step A3 can process one customer every minute (60/1). The capacity for the falafel platter is 30 customers per hour (60/2). These capacities are derived by translating the "minutes per customer" of each bottleneck activity to "customers per hour."

c. The average capacity of the car wash is [(0.75 × 60) + (0.25 × 30)] = 52.5 customers per hour.

d. Regular falafels would experience delays before steps A1, A2, and A3 because the activities that immediately precede them have a higher rate of output (i.e., smaller processing times). Falafel platter customers would experience a wait in front of steps A1 and A2 for the same reasons. A1 is included for both types of dishes because the arrival rate of customers could always exceed the capacity of A1.

SOLVED PROBLEM 2

A company is setting up an assembly line to produce 192 units per 8-hour shift. The following table identifies the work elements, times, and immediate predecessors:

Work Element	Time (sec)	Immediate Predecessor(s)
A	40	None
B	80	A
C	30	D, E, F
D	25	B
E	20	B
F	15	B
G	120	A
H	145	G
I	130	H
J	115	C, I
	Total 720	

a. What is the desired cycle time (in seconds)?

b. What is the theoretical minimum number of stations?

c. Use trial and error to work out a solution, and show your solution on a precedence diagram.

d. What are the efficiency and balance delay of the solution found?

SOLUTION

a. Substituting in the cycle-time formula, we get

$$c = \frac{1}{r} = \frac{8\ \text{hours}}{192\ \text{units}}(3{,}600\ \text{seconds/hour}) = 150\ \text{seconds/unit}$$

b. The sum of the work-element times is 720 seconds, so

$$\text{TM} = \frac{\Sigma t}{c} = \frac{720\ \text{seconds/unit}}{150\ \text{seconds/unit-station}} = 4.8\ \text{or 5 stations}$$

which may not be achievable.

c. The precedence diagram is shown in Figure 7.6. Each row in the following table shows work elements assigned to each of the five workstations in the proposed solution.

d. Calculating the efficiency, we get

$$\text{Efficiency} = \frac{\Sigma t}{nc}(100) = \frac{720\ \text{seconds/unit}}{5[150\ \text{seconds/unit}]}$$

$$= 96\%$$

Thus, the balance delay is only 4 percent (100–96).

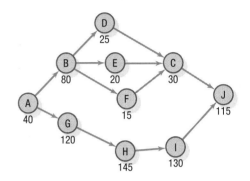

▲ FIGURE 7.6
Precedence Diagram

Station	Candidate(s)	Choice	Work-Element Time (sec)	Cumulative Time (sec)	Idle Time ($c = 150$ sec)
S1	A	A	40	40	110
	B	B	80	120	30
	D, E, F	D	25	145	5
S2	E, F, G	G	120	120	30
	E, F	E	20	140	10
S3	F, H	H	145	145	5
S4	F, I	I	130	130	20
	F	F	15	145	5
S5	C	C	30	30	120
	J	J	115	145	5

DISCUSSION QUESTIONS

1. Identify a process that you encounter on a daily basis, such as the lunch cafeteria or the journey from your home to school/work. What are the bottlenecks that limit the throughput of this process, and how could its efficiency be improved?

2. Using the same process as in question 1, identify conditions that would lead to the bottlenecks changing or shifting away from the existing bottleneck.

PROBLEMS

Software, such as OM Explorer, Active Models, and POM for Windows, is available in my**om**lab. Check with your instructor on how best to use it. In many cases, the instructor wants you to understand how to do the calculations by hand. At most, the software provides a check on your calculations. When calculations are particularly complex and the goal is interpreting the results in making decisions, the software replaces entirely the manual calculations. The software also can be a valuable resource well after your course is completed.

1. Figure 7.7 details the process flow for two types of customers who enter Barbara's Boutique shop for customized dress

alterations. After step T1, Type A customers proceed to step T2 and then to any of the three workstations at T3, followed by steps T4 and T7. After step T1, Type B customers proceed to step T5 and then steps T6 and T7. The numbers in parentheses are the minutes it takes to process a customer.

a. What is the capacity of Barbara's shop in terms of the numbers of Type A customers who can be served in an hour? Assume no customers are waiting at steps T1 or T7.

b. If 30 percent of the customers are Type A customers and 70 percent are Type B customers, what is the average capacity of Barbara's shop in customers per hour?

c. Assuming that the arrival rate is greater than five customers per hour, when would you expect Type A customers to experience waiting lines, assuming no Type B customers in the shop? Where would the Type B customers have to wait, assuming no Type A customers?

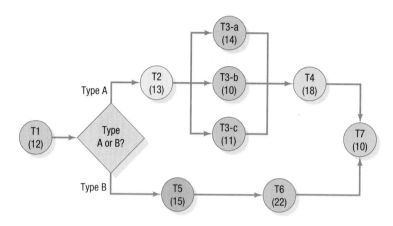

FIGURE 7.7 ▲
Process Flow for Barbara's Boutique Customers

2. Bill's Barbershop has two barbers available to cut customers' hair. Both barbers provide roughly the same experience and skill, but one is just a little bit slower than the other. The process flow in Figure 7.8 shows that all customers go through steps B1 and B2 and then can be served at either of the two barbers at step B3. The process ends for all customers at step B4. The numbers in parentheses indicate the minutes it takes that activity to process a customer.

a. How long does it take the average customer to complete this process?

b. What single activity is the bottleneck for the entire process?

c. How many customers can this process serve in an hour?

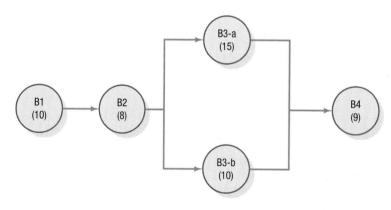

FIGURE 7.8 ▲
Process Flow for Bill's Barbershop

3. Canine Kernels Company (CKC) manufactures two different types of dog chew toys (A and B, sold in 1,000-count boxes) that are manufactured and assembled on three different workstations (W, X, and Y) using a small-batch process (see Figure 7.9). Batch setup times are negligible. The flowchart denotes the path each product follows through the manufacturing process, and each product's

price, demand per week, and processing times per unit are indicated as well. Purchased parts and raw materials consumed during production are represented by inverted triangles. CKC can make and sell up to the limit of its demand per week; no penalties are incurred for not being able to meet all the demand. Each workstation is staffed by a worker who is dedicated to work on that workstation alone and is paid $6 per hour. Total labor costs per week are fixed. Variable overhead costs are $3,500/week. The plant operates one 8-hour shift per day, or 40 hours/week.

Which of the three workstations, W, X, or Y, has the highest aggregate workload, and thus serves as the bottleneck for CKC?

▲ FIGURE 7.9
Flowchart for Canine Kernels Company (CKC)

4. Use trial and error to balance the assembly line described in the following table and Figure 7.10 so that it will produce 40 units per hour.

    a. What is the cycle time?

    b. What is the theoretical minimum number of workstations?

    c. Which work elements are assigned to each workstation?

    d. What are the resulting efficiency and balance delay percentages?

Work Element	Time (sec)	Immediate Predecessor(s)
A	40	None
B	80	A
C	30	A
D	25	B
E	20	C
F	15	B
G	60	B
H	45	D
I	10	E, G
J	75	F
K	15	H, I, J
	Total 415	

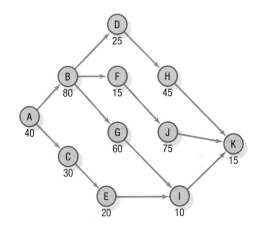

FIGURE 7.10 ▲
Precedence Diagram

5. The senior management at Canine Kernels Company (CKC) is concerned with the existing capacity limitation, so they want to accept the mix of orders that maximizes the company's profits. Traditionally, CKC has utilized a method whereby decisions are made to produce as much of the product with the highest contribution margin as possible (up to the limit of its demand), followed by the next highest contribution margin product, and so on until no more capacity is available. Because capacity is limited, choosing the proper product mix is crucial. Troy Hendrix, the newly hired production supervisor, is an avid follower of the theory of constraints philosophy and the bottleneck method for scheduling. He believes that

profitability can indeed be approved if bottleneck resources are exploited to determine the product mix.

a. What is the profit if the traditional contribution margin method is used for determining CKC's product mix?

b. What is the profit if the bottleneck method advocated by Troy is used for selecting the product mix?

c. Calculate the profit gain, both in absolute dollars as well as in terms of percentage gains, by using TOC principles for determining product mix.

6. In order to meet holiday demand, Penny's Pie Shop requires a production line that is capable of producing 50 pecan pies per week, while operating only 40 hours per week. There are only 4 steps required to produce a single pecan pie with respective processing times of 5 min, 5 min, 45 min and 15 min.

a. What should be the line's cycle time?

b. What is the smallest number of workstations Penny could hope for in designing the line considering this cycle time?

c. Suppose that Penny finds a solution that requires only four stations. What would be the efficiency of this line?

7. Johnson Cogs wants to set up a line to serve 60 customers per hour. The work elements and their precedence relationships are shown in the following table.

a. What is the theoretical minimum number of stations?

b. How many stations are required using the longest work element decision rule?

c. Suppose that a solution requiring five stations is obtained. What is its efficiency?

Work Element	Time (sec)	Immediate Predecessor(s)
A	40	None
B	30	A
C	50	A
D	40	B
E	6	B
F	25	C
G	15	C
H	20	D, E
I	18	F, G
J	30	H, I
	Total 274	

8. The *trim line* at PW is a small subassembly line that, along with other such lines, feeds into the final chassis line. The entire assembly line, which consists of more than 900 workstations, is to make PW's new E cars. The trim line itself involves only 13 work elements and must handle 20 cars per hour. In addition to the usual precedence constraints, there are two *zoning constraints*. First, work elements K and L should be assigned to the same station; both use a common component, and assigning them to the same station conserves storage space. Second, work elements H and J cannot be performed at the same station. Work-element data are as follows:

Work Element	Time (sec)	Immediate Predecessor(s)
A	1.8	None
B	0.4	None
C	1.6	None
D	1.5	A
E	0.7	A
F	0.5	E
G	0.8	B
H	1.4	C
I	1.4	D
J	1.4	F, G
K	0.5	H
L	1.0	J
M	0.8	I, K, L

a. Draw a precedence diagram.

b. What cycle time (in minutes) results in the desired output rate?

c. What is the theoretical minimum number of stations?

d. Using trial and error, balance the line as best you can.

e. What is the efficiency of your solution?

ADVANCED PROBLEMS

9. Yost-Perry Industries (YPI) manufactures a mix of affordable guitars (A, B, C) that are fabricated and assembled at four different processing stations (W, X, Y, Z). The operation is a batch process with small setup times that can be considered negligible. The product information (price, weekly demand, and processing times) and process sequences are shown in Figure 7.11. Raw materials and purchased parts (shown as a per-unit consumption rate) are represented by inverted triangles. YPI is able to make and sell up to the limit of its demand per week with no penalties incurred for

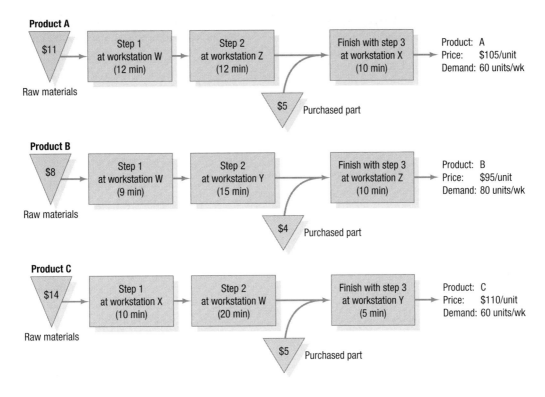

▲ **FIGURE 7.11**
Flowchart for Yost Perry Industries (YPI)

not meeting the full demand. Each workstation is staffed by one highly skilled worker who is dedicated to work on that workstation alone and is paid $15 per hour. The plant operates one 8-hour shift per day and operates on a 5-day work week (i.e., 40 hours of production per person per week). Overhead costs are $9,000/week. Which of the four workstations, W, X, Y, or Z, has the highest aggregate workload, and thus serves as the bottleneck for YPI?

10. Melissa's Photo Studio offers both individual and group portrait options. The process flow diagram in Figure 7.12 shows that all customers must first register and then pay

at one of two cashiers. Then depending on if they want a single or group portrait they go to different rooms. Finally everyone picks up their own finished portrait.

a. How long does it take to complete the entire process for a group portrait?

b. What single activity is the bottleneck for the entire process, assuming the process receives equal amounts of both groups and individuals?

c. What is the capacity of the bottleneck for both groups and individuals?

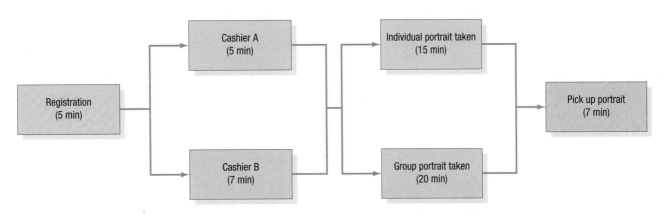

▲ **FIGURE 7.12**
Melissa's Photo Studio

11. The senior management at Davis Watercraft would like to determine if it is possible to improve firm profitability by changing their existing product mix. Currently, the product mix is determined by giving resource priority to the

highest contribution margin watercraft. Davis Watercraft always has a contingent of 10 workers on hand; each worker is paid $25 per hour. Overhead costs are $35,000 per week. The plant operates 18 hours per day and 6 days per week. Labor is considered a fixed expense because workers are paid for their time regardless of their utilization. The production manager has determined that workstation 1 is the bottleneck. Detailed production information is provided below.

	Model		
	A	B	C
Price	$450	$400	$500
Material Cost	$50	$40	$110
Weekly Demand	100	75	40
Processing Time Station 1	60 min	0 min	30 min
Processing Time Station 2	0 min	0 min	60 min
Processing Time Station 3	10 min	60 min	0 min
Processing Time Station 4	20 min	30 min	40 min

   a. Using the traditional method, which bases decisions solely on a product's contribution to profits and overhead, what is the product mix that yields the highest total profit? What is the resulting profit?

   b. Using the bottleneck-based method, what is the product mix that yields the highest total profit? What is the resulting profit?

12. A.J.'s Wildlife Emporium manufactures two unique birdfeeders (Deluxe and Super Duper) that are manufactured and assembled in up to three different workstations (X, Y, Z) using a small batch process. Each of the products is produced according to the flowchart in Figure 7.13. Additionally, the flowchart indicates each product's price, weekly demand, and processing times per unit. Batch setup times are negligible. A.J. can make and sell up to the limit of its weekly demand and there are no penalties for not being able to meet all of the demand. Each workstation is staffed by a worker who is dedicated to work on that workstation alone and is paid $16 per hour. The plant operates 40 hours per week, with no overtime. Overhead costs are $2,000 per week. Based on

the information provided, as well as the information contained in the flowchart, answer the following questions.

   a. Using the traditional method, which bases decisions solely on a product's contribution to profits and overhead, what is the optimal product mix?

   b. What is the overall profitability of the product mix found in part a?

13. Using the information found in question 12, answer the following questions.

   a. Using the bottleneck-based method, what is the optimal product mix?

   b. What is the overall profitability of the product mix found in part a?

14. Yost-Perry Industries' (YPI) senior management team wants to improve the profitability of the firm by accepting the right set of orders. Currently, decisions are made using the traditional method, which is to accept as much of the highest contribution margin product as possible (up to the limit of its demand), followed by the next highest contribution margin product, and so on until all available capacity is utilized. Because the firm cannot satisfy all the demand, the product mix must be chosen carefully. Jay Perry, the newly promoted production supervisor, is knowledgeable about the theory of constraints and the bottleneck-based method for scheduling. He believes that profitability can indeed be improved if bottleneck resources are exploited to determine the product mix. What is the change in profits if, instead of the traditional method that YPI has used thus far, the bottleneck method advocated by Jay is used for selecting the product mix?

15. Jane produces custom greeting cards using six distinct work elements. She would like to produce 10 cards in each 8-hour card-making session. Figure 7.14 details each work element and its associated durations in minutes as well as their precedence relationships.

   a. What cycle time is required to satisfy the required output rate?

FIGURE 7.13 ▲
A.J.'s Wildlife Emporium Flowchart

b. What is the theoretical minimum number of workstations required?

c. If Jane identifies a five-station solution, what is the associated efficiency and balance delay?

d. If the cycle time increased by 100 percent, would the theoretical minimum number of workstations also increase by 100 percent?

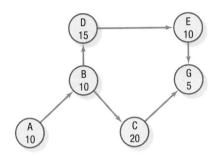

▲ **FIGURE 7.14**
Precedence Diagram for Custom Greeting Cards

16. A paced assembly line has been devised to manufacture calculators, as the following data show:

a. What is the maximum hourly output rate from this line? (*Hint*: The line can go only as fast as its slowest workstation.)

b. What cycle time corresponds to this maximum output rate?

Station	Work Element Assigned	Work Element Time (min)
S1	A	2.7
S2	D, E	0.6, 0.9
S3	C	3.0
S4	B, F, G	0.7, 0.7, 0.9
S5	H, I, J	0.7, 0.3, 1.2
S6	K	2.4

c. If a worker is at each station and the line operates at this maximum output rate, how much idle time is lost during each 10-hour shift?

d. What is the line's efficiency?

17. Greg Davis, a business major at the University of South Carolina (USC), has opened Six Points Saco (SPS), a specialty subs–taco restaurant, at the rim of the USC campus. SPS has grown in popularity over the one year that it has been in operation, and Greg is trying to perfect the business model before making it into a franchise. He wants to maximize the productivity of his staff, as well as serve customers well in a timely fashion. One area of concern is the drive-thru operation during the 11:30 A.M. to 12:30 P.M. lunch hour.

The process of fulfilling an order involves fulfilling the tasks listed below.

Greg is interested in getting a better understanding of the staffing patterns that will be needed in order to operate his restaurant. After taking a course in operations management at the university, he knows that fulfilling a customer order at SPS is very similar to operating an assembly line. He has also used the POM for Windows software before, and wants to apply it for examining different demand scenarios for serving his customers.

a. If all the seven tasks are handled by one employee, how many customers could be served per hour?

b. If Greg wants to process 45 customers per hour, how many employees will he need during the peak period?

c. With the number of employees determined in part b, what is the maximum number of customers who could be served every hour (i.e., what is the maximum output capacity)?

d. Assuming that no task is assigned to more than one employee, what is the "maximum output capacity" from this assembly line? How many employees will be needed to actually accomplish this maximum output capacity?

e. Beyond the output accomplished in part d, if Greg decides to add one additional worker to help out with a bottleneck task, where should he add that worker? With that addition, would he be able to process more customers per hour? If so, what is the new maximum output capacity for the drive-thru?

	Task	Time (seconds)	Immediate Predecessors
A.	Take an order at the booth. Most orders are for a taco and a sub.	25	
B.	Collect money at the window.	20	A
C.	Gather drinks.	35	B
D.	Assemble taco order.	32	B
E.	Assemble sub order.	30	B
F.	Put drinks, taco, and sub in a bag.	25	C, D, E
G.	Give the bag to the customer.	10	F

EXPERIENTIAL LEARNING Min-Yo Garment Company

The Min-Yo Garment Company is a small firm in Taiwan that produces sports-wear for sale in the wholesale and retail markets. Min-Yo's garments are unique because they offer fine embroidery and fabrics with a variety of striped and solid patterns. Over the 20 years of its existence, the Min-Yo Garment Company has become known as a quality producer of sports shirts with dependable deliveries. However, during that same period, the nature of the apparel industry has undergone change. In the past, firms could be success-ful producing standardized shirts in high volumes with few pattern or color choices and long production lead times. Currently, with the advent of region-alized merchandising and intense competition at the retail level, buyers of the shirts are looking for shorter lead times and much more variety in patterns and colors. Consequently, many more business opportunities are available today than ever before to a respected company such as Min-Yo.

Even though the opportunity for business success seemed bright, the management meeting last week was gloomy. Min-Yo Lee, president and owner of Min-Yo Garment, expressed concerns over the performance of the company: "We are facing strong competition for our products. Large apparel firms are driving prices down on high-volume licensed brands. Each day more firms enter the customized shirt business. Our profits are lower than expected, and delivery performance is deteriorating. We must reexamine our capabilities and decide what we can do best."

Products

Min-Yo has divided its product line into three categories: licensed brands, subcontracted brands, and special garments.

Licensed Brands

Licensed brands are brands that are owned by one company but, through a licensing agreement, are produced by another firm that also markets the brand in a specific geographic region. The licenser may have licensees all over the world. The licensee pays the licenser a fee for the privilege of mar-keting the brand in its region, and the licenser agrees to provide some adver-tising for the product, typically through media outlets that have international exposure. A key aspect of the licensing agreement is that the licensee must agree to provide sufficient quantities of product at the retail level. Running out of stock hurts the image of the brand name.

Currently, only one licensed brand is manufactured by Min-Yo. The brand, called the Muscle Shirt, is owned by a large "virtual corporation" in Italy that has no manufacturing facilities of its own. Min-Yo has been licensed to manufacture Muscle Shirts and sell them to large retail chains in Taiwan. The retail chains require prompt shipments at the end of each week. Because of competitive pressures from other licensed brands, low prices are important. Min-Yo sells each Muscle Shirt to retail chains for $6.

The demand for Muscle Shirts averages 900 shirts per week. The fol-lowing demand for Muscle Shirts has been forecasted for the next 12 weeks.

Min-Yo's forecasts of Muscle Shirts are typically accurate to within ±200 shirts per week. If demand exceeds supply in any week, the excess demand is lost. No backorders are taken, and Min-Yo incurs no cost penalty for lost sales.

Subcontracted Brands

Manufacturers in the apparel industry often face uncertain demand. To main-tain level production at their plants, many manufacturers seek subcontractors to produce their brands. Min-Yo is often considered a subcontractor because of its reputation in the industry. Although price is a consideration, the owners of subcontracted brands emphasize dependable delivery and the ability of the subcontractor to adjust order quantities on short notice.

Week	Demand	Week	Demand
1*	700	7	1,100
2	800	8	1,100
3	900	9	900
4	900	10	900
5	1,000	11	800
6	1,100	12	700

*In other words, the company expects to sell 700 Muscle Shirts at the end of week 1.

Currently, Min-Yo manufactures only one subcontracted brand, called the Thunder Shirt because of its bright colors. Thunder Shirts are manufac-tured to order for a company in Singapore. Min-Yo's price to this company is $7 per shirt. When orders are placed, usually twice a month, the customer specifies the delivery of certain quantities in each of the next two weeks. The last order the customer placed is overdue, forcing Min-Yo to pay a penalty charge. To avoid another penalty, 200 shirts must be shipped in week 1. The Singapore company is expected to specify the quantities it requires for weeks 2 and 3 at the beginning of week 1. The delivery schedule containing the orders for weeks 4 and 5 is expected to arrive at the beginning of week 3, and so on. The customer has estimated its average weekly needs for the year to be 200 shirts per week, although its estimates are frequently inaccurate.

Because of the importance of this large customer to Min-Yo and the lengthy negotiations of the sales department to get the business, manage-ment always tries to satisfy its needs. Management believes that if Min-Yo Garment ever refuses to accept an order from this customer, Min-Yo will lose the Thunder Shirt business. Under the terms of the sales contract, Min-Yo agreed to pay this customer $1 for every shirt not shipped on time for each week the shipment of the shirt is delinquent. Delinquent shipments must be made up.

Special Garments

Special garments are made only to customer order because of their low vol-ume and specialized nature. Customers come to Min-Yo Garment to manu-facture shirts for special promotions or special company occasions. Min-Yo's special garments are known as Dragon Shirts because of the elaborate embroidery and oriental flair of the designs. Because each shirt is made to a particular customer's specifications and requires a separate setup, special garments cannot be produced in advance of a firm customer order.

Although price is not a major concern for the customers of special gar-ments, Min-Yo sells Dragon Shirts for $8 a shirt to ward off other companies seeking to enter the custom shirt market. Its customers come to Min-Yo because the company can produce almost any design with high quality and deliver an entire order on time. When placing an order for a Dragon Shirt, a customer specifies the design of the shirt (or chooses from Min-Yo's catalog), supplies specific designs for logos, and specifies the quantity of the order and the delivery date. In the past, management checked to see whether such an order would fit into the schedule, and then either accepted or rejected it on that basis. If Min-Yo accepts an order for delivery at the *end* of a certain week and fails to meet this commitment, it pays a penalty of $2 per shirt for each week delivery is delayed. This penalty is incurred weekly until the delinquent order is delivered. The company tried to forecast demand for specific designs of Dragon Shirts but has given up. Last week Min-Yo had 4 Dragon Shirt opportunities of 50, 75, 200, and 60 units but chose not to accept any of the orders. Dragon Shirt orders in the past ranged from 50 units to 300 units with varying lead times.

Figure 7.15, Min-Yo's current open-order file, shows that in some prior week Min-Yo accepted an order of 400 Thunder Shirts for delivery last week. The open-order file is important because it contains the commitment management made to customers. Commitments are for a certain quantity and a date of delivery. As customer orders are accepted, management enters the quantity in the green cell representing the week that they are due. Because Dragon Shirts are unique unto themselves, they each have their own order number for future use. No Dragon Shirt orders appear in the open-order file because Min-Yo has not committed to any in the past several weeks.

Manufacturing

Process

The Min-Yo Garment Company has the latest process technology in the industry —a machine, called a garment maker, that is run by one operator on each of three shifts. This single machine process can make every garment Min-Yo produces; however, the changeover times consume a substantial amount of capacity. Company policy is to run the machine three shifts a day, five days a week. If business is insufficient to keep the machine busy, the workers are idle because Min-Yo is committed to never fire or lay off a worker. By the same token, the firm has a policy of never working on weekends. Thus, the capacity of the process is 5 days $\times$ 24 hours = 120 hours per week. The hourly wage is $10 per hour, so the firm is committed to a fixed labor cost of

MIN-YO GARMENT COMPANY

Open Order File (Record of commitments)

Product	\multicolumn{10}{c}{Week Order is Due}
	1	2	3	4	5	6	7	8	9	10
Thunder Orders	400									
Dragon Order 1										
Dragon Order 2										
Dragon Order 3										
Dragon Order 4										
Dragon Order 5										
Dragon Order 6										
Dragon Order 7										
Dragon Order 8										
Dragon Order 9										
Dragon Order 10										
Dragon Order 11										
Dragon Order 12										
Dragon Order 13										
Dragon Order 14										
Dragon Order 15										

| ▶ ▶� | Intro | **Open Order File** | Week 1 | Week 2 | Week 3 | Week 4 | Week 5 | Week 6 | Week 7 | Week 8 | Week 9 | Week 10 | S◀ ▶ |

▲ FIGURE 7.15
Min-Yo's Open Order File
Note: All orders are to be delivered at the end of the week indicated, after production for the week has been completed and before next week's production is started.

$10 $\times$ 120 = $1,200 per week. Once the machine has been set up to make a particular type of garment, it can produce that garment at the rate of 10 garments per hour, regardless of type. The cost of the material in each garment, regardless of type, is $4. Raw materials are never a problem and can be obtained overnight.

Scheduling the Garment Maker

Scheduling at Min-Yo is done once each week, after production for the week has been completed and shipped, after new orders from customers have arrived, and before production for the next week has started. Scheduling results in two documents.

The first is a production schedule, shown in Figure 7.16. The schedule shows what management wants the garment maker process to produce in a given week. Two spreadsheet entries are required for each product that is to be produced in a given week. They are in the green shaded cells. The first is the production quantity. In Figure 7.16, the schedule shows that Min-Yo produced quantities of 800 units for Muscle and 200 units for Thunder last week. The second input is a "1" if the machine is to be set up for a given product or a "blank" if no changeover is required. Figure 7.16 shows that last week changeovers were required for the Muscle and Thunder production runs. The changeover information is important because, at the end of a week, the garment maker process will be set up for the last product produced. If the same product

MIN-YO GARMENT COMPANY

PRODUCTION SCHEDULE

The two inputs to the Production Schedule table are:
1. The quantity you decide to produce this time period
2. Whether there is a setup/changeover required (1 or 0)

PRODUCT	Changeover	Quantity
Muscle	1	800
Hours		88
Thunder	1	200
Hours		30

	Changeover	Quantity		Changeover	Quantity		Changeover	Quantity
Dragon Order 1			Dragon Order 11			Dragon Order 21		
Dragon Order 2			Dragon Order 12			Dragon Order 22		
Dragon Order 3			Dragon Order 13			Dragon Order 23		
Dragon Order 4			Dragon Order 14			Dragon Order 24		
Dragon Order 5			Dragon Order 15			Dragon Order 25		
Dragon Order 6			Dragon Order 16			Dragon Order 26		
Dragon Order 7			Dragon Order 17			Dragon Order 27		
Dragon Order 8			Dragon Order 18			Dragon Order 28		
Dragon Order 9			Dragon Order 19			Dragon Order 29		
Dragon Order 10			Dragon Order 20			Dragon Order 30		

Total Dragon Hours	0
Total Dragon Production	0
Total Hours scheduled	118

Is production within capacity?   Yes

FIGURE 7.16 ▲
Min-Yo's Production Schedule

is to be produced first the following week, no new changeover will be required. Management must keep track of the sequence of production each week to take advantage of this savings. The only exception to this rule is Dragon Shirts, which are unique orders that always require a changeover. In week 0, Min-Yo did not produce any Dragon Shirts; however, it did produce 800 Muscle Shirts, followed by 200 Thunder Shirts. Finally, the spreadsheet calculates the hours required for the proposed schedule. Changeover times for Muscle, Thunder, and Dragon Shirts are 8, 10, and 25 hours respectively. Because the garment maker process produces 10 garments per hour regardless of type, the production hours required for Muscle Shirts is $8 + 800/10 = 88$ hours, and the production hours for Thunder Shirts is $10 + 200/10 = 30$ hours, as shown in Figure 7.16. The total time spent on the garment maker process on all products in a week cannot exceed 120 hours. The spreadsheet will not allow you to proceed if this constraint is violated.

The second document is a weekly profit and loss (P&L) statement that factors in sales and production costs, including penalty charges and inventory carrying costs, as shown in Figure 7.17. The inventory carrying cost for *any type of product* is $0.10 per shirt per week left in inventory after shipments for the week have been made. The spreadsheet automatically calculates the P&L statement, which links to the open-order file and the production schedule, after the demand for Muscle Shirts is known. Figure 7.17 shows that the actual demand for Muscle Shirts last week was 750 shirts.

Notes:

- The past due quantity of shirts are those shirts not shipped as promised, and appear as a negative number in the "End Inv" column.

- Available = Beginning inventory + Production

- Sales=Demand × Price when demand<available; Available × Price, otherwise

- Inventory cost = $0.10 times number of shirts in inventory. Past due cost equals past due quantity times the penalty ($1 for Thunder Shirts; $2 for Dragon Shirts). These costs are combined in the "Inv/Past Due Costs" column.

The Simulation

At Min-Yo Garment Company, the executive committee meets weekly to discuss the new order possibilities and the load on the garment maker process. The executive committee consists of top management representatives from finance, marketing, and operations. You will be asked to participate on a team and play the role of a member of the executive committee in class. During this exercise, you must decide how far into the future to plan. Some decisions, such as the markets you want to exploit, are long-term in nature. Before class, you may want to think about the markets and their implications for manufacturing. Other decisions are short-term and have an impact on the firm's ability to meet its commitments. In class, the simulation will proceed as follows.

1. Use the Min-Yo Tables spreadsheet in OM Explorer in my**om**lab. It is found in the Solver menu, under Constraint Management. You will start by specifying the production schedule for week 1, based on the forecasts for week 1 in the case narrative for Muscle Shirts and additional information on new and existing orders for the customized shirts from your instructor. *You may assume that your managerial predecessors left the garment machine set up for Thunder Shirts.* The production schedule decision is to be made in collaboration with your executive committee colleagues in class.

2. When all the teams have finalized their production plans for week 1, the instructor will supply the actual demands for Muscle Shirts in week 1. Enter that quantity in the P&L statement in the spreadsheet for week 1.

3. After the P&L statement for week 1 is completed, the instructor will announce the new order requests for Thunder Shirts and Dragon Shirts to be shipped in week 2 and the weeks beyond.

4. You should look at your order requests, accept those that you want, and reject the rest. Add those that you accept for delivery in future periods to your open-order file. Enter the quantity in the cell representing the week the order is due. You are then irrevocably committed to them and their consequences.

5. You should then make out a new production schedule, specifying what you want your garment-maker process to do in the next week (it will be for week 2 at that time).

6. The instructor will impose a time limit for each period of the simulation. When the time limit for one period has been reached, the simulation will proceed to the next week. Each week the spreadsheet will automatically update your production and financial information in the Summary Sheet.

P&L STATEMENT

Product	Price	Beg Inv	Production	Available	Demand	Sales	End Inv	Inv/Past due costs
Muscle	$6	550	800	1350	750	4500	600	60
Thunder	$7		200	200	400	1400	-200	200
Dragon Orders	$8		0	0	0	0	0	0
Totals			1000			5900		260

		Current	Cumulative
Sales Total		$5,900	$5,900
Labor	$1,200		
Materials	$4,000		
Inv/Past due	$260		
Total Cost		$5,460	
Profit Contribution		$440	$440

▲ **FIGURE 7.17**
Min-Yo's P&L Schedule

VIDEO CASE   Constraint Management at Southwest Airlines

What if you could take a commercial airline flight any time, and anywhere you wanted to go? Just show up at the airport without the need to consider time schedules or layovers. Aside from the potentially cost-prohibitive nature of such travel, there are also constraints in the airline system that preclude this kind of operation. From the lobby check-in process through to boarding at the gate and processing plane turnaround, the process of operating the airline is filled with constraints that must be managed in order for them to be successful and profitable. Flight schedules are tightly orchestrated and controlled, departure and arrival gates at airports are limited, and individual aircraft have seating capacities in each section of the plane, to name a few.

Southwest Airlines is one company that has figured out how to manage its constraints and generate positive customer experiences in the process. No other airline can claim the same level of profitability and customer satisfaction Southwest regularly achieves. What is its secret?

Talk to any loyal Southwest customer and you will hear rave reviews about its low fares, great customer service, and lack of assigned seating that gives customers a chance to choose who they sit next to onboard. From an operations perspective, it is much more than what the customer sees. Behind the scenes, operations managers carefully manage and execute—3,400 times a day in over 60 cities in the United States—a process designed to manage all potential bottleneck areas.

Passengers boarding a Southwest Airlines flight

Southwest's famous rapid gate-turnaround of 25 minutes or less demonstrates how attention to the activities that ground operations must complete to clean, fuel, and prepare a plane for flight can become bottlenecks if not properly scheduled. In the terminal at the gate, passenger boarding also can be a bottleneck if the boarding process itself is not carefully managed. Since the individual mix of passengers present a different set of issues with each flight that often are not evident until the passengers actually arrive at the gate, ranging from families with kids and strollers to large quantities of carry-on bags and passengers needing wheelchair assistance, operations managers must be ready for any and all situations to avoid a boarding bottleneck while also assuring a pleasant and stress-free gate experience for all passengers.

In 2007, as part of the company's continuous improvement activities, Southwest focused its attention on the passenger boarding process to determine whether there was a better way to board. Its existing process consisted of three groups, A, B, C, with no assigned seating. Depending on passenger check-in and arrival time, passengers were given a spot in a group. Those first to check-in received choice places in the A group. Last to check-in ended up in the C group, and usually had a choice of only middle seats in the back of the plane upon boarding. As passengers arrived at the gate, they queued up in their respective boarding group areas to await the boarding call.

Seven different alternate boarding scenarios were designed and tested. They included

- New family pre-boarding behind the "A" group of first-to-board passengers

- Family pre-boarding before anyone else but seating choices limited on-board to behind the wing

- Six boarding groups (within A-B-C groups) instead of the original three A-B-C groups

- Assigned boarding gate line positions based on both boarding group and gate arrival time

- Single boarding chute at the gate, but up to nine groups all in one queue

- Boarding with a countdown clock to give customers an incentive to get in line and board quickly; incentives given out if everyone was on time

- Educational boarding video to make the boarding process fun, inform passengers how to board efficiently, and provide the company another way to promote its brand.

QUESTIONS

1. Analyze Southwest's passenger boarding process using the Theory of Constraints.

2. Which boarding scenario among the different ones proposed would you recommend for implementation? Why?

3. How should Southwest evaluate the gate boarding and plane turnaround process?

4. How will Southwest know that the bottleneck had indeed been eliminated after the change in the boarding process?

SELECTED REFERENCES

Boyle, Matthew. "Why FedEx Is Flying High." *Fortune* (November 2004), pp. 145–150.

Corominas, Albert, Rafael Pastor, and Joan Plans. "Balancing Assembly Line with Skilled and Unskilled Workers." *Omega*, vol. 36, no.6 (2008), pp.1126–1132.

Faaland, B. H., T. D. Klastorin, T. G. Schmitt, and A. Shtub. "Assembly Line Balancing with Resource Dependent Task Times." *Decision Sciences*, vol. 23, no. 2 (1992), pp. 343–363.

Goldratt, E. M., and J. Cox. *The Goal*, 2d rev. ed. New York: North River Press, 1992.

"How Goliaths Can Act Like Davids." *Business Week/Enterprise* (1993), pp. 192–200.

"Intel's $10 Billion Gamble." *Fortune* (November 11, 2002), pp. 90–102.

"Logan's Roadhouse." *Business Week* (May 27, 1996), p. 113.

Pinto, Peter D., David Dannenbring, and Basheer Khumawala. "Assembly Line Balancing with Processing Alternatives." *Management Science*, vol. 29, no. 7 (1983), pp. 817–830.

Schultz, Kenneth L., John O. McClain, and L. Joseph Thomas. "Overcoming the Dark Side of Worker Flexibility." *Journal of Operations Management*, vol. 21, (2003), pp. 81–92.

Simons, Jacob, Jr., and Wendell P. Simpson III. "An Exposition of Multiple Constraint Scheduling as Implemented in the Goal System (Formerly Disaster™)." *Production and Operations Management*, vol. 8, no. 1 (Spring 1997), pp. 3–22.

Srikanth, M. L., H. E. Cavallaro, and H. E. Cavallaro, Jr. *Regaining Competitiveness; Putting the Goal to Work*, 2d rev. ed. Guilford, CT: Spectrum Publishing Company, 1995.

Srikanth, Mokshagundam L., and Michael Umble. *Synchronous Management: Profit-Based Manufacturing for the 21st Century*, Vol. 1. Guilford, CT: Spectrum Publishing Company, 1997.

Srinivasan, Mandyam, Darren Jones, and Alex Miller. 2004. "Applying Theory of Constraints Principles and Lean Thinking at the Marine Corps Maintenance Center." *Defense Acquisition Rev. Quart.* (August–November 2004), pp. 134–145.

Srinivasan, Mandyam, Darren Jones, and Alex Miller. "Corps Capabilities." *APICS Magazine* (March 2005), pp. 46–50.

Steele, Daniel C., Patrick R. Philipoom, Manoj K. Malhotra, and Timothy D. Fry. "Comparisons Between Drum-Buffer-Rope and Material Requirements Planning: A Case Study." *International Journal of Production Research*, vol. 43, no. 15 (2005), pp. 3181–3208.

Umble, M., E. Umble, and S. Murakami, "Implementing Theory of Constraints in a Traditional Japanese Manufacturing Environment: The Case of Hitachi Tool Engineering." *International Journal of Production Research*, vol. 44, no. 15 (2006), pp. 1863–1880.

8 DESIGNING LEAN SYSTEMS

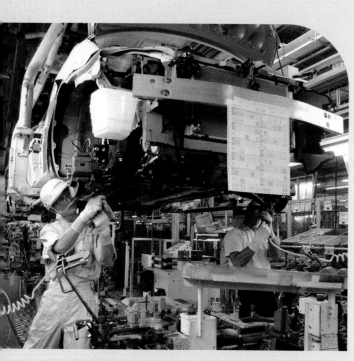

An employee helps assemble a vehicle in Toyota City, located in central Japan. Toyota's production system is among the most-admired lean manufacturing systems in the world.

TOYOTA PRODUCTION SYSTEM

If you were to select one company that exemplifies excellence in automobile manufacturing, it would probably be Toyota. Worldwide in its presence, Toyota has 13 manufacturing plants in North America alone. With 316,000 employees and sales of 8.91 million vehicles in fiscal year 2008, Toyota is poised to overtake General Motors and become the largest car manufacturer in the world. Much of this success is attributed to the famed Toyota Production System (TPS), which is one of the most admired lean manufacturing systems in existence. Replicating the system, however, is fraught with difficulties. What makes the system tick, and why has Toyota been able to use it so successfully in many different plants, whereas other automakers have not?

Most outsiders see the TPS as a set of tools and procedures that are readily visible during a plant tour. Even though they are important for the success of the TPS, they are not the key. What most people overlook is that through the process of continuous improvement, Toyota built a learning organization over the course of 50 years. Lean systems require constant improvements to increase efficiency and reduce waste. Toyota's system stimulates employees to experiment to find better ways to do their jobs. In fact, Toyota sets up all of its operations as "experiments" and teaches employees at all levels how to use the scientific method of problem solving.

Four principles form the basis of the TPS. First, all work must be completely specified as to content, sequence, timing, and outcome. Detail is important; otherwise, a foundation for improvements is missing.

LEARNING GOALS

After reading this chapter, you should be able to:

1. Identify the characteristics and strategic advantages of lean systems.
2. Describe how lean systems can facilitate the continuous improvement of processes.
3. Understand kanban systems for creating a production schedule in a lean system.
4. Understand value stream mapping and its role in waste reduction.
5. Explain the implementation issues associated with the application of lean systems.

Second, every customer–supplier connection must be direct, unambiguously specifying the people involved, the form and quantity of the services or goods to be provided, the way the requests are made by each customer, and the expected time in which the requests will be met. Customer–supplier connections can be internal (employee to employee) or external (company to company).

Third, the pathway for every service and product must be simple and direct. That is, services and goods do not flow to the next available person or machine, but to a specific person or machine. With this principle employees can determine, for example, whether a capacity problem exists at a particular workstation and then analyze ways to solve it.

The first three principles define the system in detail by specifying how employees do work, interact with each other, and how the work flows are designed. However, these specifications actually are "hypotheses" about the way the system should work. For example, if something goes wrong at a workstation enough times, the hypothesis about the methods the employee uses to do work is rejected. The fourth principle, then, is that any improvement to the system must be made in accordance with the scientific method, under the guidance of a teacher, at the lowest possible organizational level. The scientific method involves clearly stating a verifiable hypothesis of the form, "If we make the following specific changes, we expect to achieve this specific outcome." The hypothesis must then be tested under a variety of conditions. Working with a teacher, who is often the employees' supervisor, is a key to becoming a learning organization. Employees learn the scientific method and eventually become teachers of others. Finally, making improvements at the lowest level of the organization means that the employees who are actually doing the work are actively involved in making the improvements. Managers are advised only to coach employees—not to fix their problems for them.

These four principles are deceptively simple. However, they are difficult but not impossible to replicate. Those organizations that successfully implement them enjoy the benefits of a lean system that adapts to change. Toyota's lean system made it an innovative leader in the auto industry and served as an important cornerstone of its success.

Source: Steven Spear and H. Kent Bowen, "Decoding the DNA of the Toyota Production System," *Harvard Business Review* (September–October 1999), pp. 97–106; Steven J. Spear, "Learning to Lead at Toyota," *Harvard Business Review* (May 2004), pp. 78–86; www.toyota.com, July 21, 2008.

myomlab and the Companion Website at **www.pearsonglobaleditions.com/krajewski** contain many tools, activities, and resources designed for this chapter.

lean systems

Operations systems that maximize the value added by each of a company's activities by removing waste and delays from them.

COMPETING WITH OPERATIONS

Using Operations to Compete
Managing Effective Projects

DESIGNING AND
MANAGING PROCESSES

Developing a Process Strategy
Analyzing Processes
Managing Quality
Planning Capacity
Managing Process Constraints
Designing Lean Systems

DESIGNING AND
MANAGING SUPPLY CHAINS

Designing Effective Supply Chains
Integrating the Supply Chain
Locating Facilities
Managing Inventories
Forecasting Demand
Planning and Scheduling Operations
Planning Sufficient Resources

---

just-in-time (JIT) philosophy

The belief that waste can be eliminated by cutting unnecessary capacity or inventory and removing non-value-added activities in operations.

JIT system

A system that organizes the resources, information flows, and decision rules that enable a firm to realize the benefits of JIT principles.

The Toyota Production System (TPS) is an excellent example of an approach for designing supply chains known as **lean systems**. Lean systems are operations systems that maximize the value added by each of a company's activities by removing waste and delays from them. Lean systems encompass the company's operations strategy, process design, quality management, constraint management, layout design, supply chain design, and technology and inventory management, and can be used by both service and manufacturing firms. Like a manufacturer, each service business takes an order from a customer, delivers the service, and then collects revenue. Each service business purchases services or items, receives and pays for them, and hires and pays employees. Each of these activities bears considerable similarity to those in manufacturing firms. They also typically contain huge amounts of waste. In the first two parts of the text, we have discussed many ways to improve processes, regardless of whether they are manufacturing or nonmanufacturing processes. These same principles can be applied to make service processes lean, whether they are front-office, hybrid-office, or back-office designs. We conclude the second part of the text by showing how process improvement techniques can be used to make a firm lean.

We begin by discussing the continuous improvement aspect of lean systems, followed by a discussion of the characteristics of lean systems and the design of layouts needed to achieve these characteristics. We also address different types of lean systems used in practice, and some of the implementation issues that companies face.

LEAN SYSTEMS ACROSS THE ORGANIZATION

Lean systems affect a firm's internal linkages between its core and supporting processes and its external linkages with its customers and suppliers. The design of supply chains using the lean systems approach is important to various departments and functional areas across the organization. Marketing relies on lean systems to deliver high-quality services or products on time and at reasonable prices. Human resources must put in place the right incentive systems that reward teamwork, and also recruit, train, and evaluate the employees needed to create a flexible workforce that can successfully operate a lean system. Engineering must design products that use more common parts, so that fewer setups are required and focused factories can be used. Operations is responsible for maintaining close ties with suppliers, designing the lean system, and using it in the production of services or goods. Accounting must adjust its billing and cost accounting practices to provide the support needed to manage lean systems. Finally, top management must embrace the lean philosophy and make it a part of organizational culture and learning, as was done by Toyota in the opening vignette.

CONTINUOUS IMPROVEMENT USING A LEAN SYSTEMS APPROACH

One of the most popular systems that incorporate the generic elements of lean systems is the just-in-time (JIT) system. According to Taiichi Ohno, one of the earlier pioneers at Toyota, the **just-in-time (JIT) philosophy** is simple but powerful—*eliminate waste* or *muda* by cutting excess capacity or inventory and removing non-value-added activities. Table 8.1 shows the eight types of waste that often occur in firms in an interrelated fashion, and which must be eliminated in implementing lean systems.

The goals of a lean system are thus to eliminate these eight types of waste, produce services and products only as needed, and to continuously improve the value-added benefits of operations. A **JIT system** organizes the resources, information flows, and decision rules that enable a firm to realize the benefits of JIT principles.

By spotlighting areas that need improvement, lean systems lead to continuous improvement in quality and productivity. The Japanese term for this approach to process improvement is *kaizen*. The key to kaizen is the understanding that excess capacity or inventory hides underlying problems with the processes that produce a service or product. Lean systems provide the mechanism for management to reveal the problems by systematically lowering capacities or inventories until the problems are exposed. For example, Figure 8.1 characterizes the philosophy behind continuous improvement with lean systems. In services, the water surface represents service system capacity, such as staff levels. In manufacturing, the water surface represents product and component inventory levels. The rocks represent problems encountered in the fulfillment of services or products. When the water surface is high enough, the boat passes over the rocks because the high level of capacity or inventory covers up problems. As capacity or inventory shrinks,

	TABLE 8.1	THE EIGHT TYPES OF WASTE OR MUDA[1]

Waste	Definition
1. Overproduction	Manufacturing an item before it is needed, making it difficult to detect defects and creating excessive lead times and inventory.
2. Inappropriate Processing	Using expensive high precision equipment when simpler machines would suffice. It leads to overutilization of expensive capital assets. Investment in smaller flexible equipment, immaculately maintained older machines, and combining process steps where appropriate reduce the waste associated with inappropriate processing.
3. Waiting	Wasteful time incurred when product is not being moved or processed. Long production runs, poor material flows, and processes that are not tightly linked to one another can cause over 90 percent of a product's lead time to be spent waiting.
4. Transportation	Excessive movement and material handling of product between processes, which can cause damage and deterioration of product quality without adding any significant customer value.
5. Motion	Unnecessary effort related to the ergonomics of bending, stretching, reaching, lifting, and walking. Jobs with excessive motion should be redesigned.
6. Inventory	Excess inventory hides problems on the shop floor, consumes space, increases lead times, and inhibits communication. Work-in-process inventory is a direct result of overproduction and waiting.
7. Defects	Quality defects result in rework and scrap, and add wasteful costs to the system in the form of lost capacity, rescheduling effort, increased inspection, and loss of customer good will.
8. Underutilization of Employees	Failure of the firm to learn from and capitalize on its employees' knowledge and creativity impedes long-term efforts to eliminate waste.

rocks are exposed. Ultimately, the boat will hit a rock if the water surface falls far enough. Through lean systems, workers, supervisors, engineers, and analysts apply methods for continuous improvement to demolish the exposed rock. The coordination required to achieve smooth material flows in lean systems identifies problems in time for corrective action to be taken.

Maintaining low inventories, periodically stressing the system to identify problems, and focusing on the elements of the lean system lie at the heart of continuous improvement. For example, a Kawasaki plant in Nebraska periodically cuts its safety stocks almost to zero. The problems at the plant are exposed, recorded, and later assigned to employees as improvement projects. After improvements are made, inventories are permanently cut to the new level. Many firms use this trial-and-error process to develop more efficient manufacturing operations. Service processes, such as scheduling, billing, order taking, accounting, and financial planning, can be improved with lean systems, too. In service operations, a common approach used by managers is to place stress on the system by reducing the number of employees doing a particular activity or series of activities until the process begins to slow or come to a halt. The problems can be identified, and ways for overcoming them explored. Other kaizen tactics can be used as well. Eliminating the problem of too much scrap might require improving the firm's work processes, providing employees with additional training, or finding higher-quality suppliers.

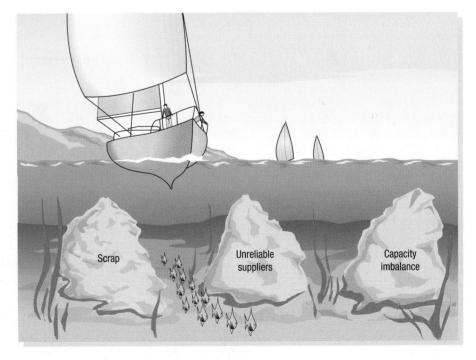

▲ **FIGURE 8.1**
Continuous Improvement with Lean Systems

---

[1] David McBride, "The Seven Manufacturing Wastes," August 29, 2003, http://www.emsstrategies.com.

Eliminating capacity imbalances might involve revising the firm's master production schedule and improving the flexibility of its workforce. Irrespective of which problem is solved, there are always new ones that can be addressed to enhance system performance.

Oftentimes, continuous improvement occurs with the ongoing involvement and input of new ideas from employees, who play an important role in implementing the JIT philosophy. In 2007 alone, about 740,000 corporate-wide improvement suggestions were received at Toyota. A large majority of them got implemented, and employees making those suggestions received rewards ranging from 500 yen (about $5) to upwards of 50,000 yen (about $500) depending upon their bottom line impact.

Managerial Practice 8.1 shows how Panasonic Corporation as a learning organization uses the philosophy of lean systems to continuously improve its operations and spread the lessons learned across the entire corporation.

SUPPLY CHAIN CONSIDERATIONS IN LEAN SYSTEMS

In this section, we discuss the two salient characteristics of lean systems that are related to creating and managing material flows in a supply chain: close supplier ties and small lot sizes.

Close Supplier Ties

Because lean systems operate with low levels of capacity slack or inventory, firms that use them need to have a close relationship with their suppliers. Supplies must be shipped frequently, have short lead times, arrive on schedule, and be of high quality. A contract might even require a supplier to deliver goods to a facility as often as several times per day.

The lean system philosophy is to look for ways to improve efficiency and reduce inventories throughout the supply chain. Close cooperation between companies and their suppliers can be a win–win situation for everyone. Better communication of component

---

MANAGERIAL PRACTICE 8.1	Continuous Improvement at Panasonic Corporation

Panasonic Corporation, which was originally founded as Matsushita Corporation in 1918 to produce lamps, has grown to become the 59th biggest firm in the world in 2007. With over 300,000 employees and 556 consolidated companies, it is the largest producer in Japan of over 15,000 electronic products under the brand names of Panasonic, National, Quasar, and Technics, among others. Renowned for its global focus on efficiency and lean operations, its pursuit of excellence is exemplified nowhere better than at the Matsushita Electric Company's factory in Saga on Japan's southern island of Kyushu, where cordless phones, fax machines, and security cameras are made in record time by machines in a spotless facility.

The plant's efficiency had doubled in the previous four years. Yet managers saw opportunities for trimming the fat and improving further. The plant's conveyor belts were replaced by a cluster of robots that could seamlessly hand off work to one another, flexibly substitute for a broken robot, and synchronize production using software. As a result, throughput time declined from 2.5 days to 40 minutes, allowing Saga to make twice as many phones per week, which in turn allowed a reduction in inventory because components such as chips and circuit boards spend much less time in the factory. Being able to make things faster means that the plant can quickly change the product mix even as customer demands shift and new products are introduced, thus allowing Panasonic to keep ahead of low cost rivals in Korea, China, and other Asian countries.

Panasonic has used the lessons learned from the Saga mother plant to change layouts and setups at six other plants in China, Malaysia, Mexico,

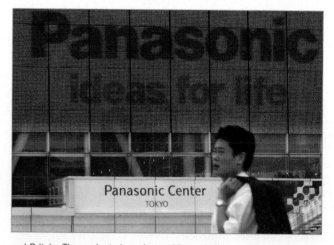

and Britain. These plants have been able to similarly cut their inventories and improve productivity, even as ideas from local staff at each plant were incorporated into the change effort. The next sets of improvements are focused on breaking assembly lines into cells and better utilizing the idle robots. In addition, standardized circuit board designs that are common to a large variety of end products are being used in order to minimize the retooling of robots for every type of board. By relentlessly focusing on minimizing waste and continuously improving efficiency, Panasonic has posted record profit growths and has become a model for other electronic firms.

Source: Kenji Hall, "No One Does Lean Like the Japanese," *BusinessWeek* (July 10, 2006), pp. 40–41; http://panasonic.net/corporate/, July 21, 2008.

requirements, for example, enables more efficient inventory planning and delivery scheduling by suppliers, thereby improving supplier profit margins. Customers can then negotiate lower component prices. Close supplier relations cannot be established and maintained if companies view their suppliers as adversaries whenever contracts are negotiated. Rather, they should consider suppliers to be partners in a venture, wherein both parties have an interest in maintaining a long-term, profitable relationship. Consequently, one of the first actions undertaken when a lean system is implemented is to pare down the number of suppliers, and make sure they are located in close geographic proximity in order to promote strong partnerships and better synchronize product flows.

A particularly close form of supplier partnerships through lean systems is the JIT II system, which was conceived and implemented by Bose Corporation, a producer of high-quality professional sound and speaker systems. In a JIT II system, the supplier is brought into the plant to be an active member of the purchasing office of the customer. The *in-plant representative* is on site full-time at the supplier's expense and is empowered to plan and schedule the replenishment of materials from the supplier. Typically, the representative's duties include issuing purchase orders to his or her own firm on behalf of the buyer, working on design ideas to help reduce costs and improve manufacturing processes, and managing production schedules for suppliers, materials contractors, and other subcontractors. The in-plant representative replaces the buyer, the salesperson, and sometimes the materials planner in a typical JIT arrangement. Thus, JIT II fosters extremely close interaction with suppliers. The qualifications for a supplier to be included in the program are stringent.

In general, JIT II can offer benefits to both buyers and suppliers because it provides the organizational structure needed to improve supplier coordination by integrating the logistics, production, and purchasing processes together. Several large corporations have implemented JIT II in their supply chains, including IBM, Intel, Honeywell, Roadway Express, Ingersoll-Rand, and Westinghouse, among others. We have more to say about supplier relationships in Chapter 10, "Integrating the Supply Chain."

Small Lot Sizes

Lean systems use lot sizes that are as small as possible. A **lot** is a quantity of items that are processed together. Small lots have the advantage of reducing the average level of inventory relative to large lots. Small lots pass through the system faster than large lots since they do not keep materials waiting. In addition, if any defective items are discovered, large lots cause longer delays because the entire lot must be examined to find all the items that need rework. Finally, small lots help achieve a uniform workload on the system and prevent overproduction. Large lots consume large chunks of capacity at workstations and, therefore, complicate scheduling. Small lots can be juggled more effectively, enabling schedulers to efficiently utilize capacities.

lot
A quantity of items that are processed together.

Although small lots are beneficial to operations, they have the disadvantage of increased setup frequency. A *setup* is the group of activities needed to change or readjust a process between successive lots of items, sometimes referred to as a *changeover*. Typically, a setup takes the same time regardless of the size of the lot. Consequently, many small lots, in lieu of several large lots, may result in waste in the form of idle employees and equipment. Setup times must be brief to realize the benefits of small-lot production.

Achieving brief setup times often requires close cooperation among engineering, management, and labor. For example, changing dies on large presses to form automobile parts from sheet metal can take 3 to 4 hours. At Honda's Marysville, Ohio, plant—where four stamping lines stamp all the exterior and major interior body panels for Accord production—teams worked on ways to reduce the changeover time for the massive dies. As a result, a complete change of dies for a giant 2,400-ton press now takes less than 8 minutes. The goal of **single-digit setup** means having setup times of less than 10 minutes. Some techniques used to reduce setup times at the Marysville plant include using conveyors for die storage, moving large dies with cranes, simplifying dies, enacting machine controls, using microcomputers to automatically feed and position work, and preparing for changeovers while a job currently in production is still being processed.

single-digit setup
The goal of having a setup time of less than 10 minutes.

PROCESS CONSIDERATIONS IN LEAN SYSTEMS

In this section, we discuss the following characteristics of lean systems: pull method of work flow, quality at the source, uniform workstation loads, standardized components and work methods, flexible workforce, automation, Five S (5S) practices, and total preventive maintenance (TPM).

Diners fill their plates at a restaurant buffet. Because the food items must be prepared in advance, the restaurant uses a push method of work flow.

Pull Method of Work Flow

Lean systems typically utilize the pull method of work flow. However, another popular method is the push method of work flow. To differentiate between these two methods, let us use a service example that involves a favorite pastime, eating. Consider a cafeteria on a busy downtown corner. During the busy periods around 12 P.M. and 5 P.M. lines develop, with hungry patrons eager to eat and then move on to other activities. The cafeteria offers choices of chicken (roasted or deep fried), roast beef, pork chops, hamburgers, hot dogs, salad, soup (chicken, pea, and clam chowder), bread (three types), beverages, and desserts (pies, ice cream, and cookies). Close coordination is required between the cafeteria's "front office," where its employees interface with customers; and its "back office," the kitchen, where the food is prepared and then placed along the cafeteria's buffet line. Because it takes substantial time to cook some of the food items, the cafeteria uses a **push method**, which involves preparing the food sold to customers prior to their ordering it. After all, shortages in food could cause riotous conditions (recall that customers are hungry), whereas preparing an excess amount of food will be wasteful because it will go uneaten. To make sure that neither of these conditions occurs and to run lean operations even with a push method, the cafeteria must accurately forecast the number of customers it expects to serve.

Now consider a five-star restaurant in which you are seated at a table and offered a menu of exquisite dishes, appetizers, soups, salads, and desserts. You can choose from filet mignon, porterhouse steak, yellowfin tuna, grouper, and lamb chops. Your choice of several salads is prepared at your table. Although some appetizers, soups, and desserts can be prepared in advance and brought to temperature just before serving, the main course and salads cannot. Your order for the salad and the main course signals the chef to begin preparing your specific requests. For these items, the restaurant is using the **pull method**. When the pull method is used, customer demand activates the production of a good or service. Firms using the pull method must be able to fulfill the customer's demands within an acceptable amount of time. The cafeteria would have a difficult time using the pull method because it could not wait until a customer asked for an item before asking the kitchen to begin processing it.

The choice between the push and pull methods is often situational. Firms with highly repetitive processes and well-defined work flows of standardized items often use the pull method because it allows closer control of inventory and output at the workstations. The five-star restaurant uses the pull method to control the freshness and taste of the meal. Firms with processes that involve long lead times and reasonably accurate forecasts of demand, a variety of products that require common processes, and customers who will not wait long for the product tend to produce using a push method. These factors are often the case with the cafeteria and many manufacturing firms. Firms using an assemble-to-order strategy sometimes use both methods: the push method to produce the standardized components and the pull method to fulfill the customer's request for a particular combination of the components.

Quality at the Source

Consistently meeting the customer's expectations is an important characteristic of lean systems. One way to achieve this goal is by adhering to a practice called *quality at the source*, which is a philosophy whereby defects are caught and corrected where they are created. The goal for workers is to act as their own quality inspectors and never pass on defective units to the next process. Automatically stopping the process when something is wrong and then fixing the problems on the line itself as they occur is also known as **jidoka** in the Toyota Production System (TPS), as described in the opening vignette. Jidoka tends to separate worker and machine activities by freeing workers from tending to machines all the time, thus allowing them to staff multiple operations simultaneously. Jidoka represents a visual management system whereby status of the system in terms of safety, quality, delivery, and cost performance relative to the goals for a given fabrication cell or workstation in an assembly line is clearly visible to workers on the floor at all times.

push method

A method in which production of the item begins in advance of customer needs.

pull method

A method in which customer demand activates production of the service or item.

jidoka

Automatically stopping the process when something is wrong and then fixing the problems on the line itself as they occur.

An alternative to jidoka or quality at the source is the traditional practice of pushing problems down the line to be resolved later. This approach is often ineffective. For example, a soldering operation at the Texas Instruments antenna department had a defect rate that varied from 0 to 50 percent on a daily basis, averaging about 20 percent. To compensate, production planners increased the lot sizes, which only increased inventory levels and did nothing to reduce the number of defective items. The company's engineers then discovered through experimentation that gas temperature was a critical variable in producing defect-free items. They subsequently devised statistical control charts for the firm's equipment operators to use to monitor the temperature and adjust it themselves. Process yields immediately improved and stabilized at 95 percent, and Texas Instruments was eventually able to implement a lean system.

One successful approach for implementing quality at the source is to use **poka-yoke**, or mistake-proofing methods aimed at designing fail-safe systems that attack and minimize human error. Poka-yoke systems work well in practice. Consider, for instance, a company that makes modular products. The company could use the poka-yoke method by making different parts of the modular product in such a way that allows them to be assembled in only one way—the correct way. Similarly, a company's shipping boxes could be designed to be packed only in a certain way to minimize damage and eliminate all chances of mistakes. At Toyota plants, every vehicle being assembled is accompanied by an RFID chip containing information on how many nuts and bolts need to be tightened on that vehicle for a given operation at a given workstation. A green light comes on when the right number of nuts have been tightened. Only then does the vehicle move forward on the assembly line.

An example of poka-yoke is the design of new fuel doors in automobiles. They are mistake proof since filling pipe insert keeps larger, leaded-fuel nozzle from being inserted. In addition, gas cap tether does not allow the motorist to drive off without the cap, and is also fitted with a ratchet to signal proper tightness and prevent over-tightening.

poka-yoke

Mistake-proofing methods aimed at designing fail-safe systems that minimize human error.

Another tool for implementing quality at the source is *andon*, which is a system that gives machines and machine operators the ability to signal the occurrence of any abnormal condition such as tool malfunction, shortage of parts, or the product being made outside the desired specifications. It can take the form of audio alarms, blinking lights, LCD text displays, or chords that can be pulled by workers to ask for help or stop the production line if needed. Stopping a production line can, however, cost a company thousands of dollars each minute production is halted. Needless to say, management must realize the enormous responsibility this method puts on employees and must prepare them properly.

Uniform Workstation Loads

A lean system works best if the daily load on individual workstations is relatively uniform. Service processes can achieve uniform workstation loads by using reservation systems. For example, hospitals schedule surgeries in advance of the actual service so that the facilities and facilitating goods can be ready when the time comes. The load on the surgery rooms and surgeons can be evened out to make the best use of these resources. Another approach is to use differential pricing of the service to manage the demand for it. Uniform loads are the rationale behind airlines promoting weekend travel or red-eye flights that begin late in the day and end in the early morning. Efficiencies can be realized when the load on the firm's resources can be managed.

For manufacturing processes, uniform loads can be achieved by assembling the same type and number of units each day, thus creating a uniform daily demand at all workstations. Capacity planning, which recognizes capacity constraints at critical workstations, and line balancing are used to develop the master production schedule. For example, at Toyota the production plan may call for 4,500 vehicles per week for the next month. That requires two full shifts, 5 days per week, producing 900 vehicles each day, or 450 per shift. Three models are produced: Camry (C), Avalon (A), and Solara (S). Suppose that Toyota needs 200 Camrys, 150 Avalons, and 100 Solaras per shift to satisfy market demand. To produce 450 units in one shift of 480 minutes, the line must roll out a vehicle every 480/450 = 1.067 minutes. The 1.067 minutes, or 64 seconds, represents the **takt time** of the process, defined as the cycle time needed to match the rate of production to the rate of sales or consumption.

takt time

Cycle time needed to match the rate of production to the rate of sales or consumption.

Toyota Motor Manufacturing, Indiana (TMMI) is building the Sienna minivan and the Sequoia sport utility vehicle on a new mixed-model assembly line in the expanded plant.

heijunka

The leveling of production load by both volume and product mix.

mixed-model assembly

A type of assembly that produces a mix of models in smaller lots.

With traditional big-lot production, all daily requirements of a model are produced in one batch before another model is started. The sequence of 200 Cs, 150 As, and 100 Ss would be repeated once per shift. Not only would these big lots increase the average inventory level, but they also would cause lumpy requirements on all the workstations feeding the assembly line.

But there are other two options for devising a production schedule for the vehicles. These options are based on the Japanese concept of **heijunka**, which is the leveling of production load by both volume and product mix. It does not build products according to the actual flow of customer orders, but levels out the total volume of orders in a period so that the same amount and mix are being made each day.[2]

Let us explore two possible heijunka options. The first option uses leveled **mixed-model assembly**, producing a mix of models in smaller lots. Note that the production requirements at Toyota are in the ratio of 4 Cs to 3 As to 2 Ss, found by dividing the model's production requirements by the greatest common divisor, or 50. Thus, the Toyota planner could develop a production cycle consisting of 9 units: 4 Cs, 3 As, and 2 Ss. The cycle would repeat in 9(1.067) = 9.60 minutes, for a total of 50 times per shift (480 min/9.60 min = 50).

The second heijunka option uses a lot size of one, such as the production sequence of C–S–C–A–C–A–C–S–A repeated 50 times per shift. The sequence would achieve the same total output as the other options; however, it is feasible only if the setup times are brief. The sequence generates a steady rate of component requirements for the various models and allows the use of small lot sizes at the feeder workstations. Consequently, the capacity requirements at those stations are greatly smoothed. These requirements can be compared to actual capacities during the planning phase, and modifications to the production cycle, production requirements, or capacities can be made as necessary.

Standardized Components and Work Methods

In highly repetitive service operations, great efficiencies can be gained by analyzing work methods and documenting the improvements for all employees to use. For example, UPS consistently monitors its work methods, from sorting packages to delivering them, and revises them as necessary to improve service. In manufacturing, the standardization of components increases the total quantity that must be produced for that component. For example, a firm producing 10 products from 1,000 different components could redesign its products so that they consist of only 100 different components with larger daily requirements. Panasonic did similar standardization with its printed circuit boards in Managerial Practice 8.1. Because the requirements per component increase, each worker performs a standardized task or work method more often each day. Productivity tends to increase because workers learn to do their tasks more efficiently with increased repetition. Standardizing components and work methods help a firm achieve the high-productivity, low-inventory objectives of a lean system.

Flexible Workforce

The role of workers is elevated in lean systems. Workers in flexible workforces can be trained to perform more than one job. A benefit of flexibility is the ability to shift workers among workstations to help relieve bottlenecks as they arise without the need for inventory buffers—an important aspect of the uniform flow of lean systems. Also, workers can step in and do the job for those who are on vacation or who are out sick. Although assigning workers to tasks they do not usually perform can temporarily reduce their efficiency, some job rotation tends to relieve boredom and refreshes workers. At some firms that have implemented lean systems, cross-trained workers may switch jobs every 2 hours.

The more customized the service or product is, the greater the firm's need for a multi-skilled workforce. For example, stereo repair shops require broadly trained personnel who can identify a wide variety of component problems when the customer brings the defective

[2] David McBride, "Heijunka, Leveling the Load," September 1, 2004, http://www.emsstrategies.com.

Employees of United Parcel Service work on a small automated package line in the $1 billion air hub in Louisville, Kentucky. The packages (in the center of the photo) are automatically deposited in the bin dedicated to their destination.

unit into the shop and who then can repair the unit. Alternatively, back-office designs, such as the mail-processing operations at a large post office, have employees with more narrowly defined jobs because of the repetitive nature of the tasks they must perform. These employees do not have to acquire as many alternative skills. In some situations, shifting workers to other jobs may require them to undergo extensive, costly training.

Automation

Automation plays a big role in lean systems and is a key to low-cost operations. Money freed up because of inventory reductions or other efficiencies can be invested in automation to reduce costs. The benefits, of course, are greater profits, greater market share (because prices can be cut), or both. Automation can play a big role when it comes to providing lean services. For example, banks offer ATMs that provide various bank services on demand 24 hours a day. Automation should be planned carefully, however. Many managers believe that if some automation is good, more is better, which is not always the case. When GM initiated Buick City, for example, it installed 250 robots, some with vision systems for mounting windshields. Unfortunately, the robots skipped black cars because they could not "see" them. New software eventually solved the problem. Nonetheless, 30 robots were replaced with humans because GM found that humans do some jobs better.

Five S Practices

Five S (5S) is a methodology for organizing, cleaning, developing, and sustaining a productive work environment. It represents five related terms, each beginning with an *S*, that describe workplace practices conducive to visual controls and lean production. These five practices of sorting, straightening, shining, standardizing, and sustaining are done systematically to achieve lean systems. They are not something that can be done as a stand-alone program. As such, they serve as an enabler and an essential foundation of lean systems. Table 8.2 shows the terms[3] that represent the 5S and what they imply.

It is commonly accepted that 5S forms an important cornerstone of waste reduction and removal of unneeded tasks, activities, and materials. 5S practices can enable workers to visually see everything differently, prioritize tasks, and achieve a greater degree of

five S (5S)

A methodology consisting of five workplace practices—sorting, straightening, shining, standardizing, and sustaining—that are conducive to visual controls and lean production.

<hr>

[3] The Japanese words for these 5S terms are *seiri, seiton, seiso, seiketsu,* and *shitsuke,* respectively.

TABLE 8.2	5S DEFINED
5S Term	**Definition**
1. Sort	Separate needed items from unneeded items (including tools, parts, materials, and paperwork), and discard the unneeded.
2. Straighten	Neatly arrange what is left, with a place for everything and everything in its place. Organize the work area so that it is easy to find what is needed.
3. Shine	Clean and wash the work area and make it shine.
4. Standardize	Establish schedules and methods of performing the cleaning and sorting. Formalize the cleanliness that results from regularly doing the first three S practices so that perpetual cleanliness and a state of readiness are maintained.
5. Sustain	Create discipline to perform the first four S practices, whereby everyone understands, obeys, and practices the rules when in the plant. Implement mechanisms to sustain the gains by involving people and recognizing them through a performance measurement system.

A monorail heads toward Cinderella's Castle and Space Mountain in Florida's Disney World. Preventive maintenance ensures reliable service to customers.

focus. They can also be applied to a diverse range of manufacturing and service settings including organizing work spaces, offices, tool rooms, shop floors, and the like. Implementation of 5S practices have been shown to lead to lowered costs, improved on-time delivery and productivity, higher product quality, better use of floor space, and a safe working environment. It also builds the discipline needed to make the lean systems work well.

Total Preventive Maintenance (TPM)

Because lean systems emphasize finely tuned flows of work and little capacity slack or buffer inventory between workstations, unplanned machine downtime can be disruptive. Total Preventive Maintenance (TPM), which is also sometimes referred to as total productive maintenance, can reduce the frequency and duration of machine downtime. After performing their routine maintenance activities, technicians can test other machine parts that might need to be replaced. Replacing parts during regularly scheduled maintenance periods is easier and quicker than dealing with machine failures during production. Maintenance is done on a schedule that balances the cost of the preventive maintenance program against the risks and costs of machine failure. Routine preventive maintenance is important for service businesses that rely heavily on machinery, such as the rides at Walt Disney World.

Another tactic is to make workers responsible for routinely maintaining their own equipment, which will develop employee pride in keeping the machines in top condition. This tactic, however, typically is limited to general housekeeping chores, minor lubrication, and adjustments. Maintaining high-tech machines requires trained specialists. Nonetheless, performing even simple maintenance tasks goes a long way toward improving the performance of machines.

For long term improvements, data can be collected for establishing trends in failure pattern of machines, which can subsequently be analyzed to establish better standards and procedures for preventive maintenance. The data can also provide failure history and costs incurred to maintain the systems. Toyota routinely follows this practice in its TPM programs.

DESIGNING LEAN SYSTEM LAYOUTS

Line flows are recommended in designing lean system layouts because they eliminate waste by reducing the frequency of setups. If volumes of specific products are large enough, groups of machines and workers can be organized into a line-flow layout to eliminate setups entirely. In a service setting, managers of back-office service processes can similarly organize their employees and equipment to provide uniform work flows through the process and, thereby, eliminate wasted employee time. Banks use this strategy in their check-processing operations, as does UPS in its parcel-sorting process.

When volumes are not high enough to justify dedicating a single line of multiple workers to a single customer type or product, managers still may be able to derive the benefits of line-flow layout—simpler materials handling, low setups, and reduced labor costs—by creating line-flow layouts in some portions of the facility. Two techniques for creating such layouts are one-worker, multiple-machines (OWMM) cells, and group technology (GT) cells.

One Worker, Multiple Machines

If volumes are not sufficient to keep several workers busy on one production line, the manager might set up a line small enough to keep one worker busy. The **one-worker, multiple-machines (OWMM) cell** is a workstation in which a worker operates several different machines simultaneously to achieve a line flow. Having one worker operate several identical machines is not unusual. However, with an OWMM cell, several different machines are in the line.

Figure 8.2 illustrates a five-machine OWMM cell that is being used to produce a flanged metal part, with the machines encircling one operator in the center. (A U-shape also is common.) The operator moves around the circle, performing tasks (typically loading and unloading) that have not been automated. Different products or parts can be produced in an OWMM cell by changing the machine setups. If the setup on one machine is especially time-consuming for a particular part, management can add a duplicate machine to the cell for use whenever that part is being produced.

An OWMM arrangement reduces both inventory and labor requirements. Inventory is cut because, rather than piling up in queues waiting for transportation to another part of the plant, materials move directly into the next operation. Labor is cut because more work is automated. The addition of several low-cost automated devices can maximize the number of machines included in an OWMM arrangement: automatic tool changers, loaders and unloaders, start and stop devices, and fail-safe devices that detect defective parts or products. Manufacturers are applying the OWMM concept widely because of their desire to achieve low inventories.

Group Technology

A second option for achieving line-flow layouts with low volume processes is **group technology (GT)**. This manufacturing technique creates cells not limited to just one worker and has a unique way of selecting work to be done by the cell. The GT method groups parts or products with similar characteristics into *families* and sets aside groups of machines for their production. Families may be based on size, shape, manufacturing or routing requirements, or demand. The goal is to identify a set of products with similar processing requirements and minimize machine changeover or setup. For example, all bolts

one-worker, multiple-machines (OWMM) cell

A one-person cell in which a worker operates several different machines simultaneously to achieve a line flow.

group technology (GT)

An option for achieving line-flow layouts with low volume processes; this technique creates cells not limited to just one worker and has a unique way of selecting work to be done by the cell.

Materials in

Finished goods out

Machine 1
Machine 2
Machine 3
Machine 4
Machine 5

◀ FIGURE 8.2
One-Worker, Multiple-Machines (OWMM) Cell

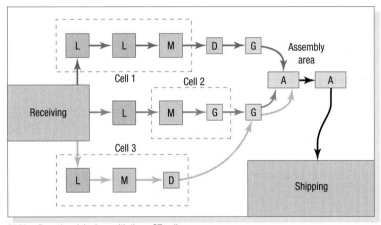

(a) Jumbled flows in a job shop without GT cells

(b) Line flows in a job shop with three GT cells

FIGURE 8.3 ▲

Process Flows Before and After the Use of GT Cells

Source: Mikell P. Groover. *Automation, Production Systems, and Computer-Aided Manufacturing.* 1st Edition, © 1980. Reprinted by permission of Pearson Education, Inc., Upper Saddle River, NJ.

might be assigned to the same family because they all require the same basic processing steps regardless of size or shape.

Once parts have been grouped into families, the next step is to organize the machine tools needed to perform the basic processes on these parts into separate cells. The machines in each cell require only minor adjustments to accommodate product changeovers from one part to the next in the same family. By simplifying product routings, GT cells reduce the time a job is in the shop. Queues of materials waiting to be worked on are shortened or eliminated. Frequently, materials handling is automated so that, after loading raw materials into the cell, a worker does not handle machined parts until the job has been completed.

Figure 8.3 compares process flows before and after creation of GT cells. Figure 8.3(a) shows a shop floor where machines are grouped according to function: lathing, milling, drilling, grinding, and assembly. After lathing, a part is moved to one of the milling machines, where it waits in line until it has a higher priority than any other job competing for the machine's capacity. When the milling operation on the part has been finished, the part is moved to a drilling machine, and so on. The queues can be long, creating significant time delays. Flows of materials are jumbled because the parts being processed in any one area of the shop have so many different routings.

By contrast, the manager of the shop shown in Figure 8.3(b) identified three product families that account for a majority of the firm's production. One family always requires two lathing operations followed by one operation at the milling machines. The second family always requires a milling operation followed by a grinding operation. The third family requires the use of a lathe, a milling machine, and a drill press. For simplicity, only the flows of parts assigned to these three families are shown. The remaining parts are produced at machines outside the cells and still have jumbled routings. Some equipment might have to be duplicated, as when a machine is required for one or more cells and for operations outside the cells. However, by creating three GT cells, the manager has definitely created more line flows and simplified routings.

Managerial Practice 8.2 shows how the principles of lean systems have been used by Porsche, the automaker.

THE KANBAN SYSTEM

kanban

A Japanese word meaning "card" or "visible record" that refers to cards used to control the flow of production through a factory.

One of the most publicized aspects of lean systems, and the TPS in particular, is the kanban system developed by Toyota. **Kanban**, meaning "card" or "visible record" in Japanese, refers to cards used to control the flow of production through a factory. In the most basic kanban system, a card is attached to each container of items produced. The container holds a given percent of the daily production requirements for an item. When the user of the parts empties a container, the card is removed from the container and put on a receiving post. The empty container is then taken to the storage area, and the card signals the need to produce another container of the part. When the container has been refilled, the card is put back on the container, which is then returned to a storage area. The cycle begins again when the user of the parts retrieves the container with the card attached.

MANAGERIAL PRACTICE 8.2	Lean Systems at Porsche

Porsche as a brand is synonymous with German-engineered automotive performance and luxury. Founded in the early 1930s by Ferdinand Porsche—an engineer known for developing, among other feats, the first electric-gas hybrid—the company has always been at the forefront of engineering innovation. Over the years Porsche has also become known for financial stability. At a time when many European car manufacturers have moved production to factories in Eastern Europe or Mexico, the presence of the Porsche factory in Germany stands as a testimony to Porsche's success. But Porsche's road to financial stability hasn't always been a smooth ride.

In the early 1990s, Porsche faced tough times. A worldwide recession cut into Porsche's sales. In the 1980s, during boom times, sales totalled more than 50,000 a year. But in 1993, sales fell to just 14,000 units. Porsche was losing millions of dollars. The family owners had to do something to save the company from bankruptcy and takeover. They hired Wendelin Wiedeking to remake the company into a profitable enterprise. Wiedeking immediately turned to the Japanese model of just-in-time lean manufacturing. In the past German automakers had tried to incorporate aspects of lean manufacturing without noticeable success. They believed in lean manufacturing, but based on their experiences, they decided such techniques would just not work in Germany. However, faced with bankruptcy, Porsche had no choice but to turn to lean manufacturing. Wiedeking took the daring step of bringing in a team of Japanese engineers—mostly former Toyota employees—to recast operations at Porsche's factory according to lean manufacturing principles.

The transition from old ways to lean manufacturing wasn't easy. According to Wiedeking, the Japanese engineers circulated through the factory production floor telling workers what to do in not-so-subtle ways. The Japanese engineers often scolded and lectured the German workers, who prided themselves as some of the world's finest craftsmen. The German workers were shocked—some even stormed off the production line—but Wiedeking wanted it this way. He knew it was the only way to rescue the company and return it to profitability. When the Japanese engineers arrived at the Porsche factory, they found a very inefficient operation. Large shelves lined with parts bordered the assembly line. Workers often had to climb ladders to get a part, which wasted time. The bins held 28 days of inventory, and sifting through this inventory slowed workers.

Compared to production times in Japanese auto plants, Porsche took almost twice as long to build vehicles.

After some growing pains, Porsche's lean manufacturing technique began to pay off. By the mid-1990s, the production line of Porsche had become much more efficient. Fewer workers were able to produce more cars at a faster rate without any loss of quality or performance. Workers no longer had to scrounge through a large inventory of parts in overhead bins. The bins were eliminated in favor of carts on a trolley system. These carts contain only those pre-selected components needed for each stage of assembly. The carts carried the parts to workers so that they never needed to leave their workstations. Since instituting lean manufacturing techniques, Porsche's fortunes as a company have risen dramatically. Recently, Porsche acquired a large stake in Volkswagen, the third largest automotive manufacturer in the world. Porsche is also building a museum in Zuffenhausen, next to its factory. The streamlined efficiency of lean manufacturing has helped return Porsche to profitability and ensured its financial stability.

Lean manufacturing techniques resulted in a dramatic rise in profitability when they were implemented at the German Porsche factory in Zuffenhausen.

Source: www.porsche.com/usa/aboutporsche/porschehistory/, Accessed September 25, 2008; Nathaniel Nash, "Putting Porsche in the Pink," New York Times, (January 20, 1996), http://query.nytimes.com/gst/fullpage.html?res=9E06E5DC1E39F933A15752C0A960958260.

Figure 8.4 shows how a single-card kanban system works when a fabrication cell feeds two assembly lines. As an assembly line needs more parts, the kanban card for those parts is taken to the receiving post, and a full container of parts is removed from the storage area. The receiving post accumulates cards for assembly lines and a scheduler sequences the production of replenishment parts. In this example, the fabrication cell will produce product 2 (red) before it produces product 1 (green). The cell consists of three different operations, but operation 2 has two workstations. Once production has been initiated in the cell, the product begins on operation 1, but could be routed to either of the workstations performing operation 2, depending on the workload at the time. Finally, the product is processed on operation 3 before being taken to the storage area.

FIGURE 8.4 ▲
Single-Card Kanban System

General Operating Rules

The operating rules for the single-card system are simple and are designed to facilitate the flow of materials while maintaining control of inventory levels.

1. Each container must have a card.

2. The assembly line always withdraws materials from the fabrication cell. The fabrication cell never pushes parts to the assembly line because, sooner or later, parts will be supplied that are not yet needed for production.

3. Containers of parts must never be removed from a storage area without a kanban first being posted on the receiving post.

4. The containers should always contain the same number of good parts. The use of non-standard containers or irregularly filled containers disrupts the production flow of the assembly line.

5. Only nondefective parts should be passed along to the assembly line to make the best use of materials and worker's time. This rule reinforces the notion of building quality at the source, which is an important characteristic of lean systems.

6. Total production should not exceed the total amount authorized on the kanbans in the system.

Toyota uses a two-card system, based on a withdrawal card and a production-order card, to control inventory quantities more closely. The withdrawal card specifies the item and the quantity the user of the item should withdraw from the producer of the item, as well as the stocking locations for both the user and the producer. The production-order card specifies the item and the quantity to be produced, the materials required and where to find them, and where to store the finished item. Materials cannot be withdrawn without a withdrawal card, and production cannot begin without a production-order card. The cards are attached to containers when production commences. By manipulating the number of withdrawal and production cards in play at any time, management can control the flow of materials in the production system.

Determining the Number of Containers

The number of authorized containers in the TPS determines the amount of authorized inventory. Management must make two determinations: (1) the number of units to be held by each container, and (2) the number of containers flowing back and forth between the supplier station and the user station. The first decision amounts to determining the size of the production lot.

The number of containers flowing back and forth between two stations directly affects the quantities of work-in-process inventory, which includes any safety stock inventory to cover for unexpected requirements.[4] The containers spend some time in production, in a line waiting, in a storage location, or in transit. The key to determining the number of containers required is to estimate the average lead time needed to produce a container of parts. The lead time is a function of the processing time per container at the supplier station, the waiting time during the production process, and the time required for materials handling. Little's Law, which says that the average work-in-process inventory (WIP) equals the average demand rate multiplied by the average time a unit spends in the manufacturing process, can be used to determine the number of containers needed to support the user station (see Supplement C, "Waiting Line Models").

WIP = (average demand rate)(average time a container spends in the manufacturing process) + safety stock

In this application of determining the number of containers needed for a part, WIP is the product of κ, the number of containers, and c, the number of units in each container. Consequently,

$$\kappa c = \overline{d}(\overline{\omega} + \overline{\rho})(1 + \alpha)$$

$$\kappa = \frac{\overline{d}(\overline{\omega} + \overline{\rho})(1 + \alpha)}{c}$$

where

κ = number of containers for a part

$\overline{d}$ = expected daily demand for the part, in units

$\overline{\omega}$ = average waiting time during the production process plus materials handling time per container, in fractions of a day

$\overline{\rho}$ = average processing time per container, in fractions of a day

c = quantity in a standard container of the part

α = a policy variable that adds safety stock to cover for unexpected circumstances (Toyota uses a value of no more than 10 percent)

The number of containers must, of course, be an integer. Rounding κ up provides more inventory than desired, whereas rounding κ down provides less.

The container quantity, c, and the efficiency factor, α, are variables that management can use to control inventory. Adjusting c changes the size of the production lot, and adjusting α changes the amount of safety stock. The kanban system allows management to fine-tune the flow of materials in the system in a straightforward way. For example, removing cards from the system reduces the number of authorized containers of the part, thus reducing the inventory of the part. Thus a major benefit is the simplicity of the system, whereby product mix or volume changes can easily be accomplished by adjusting the number of kanbans in the system.

EXAMPLE 8.1	Determining the Appropriate Number of Containers

The Pak Company in Hong Kong produces front hydraulic brake assemblies for use in the braking systems of full-size scooters or mopeds. A typical container of parts spends 0.03 day in processing and 0.07 day in materials handling and waiting during its manufacturing cycle. The daily demand for the part is 500 units. Management believes that demand for the hydraulic brake assembly is uncertain enough to warrant a safety stock equivalent to 10 percent of its authorized inventory.

a. If each container contains 5 assemblies, how many containers should be authorized each day?

b. Suppose that a proposal to use larger containers would increase the number of assemblies that can be packed to 10. Larger containers will help reduce shipping costs. However, using the larger containers increases the materials handling and wait time per container by 0.02. How many containers would be needed per day? How much inventory will be needed?

Tutor 8.1 in myomlab provides a new example of using the model to determine the number of containers.

---

[4] We discuss safety stocks, and their use, in more detail in Chapter 9, "Designing Effective Supply Chains," and Chapter 12, "Managing Inventories."

Solver-Number of Containers
Enter data in yellow-shaded area.

Daily Expected Demand	500
Quantity in Standard Container	10
Container Waiting Time (days)	0.09
Processing Time (days)	0.03
Policy Variable	10%
Containers Required	7

FIGURE 8.5 ▲
OM Explorer Solver for Number of Containers

SOLUTION

a. If $\bar{d} = 500$ units/day, $\bar{\rho} = 0.03$ day, $\alpha = 0.10$, $\bar{\omega} = 0.07$ day and $c = 5$ units,

$$\kappa = \frac{500(0.07 + 0.03)(1 + 0.10)}{5} = \frac{55}{5} = 11 \text{ containers}$$

b. See Figure 8.5. If $\bar{d} = 500$ units/day, $\bar{\rho} = 0.03$ day, $\alpha = 0.10$, $\bar{\omega} = 0.09$ day, and $c = 10$ units,

$$\kappa = \frac{500(0.09 + 0.03)(1 + 0.10)}{10} = \frac{66}{10} = 7 \text{ containers}$$

DECISION POINT

The average lead time per container is $\bar{\omega} + \bar{\rho}$. With a lead time of 0.10 day, 11 containers are needed. However, if larger containers are used that increase the materials handling time and waiting time to 0.12 day, 7 containers are needed per day. The maximum authorized inventory of the brake assembly is κC units. Thus, in part a, the maximum authorized inventory is 55 units, but in part b, it is 66 units. Increasing $\bar{\omega} + \bar{\rho}$ increases the inventory of the part. Management must balance the cost of cheaper shipping against the long-term cost of more inventory.

Other Kanban Signals

Cards are not the only way to signal the need for more production of a part. Other, less formal methods are possible, including container and containerless systems.

Container System   Sometimes the container itself can be used as a signal device: An empty container signals the need to fill it. Unisys took this approach for low-value items. The amount of inventory of the part is adjusted by adding or removing containers. This system works well when the container is specially designed for a particular part and no other parts could accidentally be put in the container. Such is the case when the container is actually a pallet or fixture used to position the part during precision processing.

Containerless System   Systems requiring no containers have been devised. In assembly-line operations, operators use their own workbench areas to put completed units on painted squares, one unit per square. Each painted square represents a container, and the number of painted squares on each operator's bench is calculated to balance the line flow. When the subsequent user removes a unit from one of the producer's squares, the empty square signals the need to produce another unit. McDonald's uses a containerless system. Information entered by the order taker at the cash register is transmitted to the cooks and assemblers, who produce the sandwiches requested by the customer.

Managerial Practice 8.3 illustrates how Mayday Healthcare used principles of kanban systems and lean management to significant improve performance.

VALUE STREAM MAPPING

value stream mapping (VSM)

A qualitative lean tool for eliminating waste or *muda* that involves a current state drawing, a future state drawing, and an implementation plan.

Value stream mapping (VSM) is a widely used qualitative lean tool aimed at eliminating waste or *muda*. Waste in many processes can be as high as 60 percent. Value stream mapping is helpful because it creates a visual "map" of every process involved in the flow of materials and information in a product's value chain. These maps consist of a *current state drawing*, a *future state drawing*, and an implementation plan. Value stream mapping spans the entire supply chain, from the firm's receipt of raw materials to the delivery of the finished good to the customer. Thus, it tends to be broader in scope, displaying far more information than a typical process map or a flowchart used with Six Sigma process improvement efforts. Creating such a big picture representation helps managers identify the source of wasteful non-value-added activities.

Value stream mapping follows the steps shown in Figure 8.6. The first step is to focus on one product family for which mapping can be done. It is then followed by drawing a current state map of the existing production situation: Analysts start from the customer end and work upstream to draw the map by hand and record actual process times rather than rely on information not obtained by firsthand observation. Information for drawing the material and information flows can be gathered

FIGURE 8.6 ▶
Value Stream Mapping Steps

Source: Mike Rother and John Shook, *Learning to See* (Brookline, MA: The Lean Enterprise Institute, 2003), p. 9.

| MANAGERIAL PRACTICE 8.3 | Lean Systems at Mayday Healthcare |

Lean management has proved so effective in the field of manufacturing that health care professionals have applied its principles to the management of hospitals and labs. The South West London Improvement Academy is an organization helping transform Mayday Healthcare in England according to lean management principles. Mayday Healthcare manages several hospitals and clinics that belong to the National Health Service, the government-funded public health care plan in Great Britain. Using lean thinking, Mayday has improved its service in several areas, including the efficiency of laboratory test results and the management of stock levels.

At one time not too long ago, the speed of test results was causing problems at Mayday. The demand for test results had risen by 20 percent and usually surged between 1 and 3 in the afternoon. The amount of requests resulted in delays and also affected staff morale. The staff often had to work unplanned overtime until 8 at night just to meet the day's requests. In response to this problem, Mayday originally planned to invest in new equipment and add additional staff. Instead, they implemented a lean system in partnership with the South West London Improvement Academy. Together they identified the small capacity of the reception area as a hindrance to the speedy turnaround of test results. So, they simplified the tasks of the reception staff, eliminating unnecessary and duplicate steps. They established a lean system in which one staff member handled the reception of a sample from start to finish. Productivity increased dramatically—by 77 percent. Previously, each of the reception staff handled 18 samples per hour. After instituting lean techniques, each handled 32 samples per hour. The increase in productivity resulted in less overtime, which in turn led to greater staff morale, all without any investment.

Mayday realized that they also had problems in managing supplies. First, they had cash tied up in excessive amounts of stock. This led to waste, as some stock in storage was damaged or expired before it could be used. Also, ordering and searching through supplies had become burdensome to the staff, mainly due to poor organization and labeling. Supplies did not have designated spaces, and some supplies were stored in multiple locations. This made it difficult for staff to locate stock or know what was available. Lastly, supply levels did not accurately reflect usage levels. The stock of items needed more often was low, while the stock of items rarely used items was high. Lean thinking again helped solve Mayday's problems. The ordering process was simplified through a reduction of paperwork. Mayday's stock was sorted and reorganized. Mayday also instituted a two-bin system of stock management. In this system two bins of the same item are stacked on top of one another. When the first bin is empty, it is placed in a designated area as a signal to restock. This system helped reduce stock by 50 percent while at the same time reducing the risk of running out of materials. By instituting lean thinking, Mayday has freed up its staff members to spend less time on administrative tasks and more time caring for patients.

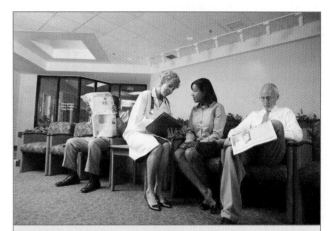

A National Health Service (NHS) doctor collects samples from a patient for testing. Simplifying processes and reducing paperwork have drastically improved performance and improved staff morale in NHS hospitals.

Sources: "Case Study: Lean Material Management in ITU and Theatres," http://www.swlia.nhs.uk/View.aspx?page=/case_studies/default.html, Accessed September 30, 2008; "Case Study: Faster Pathology Results Turnaround," http://www.swlia.nhs.uk/View.aspx?page=/case_studies/default.html, Accessed September 30, 2008; http://www.ihi.org/IHI/Results/WhitePapers/GoingLeaninHealthCare.htm; http://www.maydayhospital.org.uk/

from the shop floor, including the data related to each process: cycle time (C/T), setup or changeover time (C/O), uptime (on-demand available machine time expressed as a percentage), production batch sizes, number of people required to operate the process, number of product variations, pack size (for moving the product to the next stage), working time (minus breaks), and scrap rate. Value stream mapping uses a standard set of icons for material flow, information flow, and general information (to denote operators, safety stock buffers, and so on). Even though the complete glossary is extensive, a representative set of these icons is shown in Figure 8.7. These icons provide a common language for describing in detail how a facility should operate to create a better flow.

We use the VSM icons to illustrate in Figure 8.8 what a current state map could look like for a hypothetical bearing manufacturing company, which receives raw material sheets from Kline Steel Company every Monday for a product family of retainers (casings in which ball bearings are held), and then ships its finished product on a daily basis to a second-tier automotive manufacturing customer named GNK Enterprises. The product family of the bearing

Material Flow Icons

Information Flow Icons

FIGURE 8.7 ▲
Selected Set of Value Stream
Mapping Icons

manufacturing company under consideration consists of two types of retainers—large (L) and small (S)—that are packaged for shipping in returnable trays with 60 retainers in each tray. The manufacturing process consists of a pressing operation, a piercing and forming cell, and a finish grind operation, after which the two types of retainers are staged for shipping. The process characteristics and inventory buffers in front of each process are shown in the current state map of Figure 8.8. One worker occupies each station. Although the total processing time for each retainer is only 1 minute, it takes 16 days for the cumulative production lead time. Clearly opportunities exist for reconfiguring the existing processes and eliminating inventories.

The process flows shown at the bottom of Figure 8.8 are similar to the flowcharts discussed in Chapter 4, "Analyzing Processes," except that more detailed information is presented here for each process. However, what really sets the value stream maps apart from flowcharts is the inclusion of information flows at the top of Figure 8.8, which plan and coordinate all the process activities. The value stream maps are more comprehensive than process flowcharts, and meld together planning and control systems (discussed in detail in Chapter 15, "Planning Sufficient Resources") with detailed flowcharts (discussed in Chapter 4) to create a comprehensive supply chain view that includes both information and material flows between the firm and its suppliers and customers.

Once the current state map is done, the analysts can then use principles of lean systems such as load leveling, pull scheduling, and kanban cards to create a future state map with

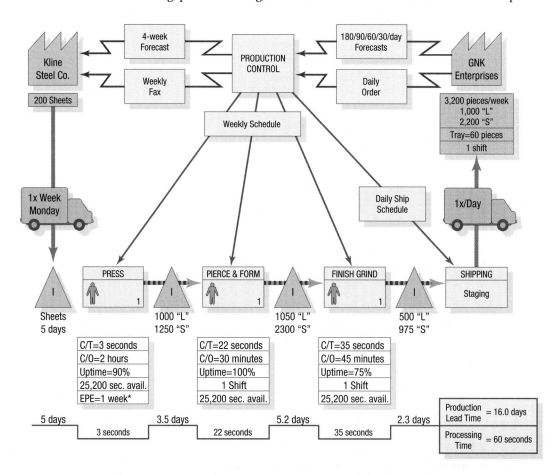

FIGURE 8.8 ▲
A Representative Current State Map for a Family of Retainers at a Bearings Manufacturing Company

more streamlined product flows. The future state drawing highlights sources of waste and how to eliminate them. The developments of the current and future state maps are overlapping efforts. Finally, the last step is aimed at preparing and actively using an implementation plan to achieve the future state. It may take only a couple of days from the creation of a future state map to the point where implementation can begin for a single product family. At this stage, the future state map essentially becomes a blueprint for implementing a lean system, and is fine-tuned as implementation progresses. As the future state becomes reality, a new future state map is drawn, thus denoting continuous improvement at the value stream level.

Unlike the theory of constraints (see Chapter 7, "Managing Process Constraints"), which accepts the existing system bottlenecks and then strives to maximize the throughput given that set of constraint(s), value stream mapping endeavors to understand through current state and future state maps how existing processes can be altered to eliminate bottlenecks and other wasteful activities. The goal is to bring the production rate of the entire process closer to the customer's desired demand rate. The benefits of applying this tool to the waste-removal process include reduced lead times and work-in-process inventories, reduced rework and scrap rates, and lower indirect labor costs.

HOUSE OF TOYOTA

A key challenge to managers seeking to implement lean systems in their organizations is to bring its underlying philosophy to their employees in an easy-to-understand fashion. Taiichi Ohno and Eiji Toyoda created a graphic representation shown in Figure 8.9[5] to define the Toyota Production System (TPS) to its employees and suppliers, and which is now known as the House of Toyota. It captures the four principles of TPS described in the opening vignette, and represents all the essential elements of lean systems that make the TPS work well. The house conveys stability. The roof, representing the primary goals of high quality, low cost, waste elimination, and short lead-times, is supported by the twin pillars of JIT and jidoka. Within JIT, TPS uses a pull system that focuses on one-piece work flow methods that can change and match the takt time of the process to the actual market demand because setup reductions and small changeover times are facilitated by cross-trained workers in cellular layouts. Implementing various tools of jidoka ensures that quality is built into the product rather than merely inspected at the end. Finally, within an environment of continuous improvement, operational stability to the house of Toyota is provided at the base by leveraging other lean concepts such as heijunka, standard work methods, 5S practices, total preventive maintenance, and elimination of waste throughout the supply chain within which the Toyota products flow to reach their eventual customers.

OPERATIONAL BENEFITS AND IMPLEMENTATION ISSUES

To gain competitive advantage and to make dramatic improvements, a lean system can be the solution. Lean systems can be an integral part of a corporate strategy based on speed because they cut cycle times, improve inventory turnover, and increase labor productivity. Recent studies also show that practices representing different components of lean systems such as JIT, TQM, Six Sigma, total preventive maintenance (TPM), and human resource management (HRM), individually as well as cumulatively, improve the performance of manufacturing plants as well as service facilities. Lean systems also involve a considerable amount of employee participation through small-group interaction sessions, which have resulted in improvements in many aspects of operations, not the least of which is service or product quality.

Even though the benefits of lean systems can be outstanding, problems can still arise after a lean system has

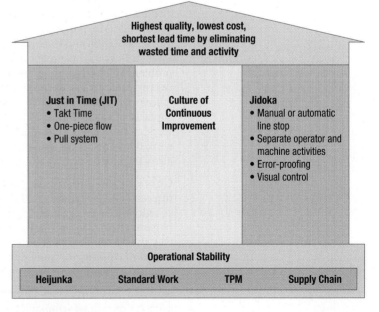

▲ FIGURE 8.9
House of Toyota

---

5 TBM Consulting Group; http://www.tbmcg.com/about/ourroots/house_toyota.php.

Single-engine Cessna airplanes roll off the assembly line at Independence, Kansas. Lean manufacturing concepts such as worker teams, manufacturing cells, group technology, and supplier managed inventories are used to build three versions of single-engine planes at the southeast Kansas plant.

long been operational. In addition, implementing a lean system can take a long time. We address below some of the issues managers should be aware of when implementing a lean system.

Organizational Considerations

Implementing a lean system requires management to consider issues of worker stress, cooperation and trust among workers and management, and reward systems and labor classifications.

The Human Costs of Lean Systems   Lean systems can be coupled with statistical process control (SPC) to reduce variations in output. However, this combination requires a high degree of regimentation and sometimes stresses the workforce. For example, in the Toyota Production System, workers must meet specified cycle times, and, with SPC, they must follow prescribed problem-solving methods. Such systems might make workers feel pushed and stressed, causing productivity losses or quality reductions. In addition, workers might feel a loss of some autonomy because of the close linkages in work flows between stations with little or no excess capacity or safety stocks. Managers can mitigate some of these effects by allowing for some slack in the system—either safety stock inventories or capacity slack—and by emphasizing work flows instead of worker pace. Managers also can promote the use of work teams and allow them to determine their task assignments within their domains of responsibility.

Cooperation and Trust   In a lean system, workers and first-line supervisors must take on responsibilities formerly assigned to middle managers and support staff. Activities such as scheduling, expediting, and improving productivity become part of the duties of lower-level personnel. Consequently, the work relationships in the organization must be reoriented in a way that fosters cooperation and mutual trust between the workforce and management. However, this environment can be difficult to achieve, particularly in light of the historical adversarial relationship between the two groups.

Reward Systems and Labor Classifications   In some instances, the reward system must be revamped when a lean system is implemented. At General Motors, for example, a plan to reduce stock at one plant ran into trouble because the production superintendent refused to cut back on the number of unneeded parts being made. Why? Because his or her salary was based on the plant's production volume.

The realignment of reward systems is not the only hurdle. Labor contracts traditionally crippled a company's ability to reassign workers to other tasks as the need arose. For example, a typical automobile plant in the United States has several unions and dozens of labor classifications. Generally, the people in each classification are allowed to do only a limited range of tasks. In some cases, companies have managed to give these employees more flexibility by agreeing to other types of union concessions and benefits. In other cases, however, companies relocated their plants to take advantage of nonunion or foreign labor.

Process Considerations

Firms using lean systems typically have some dominant work flows. To take advantage of lean practices, firms might have to change their existing layouts. Certain workstations might have to be moved closer together, and cells of machines devoted to particular component families may have to be established. However, rearranging a plant to conform to lean practices can be costly. For example, many plants currently receive raw materials and purchased parts by rail, but to facilitate smaller and more frequent shipments, truck deliveries would be preferable. Loading docks might have to be reconstructed or expanded and certain operations relocated to accommodate the change in transportation mode and quantities of arriving materials.

Inventory and Scheduling

Manufacturing firms need to have stable master production schedules, short setups, and frequent, reliable supplies of materials and components to achieve the full potential of the lean systems concept.

Schedule Stability Daily production schedules in high-volume, make-to-stock environments must be stable for extended periods. At Toyota, the master production schedule is stated in fractions of days over a three-month period and is revised only once a month. The first month of the schedule is frozen to avoid disruptive changes in the daily production schedule for each workstation; that is, the workstations execute the same work schedule each day of the month. At the beginning of each month, kanbans are reissued for the new daily production rate. Stable schedules are needed so that production lines can be balanced and new assignments found for employees who otherwise would be underutilized. Lean systems used in high-volume, make-to-stock environments cannot respond quickly to scheduling changes because little slack inventory or capacity is available to absorb these changes.

Setups If the inventory advantages of a lean system are to be realized, small lot sizes must be used. However, because small lots require a large number of setups, companies must significantly reduce setup times. Some companies have not been able to achieve short setup times and, therefore, have to use large-lot production, negating some of the advantages of lean practices. Also, lean systems are vulnerable to lengthy changeovers to new products because the low levels of finished goods inventory will be insufficient to cover demand while the system is down. If changeover times cannot be reduced, large finished goods inventories of the old product must be accumulated to compensate. In the automobile industry, every week that a plant is shut down for new-model changeover costs between $16 million and $20 million in pretax profits.

Purchasing and Logistics If frequent, small shipments of purchased items cannot be arranged with suppliers, large inventory savings for these items cannot be realized. For example, in the United States, such arrangements may prove difficult because of the geographic dispersion of suppliers.

The shipments of raw materials and components must be reliable because of the low inventory levels in lean systems. A plant can be shut down because of a lack of materials. Similarly, recovery becomes more prolonged and difficult in a lean system after supply chains are disrupted, which is what happened immediately after 9/11.

Process design and continuous improvement are key elements of a successful operations strategy. In concluding the second part of this text, we focused on lean systems as a directive for efficient process design and an approach to achieve continuous improvement. We showed how just-in-time systems (JIT), a popular lean systems approach, can be used for continuous improvement, and how kanban system can be used to control the amount of work-in-process inventory. Transforming a current process design to one embodying a lean system's philosophy is a constant challenge for management, often fraught with implementation issues. However, the transformation can be facilitated by adopting appropriate management approaches as exemplified by firms like Toyota and Panasonic among others, and by using tools such as value stream mapping. The key point to remember is that the philosophy of lean systems, applicable at the process level, is also applicable at the supply chain level. In part 3 of the text, we focus on designing and managing supply chains, which includes the design and integration of effective supply chains.

INTERNET RESOURCES

my**om**lab and the Companion Website at **www.pearsonglobaleditions.com/krajewski** contain many tools, activities, and resources designed for this chapter.

KEY EQUATION

Number of containers:

$$\kappa = \frac{\bar{d}(\bar{w} + \bar{p})(1 + \alpha)}{c}$$

KEY TERMS

five S (5S) 323
group technology 325
heijunka 322
jidoka 320
JIT system 316
just-in-time (JIT) philosophy 316

kanban 326
lean systems 316
lot 319
mixed-model assembly 322
one worker, multiple machines
   (OWMM) cell 325

poka-yoke 321
pull method 320
push method 320
single-digit setup 319
takt time 321
value stream mapping (VSM) 330

SOLVED PROBLEM

A company using a kanban system has an inefficient machine group. For example, the daily demand for part L105A is 3,000 units. The average waiting time for a container of parts is 0.8 day. The processing time for a container of L105A is 0.2 day, and a container holds 270 units. Currently, 20 containers are used for this item.

  a. What is the value of the policy variable, α?

  b. What is the total planned inventory (work-in-process and finished goods) for item L105A?

  c. Suppose that the policy variable, α, was 0. How many containers would be needed now? What is the effect of the policy variable in this example?

SOLUTION

  a. We use the equation for the number of containers and then solve for α:

$$\kappa = \frac{\bar{d}(\bar{w} + \bar{p})(1 + \alpha)}{c}$$

$$20 = \frac{3{,}000(0.8 + 0.2)(1 + \alpha)}{270}$$

and

$$(1 + \alpha) = \frac{20(270)}{3{,}000(0.8 + 0.2)} = 1.8$$

$$\alpha = 1.8 - 1 = 0.8$$

  b. With 20 containers in the system and each container holding 270 units, the total planned inventory is 20(270) = 5,400 units.

  c. If $\alpha = 0$

$$\kappa = \frac{3{,}000(0.8 + 0.2)(1 + 0)}{270} = 11.11 \ \text{ or } \ 12 \text{ containers}$$

The policy variable adjusts the number of containers. In this case, the difference is quite dramatic because $\bar{w} + \bar{p}$ is fairly large and the number of units per container is small relative to daily demand.

DISCUSSION QUESTIONS

1. Which elements of lean systems would be most troublesome for manufacturers to implement? Why?

2. Identify a service or a manufacturing process that you are familiar with, and draw a current state value stream map to depict its existing information and material flows.

3. Compare and contrast the following two situations:

   a. A company's lean system stresses teamwork. Employees feel more involved and, therefore, productivity and quality increase at the company. The problem is that workers also experience a loss of individual autonomy.

   b. A humanities professor believes that all students want to learn. To encourage students to work together and learn from each other—thereby increasing the involvement, productivity, and the quality of the learning experience—the professor announces that all students in the class will receive the same grade and that it will be based on the performance of the group.

PROBLEMS

Software, such as OM Explorer, Active Models, and POM for Windows, is available in my**om**lab. Check with your instructor on how best to use it. In many cases, the instructor wants you to understand how to do the calculations by hand. At most, the software provides a check on your calculations. When calculations are particularly complex and the goal is interpreting the results in making decisions, the software replaces entirely the manual calculations.

1. A fabrication cell at Spradley's Sprockets uses the pull method to supply gears to an assembly line. George Jitson is in charge of the assembly line, which requires 500 gears per day. Containers typically wait 0.20 day in the fabrication cell. Each container holds 20 gears, and one container requires 1.8 days in machine time. Setup times are negligible. If the policy variable for unforeseen contingencies is set at 5 percent, how many containers should Jitson authorize for the gear replenishment system?

2. The Harvey Motorcycle Company produces three models: the Tiger, a sure-footed dirt bike; the LX2000, a nimble cafe racer; and the Golden, a large interstate tourer. This month's master production schedule calls for the production of 54 Goldens, 42 LX2000s, and 30 Tigers per 7-hour shift.

   a. What average cycle time is required for the assembly line to achieve the production quota in 7 hours?

   b. If mixed-model scheduling is used, how many of each model will be produced before the production cycle is repeated?

   c. Determine a satisfactory production sequence for the ultimate in small-lot production: one unit.

   d. The design of a new model, the Cheetah, includes features from the Tiger, LX2000, and Golden models. The resulting blended design has an indecisive character and is expected to attract some sales from the other models. Determine a mixed-model schedule resulting in 52 Goldens, 39 LX2000s, 26 Tigers, and 13 Cheetahs per 7-hour shift. Although the total number of motorcycles produced per day will increase only slightly, what problem might be anticipated in implementing this change from the production schedule indicated in part (b)?

3. An assembly line requires two components: gadjits and widjits. Gadjits are produced by center 1 and widjits by center 2. Each unit of the end item, called a jit-together, requires 3 gadjits and 2 widjits, as shown in Figure 8.10. The daily production quota on the assembly line is 800 jit-togethers.

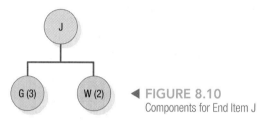

◀ **FIGURE 8.10**
Components for End Item J

The container for gadjits holds 80 units. The policy variable for center 1 is set at 0.09. The average waiting time for a container of gadjits is 0.09 day, and 0.06 day is needed to produce a container. The container for widjits holds 50 units, and the policy variable for center 2 is 0.08. The average waiting time per container of widgits is 0.14 day, and the time required to process a container is 0.20 day.

   a. How many containers are needed for gadjits?

   b. How many containers are needed for widjits?

4. You are asked to analyze the kanban system of LeWin, a French manufacturer of gaming devices. One of the workstations feeding the assembly line produces part M670N. The daily demand for M670N is 1,800 units. The average processing time per unit is 0.003 day. LeWin's records show that the average container spends 1.05 days waiting at the feeder workstation. The container for M670N can hold 300 units. Twelve containers are authorized for the part. Recall that $\bar{p}$ is the average processing time per container, not per individual part.

   a. Find the value of the policy variable, α, that expresses the amount of implied safety stock in this system.

   b. Use the implied value of α from part (a) to determine the required reduction in waiting time if one container was removed. Assume that all other parameters remain constant.

5. The Farm-4-Less tractor company produces a grain combine (GC) in addition to both a large (LT) and small size tractor (SM). Its production manager desires to produce to customer demand using a mixed model production line. The current sequence of production, which is repeated 30 times during a shift, is SM-GC-SM-LT-SM-GC-LT-SM. A new machine is produced every 2 minutes. Based on this information, answer the following questions.

   a. How long does it take the production cycle to be completed?

   b. How many of each type of machine does Farm-4-Less produce in a shift?

6. Markland First National Bank of Rolla utilizes kanban techniques in its check processing facility. The following information is known about the process. Each kanban container can hold 50 checks and spends 24 minutes a day in processing and 2 hours a day in materials handling and waiting. Finally, the facility operates 24 hours per day and utilizes a policy variable for unforeseen contingencies of 0.25.

   a. If there are 20 kanban containers in use what is the current daily demand of the check processing facility?

   b. If the muda or the waste in the system were eliminated completely, how many containers would then be needed?

7. Jitsmart is a retailer of plastic action-figure toys. The action figures are purchased from Tacky Toys, Inc., and arrive in boxes of 48. Full boxes are stored on high shelves out of reach of customers. A small inventory is maintained on child-level shelves. Depletion of the lower-shelf inventory signals the need to take down a box of action figures to replenish the inventory. A reorder card is then removed from the box and sent to Tacky Toys to authorize replenishment of a container of action figures. The average demand rate for a popular action figure, Agent 99, is 36 units per day. The total lead time (waiting plus processing) is 11 days. Jitsmart's safety stocky policy variable, α, is 0.25. What is the authorized stock level for Jitsmart?

8. The production schedule at Mazda calls for 1,200 Mazdas to be produced during each of 22 production days in January and 900 Mazdas to be produced during each of 20 production days in February. Mazda uses a kanban system to communicate with Gesundheit, a nearby supplier of tires. Mazda purchases four tires per vehicle from Gesundheit. The safety stock policy variable, α, is 0.15. The container (a delivery truck) size is 200 tires. The average waiting time plus materials handling time is 0.16 day per container. Assembly lines are rebalanced at the beginning of each month. The average processing time per container in January is 0.10 day. February processing time will average 0.125 day per container. How many containers should be authorized for January? How many for February?

9. A U.S. Postal Service supervisor is looking for ways to reduce stress in the sorting department. With the existing arrangement, stamped letters are machine-canceled and loaded into tubs with 375 letters per tub. The tubs are then pushed to postal clerks, who read and key postal codes into an automated sorting machine at the rate of 1 tub per 375 seconds. To overcome the stress caused when the stamp canceling machine outpaces the sorting clerks, a pull system is proposed. When the clerks are ready to process another tub of mail, they will pull the tub from the canceling machine area. How many tubs should circulate between the sorting clerks and the canceling machine if 90,000 letters are to be sorted during an 8-hour shift, the safety stock policy variable, α, is 0.18, and the average waiting time plus materials handling time is 25 minutes per tub?

10. Gestalt, Inc., uses a kanban system in its automobile production facility in Germany. This facility operates 8 hours per day to produce the Jitterbug, a replacement for the obsolete but immensely popular Jitney Beetle. Suppose that a certain part requires 150 seconds of processing at machine cell 33B and a container of parts average 1.6 hours of waiting time there. Management allows a 10 percent buffer for unexpected occurrences. Each container holds 30 parts, and 8 containers are authorized. How much daily demand can be satisfied with this system? (*Hint:* Recall that $\bar{p}$ is the average processing time per container, not per individual part.)

VIDEO CASE   Lean Systems at Autoliv

Autoliv is a world-class example of lean manufacturing. This Fortune 500 company makes automotive safety components such as seat belts, airbags, and steering wheels, and has over 80 plants in more than 32 countries. Revenues in 2007 topped $6.7 billion. Autoliv's lean manufacturing environment is called the Autoliv Production System (APS), and is based on the principles of lean manufacturing pioneered by Toyota, one of the world's largest automobile manufacturers, and embodied in its Toyota Production System (TPS).

At the heart of Autoliv is a system that focuses on continuous improvement. Based on the "House of Toyota," Autoliv's Ogden, Utah, airbag module plant puts the concepts embodied in the house to work every day. The only difference between the Toyota house and the one at Autoliv is that the company has added a third pillar to its house to represent employee involvement in all processes because a culture of involvement, while the norm in Japan, is not always found in the United States.

Autoliv Employee folds an air bag in a Toyota-inspired production cell

Autoliv started its lean journey back in 1995. At that time, the Ogden plant was at manufacturing capacity with 22 work cells. Company managers acknowledge that, back then, Autoliv was "broken" and in need of significant and immediate change if it was to survive. This meant that everyone—from senior management to employees and suppliers—needed to be on-board with rebuilding the company. It was not that the company could not fulfill the needs of its automaker customers; however, with increasing demand for both reliable and cost-effective component supplies, pressure to change became obvious. Recognizing the value of Toyota's approach, senior management made the commitment to embark on its own journey to bring the transformative culture of lean manufacturing to Autoliv.

In 1998, sensei Takashi Harada arrived from Japan to spend three years teaching top company managers the principles, techniques, and culture of the lean system. This helped managers create an environment in which continuous improvement could be fostered and revered as an essential activity for long-term success. Because the environment was changing, it made it difficult at first for suppliers to meet Autoliv's constantly changing and unstable processes. It also made problems visible and forced the company to address and resolve the problems instead of finding ways to work around them as had been done in the past. Daily audits, monthly training, and more in-depth education programs were created to help focus attention on where changes needed to be made. Workers and management were organized into teams that were held accountable for common goals and tasked with working toward common success.

By 2004, the lean culture was integrated into the company, and it now hosts regular visits by other corporations who want to learn from Autoliv's journey and experiences. Compared to 1995, the space required for a typical work cell has been reduced by 88.5 percent, while the number of cells has grown over 400 percent. This has allowed Autoliv to dramatically increase its production capacity with minimal investment.

Lean concepts play out every day in the each plant. For example, everyone gathers at the start of the workday for pre-shift stretching and a brief meeting—this is part of the employee involvement pillar in the APS House. Then, workers head to one of 92 work cells on the plant floor. Heijunka Room team members deliver heijunka cards to each cell to communicate the work to be done in that cell. Lot sizes may vary with each card delivered to the cell. Everything the workers need to make the lot is in the cell and regularly replenished through the kanban card system. Every 24 minutes, another heijunka card comes to the cell to signal workers what they will build next. This is part of the JIT pillar in the house.

Since a culture of continuous improvement requires employees at every level to be responsible for quality, a worker may identify an "abnormal condition" during work execution that slows down the work of the cell, or stops it altogether. This is embodied in the right pillar of the Toyota house—jidoka, which Autoliv interprets as "stop and fix." This is a rare occurrence, however, since both Autoliv and its suppliers are expected to deliver defect-free products. When a supplier is new, or has experienced quality issues, the supplier pays for inspection in Autoliv's receiving dock area until Autoliv is certain the supplier can meet quality expectations for all future deliveries. In this manner, workers in the cells know they can trust the integrity of the raw materials arriving through the kanban system into their cells for assembly. Jidoka may also come into play when a machine does not operate properly, or an employee notices a process that has deviated from the standard. When workers "stop and fix" a problem at the point of its creation, they save the company from added cost as well as lost confidence in the eyes of the customer.

To help focus worker efforts daily, Autoliv has a blue "communication wall" that everyone sees as they head to their work site. The wall contains the company's "policy deployment," which consists of company-wide goals for customer satisfaction, shareholder/financial performance, and safety and quality. The policy deployment begins with the company-wide goals, which then flow down to the plant level through the plant manager's goals, strategies, and actions for the facility. These linked activities assure that Autoliv achieves its goals. By communicating this information—and more—in a visual manner, the central pillar of the APS House is supported. Other visual communication and management methods are in place as well. For example, each cell has an overhead banner that states how that cell is doing each month in the areas of safety, quality, employee involvement, cost, and delivery. These all tie into the policy deployment shown on the communication wall.

Another visual communication method is to use a "rail" for the management of the heijunka cards in each cell. The rail has color-coded sections. As each card is delivered, it slides down a color-coded railing to the team. At the end nearest the cell, the rail is green, indicating that any cards that fall into this area can be completed within normal working hours. The middle of the rail is yellow, indicating overtime for the cell that day. The end is red, meaning weekend overtime is required to bring work processes back into harmony with customer demand. As a heijunka card slides down the rail, it stops when it hits the end or stacks up behind another card. If the cell is not performing at the required pace to meet customer demand, the cards will stack up on the rail and provide a very visual cue that the cell is not meeting expectations. This provides an opportunity for cell team members as well as management to implement immediate countermeasures to prevent required overtime if the situation is not remedied.

All aisles and walkways surrounding cells are to be clear of materials, debris, or other items. If anything appears in those areas, everyone can quickly see the abnormality. As team members work together to complete their day's work, the results of their efforts are displayed boldly on each cell's "communicube." This four-sided rotating display visually tells the story of the cell's productivity, quality, and 5S performance. The cube also contains a special section for the management of kaizen suggestions for the team itself. These kaizens enable the team to continuously improve the work environment as well as drive the achievement of team results.

Autoliv's lean journey embodied in the Autoliv Production System has led to numerous awards and achievement of its policy deployment goals. Product defects have been dramatically reduced, inventory levels are lower, and inventory turnover is approaching world-class levels of 50. Employee turnover is close to 5 percent, and remains well below that of other manufacturers in the industry. Yet the destination has not been reached. The company continues its emphasis on driving systemic improvement to avoid complacency and loss of competitive advantage. Best practices from sources beyond each immediate area of the organization are studied and integrated. And finding ways to engage and reward Autoliv's workforce in a maturing market is critical. Kaizen suggestions in the most recent year at the Ogden plant totaled 74,000, or nearly 74 per employee, indicating the culture of continuous improvement in Autoliv's APS House is alive and well.

QUESTIONS

1. Why is a visual management approach such an integral part of Autoliv's lean system?

2. Describe the JIT considerations presented in the chapter as they relate to Autoliv's manufacturing environment.

3. Which method of work flow is embodied in Autoliv's system? Why is this approach most suitable to its lean environment?

4. When Autoliv started its lean journey, a number of operational benefits and implementation issues had to be addressed. What were they, and how were they addressed?

CASE Copper Kettle Catering

Copper Kettle Catering (CKC) is a full-service catering company that provides services ranging from box lunches for picnics or luncheon meetings to large wedding, dinner, or office parties. Established as a lunch delivery service for offices in 1972 by Wayne and Janet Williams, CKC has grown to be one of the largest catering businesses in Raleigh, North Carolina. The Williamses divide customer demand into two categories: *deliver only* and *deliver and serve*.

The deliver-only side of the business delivers boxed meals consisting of a sandwich, salad, dessert, and fruit. The menu for this service is limited to six sandwich selections, three salads or potato chips, and a brownie or fruit bar. Grapes and an orange slice are included with every meal, and iced tea can be ordered to accompany the meals. The overall level of demand for this service throughout the year is fairly constant, although the mix of menu items delivered varies. The planning horizon for this segment of the business is short: Customers usually call no more than a day ahead of time. CKC requires customers to call deliver-only orders in by 10:00 A.M. to guarantee delivery the same day.

The deliver-and-serve side of the business focuses on catering large parties, dinners, and weddings. The extensive range of menu items includes a full selection of hors d'oeuvres, entrées, beverages, and special-request items. The demand for these services is much more seasonal, with heavier demands occurring in the late spring–early summer for weddings and the late fall–early winter for holiday parties. However, this segment also has a longer planning horizon. Customers book dates and choose menu items weeks or months ahead of time.

CKC's food preparation facilities support both operations. The physical facilities layout resembles that of a job process. Five major work areas consist of a stove–oven area for hot food preparation, a cold area for salad preparation, an hors d'oeuvre preparation area, a sandwich preparation area, and an assembly area where deliver-only orders are boxed and deliver-and-serve orders are assembled and trayed. Three walk-in coolers store foods requiring refrigeration, and a large pantry houses nonperishable goods. Space limitations and the risk of spoilage limit the amount of raw materials and prepared food items that can be carried in inventory at any one time. CKC purchases desserts from outside vendors. Some deliver the desserts to CKC; others require CKC to send someone to pick up desserts at their facilities.

The scheduling of orders is a two-stage process. Each Monday, the Williamses develop the schedule of deliver-and-serve orders to be processed each day. CKC typically has multiple deliver-and-serve orders to fill each day

of the week. This level of demand allows a certain efficiency in the preparation of multiple orders. The deliver-only orders are scheduled day to day, owing to the short-order lead times. CKC sometimes runs out of ingredients for deliver-only menu items because of the limited inventory space.

Wayne and Janet Williams have 10 full-time employees: 2 cooks and 8 food preparation workers, who also work as servers for the deliver-and-serve orders. In periods of high demand, the Williamses hire additional part-time servers. The position of cook is specialized and requires a high degree of training and skill. The rest of the employees are flexible and move between tasks as needed.

The business environment for catering is competitive. The competitive priorities are high-quality food, delivery reliability, flexibility, and cost—in that order. "The quality of the food and its preparation is paramount," states Wayne Williams. "Caterers with poor-quality food will not stay in business long." Quality is measured by both freshness and taste. Delivery reliability encompasses both on-time delivery and the time required to respond to customer orders (in effect, the order lead time). Flexibility focuses on both the range of catering requests that a company can satisfy and menu variety.

Recently, CKC began to notice that customers are demanding more menu flexibility and faster response times. Small specialty caterers who entered the market are targeting specific well-defined market segments. One example is a small caterer called Lunches-R-Us, which located a facility in the middle of a large office complex to serve the lunch trade and competes with CKC on cost.

Wayne and Janet Williams are impressed by the lean systems concept, especially the ideas related to increasing flexibility, reducing lead times, and lowering costs. They sound like what CKC needs to remain competitive. However, the Williamses wonder whether lean concepts and practices are transferable to a service business.

QUESTIONS

1. Are the operations of Copper Kettle Catering conducive to the application of lean concepts and practices? Explain.

2. What, if any, are the major barriers to implementing a lean system at Copper Kettle Catering?

3. What would you recommend that Wayne and Janet Williams do to take advantage of lean concepts in operating CKC?

Source: This case was prepared by Dr. Brooke Saladin, Wake Forest University, as a basis for classroom discussion.

Selected References

Ansberry, Clare. "Hurry-Up Inventory Method Hurts Where It Once Helped." *Wall Street Journal Online* (June 25, 2002).

Dixon, Lance. "Tomorrow's Ideas Take Flight in Today's Leading Edge Corporations." *APICS—The Performance Advantage* (July 1996) p. 60.

Fuime, Orrest. "Lean Accounting and Finance." *Target*, vol. 18, no. 4 (Fourth Quarter 2002), pp. 6–14.

Greenblatt, Sherwin. "Continuous Improvement in Supply Chain Management." *Chief Executive* (June 1993), pp. 40–43.

Hall, Robert W. "New Balance Athletic Shoe Company." *Target*, vol. 20, no. 5(2004), pp. 5–10.

Holweg, Matthias. "The Genealogy of Lean Production." *Journal of Operations Management*, vol. 25 (2007), pp. 420–437.

Klein, J. A. "The Human Costs of Manufacturing Reform." *Harvard Business Review* (March–April 1989), pp. 60–66.

Manufacturing Engineering Web site, www.mfgeng.com/5S.htm.

Mascitelli, Ron. "Lean Thinking: It's About Efficient Value Creation." *Target*, vol. 16, no. 2 (Second Quarter 2000), pp. 22–26.

McBride, David. "Toyota and Total Productive Maintenance." http://www.emsstrategies.com/dm050104article2.html; May 2004.

Millstein, Mitchell. "How to Make Your MRP System Flow." *APICS—The Performance Advantage* (July 2000), pp. 47–49.

Rother, Mike, and John Shook. *Learning to See*. Brookline, MA: The Lean Enterprise Institute, 2003.

Schaller, Jeff. "A 'Just Do It Now' Philosophy Rapidly Creates a Lean Culture, Produces Dramatic Results at Novametix Medical Systems." *Target*, vol. 18, no. 2 (Second Quarter 2002), pp. 48–54.

Schonberger, Richard J. "Japanese production management: An evolution—With mixed success." *Journal of Operations Management*, vol. 25 (2007), pp. 403–419.

Shah, Rachna, and Peter T. Ward. "Defining and Developing Measures of Lean Production." *Journal of Operations Management*, vol. 25 (2007), pp. 785–805.

Shah, Rachna, and Peter T. Ward. "Lean Manufacturing: Context, Practice Bundles, and Performance." *Journal of Operations Management*, vol. 21 (2003), pp. 129–149.

Spear, Steven J. "Learning to Lead at Toyota." *Harvard Business Review* (May 2004), pp. 78–86.

Stewart, Douglas M., and John R. Grout. "The Human Side of Mistake Proofing." *Production and Operations Management*, vol. 10, no. 4 (Winter 2001), pp. 440–459.

Tonkin, Lea. "System Sensor's Lean Journey." *Target*, vol. 18, no. 2 (Second Quarter 2002), pp. 44–47.

9 DESIGNING EFFECTIVE SUPPLY CHAINS

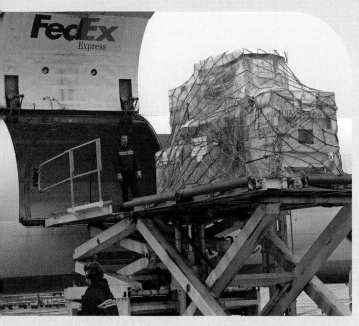

FedEx employees prepare a shipment of medical supplies from International Aid of Spring Lake, Michigan. The supplies helped victims of the Asian tsunami disaster.

FEDEX

FedEx is a $33 billion-a-year delivery service company that is used to dealing with crises. Hardly a day goes by without disruptive events such as social unrest, major storms, or unanticipated labor strikes somewhere in the world. FedEx has designed a supply chain that is flexible and responsive to unpredictable catastrophic events. This capability has made FedEx an important resource in humanitarian supply chains, which experience major mismatches of supply and demand that require a global response as quickly as possible. A wait-and-see attitude will not work; advanced planning is necessary. Such was the case with Hurricane Katrina, the costliest natural disaster in the history of the United States. Five days before Katrina hit the southeast Louisiana coast, the chief of FedEx's Global Operations Control in Memphis, Tennessee, conducted a twice-daily conference call for more than 100 people. Before the storm hit, FedEx positioned 30,000 bags of ice, 30,000 gallons of water, and 85 home generators outside Baton Rouge, Louisiana, and Tallahassee, Florida, for quick deployment to relieve employees, and 60 tons of American Red Cross equipment to strategic locations to await the storm. While the high winds were expected, the massive flooding took the company by surprise. FedEx returned 10,000 packages to their senders and had to reprogram 100,000 devices to avoid sending new shipments to closed areas. Since the New Orleans airport was closed, FedEx had to shift its hub to Lafayette, Louisiana, in only a few days, a move of 135 miles that would have normally taken

LEARNING GOALS

After reading this chapter, you should be able to:

1. Identify the nature of supply chains for service providers, as well as for manufacturers.

2. Define the key design issues associated with supply chain processes.

3. Define the critical supply chain inventory and financial measures.

4. Explain the strategic importance of supply chain design and give real examples of its application in service situations as well as in manufacturing situations.

5. Explain how efficient supply chains differ from responsive supply chains and the environments best suited for each type of supply chain.

6 months to complete. Nonetheless, within a week after the devastation, FedEx used its vast logistics network to move more than 900 tons of relief supplies to affected areas in Louisiana, Mississippi, and the Houston Astrodome.

Sources: Ellen Florian Kratz, "For FedEx, it was Time to Deliver," *Fortune* (October 3, 2005), pp. 83–84; Business Wire, www.businesswire.com, November 14, 2006; LN Van Wassenhove, "Humanitarian Aid Logistics: Supply Chain Management in High Gear," *Journal of the Operational Research Society*, 2006, Vol. 57, pp. 475–489; www.fedex.com/us/about/responsibility/katrina.html.

my**om**lab and the Companion Website at **www.pearsonglobaleditions.com/krajewski** contain many tools, activities, and resources designed for this chapter.

FedEx is an excellent example of how a firm designs its supply chain to be reactive to major disruptions and natural disasters, a capability that also gains a competitive advantage. A *supply chain* is the interrelated series of processes within a firm and across different firms that produces a service or product to the satisfaction of customers. More specifically, it is a network of service, material, monetary, and information flows that link a firm's customer relationship, order fulfillment, and supplier relationship processes to those of its suppliers and customers. It is important to note, however, that a firm such as FedEx may have multiple supply chains, depending on the mix of services or products it produces. A supplier in one supply chain may not be a supplier in another supply chain because the service or product may be different or the supplier may simply be unable to negotiate a successful contract.

The firm's operations strategy and competitive priorities guide its supply chain choices. *Supply chain management* is the synchronization of a firm's processes with those of its suppliers and customers to match the flow of materials, services, and information with demand. A key part of supply chain management is developing a strategy to mobilize and provide for all the resources in the supply chain to meet customer demand now and in the future. In this chapter we focus on **supply chain design**, an essential aspect of a supply chain strategy, which seeks to design a firm's supply chain to meet the competitive priorities of the firm's operations strategy. To get a better understanding of the importance of supply chain design, consider Figure 9.1, which conceptually shows the challenges facing supply chain managers. The blue line is an *efficiency curve*, which shows the trade-off between costs and performance for the current supply chain design if the supply chain is operated as efficiently as it can be. Now, suppose that your firm plots its actual costs and performance, as indicated by the red dot. It is far off of the efficiency curve, which is not an uncommon occurrence. The challenge is to move operations into the tinted area, as close to the curve as possible, which can be accomplished by better forecasting, inventory management, operations planning and scheduling, and resource planning. We discuss those topics in the chapters to follow. However, quantum steps in improvement can be obtained by improving the design of the supply chain in accordance with a sound supply chain strategy, which moves the curve as shown by the dashed red line. The goal is to reduce costs as well as increase performance. Design issues include placement of inventories, mass customization, outsourcing, supply chain collaboration, supplier selection, closed-loop supply chains, and facility location, which are just some of the topics we discuss in this and the next two chapters. In this chapter we will also discuss the important measures of supply chain performance and show how sound supply chain design can improve key financial measures.

supply chain design

Designing a firm's supply chain to meet the competitive priorities of the firm's operations strategy.

FIGURE 9.1 ▼
Supply Chain Efficiency Curve

SUPPLY CHAIN DESIGN ACROSS THE ORGANIZATION

Supply chains permeate the entire organization. It is hard to envision a process in a firm that is not in some way affected by the design of the supply chain. Supply chains must be managed to coordinate the inputs with the outputs in a firm to achieve the appropriate competitive priorities of the firm's enterprise processes. The Internet offers firms an alternative to traditional methods for managing the supply chain. However, the firm must be committed to redesigning its information flows throughout the organization, especially the customer relationship, order fulfillment, and supplier relationship processes. These processes intersect all of the traditional functional areas of the firm.

A supply chain strategy is essential for service as well as manufacturing firms. In fact, service providers are beginning to realize the potential benefits of redesigning their supply chain processes. For example, hospitals have notoriously held to old-fashioned approaches for purchasing and materials management. Even with the advent of group purchasing organizations and centralized buying groups, such as Premier, Inc., a typical hospital collects orders from throughout the hospital for medical supplies and equipment ranging from latex gloves to operating tables. Often the merchandise is chosen from a stack of outdated catalogs. Prices must be checked and the orders sent by phone or fax to literally thousands of distributors and suppliers.

Can this process be improved? Columbia/HCA Health Care Corporation thinks so. It funded separate ventures to create an electronic marketplace for placing orders online. The systems link to the suppliers of several hundred thousand medical and surgical supplies. Of course, to take full advantage of the marketplace, hospitals will have to redesign their supplier relationship processes to realize the benefits. Nonetheless, the potential benefits are considerable.

SUPPLY CHAINS FOR SERVICES AND MANUFACTURING

Every firm or organization is a member of some supply chain. In this section we show the similarities and differences between supply chains for services and manufacturing.

Services

Supply chain design for a service provider is driven by the need to provide support for the essential elements of the various services it delivers. Consider the example of Flowers-on-Demand, a florist with 27 retail stores in the greater Boston metropolitan area.[1] Customers can place orders for customized floral arrangements by visiting one of the stores, using a toll-free number, or going to the florist's Web page. The 800 number and the Web page are operated by a local Internet services company, which takes orders and relays them to the florist. The arrangements are produced at a distribution center, and deliveries are made using either local couriers, or FedEx, if the delivery is outside of the Boston area. Fresh flowers, flown in from all over the world, are used in the arrangements.

What differentiates Flowers-on-Demand from floral wire services, such as Teleflora or FTD, is that it assembles all the arrangements and can ship out-of-area orders for next-day delivery anywhere in the country. To do business, the florist must have a supply chain that provides retail stores, a delivery center, computers, point-of-sale equipment, and employees. It must purchase flowers that are sourced globally as well as arrangement materials, such as pots, baskets, greeting cards, and packing materials. The florist must arrange the flowers per the customer's order and ensure that the arrangement is delivered as specified by the customer, using local services or FedEx. The design of its supply chain must provide convenience, which is facilitated by the location of the retail outlets and the opportunity to place orders via the Internet or the toll-free number.

Figure 9.2 illustrates a simplified supply chain for the florist. Each of the suppliers, of course, has its own supply chain (not shown). For example, the supplier for the arrangement materials may get baskets from one supplier and pots from another. The suppliers in the

▼ FIGURE 9.2
Supply Chain for a Florist

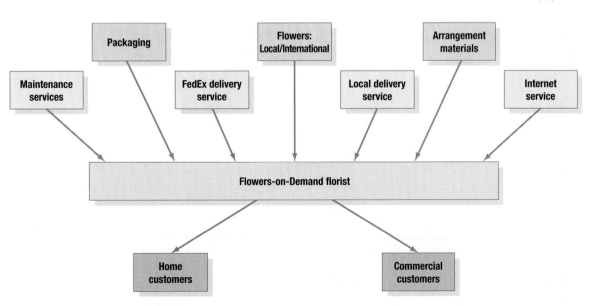

---

[1] The florist depicted is real; however, the name has been changed.

florist's supply chain play an integral role in its ability to meet its competitive priorities, such as top quality, delivery speed, and customization.

Manufacturing

A fundamental purpose of supply chain design for manufacturers is to control inventory by managing the flow of materials. The typical manufacturer spends more than 60 percent of its total income from sales on purchased services and materials, whereas the typical service provider spends only 30 to 40 percent. Because materials comprise such a large component of the sales dollar, manufacturers can reap large profits with a small reduction in the cost of materials, which makes supply chain management a key competitive weapon.

The supply chain for a manufacturing firm can be complicated, as Figure 9.3 illustrates. However, the supply chain depicted is an oversimplification because many companies have hundreds, if not thousands, of suppliers. In this example, the firm is in Ireland and deals with an international supply chain. In addition, it owns its distribution and transportation services. Suppliers are often identified by their position in the supply chain. Here, tier 1 suppliers provide major subassemblies that are assembled by the manufacturing firm, tier 2 suppliers provide tier 1 suppliers with components, and so on. Not all companies have the same number of levels in their supply chains. For example, companies that engineer products to customer specifications normally do not have distribution centers as part of their supply chains. Such companies often ship products directly to their customers.

INVENTORY AND SUPPLY CHAINS

The value of supply chain management becomes apparent when the complexity of the supply chain is recognized. The performance of numerous suppliers determines the inward flow of materials and services to a firm. The performance of the firm determines the outward flow of services or products to the next stage of the supply chain. The flow of materials, however, determines inventory levels. Too much inventory can happen to the best of companies. For example, one year Amazon.com overestimated the amount of demand for Kermit the Frog telephones and ended up with a 50-week supply, which contributed to a strain on warehouse operations and service to customers. Improved forecasting processes, selective outsourcing of warehouse operations, and state-of-the-art automation and mechanization

FIGURE 9.3 ▼
Supply Chain for a Manufacturing Firm

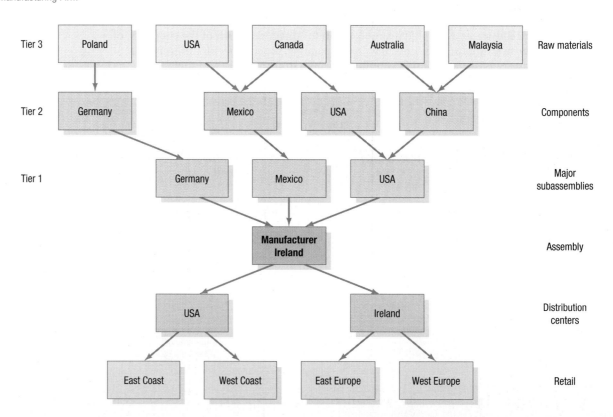

improved the flow of materials through Amazon.com's facilities and consequently improved the efficiency and performance of the supply chain.[2]

Inventory is a stock of materials used to satisfy customer demand or to support the production of services or goods. Figure 9.4 shows how inventories are created at one node in a supply chain through the analogy of a water tank. The flow of water into the tank raises the water level. The inward flow of water represents input materials, such as steel, component parts, office supplies, or a finished product. The water level represents the amount of inventory held at a plant, service facility, warehouse, or retail outlet. The flow of water from the tank lowers the water level in the tank. The outward flow of water represents the demand for materials in inventory, such as customer orders for a Huffy bicycle or service requirements for supplies such as soap, food, or furnishings. The rate of the outward flow also reflects the ability of the firm to match the demand for services or products. Another possible outward flow is that of scrap, which also lowers the level of useable inventory. Together, the difference between input flow rate and the output flow rate determines the level of inventory. Inventories rise when more material flows into the tank than flows out; they fall when more material flows out than flows in. Figure 9.4 also shows clearly why firms utilize Six Sigma and total quality management (TQM) to reduce defective materials: The larger the scrap flows, the larger the input flow of materials required for a given level of output.

A fundamental question in supply chain management is how much inventory to have. The answer to this question involves a tradeoff between the advantages and disadvantages of holding inventory. Depending on the situation, the pressures for having small inventories may or may not exceed the pressures for having large inventories.

Pressures for Small Inventories

An inventory manager's job is to balance the advantages and disadvantages of both small and large inventories and find a happy medium between the two levels. The primary reason for keeping inventories small is that inventory represents a temporary monetary investment. As such, the firm incurs an opportunity cost, which we call the cost of capital, arising from the money tied up in inventory that could be used for other purposes. The **inventory holding cost** (or *carrying cost*) is the sum of the cost of capital plus the variable costs of keeping items on hand, such as storage and handling costs and taxes, insurance, and shrinkage costs. When these components change with inventory levels, so does the holding cost.

Companies usually state an item's holding cost per period of time as a percent of its value. The annual cost to maintain one unit in inventory typically ranges from 15 to 35 percent of its value. Suppose that a firm's holding cost is 20 percent. If the average value of total inventory is 20 percent of sales, the average annual cost to hold inventory is 4 percent [0.20(0.20)] of total sales. This cost is sizable in terms of gross profit margins, which often are less than 10 percent. Thus, the components of holding cost create pressures for small inventories.

Cost of Capital   The cost of capital is the opportunity cost of investing in an asset relative to the expected return on assets of similar risk. Inventory is an asset; consequently, we should use a cost measure that adequately reflects the firm's approach to financing assets. Most firms use the *weighted average cost of capital (WACC)*, which is the average of the required return on a firm's stock equity and the interest rate on its debt, weighted by the proportion of equity and debt in its portfolio. The cost of capital usually is the largest component of holding cost, as high as 15 percent of inventory value, depending on the particular capitalization portfolio of the firm. Firms typically update the WACC on an annual basis because it is used to make many financial decisions.

Storage and Handling Costs   Inventory takes up space and must be moved into and out of storage. Storage and handling costs may be incurred when a firm rents space on either a long- or short-term basis. An inventory holding cost is incurred when a firm could use storage space productively in some other way.

Taxes, Insurance, and Shrinkage   More taxes are paid if end-of-year inventories are high, and the cost of insuring the inventories increases, too. Shrinkage takes three forms. The first, *pilferage*, or theft of inventory by customers or employees, is a significant percentage of

inventory

A stock of materials used to satisfy customer demand or to support the production of services or goods.

▲ FIGURE 9.4
Creation of Inventory

inventory holding cost

The sum of the cost of capital and the variable costs of keeping items on hand, such as storage and handling, taxes, insurance, and shrinkage.

---

[2] Nick Wingfield, "Amazon Vows to Avoid Mess of 1999 Christmas Rush: Too Many Kermit Phones," *Wall Street Journal* (September 25, 2000), p B1.

sales for some businesses. The second form of shrinkage, called *obsolescence*, occurs when inventory cannot be used or sold at full value, owing to model changes, engineering modifications, or unexpectedly low demand. Obsolescence is a big expense in the retail clothing industry. Drastic discounts on seasonal clothing frequently must be offered on many of these products at the end of a season. Finally, *deterioration* through physical spoilage or damage due to rough or excessive material handling results in lost value. Food and beverages, for example, lose value and might even have to be discarded when their shelf life is reached. When the rate of deterioration is high, building large inventories may be unwise.

Pressures for Large Inventories

Given the costs of holding inventory, why not eliminate it altogether? Let us look briefly at the pressures related to maintaining large inventories.

Customer Service Creating inventory can speed delivery and improve the firm's on-time delivery of goods. High inventory levels reduce the potential for stockouts and backorders, which are key concerns of wholesalers and retailers. A **stockout** is an order that cannot be satisfied, resulting in loss of the sale. A **backorder** is a customer order that cannot be filled when promised or demanded but is filled later. Customers do not like waiting for backorders to be filled. Many of them will take their business elsewhere. Sometimes, customers are given discounts for the inconvenience of waiting.

Ordering Cost Each time a firm places a new order, it incurs an **ordering cost**, or the cost of preparing a purchase order for a supplier or a production order for manufacturing.

Trains offer an economical way to transport large quantities of goods. The savings in shipping large quantities may offset the added costs of holding more inventory.

stockout
An order that cannot be satisfied, resulting in a loss of the sale.

backorder
A customer order that cannot be filled when promised or demanded but is filled later.

ordering cost
The cost of preparing a purchase order for a supplier or a production order for manufacturing.

setup cost
The cost involved in changing over a machine or workspace to produce a different item.

For the same item, the ordering cost is the same, regardless of the order size. The purchasing agent must take the time to decide how much to order and, perhaps, select a supplier and negotiate terms. Time also is spent on paperwork, follow-up, and receiving the item(s). In the case of a production order for a manufactured item, a blueprint and routing instructions often must accompany the order. However, the Internet streamlines the order process and reduces the costs of placing orders.

Setup Cost The cost involved in changing over a machine or workspace to produce a different item is the **setup cost**. It includes labor and time to make the changeover, cleaning, and sometimes new tools or equipment. Scrap or rework costs are also higher at the start of the production run. Setup cost also is independent of order size, which creates pressure to make or order a large supply of the items and hold them in inventory rather than order smaller batches.

Labor and Equipment Utilization By creating more inventory, management can increase workforce productivity and facility utilization in three ways. First, placing larger, less frequent production orders reduces the number of unproductive setups, which add no value to a service or product. Second, holding inventory reduces the chance of the costly rescheduling of production orders because the components needed to make the product are not in inventory. Third, building inventories improves resource utilization by stabilizing the output rate when demand is cyclical or seasonal. The firm uses inventory built during slack periods to handle extra demand in peak seasons. This approach minimizes the need for extra shifts, hiring, layoffs, overtime, and additional equipment.

Transportation Cost Sometimes, outbound transportation cost can be reduced by increasing inventory levels. Having inventory on hand allows more full carload shipments to be made and minimizes the need to expedite shipments by more expensive modes of transportation. Inbound transportation costs can also be reduced by creating more inventory. Sometimes, several items are ordered from the same supplier. Placing these orders at the same time will increase inventories because some items will be ordered before they are actually needed; nonetheless, it may lead to rate discounts, thereby decreasing the costs of transportation and raw materials.

Payments to Suppliers   A firm often can reduce total payments to suppliers if it can tolerate higher inventory levels. Suppose that a firm learns that a key supplier is about to increase its prices. In this case, it might be cheaper for the firm to order a larger quantity than usual—in effect delaying the price increase—even though inventory will increase temporarily. A firm can also take advantage of quantity discounts this way. A **quantity discount**, whereby the price per unit drops when the order is sufficiently large, is an incentive to order larger quantities. Supplement D, "Special Inventory Models," shows how to determine order quantities in such a situation.

quantity discount

A drop in the price per unit when an order is sufficiently large.

Types of Inventory

Inventory exists in three aggregate categories that are useful for accounting purposes. **Raw materials (RM)** are the inventories needed for the production of services or goods. They are considered to be inputs to the transformation processes of the firm. **Work-in-process (WIP)** consists of items, such as components or assemblies, needed to produce a final product in manufacturing. WIP is also present in some service operations, such as repair shops, restaurants, check-processing centers, and package delivery services. **Finished goods (FG)** in manufacturing plants, warehouses, and retail outlets are the items sold to the firm's customers. The finished goods of one firm may actually be the raw materials for another.

Figure 9.5 shows how inventory can be held in different forms and at various stocking points. In this example, raw materials—the finished goods of the supplier—are held both by the supplier and the manufacturer. Raw materials at the plant pass through one or more processes, which transform them into various levels of WIP inventory. Final processing of this inventory yields finished goods inventory. Finished goods can be held at the plant, the distribution center (which may be a warehouse owned by the manufacturer or the retailer), and retail locations.

Another perspective on inventory is to classify it by how it is created. In this context, inventory takes four forms: (1) cycle, (2) safety stock, (3) anticipation, and (4) pipeline. They cannot be identified physically; that is, an inventory manager cannot look at a pile of widgets and identify which ones are cycle inventory and which ones are safety stock inventory. However, conceptually, each of the four types comes into being in an entirely different way. Once you understand these differences, you can prescribe different ways to reduce inventory, which we discuss in the next section.

raw materials (RM)

The inventories needed for the production of services or goods.

work-in-process (WIP)

Items, such as components or assemblies, needed to produce a final product in manufacturing.

finished goods (FG)

The items in manufacturing plants, warehouses, and retail outlets that are sold to the firm's customers.

Raw materials — Supplier | Work-in-process — Finished goods — Manufacturing plant | Distribution center | Retailer

▲ FIGURE 9.5
Inventory at SuccessiveStocking Points

cycle inventory

The portion of total inventory that varies directly with lot size.

Cycle Inventory   The portion of total inventory that varies directly with lot size is called **cycle inventory**. Determining how frequently to order, and in what quantity, is called **lot sizing**. Two principles apply.

1. The lot size, Q, varies directly with the elapsed time (or cycle) between orders. If a lot is ordered every 5 weeks, the average lot size must equal 5 weeks' demand.

2. The longer the time between orders for a given item, the greater the cycle inventory must be.

At the beginning of the interval, the cycle inventory is at its maximum, or Q. At the end of the interval, just before a new lot arrives, cycle inventory drops to its minimum, or 0. The average cycle inventory is the average of these two extremes:

$$\text{Average cycle inventory} = \frac{Q + 0}{2} = \frac{Q}{2}$$

This formula is exact only when the demand rate is constant and uniform. However, it does provide a reasonably good estimate even when demand rates are not constant. Factors other than the demand rate (e.g., scrap losses) also may cause estimating errors when this simple formula is used.

lot sizing

The determination of how frequently and in what quantity to order inventory.

Safety Stock Inventory   To avoid customer service problems and the hidden costs of unavailable components, companies hold safety stock. **Safety stock inventory** is surplus inventory that protects against uncertainties in demand, lead time, and supply changes. Safety stocks are desirable when suppliers fail to deliver either the desired quantity on the

safety stock inventory

Surplus inventory that a company holds to protect against uncertainties in demand, lead time, and supply changes.

specified date or items of acceptable quality, or when manufactured items require significant amounts of scrap or rework. Safety stock inventory ensures that operations are not disrupted when such problems occur, allowing subsequent operations to continue.

To create safety stock, a firm places an order for delivery earlier than when the item is typically needed.[3] The replenishment order therefore arrives ahead of time, giving a cushion against uncertainty. For example, suppose that the average lead time from a supplier is 3 weeks but a firm orders 5 weeks in advance just to be safe. This policy creates a safety stock equal to a 2 weeks' supply (5–3).

Anticipation Inventory Inventory used to absorb uneven rates of demand or supply, which businesses often face, is referred to as **anticipation inventory**. Predictable, seasonal demand patterns lend themselves to the use of anticipation inventory. Uneven demand can motivate a manufacturer to stockpile anticipation inventory during periods of low demand so that output levels do not have to be increased much when demand peaks. Anticipation inventory also can help when suppliers are threatened with a strike or have severe capacity limitations.

anticipation inventory

Inventory used to absorb uneven rates of demand or supply.

Pipeline Inventory Inventory that is created when an order for an item is issued but not yet placed in inventory is called **pipeline inventory**. It exists in the form of materials that move from suppliers to a plant, from one operation to the next in the plant, from the plant to a distribution center or customer, or from the distribution center to a retailer. Longer lead times or higher demands per week create more pipeline inventory. As such, pipeline inventory between two stocking points, for either distribution or work-in-process, can be measured as the average demand during lead time, $\bar{D}_L$, which is the average demand for the item per period ($\bar{d}$) times the number of periods in the item's lead time (L) to move between the two points, or

pipeline inventory

Inventory that is created when an order for an item is issued but not yet placed in inventory.

$$\text{Pipeline inventory} = \bar{D}_L = \bar{d}L$$

The equation assumes that both $\bar{d}$ and L are constants and that L is not affected by the order or lot size, Q. Changing an item's lot size does not directly affect the average level of the pipeline inventory. Nonetheless, the lot size can *indirectly* affect pipeline inventory if it is related to the lead time. In such a case, pipeline inventory will change depending on the relationship of L to Q. Example 9.1 shows how this can happen.

EXAMPLE 9.1	Estimating Inventory Levels

Tutor 9.1 in my**om**lab provides a new example to practice the estimation of inventory levels.

A plant makes monthly shipments of electric drills to a wholesaler in average lot sizes of 280 drills. The wholesaler's average demand is 70 drills a week, and the lead time from the plant is 3 weeks. The wholesaler must pay for the inventory from the moment the plant makes a shipment. If the wholesaler is willing to increase its purchase quantity to 350 units, the plant will give priority to the wholesaler and guarantee a lead time of only 2 weeks. What is the effect on the wholesaler's cycle and pipeline inventories?

SOLUTION

The wholesaler's current cycle and pipeline inventories are

$$\text{Cycle inventory} = \frac{Q}{2} = \frac{280}{2} = 140 \text{ drills}$$

$$\text{Pipeline inventory} = \bar{D}_L = \bar{d}L = (70 \text{ drills/week})(3 \text{ weeks}) = 210 \text{ drills}$$

Figure 9.6 shows the cycle and pipeline inventories if the wholesaler accepts the new proposal.

FIGURE 9.6 ▶

Estimating Inventory Levels for Cycle and Pipeline Inventories Using Tutor 9.1

1. Enter the average lot size, average demand during a period, and the number of periods of lead time:

Average lot size	350
Average demand	70
Lead time	2

2. To compute cycle inventory, simply divide average lot size by 2. To compute pipeline inventory, multiply average demand by lead time:

Cycle inventory	175
Pipeline inventory	140

[3] When orders are placed at fixed intervals, a second way to create safety stock is used. Each new order placed is larger than the quantity typically needed through the next delivery date.

DECISION POINT

The effect of the new proposal on cycle inventories is to increase them by 35 units, or 25 percent. The reduction in pipeline inventories, however, is 70 units, or 33 percent. The proposal would reduce the total investment in cycle and pipeline inventories. Also, it is advantageous to have shorter lead times because the wholesaler only has to commit to purchases 2 weeks in advance, rather than 3 weeks.

Inventory Reduction Tactics

Managers always are eager to find cost-effective ways to reduce inventory in supply chains. In Chapter 12, we examine various ways for finding optimal lot sizes. Here, we discuss something more fundamental—the basic tactics (which we call *levers*) for reducing inventory in supply chains. A primary lever is one that must be activated if inventory is to be reduced. A secondary lever reduces the penalty cost of applying the primary lever and the need for having inventory in the first place.

Cycle Inventory   The primary lever to reduce cycle inventory is simply to reduce the lot sizes of items moving in the supply chain. However, making such reductions in Q without making any other changes can be devastating. For example, setup costs or ordering costs can skyrocket. If these changes occur, two secondary levers can be used:

1. Streamline the methods for placing orders and making setups in order to reduce ordering and setup costs and allow Q to be reduced. This may involve redesigning the infrastructure for information flows or improving manufacturing processes.

2. Increase repeatability to eliminate the need for changeovers. **Repeatability** is the degree to which the same work can be done again. Repeatability can be increased through high product demand; the use of specialization; the devotion of resources exclusively to a product; the use of the same part in many different products; the use of *flexible automation*; the use of the *one-worker, multiple-machines* concept; or through *group technology*. Increased repeatability may justify new setup methods, reduce transportation costs, and allow quantity discounts from suppliers.

repeatability

The degree to which the same work can be done again.

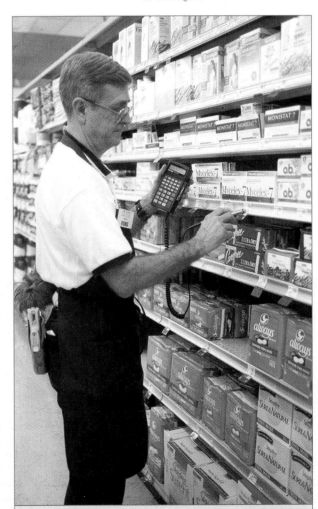

Safety Stock Inventory   The primary lever to reduce safety stock inventory is to place orders closer to the time when they must be received. However, this approach can lead to unacceptable customer service unless demand, supply, and delivery uncertainties can be minimized. Four secondary levers can be used in this case:

1. Improve demand forecasts so that fewer surprises come from customers. Design the mechanisms to increase collaboration with customers to get advanced warnings for changes in demand levels.

2. Cut the lead times of purchased or produced items to reduce demand uncertainty. For example, local suppliers with short lead times could be selected whenever possible.

3. Reduce supply uncertainties. Suppliers are likely to be more reliable if production plans are shared with them. Put in place the mechanisms to increase collaboration with suppliers. Surprises from unexpected scrap or rework can be reduced by improving manufacturing processes. Preventive maintenance can minimize unexpected downtime caused by equipment failure.

4. Rely more on equipment and labor buffers, such as capacity cushions and cross-trained workers. These buffers are important to businesses in the service sector because they generally cannot inventory their services.

Anticipation Inventory   The primary lever to reduce anticipation inventory is simply to match demand rate with production rate. Secondary levers can be used to even out customer demand in one of the following ways:

1. Add new products with different demand cycles so that a peak in the demand for one product compensates for the seasonal low for another.

Achieving good performance in supply chains begins with knowing how much inventory you have on hand, which may require changes to the infrastructure. Here a grocer uses a handheld scanner to check inventories and signal the need for replenishment from suppliers.

2. Provide off-season promotional campaigns.

3. Offer seasonal pricing plans.

Pipeline Inventory An operations manager has direct control over lead times but not demand rates. Because pipeline inventory is a function of demand during the lead time, the primary lever is to reduce the lead time. Two secondary levers can help managers cut lead times:

1. Find more responsive suppliers and select new carriers for shipments between stocking locations or improve materials handling within the plant. Improving the information system could overcome information delays between a distribution center and retailer.

2. Change Q in those cases where the lead time depends on the lot size.

Inventory Placement

A fundamental supply chain design decision that affects performance is where to locate an inventory of finished goods. Placing inventories can have strategic implications, as in the case of international companies locating *distribution centers* (DCs) in foreign countries to preempt local competition by reducing customer delivery times. However, the issue for any firm producing standardized products is where to position the inventory in the supply chain. At one extreme, the firm could use **centralized placement**, which means keeping all the inventory of a product at a single location, such as a firm's manufacturing plant or a warehouse, and shipping directly to each of its customers. The advantage would come from what is referred to as **inventory pooling**, which is a reduction in inventory and safety stock because of the merging of uncertain and variable demands from the customers. A higher-than-expected demand from one customer can be offset by a lower-than-expected demand from another so that the total demand remains fairly stable. We discuss the methods for determining the proper amount of safety stock in Chapter 12, "Managing Inventories." A disadvantage of placing inventory at a central location, however, is the added cost of shipping smaller, uneconomical quantities directly to customers over long distances.

Another approach is to use **forward placement**, which means locating stock closer to customers at a warehouse, DC, wholesaler, or retailer. Forward placement can have two advantages—faster delivery times and reduced transportation costs—that can stimulate sales. However, as inventory is placed closer to the customer, such as at a DC, the pooling effect of the inventories is reduced because safety stocks for the item must increase to take care of uncertain demands at each DC, rather than just a single location. Nonetheless, the time to get the product to the customer is reduced. Consequently, service to the customer is quicker, and the firm can take advantage of larger, less costly shipments to the DCs from the manufacturing plant, at the expense of larger overall inventories.

MEASURES OF SUPPLY CHAIN PERFORMANCE

Managers need performance measures to assess the implications of changes to a supply chain. Before discussing the major supply chain design decisions, we define the typical inventory measures and financial measures used to monitor supply chain performance and evaluate alternative supply chain designs.

Inventory Measures

All methods of measuring inventory begin with a physical count of units, volume, or weight. However, measures of inventories are reported in three basic ways: (1) average aggregate inventory value, (2) weeks of supply, and (3) inventory turnover.

The **average aggregate inventory value** is the total average value of all items held in inventory by a firm. We express the dollar values in this inventory measure at cost because we can then sum the values of individual items in raw materials, work-in-process, and finished goods. Final sales dollars have meaning only for final services or products and cannot be used for all inventory items. It is an average because it usually represents the inventory investment over some period of time. Suppose a retailer holds items A and B in stock. One unit of item A may be worth only a few dollars, whereas one unit of item B may be valued in the hundreds of dollars because of the labor, technology, and other value-added operations performed in manufacturing the product. This measure for an inventory consisting of only items A and B is

$$\begin{array}{c}\text{Average aggregate}\\\text{inventory value}\end{array} = \left(\begin{array}{c}\text{Number units of item A}\\\text{typically on hand}\end{array}\right)\left(\begin{array}{c}\text{Value of each}\\\text{unit of item A}\end{array}\right) + \left(\begin{array}{c}\text{Number of units of item B}\\\text{typically on hand}\end{array}\right)\left(\begin{array}{c}\text{Value of each}\\\text{unit of item B}\end{array}\right)$$

Summed over all items in an inventory, this total value tells managers how much of a firm's assets are tied up in inventory. Manufacturing firms typically have about 25 percent of their total assets in inventory, whereas wholesalers and retailers average about 75 percent.

To some extent, managers can decide whether the aggregate inventory value is too low or too high by historical or industry comparisons or by managerial judgment. However, a better performance measure would take demand into account because it would show how long the inventory resides in the firm. **Weeks of supply** is an inventory measure obtained by dividing the average aggregate inventory value by sales per week at cost. (In some low-inventory operations, days or even hours are a better unit of time for measuring inventory.) The formula (expressed in weeks) is

$$\text{Weeks of supply} = \frac{\text{Average aggregate inventory value}}{\text{Weekly sales (at cost)}}$$

Although the numerator includes the value of all items a firm holds in inventory (raw materials, WIP, and finished goods), the denominator represents only the finished goods sold—at cost rather than the sale price after markups or discounts. This cost is referred to as the *cost of goods sold*.

Inventory turnover (or *turns*) is an inventory measure obtained by dividing annual sales at cost by the average aggregate inventory value maintained during the year, or

$$\text{Inventory turnover} = \frac{\text{Annual sales (at cost)}}{\text{Average aggregate inventory value}}$$

The "best" inventory level, even when expressed as turnover, cannot be determined easily. A good starting point is to benchmark the leading firms in an industry.

weeks of supply

An inventory measure obtained by dividing the average aggregate inventory value by sales per week at cost.

inventory turnover

An inventory measure obtained by dividing annual sales at cost by the average aggregate inventory value maintained during the year.

EXAMPLE 9.2	**Calculating Inventory Measures**

The Eagle Machine Company averaged $2 million in inventory last year, and the cost of goods sold was $10 million. Figure 9.7 shows the breakout of raw materials, work-in-process, and finished goods inventories. The best inventory turnover in the company's industry is six turns per year. If the company has 52 business weeks per year, how many weeks of supply were held in inventory? What was the inventory turnover? What should the company do?

Tutor 9.2 in my**om**lab provides a new example to practice the calculation of inventory measures.

◀ **FIGURE 9.7**
Calculating Inventory Measures Using
Inventory Estimator Solver

| | Cost of Goods Sold | | $10,000,000 | | |
| Weeks of Operation | | 52 | | |

	Item Number	Average Level	Unit Value	Total Value
Raw Materials	1	1,400	$50.00	$70,000
	2	1,000	$32.00	$32,000
	3	400	$60.00	$24,000
	4	2,400	$10.00	$24,000
	5	800	$15.00	$12,000
Work in Process	6	320	$700.00	$224,000
	7	160	$900.00	$144,000
	8	280	$750.00	$210,000
	9	240	$800.00	$192,000
	10	400	$1,000.00	$400,000
Finished Goods	11	60	$2,000.00	$120,000
	12	40	$3,500.00	$140,000
	13	50	$2,800.00	$140,000
	14	20	$5,000.00	$100,000
	15	40	$4,200.00	$168,000
Total				$2,000,000

Average Weekly Sales at Cost	$192,308
Weeks of Supply	10.4
Inventory Turnover	5.0

SOLUTION

The average aggregate inventory value of $2 million translates into 10.4 weeks of supply and 5 turns per year, calculated as follows:

$$\text{Weeks of supply} = \frac{\$2 \text{ million}}{(\$10 \text{ million})/(52 \text{ weeks})} = 10.4 \text{ weeks}$$

$$\text{Inventory turns} = \frac{\$10 \text{ million}}{\$2 \text{ million}} = 5 \text{ turns/year}$$

DECISION POINT

The analysis indicates that management must improve the inventory turns by 20 percent. Management should improve its order fulfillment process to reduce finished goods inventory. Supply chain operations can also be improved to reduce the need to have so much raw materials and work-in-process inventory stock. It will take an inventory reduction of about 16 percent to achieve the target of 6 turns per year. However, inventories would not have to be reduced as much if sales increased. If the sales department targets an increase in sales of 8 percent ($10.8 million), inventories need only be reduced by 10 percent ($1.8 million) to get 6 turns a year. Management can now do sensitivity analyses to see what effect reductions in the inventory of specific items or increases in the annual sales have on weeks of supply or inventory turns.

Financial Measures

How the supply chain is designed and managed has a huge financial impact on the firm. Inventory is an investment because it is needed for future use. However, inventory ties up funds that might be used more profitably in other operations. Figure 9.8 shows how supply chain decisions can affect financial measures.

Total Revenue   Supply chain performance measures related to time, which is a critical dimension of supply chain operations, have financial implications. Many service providers and manufacturers measure the percent of on-time deliveries of their services or product to their customers, as well as services and materials from their suppliers. Increasing the percent of on-time deliveries to customers, for example, will increase *total revenue* because satisfied customers will buy more services and products from the firm.

Cost of Goods Sold   Being able to buy materials or services at a better price and transform them more efficiently into services or products will improve a firm's *cost of goods sold* measure and ultimately its *net income*. These improvements will also have an effect on *contribution margin*, which is the difference between price and the variable costs to produce a service or good. Reducing production, material, transportation, and poor quality costs increases the contribution margin, allowing for greater profits. Contribution margins are often used as inputs to decisions regarding the portfolio of services or products the firm offers.

Operating Expenses   Selling expenses, fixed expenses, and depreciation are considered operating expenses. Designing a supply chain with minimal capital investment can reduce depreciation charges. Changes to the supply chain infrastructure can have an effect on overhead, which is considered a fixed expense.

Cash Flow   The supply chain design can improve positive net cash flows by focusing on reducing lead times and backlogs of orders. The Internet brings another financial measure related to cash flows to the forefront: *Cash-to-cash* is the time lag between paying for the services and materials needed to produce a service or product and receiving payment for it. The shorter the time lag, the better the *cash flow* position of the firm because it needs less working capital. The firm can then use the freed-up funds for other projects or investments. Redesigning the order placement process, so that payment for the service or product by the customer is made at the time the order is placed, can reduce the time lag. By contrast, billing the customer after the service is performed or the order is shipped increases the need for working capital. The goal is to have a negative cash-to-cash situation, which is possible when the customer pays for the service or product before the firm

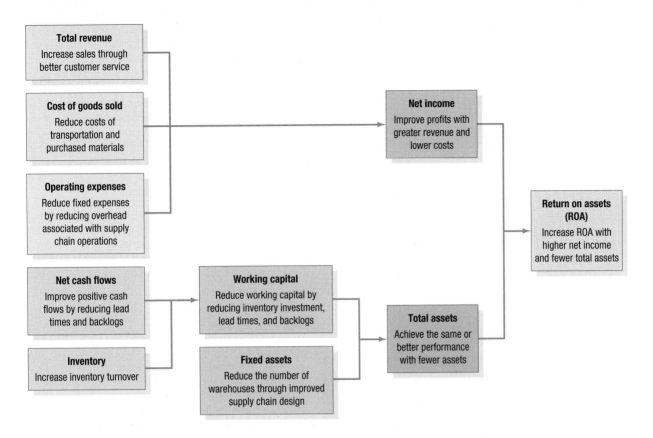

▲ FIGURE 9.8
How Supply Chain Decisions Can Affect ROA

has to pay for the resources and materials needed to produce it. In such a case, the firm must have supplier inventories on consignment, which allows it to pay for materials as it uses them.

Working Capital   Weeks of inventory and inventory turns are reflected in another financial measure, *working capital*, which is money used to finance ongoing operations. Decreasing weeks of supply or increasing inventory turns reduces the working capital needed to finance inventories. Reductions in working capital can be accomplished by improving the customer relationship, order fulfillment, or supplier relationship processes. For example, reducing supplier lead times has the effect of reducing weeks of supply and increasing inventory turns. Matching the input and output flows of materials is easier because shorter-range, more reliable forecasts of demand can be used.

Return on Assets   Designing and managing the supply chain so as to reduce the aggregate inventory investment or fixed investments such as warehouses will reduce the *total assets* portion of the firm's balance sheet. An important financial measure is *return on assets* (*ROA*), which is net income divided by total assets. Consequently, reducing aggregate inventory investment and fixed investments, or increasing net income by better cost management, will increase ROA. Techniques for reducing inventory, transportation, and operating costs related to resource usage and scheduling are discussed in the chapters to follow.

We now turn to a discussion of several major supply chain design decisions and their implications for a firm's performance.

MASS CUSTOMIZATION

A firm's supply chain must be capable of addressing certain competitive priorities that will win orders from customers. Often customers want more than a wide selection of standard services or products; they want a personalized service or product and they want it fast. For example, suppose you want to paint your living room a new color. You need to complement all of the existing furnishings, wall decorations, and carpet. You go to your local paint retail store and select a color from a stack of books that spans every color of the rainbow. The store can give you all the paint you need in your selected color while you wait. How can the store provide that service economically? Certainly the store cannot stock thousands of colors in sufficient quantities for any job. The store stocks the base colors and pigments separately and mixes them as needed, thereby supplying an unlimited variety of colors without maintaining the inventory required to match each customer's particular color needs. The paint retailer is practicing a strategy known as *mass customization*, whereby a firm's highly divergent processes generate a wide variety of customized services or products at reasonably low costs. Essentially, the firm allows customers to select from a variety of standard options to create the service or product of their choice.

Competitive Advantages

A mass customization strategy has three important competitive advantages.[4]

- *Managing Customer Relationships.* Mass customization requires detailed inputs from customers so that the ideal service or product can be produced. The firm can learn a lot about its customers from the data it receives. Once customers are in the database, the firm can keep track of them over time. A significant competitive advantage is realized through these close customer relationships based on a strategy of mass customization.

- *Eliminate Finished Goods Inventory.* Producing to a customer's order is more efficient than producing to a forecast because forecasts are not perfect. The trick is to have everything you need to produce the order quickly. A technology some firms use for their order placement process is a software system called a *configurator*, which gives firms and customers easy access to data relevant to the options available for the service or product. Dell uses a configurator that allows customers to design their own computer from a set of standard components that are in stock. Once the order is placed, the product is assembled and then delivered. Using sales promotions, the firm can exercise some control over the requirements for the inventory of components by steering customers away from options that are out of stock in favor of options that are in stock. This capability takes pressure off the supply chain while keeping the customer satisfied.

  Service providers also take advantage of mass customization to reduce the level of inventory. British Airways is trying to personalize the service of customers once they are on board. It has a software system that tracks the preferences of its most favored customers down to the magazines they read. This information allows the airline to more accurately plan what to pack on each flight. This information saves the airline a significant amount of money because it does not pack amenities passengers do not want.

- *Increase Perceived Value of Services or Products.* With mass customization, customers can have it their way. In general, mass customization often has a higher value in the mind of the customer than it actually costs to produce. This perception allows firms to charge prices that provide a nice margin.

At MyTwinn doll company, kids can create their own doll online. Artisans can even match the doll face to the child's face from a photo you supply. MyTwinn continues to market clothing accessories as the doll "grows up" with its human twin.

Supply Chain Design for Mass Customization

How does mass customization affect the design of supply chains? We address three major considerations.

---

[4] Laurie J. Flynn, "Built to Order," *Knowledge Management* (December 11, 2000), www.destinationkm.com.

Assemble to Order Strategy   The underlying process design is an assemble-to-order strategy. This strategy involves two stages in the provision of the service or product. Initially, standardized components are produced or purchased and held in stock. This stage is important because it enables the firm to produce or purchase these standard items in large volumes to keep the costs low. In the second stage the firm assembles these standard components to a specific customer order. In mass customization, this stage must be flexible to handle a large number of potential combinations, and be capable of producing the order quickly and accurately. For example, for My Twinn customized dolls, customers can choose from more than 325,000 different doll combinations. To ensure accuracy, the Web site takes the customer through the required choices and allows the customer to see the doll as the various options are chosen. Managerial Practice 9.1 shows how Lands' End implemented mass customization and how computer and process technology played a big role.

Modular Design   The service or product must have a modular design that enables the "customization" the customer desires. This approach requires careful attention to service/product designs so that the final service or product can be assembled from a set of standardized modules economically and fast in response to a customer order.

Postponement   Finally, successful mass customizers postpone the task of differentiating a service or product for a specific customer until the last possible moment. *Postponement* is a concept whereby some of the final activities in the provision of a service or product are delayed until the orders are received. Doing so allows the greatest application of standard modules before specific customization is done. Postponement is a key decision because it specifies where in the supply chain volume-oriented, standardized operations are separated from custom-oriented, assembly operations. Sometimes the final customization occurs in the last step. For example, if you wanted to buy a personal computer directly from Dell, Dell would postpone the assembly of your computer until it receives your order specifying the exact configuration you want. Dell would assemble your computer out of standardized components, which are produced in volume by suppliers, even though your computer is personalized to your specifications. Alternatively, you can buy a standardized model of a Dell computer at retail stores such as Best Buy, Staples, or Wal-Mart.

MANAGERIAL PRACTICE 9.1	Mass Customization at Lands' End

Have you ever felt that your jeans could use a little more room here, and little less room there, or be a little shorter or a little longer? Have you ever wondered what a pair of jeans made for your body would feel like? If so, Lands' End, a subsidiary of Sears, is looking for you. Here is how you can get a customized pair of jeans. You complete a brief online profile by answering a few simple questions regarding things such as height, weight, shoe size, and several other body shape details and exercise habits—nothing requiring complicated measurements. Your information is used by a sophisticated program from Archetype Solutions, Inc., to create a mathematical model of your body. The reason that you do not have to give a lot of data about your body is that the system makes use of a massive database of more than 5 million detailed sets of body measurements to calculate all of the other measurements needed for your jeans. You also select pocket options, fit styles, and colors. Click "Submit" and in two to three weeks you can expect your jeans to be delivered to your home. One more thing—you need to pay. Expect to spend $20 to $30 *more* than the standard version of your jeans.

Your part in the process is quite simple. However, behind the scenes it is quite different. Lands' End decided to try to mass customize jeans and chino slacks just to garner publicity and increase the sales of its other products. What a surprise when management discovered that online sales of customized chinos well exceeded projections and that 25 percent of new customers purchased customized clothing. How does mass customization work at Lands' End? Each night Lands' End gathers orders posted on its Web site and electronically sends them to Archetype, where the software replicates the customer's body size and weight distribution, factors in individual fit preferences, and adjusts the basic fabric patterns accordingly. The files are then sent to a contract manufacturer in Mexico. The supplier, using standard materials, transfers the individual patterns to numerically controlled cutting equipment that cuts one layer of fabric at a time. After the various pieces of the pants have been cut, they are bagged and moved to an eight-machine sewing process, where the pants flow through one at a time. The last station in the process checks five critical measurements on each pair of pants. If any are incorrect, the pants are scrapped and remade. The garments are bulk shipped to a distribution center to clear U.S. customs, and then sorted, packaged, and mailed directly to customers.

Success did not come without some headaches, however. Lands' End had to train its Mexican manufacturing partners, which had to switch to new machinery. The new manufacturing process is far different than producing mass quantities, which relied on batch processing. Nonetheless, the mass customization strategy is proving to be profitable. Lands' End is expanding the strategy to dress shirts and tailored pants with partners in the Dominican Republic and expanding jeans and chino capacity in the Far East.

Sources: David Drickhammer, "A Leg Up on Mass Customization," *Industry Week* (September 1, 2002); Anne D'Innocenzio, "Lands' End Adds More Size Options Online," *The Mercury News* (September 9, 2002); www.landsend.com (2008).

channel assembly

The process of using members of the distribution channel as if they were assembly stations in the factory.

The assemble-to-order strategy can be extended to supply chains. The costs of inventory and transportation often determine the extent to which a manufacturer uses postponement in the supply chain. With postponement, manufacturers can avoid inventory buildup. Some firms take advantage of a process called **channel assembly**, whereby members of the distribution channel act as if they were assembly stations in the factory. Distribution centers or warehouses can perform the last-minute customizing operations after specific orders have been received. This approach is particularly useful when the required customizing has some geographical rationale, such as language differences or technical requirements. Hewlett-Packard provides a good example. Hewlett-Packard postpones the assembly of its printers needing a country-specific power supply and a language-specific user's manual until the last step in the process, which is performed by the distributor in the region where the printer is being delivered. In general, beyond the inventory advantages, the advantage of postponement in the distribution channel is that the firm's plants can focus on the standardized aspects of the product, while the distributor can focus on customizing a product that may require additional components from local suppliers.

Outsourcing Processes

outsourcing

Paying suppliers and distributors to perform processes and provide needed services and materials.

make-or-buy decision

A managerial choice between whether to outsource a process or do it in-house.

All businesses buy at least some inputs to their processes (such as professional services, raw materials, or manufactured parts) from other producers. Most businesses also purchase services to get their products to their customers. How many of the processes that produce those purchased items and services should a firm own and operate instead? The answer to that question determines the extent of the firm's vertical integration. The more processes in the value chain that the organization performs itself, the more vertically integrated it is. If it does not perform some processes itself, it must rely on **outsourcing**, or paying suppliers and distributors to perform those processes and provide needed services and materials. When managers opt for more vertical integration, by definition less outsourcing occurs. These decisions are sometimes called **make-or-buy decisions**, with a *make* decision meaning more vertical integration and a *buy* decision meaning more outsourcing. After deciding what to outsource and what to do in-house, management must find ways to coordinate and integrate the various processes and suppliers involved. Example 9.3 shows how break-even analysis, which can be found in Supplement A, "Decision Making Models," can be used for the make-or-buy decision.

EXAMPLE 9.3	**Using Break-Even Analysis for the Outsourcing Decision**

Active Model A.2 in my**om**lab provides additional insight on the make-or-buy decision and its extensions.

Thompson manufacturing produces industrial scales for the electronics industry. Management is considering outsourcing the shipping operation to a logistics provider experienced in the electronics industry. Thompson's annual fixed costs of the shipping operation are $1,500,000, which includes costs of the equipment and infrastructure for the operation. The estimated variable cost of shipping the scales with the in-house operation is $4.50 per ton-mile. If Thompson outsourced the operation to Carter Trucking, the annual fixed costs of the infrastructure and management time needed to manage the contract would be $250,000. Carter would charge $8.50 per ton-mile. What is the break-even quantity?

SOLUTION

From Supplement A, "Decision Making Models," the formula for the break-even quantity yields

Tutor A.2 in my**om**lab provides a new example to practice break-even analysis on make-or-buy decisions.

$$Q = \frac{F_m - F_b}{c_b - c_m}$$

$$= \frac{1,500,000 - 250,000}{8.50 - 4.50} = 312,500 \text{ ton-miles}$$

DECISION POINT

Thompson management must now assess how many ton-miles of product will likely be shipped now and in the future. If that estimate is less than 312,500 ton-miles, the best option is to outsource the operation to Carter Trucking.

Vertical Integration

Vertical integration can be in two directions. **Backward integration** represents a firm's movement upstream in the supply chain toward the sources of raw materials, parts, and services through acquisitions, such as a major grocery chain having its own plants to produce house brands of ice cream, frozen pizza dough, and peanut butter. Backward integration has the effect of reducing the risk of supply. **Forward integration** means that the firm acquires more channels of distribution, such as its own distribution centers (warehouses) and retail stores. It can also mean that the firm goes even farther by acquiring its business customers. A firm chooses vertical integration when it has the skills, volume, and resources to hit the competitive priorities better than outsiders can. Doing the work within its organizational structure may mean better quality and more timely delivery, as well as taking better advantage of the firm's human resources, equipment, and space. Extensive vertical integration is generally attractive when input volumes are high because high volumes allow task specialization and greater efficiency. It is also attractive if the firm has the relevant skills and views the processes that it is integrating as particularly important to its future success. However, care must be exercised that excessive vertical integration does not lead to a loss of focus for the firm in delivering value in its core business.

Management must identify, cultivate, and exploit its core competencies to prevail in global competition. Recall that core competencies are the collective learning of the firm, especially its ability for coordinating diverse processes and integrating multiple technologies. They define the firm and provide its reason for existence. Management must be constantly attentive to bolstering core competencies, perhaps by looking upstream toward its suppliers and downstream toward its customers and acquiring those processes that support its core competencies—those that allow the firm to organize work and deliver value better than its competitors. To do otherwise poses a risk that the firm will lose control over critical areas of its business.

Outsourcing

Notwithstanding the arguments in favor of increased vertical integration, many firms are outsourcing important processes. The NCNB bank in Charlotte, North Carolina, outsourced the processing of card transactions and saved $5 million per year. Merrill Lynch, Sears Roebuck, and Texaco outsource their mailroom and photocopying operations to Pitney Bowes Management Services. Many firms do the same with payroll, security, cleaning, and other types of services, rather than employ personnel to provide these services. Outsourcing is a particularly attractive option to those firms that have low volumes. For example, LoanCity.com, an online mortgage company, started life with zero revenue but planned to serve more than a million customers in a few years. Any online operation of that size would require a sprawling computing center, which in turn would require a few million dollars of hardware, software licenses, and a staff of as many as 20 specialists. Instead, the company hired an application service provider (ASP) to set up and run the various business-software packages needed to handle its sales, accounting, and human resource processes. LoanCity's employees then use the Internet to connect to the applications they need housed on machines located at the ASP.

What prompted these firms to outsource rather than vertically integrate? These firms realized that another firm can perform the outsourced process more efficiently and with better quality than they can. They opted to add external suppliers to their supply chains rather than to keep internal suppliers. However, the outsourcing decision is a serious one because the firm can lose the skills and knowledge needed to conduct the process. All learning about process advancements is left to the outsourcing partner, which makes it difficult to ever bring that process back into the firm.

The strategy of globalizing a firm adds a new dimension to the development of supply chains and the use of outsourcing. **Offshoring** is a supply chain strategy that involves moving processes to another country. As such, offshoring is more encompassing than outsourcing because it also includes vertical integration by locating internal processes in other countries. Firms are motivated to initiate operations offshore by the market potential and the cost advantages it provides. The firm may be able to create new markets because of its presence in other countries and its ability to offer competitive prices due to its cost efficiencies. Competitive priorities other than low costs, such as delivery speed to distant customers, can drive the decision, too.

Benefits to Outsourcing   As for costs, several factors drive the outsourcing strategy on an international scale.

- *Comparative Labor Costs.* Some countries have a huge edge when it comes to labor costs. Two countries with a major advantage are India and China. In India, the salary for

backward integration

A firm's movement upstream toward the sources of raw materials, parts, and services through acquisitions.

forward integration

Acquiring more channels of distribution, such as distribution centers (warehouses) and retail stores, or even business customers.

offshoring

A supply chain strategy that involves moving processes to another country.

a computer programmer is much less than that of a programmer in the United States with comparable skills. It is no wonder that firms award programming processes to firms in India. In China, the average monthly wages are less than 4 percent of those in Japan. In general, firms can save from 30 to 50 percent on labor costs by outsourcing processes to low labor-cost countries.

- *Logistics Costs.* Even if labor costs are not favorable, it may still be less costly to outsource or offshore processes to other countries to reduce the logistical costs of delivering products to international customers. For example, Hewlett-Packard outsourced the final assembly of a computer server to Singapore and Australia, two higher-cost locations, to get closer to targeted customers in Australia and Southeast Asia. The savings in logistical costs offset the higher labor costs in those countries.

- *Tariffs and Taxes.* Some countries offer tax incentives to firms that do business within their borders. Tariffs can also be a stumbling block for firms looking to do business in a country. Sometimes they are high enough that the firm decides to assemble the products in that country rather than export the products in. Hewlett-Packard decided to assemble a product in India with imported parts for sale to Indian customers for that reason.

- *Labor Laws and Unions.* Some countries have fewer unions or restrictions on the flexible use of labor. The ability to use workers to perform a number of different tasks without restrictions can be important to firms trying to achieve flexibility in operations and reduce costs. Nonetheless, firms must be cognizant of local labor laws and customs and strive to achieve a high level of ethical behavior when doing business in other countries.

- *Internet.* The Internet reduces the transaction costs of managing distant partners or operations.

Pitfalls to Outsourcing Even though outsourcing appears to offer some big advantages, it also has some pitfalls that firms should carefully explore before using this strategy.

A key consideration in designing global supply chains is to focus on the total cost of manufacturing and delivering the product to customers. Often reduced logistics costs offset higher manufacturing costs offshore. Here vessels loaded with containers berth at Singapore's Keppel Port, one of the world's most efficient, and busiest, sea ports.

- *Pulling the Plug Too Quickly.* A major mistake is to decide to outsource a process before making a good-faith effort to fix the existing one. We discussed many ways to improve processes in parts 1 and 2 of this text; these methods should be explored first. It is not always the case that outsourcing is the answer, even if local labor wages far exceed those of other countries. Canon, for example, decided to keep its manufacturing in Japan rather than shift it to lower-cost countries in Southeast Asia. The strategy is to compete on technology innovations via its line of high-end cameras. To achieve that strategy, Canon kept its new product development process and its manufacturing process close to each other to support speedy new product introductions and communication between engineers and manufacturing managers. Canon improved its manufacturing process by removing its assembly lines and replacing them with manufacturing cells, thereby improving teamwork, reducing its inventory and factory costs, and increasing its ability to make innovative products faster. The message: Make sure you really need to outsource in order to accomplish your operations strategy.

- *Technology Transfer.* Often an outsourcing strategy involves creating a *joint venture* with a company in another country. With a joint venture, two firms agree to jointly produce a service or product together. Typically a transfer of technology takes place to bring one partner up to speed regarding the service or product. The danger is that the firm with the technology advantage will essentially be setting up the other firm to be a future competitor. For example, GM set up a joint venture with the Shanghai Auto Industry Corporation (SAIC) to produce Buicks. SAIC got a license to use GM's technical know-how in the form of drawings, blueprints, math data, and computer files. As GM develops local engineering design capability, it transfers technical knowledge to the Chinese staff. Because SAIC is planning to develop and produce its own cars, it is possible that GM and other joint venture partners with SAIC are creating a new competitor in China.

- *Process Integration.* Despite the power of the Internet, it is difficult to fully integrate outsourced processes with the firm's other processes. Time, distance, and communication can be formidable hurdles, especially if the supplier is on the other side of the world. Managing offshore processes will not be the same as managing processes located next door. Often considerable managerial time must be expended to coordinate offshore processes. Managerial Practice 9.2 reveals outsourcing on a global scale can be challenging for management.

MANAGERIAL PRACTICE 9.2 — Building a Supply Chain for the Dreamliner

Suppose that you had the freedom to totally design the supply chain for one of the most highly anticipated airliners of modern times. The airliner, the Boeing 787 Dreamliner, is a super-efficient commercial airplane that can carry up to 300 passengers on routes as long as 3,500 nautical miles at speeds up to 850 miles per hour. It will be constructed with carbon-fiber composite materials, which are lightweight and not susceptible to corrosion or fatigue like aluminum. This plane will be manufactured using 50 percent composite materials; Boeing used only 10 to 12 percent in the 777. Boeing's goal is to bring the most complex machine in mass production to market in just over 4 years, 2 years less time than other projects. Boeing had two options for the design of the supply chain: (1) Produce about 50 percent of the plane in-house, including the wing and fuselage as in existing Boeing planes, and run the risk that production lead times will suffer because of capacity constraints; or (2) outsource about 85 percent of the plane, essentially only constructing the vertical fin in-house, and manage the global suppliers responsible for design as well as production of major components. Boeing selected option 2.

There are some good reasons for this choice. First, a number of big customers for the 787, such as India and Japan, require that significant portions of the aircraft must be manufactured in their countries. Using major contractors within those countries satisfies the requirement. Second, a shortage of high-quality engineering talent also puts pressure on outsourcing. Third, the sheer complexity of the airplane makes it necessary to share the load. Boeing, even with all of its resources, could not build all of the components and pieces in one facility or region. Finally, work on the plane can proceed concurrently, rather than sequentially, thereby saving time and money. For example, the modular design of the plane allows Boeing to utilize flexible tooling to move planes through the factory much more quickly. The suppliers design and deliver the subsystems on a just-in-time basis where they are "snapped" together by a smaller number of factory workers in a matter of days rather than a month, the typical time for a plane of that complexity.

Boeing chose to design its supply chain with 43 top-tier suppliers on 3 continents. Outsourcing so much responsibility requires a lot of managerial attention; you have to know what is going on in each factory at all times. As expected with something so complex, major glitches popped up like

The first Boeing 787 Dreamliner takes shape in the final assembly plant in Everett, Washington. The new commercial airplane is assembled with major components produced worldwide.

gremlins. The first Dreamliner to show up at Boeing's factory was missing tens of thousands of parts. Supplier problems ranged from language barriers to problems caused by some contractors who outsourced major portions of their assigned work and then experienced problems with their suppliers. The first fuselage section, the big multi-part cylindrical barrel that encompasses the passenger seating area, failed in company testing, causing Boeing to make more sections than planned and to reexamine quality and safety concerns. Software programs designed by a variety of manufacturers had trouble talking to one another and the overall weight of the airplane was too high, especially the carbon-fiber wing. These and many other glitches caused major delays in the promised deliveries of the first 787s and which may result in penalties imposed by delivery contracts.

Will the advantages of collaboration on such a large scale outweigh the loss of logistical and design control? Boeing bets that it will; it has more than 760 orders for the Dreamliner.

Sources: Elizabeth Rennie, "Beyond Borders," *APICS Magazine* (March 2007), pp. 34–38; Stanley Holmes, "The 787 Encounters Turbulence," *Business Week* (June 19, 2006), pp. 38–40; J. Lynn Lunsford, "Boeing Scrambles to Repair Problems With New Plane," *The Wall Street Journal* (December 7, 2007), p. A1.

STRATEGIC IMPLICATIONS

A supply chain is, of course, a network of firms. Thus, each firm in the chain should design its own supply chains to support the competitive priorities of its services or products. Even though extensive technologies such as electronic data interchange (EDI), the Internet, computer-assisted design, flexible manufacturing, and automated warehousing have been applied to all stages of the supply chain, the performance of many supply chains remains dismal. A study of the U.S. food industry estimated that poor coordination among supply chain partners wastes $30 billion annually. One possible cause for failures is that managers do not understand the nature of the demand for their services or products and, therefore, cannot design supply chains to satisfy those demands. Two distinct designs used to competitive advantage are *efficient supply chains* and *responsive supply chains* (Fisher, 1997). Table 9.1 shows the environments that best suit each design.

Efficient Supply Chains

The nature of demand for the firm's services or products is a key factor in the best choice of supply chain strategy. Efficient supply chains work best in environments where demand is highly predictable, such as demand for staple items purchased at grocery stores or demand for a package delivery service. The focus of the supply chain is on efficient service, material, monetary, and information flows; and keeping inventories to a minimum. Because of the markets the firms serve, service or product designs last a long time, new introductions are infrequent, and variety is small. Such firms typically produce for markets in which price is crucial to winning an order. Contribution margins are low and efficiency is important. Consequently, the firm's competitive priorities are low-cost operations, consistent quality, and on-time delivery.

Responsive Supply Chains

Responsive supply chains are designed to react quickly in order to hedge against uncertainties in demand. They work best when firms offer a great variety of services or products and demand predictability is low. To stay competitive, firms in such a supply chain frequently introduce new services or products. Nonetheless, because of the innovativeness of their services or products, they enjoy high contribution margins. Typical competitive priorities are development speed, fast delivery times, customization, variety, volume flexibility, and top quality. The firms may not even know what services or products they need to provide until customers place orders. In addition, demand may be short-lived, as in the case of fashion goods. The focus of responsive supply chains is reaction time, which helps avoid keeping costly inventories that ultimately must be sold at deep discounts.

A firm may need to utilize both types of supply chains, especially when it focuses its operations on specific market segments or it can segment the supply chain to achieve two different requirements. For example, the supply chain for a standard product, such as an oil tanker, has different requirements than that for a customized product, such as a luxury liner, even though both are ocean-going vessels and both may be manufactured by the same company. You might also see elements of efficiency and responsiveness in the same supply chain. For example, Gillette uses an efficient supply chain to manufacture its products so that it can utilize a capital-intensive manufacturing process, and then it uses a responsive supply chain for the packaging and delivery processes to be responsive to retailers.

TABLE 9.1 | **ENVIRONMENTS BEST SUITED FOR EFFICIENT AND RESPONSIVE SUPPLY CHAINS**

Factor	Efficient Supply Chains	Responsive Supply Chains
Demand	Predictable, low forecast errors	Unpredictable, high forecast errors
Competitive priorities	Low cost, consistent quality, on-time delivery	Development speed, fast delivery times, customization, volume flexibility, variety, top quality
New-service/product introduction	Infrequent	Frequent
Contribution margins	Low	High
Product variety	Low	High

The packaging operation involves customization in the form of printing in different languages. Just as processes can be broken into parts, with different process structures for each, supply chain processes can be segmented to achieve optimal performance.

The Design of Efficient and Responsive Supply Chains

Table 9.2 contains the basic design features for efficient and responsive supply chains. The more downstream in an efficient supply chain that a firm is, the more likely it is to have a line-flow strategy that supports high volumes of standardized services or products. Consequently, suppliers in efficient supply chains should have low capacity cushions because high utilization keeps the cost per unit low. High inventory turns are desired because inventory investment must be kept low to achieve low costs. Firms should work with their suppliers to shorten lead times, but care must be taken to use tactics that do not appreciably increase costs. For example, lead times for a supplier could be shortened by switching from rail to air transportation; however, the added cost may offset the savings obtained from the shorter lead times. Suppliers should be selected with emphasis on low prices, consistent quality, and on-time delivery. Because of low capacity cushions, disruptions in an efficient supply chain can be costly and must be avoided.

By contrast, firms in a responsive supply chain should be flexible and have high capacity cushions. WIP inventories should be positioned in the chain to support delivery speed, but inventories of expensive finished goods should be avoided. Firms should aggressively work with their suppliers to shorten lead times because it allows them to wait longer before committing to a customer order—it gives them greater flexibility, in other words. Firms should select suppliers to support the competitive priorities of the services or products provided, which in this case would include the ability to provide quick deliveries, customize services or components, adjust volumes quickly to match demand cycles, offer variety, and provide top quality. Our discussion of FedEx at the beginning of this chapter is an example of the use of a responsive supply chain.

Poor supply chain performance often is the result of using the wrong supply chain design for the services or products provided. A common mistake is to use an efficient supply chain in an environment that calls for a responsive supply chain. Over time, a firm may add options to its basic service or product, or introduce variations, so that the variety of its offerings increases dramatically and demand for any given service or product predictability drops. Yet, the firm continues to measure the performance of its supply chain as it always has, emphasizing efficiency, even when contribution margins would allow a responsive supply chain design. Clearly, aligning supply chain operations to the firm's competitive priorities has strategic implications.

In this chapter we have provided an overview of supply chain design and its strategic implications. Through effective supply chain design, managers can move the supply chain efficiency curve so as to improve performance while reducing cost. Here we focused on the structural changes that can affect the efficiency curve, such as inventory placement, mass customization, and outsourcing, and their implications for inventories and competitive priorities. We also discussed the measures by which supply chain designs are judged and showed how important supply chain design and operation is to major financial measures. In the next chapter we will look into the ways that firms integrate the disparate elements of their supply chains.

TABLE 9.2	DESIGN FEATURES FOR EFFICIENT AND RESPONSIVE SUPPLY CHAINS	
Factor	**Efficient Supply Chains**	**Responsive Supply Chains**
Operation strategy	Make-to-stock or standardized services or products; emphasize high volumes	Assemble-to-order, make-to-order, or customized services or products; emphasize variety
Capacity cushion	Low	High
Inventory investment	Low; enable high inventory turns	As needed to enable fast delivery time
Lead time	Shorten, but do not increase costs	Shorten aggressively
Supplier selection	Emphasize low prices, consistent quality, on-time delivery	Emphasize fast delivery time, customization, variety, volume flexibility, top quality

INTERNET RESOURCES

my**om**lab and the Companion Website at **www.pearsonglobaleditions.com/krajewski** contain many tools, activities, and resources designed for this chapter.

KEY EQUATIONS

1. Average cycle inventory $= \dfrac{Q}{2}$

2. Pipeline inventory $= \overline{D}_L = \overline{d}L$

3. Weeks of supply $= \dfrac{\text{Average aggregate inventory value}}{\text{Weekly sales (at cost)}}$

4. Inventory turnover $= \dfrac{\text{Average sales (at cost)}}{\text{Average aggregate inventory value}}$

5. Make-or-buy break-even quantity: $Q = \dfrac{F_m - F_b}{c_b - c_m}$

KEY TERMS

anticipation inventory 350
average aggregate inventory value 352
backorder 348
backward integration 359
centralized placement 352
channel assembly 358
cycle inventory 349
finished goods (FG) 349
forward integration 359
forward placement 352

inventory 347
inventory holding cost 347
inventory pooling 352
inventory turnover 353
lot sizing 349
make-or-buy decision 358
offshoring 359
ordering cost 348
outsourcing 358
pipeline inventory 350

quantity discount 349
raw materials (RM) 349
repeatability 351
safety stock inventory 349
setup cost 348
stockout 348
supply chain design 344
weeks of supply 353
work-in-process (WIP) 349

SOLVED PROBLEM 1

A firm's cost of goods sold last year was $3,410,000, and the firm operates 52 weeks per year. It carries seven items in inventory: three raw materials, two work-in-process items, and two finished goods. The following table contains last year's average inventory level for each item, along with its value.

a. What is the average aggregate inventory value?

b. How many weeks of supply does the firm maintain?

c. What was the inventory turnover last year?

Category	Part Number	Average Level	Unit Value
Raw materials	1	15,000	$ 3.00
	2	2,500	5.00
	3	3,000	1.00
Work-in-process	4	5,000	14.00
	5	4,000	18.00
Finished goods	6	2,000	48.00
	7	1,000	62.00

SOLUTION

a.

Part Number	Average Level		Unit Value		Total Value
1	15,000	×	$3.00	=	$ 45,000
2	2,500	×	5.00	=	12,500
3	3,000	×	1.00	=	3,000
4	5,000	×	14.00	=	70,000
5	4,000	×	18.00	=	72,000
6	2,000	×	48.00	=	96,000
7	1,000	×	62.00	=	62,000
			Average aggregate inventory value	=	$360,500

b. Average weekly sales at cost = $3,410,000/52 weeks = $65,577/week

$$\text{Weeks of supply} = \frac{\text{Average aggregate inventory value}}{\text{Weekly sales (at cost)}} = \frac{\$360,500}{\$65,577} = 5.5 \text{ weeks}$$

c. $$\text{Inventory turnover} = \frac{\text{Annual sales (at cost)}}{\text{Average aggregate inventory value}} = \frac{\$3,410,000}{\$360,500} = 9.5 \text{ turns}$$

SOLVED PROBLEM 2

A distribution center experiences an average weekly demand of 50 units for one of its items. The product is valued at $650 per unit. Average inbound shipments from the factory warehouse average 350 units. Average lead time (including ordering delays and transit time) is 2 weeks. The distribution center operates 52 weeks per year; it carries a 1-week supply of inventory as safety stock and no anticipation inventory. What is the value of the average aggregate inventory being held by the distribution center?

SOLUTION

Type of Inventory	Calculation of Aggregate Average Inventory	
Cycle	$\dfrac{Q}{2} = \dfrac{350}{2}$	= 175 units
Safety stock	1-week supply	= 50 units
Anticipation	None	
Pipeline	$\bar{d}L = (50 \text{ units/week})(2 \text{ weeks})$	= 100 units
	Average aggregate inventory	= 325 units
	Value of aggregate inventory	= $650(325)
		= $211,250

DISCUSSION QUESTIONS

1. Canon, a Japanese manufacturer of photographic equipment, decided against offshoring and kept its manufacturing and new product development processes in Japan, which has relatively high labor costs. In contrast, GM, headquartered in the United States, has a joint venture with Shanghai Auto Industry Corporation to produce cars in China. Given our discussion of outsourcing, offshoring, and supply chain design, explain why these two companies chose different approaches to their supply chains and how the approaches selected support their respective operations strategies.

2. The Wal-Mart retail chain sells standardized items and enjoys great purchasing clout with its suppliers, none of

which it owns. The Limited retail chain sells fashion goods and owns Mast Industries, which is responsible for producing many of the items sold in The Limited stores. The Limited boasts that it can go from the concept for a new garment to the store shelf in 1,000 hours. Compare and contrast the implications for supply chain design for these two retail systems.

3. Form a discussion group in which each member represents a different functional area of a retailer. Suppose that cycle inventories are to be reduced. Discuss the implications of that decision for each functional area.

4. In the chapter opener we get a glimpse of how a major corporation can make a significant contribution to disaster relief by assisting in a humanitarian supply chain. Disasters often occur with little warning; humanitarian aid needs to get to the affected areas very quickly. From the perspective of supply chain design, what capabilities should humanitarian supply chains have?

PROBLEMS

Software, such as OM Explorer, Active Models, and POM for Windows, is available in my**om**lab. Check with your instructor on how best to use it. In many cases, the instructor wants you to understand how to do the calculations by hand. At most, the software provides a check on your calculations. When calculations are particularly complex and the goal is interpreting the results in making decisions, the software replaces entirely the manual calculations.

1. The Bawl Corporation supplies alloy ball bearings to auto manufacturers in Detroit. Because of its specialized manufacturing process, considerable work-in-process and raw materials are needed. The current inventory levels are $2,470,000 and $1,566,000, respectively. In addition, finished goods inventory is $1,200,000 and sales (at cost) for the current year are expected to be about $48 million. Express total inventory as
   a. Weeks of supply
   b. Inventory turns

2. One product line has 10 turns per year and an annual sales volume (at cost) of $985,000. How much inventory is being held, on average?

3. Jack Jones, the materials manager at Precision Enterprises, is beginning to look for ways to reduce inventories. A recent accounting statement shows the following inventory investment by category: raw materials, $3,129,500; work-in-process, $6,237,000; and finished goods, $2,686,500. This year's cost of goods sold will be about $32.5 million. Assuming 52 business weeks per year, express total inventory as
   a. Weeks of supply
   b. Inventory turns

4. Buzzrite, a retailer of casual clothes, ended the current year with annual sales (at cost) of $48 million. During the year, the inventory of apparel turned over six times. For the next year, Buzzrite plans to increase annual sales (at cost) by 25 percent.
   a. What is the increase in the average aggregate inventory value required if Buzzrite maintains the same inventory turnover during the next year?
   b. What change in inventory turns must Buzzrite achieve if, through better supply chain management, it wants to support next year's sales with no increase in the average aggregate inventory value?

5. Terminator, Inc., manufactures a motorcycle part in lots of 250 units. The raw materials cost for the part is $150, and the value added in manufacturing 1 unit from its components is $300, for a total cost per completed unit of $450. The lead time to make the part is 3 weeks, and the annual demand is 4,000 units. Assume 50 working weeks per year.
   a. How many units of the part are held, on average, as cycle inventory? What is its value?
   b. How many units of the part are held, on average, as pipeline inventory? What is its value?

6. Prince Electronics, a manufacturer of consumer electronic goods, has five distribution centers in different regions of the country. For one of its products, a high-speed modem priced at $350 per unit, the average weekly demand at *each* distribution center is 75 units. Average shipment size to each distribution center is 400 units, and average lead time for delivery is 2 weeks. Each distribution center carries 2 weeks' supply as safety stock but holds no anticipation inventory.
   a. On average, how many dollars of pipeline inventory will be in transit to each distribution center?
   b. How much total inventory (cycle, safety, and pipeline) does Prince hold for all five distribution centers?

7. A part is produced in lots of 1,000 units. It is assembled from 2 components worth $50 total. The value added in production (for labor and variable overhead) is $60 per unit, bringing total costs per completed unit to $110. The average lead time for the part is 6 weeks and annual demand is 3,800 units, based on 50 business weeks per year.
   a. How many units of the part are held, on average, in cycle inventory? What is the dollar value of this inventory?
   b. How many units of the part are held, on average, in pipeline inventory? What is the dollar value of this inventory? (*Hint:* Assume that the typical part in pipeline inventory is 50 percent completed. Thus, half the labor and variable overhead cost has been added, bringing the unit cost to $80, or $50 + $60/2.)

8. The following data were collected for a retailer:

Cost of goods sold	$3,500,000
Gross profit	$ 700,000
Operating costs	$ 500,000
Operating profit	$ 200,000
Total inventory	$1,200,000
Fixed assets	$ 750,000
Long-term debt	$ 300,000

Assuming 52 business weeks per year, express total inventory as

a. Weeks of supply

b. Inventory turns

ADVANCED PROBLEMS

Problems 10, 11, and 12 require prior reading of Supplement A, "Decision Making Models."

9. Sterling, Inc., operates 52 weeks per year, and its cost of goods sold last year was $6,500,000. The firm carries eight items in inventory: four raw materials, two work-in-process items, and two finished goods. Table 9.3 shows last year's average inventory levels for these items, along with their unit values.

a. What is the average aggregate inventory value?

b. How many weeks of supply does the firm have?

c. What was the inventory turnover last year?

10. At the BlueFin Bank corporate headquarters, management was discussing the potential of outsourcing the processing of credit card transactions to DataEase, an international provider of banking operational services. Processing of the transactions at BlueFin has been a costly element of the annual profit and loss statement and the continual investment in equipment to keep up to date has been draining capital reserves. Based upon initial study and negotiations, DataEase will charge $0.02 more per transaction than BlueFin's cost per transaction, and DataEase will want $12 million per year to cover equipment and overhead costs associated with the contract. BlueFin has yet to develop an estimate for the annual overhead and fixed costs associated with processing the transactions. These costs include supervision, administrative support, maintenance, equipment depreciation, and overhead. If BlueFin must process 20 million transactions per year, how high must those fixed costs be before it would pay to use DataEase?

11. A large global automobile manufacturer is considering outsourcing the manufacturing of a solenoid used in the transmission of its SUVs. The company estimates that annual fixed costs of manufacturing the part in-house, which include equipment, maintenance, and management, amounts to $6 million. The variable costs of labor and material are $5.00 per unit. The company has an offer from a major subcontractor to produce the part for $8.00 per unit. However, the subcontractor wants the company to share in the costs of the equipment. The automobile company estimates that the total cost would be $4 million, which also includes management oversight for the new supply contact.

a. How many solenoids would the automobile company need per year to make the in-house option least costly?

b. What other factors, besides costs, should the automobile company consider before revising its supply chain for SUVs?

TABLE 9.3	STERLING INVENTORY ITEMS		
Category	**Part Number**	**Average Inventory Units**	**Value per Unit**
Raw materials	RM-1	20,000	$ 1
	RM-2	5,000	5
	RM-3	3,000	6
	RM-4	1,000	8
Work-in-process	WIP-1	6,000	10
	WIP-2	8,000	12
Finished goods	FG-1	1,000	65
	FG-2	500	88

12. Black Bear Outfitters is an international supplier of outdoor gear for families. Currently, the company uses a logistical provider to provide warehouse services and handle packages destined for ground delivery. The contract calls for $9 million in annual fixed charges, which covers the provider's overhead and warehouse costs, and variable costs of $15 per package shipped. Recently, Black Bear Outfitters found a warehouse it could lease at a cost of $16 million per year, which includes lease costs, labor, and management oversight. Further, the company found another provider who would deliver packages from the warehouse for $6.00 per package. Considering only costs, how many packages must Black Bear Outfitters ship to make the vertical integration into warehouse operations beneficial?

EXPERIENTIAL LEARNING | Sonic Distributors

Scenario

Sonic Distributors produces and sells music CDs. The CDs are pressed at a single facility (factory), issued through the company's distribution center, and sold to the public from various retail stores. The goal is to operate the distribution chain at the lowest total cost.

Materials (available from instructor)

Retail and distributor purchase order forms

Factory work order forms

Factory and distributor materials delivery forms

Inventory position worksheets

A means of generating random demand (typically a pair of dice)

Setup

Each team is in the business of manufacturing music CDs and distributing them to retail stores where they are sold. Two or more people play the role of retail outlet buyers. Their task is to determine the demand for the CDs and order replenishment stock from the distributor. The distributor carries forward-placed stock obtained from the factory. The factory produces in lot sizes either to customer order or to stock.

Tasks

Divide into teams of four or five.

Two or three people operate the retail stores.

One person operates the distribution center.

One person schedules production at the factory.

Every day, as play progresses, the participants at each level of the supply chain estimate demand, fill customer orders, record inventory levels, and decide how much to order or produce and when to place orders with their supplier.

Costs and Conditions

Unless your instructor indicates otherwise, the following costs and conditions hold.

Costs

Holding cost per unit per day	Retail outlets: $1.00/CD/day
	Distribution Center: $0.50/CD/day
	Factory: $0.25/CD/day
Pipeline inventory cost	Assume that pipeline cost can be ignored for this exercise (consider it zero).
Ordering cost (retailers and distributors)	$20/order
Factory setup cost (to run an order)	$50 (Note: Cost is per order, not per day, because even though successive orders from distributors are for the same item, the factory is busy fabricating other items between orders.)
Stockout (lost margin) cost	Retail Store: $8 per CD sale lost in a period
	$0 for backorders for shortages from the factory or shipping new orders
Shipping cost	Because other products are already being distributed through this chain and because CDs are light and take up little volume, consider the cost to be zero.

Conditions

Starting inventory	Retail stores each have 15 CDs
	Distribution center has 25 CDs
	Factory has 100 CDs
Lot-sizing restrictions	Retail outlets and distribution centers—no minimum order. Any amount may be stored. Factory production lot sizes and capacity—produce in minimum lots of 20. Maximum capacity: 200/day.
Outstanding orders	None

Delays

Ordering Delay. One day to send an order from a retail store to the distributor or from the distributor to the factory (that is, 1 day is lost between placing an order and the recipient acting on it).

No delay occurs in starting up production once an order has been received (but one day is needed for delivery of an order from the distributor to the factory).

Delivery Delay. One-day shipping time between the distributor and a retail store or between the factory and the distributor (that is, 1 day is lost between shipping an order and receiving it).

Run the Exercise

For simplicity's sake, assume all transactions take place simultaneously at the middle of the day. For every simulated day, the sequence of play goes as follows.

Retailers

a. Each retailer receives any shipment due in from its distributor (1 day after shipment) and places it in sales inventory (adds the quantity indicated on any incoming Material Delivery Form from the distributor—after its 1-day delay—to the previous day's ending inventory level on the Retailer's Inventory Position Worksheet). (*Note:* For the first day of the exercise, no order will come in.)

b. The retailers each determine the day's retail demand (the quantity of CDs requested) by rolling a pair of dice. The roll determines the number demanded.

c. Retailers fill demand from available stock, if possible. Demand is filled by subtracting it from the current inventory level to develop the ending inventory level, which is recorded. If demand exceeds supply, sales are lost. Record all lost sales on the worksheet.

d. Retailers determine whether an order should be placed. If an order is required, the desired quantity of CDs is written on a Retail Store Purchase Order, which is forwarded to the distributor (who receives it after a 1-day delay). If an order is made, it should be noted on the worksheet. Retailers may also desire to keep track of outstanding orders separately.

Distributor

a. The distributor receives any shipment due in from the factory and places the CDs in available inventory (adds the quantity indicated on any incoming Material Delivery Form from the factory—after its 1-day delay—to the previous day's ending inventory level on the distributor's inventory position worksheet).

b. All outstanding backorders are filled (the quantity is subtracted from the current inventory level indicated on the worksheet) and prepared for shipment. CDs are shipped by filling out a Distribution Center Material Delivery Form indicating the quantity of CDs to be delivered.

c. The distributor uses the purchase orders received from the retail stores (after the designated 1-day delay) to prepare shipments for delivery from available inventory. Quantities shipped are subtracted from the current level to develop the ending inventory level, which is recorded. If insufficient supply exists, backorders are generated.

d. The distributor determines whether a replenishment order should be placed. If an order is required, the quantity of CDs is written on a Distribution Center Purchase Order, which is forwarded to the factory (after a 1-day delay). If an order is made, it should be noted on the worksheet. The distributor may also desire to keep track of outstanding orders separately.

Factory

a. The factory places any available new production into inventory (adds the items produced the previous day to the previous day's ending inventory level on the Factory Inventory Position Worksheet).

b. All outstanding backorders are filled (the quantity is subtracted from the current inventory level indicated on the worksheet) and prepared for shipment. CDs are shipped by filling out a Factory Material Delivery Form, indicating the quantity of CDs to be delivered.

c. The factory obtains the incoming distributor's purchase orders (after the designated 1-day delay) and ships them from stock, if it can. These amounts are subtracted from the current values on the inventory worksheet. Any unfilled orders become backorders for the next day.

d. The factory decides whether to issue a work order to produce CDs either to stock or to order. If production is required, a Factory Work Order is issued, and the order is noted on the inventory worksheet. Remember that a setup cost applies to each *production* order. It is important to keep careful track of all production in process.

Remember, once an order has been placed, it cannot be changed and no partial shipments can be made. For each day, record your ending inventory position, backorder or lost sales amount, and whether an order was made (or a production run initiated). After everyone completes the transactions for the day, the sequence repeats, beginning at retailer step (a). Your instructor will tell you how many simulated days to run the exercise.

When the play is stopped, find the cumulative amount of inventory and other costs. You can do so by summing up the numbers in each column and then multiplying these totals by the costs previously listed. Use the total of these costs to assess how well your team operated the distribution chain.

Source: This exercise was developed by Larry Meile, Carroll School of Management, Boston College.

VIDEO CASE | Supply Chain Design at Clif Bar & Company

When Gary Erickson started out on one of his typical long-distance bike treks in 1990, he expected to have a great ride. What he didn't expect was to come home with the idea for a sports nutrition energy bar that became the genesis of Clif Bar & Company.

After consuming most of his supply of Power Bars part way through the 175-mile ride, he couldn't face the prospect of consuming another one. Instead, he figured he could come up with something better. Something sports enthusiasts wouldn't mind eating in quantities while out on the road or the trail. The result? The CLIF® BAR, an all-natural combination of grains, nuts and fruit, with far more taste appeal than the standard energy bar of the time.

Today, the Berkeley, California-based company has over 100 stock-keeping units, or SKUs, in its product mix, including numerous flavorful versions of the original CLIF BAR plus brands such as LUNA®, The Whole Nutrition Bar for Women™, CLIF Kid Organic ZBaR™, The Whole Grain Energy bar for kids, CLIF Mojo™, The Sweet & Salty Trail Mix Bar, and CLIF Nectar®, an organic fruit and nut bar made with just five ingredients. CLIF BARs were originally distributed through cycling shops and other niche retail outlets, but can now be found in a wide variety of retail outlets in the United States, such as Whole Foods, Trader Joe's, REI, and even your local grocery store.

From the beginning, CLIF BARs were made from wholesome ingredients. Yet as Erickson looked at the ingredients being sourced for CLIF BAR, he realized that making a healthy food product and sourcing ingredients from farmers, ranchers and cooperatives using organic growing techniques was a "natural" fit. The company made a commitment to both sustainable growing techniques and using only organic raw ingredients back then, and by 2003, had made CLIF BAR 70 percent certified organic. Since then, six of Clif Bar & Company's CLIF and LUNA brands are now made with 70 percent organic ingredients or more.

The impact on the supply chain for sourcing organic ingredients is tremendous. First, there is a limited—but growing—number of organic growers for the ingredients Clif Bar uses. Second, growers who do not use pesticides, herbicides and genetically modified plants are sometimes at risk of producing lower crop yields. Third, it can be more costly to store the ingredients. And fourth, as more companies commit to environmentally responsible programs and organic ingredients, competition is great for the available global supply.

The company's forecasters and planners work hard to manage both the raw ingredient inventory flows from upstream suppliers, and the finished goods flows to downstream customers, to be sure products are available in the right quantities and right locations. Spending on raw materials and packaging materials is aggregated to provide efficient sourcing efficiency. Production is planned, based on both input and output forecasts, to maximize customer service and minimize inventory. Several times a year, production plans are shared with business partners at all points of the supply chain to make sure the flow of ingredients and products is smooth, and that inventories do not accumulate at any point in the supply chain beyond planned volumes. Monthly forecasts and changes to plans also are communicated to all supply chain partners.

Clif Bar & Company managers know that consumers' tastes for products change regularly, so new flavors and brands are periodically introduced into the various brands. Likewise, flavors are sometimes retired to make room for new ones. As the company's research and development team prepares to move a new product idea from the test kitchen to the manufacturing plant, supply chain managers must get to work assuring any new ingredients can be procured.

As a smaller and privately-owned company, Clif Bar does not own its manufacturing plants and distribution centers, and relies on contractual agreements with outsourcers in the United States. These supply chain business partners are carefully chosen for their ability to manufacture and distribute Clif Bar's products, their commitment to quality, and their alignment with Clif Bar's own value system. This value system, referred to as the company's "Five Aspirations," holds that Clif Bar & Company will work toward sustaining its people, brands, business, community, and the planet. Greg Ginsburg, Vice President of Supply Chain, wants to be sure all parts of the supply chain—owned or not—are in agreement with these aspirations. "We look at their energy sourcing, labor practices, and workplace environments. And where we source products from small cooperatives, we'll go as far back as possible to assure those tiny growers know about our expectations," says Ginsburg.

QUESTIONS

1. What type of supply chain does Clif Bar & Company have? Efficient, responsive, or a combination of both? How can you tell?

2. What business risks does Clif Bar & Company face with so many parts of its supply chain outsourced?

3. What issues or risks could Clif Bar & Company encounter if it chose to expand to international markets?

CASE   Brunswick Distribution, Inc.

Alex Brunswick, CEO of Brunswick Distribution, Inc. (BDI), looked out his office window at another sweltering day and wondered what could have gone wrong at his company. He just finished reviewing his company's recent financial performance and noticed something that worried him. BDI had experienced a period of robust growth over the last 4 years. "What could be going wrong?" he thought to himself. "Our sales have been growing at an average rate of 8 percent over the last 4 years but we still appear to be worse off than before." He sat back in his chair with a heavy sigh and continued reviewing the report on his desk.

Sales had risen consistently over the past 4 years but the future was uncertain. Alex Brunswick was aware that part of the past growth had largely been the result of a few competitors in the region going out of business, a situation that was unlikely to continue. Net earnings, however, had been declining for the last 3 years and were expected to decline next year.

Brunswick was determined to turn his company around within the next 3 years. He sat back from his desk and buzzed his personal assistant: "Carla, could you ask Marianna and Bradley to come up?"

Background

The distribution business, in its simplest form, involves the purchase of inventory from a variety of manufacturers and its resale to retailers. Over the last 3 to 5 years, demands on inventory changed considerably; neither manufacturers nor retailers want to handle inventory, leaving distributors to pick up the slack. In addition, an increased tendency of retailers to order directly from manufacturers placed further strain on the profitability of distributorships in general.

After humble beginnings in a shed behind Brunswick's grandmother's house, the company moved to a 10,000 square-foot leased facility. Ten years ago BDI began distributing high-end appliance products to supplement its low-margin products. BDI entered into an agreement with KitchenHelper, Corp., a large manufacturer of high-end kitchen appliances, located 35 miles from Moline, Illinois, to distribute KitchenHelper appliances to customers in the region. Over the years BDI enjoyed steady growth and expanded its area of coverage. Currently, Brunswick was covering an area with a radius of 200 miles from the company's main facility. Given the rapid growth, BDI purchased the leased facility and made additions to bring its capacity to 30,000 square feet.

The demise of several of its competitors resulted in the acquisition of new retailer customers and some new product lines. Traditional ordering in the retailer-distributor-manufacturer chain took place via fax or phone. Brunswick considered implementing an Internet-based ordering system but was unsure of the potential operational and marketing benefits that it could provide.

Concerns

Market

Direct competition from distributors increased over the past 5 years. As a result, the most successful distributors adopted a value-added strategy in order to remain competitive. Retailers want dependable delivery to support sales promotions and promises to customers. They also want the freedom to hold sales promotions at any time as competitive conditions dictate and with only short notice to distributors. They also want the opportunity to choose from a wide variety of appliances. Nonetheless, many orders are won on the basis of price and lost on the basis of delivery problems.

Financial

Manufacturers commonly demand payment in 30 to 45 days and provide no financing considerations. Retailers, on the other hand, pay in 50 to 60 days. This difference often leaves BDI in a cash-poor situation that puts an unnecessary strain on its current operating loan. The company's borrowing capacity has almost been exhausted. Any additional financing will have to be sought from alternative sources. Given BDI's financial situation, any additional financing will be issued at a higher charge than the company's existing debt.

Operations

Inventory turnover also presented a problem for the past 5 years. In the past two years, however, a significant downturn in turnover occurred. This trend seems likely to continue.

Orders from retailers come in as their customers near completion of construction or renovations. Even though historical information provided a good benchmark of future sales, the changing market lessened the reliability of the information. The changes also affect BDI's ordering. Manufacturers require projections 60, 90, and 120 days out in order to budget their production. Sometimes penalties are assessed when BDI changes an order after it is placed with a manufacturer.

Strategic Issues

As Marianna and Bradley walked into Brunswick's office, he was still pondering the report. "Grab a seat," he grunted. They knew they were going to have a long day. Brunswick quickly briefed them on why he had summoned them, and they all immediately dived into a spirited discussion. Brunswick pointed out that BDI would need to be properly structured to deal with the recession and the reality of today's market. "We need to be well-positioned for growth as the market stabilizes," he said. In order to meet this challenge, BDI must evaluate a number of alternative options. Some of the possible options might include expanding current systems and, when necessary, developing new systems that interface with suppliers, customers, and commercial transportation resources to gain total asset visibility.

Before making any investment decision, Brunswick reminded them that BDI would have to evaluate any new capital requirements, as well as the expected contribution to the company's bottom line and market share, that any option might provide. Exhibit 1 shows the income statement for the current year.

Investing in New Infrastructure

Bradley Pulaski, vice president of operations, said, "Since Associated Business Distribution, Corp., ceased operations 4 years ago, we have been inundated with phone calls and e-mails from potential customers across the Midwest looking for an alternative to ABD's services. These requests come not only from former ABD customers but also from potential customers that have not dealt with either ABD or us in the past. We cannot adequately service this market from our current warehouse because the customers do not want to wait for lengthy deliveries. We are currently servicing some customers in that region; however, I do not think we can keep them much longer because of delayed deliveries. In order to take advantage of this opportunity, we would have to construct a new storage facility to complement our already strained resources and 'forward position' inventory to shorten our delivery times to customers on short notice. We are challenged by an inadequate infrastructure far too small for our requirements. We only have the Moline warehouse at this time." The addition of new facilities would provide BDI with an opportunity for increased penetration in key industrial markets in the upper Midwest where the company has had a limited presence.

Company Income Statement ($000's)		
Revenue		33,074
Cost of Goods Sold		
Shipping costs	8,931	
Direct materials	5,963	
Direct labor and other	6,726	
Total	21,620	
Gross Profit		11,454
Operating Expenses		
Selling expenses	2,232	
Fixed expenses	2,641	
Depreciation	1,794	
Total	6,667	
Earnings before Interest and Taxes		4,787
Interest expense		838
Earnings before Taxes		3,949
Taxes @ 35%		1,382
Net Income		2,567

▲ **EXHIBIT 1**

The financing resources for this option would be a challenge, given that BDI was approaching its credit limit with its principal bank. Additional financing from larger banks in Chicago, however, was not ruled out. It would be expensive (with current interest rates for long-term loans starting at 11 percent). According to Bradley, this option would cost $2 million for property and $10 million for plant and equipment. The new warehouse facilities would be depreciated over 20 years. The 20-year loan would be repaid with a single balloon payment at the end of the loan. With the additional infrastructure, BDI would be able to increase its annual sales by $4,426,000. In addition, delivery lead times to customers in the region would be reduced from 5 days to 2 days, which would be very competitive. Because of the added warehouse capacity, BDI could also increase the number of brands and models of appliances to better serve the retailers' needs for more variety. However, certain categories in the costs of goods sold would also increase. Total annual shipping costs, which include supplier deliveries to the warehouse as well as deliveries to the customer, would increase by $955,000. Annual materials costs (for the sold appliances) and labor costs would each increase by 6 percent. Total assets would increase from $30,170,000 to $43,551,000. This increase takes into account changes to inventory investment, which would become $7,200,000, accounts receivable, property, and plant and equipment.

Streamlining the Distribution System

Marianna Jackson, the vice president of logistics, stated, "I believe there is an opportunity to capitalize on the void left by our fallen rivals by utilizing a cost-efficient distribution system. We do not need a new facility; we can continue to serve the customers in the Midwest as best as we can. However, what we do need is an efficient distribution system. We are holding a considerable amount of stock that has not moved simply because of our inefficient inventory systems. One of our top priorities is working diligently with the inventory control department to keep what we need and dispose of what we do not need. This approach will allow us to use the space recovered from the unneeded items for automated warehouse equipment that will enable us to become more efficient. Everything we do and every dollar we spend affects our customers. We need to keep our prices competitive. Our cost of operations is our customers' cost. Our goal is to enable customers to spend their resources on readiness and the tools of their trade, not logistics. This option will not help us much with product variety or delivery speed; however, it will increase our on-time delivery performance and improve our flexibility to respond to changes in retailer orders to support their sales programs."

The option of having an integrated center, comprised of sophisticated automation systems, advanced materials handling equipment, and specially developed information technology, would provide BDI with both the versatility and capacity to offer improved products and services to Brunswick's customers. The system would support real-time ordering, logistics planning and scheduling, and after-sales service. When an order is received through a call center at Brunswick's offices in Moline, it will be forwarded to a logistics center for processing. The customer is given a delivery date based on truck availability. Orders would be grouped by destination so that trucks could be efficiently loaded to maximize the truck capacity. The order would then be scheduled for delivery and the customer notified of the estimated arrival. This new information technology would improve BDI's reliability in delivering the products when promised. The system also includes an automatic storage and retrieval system (AS/RS). The AS/RS selects a customer order and moves it to a dock for loading on a truck headed for the customer's location. The capital costs for this system would be $7 million, which would be depreciated over a 10-year period. The operating costs, including training, would run at $0.5 million each year. These costs would be considered fixed expenses by Brunswick. The improved system, however, would have tremendous cost savings. Marianna estimated that the system would save up to 16 percent in shipping expenses and 16 percent in labor expenses annually. Total assets would increase from $30,170,000 to $35,932,000 to account for changes in accounts receivables and equipment. Aggregate inventories would be only $4,500,000 because of the reduced need for safety stock inventories. BDI could finance this option using a 10-year loan at a 10 percent rate of interest. The loan would be repaid with a balloon payment at the end of the loan.

These savings would come from more efficient handling of customers' orders by the call center, better planning and scheduling of shipments, and improved communication with the warehouse and the customer, resulting in a dramatic reduction in the shipping costs in the supply chain. Additional savings would result from the reduction in personnel costs; fewer operators would be required. Marianna Jackson thought that BDI could maintain its current level of service with her option while becoming much more efficient.

The Decision

Alex Brunswick pondered the two options posed by Bradley and Marianna. Bradley's option enabled the firm to increase its revenues by serving more customers. The capital outlay was sizable, however. Marianna's option focused on serving the firm's existing customers more efficiently. The value of that option was its dramatic reduction in costs; however, it was uncertain whether BDI could hold onto its current upper Midwest customers. Brunswick realized that he could not undertake both options, given the company's current financial position. Brunswick uses a 12 percent cost of capital as the discount rate when making financial decisions. How will each option affect the firm's operational and financial performance measures, which investors watch closely? Which supply chain design option would be better for the company?

SELECTED REFERENCES

Aron, Ravi, and Jitendra V. Singh. "Getting Offshoring Right." *Harvard Business Review* (December 2005), pp. 135–143.

Bowersox, D. J., and D. J. Closs. *Logistical Management: The Integrated Supply Chain Process.* New York: McGraw-Hill, 1996.

Champion, David. "Mastering the Value Chain." *Harvard Business Review* (June 2001), pp. 109–115.

Conner, Martin P. "The Supply Chain's Role in Leveraging Product Life Cycle Management." *Supply Chain Management Review* (March 2004), pp. 36–43.

Cook, Robert L., Brian Gibson, and Douglas MacCurdy. "A Lean Approach to Cross-Docking." *Supply Chain Management Review* (March 2005), pp. 54–59.

de Waart, Dick, and Steve Kemper. "5 Steps to Service Supply Chain Excellence." *Supply Chain Management Review* (January/February 2004), pp. 28–35.

Duray, Rebecca, Peter. T. Ward, Glenn W. Milligan, and William L. Berry. "Approaches to Mass Customization: Configurations and Empirical Validation." *Journal of Operations Management*, vol. 18 (2000), pp. 605–625.

Duray, Rebecca. "Mass Customization Origins: Mass or Custom Manufacturing?" *International Journal of Operations and Production Management*, vol. 22, no. 3 (2002), pp. 314–328.

Ellram, Lisa M., and Baohong Liu. "The Financial Impact of Supply Management." *Supply Chain Management Review* (November/December 2002), pp. 30–37.

Farrell, Diana. "Beyond Offshoring: Assess Your Company's Global Potential." *Harvard Business Review* (December 2004), pp. 82–90.

Fisher, Marshall L. "What Is the Right Supply Chain for Your Product?" *Harvard Business Review* (March/April 1997), pp. 105–116.

Fugate, Brian S., and John T. Mentzer. "Dell's Supply Chain DNA." *Supply Chain Management Review* (October 2004), pp. 20–24.

Grey, William, Kaan Katircioglu, Dailun Shi, Sugato Bagchi, Guillermo Gallego, Mark Adelhelm, Dave Seybold, and Stavros Stefanis. "Beyond ROI." *Supply Chain Management Review* (March/April 2003), pp. 20–27.

Hammer, Michael. "The Superefficient Company." *Harvard Business Review* (September 2001), pp. 82–91.

Handfield, Robert, S. Walton, Robert Sroufe, and Steven Melnyk. "Applying Environmental Criteria to Supplier Assessment: A Study of the Application of the Analytical Hierarchy Process." *European Journal of Operational Research*, vol. 41, no. 1 (2002), pp. 70–87.

Hartvigsen, David. *SimQuick: Process Simulation with Excel*, 2d ed. Upper Saddle River, NJ: Prentice Hall, 2004.

Lee, Hau L. "The Triple-A Supply Chain." *Harvard Business Review* (October 2004), pp. 102–112.

Lee, Hau L., and Corey Billington. "Managing Supply Chain Inventory: Pitfalls and Opportunities." *Sloan Management Review* (Spring 1992), pp. 65–73.

Martha, Joseph, and Sunil Subbakrishna. "Targeting a Just-In-Case Supply Chain for the Inevitable Next Disaster." *Supply Chain Management Review* (September/October 2002), pp. 18–23.

Metersky, Jeff, and J. Michael Kilgore. "How to Improve Your Inventory Deployment." *Supply Chain Management Review* (October 2004), pp. 26–32.

Reeve, James M., and Mandyam M. Srinivasan. "Which Supply Chain Design is Right for You?" *Supply Chain Management Review* (May/June 2005), pp. 57.

Siekman, Philip. "The Smart Car Is Looking More So." *Fortune* (April 15, 2002), pp. 310I–310P.

Slone, Reuben E., John T. Mentzer, and J. Paul Dittmann. "Are you the Weakest Link in Your Supply Chain?" *Harvard Business Review* (September 2007), pp. 116–127.

Sullivan, Laurie. "Wal-Mart's Way." *Informationweek.com* (September 27, 2004), pp. 37–50.

Tiede, Tom, and Kay Ree Lee. "What is an Optimal Distribution Network Strategy?" *Supply Chain Management Review* (November 2005), pp 32–39.

Trent, Robert J. "What Everyone Needs to Know About SCM." *Supply Chain Management Review* (March 2004), pp. 52–59.

Venkatesan, Ravi. "Strategic Sourcing: To Make or Not to Make." *Harvard Business Review* (November/December 1992), pp. 98–107.

10 INTEGRATING THE SUPPLY CHAIN

Kodak makes a diverse range of digital products, from user-friendly Picture Maker photo kiosks found in retail stores to sophisticated computer radiology equipment for trauma centers and hospitals. Here Tina Burke, author of children's books, uses the touchpad to demonstrate the Kodak digital photo printing kiosk at Delaware Camera in Williamsville, N.Y.

EASTMAN KODAK

Customer service after the sale, which requires having the right repair part in the right location in the service parts supply chain, is a key competitive dimension of business today for service providers as well as manufacturers. Overstocking the parts throughout the supply chain is not an option because of the expense. Eastman Kodak, a $13.3 billion manufacturer of digital imaging products, found this out for its digital after-market parts. These parts, which become obsolete quickly and are very expensive, included circuit boards, print head controllers, CPUs, optical drives, and monitors. Kodak faced a typical conflict: the product group managers wanted low inventories and the field engineers, who did the repair in the field and had to face the customer, wanted high inventories. Facing a need to reduce the cost of inventories while maintaining or improving service, Kodak needed to redesign its supply chain and integrate the entities for smooth operations.

Rather than allowing the expensive parts to reside with the field engineers, Kodak managers realized that centralizing expensive parts at strategic field locations and delivering them on demand to field engineers was an option worth pursuing. Kodak made three major decisions to implement the new supply chain design. First, the number of forward stock locations (FSLs) to stock the expensive parts and the inventory levels at each stock location had to be determined using software from Baxter Planning Systems. Second, UPS Supply Chain Solutions was chosen as the logistics provider to operate the more than 100 FSLs and deliver the

LEARNING GOALS

After reading this chapter, you should be able to:

1. Identify the major causes of dynamics in a supply chain.

2. Explain how integrated supply chains can mitigate supply chain dynamics.

3. Explain the nature and purpose of the key nested processes within the new service or product development, supplier relationship, order fulfillment, and customer relationship processes.

4. Use a total annual cost analysis and a preference matrix to select suppliers and the expected value decision rule to determine logistics capacity.

5. Identify key levers and performance measures useful for improving supply chain performance.

6. Explain how integrated supply chains can help firms achieve environmental goals such as sustainability.

parts as needed to the field engineers. Finally, and perhaps most importantly, Kodak fully incorporated the field engineers and service parts supply chain personnel employees in the design process and executed a four-month pilot program to help employees accept the new design.

Kodak showed that fully integrating the key elements of the new supply chain, including the software provider, logistics provider, and internal employees, can lead to significant results. During the first year of operation, the new program has reduced FSL inventory items by 66 percent, central inventory by 32 percent, priority shipments by 22 percent, and had no negative impact on call duration.

Source: Mark Brienzi and Dr. Sham Kekre, "How Kodak Transformed Its Service Parts Supply Chain," *Supply Chain Management Review* (October 2005), pp. 25–32; www.kodak.com.

my**om**lab and the Companion Website at **www.pearsonglobaleditions.com/krajewski** contain many tools, activities, and resources designed for this chapter.

supply chain integration

The effective coordination of supply chain processes through the seamless flow of information up and down the supply chain.

The development and delivery of services and products has become increasingly complex in today's global economy. The Kodak example shows how a firm can redesign its supply chain for competitive advantage by changing the location of critical stocks, adding a new supplier in the form of a logistics provider, and changing the way field engineers access that inventory. To be effective, accurate inventory and demand information had to be available along with considerable collaboration between the parties involved. Kodak was successful at **supply chain integration**, which is the effective coordination of supply chain processes through the seamless flow of information up and down the supply chain. Supply chain integration provides each member of the supply chain visibility into the capacities and inventories of other members of the supply chain to aid in planning and scheduling. It facilitates collaboration between firms in a supply chain; in effect, it is an enabler of supply chain management. In this chapter we explore the processes involved in supply chain integration, the benefits to be had, and the role supply chain integration can play in addressing environmental concerns.

SUPPLY CHAIN INTEGRATION ACROSS THE ORGANIZATION

As the Kodak example portrayed, supply chain integration involves internal as well as external processes. Figure 10.1 shows just how interconnected processes and firms in a supply chain can be. Think of a supply chain as a river that flows from raw material suppliers to consumers. For example, a ketchup factory gets its major supply from the tomato paste factories, which for the ketchup factory is a tier 1 supplier. In turn, the tomato paste factories get their major supplies from the tomato grading stations, which are tier 2 suppliers of the ketchup factory. Finally, the tomato growers ship their product directly to the tomato grading stations. The tier 1, tier 2, and tier 3 suppliers are all *upstream* from the ketchup factory, which means that they control the flow of supply to the ketchup factory. Suppose the tomato paste factory has a major process failure. The flow of tomato paste to the ketchup factory would dwindle to a trickle, as if someone built a dam across a river. Indeed, even those entities *downstream* from the ketchup factory could feel the effects after inventories of ketchup have been consumed. When a link in the supply chain fails, whether it is an internal process or one at a supplier, the rest of the chain feels the effects.

Mitigating the effects of supply chain disruptions is an important benefit of supply chain integration. Information flows, both upstream and downstream, provide visibility to supply chain members regarding supplies, capacities, and plans. Cash flows move upstream and are affected by pricing, promotional programs, and supply contracts. Understanding the implications of material, information, and cash flows in a supply chain is important for all employees in an organization.

SUPPLY CHAIN DYNAMICS

Supply chain dynamics can wreak havoc on supply chain performance. Each firm in a supply chain depends on other firms for services, materials, or the information needed to supply its immediate external customer in the chain. Because firms are typically owned and managed independently, the actions of downstream supply chain members (positioned nearer the end user of the service or product) can affect the operations of upstream members. The reason is that upstream members of a supply chain must react to the demands placed on them by downstream members of the chain. These demands are a function of the policies downstream firms have for replenishing their inventories, the actual levels of those inventories, the demands

FIGURE 10.1 ▶
Supply Chain for a Ketchup Factory

of their customers, and the accuracy of the information they have to work with. As you examine the order patterns of firms in a supply chain, you will frequently see the variability in order quantities increase as you proceed upstream. This increase in variability is referred to as the **bullwhip effect**, which gets its name from the action of a bullwhip—the handle of the whip initiates the action; however, the tip of the whip experiences the wildest action. The slightest change in customer demands can ripple through the entire chain, with each member receiving more variability in demands from the member immediately downstream. A firm contributes to the bullwhip effect if the variability of the orders to its suppliers exceeds the variability of the orders from its immediate customers.

Figure 10.2 shows the bullwhip effect in a supply chain for facial tissue. The retailer's orders to the manufacturer exhibit more variability than the actual demands from the consumers of the facial tissue. The manufacturer's orders to the package supplier have more variability than the retailer's orders. Finally, the package supplier's orders to the cardboard supplier have the most variability. Because supply patterns do not match demand patterns, inventories accumulate in some firms and shortages occur in others. The firms with too much inventory stop ordering, and those that have shortages place expedited orders. The culprits are unexpected changes in demands or supplies that are based on a number of causes.

bullwhip effect

The phenomenon in supply chains whereby ordering patterns experience increasing variance as you proceed upstream in the chain.

External Causes

A firm has the least amount of control over its external customers and suppliers, who can periodically cause disruptions. Typical external disruptions include the following:

- *Volume Changes.* Customers may change the quantity of the service or product they had ordered for a specific date or unexpectedly demand more of a standard service or product. If the market demands short lead times, the firm needs a quick reaction from its suppliers.

- *Service and Product Mix Changes.* Customers may change the mix of items in an order and cause a ripple effect throughout the supply chain. For example, a major-appliance store chain may change the mix of washing machines in its orders from 60 percent Whirlpool brand and 40 percent Kitchen Aid brand to 40 percent Whirlpool and 60 percent Kitchen Aid. This decision changes the production schedule of the Whirlpool plant that makes both brands, causing imbalances in its inventories. In addition, the tier 1 supplier that makes the face plates for the washing machines must change its schedules, thereby affecting *its* suppliers.

- *Late Deliveries.* Late deliveries of materials or delays in essential services can force a firm to switch its schedule from production of one product model to another. Firms that supply model-specific items may have their schedules disrupted. For example, the Whirlpool plant may find that a component supplier for its Model A washing machine could not supply the part on-time. To avoid shutting down the assembly line, which is an expensive action, Whirlpool may decide to switch to Model B production. Suddenly, the demand on the suppliers of Model B-specific parts increases.

▼ FIGURE 10.2
Supply Chain Dynamics for Facial Tissue

Month of April

■ *Underfilled Shipments.* Suppliers that send partial shipments do so because of disruptions at their own plants. The effects of underfilled shipments are similar to those of late shipments unless the underfilled shipment contains enough materials to allow the firm to operate until the next shipment.

Internal Causes

A famous line from a *Pogo* cartoon is "We have seen the enemy, and it is us!" Unfortunately, this statement is true for many firms when it comes to disruptions in the supply chain. A firm's own operations can be the culprit in what becomes the source of constant dynamics in the supply chain. Typical internal disruptions include the following:

■ *Internally Generated Shortages.* A shortage of parts manufactured by a firm may occur because of machine breakdowns or inexperienced workers. This shortage can cause a change in the firm's production schedule, thus affecting suppliers.

■ *Engineering Changes.* Changes to the design of services or products can have a direct impact on suppliers. For example, changing cable TV feed lines to fiber-optic technology increases the benefits to the cable company's customers but affects the demand for co-axial cable.

■ *Order Batching.* Suppliers may offer a quantity discount, which gives an incentive to firms to purchase large quantities of an item less frequently, thereby raising the variability in orders to the supplier. Order batching may also result in transportation economies; larger orders may enable full-truckload shipments and thus create more variability.

■ *New Service or Product Introductions.* New services or products always affect the supply chain. A firm decides on the number of introductions, as well as their timing, and hence introduces a dynamic in the supply chain. New services or products may even require a new supply chain or the addition of new members to an existing supply chain.

■ *Service or Product Promotions.* A common practice of firms producing standardized services or products is to use price discounts to promote sales. Price discounting creates a spike in demand that is felt throughout the supply chain.

■ *Information Errors.* Demand forecast errors can cause a firm to order too many or too few services and materials. Also, forecast errors can result in expedited orders that force suppliers to react more quickly to avoid shortages in the supply chain. In addition, errors in the physical count of items in stock can cause shortages (leading to panic purchases) or too much inventory (leading to a slowdown in purchases). Finally, communication links between buyers and suppliers can be faulty.

Many disruptions are simply caused by ineffective coordination in the supply chain because so many firms and separate operations are involved. It is therefore unrealistic to think that all disruptions can be eliminated. Nonetheless, the challenge for supply chain managers is to remove as many disruptions as possible and minimize the impact of those that cannot be eliminated. We now turn to a discussion of how this can be accomplished.

Integrated Supply Chains

A starting point for minimizing supply chain disruptions is to develop a supply chain with a high degree of functional and organizational integration. Such integration does not happen overnight; it must include linkages between the firm and its suppliers and customers, as shown in Figure 10.3. The new service or product development, supplier relationship, order fulfillment, and customer relationship processes, as well as their internal and external linkages, are integrated into the normal business routine. The firm takes on a customer orientation. However, rather than merely reacting to customer demand, the firm strives to work with its customers and suppliers so that everyone benefits from improved flows of services and materials. The firm must also develop a better understanding of its suppliers' organizations, capacities, strengths, and weaknesses—and include its suppliers earlier into the design of new services or products.

Figure 10.3 also encompasses the *supply chain operations reference model*, known as *SCOR*, developed by the Supply Chain Council[1] with the assistance of 70 of the world's leading manufacturing companies. Relative to Figure 10.3, the **SCOR model** focuses on a basic supply chain of *plan* (overall coordination represented by arrows between internal and external processes), *source* (supplier relationship), *make* (new service/product development and order fulfillment), *deliver* (order fulfillment and customer relationship), and *return*

SCOR model

A framework that focuses on a basic supply chain of plan, source, make, deliver, and return processes, repeated again and again along the supply chain.

---

[1] See www.supply-chain.org for additional details of the SCOR model.

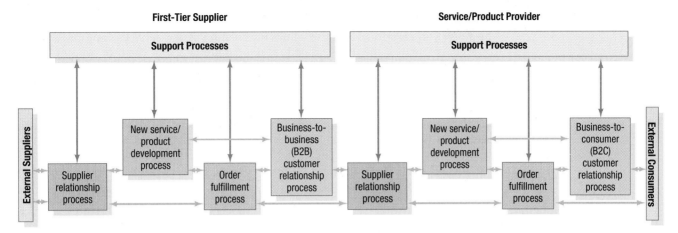

(supplier relationship, order fulfillment, and customer relationship) processes, repeated again and again along the supply chain. Much like our model shown in Figure 10.3, the SCOR model emphasizes that the design of an integrated supply chain is complex and requires a *process view*. We already provided some key insights into process design decisions in Part 1 and Part 2 of the text. These insights must be applied to the new service or product development, supplier relationship, order fulfillment, and customer relationship processes. Beyond that, these processes need to be integrated. It is important to know that an integrated supply chain, implied by Figure 10.3 and the SCOR model, provides a framework for the operating decisions in a firm and that these processes play a major role.

▲ FIGURE 10.3
External Supply Chain Linkages

New Service or Product Development Process

Competitive priorities help managers develop services and products that customers want. New services or products are essential to the long-term survival of the firm. *New* refers to both brand new services or products or major changes to existing services or products. The new service/product development process is an integral element in a firm's supply chain because it defines the nature of the materials, services, and information flows the supply chain must support. As shown in Figure 10.4, it begins with the consideration of the development strategy and ends with the launch of the new offering.

▼ FIGURE 10.4
New Service/Product Development Process

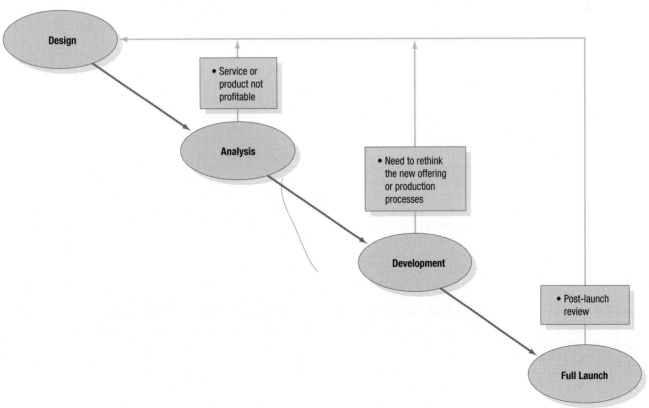

Design

The *design* stage is critical because it links the creation of new services or products to the corporate strategy of the firm and defines the requirements for the firm's supply chain. As we have already noted, the corporate strategy specifies the long-term objectives and the markets in which the firm wishes to compete. In the design stage, ideas for new offerings are proposed and screened for feasibility and market worthiness. These ideas specify how the customer connects with the service or manufacturing firm, the benefits and outcomes for the customer, and the value of the service or product. Proposals also specify how the new offering will be delivered—an important consideration for the supply chain. Even though the detailed specifics of the service or product and its processes have not yet been developed, the inputs of designers and engineers in this stage can avoid costly mistakes.

Analysis

The second stage, *analysis*, involves a critical review of the new offering and how it will be produced to make sure that it fits the corporate strategy, is compatible with regulatory standards, presents an acceptable market risk, and satisfies the needs of the intended customers. The resource requirements for the new offering must be examined from the perspective of the core capabilities of the firm and the need to acquire additional resources or expand the supply chain by forming strategic partnerships with other firms. If the analysis reveals that the new offering has good market potential and that the firm has the capability (or can acquire it), the authorization is given to proceed to the next stage.

Development

The third stage, *development*, brings more specificity to the new offering. The required competitive priorities are used as inputs to the design (or redesign) of the processes that will be involved in delivering the new offering. The processes are analyzed, including those of suppliers; each activity is designed to meet its required competitive priorities and to add value to the service or product. Once the new offering is specified and the processes have been designed, the market program can be designed. Finally, personnel are trained and some pilot runs can be conducted to iron out the kinks in production. At this stage it is possible that some unforeseen problems may arise, forcing a reconsideration of the service or product or the processes required to produce it. The supply chain might have to be redesigned as well.

To avoid costly mismatches between the design of a new offering and the capability of the processes and supply chain required to produce it, many firms engage in a concept called **concurrent engineering**, which brings product engineers, process engineers, marketers, buyers, information specialists, quality specialists, and suppliers together to design a product and the processes that will meet customer expectations. Changes are much simpler and less costly at this stage. However, problems with the design of the new offering or the capability to deliver it may be discovered during this stage. The product proposal may have to be scrapped or completely rethought.

concurrent engineering

A concept that brings product engineers, process engineers, marketers, buyers, information specialists, quality specialists, and suppliers together to design a product and the processes that will meet customer expectations.

Full Launch

The final stage, *full launch*, involves the coordination of many internal processes as well as those both upstream and downstream in the supply chain. Promotions for the new offering must be initiated, sales personnel briefed, distribution processes activated, and old services or products that the new offering is to replace withdrawn. A particular strain is placed on the supply chain during a period referred to as *ramp-up*, when the production processes must increase volume to meet demands while coping with quality problems and last-minute design changes. The more integrated the supply chain, the easier the ramp-up period.

Regardless of the service or product, a post launch review should compare the competitive priorities of the supply chain to its competitive capabilities, perhaps signaling a need to rethink the original service or product idea or even the supply chain. The review should also get inputs from customers, who may divulge their experiences and may share ideas for change.

SUPPLIER RELATIONSHIP PROCESS

The nature of the service or product determines the design requirements for the upstream supply chain. The supplier relationship process, which focuses on the interaction of the firm with upstream suppliers, includes five major nested processes: sourcing, design collaboration, negotiation, buying, and information exchange. For many firms, these processes are the organizational responsibility of **purchasing**, which is the activity that decides the suppliers to use, negotiates contracts, maintains information flows, and determines whether to buy locally.

purchasing

The activity that decides which suppliers to use, negotiates contracts, and determines whether to buy locally.

Sourcing

The sourcing process is involved in the selection, certification, and evaluation of suppliers and, in general, the management of supply contracts.

Supplier Selection   A starting point for selecting suppliers is to perform a total cost analysis. There are four key costs to consider for each supplier.

- *Material costs.* Negotiating with suppliers for the provision of a service or product results in a price per unit (or application of the service). Material costs equal annual requirements (D) multiplied by the price per unit, p.

$$\text{Annual material costs} = pD$$

- *Freight costs.* The costs of transporting the product or the equipment and personnel who will perform the service can vary greatly depending on the location of the supplier, the size of the shipments (full truckload shipments [TL] are cheaper per pound than less-than-truckload shipments [LTL]), the number of shipments per year, and the mode of transportation (air transportation is more expensive than truck or rail transportation).

- *Inventory costs.* Buyers interested in purchasing products must consider the shipping quantity and the lead time from the supplier. The shipping quantity, Q, will determine the cycle inventory the buyer must maintain until the next shipment of the product.

$$\text{Cycle inventory} = Q/2$$

The lead time, L, and the average requirements per day (or week), $\bar{d}$, will determine the level of the pipeline inventory, which also may be the responsibility of the buyer.

$$\text{Pipeline inventory} = \bar{d}L$$

The buyer must pay inventory holding costs on the cycle and pipeline inventories. Annual inventory costs equal the sum of the cycle and pipeline inventories multiplied by the annual holding cost per unit, H. See Chapter 9, "Designing Effective Supply Chains" for a review of inventory holding costs and cycle and pipeline inventories.

$$\text{Annual inventory costs} = (Q/2 + \bar{d}L)H$$

- *Administrative costs.* Supply contacts must be monitored and frequent interactions with the supplier may be required. Administrative costs include the managerial time, travel, and other variable costs associated with interacting with a supplier. These costs may vary greatly depending on the location of the supplier; more distant suppliers typically require more administrative attention.

The total annual cost for a supplier is the sum of these costs:

$$\text{Total Annual Cost} = pD + \text{Freight costs} + (Q/2 + \bar{d}L)H + \text{Administrative costs}$$

EXAMPLE 10.1   Total Cost Analysis for Supplier Selection

Compton Electronics manufactures laptops for major computer manufacturers. A key element of the laptop is the keyboard. Compton has identified three potential suppliers for the keyboard, each located in a different part of the world. Important cost considerations are the price per keyboard, freight costs, inventory costs, and contract administrative costs. The annual requirements for the keyboard are 300,000 units. Assume Compton has 250 business days a year. Managers have acquired the following data for each supplier.

Annual Freight Costs			
	Shipping Quantity (units/shipment)		
Supplier	10,000	20,000	30,000
Belfast	$380,000	$260,000	$237,000
Hong Kong	$615,000	$547,000	$470,000
Shreveport	$285,000	$240,000	$200,000

Keyboard Costs and Shipping Lead Times				
Supplier	Price/Unit	Annual Inventory Carrying Cost/Unit	Shipping Lead Time (days)	Administrative Costs
Belfast	$100	$20.00	15	$180,000
Hong Kong	$96	$19.20	25	$300,000
Shreveport	$99	$19.80	5	$150,000

Which supplier provides the lowest annual total cost to Compton?

SOLUTION

The average requirements per day are

$$\bar{d} = 300{,}000/250 = 1{,}200 \text{ keyboards.}$$

Each option must be evaluated with consideration for the shipping quantity using the following equation:

Total Annual Cost = Material costs + Freight costs + Inventory costs + Administrative costs

$$= pD + \text{Freight costs} + (Q/2 + \bar{d}L)H + \text{Administrative costs}$$

For example, consider the Belfast option for a shipping quantity of $Q = 10{,}000$ units. The costs are

Material costs $= pD = (\$100/\text{unit})(300{,}000 \text{ units}) = \$30{,}000{,}000$

Freight costs $= \$380{,}000$

Inventory costs $=$ (cycle inventory $+$ pipeline inventory)$H = Q/2 + \bar{d}L)H$

$= (10{,}000 \text{ units}/2 + 1{,}200 \text{ units/day}(15 \text{ days}))\$20/\text{unit/year} = \$460{,}000$

Administrative costs $= \$180{,}000$

Total Annual Cost $= \$30{,}000{,}000 + \$380{,}000 + \$460{,}000 + \$180{,}000 = \$31{,}020{,}000$

The total costs for all three shipping quantity options are similarly calculated and are contained in the following table.

Total Annual Costs for the Keyboard Suppliers			
	Shipping Quantity		
Supplier	10,000	20,000	30,000
Belfast	$31,020,000	$31,000,000	$31,077,000
Hong Kong	$30,387,000	$30,415,000	$30,434,000
Shreveport	$30,352,800	$30,406,800	$30,465,800

DECISION POINT

Notice that the shipping quantity plays an important role; the lowest cost for the Belfast supplier comes with a shipping quantity of 20,000 keyboards. Nonetheless, based on the total cost analysis, the Shreveport supplier will provide the lowest cost to Compton. Compton should choose a shipping quantity of 10,000 keyboards, which implies that there will be 30 shipments a year (or 300,000/10,000). While the Hong Kong supplier had the lowest price per keyboard, the Shreveport supplier could deliver the keyboards to Compton with the lowest overall cost, which includes logistics, inventory, and administrative costs.

While total cost is an important consideration in the selection of suppliers, other performance dimensions may also be important. The quality of a supplier's materials may be critical since hidden costs of poor quality may be high. Similarly, shorter lead times and on-time delivery may allow the buying firm to maintain acceptable customer service with less inventory. So management must review the market segments it wants to serve and accordingly relate its supplier selection needs to the supply chain. Competitive priorities and order winners for the firm are a good starting point in developing a list of performance criteria to be used. For example, if you were a manager of a food-service firm, in addition to total costs, you would likely use on-time delivery and quality as top criteria for selecting suppliers. These criteria reflect the requirements that food service supply chains need to meet.

Another criterion that is becoming important in the selection of suppliers is environmental impact. Many firms are engaging in **green purchasing**, which involves identifying, assessing, and managing the flow of environmental waste and finding ways to reduce it and minimize its impact on the environment. Suppliers are being asked to be environmentally conscious when designing and producing their services or products. Claims such as *green, biodegradable, natural,* and *recycled* must be substantiated when bidding on a contract. In the not-too-distant future, this criterion could be one of the most important in the selection of suppliers.

When faced with multiple criteria in the supplier selection problem, management can use a preference matrix as shown in Example 10.2. See Supplement A, "Decision Making Models" for a review of this approach.

green purchasing

The process of identifying, assessing, and managing the flow of environmental waste and finding ways to reduce it and minimize its impact on the environment.

EXAMPLE 10.2	Using a Preference Matrix for Selecting Suppliers

The management of Compton Electronics has done a total cost analysis for three international suppliers of keyboards (see Example 10.1). Compton also considers on-time delivery, consistent quality, and environmental stewardship in its selection process. Each criterion is given a weight (total of 100 points), and each supplier is given a score (1 = poor, 10 = excellent) on each criterion. The data are shown in the following table.

Criterion	Weight	Score		
		Belfast	**Hong Kong**	**Shreveport**
Total Cost	25	5	8	9
On-Time Delivery	30	9	6	7
Consistent Quality	30	8	9	6
Environment	15	9	6	8

SOLUTION

The weighted score for each supplier is calculated by multiplying the weight by the score for each criterion and arriving at a total. For example, the Belfast weighted score is

$$WS = (25 \times 5) + (30 \times 9) + (30 \times 8) + (15 \times 9) = 770$$

Similarly, the weighted score for Hong Kong is 740, and for Shreveport, 735. Consequently, Belfast is the preferred supplier.

DECISION POINT

Even though Belfast had a higher total cost based on the calculations in Example 10.1, it significantly outperformed the other suppliers on the criteria Compton considered very important. Given the weights placed on the criteria, it is clear that Compton is willing to pay extra for better delivery performance, quality, and environmental stewardship.

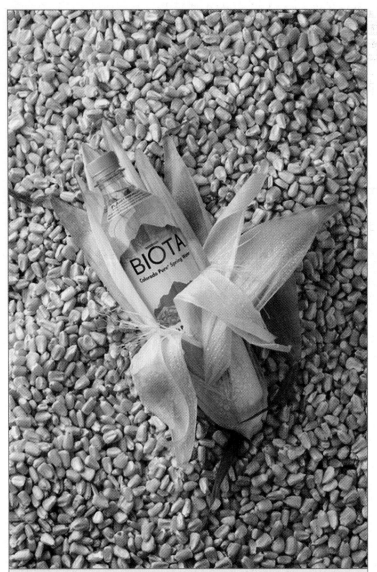

BIOTA's premium natural spring water originates from one of the world's highest protected alpine springs perched above Ouray, CO, and is packaged in the world's first biodegradable bottle. Made from corn, a 100 percent renewable resource, BIOTA bottles break down in approximately 80 days in a commercial composting environment.

early supplier involvement

A program that includes suppliers in the design phase of a service or product.

presourcing

A level of supplier involvement in which suppliers are selected early in a product's concept development stage and are given significant, if not total, responsibility for the design of certain components or systems of the product.

value analysis

A systematic effort to reduce the cost or improve the performance of services or products, either purchased or produced.

Supplier Certification and Evaluation Supplier certification programs verify that potential suppliers have the capability to provide the services or materials the buying firm requires. ISO 14000 is one such program (See Chapter 5, "Managing Quality," for more details). Nonetheless, certification typically involves site visits by a cross-functional team from the buying firm, which does an in-depth evaluation of the supplier's capability to meet cost, quality, delivery, and flexibility targets from process and information system perspectives. The team may consist of members from operations, purchasing, engineering, information systems, and accounting. Every aspect of producing the services or materials is explored. The team observes the supplier's processes in action and reviews the documentation for completeness and accuracy. Once certified, the supplier can be used by the purchasing department without its having to make background checks.

Certification does not give the supplier a free pass on future evaluation. Performance is regularly monitored and performance records are kept. Periodic visits by the certification team may take place. Recertification may be required after a certain period of time or if performance declines.

Design Collaboration

The design collaboration process focuses on jointly designing new services or products with key suppliers; it facilitates concurrent engineering by drawing key suppliers into the new service/product development process. This process seeks to eliminate costly delays and mistakes incurred when many suppliers concurrently design service packages or manufactured components.

An approach that many firms are using in their design collaboration process is called **early supplier involvement**, which is a program that includes suppliers in the design phase of a service or product. Suppliers provide suggestions for design changes and materials choices that will result in more efficient operations and higher quality. In the automotive industry, an even higher level of early supplier involvement is known as **presourcing**, whereby suppliers are selected early in a product's concept development stage and are given significant, if not total, responsibility for the design of certain components or systems of the product. Such is the case with Lear Corporation, one of the world's largest suppliers of automotive interior systems and components for the major automobile manufacturers. Presourced suppliers also take responsibility for the cost, quality, and on-time delivery of the items they produce.

Firms can also improve performance by engaging in **value analysis**, which is a systematic effort to reduce the cost or improve the performance of services or products, either purchased or produced. It is an intensive examination of the services, materials, processes, information systems, and flows of material involved in the production of a service or an item. Benefits include reduced production, materials, and distribution costs; improved profit margins; and increased customer satisfaction. Because teams involving purchasing, production, and engineering personnel from both the firm and its major suppliers play a key role in value analysis, another potential benefit is increased employee morale. Value analysis should be part of a continual effort to improve the performance of the supply chain and increase the value of the service or the item to the customer.

Negotiation

The negotiation process focuses on obtaining an effective contract that meets the price, quality, and delivery requirements of the supplier relationship process's internal customers. The nature of the relations maintained with suppliers can affect the quality, timeliness, and price of a firm's services and products. The firm's orientation toward supplier relations will affect the negotiation and design collaboration processes.

Competitive Orientation   The **competitive orientation** sees negotiations between buyer and seller as a zero-sum game: Whatever one side loses, the other side gains. Short-term advantages are prized over long-term commitments. The buyer may try to beat the supplier's price down to the lowest survival level or push demand to high levels during boom times and order almost nothing during recessions. In contrast, the supplier presses for higher prices for specific levels of quality, customer service, and volume flexibility. Which party wins depends largely on who has the most clout.

Purchasing power determines the clout that a firm has. A buyer has purchasing power when the purchasing volume represents a significant share of the supplier's sales or the purchased service or item is standardized and many substitutes are available. We refer to this condition as *economic dependency*. For example, Premier, Inc., a cooperative with 1,759 member hospitals, spends $10 billion a year on services and materials for its members. This volume makes a lot of suppliers economically dependent on the business from Premier. Suppliers are uneasy because they have to give Premier prices far lower than they do their other customers to keep its business. Premier will buy from the lowest bidder without much loyalty to any supplier. Analysts estimate that Premier helped reduce the cost of health care to its customers by $2 billion a year because of its efforts.

Economic dependency aside, firms may have other sources of power in a relationship with suppliers. These sources include:

- *Referent*–the supplier values identification with the buyer. For example, the fact that a firm is supplying IBM may open the door for business with other customers.

- *Expert*–the buyer has access to knowledge, information, and skills desired by the supplier. For example, a supplier to UPS may get access to logistics planning skills possessed by UPS.

- *Reward*–the buyer has the ability to give rewards to the supplier. Often, the rewards may involve the promise for future business or the opportunity to become a partner sometime in the future.

- *Legal*–the buyer has the legal right to prescribe behavior for the supplier. For example, the buyer may demand strict compliance to the negotiated contract or else the matter will be taken to court.

- *Coercive*–the buyer has the ability to punish the supplier. For example, the buyer may threaten to cancel future business with the supplier unless the supplier adheres to the buyer's demands.

It should be noted that the buyer does not always possess the power in a relationship. Sometimes the supplier holds the power; consequently, the supplier could exercise these sources of power as well. Should firms exercise all of the power sources they have? Most studies on power in the supply chain conclude that the use of coercive power should be minimized and a more cooperative approach to the supply relationship should be pursued.

Cooperative Orientation   The **cooperative orientation** emphasizes that the buyer and the seller are partners, each helping the other as much as possible. A cooperative orientation means long-term commitment, joint work on quality and service or product designs, and support by the buyer of the supplier's managerial, technological, and capacity development. A cooperative orientation favors fewer suppliers of a particular service or item, with just one or two suppliers being the ideal number. As order volumes increase, the supplier gains economies of scale, which lowers costs. When contracts are large and a long-term relationship is ensured, the supplier might even build a new facility and hire a new workforce, perhaps relocating close to the buyer's plant. Suppliers become almost an extension of the buyer.

A cooperative orientation means that the buyer shares more information with the supplier about its future buying intentions. This forward visibility allows suppliers to make better, more reliable forecasts of future demand. The buyer visits suppliers' plants and cultivates cooperative attitudes. The buyer may even suggest ways to improve the suppliers' operations. This close cooperation with suppliers could even mean that the buyer does not need to inspect incoming materials. It also could mean involving the supplier more in designing services or products, implementing cost-reduction ideas, and sharing in savings.

One advantage of a cooperative orientation is that of reducing the number of suppliers in the supply chain, which reduces the complexity of managing them. However, reducing the number of suppliers for a service or item may increase the risk of an interruption in supply. It also means less opportunity to drive a good bargain unless the buyer has a lot of

sole sourcing

The awarding of a contract for a service or item to only one supplier.

clout. **Sole sourcing**, which is the awarding of a contract for a service or item to only one supplier, can amplify any problems with the supplier that may crop up.

Both the competitive and cooperative orientations have their advantages and disadvantages. The key is to use the approach that serves the firm's competitive priorities best. Some companies utilize a mixed strategy, applying a competitive approach for its commodity-like supplies and a cooperative approach for its complex, high-valued, or high-volume services and materials.

Buying

The buying process relates to the actual procurement of the service or material from the supplier. This process includes the creation, management, and approval of purchase orders and determines the locus of control for purchasing decisions. Although not all purchasing opportunities involve the Internet, the emergence of the virtual marketplace has, indeed, provided firms with many opportunities to improve their buying and information exchange processes. Here we discuss four approaches to e-purchasing: (1) electronic data interchange, (2) catalog hubs, (3) exchanges, and (4) auctions, and close with the implications of choosing a locus of control.

electronic data interchange (EDI)

A technology that enables the transmission of routine business documents having a standard format from computer to computer over telephone or direct leased lines.

Electronic Data Interchange The most used form of e-purchasing today is **electronic data interchange (EDI)**, a technology that enables the transmission of routine, standardized business documents from computer to computer over telephone or direct leased lines. Special communications software translates documents into and out of a generic form, allowing organizations to exchange information even if they have different hardware and software components. Invoices, purchase orders, and payments information are some of the routine documents that EDI can handle—it replaces the phone call or mailed document.

An e-purchasing system with EDI might work as follows. Buyers browse an electronic catalog and click on items to purchase from a supplier. A computer sends the order directly to the supplier. The supplier's computer checks the buyer's credit and determines that the items are available. The supplier's warehouse and shipping departments are notified electronically, and the items are readied for shipment. Finally, the supplier's accounting department bills the buyer electronically. Savings (ranging from $5 to $125 per document) are considerable in light of the hundreds to thousands of documents many firms typically handle daily.

catalog hubs

A system whereby suppliers post their catalog of items on the Internet and buyers select what they need and purchase them electronically.

Catalog Hubs **Catalog hubs** can be used to reduce the costs of placing orders to suppliers as well as the costs of the services or goods themselves. Suppliers post their catalog of items on the hub, and buyers select what they need and purchase them electronically. The hub connects the firm to potentially hundreds of suppliers through the Internet, saving the costs of EDI, which requires one-to-one connections to individual suppliers. Moreover, the buying firm can negotiate prices with individual suppliers for items such as office supplies, technical equipment, services, and so forth. The catalog that the buying firm's employees see consists only of the approved items and the prices the buyer has prenegotiated with its suppliers. Employees use their PCs to select the items they need, and the system generates the purchase orders, which are electronically dispatched to the suppliers.

exchange

An electronic marketplace where buying firms and selling firms come together to do business.

Exchanges An **exchange** is an electronic marketplace where buying firms and selling firms come together to do business. The exchange maintains relationships with buyers and sellers, making it easy to do business without the aspect of contract negotiations or other types of long-term conditions. Exchanges are often used for "spot" purchases to satisfy an immediate need at the lowest possible cost. Commodity items such as oil, steel, or energy fit this category. However, exchanges can also be used for most any item. For example, Marriott International and Hyatt Corporation formed an exchange for purchasing hotel supplies. Hotels traditionally bought supplies from thousands of firms using faxes, telephones, and forms in quadruplicate. Placing orders was expensive, with little opportunity to do comparison shopping. The new exchange, which features thousands of supplies from many firms, makes for one-stop shopping for hotels using the service.

auction

A marketplace where firms place competitive bids to buy something.

Auctions An extension of the exchange is the **auction**, where firms place competitive bids to buy something. For example, a site may be formed for a particular industry, and firms with excess capacity or materials can offer them for sale to the highest bidder. Bids can either be closed or open to the competition. Industries where auctions have value include steel and chemicals. Examples involving consumers include eBay and Priceline.com.

An approach that has received considerable attention is the so-called *reverse auction*, where suppliers bid for contracts with buyers. Each bid is posted, so suppliers can see how much lower their next bid must be to remain in the running for the contract. Each contract has an electronic prospectus that provides all the specifications, conditions, and other requirements that are nonnegotiable. The only thing left to determine is the cost to the buyer. Savings to the buyer can be dramatic, sometime as much as 20 to 30 percent over typical contract prices. Ford, GM, and Chrysler put together a reverse auction marketplace to procure parts from suppliers. Similar marketplaces are forming around the buying and selling of paper, plastic, steel, bandwidth, chemicals, and the like.

Our discussion of these electronic purchasing approaches should not leave you with the impression that cost is the only consideration firms make. Exchanges and auctions are more useful for commodities, near-commodities, or infrequently needed items that require only short-term relationships with suppliers. Nonetheless, suppliers should be thought of as partners when the needed supply is significant and steady over extended periods of time. Supplier involvement in service or product design and supply chain performance improvement requires long-term relationships not found with competitive pricing on the Internet.

Locus of Control   When an organization has several facilities (stores, hospitals, or plants, for example), management must decide whether to buy locally or centrally. This decision has implications for the control of supply chain flows.

Centralized buying has the advantage of increasing purchasing power by creating a situation where suppliers are economically dependent on the buyer. Savings can be significant, often on the order of 10 percent or more. Increased buying power can mean getting better service, ensuring long-term supply availability, or developing new supplier capability. Companies with overseas suppliers favor centralization because the specialized skills (for example, understanding of foreign languages and cultures) needed to buy from foreign sources can be centralized in one location. Buyers also need to understand international commercial and contract law regarding the transfer of services and goods. Another trend that favors centralization is the growth of computer-based information systems and the Internet, which give specialists at headquarters access to data previously available only at the local level.

Probably the biggest disadvantage of centralized buying is loss of control at the local level. Centralized buying is undesirable for items unique to a particular facility. These items should be purchased locally whenever possible. The same holds for purchases that must be closely meshed with production schedules. Localized buying is also an advantage when the firm has major facilities in foreign countries because the managers there, often foreign nationals, have a much better understanding of the local culture than staff members at the home office. Also, centralized buying often means longer lead times.

Perhaps the best solution is a compromise strategy, whereby both local autonomy and centralized buying are possible. For example, the corporate purchasing group at IBM negotiates contracts on a centralized basis only at the request of local plants. Management at one of the plants then monitors the contract for all the participating plants.

Information Exchange

The information exchange process facilitates the exchange of pertinent operating information, such as forecasts, schedules, and inventory levels between the firm and its suppliers. New technology in the form of radio frequency identification facilitates the flow of inventory information. Beyond inventory information, the exchange of forecasts and other demand-related data facilitates integrating activities such as vendor managed inventories.

Radio Frequency Identification   An important requirement for any information exchange process in a supply chain context is accurate information regarding the quantity and location of inventories. A new application of an old technology presents some tantalizing benefits. **Radio frequency identification (RFID)** is a method for identifying items through the use of radio signals from a tag attached to an item. The tag has information about the item and sends signals to a device that can read the information and even write new information on the tag. Data from the tags can be transmitted wirelessly from one place to another through electronic product code (EPC) networks and the Internet, making it theoretically possible to uniquely identify every item a company produces and track it until the tag is destroyed.

radio frequency identification (RFID)

A method for identifying items through the use of radio signals from a tag attached to an item.

Wal-Mart, Target, Intel, Gillette, and the Department of Defense, among a number of large retailers, manufacturers, government agencies, and suppliers, are implementing RFID in their supply chains. In Wal-Mart's case, RFID tags on cases and pallets are read when inventory enters a stockroom and when those cases and pallets go to the retail floor. Wal-Mart uses the data to draw conclusions about when to bring additional stock to the floor and to figure out if too much of a product has been ordered by a store and is sitting in the stockroom or in the distribution center. The data could also help some 30,000 suppliers check inventory levels and sales. The use of RFID data can increase a supplier's service level to Wal-Mart.

RFID tags can be attached to containers or pallets of product to aid in managing the flow of inventories in a supply chain. This RFID tag card has a transponder with antenna and embedded integrated electronic circuit on a chip for receiving and transmitting Electronic Product Code signals.

Pilferage reduction is another major advantage of the RFID technology. Gillette is using RFID to reduce the amount of razor-blade theft, which amounts to as much as 30 percent of sales.

Whether RFID will be universally accepted is still unknown. Individual firms can use RFID within their own operations and avoid costly coordination with other firms in the supply chain. Benefits of using RFID internal to the firm are limited, however, and so is the investment. The larger potential gains come with application to the supply chain. To be successful, all members of the supply chain must benefit from the investment in RFID, not just the firm pushing the project. This is particularly true for global operations. Global data synchronization using industry standards is critical to ensure that accurate and consistent product information is exchanged between trading partners, a very challenging task. Much work is still to be done.

Vendor Managed Inventories   Reliable information regarding inventories up and down the supply chain allows firms to collaborate on effective ways to improve material flows. A tactic that requires a reliable information exchange process is **vendor-managed inventories (VMI)**, a system in which the supplier has access to the customer's inventory data and is responsible for maintaining the inventory level required by the customer. The inventory is on the customer's site, and often the supplier retains possession of the inventory until it is used by the customer. Companies such as Wal-Mart and Dell leverage their market position to mandate VMI. Vendor-managed inventories have several key elements.

vendor-managed inventories (VMI)

A system in which the supplier has access to the customer's inventory data and is responsible for maintaining the inventory on the customer's site.

- *Collaborative Effort.* For VMI to succeed, the customers must be willing to allow the supplier access to their inventory information, which is facilitated by RFID but must be bolstered by information on forecasts, sales promotions, and other demand related data. The implication is that the supplier assumes an important administrative role in the management of the inventory. Thus, an atmosphere of trust and accountability is required.

- *Cost Savings.* Suppliers and customers eliminate the need for excess inventory through better operational planning. VMI lowers costs by reducing administrative and inventory costs. Order placement costs are also reduced.

- *Customer Service.* The supplier is frequently on the customer's site and better understands the operations of the customer, improving response times and reducing stockouts.

- *Written Agreement.* It is important that both parties fully understand the responsibilities of each partner. Areas such as billing procedures, forecast methods, and replenishment schedules should be clearly specified. Further, the responsibility for obsolete inventory resulting from forecast revisions and changes in contract lengths should be included.

VMI can be used both by service providers as well as manufacturers. AT&T, Roadway Express, Wal-Mart, Dell, Westinghouse, and Bose are among the companies that use it.

THE ORDER FULFILLMENT PROCESS

The order fulfillment process produces and delivers the service or product to the firm's customers. There are four key nested processes: customer demand planning, supply planning, production, and logistics.

Customer Demand Planning

The customer demand planning (CDP) process facilitates the collaboration of a supplier and its customers for the purpose of forecasting customer requirements for a service or product. CDP is a business-planning process that enables sales teams (and customers) to develop demand forecasts as input to service-planning processes, production and inventory planning, and revenue planning. Forecasts must generally precede plans: It is not possible to make decisions on staffing levels, purchasing commitments, and inventory levels until forecasts are developed that give reasonably accurate views of demand over the forecasting time horizon. Chapter 13, "Forecasting Demand," provides more details on CDP and contains many practical tools for forecasting customer demands.

Supply Planning

The supply planning process takes the demand forecasts produced by the customer demand planning process and the resources provided by capacity planning to generate a plan to meet the demand. Regardless of whether the firm is producing services or a product, this process is critical for effective execution in the supply chain. It is very complex; for this reason we devote three of the following chapters to its important elements: inventory management, operations planning and scheduling, and resource planning.

Inventories exist in any supply chain to facilitate the flow of services or products. For example, Verizon must manage inventories of its "chocolate" cell phone manufactured by LG to satisfy customer demands for that item; otherwise, customers without the cell phone of their choice may go to a competing cell phone service. Similarly, a Nokia repair service facility must have enough components and materials on hand to fulfill its requirements for the repair of the various Nokia products under warranty. In Chapter 12, "Managing Inventories," we show how you can determine appropriate cycle and safety stock inventory levels and how to select the best inventory management system, which will tell you when to order inventory and how much each time.

Another important supply planning activity for a firm is planning its aggregate resource levels so that supply is in balance with demands. Usually stated at the firm or departmental level for several months to a year in advance, these aggregate plans specify output rates, workforce levels and inventory levels that are consistent with demand forecasts, capacity constraints, and inventory plans. Such plans amount to planning staffing levels for service firms and production rates and finished goods inventory levels for manufacturing firms. Once the aggregate resource levels are determined they must be scheduled to achieve the level of performance envisioned by management. In Chapter 14, "Planning and Scheduling Operations," we show how firms plan and schedule productive resources to provide an appropriate level of supply for services or products.

Finally, as the saying goes, "The devil is in the details." Planning for resources at aggregate levels is useful for making hiring decisions or acquiring capital goods so as to meet aggregate levels of demand. It ultimately becomes necessary to take each individual service or product and plan for its specific supply. With the aggregate operations plans and schedules as a basis, information such as time standards, routings, and other specific information as to how a service or product is produced is used to plan the specific inputs required. These plans are very detailed but very important for the efficient flow of services and products. In Chapter 15, "Planning Sufficient Resources," we show how this detailed level of planning is done and how the information from this planning effort is used by other functional areas in the firm.

Production

The production process executes the supply plan to produce the service or product. Nonetheless, the production process must be integrated with the processes that supply the inputs, establish the demands, and deliver the product to the customers. For example, while customers can always shop for standardized Dell computer packages at retail stores like Best Buy and Wal-Mart, order placement, buying, production, and logistics processes are tightly linked at Dell when a customized machine is being ordered directly from the computer manufacturer. The eight steps linking these processes for customer-ordered Dell computers are shown in Figure 10.5.

1. Customers communicate and buy from Dell in one of three ways: Web site, voice-to-voice, and face-to-face. The latter two ways involve actual human contact. An experienced representative takes the customer's order, reviews the information, and enters it into the system.

2. Order information is transmitted to the inventory system. Through the buying process, materials are received from suppliers and placed in racks in the manufacturing area. Dell receives only the materials it is immediately ready to use—those specified by the customer.

3. The production process begins by accessing the Traveler, which is a sheet containing all of the customer's unique product configuration information that travels with the system the customer has ordered throughout its assembly and shipping.

FIGURE 10.5 ▶
Dell's Order Fulfillment Process

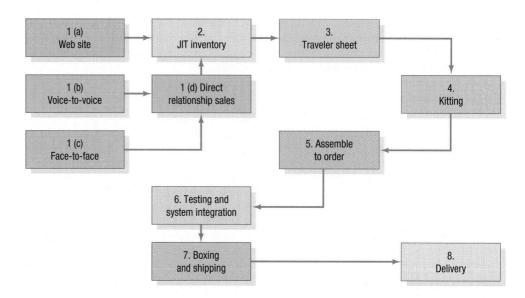

4. When the Traveler is pulled, all internal parts and components required to make the system are picked and placed in a tote, or kit. This procedure is called *kitting*.

5. A team of workers uses the kit to assemble and initially test the entire system.

6. Systems are then extensively tested using Dell diagnostic procedures. Standard or custom hardware and software is factory installed and tested.

7. The production process ends when the completed systems are placed in boxes along with documentation and manuals, then sealed and placed on trucks for shipping to the customer. The entire assemble-to-order cycle takes only a few hours.

8. The system is delivered to the customer using third-party logistics providers such as UPS.

Integrating the supply-facing and customer-facing processes to the production process is as important to service firms as it is to manufacturing firms. The best firms tightly link their production process to suppliers as well as customers.

Logistics

A key aspect of order fulfillment is the logistics process, which delivers the product or service to the customer. Five important decisions determine the design and implementation of logistics processes: degree of ownership, facility location, mode selection, capacity level, and amount of cross docking.

- *Ownership.* The firm has the most control over the logistics process if it owns and operates it, thereby becoming a *private carrier.* Although this approach may help to better achieve the firm's competitive priorities, the cost of equipment, labor, facilities, and maintenance could be high. The firm could instead leave the distribution to a *contract carrier,* negotiating with the carrier for specific services. Those services could involve taking over a major portion of the order fulfillment process. For example, UPS's Supply Chain Solutions unit controls more than 1 million square feet of warehouse space to help manage inventories for clients near Shanghai and Guangzhou in China. The clients use UPS to ship items to the warehouse, and then UPS manages the deliveries to the specific sites in China.

- *Facility Location.* A critical decision affecting the effectiveness of supply chains is the location of facilities that serve as points of service, storage, or manufacture. As the opener to this chapter showed, Kodak went though considerable analysis to arrive at its forward stocking locations. Because of the importance of this decision, we have devoted Chapter 11, "Locating Facilities," to a complete discussion of it.

- *Mode Selection.* The five basic modes of transportation are truck, train, ship, pipeline, and airplane. The drivers for the selection should be the firm's competitive priorities. Trucks provide the greatest flexibility because they can go wherever roads go. Transit times are good, and rates are usually better than trains for small quantities and short distances. Rail transportation can move large quantities cheaply; however, the transit times are long and often variable. Water transportation provides high capacity and low costs, and is necessary for overseas shipments of bulky items; however, the transit times are slow and highway or rail transportation is often needed to get the product to its ultimate destination. Pipeline transportation is highly specialized and is used for liquids, gases, or solids in slurry form. Although it has limited geographical flexibility, transporting via pipeline requires no packaging, and the operating costs per mile are low. Finally, air transportation is the fastest and most costly mode per mile. Nonetheless, getting a product to the customer fast using air transportation may actually reduce total costs when the costs of inventory and warehouse handling are considered for alternative modes. The cost of the funds tied up in some in-transit inventories can be considerable. Firms can also use mixed modal transportation, whereby a given shipment may combine two or more different modes. For example, containers can be carried by trucks, trains, or ships over different portions of their transit, and can often give the best tradeoffs between cost and delivery times.

■ *Capacity.* The performance of a logistics process is directly linked to its capacity. The ownership decision and the modal selection decision are often intertwined because the question of how much capacity is needed must be resolved. If ownership of the equipment and facilities is under consideration, capital costs as well as variable operating costs must be weighed against the costs of obtaining the logistics services from a supplier. Making things more difficult is the fact that the requirements for the logistics process are rarely known with certainty. In such cases, management can use the *expected value decision rule* to evaluate capacity alternatives. The expected value of an alternative is calculated as follows:

> *Expected value of an alternative* = (probability of a level of demand occurring)(payoff for using the alternative if that level of demand materialized) summed over all possible levels of demand.

See Supplement A, "Decision Making Models," for details on this approach. Example 10.3 demonstrates the use of the expected value decision rule for analyzing truck capacity.

EXAMPLE 10.3	**Using the Expected Value Decision Rule for Truck Capacity**

Tower Distributors provides logistical services to local manufacturers. Tower picks up products from the manufacturers, takes them to its distribution center, and then assembles shipments to retailers in the region. Tower needs to build a new distribution center; consequently, it needs to make a decision on how many trucks to use. The monthly amortized capital cost of ownership is $2,100 per truck. Operating variable costs are $1 per mile for each truck owned by Tower. If capacity is exceeded in any month, Tower can rent trucks at $2 per mile. Each truck Tower owns can be used 10,000 miles per month. The requirements for the trucks, however, are uncertain. Managers have estimated the following probabilities for several possible demand levels and corresponding fleet sizes.

Requirements (miles/month)	100,000	150,000	200,000	250,000
Fleet Size (trucks)	10	15	20	25
Probability	0.2	0.3	0.4	0.1

Notice that the sum of the probabilities must equal 1.0. If Tower Distributors wants to minimize the expected cost of operations, how many trucks should it use?

SOLUTION

We use the expected value decision rule to evaluate the alternative fleet sizes where we want to minimize the expected monthly cost. To begin, the monthly cost, C, must be determined for each possible combination of fleet size and requirements. The cost will depend on whether additional capacity must be rented for the month. For example, consider the *10 truck fleet size* alternative, which represents a capacity of 100,000 miles per month.

C = monthly capital cost of ownership + variable operating cost per month + rental costs if needed

C (100,00 miles/month) = ($2,100/truck)(10 trucks) + ($1/mile)(100,000 miles) = $121,000

C (150,000 miles/month) = ($2,100/truck)(10 trucks) + ($1/mile)(100,000 miles) + ($2 rent/mile)(150,000 miles

  − 100,000 miles) = $221,000

C (200,000 miles/month) = ($2,100/truck)(10 trucks) + ($1/mile)(100,000 miles) + ($2 rent/mile)(200,000 miles

  − 100,000 miles) = $321,000

C (250,000miles/month) = ($2,100/truck)(10 trucks) + ($1/mile)(100,000 miles) + ($2 rent/mile)(250,000 miles

  − 100,000 miles) = $421,000

Next, calculate the expected value for the *10 truck fleet size* alternative as follows:

Expected Value (10 trucks) $= 0.2(\$121,000) + 0.3(\$221,000) + 0.4(\$321,000) + 0.1(\$421,000) = \$261,000$

Using similar logic, we can calculate the expected costs for each of the other fleet-size options:

Expected Value (15 trucks) $= 0.2(\$131,500) + 0.3(\$181,500) + 0.4(\$281,500) + 0.1(\$381,500) = \$231,500$

Expected Value (20 trucks) $= 0.2(\$142,000) + 0.3(\$192,000) + 0.4(\$242,000) + 0.1(\$342,000) = \$217,000$

Expected Value (25 trucks) $= 0.2(\$152,500) + 0.3(\$202,500) + 0.4(\$252,500) + 0.1(\$302,500) = \$222,500$

Using the expected value decision rule, Tower Distributors should use a fleet of 20 trucks.

DECISION POINT

The fleet size of 20 trucks means that Tower will have enough capacity to handle 90 percent of its requirements (sum of the probabilities for 100,000 miles, 150,000 miles, and 200,000 miles). Further, there will be a 50 percent chance that it will have excess capacity (sum of the probabilities for 100,000 miles and 150,000 miles). While the decision to invest in 20 trucks will minimize expected costs, it will also provide slack capacity 50 percent of the time, which is reflective of the relatively high cost for being short of capacity.

cross-docking

The packing of products on incoming shipments so that they can be easily sorted at intermediate warehouses for outgoing shipments based on their final destinations; the items are carried from the incoming-vehicle docking point to the outgoing-vehicle docking point without being stored in inventory at the warehouse.

■ *Cross-Docking.* Low-cost operations and delivery speed can be enhanced with a technique called **cross-docking**, which is the packing of products on incoming shipments so that they can be easily sorted at intermediate warehouses for outgoing shipments based on their final destinations; the items are carried from the incoming-vehicle docking point to the outgoing-vehicle docking point without being stored in inventory at the warehouse. For example, a truck from Nebraska carrying shipments to customers in Ohio, Pennsylvania, and Virginia arrives at a warehouse in Columbus, Ohio, where warehouse personnel unload its contents and reload them on trucks headed for destinations in Ohio, Pennsylvania, and Virginia. Inbound shipments must be tightly coordinated with outbound shipments for cross-docking to work. For instance, Wal-Mart uses advanced information systems, bar coding, strategically located large-scale warehouses, and a large fleet of private trucks to make cross-docking work effectively across its vast distribution network. The warehouse becomes a short-term staging area for organizing efficient shipments to customers. The benefits of cross-docking include reductions in inventory investment, storage space requirements, handling costs, and lead times, as well as increased inventory turnover and accelerated cash flow. Management must decide where cross-docking operations are best placed, given the overall flow of items and their destinations.

THE CUSTOMER RELATIONSHIP PROCESS

The customer relationship process addresses the interface between the firm and its customers downstream in the supply chain. The purpose of the customer relationship process, which supports *customer relationship management (CRM)* programs, is to identify, attract, and build relationships with customers and to facilitate the transmission and tracking of orders. Key nested processes include the marketing, order placement, and customer service processes.

Marketing

The marketing process focuses on such issues as determining the customers to target, how to target them, what services or products to offer and how to price them, and how to manage promotional campaigns. In this regard, **electronic commerce (e-commerce)**, which is the application of information and communication technology anywhere along the supply chain of business processes, has had a huge impact up and down the supply chain. There are two e-commerce technologies that relate to the marketing process: business-to-consumer and business-to-business systems.

electronic commerce (e-commerce)

The application of information and communication technology anywhere along the supply chain of business processes.

Business-to-Consumer Systems   Business-to-consumer (B2C) systems, which allow customers to transact business over the Internet, are commonplace. B2C e-commerce offers a new distribution channel for businesses, and consumers can avoid crowded department stores with long checkout lines and parking-space shortages. Many of the advantages of e-commerce were first exploited by retail "e-businesses," such as Amazon.com, E*TRADE, and Autobytel. These three companies created Internet versions of traditional bookstores, brokerage firms, and auto dealerships. The Internet is changing operations, processes, and cost structures for even traditional retailers, and the overall growth in its usage has been dramatic. Today, anyone with an Internet connection can open a store in cyberspace.

Many leading retailers and catalog companies have opened Web "stores" with thousands of virtual aisles and millions of items. This technology allows customers to do much more shopping in an hour than they could possibly do in person at a traditional retail outlet. E-commerce is particularly attractive for products that the consumer does not have to look at carefully or touch. The Internet offers an advantage with higher-value branded convenience goods over the in-store experience.

Business-to-Business Systems   The biggest growth, however, has been in business-to-business (B2B) e-commerce systems, or commerce between firms. In fact, business-to-business e-commerce outpaces business-to-consumer transactions, with trade between businesses making up more than 70 percent of the regular economy.

Consider Fruit of the Loom, Inc., an apparel maker that depends on its wholesalers to ship products to various retailer customers. Fruit of the Loom put its wholesalers on the Web and gave each one a complete computer system that displays colorful catalogs, processes electronic orders around the clock, and manages inventories. If one of its distributors is out of stock, the company's central warehouse is notified to ship replacement stock directly to the customer. Building such an integrated e-commerce system took only a few months. The firm's retail customers need only an Internet connection and a Web browser.

Order Placement

The order placement process involves the activities required to execute a sale, register the specifics of the order request, confirm the acceptance of the order, and track the progress of the order until it is completed. Often the firm has a sales force that visits prospective and current customers to encourage a sale.

The Internet enables firms to reengineer their order placement process to benefit both the customer and the firm. For example, a traveler may arrive at the Hilton on Kauai and request a room without an advance reservation. An employee at the hotel will take the appropriate information regarding the order, including the dates of stay, suite or other type of room requested, double or single occupancy, king-size bed or double beds, smoking or nonsmoking, and then check to see which rooms (if any) are available. This approach is costly because of the time required of the employee, particularly at busy periods, not to mention the risk that the hotel will be unable to serve the customer. Alternatively, the traveler could use the hotel's Web site several weeks in advance, provide the same information, and get confirmation of the reservation. These two versions of the order placement process for the hotel involve different amounts of employee time and provide different levels of service to the customer.

The Internet provides the following advantages for a firm's order placement process.

- *Cost Reduction.* Using the Internet can reduce the costs of processing orders because it allows for greater participation by the customer. Customers can select the services or products they want and place an order with the firm without actually talking to anyone. This approach reduces the need for call centers, which are labor intensive and often take longer to place orders.

- *Revenue Flow Increase.* A firm's Web page can allow customers to enter credit card information or purchase-order numbers as part of the order placement process. This approach reduces the time lags often associated with billing the customer or waiting for checks sent in the mail.

- *Global Access.* Another advantage the Internet provides to firms is the opportunity to accept orders 24-hours a day. Traditional brick-and-mortar firms only take orders during their normal business hours. Firms with Internet access can reduce the time it takes to satisfy customers, who can shop and purchase at any time. This access gives these firms a competitive advantage over brick-and-mortar firms.

- *Pricing Flexibility.* Firms with their services and products posted on the Web can easily change prices as the need arises, thereby avoiding the cost and delay of publishing new catalogs. Customers placing orders have current prices to consider when making their choices. From the perspective of supply chains, Dell uses this capability to control for component shortages. Because of its direct-sales approach and promotional

Many firms have outsourced their customer service processes, particularly if the service can be transacted over the phone. Here Indian employees at a call center in the southern city of Bangalore, India, provide service support to international customers.

pricing, Dell can steer customers to certain configurations of computers for which ample supplies exist.

Customer Service

The customer service process helps customers with answers to questions regarding the service or product, resolves problems, and, in general, provides information to assist customers. It is an important point of contact between the firm and its customers, who may judge the firm on the basis of their experiences with this process. The age-old tradeoff between cost and quality, however, enters the picture, especially for call centers. In an effort to reduce the cost of their customer service process, many firms have opted to replace human service agents with automated systems, which often require customers to wade through an exhausting sequence of options that sometimes only lead to frustration. Other firms are using Verbots®, or "verbal robots," which are supported by sophisticated artificial intelligence. They have personalities, ask and respond to questions, and in some cases are almost indistinguishable from humans over the phone. Nonetheless, most customers and others seeking information about a service or product prefer humans. Consequently, in consideration for the cost involved, many companies have expanded their supply chain by outsourcing the customer service process to an off shore site where labor costs are low. In this regard, India has responded in a big way to the international need for low-cost call centers. For example, you might have a problem with your Hewlett-Packard ink jet printer and solve that problem by talking to a technician in Bangalore, India. Of course, the big risk in outsourcing the customer service process, or a part of it, is that the firm loses some control over a process that has direct interface with its customers. This consideration should be carefully weighed in the final analysis.

LEVERS FOR IMPROVED SUPPLY CHAIN PERFORMANCE

Now that we gave discussed a framework for integrated supply chains, we can return to the problems caused by supply chain dynamics and how integrated supply chains can mitigate the poor performance from dynamics such as the bullwhip effect. In this section we pose some levers that can be utilized with integrated supply chains to improve performance and reveal important performance measures for tracking supply chain operations.[2]

The Levers

Integrated supply chains facilitate the application of the following options for overall improvement in performance:

- *Sharing data*–one source of dynamics in supply chains is the lack of visibility of end-user demand by suppliers upstream in the supply chain. To facilitate planning at all levels in the supply chain, point-of-sale (POS) data, which records actual customer purchases of the final service or product, can be shared with all suppliers. RFID can also be used to track quantities of inventory throughout the supply chain.
- *Collaborative activities*–working closely with customers and suppliers in customer demand planning (CDP) and environmental health and safety programs as well as the design collaboration process improves information flows, improves environmental

---

[2] For more coverage of levers, see Sunil Chopra and Peter Meindl, *Supply Chain Management*, 3e (Upper Saddle River, NJ: Prentice Hall, 2007), pp. 506–511.

stewardship, and reduces surprises from demand spikes due to promotions or supply hang-ups because of poorly designed services or products.

■ *Reduce replenishment lead times*–improving internal processes and working with suppliers to reduce lead times allows the firm to wait longer before reacting to a change in demand levels, thereby mitigating the bullwhip effect. In addition, shorter lead times leads to smaller pipeline inventories.

■ *Reduce order lot sizes*–working on ways to reduce the costs associated with ordering, transporting and receiving inventory throughout the supply chain will reduce order lot sizes and thereby decrease the amount of fluctuation in the size of orders in the supply chain.

■ *Ration short supplies*–when a shortage exists, customers sometimes artificially inflate their orders to protect themselves, only to cancel them later when the shortage is relieved. To counteract this behavior, suppliers can ration short supplies to customers on the basis of their past sales, rather than their current orders.

■ *Use every day low pricing (EDLP)*–promotional or discount pricing encourages spikes in demand. Using a stable pricing program such as EDLP, as is done by Wal-Mart, discourages customers from buying excess stock at discounted prices so they can offer price promotions, a practice called *forward buying*. EDLP levels the demand.

■ *Be cooperative and trustworthy*–being cooperative in solving supply issues and providing information that can be trusted serves to reduce costs for all members of the supply chain and mitigates environmental problems and the deleterious effects of supply chain dynamics.

Performance Measures

It is important to monitor the performance of the supply chain to see where improvements can be made or to measure the impact of applying the levers. Supply chain managers monitor performance by measuring costs, time, quality, and environmental impact. Table 10.1 contains examples of commonly used performance measures for three supply chain processes. Managers periodically collect data on these measures and track them to note changes in level or direction. Statistical process control charts can be used to determine whether the changes are statistically significant.

Integrated supply chains are powerful tools for achieving competitiveness along many performance measures. Currently, concerns about the environment are prompting supply chain managers to take a careful look at their operations and those of their suppliers. In the final section of this chapter, we take a look at the impact of environmental concerns on supply chains and how integrated supply chains can be used to relieve some of those concerns and still be profitable.

TABLE 10.1	SUPPLY CHAIN PROCESS MEASURES	
Customer Relationship	**Order Fulfillment**	**Supplier Relationship**
• Percent of orders taken accurately	• Percent of incomplete orders shipped	• Percent of suppliers' deliveries on-time
• Time to complete the order placement process	• Percent of orders shipped on-time	• Suppliers' lead times
• Customer satisfaction with the order placement process	• Time to fulfill the order	• Percent defects in services and purchased materials
• Customer's evaluation of firm's environmental stewardship	• Percent of botched services or returned items	• Cost of services and purchased materials
	• Cost to produce the service or item	• Inventory levels of supplies and purchased components
	• Customer satisfaction with the order fulfillment process	• Evaluation of suppliers' collaboration on streamlining and waste conversion
	• Inventory levels of work-in-process and finished goods	• Amount of transfer of environmental technologies to suppliers
	• Amount of greenhouse gasses emitted into the air	

Supply Chains and the Environment

Environmental concerns regarding business are voiced every day in the popular media. Service providers are examining ways to increase efficiency and reduce the impact of their operations on the environment. Manufacturers are feeling pressure to take responsibility for their products from birth to death. In this section we will discuss some environmental concerns and how integrated supply chains can address them. We will also discuss the supply chain implications for implementing an approach called "reverse logistics," which responds to the need to salvage products at the end of their life cycles.

Sustainability

sustainability

A characteristic of processes that are meeting humanity's needs without harming future generations.

A growing theme among many corporations is that of environmental stewardship. Translated into a goal, these corporations strive to have services, products, and processes that have the characteristic of **sustainability**, which means that they are meeting humanity's needs without harming future generations.[3] Because of established communication and material flows, integrated supply chains can facilitate the implementation of environmentally friendly operations. Achieving sustainability is no easy task; however, firms can move closer to that goal by addressing the following environmental concerns:

- *Environmental protection*–firms should monitor their own processes and those of their suppliers to improve waste elimination methods, to reduce the pollution of the air, streams, and rivers, and to increase efforts at ecological stewardship for the protection of flora and fauna.

- *Productivity improvement*–firms should examine processes up and down the supply chain to increase material conservation, to increase energy efficiency, and to look for ways to convert waste into useful by-products.

- *Risk minimization*–as the supply chain grows, particularly on a global basis, firms should take great care to ensure that the materials that go into their services, products, or processes do not pose health or safety hazards to customers.

- *Innovation*–as new services, products, or technologies are developed, firms should strive to make sure that they support the environment while serving the needs of customers.

Sustainability is not the easiest strategy to gain approval of from most boards of directors. While seemingly intuitive, directors often need some sort of demonstrable return on investment to justify the costs. For sustainability efforts, however, managers must have a long-term view that accepts lower returns in the near future to improve the chances of survival in the future.

Reverse Logistics

reverse logistics

The process of planning, implementing, and controlling the efficient, cost effective flow of products, materials, and information from the point of consumption back to the point of origin for returns, repair, remanufacture, or recycling.

To address environmental concerns and to manage their products throughout their life cycles, firms such as Coors Brewing Company, Dell, and Caterpillar are turning to **reverse logistics**, which is the process of planning, implementing, and controlling the efficient, cost effective flow of products, materials, and information from the point of consumption back to the point of origin for returns, repair, remanufacture, or recycling. A supply chain that integrates forward logistics with reverse logistics is called a *closed-loop supply chain* because it focuses on the complete chain of operations from the birth to the death of a product. Figure 10.6 shows how a product starts its journey at the new service/product development process, makes its way to the customer, and then enters the reverse logistics chain that attempts to maximize the value of the item at the end of its useful life.

It is clear that the reverse logistics operations are considerably different from the forward logistics flows. A firm must establish convenient collection points to receive the used goods from the final customer and transport the goods to a *returns processor*, which is a facility owned by the manufacturer or outsourced to a supplier and that is proficient at disassembling products and gleaning any remaining value from them. Several options exist. If the item is inoperable, it could be repaired and returned to the customer. Another option is that it could be cleaned and refurbished for direct use and returned either to the distribution channel, which is the case with leased products, or back to customers, which is the case with a maintenance warranty. The product could be remanufactured by tearing it down, rebuilding

---

[3] For a more complete discussion of sustainability and what major corporations are doing, see Pete Engardio, "Beyond the Green Corporation," *Business Week* (January 29, 2007), pp. 50–64.

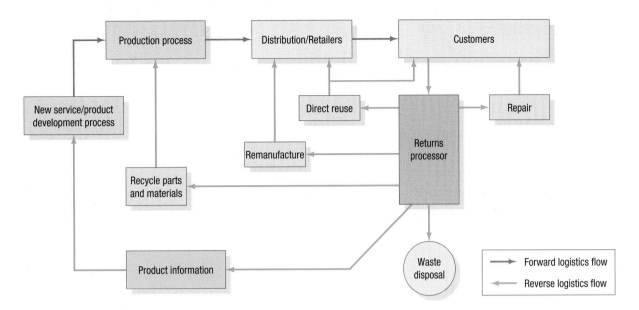

▲ FIGURE 10.6
Flows in a Closed-Loop Supply Chain

it with new parts as needed, and returning it to the distribution channel. Finally, the product could be completely disassembled and the usable parts and materials cleaned, tested, and returned to the production process. There are two important by-products of the reverse logistics process: waste, which must be properly disposed of, and product information, which is transmitted to the new service/product development process so that improvements can be made to future generations of the product.

Reverse logistics processes can be particularly important in the electronics industry. Have you ever wondered what happens to your old computer after you purchase a new one? You may have given it to the store where you purchased your new one, or merely slipped it into the household trash. More retired computers in the United States are dumped in landfills than are recycled. Old computers contain electronics components with materials that can be recycled. However, they also have toxins that leach into the soil if these components are left unprocessed: lead and cadmium in computer circuit boards, lead oxide and barium in computer monitors and cathode-ray tubes (CRT), mercury in switches and flat screens, and fire retardant on printed circuit boards and plastic casings.

Many recycling processors are located in developing countries and are typically low tech. Recyclable material is collected and processed. Workers, who usually do not wear protective gear, often toss the chemicals that come out during the processing into nearby streams and rivers. Other materials not processed often are left in the dumps, allowing the toxins to leak out. This disregard for the environment prompted a backlash against the improper disposition of electronic equipment in developed countries. The European Union (EU) passed a law requiring electronics manufacturers to take back and recycle 75 percent of the products they sell in the EU. Some states in the United States banned *e-waste*, electronic components and the chemical by-products of the recycling process, from landfills and are considering making electronics manufacturers responsible for managing e-waste. Managerial Practice 10.1 provides an example of how a company in this industry used reverse logistics to be environmentally responsive while earning a profit.

In this chapter we have provided an overview of how firms can integrate their supply chains and the advantages that accrue to them. A powerful motivator for integrating supply chains is to mitigate the debilitating effects of supply chain dynamics such as the bullwhip effect so as to develop an efficient flow of information and materials up and down the supply chain. We discussed the new service or product development, supplier relationship, order fulfillment, and customer relationship processes and their nested processes to show the extent to which these processes permeate the organization and the nature of the decisions managers must make that recognize suppliers as well as their own firms. We finished this chapter by discussing the importance of integrated supply chains for addressing environmental concerns. In the next chapter we will extend our discussion of logistics issues by examining the important topic of facility location.

MANAGERIAL PRACTICE 10.1	Reverse Logistics at Citiraya Industries Helps Recycle High-Tech Equipment

The growing need to be environmentally responsible in the electronics manufacturing industry provided a unique opportunity to deliver a service to both the manufacturers and the countries in which they do business. Citiraya Industries Ltd, a company based in Singapore, commands a 70 percent share of the corporate market for scrapped electronics. The reason for the high market share is that Citiraya created a reverse logistics supply chain that includes high-tech processes and a sophisticated tracking system that allows manufacturers to prove their compliance with environmental laws.

Citiraya uses laser technology in its Mid Glamorgan plant in the United Kingdom to separate the funnel glass of CRTs, which contains high levels of lead oxide, from the lead-free panel glass in 30 to 90 seconds, depending on the size of the tube. The remanufacturers of panel glass require a pure, uncontaminated source. Citiraya's computer recycling reverse logistics supply chain begins with its collection centers in 11 countries, including China, India, and the United Kingdom. These centers ship the electronic trash to Citiraya's premier processing plant in Singapore. Workers wearing thick boots, gloves, and breathing apparatus use heavy cutters to break up integrated-circuit chips, which are moved to a furnace designed to melt special plastics. In another section, workers use chemicals to strip out materials such as gold, copper, and plastic resins. Monitoring devices analyze the air discharged by the plant as well as the water discharged into the city's sewage system. The plant has 60 cameras to allow customers to witness the destruction of their products via the Internet. The supply chain developed by Citiraya recycles 90 percent of the products manufacturers send it, while its competitors recover only 65 percent. It is clear that environmentally friendly operations can be a competitive niche.

Source: Cris Prystay, "Recycling 'E-Waste'," Wall Street Journal (September 23, 2004); Steve Bush, "Lasers Recycle CRT Funnel Glass," ElectronicsWeekly.com (June 28, 2005); www.citiraya.co.uk, 2008.

INTERNET RESOURCES

my**om**lab and the Companion Website at **www.pearsonglobaleditions.com/krajewski** contain many tools, activities, and resources designed for this chapter.

KEY EQUATIONS

1. Total Annual Cost = pD + Freight costs + $(Q/2 + \bar{d}L)H$ + Administrative costs

2. *Expected value of an alternative* = (probability of a level of demand occurring)(payoff for using the alternative if that demand materialized) summed over all possible levels of demand.

KEY TERMS

auction 386
bullwhip effect 377
catalog hubs 386
competitive orientation 385
concurrent engineering 380
cooperative orientation 385
cross-docking 392
early supplier involvement 384

electronic commerce
  (e-commerce) 392
electronic data interchange (EDI) 386
exchange 386
green purchasing 383
presourcing 384
purchasing 381
radio frequency identification
  (RFID) 387

reverse logistics 396
SCOR model 378
sole sourcing 386
supply chain integration 376
sustainability 396
value analysis 384
vendor-managed inventories (VMI) 388

SOLVED PROBLEM 1

ABC Electric Repair wants to select a supplier based on total annual cost, consistent quality, and delivery speed. The following table shows the weights management assigned to each criterion (total of 100 points) and the scores assigned to each supplier (Excellent = 5, Poor = 1).

Criterion	Weight	Scores	
		Kramer	Sunrise
Total annual cost	30	4	5
Consistent quality	40	3	4
Delivery speed	30	5	3

Which supplier should ABC select, given these criteria and scores?

SOLUTION

Using the preference matrix approach, the weighted scores for each supplier are:

$$Kramer:\ WS = (30 \times 4) + (40 \times 3) + (30 \times 5) = 390$$

$$Sunrise:\ WS = (30 \times 5) + (40 \times 4) + (30 \times 3) = 400$$

Based on the weighted scores, ABC should select Sunrise even though delivery speed performance would be better with Kramer.

SOLVED PROBLEM 2

Schneider Logistics Company has built a new warehouse in Columbus, Ohio, to facilitate the consolidation of freight shipments to customers in the region. George Schneider must determine how many teams of dock workers he should hire to handle the cross docking operations and the other warehouse activities. Each team costs $5,000 a week in wages and overhead. Extra capacity can be subcontracted at a cost of $8,000 a team per week. Each team, whether in-house or subcontracted, can satisfy 200 labor hours of work a week. The labor hour requirements for the new facility are uncertain. Management has estimated the following probabilities for the requirements:

Requirements (hours/wk)	200	400	600
Number of teams	1	2	3
Probability	0.20	0.50	0.30

How many teams should Schneider hire?

SOLUTION

We use the expected value decision rule by first computing the cost for each option for each possible level of requirements and then using the probabilities to determine the expected value for each option. The option with the lowest expected cost is the one Schneider will implement. We demonstrate the approach using the "one team" in-house option.

One Team In-House

$$C(200) = \$5,000$$

$$C(400) = \$5,000 + \$8,000 = \$13,000$$

$$C(600) = \$5,000 + \$8,000 + \$8,000 = \$21,000$$

Expected Value

$$(\text{One Team}) = 0.20(\$5,000) + 0.50(\$13,000) + 0.30(\$21,000) = \$13,800.$$

A table of the complete results is below.

Weekly Labor Requirements				
In-House	**200 hrs**	**400 hrs**	**600 hrs**	**Expected Value**
One team	$5,000	$13,000	$21,000	$13,800
Two teams	$10,000	$10,000	$18,000	$12,400
Three teams	$15,000	$15,000	$15,000	$15,000

Based on the expected value decision rule, Schneider should employ two teams at the warehouse.

SOLVED PROBLEM 3

ABC Electric Repair is a repair facility for several major electric appliance manufacturers. ABC wants to find a low-cost supplier for an electric relay switch used in many appliances. The annual requirements for the relay switch (D) are 100,000 units. ABC operates 250 days a year. The following data are available for two suppliers, Kramer and Sunrise, for the part:

	Freight Costs Shipping Quantity (Q)					
Supplier	**2,000**	**10,000**	**Price/Unit (p)**	**Carrying Cost/Unit (H)**	**Lead Time (L) (days)**	**Administrative Costs**
Kramer	$30,000	$20,000	$5.00	$1.00	5	$10,000
Sunrise	$28,000	$18,000	$4.90	$0.98	9	$11,000

Which supplier will provide the lowest annual total costs?

SOLUTION

The daily requirements for the relay switch are:

$$\bar{d} = 100{,}000/250 = 400 \text{ units.}$$

We must calculate the total annual costs for each alternative:

Total annual cost = Material costs + Freight costs + Inventory costs + Administrative costs

$$= pD + \text{Freight costs} + (Q/2 + \bar{d}L)H + \text{Administrative costs}$$

Kramer

$Q = 2{,}000$:   ($5.00)(100,000) + $30,000 +   (2,000/2 + 400(5))($1) + $10,000 = $543,000
$Q = 10{,}000$:   ($5.00)(100,000) + $20,000 + (10,000/2 + 400(5))($1) + $10,000 = $537,000

Sunrise

$Q = 2{,}000$:   ($4.90)(100,000) + $28,000 +   (2,000/2 + 400(9))($0.98) + $11,000 = $533,508
$Q = 10{,}000$:   ($4.90)(100,000) + $18,000 + (10,000/2 + 400(9))($0.98) + $11,000 = $527,428

The analysis reveals that using Sunrise and a shipping quantity of 10,000 units will yield the lowest annual total costs.

DISCUSSION QUESTIONS

1. We discussed the inventory and supply chain considerations such as small lot sizes, close supplier ties, and quality at the source in Chapter 8, "Designing Lean Systems." What are the implications of these principles for supply chain integration?

2. Firms such as Wal-Mart, General Electric, Chase Manhattan, and Boeing have a lot of influence in their respective supply chains because of the power they have. Explain how firms with a lot of power can influence supply chain integration.

3. Chrysler and General Motors vigorously compete with each other in many automobile and truck markets. When Jose Ignacio Lopez was vice president of purchasing for GM, he made it clear that his buyers were not to accept luncheon invitations from suppliers. Thomas Stalcamp, head of purchasing for Chrysler at the time, instructed his buyers to take suppliers to lunch. Rationalize these two directives in light of supplier relations and the impact on supply chain management.

4. One of the concerns addressed by a strategy of *sustainability* is that of environmental protection, in particular the improvement of waste disposal. Such a goal is worthwhile; however, it can pose difficult choices. Take for example a major fast food restaurant chain that developed its supply chain to deliver low costs, consistent quality, and delivery speed. Operations were designed to minimize variations; consistency in operations worldwide enabled the dependable delivery of a good product at low cost to the customer. To a large extent the success of the business was due to the loyalty of the suppliers, who at times even proposed new products or better ways to produce them. One day, in an effort to be more environmentally responsible, the company decided to eliminate the Styrofoam clam containers it was using to package its hamburgers in favor of paper wrappings. This action required the certification of new suppliers for the paper wraps, the cancellation of contracts with several long-term suppliers of the clam containers, and a change to the waste disposal operations.

What are the potential benefits to the company for the elimination of the Styrofoam containers? What are the potential downsides to that decision?

PROBLEMS

Software, such as OM Explorer, Active Models, and POM for Windows, is available in my**om**lab. Check with your instructor on how best to use it. In many cases, the instructor wants you to understand how to do the calculations by hand. At most, the software provides a check on your calculations. When calculations are particularly complex and the goal is interpreting the results in making decisions, the software replaces entirely the manual calculations.

1. Eight Flags operates several amusement parks in the Midwest. The company stocks machine oil to service the machinery for the many rides at the parks. Eight Flags needs 30,000 gallons of oil annually; the parks operate 50 weeks a year. Management is unsatisfied with the current supplier of oil and has obtained two bids from other suppliers. The data are contained in the following table:

Which supplier and which shipping quantity will provide the lowest costs for Eight Flags?

	Annual Freight Costs Shipping Quantity						
Supplier	5,000	10,000	15,000	Price/Unit	Annual Holding Cost/Unit	Lead Time (wks)	Annual Administrative Cost
Sharps	$5,000	$2,600	$2,000	$4.00	$0.80	4	$4,000
Winkler	$5,500	$3,200	$2,900	$3.80	$0.76	6	$5,000

2. Horizon Cellular manufacturers cell phones for exclusive use in its communication network. Management must select a circuit board supplier for a new phone soon to be introduced to the market. The annual requirements are 50,000 units and Horizon's plant operates 250 days per year. The data for three suppliers are in the following table:

Which supplier and shipping quantity will provide the lowest total cost for Horizon Cellular?

	Annual Freight Costs Shipping Quantity					
Supplier	10,000	20,000	Price/Unit	Annual Holding Cost/Unit	Lead Time (days)	Annual Administrative Cost
Abbott	$10,000	$7,000	$30	$6.00	4	$10,000
Baker	$12,000	$9,000	$28	$5.60	7	$12,000
Carpenter	$9,000	$6,500	$31	$6.20	3	$9,000

3. Sanchez Trucking has been experiencing delays at its warehouse operations. Management hired a consultant to find out why service deliveries to local businesses have taken longer than they should. The consultant narrowed down the problem to the number of work crews loading and unloading trucks. Each crew consists of 6 employees who work as a team on a variety of tasks; each employee works a full 40 hours a week. However, costs are also a concern. The consultant advised management that they could supplement work crews with short-term employees, at a higher cost, to cover unexpected needs on a weekly basis. Each work crew permanently hired by Sanchez costs $3,200 per week in wages and benefits, while a crew of short-term employees costs $5,000 per week. Complicating the decision is the fact that the weekly hourly requirements for work crews is uncertain because of the volatility in the number of deliveries to be made. Deliberating with management, the consultant arrived at the following data:

Requirements (man-hours)	720	960	1,200	1,440
Probability	0.2	0.4	0.3	0.1
Number of crews	3	4	5	6

If the consultant wants to offer a solution that minimizes the expected weekly costs for Sanchez, how many work crews should Sanchez have on its permanent payroll?

4. Wingman Distributing Company is expanding its supply chain to include a new distribution hub in South Bend. A key decision involves the number of trucks for the facility. The particular model of truck Wingman is considering can be used 8,000 miles a month and will cost $1,500 a month in capital costs. In addition, each mile a truck is used costs $0.90 for maintenance. A local truck rental firm will rent trucks at a cost of $1.40 per mile. Given the distribution of likely requirements for trucks, management has come up with three alternatives to consider as shown in the table:

Monthly requirements (miles)	40,000	80,000	120,000
Probability	0.30	0.40	0.30
Fleet size (trucks)	5	10	15

Which fleet size will yield the lowest expected monthly costs for Wingman?

5. Beagle Clothiers uses a weighted score for the evaluation and selection of its suppliers of trendy fashion garments. Each supplier is rated on a 10-point scale (10 = highest) for four different criteria: price, quality, delivery, and flexibility (to accommodate changes in quantity and timing).

Criteria	Supplier A	Supplier B	Supplier C
Price	8	6	6
Quality	9	7	7
Delivery	7	9	6
Flexibility	5	8	9

Because of the volatility of the business in which Beagle operates, flexibility is given twice the weight of each of the other three criteria, which are equally weighted. The table shows the scores for three potential suppliers for the four performance criteria. Based on the highest weighted score, which supplier should be selected?

6. The Bennet Company purchases one of its essential raw materials from three suppliers. Bennet's current policy is to distribute purchases equally among the three. The owner's son, Benjamin Bennet, just graduated from a business college. He proposes that these suppliers be rated (high numbers mean a good performance) on six performance criteria weighted as shown in the table. A total score hurdle of 0.60 is proposed to screen suppliers. Purchasing policy would be revised to order raw materials from suppliers with performance scores greater than the total score hurdle, in proportion to their performance rating scores.

			Rating	
Performance Criterion	Weight	Supplier A	Supplier B	Supplier C
1. Price	0.2	0.6	0.5	0.9
2. Quality	0.2	0.6	0.4	0.8
3. Delivery	0.3	0.6	0.3	0.8
4. Production facilities	0.1	0.5	0.9	0.6
5. Environmental protection	0.1	0.7	0.8	0.6
6. Financial position	0.1	0.9	0.9	0.7

a. Use a preference matrix to calculate the total weighted score for each supplier.

b. Which supplier(s) survived the total score hurdle? Under the younger Bennet's proposed policy, what proportion of orders would each supplier receive?

c. What advantages does the proposed policy have over the current policy?

ADVANCED PROBLEMS

7. Wanda Lux must select a supplier for a plastic bottle and proprietary dispenser for its new hair shampoo. Three suppliers have placed bids; at Wanda's request, all bids are

for a shipping quantity of 20,000 bottles with annual requirements of 40,000 units. Wanda's factory operates 250 days a year. The first table shows each supplier's price, estimated annual freight costs, and current lead times; management has added estimates for holding costs and administrative oversight costs for each supplier.

Beyond costs, however, Wanda has three other criteria considered important in the selection of a supplier. The second table shows all the criteria, their weights, and the scores for all of them except total costs, where a score of 1.0 indicates "poor" and 10 indicates "superior." Because all three suppliers have done business with Wanda Lux

before, management will assign a score of "10" to the supplier with the lowest total annual cost, a score of "8.5" for the next lowest cost, and a score of "7.0" for the worst cost of the three.

a. Which of the three suppliers will provide the lowest annual cost to Wanda Lux?

b. Given Wanda's criteria and weighting system, which supplier should Wanda award the contract to?

Suppliers	Freight Costs	Price/Unit	Annual Holding Cost Per Unit	Lead Time (days)	Annual Administrative Costs
Dover Plastics	$3,500	$5.10	$1.02	15	$4,000
Evan & Sons	$3,000	$5.05	$1.01	12	$6,000
Farley, Inc.	$4,500	$5.00	$1.00	20	$3,000

Criterion	Weight	Score		
		Dover	Evan	Farley
Total Cost	30	?	?	?
Consistent Quality	30	9	9	7
On-Time Delivery	20	8	9	9
Environment	20	8	7	7

8. Bradley Solutions and Alexander Limited are two well-established suppliers of inexpensive tools. Weekend Projects is a national chain of retail outlets that caters to the occasional fixer-upper who would prefer to get the job done fast rather that investing in a well-appointed tool box. Weekend Projects wants to find a supplier for a particular tool set that promises to be a big seller. Expected annual sales are 100,000 units. Weekend's warehouses operate 50 weeks a year. Management collected data on the two suppliers, which are contained in the first table.

a. Which of the two suppliers would provide the lowest annual cost to Weekend Projects? What shipping quantity would you suggest?

b. Before management could make a decision, another option became available. Zelda Tools offered the tool set for only $8.00; however, the lead time is longer than the other two suppliers. Zelda is a new supplier and has not been in the industry very long. Additional data for Zelda are in the second table.

Management has begun to assess the administrative costs to manage the contract with Zelda. What is the lowest level of administrative costs at which Weekend Projects would be indifferent between using Zelda versus the option you chose in part a?

Supplier	Freight Costs Shipping Quantity			Price/Unit	Annual Holding Cost/Unit	Lead Time (wks)	Annual Administrative Cost
	10,000	25,000	50,000				
Bradley	$35,000	$25,000	$18,000	$8.10	$1.62	6	$10,000
Alexander	$40,000	$28,000	$19,000	$8.10	$1.62	4	$15,000

Supplier	Freight Costs Shipping Quantity			Price/Unit	Annual Holding Cost/Unit	Lead Time (wks)
	10,000	25,000	50,000			
Zelda	$45,000	$25,000	$17,000	$8.00	$1.60	7

VIDEO CASE   Sourcing Strategy at Starwood

Bath towels. Televisions. Fresh produce. Uniforms. On the surface, these items may not appear to have any relationship to each other. Sure, they exist in most households, even though they were probably bought independently of one another. Yet to the supply chain manager employed in the hospitality industry, they not only have a relationship, but their purchase can be critical to gaining a competitive advantage.

Just ask Paul Davis, vice president of strategic sourcing for Starwood's North American operations. With hundreds of hotels and resorts in the United States, Canada, and the Caribbean, Davis's goal is to create the hospitality industry's best supply chain organization. The items procured within his organization not only include replenishable goods such as fresh produce and food items but also extend to the sourcing of national contracts for nonperishable goods such as bath towels, electronics, staff apparel, energy, and contract services.

It is easy to confuse supply chain processes with the routine procurement of goods and services. Starwood's supply chain certainly does include contracting, but it is much more: It consists of the customer relationship, order fulfillment, and supplier relationship processes. Strong linkages exist among the company's upstream suppliers of services, materials, and information, and the customers of Starwood's hotels and resorts. If the upstream relationships are not carefully managed, downstream delivery of consistency, quality, and value to Starwood's guests may suffer. As a result, significant effort is placed on the nested processes within the supplier relationship process such as design collaboration, sourcing, negotiation, contracting, and information exchange.

Any number of events will trigger the involvement of Paul Davis's supply chain team:

- Existing contracts expire.
- Individual hotel brands seek new products.
- Hotel property design teams generate ideas.
- New categories of products emerge and need evaluation.
- A particular hotel needs help with a local service contract.

When a product or service needs to be sourced, the specifications are driven by internal customers such as restaurant chefs, housekeeping, and maintenance. If the product or service does not already exist, domestic and international suppliers that might be able to create the item are researched, as are regional and local vendors. Sometimes, sourcing an existing item simply means renewing an agreement with a current supplier. Still other situations demand creating a new category that has not been sourced before or using a third party to help locate sources.

Due diligence is always performed by sending potential suppliers a "request for information" in either paper or electronic form. The responses returned by the suppliers are entered into a database and help Starwood to prequalify the suppliers. A good match is sought, requiring the suppliers to meet minimum requirements for financial viability, quality, scope of operations, references, and legal risk avoidance. With a suitable potential supplier candidate pool, Starwood then takes one of two paths. The first one is to conduct a reverse auction where preselected vendors bid against each other. This method is used with shorter-term contracts on commodity items that have low external customer visibility. Kitchen uniforms, hotel room door keys, and paint are sourced this way. The second option is to send out a request for proposal (RFP), which requires the vendor to put its best terms forward at the outset for consideration.

After review by the supply chain team, the vendor winning the auction or emerging from the RFP review activity as the best fit is engaged in negotiations. Throughout the supplier relationship building process, Starwood gets to know the vendors, but it becomes much more personal at this point as both parties move toward concluding their contract negotiations.

Starwood maintains a cooperative orientation toward its supplier relationships, building a partnership to maximize value for each party to ensure that each side is comfortable with the price, quality, and delivery requirements it has agreed upon in the contract negotiation process. When contract negotiations are complete, the different brands are notified and the buying and information exchange processes begin.

At this point, you might think the job of the supply chain team is done. Yet managing the existing supplier relationship after the contract ink dries is perhaps the most challenging task of all. The contract involving sourcing of bed linens and terrycloth items is a perfect example. Not long after the contract was finalized, an alternate supplier approached Starwood with an offer to supply comparable quality goods at a much lower cost. Supply chain managers had a choice to make: continue to work with the existing supplier or buy out the current supplier's contract and begin sourcing with the new one.

QUESTIONS

1. Should Starwood maintain a cooperative orientation or a competitive orientation with its suppliers for the kind of items described here?

2. What types of information should Starwood exchange with its bed linens and terrycloth supplier? What does Starwood risk by sharing too much information?

3. How would you approach the sourcing of bed linens and terrycloth items? That is, would you use a reverse auction or request for proposal? Under what circumstances would you change suppliers?

4. In addition to performing value analysis on the services its properties offer, Starwood evaluates the performance of its suppliers against contract metrics. Using the bed linens and terrycloth supplier as an example, describe some of the metrics Starwood should use.

CASE | Wolf Motors

John Wolf, president of Wolf Motors, just returned to his office after visiting the company's newly acquired automotive dealership. It was the fourth Wolf Motors' dealership in a network that served a metropolitan area of 400,000 people. Beyond the metropolitan area, but within a 45-minute drive, were another 500,000 people. Each of the dealerships in the network marketed a different make of automobile and historically had operated autonomously.

Wolf was particularly excited about this new dealership because it was the first "auto supermarket" in the network. Auto supermarkets differ from traditional auto dealerships in that they sell multiple makes of automobiles at the same location. The new dealership sold a full line of Chevrolets, Nissans, and Volkswagens.

Starting 15 years ago with the purchase of a bankrupt Dodge dealership, Wolf Motors had grown steadily in size and in reputation. Wolf attributed this success to three highly interdependent factors. The first was volume. By maintaining a high volume of sales and turning over inventory rapidly, economies of scale could be achieved, which reduced costs and provided customers with a large selection. The second factor was a marketing approach called the "hassle-free buying experience." Listed on each automobile was the "one price–lowest price." Customers came in, browsed, and compared prices without being approached by pushy salespeople. If they had questions or were ready to buy, a walk to a customer service desk produced a knowledgeable salesperson to assist them. Finally, and Wolf thought perhaps most importantly, was the after-sale service. Wolf Motors established a solid reputation for servicing, diagnosing, and repairing vehicles correctly and in a timely manner—the first time.

High-quality service after the sale depended on three essential components. First was the presence of a highly qualified, well-trained staff of service technicians. Second was the use of the latest tools and technologies to support diagnosis and repair activities. Third was the availability of the full range of parts and materials necessary to complete the service and repairs without delay. Wolf invested in training and equipment to ensure that the trained personnel and technology were provided. What he worried about, as Wolf Motors grew, was the continued availability of the right parts and materials. This concern caused him to focus on the supplier relationship process and management of the service parts and materials flows in the supply chain.

Wolf thought back on the stories in the newspaper's business pages describing the failure of companies that had not planned appropriately for growth. These companies outgrew their existing policies, procedures, and control systems. Lacking a plan to update their systems, the companies experienced myriad problems that led to inefficiencies and an inability to compete effectively. He did not want that to happen to Wolf Motors.

Each of the four dealerships purchased its own service parts and materials. Purchases were based on forecasts derived from historical demand data, which accounted for factors such as seasonality. Batteries and alternators had a high failure rate in the winter, and air-conditioner parts were in great demand during the summer. Similarly, coolant was needed in the spring to service air conditioners for the summer months, whereas antifreeze was needed in the fall to winterize automobiles. Forecasts also were adjusted for special vehicle sales and service promotions, which increased the need for materials used to prep new cars and service other cars.

One thing that made the purchase of service parts and materials so difficult was the tremendous number of different parts that had to be kept on hand. Some of these parts would be used to service customer automobiles, and others would be sold over the counter. Some had to be purchased from the automobile manufacturers or their certified wholesalers, and to support, for example, the "guaranteed GM parts" promotion. Still, other parts and materials such as oils, lubricants, and fan belts could be purchased from any number of suppliers. The purchasing department had to remember that the success of the dealership depended on (1) lowering costs to support the hassle-free, one price–lowest price concept and (2) providing the right parts at the right time to support fast, reliable after-sale service.

As Wolf thought about the purchasing of parts and materials, two things kept going through his mind: the amount of space available for parts storage and the level of financial resources available to invest in parts and materials. The acquisition of the auto supermarket dealership put an increased strain on both finances and space, with the need to support three different automobile lines at the same facility. Investment dollars were becoming scarce, and space was at a premium. Wolf wondered what could be done in the purchasing area to address some of these concerns and alleviate some of the pressures.

QUESTIONS

1. What recommendations would you make to John Wolf with respect to structuring the supplier relationship process for the Wolf Motors dealership network?

2. How might purchasing policies and procedures differ as the dealerships purchase different types of service parts and materials (for example, lubricants versus genuine GM parts)?

3. How can supply chain design and integration help John Wolf reduce investment and space requirements while maintaining adequate service levels?

Source: This case was prepared by Dr. Brooke Saladin, Wake Forest University, as a basis for classroom discussion.

SELECTED REFERENCES

Bowersox, D. J., and D. J. Closs. *Logistical Management: The Integrated Supply Chain Process.* New York: McGraw-Hill, 1996.

Brienzi, Mark, and Dr. Sham Kekre. "How Kodak Transformed its Service Parts Supply Chain." *Supply Chain Management Review* (October 2005), pp. 25–32.

Chopra, Sunil, and ManMohan S. Sodhi. "Looking for the Bang from the RFID Buck." *Supply Chain Management Review* (May/June 2007), pp. 34–41.

Conner, Martin P. "The Supply Chain's Role in Leveraging Product Life Cycle Management." *Supply Chain Management Review* (March 2004), pp. 36–43.

Cook, Robert L., Brian Gibson, and Douglas MacCurdy. "A Lean Approach to Cross-Docking." *Supply Chain Management Review* (March 2005), pp. 54–59.

Engardio, Pete. "Beyond the Green Corporation." *BusinessWeek* (January 29, 2007), pp. 50–64.

Fiksel, Joseph, Douglas Lambert, Les B. Artman, John A. Harris, and Hugh M. Share. "Environmental Excellence: The New Supply Chain Edge." *Supply Chain Management Review* (July/August 2004), pp. 50–57.

Fleck, Thomas. "Supplier Collaboration in Action at IBM." *Supply Chain Management Review.* (March 2008), pp. 30–37.

Freund, Brian C., and June M. Freund. "Hands-On VMI." *APICS—The Performance Advantage* (March 2003), pp. 34–39.

Fugate, Brian S., and John T. Mentzer. "Dell's Supply Chain DNA." *Supply Chain Management Review* (October 2004), pp. 20–24.

Hammer, Michael. "The Superefficient Company." *Harvard Business Review* (September 2001), pp. 82–91.

Handfield, Robert B., and Kevin McCormack. "What you Need to Know About Sourcing From China." *Supply Chain Management Review* (September 2005), pp. 28–33.

Handfield, Robert, S. Walton, Robert Sroufe, and Steven Melnyk. "Applying Environmental Criteria to Supplier Assessment: A Study of the Application of the Analytical Hierarchy Process." *European Journal of Operational Research*, vol. 41, no. 1 (2002), pp. 70–87.

Hartvigsen, David. *SimQuick: Process Simulation with Excel*, 2d ed. Upper Saddle River, NJ: Prentice Hall, 2004.

Hindo, Brian. "Everything Old is New Again." *BusinessWeek* (September 25, 2006), pp. 64–70.

Kulwiec, Ray. "Reverse Logistics Provides Green Benefits." *Target*, vol. 22, no. 3 (Third Issue 2006), pp. 11–20.

Lee, Hau L. "The Triple-A Supply Chain." *Harvard Business Review* (October 2004), pp. 102–112.

Lee, Hau L., and Corey Billington. "Managing Supply Chain Inventory: Pitfalls and Opportunities." *Sloan Management Review* (Spring 1992), pp. 65–73.

Liker, Jeffrey K., and Thomas Y. Choi. "Building Deep Supplier Relationships." *Harvard Business Review* (December 2004), pp. 104–113.

Maloni, M., and W. C. Benton. "Power Influences in the Supply Chain." *Journal of Business Logistics*, vol. 21 (2000), pp. 49–73.

Melnyk, Steven, and Robert Handfield. "Green Speak." *Purchasing Today*, vol. 7, no. 7 (1996), pp. 32–36.

Melnyk, Steven, Robert Sroufe, and Roger Calantone. "Assessing the Impact of Environmental Management Systems on Corporate and Environmental Performance." *Journal of Operations Management*, vol. 21, no. 3 (2003).

Miller, Jamey. "Shared Success: Working Together to Find the Value of VMI." *APICS Magazine* (November/December 2007), pp. 37–39.

Moeeni, Farhad. "Quality Decision Making, Input Technologies, and IT Education." *Decision Line* (May 2004), pp. 14–17.

Mollenkopf, Diane A., and David J. Closs. "The Hidden Value in Reverse Logistics." *Supply Chain Management Review* (July/August 2005), pp. 34–43.

Murphy-Hoye, Mary, Hau L. Lee, and James B. Rice, Jr. "A Real-World Look at RFID." *Supply Chain Management Review* (July/August 2005), pp. 18–26.

Plambeck, Erica L. "The Greening of Wal-Mart's Supply Chain." *Supply Chain Management Review* (July/August 2007), pp. 18–25.

Randall, Taylor, Serguei Netessine, and Nils Rudi. "Should You Take the Virtual Fulfillment Path?" *Supply Chain Management Review* (November/December 2002), pp. 54–58.

Sullivan, Laurie. "Wal-Mart's Way." *Informationweek.com* (September 27, 2004), pp. 37–50.

Trent, Robert J. "What Everyone Needs to Know About SCM." *Supply Chain Management Review* (March 2004), pp. 52–59.

Venkatesan, Ravi. "Strategic Sourcing: To Make or Not to Make." *Harvard Business Review* (November/December 1992), pp. 98–107.

11 LOCATING FACILITIES

Fluctuating exchange rates and other economic factors led Bavarian Motor Works (BMW) to consider manufacturing outside of Europe. The question was, where? After an extensive study and numerous government concessions, the Spartanburg, South Carolina, location was chosen. The plant is now an exclusive manufacturer of the X series vehicles.

BAVARIAN MOTOR WORKS (BMW)

Bavarian Motor Works (BMW), founded in 1917 and headquartered in Munich, Germany, is a manufacturer of select premium segment brands such as BMW, MINI, and Rolls-Royce Motor Cars in the international automobile market. When faced with fluctuating exchange rates and increasing production costs in the late 1980s, BMW decided that it was time to consider operating a new production facility outside the European borders. A "blank page" approach was used to compile a list of 250 potential worldwide plant sites. Further analysis pared the list down to 10 viable options; a plant location in the United States was preferred due to its proximity to a large market segment for BMW's automobiles.

The selection of the plant site involved many factors that had to be analyzed prior to its construction. BMW considered the labor climate in each country, geographical requirements and constraints, and its relations with the governments of the countries in which the prospective sites were located. In terms of the labor climate, a technologically capable workforce was needed due to the complex nature of the automotive manufacturing process. Because the cost to train a single worker in the automotive industry is between $10,000 and $20,000, this factor was especially critical. Additionally, BMW decided that if the plant were located in the United States, it should be in a "right-to-work" state in which workers could decide for themselves whether they want to join or financially support a union. Geographical factors had to be examined because thousands of automobile parts needed to be delivered from both domestic and foreign suppliers. In order to keep the supply

LEARNING GOALS

After reading this chapter, you should be able to:

1. Explain how location decisions relate to the design of supply chains.
2. Identify factors affecting location choices.
3. Understand the role of geographical information systems in making location decisions.
4. Understand single facility location techniques.
5. Explain how to apply the load-distance method, center of gravity, break-even analysis, and multiple facilities location methods.

chain costs down, it was decided that the new location should have ample highway/interstate access and be reasonably close to a port from which both supplies and finished automobiles could be easily transported. Another consideration was easy access to an airport for BMW's executives traveling back and forth to its headquarters in Germany. The final location factor was government related. BMW wanted to move to a location that was "business friendly" in terms of making concessions on issues such as infrastructural improvements, tax abatements, and employee screening and education programs. The overall goal was to make the relationship between BMW and the local community as mutually beneficial as possible through a coordinated improvement effort.

After a 3 1/2-year search process that stringently evaluated the 10 viable options across these location factors, BMW finally decided to build a new 2 million square-foot production facility in Spartanburg, South Carolina. The final decision was made based on a good match between the aforementioned selection criteria and the environment in Spartanburg. South Carolina lawmakers proved flexible and open as to how the state would address the needs set forth by BMW. For instance, they agreed to acquire the 500 acres necessary to build the plant (requiring a $25 million bond package be passed), improve the highway system around the facility (requiring

$10 million), and lengthen the runway and modernize the terminal at the Spartanburg airport ($40 million expenditure). The legislature also agreed to provide tax incentives, property tax relief, and establish an employee screening and training program to ensure the right mix of workers were available. (Processing the applications alone proved to be a daunting task because more than 50,000 applications were received.) South Carolina may not have scored the highest on each decision criterion, but taken as a whole, the Spartanburg location was best for BMW.

This location proved to be a good one. The plant, which opened in 1994, subsequently underwent a $200 million expansion in 1996, a $50 million expansion in 1999, and a $300 million expansion in 2000. Another $750 million dollar expansion was announced in March 2008 that will add 1.5 million square feet of manufacturing space and 500 new full-time jobs by 2012. BMW Manufacturing Corporation in South Carolina today is part of BMW Group's global manufacturing network and will soon become the exclusive manufacturing plant for all its X series vehicles. South Carolina also reaped rewards in the form of business growth (BMW brought along 39 of its suppliers), employment, and community improvements—a success story all around.

Sources: "Manager's Journal: Why BMW Cruised into Spartanburg," *Wall Street Journal* (July 6, 1992), p. A10; "BMW Announces Its Plans for a Plant in South Carolina," *Wall Street Journal* (June 24, 1992), p. B2; P. Galuszka, "The South Shall Rise Again," *Chief Executive* (November 2004), pp. 50–54; Southern Business & Development, www.sb-d.com (June 2005); www.bmwusfactory.com, July 2008.

my**om**lab and the Companion Website at **www.pearsonglobaleditions.com/krajewski** contain many tools, activities, and resources designed for this chapter.

facility location

The process of determining geographic sites for a firm's operations.

Facility location is the process of determining geographic sites for a firm's operations. Location choices can be critically important for firms, and have a profound impact on its supply chain. For example, they can affect the supplier relationship process: The expanding global economy gives firms greater access to suppliers around the world, many of whom can offer lower input costs or better-quality services and products. Nonetheless, when manufacturing facilities are off-shored, locating far from one's suppliers can lead to higher transportation costs and coordination difficulties. The customer relationship process can also be affected by the firm's location decisions. If the customer must be physically present at the process, it is unlikely that a location will be acceptable if the time or distance between the service provider and customer is great. If, on the other hand, customer contact is more passive and impersonal, or if materials or information is processed rather than people, then location may be less of an issue. Information technology and the Internet can sometimes help overcome the disadvantages related to a company's location. Still, one thing is clear: The location of a business's facilities has a significant impact on the company's operating costs, the prices it charges for services and goods, and its ability to compete in the marketplace and penetrate new customer segments.

Analyzing location patterns to discover a firm's underlying strategy is fascinating. For example, why do competing new-car sales showrooms cluster near one another? Managers of new-car showrooms deliberately locate near one another because customers prefer to do their comparison shopping in one area. Recognizing the strategic impact location decisions have on implementing a firm's strategy and supply chain design, we first consider the qualitative factors that influence location choices and their implications across the organization. Subsequently we examine an important trend in location patterns: the use of geographical information systems (GIS) to identify market segments and how serving each segment can profitably affect the firm's location decisions. We end by presenting some analytic and GIS-based techniques for making single- and multiple-facility location decisions.

Wal-Mart Stores, the world's largest retailer, is a global player. Here, a Chinese couple cycle past Wal-Mart Supercenter in Jinan, the capital city of Shandong Province on China's east coast. Wal-Mart's trademark yellow smiley face, low prices, and focus on customer service was first introduced to large US cities and then abroad to Canada, Puerto Rico, Brazil, the United Kingdom, Germany, South Korea, Japan, China, and Mexico.

LOCATION DECISIONS ACROSS THE ORGANIZATION

Location decisions affect processes and departments throughout the organization. When locating new retail facilities, such as Wendy's stores, marketing must carefully assess how the location will appeal to customers and possibly open up new markets. Relocating all or part of an organization can significantly affect the attitudes of the firm's workforce and the organization's ability to operate effectively across departmental lines. Location also has implications for a firm's human resources department, which must be attuned to the firm's hiring and training needs. Locating new facilities or relocating existing facilities is usually costly; therefore, these decisions must be carefully evaluated by the organization's accounting and finance departments. For instance, when BMW located its manufacturing plant in South Carolina, the economic environment of the state and the monetary incentives offered by its legislators played a role in the financial payoff associated with the proposed new plant. Finally, operations also has an important stake in location decisions because the location needs to be able to meet current customer demand and provide the right amount of customer contact (for both external and internal customers). International operations, like those of McDonald's, Toyota, and Wal-Mart, introduce a new set of challenges because setting up and managing facilities and employees in foreign countries can be extremely time-consuming and difficult.

FACTORS AFFECTING LOCATION DECISIONS

Managers of both service and manufacturing organizations must weigh many factors when assessing the desirability of particular locations, including their proximity to customers and suppliers, labor costs, and transportation costs. Managers generally can disregard factors that fail to meet at least one of the following two conditions:

1. *The Factor Must Be Sensitive to Location.* In other words, managers should not consider a factor not affected by the location decision. For example, if community attitudes are uniformly good at all the locations under consideration, community attitudes should not be considered as a factor.

2. *The Factor Must Have a High Impact on the Company's Ability to Meet Its Goals.* For example, although different facilities will be located at different distances from suppliers, if the shipments from them can take place overnight and the communication with them is done via fax or e-mail, the distance is not likely to have a large impact on the firm's ability to meet its goals. It should therefore not be considered as a factor.

Managers can divide location factors into dominant and secondary factors. Dominant factors are derived from competitive priorities (cost, quality, time, and flexibility) and have a particularly strong impact on sales or costs. For example, a favorable labor climate and monetary incentives were dominant factors affecting the decision to locate the BMW plant in Spartanburg, South Carolina. Secondary factors also are important, but management may downplay or even ignore some of these secondary factors if other factors are more important. Thus, for GM's Saturn plant, which makes many of its parts onsite, inbound transportation costs were considered less important and therefore were a secondary factor.

Dominant Factors in Manufacturing

The following six groups of factors dominate the decisions firms, including BMW, make about the location of new manufacturing plants. Often there is a trade-off among factors. Locating facilities in, say, a location with high labor costs might make sense if other factors such as logistics, taxes, and proximity to customers are favorable. Lowering the total costs of designing, developing, manufacturing, and distributing a product to its market becomes especially important in developing international supply chains and finding locations for plants, distribution centers, software design studios, and the like.

Favorable Labor Climate A favorable labor climate may well be the most important factor for labor-intensive firms in industries such as textiles, furniture, and consumer electronics. Labor climate is a function of wage rates, training requirements, attitudes toward work, worker productivity, and union strength. Many executives perceive weak unions or a low probability of union organizing efforts as a distinct advantage. Having a favorable climate applies not only to the workforce already on site, but also to the employees that a firm hopes will transfer to or will be attracted to the new site.

Proximity to Markets After determining where the demand for services and goods is greatest, management must select a location for the facility that will supply that demand. Locating near markets is particularly important when the final goods are bulky or heavy and *outbound* transportation rates are high. For example, manufacturers of products such as plastic pipe and heavy metals require proximity to their markets.

Quality of Life Good schools, recreational facilities, cultural events, and an attractive lifestyle contribute to **quality of life**. This factor can make the difference in location decisions. In the United States during the past 2 decades, more than 50 percent of new industrial jobs went to nonurban regions. A similar shift is taking place in Japan and Europe. Reasons for this movement include high costs of living, high crime rates, and general decline in the quality of life in many large cities.

Proximity to Suppliers and Resources Firms dependent on inputs of bulky, perishable, or heavy raw materials emphasize proximity to their suppliers and resources. In such cases, *inbound*

COMPETING WITH OPERATIONS

Using Operations to Compete
Managing Effective Projects

DESIGNING AND
MANAGING PROCESSES

Developing a Process Strategy
Analyzing Processes
Managing Quality
Planning Capacity
Managing Process Constraints
Designing Lean Systems

DESIGNING AND
MANAGING SUPPLY CHAINS

Designing Effective Supply Chains
Integrating the Supply Chain
Locating Facilities
Managing Inventories
Forecasting Demand
Planning and Scheduling Operations
Planning Sufficient Resources

quality of life

A factor that considers the availability of good schools, recreational facilities, cultural events, and an attractive lifestyle.

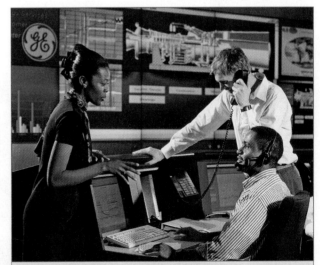

A GE Energy Division employee works at the company's remote diagnostics center located inside its new division headquarters building in Atlanta, Georgia. Despite a 100-year history in Schenectady, New York, the division relocated to Atlanta in 2001. Among the factors that led to the move: GE's customers are concentrated in and around Atlanta, and the city has a deep talent base of technologically oriented workers.

transportation costs become a dominant factor, encouraging such firms to locate facilities near suppliers. For example, locating paper mills near forests and food-processing facilities near farms is practical. Another advantage of locating near suppliers is the ability to maintain lower inventories (see Chapter 8, "Designing Lean Systems," and Chapter 9, "Designing Effective Supply Chains").

Proximity to the Parent Company's Facilities   In many companies, plants supply parts to other facilities or rely on other facilities for management and staff support. These ties require frequent coordination and communication, which can become more difficult as distance increases.

Utilities, Taxes, and Real Estate Costs   Other location decision factors include utility costs (telephone, energy, and water), local and state taxes, financing incentives offered by local or state governments, relocation costs, and land costs. For example, the location of the Daimler plant in Alabama for manufacturing its "M series" vehicles, the BMW plant in South Carolina in the opening vignette, and a Toyota plant in Georgetown, Kentucky, were all attractive to these companies in part due to the incentives from local governments.

Other Factors   Still other secondary factors may need to be considered, including room for expansion, construction costs, accessibility to multiple modes of transportation, the cost of shuffling people and materials between plants, insurance costs, competition from other firms for the workforce, local ordinances (such as pollution or noise control regulations), community attitudes, and many others. For global operations, firms need a good local infrastructure and local employees who are educated and have good skills. Many firms are concluding that large, centralized manufacturing facilities in low-cost countries with poorly trained workers are not sustainable. Smaller, flexible facilities located in the countries that the firm serves allow it to avoid problems related to trade barriers like tariffs and quotas and the risk that changing exchange rates will adversely affect its sales and profits.

Dominant Factors in Services

The factors mentioned for manufacturers also apply to service providers with one important addition: the impact of location on sales and customer satisfaction. Customers usually care about how close a service facility is, particularly if the process requires considerable customer contact.

Proximity to Customers   Location is a key factor in determining how conveniently customers can carry on business with a firm. For example, few people will patronize a remotely located supermarket if another is more convenient. Thus, the influence of location on revenues tends to be the dominant factor. In addition, customer proximity by itself is not enough—the key is proximity to customers who will actively patronize the facility. For instance, Mirage opened the opulent Beau Rivage resort and casino in Biloxi, Mississippi, in 1999. Its revenues turned out lower than expectations because the new casino did not cater as well to the needs of local customers, who came there to view and admire it but gambled elsewhere. Revenues picked up only after the cuisine at Beau Rivage was tailored to local tastes, costs were slashed, and other changes were made. Being close to customers who match a firm's target market and service offerings is thus important for profitability.

Transportation Costs and Proximity to Markets   For warehousing and distribution operations, transportation costs and proximity to markets are extremely important. With a warehouse nearby, many firms can hold inventory closer to the customer, thus reducing delivery time and promoting sales. For example, Invacare Corporation of Elyria, Ohio, gained a competitive edge in the distribution of home health care products by decentralizing inventory into 32 warehouses across the United States. Invacare sells wheelchairs, hospital beds, and other patient aids—some of which it produces and some of which it buys from other firms—to small dealers who sell to consumers. Previously the dealers, often small operations, had to wait three weeks for deliveries, which meant their cash was tied up in excess inventory. With Invacare's new distribution network, the

This Scottrade office in Indianapolis, Indiana, is among 363 local brokerage branches located near where their customers live and work.

dealers get daily deliveries of products from one source. Invacare's location strategy shows how timely delivery can be a competitive advantage.

Location of Competitors   One complication related to estimating the sales potential of different locations is the impact of competitors. Management must not only consider the current location of competitors but also try to anticipate their reaction to the firm's new location. Avoiding areas where competitors are already well-established often pays off. However, in some industries, such as new-car sales showrooms and fast-food chains, locating near competitors is actually advantageous. The strategy is to create a **critical mass**, whereby several competing firms clustered in one location attract more customers than the total number who would shop at the same stores at scattered locations. Recognizing this effect, some firms use a follow-the-leader strategy when selecting new sites.

Site-Specific Factors   Retailers also must consider the level of retail activity, residential density, traffic flow, and site visibility. Retail activity in the area is important because shoppers often decide on impulse to go shopping or to eat in a restaurant. Traffic flows and visibility are important because businesses' customers arrive in cars. Management considers possible traffic tie-ups, traffic volume and direction by time of day, traffic signals, intersections, and the position of traffic medians. Visibility involves distance from the street and the size of nearby buildings and signs. A high residential density increases nighttime and weekend business if the population in the area fits the firm's competitive priorities and target market segment.

critical mass

A situation whereby several competing firms clustered in one location attract more customers than the total number who would shop at the same stores at scattered locations.

GEOGRAPHICAL INFORMATION SYSTEMS AND LOCATION DECISIONS

A **geographical information system (GIS)** is a system of computer software, hardware, and data that the firm's personnel can use to manipulate, analyze, and present information relevant to a location decision. A GIS can also integrate different systems to create a visual representation of a firm's location choices. Among other things, it can be used to (1) store databases, (2) display maps, and (3) create models that can take information from existing datasets, apply analytic functions, and write results into newly derived datasets. Together, these three functionalities of data storage, map displays, and modeling are critical parts of an intelligent GIS, and are used to a varying extent in all GIS applications.

A GIS system can be a really useful decision-making tool because many of the decisions made by businesses today have a geographical aspect. A GIS stores information in several databases that can be naturally linked to places, such as customer sales and locations, or a census tract, or the percentage of residents in the tract that make a certain amount of money a year. The demographics of an area include the number of people in the metropolitan statistical area, city, or postal code; average income; number of families with children; and so forth. These demographics may all be important variables in the decision of how best to reach the target market. Similarly, the road system, including bridges and highways, location of nearby airports and seaports, and the terrain (mountains, forests, lakes, and so forth), play an important role in facility location decisions. As such, a GIS can have a diverse set of location-related applications in different industries such as the retail, real estate, government, transportation, and logistics industries.

Managerial Practice 11.1 illustrates how fast-food chains use GIS to select their sites.

As highlighted in Managerial Practice 11.1, governmental data can provide a statistical mother lode of information used to make better GIS-based location decisions. For example, the U.S. Census Bureau has a minutely detailed computerized map of the entire United States—the so-called Tiger file. Its formal name is the Topologically Integrated Geographic Encoding and Reference file. It lists in digital form every highway, street, bridge, and tunnel in the nation's 50 states. When combined with a database, such as the results of the census or a company's own customer files, Tiger provides GIS-type of functionalities and gives desktop computer users the ability to ask various "what-if" questions about different location alternatives. Internet sites on Yahoo!, MapQuest, and Expedia, among others, allow people to pull up maps, distances and travel times, and routes between locations, such as between Toronto, Ontario, and San Diego, California. In addition, search engines such as Google can be integrated with population demographics to create information of interest in social and business domains. Web sites are using Google maps to display high crime areas, the location of cheap gas, and apartments for rent.

Many different types of GIS packages are available, such as ArcInfo (from ESRI), MapInfo (from MapInfo), SAS/GIS (from SAS Institute, Inc.), and SiteAmerica (from Tactician). Many of these systems are tailored to a specific application such as locating retail stores, redistricting

geographical information system (GIS)

A system of computer software, hardware, and data that the firm's personnel can use to manipulate, analyze, and present information relevant to a location decision.

MANAGERIAL PRACTICE 11.1 — How Fast-Food Chains Use GIS to Select Their Sites

Until recently, fast-food chains used consultants to analyze geodemographic data (description of different characteristics about people based upon the location where they live or work) for strategic planning and making franchise location and marketing decisions. Now with the availability of easy-to-use GIS systems that cost less than $5,000 and can be operated on a regular PC, small and large fast-food chains are doing it on their own. For instance, Marco's Franchising, headquartered in Toledo, Ohio, uses MapInfo's GIS solutions to identify new markets where the customer and competitor landscape are best for new sites. MapInfo's Smart Site Solutions and AnySite Online technologies supply interactive mapping and reporting functionality to examine market level deployment strategies and individual site opportunities. These programs can estimate the total dollars up for grabs in a market by analyzing local age and income data from the U.S. Census Bureau as well as sales data from stores in an area—numbers that are commonly available through third-party vendors. The programs can also tell the optimal number and locations of stores in a market, and how much in sales a store can expect. Analyses can be run for any U.S. market and can rank markets in order of viability. A list of realistic sites with high sales potential can be put together at times in less than one minute. Other small fast-food chains in the United States, like Cousins Subs and 99 Restaurants and Pubs, are using in-house GIS and getting a handsome return on the investments. For instance, 99 Restaurants and Pubs found that it was able to recoup its GIS-related investment in a single week.

Bigger nationwide fast-food chains such as Domino's Pizza use GIS software to screen alternative sites for new franchises, determine how moving a store a few blocks away can affect sales, and decide when they should relocate or remodel existing stores. They can also use GIS to identify overlapping delivery zones and zones that are not being covered. AFC Enterprises, which owns and franchises the Popeye's and Church's chains

of restaurants, uses GIS to help it sell franchises. The level of detailed information that it can provide to prospective franchisees can make all the difference when it comes to closing the deal.

Because of its ability to provide these insights, GIS is a useful tool for expanding fast-food chains that need to quickly master the demographic details of competitive terrains in thousands of locations across the U.S.

A Domino's Pizza store in the NYC neighborhood of Chelsea.

Sources: www.gis.com/whatisgis/index.html; Ed Rubinstein, "Chains Chart Their Course of Actions with Geographic Information Systems," *Nation's Restaurant News,* vol. 32, no. 6 (1998), p. 49; "MapInfo Delivers Location Intelligence for Marco's Pizza," *Directions Magazine* (December 14, 2004), www.directionsmag.com/press.releases/?duty=Show&id=10790; Ryan Chittum, "Location, Location, and Technology: Where to Put That New Store? Site-Selection Software May Be Able to Help," *Wall Street Journal* (July 18, 2005), p. R7.

The Starbucks video in my**om**lab shows how to perform geodemographic analysis using MapPoint 2004.

legislative districts, analyzing logistics and marketing data, environmental management, and so forth. However, in this chapter, we explore the use of a particular GIS, Microsoft's MapPoint 2004. One of the nice features of MapPoint is that the maps and much of the census data come with the software itself, while in many other systems, the maps and the data are purchased separately from the GIS software vendor. MapPoint is an easy-to-use and fairly inexpensive GIS that mainly focuses on everyday business use by nontechnical analysts. Its ability to display information on maps can be a powerful decision-making tool.

GIS can be useful for identifying locations that relate well to a firm's target market based on customer demographics. When coupled with other location models, sales forecasting models, and geodemographic systems, it can give a firm such as Starbucks and many others a formidable array of decision-making tools for its location decisions.

LOCATING A SINGLE FACILITY

Having examined trends and important factors in location, we now consider more specifically how a firm can make location decisions. In this section, we consider the case of locating only one new facility. Managers must first decide whether to expand onsite, build another facility, or relocate to another site. Onsite expansion has the advantage of keeping people together, reducing construction time and costs, and avoiding splitting up operations. However, as a firm expands a facility, at some point diseconomies of scale set in. Poor materials handling, increasingly complex production control, and simple lack of space are reasons for building a new plant or relocating the existing plant.

The advantages of building a new plant or moving to a new retail or office space are that the firm does not have to rely on the production from a single plant. A new plant allows it to hire more employees, install newer, more productive machinery and better technology, and reduce transportation costs. Most firms that choose to relocate are small (comprised of fewer than 10 employees). They tend to be single-location companies cramped for space and needing to redesign their production processes and layouts. More than 80 percent of all relocations are made within 20 miles of companies' original locations, which enables the firms to retain their current employees.

On an average, it is less costly to relocate a service-oriented business than a manufacturing business. For instance, relocating a major check or credit card transaction processing facility for a bank may not be as difficult as moving a manufacturing plant. Because proximity to customers is important, the location of service facilities must constantly be reevaluated in the context of shifting populations and their changing needs. At times, a combination of all three options—staying at the same location, relocating, and opening a new facility—might simultaneously be considered.

When the facility is part of a firm's larger network of facilities, we assume that it is not interdependent; that is, a decision to open a restaurant in Tampa, Florida, is independent of whether the chain has a restaurant in Austin, Texas. Let us begin by considering how to decide whether a new location is needed, and then examine a systematic selection process aided by what is known as the *load–distance method* to deal with proximity.

The Tyler EMS video in my**om**lab shows how to do relocation analysis using MapPoint 2004.

Comparing Several Sites

A systematic selection process begins after perception or evidence indicates that opening a retail outlet, warehouse, office, or plant in a new location will improve performance. The process of selecting a new facility location involves a series of steps.

1. Identify the important location factors and categorize them as dominant or secondary.

2. Consider alternative regions; then narrow the choices to alternative communities and finally to specific sites.

3. Collect data on the alternatives from location consultants, provincial development agencies, city and county planning departments, chambers of commerce, land developers, electric power companies, banks, and onsite visits. Some of these data and information may also be contained inside the GIS.

4. Analyze the data collected, beginning with the *quantitative* factors—factors that can be measured in dollars, such as annual transportation costs or taxes. The quantitative factors can also be measured in terms other than dollars, such as driving time and miles. These dollar values may be broken into separate cost categories (for example, inbound and outbound transportation, labor, construction, and utilities) and separate revenue sources (say sales, stock or bond issues, and interest income). These financial factors can the n be converted to a single measure of financial merit such as total costs, return on investment (ROI), or net present value (NPV), and used to compare two or more sites, especially if capital costs for the new facility are also considered.

5. Bring the qualitative factors pertaining to each site into the evaluation. A *qualitative* factor is one that cannot be evaluated in dollar terms, such as community attitudes or quality of life. To merge quantitative and qualitative factors, some managers review the expected performance of each factor, while others assign each factor a weight of relative importance and calculate a weighted score for each site, using a preference matrix. What is important in one situation may be unimportant or less important in another. The site with the highest weighted score is best.

After thoroughly evaluating all potential sites, those making the study prepare a final report containing site recommendations, along with a summary of the data and analyses on which they are based. An audiovisual presentation of the key findings usually is delivered to top management in large firms.

EXAMPLE 11.1	**Calculating Weighted Scores in a Preference Matrix**

A new medical facility, Health-Watch, is to be located in Erie, Pennsylvania. The following table shows the location factors, weights, and scores (1 = poor, 5 = excellent) for one potential site. The weights in this case add up to 100 percent. A weighted score (*WS*) will be calculated for each site. What is the *WS* for this site?

Location Factor	Weight	Score
Total patient miles per month	25	4
Facility utilization	20	3
Average time per emergency trip	20	3
Expressway accessibility	15	4
Land and construction costs	10	1
Employee preferences	10	5

SOLUTION

The *WS* for this particular site is calculated by multiplying each factor's weight by its score and adding the results:

$$WS = (25 \times 4) + (20 \times 3) + (20 \times 3) + (15 \times 4) + (10 \times 1) + (10 \times 5)$$
$$= 100 + 60 + 60 + 60 + 10 + 50$$
$$= 340$$

The total *WS* of 340 can be compared with the total weighted scores for other sites being evaluated.

Tutor 11.1 in my**om**lab provides another example to practice with a preference matrix for location decisions.

Applying the Load–Distance Method

In the systematic selection process, the analyst must identify attractive candidate locations and compare them on the basis of quantitative factors. The load–distance method is one way to facilitate this step. It works much like the weighted-distance method does for designing layouts for divergent processes (see Chapter 3, "Developing a Process Strategy"), whereby loads represent the weights. Several location factors relate directly to distance: proximity to markets, average distance to target customers, proximity to suppliers and resources, and proximity to other company facilities. The **load–distance method** is a mathematical model used to evaluate locations based on proximity factors. The objective is to select a location that minimizes the sum of the loads times the distance the load travels. Time may be used instead of distance if so desired.

load–distance method

A mathematical model used to evaluate locations based on proximity factors.

Calculating a Load–Distance Score
Suppose that a firm planning a new location wants to select a site that minimizes the distances that loads, particularly the larger ones, must travel to and from the site. Depending on the industry, a *load* may be shipments from suppliers, shipments between plants or to customers, or it may be customers or employees traveling to and from the facility. The firm seeks to minimize its load–distance (*ld*) score, generally by choosing a location that ensures loads go short distances.

To calculate the *ld* score for any potential location, we use the actual distance between any two points using a GIS system and simply multiply the loads flowing to and from the facility by the distances traveled. Alternately, rectilinear or Euclidean distance as calculated in Chapter 3, "Developing a Process Strategy," can also be used as an approximation for distance using the *x* coordinate and *y* coordinate. Travel time, actual miles, or rectilinear distances when using a grid approach are all appropriate measures for distance. The formula for the *ld* score is

$$ld = \sum_i l_i d_i$$

These loads may be expressed as the number of potential customers needing physical presence for a service facility; loads may be tons or number of trips per week for a manufacturing facility. The score is the sum of these load–distance products. By selecting a new location based on *ld* scores, customer service is improved or transportation costs reduced.

The goal is to find one acceptable facility location that minimizes the score, where the location is defined by its *x* coordinate and *y* coordinate or the longitude and the latitude. Practical considerations rarely allow managers to select the exact location with the lowest possible score. For example, land might not be available there at a reasonable price, or other location factors may make the site undesirable.

center of gravity

A good starting point to evaluate locations in the target area using the load–distance model.

Center of Gravity
Testing different locations with the load–distance model is relatively simple if some systematic search process is followed. **Center of gravity** is a good starting point to evaluate locations in the target area using the load–distance method. The first step is to determine the *x* and *y* coordinates of different locations either in the form of the longitude and latitude of the locations, or by creating an (*x*, *y*) grid as was used in constructing

layouts in Chapter 3, "Developing a Process Strategy." The center of gravity's x coordinate, denoted x^*, is found by multiplying each point's x coordinate (either the longitude of the location or the x coordinate on a grid), by its load (l_i), summing these products ($\sum_i l_i x_i$), and then dividing by the sum of the loads ($\sum_i l_i$). The center of gravity's y coordinate (either the latitude or the y coordinate on a grid), denoted y^*, is found the same way. The formulas are as follows:

$$x^* = \frac{\sum_i l_i x_i}{\sum_i l_i} \quad \text{and} \quad y^* = \frac{\sum_i l_i y_i}{\sum_i l_i}$$

This location generally is not the optimal one for the distance measures, but it still is an excellent starting point. The load–distance scores for locations in its vicinity can be calculated until the solution is near optimal.

EXAMPLE 11.2	Finding the Center of Gravity for an Electric Utilities Supplier

A supplier to the electric utility industry produces power generators; the transportation costs are high. One market area includes the lower part of the Great Lakes region and the upper portion of the southeastern region. More than 600,000 tons are to be shipped to eight major customer locations as shown below:

Customer Location	Tons Shipped	x, y Coordinates
Three Rivers, MI	5,000	(7, 13)
Fort Wayne, IN	92,000	(8, 12)
Columbus, OH	70,000	(11, 10)
Ashland, KY	35,000	(11, 7)
Kingsport, TN	9,000	(12, 4)
Akron, OH	227,000	(13, 11)
Wheeling, WV	16,000	(14, 10)
Roanoke, VA	153,000	(15, 5)

What is the center of gravity for the electric utilities supplier?   Using rectilinear distance, what is the resulting load–distance score for this location?

SOLUTION

The center of gravity is calculated as shown below:

$$\sum_i l_i = 5 + 92 + 70 + 35 + 9 + 227 + 16 + 153 = 607$$

$$\sum_i l_i x_i = 5(7) + 92(8) + 70(11) + 35(11) + 9(12) + 227(13) + 16(14) + 153(15)$$
$$= 7{,}504$$

$$x^* = \frac{\sum_i l_i x_i}{\sum_i l_i} = \frac{7{,}504}{607} = 12.4$$

$$\sum_i l_i y_i = 5(13) + 92(12) + 70(10) + 35(7) + 9(4) + 227(11) + 16(10) + 153(5) = 5{,}572$$

$$y^* = \frac{\sum_i l_i y_i}{\sum_i l_i} = \frac{5{,}572}{607} = 9.2$$

The resulting load–distance score is

$$id = \sum_i l_i d_i = 5(5.4 + 3.8) + 92(4.4 + 2.8) + 70(1.4 + 0.8) + 35(1.4 + 2.2)$$

$$+ 9(0.4 + 5.2) + 227(0.6 + 1.8) + 16(1.6 + 0.8) + 153(2.6 + 4.2)$$

$$= 2,662.4$$

where

$$d_i = |x_i - x^*| + |y_i - y^*|$$

Tutor 11.2 in my**om**lab provides another example on how to calculate the center of gravity.

DECISION POINT

The center of gravity is (12.4, 9.2) and the load distance score is 2662.4. Solved Problem 2 at the end of this chapter illustrates an example of using latitude and longitude rather than grid coordinates for finding center of gravity.

Amazon.com and Target recently announced they would both open fulfillment centers in Arizona, due in part to the availability of affordable real estate.

Using Break-Even Analysis

Break-even analysis can help a manager compare location alternatives on the basis of quantitative factors that can be expressed in terms of total cost. It is particularly useful when the manager wants to define the ranges over which each alternative is best. The basic steps for graphic and algebraic solutions are as follows:

1. Determine the variable costs and fixed costs for each site. Recall that *variable costs* are the portion of the total cost that varies directly with the volume of output. Recall that *fixed costs* are the portion of the total cost that remains constant regardless of output levels.

2. Plot the total cost lines—the sum of variable and fixed costs—for all the sites on a single graph (for assistance, see Tutors A.1 and A.2 in OM Explorer).

3. Identify the approximate ranges for which each location has the lowest cost.

4. Solve algebraically for the break-even points over the relevant ranges.

EXAMPLE 11.3	Break-Even Analysis for Location

Active Model 11.1 in my**om**lab provides insight on defining the three relevant ranges for this example.

Tutor 11.3 in my**om**lab provides another example to practice break-even analysis for location decisions.

An operations manager narrowed the search for a new facility location to four communities. The annual fixed costs (land, property taxes, insurance, equipment, and buildings) and the variable costs (labor, materials, transportation, and variable overhead) are as follows:

Community	Fixed Costs per Year	Variable Costs per Unit
A	$150,000	$62
B	$300,000	$38
C	$500,000	$24
D	$600,000	$30

Step 1: Plot the total cost curves for all the communities on a single graph. Identify on the graph the approximate range over which each community provides the lowest cost.

Step 2: Using break-even analysis, calculate the break-even quantities over the relevant ranges. If the expected demand is 15,000 units per year, what is the best location?

SOLUTION

Step 1:   To plot a community's total cost line, let us first compute the total cost for two output levels: $Q = 0$ and $Q = 20,000$ units per year. For the $Q = 0$ level, the total cost is simply the fixed costs. For the $Q = 20,000$ level, the total cost (fixed plus variable costs) is as follows:

Community	Fixed Costs	Variable Costs (Cost per Unit) (No. of Units)	Total Cost (Fixed + Variable)
A	$150,000	$62(20,000) = $1,240,000	$1,390,000
B	$300,000	$38(20,000) = $ 760,000	$1,060,000
C	$500,000	$24(20,000) = $ 480,000	$ 980,000
D	$600,000	$30(20,000) = $ 600,000	$1,200,000

Figure 11.1 shows the graph of the total cost lines. The line for community A goes from (0, 150) to (20, 1,390). The graph indicates that community A is best for low volumes, B for intermediate volumes, and C for high volumes. We should no longer consider community D, because both its fixed *and* its variable costs are higher than community C's.

Step 2:   The break-even quantity between A and B lies at the end of the first range, where A is best, and the beginning of the second range, where B is best. We find it by setting both communities' total cost equations equal to each other and solving:

(A)	(B)
$150,000 + $62Q = $300,000 + $38Q	
Q = 6,250 units	

The break-even quantity between B and C lies at the end of the range over which B is best and the beginning of the final range where C is best. It is

(B)	(C)
$300,000 + $38Q = $500,000 + $24Q	
Q = 14,286 units	

No other break-even quantities are needed. The break-even point between A and C lies above the shaded area, which does not mark either the start or the end of one of the three relevant ranges.

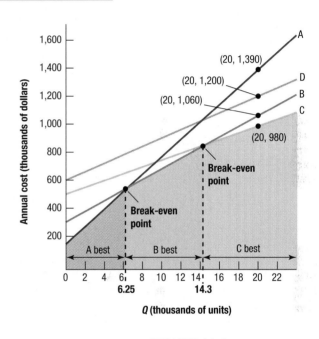

▲ FIGURE 11.1
Break-Even Analysis of Four Candidate Locations

DECISION POINT

Management located the new facility at community C, because the 15,000 units-per-year demand forecast lies in the high-volume range. These results can also be used as an input for a final decision using a preference matrix, where other non-quantitative factors could also be incorporated into the decision-making process.

LOCATING A FACILITY WITHIN A NETWORK OF FACILITIES

When a firm with a network of existing facilities plans a new facility, one of two conditions exists: Either the facilities operate independently (examples include a chain of restaurants, health clinics, banks, or retail establishments) or the facilities interact (examples include component manufacturing plants, assembly plants, and warehouses). Independently operating units can be located by treating each as a separate single facility, as described in the preceding section. Locating interacting facilities introduces new issues, such as how to allocate

On March 12, 2007, Raving Brands, owners of Moe's Southwest Grill, announced it inked development agreements for the Middle East, Singapore, and Canada. According to the announcement, these three independent deals will result in 150 restaurants. Moe's will subsequently determine specific locations for these multiple facilities.

transportation method

A quantitative approach that can help solve multiple-facility location problems.

work between the facilities and how to determine the best capacity for each. In addition, the facilities may be scattered internationally around the globe. Changing the work allocations in turn affects the size (or capacity utilization) of the various facilities. Thus, the multiple-facility location problem has three dimensions—location, allocation, and capacity—that must be solved simultaneously. In many cases, the analyst can identify a workable solution merely by looking for patterns in the cost, demand, and capacity data and using trial-and-error calculations. In other cases, more formal approaches are needed.

The GIS Method for Locating Multiple Facilities

The **transportation method** is a quantitative approach that can help solve multiple-facility location problems. We cover it as part of Supplement E, "Linear Programming Models." What we instead cover here are GIS tools, which are another option to help the search for a solution. GIS helps visualize customer locations and data, as well as the transportation structure of roads and highways. These capabilities allow the analyst to quickly arrive at a reasonable solution to the multiple-facility location problems. Load–distance score and center of gravity data can be merged with customer databases in Excel to arrive at trial locations for facilities, which can then be evaluated for annual driving time or distance using a GIS such as MapPoint and Excel. A five-step framework that captures the use of GIS for locating multiple facilities is outlined here.

1. Map the data for existing customers and facilities in the GIS.

2. Visually split the entire operating area into the number of parts or subregions that equal the number of facilities to be located.

3. Assign a facility location for each region based on the visual density of customer concentration or other factors. Alternately, determine the center of gravity for each part or subregion identified in step 2 as the starting location point for the facility in that subregion.

4. Search for alternate sites around the center of gravity to pick a feasible location that meets the firm's managerial criteria such as proximity to major metropolitan areas or highways.

5. Compute total load–distance scores and perform capacity checks before finalizing the locations for each region.

Such an approach can have many applications, including the design of supply chain distribution networks as illustrated in Example 11.4 and the accompanying video in my**om**lab.

EXAMPLE 11.4	**Locating Multiple Facilities for Witherspoon Automotive**

Witherspoon Automotive, a remanufacturer of automotive components and subassemblies, delivers full truckloads of parts to its customers, and returns with a shipment of used automotive parts for disassembly and remanufacturing. The company currently operates out of two locations in the Southeast: Spartanburg, South Carolina, and Orlando, Florida. Each of these locations has a remanufacturing facility, along with an attached warehouse that serves as a distribution center (DC). The Spartanburg facility covers a total of 362 customers in Georgia, North Carolina, South Carolina, and parts of Alabama, Tennessee, and Virginia. The Orlando facility covers a total of 66 customers mostly in Florida, and a small portion of Alabama and Georgia. The Spartanburg DC and Orlando DC shipped 17,219 and 4,629 full truckloads, respectively, to their customers last year. The operating regions and the specific customer locations (in the form of pushpins) covered by both these facilities are shown in Figure 11.2.

The senior management at Witherspoon Automotive decided to close the Spartanburg facility because of its age and obsolescence, and instead split the Spartanburg region into two new regions, each with its own manufacturing and distribution center. In addition, the following five important location factors affect their final decision:

1. In order to promote a better quality of life for its workers, the new facilities should be located in a major metropolitan area.

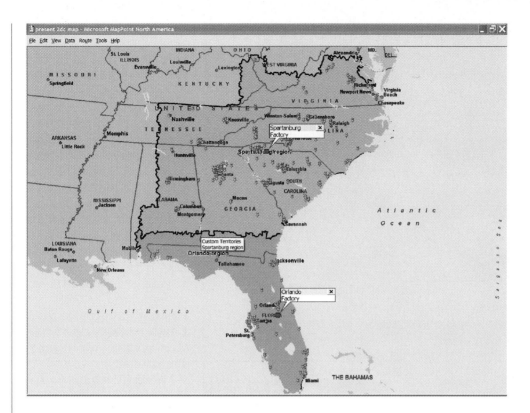

▲ FIGURE 11.2
Operating Regions and Customer Location for Witherspoon Automotive

2. Distribution costs are a major determinant of profits, and so the total load–distance score should be minimized in order to minimize the distribution costs.

3. Because of the diseconomies of scale previously experienced with the Spartanburg plant, the size of the two new facilities should not exceed a maximum of 9,500 truckloads of output per year.

4. The customer truckloads allocated between the two facilities should be fairly balanced given the previous year's demand data.

5. Marketing indicated that they are going to develop the northern Alabama market. Consequently, the new distribution network should be able to accommodate up to an additional 1,000 full truckload shipments per year from the Alabama market.

Where should the two new facilities be opened, assuming that the Orlando DC will stay where it is, and that fixed cost differences in opening a new facility are comparable across most potential sites in the region?

SOLUTION

Using the data in their system and MapPoint, the managers at Witherspoon automotive overlaid the locations and the number of full truckload shipments delivered last year for each customer in the Spartanburg region onto a map. The Witherspoon Automotive video on my**om**lab shows how to perform this analysis using MapPoint. To achieve a greater degree of aggregation in customer base and to also give due consideration to the quality of life location factor, the map was changed from displaying data for each street address (customer) to an aggregate view that displays data for each Metropolitan Statistical Area (MSA). The darker the shade, the greater the number of truckloads in the MSA. It was visually clear that Atlanta and Charlotte were the major markets, with Columbia, South Carolina; Greenville, South Carolina; and Richmond, Virginia, also having a heavy concentration of customers. From this map in Figure 11.3, it was easy to see that the dark green shaded area in Atlanta has a heavy customer-trips concentration. It represents 4,475 full truckloads, which would easily support half a facility. It seems reasonable for the management to locate one of the two new facilities near Atlanta. This decision will also achieve two other management objectives, in that the facility is near a major metropolitan area and is also well placed to serve the proposed expansion of the northern Alabama market. Management stated that if it decides to locate a facility near the Atlanta area, it would be in Buford, Georgia.

 The next step was to partition the customers into 2 regions, each with a total demand of less than 9,500 truckloads. Because it seemed clear that the Atlanta area would have a facility, one region was circled around Atlanta as

The Witherspoon Automotive video in my**om**lab shows how to locate multiple facilities using MapPoint 2004.

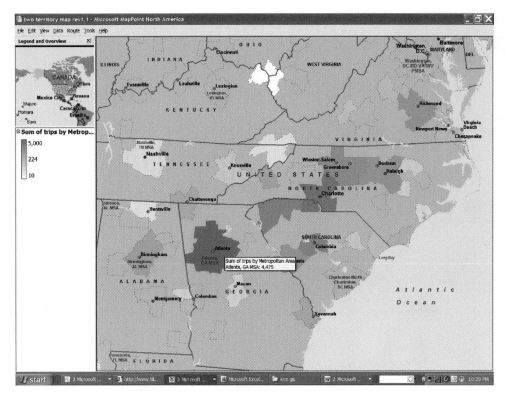

FIGURE 11.3 ▲
Truckload Concentration for Witherspoon

shown in Figure 11.4. Furthermore, if the northern Alabama market develops as hoped, it will handle an additional 1,000 truckloads. Because of this potential, the Atlanta region can only handle 8,500 truckloads for current customers. After a careful look at the map data, it was decided that Georgia, Tennessee, Alabama, and the parts of South Carolina that were within 2.5 hours of the Atlanta facility would be assigned to the Atlanta region. The Augusta/Aiken MSA that straddles the Georgia/South Carolina border was also added to this region to balance the two regions. This scenario results in the Atlanta region being assigned 8,397 truckloads and the second region having 8,822 trips, and achieving a 48.8 percent to 51.2 percent split while still allowing capacity in the Atlanta region for the proposed expansion of the northern Alabama market.

In order to identify a good location for the second facility, the center of gravity for the second region was determined to find a good starting point. Looking at the map in Figure 11.4, it appears that the center of the second region is around Durham, North Carolina. However, the center of gravity for the second region is close to a National Forest in Randolph County, North Carolina—not too far from Charlotte but considerably south and west of Durham. Such an outcome is to be expected because the Charlotte and to a lesser extent Columbia, South Carolina, markets have such a large percentage of the truckload volume for this region. However, the center of gravity does not appear to be a promising site because it is only near one customer.

Given this dilemma, the management of Witherspoon Automotive decided to pick a site next to the center of gravity as well as several sites in the general area of the center of gravity that are near Interstate I-85

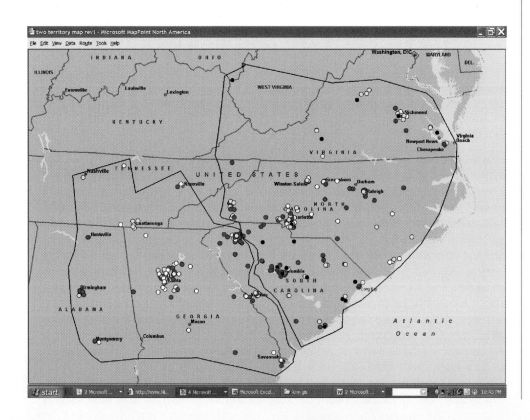

FIGURE 11.4 ▶
Witherspoon's Facilities Areas

(because almost every trip will require the truck driver to first drive to or go near Interstate I-85). Load–distance scores were computed using driving mileage and driving time based on last year's demand for each of the possible locations. The following results were obtained for load–distance calculations based on one-way trips:

Site	City	Load–Distance Using One-Way Mileage	Load–Distance Using One-Way Travel Hours
1	Albemarle	1,331,608	22,194
2	Salisbury	1,075,839	18,541
3	Greensboro	1,222,675	20,378
4	Concord	1,037,424	17,938

As the Witherspoon Automotive managers reviewed the results, they noted that Concord will provide the minimum mileage and drive time, and have the additional advantage of being near Charlotte—fulfilling the managerial objective of being located near a major city. Another attractive feature of this solution is that the Greenville, South Carolina, and Augusta, Georgia, markets are almost as close to the Concord facility as they are to the Buford facility. Management can reassign customers in these markets to the Charlotte region at little additional cost if the northern Alabama market grows faster than expected.

DECISION POINT

The Witherspoon Automotive management decided to locate the first facility in Buford, and the second one in Concord along the I-85 corridor. These locations are within the MSA of Atlanta and Charlotte, respectively, and reflect the wishes of management to be near a major metropolitan area. Creating two distribution centers in what is currently the Spartanburg region will reduce total mileage for Witherspoon Automotive by more than 3.5 million miles, and reduce annual drive time by almost 57,000 hours. These logistical savings are substantial, and meet all the specified location criteria.

Other Methods of Location Analysis

Many location analysis problems are even more complex than those discussed so far. Consider the complexity that a medium-sized manufacturer faces when distributing products through warehouses, or *distribution centers*, to various demand centers. The problem is to determine the number, size, allocation pattern, and location of the warehouses. The situation may involve thousands of demand centers, hundreds of potential warehouse locations, several plants, and multiple product lines. Transportation rates depend on the direction of shipment, product, quantity, rate breaks, and geographic area.

Such complexity requires the use of a computer for a comprehensive evaluation. Three basic types of computer models, in addition to the transportation method, have been developed for this purpose: (1) heuristics, (2) simulation, and (3) optimization.

Heuristics   Solution guidelines, or rules of thumb, that find feasible—but not necessarily the best—solutions to problems are called **heuristics**. Their advantages include efficiency and an ability to handle large problems. The systematic search procedure utilizing a target area's center of gravity, described earlier for single-facility location problems, is a typical heuristic procedure. One of the first heuristics to be computerized for location problems was proposed four decades ago to handle several hundred potential warehouse sites and several thousand demand centers. Many other heuristic models are available now for analyzing a variety of situations.

heuristics

Solution guidelines, or rules of thumb, that find feasible—but not necessarily the best—solutions to problems.

Simulation   A modeling technique that reproduces the behavior of a system is called simulation. Simulation models allow the analyst to evaluate different location alternatives by trial and error. A simulation model can handle more realistic views of a problem and involves the analyst who can propose and test the most reasonable alternatives. For each run, the analyst inputs the facilities to be opened and the simulator typically makes the allocation decisions based on some reasonable assumptions that have been written into the computer program.

The Ralston-Purina Company used simulation to assist the company in locating warehouses to serve 137 demand centers, 5 field warehouses, and 4 plants. Random demand at each demand center by product type was simulated over a period of time. Demand was met by the closest warehouse that had available inventory. Data were produced by simulating inventory levels, transportation costs, warehouse operating costs, and backorders. Ralston-Purina implemented the result of the simulation, which showed that the least-cost alternative would be to consolidate the five field warehouses into only three.

optimization

A procedure used to determine the "best" solution; generally utilizes simplified and less realistic views of a problem.

Optimization   The transportation method was one of the first optimization procedures for solving one part (the allocation pattern) of multiple-facility location problems. In contrast to heuristics and simulation, **optimization** involves procedures to determine the *best* solution. Even though this approach might appear to be preferable, it has a limitation: Optimization procedures generally utilize simplified and less realistic views of a problem. However, the payoffs can be substantial.

INTERNET RESOURCES

my**om**lab and the Companion Website at **www.pearsonglobaleditions.com/krajewski** contain many tools, activities, and resources designed for this chapter.

KEY EQUATIONS

1. Load–distance score:

$$ld = \sum_i l_i d_i$$

2. Center of gravity:

$$x^* = \frac{\sum_i l_i x_i}{\sum_i l_i} \text{ and } y^* = \frac{\sum_i l_i y_i}{\sum_i l_i}$$

KEY TERMS

center of gravity 416
critical mass 413
facility location 410

geographical information system
 (GIS) 413
heuristics 423
load–distance method 416

optimization 424
quality of life 411
transportation method 420

SOLVED PROBLEM 1

The operations manager for Mile-High Lemonade narrowed the search for a new facility location to seven communities. Annual fixed costs (land, property taxes, insurance, equipment, and buildings) and variable costs (labor, materials, transportation, and variable overhead) are shown in Table 11.1.

a. Which of the communities can be eliminated from further consideration because they are dominated (both variable and fixed costs are higher) by another community?

b. Plot the total cost curves for all remaining communities on a single graph. Identify on the graph the approximate range over which each community provides the lowest cost.

TABLE 11.1	FIXED AND VARIABLE COSTS FOR MILE-HIGH LEMONADE

Community	Fixed Costs per Year	Variable Costs per Barrel
Aurora	$1,600,000	$17.00
Boulder	$2,000,000	$12.00
Colorado Springs	$1,500,000	$16.00
Denver	$3,000,000	$10.00
Englewood	$1,800,000	$15.00
Fort Collins	$1,200,000	$15.00
Golden	$1,700,000	$14.00

c. Using break-even analysis, calculate the break-even quantities to determine the range over which each community provides the lowest cost.

SOLUTION

a. Aurora and Colorado Springs are dominated by Fort Collins, because both fixed and variable costs are higher for those communities than for Fort Collins. Englewood is dominated by Golden.

b. Figure 11.5 shows that Fort Collins is best for low volumes, Boulder for intermediate volumes, and Denver for high volumes. Although Golden is not dominated by any community, it is the second or third choice over the entire range. Golden does not become the lowest-cost choice at any volume.

c. The break-even point between Fort Collins and Boulder is

$$\$1,200,000 \ + \ \$15Q \ = \ \$2,000,000 \ + \ \$12Q$$

$$Q \ = \ 266{,}667 \text{ barrels per year}$$

The break-even point between Denver and Boulder is

$$\$3,000,000 \ + \ \$10Q \ = \ \$2,000,000 \ + \ \$12Q$$
$$Q \ = \ 500{,}000 \text{ barrels per year}$$

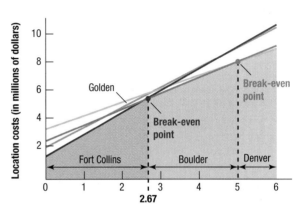

FIGURE 11.5 ▲
Break-Even Analysis of Four Candidate Locations

SOLVED PROBLEM 2

The new Health-Watch facility is targeted to serve seven census tracts in Erie, Pennsylvania, whose latitudes and longitudes are shown in Table 11.2. Customers will travel from the seven census-tract centers to the new facility when they need health care. What is the target area's center of gravity for the Health-Watch medical facility?

SOLUTION

We use MapPoint in this solution, with coordinates represented in the form of latitude and longitude rather than an (x, y) grid, to calculate the center of gravity. First the target area is displayed on the map of Erie, Pennsylvania, using MapPoint. In Figure 11.6 a pushpin is placed in the approximate geographical center of the census tracts. The location sensor is then turned on. By moving the cursor over the pushpin, the location sensor will register the longitude and latitude for the pushpin. The population of each census tract is added to the map using MapPoint's built-in demographic data. Thus, we obtain the following table in which latitudes and longitudes for each of the seven census-tracts are given, along with their actual populations, in thousands.

TABLE 11.2	LOCATION DATA AND CALCULATIONS FOR HEALTH WATCH				
Census Tract	Population	Latitude	Longitude	Population × Latitude	Population × Longitude
15	2,711	42.134	−80.041	114,225.27	−216,991.15
16	4,161	42.129	−80.023	175,298.77	−332,975.70
17	2,988	42.122	−80.055	125,860.54	−239,204.34
25	2,512	42.112	−80.066	105,785.34	−201,125.79
26	4,342	42.117	−80.052	182,872.01	−347,585.78
27	6,687	42.116	−80.023	281,629.69	−535,113.80
28	6,789	42.107	−80.051	285,864.42	−543,466.24
Total	**30,190**			**1,271,536.04**	**−2,416,462.80**

FIGURE 11.6 ▶
Center of Gravity for Health-Watch

Next we solve for the center of gravity x^* and y^*. Because the coordinates are given as longitude and latitude, x^* is the longitude and y^* is the latitude for the center of gravity.

$$x^* = \frac{1,271,536.05}{30,190} = 42.1178$$

$$y^* = \frac{-2,416,462.81}{30,190} = -80.0418$$

The center of gravity is (42.12 North, 80.04 West), and is shown on the map to be fairly central to the target area.

Active Model 11.2 in my**om**lab confirms these calculations for the center of gravity, and allows us to explore other alternative locations as well.

Active Model 11.2 in my**om**lab explores the *ld* scores of locations in the vicinity of the center of gravity.

SOLVED PROBLEM 3

The RiTech Company makes plasma televisions to serve distribution centers in Los Angeles, Chicago, and Boston from existing plants in New Delhi and Calcutta. Annual demand is expected to increase as projected in the bottom row of the tableau shown in Table 11.3. RiTech is considering expanding their operations and building a plant outside Shanghai. Annual capacity for each plant is shown in the right-hand column of the tableau. Transportation costs per television are shown in the tableau in brackets. For example, the cost to ship one television from New Delhi to Los Angeles is $20.37. The optimal allocations are also shown. For example, New Delhi ships 12,000 units to Chicago. What are the estimated transportation costs associated with this allocation pattern?

TABLE 11.3	OPTIMAL SOLUTION FOR RITECH COMPANY		
	Destination		
Source	**Los Angeles**	**Chicago**	**Boston**	**Capacity**
New Delhi	[$20.37]	[$22.25] **12,000**	[$28.89]	12,000
Calcutta	[$22.00] **6,000**	[$24.00] **4,000**	[$26.27]	10,000
Shanghai	[$21.13]	[$21.50] **6,000**	[$23.75] **12,000**	18,000
Demand	6,000	22,000	12,000	40,000

SOLUTION

The total cost is $909,000.

Ship 12,000 units from New Delhi to Chicago @ $22.25.   Cost = $267,000
Ship 6,000 units from Calcutta to Los Angeles @ $22.00.   Cost = $132,000
Ship 4,000 units from Calcutta to Chicago @ $24.00.   Cost = $96,000
Ship 6,000 units from Shanghai to Chicago @ $21.50.   Cost = $129,000
Ship 12,000 units from Shanghai to Boston @ $23.75.   Cost = $285,000

Total $909,000

DISCUSSION QUESTIONS

1. The owner of a Major League Baseball team is considering moving his team from its current city in the upper Midwest to a city in the Southeast that offers a larger television market, a new stadium, and holds the potential for greater fan support. What other factors should the owner consider before actually making the decision to relocate?

2. Break into teams. Select two organizations, one in services and one in manufacturing, that are known to some of your team members. What are the key factors that each organization would consider in locating a new facility? What data would you want to collect before evaluating the location options, and how would you collect the data? Explain.

PROBLEMS

Software, such as OM Explorer, Active Models, and POM for Windows, is available in my**om**lab. Check with your instructor on how best to use it. In many cases, the instructor wants you to understand how to do the calculations by hand. At most, the software provides a check on your calculations. When calculations are particularly complex and the goal is interpreting the results in making decisions, the software replaces entirely the manual calculations.

1. Fall-Line, Inc., is a Great Falls, Montana, manufacturer of a variety of downhill skis. Fall-Line is considering four locations for a new plant: Aspen, Colorado; Medicine Lodge, Kansas; Broken Bow, Nebraska; and Wounded Knee, South Dakota. Annual fixed costs and variable costs per pair of skis are shown in the following table:

Location	Annual Fixed Costs	Variable Cost per Pair
Aspen	$8,000,000	$250
Medicine Lodge	$2,400,000	$130
Broken Bow	$3,400,000	$ 90
Wounded Knee	$4,500,000	$ 65

a. Plot the total cost curves for all the communities on a single graph (see Solved Problem 1). Identify on the graph the range in volume over which each location would be best.

b. What break-even quantity defines each range?

Although Aspen's fixed and variable costs are dominated by those of the other communities, Fall-Line believes that both the demand and the price would be higher for skis made in Aspen than for skis made in the other locations. The following table shows those projections:

Location	Price per Pair	Forecast Demand per Year
Aspen	$500	60,000 pairs
Medicine Lodge	$350	45,000 pairs
Broken Bow	$350	43,000 pairs
Wounded Knee	$350	40,000 pairs

c. Determine which location yields the highest total profit per year.

d. Is this location decision sensitive to forecast accuracy? At what minimum sales volume does Aspen become the location of choice?

2. Two alternative locations are under consideration for a new plant: Jackson, Mississippi, and Dayton, Ohio. The Jackson location is superior in terms of costs. However, management believes that sales volume would decline if this location were chosen because it is farther from the market, and the firm's customers prefer local suppliers.

The selling price of the product is $250 per unit in either case. Use the following information to determine which location yields the higher total profit per year:

Location	Annual Fixed Cost	Variable Cost per Unit	Forecast Demand per Year
Jackson	$1,500,000	$50	30,000 units
Dayton	$2,800,000	$85	40,000 units

3. Calculate the weighted score for each location (A, B, C, and D) shown in Table 11.4. Which location would you recommend?

4. John and Jane Darling are newlyweds trying to decide among several available rentals. Alternatives were scored on a scale of 1 to 5 (5 = best) against weighted performance criteria, as shown in Table 11.5. The criteria included rent, proximity to work and recreational opportunities, security, and other neighborhood characteristics associated with the couple's values and lifestyle. Alternative A is an apartment, B is a bungalow, C is a condo, and D is a downstairs apartment in Jane's parents' home.

Which location is indicated by the preference matrix? What qualitative factors might cause this preference to change?

5. Centura High School is to be located at the population center of gravity of three communities: Boelus, population 228; Cairo, population 737; and Dannebrog, population 356. The Boelus community is located at 106.72°E, 46.31°N; Cairo is located at 106.68°E, 46.37°N; and Dannebrog is located at 106.77°E, 46.34°N. Where should Centura High School be located?

6. The following three points are the locations of important facilities in a transportation network: (20, 20), (50, 10), and (50, 60). The coordinates are in miles.

a. Calculate the Euclidean distances (in miles) between each of the three pairs of facilities.

b. Calculate these distances using rectilinear distances.

TABLE 11.4 | FACTORS FOR LOCATIONS A–D

Location Factor	Factor Weight	A	B	C	D
1. Labor climate	5	5	4	3	5
2. Quality of life	30	2	3	5	1
3. Transportation system	5	3	4	3	5
4. Proximity to markets	25	5	3	4	4
5. Proximity to materials	5	3	2	3	5
6. Taxes	15	2	5	5	4
7. Utilities	15	5	4	2	1
Total	100				

TABLE 11.5	FACTORS FOR NEWLYWEDS					
			Factor Score for Each Location			
Location Factor	Factor Weight	A	B	C	D
1. Rent	25	3	1	2	5
2. Quality of life	20	2	5	5	4
3. Schools	5	3	5	3	1
4. Proximity to work	10	5	3	4	3
5. Proximity to recreation	15	4	4	5	2
6. Neighborhood security	15	2	4	4	4
7. Utilities	10	4	2	3	5
Total	100				

7. Sam Hutchins is planning to operate a specialty bagel sandwich kiosk but is undecided about whether to locate in the downtown shopping plaza or in a suburban shopping mall. Based on the following data, which location would you recommend?

Location	Downtown	Suburban
Annual rent, including utilities	$12,000	$8,000
Expected annual demand (sandwiches)	30,000	25,000
Average variable costs per sandwich	$1.50	$1.00
Average selling price per sandwich	$3.25	$2.85

8. Wiebe Trucking, Inc., is planning a new warehouse to serve the west. Denver, Santa Fe, and Salt Lake City are under consideration. For each location, annual fixed costs (rent, equipment, and insurance) and average variable costs per shipment (labor, transportation, and utilities) are listed in the following table. Sales projections range from 550,000 to 600,000 shipments per year.

Location	Annual Fixed Costs	Variable Costs per Shipment
Denver	$5,000,000	$4.65
Santa Fe	$4,200,000	$6.25
Salt Lake City	$3,500,000	$7.25

a. Plot the total cost curves for all the locations on a single graph.

b. Which city provides the lowest overall costs?

QUESTIONS 9, 10, AND 15 REQUIRE THE MS MAPPOINT 2004 SOFTWARE

9. Office Warehouse has decided to locate its new facility in Red Bluff, California. A map of its customers can be found in the "Office Warehouse.ptm" file in my**om**lab. The loads delivered annually to each customer (expressed in tons of material) are shown in the following table.

   Determine the center of gravity for Office Warehouse's customers in Red Bluff. Use the location sensor in MapPoint to determine the longitude and latitude for each of its customers and then use Active Model 11.2.

10. Snappy Pizza decided to locate a pizza and take-out delivery restaurant in Fargo, North Dakota. It wants to locate near the densely populated areas of the town. Snappy management created a map of the population density of the various census tracts in Fargo. The map can be found in the file "Snappy.ptm" in my**om**lab.

Customer Name	Address	Tons of Material Delivered Annually
Standard Products	2808 Live Oak Road Red Bluff, CA 96080	4,000
National Products	1437 Warren Ave Red Bluff, CA 96080	3,000
Golf Cart, Inc.	630 Nicklaus Avenue Red Bluff, CA 96080	7,000
Acme Corp.	277 Gurnsey Dr. Red Bluff, CA 96080	2,000
Speedy Electronics	1371 Trinity Avenue Red Bluff, CA 96080	1,000

Choose a site that has as many people as possible within a 5-minute drive time zone. Print the map with your 5-minute drive time zone. You may wish to watch the Tyler EMS video on myomlab before starting this problem.

11. Paramount Manufacturing is investigating which location would best position its new plant relative to two suppliers (located in cities A and B) and one market area (represented by city C). Management limited the search for this plant to those three locations and compiled the following information:

Location	Coordinates (miles)	Tons per Year	Freight Rate ($/ton-mile)
A	(100, 200)	4,000	$3.00
B	(400, 100)	3,000	$1.00
C	(100, 100)	4,000	$3.00

a. Which of the three locations gives the lowest total cost, based on Euclidean distances? [*Hint:* The annual cost of inbound shipments from supplier A to the new plant is $12,000 per mile (4,000 tons per year × $3.00 per ton-mile).]

b. Which location is best, based on rectilinear distances?

c. What are the coordinates of the center of gravity?

12. A larger and more modern main post office is to be constructed at a new location in Davis, California. Growing suburbs caused a shift in the population density from where it was 40 years ago, when the current facility was built. Annette Werk, the postmaster, asked her assistants to draw a grid map of the seven points where mail is picked up and delivered in bulk. The coordinates and trips per day to and from the seven mail source points and the current main post office, M, are shown in the following table. M will continue to act as a mail source point after relocation.

Mail Source Point	Round Trips Per Day	x, y Coordinates (miles)
1	6	(2, 8)
2	3	(6, 1)
3	3	(8, 5)
4	3	(13, 3)
5	2	(15, 10)
6	7	(6, 14)
7	5	(18, 1)
M	3	(10, 3)

a. Calculate the center of gravity as a possible location for the new facility (round to the nearest whole number).

b. Compare the load–distance scores for the location in part (a) and the current location, using rectilinear distance.

13. Val's Pizza is looking for a single central location to make pizza for delivery only. This college town is arranged on a grid with arterial streets, as shown in Figure 11.7. The main campus (A), located at 14th and R, is the source of 4,000 pizza orders per week. Three smaller campuses (B, C, and D) are located at 52nd and V, at 67th and Z, and at 70th and South. Orders from the smaller campuses average 1,000 pizzas per week. In addition, the State Patrol headquarters (E) at 10th and A orders 500 pizzas per week.

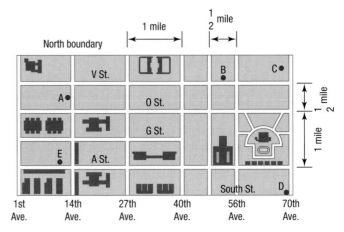

FIGURE 11.7 ▲
Map of Campus Area

a. At about what intersection should Val start looking for a suitable site? (Estimate coordinates for the major demands accurate to the nearest one-quarter mile, and then find the center of gravity.)

b. What is the rectilinear weekly load–distance score for this location?

c. If the delivery person can travel 1 mile in 2 minutes on arterial streets and ¼; mile per minute on residential streets, going from the center of gravity location to the farthest demand location will take how long?

14. A personal computer manufacturer plans to locate its assembly plant in Taiwan and to ship its computers back to the United States through either Los Angeles or San Francisco. It has distribution centers in Atlanta, New York, and Chicago and will ship to them from whichever city is chosen as the port of entry on the West Coast. Overall transportation cost is the only criterion for choosing the port. Use the load–distance model and the information in Table 11.6 to select the more cost-effective city.

TABLE 11.6	DISTANCES AND COSTS FOR PC MANUFACTURER		
	Distribution Center (units/year)		
	Chicago	**Atlanta**	**New York**
	(10,000)	**(7,500)**	**(12,500)**
Los Angeles			
Distance (miles)	1,800	2,600	3,200
Shipping cost ($/unit)	0.0017/mile	0.0017/mile	0.0017/mile
PORT OF ENTRY			
San Francisco			
Distance (miles)	1,700	2,800	3,000
Shipping cost ($/unit)	0.0020/mile	0.0020/mile	0.0020/mile

ADVANCED PROBLEMS

15. Metro Supply decided to relocate its warehouse. Determine a good location for its new warehouse based on minimizing the number of miles traveled. The addresses and number of trips made to each of its customers last year can be found in the "Metro Supply.xls" file and displayed in a "Metro Supply.ptm" file (a MapPoint map) in myomlab. For your convenience, the center of gravity is displayed on the map. Enter the street address of your proposed warehouse location on the "Distribution Centers" worksheet in the "Metro Supply.xls" file and run the macro by selecting the button on the "Customers" worksheet to determine the total one-way mileage (which is essentially the load–distance score). You may wish to watch the Witherspoon Automotive video on myomlab before starting this problem.

16. Oscar's Bowling, Inc., wants to break into the Phoenix metropolitan market with one of its super-sized 200 lane, 24-hour bowling alleys. It, however, only has enough capital to build one facility. Oscar wants it to be centered by population, as determined by the center of gravity method. The following information is given:

City	Population	x coordinate	y coordinate
Tempe	250,000	5	5
Scottsdale	400,000	5	10
Chandler	300,000	5	0
Mesa	700,000	10	1
Glendale	350,000	1	10

a. Where should Oscar build?

b. If Oscar wanted to relocate to the closest city near his new facility—where would he live?

17. Darren's Custom Guitars has narrowed its potential choices for its new manufacturing facility to four cities. The following information is known about each of these four cities:

	Fixed Costs per Year	Variable Costs per Unit
Phoenix	$300,000	$75.00
Buffalo	$600,000	$60.00
Seattle	$1,500,000	$38.00
Atlanta	$1,750,000	$47.00

a. Use breakeven point analysis to determine where Darren should locate.

b. Based solely on breakeven quantity, if Darren's manufacturing forecast for the foreseeable future is 40,000 units annually, where should he locate?

ACTIVE MODEL EXERCISE

Active Model 11.2 appears in myomlab. It allows you to find the location that minimizes the total load–distance score.

QUESTIONS

1. What is the total load–distance score to the new Health-Watch medical facility if it is located at the center of gravity?

2. Fix the y coordinate, and use the scroll bar to modify the x coordinate. Can you reduce the total load–distance score?

3. Fix the x coordinate, and use the scroll bar to modify the y coordinate. Can you reduce the total load–distance score?

4. The center of gravity does not necessarily find the site with the minimum total load–distance score. Use both scroll bars to move the trial location, and see whether you can improve (lower) the total load–distance score.

CASE	Industrial Repair, Inc.

For 25 years, Industrial Repair (IR) operated its industrial machine repair business out of its main office located at 26 Arbor Street, Hartford, Connecticut. Initially, almost all of its customers were based in Hartford only. However, its good reputation for timely service allowed IR to grow, and as a result it currently serves customers throughout the U.S. state of Connecticut. When its customers' heavy industrial machines break down, IR is called in to fix them. Upon receiving a service request, IR sends a crew of two technicians and a truck to the customer site as quickly as possible. Because downtime on machines is expensive for IR's customers, it is important that IR responds quickly to customers' calls.

IR noticed a number of changes in the industrial repair market over the past couple of years. Several other companies entered the market and increased the level of competition. Also, as customers become more just-in-time oriented, they are less tolerant of long delays in the arrival of repair crews. IR's management believes that it will be increasingly difficult to keep or attract customers that are more than a 30-minute drive away from its facility. Because so many of its customers are farther than a 30-minute drive, IR's managers realize that they will have to look more closely at IR's location choices. Ideally, management would like to simply relocate the current facility. However, it may be necessary to operate two facilities to cover the entire customer base and also provide for future expansion. If IR operates two facilities, IR will keep its current facility and open a new one elsewhere. To help with their analysis, managers gathered the address and the number of repairs performed last year for each customer.

IR's accountants determined that the technicians cost the company approximately $75 per hour including pay, fringe benefits, and frequent training workshops. Since technicians always work in teams of two, one hour of driving time costs IR $150. Additionally, after taking into account all fixed and variable costs associated with its trucks, IR figures that the trucks cost $2 per mile to operate

If IR opens a facility, the cost will be $100,000 in initial expenses (which IR must depreciate over 10 years using straight-line depreciation). If IR decides to operate two facilities, the cost will be an extra $70,000 per year in operating expenses. IR uses a 12 percent discount rate in its investment decisions. Its tax rate is 40 percent.

IR management assigned Andrew Morgan, the facility manager, to the task of investigating and making recommendations on the best locations if IR uses a single facility or two facilities. As mentioned earlier, IR decided that for the two facilities option, it would retain its present facility and open up one new facility. Management also requested that Morgan's recommendations consider both the transportation costs and the percent of customers within a 30-minute drive time zone of IR's facilities.

(The addresses and the number of repairs for each customer last year have already been entered in the *OM Explorer* Solver for "Center of Gravity Using MS MapPoint 2004-IR Case" and *OM Explorer* Solver for "Multiple Facilities Location-Driving Time and Distance Calculator Using MS MapPoint 2004-IR Case." Note that the latter *OM Explorer* Solver displays the travel time for each customer to the nearest facility. For the case in which you use the current facility in conjunction with a new facility, you can enter both locations into the *OM Explorer* Solver to determine the travel time to the closest facility.)

QUESTIONS

1. Determine the best location if IR decides to use only one facility. Be sure to report the net present value (NPV) using a 10-year horizon and the *Financial Analysis-Straight Line Depreciation (SLD)* Solver for this relocation, as well as the percentage of repairs that are within 30 minutes of the chosen location.

2. Determine the best location for the new site if IR decides to use two facilities (retaining the existing site for the first one). Be sure to report the NPV using a 10-year horizon and the *Financial Analysis-Straight Line Depreciation (SLD)* Solver for this relocation and the percentage of repairs that are within 30 minutes of the chosen locations.

3. What should Andrew recommend? Provide an explanation for supporting the recommendation.

Source: This case was prepared by Dr. Patrick R. Philipoom, University of South Carolina, as a basis for classroom discussion.

SELECTED REFERENCES

Andel, T. "Site Selection Tools Dig Data." *Transportation & Distribution*, vol. 37, no. 6 (1996), pp. 77–81.

Bartness, A. D. "The Plant Location Puzzle." *Harvard Business Review* (March–April 1994), pp. 20–30.

"BMW Announces Its Plans for a Plant in South Carolina." *Wall Street Journal* (June 24, 1992), p. B2.

Chittum, Ryan. "Location, Location, and Technology: Where to Put That New Store? Site-Selection Software May Be Able to Help." *Wall Street Journal* (July 18, 2005), p. R7.

Cook, David P., Chon-Huat Goh, and Chen H. Chung. "Service Typologies: A State of the Art Survey." *Production and Operations Management*, vol. 8, no. 3 (1999), pp. 318–338.

Cook, Thomas M., and Robert A. Russell. *Introduction to Management Sciences*. Englewood Cliffs, NJ: Prentice Hall, 1993.

DeForest, M. E. "Thinking of a Plant in Mexico?" *The Academy of Management Executive*, vol. 8, no. 1 (1994), pp. 33–40.

"Doing Well by Doing Good." *The Economist* (April 22, 2000), pp. 65–67.

Drezner, Z. *Facility Location: A Survey of Applications and Methods*. Secaucus, NJ: Springer-Verlag, 1995.

Ferdows, Kasra, "Making the Most of Foreign Factories." *Fortune* (March–April 1997), pp. 73–88.

Galuszka, P. "The South Shall Rise Again." *Chief Executive*, November 2004, pp. 50–54.

"How Legend Lives Up to Its Name." *Business Week* (February 15, 1999), pp. 75–78.

"Location Analysis Tools Help Starbucks Brew Up New Ideas." *Business Geographics*, www.geoplace.com.

Love, Robert F., James G. Morris, and George O. Weslowsky. *Facilities Location: Models and Methods.* New York: North-Holland, 1988.

Lovelock, Christopher H., and George S, Yip. "Developing Global Strategies for Service Businesses." *California Management Review*, vol. 38, no. 2 (1996), pp. 64–86.

"Manager's Journal: Why BMW Cruised into Spartanburg." *Wall Street Journal* (July 6, 1992), p. A10.

"MapInfo Delivers Location Intelligence for Marco's Pizza." *Directions Magazine* (December 14, 2004), www.directions mag.com/press.releases/?duty=Show&id=10790.

Porter, Michael E. "The Competitive Advantage of Nations." *Harvard Business Review* (March–April 1990), pp. 73–93.

Roth, Aleda. "The Second Generation of Quality: Global Supply-Chain Integration in Japan and the United States." *The Quality Yearbook: 1998 Edition*, J. W. Cortada and J. A. Woods (eds.). New York: McGraw-Hill, 1998.

Rubinstein, Ed. "Chain Chart Their Course of Actions with Geographic Information Systems." *Nation's Restaurant News*, vol. 32, no. 6 (1998), p. 49.

"The Science of Site Selection." *National Real Estate Investor* (October 11, 2002).

Vishwanath, Vijay, and David Hardling. "The Starbucks Effect." *Harvard Business Review* (March–April 2000), pp. 17–18.

12 MANAGING INVENTORIES

State-of-the-art technology, including new RFID tags, help move merchandise efficiently through Wal-Mart's distribution centers.

INVENTORY MANAGEMENT AT WAL-MART

In the market for shaver blade replacements? A printer? First-aid supplies? Dog food? Hair spray? If so, you expect that the store you shop at will have what you want. However, making sure that the shelves are stocked with tens of thousands of products is no simple matter for inventory managers at Wal-Mart, which has 7,357 Wal-Mart stores and Sam's Club locations in 14 markets, employs more than 2 million associates, serves 180 million customers per week worldwide, and uses 56,000 suppliers. You can imagine in an operation this large that some things can get lost. Linda Dillman, CIO at Wal-Mart, recounts the story of the missing hair spray at one of the stores. The shelf needed to be restocked with a specific hair spray; however, it took three days to find the case in the backroom. Most customers will not swap hair sprays, so Wal-Mart lost three days of sales on that product.

Knowing what is in stock, in what quantity, and where it is being held is critical to effective inventory management. Without accurate inventory information, companies can make major mistakes by ordering too much, not enough, or shipping products to the wrong location. Companies can have large inventories and still have stockouts of product because they have too much inventory of some products and not enough of others. Wal-Mart, with inventories in excess of $36 billion, is certainly aware of the potential benefits from improved inventory management and is constantly experimenting with ways to reduce inventory investment. Knowing when

LEARNING GOALS

After reading this chapter, you should be able to:

1. Determine the items deserving most attention and tightest inventory control.

2. Calculate the economic order quantity and apply it to various situations.

3. Determine the order quantity and reorder point for a continuous review inventory control system.

4. Determine the review interval and target inventory level for a periodic review inventory control system.

5. Define the key factors that determine the appropriate choice of an inventory system.

to replenish inventory stocks and how much to order each time is critical when dealing with so much inventory investment. The application of technology is also important, such as using radio frequency identification (RFID) to track inventory shipments and stock levels at stores and warehouses throughout the supply chain. One handheld RFID reader could have found the missing case of hair spray in a few minutes.

Sources: Laurie Sullivan, "Wal-Mart's Way," Informationweek.com (September 27, 2004), pp. 36–50; Gus Whitcomb and Christi Gallagher, "Wal-Mart Begins Roll-Out of Electronic Product Codes in Dallas/Fort Worth Area," www.walmartstores.com (June, 2008), and Investor Information, 2008 Financial Reports.

myomlab and the Companion Website at **www.pearsonglobaleditions.com/krajewski** contain many tools, activities, and resources designed for this chapter.

Inventory management, the planning and controlling of inventories in order to meet the competitive priorities of the organization, is an important concern for managers in all types of businesses. Effective inventory management is essential for realizing the full potential of any supply chain. The challenge is not to pare inventories to the bone to reduce costs or to have plenty around to satisfy all demands, but to have the right amount to achieve the competitive priorities of the business most efficiently. This type of efficiency can only happen if the right amount of inventory is flowing through the supply chain—through suppliers, the firm, warehouses or distribution centers, and customers. These decisions were so important for Wal-Mart that it decided to use RFID to improve the information flows in the supply chain. Much of inventory management involves *lot sizing*, which is the determination of how frequently and in what quantity to order inventory. We make ample reference to the term **lot size**, which is the quantity of an inventory item management either buys from a supplier or manufactures using internal processes. In this chapter we focus on the decision-making aspects of inventory management. We begin with an overview of the importance of inventory management to the organization and how to choose the items most deserving of management attention. We then introduce the basics of inventory decision making by exploring the economic order quantity and how it can be used to balance inventory holding costs with ordering costs. A major segment of the chapter is devoted to retail and distribution inventory control systems and how to use them.

INVENTORY MANAGEMENT ACROSS THE ORGANIZATION

Inventories are important to all types of organizations, their employees, and their supply chains. Inventories profoundly affect everyday operations because they must be counted, paid for, used in operations, used to satisfy customers, and managed. Inventories require an investment of funds, as does the purchase of a new machine. Monies invested in inventory are not available for investment in other things; thus, they represent a drain on the cash flows of an organization. Nonetheless, companies realize that the availability of products is a key selling point in many markets and downright critical in many more.

So, is inventory a boon or a bane? Certainly, too much inventory on hand reduces profitability, and too little inventory on hand creates shortages in the supply chain and ultimately damages customer confidence. Inventory management, therefore, involves trade-offs. Let us discover how companies can effectively manage inventories across the organization.

ABC Analysis

Thousands of items, often referred to as stock-keeping units, are held in inventory by a typical organization, but only a small percentage of them deserve management's closest attention and tightest control. A **stock-keeping unit (SKU)** is an individual item or product that has an identifying code and is held in inventory somewhere along the supply chain. **ABC analysis** is the process of dividing SKUs into three classes according to their dollar usage so that managers can focus on items that have the highest dollar value. This method is the equivalent of creating a *Pareto chart* except that it is applied to inventory rather than to process errors. As Figure 12.1 shows, class A items typically represent only about 20 percent of the SKUs but account for 80 percent of the dollar usage. Class B items account for another 30 percent of the SKUs but only 15 percent of the dollar usage. Finally, 50 percent of the SKUs fall in class C, representing a mere 5 percent of the dollar usage. The goal of ABC analysis is to identify the class A SKUs so management can control their inventory levels.

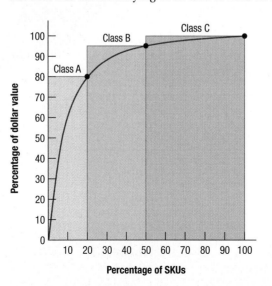

FIGURE 12.1 ▶
Typical Chart Using ABC Analysis

The analysis begins by multiplying the annual demand rate for an SKU by the dollar value (cost) of one unit of that SKU to determine its dollar usage. After ranking the SKUs on the basis of dollar usage and creating the Pareto chart, the analyst looks for "natural" changes in slope. The dividing lines in Figure 12.1 between classes are inexact. Class A SKUs could be somewhat higher or lower than 20 percent of all SKUs but normally account for the bulk of the dollar usage.

Class A SKUs are reviewed frequently to reduce the average lot size and to ensure timely deliveries from suppliers. It is important to maintain high inventory turnover for these items. By contrast, class B SKUs require an intermediate level of control. Here, less frequent monitoring of suppliers coupled with adequate safety stocks can provide cost-effective coverage of demands. For class C SKUs, much looser control is appropriate. While a stockout of a class C SKU can be as crucial as for a class A SKU, the inventory holding cost of class C SKUs tends to be low. These features suggest that higher inventory levels can be tolerated and that more safety stock and larger lot sizes may suffice for class C SKUs. See Solved Problem 4 for a detailed example of ABC analysis.

Creating ABC inventory classifications is useless unless inventory records are accurate. Technology can help; many companies are going to RFID to track inventory wherever it exists in the supply chain. Chips imbedded in product packaging contain information on the product and send signals that can be accessed by sensitive receivers and transmitted to a central location for processing. There are other, less sophisticated approaches of achieving accuracy that can be used. One way is to assign responsibility to specific employees for issuing and receiving materials and accurately reporting each transaction. Another method is to secure inventory behind locked doors or gates to prevent unauthorized or unreported withdrawals. This method also guards against accidentally storing newly received inventory in the wrong locations, where it can be lost for months. **Cycle counting** can also be used, whereby storeroom personnel physically count a small percentage of the total number of SKUs each day, correcting errors that they find. Class A SKUs are counted most frequently. A final method, for computerized systems, is to make logic error checks on each transaction reported and fully investigate any discrepancies. The discrepancies can include (1) actual receipts when no receipts are scheduled, (2) disbursements that exceed the current on-hand inventory balance, and (3) receipts with an inaccurate (nonexistent) SKU number.

Now that we have identified the inventory items deserving of most attention, we devote the remainder of the chapter to the decisions of how much to order and when.

Tutor 12.1 in myomlab provides a new example to practice ABC analysis.

cycle counting

An inventory control method, whereby storeroom personnel physically count a small percentage of the total number of items each day, correcting errors that they find.

ECONOMIC ORDER QUANTITY

Recall from our discussion in Chapter 9, "Designing Effective Supply Chains," that managers face conflicting pressures to keep inventories low enough to avoid excess inventory holding costs but high enough to reduce ordering and setup costs. *Inventory holding cost* is the sum of the cost of capital and the variable costs of keeping items on hand, such as storage and handling, taxes, insurance, and shrinkage. *Ordering cost* is the cost of preparing a purchase order for a supplier or a production order for the shop, while *setup cost* is the cost of changing over a machine to produce a different item. In this section we will address the *cycle inventory*, which is that portion of total inventory that varies directly with lot size. A good starting point for balancing these conflicting pressures and determining the best cycle-inventory level for an item is finding the **economic order quantity (EOQ)**, which is the lot size that minimizes total annual cycle-inventory holding and ordering costs. The approach to determining the EOQ is based on the following assumptions:

economic order quantity (EOQ)

The lot size that minimizes total annual inventory holding and ordering costs.

1. The demand rate for the item is constant (for example, always 10 units per day) and known with certainty.

2. No constraints are placed (such as truck capacity or materials handling limitations) on the size of each lot.

3. The only two relevant costs are the inventory holding cost and the fixed cost per lot for ordering or setup.

4. Decisions for one item can be made independently of decisions for other items. In other words, no advantage is gained in combining several orders going to the same supplier.

5. The lead time is constant (e.g., always 14 days) and known with certainty. The amount received is exactly what was ordered and it arrives all at once rather than piecemeal.

The economic order quantity will be optimal when all five assumptions are satisfied. In reality, few situations are so simple. Nonetheless, the EOQ is often a reasonable approximation of the appropriate lot size, even when several of the assumptions do not quite apply. Here are some guidelines on when to use or modify the EOQ.[1]

- **Do not use the EOQ**
  - If you use the "make-to-order" strategy and your customer specifies that the entire order be delivered in one shipment
  - If the order size is constrained by capacity limitations such as the size of the firm's ovens, amount of testing equipment, or number of delivery trucks
- **Modify the EOQ**
  - If significant quantity discounts are given for ordering larger lots
  - If replenishment of the inventory is not instantaneous, which can happen if the items must be used or sold as soon as they are finished without waiting until the entire lot has been completed (see Supplement D, "Special Inventory Models," for several useful modifications to the EOQ)
- **Use the EOQ**
  - If you follow a "make-to-stock" strategy and the item has relatively stable demand
  - If your carrying costs per unit and setup or ordering costs are known and relatively stable

The EOQ was never intended to be an optimizing tool. Nonetheless, if you need to determine a reasonable lot size, it can be helpful in many situations.

Calculating the EOQ

We begin by formulating the total cost for any lot size Q for a given SKU. Next, we derive the EOQ, which is the Q that minimizes total annual cycle-inventory cost. Finally, we describe how to convert the EOQ into a companion measure, the elapsed time between orders.

When the EOQ assumptions are satisfied, cycle inventory behaves as shown in Figure 12.2. A cycle begins with Q units held in inventory, which happens when a new order is received. During the cycle, on-hand inventory is used at a constant rate and, because demand is known with certainty and the lead time is a constant, a new lot can be ordered so that inventory falls to 0 precisely when the new lot is received. Because inventory varies uniformly between Q and 0, the average cycle inventory equals half the lot size, Q.

FIGURE 12.2 ▶
Cycle-Inventory Levels

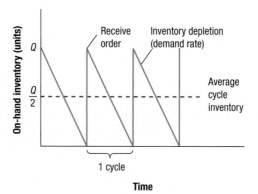

---

[1] See Alan R. Cannon and Richard E. Crandall, "The Way Things Never Were," *APICS—The Performance Advantage* (January 2004), pp. 32–35, for a more detailed discussion of the EOQ, its relevance to the just-in-time (JIT) philosophy, and when to use the EOQ.

The annual holding cost for this amount of inventory, which increases linearly with Q, as Figure 12.3(a) shows, is

Annual holding cost = (Average cycle inventory)(Unit holding cost)

The annual ordering cost is

Annual ordering cost = (Number of orders/Year)(Ordering or setup cost)

The average number of orders per year equals annual demand divided by Q. For example, if 1,200 units must be ordered each year and the average lot size is 100 units, then 12 orders will be placed during the year. The annual ordering or setup cost decreases nonlinearly as Q increases, as shown in Figure 12.3(b), because fewer orders are placed.

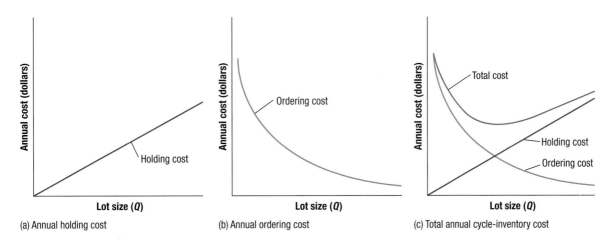

(a) Annual holding cost   (b) Annual ordering cost   (c) Total annual cycle-inventory cost

▲ FIGURE 12.3
Graphs of Annual Holding, Ordering, and Total Costs

The total annual cycle-inventory cost,[2] as graphed in Figure 12.4(c), is the sum of the two cost components:

Total cost = Annual holding cost + Annual ordering or setup cost[3]

$$C = \frac{Q}{2}(H) + \frac{D}{Q}(S)$$

where

C = total annual cycle-inventory cost

Q = lot size, in units

H = cost of holding one unit in inventory for a year, often expressed as a percentage of the item's value

D = annual demand, in units per year

S = cost of ordering or setting up one lot, in dollars per lot

---

[2] Expressing the total cost on an annual basis usually is convenient (although not necessary). Any time horizon can be selected, as long as D and H cover the same time period. If the total cost is calculated on a monthly basis, D must be monthly demand and H must be the cost of holding a unit for 1 month.

[3] The number of orders actually placed in any year is always a whole number, although the formula allows the use of fractional values. However, rounding is not needed because what is being calculated is an average for multiple years. Such averages often are nonintegers.

EXAMPLE 12.1 | **The Cost of a Lot-Sizing Policy**

A museum of natural history opened a gift shop two years ago. Managing inventories has become a problem. Low inventory turnover is squeezing profit margins and causing cash-flow problems.

One of the top-selling SKUs in the container group at the museum's gift shop is a bird feeder. Sales are 18 units per week, and the supplier charges $60 per unit. The cost of placing an order with the supplier is $45. Annual holding cost is 25 percent of a feeder's value, and the museum operates 52 weeks per year. Management chose a 390-unit lot size so that new orders could be placed less frequently. What is the annual cycle-inventory cost of the current policy of using a 390-unit lot size? Would a lot size of 468 be better?

SOLUTION

We begin by computing the annual demand and holding cost as

$$D = (18 \text{ units/week})(52 \text{ weeks/year}) = 936 \text{ units}$$
$$H = 0.25(\$60/\text{unit}) = \$15$$

The total annual cycle-inventory cost for the current policy is

$$C = \frac{Q}{2}(H) + \frac{D}{Q}(S)$$

$$= \frac{390}{2}(\$15) + \frac{936}{390}(\$45) = \$2,925 + \$108 = \$3,033$$

The total annual cycle-inventory cost for the alternative lot size is

$$C = \frac{468}{2}(\$15) + \frac{936}{468}(\$45) = \$3,510 + \$90 = \$3,600$$

DECISION POINT

The lot size of 468 units, which is a half-year supply, would be a more expensive option than the current policy. The savings in ordering costs are more than offset by the increase in holding costs. Management should use the total annual cycle-inventory cost function to explore other lot-size alternatives.

Figure 12.4 displays the impact of using several Q values for the bird feeder in Example 12.1. Eight different lot sizes were evaluated in addition to the current one. Both holding and ordering costs were plotted, but their sum—the total annual cycle-inventory cost curve—is the important feature. The graph shows that the best lot size, or EOQ, is the lowest point on the total annual cost curve, or between 50 and 100 units. Obviously, reducing the current lot-size policy ($Q = 390$) can result in significant savings.

A more efficient approach is to use the EOQ formula:

$$EOQ = \sqrt{\frac{2DS}{H}}$$

We use calculus to obtain the EOQ formula from the total annual cycle-inventory cost function. We take the first derivative of the total annual cycle-inventory cost function with respect to Q, set it equal to 0, and solve for Q. As Figure 12.4 indicates, the EOQ is the order quantity for which annual holding cost equals annual ordering cost. Using this insight, we can also obtain the EOQ formula by equating the formulas for annual ordering cost and annual holding cost and solving for Q. The graph in

FIGURE 12.4 ▶
Total Annual Cycle-Inventory Cost Function for the Bird Feeder

Figure 12.4 also reveals that when the annual holding cost for any Q exceeds the annual ordering cost, as with the 390-unit order, we can immediately conclude that Q is too big. A smaller Q reduces holding cost and increases ordering cost, bringing them into balance. Similarly, if the annual ordering cost exceeds the annual holding cost, Q should be increased.

Sometimes, inventory policies are based on the time between replenishment orders, rather than on the number of units in the lot size. The **time between orders (TBO)** for a particular lot size is the average elapsed time between receiving (or placing) replenishment orders of Q units. Expressed as a fraction of a year, the TBO is simply Q divided by annual demand. When we use the EOQ and express time in terms of months, the TBO is

time between orders (TBO)

The average elapsed time between receiving (or placing) replenishment orders of Q units for a particular lot size.

$$\text{TBO}_{\text{EOQ}} = \frac{\text{EOQ}}{D}(12 \text{ months/year})$$

In Example 12.2, we show how to calculate TBO for years, months, weeks, and days.

EXAMPLE 12.2   **Finding the EOQ, Total Cost, and TBO**

For the bird feeders in Example 12.1, calculate the EOQ and its total annual cycle-inventory cost. How frequently will orders be placed if the EOQ is used?

Tutor 12.2 in my**om**lab provides a new example to practice the application of the EOQ model.

SOLUTION

Using the formulas for EOQ and annual cost, we get

$$\text{EOQ} = \sqrt{\frac{2DS}{H}} = \sqrt{\frac{2(936)(45)}{15}} = 74.94 \text{ or } 75 \text{ units}$$

Figure 12.5 shows that the total annual cost is much less than the $3,033 cost of the current policy of placing 390-unit orders.

Parameters			
Current Lot Size (Q)	390	Economic Order Quantity	75
Demand (D)	936		
Order Cost (S)	$45		
Unit Holding Cost (H)	$15		

Annual Costs		Annual Costs based on EOQ	
Orders per Year	2.4	Orders per Year	12.48
Annual Ordering Cost	$108.00	Annual Ordering Cost	$561.60
Annual Holding Cost	$2,925.00	Annual Holding Cost	$562.50
Annual Inventory Cost	$3,033.00	Annual Inventory Cost	$1,124.10

◀ **FIGURE 12.5**
Total Annual Cycle-Inventory Costs Based on EOQ Using Tutor 12.2

When the EOQ is used, the TBO can be expressed in various ways for the same time period.

$$\text{TBO}_{\text{EOQ}} = \frac{\text{EOQ}}{D} = \frac{75}{936} = 0.080 \text{ year}$$

$$\text{TBO}_{\text{EOQ}} = \frac{\text{EOQ}}{D}(12 \text{ months/year}) = \frac{75}{936}(12) = 0.96 \text{ month}$$

$$\text{TBO}_{\text{EOQ}} = \frac{\text{EOQ}}{D}(52 \text{ weeks/year}) = \frac{75}{936}(52) = 4.17 \text{ weeks}$$

$$\text{TBO}_{\text{EOQ}} = \frac{\text{EOQ}}{D}(365 \text{ days/year}) = \frac{75}{936}(365) = 29.25 \text{ days}$$

Active Model 12.1 in my**om**lab provides additional insight on the EOQ model and its uses.

DECISION POINT

Using the EOQ, about 12 orders per year will be required. Using the current policy of 390 units per order, an average of 2.4 orders will be needed each year (every 5 months). The current policy saves on ordering costs but incurs a much larger cost for carrying the cycle inventory. Although it is easy to see which option is best on the basis of total ordering and holding costs, other factors may affect the final decision. For example, if the supplier would reduce the price per unit for large orders, it may be better to order the larger quantity.

Managerial Insights from the EOQ

Subjecting the EOQ formula to *sensitivity analysis* can yield valuable insights into the management of inventories. Sensitivity analysis is a technique for systematically changing crucial parameters to determine the effects of a change. Table 12.1 shows the effects on the EOQ when we substitute different values into the numerator or denominator of the formula.

TABLE 12.1	SENSITIVITY ANALYSIS OF THE EOQ			
Parameter	**EOQ**	**Parameter Change**	**EOQ Change**	**Comments**
Demand	$\sqrt{\dfrac{2DS}{H}}$	↑	↑	Increase in lot size is in proportion to the square root of D.
Order/Setup Costs	$\sqrt{\dfrac{2DS}{H}}$	↓	↓	Weeks of supply decreases and inventory turnover increases because the lot size decreases.
Holding Costs	$\sqrt{\dfrac{2DS}{H}}$	↓	↑	Larger lots are justified when holding costs decrease.

As Table 12.1 shows, the EOQ provides support for some of the intuition you may have about inventory management. However, the effect of ordering or setup cost changes on inventories is especially important for *lean systems*. This relationship explains why manufacturers are so concerned about reducing setup time and costs; it makes small lot production economic. Actually, lean systems provide an environment conducive to the use of the EOQ. For example, yearly, monthly, daily, or hourly demand rates are known with reasonable certainty in lean systems, and the rate of demand is relatively uniform. Lean systems (see Chapter 8, "Designing Lean Systems") may have few process constraints if the firm practices *constraint management* (see Chapter 7, "Managing Process Constraints"). In addition, lean systems strive for constant delivery lead times and dependable delivery quantities from suppliers, both of which are assumptions of the EOQ. Consequently, the EOQ as a lot sizing tool is quite compatible with the principles of lean systems.

INVENTORY CONTROL SYSTEMS

The EOQ and other lot-sizing methods answer the important question: *How much* should we order? Another important question that needs an answer is: *When* should we place the order? An inventory control system responds to both questions. In selecting an inventory control system for a particular application, the nature of the demands imposed on the inventory items is crucial. An important distinction between types of inventory is whether an item is subject to dependent or independent demand. Retailers, such as JCPenney, and distributors must manage **independent demand items**—that is, items for which demand is influenced by market conditions and is not related to the inventory decisions for any other item held in stock or produced. Independent demand inventory includes

independent demand items

Items for which demand is influenced by market conditions and is not related to the inventory decisions for any other item held in stock or produced.

- Wholesale and retail merchandise
- Service support inventory, such as stamps and mailing labels for post offices, office supplies for law firms, and laboratory supplies for research universities
- Product and replacement-part distribution inventories
- Maintenance, repair, and operating (MRO) supplies—that is, items that do not become part of the final service or product, such as employee uniforms, fuel, paint, and machine repair parts

Managing independent demand inventory can be tricky because demand is influenced by external factors. For example, the owner of a bookstore may not be sure how many copies of the latest best-seller novel customers will purchase during the coming month. As a result, the manager may decide to stock extra copies as a safeguard. Independent demand, such as the demand for various book titles, must be *forecasted*.

In this chapter, we focus on inventory control systems for independent demand items, which is the type of demand the bookstore owner, other retailers, service providers, and distributors face. Even though demand from any one customer is difficult to predict, low demand from some customers for a particular item often is offset by high demand from others. Thus, total demand for any independent demand item may follow a relatively smooth pattern, with some random fluctuations. *Dependent demand items* are those required as components or inputs to a service or product. Dependent demand exhibits a pattern very different from that of independent demand and must be managed with different techniques (see Chapter 15, "Planning Sufficient Resources").

In this section, we discuss and compare two inventory control systems: (1) the continuous review system, called a *Q* system, and (2) the periodic review system, called a *P* system. We close with a look at hybrid systems, which incorporate features of both the *P* and *Q* systems.

A shopper peruses the shoes display at a Macy's Department Store. Shoes experience an independent demand at the retail level.

Continuous Review System

A **continuous review (Q) system**, sometimes called a **reorder point (ROP) system** or *fixed order-quantity system*, tracks the remaining inventory of a SKU each time a withdrawal is made to determine whether it is time to reorder. In practice, these reviews are done frequently (e.g., daily) and often continuously (after each withdrawal). The advent of computers and electronic cash registers linked to inventory records has made continuous reviews easy. At each review, a decision is made about a SKU's inventory position. If it is judged to be too low, the system triggers a new order. The **inventory position (IP)** measures the SKU's ability to satisfy future demand. It includes **scheduled receipts (SR)**, which are orders that have been placed but have not yet been received, plus on-hand inventory (OH) minus backorders (BO). Sometimes scheduled receipts are called **open orders**. More specifically,

$$\text{Inventory position} = \text{On-hand inventory} + \text{Scheduled receipts} - \text{Backorders}$$

$$\text{IP} = \text{OH} + \text{SR} - \text{BO}$$

When the inventory position reaches a predetermined minimum level, called the **reorder point (R)**, a fixed quantity Q of the SKU is ordered. In a continuous review system, although the order quantity Q is fixed, the time between orders can vary. Hence, Q can be based on the EOQ, a price break quantity (the minimum lot size that qualifies for a quantity discount), a container size (such as a truckload), or some other quantity selected by management.

Selecting the Reorder Point When Demand and Lead Time Are Constant To demonstrate the concept of a reorder point, suppose that the demand for feeders at the museum gift shop in Example 12.2 is always 18 per week, the lead time is a constant 2 weeks, and the supplier always ships the exact number ordered on time. With both demand and lead time constant, the museum's buyer can wait until the inventory position drops to 36 units, or (18 units/week) (2 weeks), to place a new order. Thus, in this case, the reorder point, *R*, equals the *total demand during lead time*, with no added allowance for safety stock.

Figure 12.6 shows how the system operates when demand and lead time are constant. The

continuous review (Q) system

A system designed to track the remaining inventory of a SKU each time a withdrawal is made to determine whether it is time to reorder.

reorder point (ROP) system

See continuous review (Q) system.

inventory position (IP)

The measurement of a SKU's ability to satisfy future demand.

scheduled receipts (SR)

Orders that have been placed but have not yet been received.

open orders

See scheduled receipts (SR).

reorder point (R)

The predetermined minimum level that an inventory position must reach before a fixed quantity Q of the SKU is ordered.

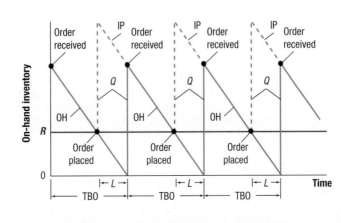

◀ **FIGURE 12.6**
Q System When Demand and Lead Time Are Constant and Certain

downward-sloping line represents the on-hand inventory, which is being depleted at a constant rate. When it reaches reorder point R (the horizontal line), a new order for Q units is placed. The on-hand inventory continues to drop throughout lead time L until the order is received. At that time, which marks the end of the lead time, on-hand inventory jumps by Q units. A new order arrives just when inventory drops to 0. The TBO is the same for each cycle.

The inventory position, IP, shown in Figure 12.6 corresponds to the on-hand inventory, except during the lead time. Just after a new order is placed, at the start of the lead time, IP increases by Q, as shown by the dashed line. The IP exceeds OH by this same margin throughout the lead time.[4] At the end of the lead time, when the scheduled receipts convert to on-hand inventory, IP = OH once again. The key point here is to compare IP, not OH, with R in deciding whether to reorder. A common error is to ignore scheduled receipts or backorders.

EXAMPLE 12.3	Placing a New Order When Demand and Lead Time Are Constant

Demand for chicken soup at a supermarket is always 25 cases a day and the lead time is always 4 days. The shelves were just restocked with chicken soup, leaving an on-hand inventory of only 10 cases. No backorders currently exist, but there is one open order in the pipeline for 200 cases. What is the inventory position? Should a new order be placed?

SOLUTION

$$R = \text{Total demand during lead time} = (25)(4) = 100 \text{ cases}$$
$$\text{IP} = \text{OH} + \text{SR} - \text{BO}$$
$$= 10 + 200 - 0 = 210 \text{ cases}$$

DECISION POINT

Because IP exceeds R (210 versus 100), do not reorder. Inventory is almost depleted, but a new order need not be placed because the scheduled receipt is in the pipeline.

Selecting the Reorder Point When Demand Is Variable and Lead Time Is Constant   In reality demand is not always predictable. For instance, the museum's buyer knows that *average* demand is 18 feeders per week. That is, a variable number of feeders may be purchased during the lead time, with an average demand during lead time of 36 feeders (assuming that each week's demand is identically distributed and lead time is a constant 2 weeks). This situation gives rise to the need for safety stocks. Suppose that the museum's buyer sets R at 46 units, thereby placing orders before they typically are needed. This approach will create a safety stock, or stock held in excess of expected demand, of 10 units (46 − 36) to buffer against uncertain demand. In general

$$\text{Reorder point} = \text{Average demand during lead time} + \text{Safety stock}$$
$$= \bar{d}L + \text{safety stock}$$

where

$$\bar{d} = \text{average demand per week (or day or month)}$$
$$L = \text{constant lead time in weeks (or days or months)}$$

Figure 12.7 shows how the Q system operates when demand is variable and lead time is constant. The wavy downward-sloping line indicates that demand varies from day to day. Its slope is steeper in the second cycle, which means that the demand rate is higher during this time period. The changing demand rate means that the time between orders changes, so $\text{TBO}_1 \neq \text{TBO}_2 \neq \text{TBO}_3$. Because of uncertain demand, sales during the lead time are unpredictable, and safety stock is added to hedge against lost sales. This addition is why R is

---

[4] A possible exception is the unlikely situation when more than one scheduled receipt is open at the same time because of long lead times.

higher in Figure 12.7 than in Figure 12.6. It also explains why the on-hand inventory usually does not drop to 0 by the time a replenishment order arrives. The greater the safety stock and thus the higher reorder point R, the less likely a stockout.

Because the average demand during lead time is variable, the real decision to be made when selecting R concerns the safety stock level. Deciding on a small or large safety stock is a trade-off between customer service and inventory holding costs. Cost minimization models can be used to find the best safety stock, but they require estimates of stockout and back-order costs, which are usually difficult to make with any precision because it is hard to estimate the effect of lost sales, lost customer confidence, future loyalty of customers, and market share because the customer went to a competitor. The usual approach for determining R is for management—based on judgment—to set a reasonable service-level policy for the inventory and then determine the safety stock level that satisfies this policy. There are three steps to arrive at a reorder point:

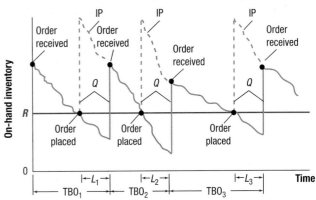

▲ **FIGURE 12.7**
Q System When Demand Is Uncertain

1. Choose an appropriate service-level policy.
2. Determine the demand during lead time probability distribution.
3. Determine the safety stock and reorder point levels.

Step 1: Service level policy.   Select a **service level**, or **cycle-service level** (the desired probability of not running out of stock in any one ordering cycle), which begins at the time an order is placed and ends when it arrives in stock. The intent is to provide coverage over the **protection interval**, or the period over which safety stock must protect the user from running out of stock. For the Q system, the lead time is the protection interval. For example, in a bookstore the manager may select a 90 percent cycle-service level for a book. In other words, the probability is 90 percent that demand will not exceed the supply during the lead time. The probability of running short *during the protection interval*, creating a stockout or backorder, is only 10 percent ($100 - 90$) in our example. This stockout risk, which occurs only during the lead time in the Q system, is greater than the overall risk of a stockout because the risk is nonexistent outside the ordering cycle.

Step 2: Demand during lead time distribution.   Determine the demand during lead time probability distribution, which requires the specification of its mean and standard deviation. To translate a cycle-service level policy into a specific safety stock level, we must know how demand during the lead time is distributed. If demand and lead times vary little around their averages, the safety stock can be small. Conversely, if they vary greatly from one order cycle to the next, the safety stock must be large. Variability is measured by the demand during lead time distribution. Sometimes average demand during the lead time and the standard deviation of demand during the lead time are not directly available and must be calculated by combining information on the demand rate with information on the lead time. Suppose that lead time is constant and demand is variable, but records on demand are not collected for a time interval that is exactly the same as the lead time. The same inventory control system may be used to manage thousands of different SKUs, each with a different lead time. For example, if demand is reported *weekly*, these records can be used directly to compute the average and the standard deviation of demand during the lead time if the lead time is exactly one week. However, if the lead time is three weeks, the computation is more difficult.

We can determine the demand during the lead time distribution by making some reasonable assumptions. Suppose that the average demand, $\bar{d}$, is known along with the standard deviation of demand, σ_d, over some time interval such as days or weeks. Also, suppose that the probability distributions of demand for each time interval are identical and independent of each other. For example, if the time interval is a week, the probability distributions of demand are assumed to be the same each week (identical $\bar{d}$ and σ_d), and the total demand in one week does not affect the total demand in another week. Let L be the constant lead time, expressed in the same time units as the demand. Under these assumptions, average demand during the lead time will be the sum of the averages for each of the L identical and independent distributions of demand, or $\bar{d} + \bar{d} + \bar{d} + \ldots = \bar{d}L$. In addition, the variance of the demand during lead time distribution will be the sum of the variances of the L identical and independent distributions of demand, or

$$\sigma_d^2 + \sigma_d^2 + \sigma_d^2 + \ldots = \sigma_d^2 L$$

Finally, the standard deviation of the demand during lead time distribution is

$$\sigma_{dLT} = \sqrt{\sigma_d^2 L} = \sigma_d \sqrt{L}$$

Figure 12.8 shows how the demand distribution of the lead time is developed from the individual distributions of weekly demands, where $\bar{d} = 75$, $\sigma_d = 15$, and $L = 3$ weeks. In this example, average demand during the lead time is $(75)(3) = 225$ units and $\sigma_{dLT} = 15\sqrt{3} = 25.98$.

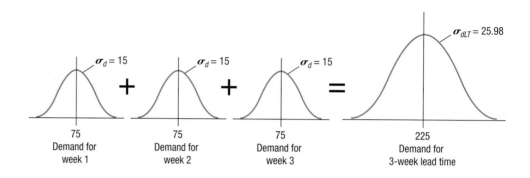

FIGURE 12.8 ▲
Development of Demand Distribution for the Lead Time

Step 3: Safety stock and reorder point. When selecting the safety stock, the inventory planner often assumes that demand during the lead time is normally distributed, as shown in Figure 12.9. The average demand during the lead time is the centerline of the graph, with 50 percent of the area under the curve to the left and 50 percent to the right. Thus, if a cycle-service level of 50 percent were chosen, the reorder point R would be the quantity represented by this centerline. Because R equals the average demand during the lead time plus the safety stock, the safety stock is 0 when R equals this average demand. Demand is less than average 50 percent of the time and, thus, having no safety stock will be sufficient only 50 percent of the time.

To provide a service level above 50 percent, the reorder point must be greater than the average demand during the lead time. As Figure 12.9 shows, that requires moving the reorder point to the right of the centerline so that more than 50 percent of the area under the curve is to the left of R. An 85 percent cycle-service level is achieved in Figure 12.9 with 85 percent of the area under the curve to the left of R (in blue) and only 15 percent to the right (in pink). We compute the safety stock as follows:

$$\text{Safety stock} = z\sigma_{dLT}$$

where

z = the number of standard deviations needed to achieve the cycle-service level

σ_{dLT} = standard deviation of demand during the lead time

The reorder point becomes

$$R = \bar{d}L + \text{safety stock}$$

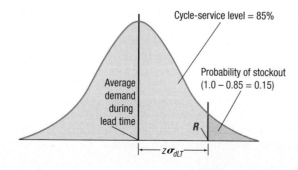

FIGURE 12.9 ▶
Finding Safety Stock with a Normal Probability Distribution for an 85 Percent Cycle-Service Level

The higher the value of z, the higher the safety stock and the cycle-service level should be. If $z = 0$, there is no safety stock, and stockouts will occur during 50 percent of the order cycles. For a cycle-service level of 85 percent, $z = 1.04$. Example 12.4 shows how to use the Normal Distribution appendix to find the appropriate z value, safety stock, and reorder point.

EXAMPLE 12.4   **Reorder Point for Variable Demand and Constant Lead Time**

Let us return to the bird feeder in Example 12.2. The EOQ is 75 units. Suppose that the average demand is 18 units per week with a standard deviation of 5 units. The lead time is constant at two weeks. Determine the safety stock and reorder point if management wants a 90 percent cycle-service level.

Tutor 12.3 in my**om**lab provides a new example to determine the safety stock and the reorder point for a Q system.

SOLUTION

In this case, $\sigma_d = 5$, $\bar{d} = 18$ units, and $L = 2$ weeks, so $\sigma_{dLT} = \sigma_d\sqrt{L} = 5\ \sqrt{2} = 7.07$. Consult the body of the table in the Normal Distribution appendix for 0.9000, which corresponds to a 90 percent cycle-service level. The closest number is 0.8997, which corresponds to 1.2 in the row heading and 0.08 in the column heading. Adding these values gives a z value of 1.28. With this information, we calculate the safety stock and reorder point as follows:

$$\text{Safety stock} = z\sigma_{dLT} = 1.28(7.07) = 9.05 \text{ or 9 units}$$

$$\text{Reorder point} = \bar{d}L + \text{Safety stock}$$

$$= 2(18) + 9 = 45 \text{ units}$$

DECISION POINT

The Q system for the bird feeder operates as follows: Whenever the inventory position reaches 45 units, order the EOQ of 75 units. Various order quantities and safety stock levels can be used in a Q system. For example, management could specify a different order quantity (because of shipping constraints) or a different safety stock (because of storage limitations).

Selecting the Reorder Point When Both Demand and Lead Time Are Variable   In practice it is often the case that both the demand and the lead time are variable. Unfortunately, the equations for the safety stock and reorder point become more complicated. In the model below we make two simplifying assumptions. First, the demand distribution and the lead time distribution are measured in the same time units. For example, both demand and lead time are measured in weeks. Second, demand and lead time are *independent*. That is, demand per week is not affected by the length of the lead time.

$$\text{Safety stock} = z\sigma_{dLT}$$

$$R = (\text{Average weekly demand} \times \text{Average lead time in weeks}) + \text{Safety stock}$$

$$= \bar{d}\,\bar{L} + \text{Safety stock}$$

where

$\bar{d}$ = Average weekly (or daily or monthly) demand

$\bar{L}$ = Average weekly (or daily or monthly) lead time

σ_d = Standard deviation of weekly (or daily or monthly) demand

σ_{LT} = Standard deviation of the lead time, and

$\sigma_{dLT} = \sqrt{\bar{L}\sigma_d^2 + \bar{d}^2\sigma_{LT}^2}$

Now that we have determined the mean and standard deviation of the demand during lead time distribution under these more complicated conditions, we can select the reorder point as we did before for the case where the lead time was constant.

EXAMPLE 12.5   **Reorder Point for Variable Demand and Variable Lead Time**

The Office Supply Shop estimates that the average demand for a popular ball-point pen is 12,000 pens per week with a standard deviation of 3,000 pens. The current inventory policy calls for replenishment orders of 156,000 pens. The average lead time from the distributor is 5 weeks, with a standard deviation of 2 weeks. If management wants a 95 percent cycle-service level, what should the reorder point be?

SOLUTION

We have $\bar{d} = 12{,}000$ pens, $\sigma_d = 3{,}000$ pens, $\bar{L} = 5$ weeks, and $\sigma_{LT} = 2$ weeks.

$$\sigma_{dLT} = \sqrt{\bar{L}\sigma_d^2 + \bar{d}^2\,\sigma_{LT}^2} = \sqrt{(5)(3{,}000)^2 + (12{,}000)^2(2)^2} = 24{,}919.87 \text{ pens}$$

Consult the body of the Normal Distribution appendix for 0.9500, which corresponds to a 95 percent cycle-service level. That value falls exactly in the middle of the tabular values of 0.9495 (for a z value of 1.64) and 0.9505 (for a z value of 1.65). Consequently, we will use the more conservative value of 1.65. We calculate the safety stock and reorder point as follows:

$$\text{Safety stock} = z\sigma_{dLT} = (1.65)(24{,}919.87) = 41{,}117.79, \text{ or } 41{,}118 \text{ pens}$$

$$\text{Reorder point} = \bar{d}\bar{L} + \text{Safety stock} = (12{,}000)(5) + 41{,}118 = 101{,}118 \text{ pens}$$

DECISION POINT

Whenever the stock of ball-point pens drops to 101,118, management should place another replenishment order of 156,000 pens to the distributor.

Sometimes the theoretical distributions for demand and lead time are not known. In those cases, we can use simulation to find the distribution of demand during lead time using discrete distributions for demand and lead times. Simulation can also be used to estimate the performance of an inventory system. Solved Problems 6 and 7 show how the Demand During Lead Time Simulator and the Q System Simulator in OM Explorer can be used to determine the appropriate inventory system parameters and to see how the system might work in practice. More discussion, and an example, can be found in my**om**lab.

visual system

A system that allows employees to place orders when inventory visibly reaches a certain marker.

Two-Bin System   The concept of a Q system can be incorporated in a **visual system**, that is, a system that allows employees to place orders when inventory visibly reaches a certain marker. Visual systems are easy to administer because records are not kept on the current inventory position. The historical usage rate can simply be reconstructed from past purchase orders. Visual systems are intended for use with low-value SKUs that have a steady demand, such as nuts and bolts or office supplies. Overstocking is common, but the extra inventory holding cost is minimal because the items have relatively little value.

two-bin system

A visual system version of the Q system in which a SKU's inventory is stored at two different locations.

A visual system version of the Q system is the **two-bin system** in which a SKU's inventory is stored at two different locations. Inventory is first withdrawn from one bin. If the first bin is empty, the second bin provides backup to cover demand until a replenishment order arrives. An empty first bin signals the need to place a new order. Premade order forms placed near the bins let workers send one to purchasing or even directly to the supplier. When the new order arrives, the second bin is restored to its normal level and the rest is put in the first bin. The two-bin system operates like a Q system, with the normal level in the second bin being the reorder point R. The system also may be implemented with just one bin by marking the bin at the reorder point level.

Calculating Total Q System Costs   Total costs for the continuous review (Q) system is the sum of three cost components:

Total cost = Annual cycle inventory holding cost + annual ordering cost

+ annual safety stock holding cost

$$C = \frac{Q}{2}(H) + \frac{D}{Q}(S) + (H)(\text{Safety stock})$$

The annual cycle-inventory holding cost and annual ordering cost are the same equations we used for computing the total annual cycle-inventory cost in Example 12.1. The annual cost of holding the safety stock is computed under the assumption that the safety stock is on hand at all times. Referring to Figure 12.7 in each order cycle, we will sometimes experience a demand greater than the average demand during lead time, and sometimes we will experience less. On average over the year, we can assume the safety stock will be on hand. See Solved Problem 1 at the end of this chapter for an example of calculating the total costs for a Q system.

Periodic Review System

An alternative inventory control system is the **periodic review (P) system**, sometimes called a *fixed interval reorder system* or *periodic reorder system*, in which an item's inventory position is reviewed periodically rather than continuously. Such a system can simplify delivery scheduling because it establishes a routine. A new order is always placed at the end of each review, and the time between orders (TBO) is fixed at P. Demand is a random variable, so total demand between reviews varies. In a P system, the lot size, Q, may change from one order to the next, but the time between orders is fixed. An example of a periodic review system is that of a soft-drink supplier making weekly rounds of grocery stores. Each week, the supplier reviews the store's inventory of soft drinks and restocks the store with enough items to meet demand and safety stock requirements until the next week.

Under a P system, four of the original EOQ assumptions are maintained: (1) no constraints are placed on the size of the lot, (2) the relevant costs are holding and ordering costs, (3) decisions for one SKU are independent of decisions for other SKUs, and (4) lead times are certain and supply is known. However, demand uncertainty is again allowed for. Figure 12.10 shows the periodic review system under these assumptions. The downward-sloping line again represents on-hand inventory. When the predetermined time, P, has elapsed since the last review, an order is placed to bring the inventory position, represented by the dashed line, up to the target inventory level, T. The lot size for the first review is Q_1, or the difference between inventory position IP_1 and T. As with the continuous review system, IP and OH differ only during the lead time. When the order arrives at the end of the lead time, OH and IP again are identical. Figure 12.10 shows that lot sizes vary from one order cycle to the next. Because the inventory position is lower at the second review, a greater quantity is needed to achieve an inventory level of T.

periodic review (P) sytem

A system in which an item's inventory position is reviewed periodically rather than continuously.

▼ FIGURE 12.10
P System When Demand Is Uncertain

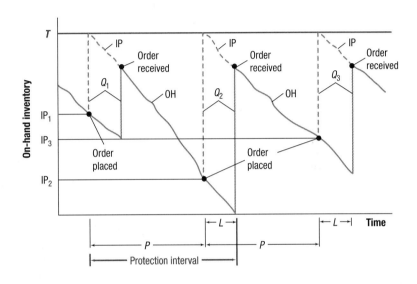

EXAMPLE 12.6	Determining How Much to Order in a P System

A distribution center has a backorder for five 46-inch LCD TV sets. No inventory is currently on hand, and now is the time to review. How many should be reordered if $T = 400$ and no receipts are scheduled?

SOLUTION

$$IP = OH + SR - BO$$
$$= 0 + 0 - 5 = -5 \text{ sets}$$
$$T - IP = 400 - (-5) = 405 \text{ sets}$$

That is, 405 sets must be ordered to bring the inventory position up to T sets.

Selecting the Time between Reviews   To run a P system, managers must make two decisions: the length of time between reviews, P, and the target inventory level, T. Let us first consider the time between reviews, P. It can be any convenient interval, such as each Friday or every other Friday. Another option is to base P on the cost trade-offs of the EOQ. In other words, P can be set equal to the average time between orders for the economic order quantity, or TBO_{EOQ}. Because demand is variable, some orders will be larger than the EOQ and some will be smaller. However, over an extended period of time, the average lot size should be close to the EOQ. If other models are used to determine the lot size (e.g., those described in Supplement D, "Special Inventory Models"), we divide the lot size chosen by the annual demand, D, and use this ratio as P. It will be expressed as the fraction of a year between orders, which can be converted into months, weeks, or days as needed.

Selecting the Target Inventory Level When Demand Is Variable and Lead Time Is Constant   Now let us calculate the target inventory level, T, when demand is variable but the lead time is constant. Figure 12.10 reveals that an order must be large enough to make the inventory position, IP, last beyond the next review, which is P time periods away. The checker must wait P periods to revise, correct, and reestablish the inventory position. Then, a new order is placed, but it does not arrive until after the lead time, L. Therefore, as Figure 12.10 shows, a protection interval of $P + L$ periods is needed. A fundamental difference between the Q and P systems is the length of time needed for stockout protection. A Q system needs stockout protection only during the lead time because orders can be placed as soon as they are needed and will be received L periods later. A P system, however, needs stockout protection for the longer $P + L$ protection interval because orders are placed only at fixed intervals, and the inventory is not checked until the next designated review time.

As with the Q system, we need to develop the appropriate distribution of demand during the protection interval to specify the system fully. In a P system, we must develop the distribution of demand for $P + L$ time periods. The target inventory level T must equal the expected demand during the protection interval of $P + L$ periods, plus enough safety stock to protect against demand uncertainty over this same protection interval. We assume that lead time is constant and that demand in one period is independent of demand in the next period. Thus, the average demand during the protection interval is $\bar{d}(P + L)$, or

$$T = \bar{d}(P + L) + \text{Safety stock for the protection interval}$$

We compute safety stock for a P system much as we did for the Q system. However, the safety stock must cover demand uncertainty for a longer period of time. When using a normal probability distribution, we multiply the desired standard deviations to implement the cycle-service level, z, by the standard deviation of demand during the protection interval, σ_{P+L}. The value of z is the same as for a Q system with the same cycle-service level. Thus,

$$\text{Safety stock} = z\sigma_{P+L}$$

Based on our earlier logic for calculating σ_{dLT}, we know that the standard deviation of the distribution of demand during the protection interval is

$$\sigma_{P+L} = \sigma_d \sqrt{P + L}$$

Because a P system requires safety stock to cover demand uncertainty over a longer time period than a Q system, a P system requires more safety stock; that is, σ_{P+L} exceeds σ_{dLT}. Hence, to gain the convenience of a P system requires that overall inventory levels be somewhat higher than those for a Q system.

EXAMPLE 12.7	Calculating *P* and *T*

Tutor 12.4 in my**om**lab provides a new example to determine the review interval and the target inventory for a *P* system.

Again, let us return to the bird feeder example. Recall that demand for the bird feeder is normally distributed with a mean of 18 units per week and a standard deviation in weekly demand of 5 units. The lead time is 2 weeks, and the business operates 52 weeks per year. The *Q* system developed in Example 12.4 called for an EOQ of 75 units and a safety stock of 9 units for a cycle-service level of 90 percent. What is the equivalent *P* system? Answers are to be rounded to the nearest integer.

SOLUTION

We first define *D* and then *P*. Here, *P* is the time between reviews, expressed in weeks because the data are expressed as demand *per week*:

$$D = (18 \text{ units/week})(52 \text{ weeks/year}) = 936 \text{ units}$$

$$P = \frac{EOQ}{D}(52) = \frac{75}{936}(52) = 4.2 \text{ or } 4 \text{ weeks}$$

With $\bar{d} = 18$ units per week, an alternative approach is to calculate *P* by dividing the EOQ by $\bar{d}$ to get 75/18=4.2 or 4 weeks. Either way, we would review the bird feeder inventory every 4 weeks. We now find the standard deviation of demand over the protection interval $(P + L = 6)$:

$$\sigma_{P+L} = \sigma_d \sqrt{P + L} = 5\sqrt{6} = 12.25 \text{ units}$$

Before calculating *T*, we also need a *z* value. For a 90 percent cycle-service level, $z = 1.28$ (see the Normal Distribution appendix). The safety stock becomes

$$\text{safety stock} = z\sigma_{P+L} = 1.28(12.25) = 15.68, \text{ or } 16 \text{ units}$$

We now solve for T:

$$T = \text{Average demand during the protection interval} + \text{Safety stock}$$
$$= \bar{d}(P + L) + \text{safety stock}$$
$$= (18 \text{ units/week})(6 \text{ weeks}) + 16 \text{ units} = 124 \text{ units}$$

DECISION POINT

Every 4 weeks we would order the number of units needed to bring inventory position IP (counting the new order) up to the target inventory level of 124 units. The P system requires 16 units in safety stock, while the Q system only needs 9 units. If cost were the only criterion, the Q system would be the choice for the bird feeder. As we discuss later, other factors may sway the decision in favor of the P system.

Selecting the Target Inventory Level When Demand and Lead Time Are Variable A useful approach for finding P and T in practice is simulation. Given discrete probability distributions for demand and lead time, simulation can be used to estimate the demand during the protection interval distribution. The Demand During the Protection Interval Simulator in OM Explorer can be used to determine the distribution. Once determined, the distribution can be used to select a value for T, given a desired cycle-service level. Solved Problem 7 demonstrates this approach. More discussion, and an example, can be found in my**om**lab.

Managerial Practice 12.1 shows how the use of periodic inventory review systems is important in supply chains in the chemical industry.

Single-Bin System The concept of a P system can be translated into a simple visual system of inventory control. In the **single-bin system**, a maximum level is marked on the storage shelf or bin, and the inventory is brought up to the mark periodically—say, once a week. The single bin may be, for example, a gasoline storage tank at a service station or a storage bin for small parts at a manufacturing plant.

single-bin system

A system of inventory control in which a maximum level is marked on the storage shelf or bin, and the inventory is brought up to the mark periodically.

Calculating Total P System Costs The total costs for the P system are the sum of the same three cost elements for the Q system. The differences are in the calculation of the order quantity and the safety stock. As shown in Figure 12.10, the average order quantity will be the average consumption of inventory during the P periods between orders. Consequently, $Q = \bar{d}P$. Total costs for the P system are

$$C = \frac{\bar{d}P}{2}(H) + \frac{D}{\bar{d}P}(S) + (H)(\text{Safety stock})$$

See Solved Problem 1 at the end of this chapter for an example of calculating total P system costs.

Comparative Advantages of the Q and P Systems

Neither the Q nor the P system is best for all situations. Three P-system advantages must be balanced against three Q-system advantages. The advantages of one system are implicitly disadvantages of the other system.

The primary advantages of P systems are the following:

1. The system is convenient because replenishments are made at fixed intervals. Fixed replenishment intervals allow for standardized pickup and delivery times.

2. Orders for multiple items from the same supplier can be combined into a single purchase order. This approach reduces ordering and transportation costs and can result in a price break from the supplier.

3. The inventory position, IP, needs to be known only when a review is made (not continuously, as in a Q system). However, this advantage is moot for firms using computerized record-keeping systems, in which a transaction is reported upon each receipt or withdrawal. When inventory records are always current, the system is called a **perpetual inventory system**.

perpetual inventory system

A system of inventory control in which the inventory records are always current.

| MANAGERIAL PRACTICE 12.1 | The Supply Chain Implications of Periodic Review Inventory Systems at Celanese |

What do products such as paints, adhesives, coatings, plastics, medicines, cosmetics, detergents, textiles, or fragrances have in common? All of these products use acetic acid as a major component. Celanese, a $6.5 billion chemical company with $640 million in total inventories, is a major supplier of acetic acid in the world. The large investment in inventory forces Celanese to take a hard look at inventory policies for all products, including acetic acid. The key to successful management of the inventories was to acknowledge the interaction between the inventory policies at each stage of the supply chain with the realities of material flows and logistics in the chemical industry.

The supply chain for acetic acid is complex, involving 90 stages. For example, the supply chain is comprised of stages such as vendors supplying a liner to transport the acid, manufacturing sites producing the acid, transportation modes moving acid, warehouses storing it, and customer demand locations to which the acid is finally shipped. There are four manufacturing facilities, three in the United States and one in Singapore, each of which supplies several storage locations worldwide. Transportation stages correspond to rail, barges, trucks, and ocean vessels. Material typically moves in large quantities because of economies of scale and transportation schedules. Storage facilities may be supplied by multiple upstream facilities as well as the manufacturing plant itself.

The use of periodic review inventory systems at the storage and demand locations in this supply chain scenario makes sense for several reasons. First, the transportation modes have defined schedules of operation. Review periods at storage facilities reflect the schedule of the supplying transportation mode. Second, customer orders are typically batched and timed with weekly, bi-weekly, or monthly frequencies. Celanese often assigns customers and storage facilities specific days to place orders so that their own production schedules can be coordinated. Finally, the cyclic ordering is often a function of the capital intensity of the industry. Long production runs are scheduled to gain production efficiency; it is costly to set up the equipment for another product.

Specifying the best review period and target inventory levels for the various stages of the supply chain takes sophisticated mathematical models. Regardless of the effort required, it is important to recognize the implications of the supply chain when determining inventory policies.

Large manufacturers of chemicals often assign schedules to customers and storage facilities for ordering and picking up chemicals. Such a practice facilitates the coordination of the manufacturer's production schedules. Here a tank truck is loaded at its assigned time.

Source: John M. Bossert and Sean P. Williams, "A Periodic-Review Modeling Approach for Guaranteed Service Supply Chains," *Interfaces*, Vol. 37, No. 5 (September/October 2007), pp. 420–435; http://finance.yahoo.com; www.Celanese.com, 2008.

The primary advantages of Q systems are the following:

1. The review frequency of each SKU may be individualized. Tailoring the review frequency to the SKU can reduce total ordering and holding costs.

2. Fixed lot sizes, if large enough, can result in quantity discounts. The firm's physical limitations, such as its truckload capacities, materials handling methods, and shelf space might also necessitate a fixed lot size.

3. Lower safety stocks result in savings.

In conclusion, the choice between Q and P systems is not clear cut. Which system is better depends on the relative importance of its advantages in various situations.

Hybrid Systems

Various hybrid inventory control systems merge some but not all the features of the P and Q systems. We briefly examine two such systems: (1) optional replenishment and (2) base stock.

Optional Replenishment System   Sometimes called the optional review, min–max, or (s, S) system, the **optional replenishment system** is much like the P system. It is used to review the inventory position at fixed time intervals and, if the position has dropped to (or below) a predetermined level, to place a variable-sized order to cover expected needs. The new order is large enough to bring the inventory position up to a target inventory, similar to T for the P system. However, orders are not placed after a review unless the inventory position has dropped to the predetermined minimum level. The minimum level acts as the reorder point R does in a Q system. If the target is 100 and the minimum level is 60, the minimum order size is 40 (or 100 – 60). Because continuous reviews need not be made, this system is particularly attractive when both review and ordering costs are high.

Base-Stock System   In its simplest form, the **base-stock system** issues a replenishment order, Q, each time a withdrawal is made, for the same amount as the withdrawal. This one-for-one replacement policy maintains the inventory position at a base-stock level equal to expected demand during the lead time plus safety stock. The base-stock level, therefore, is equivalent to the reorder point in a Q system. However, order quantities now vary to keep the inventory position at R at all times. Because this position is the lowest IP possible that will maintain a specified service level, the base-stock system may be used to minimize cycle inventory. More orders are placed, but each order is smaller. This system is appropriate for expensive items, such as replacement engines for jet airplanes. No more inventory is held than the maximum demand expected until a replacement order can be received.

Inventory management is a critical activity for the efficient operation of supply chains. Whether the firm is a service provider or a manufacturer, inventories are a necessity. In this chapter we focused on the systems firms can use to maintain levels of inventory that balance cost with customer service. ABC analysis identifies inventory categories so that management can focus attention on the most critical items. We explored the economic order quantity (EOQ) as a starting point for the determination of the best cycle-inventory level, its assumptions, and it usefulness for gaining insight into the management of inventory. We then showed how to develop and use the continuous review system and the periodic review system and identified the benefits and shortcomings of each one. There are also visual systems and hybrid systems that managers can use to fit certain situations. In Supplement D, "Special Inventory Models," we show models that can be useful for quantity discounts, production lot sizes, and one-period decisions.

INTERNET RESOURCES

myomlab and the Companion Website at **www.pearsonglobaleditions.com/krajewski** contain many tools, activities, and resources designed for this chapter.

KEY EQUATIONS

1. Total annual cycle-inventory cost = Annual holding cost + Annual ordering or setup cost

$$C = \frac{Q}{2}(H) + \frac{D}{Q}(S)$$

2. Economic order quantity:

$$EOQ = \sqrt{\frac{2DS}{H}}$$

3. Time between orders, expressed in weeks:

$$TBO_{EOQ} = \frac{EOQ}{D}(52 \text{ weeks/year})$$

4. Inventory position = On-hand inventory + Scheduled receipts – Backorders

$$IP = OH + SR - BO$$

5. Continuous review system:

   Protection interval = Lead time (L)

   Standard deviation of demand during the lead time (constant L) = $\sigma_{dLT} = \sigma_d\sqrt{L}$

   Standard deviation of demand during the lead time (variable L) =
   $$\sigma_{dLT} = \sqrt{L\sigma_d^2 + \bar{d}^2\,\sigma_{LT}^2}$$

   Safety stock = $z\sigma_{dLT}$

   Reorder point (R) for constant lead time = $\bar{d}L$ + Safety stock

   Reorder point (R) for variable lead time = $\bar{d}\bar{L}$ + Safety stock

   Order quantity = EOQ

   Replenishment rule: Order EOQ units when IP $\leq R$

   Total Q system cost: $C = \dfrac{Q}{2}(H) + \dfrac{D}{Q}(S) + (H)(\text{Safety stock})$

6. Periodic review system:

   Review interval = Time between orders = P

   Protection interval = Time between orders + Lead time
   $$= P + L$$

   Standard deviation of demand during the protection interval = $\sigma_{P+L} = \sigma_d\sqrt{P+L}$

   Safety stock = $z\sigma_{P+L}$

   Target inventory level (T) = Average demand during the protection interval + Safety stock
   $$= \bar{d}(P + L) + \text{Safety stock}$$

   Order quantity = Target inventory level – Inventory position = T – IP

   Replenishment rule: Every P time periods, order T – IP units

   Total P system cost: $C = \dfrac{\bar{d}P}{2}(H) + \dfrac{D}{\bar{d}P}(S) + (H)(\text{Safety stock})$

KEY TERMS

ABC analysis 436
base-stock system 453
continuous review (Q) system 443
cycle counting 437
cycle-service level 445
economic order quantity (EOQ) 437
independent demand items 442
inventory management 436

inventory position (IP) 443
lot size 436
open orders 443
optional replenishment system 453
periodic review (P) system 449
perpetual inventory system 451
protection interval 445
reorder point (R) 443

reorder point (ROP) system 443
scheduled receipts (SR) 443
service level 445
single-bin system 451
stock-keeping unit (SKU) 436
time between orders (TBO) 441
two-bin system 448
visual system 448

SOLVED PROBLEM 1

A regional distributor purchases discontinued appliances from various suppliers and then sells them on demand to retailers in the region. The distributor operates 5 days per week, 52 weeks per year. Only when it is open for business can orders be received. Management wants to reevaluate its current inventory policy, which calls for order quantities of 440 counter-top mixers. The following data are estimated for the mixer:

Average daily demand ($\bar{d}$) = 100 mixers

Standard deviation of daily demand (σ_d) = 30 mixers

Lead time (L) = 3 days

Holding cost $(H) = \$9.40/\text{unit/year}$

Ordering cost $(S) = \$35/\text{order}$

Cycle-service level = 92 percent

The distributor uses a continuous review (Q) system.

a. What order quantity Q, and reorder point, R, should be used?

b. What is the total annual cost of the system?

c. If on-hand inventory is 40 units, one open order for 440 mixers is pending, and no backorders exist, should a new order be placed?

SOLUTION

a. Annual demand is

$$D = (5 \text{ days/week})(52 \text{ weeks/year})(100 \text{ mixers/day}) = 26{,}000 \text{ mixers/year}$$

The order quantity is

$$\text{EOQ} = \sqrt{\frac{2DS}{H}} = \sqrt{\frac{2(26{,}000)(\$35)}{\$9.40}} = \sqrt{193{,}167} = 440.02 \text{ or } 440 \text{ mixers}$$

The standard deviation of the demand during lead time distribution is

$$\sigma_{dLT} = \sigma_d\sqrt{L} = 30\sqrt{3} = 51.96$$

A 92 percent cycle-service level corresponds to $z=1.41$ (see the Normal Distribution appendix). Therefore,

$$\text{Safety stock} = z\sigma_{dLT} = 1.41(51.96 \text{ mixers}) = 73.26 \text{ or } 73 \text{ mixers}$$

$$\text{Average demand during the lead time} = \bar{d}L = 100(3) = 300 \text{ mixers}$$

$$\text{Reorder point } (R) = \text{Average demand during the lead time} + \text{Safety stock}$$

$$= 300 \text{ mixers} + 73 \text{ mixers} = 373 \text{ mixers}$$

With a continuous review system, $Q = 440$ and $R = 373$.

b. The total annual cost for the Q systems is

$$C = \frac{Q}{2}(H) + \frac{D}{Q}(S) + (H)(\text{Safety stock})$$

$$C = \frac{440}{2}(\$9.40) + \frac{26{,}000}{440}(35) + (\$9.40)(73) = \$4{,}822.38$$

c. Inventory position = On-hand inventory + Scheduled receipts − Backorders

$$\text{IP} = \text{OH} + \text{SR} - \text{BO} = 40 + 440 - 0 = 480 \text{ mixers}$$

Because IP (480) exceeds R (373), do not place a new order.

SOLVED PROBLEM 2

Suppose that a periodic review (P) system is used at the distributor in Solved Problem 2, but otherwise the data are the same.

a. Calculate the P (in workdays, rounded to the nearest day) that gives approximately the same number of orders per year as the EOQ.

b. What is the target inventory level, T? Compare the P system to the Q system in Solved Problem 2.

c. What is the total annual cost of the P system?

d. It is time to review the item. On-hand inventory is 40 mixers; receipt of 440 mixers is scheduled, and no backorders exist. How much should be reordered?

SOLUTION

a. The time between orders is

$$P = \frac{\text{EOQ}}{D}(260 \text{ days/year}) = \frac{440}{26{,}000}(260) = 4.4 \text{ or } 4 \text{ days}$$

b. Figure 12.11 shows that $T = 812$ and safety stock $= (1.41)(79.37) = 111.91$ or about 112 mixers. The corresponding Q system for the counter-top mixer requires less safety stock.

c. The total annual cost of the P system is

$$C = \frac{\overline{dP}}{2}(H) + \frac{D}{dP}(S) + (H)(\text{Safety stock})$$

$$C = \frac{(100)(4)}{2}(\$9.40) + \frac{26,000}{(100)(4)}(\$35) + (\$9.40)(1.41)(79.37)$$

$$= \$\,5,207.80$$

d. Inventory position is the amount on hand plus scheduled receipts minus backorders, or

$$IP = OH + SR - BO = 40 + 440 - 0 = 480 \text{ mixers}$$

The order quantity is the target inventory level minus the inventory position, or

$$Q = T - IP = 812 \text{ mixers} - 480 \text{ mixers} = 332 \text{ mixers}$$

An order for 332 mixers should be placed.

FIGURE 12.11 ▶
OM Explorer Solver for Inventory Systems

Continuous Review (Q) System	
z	1.41
Safety Stock	73
Reorder Point	373
Annual Cost	$4,822.38

Periodic Review (P) System	
Time Between Reviews (P)	4.00 Days
	☑ Enter manually
Standard Deviation of Demand During Protection Interval	79.37
Safety Stock	112
Average Demand During Protection Interval	700
Target Inventory Level (T)	812
Annual Cost	$5,207.80

SOLVED PROBLEM 3

Nelson's Hardware Store stocks a 19.2 volt cordless drill that is a popular seller. Annual demand is 5,000 units, the ordering cost is $15, and the inventory holding cost is $4/unit/year.

a. What is the economic order quantity?

b. What is the total annual cost for this inventory item?

SOLUTION

a. The order quantity is

$$EOQ = \sqrt{\frac{2DS}{H}} = \sqrt{\frac{2(5,000)(\$15)}{\$4}} = \sqrt{37,500} = 193.65 \text{ or } 194 \text{ drills}$$

b. The total annual cost is

$$C = \frac{Q}{2}(H) + \frac{D}{Q}(S) = \frac{194}{2}(\$4) + \frac{5,000}{194}(\$15) = \$774.60$$

SOLVED PROBLEM 4

Booker's Book Bindery divides SKUs into three classes, according to their dollar usage. Calculate the usage values of the following SKUs and determine which is most likely to be classified as class A.

SOLUTION

The annual dollar usage for each SKU is determined by multiplying the annual usage quantity by the value per unit. As shown in Figure 12.12, the SKUs are then sorted by annual dollar

SKU Number	Description	Quantity Used per Year	Unit Value ($)
1	Boxes	500	3.00
2	Cardboard (square feet)	18,000	0.02
3	Cover stock	10,000	0.75
4	Glue (gallons)	75	40.00
5	Inside covers	20,000	0.05
6	Reinforcing tape (meters)	3,000	0.15
7	Signatures	150,000	0.45

usage, in declining order. Finally, A–B and B–C class lines are drawn roughly, according to the guidelines presented in the text. Here, class A includes only one SKU (signatures), which represents only 1/7, or 14 percent, of the SKUs but accounts for 83 percent of annual dollar usage. Class B includes the next two SKUs, which taken together represent 28 percent of the SKUs and account for 13 percent of annual dollar usage. The final four SKUs, class C, represent over half the number of SKUs but only 4 percent of total annual dollar usage.

SKU Number	Description	Quantity Used per Year		Unit Value($)		Annual Dollar Usage($)
1	Boxes	500	×	3.00	=	1,500
2	Cardboard (square feet)	18,000	×	0.02	=	360
3	Cover stock	10,000	×	0.75	=	7,500
4	Glue (gallons)	75	×	40.00	=	3,000
5	Inside covers	20,000	×	0.05	=	1,000
6	Reinforcing tape (meters)	3,000	×	0.15	=	450
7	Signatures	150,000	×	0.45	=	67,500
					Total	81,310

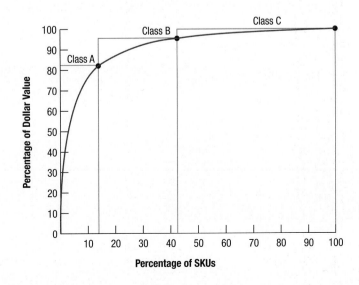

SKU #	Description	Qty Used/Year	Value	Dollar Usage	Pct of Total	Cumulative % of Dollar Value	Cumulative % of SKU	Class
7	Signatures	150,000	$0.45	$67,500	83.0%	83.0%	14.3%	A
3	Cover stock	10,000	$0.75	$7,500	9.2%	92.2%	28.6%	B
4	Glue	75	$40.00	$3,000	3.7%	95.9%	42.9%	B
1	Boxes	500	$3.00	$1,500	1.8%	97.8%	57.1%	C
5	Inside covers	20,000	$0.05	$1,000	1.2%	99.0%	71.4%	C
6	Reinforcing tape	3,000	$0.15	$450	0.6%	99.6%	85.7%	C
2	Cardboard	18,000	$0.02	$360	0.4%	100.0%	100.0%	C
Total				$81,310				

◀ FIGURE 12.12
Annual Dollar Usage for Class A, B, and C SKUs Using Tutor 12.2

SOLVED PROBLEM 5

A distribution center experiences an average weekly demand of 60 units for one of its items. The product is valued at $700 per unit. Average inbound shipments from the factory warehouse average 350 units. Average lead time (including ordering delays and transit time) is 2 weeks. The distribution center operates 52 weeks per year. It carries a 1-week supply of inventory as safety stock and no anticipation inventory. What is the average aggregate inventory that the distribution center holds?

SOLUTION

Type of Inventory	Calculation of Average Inventory	Quantity
Cycle	$\frac{Q}{2} = \frac{350}{2} =$	175 units
Safety stock	1-week supply =	60 units
Anticipation	None	
Pipeline	$\bar{d}L = (60 \text{ units/week})(2 \text{ weeks}) =$	120 units
	Average aggregate inventory =	355 units

SOLVED PROBLEM 6

Zeke's Hardware Store sells furnace filters. The cost to place an order to the distributor is $25 and the annual cost to hold a filter in stock is $2. The average demand per week for the filters is 32 units, and the store operates 50 weeks per year. The weekly demand for filters has the probability distribution shown on the left below. The delivery lead time from the distributor is uncertain and has the probability distribution shown on the right below.

Suppose Zeke wants to use a P system with $P = 6$ weeks and a cycle-service level of 90 percent. What is the appropriate value for T and the associated annual cost of the system?

Demand	Probability
24	0.15
28	0.20
32	0.30
36	0.20
40	0.15

Lead Time (wks)	Probability
1	0.05
2	0.25
3	0.40
4	0.25
5	0.05

SOLUTION

Figure 12.13 contains output from the Demand During the Protection Interval Simulator from OM Explorer.

FIGURE 12.13 ▶
OM Explorer Solver for Demand during the Protection Interval Simulator

Demand During Protection Interval Distribution

Bin Upper Bound	Demand	Frequency	Cumulative Percentage
196	182	0	0.0%
224	210	17	3.4%
252	138	66	16.6%
280	266	135	43.6%
308	294	140	71.6%
336	322	109	93.4%
364	350	30	99.4%
392	378	3	100.0%
420	406	0	100.0%
448	More	0	100.0%
Total		**500**	

Average Demand During Protection Interval
289

Given the desired cycle-service level of 90 percent, the appropriate T value is 322 units. The simulation estimated the average demand during the protection interval to be 289 units, consequently the safety stock is $322 - 289 = 33$ units.

The annual cost of this P system is

$$C = \frac{6(32)}{2}(\$2) + \frac{50(32)}{6(32)}(\$25) + 33(\$2) = \$192.00 + \$208.33 + \$66.00 = \$466.33$$

Solved Problem 7

Consider Zeke's inventory in Solved Problem 7. Suppose that he wants to use a continuous review (Q) system for the filters, with an order quantity of 200 and a reorder point of 140. Initial inventory is 170 units. If the stockout cost is $5 per unit, and all of the other data in Solved Problem 7 are the same, what is the expected cost per week of using the Q system?

SOLUTION

Figure 12.14 shows output from the Q System Simulator in OM Explorer. Only weeks 1 through 13 and weeks 41 through 50 are shown in the figure. The average total cost per week is $305.62. Notice that no stockouts occurred in this simulation. These results are dependent on Zeke's choices for the reorder point and lot size. It is possible that stockouts would occur if the simulation were run for more than 50 weeks.

	D	E	F	G	H	I	J	K	L	M	N	O
14	Week	Beginning Inventory	Simulated Demand	Ending Inventory	Stockout Units	Place Order?	Simulated Lead Time	Weeks to Receive Order	Holding Cost	Ordering Cost	Stockout Cost	Total Cost
15	1	170	36	134	0	Yes	4	4	$ 304	$ 25	$ -	$ 329
16	2	134	32	102	0	No	-	3	$ 236	$ -	$ -	$ 236
17	3	102	40	62	0	No	-	2	$ 164	$ -	$ -	$ 164
18	4	62	28	34	0	No	-	1	$ 96	$ -	$ -	$ 96
19	5	234	32	202	0	No	-	0	$ 436	$ -	$ -	$ 436
20	6	202	40	162	0	No	-	-	$ 364	$ -	$ -	$ 364
21	7	162	28	134	0	Yes	2	2	$ 296	$ 25	$ -	$ 321
22	8	134	40	94	0	No	-	1	$ 228	$ -	$ -	$ 228
23	9	294	32	262	0	No	-	0	$ 556	$ -	$ -	$ 556
24	10	262	24	238	0	No	-	-	$ 500	$ -	$ -	$ 500
25	11	238	32	206	0	No	-	-	$ 444	$ -	$ -	$ 444
26	12	206	40	166	0	No	-	-	$ 372	$ -	$ -	$ 372
27	13	166	24	142	0	No	-	-	$ 308	$ -	$ -	$ 308
55	41	262	28	234	0	No	-	0	$ 496	$ -	$ -	$ 496
56	42	234	40	194	0	No	-	-	$ 428	$ -	$ -	$ 428
57	43	194	36	158	0	No	-	-	$ 352	$ -	$ -	$ 352
58	44	158	36	122	0	Yes	3	3	$ 280	$ 25	$ -	$ 305
59	45	122	36	86	0	No	-	2	$ 208	$ -	$ -	$ 208
60	46	86	28	58	0	No	-	1	$ 144	$ -	$ -	$ 144
61	47	258	36	222	0	No	-	0	$ 480	$ -	$ -	$ 480
62	48	222	36	186	0	No	-	-	$ 408	$ -	$ -	$ 408
63	49	186	40	146	0	No	-	-	$ 332	$ -	$ -	$ 332
64	50	146	32	114	0	Yes	2	2	$ 260	$ 25	$ -	$ 285
65	**Averages**	**167.12**	**33.12**	**134.00**	**0.00**		**3.00**		**$301.12**	**$4.50**	**$0.00**	**$305.62**

▲ FIGURE 12.14
OM Explorer Q System Simulator

DISCUSSION QUESTIONS

1. Will organizations ever get to the point where they will no longer need inventories? Why or why not?

2. What is the relationship between inventory and the nine competitive priorities we discussed in Chapter 1, "Using Operations to Compete?" Suppose that two competing manufacturers, Company H and Company L, are similar except that Company H has much higher investments in raw materials, work-in-process, and finished goods inventory than Company L. In which of the nine competitive priorities will Company H have an advantage?

3. Suppose that a large discount retailer with a lot of purchasing power in a supply chain requires that all suppliers incorporate a new information system that will reduce the cost of placing orders between the retailer and its suppliers as well as between the suppliers and their suppliers. Suppose also that order quantities and lead times are related; the smaller the order quantity the shorter the lead time from suppliers. Assume that all members of the supply chain use a continuous review system and EOQ order quantities. Explain the implications of the new information system for the supply chain in general and the inventory systems of the supply chain members in particular.

PROBLEMS

It will be helpful to review the section Inventory and Supply Chains in Chapter 9, "Designing Effective Supply Chains" before attempting these problems. Software, such as OM Explorer, Active Models, and POM for Windows, is in my**om**lab. Check with your instructor on how best to use it. In many cases, the instructor wants you to understand how to do the calculations by hand. At most, the software provides a check on your calculations. When calculations are particularly complex and the goal is interpreting the results in making decisions, the software replaces entirely the manual calculations.

1. Stock-Rite, Inc., is considering the use of ABC analysis to focus on the most critical SKUs in its inventory. For a random sample of eight SKUs, the following table shows the SKU's unit value and annual demand. Categorize these SKUs as A, B, and C classes.

SKU Code	Unit Value	Demand (units)
A104	$40.25	80
D205	80.75	120
X104	10.00	150
U404	40.50	150
L205	60.70	50
S104	80.20	20
X205	80.15	20
L104	20.05	100

2. Lockwood Industries is considering the use of ABC analysis to focus on the most critical SKUs in its inventory. For a random sample of eight SKUs, the following table shows the annual dollar usage. Rank the SKUs, and assign them to the A, B, or C class.

SKU	Dollar Value	Annual Usage
1	$0.01	1,200
2	$0.03	120,000
3	$0.45	100
4	$1.00	44,000
5	$4.50	900
6	$0.90	350
7	$0.30	70,000
8	$1.50	200

3. Leaky Pipe, a local retailer of plumbing supplies, faces demand for one of its SKUs at a constant rate of 30,000 units per year. It costs Leaky Pipe $10 to process an order to replenish stock and $1 per unit per year to carry the item in stock. Stock is received four working days after an order is placed. No backordering is allowed. Assume 300 working days a year.

   a. What is Leaky Pipe's optimal order quantity?

   b. What is the optimal number of orders per year?

c. What is the optimal interval (in working days) between orders?

d. What is the demand during the lead time?

e. What is the reorder point?

f. What is the inventory position immediately after an order has been placed?

4. At Dot Com, a large retailer of popular books, demand is constant at 32,000 books per year. The cost of placing an order to replenish stock is $10, and the annual cost of holding is $4 per book. Stock is received five working days after an order has been placed. No backordering is allowed. Assume 300 working days a year.

a. What is Dot Com's optimal order quantity?

b. What is the optimal number of orders per year?

c. What is the optimal interval (in working days) between orders?

d. What is demand during the lead time?

e. What is the reorder point?

f. What is the inventory position immediately after an order has been placed?

5. Babble, Inc., buys 400 blank cassette tapes per month for use in producing foreign language courseware. The ordering cost is $12.50. Holding cost is $0.12 per cassette per year.

a. How many tapes should Babble order at a time?

b. What is the time between orders?

6. Yellow Press, Inc., buys paper in 1,500-pound rolls for printing. Annual demand is 2,500 rolls. The cost per roll is $800, and the annual holding cost is 15 percent of the cost. Each order costs $50.

a. How many rolls should Yellow Press order at a time?

b. What is the time between orders?

7. Sam's Cat Hotel operates 52 weeks per year, 6 days per week, and uses a continuous review inventory system. It purchases kitty litter for $11.70 per bag. The following information is available about these bags.

Demand = 90 bags/week

Order cost = $54/order

Annual holding cost = 27 percent of cost

Desired cycle-service level= 80 percent

Lead time = 3 weeks (18 working days)

Standard deviation of weekly demand = 15 bags

Current on-hand inventory is 320 bags, with no open orders or backorders.

a. What is the EOQ? What would be the average time between orders (in weeks)?

b. What should R be?

c. An inventory withdrawal of 10 bags was just made. Is it time to reorder?

d. The store currently uses a lot size of 500 bags (i.e., $Q = 500$). What is the annual holding cost of this policy? Annual ordering cost? Without calculating the EOQ, how can you conclude from these two calculations that the current lot size is too large?

e. What would be the annual cost saved by shifting from the 500-bag lot size to the EOQ?

8. In a Q system, the demand rate for strawberry ice cream is normally distributed, with an average of 300 pints *per week*. The lead time is 9 weeks. The standard deviation of *weekly* demand is 15 pints.

a. What is the standard deviation of demand during the 9-week lead time?

b. What is the average demand during the 9-week lead time?

c. What reorder point results in a cycle-service level of 99 percent?

9. Consider again the kitty litter ordering policy for Sam's Cat Hotel in Problem 7.

a. Suppose that the weekly demand forecast of 90 bags is incorrect and actual demand averages only 60 bags per week. How much higher will total costs be, owing to the distorted EOQ caused by this forecast error?

b. Suppose that actual demand is 60 bags but that ordering costs are cut to only $6 by using the Internet to automate order placing. However, the buyer does not tell anyone, and the EOQ is not adjusted to reflect this reduction in S. How much higher will total costs be, compared to what they could be if the EOQ were adjusted?

10. Suppose that Sam's Cat Hotel in Problem 7 uses a P system instead of a Q system. The average daily demand is 15 bags (90/6), and the standard deviation of *daily* demand is 6.124 bags ($15/\sqrt{6}$).

a. What P (in working days) and T should be used to approximate the cost trade-offs of the EOQ?

b. How much more safety stock is needed than with a Q system?

c. It is time for the periodic review. How much kitty litter should be ordered?

11. You are in charge of inventory control of a highly successful product retailed by your firm. Weekly demand for this item varies, with an average of 200 units and a standard deviation of 16 units. It is purchased from a wholesaler at a cost of $12.50 per unit. The supply lead time is 4 weeks. Placing an order costs $50, and the inventory carrying rate per year is 20 percent of the item's cost. Your firm operates 5 days per week, 50 weeks per year.

a. What is the optimal ordering quantity for this item?

b. How many units of the item should be maintained as safety stock for 99 percent protection against stockouts during an order cycle?

c. If supply lead time can be reduced to 2 weeks, what is the percent reduction in the number of units maintained as safety stock for the same 99 percent stockout protection?

d. If through appropriate sales promotions, the demand variability is reduced so that the standard deviation of weekly demand is 8 units instead of 16, what is the percent reduction (compared to that in part [b]) in the number of units maintained as safety stock for the same 99 percent stockout protection?

12. In a *P* system, the lead time for a box of weed-killer is two weeks and the review period is one week. Demand during the protection interval averages 218 boxes, with a standard deviation of 40 boxes. What is the cycle-service level when the target inventory level is set at 300 boxes?

13. Nationwide Auto Parts uses a periodic review inventory control system for one of its stock items. The review interval is six weeks, and the lead time for receiving the materials ordered from its wholesaler is three weeks. Weekly demand is normally distributed, with a mean of 100 units and a standard deviation of 20 units.

a. What is the average and the standard deviation of demand during the protection interval?

b. What should be the target inventory level if the firm desires 97.5 percent stockout protection?

c. If 350 units were in stock at the time of a periodic review, how many units should be ordered?

14. In a two-bin inventory system, the demand for three-inch lag bolts during the two-week lead time is normally distributed, with an average of 53 units per week. The standard deviation of weekly demand is 5 units. What cycle-service level is provided when the normal level in the second bin is set at 120 units?

15. In a continuous review inventory system, the lead time for door knobs is five weeks. The standard deviation of demand during the lead time is 85 units. The desired cycle-service level is 99 percent. The supplier of door knobs streamlined its operations and now quotes a one-week lead time. How much can safety stock be reduced without reducing the 99 percent cycle-service level?

16. Petromax Enterprises uses a continuous review inventory control system for one of its SKUs. The following information is available on the item. The firm operates 50 weeks in a year.

Demand = 50,000 units/year

Ordering cost = $35/order

Holding cost = $2/unit/year

Average lead time = 3 weeks

Standard deviation of weekly demand = 125 units

a. What is the economic order quantity for this item?

b. If Petromax wants to provide a 90 percent cycle-service level, what should be the safety stock and the reorder point?

17. Your firm uses a continuous review system and operates 52 weeks per year. One of the SKUs has the following characteristics.

Demand (D) = 20,000 units/year

Ordering cost (S) = $40/order

Holding cost (H) = $2/unit/year

Lead time (L) = 2 weeks

Cycle-service level = 95%

Demand is normally distributed, with a standard deviation of *weekly* demand of 100 units.

Current on-hand inventory is 1,040 units, with no scheduled receipts and no backorders.

a. Calculate the item's EOQ. What is the average time, in weeks, between orders?

b. Find the safety stock and reorder point that provide a 95 percent cycle-service level.

c. For these policies, what are the annual costs of (i) holding the cycle inventory and (ii) placing orders?

d. A withdrawal of 15 units just occurred. Is it time to reorder? If so, how much should be ordered?

18. Suppose that your firm uses a periodic review system, but otherwise the data are the same as in Problem 17.

a. Calculate the *P* that gives approximately the same number of orders per year as the EOQ. Round your answer to the nearest week.

b. Find the safety stock and the target inventory level that provide a 95 percent cycle-service level.

c. How much larger is the safety stock than with a *Q* system?

19. A company begins a review of ordering policies for its continuous review system by checking the current policies for a sample of SKUs. Following are the characteristics of one item.

Demand (D) = 64 units/week (Assume 52 weeks per year)

Ordering and setup cost (S) = $50/order

Holding cost (H) = $13/unit/year

Lead time (L) = 2 weeks

Standard deviation of *weekly* demand = 12 units

Cycle-service level = 88 percent

a. What is the EOQ for this item?

b. What is the desired safety stock?

c. What is the reorder point?

d. What are the cost implications if the current policy for this item is $Q = 200$ and $R = 180$?

20. Using the same information as in Problem 19, develop the best policies for a periodic review system.

    a. What value of P gives the same approximate number of orders per year as the EOQ? Round to the nearest week.

    b. What safety stock and target inventory level provide an 88 percent cycle-service level?

21. The Farmer's Wife is a country store specializing in knick-knacks suitable for a farm-house décor. One item experiencing a considerable buying frenzy is a miniature Holstein cow. Average weekly demand is 30 cows, with a standard deviation of 5 cows. The cost to place a replenishment order is $15 and the holding coast is $0.75/cow/year. The supplier, however, is in China. The lead time for new orders is 8 weeks, with a standard deviation of 2 weeks. The Farmer's Wife, which is open only 50 weeks a year, wants to develop a continuous review inventory system for this item with a cycle-service level of 90 percent.

    a. Specify the continuous review system for the cows. Explain how it would work in practice.

    b. What is the total annual cost for the system you developed?

22. Osprey Sports stocks everything that a musky fisherman could want in the Great North Woods. A particular musky lure has been very popular with local fishermen as well as those who buy lures on the Internet from Osprey Sports. The cost to place orders with the supplier is $30/order; the demand averages 4 lures per day, with a standard deviation of 1 lure; and the inventory holding cost is $1.00/lure/year. The lead time form the supplier is 10 days, with a standard deviation of 3 days. It is important to maintain a 97 percent cycle-service level to properly balance service with inventory holding costs. Osprey Sports is open 350 days a year to allow the owners the opportunity to fish for muskies during the prime season.

The owners want to use a continuous review inventory system for this item.

    a. What order quantity should be used?

    b. What reorder point should be used?

    c. What is the total annual cost for this inventory system?

23. A golf specialty wholesaler operates 50 weeks per year. Management is trying to determine an inventory policy for its 1-irons, which have the following characteristics:

Demand (D) = 2,000 units/year

Demand is normally distributed

Standard deviation of *weekly* demand = 3 units

Ordering cost = $40/order

Annual holding cost (H) = $5/units

Desired cycle-service level = 90%

Lead time (L) = 4 weeks

    a. If the company uses a periodic review system, what should P and T be? Round P to the nearest week.

    b. If the company uses a continuous review system, what should R be?

24. Wood County Hospital consumes 1,000 boxes of bandages per week. The price of bandages is $35 per box, and the hospital operates 52 weeks per year. The cost of processing an order is $15, and the cost of holding one box for a year is 15 percent of the value of the material.

    a. The hospital orders bandages in lot sizes of 900 boxes. What *extra* cost does the hospital incur, which it could save by using the EOQ method?

    b. Demand is normally distributed, with a standard deviation of weekly demand of 100 boxes. The lead time is 2 weeks. What safety stock is necessary if the hospital uses a continuous review system and a 97 percent cycle-service level is desired? What should be the reorder point?

    c. If the hospital uses a periodic review system, with $P = 2$ weeks, what should be the target inventory level, T?

ADVANCED PROBLEMS

It may be helpful to review Supplement B, "Simulation Models," before working Problem 25.

25. The Georgia Lighting Center stocks more than 3,000 lighting fixtures, including chandeliers, swags, wall lamps, and track lights. The store sells at retail, operates six days per week, and advertises itself as the "brightest spot in town." One expensive fixture is selling at an average rate of five units per day. The reorder policy is $Q = 40$ and $R = 15$. A new order is placed on the day the reorder point is reached. The lead time is three business days. For example, an order placed on Monday will be delivered on Thursday. Simulate the performance of this Q system for the next 3 weeks (18 workdays). Any stockouts result in lost sales (rather than backorders). The beginning inventory is 19 units, and no receipts are scheduled. Table 12.2 simulates the first week of operation. Extend Table 12.2 to simulate operations for the next 2 weeks if demand for the next 12 business days is 7, 4, 2, 7, 3, 6, 10, 0, 5, 10, 4, and 7.

    a. What is the average daily ending inventory over the 18 days?

    b. How many stockouts occurred?

26. Muscle Bound is chain of fitness stores located in many large shopping centers. Recently, an internal memo from the CEO to all operations personnel complained about the budget overruns at Muscle Bound's central warehouse. In particular, she said that inventories were too high and that the budget will be cut dramatically and proportionately equal for all items in stock. Consequently, warehouse management set up a pilot study to see what effect the budget cuts would have on customer service. They chose 5-pound barbells, which are a high volume SKU and consume considerable warehouse space. Daily demand for the barbells is 1,000 units, with a standard deviation of 150 units. Ordering costs are $40 per order. Holding costs are $2/unit/year. The supplier is located in the Philippines; consequently, the lead time is 35 days with a standard deviation of 5 days. Muscle Bound stores operate 313 days a year (no Sundays).

    Suppose that the barbells are allocated a budget of $16,000 for total annual costs. If Muscle Bound uses a continuous review system for the barbells and cannot change the ordering costs and holding costs or the distributions of demand or lead time, what is the best cycle-service level management can expect from their system?

TABLE 12.2 | **FIRST WEEK OF OPERATION**

Workday	Beginning Inventory	Orders Received	Daily Demand	Ending Inventory	Inventory Position	Order Quantity
1. Monday	19	—	5	14	14	40
2. Tuesday	14	—	3	11	51	—
3. Wednesday	11	—	4	7	47	—
4. Thursday	7	40	1	46	46	—
5. Friday	46	—	10	36	36	—
6. Saturday	36	—	9	27	27	—

ACTIVE MODEL EXERCISE

This Active Model appears in my**om**lab. It allows you to evaluate the sensitivity of the EOQ and associated costs to changes in the demand and cost parameters.

QUESTIONS

1. What is the EOQ and what is the lowest total cost?

2. How much does the total cost increase if the store manager orders twice as many bird feeders as the EOQ? How much does the total cost increase if the store manager orders half as many bird feeders as the EOQ?

3. From the graph, what can you conclude about the relationship between the lowest total cost and the costs of ordering and holding inventory?

4. What is the annual cost of holding inventory at the EOQ and the annual cost of ordering inventory at the EOQ?

5. What happens to the EOQ and the total cost when demand is doubled? What happens to the EOQ and the total cost when unit price is doubled?

6. Comment on the sensitivity of the EOQ model to errors in demand or cost estimates.

7. Scroll through the lower order cost values and describe the changes to the graph. What happens to the EOQ?

Economic Order Quantity (EOQ) Model

Reset Data | Questions

		Optimal	Other
Annual demand rate, D	936		
Order cost, S	45		
Holding cost percent	25%		
Unit price, P	60		

	Optimal	Other	
Order quantity, Q*	75	390	
Maximum inventory	75	390	
Average Inventory	37	195	
Num orders per year	12.49	2.40	

	Optimal	Other
Annual holding cost	$ 562.05	$ 2,925.00
Annual ordering cost	$ 562.05	$108.00
Total	$1,124.10	$3,033.00

Difference	$1,908.90
% Difference	169.82%

Inventory: Cost vs Quantity

The Economic Order Quantity Model using Data from Example 12.1

EXPERIENTIAL LEARNING Swift Electronic Supply, Inc.

It was a typical fall afternoon in Southern California, with thousands of tourists headed to the beaches to have fun. About 40 miles away, however, Steven Holland, the CEO of the Swift Electronic Supply, Inc., faced a severe problem with Swift's inventory management.

An Intel veteran, Steven Holland worked in the electronic components distribution industry for more than 20 years. Seven years ago, he founded the Swift Electronic Supply, Inc., an electronic distributor. After several successful years, the company is now troubled with eroding profit margins. Recent economic downturns worsened the situation further. Factors such as the growth of B2B e-commerce, the globalization of markets, the increased popularity of value-added services, and ongoing consolidations among electronic distributors affect the future of Swift.

To reverse these influences, Holland talked to a prestigious local university. After consultation, Holland found the most effective way to increase profitability is to cut inventory costs. As a starting point, he studied in detail a representative product, dynamic random access memory (DRAM), as the basis for his plan.

Industry and Company Preview

Owing to a boom in the telecommunications industry and the information technology revolution, electronics distributors experienced double-digit annual growth over the last decade. To cut the cost of direct purchasing forces, large component manufacturers such as Intel, Cisco, and Texas Instruments decided to outsource their procurement so that they could focus on product development and manufacturing. Therefore, independent electronic distributors like Swift started offering procurement services to these companies.

Swift serves component manufacturers in California and Arizona. Working as the intermediary between its customers and overseas original equipment manufacturers (OEMs), Swift's business model is quite simple. Forecasting customer demand, Swift places orders to a number of OEMs, stocks those products, breaks the quantities down, and delivers the products to its end customers.

Recently, due to more intense competition and declines in demand, Swift offered more flexible delivery schedules and was willing to accommodate small order quantities. However, customers can always shift to Swift's competitors should Swift not fulfill their orders. Steven Holland was in a dilemma: The intangible costs of losing customers can be enormous; however, maintaining high levels of inventory can also be costly.

DRAM

Holland turned his attention to DRAM as a representative product. Previously, the company ordered a big amount every time it felt it was necessary. Holland's assistant developed a table (Table 12.3) that has two months of demand history. From Holland's experience, the demand for DRAM is relatively stable in the company's product line and it had no sales seasonality. The sales staff agrees that conditions in the current year will not be different from those of past years, and historical demand will be a good indicator of what to expect in the future.

TABLE 12.3 | HISTORICAL DEMAND DATA FOR THE DRAM (UNITS)

Day	Demand	Day	Demand	Day	Demand
1	869	21	663	41	959
2	902	22	1,146	42	703
3	1,109	23	1,016	43	823
4	947	24	1,166	44	862
5	968	25	829	45	966
6	917	26	723	46	1,042
7	1,069	27	749	47	889
8	1,086	28	766	48	1,002
9	1,066	29	996	49	763
10	929	30	1,122	50	932
11	1,022	31	962	51	1,052
12	959	32	829	52	1,062
13	756	33	862	53	989
14	882	34	793	54	1,029
15	829	35	1,039	55	823
16	726	36	1,009	56	942
17	666	37	979	57	986
18	879	38	976	58	736
19	1,086	39	856	59	1,009
20	992	40	1,036	60	852

The primary manufacturers of DRAM are those in Southeast Asia. Currently, Swift can purchase one unit of 128M DRAM for $10. After negotiation with a reputable supplier, Holland managed to sign a long-term agreement, which kept the price at $10 and allowed Swift to place orders at any time. The supplier also supplies other items in Swift's inventory. In addition, it takes the supplier of the DRAM two days to deliver the goods to Swift's warehouse using air carriers.

When Swift does not have enough inventory to fill a customer's order, the sales are lost; that is, Swift is not able to backorder the shortage because its customers fill their requirements through competitors. The customers will accept partial shipments, however.

It costs Swift $200 to place an order with the suppliers. This amount covers the corresponding internal ordering costs and the costs of delivering the products to the company. Holland estimates that the cost of lost sales amounts to $2 per unit of DRAM. This rough estimate includes the loss of profits, as well as the intangible damage to customer goodwill.

To simplify its inventory management system, Swift has a policy of maintaining a cycle-service level of 95 percent. The holding cost per day per unit is estimated to be 0.5 percent of the cost of goods, regardless of the product. Inventory holding costs are calculated on the basis of the ending inventory each day. The current balance is 1,700 units of DRAM in stock.

The daily purchasing routine is as follows. Orders are placed at the *beginning* of the day, before Swift is open for customer business. The orders arrive at the beginning of the day, two days later, and can be used for sales that day. For example, an order placed at the beginning of day 1 will arrive at Swift before Swift is open for business on day 3. The actual daily demand is always recorded at the *end* of the day, after Swift has closed for customer business. All cost computations are done at the end of the day after the total demand has been recorded.

Simulation

Holland believes that simulation is a useful approach to assess various inventory control alternatives. The historical data from Table 12.3 could be used to develop attractive inventory policies. The table was developed to record various costs and evaluate different alternatives. An example showing some recent DRAM inventory decisions is shown in Table 12.4.

1. Design a new inventory system for Swift Electronic Supply, Inc., using the data provided.

2. Provide the rationale for your system, which should include the decision rules you would follow to determine how much to order and when.

3. Simulate the use of your inventory system and record the costs. Develop a table such as Table 12.4 to record your results. Your instructor will provide actual demands on a day-to-day basis during the simulation.

TABLE 12.4	EXAMPLE SIMULATION									
Day	**1**	**2**	**3**	**4**	**5**	**6**	**7**	**8**	**9**	**10**
Beginning inventory position	1,700	831	1,500	391	3,000	3,232	2,315			
Number ordered	1,500		3,000	1,200			1,900			
Daily demand	869	902	1,109	947	968	917	1,069			
Day-ending inventory	831	−71	391	−556	2,032	2,315	1,246			
Ordering costs ($200 per order)	200		200	200			200			
Holding costs ($0.05 per piece per day)	41.55	0.00	19.55	0.00	101.60	115.75	62.30			
Shortage costs ($2 per piece)	0	142	0	1,112	0	0	0			
Total cost for day	241.55	142.00	219.55	1,312.00	101.60	115.75	262.30			
Cumulative cost from last day	0.00	241.55	383.55	603.10	1,915.10	2,016.70	2,132.45			
Cumulative costs to date	241.55	383.55	603.10	1,915.10	2,016.70	2,132.45	2,394.75			

CASE | Parts Emporium

Parts Emporium, Inc., is a wholesale distributor of automobile parts formed by two disenchanted auto mechanics, Dan Block and Ed Spriggs. Originally located in Block's garage, the firm showed slow but steady growth for 7 years before it relocated to an old, abandoned meat-packing warehouse on Chicago's South Side. With increased space for inventory storage, the company was able to begin offering an expanded line of auto parts. This increased selection, combined with the trend toward longer car ownership, led to an explosive growth of the business. Fifteen years later, Parts Emporium was the largest independent distributor of auto parts in the north central region.

Recently, Parts Emporium relocated to a sparkling new office and warehouse complex off Interstate 55 in suburban Chicago. The warehouse space alone occupied more than 100,000 square feet. Although only a handful of new products have been added since the warehouse was constructed, its utilization increased from 65 percent to more than 90 percent of capacity. During this same period, however, sales growth stagnated. These conditions motivated Block and Spriggs to hire the first manager from outside the company in the firm's history.

It is June 6, Sue McCaskey's first day in the newly created position of materials manager for Parts Emporium. A recent graduate of a prominent business school, McCaskey is eagerly awaiting her first real-world problem. At approximately 8:30 A.M., it arrives in the form of status reports on inventory and orders shipped. At the top of an extensive computer printout is a handwritten note from Joe Donnell, the purchasing manager: "Attached you will find the inventory and customer service performance data. Rest assured that the individual inventory levels are accurate because we took a complete physical inventory count at the end of last week. Unfortunately, we do not keep compiled records in some of the areas as you requested. However, you are welcome to do so yourself. Welcome aboard!"

A little upset that aggregate information is not available, McCaskey decides to randomly select a small sample of approximately 100 items and compile inventory and customer service characteristics to get a feel for the "total picture." The results of this experiment reveal to her why Parts Emporium decided to create the position she now fills. It seems that the inventory is in all the wrong places. Although an *average* of approximately 60 days of inventory is on hand, the firm's customer service is inadequate. Parts Emporium tries to backorder the customer orders not immediately filled from stock, but some 10 percent of demand is being lost to competing distributorships. Because stockouts are costly, relative to inventory holding costs, McCaskey believes that a cycle-service level of at least 95 percent should be achieved.

McCaskey knows that although her influence to initiate changes will be limited, she must produce positive results immediately. Thus, she decides to concentrate on two products from the extensive product line: the EG151 exhaust gasket and the DB032 drive belt. If she can demonstrate significant gains from proper inventory management for just two products, perhaps Block and Spriggs will give her the backing needed to change the total inventory management system.

The EG151 exhaust gasket is purchased from an overseas supplier, Haipei, Inc. Actual demand for the first 21 weeks of this year is shown in the following table:

Week	Actual Demand	Week	Actual Demand
1	104	12	97
2	103	13	99
3	107	14	102
4	105	15	99
5	102	16	103
6	102	17	101
7	101	18	101
8	104	19	104
9	100	20	108
10	100	21	97
11	103		

A quick review of past orders, shown in another document, indicates that a lot size of 150 units is being used and that the lead time from Haipei is fairly constant at 2 weeks. Currently, at the end of week 21, no inventory is on hand, 11 units are backordered, and the company is awaiting a scheduled receipt of 150 units.

The DB032 drive belt is purchased from the Bendox Corporation of Grand Rapids, Michigan. Actual demand so far this year is shown in the following table:

Week	Actual Demand	Week	Actual Demand
11	18	17	50
12	33	18	53
13	53	19	54
14	54	20	49
15	51	21	52
16	53		

Because this product is new, data are available only since its introduction in week 11. Currently, 324 units are on hand, with no backorders and no scheduled receipts. A lot size of 1,000 units is being used, with the lead time fairly constant at 3 weeks.

The wholesale prices that Parts Emporium charges its customers are $12.99 for the EG151 exhaust gasket and $8.89 for the DB032 drive belt. Because no quantity discounts are offered on these two highly profitable items, gross margins based on current purchasing practices are 32 percent of the wholesale price for the exhaust gasket and 48 percent of the wholesale price for the drive belt.

Parts Emporium estimates its cost to hold inventory at 21 percent of its inventory investment. This percentage recognizes the opportunity cost of tying money up in inventory and the variable costs of taxes, insurance, and shrinkage. The annual report notes other warehousing expenditures for utilities and maintenance and debt service on the 100,000-square-foot warehouse, which was built for $1.5 million. However, McCaskey reasons that these warehousing costs can be ignored because they will not change for the range of inventory policies that she is considering.

Out-of-pocket costs for Parts Emporium to place an order with suppliers are estimated to be $20 per order for exhaust gaskets and $10 per order for drive belts. On the outbound side, the company can charge a delivery fee. Although most customers pick up their parts at Parts Emporium, some orders are delivered to customers. To provide this service, Parts Emporium contracts with a local company for a flat fee of $21.40 per order, which is added to the customer's bill. McCaskey is unsure whether to increase the ordering costs for Parts Emporium to include delivery charges.

QUESTIONS

1. Put yourself in Sue McCaskey's position and prepare a detailed report to Dan Block and Ed Spriggs on managing the inventory of the EG151 exhaust gasket and the DB032 drive belt. Be sure to present a proper inventory system and recognize all relevant costs.

2. By how much do your recommendations for these two items reduce annual cycle inventory, stockout, and ordering costs?

SELECTED REFERENCES

Bastow, B. J. "Metrics in the Material World." *APICS—The Performance Advantage* (May 2005), pp. 49–52.

Berlin, Bob. "Solving the OEM Puzzle at Valleylab." *APICS—The Performance Advantage* (March 1997), pp. 58–63.

Callioni, Gianpaolo, Xavier de Montgros, Regine Slagmulder, Luk N. Van Wassenhove, and Linda Wright. "Inventory-Driven Costs." *Harvard Business Review* (March 2005), pp. 135–141.

Cannon, Alan R., and Richard E. Crandall. "The Way Things Never Were." *APICS—The Performance Advantage* (January 2004), pp. 32–35.

Chikan, A., A. Milne, and L. G. Sprague. "Reflections on Firm and National Inventories." Budapest: International Society for Inventory Research, 1996.

Greene, James H. *Production and Inventory Control Handbook*, 3d ed. New York: McGraw-Hill, 1997.

Hartvigsen, David. *SimQuick: Process Simulation with Excel*, 2d ed. Upper Saddle River, NJ: Prentice Hall, 2004.

Inventory Management Reprints. Falls Church, VA: American Production and Inventory Control Society, 1993.

Krupp, James A. G. "Are ABC Codes an Obsolete Technology?" *APICS—The Performance Advantage* (April 1994), pp. 34–35.

Silver, Edward A. "Changing the Givens in Modeling Inventory Problems: The Example of Just-in-Time Systems." *International Journal of Production Economics*, vol. 26 (1996), pp. 347–351.

Silver, Edward A., D. E. Pyke, and Rein Peterson. *Inventory Management, Production Planning, and Scheduling*, 3d ed. New York: John Wiley & Sons, 1998.

Tersine, Richard J. *Principles of Inventory and Materials Management*, 4th ed. Upper Saddle River, NJ: Prentice Hall, 1994.

Timme, Stephen G., and Christine Williams-Timme. "The Real Cost of Holding." *Supply Chain Management Review* (July/August 2003), pp. 30–37.

D SPECIAL INVENTORY MODELS

LEARNING GOALS

After reading this supplement, you should be able to:

1. Define the relevant costs that should be considered to determine the order quantity when discounts are available.

2. Identify the situations where the economic lot size should be used rather than the economic order quantity.

3. Calculate the optimal lot size when replenishment is not instantaneous.

4. Determine the optimal order quantity when materials are subject to quantity discounts.

5. Calculate the order quantity that maximizes the expected profits for a one-period inventory decision.

Many real world problems require relaxation of certain assumptions on which the economic order quantity (EOQ) model is based. This supplement addresses three realistic situations that require going beyond the simple EOQ formulation.

1. Noninstantaneous Replenishment. Particularly in situations in which manufacturers use a continuous process to make a primary material, such as a liquid, gas, or powder, production is not instantaneous. Thus, inventory is replenished gradually, rather than in lots.

2. Quantity Discounts. Three annual costs are the inventory holding cost, the fixed cost for ordering and setup, and the cost of materials. For service providers and for manufacturers alike, the unit cost of purchased materials sometimes depends on the order quantity.

3. One-Period Decisions. Retailers and manufacturers of fashion goods often face a situation in which demand is uncertain and occurs during just one period or season.

This supplement assumes you have read Chapter 12, "Managing Inventories," and Supplement A, "Decision Making Models."

myomlab and the Companion Website at **www.pearsonglobaleditions.com/krajewski** contain many tools, activities, and resources designed for this supplement.

Noninstantaneous Replenishment

If an item is being produced internally rather than purchased, finished units may be used or sold as soon as they are completed, without waiting until a full lot is completed. For example, a restaurant that bakes its own dinner rolls begins to use some of the rolls from the first pan even before the baker finishes a five-pan batch. The inventory of rolls never reaches the full five-pan level, the way it would if the rolls all arrived at once on a truck sent by a supplier.

Figure D.1 depicts the usual case, in which the production rate, p, *exceeds* the demand rate, d.[1] *Cycle* inventory accumulates faster than demand occurs; that is, a buildup *of $p - d$* units occurs per time period. For example, if the production rate is 100 units per day and the demand is 5 units per day, the buildup is 95 (or 100 − 5) units each day. This buildup continues until the lot size, Q, has been produced, after which the inventory depletes at a rate of 5 units per day. Just as the inventory reaches 0, the next production interval begins. To be consistent, both p and d must be expressed in units of the same time period, such as units per day or units per week. Here, we assume that they are expressed in units per day.

The $p - d$ buildup continues for Q/p days because Q is the lot size and p units are produced each day. In our example, if the lot size is 300 units, the production interval is 3 days (300/100). For the given rate of buildup over the production interval, the maximum cycle inventory, I_{max}, is

$$I_{max} = \frac{Q}{p}(p - d) = Q\left(\frac{p - d}{p}\right)$$

Cycle inventory is no longer $Q/2$, as it was with the basic EOQ method; instead, it is $I_{max}/2$. Setting up the total annual cost equation for this production situation, where D is annual demand, as before, and d is daily demand, we get

Total annual cost = Annual holding cost + Annual ordering or setup cost

$$C = \frac{I_{max}}{2}(H) + \frac{D}{Q}(S) = \frac{Q}{2}\left(\frac{p - d}{p}\right)(H) + \frac{D}{Q}(S)$$

Based on this cost function, the optimal lot size, often called the **economic production lot size (ELS)**, is

$$ELS = \sqrt{\frac{2DS}{H}}\sqrt{\frac{p}{p - d}}$$

Because the second term is a ratio greater than 1, the ELS results in a larger lot size than the EOQ.

economic production lot size (ELS)

The optimal lot size in a situation in which replenishment is not instantaneous.

◀ **FIGURE D.1**
Lot Sizing with Noninstantaneous Replenishment

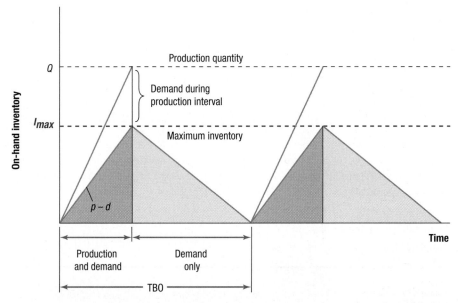

---

[1] If demand and production were equal, production would be continuous with no buildup of cycle inventory. If the production rate is lower than the demand rate, sales opportunities are being missed on an ongoing basis. We assume that $p > d$ in this supplement.

| EXAMPLE D.1 | Finding the Economic Production Lot Size |

Tutor D.1 in my**om**lab provides a new example to determine the ELS.

Active Model D.1 in my**om**lab provides additional insight on the ELS model and its uses.

A plant manager of a chemical plant must determine the lot size for a particular chemical that has a steady demand of 30 barrels per day. The production rate is 190 barrels per day, annual demand is 10,500 barrels, setup cost is $200, annual holding cost is $0.21 per barrel, and the plant operates 350 days per year.

a.   Determine the economic production lot size (ELS).

b.   Determine the total annual setup and inventory holding cost for this item.

c.   Determine the time between orders (TBO), or cycle length, for the ELS.

d.   Determine the production time per lot.

What are the advantages of reducing the setup time by 10 percent?

SOLUTION

a.   Solving first for the ELS, we get

$$\text{ELS} = \sqrt{\frac{2DS}{H}}\sqrt{\frac{p}{p-d}} = \sqrt{\frac{2(10,500)(\$200)}{\$0.21}}\sqrt{\frac{190}{190-30}}$$

$$= 4,873.4 \text{ barrels}$$

b.   The total annual cost with the ELS is

$$C = \frac{Q}{2}\left(\frac{p-d}{p}\right)(H) + \frac{D}{Q}(S)$$

$$= \frac{4,873.4}{2}\left(\frac{190-30}{190}\right)(\$0.21) + \frac{10,500}{4,873.4}(\$200)$$

$$= \$430.91 + \$430.91 = \$861.82$$

c.   Applying the TBO formula to the ELS, we get

$$\text{TBO}_{\text{ELS}} = \frac{\text{ELS}}{D}(350 \text{ days/year}) = \frac{4,873.4}{10,500}(350)$$

$$= 162.4 \quad \text{or} \quad 162 \text{ days}$$

d.   The production time during each cycle is the lot size divided by the production rate:

$$\frac{\text{ELS}}{p} = \frac{4,873.4}{190} = 25.6 \quad \text{or} \quad 26 \text{ days}$$

DECISION POINT

As OM Explorer shows in Figure D.2, the net effect of reducing the setup cost by 10 percent is to reduce the lot size, the time between orders, and the production cycle time. Consequently, total annual costs are also reduced. This adds flexibility to the manufacturing process because items can be made more quickly with less expense. Management must decide whether the added cost of improving the setup process is worth the added flexibility and inventory cost reductions.

FIGURE D.2 ▶
OM Explorer Solver for the Economic Production Lot Size Showing the Effect of a 10 Percent Reduction in Setup Cost

Period Used in Calculations	Day ▼

Demand per Day	30
Production Rate/Day	190
Annual Demand	10,500
Setup Cost	$180
Annual Holding Cost ($)	$0.21
Operating Days per Year	350

⦿ Enter Holding Cost Manually   ◯ Holding Cost As % of Value

Economic Lot Size (ELS)	4,623
Annual Total Cost	$817.60
Time Between Orders (days)	154.1
Production Time	24.3

QUANTITY DISCOUNTS

Quantity discounts, which are price incentives to purchase large quantities, create pressure to maintain a large inventory. For example, a supplier may offer a price of $4.00 per unit for orders between 1 and 99 units, a price of $3.50 per unit for orders between 100 and 199 units, and a price of $3.00 per unit for orders of 200 or more units. The item's price is no longer fixed, as assumed in the EOQ derivation; instead, if the order quantity is increased enough, the price is discounted. Hence, a new approach is needed to find the best lot size—one that balances the advantages of lower prices for purchased materials and fewer orders (which are benefits of large order quantities) against the disadvantage of the increased cost of holding more inventory.

The total annual cost now includes not only the holding cost, *(Q/2)(H)*, and the ordering cost, *(D/Q)(S)*, but also the cost of purchased materials. For any per-unit price level, *P*, the total cost is

$$\text{Total annual cost} = \text{Annual holding cost} + \text{Annual ordering or setup cost}$$
$$+ \text{Annual cost of materials}$$

$$C = \frac{Q}{2}(H) + \frac{D}{Q}(S) + PD$$

The unit holding cost, *H*, usually is expressed as a percent of the unit price because the more valuable the item held in inventory, the higher the holding cost is. Thus, the lower the unit price, *P*, the lower *H* is. Conversely, the higher *P* is, the higher *H* is.

The total cost equation yields U-shaped total cost curves. Adding the annual cost of materials to the total cost equation raises each total cost curve by a fixed amount, as shown in Figure D.3(a). The three cost curves illustrate each of the price levels. The top curve applies when no discounts are received; the lower curves reflect the discounted price levels. No single curve is relevant to all purchase quantities. The relevant, or feasible, total cost begins with the top curve, then drops down, curve by curve, at the price breaks. A price break is the minimum quantity needed to get a discount. In Figure D.3, two price breaks occur at *Q* = 100 and *Q* = 200. The result is a total cost curve, with steps at the price breaks.

Figure D.3(b) also shows three additional points—the minimum point on each curve—obtained with the EOQ formula at each price level. These EOQs do not necessarily produce the best lot size for two reasons.

1. The EOQ at a particular price level may not be feasible. The lot size may not lie in the range corresponding to its per-unit price. Figure D.3(b) illustrates two instances of an infeasible EOQ. First, the minimum point for the $3.00 curve appears to be fewer than 200 units. However, the supplier's quantity discount schedule does not allow purchases of that small a quantity at the $3.00 unit price. Similarly, the EOQ for the $4.00 price level is greater than the first price break, so the price charged would be only $3.50.

▼ FIGURE D.3
Total Cost Curves with Quantity Discounts

(a) Total cost curves with purchased materials added

(b) EOQs and price break quantities

2. The EOQ at a particular price level may be feasible but may not be the best lot size. The feasible EOQ may have a higher cost than is achieved by the EOQ or price break quantity on a lower price curve. In Figure D.3(b), for example, the 200-unit price break quantity for the $3.00 price level has a lower total cost than the feasible EOQ for the $3.50 price level. A feasible EOQ always is better than any feasible point on cost curves with higher price levels, but not necessarily those with lower levels. Thus, the only time we can immediately conclude, without comparing total costs, that a feasible EOQ is the best order quantity is when it is on the curve for the lowest price level. This conclusion is not possible in Figure D.3(b) because the only feasible EOQ is at the middle price level, $P = \$3.50$.

We must, therefore, pay attention only to feasible price–quantity combinations, shown as solid lines in Figure D.3(b), as we search for the best lot size. The following two-step procedure may be used to find the best lot size.

Step 1. Beginning with the lowest price, calculate the EOQ for each price level until a feasible EOQ is found. It is feasible if it lies in the range corresponding to its price. Each subsequent EOQ is smaller than the previous one because P, and thus H, gets larger and because the larger H is in the denominator of the EOQ formula.

Step 2. If the first feasible EOQ found is for the lowest price level, this quantity is the best lot size. Otherwise, calculate the total cost for the first feasible EOQ and for the larger price break quantity at each lower price level. The quantity with the lowest total cost is optimal.

EXAMPLE D.2	Finding Q with Quantity Discounts at St. LeRoy Hospital

Tutor D.2 in my**om**lab provides a new example for choosing the best order quantity when discounts are available.

Active Model D.2 in my**om**lab provides additional insight on the quantity discount model and its uses.

A supplier for St. LeRoy Hospital has introduced quantity discounts to encourage larger order quantities of a special catheter. The price schedule is

Order Quantity	Price per Unit
0 to 299	$60.00
300 to 499	$58.80
500 or more	$57.00

The hospital estimates that its annual demand for this item is 936 units, its ordering cost is $45.00 per order, and its annual holding cost is 25 percent of the catheter's unit price. What quantity of this catheter should the hospital order to minimize total costs? Suppose the price for quantities between 300 and 499 is reduced to $58.00. Should the order quantity change?

SOLUTION

Step 1: Find the first feasible EOQ, starting with the lowest price level:

$$EOQ_{57.00} = \sqrt{\frac{2DS}{H}} = \sqrt{\frac{2(936)(\$45.00)}{0.25(\$57.00)}} = 77 \text{ units}$$

A 77-unit order actually costs $60.00 per unit, instead of the $57.00 per unit used in the EOQ calculation, so this EOQ is infeasible. Now try the $58.80 level:

$$EOQ_{58.80} = \sqrt{\frac{2DS}{H}} = \sqrt{\frac{2(936)(\$45.00)}{0.25(\$58.80)}} = 76 \text{ units}$$

This quantity also is infeasible because a 76-unit order is too small to qualify for the $58.80 price. Try the highest price level:

$$EOQ_{60.00} = \sqrt{\frac{2DS}{H}} = \sqrt{\frac{2(936)(\$45.00)}{0.25(\$60.00)}} = 75 \text{ units}$$

This quantity is feasible because it lies in the range corresponding to its price, $P = \$60.00$.

Step 2: The first feasible EOQ of 75 does not correspond to the lowest price level. Hence, we must compare its total cost with the price break quantities (300 and 500 units) at the lower price levels ($58.80 and $57.00):

$$C = \frac{Q}{2}(H) \; + \; \frac{D}{Q}(S) \; + \; PD$$

$$C_{75} = \frac{75}{2}[(0.25)(\$60.00)] \quad + \quad \frac{936}{75}(\$45.00) \; + \; \$60.00(936) = \$57,284$$

$$C_{300} = \frac{300}{2}[(0.25)(\$58.80)] \quad + \quad \frac{936}{300}(\$45.00) \; + \; \$58.80(936) = \$57,382$$

$$C_{500} = \frac{500}{2}[(0.25)(\$57.00)] \quad + \quad \frac{936}{500}(\$45.00) \; + \; \$57.00(936) = \$56,999$$

The best purchase quantity is 500 units, which qualifies for the deepest discount.

DECISION POINT

If the price per unit for the range of 300 to 499 units is reduced to $58.00, the best decision is to order 300 catheters, as shown by OM Explorer in Figure D.4. This result shows that the decision is sensitive to the price schedule. A reduction of slightly more than 1 percent is enough to make the difference in this example. In general, however, it is not always the case that you should order more than the economic order quantity when given price discounts. When discounts are small, holding cost H is large, and demand D is small, small lot sizes are better even though price discounts are forgone.

◀ **FIGURE D.4**
OM Explorer Solver for Quantity Discounts Showing the Best Order Quantity

	More	Fewer	
Min. Amount Req'd for Price Point	Lot Sizes	Price/Unit	
...	0–299	$60.00	
300	300–499	$58.00	
500	500 or more	$57.00	

Annual Demand	936	
Order Cost	$45	
Holding Cost (% or price)	25%	

Best Order Quantity	300

	Price Point	EOQ or Req'd Order for Price Point	Inventory Cost	Order Cost	Purchase Cost	Total Cost	
	$60.00	75	$562.50	$561.60	$56,160	$57,284	
>>	$58.00	300	$2,175	$140.40	$54,288	$56,603	<<
	$57.00	500	$3,563	$84.24	$53,352	$56,999	

ONE-PERIOD DECISIONS

One of the dilemmas facing many retailers is how to handle seasonal goods, such as winter coats. Often, they cannot be sold at full markup the next year because of changes in styles. Furthermore, the lead time can be longer than the selling season, allowing no second chance to rush through another order to cover unexpectedly high demand. A similar problem exists for manufacturers of fashion goods.

This type of situation is often called the newsboy problem. If the newspaper seller does not buy enough newspapers to resell on the street corner, sales opportunities are lost. If the seller buys too many newspapers, the overage cannot be sold because nobody wants yesterday's newspaper.

The following process is a straightforward way to analyze such problems and decide on the best order quantity.

1. List the different levels of demand that are possible, along with the estimated probability of each.

2. Develop a *payoff* table that shows the profit for each purchase quantity, Q, at each assumed demand level, D. Each row in the table represents a different order quantity, and each column represents a different demand level. The payoff for a given quantity–demand combination depends on whether all units are sold at the regular profit margin during the regular season, which results in two possible cases.

a. If demand is high enough ($Q \leq D$), then all units are sold at the full profit margin, p, during the regular season,

$$\text{Payoff} = (\text{Profit per unit})(\text{Purchase quantity}) = pQ$$

b. If the purchase quantity exceeds the eventual demand ($Q > D$), only D units are sold at the full profit margin, and the remaining units purchased must be disposed of at a loss, l, after the season. In this case,

$$\text{Payoff} = \left(\begin{array}{c} \text{Profit per unit sold} \\ \text{during season} \end{array} \right)(\text{Demand}) - \left(\begin{array}{c} \text{Loss per} \\ \text{unit} \end{array} \right)\left(\begin{array}{c} \text{Amount disposed of} \\ \text{after season} \end{array} \right)$$

$$= pD - l(Q - D)$$

3. Calculate the expected payoff for each Q (or row in the payoff table) by using the *expected value* decision rule. For a specific Q, first multiply each payoff in the row by the demand probability associated with the payoff, and then add these products.

4. Choose the order quantity Q with the highest expected payoff.

Using this decision process for all such items over many selling seasons will maximize profits. However, it is not foolproof, and it can result in an occasional bad outcome.

EXAMPLE D.3	Finding Q for One-Period Inventory Decisions

Tutor D.3 in my**om**lab provides a new example to practice the one-period inventory decision.

Active Model D.3 in my**om**lab provides additional insight on the one-period inventory decision model and its uses.

FIGURE D.5 ▼
OM Explorer Solver for One-Period Inventory Decisions Showing the Payoff Table

One of many items sold at a museum of natural history is a Christmas ornament carved from wood. The gift shop makes a $10 profit per unit sold during the season, but it takes a $5 loss per unit after the season is over. The following discrete probability distribution for the season's demand has been identified:

Demand	10	20	30	40	50
Demand Probability	0.2	0.3	0.3	0.1	0.1

How many ornaments should the museum's buyer order?

SOLUTION

Each demand level is a candidate for best order quantity, so the payoff table should have five rows. For the first row, where $Q = 10$, demand is at least as great as the purchase quantity. Thus, all five payoffs in this row are

$$\text{Payoff} = pQ = (\$10)(10) = \$100$$

This formula can be used in other rows but only for those quantity–demand combinations where all units are sold during the season. These combinations lie in the upper-right portion of the payoff table, where $Q \leq D$. For example, the payoff when $Q = 40$ and $D = 50$ is

$$\text{Payoff} = pQ = (\$10)(40) = \$400$$

The payoffs in the lower-left portion of the table represent quantity–demand combinations where some units must be disposed of after the season ($Q > D$). For this case, the payoff must be calculated with the second formula. For example, when $Q = 40$ and $D = 30$,

$$\text{Payoff} = pD - l(Q - D) = (\$10)(30) - (\$5)(40 - 30) = \$250$$

Using OM Explorer, we obtain the payoff table in Figure D.5.

Profit	$10.00	(if sold during preferred period)
Loss	$5.00	(if sold after preferred period)

Enter the possible demands along with the probability of each occuring. Use the buttons to increase or decrease the number of allowable demand forecasts. NOTE: Be sure to enter demand forecasts and probablities in all tinted cells, and be sure probabilities add up to 1.

	<	>			
Demand	10	20	30	40	50
Profitability	0.2	0.3	0.3	0.1	0.1

Payoff Table

		Demand				
		10	20	30	40	50
Quantity	10	100	100	100	100	100
	20	50	200	200	200	200
	30	0	150	300	300	300
	40	−50	100	250	400	400
	50	−100	50	200	350	500

Now we calculate the expected payoff for each Q by multiplying the payoff for each demand quantity by the probability of that demand and then adding the results. For example, for $Q = 30$,

$$\text{Payoff} = 0.2(\$0) + 0.3(\$150) + 0.3(\$300) + 0.1(\$300) + 0.1(\$300) = \$195$$

Using OM Explorer, Figure D.6 shows the expected payoffs.

Weighted Payoffs

Order Quantity	Expected Payoff
10	100
20	170
30	195
40	175
50	140

Greatest Expected Payoff   195

Associated with Order Quantity   30

◀ **FIGURE D.6**
OM Explorer Solver Showing the Expected Payoffs

DECISION POINT

Because $Q = 30$ has the highest payoff at $195, it is the best order quantity. Management can use OM Explorer to do sensitivity analysis on the demands and their probabilities to see how confident they are with that decision.

The need for one-time inventory decisions also can arise in manufacturing plants when (1) customized items are made (or purchased) to a single order, and (2) scrap quantities are high.[2] A customized item produced for a single order is never intentionally held in stock because the demand for it is too unpredictable. In fact, it may never be ordered again so the manufacturer would like to make just the amount requested by the customer—no more, no less. The manufacturer also would like to satisfy an order in just one run to avoid an extra setup and a delay in delivering goods ordered. These two goals may conflict if the likelihood of some units being scrapped is high. Suppose that a customer places an order for 20 units. If the manager orders 20 units from the shop or from the supplier, one or two units may have to be scrapped. This shortage will force the manager to place a second (or even third) order to replace the defective units. Replacement can be costly if setup time is high and can also delay shipment to the customer. To avoid such problems, the manager could order more than 20 units the first time. If some units are left over, the customer might be willing to buy the extras or the manager might find an internal use for them. For example, some manufacturing companies set up a special account for obsolete materials. These materials can be "bought" by departments within the company at less than their normal cost, as an incentive to use them.

INTERNET RESOURCES

my**om**lab and the Companion Website at **www.pearsonglobaleditions.com/krajewski** contain many tools, activities, and resources designed for this supplement.

KEY EQUATIONS

1. Noninstantaneous replenishment:

Maximum inventory: $I_{\max} = Q\left(\dfrac{p - d}{p}\right)$

Total annual cost = Annual holding cost + Annual ordering or setup cost

$$C = \frac{Q}{2}\left(\frac{p - d}{p}\right)(H) + \frac{D}{Q}(S)$$

---

[2] One goal of total quality management (TQM) and Six Sigma is to eliminate scrap. Achievement of that goal makes this discussion moot.

Economic production lot size: $\text{ELS} = \sqrt{\dfrac{2\,D\,S}{H}}\sqrt{\dfrac{p}{p-d}}$

Time between orders, expressed in years: $\text{TBO}_{\text{ELS}} = \dfrac{\text{ELS}}{D}$

2. Quantity discounts:

Total annual cost = Annual holding cost + Annual ordering or setup cost + Annual cost of material

$$C = \frac{Q}{2}(H) + \frac{D}{Q}(S) + PD$$

3. One-period decisions:

Payoff matrix: $\text{Payoff} = \begin{cases} pQ & \text{if } Q \le D \\ pD - l(Q-D) & \text{if } Q > D \end{cases}$

SOLVED PROBLEM 1

A hospital buys disposable surgical packages from Pfisher, Inc. Pfisher's price schedule is $50.25 per package on orders of 1 to 199 packages and $49.00 per package on orders of 200 or more packages. Ordering cost is $64 per order, and annual holding cost is 20 percent of the per-unit purchase price. Annual demand is 490 packages. What is the best purchase quantity?

SOLUTION

We first calculate the EOQ at the *lowest* price:

$$\text{EOQ}_{49.00} = \sqrt{\frac{2\,D\,S}{H}} = \sqrt{\frac{2(490)\,(\$64.00)}{0.20(\$49.00)}} = \sqrt{6{,}400} = 80 \text{ packages}$$

This solution is infeasible because, according to the price schedule, we cannot purchase 80 packages at a price of $49.00 each. Therefore, we calculate the EOQ at the next lowest price ($50.25):

$$\text{EOQ}_{50.25} = \sqrt{\frac{2\,D\,S}{H}} = \sqrt{\frac{2(490)\,(\$64.00)}{0.20(\$50.00)}} = \sqrt{6{,}241} = 79 \text{ packages}$$

This EOQ is feasible, but $50.25 per package is not the lowest price. Hence, we have to determine whether total costs can be reduced by purchasing 200 units and thereby obtaining a quantity discount.

$$C = \frac{Q}{2}(H) + \frac{D}{Q}(S) + PD$$

$$C_{79} = \frac{79}{2}(0.20 \times \$50.25) + \frac{490}{79}(\$64.00) + \$50.25(490)$$

$$= \$396.98/\text{year} + \$396.68/\text{year} + \$24{,}622.50/\text{year} = \$25{,}416.44/\text{year}$$

$$C_{200} = \frac{200}{2}(0.20 \times \$49.00) + \frac{490}{200}(\$64.00) + \$49.00(490)$$

$$= \$980.00/\text{year} + \$156.80/\text{year} + \$24{,}010.00/\text{year} = \$25{,}146.80/\text{year}$$

Purchasing 200 units per order will save $269.64/year, compared to buying 79 units at a time.

SOLVED PROBLEM 2

Peachy Keen, Inc., makes mohair sweaters, blouses with Peter Pan collars, pedal pushers, poodle skirts, and other popular clothing styles of the 1950s. The average demand for mohair sweaters is 100 per week. Peachy's production facility has the capacity to sew 400 sweaters per week. Setup cost is $351. The value of finished goods inventory is $40 per sweater. The annual per-unit inventory holding cost is 20 percent of the item's value.

a. What is the economic production lot size (ELS)?

b. What is the average time between orders (TBO)?

c. What is the total of the annual holding cost and setup cost?

SOLUTION

a. The production lot size that minimizes total cost is

$$\text{ELS} = \sqrt{\frac{2DS}{H}}\sqrt{\frac{p}{p-d}} = \sqrt{\frac{2(100 \times 52)(\$351)}{0.20(\$40)}}\sqrt{\frac{400}{(400-100)}}$$

$$= \sqrt{456,300}\sqrt{\frac{4}{3}} = 780 \text{ sweaters}$$

b. The average time between orders is

$$\text{TBO}_{\text{ELS}} = \frac{\text{ELS}}{D} = \frac{780}{5,200} = 0.15 \text{ year}$$

Converting to weeks, we get

$$\text{TBO}_{\text{ELS}} = (0.15 \text{ year})(52 \text{ weeks/year}) = 7.8 \text{ weeks}$$

c. The minimum total of setup and holding costs is

$$C = \frac{Q}{2}\left(\frac{p-d}{p}\right)(H) + \frac{D}{Q}(S) = \frac{780}{2}\left(\frac{400-100}{400}\right)(0.20 \times \$40) + \frac{5,200}{780}(\$351)$$

$$= \$2,340/\text{year} + \$2,340/\text{year} = \$4,680/\text{year}$$

SOLVED PROBLEM 3

Swell Productions is sponsoring an outdoor conclave for owners of collectible and classic Fords. The concession stand in the T-Bird area will sell clothing such as T-shirts and official Thunderbird racing jerseys. Jerseys are purchased from Columbia Products for $40 each and are sold during the event for $75 each. If any jerseys are left over, they can be returned to Columbia for a refund of $30 each. Jersey sales depend on the weather, attendance, and other variables. The following table shows the probability of various sales quantities. How many jerseys should Swell Productions order from Columbia for this one-time event?

Sales Quantity	Probability	Quantity Sales	Probability
100	0.05	400	0.34
200	0.11	500	0.11
300	0.34	600	0.05

SOLUTION

Table D.1 is the payoff table that describes this one-period inventory decision. The upper-right portion of the table shows the payoffs when the demand, D, is greater than or equal to

TABLE D.1 | PAYOFFS

				Demand, D			
Q	100	200	300	400	500	600	Expected Payoff
100	$3,500	$3,500	$ 3,500	$ 3,500	$ 3,500	$ 3,500	$ 3,500
200	$2,500	$7,000	$ 7,000	$ 7,000	$ 7,000	$ 7,000	$ 6,775
300	$1,500	$6,000	$10,500	$10,500	$10,500	$10,500	$ 9,555
400	$ 500	$5,000	$ 9,500	$14,000	$14,000	$14,000	$10,805
500	($ 500)	$4,000	$ 8,500	$13,000	$17,500	$17,500	$10,525
600	($1,500)	$3,000	$ 7,500?	$12,000	$16,500	$21,000	$ 9,750

the order quantity, Q. The payoff is equal to the per-unit profit (the difference between price and cost) multiplied by the order quantity. For example, when the order quantity is 100 and the demand is 200,

$$\text{Payoff} = (p - c)\,Q = (\$75 - \$40)100 = \$3,500$$

The lower-left portion of the payoff table shows the payoffs when the order quantity exceeds the demand. Here the payoff is the profit from sales, pD, minus the loss associated with returning overstock, $l(Q - D)$, where l is the difference between the cost and the amount refunded for each jersey returned and $Q - D$ is the number of jerseys returned. For example, when the order quantity is 500 and the demand is 200,

$$\text{Payoff} = pD - l(Q - D) = (\$75 - \$40)200 - (\$40 - \$30)(500 - 200) = \$4,000$$

The highest expected payoff occurs when 400 jerseys are ordered:

$$\text{Expected payoff}_{400} = (\$500 \times 0.05) + (\$5,000 \times 0.11) + (\$9,500 \times 0.34)$$
$$+ (\$14,000 \times 0.34) + (\$14,000 \times 0.11) + (\$14,000 \times 0.05)$$
$$= \$10,805$$

PROBLEMS

Software, such as OM Explorer, Active Models, and POM for Windows, is available in my**om**lab. Check with your instructor on how best to use it. In many cases, the instructor wants you to understand how to do the calculations by hand. At most, the software provides a check on your calculations. When calculations are particularly complex and the goal is interpreting the results in making decisions, the software replaces entirely the manual calculations. The software also can be a valuable resource well after your course is completed.

1. Based on advance ticket sales, the athletic department has forecast hot dog sales for an upcoming football game to be as shown in the following table. The school buys premium hot dogs for $1.50 and sells them during the game at $3.00 each. Hot dogs left over after the game will be sold for $0.50 each to the Aggie student cafeteria to be used in making hotdog casserole.

Sales Quantity	Probability
2,000	0.10
3,000	0.30
4,000	0.30
5,000	0.20
6,000	0.10

Use a payoff matrix to determine the number of hot dogs to buy for the game.

2. Dorothy's pastries are freshly baked and sold at several specialty shops throughout Perth. When they are a day old, they must be sold at reduced prices. Daily demand is distributed as follows:

Demand	Probability
50	0.25
150	0.50
200	0.25

Each pastry sells for $1.00 and costs $0.60 to make. Each one not sold at the end of the day can be sold the next day for $0.30 as day-old merchandise. How many pastries should be baked each day?

3. National Printing Company must decide how many wall calendars it should produce for sale during the upcoming sale season. Each calendar sells for $8.50 and costs $2.50 to produce. The local school district has agreed to buy all unsold calendars at a unit price of $1.50. National estimates the following probability distribution for the season's demand:

Demand	Probability
2,000	0.05
3,000	0.20
4,000	0.25
5,000	0.40
6,000	0.10

How many calendars should National produce to maximize its expected profit?

4. As inventory manager, you must decide on the order quantity for an item that has an annual demand of 2,000 units. Placing an order costs you $20 each time. Your annual holding cost, expressed as a percentage of average inventory value, is 20 percent. Your supplier has provided the following price schedule:

Minimum Order Quantity	Price per Unit
1	$2.50
200	$2.40
300	$2.25
1,000	$2.00

What ordering policy do you recommend?

5. Mac-in-the-Box, Inc., sells computer equipment by mail and telephone order. Mac sells 1,200 flat-bed scanners per year. Ordering cost is $300, and annual holding cost is 16 percent of the item's price. The scanner manufacturer offers the following price structure to Mac-in-the-Box:

Order Quantity	Price per Unit
0 to 11	$520
12 to 143	$500
144 or more	$400

What order quantity minimizes total annual costs?

6. The University Bookstore at a prestigious private university buys mechanical pencils from a wholesaler. The wholesaler offers discounts for large orders according to the following price schedule:

Order Quantity	Price per Unit
0 to 200	$4.00
201 to 2,000	$3.50
2,001 or more	$3.25

The bookstore expects an annual demand of 2,500 units. It costs $10 to place an order, and the annual cost of holding a unit in stock is 30 percent of the unit's price. Determine the best order quantity.

7. To boost sales, Pfisher (refer to Solved Problem 1) announces a new price structure for disposable surgical packages. Although the price break no longer is available at 200 units, Pfisher now offers an even greater discount if larger quantities are purchased. On orders of 1 to 499 packages, the price is $50.25 per package. For orders of 500 or more, the price per unit is $47.80. Ordering costs, annual holding costs, and annual demand remain at $64 per order, 20 percent of the per-unit cost, and 490 packages per year, respectively. What is the new lot size?

8. The Bucks Grande major league baseball team breaks an average of four bats per week. The team orders baseball bats from Corky's, a bat manufacturer noted for its access to the finest hardwood. The order cost is $70, and the annual holding cost per bat per year is 38 percent of the purchase price. Corky's price structure is

Order Quantity	Price per Unit
0 to 11	$54.00
12 to 143	$51.00
144 or more	$48.50

a. How many bats should the team buy per order?

b. What are the total annual costs associated with the best order quantity?

c. Corky discovers that, owing to special manufacturing processes required for the Bucks's bats, it has underestimated setup costs. Rather than raise prices, Corky adds another category to the price structure to provide an incentive for larger orders and reduce the number of setups required. If the Bucks buy 180 bats or more, the price will drop to $45.00 each. Should the Bucks revise the order quantity to 180 bats?

9. Suds's Bottling Company does bottling, labeling, and distribution work for several local microbreweries. The demand rate for Wortman's beer is 600 cases (24 bottles each) per week. Suds's bottling production rate is 2,400 cases per week, and the setup cost is $800. The value of inventory is $12.50 per case, and the annual holding cost is 30 percent of the inventory value. What is the economic production lot size?

10. Sharpe Cutter is a small company that produces specialty knives for paper cutting machinery. The annual demand for a particular type of knife is 100,000 units. The demand is uniform over the 250 working days in a year. Sharpe Cutter produces this type of knife in lots and, on average, can produce 450 knives a day. The cost to set up a production lot is $300, and the annual holding cost is $1.20 per knife.

a. Determine the economic production lot size (ELS).

b. Determine the total annual setup and inventory holding cost for this item.

c. Determine the TBO, or cycle length, for the ELS.

d. Determine the production time per lot.

11. Bold Vision, Inc., makes laser printer and photocopier toner cartridges. The demand rate is 625 EP cartridges per week. The production rate is 1,736 EP cartridges per week, and the setup cost is $100. The value of inventory is $130 per unit, and the holding cost is 20 percent of the inventory value. What is the economic production lot size?

Selected References

"Factors That Make or Break Season Sales." *Wall Street Journal* (December 9, 1991).

Greene, James H. *Production and Inventory Control Handbook*, 3d ed. New York: McGraw-Hill, 1997.

Inventory Management Reprints. Falls Church, VA: American Production and Inventory Control Society, 1993.

Manikas, Andrew. "Fighting Pests with the EOQ," *APICS Magazine* (April 2007), pp. 34–37.

Silver, Edward A., D. F. Pyke, and Rein Peterson. *Inventory Management, Production Planning, and Scheduling*, 3d ed. New York: John Wiley & Sons, 1998.

Sipper, Daniel, and Robert L. Bulfin, Jr. *Production Planning, Control, and Integration*. New York: McGraw-Hill, 1997.

Tersine, Richard J. *Principles of Inventory and Materials Management*, 4th ed. Upper Saddle River, NJ: Prentice Hall, 1994.

13 FORECASTING DEMAND

Lipton tea is one of many Unilever products, and its demand around the world must be forecasted. For centuries, globalism's story traveled with merchants who shepherded spices along Eurasian trade routes. Now it travels over wires and radio waves, satellites, airplanes, and gigabytes.

UNILEVER

Unilever, the fast-moving consumer products supplier, has a state-of-the-art customer demand planning (CDP) system. CDP, first introduced in Chapter 10, "Integrating the Supply Chain," is a business-planning process that enables sales teams (and customers) to develop demand forecasts. Using software from Manugistics, the system blends historical shipment data with promotional data, allowing information sharing and collaboration with important customers. The system begins with shipment history and current order information. This baseline forecast depends solely on past and present information, so reliable data is a critical requirement. However, statistical information is not useful in forecasting the outcomes of certain events, promotions, rollouts, and special packages, which are common in the industry. To overcome this problem, planners at Unilever must adjust the statistical forecasts with planned promotion predictions conducted by special sales teams. For each promotion, the sales-planning system predicts the "lift," or projected increase in sales, and routes it to the demand-planning system, which applies it to appropriate stock-keeping units (SKUs) and distribution centers each week. In turn, these forecasts are reviewed and adjusted if needed.

Unilever also conducts external market research and internal sales projections that are analyzed, combined with the retail customer promotions, and fed into the demand-planning system. To further improve the accuracy of its forecasts and reduce inventory lead times, Unilever—the purveyor of Dove, Lipton, Hellmann's, and hundreds of other

LEARNING GOALS

After reading this chapter, you should be able to:

1. Identify the various forecasting methods available to customer demand planning systems.

2. Explain collaborative planning, forecasting, and replenishment (CPFR).

3. Use regression to make forecasts.

4. Make forecasts using the most common approaches for time-series analysis.

5. Identify the various measures of forecast errors.

6. Describe a typical forecasting process used by businesses.

brands—compares point-of-sale (POS) data with its own forecasts. Most companies, including Unilever, only collect POS data from their largest customers. Ultimately, planners at Unilever negotiate the final numbers each week and feed these forecasts into the demand-planning system.

Overall, the current CDP system has been a success. Unilever has reduced its inventory and improved its customer service. However, if collaboration and the usage of POS data were to increase, Unilever would likely reap even larger benefits.

Sources: Robert L. Mitchell, "Case Study: Unilever Crosses the Data Streams," *Computerworld* (December 17, 2001); Robert L. Mitchell, "Tech Check: Getting Demand Planning Right," *Computerworld* (December 17, 2001); www.unilever.com, July 6, 2008.

myomlab and the Companion Website at **www.pearsonglobaledions.com/krajewski** contain many tools, activities, and resources designed for this chapter.

forecast

A prediction of future events used for planning purposes.

COMPETING WITH OPERATIONS

↓

Using Operations to Compete
Managing Effective Projects

DESIGNING AND
MANAGING PROCESSES

↓

Developing a Process Strategy
Analyzing Processes
Managing Quality
Planning Capacity
Managing Process Constraints
Designing Lean Systems

DESIGNING AND
MANAGING SUPPLY CHAINS

↓

Designing Effective Supply Chains
Integrating the Supply Chain
Locating Facilities
Managing Inventories
Forecasting Demand
Planning and Scheduling Operations
Planning Sufficient Resources

---

time series

The repeated observations of demand for a service or product in their order of occurrence.

Balancing supply and demand begins with making accurate forecasts. A **forecast** is a prediction of future events used for planning purposes. Planning, on the other hand, is the process of making management decisions on how to deploy resources to best respond to the demand forecasts. Forecasting methods may be based on mathematical models that use available historical data or on qualitative methods that draw on managerial experience and judgments, or they may be based on a combination of both. Unilever's CDP system illustrates the value of merging forecasts from multiple sources.

In this chapter, our focus is on demand forecasts. We begin with different types of demand patterns and designing the forecasting system. We examine forecasting methods in three basic categories: judgment, causal, and time-series methods. Forecast errors are defined, providing important clues for making better forecasts. We conclude with multiple techniques, which bring together insights from several sources, and an overall process for making forecasts.

Forecasts are useful for both managing processes and managing supply chains. At the supply chain level, a firm needs forecasts to coordinate with its customers and suppliers. At the process level, output forecasts are needed to design the various processes throughout the organization, including identifying and dealing with in-house bottlenecks. For example, Hewlett-Packard produces network cards that turn dedicated HP printers into network-shared printers. Changing its forecasting process reduced its inventory levels by 20 to 30 percent reduction while maintaining high levels of product availability. Recognizing the important role of the forecasting process resulted in better overall performance of the supply chain.

FORECASTING ACROSS THE ORGANIZATION

As the Hewlett-Packard example shows, the organization-wide forecasting process cuts across functional areas. Forecasting overall demand typically originates with marketing, but internal customers throughout the organization depend on forecasts to formulate and execute their plans as well. Forecasts are critical inputs to business plans, annual plans, and budgets. Finance needs forecasts to project cash flows and capital requirements. Human resources needs forecasts to anticipate hiring and training needs. Marketing is an important source for sales forecast information because it is closest to external customers. Operations and supply chain managers need forecasts to plan output levels, purchases of services and materials, workforce and output schedules, inventories, and long-term capacities.

Managers throughout the organization make forecasts on many variables other than future demand, such as competitor strategies, regulatory changes, technological changes, processing times, supplier lead times, and quality losses. Tools for making these forecasts are basically the same tools covered here for demand: judgment, opinions of knowledgeable people, averages of experience, regression, and time-series techniques. Using these tools, forecasting can be improved. Still, forecasts are rarely perfect. As Samuel Clemens (Mark Twain) said in *Following the Equator*, "Prophesy is a good line of business, but it is full of risks." Smart managers recognize this reality and find ways to update their plans when the inevitable forecast error or unexpected event occurs.

DEMAND PATTERNS

Forecasting customer demand is a difficult task because the demand for services and goods can vary greatly. For example, demand for lawn fertilizer predictably increases in the spring and summer months; however, the particular weekends when demand is heaviest may depend on uncontrollable factors such as the weather. Sometimes patterns are more predictable. Thus, the peak hours of the day for a large bank's call center are from 9:00 A.M. to 12:00 P.M., and the peak day of the week is Monday. For its statement-rendering processes, the peak months are January, April, July, and October, which is when the quarterly statements are sent out. Forecasting demand in such situations requires uncovering the underlying patterns from available information. In this section, we discuss the basic patterns of demand.

The repeated observations of demand for a service or product in their order of occurrence form a pattern known as a **time series**. There are five basic patterns of most demand time series:

1. *Horizontal.* The fluctuation of data around a constant mean.

2. *Trend.* The systematic increase or decrease in the mean of the series over time.

3. *Seasonal.* A repeatable pattern of increases or decreases in demand, depending on the time of day, week, month, or season.

4. *Cyclical.* The less predictable gradual increases or decreases in demand over longer periods of time (years or decades).

5. *Random.* The unforecastable variation in demand.

Cyclical patterns arise from two influences. The first is the business cycle, which includes factors that cause the economy to go from recession to expansion over a number of years. The other influence is the service or product life cycle, which reflects the stages of demand from development through decline. Business cycle demand is difficult to predict because it is affected by national or international events.

Four of the patterns of demand—horizontal, trend, seasonal, and cyclical—combine in varying degrees to define the underlying time pattern of demand for a service or product. The fifth pattern, random variation, results from chance causes and thus cannot be predicted. Random variation is an aspect of demand that makes every forecast ultimately wrong. Figure 13.1 shows the first four patterns of a demand time series, all of which contain random variations.

Key Decisions on Making Forecasts

Before using forecasting techniques, a manager must make three decisions: (1) what to forecast, (2) what forecasting system to use, and (3) what type of forecasting technique to select for different items.

Deciding What to Forecast

Although some sort of demand estimate is needed for the individual services or goods produced by a company, forecasting total demand for groups or clusters and then deriving individual service or product forecasts may be easiest. Also, selecting the correct unit of measurement (e.g., service or product units or machine-hours) for forecasting may be as important as choosing the best method.

Level of Aggregation   Few companies err by more than 5 percent when forecasting the annual total demand for all their services or products. However, errors in forecasts for individual items and shorter time periods may be much higher. Recognizing this reality, many companies use a two-tier forecasting system. They first cluster (or "roll up") several similar services or products in a process called **aggregation**, making forecasts for families of services or goods that have similar demand requirements and common processing, labor, and materials requirements. Next they derive forecasts for individual items, which are sometimes called stock-keeping units. A *stock-keeping unit (SKU)* is an individual item or product

aggregation

The act of clustering several similar services or products so that forecasts and plans can be made for whole families.

◄ FIGURE 13.1
Patterns of Demand

(a) Horizontal: Data cluster about a horizontal line.

(b) Trend: Data consistently increase or decrease.

(c) Seasonal: Data consistently show peaks and valleys.

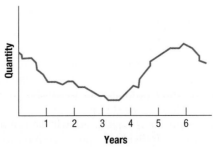

(d) Cyclical: Data reveal gradual increases and decreases over extended periods of time.

that has an identifying code and is held in inventory somewhere along the supply chain, such as in a distribution center.

Units of Measurement   Rather than using dollars as the initial unit of measurement, forecasts often begin with service or product units, such as SKUs, express packages to deliver, or customers needing maintenance service or repairs for their cars. Forecasted units can then be translated to dollars by multiplying them by the unit price. If accurately forecasting demand units for a service or product is not possible, forecast the standard labor or machine-hours required of each of the critical resources.

Choosing a Forecasting System

Often companies must prepare forecasts for hundreds or even thousands of services or products repeatedly. For example, a large network of health care facilities must calculate demand forecasts for each of its services for every department. This undertaking involves voluminous data that must be manipulated frequently. However, software such as Unilever's CDP system can ease the burden of making these forecasts and coordinating the forecasts between retailers and suppliers. Many forecasting software packages are available, including Manugistics, Forecast Pro, and SAS. The forecasting routines in OM Explorer and POM for Windows give some hint of their capabilities.

Many firms, including Wal-Mart and Campbell Soup, use a specific CDP process called **collaborative planning, forecasting, and replenishment (CPFR)** for supply chain integration that allows a supplier and its customers to collaborate on making demand forecasts by using the Internet. Managerial Practice 13.1 describes Wal-Mart's experience with this approach.

Choosing the Type of Forecasting Technique

CDP systems offer a variety of forecasting techniques, and no one of them is best for all items and situations. The forecaster's objective is to develop a useful forecast from the information at hand with the technique that is appropriate for the different patterns of demand. Two general types of forecasting techniques are used: judgment methods and quantitative methods. **Judgment methods** translate the opinions of managers, expert opinions, consumer surveys, and salesforce estimates into quantitative estimates. Quantitative methods include causal methods and time-series analysis. **Causal methods** use historical data on independent variables, such as promotional campaigns, economic conditions, and competitors' actions, to predict demand. **Time-series analysis** is a statistical approach that relies heavily on historical demand data to project the future size of demand and recognizes trends and seasonal patterns.

JUDGMENT METHODS

Forecasts from quantitative methods are possible only when there is adequate historical data, often called the *history file* by various commercial software packages. However, the history file may be nonexistent when a new product is introduced or when technology is expected to change. The history file might exist but be less useful when certain events (such as rollouts or special packages) are reflected in the past data, or when certain events are expected to occur in the future. In some cases, judgment methods are the only practical way to make a forecast. In other cases, judgment methods can also be used to modify forecasts that are generated by quantitative methods. Such adjustments are particularly important when the forecaster has important contextual knowledge. *Contextual knowledge* is knowledge that practitioners gain through experience, such as cause-and-effect relationships, environmental cues, and organizational information that may have an effect on the variable being forecast. Finally, judgment methods can be used to adjust the history file that will be analyzed with quantitative methods to discount the impact of special one-time events that occurred in the past. Four of the more successful judgment methods are as follows: (1) salesforce estimates, (2) executive opinion, (3) market research, and (4) the Delphi method.

Salesforce estimates are forecasts compiled from estimates made periodically by members of a company's salesforce. The salesforce is the group most likely to know which services or products customers will be buying in the near future and in what quantities. Forecasts of individual salesforce members can be combined easily to get regional or national sales estimates. However, individual biases of the salespeople may taint the forecast. For example, some people are naturally optimistic, whereas others are more cautious. Adjustments in forecasts may need to be made.

---

collaborative planning, forecasting, and replenishment (CPFR)

A nine-step process for supply chain integration that allows a supplier and its customers to collaborate on making the forecast by using the Internet.

judgment methods

A forecasting method that translates the opinions of managers, expert opinions, consumer surveys, and salesforce estimates into quantitative estimates.

causal methods

A quantitative forecasting method that uses historical data on independent variables, such as promotional campaigns, economic conditions, and competitors' actions, to predict demand.

time-series analysis

A statistical approach that relies heavily on historical demand data to project the future size of demand and recognizes trends and seasonal patterns.

salesforce estimates

The forecasts that are compiled from estimates of future demands made periodically by members of a company's salesforce.

MANAGERIAL PRACTICE 13.1

Wal-Mart Uses CPFR and the Internet to Improve Demand Planning Performance

Wal-Mart has long been known for its careful analysis of cash register receipts and for working with suppliers to reduce inventories. In the past, like many other retailers, Wal-Mart did not share its forecasts with its suppliers. The result was forecast errors as much as 60 percent of actual demand. Retailers ordered more than they needed, and suppliers produced more than they could sell.

To combat the ill effects of forecast errors on inventories, Benchmarking Partners, Inc., was funded in the mid-1990s by Wal-Mart, IBM, SAP, and Manugistics to develop a software package. A key benefit of the package was the capability of providing more reliable medium-term forecasts. The system allowed manufacturers and merchants to work together on forecasts by using the Internet rather than fax or phone, which would have been a heavy burden with the thousands of items stocked at each store requiring weekly forecasts.

Wal-Mart initiated this new approach with Listerine, a primary product of Warner-Lambert that in 2000 joined with Pfizer. Listerine is currently produced and distributed by Johnson & Johnson, which acquired Pfizer's consumer health care division in 2006. The system worked in the following way during this pilot period. Wal-Mart and Warner-Lambert independently calculated the demand they expected for Listerine six months into the future, taking into consideration factors such as past sales trends and promotion plans. They then exchanged their forecasts over the Internet. If the forecasts differed by more than a predetermined percentage, the retailer and the manufacturer used the Internet to exchange written comments and supporting data. The parties went through as many cycles as needed to converge on an acceptable forecast. After the pilot ended, the benefits to Wal-Mart included a reduction in stockouts from 15 percent to 2 percent as well as significant increases in sales and reductions in inventory costs. Likewise, Warner-Lambert benefited by having a smoother production plan and lower average costs. This system was later generalized and dubbed CPFR, which stands for collaborative planning, forecasting, and replenishment.

Following the pilot with Warner-Lambert, Wal-Mart had a CPFR pilot with Sara Lee in which the firms exchanged information such as forecasts and replenishment data. In return, Wal-Mart benefited by ensuring that it had the right item at the right time and at the right place, thus increasing customer satisfaction and profitability.

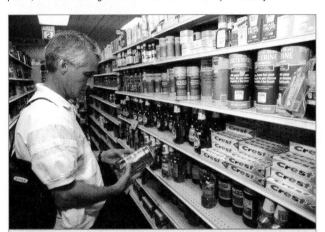

A customer examining a bottle of Listerine at a drug store. Listerine was the "test case" for a new forecasting standard called CPFR, which stands for "collaborative planning, forecast, and replenishment." Using the Internet, retailers such as Wal-Mart and manufacturers exchange their forecasts for products such as Listerine and are much better able to match supply with demand.

Sources: VICS (2002), "Collaborative Planning, Forecasting, and Replenishment," Version 2.0, www.cpfr.org; Jerold P. Cederlund, Rajiv Kohli, Susan A. Sherer, and Yuliang Yao, "How Motorola Put CPFR into Action," *Supply Chain Management Review* (October 2007), pp. 28–35.

Executive opinion is a forecasting method in which the opinions, experience, and technical knowledge of one or more managers or customers (as with CPFR) are summarized to arrive at a single forecast. As we discuss later, executive opinion can be used to modify an existing sales forecast to account for unusual circumstances, such as a new sales promotion or unexpected international events. Executive opinion can also be used for **technological forecasting**. The quick pace of technological change makes keeping abreast of the latest advances difficult.

Market research is a systematic approach to determine external consumer interest in a service or product by creating and testing hypotheses through data-gathering surveys. Conducting a market research study includes designing a questionnaire, deciding how to administer it, selecting a representative sample, and analyzing the information using judgment and statistical tools to interpret the responses. Although market research yields important information, it typically includes numerous qualifications and hedges in the findings.

The **Delphi method** is a process of gaining consensus from a group of experts while maintaining their anonymity. This form of forecasting is useful when no historical data are available from which to develop statistical models and when managers inside the firm have no experience on which to base informed projections. A coordinator sends questions to each member of the group of outside experts, who may not even know who else is participating. The coordinator prepares a statistical summary of the responses along with a summary of arguments for particular

executive opinion

A forecasting method in which the opinions, experience, and technical knowledge of one or more managers are summarized to arrive at a single forecast.

technological forecasting

An application of executive opinion to keep abreast of the latest advances in technology.

market research

A systematic approach to determine external consumer interest in a service or product by creating and testing hypotheses through data-gathering surveys.

Delphi method

A process of gaining consensus from a group of experts while maintaining their anonymity.

responses. The report is sent to the same group for another round, and the participants may choose to modify their previous responses. These rounds continue until consensus is obtained.

In the remainder of this chapter, we turn to the commonly used quantitative forecasting approaches.

CAUSAL METHODS: LINEAR REGRESSION

Causal methods are used when historical data are available and the relationship between the factor to be forecasted and other external or internal factors (e.g., government actions or advertising promotions) can be identified. These relationships are expressed in mathematical terms and can be complex. Causal methods are good for predicting turning points in demand and for preparing long-range forecasts. We focus on linear regression, one of the best known and most commonly used causal methods.

In **linear regression**, one variable, called a dependent variable, is related to one or more independent variables by a linear equation. The **dependent variable** (such as demand for doorknobs) is the one the manager wants to forecast. The **independent variables** (such as advertising expenditures and new housing starts) are assumed to affect the dependent variable and thereby "cause" the results observed in the past. Figure 13.2 shows how a linear regression line relates to the data. In technical terms, the regression line minimizes the squared deviations from the actual data.

In the simplest linear regression models, the dependent variable is a function of only one independent variable and, therefore, the theoretical relationship is a straight line:

$$Y = a + bX$$

where

Y = dependent variable

X = independent variable

a = Y-intercept of the line

b = slope of the line

linear regression

A causal method in which one variable (the dependent variable) is related to one or more independent variables by a linear equation.

dependent variable

The variable that one wants to forecast.

independent variables

Variables that are assumed to affect the dependent variable and thereby "cause" the results observed in the past.

The objective of linear regression analysis is to find values of a and b that minimize the sum of the squared deviations of the actual data points from the graphed line. Computer programs are used for this purpose. For any set of matched observations for Y and X, the program computes the values of a and b and provides measures of forecast accuracy. Three measures commonly reported are the sample correlation coefficient, the sample coefficient of determination, and the standard error of the estimate.

The *sample correlation coefficient, r,* measures the direction and strength of the relationship between the independent variable and the dependent variable. The value of r can range from −1.00 to +1.00. A correlation coefficient of +1.00 implies that period-by-period changes in direction (increases or decreases) of the independent variable are always accompanied by changes in the same direction by the dependent variable. An r of −1.00 means that decreases in the independent variable are always accompanied by increases in the dependent variable, and vice versa. A zero value of r means no linear relationship exists between the variables. The closer the value of r is to ±1.00, the better the regression line fits the points.

The *sample coefficient of determination* measures the amount of variation in the dependent variable about its mean that is explained by the regression line. The coefficient of determination is the square of the correlation coefficient, or r^2. The value of r^2 ranges from 0.00 to 1.00. Regression equations with a value of r^2 close to 1.00 mean a close fit.

The *standard error of the estimate,* s_{yx}, measures how closely the data on the dependent variable cluster around the regression line. Although it is similar to the sample standard deviation, it measures the error from the dependent variable, Y, to the regression line, rather than to the mean. Thus, it is the standard deviation of the difference between the actual demand and the estimate provided by the regression equation. When determining which independent variable to include in the regression equation, you should choose the one with the smallest standard error of the estimate.

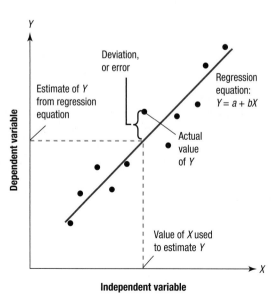

FIGURE 13.2 ▲
Linear Regression Line Relative to Actual Data

EXAMPLE 13.1	Using Linear Regression to Forecast Product Demand

The supply chain manager seeks a better way to forecast the demand for door hinges and believes that the demand is related to advertising expenditures. The following are sales and advertising data for the past 5 months:

Active Model 13.1 in my**om**lab provides insight on varying the intercept and slope of the model.

Month	Sales (thousands of units)	Advertising (thousands of $)
1	264	2.5
2	116	1.3
3	165	1.4
4	101	1.0
5	209	2.0

The company will spend $1,750 next month on advertising for the product. Use linear regression to develop an equation and a forecast for this product.

SOLUTION

We used POM for Windows to determine the best values of a, b, the correlation coefficient, the coefficient of determination, and the standard error of the estimate.

$$a = -8.135$$
$$b = 109.229X$$
$$r = 0.980$$
$$r^2 = 0.960$$
$$s_{yx} = 15.603$$

The regression equation is

$$Y = -8.135 + 109.229X$$

and the regression line is shown in Figure 13.3. The sample correlation coefficient, r, is 0.98, which is close to 1.00 and suggests an unusually strong positive relationship exists between sales and advertising expenditures. The sample coefficient of determination, r^2, implies that 96 percent of the variation in sales is explained by advertising expenditures.

◀ FIGURE 13.3
Linear Regression Line for the Sales and Advertising Data Using POM for Windows

DECISION POINT

The supply chain manager decided to use the regression model as input to planning production levels for month 6. As the advertising expenditure will be $1,750, the forecast for month 6 is $Y = -8.135 + 109.229(1.75)$ = 183.016 or 183,016 units.

Often several independent variables may affect the dependent variable. For example, advertising expenditures, new corporation start-ups, and residential building contracts all may be important for estimating the demand for door hinges. In such cases, *multiple regression analysis* is helpful in determining a forecasting equation for the dependent variable as a function of several independent variables. Such models can be analyzed with POM for Windows or OM Explorer and can be quite useful for predicting turning points and solving many planning problems.

TIME-SERIES METHODS

Rather than using independent variables for the forecast as regression models do, time-series methods use historical information regarding only the dependent variable. These methods are based on the assumption that the dependent variable's past pattern will continue in the future. Time-series analysis identifies the underlying patterns of demand that combine to produce an observed historical pattern of the dependent variable and then develops a model to replicate it. In this section, we focus on time-series methods that address the horizontal, trend, and seasonal patterns of demand. Before we discuss statistical methods, let us take a look at the simplest time-series method for addressing all patterns of demand—the naive forecast.

Naive Forecast

naive forecast

A time-series method whereby the forecast for the next period equals the demand for the current period, or Forecast = D_t.

A method often used in practice is the **naive forecast**, whereby the forecast for the next period equals the demand for the current period (D_t). So if the actual demand for Wednesday is 35 customers, the forecasted demand for Thursday is 35 customers. Despite its name, the naive forecast can perform well.

The naive forecast method may be adapted to take into account a demand trend. The increase (or decrease) in demand observed between the last two periods is used to adjust the current demand to arrive at a forecast. Suppose that last week the demand was 120 units and the week before it was 108 units. Demand increased 12 units in 1 week, so the forecast for next week would be 120 + 12 = 132 units. The naive forecast method also may be used to account for seasonal patterns. If the demand last July was 50,000 units, the forecast for this July would be 50,000 units. The method works best when the horizontal, trend, or seasonal patterns are stable and random variation is small.

Estimating the Average

We begin our discussion of statistical methods of time-series forecasting with demand that has no trend, seasonal, or cyclical patterns. The horizontal pattern in a time series is based on the mean of the demands, so we focus on forecasting methods that estimate the average of a time series of data. The forecast of demand for *any* period in the future is the average of the time series computed in the current period. For example, if the average of past demand calculated on Tuesday is 65 customers, the forecasts for Wednesday, Thursday, and Friday are 65 customers each day.

Consider Figure 13.4, which shows patient arrivals at a medical clinic over the past 28 weeks. Assuming that the time series has only a horizontal and random pattern, the statistical techniques useful for forecasting such a time series are (1) simple moving averages, (2) weighted moving averages, and (3) exponential smoothing.

Simple Moving Averages   The **simple moving average method** simply involves calculating the average demand for the *n* most recent time periods and using it as the forecast for future time periods. For the next period, after the demand is known, the oldest demand from the previous average is replaced with the most recent demand and the average is recalculated. In this way, the *n* most recent demands are used, and the average "moves" from period to period.

Specifically, the forecast for period *t* + 1 can be calculated at the end of period *t* (after the actual demand for period *t* is known) as

$$F_{t+1} = \frac{\text{Sum of last } n \text{ demands}}{n} = \frac{D_t + D_{t-1} + D_{t-2} + \cdots + D_{t-n+1}}{n}$$

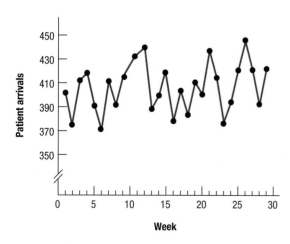

FIGURE 13.4 ▲
Weekly Patient Arrivals at a Medical Clinic

where

$$D_t = \text{actual demand in period } t$$

$$n = \text{total number of periods in the average}$$

$$F_{t+1} = \text{forecast for period } t+1$$

For any forecasting method, it is important to measure the accuracy of its forecasts. **Forecast error** is simply the difference found by subtracting the forecast from actual demand for a given period, or

$$E_t = D_t - F_t$$

where

$$E_t = \text{forecast error for period } t$$

$$D_t = \text{actual demand for period } t$$

$$F_t = \text{forecast for period } t$$

EXAMPLE 13.2	Using the Moving Average Method to Estimate Average Demand

a. Compute a *three-week* moving average forecast for the arrival of medical clinic patients in week 4. The numbers of arrivals for the past three weeks were as follows:

Week	Patient Arrivals
1	400
2	380
3	411

b. If the actual number of patient arrivals in week 4 is 415, what is the forecast error for week 4?

c. What is the forecast for week 5?

Active Model 13.2 in my**om**lab provides insight on the impact of varying n using the example in Figure 13.4.

Tutor 13.1 in my**om**lab provides another example to practice making forecasts with the moving average method.

SOLUTION

a. The moving average forecast at the end of week 3 is

$$F_4 = \frac{411 + 380 + 400}{3} = 397.0$$

b. The forecast error for week 4 is

$$E_4 = D_4 - F_4 = 415 - 397 = 18$$

c. The forecast for week 5 requires the actual arrivals from weeks 2 through 4, the three most recent weeks of data.

$$F_5 = \frac{415 + 411 + 380}{3} = 402.0$$

DECISION POINT

Thus, the forecast at the end of week 3 would have been 397 patients for week 4, which fell short of actual demand by 18 patients. The forecast for week 5, made at the end of week 4, would be 402 patients. In addition, at the end of week 4, the forecast for week 6 and beyond is also 402 patients.

The moving average method may involve the use of as many periods of past demand as desired. Large values of n should be used for demand series that are stable, and small values of n should be used for those that are susceptible to changes in the underlying average.

weighted moving average method

A time-series method in which each historical demand in the average can have its own weight; the sum of the weights equals 1.0.

Tutor 13.2 in my**om**lab provides a new practice example for making forecasts with the weighted moving average method.

exponential smoothing method

A weighted moving average method that calculates the average of a time series by giving recent demands more weight than earlier demands.

Weighted Moving Averages   In the simple moving average method, each demand has the same weight in the average—namely, $1/n$. In the **weighted moving average method**, each historical demand in the average can have its own weight. The sum of the weights equals 1.0. For example, in a *three-period* weighted moving average model, the most recent period might be assigned a weight of 0.50, the second most recent might be weighted 0.30, and the third most recent might be weighted 0.20. The average is obtained by multiplying the weight of each period by the value for that period and adding the products together:

$$F_{t+1} = 0.50D_t + 0.30D_{t-1} + 0.20D_{t-2}$$

For a numerical example of using the weighted moving average method to estimate average demand, see Solved Problem 2 and Tutor 13.2 of OM Explorer in my**om**lab.

The advantage of a weighted moving average method is that it allows you to emphasize recent demand over earlier demand. (It can even handle seasonal effects by putting higher weights on prior years in the same season.) The forecast will be more responsive to changes in the underlying average of the demand series than the simple moving average forecast.

Exponential Smoothing   The **exponential smoothing method** is a sophisticated weighted moving average method that calculates the average of a time series by giving recent demands more weight than earlier demands. It is the most frequently used formal forecasting method because of its simplicity and the small amount of data needed to support it. Unlike the weighted moving average method, which requires n periods of past demand and n weights, exponential smoothing requires only three items of data: the last period's forecast; the actual demand for this period; and a smoothing parameter, alpha (α), which has a value between 0 and 1.0. To obtain an exponentially smoothed forecast, we simply calculate a weighted average of the most recent demand and the forecast calculated last period. The equation for the forecast is

$$F_{t+1} = \alpha(\text{Demand this period}) + (1-\alpha)(\text{Forecast calculated last period})$$
$$= \alpha D_t + (1-\alpha)F_t$$

An equivalent equation is

$$F_{t+1} = F_t + \alpha(D_t - F_t)$$

This form of the equation shows that the forecast for the next period equals the forecast for the current period plus a proportion of the forecast error for the current period.

The emphasis given to the most recent demand levels can be adjusted by changing the smoothing parameter. Larger α values emphasize recent levels of demand and result in forecasts more responsive to changes in the underlying average. Smaller α values treat past demand more uniformly and result in more stable forecasts. This approach is analogous to adjusting the value of n in the moving average method except that in that method, smaller values of n emphasize recent demand and larger values give greater weight to past demand. In practice, various values of α are tried and the one producing the best forecasts is chosen.

Exponential smoothing requires an initial forecast to get started. There are several ways to get this initial forecast, such as by using last period's actual demand or, if some historical data are available, by calculating the average of several recent periods of demand. The effect of the initial estimate of the average on successive estimates of the average diminishes over time.

EXAMPLE 13.3	**Using Exponential Smoothing to Estimate Average Demand**

Active Model 13.3 in my**om**lab provides insight on the impact of varying α in Figure 13.4.

Tutor 13.3 in my**om**lab provides a new practice example of how to make forecasts with the exponential smoothing method.

a.   Reconsider the patient arrival data in Example 13.2. It is now the end of week 3. Using $\alpha = 0.10$, calculate the exponential smoothing forecast for week 4.

b.   What was the forecast error for week 4 if the actual demand turned out to be 415?

c.   What is the forecast for week 5?

SOLUTION

a.   The exponential smoothing method requires an initial forecast. Suppose that we take the demand data for the first two weeks and average them, obtaining $(400 + 380)/2 = 390$ as an initial forecast. (POM for Windows and OM Explorer simply use the actual demand for the first week as a default setting for the initial forecast for period 1, and do not begin tracking forecast errors until the second period). To obtain the forecast for week 4, using exponential smoothing with $\alpha = 0.10$ and the initial forecast of 390, we calculate the average at the end of week 3 as

$$F_4 = 0.10(411) + 0.90(390) = 392.1$$

Thus, the forecast for week 4 would be 392 patients.

b. The forecast error for week 4 is

$$E_4 = 415 - 392 = 23$$

c. The new forecast for week 5 would be

$$F_5 = 0.10(415) + 0.90(392.1) = 394.4$$

or 394 patients. Note that we used F_4, not the integer-value forecast for week 4, in the computation for F_5. In general, we round off (when it is appropriate) only the final result to maintain as much accuracy as possible in the calculations.

DECISION POINT

Using this exponential smoothing model, the analyst's forecasts would have been 392 patients for week 4 and then 394 patients for week 5 and beyond. As soon as the actual demand for week 5 is known, then the forecast for week 6 will be updated.

Because exponential smoothing is simple and requires minimal data, it is inexpensive and attractive to firms that make thousands of forecasts for each time period. However, its simplicity also is a disadvantage when the underlying average is changing, as in the case of a demand series with a trend. Like any method geared solely to the assumption of a stable average, exponential smoothing results will lag behind changes in the underlying average of demand. Higher α values may help reduce forecast errors when there is a change in the average; however, the lags will still occur if the average is changing systematically. Typically, if large α values (e.g., > 0.50) are required for an exponential smoothing application, chances are good that another model is needed because of a significant trend or seasonal influence in the demand series.

Including a Trend

Let us now consider a demand time series that has a trend. A *trend* in a time series is a systematic increase or decrease in the average of the series over time. Where a significant trend is present, exponential smoothing approaches must be modified; otherwise, the forecasts tend to be below or above the actual demand.

To improve the forecast, we need to calculate an estimate of the trend. We start by calculating the *current* estimate of the trend, which is the difference between the average of the series computed in the current period and the average computed last period. To obtain an estimate of the long-term trend, you can average the current estimates. The method for estimating a trend is similar to that used for estimating the demand average with exponential smoothing.

The method for incorporating a trend in an exponentially smoothed forecast is called the **trend-adjusted exponential smoothing method**. With this approach, the estimates for both the average and the trend are smoothed, requiring two smoothing constants. For each period, we calculate the average and the trend:

> **trend-adjusted exponential smoothing method**
>
> The method for incorporating a trend in an exponentially smoothed forecast.

$$A_t = \alpha(\text{Demand this period}) + (1 - \alpha)(\text{Average } + \text{ Trend estimate last period})$$

$$= \alpha D_t + (1 - \alpha)(A_{t-1} + T_{t-1})$$

$$T_t = \beta(\text{Average this period} - \text{Average last period})$$

$$+ (1 - \beta)(\text{Trend estimate last period})$$

$$= \beta(A_t - A_{t-1}) + (1 - \beta)T_{t-1}$$

$$F_{t+1} = A_t + T_t$$

where

A_t = exponentially smoothed average of the series in period t

T_t = exponentially smoothed average of the trend in period t

α = smoothing parameter for the average, with a value between 0 and 1

β = smoothing parameter for the trend, with a value between 0 and 1

F_{t+1} = forecast for period $t + 1$

To make forecasts for periods beyond the next period, we multiply the trend estimate (T_t) by the number of additional periods that we want in the forecast, and add the results to the current average (A_t). Thus, trend-adjusted exponential smoothing differs from the previous methods covered. For those methods, the forecast for all future periods is the same as the forecast for the next period.

Estimates for last period's average and trend needed for the first forecast can be derived from past data or they can be based on an educated guess if no historical data exist. (POM for Windows and OM Explorer simply use the actual demand for the first week as a default setting for the initial average and 0 for the initial trend, and do not begin tracking forecast errors until the second period). To find values for α and β, often an analyst systematically adjusts α and β until the forecast errors are lowest. This process can be carried out in an experimental setting with the model used to forecast historical demands.

EXAMPLE 13.4	Using Trend-Adjusted Exponential Smoothing to Forecast a Demand Series with a Trend

Active Model 13.4 in my**om**lab provides insight on varying α and β using the example in Figure 13.5.

Tutor 13.4 in my**om**lab provides another practice example and explanation of how to make forecasts with the trend-adjusted exponential smoothing method.

Medanalysis, Inc., provides medical laboratory services to patients of Health Providers, a group of 10 family-practice doctors associated with a new health maintenance program. Managers are interested in forecasting the number of blood analysis requests per week. Supplies must be purchased and a decision made regarding the number of blood samples to be sent to another laboratory because of capacity limitations at the main laboratory. Recent publicity about the damaging effects of cholesterol on the heart has caused a national increase in requests for standard blood tests. Medanalysis recently ran an average of 28 blood tests per week. The trend has been about three additional patients per week. This week's demand was for 27 blood tests. We use $\alpha = 0.20$ and $\beta = 0.20$ to calculate the forecast for next week.

SOLUTION

$$A_0 = 28 \text{ patients and } T_0 = 3 \text{ patients}$$

The forecast for week 2 (next week) is

$$A_1 = 0.20(27) + 0.80(28 + 3) = 30.2$$
$$T_1 = 0.20(30.2 - 28) + 0.80(3) = 2.8$$
$$F_2 = 30.2 + 2.8 = 33 \text{ blood tests}$$

If the actual number of blood tests requested in week 2 proved to be 44, the updated forecast for week 3 would be

$$A_2 = 0.20(44) + 0.80(30.2 + 2.8) = 35.2$$
$$T_2 = 0.2(35.2 - 30.2) + 0.80(2.8) = 3.2$$
$$F_3 = 35.2 + 3.2 = 38.4 \text{ or } 38 \text{ blood tests}$$

DECISION POINT

Using this trend-adjusted exponential smoothing model, the forecast for week 2 was 33 blood tests, and then 38 blood tests for week 3. If the analyst makes forecasts at the end of week 2 for periods beyond week 3, the forecast would be even greater because of the upward trend estimated to be 3.2 blood tests per week.

Figure 13.5 shows the trend-adjusted forecast (the blue line) for Medanalysis for a period of 15 weeks. We set α at 0.20, β at 0.20, the initial average at 28, and the initial estimate of the trend at 3. Table 13.1 shows the calculations and forecasts for a period of 15 weeks. At the end of each week, we calculated a forecast for the next week, using the number of blood tests for the current week. Note that they vary less than actual demand because of the smoothing effect of the procedure for calculating the estimates for the average and the trend. By adjusting α and β, we may be able to come up with a better forecast.

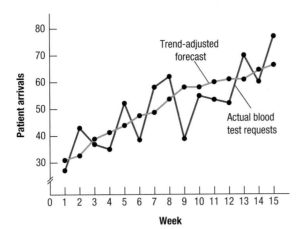

◄ **FIGURE 13.5**
Trend-Adjusted Forecast for
Medanalysis

To make forecasts for periods beyond the next period, we multiply the trend estimate by the number of additional periods that we want in the forecast and add the result to the current average. For example, if we were at the end of week 2 and wanted to estimate the demand for blood tests in week 6 (i.e., 4 weeks ahead), the forecast would be 35.23 + 4(3.28) = 48 tests.

TABLE 13.1	FORECASTS FOR MEDANALYSIS USING THE TREND-ADJUSTED EXPONENTIAL SMOOTHING MODEL			
Week	**Arrivals**	**Calculations to Forecast Arrivals for Next Week**		**Forecast for This Week**	**Forecast Error**
		Smoothed Average	**Trend Average**		
0	28	28.00	3.00		
1	27	30.20	2.84	28.00 + 3.00 = 31.00	−4
2	44	35.23	3.28	30.20 + 2.84 = 33.04	10.96
3	37	38.21	3.22	35.23 + 3.28 = 38.51	−1.51
4	35	40.14	2.96	38.21 + 3.22 = 41.43	−6.43
5	53	45.08	3.36	40.14 + 2.96 = 43.10	9.90
6	38	46.35	2.94	45.08 + 3.36 = 48.44	−10.44
7	57	50.83	3.25	46.35 + 2.94 = 49.29	7.71
8	61	55.46	3.52	50.83 + 3.25 = 54.08	6.92
9	39	54.99	2.72	55.46 + 3.52 = 58.98	−19.98
10	55	57.17	2.62	54.99 + 2.72 = 57.71	−2.71
11	54	58.63	2.38	57.17 + 2.62 = 59.79	−5.79
12	52	59.21	2.02	58.63 + 2.38 = 61.01	−9.01
13	60	60.99	1.97	59.21 + 2.02 = 61.23	−1.23
14	60	62.37	1.86	60.99 + 1.97 = 62.96	−2.96
15	75	66.38	2.29	62.37 + 1.86 = 64.23	10.77

The trend-adjusted exponential smoothing method accounts for both the average and trend, and might be considered to be a better performer than the ones already covered. This is not necessarily true, and the simpler models can sometimes be better performers.

Seasonal Patterns

Seasonal patterns are regularly repeating upward or downward movements in demand measured in periods of less than one year (hours, days, weeks, months, or quarters). In this context, the time periods are called *seasons*. For example, customer arrivals at a fast-food shop on any day may peak between 11 A.M. and 1 P.M and again from 5 P.M. to 7 P.M.

An easy way to account for seasonal effects is to use one of the techniques already described but to limit the data in the time series to those time periods in the same season. For example, for a day-of-the-week seasonal effect, one time series would be for Mondays, one for Tuesdays, and so on. Such an approach accounts for seasonal effects, but has the disadvantage of discarding considerable information on past demand.

Other methods are available that analyze all past data, using one model to forecast demand for all of the seasons. We describe only the **multiplicative seasonal method**, whereby seasonal factors are multiplied by an estimate of average demand to arrive at a seasonal forecast. The four-step procedure presented here involves the use of simple averages of past demand, although more sophisticated methods for calculating averages, such as a moving average or exponential smoothing approach, could be used. The following description is based on a seasonal pattern lasting one year and seasons of one month, although the procedure can be used for any seasonal pattern and season of any length.

multiplicative seasonal method

A method whereby seasonal factors are multiplied by an estimate of average demand to arrive at a seasonal forecast.

1. For each year, calculate the average demand per season by dividing annual demand by the number of seasons per year.

2. For each year, divide the actual demand for a season by the average demand per season. The result is a *seasonal index* for each season in the year, which indicates the level of demand relative to the average demand. For example, a seasonal index of 1.14 calculated for April implies that April's demand is 14 percent greater than the average demand per month.

3. Calculate the average seasonal index for each season, using the results from step 2. Add the seasonal indices for a season and divide by the number of years of data.

4. Calculate each season's forecast for next year. Begin by forecasting next year's annual demand using the naive method, moving averages, exponential smoothing, trend-adjusted exponential smoothing, or linear regression. Then divide annual demand by the number of seasons per year to get the average demand per season. Finally, make the seasonal forecast by multiplying the average demand per season by the appropriate seasonal index found in step 3.

EXAMPLE 13.5   **Using the Multiplicative Seasonal Method to Forecast the Number of Customers**

The manager of the Stanley Steemer carpet cleaning company needs a quarterly forecast of the number of customers expected next year. The carpet cleaning business is seasonal, with a peak in the third quarter and a trough in the first quarter. Following are the quarterly demand data from the past 4 years:

Quarter	Year 1	Year 2	Year 3	Year 4
1	45	70	100	100
2	335	370	585	725
3	520	590	830	1,160
4	100	170	285	215
Total	1,000	1,200	1,800	2,200

The manager wants to forecast customer demand for each quarter of year 5, based on an estimate of total year 5 demand of 2,600 customers.

SOLUTION

Figure 13.6 shows the solution using the *Seasonal Forecasting* Solver in OM Explorer. (For a numerical example calculated manually, see Solved Problem 4 at the end of this chapter.) For the Inputs sheet (a), forecast for the total demand in year 5 is needed. The annual demand has been increasing by an average of 400 customers each year (from 1,000 in year 1 to 2,200 in year 4, or 1,200/3 = 400). The computed forecast demand is found by extending that trend, and projecting an annual demand in year 5 of 2,200 + 400 = 2,600 customers. The option of a user-supplied forecast is also available if the manager wishes to make a judgmental forecast based on additional information.

The results sheet, sheet (b), shows quarterly forecasts by multiplying the seasonal factors by the average demand per quarter. For example, the average demand forecast in year 5 is 650 customers (or 2,600/4 = 650). Multiplying that by the seasonal index computed for the first quarter gives a forecast of 133 customers (or 650 × 0.2043 = 132.795).

◀ FIGURE 13.6
Demand Forecasts Using the *Seasonal Forecast* Solver of OM Explorer

Period   Quarters ▼

Starting Year   1   Years   4 ▲▼

Computed Forecast Demand for Year 5   2600

User-supplied Forecast Demand for Year 5   2600

Year

Quarter	1	2	3	4
1	45	70	100	100
2	335	370	585	725
3	520	590	830	1160
4	100	170	285	215

(a) Inputs sheet

Quarter	Seasonal Index	Forecast
1	0.2043	132.795
2	1.2979	843.635
3	2.0001	1300.065
4	0.4977	323.505

(b) Results

DECISION POINT

Using this seasonal method, the analyst makes a demand forecast as low as 133 customers in the first quarter and as high as 1,300 customers in the third quarter. The season of the year clearly makes a difference.

An alternative to the multiplicative seasonal method is the **additive seasonal method**, whereby seasonal forecasts are generated by adding or subtracting a seasonal constant (say, 50 units) to the estimate of average demand per season. This approach is based on the assumption that the seasonal pattern is constant, regardless of average demand. The amplitude of the seasonal adjustment remains the same regardless of the level of demand.

> **additive seasonal method**   A method in which seasonal forecasts are generated by adding a constant to the estimate of average demand per season.

CHOOSING A TIME-SERIES METHOD

We now turn to factors that managers must consider in selecting a forecasting technique for a particular time series. One important consideration is forecast performance, as determined by forecast errors. Managers need to know how to measure forecast errors and how to detect when something is going wrong with the forecasting system. After examining forecast errors and their detection, we discuss criteria that managers can use to choose an appropriate time-series forecasting method.

Forecast Error

Forecasts almost always contain errors. Forecast errors can be classified as either *bias errors* or *random errors*. Bias errors are the result of consistent mistakes—the forecast is always too high or too low. The other type of forecast error, random error, results from unpredictable factors that cause the forecast to deviate from the actual demand. Forecasting analysts try to minimize the effects of bias and random errors by selecting appropriate forecasting models, but eliminating all forms of errors is impossible.

Measures of Forecast Error   Our earlier definition of forecast error for a given time period ($E_t = D_t - F_t$) is the starting point for creating several measures of forecast error that cover a relatively long period of time.

The **cumulative sum of forecast errors (CFE)** measures the total forecast error:

$$\text{CFE} = \Sigma E_t$$

> **cumulative sum of forecast errors (CFE)**
>
> A measurement of the total forecast error that assesses the bias in a forecast.

Large positive errors tend to be offset by large negative errors in the CFE measure. Nonetheless, CFE is useful in assessing *bias* in a forecast. For example, if a forecast is always lower than actual demand, the value of CFE will gradually get larger and larger. This increasingly large error indicates some systematic deficiency in the forecasting approach. The average forecast error, sometimes called the *mean bias*, is simply

$$\bar{E} = \frac{\text{CFE}}{n}$$

mean squared error (MSE)

A measurement of the dispersion of forecast errors.

standard deviation (σ)

A measurement of the dispersion of forecast errors.

mean absolute deviation (MAD)

A measurement of the dispersion of forecast errors.

The **mean squared error (MSE)**, **standard deviation (σ)**, and **mean absolute deviation (MAD)** measure the dispersion of forecast errors:

$$\text{MSE} = \frac{\Sigma E_t^2}{n}$$

$$\sigma = \sqrt{\frac{\Sigma (E_t - \bar{E})^2}{n - 1}}$$

$$\text{MAD} = \frac{\Sigma |E_t|}{n}$$

The mathematical symbol $|\ |$ is used to indicate the absolute value—that is, it tells you to disregard positive or negative signs. If MSE, σ, or MAD is small, the forecast is typically close to actual demand; by contrast, a large value indicates the possibility of large forecast errors. The two measures differ in the way they emphasize errors. Large errors get far more weight in MSE and σ because the errors are squared. MAD is a widely used measure of forecast error and is easily understood; it is merely the mean of the forecast errors over a series of time periods, without regard to whether the error was an overestimate or an underestimate.

mean absolute percent error (MAPE)

A measurement that relates the forecast error to the level of demand and is useful for putting forecast performance in the proper perspective.

The **mean absolute percent error (MAPE)** relates the forecast error to the level of demand and is useful for putting forecast performance in the proper perspective:

$$\text{MAPE} = \frac{(\Sigma |E_t|/D_t)\,(100)}{n} \quad \text{(expressed as a percentage)}$$

For example, an absolute forecast error of 100 results in a larger percentage error when the demand is 200 units than when the demand is 10,000 units. MAPE is the best error measure to use when making comparisons between time series for different SKUs.

EXAMPLE 13.6	Calculating Forecast Error Measures

The following table shows the actual sales of upholstered chairs for a furniture manufacturer and the forecasts made for each of the last eight months. Calculate CFE, MSE, σ, MAD, and MAPE for this product.

Month, t	Demand, D_t	Forecast, F_t	Error, E_t	Error, Squared, E_t^2	Absolute Error $|E_t|$	Absolute Percent Error, $(|E_t|/D_t)(100)$
1	200	225	−25	625	25	12.5%
2	240	220	20	400	20	8.3
3	300	285	15	225	15	5.0
4	270	290	−20	400	20	7.4
5	230	250	−20	400	20	8.7
6	260	240	20	400	20	7.7
7	210	250	40	1,600	40	19.0
8	275	240	35	1,225	35	12.7
		Total	−15	5,275	195	81.3%

SOLUTION

Using the formulas for the measures, we get

Cumulative forecast error (bias):

CFE = −15

Average forecast error (mean bias):

$$\bar{E} = \frac{\text{CFE}}{n} = \frac{-15}{8} = -1.875$$

Mean squared error:

$$\text{MSE} = \frac{\Sigma E_t^2}{n} = \frac{5,275}{8} = 659.4$$

Standard deviation:

$$\sigma = \sqrt{\frac{\Sigma[E_t - (-1.875)]^2}{7}} = 27.4$$

Mean absolute deviation:

$$\text{MAD} = \frac{\Sigma|E_t|}{n} = \frac{195}{8} = 24.4$$

Mean absolute percent error:

$$\text{MAPE} = \frac{[\Sigma|E_t|/D_t]\,100}{n} = \frac{81.3\%}{8} = 10.2\%$$

A CFE of −15 indicates that the forecast has a slight bias to overestimate demand. The MSE, σ, and MAD statistics provide measures of forecast error variability. A MAD of 24.4 means that the average forecast error was 24.4 units in absolute value. The value of σ, 27.4, indicates that the sample distribution of forecast errors has a standard deviation of 27.4 units. A MAPE of 10.2 percent implies that, on average, the forecast error was about 10 percent of actual demand. These measures become more reliable as the number of periods of data increases.

DECISION POINT

Although reasonably satisfied with these forecast performance results, the analyst decided to test out a few more forecasting methods before reaching a final forecasting method to use for the future.

Tracking Signals   A **tracking signal** is a measure that indicates whether a method of forecasting is accurately predicting actual changes in demand. The tracking signal measures the number of MADs represented by the cumulative sum of forecast errors, the CFE. The CFE tends to be 0 when a correct forecasting system is being used. At any time, however, random errors can cause the CFE to be a nonzero number. The tracking signal formula is

tracking signal
A measure that indicates whether a method of forecasting is accurately predicting actual changes in demand.

$$\text{Tracking signal} = \frac{\text{CFE}}{\text{MAD}}$$

Each period, the CFE and MAD are updated to reflect current error, and the tracking signal is compared to some predetermined limits. The MAD can be calculated in one of two ways: (1) as the simple average of all absolute errors (as demonstrated in Example 13.6) or (2) as a weighted average determined by the exponential smoothing method:

$$\text{MAD}_t = \alpha|E_t| + (1 - \alpha)\text{MAD}_{t-1}$$

If forecast errors are normally distributed with a mean of 0, the relationship between σ and MAD is simple:

$$\sigma = (\sqrt{\pi/2})(\text{MAD}) \cong 1.25(\text{MAD})$$

$$\text{MAD} = 0.7978\sigma \cong 0.8\sigma$$

where

$$\pi = 3.1416$$

This relationship allows use of the normal probability tables to specify limits for the tracking signal. If the tracking signal falls outside those limits, the forecasting model no longer is tracking demand adequately. A tracking system is useful when forecasting systems are

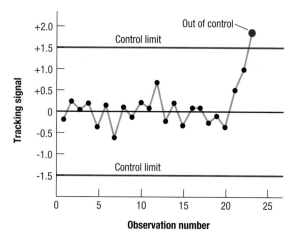

FIGURE 13.7 ▲
Tracking Signal

computerized because it alerts analysts when forecasts are getting far from desirable limits. Figure 13.7 shows tracking signal results for 23 periods plotted on a *control chart*. The control chart is useful for determining whether any action needs to be taken to improve the forecasting model. In the example, the first 20 points cluster around 0, as we would expect if the forecasts are not biased. The CFE will tend toward 0. When the underlying characteristics of demand change but the forecasting model does not, the tracking signal eventually goes out of control. The steady increase after the 20th point in Figure 13.7 indicates that the process is going out of control. The 21st and 22nd points are acceptable, but the 23rd point is not.

Computer Support Computer support, such as from OM Explorer or POM for Windows, makes error calculations easy when evaluating how well forecasting models fit with past data (i.e., the *history file*). They show the various error measures across the entire history file for each method evaluated. They also make forecasts into the future, based on the method selected.

Criteria for Selecting Time-Series Methods

Forecast error measures provide important information for choosing the best forecasting method for a service or product. They also guide managers in selecting the best values for the parameters needed for the method: n for the moving average method, the weights for the weighted moving average method, and α for the exponential smoothing method. The criteria to use in making forecast method and parameter choices include (1) minimizing bias; (2) minimizing MAPE, MAD, or MSE; (3) meeting managerial expectations of changes in the components of demand; and (4) minimizing the forecast error last period. The first two criteria relate to statistical measures based on historical performance, the third reflects expectations of the future that may not be rooted in the past, and the fourth is a way to use whatever method seems to be working best at the time a forecast must be made.

Using Statistical Criteria Statistical performance measures can be used in the selection of a forecasting method. The following guidelines will help when searching for the best time-series models:

1. For projections of more stable demand patterns, use lower α and β values or larger n values to emphasize historical experience.

2. For projections of more dynamic demand patterns using the models covered in this chapter, try higher α and β values or smaller n values. When historical demand patterns are changing, recent history should be emphasized.

Often, the forecaster must make trade-offs between bias (CFE) and the measures of forecast error dispersion (MAPE, MAD, and MSE). Managers also must recognize that the best technique in explaining the past data is not necessarily the best technique to predict the future, and that "overfitting" past data can be deceptive. A forecasting method may have small errors relative to the history file, but may generate high errors for future time periods. For this reason, some analysts prefer to use a **holdout set** as a final test. To do so, they set aside some of the more recent periods from the time series and use only the earlier time periods to develop and test different models. Once the final models have been selected in the first phase, they are tested again with the holdout set. Performance measures, such as MAPE and CFE, would still be used but they would be applied to the holdout sample. Whether this idea is used or not, managers should monitor future forecast errors, perhaps with tracking signals, and modify their forecasting approaches as needed. Maintaining data on forecast performance is the ultimate test of forecasting power—rather than how well a model fits past data or holdout samples.

holdout set

Actual demands from the more recent time periods in the time series, that are set aside to test different models developed from the earlier time periods.

Using Multiple Techniques

We described several individual forecasting methods and showed how to assess their forecast performance. However, we need not rely on a single forecasting method. Several different forecasts can be used to arrive at a final forecast. Initial statistical forecasts using several time-series methods and regression are distributed to knowledgeable individuals, such as marketing directors and sales teams, for their adjustments. They can account for current market and customer conditions that are not necessarily reflected in past data. Multiple forecasts may come from different sales teams, and some teams may have a better record on forecast errors than others. Finally, the collaborative process of CPFR introduces forecasts from customers and even suppliers.

Research during the last two decades suggests that combining forecasts from multiple sources often produces more accurate forecasts. **Combination forecasts** are forecasts that are produced by averaging independent forecasts based on different methods or different data or both. It is intriguing that combination forecasts often perform better over time than even the *best* single forecasting procedure. For example, suppose that the forecast for the next period is 100 units from technique 1 and 120 units from technique 2 and that technique 1 has provided more accurate forecasts to date. The combination forecast for next period, giving equal weight to each technique, is 110 units (or $0.5 \times 100 + 0.5 \times 120$). When this averaging technique is used consistently into the future, its combination forecasts often will be much more accurate than those of any single best forecasting technique (in this example, technique 1). Combining is most effective when the individual forecasts bring different kinds of information into the forecasting process. Forecasters have achieved excellent results by weighting forecasts equally, and this is a good starting point. However, unequal weights may provide better results under some conditions.

OM Explorer and POM for Windows allow you to evaluate several forecasting models, and then you can create combination forecasts from them. The models can be the ones evaluated separately, but they can also include forecasts from the regression, judgment, or naive method. For example, you can create a simple Excel spreadsheet that combines forecasts generated by OM Explorer or POM for Windows to create combination forecasts. To evaluate the judgment method, the forecaster should be given actual demand just one period at a time, preferably as the actual events are happening, and then commit to a forecast for the next period. To be informed, the forecaster should also be aware of how well the other forecasting methods have been performing, particularly in the recent past. Managerial Practice 13.2 describes how Fiskars Brands uses combination forecasts as part of its demand planning system.

Another way to take advantage of multiple techniques is **focus forecasting**, which selects the best forecast (based on past error measures) from a group of forecasts generated by individual techniques. Every period, all techniques are used to make forecasts for each item. The forecasts are made with a computer because there can be 100,000 SKUs at a company, each needing to be forecast. Using the history file as the starting point for each method, the computer generates forecasts for the current period. The forecasts are compared to actual demand, and the method that produces the forecast with the least error is used to make the forecast for the next period. The method used for each item may change from period to period.

combination forecasts

Forecasts that are produced by averaging independent forecasts based on different methods or different data or both.

focus forecasting

A method of forecasting that selects the best forecast from a group of forecasts generated by individual techniques.

PUTTING IT ALL TOGETHER: FORECASTING AS A PROCESS

Forecasting is not just a set of techniques, but instead a process that must be designed and managed. While there is no one process that works for everyone, here we describe a comprehensive process that can be quite effective in managing operations and the supply chain.

A Typical Forecasting Process

Many *inputs* to the forecasting process are informational, beginning with the *history file* on past demand. The history file is kept up-to-date with the actual demands. Clarifying notes and adjustments are made to the database to explain unusual demand behavior, such as the impact of special promotions and closeouts. Often the database is separated into two parts: *base* data and *nonbase* data. The second category reflects irregular demands. Final forecasts just made at the end of the prior cycle are entered in the history file, so as to track forecast errors. Other information sources are from salesforce estimates, outstanding bids on new orders, booked orders, market research studies, competitor behavior, economic outlook, new product introductions, pricing, and promotions. If CPFR is used, considerable information sharing will take place with customers and suppliers. For new products, a history database is fabricated based on the firm's experience with prior products and the judgment of personnel.

Outputs of the process are forecasts for multiple time periods into the future. Typically they are on a monthly basis and are projected out from six months to two years. Most software packages have the ability to "roll up" or "aggregate" forecasts for individual stock-keeping units (SKUs) into forecasts for whole product families. Forecasts can also be "blown down" or "disaggregated" into smaller pieces. In a make-to-stock environment, forecasts tend to be more detailed and can get down to specific individual products. In a

MANAGERIAL PRACTICE 13.2 | Combination Forecasts and the Forecasting Process

Fiskars Brands, Inc., totally overhauled its forecasting process. It serves 2,000 customers ranging from large discounters to local craft stores providing about 2,300 finished SKUs. Its parent company, Fiskars Corporation, is the second oldest incorporated entity in the world and produces a variety of high-quality products such as garden shears, pruners, hand tools, scissors for preschoolers, ratchet tools, screwdrivers, and the like. Business is highly seasonal and prices quite variable. About 10 percent to 15 percent of the annual revenue comes from one-time promotions, and 25 percent to 35 percent of its products are new every year.

It introduced a statistical-based analysis along with a Web-based business intelligence tool for reporting. It put much more emphasis on combination forecasts. Instead of asking members of the sales staff to provide their own forecasts, forecasts were sent to them, and they were asked for their validation and refinement. Their inputs are most useful relative to additions, deletions, and promotions. Converting multiple forecasts into one number (forecasts from time-series techniques, sales input, and customer input) creates more accurate forecasts by SKU. Fiskars's software has the ability to weigh each input. It gives more weight to a statistical forecast for in-line items, and inputs from the sales staff get much more weight for promoted products and new items.

It also segments SKUs by value and forecastability so as to focus forecasting efforts on SKUs that have the biggest impact on the business. High-value items ("A" items identified with ABC analysis in Chapter 12, "Managing Inventories") that also have high forecastability (stable demand with low forecast errors to date) tend to do well with the time-series techniques, and judgmental adjustments are made with caution. High-value items with low forecastability get top priority in the forecasting effort, such as with CPFR. Much less attention is given to improving forecasts for "C" items for which there is some history and fairly steady demand.

Finally, Fiskars instituted a Web-based program that gives the entire company visibility to forecast information in whatever form it needs. For example, Finance wants monthly, quarterly, and yearly projections in dollars, whereas Operations wants projections in units as well as accuracy measures. Everybody can track updated forecast information by customer, brand, and SKU.

This power-point bypass pruner is one of 2,300 SKUs for which Fiskars Brands needs demand forecasts. Sales are quite seasonal and one-time promotions can be a factor. This garden tool is especially designed for people with limited hand strength. Combination forecasts that modify statistical forecasts with judgmental inputs from the sales staff improved their forecasting process.

Sources: David Montgomery, "Flashpoints for Changing Your Forecasting Process," *The Journal of Business Forecasting*, (Winter 2006–2007), pp. 35–37; http://www.fiskars.com, July 6, 2008.

make-to-order environment, the forecasts tend to be for groups of products. Similarly, if the lead times to buy raw materials and manufacture a product or provide a service are long, the forecasts go further out into the future.

The forecast process itself, typically done on a monthly basis, consists of structured steps. These steps often are facilitated by someone who might be called a demand manager, forecast analyst, or demand/supply planner. However, many other people are typically involved before the plan for the month is authorized.

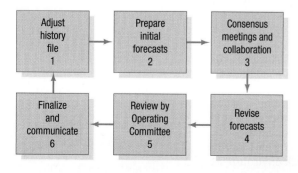

Step 1. The cycle begins mid-month just after the forecasts have been finalized and communicated to the stakeholders. Now is the time to update the history file and review forecast accuracy. At the end of the month, enter actual demand and review forecast accuracy.

Step 2. Prepare initial forecasts using some forecasting software package and judgment. Adjust the parameters of the software to find models that fit the past demand well and yet reflect the demand manager's judgment on irregular events and information about future sales pulled from various sources and business units.

Step 3. Hold consensus meetings with the stakeholders, such as marketing, sales, supply chain planners, and finance. Make it easy for business unit and field sales personnel to make inputs. Use the Internet to get collaborative information from key customers and suppliers. The goal is to arrive at consensus forecasts from all of the important players.

Step 4. Revise the forecasts using judgment, considering the inputs from the consensus meetings and collaborative sources.

Step 5. Present the forecasts to the operating committee for review and to reach a final set of forecasts. It is important to have a set of forecasts that everybody agrees upon and will work to support.

Step 6. Finalize the forecasts based on the decisions of the operating committee and communicate them to the important stakeholders. Supply chain planners are usually the biggest users.

As with all work activity, forecasting is a process and should be continually reviewed for improvements. A better process will foster better relationships between departments such as marketing, sales, and operations. It will also produce better forecasts. This principle is the first one in Table 13.2 to guide process improvements.

Forecasting as a Nested Process

Forecasting is not a stand-alone activity, but instead part of a larger process that encompasses the remaining chapters. After all, demand is only half of the equation—the other half is supply. Future plans must be developed to supply the resources needed to meet the forecasted demand. Resources include the workforce, materials, inventories, dollars, and equipment capacity. Making sure that demand and supply plans are in balance begins in the next chapter, Chapter 14, "Planning and Scheduling Operations" and continues with Chapter 15, "Planning Sufficient Resources."

TABLE 13.2	SOME PRINCIPLES FOR THE FORECASTING PROCESS

- Better processes yield better forecasts.
- Demand forecasting is being done in virtually every company, either formally or informally. The challenge is to do it well—better than the competition.
- Better forecasts result in better customer service and lower costs, as well as better relationships with suppliers and customers.
- The forecast can and must make sense based on the big picture, economic outlook, market share, and so on.
- The best way to improve forecast accuracy is to focus on reducing forecast error.
- Bias is the worst kind of forecast error; strive for zero bias.
- Whenever possible, forecast at more aggregate levels. Forecast in detail only where necessary.
- Far more can be gained by people collaborating and communicating well than by using the most advanced forecasting technique or model.

Source: Adapted from Thomas F. Wallace and Robert A. Stahl, *Sales Forecasting: A New Approach* (Cincinnati, OH: T. E. Wallace & Company, 2002), p. 112.

INTERNET RESOURCES

my**om**lab and the Companion Website at **www.pearsonglobaleditions.com/krajewski** contain many tools, activities, and resources designed for this chapter.

KEY EQUATIONS

1. Linear regression: $Y = a + bX$
2. Naive forecasting: Forecast = D_t
3. Simple moving average:
$$F_{t+1} = \frac{D_t + D_{t-1} + D_{t-2} + \cdots + D_{t-n+1}}{n}$$

4. Weighted moving average:

$$F_{t+1} = \text{Weight}_1(D_t) + \text{Weight}_2(D_{t-1}) +$$
$$\text{Weight}_3(D_{t-2}) + \cdots + \text{Weight}_n(D_{t-n+1})$$

5. Exponential smoothing:

$$F_{t+1} = \alpha D_t + (1-\alpha)F_t$$

$$F_{t+1} = F_t + \alpha(D_t - F_t)$$

6. Trend-adjusted exponential smoothing:

$$A_t = \alpha D_t + (1-\alpha)(A_{t-1}+T_{t-1})$$

$$T_t = \beta(A_t - A_{t-1}) + (1-\beta)T_{t-1}$$

$$F_{t+1} = A_t + T_t$$

7. Forecast error:

$$E_t = D_t - F_t$$
$$\text{CFE} = \Sigma E_t$$
$$\bar{E} = \frac{\text{CFE}}{n}$$
$$\text{MSE} = \frac{\Sigma E_t^2}{n}$$
$$\sigma = \sqrt{\frac{\Sigma(E_t-\bar{E})^2}{n-1}}$$
$$\text{MAD} = \frac{\Sigma|E_t|}{n}$$
$$\text{MAPE} = \frac{(\Sigma|E_t|/D_t)(100\%)}{n}$$

8. Tracking signal: $\dfrac{\text{CFE}}{\text{MAD}}$ or $\dfrac{\text{CFE}}{\text{MAD}_t}$

9. Exponentially smoothed error:

$$\text{MAD}_t = \alpha|E_t| + (1-\alpha)\text{MAD}_{t-1}$$

KEY TERMS

additive seasonal method 497
aggregation 485
causal methods 486
collaborative planning, forecasting, and replenishment (CPFR) 486
combination forecasts 501
cumulative sum of forecast errors (CFE) 497
Delphi method 487
dependent variable 488
executive opinion 487
exponential smoothing method 492

focus forecasting 501
forecast 484
forecast error 491
holdout set 500
independent variables 488
judgment methods 486
linear regression 488
market research 487
mean absolute deviation (MAD) 498
mean absolute percent error (MAPE) 498
mean squared error (MSE) 498

multiplicative seasonal method 496
naive forecast 490
salesforce estimates 486
simple moving average method 491
standard deviation (σ) 498
technological forecasting 487
time series 484
time-series analysis 486
tracking signal 499
trend-adjusted exponential smoothing method 493
weighted moving average method 492

SOLVED PROBLEM 1

The monthly demand for units manufactured by the Acme Rocket Company has been as follows:

Month	Units	Month	Units
May	100	September	105
June	80	October	110
July	110	November	125
August	115	December	120

a. Use the exponential smoothing method to forecast the number of units for June to January. The initial forecast for May was 105 units; $\alpha = 0.2$.

b. Calculate the absolute percentage error for each month from June through December and the MAD and MAPE of forecast error as of the end of December.

c. Calculate the tracking signal as of the end of December. What can you say about the performance of your forecasting method?

SOLUTION

a.

Current Month, t	Calculating Forecast for <u>Next</u> Month $F_{t+1} = \alpha D_t + (1-\alpha) F_t$	Forecast for Month $t + 1$
May	$0.2(100) + 0.8(105) = 104.0$ or 104	June
June	$0.2(80) + 0.8(104.0) = 99.2$ or 99	July
July	$0.2(110) + 0.8(99.2) = 101.4$ or 101	August
August	$0.2(115) + 0.8(101.4) = 104.1$ or 104	September
September	$0.2(105) + 0.8(104.1) = 104.3$ or 104	October
October	$0.2(110) + 0.8(104.3) = 105.4$ or 105	November
November	$0.2(125) + 0.8(105.4) = 109.3$ or 109	December
December	$0.2(120) + 0.8(109.3) = 111.4$ or 111	January

b.

Month, t	Actual Demand, D_t	Forecast, F_t	Error, $E_t = D_t - F_t$	Absolute Error, $|E_t|$	Absolute Percentage Error, $(|E_t|/D_t)$ (100%)
June	80	104	−24	24	30.0%
July	110	99	11	11	10.0
August	115	101	14	14	12.0
September	105	104	1	1	1.0
October	110	104	6	6	5.5
November	125	105	20	0	16.0
December	<u>120</u>	109	<u>11</u>	<u>11</u>	<u>9.2</u>
Total	765		39	87	83.7%

$$\text{MAD} = \frac{\Sigma |E_t|}{n} = \frac{87}{7} = 12.4 \text{ and } \text{MAPE} = \frac{(\Sigma |E_t|/D_t)(100)}{n} = \frac{83.7\%}{7} = 11.96\%$$

c. As of the end of December, the cumulative sum of forecast errors (CFE) is 39. Using the mean absolute deviation calculated in part (b), we calculate the tracking signal:

$$\text{Tracking signal} = \frac{\text{CFE}}{\text{MAD}} = \frac{39}{12.4} = 3.14$$

The probability that a tracking signal value of 3.14 could be generated completely by chance is small. Consequently, we should revise our approach. The long string of forecasts lower than actual demand suggests use of a trend method.

SOLVED PROBLEM 2

The Polish General's Pizza Parlor is a small restaurant catering to patrons with a taste for European pizza. One of its specialties is Polish Prize pizza. The manager must forecast weekly demand for these special pizzas so that he can order pizza shells weekly. Recently, demand has been as follows:

Week	Pizzas	Week	Pizzas
June 2	50	June 23	56
June 9	65	June 30	55
June 16	52	July 7	60

a. Forecast the demand for pizza for June 23 to July 14 by using the simple moving average method with $n = 3$. Then repeat the forecast by using the weighted moving average method with $n = 3$ and weights of 0.50, 0.30, and 0.20, with 0.50 applying to the most recent demand.

b. Calculate the MAD for each method.

SOLUTION

a. The simple moving average method and the weighted moving average method give the following results:

Current Week	Simple Moving Average Forecast for Next Week	Weighted Moving Average Forecast for Next Week
June 16	$\dfrac{52 + 65 + 50}{3} = 55.7$ or 56	$[(0.5 \times 52) + (0.3 \times 65) + (0.2 \times 50)] = 55.5$ or 56
June 23	$\dfrac{56 + 52 + 65}{3} = 57.7$ or 58	$[(0.5 \times 56) + (0.3 \times 52) + (0.2 \times 65)] = 56.6$ or 57
June 30	$\dfrac{55 + 56 + 52}{3} = 54.3$ or 54	$[(0.5 \times 55) + (0.3 \times 56) + (0.2 \times 52)] = 54.7$ or 55
July 7	$\dfrac{60 + 55 + 56}{3} = 57.0$ or 57	$[(0.5 \times 60) + (0.3 \times 55) + (0.2 \times 56)] = 57.7$ or 58

Forecasts in each row are for the next week's demand. For example, the simple moving average and weighted moving average forecasts (both are 56 units) calculated after learning the demand on June 16 apply to June 23's demand forecast.

b. The mean absolute deviation is calculated as follows:

Week	Actual Demand	Simple Moving Average		Weighted Moving Average	
		Forecast for This Week	Absolute Errors $\lvert E_t \rvert$	Forecast for This Week	Absolute Errors $\lvert E_t \rvert$
June 23	56	56	$\lvert 56 - 56 \rvert = 0$	56	$\lvert 56 - 56 \rvert = 0$
June 30	55	58	$\lvert 55 - 58 \rvert = 3$	57	$\lvert 55 - 57 \rvert = 2$
July 7	60	54	$\lvert 60 - 54 \rvert = 6$	55	$\lvert 60 - 55 \rvert = 5$
			$\text{MAD} = \dfrac{0 + 3 + 6}{3} = 3.0$		$\text{MAD} = \dfrac{0 + 2 + 5}{3} = 2.3$

For this limited set of data, the weighted moving average method resulted in a slightly lower mean absolute deviation. However, final conclusions can be made only after analyzing much more data.

SOLVED PROBLEM 3

Chicken Palace periodically offers carryout five-piece chicken dinners at special prices. Let Y be the number of dinners sold and X be the price. Based on the historical observations and calculations in the following table, determine the regression equation, correlation coefficient, and coefficient of determination. How many dinners can Chicken Palace expect to sell at $3.00 each?

Observation	Price (X)	Dinners Sold (Y)
1	$ 2.70	760
2	$ 3.50	510
3	$ 2.00	980
4	$ 4.20	250
5	$ 3.10	320
6	$ 4.05	480
Total	$19.55	3,300
Average	$ 3.258	550

SOLUTION

We use the computer to calculate the best values of a, b, the correlation coefficient, and the coefficient of determination.

$$a = 1{,}454.60$$
$$b = -277.63$$
$$r = -0.84$$
$$r^2 = 0.71$$

The regression line is

$$Y = a + bX = 1{,}454.60 - 277.63X$$

The correlation coefficient ($r = -0.84$) shows a negative correlation between the variables. The coefficient of determination ($r^2 = 0.71$) is relatively small, which suggests that other variables (in addition to price) might appreciably affect sales.

If the regression equation is satisfactory to the manager, estimated sales at a price of $3.00 per dinner may be calculated as follows:

$$Y = a + bX = 1,454.60 - 277.63(3.00)$$

$$= 621.71 \text{ or } 622 \text{ dinners}$$

SOLVED PROBLEM 4

The Northville Post Office experiences a seasonal pattern of daily mail volume every week. The following data for two representative weeks are expressed in thousands of pieces of mail:

Day	Week 1	Week 2
Sunday	5	8
Monday	20	15
Tuesday	30	32
Wednesday	35	30
Thursday	49	45
Friday	70	70
Saturday	15	10
Total	224	210

a. Calculate a seasonal factor for each day of the week.

b. If the postmaster estimates 230,000 pieces of mail to be sorted next week, forecast the volume for each day of the week.

SOLUTION

a. Calculate the average daily mail volume for each week. Then for each day of the week divide the mail volume by the week's average to get the seasonal factor. Finally, for each day, add the two seasonal factors and divide by 2 to obtain the average seasonal factor to use in the forecast (see part [b]).

Day	Week 1 Mail Volume	Week 1 Seasonal Factor (1)	Week 2 Mail Volume	Week 2 Seasonal Factor (2)	Average Seasonal Factor [(1) + (2)]/2
Sunday	5	5/32 = 0.15625	8	8/30 = 0.26667	0.21146
Monday	20	20/32 = 0.62500	15	15/30 = 0.50000	0.56250
Tuesday	30	30/32 = 0.93750	32	32/30 = 1.06667	1.00209
Wednesday	35	35/32 = 1.09375	30	30/30 = 1.00000	1.04688
Thursday	49	49/32 = 1.53125	45	45/30 = 1.50000	1.51563
Friday	70	70/32 = 2.18750	70	70/30 = 2.33333	2.26042
Saturday	15	15/32 = 0.46875	10	10/30 = 0.33333	0.40104
Total	224		210		
Average	224/7 = 32		210/7 = 30		

b. The average daily mail volume is expected to be 230,000/7 = 32,857 pieces of mail. Using the average seasonal factors calculated in part (a), we obtain the following forecasts:

Day	Calculation	Forecast
Sunday	0.21146(32,857) =	6,948
Monday	0.56250(32,857) =	18,482
Tuesday	1.00209(32,857) =	32,926
Wednesday	1.04688(32,857) =	34,397
Thursday	1.51563(32,857) =	49,799
Friday	2.26042(32,857) =	74,271
Saturday	0.40104(32,857) =	13,177
	Total	230,000

DISCUSSION QUESTIONS

1. Kay and Michael Passe publish *What's Happening?*—a biweekly newspaper to publicize local events. *What's Happening?* has few subscribers; it typically is sold at checkout stands. Much of the revenue comes from advertisers of garage sales and supermarket specials. In an effort to reduce costs associated with printing too many papers or delivering them to the wrong location, Michael implemented a computerized system to collect sales data. Sales-counter scanners accurately record sales data for each location. Since the system was implemented, total sales volume has steadily declined. Selling advertising space and maintaining shelf space at supermarkets are getting more difficult.

   Reduced revenue makes controlling costs all the more important. For each issue, Michael carefully makes a forecast based on sales data collected at each location. Then he orders papers to be printed and distributed in quantities matching the forecast. Michael's forecast reflects a downward trend, which *is* present in the sales data. Now only a few papers are left over at only a few locations. Although the sales forecast accurately predicts the actual sales at most locations, *What's Happening?* is spiraling toward oblivion. Kay suspects that Michael is doing something wrong in preparing the forecast but can find no mathematical errors. Tell her what is happening.

2. Figure 13.8 shows summer air visibility measurements for Denver, Colorado. The acceptable visibility standard is 100, with readings above 100 indicating clean air and good visibility, and readings below 100 indicating temperature inversions caused by forest fires, volcanic eruptions, or collisions with comets.

   a. Is a trend evident in the data? Which time-series techniques might be appropriate for estimating the average of these data?

   b. A medical center for asthma and respiratory diseases located in Denver has great demand for its services when air quality is poor. If you were in charge of developing a short-term (say, three-day) forecast of

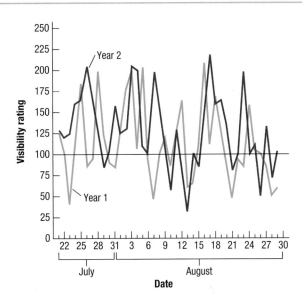

▲ **FIGURE 13.8**

visibility, which causal factor(s) would you analyze? In other words, which external factors hold the potential to significantly affect visibility in the *short term*?

   c. Tourism, an important factor in Denver's economy, is affected by the city's image. Air quality, as measured by visibility, affects the city's image. If you were responsible for development of tourism, which causal factor(s) would you analyze to forecast visibility for the *medium term* (say, the next two summers)?

   d. The U.S. government threatens to withhold several hundred million dollars in Department of Transportation funds unless Denver meets visibility standards within eight years. How would you proceed to generate a *long-term* judgment forecast of technologies that will be available to improve visibility in the next 10 years?

PROBLEMS

Software, such as OM Explorer, Active Models, and POM for Windows, is available in my**om**lab. Check with your instructor on how best to use it. In many cases, the instructor wants you to understand how to do the calculations by hand. At most, the software provides a check on your calculations. When calculations are particularly complex and the goal is interpreting the results in making decisions, the software replaces entirely the manual calculations.

1. A convenience store recently started to carry a new brand of soft drink in its territory. Management is interested in estimating future sales volume to determine whether it should continue to carry the new brand or replace it with another brand. At the end of April, the average monthly sales volume of the new soft drink was 700 cans and the trend was +50 cans per month. The actual sales volume figures for May, June, and July are 760, 800, and 820, respectively. Use trend-adjusted exponential smoothing with $\alpha = 0.2$ and $\beta = 0.1$ to forecast usage for June, July, and August.

2. Sales for the past 12 months at Dalworth Company are given here.

Month	Sales ($ millions)	Month	Sales ($millions)
January	20	July	53
February	24	August	62
March	27	September	54
April	31	October	36
May	37	November	32
June	47	December	29

   a. Use a three-month moving average to forecast the sales for the months May through December.

   b. Use a four-month moving average to forecast the sales for the months May through December.

   c. Compare the performance of the two methods by using the mean absolute deviation as the performance criterion. Which method would you recommend?

   d. Compare the performance of the two methods by using the mean absolute percent error as the performance criterion. Which method would you recommend?

   e. Compare the performance of the two methods by using the mean squared error as the performance criterion. Which method would you recommend?

3. Consider the sales data for Dalworth Company given in Problem 2.

   a. Use a three-month weighted moving average to forecast the sales for the months April through December. Use weights of (3/6), (2/6), and (1/6), giving more weight to more recent data.

   b. Use exponential smoothing with $\alpha = 0.6$ to forecast the sales for the months April through December. Assume that the initial forecast for January was $20 million. Start error measurement in April.

   c. Compare the performance of the two methods by using the mean absolute deviation as the performance criterion, with error measurement beginning in April. Which method would you recommend?

   d. Compare the performance of the two methods by using the mean absolute percent error as the performance criterion, with error measurement beginning in April. Which method would you recommend?

   e. Compare the performance of the two methods by using the mean squared error as the performance criterion, with error measurement beginning in April. Which method would you recommend?

4. Karl's Copiers sells and repairs photocopy machines. The manager needs weekly forecasts of service calls so that he can schedule service personnel. Use the actual demand in the first period for the forecast for the first week so error measurement begins in the second week. The manager uses exponential smoothing with $\alpha = 0.20$. Forecast the number of calls for week 6, which is next week.

Week	Actual Service Calls
1	24
2	32
3	36
4	23
5	25

5. The owner of a computer store rents printers to some of her preferred customers. She is interested in arriving at a forecast of rentals so that she can order the correct quantities of supplies that go with the printers. Data for the last 10 weeks are shown here.

Week	Rentals	Week	Rentals
1	23	6	28
2	24	7	32
3	32	8	35
4	26	9	26
5	31	10	24

   a. Prepare a forecast for weeks 6 through 10 by using a five-week moving average. What is the forecast for week 11?

   b. Calculate the mean absolute deviation as of the end of week 10.

6. Community Federal Bank in Dothan, Alabama, recently installed a new automatic teller machine to perform the standard banking services and handle loan applications

and investment transactions. The new machine is a bit complicated to use, so management is interested in tracking its past use and projecting its future use. Additional machines may be needed if projected use is high enough.

At the end of April, the average monthly use was 600 customers and the trend was +60 customers per month. The actual use figures for May, June, and July are 680, 710, and 790, respectively. Use trend-adjusted exponential smoothing with $\alpha = 0.3$ and $\beta = 0.2$ to forecast usage for June, July, and August.

7. Forrest and Dan make boxes of chocolates for which the demand is uncertain. Forrest says, "That's life." On the other hand, Dan believes that some demand patterns exist that could be useful for planning the purchase of sugar, chocolate, and shrimp. Forrest insists on placing a surprise chocolate-covered shrimp in some boxes so that "You never know what you'll get." Quarterly demand (in boxes of chocolates) for the last three years follows:

Quarter	Year 1	Year 2	Year 3
1	3,000	3,300	3,502
2	1,700	2,100	2,448
3	900	1,500	1,768
4	4,400	5,100	5,882
Total	10,000	12,000	13,600

a. Use intuition and judgment to estimate quarterly demand for the fourth year.

b. If the expected sales for chocolates are 14,800 cases for year 4, use the multiplicative seasonal method to prepare a forecast for each quarter of the year. Are any of the quarterly forecasts different from what you thought you would get in part (a)?

8. The demand for Krispee Crunchies, a favorite breakfast cereal of people born in the 1940s, is experiencing a decline. The company wants to monitor demand for this product closely as it nears the end of its life cycle. The trend-adjusted exponential smoothing method is used with $\alpha = 0.1$ and $\beta = 0.2$. At the end of December, the updated estimate for the average number of cases sold per month, A_t, was 900,000 and the updated trend, T_t, was –50,000 per month. The following table shows the actual sales history for January, February, and March. Generate forecasts for February, March, and April.

Month	Sales
January	890,000
February	800,000
March	825,000

9. The following data are for calculator sales in units at an electronics store over the past five weeks:

Week	Sales
1	46
2	49
3	43
4	50
5	53

Use trend-adjusted exponential smoothing with $\alpha = 0.2$ and $\beta = 0.2$ to forecast sales for weeks 3 through 6. Assume that the average of the time series was 45 units and that the average trend was +2 units per week just before week 1.

10. The number of heart surgeries performed at Heartville General Hospital has increased steadily over the past several years. The hospital's administration is seeking the best method to forecast the demand for such surgeries in year 6. The data for the past five years are shown.

Year	Demand
1	45
2	50
3	52
4	56
5	8

The hospital's administration is considering the following forecasting methods. Begin error measurement in year 3, so all methods are compared for the same years.

i. Exponential smoothing, with $\alpha = 0.6$. Let the initial forecast for year 1 be 45, the same as the actual demand.

ii. Exponential smoothing, with $\alpha = 0.9$. Let the initial forecast for year 1 be 45, the same as the actual demand.

iii. Trend-adjusted exponential smoothing, with $\alpha = 0.6$ and $\beta = 0.1$. Use the actual demand for year 1 for the initial average for the first year and 0 for the initial trend.

iv. Two-year moving average.

v. Two-year weighted moving average, using weights 0.6 and 0.4, with more recent data given more weight.

vi. Regression model, $Y = 42.6 + 3.2X$, where Y is the number of surgeries and X is the index for the year (e.g., $X = 1$ for year 1, $X = 2$ for year 2, and so forth).

a. If MAD is the performance criterion chosen by the administration, which forecasting method should it choose?

b. If MSE is the performance criterion chosen by the administration, which forecasting method should it choose?

c. If MAPE is the performance criterion chosen by the administration, which forecasting method should it choose?

11. Ohio Swiss Milk Products manufactures and distributes ice cream in Ohio, Kentucky, and West Virginia. The company wants to expand operations by locating another plant in northern Ohio. The size of the new plant will be a function of the expected demand for ice cream within the area served by the plant. A market survey is currently under way to determine that demand.

    Ohio Swiss wants to estimate the relationship between the manufacturing cost per gallon and the number of gallons sold in a year to determine the demand for ice cream and, thus, the size of the new plant. The following data have been collected:

    a. Develop a regression equation to forecast the cost per gallon as a function of the number of gallons produced.

    b. What are the correlation coefficient and the coefficient of determination? Comment on your regression equation in light of these measures.

    c. Suppose that the market survey indicates a demand of 325,000 gallons in the Bucyrus, Ohio, area. Estimate the manufacturing cost per gallon for a plant producing 325,000 gallons per year.

Plant	Cost per Thousand Gallons (Y)	Thousands of Gallons Sold (X)
1	$ 1,015	416.9
2	973	472.5
3	1,046	250.0
4	1,006	372.1
5	1,058	238.1
6	1,068	258.6
7	967	597.0
8	997	414.0
9	1,044	263.2
10	1,008	372.0
Total	$10,182	3,654.4

12. At a hydrocarbon processing factory, process control involves periodic analysis of samples for a certain process quality parameter. The analytic procedure currently used is costly and time consuming. A faster and more economical alternative procedure has been proposed. However, the numbers for the quality parameter given by the alternative procedure are somewhat different from those given by the current procedure, not because of any inherent errors but because of changes in the nature of the chemical analysis.

Management believes that if the numbers from the new procedure can be used to forecast reliably the corresponding numbers from the current procedure, switching to the new procedure would be reasonable and cost effective. The following data were obtained for the quality parameter by analyzing samples using both procedures:

Current (Y)	Proposed (X)	Current (Y)	Proposed (X)
3.0	3.1	3.1	3.1
3.1	3.9	2.7	2.9
3.0	3.4	3.3	3.6
3.6	4.0	3.2	4.1
3.8	3.6	2.1	2.6
2.7	3.6	3.0	3.1
2.7	3.6	2.6	2.8

a. Use linear regression to find a relation to forecast Y, which is the quality parameter from the current procedure, using the values from the proposed procedure, X.

b. Is there a strong relationship between Y and X? Explain.

13. Demand for oil changes at Garcia's Garage has been as follows:

Month	Number of Oil Changes
January	41
February	46
March	57
April	52
May	59
June	51
July	60
August	62

a. Use simple linear regression analysis to develop a forecasting model for monthly demand. In this application, the dependent variable, Y, is monthly demand and the independent variable, X, is the month. For January, let $X = 1$; for February, let $X = 2$; and so on.

b. Use the model to forecast demand for September, October, and November. Here, $X = 9$, 10, and 11, respectively.

14. The manager of a utility company in the Texas panhandle wants to develop quarterly forecasts of power loads for the next year. The power loads are seasonal, and the data on the quarterly loads in megawatts (MW) for the last four years are as follows:

Quarter	Year 1	Year 2	Year 3	Year 4
1	103.5	94.7	118.6	109.3
2	126.1	116.0	141.2	131.6
3	144.5	137.1	159.0	149.5
4	166.1	152.5	178.2	169.0

The manager estimates the total demand for the next year at 600 MW. Use the multiplicative seasonal method to develop the forecast for each quarter.

15. The manager of Snyder's Garden Center must make the annual purchasing plans for rakes, gloves, and other gardening items. One of the items the company stocks is Fast-Grow, a liquid fertilizer. The sales of this item are seasonal, with peaks in the spring, summer, and fall months. Quarterly demand (in cases) for the past two years follows:

Quarter	Year 1	Year 2
1	40	60
2	350	440
3	290	320
4	210	280
Total	890	1,100

If the expected sales for Fast-Grow are 1,150 cases for year 3, use the multiplicative seasonal method to prepare a forecast for each quarter of the year.

ADVANCED PROBLEMS

16. The director of a large public library must schedule employees to reshelve books and periodicals checked out of the library. The number of items checked out will determine the labor requirements. The following data reflect the number of items checked out of the library for the past three years:

Month	Year 1	Year 2	Year 3
January	1,847	2,045	1,986
February	2,669	2,321	2,564
March	2,467	2,419	2,635
April	2,432	2,088	2,150
May	2,464	2,667	2,201
June	2,378	2,122	2,663
July	2,217	2,206	2,055
August	2,445	1,869	1,678
September	1,894	2,441	1,845
October	1,922	2,291	2,065
November	2,431	2,364	2,147
December	2,274	2,189	2,451

The director needs a time-series method for forecasting the number of items to be checked out during the next month. Find the best simple moving average forecast you can. Decide what is meant by "best" and justify your decision.

17. The past demands at a medical clinic follow:

Week	Demand	Week	Demand
1	400	15	383
2	380	16	402
3	411	17	387
4	415	18	410
5	393	19	398
6	375	20	433
7	410	21	415
8	395	22	380
9	406	23	394
10	424	24	412
11	433	25	439
12	391	26	416
13	396	27	395
14	417	28	419

The clinic's administration is considering the following forecasting methods. Use OM Explorer or POM for Windows to evaluate each one. Start error measurement in the fourth week, so all methods are evaluated over the same periods.

(i) Naive (1-Period Moving Average)

(ii) 3-Period Weighted Moving Average, using weights of 0.70, 0.20, and 0.10, with more recent data given more weight

(iii) Exponential smoothing, with $\alpha = 0.10$

(iv) Trend-adjusted exponential smoothing, with $\alpha = 0.10$ and $\beta = 0.10$. Use 400 for the initial average and an initial trend of 0.

a. If CFE (or mean bias) is the performance criterion chosen by the administration, which forecasting method should it choose?

b. If MAD is the performance criterion chosen by the administration, which forecasting method should it choose?

c. If MSE is the performance criterion chosen by the administration, which forecasting method should it choose?

d. If MAPE is the performance criterion chosen by the administration, which forecasting method should it choose?

18. Create an Excel spreadsheet on your own that can create a combination forecast for Problem 17, using the three techniques that seem best based on MAD. Give equal weight to each technique. Calculate MAD for the combination forecast. Is it better or worse than the forecasting techniques identified in Problem 17?

19. Using the data in Problem 16, find the best trend-adjusted exponential smoothing solution you can. Compare the performance of this method with those of the best moving average method and the exponential smoothing method. Which of the three methods would you choose?

20. Using the data in Problem 16, find the best exponential smoothing solution you can. Justify your choice.

21. Cannister, Inc., specializes in the manufacture of plastic containers. The data on the monthly sales of 10-ounce shampoo bottles for the past five years are as follows:

Year	1	2	3	4	5
January	742	741	896	951	1,030
February	697	700	793	861	1,032
March	776	774	885	938	1,126
April	898	932	1,055	1,109	1,285
May	1,030	1,099	1,204	1,274	1,468
June	1,107	1,223	1,326	1,422	1,637
July	1,165	1,290	1,303	1,486	1,611
August	1,216	1,349	1,436	1,555	1,608
September	1,208	1,341	1,473	1,604	1,528
October	1,131	1,296	1,453	1,600	1,420
November	971	1,066	1,170	1,403	1,119
December	783	901	1,023	1,209	1,013

a. Using the multiplicative seasonal method, calculate the monthly seasonal indices.

b. Develop a simple linear regression equation to forecast annual sales. For this regression, the dependent variable, Y, is the demand in each year and the independent variable, X, is the index for the year (i.e., $X = 1$ for year 1, $X = 2$ for year 2, and so on until $X = 5$ for year 5).

c. Forecast the annual sales for year 6 by using the regression model you developed in part (b).

d. Prepare the seasonal forecast for each month by using the monthly seasonal indices calculated in part (a).

22. A certain food item at P&Q Supermarkets has the demand pattern shown in the table at the bottom of the next page. Find the "best" forecast you can for month 25 and justify your methodology. You may use some of the data to find the best parameter value(s) for your method and the rest to test the forecast model. Your justification should include both quantitative and qualitative considerations.

Month	Demand	Month	Demand
1	33	13	37
2	37	14	43
3	31	15	56
4	39	16	41
5	54	17	36
6	38	18	39
7	42	19	41
8	40	20	58
9	41	21	42
10	54	22	45
11	43	23	41
12	39	24	38

23. The Midwest Computer Company serves a large number of businesses in the Great Lakes region. The company sells supplies and replacements and performs service on all computers sold through seven sales offices. Many items are stocked, so close inventory control is necessary to assure customers of efficient service. Recently, business has been increasing, and management is concerned about stockouts. A forecasting method is needed to estimate requirements several months in advance so that adequate replenishment quantities can be purchased. An example of the sales growth experienced during the last 50 months is the growth in demand for item EP-37, a laser printer cartridge, shown in Table 13.3.

a. Develop a trend-adjusted exponential smoothing solution using POM for Windows for forecasting demand. Find the "best" parameters and justify your choices. Forecast demand for month 51.

b. A consultant to Midwest's management suggested that new office building leases would be a good leading indicator for company sales. The consultant quoted a recent university

TABLE 13.3 | EP-37 SALES AND LEASE DATA

Month	EP-37 Sales	Leases	Month	EP-37 Sales	Leases
1	80	32	26	1,296	281
2	132	29	27	1,199	298
3	143	32	28	1,267	314
4	180	54	29	1,300	323
5	200	53	30	1,370	309
6	168	89	31	1,489	343
7	212	74	32	1,499	357
8	254	93	33	1,669	353
9	397	120	34	1,716	360
10	385	113	35	1,603	370
11	472	147	36	1,812	386
12	397	126	37	1,817	389
13	476	138	38	1,798	399
14	699	145	39	1,873	409
15	545	160	40	1,923	410
16	837	196	41	2,028	413
17	743	180	42	2,049	439
18	722	197	43	2,084	454
19	735	203	44	2,083	441
20	838	223	45	2,121	470
21	1,057	247	46	2,072	469
22	930	242	47	2,262	490
23	1,085	234	48	2,371	496
24	1,090	254	49	2,309	509
25	1,218	271	50	2,422	522

study finding that new office building leases precede office equipment and supply sales by three months. According to the study findings, leases in month 1 would affect sales in month 4, leases in month 2 would affect sales in month 5, and so on. Use POM for Windows' linear regression module to develop a forecasting model for sales, with leases as the independent variable. Forecast sales for month 51.

c. Which of the two models provides better forecasts? Explain.

24. The materials handling manager of a manufacturing company is trying to forecast the cost of maintenance for the company's fleet of over-the-road tractors. The manager believes that the cost of maintaining the tractors increases with their age. The following data was collected:

Age (years)	Yearly Maintenance Cost ($)	Age (years)	Yearly Maintenance Cost ($)
4.5	619	5.0	1,194
4.5	1,049	0.5	163
4.5	1,033	0.5	182
4.0	495	6.0	764
4.0	723	6.0	1,373
4.0	681	1.0	978
5.0	890	1.0	466
5.0	1,522	1.0	549
5.5	987		

a. Use POM for Windows' least squares-linear regression module to develop a relationship to forecast the yearly maintenance cost based on the age of a tractor.

b. If a section has 20 three-year-old tractors, what is the forecast for the annual maintenance cost?

25. The data for the visibility chart in Discussion Question 1 are shown in Table 13.4. The visibility standard is set at 100. Readings below 100 indicate that air pollution has reduced visibility, and readings above 100 indicate that the air is clearer.

a. Use several methods to generate a visibility forecast for August 31 of the second year. Which method seems to produce the best forecast?

b. Use several methods to forecast the visibility index for the summer of the third year. Which method seems to produce the best forecast? Support your choice.

26. A manufacturing firm has developed a skills test, the scores from which can be used to predict workers' production rating factors. Data on the test scores of various workers and their subsequent production ratings are shown.

a. Using POM for Windows' least squares-linear regression module, develop a relationship to forecast production ratings from test scores.

b. If a worker's test score was 80, what would be your forecast of the worker's production rating?

c. Comment on the strength of the relationship between the test scores and production ratings.

Worker	Test Score	Production Rating	Worker	Test Score	Production Rating
A	53	45	K	54	59
B	36	43	L	73	77
C	88	89	M	65	56
D	84	79	N	29	28
E	86	84	O	52	51
F	64	66	P	22	27
G	45	49	Q	76	76
H	48	48	R	32	34
I	39	43	S	51	60
J	67	76	T	37	32

27. Tom Glass forecasts electrical demand for the Flatlands Public Power District (FPPD). The FPPD wants to take its Comstock power plant out of service for maintenance when demand is expected to be low. After shutdown, performing maintenance and getting the plant back on line takes two weeks. The utility has enough other generating capacity to satisfy 1,550 megawatts (MW) of demand while Comstock is out of service. Table 13.5 shows weekly peak demands (in MW) for the past several autumns. When next fall should the Comstock plant be scheduled for maintenance?

TABLE 13.4		VISIBILITY DATA							
Date	**Year 1**	**Year 2**	**Date**	**Year 1**	**Year 2**	**Date**	**Year 1**	**Year 2**
July 22	125	130	Aug 5	105	200	Aug. 19	170	160
23	100	120	6	205	110	20	125	165
24	40	125	7	90	100	21	85	135
25	100	160	8	45	200	22	45	80
26	185	165	9	100	160	23	95	100
27	85	205	10	120	100	24	85	200
28	95	165	11	85	55	25	160	100
29	200	125	12	125	130	26	105	110
30	125	85	13	165	75	27	100	50
31	90	105	14	60	30	28	95	135
Aug 1	85	160	15	65	100	29	50	70
2	135	125	16	110	85	30	60	105
3	175	130	17	210	150			
4	200	205	18	110	220			

TABLE 13.5 | WEEKLY PEAK POWER DEMANDS

Year	August			September				October				November	
	1	2	3	4	5	6	7	8	9	10	11	12	13
1	2,050	1,925	1,825	1,525	1,050	1,300	1,200	1,175	1,350	1,525	1,725	1,575	1,925
2	2,000	2,075	2,225	1,800	1,175	1,050	1,250	1,025	1,300	1,425	1,625	1,950	1,950
3	1,950	1,800	2,150	1,725	1,575	1,275	1,325	1,100	1,500	1,550	1,375	1,825	2,000
4	2,100	2,400	1,975	1,675	1,350	1,525	1,500	1,150	1,350	1,225	1,225	1,475	1,850
5	2,275	2,300	2,150	1,525	1,350	1,475	1,475	1,175	1,375	1,400	1,425	1,550	1,900

VIDEO CASE   Forecasting and Supply Chain Management at Deckers Outdoor Corporation

Deckers Outdoor Corporation's footwear products are among some of the most well-known brands in the world. From UGG sheepskin boots and Teva sport sandals to Simple shoes, Deckers flip-flops, and Tsubo footwear, Deckers is committed to building niche footwear brands into global brands with market leadership positions. Net sales for fiscal year 2007 were close to $449 million. In addition to traditional retail store outlets for Deckers' footwear styles, the company maintains an active and growing "direct to consumer" e-commerce business. Since most retail stores cannot carry every style in every color and size, the company offers the full line for each of its brands directly to consumers through the brands' individual Web sites. Online sales at its virtual store are handled by its e-commerce group. Customers who want a pair of shoes not available at the retail store can always buy from the virtual store.

Founded in 1973, the company manufactured a single line of sandals in a small factory in Southern California. The challenges of managing the raw materials and finished goods inventories were small compared to today's global sourcing and sales challenges for the company's various brands. Today, each brand has its own development team and brand managers who generate, develop, and test-market the seasonal styles that appear on the shelves of retailers such as Nordstrom, Lord & Taylor, REI, the Walking Company, and the company's own UGG brand retail stores in the United States and Japan.

At Deckers, forecasting is the starting point for inventory management, sales and operations planning, resource planning, and scheduling—in short, managing its supply chain. It carries a considerable amount of seasonal stock. Shoes with seasonal demand that are left over at the end of their season must be sold at heavily discounted prices. Its products fall into three categories: (1) carry-over items that were sold in prior years, (2) new items that look similar to past models, and (3) completely new designs that are fashionable with no past history.

Twice a year, the brand development teams work on the fall and spring product lines. They come up with new designs about one year in advance of each season. Each brand (UGG, Teva, Simple, Tsubo, and Deckers) contains numerous products, called stock keeping units (SKUs). The materials for new designs are selected and tested in prototypes. Approved designs are put into the seasonal line-up. Forecasts must be made at both the SKU and aggregate levels months before the season begins. "Bottoms-up" forecasts for each SKU begin by analyzing any available history files of past demand. Judgment forecasts are also important inputs, particularly for the second and third categories of shoes that are not carry-overs. For example, Char Nicanor-Kimball is an expert in spotting trends in shoe sales and makes forecasts for the virtual store. For new designs, historical sales on similar items are used to make a best guess on demand for those items. This process is facilitated by a forecasting and inventory system on the company's Intranet. At the same time, the sales teams for each brand call on their retail accounts and secure customer orders of approved designs for the coming season. Then the virtual store forecasts are merged with orders from the retail store orders to get the

The Deckers Family.

total seasonal demand forecasted by SKU. Next, the SKU forecasts are "rolled up" by category and "top down" forecasts are also made.

These forecasts then go to top management where some adjustments may be made to account for financial market conditions, consumer credit, weather, demographic factors, and customer confidence. The impact of public relations and advertising must also be considered.

Actually, forecasting continues on throughout the year on a daily and weekly basis to "get a handle" on demand. Comparing actual demand with what was forecasted for different parts of the season also helps the forecasters make better forecasts for the future and better control inventories.

Based on initial demand forecasts, the company must begin sourcing the materials needed to produce the footwear. The company makes most of its products in China and sources many of the raw materials there as well. For UGG products sheepskin sourcing occurs in Australia with top grade producers, but the rawhide tanning still takes places in China. With potential suppliers identified and assurance from internal engineering that the footwear can be successfully made, the engineering and material data are handed over to the manufacturing department to determine how best to make the footwear in mass quantities. At this point, Deckers places a seasonal "buy" with its suppliers.

The orders for each SKU are fed into the manufacturing schedules at the Chinese factories. All the SKUs for a given brand are manufactured at the same factory. While Deckers agents negotiate the raw materials contracts early in the development process, the factories only place the orders for the raw materials when the company sends in the actual orders for the finished goods. No footwear is made by the factories until orders are received.

At the factories, finished goods footwear is inspected and packaged for the month-long ocean voyage from Hong Kong to ports in the United States. Deckers ships fifty containers a week from its Chinese manufacturing sources, each holding approximately 5,000 pairs of shoes. Ownership of the finished goods transfers from the factories to Deckers in Hong Kong.

When the shipping containers arrive in the United States, the footwear is transferred to Deckers' distribution centers in Southern California. Teva products are warehoused in Ventura, California; all other products are handled by the company's state-of-the-art facility in Camarillo, California. Typically, Deckers brings product into the distribution centers two to three months in advance of expected needs so that the production at the suppliers' factories and the labor activities at the distribution centers are leveled. There are definitive spikes in the demand for footwear, with Teva spiking in Quarter 1 and UGG spiking in Quarter 4. The leveling approach works to keep costs low in the supply chain. However, it also means that Deckers must maintain sizeable inventories. Most shipments from suppliers come in to the distribution centers and are stored in inventory for one to two months awaiting a customer order. By the time the footwear is stocked in the distribution center, the company knows which retail customers will be getting the various products, based on the orders booked months earlier. Then, according to delivery schedules negotiated with the customers, the company begins filling orders and shipping products to retail locations. The warehouse tracks incoming shipments, goods placed on the shelves for customers, and outgoing orders. The inventory system helps manage the customer order filling process.

Because the booked orders are a relatively large proportion of the total orders from retailers, and the number of unanticipated orders is very small, only small safety stocks are needed to service the retailers. Occasionally, the purchase order from Deckers to one of its suppliers matches the sales order from the customer. In such a case, Deckers uses a "cross-dock" system. When the shipment is received at the distribution center, it is immediately checked in and loaded on another truck for delivery to customers. Cross docking reduces the need to store vast quantities of product for long periods of time and cuts down on warehousing expenses for Deckers. The company has been successful in turning its inventory over about four times a year, which is in line with footwear industry standards.

The online sales traffic is all managed centrally. In fact, for ordering and inventory management purposes, the online side of the business is treated just like another major retail store account. As forecasted seasonal orders are generated by each brand's sales team, a manufacturing order for the online business is placed by the e-commerce sales team at the same time. However, unlike the retail outlets that take delivery of products on a regular schedule, the inventory pledged to the online business is held in the distribution center until a Web site order is received. Only then is it shipped directly to the consumer who placed the online order. If actual demand exceeds expected demand, Char checks if more inventory can be secured from other customer orders that have scaled back.

The forecasting and supply chain management challenges now facing Deckers are two-fold. First, the company plans to grow the brands that have enjoyed seasonal sales activity into year-round footwear options for consumers by expanding the number of SKUs for those brands. For example, most sales for UGG footwear occur in the fall/winter season. Sales for Teva historically have been in the spring and summer. Product managers are now working to develop styles that will allow the brands to cross over the seasons. Second, the company plans to expand internationally, and will have retail outlets in Europe, China, and other Asian locations in the very near future. Company managers are well aware of the challenges and opportunities such global growth will bring, and are taking steps now to assure that the entire supply chain is prepared to forecast and handle the demand when the time comes.

QUESTIONS

1. How much does the forecasting process at Deckers correspond with the "typical forecasting process" described at the end of this chapter?

2. Based on what you see in the video, what kinds of information technology are used to make forecasts, maintain accurate inventory records, and project future inventory levels?

3. What factors make forecasting at Deckers particularly challenging? How can forecasts be made for seasonal, fashionable products for which there is no history file? What are the costs of over-forecasting demand for such items? Under-forecasting?

4. How does the concept of *postponement* get implemented at Deckers by having online sales and positioning inventory at the DCs for every model, color, and size?

5. Where in the supply chain are cycle, pipeline, safety stock, and anticipation inventories being created?

6. What are the benefits of leveling aggregate demand by having a portfolio of SKUs that create 365-day demand?

7. Deckers plans to expand internationally, thereby increasing the volume of shoes it must manage in the supply chain and the pattern of material flows. What implications does this strategy have on forecasting, order quantities, logistics, and relationships with its suppliers and customers?

CASE   Forecasting at TNN Hire Centres

"I would like to welcome you to the launch of www.tnn.com, mark II, a completely revamped Web site," said Alan Clark, chief executive of TNN Plant and Equipment Hire Centres. His attentive audience was made up of local business people and past customers. "Just one of the ways we make sure you have access to the Right Tool, in the Right Place, at the Right Time ... Every Time!" he said. He then went on to say, "We have developed this new interactive Web site to help our customers to succeed in getting the job done. It's full of facts about our comprehensive range of tools and it enables you to hire online from your home or office—24 hours a day."

TNN is the United Kingdom's largest tool hire company, with 50 years of experience and knowledge. It employs over 2,000 staff dedicated to providing hire, sales, and service. TNN has over 300 outlets with more than 1,000 different products for hire. "Service quality, product innovation, and customer satisfaction has kept TNN at the forefront of the tool hire industry for nearly half a century and we have been the first choice for many professionals because we've focused on top quality tools and, above all, experienced, well-trained staff," Clark said.

"Please browse our Web pages to check out updated product information, training courses, and the latest health and safety advice. You'll also find details of our services for new equipment sales and repairs to customer-owned tools."

Its 2,300 strong workforce and fleet of over 800 vehicles reflect TNN's leading position in the market. Throughout its history, TNN has maintained a policy of strong organic growth. Its founder, an entrepreneurial stallholder, Bert Taylor, never dreamt that his brainchild would grow into the country's most extensive network of hire shops servicing trade, industrial, and home-owner customers. It all started when Taylor was pestered by his sister, who wanted to borrow a stepladder. He realized that there was potentially a larger group of customers who needed equipment for special tasks but who actually did not want to buy products that they may use only rarely. TNN continues to expand the network both organically and by establishing agency partnerships for TNN Hire Shops within independent builders' merchants. Overseas, TNN Hire is developing its operations by means of franchise partnerships. The company already has licensees in Greece, Holland, Italy, Norway, Spain, Trinidad, and the United Arab Emirates, and is seeking further to expand its network. In the United Kingdom, the tool hire market is estimated to be worth over $1 billion.

Throughout the 1960s, growth continued and was already beginning to attract trade sales with builders, plumbers, decorators, and other professionals. Having celebrated its 40th year in 1997, TNN continued its major expansion. Throughout 2004, to enable the company to concentrate on its core business strength of tool and equipment hire in the United Kingdom, various service divisions were sold, for example, the Event Hire division. In 2005, TNN won its largest ever contract, securing a multi-million pound deal with Network Rail to supply non-rail specific plant to all Network Rail regions—the first time one contract had been awarded to cover all 18 regions. A revamped Web site marked the start of 2008, enabling customers to hire any item from the entire catalogue range online. Additionally, a network of supercenters around the country opened, including locations in Manchester, Beckton, Inverness, and Solihull.

One of the biggest issues that continually confront TNN is the ability to forecast demand. Too much stock means expensive equipment sitting on the shelf not paying for itself, and equipment not available means a lost customer. Alan Clark is acutely aware that numerous factors affect the hire of his products—national economic conditions, house builds, disposable income, and weather conditions, to name just a few. Basic patterns of demand follow classic lines of horizontal, trend, seasonal, cyclical, and random variation. The tool hire market comprises customer sectors ranging from the occasional DIY user to the largest national construction companies. In between falls just about every other industrial group, public sector organization and specialist trade contractor. TNN's considerable investment in computer technology has enabled each branch to link into a national network so that equipment can be quickly located and supplied to customers wherever they are based. Nevertheless, it has become noticeable of late that market requirements have become increasingly difficult to predict, and therefore, Clark has decided to investigate how forecasting demand might be improved.

Historically, stock has been identified by its function, for example, access that relates to towers, lifts, ladders, etc. However, it is noticeable that frequently groups of equipment are hired as a set. In addition, more recently the over-riding factor that appears to impact hire sales is "economic factors." Currently, forecasting of plant and equipment hire is categorized under 16 main headings, with each main heading having up to 10 sub-categories, totaling some 160 products. The list below shows some of the categories:

[1] Access

<1> Access Towers

<2> Boom Lifts

<3> Ladders

<4> Scissor Lifts

<5> Self-Propelled Boom

<6> Towers and Platforms

<7> Trestles, Staging, and Steps

<8> Work Platforms

[2] Breaking and Drilling

[3] Building and Siteworks

[4] Cleaning and Floorcare

[5] Concreting and Preparation

[6] Gardening and Event

[7] Heating, Cooling, Drying

[8] Lifting and Handling

[9] Lighting and Power

[10] Painting and Decorating

[11] Plumbing and Pumping

[12] Safety and Protection

[13] Sanding and Fixing

[14] Sawing and Cutting

[15] Surveying and Location

[16] Welding

Alan Clark said, "It has become obvious from our sales figures that using historical information is insufficient for predicting the future. We need far more sophisticated methods of forecasting." The majority of the 90 percent of business within the trade sector is derived from the Build, Maintain, and Operate segments of the construction and facilities management industries, along with utilities and industrial users. Domestic customers account for less than 10 percent of turnover and increasingly that turnover is online. Moreover, TNN is moving increasingly beyond a traditional hire contract. For its largest customers it provides a managed service, owning specialist equipment, providing planned maintenance programs, and training operators. "We see our future as a logistical and technical partner of our customers in industries where the provision of safe and effective equipment on time is mission critical to their success and profit," Alan said. "We therefore need to be far more accurate with calculating future demands."

QUESTIONS

1. If you were Alan Clark, would you continue to categorize and forecast your stock based on the current product families, or would you use other classifications to obtain a level of aggregated data?

2. Of the various forecasting methods available, which techniques would you advise Alan to use? Why?

3. Would time-series analysis, exponential smoothing techniques, and linear regression analysis be most applicable in this situation, or would judgment methods and the Delphi method be better suited?

Source: This fictional case was prepared by Dr. David Parker, The University of Queensland, Business School, as a basis for classroom discussion.

EXPERIENTIAL LEARNING	Forecasting with Holdout Sample

A company's history file, as shown in the following table, gives monthly sales in thousands of dollars "rolled up" into aggregated totals for one of its major product lines.

Your team should input this data into a forecasting routine for POM for Windows. Seek out three models to use in making in-class forecasts of monthly sales for year 9. You should bring to class at least one computer for your team that has loaded on it an Excel spreadsheet for making combination forecasts (see Problem 18). Also bring a one-page document that

- characterizes the monthly sales of the product line in terms of its forecastability.

- identifies the relative importance of four demand patterns: horizontal, trend, seasonal, and cyclical.

- states how much importance you think should be placed on judgmental forecasts in year 9, justifying how you reached this conclusion.

- identifies the forecasting model (models in the case of combination forecasts) that you will use to make the forecasts for year 9. Explain

why you made this selection, given that MAD will be used as our error measure.

- makes the January forecast for year 9.

After you hand in your document that gives your January forecast, the month's actual sales for January will be revealed from a *holdout sample*. Using that additional information you will then generate February forecasts using your three models that you selected before class, as well as the combination forecast derived from them. The process will repeat itself until all of the forecasts have been made for year 9. Update your model(s) from one period to the next. At the end of this exercise, create a second one-page document that reports your forecasts for year 9, the corresponding average MAD for last year, whether (and how) you modified your forecasting model as the exercise progressed, and what you learned from this exercise. Submit your report to your instructor at the end of the class session.

Your grade on this exercise will be based on (1) the insights provided in the two documents (50 percent of grade) and (2) the average MAD for year 9 (50 percent of grade).

Yr	Jan	Feb	Mar	Apr	May	Jun	Jul	Aug	Sep	Oct	Nov	Dec
1	3,255	3,420	3,482	3,740	3,713	3,785	3,817	3,900	3,878	3,949	4,004	4,035
2	3,892	3,730	4,115	4,054	4,184	4,321	4,307	4,481	4,411	4,443	4,395	4,403
3	4,507	4,400	4,099	4,064	4,002	3,963	4,037	4,162	4,312	4,395	4,540	4,471
4	4,589	4,688	4,566	4,485	4,385	4,377	4,309	4,276	4,280	4,144	4,219	4,052
5	4,084	4,158	4,174	4,225	4,324	4,220	4,267	4,187	4,239	4,352	4,331	4,371
6	4,535	4,477	4,601	4,648	4,860	4,998	5,003	4,960	4,943	5,052	5,107	5,100
7	5,303	5,550	5,348	5,391	5,519	5,602	5,557	5,608	5,663	5,497	5,719	5,679
8	5,688	5,604	5,703	5,899	5,816	5,745	5,921	5,900	5,911	5,987	6,074	6,045

Source: This experiential exercise was adapted from in in-class exercise prepared by Dr. Richard J. Penlesky, Carroll University, as a basis for classroom discussion.

SELECTED REFERENCES

Armstrong, J. S. *Long-Range Forecasting: From Crystal Ball to Computer.* New York: John Wiley & Sons, 1995.

Armstrong, J. Scott, and F. Collopy. "Integration of Statistical Methods and Judgment for Time Series Forecasting: Principles from Empirical Research," in G. Wright and P. Goodwin (eds.), *Forecasting with Judgment*, New York: John Wiley and Sons, 1998.

Blattberg, R. C., and S. J. Hoch. "Database Models and Managerial Intuition: 50% Model + 50% Manager." *Management Science*, vol. 36 (1990), pp. 887–899.

Bowerman, Bruce L., and Richard T. O'Connell. *Forecasting and Time Series: An Applied Approach*, 3d ed., Belmont, CA: Duxbury Press, 1993.

Bowman, Robert J. "Access to Data in Real Time: Seeing Isn't Everything." *Global Logistics and Supply-Chain Strategies* (May 2002).

Cederlund, Jerold P., Rajiv Kohli, Susan A. Sherer, and Yuliang Yao. "How Motorola Put CPFR into Action." *Supply Chain Management Review* (October 2007), pp. 28–35.

"Clearing the Cobwebs from the Stockroom." *Business Week* (October 21, 1996), p. 140.

Clemen, R. T. "Combining Forecasts: A Review and Annotated Bibliography." *International Journal of Forecasting*, vol. 5 (1989), pp. 559–583.

Hudson, William J. *Executive Economics: Forecasting and Planning for the Real World of Business.* New York: John Wiley & Sons, 1993.

Jenkins, Carolyn. "Accurate Forecasting Reduces Inventory and Increases Output at Henredon." *APIC—The Performance Advantage* (September 1992), pp. 37–39.

Kakouros, Steve, Dorothea Kuettner, and Brian Cargille. "Measure, Then Manage." *APICS—The Performance Advantage* (October 2002), pp. 25–29.

Kimes, Sheryl E., and James A. Fitzsimmons. "Selecting Profitable Hotel Sites at La Quinta Motor Inns." *Interfaces*, vol. 20, no. 2 (1990), pp. 12–20.

Li, X. "An Intelligent Business Forecaster for Strategic Business Planning." *Journal of Forecasting*, vol. 18, no. 3 (1999), pp. 181–205.

Lim, J. S., and M. O'Connor. "Judgmental Forecasting with Time Series and Causal Information." *International Journal of Forecasting*, vol. 12 (1996), pp. 139–153.

Melnyk, Steven. "1997 Forecasting Software Product Listing." *APICS—The Performance Advantage* (April 1997), pp. 62–65.

Mitchell, Robert L. "Case Study: Unilever Crosses the Data Streams." *Computerworld* (December 17, 2001).

Moon, Mark A., John T. Mentzer, and Dwight E. Thomas Jr. "Customer Demand Planning at Lucent Technologies: A Case Study in Continuous Improvement Through Sales Forecast Auditing." *Industrial Marketing Management*, vol. 29, no. 1 (2000).

Principles of Forecasting: A Handbook for Researchers and Practitioners. J. Scott Armstrong (ed.). Norwell, MA: Kluwer Academic Publishers, 2001. Also visit http://www.forecastingprinciples.com for valuable information on forecasting, including frequently asked questions, a forecasting methodology tree, and a dictionary.

Raghunathan, Srinivasan. "Interorganizational Collaborative Forecasting and Replenishment Systems and Supply-Chain Implications." *Decision Sciences*, vol. 30, no. 5 (1999), pp. 1053–1067.

Sanders, Nada R., and L. P. Ritzman. "Bringing Judgment into Combination Forecasts." *Journal of Operations Management*, vol. 13 (1995), pp. 311–321.

Sanders, Nada R., and Karl B. Manrodt. "Forecasting in Practice: Use, Satisfaction, and Performance." *Interfaces*, vol. 33, no. 5 (2003), pp. 90–93.

Sanders, Nada R., and Larry P. Ritzman. "The Need for Contextual and Technical Knowledge in Judgmental Forecasting." *Journal of Behavioral Decision Making*, vol. 5, no. 1 (1992), pp. 39–52.

Schachtman, Noah. "Trading Partners Collaborate to Increase Sales." *Information Week.com* (October 9, 2000), www.informationweek.com/807/cpfr.htm.

Schoenberger, Chana R. "The Weakest Link." *Forbes* (October 1, 2001), www.forbes.com/forbes/2001/1001/114.print.html.

Seifert, Dirk. *Collaborative Planning, Forecasting, and Replenishment: How to Create a Supply-Chain Advantage.* Bonn, Germany: Galileo Press, 2002.

Smith, Larry. "West Marine: A CPFR Success Story." *Supply Chain Management Review* (March 2006), pp. 29–36.

Smith, Bernard. *Focus Forecasting: Computer Techniques for Inventory Control.* Boston: CBI Publishing, 1984.

Steerman, Hank. "A Practical Look at CPFR: The Sears-Michelin Experience." *Supply Chain Management Review* (July/August 2003), pp. 46–53.

VICS (2002) "Collaborative Planning, Forecasting, and Replenishment," Version 2.0, www.cpfr.org.

Wallace, Thomas F., and Robert A. Stahl. *Sales Forecasting: A New Approach.* Cincinnati, OH: T. E. Wallace & Company, 2002.

Yurkiewicz, Jack. "Forecasting 2000." *OR/MS Today*, vol. 27, no. 1 (2000), pp. 58–65.

Yurkiewicz, Jack. "2003 Forecasting Software Survey." *OR/MS Today* (February 2003).

14 PLANNING AND SCHEDULING OPERATIONS

Operations planning and scheduling at an airline like Air New Zealand goes through several stages to match supply with demand, from aggregate plans to short-term schedules. Even after finalizing flights and crew roster schedules, severe weather conditions or mechanical failures can cause last-minute changes. Long-term competitive strength depends on how well it performs this process.

AIR NEW ZEALAND

How important is scheduling to an airline company? Certainly, customer satisfaction regarding on-time schedule performance is critical in a highly competitive industry such as air transportation. In addition, airlines lose a lot of money when expensive equipment, such as an aircraft, is idle. Flight and crew scheduling, however, is a complex process. For example, Air New Zealand is a group of five airlines with a combined fleet of 96 aircraft. It directly serves 50 ports—26 domestic and 24 international within 15 countries. It carries 11.7 million passengers annually, and its network incorporates flight times ranging from 15 minutes to 13 hours. Operations planning and scheduling at the aggregate level begins with a market plan that identifies the new and existing flight segments that are needed to remain competitive. This general plan is further refined to a three-year plan, and then is put into an annual budget in which flight segments have specific departure and arrival times.

Next, crew availability must be matched to the flight schedules. The two types of crews—pilots and attendants—each comes with its own set of constraints. Pilots, for example, cannot be scheduled for more than 35 hours in a 7-day week and no more than 100 hours in a 28-day cycle. They also must have a 36-hour break every 7 days and 30 days off in an 84-day cycle. Each pilot's tour of duty begins and ends at a crew base and consists of an alternating sequence of duty periods and rest periods, with duty periods including one or more flights. The schedule must ensure that each flight has a qualified crew and

LEARNING GOALS

After reading this chapter, you should be able to:

1. Describe the operations planning and scheduling process.
2. Explain why the process of matching supply with demand begins with aggregation.
3. Identify the different demand and supply options.
4. Explain how operations plans and schedules relate to other plans.
5. Use spreadsheets to create sales and operations plans.
6. Develop employee schedules.
7. Develop schedules for single workstations.

that each crew member has a feasible tour of duty over the roster period. From the crew's point of view, it is also important to satisfy as many crew requests and preferences as possible.

Source: "Service Scheduling at Air New Zealand," *Operations Management 9e Video Library* (Upper Saddle River, NJ: Prentice Hall, 2010); http://www. pacificislands.airnewzealand.com/aboutus/consulting/history.htm (2008)

my**om**lab and the Companion Website at **www.pearsonglobaleditions.com/krajewski** contain many tools, activities, and resources designed for this chapter.

operations planning and scheduling

The process of balancing supply with demand, from the aggregate level down to the short-term scheduling level.

COMPETING WITH OPERATIONS

↓

Using Operations to Compete
Managing Effective Projects

DESIGNING AND
MANAGING PROCESSES

↓

Developing a Process Strategy
Analyzing Processes
Managing Quality
Planning Capacity
Managing Process Constraints
Designing Lean Systems

DESIGNING AND
MANAGING SUPPLY CHAINS

↓

Designing Effective Supply Chains
Integrating the Supply Chain
Locating Facilities
Managing Inventories
Forecasting Demand
Planning and Scheduling Operations
Planning Sufficient Resources

Managing supply chains effectively requires more than just good demand forecasts. Demand is the first half of the equation, and the other half is supply. The firm must develop plans to supply the resources needed to meet the forecasted demand. These resources include the workforce, materials, inventories, dollars, and equipment capacity.

Operations planning and scheduling is the process of making sure that demand and supply plans are in balance, from the aggregate level down to the short-term scheduling level. As we saw with Air New Zealand, the process begins at the aggregate level and gets progressively more specific until all crew members know their tour of duty. Operations planning and scheduling lies at the core of supply chain integration, around which plans are made up and down the supply chain, from supplier deliveries to customer due dates and services. Table 14.1 defines several types of plans related to operations planning and scheduling.

In this chapter, we focus on two major parts of the overall process: (1) sales and operations planning and (2) scheduling. We begin with the purpose of aggregation in sales and operations planning. We examine how S&OP relates with other plans and functional areas within the firm. We describe a typical planning process, and various strategies to cope with uneven demand. We show how spreadsheets can help find good solutions. Then we conclude with scheduling, including performance measures and some basic techniques for creating schedules. Supplement J, "Operations Scheduling" in my**om**lab, provides additional help with scheduling problems.

OPERATIONS PLANNING AND SCHEDULING ACROSS THE ORGANIZATION

Operations planning and scheduling is meaningful for each organization along the supply chain. First, it requires managerial inputs from all of the firm's functions. Marketing provides inputs on demand and accounting provides important cost data and a firm's financial condition. Second, each function is affected by the plan. A plan that calls for expanding the workforce has a direct impact on the hiring and training requirements for the human resources function. As the plan is implemented, it creates revenue and cost streams that finance must deal with as it manages the firm's cash flows. Third, each department and group in a firm has its own workforce. Managers of these departments must make choices on hiring, overtime, and vacations.

Scheduling is important for both service and manufacturing processes. Whether the business is an airline, hotel, computer manufacturer, or university, schedules are a part of everyday life. Schedules involve an enormous amount of detail and affect every process in a firm. For example, service, product, and employee schedules determine specific cash flow requirements, trigger the firm's billing process, and initiate requirements for the employee training process. Firms use the scheduling process to lower their costs and improve their responsiveness, affecting operations up and down the supply chain worldwide.

TABLE 14.1	**TYPES OF PLANS WITH OPERATIONS PLANNING AND SCHEDULING**
Key Term	**Definition**
sales and operations plan (S&OP)	A plan of future aggregate resource levels so that supply is in balance with demand. It states a company's or department's production rates, workforce levels, and inventory holdings that are consistent with demand forecasts and capacity constraints. The S&OP is time-phased, meaning that it is projected for several time periods (such as months or quarters) into the future.
aggregate plan	Another term for the sales and operations plan.
production plan	A manufacturing firm's sales and operations plan that centers on production rates and inventory holdings.
staffing plan	A sales and operations plan for a service firm, which centers on staffing and on other human resource-related factors.
resource plan	An intermediate step in the planning process that lies between S&OP and scheduling. It determines requirements for materials and other resources on a more detailed level than the S&OP. It is covered in the next chapter.
schedule	A detailed plan that allocates resources over shorter time horizons to accomplish specific tasks.

Stages in Operations Planning and Scheduling

In this section, we explain why companies begin with plans that take a macro, or big picture, view of their business. We also describe how these plans relate to their other plans, and how the long-term plans ultimately are translated into detailed schedules ready for immediate action.

Aggregation

The sales and operations plan is useful because it focuses on a general course of action, consistent with the company's strategic goals and objectives, without getting bogged down in details. We must first aggregate, and then use the targets and resources from the plan to create effective, coordinated schedules. A company's managers must determine whether they can satisfy budgetary goals without having to schedule each of the company's thousands of products and employees individually. While schedules with such detail are the goal, the operations planning and scheduling process begins at the aggregate level.

In general, companies perform aggregation along three dimensions: services or products, workforce, and time.

Product Families   A group of customers, services, or products that have similar demand requirements and common process, workforce, and materials requirements is called a **product family**. Sometimes, product families relate to market groupings or to specific processes. A firm can aggregate its services or products into a set of relatively broad families, avoiding too much detail at this stage of the planning process. For instance, a manufacturer of bicycles that produces 12 different models of bikes might divide them into two groups, mountain bikes and road bikes, for the purpose of preparing the sales and operations plan. Common and relevant measurements should be used.

Workforce   A company can aggregate its workforce in various ways as well, depending on its flexibility. For example, if workers at the bicycle manufacturer are trained to work on either mountain bikes or road bikes, for planning purposes management can consider its workforce to be a single aggregate group, even though the skills of individual workers may differ.

Time   The planning horizon covered by a sales and operations plan typically is one year, although it can differ in various situations. To avoid the expense and disruptive effect of frequent changes in output rates and the workforce, adjustments usually are made monthly or quarterly. In other words, the company looks at time in the aggregate—months, quarters, or seasons—rather than in weeks, days, or hours.

The Relationship of Operations Plans and Schedules to Other Plans

A financial assessment of the organization's near future—that is, for 1 or 2 years ahead—is called either a business plan (in for-profit firms) or an annual plan (in nonprofit service organizations). A **business plan** is a projected statement of income, costs, and profits. It usually is accompanied by budgets, a projected (pro forma) balance sheet, and a projected cash flow statement, showing sources and allocations of funds. The business plan unifies the plans and expectations of a firm's operations, finance, sales, and marketing managers. In particular, it reflects plans for market penetration, new product introduction, and capital investment. Manufacturing firms and for-profit service organizations, such as a retail store, a firm of attorneys, or a hospital, prepare such plans. A nonprofit service organization, such as the United Way or a municipal government, prepares a different type of plan for financial assessment, called an **annual plan or financial plan**.

Figure 14.1 illustrates the relationships among the business or annual plan, sales and operations plan, and detailed plans and schedules derived from it. For service providers in the supply chain, top management sets the organization's direction and objectives in the business plan (in a for-profit organization) or annual plan (in a not-for-profit organization). This plan then provides the framework for developing the sales and operations plan, which typically focuses on staffing and other human resource-related factors at a more aggregate level. It presents the number and types of employees needed to meet the objectives of the business or annual plan.

Based on the sales and operations plan for a service provider, the next planning level is *resource planning* to determine the firm's workforce schedules and other resource requirements, such as materials and facilities, on a more detailed level. The *workforce schedule* details the specific work schedule for each category of employee. For example, a sales and operations plan might allocate 10 police officers for the day shift in a particular district; the

product family

A group of customers, services, or products that have similar demand requirements and common process, labor, and materials requirements.

business plan

A projected statement of income, costs, and profits.

annual plan or financial plan

A plan for financial assessment used by a nonprofit service organization.

FIGURE 14.1 ▶
The Relationship of Sales and Operations
Plans and Schedules to Other Plans

workforce schedule might assign 5 of them to work Monday through Friday and the other 5 to work Wednesday through Sunday to meet the varying daily needs for police protection in that district. The lowest planning level is *scheduling*, which puts together day-to-day schedules for individual employees and customers.

For manufacturing firms in the supply chain, top management sets the company's strategic objectives for at least the next year in the business plan. It provides the overall framework, along with inputs coming from operations strategy, forecasting, and capacity constraint management. The sales and operations plan specifies product family production rates, inventory levels, and workforce levels. The next planning level beneath the sales and operations plan is resource planning, which we cover in the next chapter. Resource planning gets specific as to individual products within each product family, purchased materials, and resources on a detailed level. The *master production schedule* specifies the timing and size of production quantities for each product in the product families. The *material requirements planning* process then derives plans for components, purchased materials, and workstations. As with service providers, the lowest and most detailed planning level is scheduling. It puts together day-to-day schedules or priorities for employees, equipment, and production or purchase orders. Thus, the sales and operations plan plays a key role in translating the strategies of the business plan into an operational plan for the manufacturing process.

As the arrows in Figure 14.1 indicate, information flows in two directions: from the top down (broad to detailed) and from the bottom up (detailed to broad). If a sales and operations plan cannot be developed to satisfy the objectives of the business or annual plan with the existing resources, the business or annual plan might need some adjustment. Similarly, if a feasible master production schedule or workforce schedule cannot be developed, the sales and operations plan might need some adjustment. The planning process is dynamic, with periodic plan revisions or adjustments based on two-way information flows, typically on a monthly basis.

MANAGING DEMAND

Matching supply with demand becomes a challenge when forecasts call for uneven demand patterns—and uneven demand is more the rule than the exception. Demand swings can be from one month to the next, one week to the next, or even one hour to the next. Peaks and valleys in demand are costly or can cause poor customer service. Air New Zealand can lose sales because capacity is exceeded for one of its flights, while another of its flights to the same destination at about the same time has many empty seats. If nothing is done to even out demand, sales are lost or greater capacity cushions might be needed. For other companies, the supply options for handing uneven demand could be overtime, hiring and curtailing the workforce, and anticipation inventories. All come at an extra cost. Here we deal with

demand management, the process of changing demand patterns using one or more demand options.

demand management

The process of changing demand patterns using one or more demand options.

Demand Options

Various options are available in managing demand, including complementary products, promotional pricing, prescheduled appointments, reservations, revenue management, backlogs, backorders, and stockouts. The manager may select one or more of them, as we illustrate below.

Complementary Products   One demand option for a company to even out the load on resources is to produce **complementary products**, or services that have similar resource requirements but different demand cycles. For example, manufacturers of matzoh balls for the Jewish Passover holiday are in a seasonal business. The B. Manischewitz Company, a kosher foods manufacturer in Jersey City, New Jersey, previously experienced 40 percent of its annual sales for the 8-day Passover holiday alone. It expanded toward markets with year-round appeal such as low-carb, low-fat foods, including canned soups and crackers, borscht, cake mixes, dressing and spreads, juices, and condiments.

complementary products

Services or products that have similar resource requirements but different demand cycles.

For service providers, a city parks and recreation department can counterbalance seasonal staffing requirements for summer activities by offering ice skating, tobogganing, or indoor activities during the winter months. The key is to find services and products that can be produced with the existing resources and can level off the need for resources over the year.

Promotional Pricing   Promotional campaigns are designed to increase sales with creative pricing. Examples include automobile rebate programs, price reductions for winter clothing in the late summer months, reduced prices for hotel rooms during off-peak periods, and "two-for-the-price-of-one" automobile tire sales. Lower prices can increase demand for the product or service from new and existing customers, take sales from competitors, or encourage customers to move up future buying. The first two outcomes increase overall demand, while the third shifts demand to the current period.

Prescheduled Appointments   Service providers often can schedule customers for definite periods of order fulfillment. With this approach, demand is leveled to not exceed supply capacity. An appointment system assigns specific times for service to customers. The advantages of this method are timely customer service and the high utilization of service personnel.

Doctors, dentists, lawyers, and automobile repair shops are examples of service providers that use appointment systems. Doctors can use the system to schedule parts of their day to visit hospital patients, and lawyers can set aside time to prepare cases. Care must be taken to tailor the length of appointments to individual customer needs rather than merely scheduling customers at equal time intervals.

Reservations   Reservation systems, although quite similar to appointment systems, are used when the customer actually occupies or uses facilities associated with the service. For example, customers reserve hotel rooms, automobiles, airline seats, and concert seats. The major advantage of reservation systems is the lead time they give service managers and the ability to level demand. Managers can deal with no-shows with a blend of overbooking, deposits, and cancellation penalties. Sometimes overbooking means that a customer with reservations cannot be served as promised. In such cases, bonuses can be offered for compensation. For example, an airline passenger might not only get on the next available flight, but also may be given a free ticket for a second flight sometime in the future.

Revenue Management   A specialized combination of the pricing and reservation options for service providers is revenue management. **Revenue management** (sometimes called *yield management*) is the process of varying price at the right time for different customer segments to maximize revenues generated from existing supply capacity. It works best if customers can be segmented, prices can be varied by segment, fixed costs are high, variable costs are low, service duration is predictable, and capacity is lost if not used (sometimes called *perishable capacity*). Airlines, hotels, cruise lines, restaurants (early-bird specials), and rental cars are good examples. Computerized reservation systems can make hour-by-hour updates, using decision rules for opening or closing price classes depending on the difference between supply and continually updated demand forecasts. In the airlines industry, prices are lowered if a particular airline flight is not selling as fast as expected, until more seats are booked. Alternately, if larger than expected demand is developing, prices for the remaining seats may be increased. Last-minute business travelers pay the higher prices, whereas leisure travelers making reservations well in advance and staying over the weekend get the bargain prices. Managerial Practice 14.1 describes how techniques for segmenting customers are used in the airline and rail industry.

revenue management

Varying price at the right time for different customer segments to maximize revenues yielded by existing supply capacity.

MANAGERIAL PRACTICE 14.1   Management in Airlines and Rail Industries

Lufthansa: Premium Service for a Premium Price

For German airline Lufthansa, offering its first-class customers larger seats and better in-flight food was not enough to keep its first-class section full. Under a plan implemented in 2004, those customers willing to pay the extra price for a first-class ticket or members of the HON Circle, a status given to passengers who accumulate 600,000 HON Circle miles, Lufthansa offers many unique services, several of which are not offered by competitors. Customers can wait for their flights in a stylish first-class terminal and have access to amenities such as private relaxation quarters, office areas, personal shower and bath accommodations, and à la carte meals. Lufthansa even makes getting to the first-class terminal easier for its valued customers. A valet service will accompany customers through airport customs and security checkpoints. Once inside the first-class terminal, customers are offered a personal assistant to help them with any needs they may have before their flights depart. Although this kind of attention is costly for customers, the differentiated price allows Lufthansa to offer a unique service to those passengers who wish to avoid the hassles of air travel.

Eurail Offers Discounts to Select Groups

Eurail is a cooperation of 30 European railway companies that traverse numerous countries in Europe. The organization sells travelers train passes that are accepted by all participating railways. In an attempt to keep train seats full and avoid losing revenue on below-capacity services, Eurail offers a variety of discounts to select groups. Travelers under the age of 25 are eligible for a considerable discount. The Eurail Youth Pass is on average only 65 percent of the standard adult fare, allowing students, backpackers, and other young travelers to tour numerous countries at an affordable price. Although Youth Pass is not available for all travel packages and is only offered in second-class for most travel routes, it is still a value to young travelers. For travelers over the age of 25 who travel on a budget, Eurail offers early bird specials. Travelers must buy their passes several months in

German airline Lufthansa is one of a number of airlines that offer a differentiated price scheme to its customers. To boost sales of first class bookings the airline introduced additional luxury services that are not offered by rival airlines.

advance and are typically required to ride during slower travel months such as March, April, and May; however, they can benefit from a significant price reduction. Eurail also attempts to maximize its passenger capacity by offering a group rate. Known as a Saver Pass, groups of two or more people are eligible for a pass that offers a 15 percent discount off the standard pass price if all members of thegroup travel at the same time. By segmenting the pass prices for different groups, Eurail is able to gain customers who may otherwise choose a different travel option and leave railway companies with empty seats and lost revenue.

Sources: Lufthansa, http://www.lufthansa-financials.de/servlet/PB/menu/1016703_l2/index.html; Eurail About Us, http://www.eurail.com/1_about_us.

backlog

An accumulation of customer orders that a manufacturer has promised for delivery at some future date.

Backlogs   Much like the appointments or reservations of service providers, a **backlog** is an accumulation of customer orders that a manufacturer has promised for delivery at some future date. Manufacturers in the supply chain that maintain a backlog of orders as a normal business practice can allow the backlog to grow during periods of high demand and then reduce it during periods of low demand. Airplane manufacturers do not promise instantaneous delivery, as do wholesalers or retailers farther forward in the supply chain. Instead, they impose a lead time between when the order is placed and when it is delivered. For example, an automotive parts manufacturer may agree to deliver to the repair department of a car dealership a batch of 100 door latches for a particular car model next Tuesday. The parts manufacturer uses that due date to plan its production of door latches within its capacity limits. Firms that are most likely to use backlogs—and increase the size of them during periods of heavy demand—make customized products and tend to have a make-to-order strategy. Backlogs reduce the uncertainty of future production requirements and also can be used to level demand. However, they become a competitive disadvantage if they get too big.

Backorders and Stockouts   A last resort in demand management is to set lower standards for customer service, either in the form of backorders or stockouts (see Chapter 9, "Designing Effective Supply Chains"). Not to be confused with a backlog, a *backorder* is a customer order that cannot be filled immediately but is filled as soon as possible. Demand may be too unpredictable or the item may be too costly to hold it in inventory. Although the customer is not pleased with the delay, the customer order is not lost and it is filled at a later date. In contrast, a *stockout* is much the same, except that the order is lost and the customer goes elsewhere. A backorder adds to the next period's demand requirement, whereas a stockout does not. Backorders and stockouts can lead dissatisfied customers to do their future business with another firm. Generally, backorders and stockouts are to be avoided.

Combinations of demand options can also be used. For example, a manufacturer of lighting equipment had several products characterized as "slow movers with spikes," where only 2 or 3 units were sold for several weeks, and then suddenly there was a huge order for 10,000 units the next week. The reason is that their product was purchased by commercial property managers who might be upgrading the lighting in a large office building. The result was a forecasting nightmare and having to resort to high cost supply options to meet the demand spikes. The breakthrough in solving this problem was to combine the pricing and backlog options. Contractors are now offered a 3 percent discount (the pricing option) on any order in excess of 10,000 units that are placed five or more weeks before they are needed (the backlog option). The advanced warning allows the manufacturer to smooth out its production processes, saving millions of dollars annually.

The left side of Table 14.2 summarizes the demand options for operations planning and scheduling, and the right side lists the supply options for balancing supply with demand. The following two sections on sales and operations planning and scheduling cover the supply options.

TABLE 14.2	DEMAND AND SUPPLY OPTIONS FOR OPERATIONS PLANNING AND SCHEDULING
Demand Options	**Supply Options**
Complementary products	Anticipation inventory
Promotional pricing	Workforce adjustment (hiring and layoffs)
Prescheduled appointments	Workforce utilization (overtime and undertime)
Reservations	Part-time workers and subcontractors
Revenue management	Vacation schedules
Backlogs	Workforce schedules
Backorders	Job and customer sequences
Stockouts	Expediting

SALES AND OPERATIONS PLANS

Developing sales and operations plans means making decisions. In this section, we concentrate on the information inputs, the supply options themselves, and strategies that go into the sales and operations planning (S&OP) decisions.

Information Inputs

Just as it is needed to manage the demand side, consensus is needed among the firm's departments when decisions for the supply side are made. Information inputs are sought to create a plan that works for all. Figure 14.2 lists inputs from each functional area. They must be accounted for to make sure that the plan is a good one and also doable. Such coordination helps synchronize the flow of services, materials, and information through the supply chain to best balance supply with customer demand.

Supply Options

Given demand forecasts, as modified by demand management choices, operations managers must develop a plan to meet the demand, drawing from the supply options listed in Table 14.2.

Anticipation Inventory   *Anticipation inventory* can be used to absorb uneven rates of demand or supply. For example, a plant facing seasonal demand can stock anticipation inventory during light demand periods and use it during heavy demand periods.

FIGURE 14.2 ▶
Managerial Inputs from Functional Areas
to Sales and Operations Plans

Manufacturers of air conditioners, such as Whirlpool (see Managerial Practice 14.2), can experience 90 percent of their annual demand during just three months of a year. Extra, or anticipation inventory, also can help when supply, rather than demand, is uneven. For example, a company can stock up on a certain purchased item if the company's suppliers expect severe capacity limitations. Despite its advantages, anticipation inventory can be costly to hold, particularly if stocked in its finished state. Moreover, when services or products are customized, anticipation inventory is not usually an option. Service providers in the supply chain generally cannot use anticipation inventory because services cannot be stocked.

Workforce Adjustment   Management can adjust workforce levels by hiring or laying off employees. The use of this alternative can be attractive if the workforce is largely unskilled or semiskilled and the labor pool is large. These conditions are more likely found in some

---

MANAGERIAL PRACTICE 14.2   Anticipation Inventory at Whirpool Corporation

Whirlpool Corporation, with annual sales of more than $18 billion, 73,000 employees, and nearly 70 manufacturing and technology research centers around the globe, manufactures and markets major home appliances. It is also a leading producer of room air conditioners. The demand for window units is highly seasonal and also depends on variations in the weather. Typically, Whirlpool begins production of room air conditioners in the fall and holds them as inventory until they are shipped in the spring. Building inventory in the slack season allows the company to even out production rates over much of the year and still satisfy demand in the peak periods (spring and summer) when retailers are placing most of their orders. However, when summers are hotter than usual, demand increases dramatically and stockouts can occur. If Whirlpool increases its output and the summer is hot, it stands to increase its sales and market share. But if the summer is cool, the company is stuck with expensive inventories of unsold machines.

An employee stocks a Whirlpool air conditioner at a Lowe's store in Westborough, Massachusetts. The demand for window-unit air conditioners not only fluctuates by season but by year—some summers are hotter or cooler than others. Instead of ramping up or ramping down production based on a particular year, Whirlpool bases its sales and operations plans on the *average* year.

Source: Based on "An Industry's Race with Summer," *New York Times,* February 23, 1989; www.whirlpoolcorp.com/about/default.asp, March 2008.

countries than in others. However, for a particular company, the size of the qualified labor pool may limit the number of new employees that can be hired at any one time. Also, new employees must be trained, and the capacity of the training facilities themselves might limit the number of new hires at any one time. In some industries, laying off employees is difficult or unusual for contractual reasons (unions); in other industries, such as tourism and agriculture, seasonal layoffs and hirings are the norm. Hallmark is a good example of a company that does not choose this supply option.

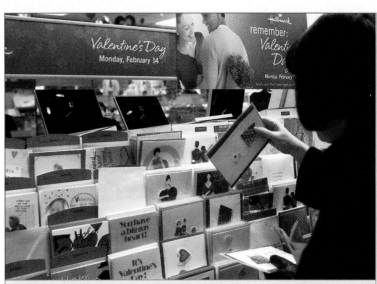

Even though Hallmark's business is seasonal, the company has never laid off employees. Instead the company's employees are trained to do different jobs at different times, and at different plants, if need be. Because they know they have greater job security, they work hard to keep setup times short and Hallmark's costs low.

Workforce Utilization An alternative to a workforce adjustment is a change in workforce utilization involving overtime and undertime. **Overtime** means that employees work longer than the regular workday or workweek and receive additional pay for the extra hours. It can be used to satisfy output requirements that cannot be completed on regular time. However, overtime is expensive (typically 150 percent of the regular-time pay rate). Moreover, workers often do not want to work a lot of overtime for an extended period of time, and excessive overtime may result in declining quality and productivity.

Undertime means that employees do not have enough work for the regular-time workday or workweek. For example, they cannot be fully utilized for eight hours per day or for five days per week. Undertime occurs when labor capacity exceeds demand requirements (net of anticipation inventory), and this excess capacity cannot or should not be used productively to build up inventory or to satisfy customer orders earlier than the delivery dates already promised.

Undertime can either be paid or unpaid. An example of *paid undertime* is when employees are kept on the payroll rather than being laid off. In this scenario, employees work a full day and receive their full salary but are not as busy because of the light workload. Some companies use paid undertime (though they do not call it that) during slack periods, particularly with highly skilled, hard-to-replace employees or when there are obstacles to laying off workers. The disadvantages of paid undertime include the cost of paying for work not performed and lowered productivity.

Part-Time Workers Another option apart from undertime is to hire part-time workers, who are paid only for the hours and days worked. Perhaps they only work during the peak times of the day or peak days of the week. Sometimes, part-time arrangements provide predictable work schedules, but in other cases workers are not called in if the workload is light. Such arrangements are more common in low-skill positions or when the supply of workers seeking such an arrangement is sufficient. Part-time workers typically do not receive fringe benefits.

Subcontractors Subcontractors can be used to overcome short-term capacity shortages, such as during peaks of the season or business cycle. Subcontractors can supply services, make components and subassemblies, or even assemble an entire product.

Vacation Schedules A manufacturer can shut down during an annual lull in sales, leaving a skeleton crew to cover operations and perform maintenance. Hospital employees might be encouraged to take all or part of their allowed vacation time during slack periods. The use of this alternative depends on whether the employer can mandate the vacation schedules of its employees. In any case, employees may be strongly discouraged from taking vacations during peak periods or encouraged to take vacations during slack periods.

Planning Strategies

Here we focus on supply options that define output rates and workforce levels. Two basic strategies are useful starting points in searching for the best plan.

1. *Chase Strategy*. The **chase strategy** involves hiring and laying off employees to match the demand forecast over the planning horizon. Varying the workforce's regular-time

overtime

The time that employees work that is longer than the regular workday or workweek for which they receive additional pay.

undertime

The situation that occurs when employees do not have enough work for the regular-time workday or workweek.

chase strategy

A strategy that involves hiring and laying off employees to match the demand forecast.

capacity to equate supply to demand requires no inventory investment, overtime, or undertime. The drawbacks are the expense of continually adjusting workforce levels, the potential alienation of the workforce, and the loss of productivity and quality because of constant changes in the workforce.

level strategy

A strategy that keeps the workforce constant, but varies its utilization via overtime, undertime, and vacation planning to match the demand forecast.

2. *Level Strategy.* The **level strategy** involves keeping the workforce constant (except possibly at the beginning of the planning horizon). It can vary its utilization to match the demand forecast via overtime, undertime (paid or unpaid), and vacation planning (i.e., paid vacations when demand is low). A constant workforce can be sized at many levels: Managers can choose to maintain a large workforce so as to minimize the planned use of overtime during peak periods (which, unfortunately, also maximizes the need for undertime during slack periods). Alternately, they can choose to maintain a smaller workforce and rely heavily on overtime during the peak periods (which places a strain on the workforce and endangers quality).

mixed strategy

A strategy that considers the full range of supply options.

These two "pure" strategies used alone usually do not produce the best sales and operations plan. It might not be best to keep the workforce exactly level, or to vary it to exactly match forecasted demand on a period-by-period basis. The best strategy, therefore, usually is a **mixed strategy** that considers the full range of supply options. The chase strategy is limited to just hiring and laying off employees. The level strategy is limited to overtime, undertime, and vacation schedules. The mixed strategy opens things up to all options, including anticipation inventory, part-time workers, subcontractors, backorders, and stockouts.

Constraints and Costs

An acceptable sales and operations plan must recognize relevant constraints or costs. Constraints can be either physical limitations or related to managerial policies. Examples of physical constraints might be machine capacities that limit maximum output or inadequate inventory storage space. Policy constraints might include limitations on the number of backorders or the use of subcontractors or overtime, as well as the minimum inventory levels needed to achieve desired safety stocks.

Typically, many plans can contain a number of constraints. Table 14.3 lists the costs that the planner considers when preparing sales and operations plans.

Sales and Operations Planning as a Process

Sales and operations planning is a decision-making process, involving both planners and management. It is dynamic and continuing, as aspects of the plan are updated periodically when new information becomes available and new opportunities emerge. It is a cross-functional process that seeks a set of plans that all of a firm's functions can support. For each product family, decisions are made based on cost trade-offs, recent history, recommendations by planners and middle management, and the executive team's judgment.

Figure 14.3 shows a typical plan for a manufacturer. The plan is for one of the manufacturer's make-to-stock product families expressed in aggregate units. This simple spreadsheet shows the interplay between demand and supply. The history on the left for January through

TABLE 14.3	TYPES OF COSTS WITH SALES AND OPERATIONS PLANNING
Cost	**Definition**
regular time	Regular-time wages paid to employees plus contributions to benefits, such as health insurance, dental care, Social Security, retirement funds, and pay for vacations, holidays, and certain other types of absences.
overtime	Wages paid for work beyond the normal workweek, typically 150 percent of regular-time wages (sometimes up to 200 percent for Sundays and holidays), exclusive of fringe benefits. Overtime can help avoid the extra cost of fringe benefits that come with hiring another full-time employee.
hiring and layoff	Costs of advertising jobs, interviews, training programs for new employees, scrap caused by the inexperience of new employees, loss of productivity, and initial paperwork. Layoff costs include the costs of exit interviews, severance pay, retaining and retraining remaining workers and managers, and lost productivity.
inventory holding	Costs that vary with the level of inventory investment: the costs of capital tied up in inventory, variable storage and warehousing costs, pilferage and obsolescence costs, insurance costs, and taxes.
backorder and stockout	Additional costs to expedite past-due orders, the costs of lost sales, and the potential cost of losing a customer to a competitor (sometimes called loss of goodwill).

Artic Air Company—April Sales and Operations Plan

Family: Medium window units (make-to-stock)　　　　　　　　　　　*Unit of measure:* 100 units

SALES	HISTORY J	F	M	A*	M	J	J	A	S	3rd 3 Mos**	4th 3 Mos	Mos 13–18	Fiscal Year Projection ($000)	Business Plan ($000)
New forecast	45	55	60	70	85	95	130	110	70	150	176	275	$8,700	$8,560
Actual sales	52	40	63											
Diff for month	7	–15	3											
Cum		–8	–5											
OPERATIONS														
New Plan	75	75	75	75	75	85	85	85	75	177	225			
Actual	75	78	76											
Diff for month	0	3	1											
Cum		3	4											
INVENTORY														
Plan	85	105	120	125	115	105	60	35	40	198	321			
Actual	92	130	143											

DEMAND ISSUES AND ASSUMPTIONS
1. New product design to be launched in January of next year.

SUPPLY ISSUES
1. Vacations primarily in November and December.
2. Overtime in July–August.

* April is the first month of the planning horizon for this current plan. When next month's plan is developed, its first month in the planning horizon will be May, and the most recent month of the history will be April (with January no longer shown in the history).

** This column provides the sales, operations, and inventory totals for October through December. For example, the forecast of 150 units translates into an average of 50 units per month (or 150/3 = 50).

◀ FIGURE 14.3
Sales and Operations Plan for Make-to-Stock Product Family

March shows how forecasts are tracking actual sales, and how well actual production conforms to the plan. The inventory projections are of particular interest to finance because they significantly affect the manufacturer's cash requirements. The last two columns on the top right show how current fiscal year sales projections match up with the current business plan.

This particular plan is projected out for 18 months, beginning with April. The forecast, operations, and inventory sections for the first 6 months are shown on a month-by-month basis. They then are shown on a quarterly basis for the second 6 months. Finally, the totals for the last 6 months in the time horizon are given in just one column. This display gives more precision to the short term and yet gives coverage well into the future—all with a limited number of columns.

This particular make-to-stock family experiences highly seasonal demand. The operations plan is to build up seasonal inventory in the slack season, schedule vacations as much as possible in November and December, and use overtime in the peak season of June, July, and August. For example, the Operations plan increases monthly production from 75 to 85 for June through August, returns to 75 for September, and then drops to an average of only 59 (or 177/3) for October through December. Plan spreadsheets use different formats depending on production and inventory strategy. For an assemble-to-order strategy, the inventory does not consist of finished goods. Instead, it is inventory of standardized components and subassemblies built for the finishing and assembly operations. For the make-to-order strategy, the inventory section in the plan of Figure 14.3 is replaced by a section showing the planned and actual order backlog quantities.

Plans for service providers are quite different. For one thing, their plan does not contain an inventory section, but focuses instead on the demand and supply of human resources. Forecasts are typically expressed in terms of employees required, with separate rows for regular time, overtime, vacations, part-time workers, and so on. Different departments or worker classifications replace product families.

The process itself, typically done on a monthly basis, consists of six basic steps. They are much like the steps we discussed in Chapter 13, "Forecasting Demand."

Step 1. Begin to "roll forward" the plan for the new planning horizon. Start preliminary work right after the month's end. Update files with actual sales, production, inventory, costs, and constraints.

Step 2. Participate in the forecasting and demand planning to create the authorized demand forecasts. For service providers, the forecasts are staff requirements for each workforce group. For example, a director of nursing in a hospital can develop a workload index for a nursing staff and translate a projection of the month-to-month patient load into an equivalent total amount of nursing care time—and thus the number of nurses—required for each month of the year.

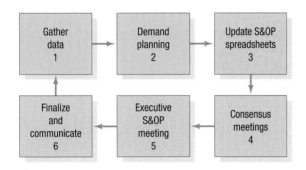

Step 3. Update the sales and operations planning spreadsheet for each family, recognizing relevant constraints and costs including availability of materials from suppliers, training facilities capable of handling only so many new hires at a time, machine capacities, or limited storage space. Policy constraints might include limitations on the number of backorders, or the use of subcontractors or overtime, as well as the minimum inventory levels needed to achieve desired safety stocks. Typically, many plans can satisfy a specific set of constraints. The planner searches for a plan that best balances costs, customer service, workforce stability, and the like. This process may necessitate revising the plan several times.

Step 4. Have one or more consensus meetings with the stakeholders on how best to balance supply with demand. Participants could include the supply chain manager, plant manager, controller, purchasing manager, production control manager, or logistics manager. The goal is one set of recommendations to present at the firm's executive sales and operations planning (S&OP) meeting. Where agreement cannot be reached, prepare scenarios of alternative plans. Also prepare an updated financial view of business by rolling up the plans for all product families into a spreadsheet expressed in total dollars.

Step 5. Present recommendations by product family at the executive S&OP meeting, which typically includes the firm's president and the vice presidents of functional areas. The plan is reviewed relative to the business plan, new product issues, special projects, and other relevant factors. The executives may ask for final changes to the plan, such as to balance conflicting objectives better. Acceptance of this authorized plan does not necessarily mean that everyone is in total agreement, but it does imply that everyone will work to achieve the plan.

Step 6. Update the spreadsheets to reflect the authorized plan, and communicate the plans to the important stakeholders for implementation. Important recipients include those who do resource planning, covered in the next chapter.

FUJIFILM Imaging Colorants makes inks and dyes, primarily for inkjet printer cartridges, and operates an effective S&OP process. It must coordinate between a U.S. finishing plant and a UK bulk manufacturing plant. The photo shows managers from all functions, who are teleconferencing at the U.S. site with seven other UK managers. At this Partnership meeting (step 4 in the S&OP process), they are reviewing the demand, production, and inventory plans, as well as the projected working capital plan. The image on the screen is their 18-month business plan approved by the Partnership. It shows the inventory target and inventory plan (top two lines), and the production and demand plan (bottom two lines). They are always looking at ways to reduce the top two lines (inventory).

Using Spreadsheets

The sales and operations plan in Figure 14.3 does not show much on the supply options used in the operations plan or their cost implications. Here we discuss using spreadsheets that do just that. Supplement E, "Linear Programming Models," describes using the transportation method for production planning. Both techniques could be used on the side as a planner develops prospective plans in step 3 of the planning process.

Various spreadsheets can be used, including ones that you develop on your own. Here we work with the *Sales and Operations Planning with Spreadsheets* Solver in OM Explorer. Figure 14.4 shows a plan for a manufacturer, which uses all supply options except overtime.

Spreadsheets for a Manufacturer　The top part of the spreadsheet shows the *input values* that give the forecasted demand requirements and the supply option choices period by period. Vary these "levers" as you search for better plans.

The next part of the spreadsheet (in green) shows the *derived values* that must follow from the input values. The first row of derived values is called *utilized time*, which is that portion of the workforce's regular time that is paid for and productively used. In any period, the utilized time equals the workforce level minus undertime and vacation time. For example, in period 1 the utilized time is 94 (or 120 − 6 − 20). The hires and layoffs rows can be derived from the workforce

	1	2	3	4	5	6	Total
Inputs							
Forecasted demand	24	142	220	180	136	168	870
Workforce level	120	158	158	158	158	158	910
Undertime	6	0	0	0	0	0	6
Overtime	0	0	0	0	0	0	0
Vacation time	20	6	0	0	4	10	40
Subcontracting time	0	0	0	0	0	6	6
Backorders	0	0	0	4	0	0	4
Derived							
Utilized time	94	152	158	158	154	148	864
Inventory	70	80	18	0	14	0	182
Hires	0	38	0	0	0	0	38
Layoffs	0	0	0	0	0	0	0
Calculated							
Utilized time cost	$376,000	$608,000	$632,000	$632,000	$616,000	$592,000	$3,456,000
Undertime cost	$24,000	$0	$0	$0	$0	$0	$24,000
Overtime cost	$0	$0	$0	$0	$0	$0	$0
Vacation time cost	$80,000	$24,000	$0	$0	$16,000	$40,000	$160,000
Inventory cost	$2,800	$3,200	$720	$0	$560	$0	$7,280
Backorders cost	$0	$0	$0	$4,000	$0	$0	$4,000
Hiring cost	$0	$91,200	$0	$0	$0	$0	$91,200
Layoff cost	$0	$0	$0	$0	$0	$0	$0
Subcontracting cost	$0	$0	$0	$0	$0	$43,200	$43,200
Total cost	$482,800	726,400	632,720	636,000	632,560	675,200	$3,785,680

▲ **FIGURE 14.4**
Manufacturer's Plan Using a Spreadsheet and Mixed Strategy

levels. In this example, the workforce is increased for period 2 from its initial size of 120 employees to 158, which means that 38 employees are hired. Because the workforce size remains constant at 158 throughout the rest of the planning horizon, no other hirings or lay-offs happen. When additional alternatives, such as vacations, inventory, and backorders are all possible, the overtime and undertime cannot be derived just from information on forecasted demand and workforce levels. Thus, undertime and overtime are shown as input values (rather than derived values) in the spreadsheet, and the user must be careful to specify consistent input values.

The final part of the spreadsheet, the *calculated values* of the plan, shows the plan's cost consequences. Along with qualitative considerations, the cost of each plan determines whether the plan is satisfactory or whether a revised plan should be considered. When seeking clues about how to improve a plan already evaluated, we identify its highest cost elements. Revisions that would reduce these specific costs might produce a new plan with lower overall costs. Spreadsheet programs make analyzing these plans easy, and they present a whole new set of possibilities for developing sound sales and operations plans.

The plan in Figure 14.4 definitely is for a manufacturer because it uses inventory to advantage, particularly in the first two periods. It is a mixed strategy, and not just because it uses anticipation inventory, backorders, and subcontracting. The workforce level changes in period 2, but it does not exactly match the forecasted demand as with a chase strategy. It has some elements of the level strategy, because undertime and vacation time are part of the plan, but it does not rely exclusively on these supply options.

Care must be taken to recognize differences in how inputs are measured. The workforce level might be expressed as the number of employees, but the forecasted demand and inventory are expressed as units of the product. The OM Explorer spreadsheets require a common unit of measure, so we must translate some of the data prior to entering the input values. Perhaps the easiest approach is to express the forecasted demand and supply options as *employee-period equivalents*. If demand forecasts are given as units of product, we can convert them to employee-period equivalents by dividing them by the productivity of a worker. For example, if the demand is for 1,500 units of product and the average employee produces 100 units in one period, the demand requirement is 15 employee-period equivalents.

Spreadsheets for a Service Provider   The same spreadsheets can be used by service providers, except anticipation inventory is not an option. Whereas Figure 14.4 shows a good plan found after several revisions, here we illustrate with Example 14.1 how to find a good plan for a service provider beginning with the chase and level (ignoring vacations) strategies. These plans can provide insights that lead to even better mixed strategy plans.

EXAMPLE 14.1   **Using the Chase and Level Strategies as Starting Points**

The manager of a large distribution center must determine how many part-time stockpickers to maintain on the payroll. She wants to develop a staffing plan that minimizes total costs, and wants to begin with the chase strategy and level strategy. For the level strategy, she wants to first try the workforce level that meets demand with the minimum use of undertime and not consider vacation scheduling.

First, the manager divides the next year into six time periods, each one 2 months long. Each part-time employee can work a maximum of 20 hours per week on regular time, but the actual number can be less. Instead of paying undertime, each worker's day is shortened during slack periods. Once on the payroll, each worker is used each day, but they may work only a few hours. Overtime can be used during peak periods.

The distribution center's forecasted demand is shown as the number of part-time employees required for each time period at the maximum regular time of 20 hours per week. For example, in period 3, an estimated 18 part-time employees working 20 hours per week on regular time will be needed.

	1	2	3	4	5	6	Total
Forecasted demand*	6	12	18	15	13	14	78

*Number of part-time employees

Currently, 10 part-time clerks are employed. They have not been subtracted from the forecasted demand shown. Constraints and cost information are as follows:

a. The size of training facilities limits the number of new hires in any period to no more than 10.

b. No backorders are permitted; demand must be met each period.

c. Overtime cannot exceed 20 percent of the regular-time capacity (that is, 4 hours) in any period. Therefore, the most that any part-time employee can work is 1.20(20) = 24 hours per week.

d. The following costs can be assigned:

Regular-time wage rate	$2,000 per time period at 20 hours per week
Overtime wages	150 percent of the regular-time rate
Hires	$1,000 per person
Layoffs	$500 per person

Framed by thousands of ski poles, a part-time worker sorts and inventories new products in the receiving department of REI's Distribution Center in Sumner, Washington. REI employs a high percentage of part-time workers, many of whom are college students. They tend to be young people who participate in outdoor sports and are familiar with the equipment that REI sells.

SOLUTION

a.   Chase Strategy

This strategy simply involves adjusting the workforce as needed to meet demand, as shown in Figure 14.5. Rows in the spreadsheet that do not apply (such as inventory and vacations) are hidden. The workforce level row is identical to the forecasted demand row. A large number of hirings and layoffs begin with laying off 4 part-time employees immediately because the current staff is 10 and the staff level required in period 1 is only 6. However, many employees, such as college students, prefer part-time work. The total cost is $173,500, and most of the cost increase comes from frequent hiring and layoffs, which add $17,500 to the cost of utilized regular-time costs.

Tutor 14.1 in my**om**lab provides a new example for planning using the chase strategy with hiring and layoffs.

	1	2	3	4	5	6	Total
Inputs							
Forecasted demand	6	12	18	15	13	14	78
Workforce level	6	12	18	15	13	14	78
Undertime	0	0	0	0	0	0	0
Overtime	0	0	0	0	0	0	0
Derived							
Utilized time	6	12	18	15	13	14	78
Hires	0	6	6	0	0	1	13
Layoffs	4	0	0	3	2	0	9
Calculated							
Utilized time cost	$12,000	$24,000	$36,000	$30,000	$26,000	$28,000	$156,000
Undertime cost	$0	$0	$0	$0	$0	$0	$0
Hiring cost	$0	$6,000	$6,000	$0	$0	$1,000	$13,000
Layoff cost	$2,000	$0	$0	$1,500	$1,000	$0	$4,500
Total cost	$14,000	30,000	42,000	31,500	27,000	29,000	$173,500

◀ **FIGURE 14.5**
Spreadsheet for Chase Strategy

b.   Level Strategy

In order to minimize undertime, the maximum use of overtime possible must occur in the peak period. For this particular level strategy (other workforce options are possible), the most overtime that the manager can use is 20 percent of the regular-time capacity, w, so

$$1.20w = 18 \text{ employees required in peak period (period 3)}$$

$$w = \frac{18}{1.20} = 15 \text{ employees}$$

A 15-employee staff size minimizes the amount of undertime for this level strategy. Because the staff already includes 10 part-time employees, the manager should immediately hire 5 more. The complete plan is shown in Figure 14.6. The total cost is $164,000, which seems reasonable because the minimum conceivable cost is only $156,000 (78 periods × $2,000/period). This cost could be achieved only if the manager found a way to cover the forecasted demand for all 78 periods with regular time. The plan seems reasonable primarily because it involves the use of large amounts of undertime (15 periods), which in this example are unpaid.

Tutor 14.2 in my**om**lab provides a new example for planning using the level strategy with overtime and undertime.

	1	2	3	4	5	6	Total
Inputs							
Forecasted demand	6	12	18	15	13	14	78
Workforce level	15	15	15	15	15	15	90
Undertime	9	3	0	0	2	1	15
Overtime	0	0	3	0	0	0	3
Derived							
Utilized time	6	12	15	15	13	14	75
Hires	5	0	0	0	0	0	5
Layoffs	0	0	0	0	0	0	0
Calculated							
Utilized time cost	$12,000	$24,000	$30,000	$30,000	$26,000	$28,000	$150,000
Undertime cost	$0	$0	$0	$0	$0	$0	$0
Overtime cost	$0	$0	$9,000	$0	$0	$0	$9,000
Hiring cost	$5,000	$0	$0	$0	$0	$0	$5,000
Layoff cost	$0	$0	$0	$0	$0	$0	$0
Total cost	$17,000	24,000	39,000	30,000	26,000	28,000	$164,000

◀ **FIGURE 14.6**
Spreadsheet for Level Strategy

Active Model 14.1 in my**om**lab shows the impact of changing the workforce level, the cost structure, and overtime capacity.

DECISION POINT

The manager, now having a point of reference with which to compare other plans, decided to evaluate some other plans before making a final choice, beginning with the chase strategy. The only way to reduce costs is somehow to reduce the premium for 3 overtime employee periods (3 periods × $3,000/period) or to reduce the hiring cost of 5 employees (5 hires × $1,000/person). Nonetheless, better solutions may be possible. For example, undertime can be reduced by delaying the hiring until period 2 because the current workforce is sufficient until then. This delay would decrease the amount of unpaid undertime, which is a qualitative improvement. See Active Model 14.1 for additional insights.

SCHEDULING

Scheduling is the last step in Figure 14.1. It takes the operations and scheduling process from planning to execution, and is where the "rubber meets the road." This important aspect of supply chain management is itself a process. It requires gathering data from sources such as demand forecasts or specific customer orders, resource availability from the sales and operations plan, and specific constraints to be reckoned with from employees and customers. It then involves generating a work schedule for employees or sequences of jobs or customers at workstations. The schedule has to be coordinated with the employees and suppliers to make sure that all constraints are satisfied. Here we cover Gantt charts, employee schedules, job sequencing at workstations, and software support.

Gantt Charts

Schedules can be displayed in various ways. For different jobs or activities they can simply list their due dates, show in a table their start and finish times, or show in a graph their start and finish times. The *Gantt chart* uses the third approach. Figure 2.5 back in Chapter 2 demonstrates how a "picture can be worth a thousand words" in managing projects. Associates not familiar with scheduling techniques can still grasp the essence of the plan. This tool can be used to monitor the progress of work and to view the load on workstations. The chart takes two basic forms: (1) the job or activity progress chart and (2) the workstation chart. The *Gantt progress chart* graphically displays the current status of each job or activity relative to its scheduled completion date. For example, suppose that an automobile parts manufacturer has three jobs under way, one each for Ford, Nissan, and Pontiac. The actual status of these orders is shown by the colored bars in Figure 14.7; the red lines indicate the desired schedule for the start and finish of each job. For the current date, April 21, this Gantt chart shows that the Ford order is behind schedule because operations has completed only the work scheduled through April 18. The Nissan order is exactly on schedule, and the Pontiac order is ahead of schedule.

FIGURE 14.7 ▲
Gantt Progress Chart for an Auto Parts Company

Figure 14.8 shows a *Gantt workstation chart* of the operating rooms at a hospital for a particular day. Using the same notation as in Figure 14.7, the chart shows the load on the operating rooms and the nonproductive time. The time slots assigned to each doctor include the time needed to clean the room prior to the next surgery. The chart can be used to identify time slots for unscheduled emergency surgeries. It can also be used to accommodate requests to change the time of surgeries. For example, Dr. Flowers may be able to change the start of her surgery to 2 P.M. by swapping time slots with Dr. Gillespie in operating room C or by asking Dr. Brothers to start her surgery one hour earlier in operating room A and asking Dr. Bright to schedule her surgery for the morning in operating room C. In any event, the hospital administrator would have to get involved in rescheduling the surgeries.

▲ FIGURE 14.8
Gantt Workstation Chart for Operating Rooms at a Hospital

Scheduling Employees

Another way to manage capacity is **workforce scheduling**, which is a type of scheduling that determines when employees work. It specifies the on-duty and off-duty periods for each employee over a certain time period, as in assigning postal clerks, nurses, pilots, attendants, or police officers to specific workdays and shifts. This approach is used when customers demand quick response and total demand can be forecasted with reasonable accuracy. In these instances, capacity is adjusted to meet the expected loads on the service system.

workforce scheduling

A type of scheduling that determines when employees work.

Workforce schedules translate the staffing plan into specific schedules of work for each employee. Determining the workdays for each employee in itself does not make the staffing plan operational. Daily workforce requirements, stated in aggregate terms in the staffing plan, must be satisfied. The workforce capacity available each day must meet or exceed daily workforce requirements. If it does not, the scheduler must try to rearrange days off until the requirements are met. If no such schedule can be found, management might have to change the staffing plan and hire more employees, authorize overtime hours, or allow for larger backlogs.

Constraints The technical constraints imposed on the workforce schedule are the resources provided by the staffing plan and the requirements placed on the operating system. However, other constraints, including legal and behavioral considerations, also can be imposed. For example, Air New Zealand is required to

When it comes to services like firefighting, schedulers cannot manage the customer demand. Fires will occur whenever they occur, of course. The workforce capacity available each day at a firehouse must, therefore, always meet or exceed daily requirements.

have at least a minimum number of flight attendants on duty at all times. Similarly, a minimum number of fire and safety personnel must be on duty at a fire station at all times. Such constraints limit management's flexibility in developing workforce schedules.

The constraints imposed by the psychological needs of workers complicate scheduling even more. Some of these constraints are written into labor agreements. For example, an employer might agree to give employees a certain number of consecutive days off per week or to limit employees' consecutive workdays to a certain maximum. Other provisions might govern the allocation of vacations, days off for holidays, or rotating shift assignments. In addition, the preferences of the employees themselves need to be considered.

One way that managers deal with certain undesirable aspects of scheduling is to use a **rotating schedule**, which rotates employees through a series of workdays or hours. Thus, over a period of time, each person has the same opportunity to have weekends and holidays off and to work days, as well as evenings and nights. A rotating schedule gives each employee the next employee's schedule the following week. In contrast, a **fixed schedule** calls for each employee to work the same days and hours each week.

rotating schedule

A schedule that rotates employees through a series of workdays or hours.

fixed schedule

A schedule that calls for each employee to work the same days and hours each week.

Developing a Workforce Schedule Suppose that we are interested in developing a workforce schedule for a company that operates seven days a week and provides each employee with two consecutive days off. In this section, we demonstrate a method that recognizes this constraint. The objective is to identify the two consecutive days off for each employee that will minimize the amount of total slack capacity, thereby maximizing the utilization of the workforce. The work schedule for each employee, then, is the five days that remain after the two days off have been determined. The procedure involves the following steps.

Step 1. From the schedule of net requirements for the week, find all the pairs of consecutive days, excluding the day (or days) with the maximum daily requirement. Select the unique pair that has the lowest total requirements for the two days. In some unusual situations, all pairs may contain a day with the maximum requirements. If so, select the pair with the lowest total requirements. Suppose that the numbers of employees required are

Monday: 8	Thursday: 12	Saturday: 4
Tuesday: 9	Friday: 7	Sunday: 2
Wednesday: 2		

The maximum daily requirement is 12 employees, on Thursday. The consecutive pair with the lowest total requirements is Saturday and Sunday, with $4 + 2 = 6$.

Step 2. If a tie occurs, choose one of the tied pairs, consistent with the provisions written into the labor agreement, if any. Alternatively, the tie could be broken by asking the employee being scheduled to make the choice. As a last resort, the tie could be broken arbitrarily. For example, preference could be given to Saturday–Sunday pairs.

Step 3. Assign the employee the selected pair of days off. Subtract the requirements satisfied by the employee from the net requirements for each day the employee is to work. In this example, the employee is assigned Saturday and Sunday off. After requirements are subtracted, Monday's requirement is 7, Tuesday's is 8, Wednesday's is 1, Thursday's is 11, and Friday's is 6. Saturday's and Sunday's requirements do not change because no employee is yet scheduled to work those days.

Step 4. Repeat steps 1 through 3 until all the requirements have been satisfied or a certain number of employees have been scheduled.

This method reduces the amount of slack capacity assigned to days with low requirements and forces the days with high requirements to be scheduled first. It also recognizes some of the behavioral and contractual aspects of workforce scheduling in the tie-breaking rules.

EXAMPLE 14.2	Developing a Workforce Schedule

The Amalgamated Parcel Service is open seven days a week. The schedule of requirements is

Day	M	T	W	Th	F	S	Su
Required number of employees	6	4	8	9	10	3	2

The manager needs a workforce schedule that provides two consecutive days off and minimizes the amount of total slack capacity. To break ties in the selection of off days, the scheduler gives preference to Saturday and Sunday if it is one of the tied pairs. If not, she selects one of the tied pairs arbitrarily.

myomlab

Tutor 14.3 in myomlab provides a new example to practice workforce scheduling.

SOLUTION

Friday contains the maximum requirements, and the pair S–Su has the lowest total requirements. Therefore, Employee 1 is scheduled to work Monday through Friday.

Note that Friday still has the maximum requirements and that the requirements for the S–Su pair are carried forward because these are Employee 1's days off. These updated requirements are the ones the scheduler uses for the next employee.

The day-off assignments for the employees are shown in the following table.

Scheduling Days Off

M	T	W	Th	F	S	Su	Employee	Comments
6	4	8	9	10	3	2	**1**	The S–Su pair has the lowest total requirements. Assign Employee **1** to a Monday through Friday schedule and update the requirements.
5	3	7	8	9	3	2	**2**	The S–Su pair has the lowest total requirements. Assign Employee **2** to a Monday through Friday schedule and update the requirements.
4	2	6	7	8	3	2	**3**	The S–Su pair has the lowest total requirements. Assign Employee **3** to a Monday through Friday schedule and update the requirements.
3	1	5	6	7	3	2	**4**	The M–T pair has the lowest total requirements. Assign Employee **4** to a Wednesday through Sunday schedule and update the requirements.
3	1	4	5	6	2	1	**5**	The S–Su pair has the lowest total requirements. Assign Employee **5** to a Monday through Friday schedule and update the requirements.
2	0	3	4	5	2	1	**6**	The M–T pair has the lowest total requirements. Assign Employee **6** to a Wednesday through Sunday schedule and update the requirements.
2	0	2	3	4	1	0	**7**	The S–Su pair has the lowest total requirements. Assign Employee **7** to a Monday through Friday schedule and update the requirements.
1	0	1	2	3	1	0	**8**	Four pairs have the minimum requirement and the lowest total: S–Su, Su–M, M–T, and T–W. Choose the S–Su pair according to the tie-breaking rule. Assign Employee **8** to a Monday through Friday schedule and update the requirements.
0	0	0	1	2	1	0	**9**	Arbitrarily choose the Su–M pair to break ties because the S–Su pair does not have the lowest total requirements. Assign Employee **9** to a Tuesday through Saturday schedule and update the requirements.
0	0	0	0	1	0	0	**10**	Choose the S–Su pair according to the tie-breaking rule. Assign Employee **10** to a Monday through Friday schedule.

In this example, Friday always has the maximum requirements and should be avoided as a day off. The final schedule for the employees is shown in the following table.

Employee	M	T	W	Th	F	S	Su	Total
			Final Schedule					
1	X	X	X	X	X	off	off	
2	X	X	X	X	X	off	off	
3	X	X	X	X	X	off	off	
4	off	off	X	X	X	X	X	
5	X	X	X	X	X	off	off	
6	off	off	X	X	X	X	X	
7	X	X	X	X	X	off	off	
8	X	X	X	X	X	off	off	
9	off	X	X	X	X	X	off	
10	X	X	X	X	X	off	off	
Capacity, C	7	8	10	10	10	3	2	50
Requirements, R	6	4	8	9	10	3	2	42
Slack, C − R	1	4	2	1	0	0	0	8

DECISION POINT

With its substantial amount of slack capacity, the schedule is not unique. Employee 9, for example, could have Sunday and Monday, Monday and Tuesday, or Tuesday and Wednesday off without causing a capacity shortage. Indeed, the company might be able to get by with one fewer employee because of the total of eight slack days of capacity. However, all 10 employees are needed on Fridays. If the manager were willing to get by with only nine employees on Fridays or if someone could work one day of overtime on a rotating basis, he would not need Employee 10. As indicated in the table, the net requirement left for Employee 10 to satisfy amounts to only one day, Friday. Thus, Employee 10 can be used to fill in for vacationing or sick employees.

Managers try to staff their call centers to meet certain performance measures. One such measure is the percentage of calls answered (PCA) within a specified time interval, termed the service objective (SO). Typically in a call center, the PCA is in the range of 80 to 90 percent, and the SO is 15 to 30 seconds. The problem is that the requirements for agents change over time, depending on the time of day and day of the year. Also, the callers are likely to speak different languages. Determining how many of each group of agents to have on hand at all times is not easy. Fortunately, employee scheduling software is available to estimate call volumes, project skill requirements, and identify employee start and end times or preferred days off.

Sequencing Jobs at a Workstation

Another aspect of scheduling is sequencing work at workstations. **Sequencing** determines the order in which jobs or customers are processed in the waiting line at a workstation. When combined with the expected processing time, the sequence allows you to estimate the start and finish times of each job.

Priority Sequencing Rules   One way to determine what job or customer to process next is with the help of a **priority sequencing rule**. The following two priority sequencing rules are commonly used in practice.

- *First-Come, First-Served.* The job or customer arriving at the workstation first has the highest priority under a **first-come, first-served (FCFS)** rule. This rule is the most "democratic" in that each job is treated equally, with no one stepping ahead of others already in line. It is commonly used at service facilities, and is the rule that was assumed in Supplement C, "Waiting Line Models."

- *Earliest Due Date.* The job or customer with the **earliest due date (EDD)** is the next one to be processed. The *due date* specifies when work on a job or customer should be finished. Due dates are commonly used by manufacturers and suppliers in the supply chain. For example, a product cannot be assembled until all of its purchased and produced components are available. If these components were not already in inventory, they must be ordered prior to when the product assembly can begin. Their due date is the start date for assembling the product to be assembled. This simple relationship is fundamental to coordinating with suppliers and with the manufacturer's own shops in the supply chain. It is also the key to **expediting**, which is the process of completing a job sooner than would otherwise be done. Expediting can be done by revising the due date, moving the job to the front of the waiting line, making a special appeal by phone or e-mail to the supplier, adding extra capacity, or even putting a red tag on the job that says the job is urgent.

Neither rule guarantees finding an optimal solution. Different sequences found by trial and error can produce better schedules. In fact, there are multiple performance measures for judging a schedule. A schedule that does well on one measure may do poorly on another.

Performance Measures   The quality of a schedule can be judged in various ways. Two commonly used performance measures are flow time and past due.

- *Flow Time.* The amount of time a job spends in the service or manufacturing system is called **flow time**. It is the sum of the waiting time for servers or machines; the process time, including setups; the time spent moving between operations; and delays resulting from machine breakdowns, unavailability of facilitating goods or components, and the like. Flow time is sometimes referred to as *throughput time* or *time spent in the system, including service.* For a set of jobs to be processed at a single workstation. a job's flow time is

$$\text{Flow time} = \text{Finish time} + \text{Time since job arrived at workstation}$$

When using this equation, we assume for convenience that the first job scheduled starts at time zero (0). At time 0, all the jobs were available for processing at the workstation.

- *Past Due.* The measure **past due** can be expressed as the amount of time by which a job missed its due date (also referred to as **tardiness**) or as the percentage of total jobs processed over some period of time that missed their due dates. Minimizing the past due measure supports the competitive priorities of cost (penalties for missing due dates), quality (perceptions of poor service), and time (on-time delivery).

---

sequencing

Determining the order in which jobs or customers are processed in the waiting line at a workstation.

priority sequencing rule

A rule that specifies the job or customer processing sequence when several jobs are waiting in line at a workstation.

first-come, first served (FCFS)

A priority sequencing rule that specifies that the job or customer arriving at the workstation first has the highest priority.

earliest due date (EDD)

A priority sequencing rule that specifies that the job or customer with the earliest due date is the next job to be processed.

expediting

The process of completing a job or finishing with a customer sooner than would otherwise be done.

flow time

The amount of time a job spends in the service or manufacturing system.

past due

The amount of time by which a job missed its due date.

tardiness

See **past due**.

EXAMPLE 14.3	Using the FCFS Rule

Currently a consulting company has five jobs in its backlog. The time since the order was placed, processing time, and promised due dates are given in the following table. Determine the schedule by using the FCFS rule, and calculate the average days past due and flow time. How can the schedule be improved, if average flow time is the most critical?

Customer	Time Since Order Arrived (days ago)	Processing Time (days)	Due Date (days from now)
A	15	25	29
B	12	16	27
C	5	14	68
D	10	10	48
E	0	12	80

SOLUTION

a. The FCFS rule states that Customer A should be the first one in the sequence, because that order arrived earliest—15 days ago. Customer E's order arrived today, so it is processed last. The sequence is shown in the following table, along with the days past due and flow times.

Customer Sequence	Start Time (days)		Processing Time (days)		Finish Time (days)	Due Date	Days Past Due	Days Ago Since Order Arrived	Flow Time (days)
A	0	+	25	=	25	29	0	15	40
B	25	+	16	=	41	27	14	12	53
D	41	+	10	=	51	48	3	10	61
C	51	+	14	=	65	68	0	5	70
E	65	+	12	=	77	80	0	0	77

The *finish time* for a job is its start time plus the processing time. Its finish time becomes the start time for the next job in the sequence, assuming that the next job is available for immediate processing. The days past due for a job is zero (0) if its due date is equal to or exceeds the finish time. Otherwise it equals the shortfall. The flow time for each job equals its finish time plus the number of days ago since the order first arrived at the workstation. For example, Customer C's flow time is its scheduled finish time of 65 days plus the 5 days since the order arrived, or 70 days. The days past due and average flow time performance measures for the FCFS schedule are

$$\text{Average days past due} = \frac{0 + 14 + 3 + 0 + 0}{5} = 3.4 \text{ days}$$

$$\text{Average flow time} = \frac{40 + 53 + 61 + 70 + 77}{5} = 60.2 \text{ days}$$

b. The average flow time can be reduced. One possibility is the sequence shown in the following table, which uses one of the rules introduced in Supplement J, "Operations Scheduling." (For still another possibility see Solved Problem 3, which applies the EDD rule.)

Customer Sequence	Start Time (days)		Processing Time (days)		Finish Time (days)	Due Date	Days Past Date	Days Ago Since Order Arrived	Flow Time (days)
D	0	+	10	=	10	48	**0**	10	**20**
E	10	+	12	=	22	80	**0**	0	**22**
C	22	+	14	=	36	68	**0**	5	**41**
B	36	+	16	=	52	27	**25**	12	**64**
A	52	+	25	=	77	29	**48**	15	**92**

$$\text{Average days past due} = \frac{0 + 0 + 0 + 25 + 48}{5} = 14.6 \text{ days}$$

$$\text{Average flow time} = \frac{20 + 22 + 41 + 64 + 92}{5} = 47.8 \text{ days}$$

This schedule reduces the average flow time from 60.2 to 47.8 days—a 21 percent improvement. However, the past due times for jobs A and B have increased.

DECISION POINT

Management decided to use a modified version of the second schedule, adding overtime when Customer B is processed. Further, Customer A agreed to extend its due date to 77 days, because in this case the advanced warning allowed it to reschedule its own operations with little problem.

Software Support

Computerized scheduling systems are available to cope with the complexity of workforce scheduling, such as the myriad constraints and concerns at Air New Zealand. In some types of firms, such as telephone companies, mail-order catalog houses, or emergency hotline agencies, employees must be on duty 24 hours a day, 7 days a week.

Sometimes a portion of the staff is part time, which allows management a great deal of flexibility but adds considerable complexity to the scheduling requirements. The flexibility comes from the opportunity to match anticipated loads closely through the use of overlapping shifts or odd shift lengths; the complexity comes from the need to evaluate the numerous possible alternatives. Management also must consider the timing of lunch breaks and rest periods, the number and starting times of shift schedules, and the days off for each employee. The programs select the schedule that minimizes the sum of expected costs of over- and understaffing.

Software is also available for sequencing jobs at workstations. They help firms design and manage the linkages between customers and suppliers in the supply chain. True integration requires the manipulation of large amounts of complex data in real time because the customer order work flow must be synchronized with the required material, manufacturing, and distribution activity. Coupled with the Internet and improved data storage and manipulation methods, such computer software has given rise to **advanced planning and scheduling (APS) systems**, which seek to optimize resources across the supply chain and align daily operations with strategic goals. A firm's ability to change its schedules quickly and still keep the goods and services flowing smoothly through the supply chain provides a competitive edge.

When Nissan introduced the Almera to the European market, it decided to produce it at the most efficient Sunderland plant in the United Kingdom. It already manufactured the Micra and Primera models there. Multi-vehicle scheduling is quite complex because of the many constraints involved. The painting portion of the job is particularly time consuming, but is only one of thousands of tasks the plant must efficiently schedule. A sophisticated software package, called ILOG Solver, assists the scheduling process for a coordinated flow.

advanced planning and scheduling (APS) systems

Computer software systems that seek to optimize resources across the supply chain and align daily operations with strategic goals.

INTERNET RESOURCES

my**om**lab and the Companion Website at **www.pearsonglobaleditions.com/krajewski** contain many tools, activities, and resources designed for this chapter.

KEY TERMS

advanced planning and scheduling
    (APS) systems 545
aggregate plan 524
annual plan or financial plan 525
backlog 528
backorder and stockout 532
business plan 525
chase strategy 531
complementary products 527
demand management 527
earliest due date (EDD) 543
expediting 543
first-come, first-served (FCFS) 543

fixed schedule 540
flow time 543
hiring and layoff 532
inventory holding 532
level strategy 532
mixed strategy 532
operations planning and scheduling 524
overtime 531
past due 543
priority sequencing rule 543
product family 525
production plan 524

regular time 532
resource plan 524
revenue management 527
rotating schedule 540
sales and operations planning
    (S&OP) 524
schedule 524
sequencing 543
staffing plan 524
tardiness 543
undertime 531
workforce scheduling 539

SOLVED PROBLEM 1

The Food Bin grocery store operates 24 hours per day, 7 days per week. Fred Bulger, the store manager, has been analyzing the efficiency and productivity of store operations recently. Bulger decided to observe the need for checkout clerks on the first shift for a one-month period. At the end of the month, he calculated the average number of checkout registers that should be open during the first shift each day. His results showed peak needs on Saturdays and Sundays.

Day	M	T	W	Th	F	S	Su
Number of Clerks Required	3	4	5	5	4	7	8

Bulger now has to come up with a workforce schedule that guarantees each checkout clerk two consecutive days off but still covers all requirements.

a. Develop a workforce schedule that covers all requirements while giving two consecutive days off to each clerk. How many clerks are needed? Assume that the clerks have no preference regarding which days they have off.

b. Plans can be made to use the clerks for other duties if slack or idle time resulting from this schedule can be determined. How much idle time will result from this schedule, and on what days?

SOLUTION

a. We use the method demonstrated in Example 14.2 to determine the number of clerks needed. The minimum number of clerks is eight.

	Day						
	M	**T**	**W**	**Th**	**F**	**S**	**Su**
Requirements	3	4	5	5	4	7	8*
Clerk 1	off	off	X	X	X	X	X
Requirements	3	4	4	4	3	6	7*
Clerk 2	off	off	X	X	X	X	X
Requirements	3	4	3	3	2	5	6*
Clerk 3	X	X	X	off	off	X	X
Requirements	2	3	2	3	2	4	5*
Clerk 4	X	X	X	off	off	X	X
Requirements	1	2	1	3	2	3	4*
Clerk 5	X	off	off	X	X	X	X
Requirements	0	2	1	2	1	2	3*
Clerk 6	off	off	X	X	X	X	X
Requirements	0	2*	0	1	0	1	2*
Clerk 7	X	X	off	off	X	X	X
Requirements	0	1*	0	1*	0	0	1*
Clerk 8	X	X	X	X	off	off	X
Requirements	0	0	0	0	0	0	0

* Maximum requirements

b. Based on the results in part (a), the number of clerks on duty minus the requirements is the number of idle clerks available for other duties:

	M	**T**	**W**	**Th**	**F**	**S**	**Su**
Number on duty	5	4	6	5	5	7	8
Requirements	3	4	5	5	4	7	8
Idle clerks	2	0	1	0	1	0	0

The slack in this schedule would indicate to Bulger the number of employees he might ask to work part time (fewer than five days per week). For example, Clerk 7 might work Tuesday, Saturday, and Sunday and Clerk 8 might work Tuesday, Thursday, and Sunday. That would eliminate slack from the schedule.

SOLVED PROBLEM 2

The Cranston Telephone Company employs workers who lay telephone cables and perform various other construction tasks. The company prides itself on good service and strives to complete all service orders within the planning period in which they are received.

Each worker puts in 600 hours of regular time per planning period and can work as many as an additional 100 hours of overtime. The operations department has estimated the following workforce requirements for such services over the next four planning periods:

Planning Period	1	2	3	4
Demand (hours)	21,000	18,000	30,000	12,000

Cranston pays regular-time wages of $6,000 per employee per period for any time worked up to 600 hours (including undertime). The overtime pay rate is $15 per hour over 600 hours. Hiring, training, and outfitting a new employee costs $8,000. Layoff costs are $2,000 per employee. Currently, 40 employees work for Cranston in this capacity. No delays in service, or backorders, are allowed. Use the spreadsheet approach to answer the following questions:

a. Prepare a chase strategy using only hiring and layoffs. What are the total numbers of employees hired and laid off?

b. Develop a workforce plan that uses the level strategy, relaying only on overtime and undertime. Maximize the use of overtime during the peak period so as to minimize the workforce level and amount of undertime.

c. Propose an effective mixed-strategy plan.

d. Compare the total costs of the three plans.

SOLUTION

a. The chase strategy workforce is calculated by dividing the demand for each period by 600 hours, or the amount or regular-time work for one employee during one period. This strategy calls for a total of 20 workers to be hired and 40 to be laid off during the four-period plan. Figure 14.9 shows the "chase strategy" solution that OM Explorer's *Sales and Operations Planning with Spreadsheets* Solver produces. We simply hide any unneeded columns and rows in this general-purpose solver.

FIGURE 14.9 ▶
Spreadsheet for Chase Strategy

	1	2	3	4	Total
Inputs					
Forecasted demand	35	30	50	20	135
Workforce level	35	30	50	20	135
Undertime	0	0	0	0	0
Overtime	0	0	0	0	0
Derived					
Utilized time	35	30	50	20	135
Hires	0	0	20	0	20
Layoffs	5	5	0	30	40
Calculated					
Utilized time cost	$210,000	$180,000	$300,000	$120,000	$810,000
Undertime cost	$0	$0	$0	$0	$0
Overtime cost	$0	$0	$0	$0	$0
Hiring cost	$0	$0	$160,000	$0	$160,000
Layoff cost	$10,000	$10,000	$0	$60,000	$80,000
Total cost	$220,000	190,000	460,000	180,000	$1,050,000

b. The peak demand is 30,000 hours in period 3. As each employee can work 700 hours per period (600 on regular time and 100 on overtime), the workforce level of the level strategy that minimizes undertime is 30,000/700 = 42.86, or 43 employees. This strategy calls for three employees to be hired in the first quarter and for none to be laid off. To convert the demand requirements into employee-period equivalents, divide the demand in hours by 600. For example, the demand of 21,000 hours in period 1 translates into 35 employee-period equivalents (21,000/600) and demand in period 3 translates into 50 employee-period equivalents (30,000/600). Figure 14.10 shows OM Explorer's spreadsheet for this level strategy that minimizes undertime.

◀ FIGURE 14.10
Spreadsheet for Level Strategy

	1	2	3	4	Total
Inputs					
Forecasted demand	35	30	50	20	135
Workforce level	43	43	43	43	172
Undertime	8	13	0	23	44
Overtime	0	0	7	0	7
Derived					
Utilized time	35	30	43	20	128
Hires	3	0	0	0	3
Layoffs	0	0	0	0	0
Calculated					
Utilized time cost	$210,000	$180,000	$258,000	$120,000	$768,000
Undertime cost	$48,000	$78,000	$0	$138,000	$264,000
Overtime cost	$0	$0	$63,000	$0	$63,000
Hiring cost	$24,000	$0	$0	$0	$24,000
Layoff cost	$0	$0	$0	$0	$0
Total cost	$282,000	258,000	321,000	258,000	$1,119,000

c. The mixed-strategy plan that we propose uses a combination of hires, layoffs, and overtime to reduce total costs. The workforce is reduced by 5 at the beginning of the first period, increased by 8 in the third period, and reduced by 13 in the fourth period. Figure 14.11 shows the results.

◀ FIGURE 14.11
Spreadsheet for Mixed Strategy

	1	2	3	4	Total
Inputs					
Forecasted demand	35	30	50	20	135
Workforce level	35	35	43	30	143
Undertime	0	5	0	10	15
Overtime	0	0	7	0	7
Derived					
Utilized time	35	30	43	20	128
Hires	0	0	8	0	8
Layoffs	5	0	0	13	18
Calculated					
Utilized time cost	$210,000	$180,000	$258,000	$120,000	$768,000
Undertime cost	$0	$30,000	$0	$60,000	$90,000
Overtime cost	$0	$0	$63,000	$0	$63,000
Hiring cost	$0	$0	$64,000	$0	$64,000
Layoff cost	$10,000	$0	$0	$26,000	$36,000
Total cost	$220.000	210,000	385,000	206,000	$1,021,000

d. The total cost of the chase strategy is $1,050,000. The level strategy results in a total cost of $1,119,000. The mixed-strategy plan was developed by trial and error and results in a total cost of $1,021,000. Further improvements are possible.

SOLVED PROBLEM 3

Revisit Example 14.3, where the consulting company has five jobs in its backlog. Create a schedule using the EDD rule, calculating the average days past due and flow time. In this case, does EDD outperform the FCFS rule?

SOLUTION

Customer Sequence	Start Time (days)		Processing Time (days)		Finish Time (days)	Due Date	Days Past Due	Days Ago Since Order Arrived	Flow Time (days)
B	0	+	16	=	16	27	0	12	**28**
A	16	+	25	=	41	29	**12**	15	**56**
D	41	+	10	=	51	48	**3**	10	**61**
C	51	+	14	=	65	68	0	5	**70**
E	65	+	12	=	77	80	0	0	**77**

The days past due and average flow time performance measures for the EDD schedule are

$$\text{Average days past due} = \frac{0 + 12 + 3 + 0 + 0}{5} = 3.0 \text{ days}$$

$$\text{Average flow time} = \frac{28 + 56 + 61 + 70 + 77}{5} = 58.4 \text{ days}$$

By both measures, EDD outperforms the FCFS (3.0 versus 3.4 past due and 58.4 versus 60.2 flow time). However, the solution found in part (b) of Example 14.3 still has the best average flow time of only 47.8 days.

DISCUSSION QUESTIONS

1. Explain why management should be concerned about priority systems in service and manufacturing organizations.

2. In your community, some employers maintain stable workforces at all costs, and others furlough and recall workers seemingly at the drop of a hat. What are the differences in markets, management, products, financial position, skills, costs, and competition that could explain these two extremes in personnel policy?

3. Consider the revenue management policies used by Lufthansa, as described in Managerial Practice 14.1. From a business perspective, what other industries might successfully implement these strategies? Give an example of one benefit and one challenge.

4. Quantitative methods can help managers evaluate alternative sales and operations plans on the basis of cost. These methods require cost estimates for each of the controllable variables, such as overtime, subcontracting, hiring, firing, and inventory investment. Say that the existing workforce is made up of 10,000 workers, each having skills valued at $40,000 per year. The plan calls for "creating alternative career opportunities"—in other words, laying off 500 employees. List the types of costs incurred when employees are laid off, and make a rough estimate of the length of time required for payroll savings to recover restructuring costs. If business is expected to improve in one year, are layoffs financially justified? What costs are incurred in a layoff that are difficult to estimate in monetary terms?

PROBLEMS

Software, such as OM Explorer, Active Models, and POM for Windows, is available in my**om**lab. Check with your instructor on how best to use it. In many cases, the instructor wants you to understand how to do the calculations by hand. At most, the software provides a check on your calculations. When calculations are particularly complex and the goal is interpreting the results in making decisions, the software replaces entirely the manual calculations.

1. Bob Carlton's golf camp estimates the following workforce requirements for its services over the next two years.

Quarter	1	2	3	4
Demand (hours)	4,200	6,400	3,000	4,800
Quarter	5	6	7	8
Demand (hours)	4,400	6,240	3,600	4,800

Each certified instructor puts in 480 hours per quarter regular time and can work an additional 120 hours overtime. Regular-time wages and benefits cost Carlton $7,200 per employee per quarter for regular time worked up to 480 hours, with an overtime cost of $20 per hour. Unused regular time for certified instructors is paid at $15 per hour. There is no cost for unused overtime capacity. The cost of hiring, training, and certifying a new employee is $10,000. Layoff costs are $4,000 per employee. Currently, eight employees work in this capacity.

a. Find a workforce plan using the level strategy that allows for no delay in service. It should rely only on overtime and the minimum amount of undertime necessary. What is the total cost of this plan?

b. Use a chase strategy that varies the workforce level without using overtime or undertime. What is the total cost of this plan?

c. Propose a better plan and calculate its total cost.

2. Continuing Problem 1, now assume that Carlton is permitted to employ some uncertified, part-time instructors, provided they represent no more than 15 percent of the total workforce hours in any quarter. Each part-time instructor can work up to 240 hours per quarter, with no overtime or undertime cost. Labor costs for part-time instructors are $12 per hour. Hiring and training costs are $2,000 per uncertified instructor, and there are no layoff costs.

a. Propose a low-cost, mixed-strategy plan and calculate its total cost.

b. What are the primary advantages and disadvantages of having a workforce consisting of both regular and temporary employees?

3. The Barberton Municipal Division of Road Maintenance is charged with road repair in the city of Barberton and the surrounding area. Cindy Kramer, road maintenance director, must submit a staffing plan for the next year based on a set schedule for repairs and on the city budget. Kramer

estimates that the labor hours required for the next four quarters are 6,000, 12,000, 19,000, and 9,000, respectively. Each of the 11 workers on the workforce can contribute 500 hours per quarter. Payroll costs are $6,000 in wages per worker for regular time worked up to 500 hours, with an overtime pay rate of $18 for each overtime hour. Overtime is limited to 20 percent of the regular-time capacity in any quarter. Although unused overtime capacity has no cost, unused regular time is paid at $12 per hour. The cost of hiring a worker is $3,000, and the cost of laying off a worker is $2,000. Subcontracting is not permitted.

a. Find a level workforce plan that relies just on overtime and the minimum amount of undertime possible. Overtime can be used to its limits in any quarter. What is the total cost of the plan and how many undertime hours does it call for?

b. Use a chase strategy that varies the workforce level without using overtime or undertime. What is the total cost of this plan?

c. Propose a plan of your own. Compare your plan with those in part (a) and part (b) and discuss its comparative merits.

4. The Twilight Clothing Company makes jeans for children. Management prepared a forecast of sales (in pairs of jeans) for next year and now must prepare a production plan. The company has traditionally maintained a level workforce strategy. Currently, all eight workers have been with the company for a number of years. Each employee can produce 2,000 pairs of jeans during a 2-month planning period. Every year management authorizes overtime in periods 1, 5, and 6, up to a maximum of 20 percent of regular-time capacity. Management wants to avoid stockouts and backorders and will not accept any plan that calls for such shortages. It also does not want to consider vacation scheduling as a supply option. At present, finished goods inventory holds 12,000 pairs of jeans. The demand forecast is as follows:

Period	1	2	3
Sales	25,000	6,500	15,000
Period	4	5	6
Sales	19,000	32,000	29,000

a. Is it feasible to hold the workforce constant, assuming that overtime is used only in periods 1, 5, and 6? Explain.

b. Find two alternative plans that would satisfy management's concern over stockouts and backorders, disregarding costs. What trade-offs between these two plans must be considered?

5. The Flying Frisbee Company has forecasted the following staffing requirements for full-time employees. Demand is seasonal, and management wants three alternative staffing plans to be developed.

Month	1	2	3	4
Requirement	2	2	4	6
Month	5	6	7	8
Requirement	18	20	12	18
Month	9	10	11	12
Requirement	7	3	2	1

The company currently has 10 employees. No more than 10 new hires can be accommodated in any month because of limited training facilities. No backorders are allowed, and overtime cannot exceed 25 percent of regular-time capacity in any month. There is no cost for unused overtime capacity. Regular-time wages are $1,500 per month, and overtime wages are 150 percent of regular-time wages. Undertime is paid at the same rate as regular time. The hiring cost is $2,500 per person, and the layoff cost is $2,000 per person.

a. Prepare a staffing plan utilizing a level workforce strategy, minimizing undertime. The plan may call for a one-time adjustment of the workforce before month 1.

b. Using a chase strategy as much as possible, prepare a plan that is consistent with the constraint on hiring and minimizes use of overtime.

c. Prepare a low-cost, mixed-strategy plan.

d. Which strategy is most cost-effective? What are the advantages and disadvantages of each plan?

6. Management at the Davis Corporation has determined the following demand schedule (in units):

Month	1	2	3	4
Demand	500	800	1,000	1,400
Month	5	6	7	8
Demand	2,000	1,600	1,400	1,200
Month	9	10	11	12
Demand	1,000	2,400	3,000	1,000

An employee can produce an average of 10 units per month. Each worker on the payroll costs $2,000 in regular-time wages per month. Undertime is paid at the same rate as regular time. In accordance with the labor contract in force, Davis Corporation does not work overtime or use subcontracting. Davis can hire and train a new employee for $2,000 and lay off one for $500. Inventory costs $32 per unit on hand at the end of each month. At present, 140 employees are on the payroll and anticipation inventory is zero.

a. Prepare a production plan using a mixed strategy that only uses a level workforce and anticipation inventory as its supply options. Minimize the inventory left over at the end of the year. Layoffs, undertime, vacations, subcontracting, backorders, and stockouts are not options. The plan may call for a one-time adjustment of the workforce before month 1.

b. Prepare a production plan with the chase strategy, relying only on hires and layoffs.

c. Compare and contrast these two plans on the basis of annual costs and other factors that you believe to be important.

d. Propose a better plan than these two plans, and explain why you believe it is better.

7. The Donald Fertilizer Company produces industrial chemical fertilizers. The projected manufacturing requirements (in thousands of gallons) for the next four quarters are 80, 50, 80, and 130, respectively. A level workforce is desired, relying only on anticipation inventory as a supply option. Stockouts and backorders are to be avoided, as are overtime and undertime.

a. Determine the quarterly production rate required to meet total demand for the year, and minimize the anticipation inventory that would be left over at the end of the year. Beginning inventory is zero.

b. Specify the anticipation inventory that will be produced.

c. Suppose that the requirements for the next four quarters are revised to 80, 130, 50, and 80, respectively. If total demand is the same, what level of production rate is needed now, using the same strategy as part (a)?

8. The Kool King Company has followed a policy of no layoffs for most of the manufacturer's life, even though the demand for its air conditioners is highly seasonal. Management wants to evaluate the cost-effectiveness of this policy. Competitive pressures are increasing, and ways need to be found to reduce costs. The following demand (expressed in employee–month equivalents) has been forecast for next year:

Jan.	70	May	130	Sept.	110
Feb.	90	June	170	Oct.	60
Mar.	100	July	170	Nov.	20
Apr.	100	Aug.	150	Dec.	40

Additional planning data follow, with costs, inventory, and backorders expressed in employee–month equivalents:

Regular-time production cost	$1,500	Hire cost	$500/person
Overtime production cost	150% of regular-time production cost	Layoff cost	$2,000/person
Subcontracting cost	$2,500	Current backorders	10
Inventory holding cost	$100	Current inventory	0
Backorder cost	$1,000	Desired ending inventory	0
Maximum overtime	20% of regular-time capacity	Current employment	130 employees

Hiring costs are lower than layoff costs because the facility is located near a Technical Training School. Undertime is paid at the rate equivalent to regular-time production. Each employee who has been with the company at least one year also received 0.5 months of paid vacation. All 130 employees currently employed qualify for vacations next year, assuming that they remain on the workforce. Answer the following questions using *Sales and Operations Planning with Spreadsheets* Solver in OM Explorer, or an Excel spreadsheet that you developed on your own.

a. Develop an S&OP with the level strategy using overtime, undertime, and vacations as the only supply options. Use the maximum amount of overtime so as to minimize undertime. What is the total cost of this plan, and what are its advantages and disadvantages?

b. Develop an S&OP with the chase strategy. Part of your decision will be when and how many vacation periods to grant. What is the total cost of this plan, and what are its advantages and disadvantages?

c. Develop an S&OP with a lower cost than found with either the level or chase strategy, being open to the full range of supply options (including anticipation inventory). Subcontractors can supply up to 50 employee–month equivalents. What is the total cost of this plan, and what are its advantages and disadvantages?

9. Gretchen's Kitchen is a fast-food restaurant located in an ideal spot near the local high school. Gretchen Lowe must prepare an annual staffing plan. The only menu items are hamburgers, chili, soft drinks, shakes, and french fries. A sample of 1,000 customers taken at random revealed that they purchased 2,100 hamburgers, 200 pints of chili, 1,000 soft drinks and shakes, and 1,000 bags of french fries. Thus, for purposes of estimating staffing requirements, Lowe assumes that each customer purchases 2.1 hamburgers, 0.2 pint of chili, 1 soft drink or shake, and 1 bag of french fries. Each hamburger requires 4 minutes of labor, a pint of chili requires 3 minutes, and a soft drink or shake and a bag of fries each take 2 minutes of labor.

The restaurant currently has 10 part-time employees who work 80 hours a month on staggered shifts. Wages are $400 per month for regular time and $7.50 per hour for overtime. Hiring and training costs are $250 per new employee, and layoff costs are $50 per employee.

Lowe realizes that building up seasonal inventories of hamburgers (or any of the products) would not be wise because of shelf-life considerations. Also, any demand not satisfied is a lost sale and must be avoided. Three strategies come to mind.

- Use a level strategy relying on overtime and undertime, with up to 20 percent of regular-time capacity on overtime.

- Maintain a base of 10 employees, hiring and laying off as needed to avoid any overtime.

- Utilize a chase strategy, hiring and laying off employees as demand changes to avoid overtime.

When performing her calculations, Lowe always rounds to the next highest integer for the number of employees. She also follows a policy of not using an employee more than 80 hours per month, except when overtime is needed. The projected demand by month (number of customers) for next year is as follows:

Jan.	3,200	July	4,800
Feb.	2,600	Aug.	4,200
Mar.	3,300	Sept.	3,800
Apr.	3,900	Oct.	3,600
May	3,600	Nov.	3,500
June	4,200	Dec.	3,000

a. Develop the schedule of service requirements for the next year.

b. Which strategy is most effective?

c. Suppose that an arrangement with the high school enables the manager to identify good prospective employees without having to advertise in the local newspaper. This source reduces the hiring cost to $50, which is mainly the cost of charred hamburgers during training. If cost is her only concern, will this method of hiring change Gretchen Lowe's strategy?

Considering other objectives that may be appropriate, do you think she should change strategies?

10. Little 6, Inc., an accounting firm, forecasts the following weekly workload during the tax season:

	Day						
	M	T	W	Th	F	S	Su
Personal Tax Returns	24	14	18	18	10	28	16
Corporate Tax Returns	18	10	12	15	24	12	4

Corporate tax returns each require 4 hours of an accountant's time, and personal returns each require 90 minutes. During tax season, each accountant can work up to 10 hours per day. However, error rates increase to unacceptable levels when accountants work more than 5 consecutive days per week.

a. Create an effective and efficient work schedule.

b. Assume that Little 6 has 3 part-time employees available to work 3 days per week. How could these employees be effectively utilized?

11. The mayor of Cambridge, Colorado, wanting to be environmentally progressive, decides to implement a recycling plan. All residents of the city will receive a special three-part bin to separate their glass, plastic, and aluminum, and the city will be responsible for picking up the materials. A young city and regional planning graduate, Michael Duffy, has been hired to manage the recycling program. After carefully studying the city's population density, Duffy decides that the following numbers of recycling collectors will be needed:

Day	M	T	W	Th	F	S	Su
Requirements	12	7	9	9	5	3	6

The requirements are based on the populations of the various housing developments and subdivisions in the city and surrounding communities. To motivate residents of some areas to have their pickups scheduled on weekends, a special tax break will be given.

a. Find the minimum number of recycling collectors required if each employee works 5 days a week and has 2 consecutive days off. Give preference to the S–Su pair when that pair is involved in a tie.

b. Specify the work schedule for each employee. How much slack does your schedule generate for each day?

c. Suppose that Duffy can smooth the requirements further through greater tax incentives. The requirements then will be eight collectors on Monday and seven on the other days of the week. How many collectors will be needed now? Does smoothing of requirements have capital investment implications? If so, what are they?

12. Cara Ryder manages a ski school in a large resort and is trying to develop a schedule for instructors. The instructors receive little salary and work just enough to earn room and board. They receive free skiing and spend most of their free time tackling the resort's notorious double black-diamond slopes. Hence, the instructors work only 4 days a week. One of the lesson packages offered at the resort is a 4-day beginner package. Ryder likes to keep the same instructor with a group over the 4-day period, so she schedules the instructors for 4 consecutive days and then 3 days off. Ryder uses years of experience with demand forecasts provided by management to formulate her instructor requirements for the upcoming month.

Day	M	T	W	Th	F	S	Su
Requirements	7	5	4	5	6	9	8

   a. Determine how many instructors Ryder needs to employ. Give preference to Saturday and Sunday off. (*Hint:* Look for the group of *3* days with the lowest requirements.)

   b. Specify the work schedule for each employee. How much slack does your schedule generate for each day?

13. Gerald Glynn manages the Michaels Distribution Center. After careful examination of his database information, he has determined the daily requirements for part-time loading dock personnel. The distribution center operates 7 days a week, and the daily part-time staffing requirements are

Day	M	T	W	Th	F	S	Su
Requirements	6	3	5	3	7	2	3

   Find the minimum number of workers Glynn must hire. Prepare a workforce schedule for these individuals so that each will have 2 consecutive days off per week and all staffing requirements will be satisfied. Give preference to the S–Su pair in case of a tie.

14. A manager faces peak [weekly] demand for one of her operations, but is not sure how long the peak will last. She can either use overtime from the current workforce, or hire/lay off and just pay regular-time wages. Regular-time pay is $500 per week, overtime is $750 per week, the hiring cost is $2,000, and the layoff cost is $3,000. Assuming that people are available seeking such a short-term arrangement, how many weeks must the surge in demand last to justify a temporary hire? *Hint:* Use break-even analysis (see Supplement A, "Decision Making Models"). Let w be the number of weeks of the high demand (rather than using Q for the break-even quantity). What is the fixed cost for the regular-time option? Overtime option?

15. Return to Problem 13 and the workforce schedule for part-time loading dock workers. Suppose that each part-time worker can work only 3 days, but the days must be consecutive. Devise an approach to this workforce scheduling problem. Your objective is to minimize total slack capacity. What is the minimum number of loaders needed now and what are their schedules?

16. The Mowry Machine Shop still has five jobs to be processed as of 8 A.M. today (day 23) at its bottleneck operation. The day when the order arrived, processing time, and promised due dates are given in the following table. The jobs are listed in the order of arrival.

Job	Day Order Arrived	Processing Time (days)	Due Date
A	12	10	45
B	13	8	36
C	15	4	42
D	17	4	39
E	22	3	53

   a. Develop separate schedules by using the FCFS and EDD rules. Compare the schedules on the basis of average flow time and average days past due.

   b. Which rule gives the best schedule, in your judgment? Why?

17. Currently a company that designs Web sites has five customers in its backlog. The day when the order arrived, processing time, and promised due dates are given in the following table. The customers are listed in the order of when they arrived. They are ready to be scheduled today, which is the start of day 190.

Customer	Day Order Arrived	Processing Time (days)	Due Date
A	180	20	216
B	182	12	240
C	184	28	256
D	187	24	248
E	188	32	290

   a. Develop separate schedules by using the FCFS and EDD rules. Compare the schedules on the basis of average flow time and average days past due.

   b. Comment on the performance of the two rules relative to these measures. Which one gives the best schedule? Why?

18. The Hickory Company manufactures wooden desks. Management schedules overtime every weekend to reduce the backlog on the most popular models. The automatic routing machine is used to cut certain types of edges on the desktops. The following orders need to be scheduled for the routing machine:

Order	Time Since Order Arrived (hours ago)	Estimated Machine Time (hours)	Due Date (hours from now)
1	6	10	12
2	5	3	8
3	3	15	18
4	1	9	20
5	0	7	21

The due dates reflect the need for the order to be at its next operation.

a. Develop separate schedules by using the FCFS and EDD rules. Compare the schedules on the basis of average flow time and average past due hours.

b. Comment on the performance of the two rules relative to these measures.

ACTIVE MODEL EXERCISE

This Active Model appears in my**om**lab. It allows you to evaluate the effects of modifying the size of a constant workforce.

QUESTIONS

1. Suppose the hiring cost is $1,100. What happens as the number of workers increases?

2. Suppose the overtime cost is $3,300. What happens as the number of workers increases?

3. Suppose the undertime cost is the same as the regular-time cost (i.e., paid undertime). What is the best number of workers to have in each month and still meet the demand?

4. If the overtime capacity increases to 30 percent, what is the minimum number of workers that meets the demand in every month?

5. If we use the same number of workers in each period, what happens as the number of workers increases from 15?

6. If we use the same number of workers in each period, what happens as the number of workers decreases from 15?

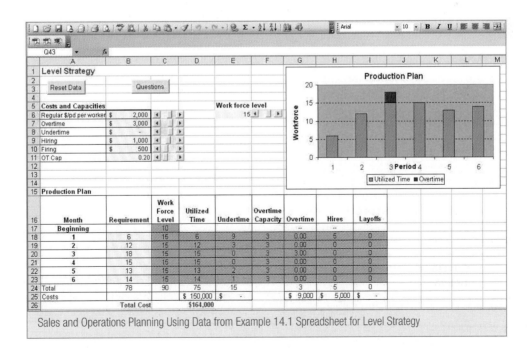

Sales and Operations Planning Using Data from Example 14.1 Spreadsheet for Level Strategy

VIDEO CASE | Sales and Operations Planning at Starwood

Business travel often means staying overnight in a hotel. Upon arrival, you may be greeted by a doorman or valet to assist you with your luggage. Front desk staff awaits your check-in. Behind the scenes, housekeeping, maintenance, and culinary staff prepare for your stay. Making a reservation gives the hotel notice of your plan to stay, but even before your trip is ever conceived, the hotel is staffed and ready. How? Through a process called *sales and operations planning*.

Sales and operations planning is a process every organization performs to some degree. Called a staffing plan (or service resource plan if more detailed) in service organizations, the plan must strike the right level of customer service while maintaining workforce stability and cost control so as to achieve the organization's profit expectations. So where do companies begin? Let us take a look at Starwood Hotels and Resorts to see how it is done.

Starwood operates in more than 750 locations around the globe. At the highest levels, Starwood engages in sales and operations planning on an annual basis, with adjustments made as needed each month by region and by property. Budgeted revenues and other projections come from headquarters; the regions and individual properties then break down the forecasts to meet their expected occupancies. Typically, the director of human resources determines the staffing mix needed across divisions such as food and beverage service, rooms (including housekeeping, spa, and guest services), engineering, Six Sigma (see Chapter 5, "Managing Quality"), revenue management, and accounting.

At the property level, general managers and their staff must provide input into next year's plan while implementing and monitoring activity in the current year. For most properties, payroll is close to 40 percent of budgeted revenues and represents the largest single expense the hotel incurs. It is also the most controllable expense. Many of Starwood's hotels and most resorts experience patterns of seasonality that affect demand for rooms and services. This seasonality, in turn, significantly affects the organization's staffing plan.

To determine the staffing levels, the company uses a proprietary software program that models occupancy demand based on historical data. The key drivers of staffing are occupied rooms and restaurant meals, called "covers." Starwood knows on a *per room* and *per cover* basis how many staff are required to function properly. When occupancy and covers are entered into the software program, the output models a recommended staffing level for each division. This recommendation is then reviewed by division managers and adjusted, as needed, to be sure staffing is in line with budgeted financial plans. Job fairs to recruit nonmanagement staff are held several times a year so a qualified candidate pool of both part-time and full-time staff is ready when needed. Most hotels maintain a pool of part-time workers who can contract or expand the hours worked if required by property guest levels. Vacations for management are scheduled for the low season. Overtime will be worked as needed, but is less desirable than scheduling the appropriate level of staff in each division.

The program also takes into account both the complexity and positioning of the property within Starwood. For example, a 400-room city hotel that is essentially a high-rise building is not as complex as a 400-room sprawling resort with golf, spa, convention, and other services not offered by the city hotel. Positioning also is important. A five-star resort hotel's customer service expectations are much greater than a three-star airport hotel location and requires much higher ratios of staff to guests. Finally, if the hotel is a brand new property, historical data from similar properties is used to model staffing for the first year or two of operation.

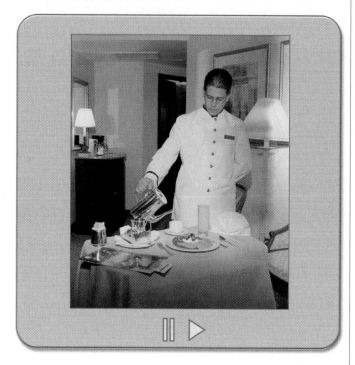

A software program that models occupancy based on historical data helps Starwood maintain proper staffing levels at its hotels. Managers know on a per-room, and "per-cover," basis how many hotel employees should be scheduled so that customers get good service.

Starwood attempts to modify demand and smooth out the peaks and valleys of its demand patterns. Many of the company's hotels experience three seasons: high, mid (called "shoulder"), and low season. Starwood, like its competitors, offers special rates, family packages, and weekend specials to attract different segments of the market during slower business periods. Staff is cross-trained to work in multiple areas, such as front reception and the concierge desk, so additional staff does not have to be added across seasons. Employees may also be temporarily redeployed among Starwood's properties to help out during peak periods. For example, when occupancy is forecast to be high in one region, staff from areas entering their low season will be assigned to cover the demand.

QUESTIONS

1. At what points in the planning process would you expect accounting/finance, marketing, information systems, and operations to play a role? What inputs should these areas provide, and why?

2. Does Starwood employ a chase, level, or mixed strategy? Why is this approach the best choice for the company?

3. How would staffing for the opening of a new hotel or resort differ from that of an existing property? What data might Starwood rely upon to make sure the new property is not over- or understaffed in its first year of operation?

CASE	Memorial Hospital

Memorial Hospital is a 265-bed regional health care facility located in the mountains of western North Carolina. The mission of the hospital is to provide quality health care to the people of Ashe County and the six surrounding counties. To accomplish this mission, Memorial Hospital's CEO has outlined three objectives: (1) maximize customer service to increase customer satisfaction, (2) minimize costs to remain competitive, and (3) minimize fluctuations in workforce levels to help stabilize area employment.

The hospital's operations are segmented into eight major wards for the purposes of planning and scheduling the nursing staff. These wards are listed in Table 14.4, along with the number of beds, targeted patient-to-nurse ratios, and average patient census for each ward. The overall demand for hospital services remained relatively constant over the past few years even though the population of the seven counties served increased. This stable demand can be attributed to increased competition from other hospitals in the area and the rise in alternative health care delivery systems, such as health maintenance organizations (HMOs). However, demand for Memorial Hospital's services does vary considerably by type of ward and time of year. Table 14.5 provides a historical monthly breakdown of the average daily patient census per ward.

The director of nursing for Memorial Hospital is Darlene Fry. Each fall she confronts one of the most challenging aspects of her job: planning the nurse-staffing levels for the next calendar year. Although the average demand for nurses has remained relatively stable over the past couple of years, the staffing plan usually changes because of changing work policies, changing pay structures, and temporary nurse availability and cost. With fall quickly approaching, Fry is collecting information to plan next year's staffing levels.

The nurses at Memorial Hospital work a regular schedule of four 10-hour days per week. The average regular-time pay across all nursing grades is $12.00 per hour. Overtime may be scheduled when necessary. However, because of the intensity of the demands placed on nurses, only a limited amount of overtime is permitted per week. Nurses may be scheduled for as many as 12 hours per day, for a maximum of 5 days per week. Overtime is compensated at a rate of $18.00 per hour. In periods of extremely high demand, temporary part-time nurses may be hired for a limited period of time. Temporary nurses are paid $15.00 per hour. Memorial Hospital's policy limits the proportion of temporary nurses to 15 percent of the total nursing staff.

Finding, hiring, and retaining qualified nurses is an ongoing problem for hospitals. One reason is that various forms of private practice lure many nurses away from hospitals with higher pay and greater flexibility. This situation has caused Memorial to guarantee its full-time staff nurses pay for a minimum of 30 hours per week, regardless of the demand placed on nursing services. In addition, each nurse receives 4 weeks of paid vacation each year. However, vacation scheduling may be somewhat restricted by the projected demand for nurses during particular times of the year.

TABLE 14.4	WARD CAPACITY DATA

Ward	Number of Beds	Patients per Nurse	Patient Census*
Intensive Care	20	2	10
Cardiac	25	4	15
Maternity	30	4	10
Pediatric	40	4	22
Surgery	5	†	†
Post-Op	15	5	8 (T–F daily equivalent)‡
Emergency	10	3	5 (daily equivalent)‡
General	120	8	98

* Yearly average per day

† The hospital employs 20 surgical nurses. Routine surgery is scheduled on Tuesdays and Fridays; five surgeries can be scheduled per day per operating room (bed) on these days. Emergency surgery is scheduled as needed.

‡ Daily equivalents are used to schedule nurses because patients flow through these wards in relatively short periods of time. A daily equivalent of 5 indicates that throughout a typical day, an average of five patients are treated in the ward.

At present, the hospital employs 130 nurses, including 20 surgical nurses. The other 110 nurses are assigned to the remaining seven major areas of the hospital. The personnel department informed Fry that the average cost to the hospital for hiring a new full-time nurse is $400 and for laying off or firing a nurse is $150. Although layoffs are an option, Fry is aware of the hospital's objective of maintaining a level workforce.

After looking over the information that she collected, Darlene Fry wants to consider staffing changes in all areas except the surgery ward, which is already correctly staffed.

QUESTIONS

1. Explain the alternatives available to Darlene Fry as she develops a nurse staffing plan for Memorial Hospital. How does each alternative plan meet the objective stated by the CEO?

2. Based on the data presented, develop a nurse staffing plan for Memorial Hospital. Explain your rationale for this plan.

TABLE 14.5	AVERAGE DAILY PATIENT CENSUS PER MONTH											
	Month											
Ward	**J**	**F**	**M**	**A**	**M**	**J**	**J**	**A**	**S**	**O**	**N**	**D**
Intensive Care	13	10	8	7	7	6	11	13	9	10	12	14
Cardiac	18	16	15	13	14	12	13	12	13	15	18	20
Maternity	8	8	12	13	10	8	13	13	14	10	8	7
Pediatric	22	23	24	24	25	21	22	20	18	20	21	19
Surgery*	20	18	18	17	16	16	22	21	17	18	20	22
Post-Opt†	10	8	7	7	6	6	10	10	7	8	9	10
Emergency†	6	4	4	7	8	5	5	4	4	3	4	6
General	110	108	100	98	95	90	88	92	98	102	107	94

*Average surgeries per day on Tuesday and Thursday.

† Daily equivalents

Source: This case was prepared by Dr. Brooke Saladin, Wake Forest University, North Carolina, as a basis for classroom discussion.

SELECTED REFERENCES

Baker, K. R. *Elements of Sequencing and Scheduling.* Hanover, NH: Baker Press, 2002.

Brandimarte, P., and A. Villa (eds.). *Modeling Manufacturing Systems: From Aggregate Planning to Real-Time Control.* New York: Springer, 1999.

Browne, J. J. "Simplified Scheduling of Routine Work Hours and Days Off." *Industrial Engineering* (December 1979), pp. 27–29.

Buxey, G. "Production Planning and Scheduling for Seasonal Demand." *International Journal of Operations and Production Management,* vol. 13, no. 7 (1993), pp. 4–21.

Chiang, Wen-Chyuan, Jason C. H. Chen, and Xiaojing Xu. "An Overview of Research on Revenue Management: Current Issues and Future Research." *International Journal of Revenue Management,* vol. 1, no. 1 (2007), pp. 97–128.

"Cycle Management—Cycle Proficiency." *Post Magazine* (July 1, 2004), p. 22.

Dougherty, John R. "Lessons from the Pros." *APICS Magazine* (November/December, 2007), pp. 31–33.

Dougherty, John R., and Christopher Gray. *Sales & Operations Planning—Best Practices.* Victoria, Canada: Trafford Publishing, 2006.

Fisher, M. L., J. H. Hammond, W. R. Obermeyer, and A. Raman. "Making Supply Meet Demand in an Uncertain World." *Harvard Business Review,* vol. 72, no. 3 (1994), pp. 83–93.

Fogarty, Donald W., John H. Blackstone Jr., and Thomas R. Hoffman. *Production and Inventory Management.* Cincinnati, OH: South-Western Publishing, 1991.

Gray, Christopher. *Sales & Operations Planning—Standard System.* Victoria, Canada: Trafford Publishing, 2007.

Heskett, J., W. E. Sasser, and C. Hart. *Service Breakthroughs: Changing the Rules of the Game.* New York: The Free Press, 1990.

Jim Hogan. "Workforce Management Software: A Mission-Critical Call Center Component." *Call Center CRM Solutions,* www.tmcnet.com/articles (July 2000).

Hopp, Wallace J., and Mark L. Spearman. *Factory Physics,* 2d ed. New York: Irwin/McGraw-Hill, 2001.

Kimes, Sheryl E., and Richard B. Chase. "The Strategic Levers of Yield Management." *Journal of Service Research,* vol. 1, no. 2 (1998), pp. 298–308.

LaForge, R. Lawrence, and Christopher W. Craighead. "Computer-Based Scheduling in Manufacturing Firms: Some Indicators of Successful Practice." *Production and Inventory Management Journal* (First Quarter 2000), pp. 29–34.

Lesaint, David, Christos Voudouris, and Nader Azarmi. "Dynamic Workforce Scheduling for British Telecommunications plc." *Interfaces* (January–February 2000), pp. 45–56.

Mentzer, John T., and Mark A. Moon. "Understanding Demand." *Supply Chain Management* (May/June 2004), pp. 38–45.

Metters, Richard, and Vincente Vargas. "A Comparison of Production Scheduling Policies on Costs, Service Levels, and Schedule Changes." *Production and Operations Management*, vol. 17, no. 3 (1999), pp. 76–91.

Muzumdar, Maha, and John Fontanella. "The Secrets to S&OP Success." *Supply Chain Management* (April 2006), pp. 34–41.

Narasimhan, S., D. W. McLeavey, and P. J. Billington. *Production Planning and Inventory Control*. Englewood Cliffs, NJ: Prentice Hall, 1995.

Ramani, K. V. "Scheduling Doctors' Activities at a Large Teaching Hospital." *Production and Inventory Management Journal* (First/Second Quarter 2002), pp. 56–62.

Rennie, Elizabeth. "All Fired UP: Why Food and Beverage Professionals Must Put S&OP on the Menu." *APICS Magazine* (July/August 2006), pp. 32–35.

Rennie, Elizabeth. "Remote Possibilities: Improved Logistics Management Leads to Promising New Distribution Activities." *APICS Magazine* (July/August 2006), pp. 36–37.

Silver, E. A., F. F. Pyke, and R. Peterson. *Inventory Management and Production Planning and Scheduling*. New York: Wiley, 1998.

Sipper, D., and R. Bulfin. *Production: Planning, Control, and Integration*. New York: McGraw-Hill, 1997.

"Skill Set Scheduling," www.pipkins.com/articles, 2005.

Smith-Daniels, V., S. Scheweikhar, and D. Smith-Daniels. "Capacity Management in Health Care Services: Review and Future Research Directions." *Decision Sciences*, vol. 91 (1988), pp. 889–919.

Tibrewala, R. K., D. Philippe, and J. J. Browne. "Optimal Scheduling of Two Consecutive Idle Periods." *Management Science*, vol. 19, no. 1 (1972), pp. 71–75.

Trottman, Melanie. "Choices in Stormy Weather: How Airline Employees Make Hundreds of Decisions to Cancel or Reroute Flights." *Wall Street Journal* (February 14, 2006), pp. B1–B3.

Vollmann, Thomas E., William Berry, D. Clay Whybark, and Robert Jacobs. *Manufacturing Planning and Control Systems for Supply Chain Management*, 5th ed. New York: McGraw-Hill/Irwin, 2005.

Wallace, Thomas F. *Sales & Operations Planning: The How-To Handbook*, 3rd ed. Cincinnati, OH: T. E. Wallace & Company, 2008.

Wallace, Thomas F., and Robert A. Stahl. *Sales Forecasting: A New Approach*. Cincinnati, OH: T. E. Wallace & Company, 2002.

15 PLANNING SUFFICIENT RESOURCES

Dow Corning scientist research next generation solar technologies at the company's Solar Application Center.

DOW CORNING

Dow Corning, created as a joint venture between Corning Incorporated and the Dow Chemical Company in 1943, is a global leader that offers over 7,000 innovative products and services using silicon-based technology in diverse industries such as electronics, aviation and aerospace, textile, automotive, and health care, among others. As an example, Dow Corning's Electrical Insulating Compounds are used for creating moisture proof seals for aircraft, automotive, and marine ignition systems. With 10,000 employees, over 20,000 customers, and 45 manufacturing and warehouse locations worldwide, its annual revenues of $4.94 billion generated an income of $690 million in 2007. In order to integrate different business functions and enhance resource planning across the entire firm and its supply chain, Dow Corning turned to a leading provider of enterprise resource planning (ERP) software solutions. It installed the SAP R/3 and mySAP Supply Chain Management solution, with SAP Advanced Planner and Optimizer (APO) at its core.

Prior to the ERP implementation, limited transparency and redundancy within the existing legacy systems made it difficult to access and analyze data needed for effective resource planning, and also hampered decision making and responsiveness. A sequenced implementation of the SAP modules facilitated the linking of key processes from order generation to production planning to warehousing to delivery and final billing. The SAP APO solution enabled the SCOR model of plan, source, make, and deliver (see Chapter 10, "Integrating the Supply Chain"),

LEARNING GOALS

After reading this chapter, you should be able to:

1. Explain how enterprise resource planning (ERP) systems can foster better resource planning.
2. Explain how the concept of dependent demand is fundamental to resource planning.
3. Describe a master production schedule (MPS) and the information it provides.
4. Create an MPS and compute available-to-promise quantities.
5. Discuss the logic of a material requirements planning (MRP) system.
6. Identify production and purchase orders needed for dependent demand items.
7. Apply MRP principles to the provision of services and distribution inventories.

which allowed the linkage of shop floor processes and manufacturing operations with the rest of the business. With a transparent view of orders, materials, equipment, product quality, and cost information, Dow Corning can now coordinate plants and processes with greater ease and better match production to market requirements on a global scale. Employee productivity and satisfaction are also up, due mostly to faster response times and accurate on-time deliveries.

Sources: End to End Supply Chain Management at Dow Corning, http://www.sap.com/usa/solutions/business-suite/erp/operations/pdf/CS_Dow_Corning. pdf; Dow Corning, Optimizing Operational Performance to Sharpen Competitive Advantage, www.sap.com; http://www.dowcorning.com/content/about/aboutmedia/fastfacts.asp; July 2008.

my**om**lab and the Companion Website at **www.pearsonglobaleditions.com/krajewski** contain many tools, activities, and resources designed for this chapter.

resource planning

A process that takes sales and operations plans; processes information in the way of time standards, routings, and other information on how the firm produces its services or products; and then plans the input requirements.

enterprise process

A companywide process that cuts across functional areas, business units, geographical regions, and product lines.

enterprise resource planning (ERP) systems

Large, integrated information systems that support many enterprise processes and data storage needs.

ow Corning demonstrates that companies can gain a competitive edge by using an effective information system to help with their resource planning. Companies must ensure that all of the resources they need to produce finished services or products are available at the right time. If they are not, a firm risks losing business. For a manufacturer, this task can mean keeping track of thousands of subassemblies, components, and raw materials as well as key equipment capacities. For a service provider, this task can mean keeping track of numerous supplies and carefully scheduling the time and capacity requirements of different employees and types of equipment.

We begin this chapter by describing enterprise resource planning (ERP) systems, which have become a valuable tool for, among other things, resource planning. We then examine a specific approach to resource planning, called material requirements planning (MRP). The concluding section of the chapter illustrates how service providers manage their supplies, human resources, equipment, and financial resources.

RESOURCE PLANNING ACROSS THE ORGANIZATION

Resource planning lies at the heart of any organization, cutting across all of its different functional areas. It takes sales and operations plans; processes information in the way of time standards, routings, and other information on how services or products are produced; and then plans the input requirements. It also can create reports for managers of the firm's major functional areas, such as human resources, purchasing, sales and marketing, and finance and accounting. In essence, resource planning is a process in and of itself that can be analyzed relative to the firm's competitive priorities.

ENTERPRISE RESOURCE PLANNING

An **enterprise process** is a companywide process that cuts across functional areas, business units, geographic regions, and product lines. **Enterprise resource planning (ERP) systems** are large, integrated information systems that support many enterprise processes and data storage needs. By integrating the firm's functional areas, ERP systems allow an organization to view its operations as a whole rather than having to try to put together the different information pieces produced by its various functions and divisions. Today, ERP systems are being used by traditional brick-and-mortar organizations such as manufacturers, restaurants, hospitals, and hotels, as well as by Internet companies that rely extensively on Web connectivity to link their customers and suppliers.

How ERP Systems Are Designed

ERP revolves around a single comprehensive database that can be made available across the entire organization (or enterprise). Passwords are generally issued to allow certain personnel to access certain areas of the system. Having a single database for all of the firm's information makes it much easier for managers to monitor all of the company's products at all locations and at all times. The database collects data and feeds them into the various modular applications (or suites) of the software system. As new information is entered as a *transaction* in one application, related information is automatically updated in the other applications, including the firm's financial and accounting databases, its human resource and payroll databases, sales and customer databases, and so forth. In this way, the ERP system streamlines the data flows throughout the organization and provides employees with direct access to a wealth of real-time operating information. This process eliminates many of the cross-functional coordination problems older, nonintegrated systems suffered from. Figure 15.1 shows some of the typical applications with a few subprocesses nested within each one. Some of the applications are for back-office operations such as manufacturing and payroll, while others are for front-office operations such as customer service.

Amazon.com is one company that uses an ERP system. The supply chain application of Amazon's system is particularly important because it allows Amazon.com to link customer orders to warehouse shipments and, ultimately, to supplier replenishment orders. Other applications are more important in other businesses. For example, universities put particular emphasis on the human resources and accounting and finance applications, and manufacturers have an interest in almost every application suite. Not all applications in Figure 15.1 need to be integrated into an ERP system, but those left out will not share their information with the ERP system. Sometimes, however, ERP systems are designed to interface with a firm's existing, older information systems (called "legacy systems").

◀ **FIGURE 15.1**
ERP Application Modules

Source: Reprinted by permission of Harvard Business School Press. From *Enterprise Resource Planning (ERP)* by Scalle and Cotteleer. Boston, MA, 1999, No. 9-699-020. Copyright © 1999 by the Harvard Business School Publishing Corporation; all rights reserved.

Designing an ERP system requires that a company carefully analyze its major processes so that appropriate decisions about the coordination of legacy systems and new software can be made. Sometimes, a company's processes must be completely reengineered before the firm can enjoy the benefits of an integrated information system. However, a recent study showed that companies reap the greatest rewards when they keep their ERP implementations simple, work with a small number of vendors, and use standardized systems rather than customizing them extensively. Firms can otherwise end up spending excessive amounts of money on ERP systems that are complex to use and costly to manage.

Most ERP systems today use a graphical user interface, although the older, keyboard-driven, text-based systems are still popular because of their dependability and technical simplicity. Users navigate through various screens and menus. Training, such as during ERP implementation, focuses on these screens and how users can utilize them to get their jobs done. The biggest suppliers of these off-the-shelf commercial ERP packages are SAP AG, a German company that was also used by Dow Corning in the opening vignette, followed by Oracle Corporation.

ERP systems have undergone significant changes over the past several years. One direction relates to their **interoperability**—the ability of one piece of software to interact with others. Electronic data interchange, a system that allows data to be transferred between companies on a batch basis, and XML (Extensible Markup Language) let companies structure and exchange information without rewriting their existing software or having to purchase new software or hardware. The goal of these and other such methods is to automate, in almost real time, the sharing of information across enterprise boundaries.

interoperability

The ability of one piece of software to interact with others.

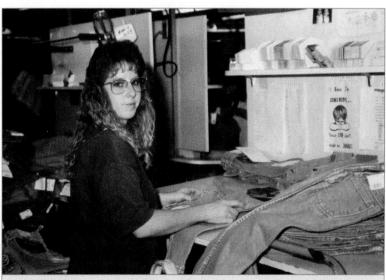

VF Corporation is the world's largest apparel producer, with more than 50,000 workers and $6 billion in sales. Data on quality are important inputs for VF's ERP system. Here an employee inspects jeans to assure they conform to VF's quality standards and meet customer expectations.

Material Requirements Planning

The Manufacturing and Supply Chain Management modules in Figure 15.1 deal with resource planning. Understanding resource planning begins with the concept of *dependent demand*, which sets it apart from the techniques covered in Chapter 12, "Managing Inventories." **Material requirements planning (MRP)** is a computerized information system developed specifically to help manufacturers manage dependent demand inventory and schedule replenishment orders. The key inputs of an MRP system are a bill of materials database, a master production schedule, and an inventory record database, as shown in Figure 15.2. Using this information, the MRP system identifies the actions planners must take to stay on schedule, such as releasing new production orders, adjusting order quantities, and expediting late orders.

An MRP system translates the master production schedule and other sources of demand, such as independent demand for replacement parts and maintenance items, into the requirements for all subassemblies, components, and raw materials needed to produce the required parent items. This process is called an **MRP explosion** because it converts the requirements of various final products into a material requirements plan that specifies the replenishment schedules of all the subassemblies, components, and raw materials needed to produce final products.

We first explore the nature of dependent demand and how it differs from independent demand, followed by a discussion of each of the key inputs to the MRP system shown in Figure 15.2.

Dependent Demand

For years, many companies tried to manage production and their dependent demand inventories using independent demand systems similar to those discussed in Chapter 12, "Managing Inventories," but the outcome was seldom satisfactory because dependent demand is fundamentally different from independent demand. To illustrate the concept of dependent demand, let us consider a Huffy bicycle produced for retail outlets. Demand for a final product, such as a bicycle, is called *independent demand* because it is influenced only by market conditions. In contrast, the demand for spokes going into the bicycle "depends" on the production planned for its wheels. Huffy must forecast this demand using techniques such as those discussed in Chapter 13, "Forecasting Demand." However, Huffy also keeps many other items in inventory—handlebars, pedals, frames, and wheel rims—used to make completed bicycles. Each of these items has a **dependent demand** because the quantity required varies with the production plans for other items held in the firm's inventory— finished bikes, in this case. For example, the demand for frames, pedals, and wheel rims is *dependent* on the production of completed bicycles. Operations can calculate the demand for dependent demand items once the bicycle production levels are laid out in the sales and operations plan. For example, every bicycle needs 2 wheel rims, so 1,000 completed bicycles need 1,000(2) = 2,000 rims. Forecasting techniques are not needed for these items.

The bicycle, or any other product that is manufactured from one or more components, is called a **parent**. The wheel rim is an example of a **component**—an item that goes through one or more operations to be transformed into or become part of one or more parents. A wheel rim, for example, will have several different parents if the rim is used to make more than one style of bicycle. This parent–component relationship can cause erratic dependent demand patterns for components. Suppose that every time inventory falls to 500 units (a reorder point), an order for 1,000 more bicycles is placed, as shown in Figure 15.3(a). The assembly supervisor then authorizes the withdrawal of 2,000 rims from inventory, along with other components for the finished product. The demand for the rim is shown in Figure 15.3(b). So, even though customer demand for the finished bicycle is continuous and reasonably uniform, the production demand for wheel rims is "lumpy"; that is, it occurs sporadically, usually in relatively large quantities. Thus, the production decisions for the assembly of bicycles, which account for the costs of assembling the bicycles and the projected assembly capacities at the time the decisions are made, determine the demand for wheel rims.

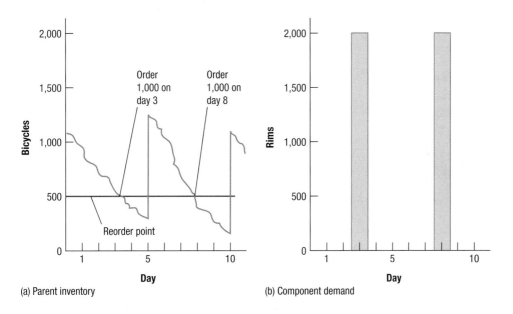

◀ FIGURE 15.3
Lumpy Dependent Demand Resulting from Continuous Independent Demand

(a) Parent inventory   (b) Component demand

Managing dependent demand inventories is complicated because some components may be subject to both dependent and independent demand. For example, the shop floor needs 2,000 wheel rims for the new bicycles, but the company also sells replacement rims for old bicycles directly to retail outlets. This practice places an independent demand on the inventory of wheel rims. Materials requirements planning can be used in complex situations involving components that may have independent demand as well as dependent demand inventories.

Bill of Materials

The replenishment schedule for a component is determined from the production schedules of its parents. Hence, the system needs accurate information on parent–component relationships. A **bill of materials (BOM)** is a record of all the components of an item, the parent–component relationships, and the usage quantities derived from engineering and process designs. In Figure 15.4, the BOM of a simple ladder-back chair shows that the chair is made from a ladder-back subassembly, a seat subassembly, front legs, and leg supports. In turn, the ladder-back subassembly is made from back legs and back slats, and the seat subassembly is made from a seat frame and a seat cushion. Finally, the seat frame is made from seat-frame boards. For convenience, we refer to these items by the letters shown in Figure 15.4.

All items except item A are components because they are needed to make a parent. Items A, B, C, and H are parents because they all have at least one component. The BOM also specifies the **usage quantity**, or the number of units of a component that are needed to make one unit of its immediate parent. Figure 15.4 shows usage quantities for each parent–component relationship in parentheses. Note that one chair (item A) is made from one ladder-back subassembly (item B), one seat subassembly (item C), two front legs (item D), and four leg supports (item E). In addition, item B is made from two back legs (item F) and four back slats (item G). Item C needs one seat frame (item H) and one seat cushion (item I). Finally, item H needs four seat-frame boards (item J).

Four terms frequently used to describe inventory items are *end items, intermediate items, subassemblies,* and *purchased items*. An **end item** typically is the final product sold to the customer; it is a parent but not a component. Item A in Figure 15.4, the completed

bill of materials (BOM)

A record of all the components of an item, the parent–component relationships, and the usage quantities derived from engineering and process designs.

usage quantity

The number of units of a component that are needed to make one unit of its immediate parent.

end item

The final product sold to a customer.

FIGURE 15.4 ▶
BOM for a Ladder-Back Chair

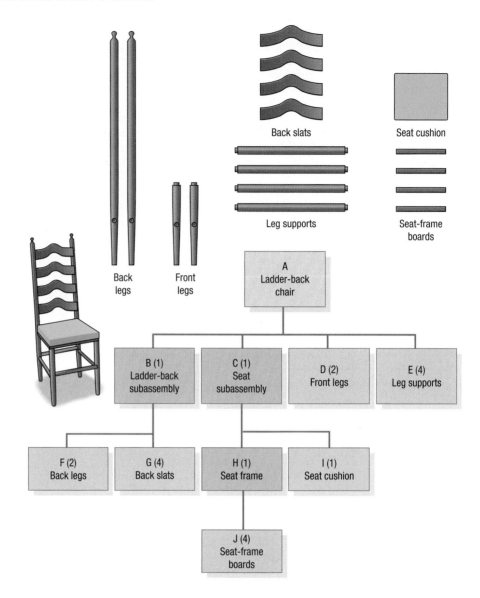

ladder-back chair, is an end item. Accounting statements classify inventory of end items as either work-in-process (WIP), if work remains to be done, or finished goods. An **intermediate item** is one such as item B, C, or H that has at least one parent and at least one component. Some products have several levels of intermediate items; the parent of one intermediate item can also be an intermediate item. Inventory of intermediate items—whether completed or still on the shop floor—is classified as WIP. A **subassembly** is an intermediate item that is assembled (as opposed to being transformed by other means) from more than one component. Items B and C are subassemblies. A **purchased item** has no components because it comes from a supplier, but it has one or more parents. Examples are items D, E, F, G, I, and J in Figure 15.4. Inventory of purchased items is treated as raw materials in accounting statements.

A component may have more than one parent. **Part commonality**, sometimes called *standardization of parts* or *modularity*, is the degree to which a component has more than one immediate parent. As a result of commonality, the same item may appear in several places in the bill of materials for a product, or it may appear in the bills of materials for several different products. For example, the seat subassembly in Figure 15.4 is a component of the ladder-back chair and of a kitchen chair that is part of the same family of products. The usage quantity specified in the bill of materials relates to a specific parent–component relationship. The usage quantity for any component can therefore change, depending on the parent item. Part commonality, or using the same part in many parents, increases its volume and repeatability, which provides several process advantages and helps minimize inventory costs.

intermediate item

An item that has at least one parent and at least one component.

subassembly

An intermediate item that is *assembled* (as opposed to being transformed by other means) from more than one component.

purchased item

An item that has one or more parents but no components because it comes from a supplier.

part commonality

The degree to which a component has more than one immediate parent.

Master Production Scheduling

The second input into a material requirements plan is the **master production schedule (MPS)**, which details how many end items will be produced within specified periods of time. It breaks the sales and operations plan into specific product schedules. Figure 15.5 shows how a sales and operations plan for a family of chairs breaks down into the weekly MPS for each specific chair type (the time period can be hours, days, weeks, or months). The chair example demonstrates the following aspects of master scheduling:

1. The sums of the quantities in the MPS must equal those in the sales and operations plan. This consistency between the plans is desirable because of the economic analysis done to arrive at the sales and operations plan.

2. The production quantities must be allocated efficiently over time. The specific mix of chair types—the number of each type as a percent of the total family's quantity—is based on historic demand and on marketing and promotional considerations. The planner must select lot sizes for each chair type, taking into consideration economic factors such as production setup costs and inventory carrying costs.

3. Capacity limitations and bottlenecks, such as machine or labor capacity, storage space, or working capital, may determine the timing and size of MPS quantities. The planner must acknowledge these limitations by recognizing that some chair styles require more resources than others and setting the timing and size of the production quantities accordingly.

> **master production schedule (MPS)**
>
> A part of the material requirements plan that details how many end items will be produced within specified periods of time.

▼ **FIGURE 15.5**
MPS for a Family of Chairs

	April				May			
	1	2	3	4	5	6	7	8
Ladder-back chair	150					150		
Kitchen chair				120			120	
Desk chair		200	200		200			200
Sales and operations plan for chair family	670				670			

Figure 15.6 shows the master production scheduling process. Operations must first create a prospective MPS to test whether it meets the schedule with the resources (e.g., machine capacities, workforce, overtime, and subcontractors) provided for in the sales and operations plan. Operations then revises the MPS until a schedule that satisfies all of the resource limitations is developed or until it is determined that no feasible schedule can be developed. In the latter event, the production plan must be revised to adjust production requirements or increase authorized resources. Once a feasible prospective MPS has been accepted by the firm's managers, operations uses the authorized MPS as input to material requirements planning. Operations can then determine specific schedules for component production and assembly. Actual performance data such as inventory levels and shortages are inputs to preparing the prospective MPS for the next period, and so the master production scheduling process is repeated from one period to the next.

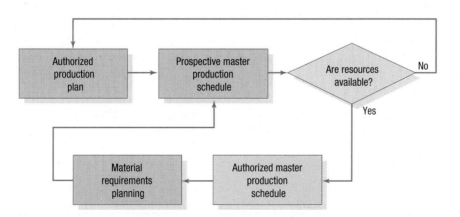

◄ **FIGURE 15.6**
Master Production Scheduling Process

Developing a Master Production Schedule

The process of developing a master production schedule includes (1) calculating the projected on-hand inventory and (2) determining the timing and size of the production quantities of specific products. We use the manufacturer of the ladder-back chair to illustrate the process. For simplicity, we assume that the firm does not utilize safety stocks for end items, even though many firms do. In addition, we use weeks as our planning periods, even though hours, days, or months could be used.

Step 1. *Calculate Projected On-Hand Inventories.* The first step is to calculate the projected on-hand inventory, which is an estimate of the amount of inventory available each week after demand has been satisfied:

$$\begin{pmatrix} \text{Projected on-hand} \\ \text{inventory at end} \\ \text{of this week} \end{pmatrix} = \begin{pmatrix} \text{On-hand} \\ \text{inventory at} \\ \text{end of last week} \end{pmatrix} + \begin{pmatrix} \text{MPS quantity} \\ \text{due at start} \\ \text{of this week} \end{pmatrix} - \begin{pmatrix} \text{Projected} \\ \text{requirements} \\ \text{this week} \end{pmatrix}$$

In some weeks, no MPS quantity for a product may be needed because sufficient inventory already exists. For the projected requirements for this week, the scheduler uses whichever is larger—the forecast or the customer orders booked—recognizing that the forecast is subject to error. If actual booked orders exceed the forecast, the projection will be more accurate if the scheduler uses the booked orders because booked orders are a known quantity. Conversely, if the forecast exceeds booked orders for a week, the forecast will provide a better estimate of the requirements needed for that week because some orders are yet to come in.

The manufacturer of the ladder-back chair produces the chair to stock and needs to develop an MPS for it. Marketing has forecasted a demand of 30 chairs for the first week of April, but actual customer orders booked are for 38 chairs. The current on-hand inventory is 55 chairs. No MPS quantity is due in week 1. Figure 15.7 shows an MPS record with these quantities listed. Because actual orders for week 1 are greater than the forecast, the scheduler uses that figure for actual orders to calculate the projected inventory balance at the end of week 1:

$$\text{Inventory} = \begin{pmatrix} 55 \text{ chairs} \\ \text{currently} \\ \text{in stock} \end{pmatrix} + \begin{pmatrix} \text{MPS quantity} \\ (0 \text{ for week 1}) \end{pmatrix} - \begin{pmatrix} 38 \text{ chairs already} \\ \text{promised for} \\ \text{delivery in week 1} \end{pmatrix} = 17 \text{ chairs}$$

FIGURE 15.7 ▶
Master Production Schedule for Weeks 1 and 2

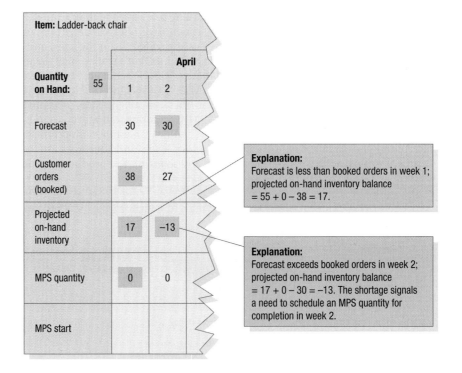

Item: Ladder-back chair

		April	
Quantity on Hand: 55		1	2
Forecast		30	30
Customer orders (booked)		38	27
Projected on-hand inventory		17	−13
MPS quantity		0	0
MPS start			

Explanation:
Forecast is less than booked orders in week 1; projected on-hand inventory balance = 55 + 0 − 38 = 17.

Explanation:
Forecast exceeds booked orders in week 2; projected on-hand inventory balance = 17 + 0 − 30 = −13. The shortage signals a need to schedule an MPS quantity for completion in week 2.

In week 2, the forecasted quantity exceeds actual orders booked, so the projected on-hand inventory for the end of week 2 is 17 + 0 − 30 = −13. The shortage signals the need for more chairs to be produced and available for week 2.

Step 2. *Determine the Timing and Size of MPS Quantities.* The goal of determining the timing and size of MPS quantities is to maintain a nonnegative projected on-hand inventory balance. As shortages in inventory are detected, MPS quantities should be scheduled to cover them. The first MPS quantity should be scheduled for the week when the projected on-hand inventory reflects a shortage, such as week 2 in Figure 15.7.[1] The scheduler adds the MPS quantity to the projected on-hand inventory and searches for the next period when a shortage occurs. This shortage signals a need for a second MPS quantity, and so on.

Figure 15.8 shows a master production schedule for the ladder-back chair for the next 8 weeks. The order policy requires production lot sizes of 150 units. A shortage of 13 chairs in week 2 will occur unless the scheduler provides for an MPS quantity for that period. Our convention is to show blanks instead of zeroes in all rows, which improves readability and is often used in practice. The only exception is in the projected on-hand inventory row, where a number is always shown, even if it is a 0 or negative number.

Once the MPS quantity is scheduled, the updated projected inventory balance for week 2 is

$$\text{Inventory} = \begin{pmatrix} 17 \text{ chairs in} \\ \text{inventory at the} \\ \text{end of week 1} \end{pmatrix} + \begin{pmatrix} \text{MPS quantity} \\ \text{of 150 chairs} \end{pmatrix} - \begin{pmatrix} \text{Forecast of} \\ 30 \text{ chairs} \end{pmatrix} = 137 \text{ chairs}$$

The scheduler proceeds column by column through the MPS record until it reaches the end, filling in the MPS quantities as needed to avoid shortages. The 137 units will satisfy forecasted demands until week 7, when the inventory shortage in the absence of an MPS quantity is $7 + 0 - 35 = 28$. This shortage signals the need for another MPS quantity of 150 units. The updated inventory balance is $7 + 150 - 35 = 122$ chairs for week 7.

The last row in Figure 15.8 indicates the periods in which production of the MPS quantities must *begin* so that they will be available when indicated in the MPS quantity row. In the upper-right portion of the MPS record, a lead time of 1 week is indicated for the ladder-back chair; that is, 1 week is needed to assemble 150 ladder-back chairs, assuming that items B, C, D, and E are available. For each MPS quantity, the scheduler works backward through the lead time to determine when the assembly department must start producing chairs. Consequently, a lot of 150 units must be started in week 1 and another in week 6.

Available-to-Promise Quantities In addition to providing manufacturing with the timing and size of production quantities, the MPS provides marketing with information useful for negotiating delivery dates with customers. The quantity of end items that marketing can promise to deliver on specified dates is called **available-to-promise (ATP) inventory**. It is the difference between the customer orders already booked and the quantity that operations is planning to produce. As new customer orders are accepted, the ATP inventory is reduced to reflect the commitment of the firm to ship those quantities, but the actual inventory stays unchanged until the order is removed from inventory and shipped to the customer. An available-to-promise inventory is associated with each MPS quantity because the MPS quantity specifies the timing and size of new stock that can be earmarked to meet future bookings.

Figure 15.9 shows an MPS record with an additional row for the available-to-promise quantities. The ATP in week 2 is the MPS quantity minus booked customer orders until the next MPS quantity, or $150 - (27 + 24 + 8 + 0 + 0) = 91$ units. The ATP indicates to marketing that, of the 150 units scheduled for completion in week 2, 91 units are uncommitted, and

available-to-promise (ATP) inventory

The quantity of end items that marketing can promise to deliver on specified dates.

▼ FIGURE 15.8
Master Production Schedule for Weeks 1–8

Item: Ladder-back chair				April				May		
							Order Policy: 150 units **Lead Time:** 1 week			
Quantity on Hand: 55		1	2	3	4	5	6	7	8
Forecast		30	30	30	30	35	35	35	35
Customer orders (booked)		38	27	24	8	0	0	0	0
Projected on-hand inventory		17	137	107	77	42	7	122	87
MPS quantity		0	150	0	0	0	0	150	0
MPS start		150	0	0	0	0	150	0	0

Explanation:
The time needed to assemble 150 chairs is 1 week. The assembly department must start assembling chairs in week 1 to have them ready by week 2.

Explanation:
On-hand inventory balance
$= 17 + 150 - 30 = 137$. The MPS quantity is needed to avoid a shortage of $30 - 17 = 13$ chairs in week 2.

---

[1] In some cases, new orders will be planned before a shortage is encountered. Two such instances occur when safety stocks and anticipation inventories are built up.

Item: Ladder-back chair					Order Policy: 150 units Lead Time: 1 week			
			April				May	
Quantity on Hand:	55	1	2	3	4	5	6	7	8
Forecast		30	30	30	30	35	35	35	35
Customer orders (booked)		38	27	24	8	0	0	0	0
Projected on-hand inventory		17	137	107	77	42	7	122	87
MPS quantity		0	150	0	0	0	0	150	0
MPS start		150	0	0	0	0	150	0	0
Available-to- promise (ATP) inventory		17	91						150

Explanation:
The total of customer orders booked until the next MPS receipt is 38 units. The ATP = 55 (on-hand) + 0 (MPS quantity) − 38 = 17.

Explanation:
The total of customer orders booked until the next MPS receipt is 27 + 24 + 8 = 59 units. The ATP = 150 (MPS quantity) − 59 = 91 units.

FIGURE 15.9 ▲
MPS Record with an ATP Row

Tutor 15.1 in myomlab provides a new example to practice completing a master production schedule.

total new orders up to that quantity can be promised for delivery as early as week 2. In week 7, the ATP is 150 units because there are no booked orders in week 7 and beyond.

The procedure for calculating available-to-promise information is slightly different for the first (current) week of the schedule than for other weeks because it accounts for the inventory currently in stock. The ATP inventory for the first week equals *current on-hand inventory* plus the MPS quantity for the first week, minus the cumulative total of booked orders up to (but not including) the week in which the next MPS quantity arrives. So, in Figure 15.9, the ATP for the first week is 55 + 0 − 38 = 17. This information indicates to the sales department that it can promise as many as 17 units this week, 91 more units sometime in weeks 2 through 6, and 150 more units in week 7 or 8. If customer order requests exceed ATP quantities in those time periods, the MPS must be changed before the customer orders can be booked or the customers must be given a later delivery date—when the next MPS quantity arrives. See Solved Problem 2 at the end of this chapter for an example of decision making using the ATP quantities.

Freezing the MPS   The master production schedule is the basis of all end item, sub-assembly, component, and materials schedules. For this reason, changes to the MPS can be costly, particularly if they are made to MPS quantities soon to be completed. Increases in an MPS quantity can result in material shortages, delayed shipments to customers, and excessive expediting costs. Decreases in MPS quantities can result in unused materials or components (at least until another need for them arises) and valuable capacity being used to create products not needed. Similar costs occur when forecasted need dates for MPS quantities are changed. For these reasons, many firms, particularly those with a make-to-stock strategy and a focus on low-cost operations, *freeze*, or disallow changes to, the near-term portion of the MPS.

Reconciling the MPS with Sales and Operations Plans   Because the master production schedule is based on both forecasts as well as actual orders received, it can differ from the sales and operations plan when summed across different periods in a month. For instance, in Figure 15.5, if the sum total MPS quantities of the three models of chairs in the month of April was 725 instead of 670, then either the management must revise the sales and operations plan upwards by authorizing additional resources to match supply with demand, or reduce the quantities of MPS in the month of April to match the sales and operations plan. Master production schedules drive plant and supplier activity, so they must be synchronized with the sales and operations plans to ensure that the firm's planning decisions are actually being implemented on an ongoing basis.

As Managerial Practice 15.1 illustrates, firms may also use commercial software solutions to manage the complexity of their master production scheduling processes.

Inventory Record

Inventory records are a third major input to MRP, and inventory transactions are the basic building blocks of up-to-date records (see Figure 15.2). These transactions include releasing new orders, receiving scheduled receipts, adjusting due dates for scheduled receipts, withdrawing inventory, canceling orders, correcting inventory errors, rejecting shipments, and verifying scrap losses and stock returns. Recording the transactions accurately is essential if the firm's on-hand inventory balances are to be correct and its MRP system is to operate effectively.

MANAGERIAL PRACTICE 15.1 | Master Production Scheduling at Truvo Nederland BV

Truvo Nederland BV (formerly known as Gouden Gids) is a company that publishes classified directories, or yellow pages, that advertise for more than 700,000 Dutch companies and organizations. As a subsidiary of Truvo (formerly known as World Directories), a global leader in classified advertising, Truvo Nederland BV employs nearly 650 people and has a print run of more than 7.5 million copies. Recently, in an attempt to make production more streamlined, Truvo Nederland BV decided to create a master production schedule with the help of a commercial software solution application.

Creating a master production schedule is complex; translating production plans into detailed schedules can be an error-prone and maintenance-heavy process. Truvo Nederland BV found it especially difficult to find a software application that would help create batch schedules because the software had to coordinate with the company's current computing systems. On the suggestion of its sister company Paginas Amarelas in Portugal, Truvo Nederland BV deployed ActiveBatch job scheduler from Advanced Systems Concepts. ActiveBatch coordinates the operations of computing systems, production, and standalone tasks and identifies any "slack time" that may keep operations from working efficiently. It also keeps track of program interdependencies, monitors for errors, sends alerts if human intervention is needed, and writes reports and distributes them to the right parties.

By implementing a batch scheduling software like ActiveBatch, Truvo Nederland BV has been able to improve service levels and reduce job-related errors. The company was also able to eliminate the man-hours previously committed to job scheduling tasks and use the surplus resources to troubleshoot other challenges. Overall, the software solution application has helped the book production system at Truvo Nederland BV work more efficiently and continues to improve the financial health of the company.

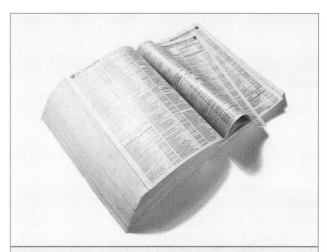

Dutch company Trudo Nederland BV deployed the ActiveBatch job scheduler to create batch schedules for the classified directories it publishes. The implementation of a master production schedule reduced scheduling inefficiencies and allowed valuable time and resources to be allocated elsewhere.

Sources: "Yellow Pages Business Directories: Products and Services," Gouden Gids, http://www.goudengids.nl/content/en_NL/Adverteren/Gouden_Gids_directory.html; "ActiveBatch Case Study: Truvo Nederland BV," https://www.advsyscon.com/pdf/ActiveBatch%20and%20Truvo%20Case%20Study%20Final.pdf.

The **inventory record** divides the future into time periods called *time buckets*. In our discussion, we use weekly time buckets for consistency with our MPS example, although other time periods could as easily be used. The inventory record shows an item's lot-size policy, lead time, and various time-phased data. The purpose of the inventory record is to keep track of inventory levels and component replenishment needs. The time-phased information contained in the inventory record consists of (1) *gross requirements*, (2) *scheduled receipts*, (3) *projected on-hand inventory*, (4) *planned receipts*, and (5) *planned order releases*.

We illustrate the discussion of inventory records with the seat subassembly, item C, that was shown in Figure 15.4. It is used in two products: a ladder-back chair and a kitchen chair.

Gross Requirements The **gross requirements** are the total demand derived from *all* parent production plans. They also include demand not otherwise accounted for, such as demand for replacement parts for units already sold. Figure 15.10 shows an inventory record for item C, the seat subassembly. Item C is produced in lots of 230 units and has a lead time of 2 weeks. The inventory record also shows item C's gross requirements for the next 8 weeks, which come from the master production schedule for the ladder-back and kitchen chairs (see Figure 15.5). The MPS start quantities for each parent are added to arrive at each week's gross requirements. The seat subassembly's gross requirements exhibit lumpy demand: Operations will withdraw seat subassemblies from inventory in only four of the 8 weeks.

The MRP system works with release dates to schedule production and delivery for components and subassemblies. Its program logic anticipates the removal of all materials required by a parent's production order from inventory at the beginning of the parent item's lead time—when the scheduler first releases the order to the shop.

inventory record

A record that shows an item's lot-size policy, lead time, and various time-phased data.

gross requirements

The total demand derived from *all* parent production plans.

Item: C Description: Seat subassembly					Lot Size: 230 units Lead Time: 2 weeks			
	Week							
	1	2	3	4	5	6	7	8
Gross requirements	150	0	0	120	0	150	120	0
Scheduled receipts	230	0	0	0	0	0	0	0
Projected on-hand inventory 37	117	117	117	−3	−3	−153	−273	−273
Planned receipts								
Planned order releases								

Explanation:
Gross requirements are the total demand for the two chairs. Projected on-hand inventory in week 1 is 37 + 230 − 150 = 117 units.

FIGURE 15.10 ▲
MRP Record for the Seat Subassembly

projected on-hand inventory

An estimate of the amount of inventory available each week after gross requirements have been satisfied.

planned receipts

Orders that are not yet released to the shop or the supplier.

Scheduled Receipts   Recall that *scheduled receipts* (sometimes called *open orders*) are orders that have been placed but not yet completed. For a purchased item, the scheduled receipt could be in one of several stages: being processed by a supplier, being transported to the purchaser, or being inspected by the purchaser's receiving department. If the firm is making the item in-house, the order could be on the shop floor being processed, waiting for components, waiting for a machine to become available, or waiting to be moved to its next operation. According to Figure 15.10 one 230-unit order of item C is due in week 1. Given the 2-week lead time, the inventory planner probably released the order 2 weeks ago. Scheduled receipts due in beyond the item's lead time are unexpected, caused by events such as a last-minute change in the MPS.

Projected On-Hand Inventory   The **projected on-hand inventory** is an estimate of the amount of inventory available each week after gross requirements have been satisfied. The beginning inventory, shown as the first entry (37) in Figure 15.10, indicates the on-hand inventory available at the time the record was computed. As with scheduled receipts, entries are made for each actual withdrawal and receipt to update the MRP database. Then, when the MRP system produces the revised record, the correct inventory will appear.

Other entries in the row show inventory expected in future weeks. Projected on-hand inventory is calculated as

$$\begin{pmatrix} \text{Projected on-hand} \\ \text{inventory balance} \\ \text{at end of week } t \end{pmatrix} = \begin{pmatrix} \text{Inventory on} \\ \text{hand at end of} \\ \text{week } t-1 \end{pmatrix} + \begin{pmatrix} \text{Scheduled} \\ \text{or planned} \\ \text{receipts in} \\ \text{week } t \end{pmatrix} - \begin{pmatrix} \text{Gross} \\ \text{requirements} \\ \text{in week } t \end{pmatrix}$$

The projected on-hand calculation includes the consideration of **planned receipts**, which are orders not yet released to the shop or the supplier. Planned receipts should not be confused with scheduled receipts. Planned receipts are still at the planning stage and can still change from 1 week to the next, whereas scheduled receipts are actual orders that are being acted upon by the shop or supplier. In Figure 15.10, the planned receipts are all zero. The on-hand inventory calculations for each week are as follows:

Week 1:	$37 + 230 - 150 = 117$
Weeks 2 and 3:	$117 + 0 - 0 = 117$
Week 4:	$117 + 0 - 120 = -3$
Week 5:	$-3 + 0 - 0 = -3$
Week 6:	$-3 + 0 - 150 = -153$
Week 7:	$-153 + 0 - 120 = -273$
Week 8:	$-273 + 0 - 0 = -273$

In week 4, the balance drops to –3 units, which indicates that a shortage of 3 units will occur unless more seat subassemblies are built. This condition signals the need for a planned receipt to arrive in week 4. In addition, unless more stock is received, the shortage will grow to 273 units in weeks 7 and 8.[2]

---

[2] There is an exception to the rule of scheduling a planned receipt whenever the projected inventory otherwise becomes negative. When a scheduled receipt is coming in *after* the inventory becomes negative, the first recourse is to expedite the scheduled receipt (giving it an earlier due date), rather than scheduling a new planned receipt.

Planned Receipts Planning for the receipt of new orders will keep the projected on-hand balance from dropping below zero. The planned receipt row is developed as follows:

1. Weekly on-hand inventory is projected until a shortage appears. Completion of the initial planned receipt is scheduled for the week in which the shortage is projected. The addition of the newly planned receipt should increase the projected on-hand balance so that it equals or exceeds zero. It will exceed zero when the lot size exceeds requirements in the week it is planned to arrive.

2. The projection of on-hand inventory continues until the next shortage occurs. This shortage signals the need for the second planned receipt.

This process is repeated until the end of the planning horizon by proceeding column by column through the MRP record—filling in planned receipts as needed and completing the projected on-hand inventory row. Figure 15.11 shows the planned receipts for the seat subassembly. In week 4, the projected on-hand inventory will drop below zero, so a planned receipt of 230 units is scheduled for week 4. The updated inventory on-hand balance is 117 (inventory at end of week 3) + 230 (planned receipts) –120 (gross requirements)=227 units. The projected on-hand inventory remains at 227 for week 5 because no scheduled receipts or gross requirements are anticipated. In week 6, the projected on-hand inventory is 227 (inventory at end of week 5) −150 (gross requirements) = 77 units. This quantity is greater than zero, so no new planned receipt is needed. In week 7, however, a shortage will occur unless more seat subassemblies are received. With a planned receipt in week 7, the updated inventory balance is 77 (inventory at end of week 6) + 230 (planned receipts)−120 (gross requirements) = 187 units.

Item: C Description: Seat subassembly								Lot Size: 230 units Lead Time: 2 weeks	
		Week							
		1	2	3	4	5	6	7	8
Gross requirements		150	0	0	120	0	150	120	0
Scheduled receipts		230	0	0	0	0	0	0	0
Projected on-hand inventory	37	117	117	117	227	227	77	187	187
Planned receipts					230			230	
Planned order releases			230			230			

Explanation:
Without a planned receipt in week 4, a shortage of 3 units will occur: 117 + 0 + 0 − 120 = −3 units. Adding the planned receipt brings the balance to 117 + 0 + 230 − 120 = 227 units. Offsetting for a 2-week lead time puts the corresponding planned order release back to week 2.

Explanation:
The first planned receipt lasts until week 7, when projected inventory would drop to 77 + 0 + 0 − 120 = −43 units. Adding the second planned receipt brings the balance to 77 + 0 + 230 − 120 = 187 units. The corresponding planned order release is for week 5 (or week 7 minus 2 weeks).

▲ FIGURE 15.11
Completed Inventory Record for the Seat Subassembly

Planned Order Releases A **planned order release** indicates when an order for a specified quantity of an item is to be issued. We must place the planned order release quantity in the proper time bucket. To do so, we must assume that all inventory flows—scheduled receipts, planned receipts, and gross requirements—occur at the same point of time in a time period. Some firms assume that all flows occur at the beginning of a time period; other firms assume that they occur at the end of a time period or at the middle of the time period. Regardless of when the flows are assumed to occur, we find the release date by subtracting the lead time from the receipt date. For example, the release date for the first planned order release in Figure 15.11 is 4 (planned receipt date) – 2 (lead time) = 2 (planned order release date). Figure 15.11 shows the planned order releases for the seat subassembly. If all goes according to the plan, we will release an order for 230 seat assemblies next week (in week 2). This order release sets off a series of updates to the inventory record. First, the planned order release for the order is removed. Next, the planned receipt for 230 units in week 4 is also removed. Finally, a new scheduled receipt for 230 units will appear in the scheduled receipt row for week 4.

planned order release

An indication of when an order for a specified quantity of an item is to be issued.

Planning Factors

The planning factors in a MRP inventory record play an important role in the overall performance of the MRP system. By manipulating these factors, managers can fine-tune inventory operations. In this section, we discuss planning lead time, lot-sizing rules, and safety stock.

Planning Lead Time Planning lead time is an estimate of the time between placing an order for an item and receiving the item in inventory. Accuracy is important in planning lead time. If an item arrives in inventory sooner than needed, inventory holding costs increase. If an item arrives too late, stockouts, excessive expediting costs, or both may occur.

For purchased items, the planning lead time is the time allowed for receiving a shipment from the supplier after the order has been sent, including the normal time to place the order. Often, the purchasing contract stipulates the delivery date. For items manufactured in-house, the planning lead time consists of estimates for the following factors:

- Setup time
- Processing time
- Materials handling time between operations
- Waiting time

Each of these times must be estimated for every operation along the item's route. Estimating setup, processing, and materials handling times can be relatively easy, but estimating the waiting time for materials handling equipment or for a workstation to perform a particular operation can be more difficult. In a facility that uses a make-to-order strategy, such as a machine shop, the load on the shop varies considerably over time, causing actual waiting times for a particular order to fluctuate widely. Therefore, being able to accurately estimate the waiting time is especially important when it comes to estimating the planning lead time. However, in a facility that uses a make-to-stock strategy, such as an assembly plant, product routings are more standard and waiting time is more predictable; hence, waiting time generally is a less-troublesome part of planning lead times.

Lot-Sizing Rules   A lot-sizing rule determines the timing and size of order quantities. A lot-sizing rule must be assigned to each item before planned receipts and planned order releases can be computed. The choice of lot-sizing rules is important because they determine the number of setups required and the inventory holding costs for each item. We present three lot-sizing rules: (1) fixed order quantity, (2) periodic order quantity, and (3) lot-for-lot.

fixed order quantity (FOQ)

A rule that maintains the same order quantity each time an order is issued.

Fixed Order Quantity   The **fixed order quantity (FOQ)** rule maintains the same order quantity each time an order is issued.[3] For example, the lot size might be the size dictated by equipment capacity limits, such as when a full lot must be loaded into a furnace at one time. For purchased items, the FOQ could be determined by the quantity discount level, truckload capacity, or minimum purchase quantity. Alternatively, the lot size could be determined by the economic order quantity (EOQ) formula. Figure 15.11 illustrated the FOQ rule. However, if an item's gross requirement within a week is particularly large, the FOQ might be insufficient to avoid a shortage. In such unusual cases, the inventory planner must increase the lot size beyond the FOQ, typically to a size large enough to avoid a shortage. Another option is to make the order quantity an integer multiple of the FOQ. This option is appropriate when capacity constraints limit production to FOQ sizes (at most).

periodic order quantity (POQ)

A rule that allows a different order quantity for each order issued but issues the order for predetermined time intervals.

Periodic Order Quantity   The **periodic order quantity (POQ)** rule allows a different order quantity for each order issued but issues the order for predetermined time intervals, such as every 2 weeks. The order quantity equals the amount of the item needed during the predetermined time between orders and must be large enough to prevent shortages. Specifically, the POQ is

$$\begin{pmatrix} \text{POQ lot size} \\ \text{to arrive in} \\ \text{week } t \end{pmatrix} = \begin{pmatrix} \text{Total gross requirements} \\ \text{for } P \text{ weeks, including} \\ \text{week } t \end{pmatrix} - \begin{pmatrix} \text{Projected on-hand} \\ \text{inventory balance at} \\ \text{end of week } t{-}1 \end{pmatrix}$$

This amount exactly covers P weeks' worth of gross requirements. That is, the projected on-hand inventory should equal zero at the end of the Pth week.

Suppose that we want to switch from the FOQ rule used in Figure 15.11 to the POQ rule. Figure 15.12 shows the application of the POQ rule, with $P = 3$ weeks, to the seat subassembly inventory. The first order is required in week 4 because it is the first week that projected inventory balance will fall below zero. The first order using $P = 3$ weeks is

$$\text{(POQ lot size)} = \begin{pmatrix} \text{Gross requirements} \\ \text{for weeks} \\ 4, 5, \text{ and } 6 \end{pmatrix} - \begin{pmatrix} \text{Inventory at} \\ \text{end of week 3} \end{pmatrix}$$

$$= (120 + 0 + 150) - 117 = 153 \text{ units}$$

Tutor 15.2 in my**om**provides a new example to practice lot-sizing decisions using FOQ, POQ, and L4L rules.

---

[3] The kanban system essentially uses a FOQ rule, except that the order quantity is very small.

Periods	8								
Item	Seat Assembly			Period (P) for POQ		3	Lot Size (FOQ)		
Description							Lead Time		2
POQ Rule	▼								
	1	2	3	4	5	6	7	8
Gross requirements		150			120		150	120	
Scheduled receipts		230							
Projected on-hand inventory	37	117	117	117	150	150			
Planned receipts					153			120	
Planned order releases			153			120			

◀ FIGURE 15.12
The POQ (P = 3) Rule for the Seat Subassembly

The second order must arrive in week 7 with a lot size of $(120 + 0) - 0 = 120$ units. This second order reflects only two weeks' worth of gross requirements—to the end of the planning horizon.

The POQ rule does not mean that the planner must issue a new order every P weeks. Rather, when an order is planned, its lot size must be enough to cover P successive weeks. One way to select a P value is to divide the average lot size desired, such as the EOQ or some other applicable lot size, by the average weekly demand. That is, express the target lot size as the desired weeks of supply (P) and round to the nearest integer.

Lot for Lot A special case of the POQ rule is the **lot-for-lot (L4L) rule**, under which the lot size ordered covers the gross requirements of a single week. Thus, $P = 1$, and the goal is to minimize inventory levels. This rule ensures that the planned order is just large enough to prevent a shortage in the single week it covers. The L4L lot size is

lot-for-lot (L4L) rule

A rule under which the lot size ordered covers the gross requirements of a single week.

$$\begin{pmatrix} \text{L4L lot size} \\ \text{to arrive in} \\ \text{week } t \end{pmatrix} = \begin{pmatrix} \text{Gross requirements} \\ \text{for week } t \end{pmatrix} - \begin{pmatrix} \text{Projected on-hand} \\ \text{inventory balance at} \\ \text{end of week } t-1 \end{pmatrix}$$

The projected on-hand inventory combined with the new order will equal zero at the end of week t. Following the first planned order, an additional planned order will be used to match each subsequent gross requirement.

This time we want to switch from the FOQ rule to the L4L rule. Figure 15.13 shows the application of the L4L rule to the seat subassembly inventory. As before, the first order is needed in week 4:

$$\begin{aligned} (\text{L4L lot size}) &= \begin{pmatrix} \text{Gross requirements} \\ \text{in week 4} \end{pmatrix} - \begin{pmatrix} \text{Inventory balance} \\ \text{at end of week 3} \end{pmatrix} \\ &= 120 - 117 = 3 \end{aligned}$$

The stockroom must receive additional orders in weeks 6 and 7 to satisfy each of the subsequent gross requirements. The planned receipt for week 6 is 150 and for week 7 is 120.

Comparing Lot-Sizing Rules Choosing a lot-sizing rule can have important implications for inventory management. Lot-sizing rules affect inventory costs and setup and ordering costs. The FOQ, POQ, and L4L rules differ from one another in one or both respects. In our example, each rule took effect in week 4, when the first order was placed. Let us compare

Periods	8								
Item	Seat Assembly			Period (P) for POQ			Lot Size (FOQ)		
Description							Lead Time		2
L4L Rule	▼								
	1	2	3	4	5	6	7	8
Gross requirements		150			120		150	120	
Scheduled receipts		230							
Projected on-hand inventory	37	117	117	117					
Planned receipts					3		150	120	
Planned order releases			3		150	120			

◀ FIGURE 15.13
The L4L Rule for the Seat Subassembly

the projected on-hand inventory averaged over weeks 4 through 8 of the planning horizon. The data are shown in Figures 15.11, 15.12, and 15.13, respectively.

$$\text{FOQ: } \frac{227 + 227 + 77 + 187 + 187}{5} = 181 \text{ units}$$

$$\text{POQ: } \frac{150 + 150 + 0 + 0 + 0}{5} = 60 \text{ units}$$

$$\text{L4L: } \frac{0 + 0 + 0 + 0 + 0}{5} = 0 \text{ units}$$

The performance of the L4L rule with respect to average inventory levels comes at the expense of an additional planned order and its accompanying setup time and cost. We can draw three conclusions from this comparison:

1. The FOQ rule generates a high level of average inventory because it creates inventory *remnants*. A remnant is inventory carried into a week, but it is too small to prevent a shortage. Remnants occur because the FOQ does not match requirements exactly. For example, according to Figure 15.11, the stockroom must receive a planned order in week 7, even though 77 units are on hand at the beginning of that week. The remnant is the 77 units that the stockroom will carry for 3 weeks, beginning with receipt of the first planned order in week 4. Although they increase average inventory levels, inventory remnants introduce stability into the production process by buffering unexpected scrap losses, capacity bottlenecks, inaccurate inventory records, or unstable gross requirements.

2. The POQ rule reduces the amount of average on-hand inventory because it does a better job of matching order quantity to requirements. It adjusts lot sizes as requirements increase or decrease. Figure 15.12 shows that in week 7, when the POQ rule has fully taken effect, the projected on-hand inventory is zero—no remnants.

3. The L4L rule minimizes inventory investment, but it also maximizes the number of orders placed. This rule is most applicable to expensive items or items with small ordering or setup costs. It is the only rule that can be used for a low-volume item made to order. It can also approximate the small-lot inventory levels of a lean system.

By avoiding remnants, both the POQ and the L4L rule may introduce instability by tying the lot-sizing decision so closely to requirements. If any requirement changes, so must the lot size, which can disrupt component schedules. Last-minute increases in parent orders may be hindered by missing components.

Safety Stock An important managerial decision is the quantity of safety stock to carry. It is more complex for dependent demand items than for independent demand items. Safety stock for dependent demand items with lumpy demand (gross requirements) is helpful only when future gross requirements, the timing or size of scheduled receipts, and the amount of scrap that will be produced are uncertain. As these uncertainties are resolved, safety stock should be reduced and ultimately eliminated. The usual policy is to use safety stock for end items and purchased items to protect against fluctuating customer orders and unreliable suppliers of components but to avoid using it as much as possible for intermediate items. Safety stocks can be incorporated in the MRP logic by using the following rule: Schedule a planned receipt whenever the projected on-hand inventory balance drops below the desired safety stock level (rather than zero, as before). The objective is to keep a minimum level of planned inventories equal to the safety stock quantity. Figure 15.14 shows what happens when the safety stock requirement has just been increased from 0 units to 80 units of safety stock for the seat assembly using an FOQ of 230 units. Compare these results to Figure 15.11. The net effect is to move the second planned order release from week 5 to week 4 to avoid dropping below 80 units in week 6.

FIGURE 15.14 ▼
Inventory Record for the Seat Subassembly Showing the Application of a Safety Stock

FOQ Rule							Lot Size	230
							Lead Time	2
							Safety Stock	80
	1	2	3	4	5	6	7	8
Gross requirements	150	0	0	120	0	150	120	0
Scheduled receipts	230	0	0	0	0	0	0	0
Projected on-hand inventory 37	117	117	117	227	227	307	187	187
Planned receipts	0	0	0	230	0	230	0	0
Planned order releases	0	230	0	230	0	0	0	0

Outputs from MRP

MRP systems provide many reports, schedules, and notices to help planners control dependent demand inventories, as indicated in Figure 15.15. In this section, we discuss the MRP explosion

▲ FIGURE 15.15
MRP Outputs

process, notices that alert planners to items needing attention, resource requirement reports, and performance reports.

MRP Explosion   MRP translates, or *explodes*, the MPS and other sources of demand into the requirements needed for all of the subassemblies, components, and raw materials the firm needs to produce parent items. This process generates the material requirements plan for each component item.

An item's gross requirements are derived from three sources:

1. The MPS for immediate parents that are end items
2. The planned order releases (*not* the gross requirements, scheduled receipts, or planned receipts) for immediate parents below the MPS level
3. Any other requirements not originating in the MPS, such as the demand for replacement parts

Consider the seat subassembly and its inventory record shown in Figure 15.11. The seat subassembly requires a seat cushion and a seat frame, which in turn needs four seat-frame boards. Its BOM is shown in Figure 15.16 (see also Figure 15.4, which shows how the seat subassembly BOM relates to the product as a whole). How many seat cushions should we order from the supplier? How many seat frames should we produce to support the seat subassembly schedule? How many seat-frame boards do we need to make? The answers to these questions depend on the existing inventories of these items and the replenishment orders already in progress. MRP can help answer these questions through the explosion process.

Figure 15.17 shows the MRP records for the seat subassembly and its components. We already showed how to develop the MRP record for the seat subassembly. We now concentrate on the MRP records of its components. The lot-size rules are an FOQ of 300 units for the seat frame, L4L for the seat cushion, and an FOQ of 1,500 for the seat-frame boards. All three components have a 1-week lead time. The key to the explosion process is to determine the proper timing and size of the gross requirements for each component. After we make those determinations, we can derive the planned order release schedule for each component by using the logic already demonstrated.

In our example, the components have no independent demand for replacement parts. Consequently, in Figure 15.17 the gross requirements of a component come from the planned order releases of its parents. The seat frame and the seat cushion get their gross requirements from the planned order release schedule of the seat subassembly. Both components have gross requirements of 230 units in weeks 2 and 5, the same weeks in which we will be releasing orders to make more seat subassemblies. In week 2, for example, the materials handler for the assembly department will withdraw 230 seat frames and 230 seat cushions from inventory so that the assembly department can

▼ FIGURE 15.16
BOM for the Seat Subassembly

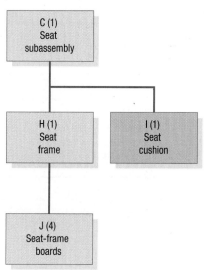

Item: Seat subassembly
Lot size: 230 units

Lead time: 2 weeks	Week							
	1	2	3	4	5	6	7	8
Gross requirements	150	0	0	120	0	150	120	0
Scheduled receipts	230	0	0	0	0	0	0	0
Projected inventory 37	117	117	117	227	227	77	187	187
Planned receipts				230			230	
Planned order releases		230			230			

Usage quantity: 1   Usage quantity: 1

Item: Seat frames
Lot size: 300 units

Lead time: 1 week	Week							
	1	2	3	4	5	6	7	8
Gross requirements	0	230	0	0	230	0	0	0
Scheduled receipts	0	300	0	0	0	0	0	0
Projected inventory 40	40	110	110	110	180	180	180	180
Planned receipts					300			
Planned order releases				300				

Item: Seat cushion
Lot size: L4L

Lead time: 1 week	Week							
	1	2	3	4	5	6	7	8
Gross requirements	0	230	0	0	230	0	0	0
Scheduled receipts	0	0	0	0	0	0	0	0
Projected inventory 0	0	0	0	0	0	0	0	0
Planned receipts		230			230			
Planned order releases	230			230				

Usage quantity: 4

Item: Seat-frame boards
Lot size: 1,500 units

Lead time: 1 week	Week							
	1	2	3	4	5	6	7	8
Gross requirements	0	0	0	1,200	0	0	0	0
Scheduled receipts	0	0	0	0	0	0	0	0
Projected inventory 200	200	200	200	500	500	500	500	500
Planned receipts				1,500				
Planned order releases			1,500					

FIGURE 15.17 ▲
MRP Explosion of Seat Assembly Components

produce the seat subassemblies in time to avoid a stockout in week 4. The materials plans for the seat frame and the seat cushion must allow for that.

Using the gross requirements in weeks 2 and 5, we can develop the MRP records for the seat frame and the seat cushion, as shown in Figure 15.17. For a scheduled receipt of 300 seat frames in week 2, an on-hand quantity of 40 units, and a lead time of 1 week, we need to release an order of 300 seat frames in week 4 to cover the assembly schedule for the seat sub-assembly. The seat cushion has no scheduled receipts and no inventory on hand; consequently, we must place orders for 230 units in weeks 1 and 4, using the L4L logic with a lead time of 1 week.

After determining the replenishment schedule for the seat frame, we can calculate the gross requirements for the seat-frame boards. We plan to begin producing 300 seat frames in week 4. Each frame requires 4 boards, so we need to have 300(4) = 1,200 boards available in week 4. Consequently, the gross requirement for seat-frame boards is 1,200 in week 4. Given no scheduled receipts, 200 boards in stock, a lead time of 1 week, and an FOQ of 1,500 units, we need a planned order release of 1,500 in week 3.

The questions posed earlier can now be answered. We should plan to release the following orders: 300 seat frames in week 4; 230 seat cushions in each of weeks 1 and 4; and 1,500 seat-frame boards in week 3. If MRP plans are updated weekly, only the planned order for week 1 should be released now. Releasing it creates a scheduled receipt of 230 seat cushions that will appear in the updated inventory record. The other orders remain in the planning stage, and even might be revised by the MRP explosion done next week.

Other Important Reports   Once computed, inventory records for any item appearing in the BOM can be printed in hard copy or displayed on a computer video screen. Inventory planners use a computer-generated memo called an **action notice** to make decisions about releasing new orders and adjusting the due dates of scheduled receipts. These notices are generated every time the system is updated, such as once per week. The action notice alerts planners to only the items that need their attention, such as those items that have a planned order release in the current period or a scheduled receipt that needs its due date revised. Planners can then view the full records for those items and take the necessary actions. An action notice can simply be a list of part numbers for items that need attention; or it can be the full record for such items, with a note at the bottom identifying the action needed.

By itself, the MRP system does not recognize capacity limitations when computing planned orders; that is, it may call for a planned order release that exceeds the amount that can be physically produced. An essential role of planners is to monitor the capacity requirements of material requirements plans, adjusting a plan when it cannot be met. Particular attention is paid to bottlenecks. The planner can apply theory of constraints (TOC) principles (see Chapter 7, "Managing Process Constraints") to keep bottleneck operations fed by adjusting some lot sizing rules or occasionally overriding planned order releases. To facilitate this process, various types of capacity reports can be provided. For example, **capacity requirements planning (CRP)** reports project time-phased capacity requirements for workstations. They calculate workload according to the work required to complete the scheduled receipts already in the shop and to complete the planned order releases not yet released. Bottlenecks are those workstations at which the projected loads exceed station capacities.

Other types of outputs are also possible, such as priority reports on orders already placed to the shop or with suppliers. Priority reports begin with the due dates assigned to scheduled receipts, which planners keep up to date so that they continue to reflect when receipt is really needed. On a broader scale, the information in an MRP system is useful to functional areas other than operations. MRP evolved into **manufacturing resource planning (MRP II)**, a system that ties the basic MRP system to the company's financial system and to other core and supporting processes. For example, management can project the dollar value of shipments, product costs, overhead allocations, inventories, backlogs, and profits by using the MRP plan along with prices and product and activity costs from the accounting system. Also, information from the MPS, scheduled receipts, and planned orders can be converted into cash flow projections, which are broken down by product families. Similar computations are possible for other performance measures of interest to management. In fact, MRP II ultimately evolved into enterprise resource planning (ERP), which was introduced at the beginning of this chapter. Some firms may, however, forego the cost of vendor-delivered MRP and ERP systems because of the huge budgets and company resources involved in their deployment, and instead create their own MRP system implementations in-house. Managerial Practice 15.2 illustrates how Winnebago created and adapted its own homegrown software for the MRP system to achieve business self sufficiency.

action notice

A computer-generated memo alerting planners about releasing new orders and adjusting the due dates of scheduled receipts.

capacity requirements planning (CRP)

A technique used for projecting time-phased capacity requirements for workstations; its purpose is to match the material requirements plan with the capacity of key processes.

manufacturing resource planning (MRP II)

A system that ties the basic MRP system to the company's financial system and to other core and supporting processes.

| MANAGERIAL PRACTICE 15.2 | Material Requirements Planning at Winnebago Industries |

Winnebago Industries, based in Forest City, Iowa, is a leading manufacturer of motor homes and related products and services in the United States, with sales of $870 million in 2007. In a challenging business environment, the firm improves the quality of its products at lowered production costs by emphasizing employee teamwork and involvement. So it is no surprise that Winnebago has for decades kept away from software packages, preferring instead to create and adapt its own applications. It can thereby achieve a closer fit to the company's business needs, an objective that is at times not met by the ERP vendors described at the beginning of this chapter. It can also be more responsive to users of its systems at lowered costs since it can reuse its code as needed.

Winnebago Industries keeps innovating with its motor home products, and introduced several new models in 2009 to celebrate 50 years of its existence.

An example of Winnebago's homegrown approach is its MRP system, which runs on an IBM zSeries mainframe and is used to plan material needs and schedule production orders. When the company added a new model to its fleet of motor homes, it took only a few hundred hours of development, including a new bill of materials, to make the required changes to the MRP system in order to support production of the new vehicle. Such agility in adapting the MRP system to manufacturing and supplier needs can be especially rewarding in an environment where the change in product variety is constant. For the 2007 model year alone, Winnebago offered 20 different models in 86 different floor plans, each of which can be outfitted with a variety of options including colors, wood stains, and drawer pulls. When you are in the business of building customized homes-on-wheels ranging in prices from $60,000 to $285,000, combining cost consciousness with common sense and employee involvement in developing your own MRP, sales order management, and purchasing systems can prove valuable.

Sources: "Road Rules: Creating and Adapting Homegrown Software is the key to Winnebago's Drive for Business Self Sufficiency," October 15, 2006; http://www.winnebagoind.com/ (accessed July 2008).

MRP and the Environment

Consumer and governmental concern about the deterioration of the natural environment has driven manufacturers to reengineer their processes to become more environmentally friendly. The recycling of base materials is becoming more commonplace, and products are being designed in such a way that they can be remanufactured after their useful lives. Nonetheless, manufacturing processes often produce a number of waste materials that need to be properly disposed of. Wastes come in many forms:

- Effluents, such as carbon monoxide, sulfur dioxide, and hazardous chemicals associated with the processes used to manufacture the product
- Materials, such as metal shavings, oils, and chemicals associated with specific operations
- Packaging materials, such as unusable cardboard and plastics associated with certain products or purchased items
- Scrap associated with unusable products or component defects generated by the manufacturing process

Companies can modify their MRP systems to help them track these wastes and plan for their disposal. The type and amount of waste associated with each item can be entered into its BOM by treating the waste much like you would a component of the item. When the MPS is developed for a product, reports can be generated that project the amount of waste expected during the production process and when it will occur. Although this approach can require that a firm's BOM be modified substantially, the benefits are also substantial. Firms can identify their waste problems in advance to eliminate them in some cases (though process improvement efforts) or plan for their proper disposal in others. It also gives the firm a way to generate any formal documentation required by the government to verify that it has complied with environmental laws and policies.

RESOURCE PLANNING FOR SERVICE PROVIDERS

We have seen how manufacturing companies can disaggregate an MPS of finished products, which in turn must be translated into the needs for resources, such as staff, equipment, components, and financial assets. The driver for these resource requirements is a material requirements plan. Service providers, of course, must plan their resources just as manufacturers do. However, unlike finished goods, services cannot be inventoried. They must be provided on demand. In terms of resource planning then, service organizations must focus on maintaining the *capacity* to serve their customers. In this section, we will discuss how service providers use the concept of dependent demand and a bill of resources in managing capacity.

A concierge for the Hotel Gritti Palace greets a rowing team competing in the Volgalonga. Boaters must row from the Piazza San Marco to Buranoa and back, a total distance of 20 miles. The Hotel Gritti Palace is one of many properties of Starwood Hotels and Resorts Worldwide that faces complex resource planning issues.

Dependent Demand for Services

When we discussed planning and control systems for manufacturers earlier in this chapter, we introduced the concept of *dependent demand*, which is demand for an item that is a function of the production plans for some other item the company produces. For service resource planning, it is useful to define the concept of dependent demand to include demands for resources that are driven by forecasts of customer requests for services or by plans for various activities in support of the services the company provides. Here are some other examples of dependent demands for service providers.

Restaurants Every time you order from the menu at a restaurant, you initiate the restaurant's need for certain types of goods (uncooked food items, plates, and napkins), staff (chef, servers, and dishwashers), and equipment (stoves, ovens, and cooking utensils). Using a forecast of the demand for each type of meal, the manager of the restaurant can estimate the need for these resources. Many restaurants, for example, feature "specials" on certain days, say, fish on Fridays or prime rib on Saturdays. Specials improve the accuracy of the forecasts managers need to make for different types of meals (and the food products that are required to make them) and typically signal the need for above-average staffing levels. How much of these resources will be needed, however, depends on the number of meals the restaurant ultimately expects to serve. As such, these items—food products and staff members—are dependent demands.

A couple enjoys eating at a fine restaurant. Each meal initiates the need for facilitating goods, staff, and equipment.

Airlines Whenever an airline schedules a flight, certain supporting goods are needed (beverages, snacks, and fuel), labor (pilots, flight attendants, and airport services), and equipment (a plane and airport gate). The number of flights and passengers the airline forecasts it will serve determines the amount of these resources needed. Just like a manufacturer, the airline can explode its master schedule of flights to make this determination.

Hospitals With the exception of the emergency room services, hospitals can use their admission appointments to create a master schedule. The master schedule can be exploded to determine the resources the hospital will need during a certain period. For example, when you schedule a surgical procedure, you generate a need for facilitating goods such as medicines, surgical gowns, linens, staff (a surgeon, nurses, and anesthesiologist), and equipment (an operating room, surgical tools, and recovery bed). As they build their master schedules, hospitals must ensure that certain equipment and personnel do not become overcommitted—that capacity is maintained, in other words. For example, an appointment for a key operation might have to be scheduled in advance at a time a surgeon is available to do it, even though the hospital's other resources—operating room, nurses, and so forth—might be currently be available.

Hotels A traveler who makes a reservation at a hotel generates demand for facilitating goods (soap and towels), staff (front desk, housekeeping, and concierge), and equipment (fax, television, and exercise bicycle). To determine its dependent resource needs, a hotel adds the number of reservations already booked to the number of "walk-in" customers it forecasts it will have. This figure is used to create the hotel's master schedule. One resource a hotel cannot easily adjust, however, is the number of rooms it has. If the hotel is overbooked, for instance, it cannot simply add more rooms. If it has too few guests, it cannot "downsize" its number of rooms. Given the high capital costs needed for this resource, hotels try to maintain as high a utilization rate as possible by offering group rates or special promotions at certain times of the year. In other words, they try to drive up dependent demand for this particular resource.

Bill of Resources

bill of resources (BOR)

A record of a service firm's parent–component relationships and all of the materials, equipment time, staff, and other resources associated with them, including usage quantities.

The service analogy to the bill of materials in a manufacturing company is the **bill of resources (BOR)**, which is a record of a service firm's parent–component relationships and all of the materials, equipment time, staff, and other resources associated with them, including usage quantities. Once the service firm has completed its master schedule, the BOR can be used to determine what resources the firm will need, how much of them it will need, and when. A BOR for a service provider can be as complex as a BOM for a manufacturer. Consider a hospital that just scheduled treatment of a patient with an aneurysm. As shown in Figure 15.18 the BOR for treatment of an aneurysm has seven levels, starting at the top (end item): (1) discharge, (2) intermediate care, (3) postoperative care (step down), (4) postoperative care (intensive), (5) surgery, (6) preoperative care (angiogram), and (7) preoperative care (testing). Each level of the BOR has a set of material and resource requirements and an associated lead time. For example, at level 6, shown in Figure 15.18(b), the patient needs 6 hours of nurses' time, 1 hour of the primary MD's time, 1 hour of the respiratory therapist's time, 24 hours of bed time, 3 different lab tests, 1 meal, and 10 different medicines from the pharmacy. The lead time for this level is 1 day. The lead time for the entire stay for treatment of the aneurysm is 12.2 days. A master schedule of patient admissions and the BORs for each illness enable the hospital to manage its critical resources. Reports analogous to the MRP II reports we discussed earlier in the chapter can be generated for the people who manage the various functional areas of the hospital.

One resource every service provider needs, however, is cash. Service organizations have to forecast the number of customers they expect to serve so that they have enough cash on hand to purchase materials that support the services—labor and other products. Purchasing these items increases the firm's accounts payable. As services are actually completed for customers, the firm's accounts receivable increases. The firm's master schedule and its accounts receivable and payable help a company predict the amount and timing of its cash flows.

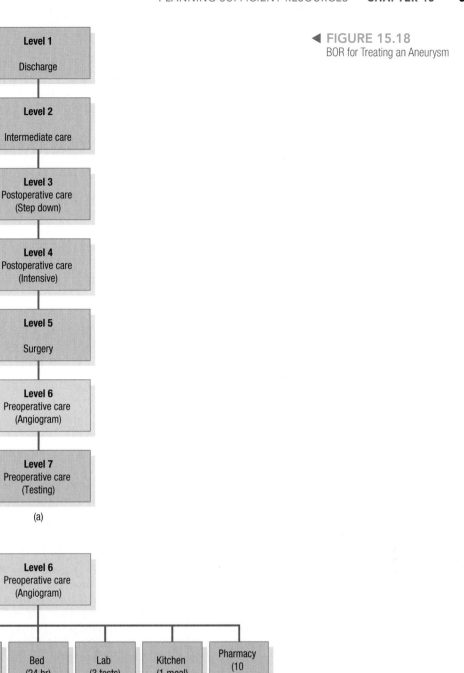

◀ FIGURE 15.18
BOR for Treating an Aneurysm

INTERNET RESOURCES

my**om**lab and the Companion Website at **www.pearsonglobaleditions.com/krajewski** contain many tools, activities, and resources designed for this chapter.

KEY TERMS

action notice 579
available-to-promise (ATP)
    inventory 569
bill of materials (BOM) 565
bill of resources (BOR) 582

capacity requirements planning
    (CRP) 579
component 564
dependent demand 564
end item 565
enterprise process 562

enterprise resource planning (ERP)
    systems 562
fixed order quantity (FOQ) 574
gross requirements 571
intermediate item 566
interoperability 563

SOLVED PROBLEM 1

Refer to the bill of materials for product A shown in Figure 15.19.

FIGURE 15.19 ▶
BOM for Product A

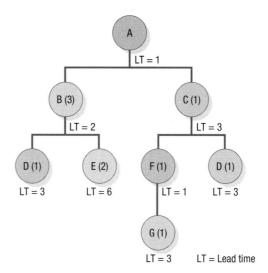

If there is no existing inventory and no scheduled receipts, how many units of items G, E, and D must be purchased to produce 5 units of end item A?

SOLUTION

Five units of item G, 30 units of item E, and 20 units of item D must be purchased to make 5 units of A. The usage quantities shown in Figure 15.21 indicate that 2 units of E are needed to make 1 unit of B and that 3 units of B are needed to make 1 unit of A; therefore, 5 units of A require 30 units of E $(2 \times 3 \times 5 = 30)$. One unit of D is consumed to make 1 unit of B, and 3 units of B per unit of A result in 15 units of D $(1 \times 3 \times 5 = 15)$; 1 unit of D in each unit of C and 1 unit of C per unit of A result in another 5 units of D $(1 \times 1 \times 5 = 5)$. The total requirements to make 5 units of A are 20 units of D $(15 + 5)$. The calculation of requirements for G is simply $1 \times 1 \times 1 \times 5 = 5$ units.

SOLVED PROBLEM 2

The order policy is to produce end item A in lots of 50 units. Using the data shown in Figure 15.20 and the FOQ lot-sizing rule, complete the projected on-hand inventory and MPS quantity rows. Then complete the MPS start row by offsetting the MPS quantities for the final assembly lead time. Finally, compute the available-to-promise inventory for item A. If in week 1 a customer requests a new order for 30 units of item A, when is the earliest date the entire order could be shipped?

SOLUTION

The projected on-hand inventory for the second week is

$$\begin{pmatrix} \text{Projected on-hand} \\ \text{inventory at end} \\ \text{of week 2} \end{pmatrix} = \begin{pmatrix} \text{On-hand} \\ \text{inventory in} \\ \text{week 1} \end{pmatrix} + \begin{pmatrix} \text{MPS quantity} \\ \text{due in week 2} \end{pmatrix} - \begin{pmatrix} \text{Requirements} \\ \text{in week 2} \end{pmatrix}$$

$$= 25 + 0 - 20 = 5 \text{ units}$$

Item: A								Order Policy: 50 units Lead Time: 1 week			
		Week										
Quantity on Hand: 5		1	2	3	4	5	6	7	8	9	10
Forecast		20	10	40	10	0	0	30	20	40	20
Customer orders (booked)		30	20	5	8	0	2	0	0	0	0
Projected on-hand inventory		25									
MPS quantity		50									
MPS start											
Available-to- promise (ATP) inventory											

◀ **FIGURE 15.20**
MPS Record for End Item A

where requirements are the larger of the forecast or actual customer orders booked for shipment during this period. No MPS quantity is required.

Without an MPS quantity in the third period, a shortage of item A will occur: $5 + 0 - 40 = -35$. Therefore, an MPS quantity equal to the lot size of 50 must be scheduled for completion in the third period. Then the projected on-hand inventory for the third week will be $5 + 50 - 40 = 15$.

Figure 15.21 shows the projected on-hand inventories and MPS quantities that would result from completing the MPS calculations. The MPS start row is completed by simply shifting a copy of the MPS quantity row to the left by one column to account for the 1-week final assembly lead time. Also shown are the available-to-promise quantities. In week 1, the ATP is

$$\begin{pmatrix} \text{Available-to-} \\ \text{promise in} \\ \text{week 1} \end{pmatrix} = \begin{pmatrix} \text{On-hand} \\ \text{quantity in} \\ \text{week 1} \end{pmatrix} + \begin{pmatrix} \text{MPS quantity} \\ \text{in week 1} \end{pmatrix} - \begin{pmatrix} \text{Orders booked up} \\ \text{to week 3 when the} \\ \text{next MPS arrives} \end{pmatrix}$$

$$= 5 + 50 - (30 + 20) = 5 \text{ units}$$

The ATP for the MPS quantity in week 3 is

$$\begin{pmatrix} \text{Available-to-} \\ \text{promise in} \\ \text{week 3} \end{pmatrix} = \begin{pmatrix} \text{MPS quantity} \\ \text{in week 3} \end{pmatrix} - \begin{pmatrix} \text{Orders booked up} \\ \text{to week 7 when the} \\ \text{next MPS arrives} \end{pmatrix}$$

$$= 50 - (5 + 8 + 0 + 2) = 35 \text{ units}$$

The other ATPs equal their respective MPS quantities because no orders are booked for those weeks. As for the new order for 30 units in week 1, the earliest it can be shipped is week 3 because the ATP for week 1 is insufficient. If the customer accepts the delivery date of week 3, the ATP for week 1 will stay at 5 units and the ATP for week 3 will be reduced to 5 units. This acceptance allows the firm the flexibility to immediately satisfy an order for 5 units or less, if one comes in. When the MPS is updated next, the customer orders booked for week 3 would be increased to 35 to reflect the new order's shipping date.

Lot Size	50															
Lead Time	1															
Quantity on Hand	5	1	2	3	4	5	6	7	8	9	10	11	12	13	14	15
Forecast		20	10	40	10			30	20	40	20					
Customer Orders (Booked)		30	20	5	8		2									
Projected On-Hand Inventory		25	5	15	5	5	3	23	3	13	43					
MPS Quantity		50		50				50		50	50					
MPS Start			50				50		50	50						
Available-to-Promise Inv (ATP)		5		35				50		50	50					

FIGURE 15.21 ▲
Completed MPS Record for End Item A

Solved Problem 3

Active Model 15.1 in my**om**lab provides additional insight on lot-sizing decisions for this problem.

FIGURE 15.22 ▶
BOM for Product A

The MPS start quantities for product A calls for the assembly department to begin final assembly according to the following schedule: 100 units in week 2; 200 units in week 4; 120 units in week 6; 180 units in week 7; and 60 units in week 8. Develop a material requirements plan for the next 8 weeks for items B, C, and D. The BOM for A is shown in Figure 15.22, and data from the inventory records are shown in Table 15.1.

SOLUTION

We begin with items B and C and develop their inventory records, as shown in Figure 15.23. The MPS for product A must be multiplied by 2 to derive the gross requirements for item C because of the usage quantity. Once the planned order releases for item C are found, the gross requirements for item D can be calculated.

TABLE 15.1	INVENTORY RECORD DATA		
		Item	
Data Category	**B**	**C**	**D**
Lot-sizing rule	POQ ($P = 3$)	L4L	FOQ = 500 units
Lead time (LT)	1 week	2 weeks	3 weeks
Scheduled receipts	None	200 (week 1)	None
Beginning (on-hand) inventory	20	0	425

◀ **FIGURE 15.23**
Inventory Records for Items B, C, and D

Item: B
Description:
Lot Size: POQ (P = 3)
Lead Time: 1 week

		Week									
		1	2	3	4	5	6	7	8	9	10
Gross requirements			100		200		120	180	60		
Scheduled receipts											
Projected on-hand inventory	20	20	200	200	0	0	240	60	0	0	0
Planned receipts			280				360				
Planned order releases		280				360					

Item: C
Description:
Lot Size: L4L
Lead Time: 2 weeks

		Week									
		1	2	3	4	5	6	7	8	9	10
Gross requirements			200		400		240	360	120		
Scheduled receipts		200									
Projected on-hand inventory	0	200	0	0	0	0	0	0	0	0	0
Planned receipts					400		240	360	120		
Planned order releases			400		240	360	120				

Item: D
Description:
Lot Size: FOQ = 500 units
Lead Time: 3 weeks

		Week									
		1	2	3	4	5	6	7	8	9	10
Gross requirements			400		240	360	120				
Scheduled receipts											
Projected on-hand inventory	425	425	25	25	285	425	305	305	305	305	305
Planned receipts					500	500					
Planned order releases		500	500								

DISCUSSION QUESTIONS

1. Consider the master flight schedule of a major airline, such as Air New Zealand. Discuss the ways in which it is analogous to a master production schedule for a manufacturer.

2. Consider a service provider that is in the delivery business, such as UPS or FedEx. How can the principles of MRP be useful to such a company?

3. For an organization of your choice, such as where you previously worked, discuss how an ERP system could be used and whether it would increase effectiveness.

4. Form a group in which each member represents a different functional area of a firm. Provide a priority list of the information that could be generated from an MPS, from the most important to the least important, for each functional area. Rationalize the differences in the lists.

PROBLEMS

Software, such as OM Explorer, Active Models, and POM for Windows, is available in my**om**lab. Check with your instructor on how best to use it. In many cases, the instructor wants you to understand how to do the calculations by hand. At most, the software provides a check on your calculations. When calculations are particularly complex and the goal is interpreting the results in making decisions, the software replaces entirely the manual calculations.

1. Consider the bill of materials (BOM) in Figure 15.24.

   a. How many immediate parents (one level above) does item I have? How many immediate parents does item E have?

   b. How many unique components does product A have at all levels?

   c. Which of the components are purchased items?

   d. How many intermediate items does product A have at all levels?

   e. Given the lead times (LT) noted on Figure 15.24, how far in advance of shipment must a purchase commitment be for any of the purchased items identified in part (c)?

2. Product A is made from components B, C, and D. Item B is a subassembly that requires 2 units of C and 1 unit of E. Item D also is an intermediate item, made from F. All other usage quantities are 2. Draw the BOM for product A.

3. What is the lead time (in weeks) to respond to a customer order for product A, based on the BOM shown in Figure 15.25, assuming no existing inventories or scheduled receipts?

4. Product A is made from components B and C. Item B, in turn, is made from D and E. Item C also is an intermediate item, made from F and H. Finally, intermediate item E is made from H and G. Note that item H has two parents. The following are item lead times:

Item	A	B	C	D	E	F	G	H
Lead Time (weeks)	1	2	2	6	5	6	4	3

   a. What lead time (in weeks) is needed to respond to a customer order for product A, assuming no existing inventories or scheduled receipts?

   b. What is the customer response time if all purchased items (i.e., D, F, G, and H) are in inventory?

   c. If you are allowed to keep just one purchased item in stock, which one would you choose?

5. Refer to Figure 15.19 and Solved Problem 1. If inventory consists of 2 units of B, 1 unit of F, and 3 units of G, how many units of G, E, and D must be purchased to produce 5 units of product A?

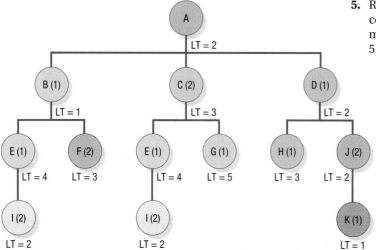

FIGURE 15.24 ▲
BOM for Product A

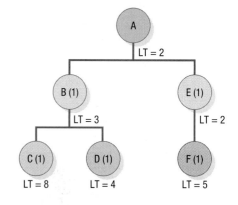

FIGURE 15.25 ▲
BOM for Product A

6. Complete the MPS record shown in Figure 15.26 for a single item.

Item: A						Order Policy: 100 units Lead Time: 1 week		
		January				February		
Quantity on Hand: 75	1	2	3	4	5	6	7	8
Forecast	65	65	65	45	50	50	50	50
Customer orders (booked)	40	10	85	0	35	70	0	0
Projected on-hand inventory								
MPS quantity								
MPS start								

◀ **FIGURE 15.26**
MPS Record for Single Item

7. Complete the MPS record in Figure 15.27 for a single item.

Item: A						Order Policy: 60 units Lead Time: 1 week		
				Week				
Quantity on Hand: 35	1	2	3	4	5	6	7	8
Forecast	20	18	28	28	23	30	33	38
Customer orders (booked)	15	17	9	14	9	0	7	0
Projected on-hand inventory								
MPS quantity								
MPS start								

◀ **FIGURE 15.27**
MPS Record for Single Item

8. An end item's demand forecasts for the next 10 weeks are 30, 20, 35, 50, 25, 25, 0, 40, 0, and 50 units. The current on-hand inventory is 80 units. The order policy is to produce in lots of 100. The booked customer orders for the item, starting with week 1, are 22, 30, 15, 9, 0, 0, 5, 3, 7, and 0 units. At present, no MPS quantities are on-hand for this item. The lead time is 2 weeks. Develop an MPS for this end item.

9. Morrison Electronics forecasted the following demand for one of its products for the next 8 weeks: 70, 70, 65, 60, 55, 85, 75, and 85. The booked customer orders for this product, starting in week 1, are 50, 60, 55, 40, 35, 0, 0, and 0 units. The current on-hand inventory is 100 units, the order quantity is 150 units, and the lead time is one week.

   a. Develop an MPS for this product.

   b. The marketing department at Morrison revised its forecasts. Starting with week 1, the new forecasts are 70, 70, 75, 70, 70, 100, 100, and 110 units. Assuming that the prospective MPS you developed in part (a) does not change, prepare a revised MPS record. Comment on the situation that Morrison now faces.

10. Figure 15.28 shows a partially completed MPS record for ball bearings.

   a. Develop the MPS for ball bearings.

   b. Four customer orders arrived in the following sequence:

Order	Quantity	Week Desired
1	500	4
2	400	5
3	300	1
4	300	7

   Assume that you must commit to the orders in the sequence of arrival and cannot change the desired shipping dates or your MPS. Which orders should you accept?

11. Figure 15.29 shows a partially completed MPS record for 2" pneumatic control valves. Suppose that you receive the following orders for the valves (shown in the order of their arrival). As they arrive, you must decide whether to accept or reject them. Which orders would you accept for shipment?

Order	Amount (units)	Week Requested
1	15	2
2	30	5
3	25	3
4	75	7

12. A forecast of 240 units in January, 320 units in February, and 240 units in March has been approved for the seismic-sensory product family manufactured at the Rockport facility of Maryland Automated, Inc. Three products, A, B, and C, comprise this family. The product mix ratio for products A, B, and C for the past 2 years has been 35 percent, 40 percent, and 25 percent, respectively. Management believes that the monthly forecast requirements are evenly spread over the 4 weeks of each month. Currently, 10 units of product C are on hand. The company produces product C in lots of 40, and the lead time is 2 weeks. A production quantity of 40 units from the previous period is scheduled to arrive in week 1. The company has accepted orders of 25, 12, 8, 10, 2, and 3 units of product C in weeks 1 through 6, respectively. Prepare a prospective MPS for product C and calculate the available-to-promise inventory quantities.

FIGURE 15.28 ▶
MPS Record for Ball Bearings

Item: Ball bearings									Order Policy: 500 units		
									Lead Time: 1 week		

		Week									
Quantity on Hand:	400	1	2	3	4	5	6	7	8	9	10
Forecast		550	300	400	450	300	350	200	300	450	400
Customer orders (booked)		300	350	250	250	200	150	100	100	100	100
Projected on-hand inventory											
MPS quantity		500									
MPS start											
Available-to-promise (ATP) inventory											

Item: 2" Pneumatic control valve						Order Policy: 75 units Lead Time: 1 week			
		Week							
Quantity on Hand: 10		1	2	3	4	5	6	7	8
Forecast		40	40	40	40	30	30	50	50
Customer orders (booked)		60	45	30	35	10	5	5	0
Projected on-hand inventory									
MPS quantity		75	75						
MPS start		75							
Available-to-promise (ATP) inventory									

◀ **FIGURE 15.29**
MPS Record for 2" Pneumatic Control Valve

13. The forecasted requirements for an electric hand drill for the next 6 weeks are 15, 40, 10, 20, 50, and 30 units. The marketing department has booked orders totaling 20, 25, 10, and 20 units for delivery in the first (current), second, third, and fourth weeks. Currently, 30 hand drills are in stock. The policy is to order in lots of 60 units. Lead time is one week.

  a. Develop the MPS record for the hand drills.

  b. A distributor of the hand drills places an order for 15 units. What is the appropriate shipping date for the entire order?

14. The partially completed inventory record for the rotor subassembly in Figure 15.30 shows gross requirements, scheduled receipts, lead time, and current on-hand inventory.

  a. Complete the last three rows of the record for an FOQ of 150 units.

  b. Complete the last three rows of the record by using the L4L lot-sizing rule.

  c. Complete the last three rows of the record by using the POQ lot-sizing rule, with $P = 2$.

◀ **FIGURE 15.30**
Inventory Record for the Rotor Subassembly

Item: Rotor subassembly						Lot Size: Lead Time: 2 weeks			
		Week							
		1	2	3	4	5	6	7	8
Gross requirements		65	15	45	40	80	80	80	80
Scheduled receipts		150							
Projected on-hand inventory	20								
Planned receipts									
Planned order releases									

15. The partially completed inventory record for the tabletop subassembly in Figure 15.31 shows gross requirements, scheduled receipts, lead time, and current on-hand inventory.

    a. Complete the last three rows of the record for an FOQ of 110 units.

    b. Complete the last three rows of the record by using the L4L lot-sizing rule.

    c. Complete the last three rows of the record by using the POQ lot-sizing rule, with $P = 2$.

FIGURE 15.31 ▶
Inventory Record for the Tabletop Subassembly

Item: M405—X Description: Tabletop subassembly											Lot Size: Lead Time: 2 weeks	
	Week											
	1	2	3	4	5	6	7	8	9	10		
Gross requirements	90		85		80		45	90				
Scheduled receipts	110											
Projected on-hand inventory 40												
Planned receipts												
Planned order releases												

16. Figure 15.32 shows a partially completed inventory record for the rear wheel subassembly. Gross requirements, scheduled receipts, lead time, and current on-hand inventory are shown.

    a. Complete the last three rows of the record for an FOQ of 300 units.

    b. Complete the last three rows of the record by using the L4L rule.

    c. Complete the last three rows of the record by using the POQ rule, with $P = 4$.

17. The partially completed inventory record for the driveshaft subassembly in Figure 15.33 shows gross requirements, scheduled receipts, lead time, and current on-hand inventory.

    a. Complete the last three rows of the record for an FOQ of 50 units.

    b. Complete the last three rows of the record by using the L4L lot-sizing rule.

    c. Complete the last three rows of the record by using the POQ lot-sizing rule, with $P = 4$.

FIGURE 15.32 ▶
Inventory Record for the Rear Wheel Subassembly

Item: MQ—09 Description: Rear wheel subassembly											Lot Size: Lead Time: 1 week	
	Week											
	1	2	3	4	5	6	7	8	9	10		
Gross requirements	205		130	85		70	60	95				
Scheduled receipts	300											
Projected on-hand inventory 100												
Planned receipts												
Planned order releases												

Item: Driveshaft subassembly							Lot Size:		
							Lead Time: 3 weeks		

	Week							
	1	2	3	4	5	6	7	8
Gross requirements	35	25	15	20	40	40	50	50
Scheduled receipts	80							
Projected on-hand inventory 10								
Planned receipts								
Planned order releases								

◀ **FIGURE 15.33**
Inventory Record for the Driveshaft Subassembly

18. A partially completed inventory record for the motor sub-assembly is shown in Figure 15.34.

  a. Complete the last three rows of the record for an FOQ of 60 units.

  b. Revise the planned order release row by using the L4L rule.

  c. Revise the planned order release row by using the POQ rule. Find the value of P that should (in the long run) yield an average lot size of 60 units. Assume that the average weekly demand for the foreseeable future is 15 units.

Item: GF—4									Lot Size:			
Description: Motor subassembly									Lead Time: 3 weeks			

	Week											
	1	2	3	4	5	6	7	8	9	10	11	12
Gross requirements		50		35		55		30		10		25
Scheduled receipts		60										
Projected on-hand inventory 40												
Planned receipts												
Planned order releases												

▲ **FIGURE 15.34**
Inventory Record for the Motor Subassembly

ADVANCED PROBLEMS

19. The BOM for product A is shown in Figure 15.35, and data from the inventory records are shown in Table 15.2. In the master production schedule for product A, the MPS start row has 500 units in week 6. Develop the material requirements plan for the next 6 weeks for items B, C, and D. (*Hint:* You cannot derive an item's gross requirements unless you know the planned order releases of all its parents, or the MPS start row if one of its immediate parents is an end item.)

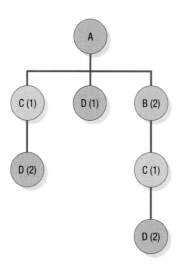

▲ FIGURE 15.35
BOM for Product A

TABLE 15.2	INVENTORY RECORD DATA		
	Item		
Data Category	**B**	**C**	**D**
Lot-sizing rule	L4L	L4L	FOQ = 2,000
Lead time	3 weeks	1 week	1 week
Scheduled receipts	None	None	2,000 (week 1)
Beginning inventory	0	0	200

20. The BOMs for products A and B are shown in Figure 15.36. Data from inventory records are shown in Table 15.3. The MPS calls for 85 units of product A to be started in week 3 and 100 units in week 6. The MPS for product B calls for 180 units to be started in week 5. Develop the material requirements plan for the next 6 weeks for items C, D, E, and F.

FIGURE 15.36 ▶
BOMs for Product A and Product B

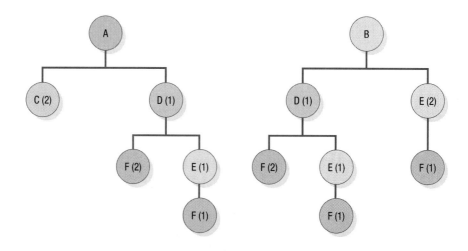

TABLE 15.3	INVENTORY RECORD DATA			
	Item			
Data Category	**C**	**D**	**E**	**F**
Lot-sizing rule	FOQ = 220	L4L	FOQ = 300	POQ ($P = 2$)
Lead time	3 weeks	2 weeks	3 weeks	2 weeks
Scheduled receipts	280 (week 1)	None	300 (week 3)	None
Beginning inventory	25	0	150	600

21. Figure 15.37 illustrates the BOM for product A. The MPS start row in the master production schedule for product A calls for 50 units in week 2, 65 units in week 5, and 80 units in week 8. Item C is produced to make A and to meet the forecasted demand for replacement parts. Past replacement part demand has been 20 units per week (add 20 units to C's gross requirements). The lead times for items F and C are 1 week, and for the other items the lead time is 2 weeks. No safety stock is required for items B, C, D, E, and F. The L4L lot-sizing rule is used for items B and F; the POQ lot-sizing rule ($P = 3$) is used for C. Item E has an FOQ of 600 units, and D has an FOQ of 250 units. On-hand inventories are 50 units of B, 50 units of C, 120 units of D, 70 units of E, and 250 units of F. Item B has a scheduled receipt of 50 units in week 2.

Develop a material requirements plan for the next 8 weeks for items B, C, D, E, and F.

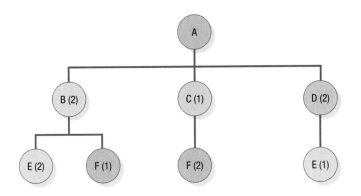

▲ FIGURE 15.37
BOM for Product A

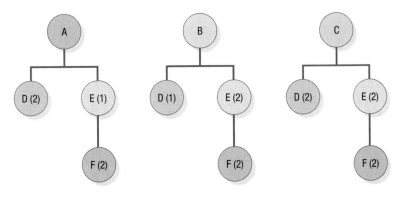

22. The following information is available for three MPS items:

Product A	An 80-unit order is to be started in week 3.
	A 55-unit order is to be started in week 6.
Product B	A 125-unit order is to be started in week 5.
Product C	A 60-unit order is to be started in week 4.

Develop the material requirements plan for the next 6 weeks for items D, E, and F. The BOMs are shown in Figure 15.38, and data from the inventory records are shown in Table 15.4. (*Warning:* A safety stock requirement applies to item F. Be sure to plan a receipt for any week in which the projected on-hand inventory becomes less than the safety stock.)

◄ FIGURE 15.38
BOMs for Products A, B, and C

TABLE 15.4 | INVENTORY RECORD DATA

| | Item | | |
Data Category	D	E	F
Lot-sizing rule	FOQ = 150	L4L	POQ (P = 2)
Lead time	3 weeks	1 week	2 weeks
Safety stock	0	0	30
Scheduled receipts	150 (week 3)	120 (week 2)	None
Beginning inventory	150	0	100

23. Figure 15.39 shows the BOMs for two products, A and B. Table 15.5 shows the MPS quantity start date for each one. Table 15.6 contains data from inventory records for items C, D, and E. There are no safety stock requirements for any of the items. Determine the material requirements plan for items C, D, and E for the next 8 weeks.

24. The BOM for product A is shown in Figure 15.40. The MPS for product A calls for 120 units to be started in weeks 2, 4, 5, and 8. Table 15.7 shows data from the inventory records. Develop the material requirements plan for the next 8 weeks for each item.

▼ FIGURE 15.39
BOMs for Products A and B

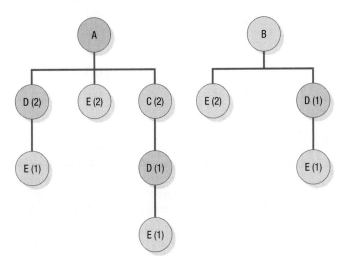

TABLE 15.5 | MPS QUANTITY START DATES

Product	1	2	3	4	5	6	7	8
					Date			
A		125		95		150		130
B			80			70		

TABLE 15.6 | INVENTORY RECORD DATA

Data Category	Item C	D	E
Lot-sizing rule	L4L	POQ ($P = 3$)	FOQ = 800
Lead time	3 weeks	2 weeks	1 week
Scheduled receipts	200 (week 2)	None	800 (week 1)
Beginning inventory	85	625	350

FIGURE 15.40 ▶
BOM for Product A

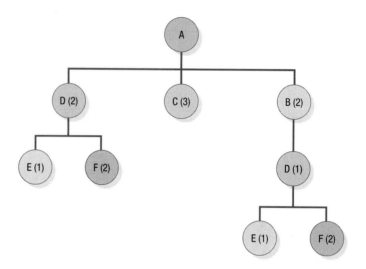

TABLE 15.7 | INVENTORY RECORD DATA

Data Category	B	C	D	E	F
			Item		
Lot-sizing rule	L4L	FOQ = 700	FOQ = 700	L4L	L4L
Lead time	3 weeks	3 weeks	4 weeks	2 weeks	1 week
Safety stock	0	0	0	50	0
Scheduled receipts	150 (week 2)	450 (week 2)	700 (week 1)	None	1,400 (week 1)
Beginning inventory	125	0	235	750	0

25. An end item's demand forecasts for the next 6 weeks are 30 units, followed by forecasts of 25 units for weeks 7 though 10. The current on-hand inventory is 60 units. The order policy is to produce in lots of 100. The booked customer orders for the item, starting with week 1, are 22, 30, 15, 11, 0, 0, 9, 0, 0, and 0 units. The lead time is 2 weeks.

    a. Develop an MPS for this end item.

    b. The marketing department has received six orders for this item in the following sequence:

    Order 1 is for 40 units to be delivered in period 3

    Order 2 is for 60 units to be delivered in period 4

    Order 3 is for 70 units to be delivered in period 6

    Order 4 is for 40 units to be delivered in period 3

TABLE 15.8	INVENTORY RECORD DATA					
	Item					
Data Category	B	C	D	E	F	G
Lot-sizing rule	L4L	L4L	POQ ($P = 2$)	L4L	L4L	FOQ = 100
Lead time	2 weeks	3 weeks	3 weeks	6 weeks	1 week	3 weeks
Safety stock	30	10	0	0	0	0
Scheduled receipts	150 (week 2)	50 (week 2)	None	400 (week 6)	40 (week 3)	None
Beginning inventory	30	20	60	400	0	0

Order 5 is for 20 units to be delivered in period 5

Order 6 is for 115 units to be delivered in period 9

Assuming that the prospective MPS you developed in part (a) does not change, which orders would you be able to accept based on the available to promise (ATP)?

26. Develop the material requirements plan for all components and intermediate items associated with product A for the next 10 weeks. Refer to Solved Problem 1 (Figure 15.19) for the bill of materials and Table 15.8 for component inventory record information. The MPS for product A calls for 50 units to be started in weeks 2, 6, 8, and 9. (*Warning:* Safety stock requirements apply to items B and C.)

27. The bill of materials and the data from the inventory records for product A are shown in Figure 15.41. Assume that the MPS start quantities for A are 100 units in weeks 1, 2, and 7. Derive an MRP plan for the components going into product A using the data in Table 15.9.

28. The bill of materials and the data from the inventory records for product A are shown in Figure 15.42. Assume that the MPS start quantities for A are 50 units in weeks 2 and 3, and 150 units in week 6. Derive an MRP plan for the components going into product A using the data in Table 15.10.

29. An end item's demand forecasts for the next 10 weeks are 30, 30, 30, 30, 20, 20, 30, 30, 30, and 30 units. The current on-hand inventory is 100 units. The order policy is to produce in lots of 75. The booked customer orders for the item, starting with week 1, are 15, 38, 7, 5, 0, 3, 10, 0, 0, and 0 units. The lead time is 2 weeks.

   a. Develop an MPS for this end item.

   b. The marketing department has received five orders for this item in the following sequence:

   Order 1 is for 20 units to be delivered in period 1

   Order 2 is for 75 units to be delivered in period 4

   Order 3 is for 90 units to be delivered in period 6

   Order 4 is for 75 units to be delivered in period 7

   Order 5 is for 90 units to be delivered in period 10

   Assuming that the prospective MPS you developed in part (a) does not change, which orders would you be able to accept based on the available to promise (ATP)?

TABLE 15.9	INVENTORY RECORD DATA		
	Item		
Data Category	B	C	D
Lot-sizing rule	L4L	L4L	FOQ=300
Lead time	1 week	2 weeks	2 weeks
Scheduled receipts		100 (week 2)	
Beginning inventory	225	350	250

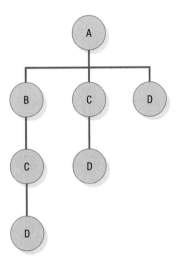

▲ FIGURE 15.41
BOM for Product A

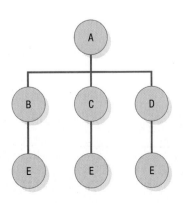

▲ FIGURE 15.42
BOM for Product A

TABLE 15.10	INVENTORY RECORD DATA			
		Item		
Data Category	**B**	**C**	**D**	**E**
Lot-sizing rule	POQ (*P*=2)	L4L	FOQ=300	FOQ=400
Lead time	1 week	1 week	2 weeks	4 weeks
Scheduled receipts		100 (week 2)		400 (week 2)
Beginning inventory	100	0	110	40

ACTIVE MODEL EXERCISE

This Active Model appears in my**om**lab. It allows you to evaluate the relationship between the inventory record data and the planned order releases.

QUESTIONS

1. As the lead time for item C changes, what happens to the order releases for items B, C, and D?

2. Suppose that the POQ for item B is changed from 3 weeks to 2 weeks. How does this change affect the order releases for items B, C, and D?

3. As the on-hand inventory for item C increases from 0 to 200, what happens to the order releases for items B, C, and D?

4. As the fixed order quantity (FOQ) for item D increases from 500 to 750, what happens to the order releases for items B, C, and D?

ACTIVE MODEL 15.1 ▲

Material Requirements Planning Using Data from Solved Problem 3 and Table 15.1

CASE | Materials Requirement Planning (MRP) Gives Dyson the Edge

In 1978, James Dyson developed the technology for the first vacuum cleaner with constant suction. Known as the "G Force," it won the 1991 International Design Fair prize in Japan. The Japanese were so impressed by its performance that the G Force became a status symbol, selling for as much as $2,000 each. The famous Dual Cyclone system was a major breakthrough, eliminating the need for a bag to collect the dust. The traditional bag was replaced by two cyclone chambers: After the outer cyclone has spun-out the larger dust and dirt particles, the inner cyclone accelerates the air further to remove health-threatening smaller particles. Since those early designs, there have been significant improvements to the cyclone system, with the new Radix Cyclone getting 45 percent more suction by using eight smaller cyclones. The Dyson brand has become synonymous with innovative quality design and practical functionality.

As well as excellent design and application of advanced technology, Dyson prides itself in applying state-of-the-art production methods. Central to the manufacturing system is Materials Requiring Planning (MRP). However, it has become apparent to senior operations management that there is not a general understanding of how, if the correct use of MRP is made when planning the launch of a new product's production, it can save significant cost and eliminate material waste. Consequently, you have been requested to lead a one-day workshop to explain the key features of MRP and describe its benefits. The attendees will include people from Dyson's production planning and procurement section and key suppliers. The order of topics that you have asked to address includes the following:

- Demand Patterns

- Comparison of Lot-sizing Rules
- Bill of Materials (BOM)
- Master Production Schedule (MPS)
- Inventory Records
- Planned Orders

You have decided, therefore, to use the famous Dyson roller ball subassembly as a central example to your workshop. Annually, some 20,000 of these subassemblies are needed, requiring component details to be purchased from external suppliers and subassemblies to be fabricated in-house prior to final assembly to the vacuum cleaner. It is apparent, however, that the monthly demands over the years have fluctuated due to seasonal factors, for example, Christmas and other holidays, and economic pressure. Therefore, you have decided to illustrate issues of demand patterns based on Figure 15.43.

To explain how orders are currently placed on suppliers, you use Figure 15.44.

You next describe the different lot-sizing rules. To help in your explanation, you hand out to each participant the partly completed information shown in Figure 15.45 and ask each person to fill in the missing words.

- The fixed order quantity (FOQ) rule generates high average inventory because it ....

FIGURE 15.43 ▲
Demand Patterns

- The periodic order quantity (POQ) rule reduces average on-hand inventory because it does a better job of matching order quantity to................

- The lot-for-lot (L4L) rule minimizes .... but maximizes the number of orders placed.

  Complete the missing words.

The bill of materials for the Dyson roller ball subassembly is shown in Figure 15.46. To calculate the gross requirements for each component, it will be necessary to determine the quantity for B, C, D, E, F, G, H, I, J, K, and L for one roller ball subassembly (A). You therefore decide to ask the workshop participants to calculate these answers.

To illustrate the importance of the master production schedule (MPS) for the roller ball subassembly, you refer to Figure 15.46.

There are currently three vacuum cleaners that use this particular roller ball subassembly, the Classic, Zoom, and Elite. The aggregated total quantity for the month of January and February is 1,030 and 620, respectively. During your presentation, you take the time to emphasize that the design department has always tried, if possible, to incorporate standard units such as the roller ball subassembly to reduce complexity, gain economy of scale, and enhance performance reliability. Dyson periodically carries out rationalization and consolidation exercises to wean out components that are unique to a single vacuum and use standard components.

The calculation of inventory records (IR) is another important stage in MRP. Using Table 15.11 for illustrative purposes only, you need to identify the lot-sizing rule to be used, lead time (LT), scheduled receipts, and on-hand inventory for components B, C, D, E, F, G, H, I, J, K, and L.

To minimize the amount of time and effort that would be required by the workshop participants to discuss all the information, you should focus on item B, Plastic Ball. In particular, you should draw attention to the affect of using alternative lot-sizing rules on the final outcome.

$$\begin{pmatrix} \text{POQ lot} \\ \text{size} \end{pmatrix} = \begin{pmatrix} \text{Gross requirements} \\ \text{for weeks 4, 5, and 6} \end{pmatrix} = \begin{pmatrix} \text{Inventory at} \\ \text{end of week 3} \end{pmatrix}$$

$$\begin{pmatrix} \text{L4L lot} \\ \text{size} \end{pmatrix} = \begin{pmatrix} \text{Gross requirements} \\ \text{in week 4} \end{pmatrix} - \begin{pmatrix} \text{Inventory balance} \\ \text{at end of week 3} \end{pmatrix}$$

The resultant Planned Order for item B, the Plastic Ball, is then discussed at length (see Figure 15.47).

You should explain that the gross requirements are the total demand for the three vacuums. Projected on-hand inventory in week 1 is 37 + 230 − 150 = 117 units.

The next step is to calculate the projected on-hand inventory balance at the end of each week (t).

$$\begin{pmatrix} \text{Projected} \\ \text{on-hand inventory} \\ \text{balance at end} \\ \text{of week } t \end{pmatrix} = \begin{pmatrix} \text{Inventory} \\ \text{on hand} \\ \text{at end of} \\ \text{week } t-1 \end{pmatrix} + \begin{pmatrix} \text{Scheduled} \\ \text{or planned} \\ \text{receipts} \\ \text{in week } t \end{pmatrix} - \begin{pmatrix} \text{Gross} \\ \text{requirements} \\ \text{in week } t \end{pmatrix}$$

Without a new order in week 4, there will be a shortage of three units: 117 + 0 + 0 − 120 = −3 units.

The concluding remarks of the workshop might include discussion of how the output information is reported. This type of report gives a range of information upon which operational management and supply management can take proactive action if necessary.

YOUR ASSIGNMENT

The leading of this workshop will require both clearness in explanation as well as the ability to answer questions and points of clarification. Therefore, it will be necessary for you to work through the challenges that you have posed for your audience and supply fully prepared answers and explanations.

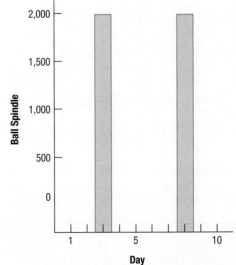

FIGURE 15.44 ▲
Orders Placed On Suppliers

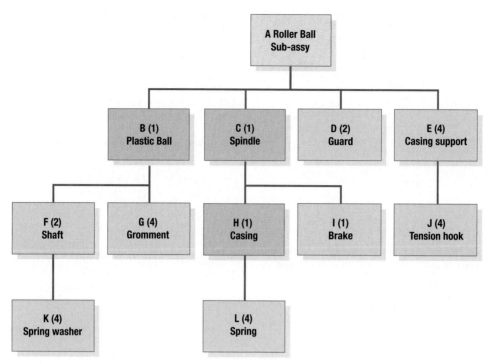

FIGURE 15.45 ▲
Comparlson of Lot-Sizing Rules

		January				February		
	1	2	3	4	5	6	7	8
Dyson Classic	265					100		
Dyson Zoom				115			120	
Dyson Elite		300	350		200			200
Aggregate production plan for all Vacuums			1030				620	

FIGURE 15.46 ▲
Bill of Materials (BOM)

TABLE 15.11 | INVENTORY RECORD DATA

	Item										
Data category	P Ball B	Spindle C	Guard D	Casing E	Shaft F	Grom G	Casing H	Brake I	Tensn Hook J	SWash K	Sprng L
Lot-sizing rule)	POQ (P = 230)	LFL	FOQ = 6	LFL	LFL	FOQ = 6	LFL	FOQ = 6	LFL	LFL	FOQ = 6
Lead time (LT)	2 weeks	2 weeks	1 week	2 weeks	2 weeks	1 week	2 weeks	1 week	2 weeks	2 weeks	1 week
Scheduled receipts	None	10 (week 1)	None	10 (week 1)	10 (week 1)	None	10 (week 1)	None	10 (week 1)	10 (week 1)	None
Beginning (on-hand) inventory	37	25	0	25	25	0	35	0	25	25	0

Terms: POQ (periodic order quantity)
L4L (lot for lot)
FOQ (fixed order quantity)

Item: B Description: Plastic ball							Lot Size: 230 units Lead Time: 2 weeks		
	Week								
		1	2	3	4	5	6	7	8
Gross requirements		150	0	0	120	0	150	120	0
Scheduled receipts		230	0	0	0	0	0	0	0
Projected on-hand inventory	37	117	117	117	227	227	77	187	187
Planned receipts					230			230	
Planned order releases			230			230			

FIGURE 15.47 ▲
Planned Order and Explosion for Item B

Source: This case was prepared by Dr. David Parker, The University of Queensland, Business School, as a basis for classroom discussion.

SELECTED REFERENCES

Conway, Richard W. "Linking MRP II and FCS." *APICS—The Performance Advantage* (June 1996), pp. 40–44.

Cotten, Jim. "Starting from Scratch." *APICS—The Performance Advantage* (November 1996), pp. 34–37.

Davenport, Thomas H. "Putting the Enterprise into the Enterprise System." *Harvard Business Review* (July–August 1998), pp. 121–131.

Dollries, Joseph. "Don't Pick a Package—Match One." *APICS—The Performance Advantage* (May 1996), pp. 50–52.

Goddard, Walter, and James Correll. "MRP II in the Year 2000." *APICS—The Performance Advantage* (March 1994), pp. 38–42.

Hendricks, Kevin B., Vinod R. Singhal and Jeff K. Stratman. "The Impact of Enterprise Systems on Corporate Performance: A Study of ERP, SCM and CRM System Implementations." *Journal of Operations Management*, vol. 25, no. 1 (2007), pp. 65–82.

Hoy, Paul A. "The Changing Role of MRP II." *APICS—The Performance Advantage* (June 1996), pp. 50–53.

Jacobs, F. Robert, and Weston, F.C. (Ted) Jr. "Enterprise Resource Planning (ERP)—A Brief History." *Journal of Operations Management*, vol.25, no. 2 (2007), pp. 357–363.

Jacobs, F. Robert, and D. Clay Whybark. *Why ERP?* New York: Irwin McGraw-Hill, 2000.

Jemigan, Jeff. "Comprehensiveness, Cost-Effectiveness Sweep Aside Operations Challenges." *APICS—The Performance Advantage* (March 1993), pp. 44–45.

Mabert, Vincent A. "The Early Road to Materials Requirements Planning." *Journal of Operations Management*, vol. 25, no. 2 (2007), pp. 346–356.

Melnyk, Steven A., Robert Sroufe, Frank Montabon, Roger Calantone, R. Lal Tummala, and Timothy J. Hinds. "Integrating Environmental Issues into Material Planning: 'Green' MRP." *Production and Inventory Management Journal* (Third Quarter 1999), pp. 36–45.

Prouty, Dave. "Shiva Finite Capacity Scheduling System." *APICS—The Performance Advantage* (April 1997), pp. 58–61.

Ptak, Carol. *MRP and Beyond.* Homewood, IL: Irwin Professional Publishing, 1996.

Roth, Aleda V., and Roland Van Dierdonck. "Hospital Resource Planning: Concepts, Feasibility, and Framework." *Production and Operations Management*, vol. 4, no. 1 (1995), pp. 2–29.

Scalle, Cedric X., and Mark J. Cotteleer. *Enterprise Resource Planning (ERP).* Boston, MA: Harvard Business School Publishing, 1999, No. 9-699-020.

Turbide, David A. "This Is Not Your Father's MRP!" *APICS—The Performance Advantage* (March 1994), pp. 28–37.

Vollmann, T. E., W. L. Berry, D. C. Whybark, and F. R. Jacobs. *Manufacturing Planning and Control for Supply Chain Management*, 5th ed. New York: Irwin/McGraw-Hill, 2004.

Wallace, Thomas F. *Sales & Operations Planning: The How-To Handbook*, 3rd ed. Cincinnati, OH: T. E. Wallace & Company, 2008.

Wallace, Thomas F., and Robert A. Stahl. *Master Scheduling in the 21st Century.* Cincinnati, OH: T. E. Wallace & Company, 2003.

ZDWire Plus. "Customization, Complexity Still Dog ERP Efforts." Thompson Dialogue, July 19, 2005.

E LINEAR PROGRAMMING MODELS

LEARNING GOALS

After reading this supplement, you should be able to:

1. Describe formulating models for various problems.

2. Demonstrate graphic analysis and solutions for two-variable problems.

3. Define slack variables, surplus variables, and sensitivity analysis.

4. Interpret computer output of a linear programming solution.

5. Apply the transportation method to location problems.

6. Apply the transportation method to Sales and Operations Planning (S&OP) problems.

In many business situations, resources are limited and demand for them is great. For example, a limited number of vehicles may have to be scheduled to make multiple trips to customers, the best location for a facility may have to be selected to minimize transportation costs, or a staffing plan may have to be developed to cover expected variable demand with the fewest employees. In this supplement, we describe a technique called **linear programming**, which is useful for allocating scarce resources among competing demands. The resources may be time, money, or materials, and the limitations are known as constraints. Linear programming can help managers find the best allocation solution and provide information about the value of additional resources.

myomlab and the Companion Website at **www.pearsonglobaleditions.com/krajewski** contain many tools, activities, and resources designed for this supplement.

BASIC CONCEPTS

Before we can demonstrate how to solve problems in operations and supply chain management with linear programming, we must first explain several characteristics of all linear programming models and mathematical assumptions that apply to them: (1) objective function, (2) decision variables, (3) constraints, (4) feasible region, (5) parameters, (6) linearity, and (7) nonnegativity.

Linear programming is an *optimization* process. A single **objective function** states mathematically what is being maximized (e.g., profit or present value) or minimized (e.g., cost or scrap). The objective function provides the scorecard on which the attractiveness of different solutions is judged.

Decision variables represent choices that the decision maker can control. Solving the problem yields their optimal values. For example, a decision variable could be the number of units of a product to make next month or the number of units of inventory to hold next month. Linear programming is based on the assumption that decision variables are *continuous*; they can be fractional quantities and need not be whole numbers. Often, this assumption is realistic, as when the decision variable is expressed in dollars, hours, or some other continuous measure. Even when the decision variables represent nondivisible units, such as workers, tables, or trucks, we sometimes can simply round the linear programming solution up or down to get a reasonable solution that does not violate any constraints, or we can use a more advanced technique, called *integer programming*.

Constraints are limitations that restrict the permissible choices for the decision variables. Each limitation can be expressed mathematically in one of three ways: a less-than-or-equal-to ($\leq$), an equal-to ($=$), or a greater-than-or-equal-to ($\geq$) constraint. A $\leq$ constraint puts an upper limit on some function of decision variables and most often is used with maximization problems. For example, a $\leq$ constraint may specify the maximum number of customers who can be served or the capacity limit of a machine. An $=$ constraint means that the function must equal some value. For example, 100 (not 99 or 101) units of one product must be made. An $=$ constraint often is used for certain mandatory relationships, such as the fact that ending inventory always equals beginning inventory plus production minus sales. A $\geq$ constraint puts a lower limit on some function of decision variables. For example, a $\geq$ constraint may specify that production of a product must exceed or equal demand.

Every linear programming problem must have one or more constraints. Taken together, the constraints define a **feasible region**, which represents all permissible combinations of the decision variables. In some unusual situations, the problem is so tightly constrained that there is only one possible solution—or perhaps none. However, in the usual case, the feasibility region contains infinitely many possible solutions, assuming that the feasible combinations of the decision variables can be fractional values. The goal of the decision maker is to find the best possible solution.

The objective function and constraints are functions of decision variables and parameters. A **parameter**, also known as a *coefficient* or *given constant*, is a value that the decision maker cannot control and that does not change when the solution is implemented. Each parameter is assumed to be known with **certainty**. For example, a computer programmer may know that running a software program will take three hours—no more, no less.

The objective function and constraint equations are assumed to be linear. **Linearity** implies proportionality and additivity—there can be no products (e.g., $10x_1x_2$) or powers (e.g., x_1^3) of decision variables. Suppose that the profit gained by producing two types of products (represented by decision variables x_1 and x_2) is $2x_1 + 3x_2$. Proportionality implies that one unit of x_1 contributes $2 to profits and two units contribute $4, regardless of how much of x_1 is produced. Similarly, each unit of x_2 contributes $3, whether it is the first or the tenth unit produced. Additivity means that the total objective function value equals the profits from x_1 plus the profits from x_2.

Finally, we make an assumption of **nonnegativity**, which means that the decision variables must be positive or zero. A firm that makes spaghetti sauce, for example, cannot produce a negative number of jars. To be formally correct, a linear programming formulation should show a ≥ 0 constraint for each decision variable.

Although the assumptions of linearity, certainty, and continuous variables are restrictive, linear programming can help managers analyze many complex resource allocation problems. The process of building the model forces managers to identify the important decision variables and constraints, which is a useful step in its own right. Identifying the nature and scope of the problem represents a major step toward solving it. In a later section, we show how sensitivity analysis can help the manager deal with uncertainties in the parameters and answer "what-if" questions.

---

linear programming
A technique that is useful for allocating scarce resources among competing demands.

objective function
An expression in linear programming models that states mathematically what is being maximized (e.g., profit or present value) or minimized (e.g., cost or scrap).

decision variables
The variables that represent choices the decision maker can control.

constraints
The limitations that restrict the permissible choices for the decision variables.

feasible region
A region that represents all permissible combinations of the decision variables in a linear programming model.

parameter
A value that the decision maker cannot control and that does not change when the solution is implemented.

certainty
The word that is used to describe that a fact is known without doubt.

linearity
A characteristic of linear programming models that implies proportionality and additivity—there can be no products or powers of decision variables.

nonnegativity
An assumption that the decision variables must be positive or zero.

Formulating a Problem

Linear programming applications begin with the formulation of a *model* of the problem with the general characteristics just described. We illustrate the modeling process here with the **product-mix problem**, which is a one-period type of planning problem, the solution of which yields optimal output quantities (or product mix) of a group of services or products subject to resource capacity and market demand constraints. Formulating a model to represent each unique problem, using the following three-step sequence, is the most creative and perhaps the most difficult part of linear programming.

product-mix problem
A one-period type of planning problem, the solution of which yields optimal output quantities (or product mix) of a group of services or products subject to resource capacity and market demand constraints.

Step 1. Define the Decision Variables. What must be decided? Define each decision variable specifically, remembering that the definitions used in the objective function must be equally useful in the constraints. The definitions should be as specific as possible. Consider the following two alternative definitions:

x_1 = product 1
x_1 = number of units of product 1 to be produced and sold next month

The second definition is much more specific than the first, making the remaining steps easier.

Step 2. Write Out the Objective Function. What is to be maximized or minimized? If it is next month's profits, write out an objective function that makes next month's profits a linear function of the decision variables. Identify parameters to go with each decision variable. For example, if each unit of x_1 sold yields a profit of $7, the total profit from product x_1 = $7x_1$. If a variable has no impact on the objective function, its objective function coefficient is 0. The objective function often is set equal to Z, and the goal is to maximize or minimize Z.

Step 3. Write Out the Constraints. What limits the values of the decision variables? Identify the constraints and the parameters for each decision variable in them. As with the objective function, the parameter for a variable that has no impact in a constraint is 0. To be formally correct, also write out the nonnegativity constraints.

As a consistency check, make sure that the same unit of measure is being used on both sides of each constraint and in the objective function. For example, suppose that the right-hand side of a constraint is hours of capacity per month. Then, if a decision variable on the left-hand side of the constraint measures the number of units produced per month, the dimensions of the parameter that is multiplied by the decision variable must be hours per unit because

$$\left(\frac{\text{Hours}}{\text{Unit}}\right)\left(\frac{\text{Units}}{\text{Month}}\right) = \left(\frac{\text{Hours}}{\text{Month}}\right)$$

Of course, you can also skip around from one step to another, depending on the part of the problem that has your attention. If you cannot get past step 1, try a new set of definitions for the decision variables. Often the problem can be modeled correctly in more than one way.

EXAMPLE E.1	Formulating a Linear Programming Model

The Stratton Company produces two basic types of plastic pipe. Three resources are crucial to the output of pipe: extrusion hours, packaging hours, and a special additive to the plastic raw material. The following data represent next week's situation. All data are expressed in units of 100 feet of pipe.

	Product		
Resource	**Type 1**	**Type 2**	**Resource Availability**
Extrusion	4 hr	6 hr	48 hr
Packaging	2 hr	2 hr	18 hr
Additive mix	2 lb	1 lb	16 lb

The contribution to profits and overhead per 100 feet of pipe is $34 for type 1 and $40 for type 2. Formulate a linear programming model to determine how much of each type of pipe should be produced to maximize contribution to profits and to overhead.

SOLUTION

Step 1: To define the decision variables that determine product mix, we let

x_1 = amount of type 1 pipe to be produced and sold next week,

measured in 100-foot increments (e.g., $x_1 = 2$ means 200 feet of type 1 pipe)

and

x_2 = amount of type 2 pipe to be produced and sold next week, measured in 100-foot increments

Step 2: Next, we define the objective function. The goal is to maximize the total contribution that the two products make to profits and overhead. Each unit of x_1 yields \$34, and each unit of x_2 yields \$40. For specific values of x_1 and x_2, we find the total profit by multiplying the number of units of each product produced by the profit per unit and adding them. Thus, our objective function becomes

Maximize: $\$34x_1 + \$40x_2 = Z$

Step 3: The final step is to formulate the constraints. Each unit of x_1 and x_2 produced consumes some of the critical resources. In the extrusion department, a unit of x_1 requires 4 hours and a unit of x_2 requires 6 hours. The total must not exceed the 48 hours of capacity available, so we use the $\leq$ sign. Thus, the first constraint is

$$4x_1 + 6x_2 \leq 48$$

Similarly, we can formulate constraints for packaging and raw materials:

$$2x_1 + 2x_2 \leq 18 \text{ (packaging)}$$

$$2x_1 + x_2 \leq 16 \text{ (additive mix)}$$

These three constraints restrict our choice of values for the decision variable because the values we choose for x_1 and x_2 must satisfy all of the constraints. Negative values for x_1 and x_2 do not make sense, so we add nonnegativity restrictions to the model:

$$x_1 \geq 0 \text{ and } x_2 \geq 0 \text{ (nonnegativity restrictions)}$$

We can now state the entire model, made complete with the definitions of variables.

Maximize: $\$34x_1 + \$40x_2 = Z$

Subject to: $4x_1 + 6x_2 \leq 48$

$2x_1 + 2x_2 \leq 18$

$2x_1 + x_2 \leq 16$

$x_1 \geq 0 \text{ and } x_2 \geq 0$

where

x_1 = amount of type 1 pipe to be produced and sold next week, measured in 100-foot increments

x_2 = amount of type 2 pipe to be produced and sold next week, measured in 100-foot increments

GRAPHIC ANALYSIS

With the model formulated, we now seek the optimal solution. In practice, most linear programming problems are solved with a computer. However, insight into the meaning of the computer output—and linear programming concepts in general—can be gained by analyzing a simple two-variable problem with the **graphic method of linear programming**. Hence, we begin with the graphic method, even though it is not a practical technique for solving problems that have three or more decision variables. The five basic steps are (1) *plot the constraints*, (2) *identify the feasible region*, (3) *plot an objective function line*, (4) *find the visual solution*, and (5) *find the algebraic solution*.

Plot the Constraints

We begin by plotting the constraint equations, disregarding the inequality portion of the constraints (< or >). Making each constraint an equality (=) transforms it into the equation for a straight line. The line can be drawn as soon as we identify two points on it. Any two points reasonably spread out may be chosen; the easiest ones to find are the *axis intercepts*, where the line intersects each axis. To find the x_1 axis intercept, set x_2 equal to 0 and solve

graphic method of linear programming
A type of graphic analysis that involves the following five steps: plotting the constraints, identifying the feasible region, plotting an objective function line, finding a visual solution, and finding the algebraic solution.

the equation for x_1. For the Stratton Company in Example E.1, the equation of the line for the extrusion process is

$$4x_1 + 6x_2 = 48$$

For the x_1 axis intercept, $x_2 = 0$, so

$$4x_1 + 6(0) = 48$$
$$x_1 = 12$$

To find the x_2 axis intercept, set $x_1 = 0$ and solve for x_2:

$$4(0) + 6x_2 = 48$$
$$x_2 = 8$$

We connect points (0, 8) and (12, 0) with a straight line, as shown in Figure E.1.

FIGURE E.1 ▶
Graph of the Extrusion Constraint

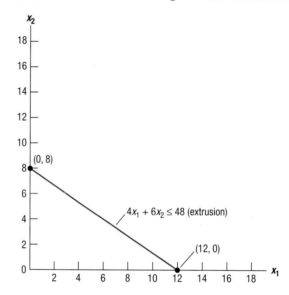

EXAMPLE E.2	**Plotting the Constraints**

Active Model E.1 in my**om**lab offers many insights on graphic analysis and sensitivity analysis. Use it when studying Examples E.2 through E.4.

Tutor E.1 in my**om**lab provides a new practice example for plotting the constraints.

For the Stratton Company problem, plot the other constraints: one constraint for packaging and one constraint for the additive mix.

SOLUTION

The equation for the packaging process's line is $2x_1 + 2x_2 = 18$. To find the x_1 intercept, set $x_2 = 0$:

$$2x_1 + 2(0) = 18$$
$$x_1 = 9$$

To find the x_2 axis intercept, set $x_1 = 0$:

$$2(0) + 2x_2 = 18$$
$$x_2 = 9$$

The equation for the additive mix's line is $2x_1 + x_2 = 16$. To find the x_1 intercept, set $x_2 = 0$:

$$2x_1 + 0 = 16$$
$$x_1 = 8$$

To find the x_2 axis intercept, set $x_1 = 0$:

$$2(0) + x_2 = 16$$
$$x_2 = 16$$

With a straight line, we connect points (0, 9) and (9, 0) for the packaging constraint and points (0, 16) and (8, 0) for the additive mix constraint. Figure E.2 shows the graph with all three constraints plotted.

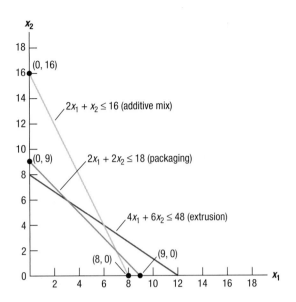

Identify the Feasible Region

The feasible region is the area on the graph that contains the solutions that satisfy all the constraints simultaneously, including the nonnegativity restrictions. To find the feasible region, first locate the feasible points for each constraint and then the area that satisfies all constraints. Generally, the following three rules identify the feasible points for a given constraint:

1. For the = constraint, only the points on the line are feasible solutions.
2. For the ≤ constraint, the points on the line and the points below or to the left of the line are feasible solutions.
3. For the ≥ constraint, the points on the line and the points above or to the right of the line are feasible solutions.

Exceptions to these rules occur when one or more of the parameters on the left-hand side of a constraint are negative. In such cases, we draw the constraint line and test a point on one side of it. If the point does not satisfy the constraint, it is in the infeasible part of the graph. Suppose that a linear programming model has the following five constraints plus the two nonnegativity constraints:

$$2x_1 + x_2 \geq 10$$
$$2x_1 + 3x_2 \geq 18$$
$$x_1 \leq 7$$
$$x_2 \leq 5$$
$$-6x_1 + 5x_2 \leq 5$$
$$x_1, x_2 \geq 0$$

The feasible region is the shaded portion of Figure E.3. The arrows shown on each constraint identify which side of each line is feasible. The rules work for all but the fifth constraint, which has a negative parameter, -6, for x_1. We arbitrarily select $(2, 2)$ as the test point, which Figure E.3 shows is below the line and to the right. At this point, we find $-6(2) + 5(2) = -2$. Because -2 does not exceed 5, the portion of the figure containing $(2, 2)$ is feasible, at least for this fifth constraint.

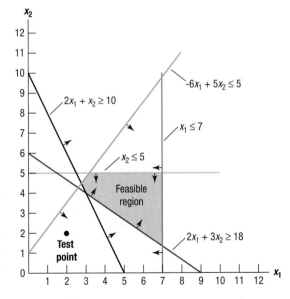

EXAMPLE E.3	Identifying the Feasible Region

Identify the feasible region for the Stratton Company problem.

SOLUTION

Because the problem contains only $\leq$ constraints, and the parameters on the left-hand side of each constraint are not negative, the feasible portions are to the left of and below each constraint. The feasible region, shaded in Figure E.4, satisfies all three constraints simultaneously.

FIGURE E.4 ▶
The Feasible Region

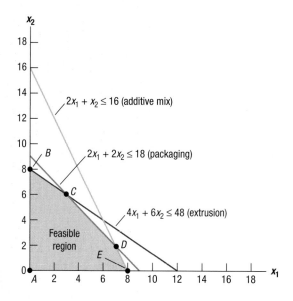

Plot an Objective Function Line

Now we want to find the solution that optimizes the objective function. Even though all the points in the feasible region represent possible solutions, we can limit our search to the corner points. A **corner point** lies at the intersection of two (or possibly more) constraint lines on the boundary of the feasible region. No interior points in the feasible region need be considered because at least one corner point is better than any interior point. Similarly, other points on the boundary of the feasible region can be ignored because a corner point is at least as good as any of them.

In Figure E.4 the five corner points are marked A, B, C, D, and E. Point A is the origin $(0, 0)$ and can be ignored because any other feasible point is a better solution. We could try each of the other corner points in the objective function and select the one that maximizes Z. For example, corner point B lies at $(0, 8)$. If we substitute these values into the objective function, the resulting Z value is 320:

$$34x_1 + 40x_2 = Z$$

$$34(0) + 40(8) = 320$$

However, we may not be able to read accurately the values of x_1 and x_2 for some of the points (e.g., C or D) on the graph. Algebraically solving two linear equations for each corner point also is inefficient when there are many constraints and, thus, many corner points.

The best approach is to plot the objective function on the graph of the feasible region for some arbitrary Z values. From these objective function lines, we can spot the best solution visually. If the objective function is profits, each line is called an *iso-profit line* and every point on that line will yield the same profit. If Z measures cost, the line is called an *iso-cost line* and every point on it represents the same cost. We can simplify the search by plotting the first line in the feasible region—somewhere near the optimal solution, we hope. For the Stratton Company example, let us pass a line through point E (8, 0). This point is a corner point. It might even be the optimal solution because it is far from the origin. To draw the line, we first identify its Z value as $34(8) + 40(0) = 272$. Therefore, the equation for the objective function line passing through E is

$$34x_1 + 40x_2 = 272$$

corner point
A point that lies at the intersection of two (or possibly more) constraint lines on the boundary of the feasible region.

Every point on the line defined by this equation has an objective function Z value of 272. To draw the line, we need to identify a second point on it and then connect the two points. Let us use the x_2 intercept, where $x_1 = 0$:

$$34(0) + 40x_2 = 272$$

$$x_2 = 6.8$$

Figure E.5 shows the iso-profit line that connects points $(8, 0)$ and $(0, 6.8)$. A series of other dashed lines could be drawn parallel to this first line. Each would have its own Z value. Lines above the first line we drew would have higher Z values. Lines below it would have lower Z values.

▲ FIGURE E.5
Passing an Iso-Profit Line Through (8, 0)

▲ FIGURE E.6
Drawing the Second Iso-Profit Line

Find the Visual Solution

We now eliminate corner points A and E from consideration as the optimal solution because better points lie above and to the right of the $Z = 272$ iso-profit line. Our goal is to maximize profits, so the best solution is a point on the iso-profit line *farthest* from the origin but still touching the feasible region. (For minimization problems, it is a point in the feasible region on the iso-cost line *closest* to the origin.) To identify which of the remaining corner points is optimal (*B*, *C*, or *D*), we draw, parallel to the first line, one or more iso-profit lines that give better Z values (higher for maximization and lower for minimization). The line that just touches the feasible region identifies the optimal solution. For the Stratton Company problem, Figure E.6 shows the second iso-profit line. The optimal solution is the last point touching the feasible region: point *C*. It appears to be in the vicinity of $(3, 6)$, but the visual solution is not exact.

A linear programming problem can have more than one optimal solution. This situation occurs when the objective function is parallel to one of the faces of the feasible region. Such would be the case if our objective function in the Stratton Company problem were $\$38x_1 + \$38x_2$. Points $(3, 6)$ and $(7, 2)$ would be optimal, as would any other point on the line connecting these two corner points. In such a case, management probably would base a final decision on nonquantifiable factors. It is important to understand, however, that we need to consider only the corner points of the feasible region when optimizing an objective function.

Find the Algebraic Solution

To find an exact solution, we must use algebra. We begin by identifying the pair of constraints that define the corner point at their intersection. We then list the constraints as equations and solve them simultaneously to find the coordinates x_1, x_2 of the corner point.

Simultaneous equations can be solved several ways. For small problems, the easiest way is as follows:

Step 1. Develop an equation with just one unknown. Start by multiplying both sides of one equation by a constant so that the coefficient for one of the two decision variables is *identical* in both equations. Then subtract one equation from the other and solve the resulting equation for its single unknown variable.

Step 2. Insert this decision variable's value into either one of the original constraints and solve for the other decision variable.

EXAMPLE E.4   Finding the Optimal Solution Algebraically

Tutor E.2 in my**om**lab provides a new practice example for finding the optimal solution.

Find the optimal solution algebraically for the Stratton Company problem. What is the value of Z when the decision variables have optimal values?

SOLUTION

Step 1: Figure E.6 showed that the optimal corner point lies at the intersection of the extrusion and packaging constraints. Listing the constraints as equalities, we have

$$4x_1 + 6x_2 = 48 \text{ (extrusion)}$$
$$2x_1 + 2x_2 = 18 \text{ (packaging)}$$

We multiply each term in the packaging constraint by 2. The packaging constraint now is $4x_1 + 4x_2 = 36$. Next, we subtract the packaging constraint from the extrusion constraint. The result will be an equation from which x_1 has dropped out. (Alternatively, we could multiply the second equation by 3 so that x_2 drops out after the subtraction.) Thus,

$$
\begin{aligned}
4x_1 + 6x_2 &= 48 \\
-(4x_1 + 4x_2 &= 36) \\
\hline
2x_2 &= 12 \\
x_2 &= 6
\end{aligned}
$$

Step 2: Substituting the value of x_2 into the extrusion equation, we get

$$4x_1 + 6(6) = 48$$
$$4x_1 = 12$$
$$x_1 = 3$$

Thus, the optimal point is (3, 6). This solution gives a total profit of $34(3) + 40(6) = \$342$.

DECISION POINT

Management at the Stratton Company decided to produce 300 feet of type 1 pipe and 600 feet of type 2 pipe for the next week for a total profit of \$342.

Slack and Surplus Variables

Figure E.6 shows that the optimal product mix will exhaust all the extrusion and packaging resources because at the optimal corner point (3, 6) the two constraints are equalities. Substituting the values of x_1 and x_2 into these constraints shows that the left-hand sides equal the right-hand sides:

$$4(3) + 6(6) = 48 \text{ (extrusion)}$$

$$2(3) + 2(6) = 18 \text{ (packaging)}$$

binding constraint

A constraint that helps form the optimal corner point; it limits the ability to improve the objective function.

A constraint (such as the one for extrusion) that helps form the optimal corner point is called a **binding constraint** because it limits the ability to improve the objective function. If a binding constraint is relaxed, or made less restrictive, a better solution is possible. Relaxing a constraint means increasing the right-hand-side parameter for a ≤ constraint or decreasing it for a ≥ constraint. No improvement is possible from relaxing a constraint that is not binding, such as the additive mix constraint in Figure E.6. If the right-hand side was increased from 16 to 17 and the problem solved again, the optimal solution would not change. In other words, there is already more additive mix than needed.

For nonbinding inequality constraints, knowing how much the left and right sides differ is helpful. Such information tells us how close the constraint is to becoming binding. For a $\leq$ constraint, the amount by which the left-hand side falls short of the right-hand side is called **slack**. For a $\geq$ constraint, the amount by which the left-hand side exceeds the right-hand side is called **surplus**. To find the slack for a $\leq$ constraint algebraically, we *add* a slack variable to the constraint and convert it to an equality. Then we substitute in the values of the decision variables and solve for the slack. For example, the additive mix constraint in Figure E.6, $2x_1 + x_2 \leq 16$, can be rewritten by adding slack variable s_1:

$$2x_1 + x_2 + s_1 = 16$$

We then find the slack at the optimal solution (3, 6):

$$2(3) + 6 + s_1 = 16$$

$$s_1 = 4$$

The procedure is much the same to find the surplus for a $\geq$ constraint, except that we *subtract* a surplus variable from the left-hand side. Suppose that $x_1 + x_2 \geq 6$ was another constraint in the Stratton Company problem, representing a lower bound on the number of units produced. We would then rewrite the constraint by subtracting a surplus variable s_2:

$$x_1 + x_2 - s_2 = 6$$

The slack at the optimal solution (3, 6) would be

$$3 + 6 - s_2 = 6$$

$$s_2 = 3$$

slack
The amount by which the left-hand side of a linear programming constraint falls short of the right-hand side.

surplus
The amount by which the left-hand side of a linear programming constraint exceeds the right-hand side.

Tutor E.3 in my**om**lab provides another practice example for finding slack.

SENSITIVITY ANALYSIS

Rarely are the parameters in the objective function and constraints known with certainty. Often, they are just estimates of actual values. For example, the available packaging and extrusion hours for the Stratton Company are estimates that do not reflect the uncertainties associated with absenteeism or personnel transfers, and the required hours per unit to package and extrude may be time estimates that essentially are averages. Likewise, profit contributions used for the objective function coefficients do not reflect uncertainties in selling prices and such variable costs as wages, raw materials, and shipping.

Despite such uncertainties, initial estimates are needed to solve the problem. Accounting, marketing, and time-standard information systems often provide these initial estimates. After solving the problem using these estimated values, the analyst can determine how much the optimal values of the decision variables and the objective function value Z would be affected if certain parameters had different values. This type of postsolution analysis for answering "what-if" questions is called *sensitivity analysis*.

One way of conducting sensitivity analysis for linear programming problems is the brute-force approach of changing one or more parameter values and resolving the entire problem. This approach may be acceptable for small problems, but it is inefficient if the problem involves many parameters. For example, brute-force sensitivity analysis using 3 separate values for each of 20 objective function coefficients requires 3^{20}, or 3,486,784,401, separate solutions! Fortunately, efficient methods are available for getting sensitivity information without resolving the entire problem, and they are routinely used in most linear programming computer software packages. Table E.1, on the following page, describes the four basic types of sensitivity analysis information provided by linear programming.

COMPUTER SOLUTION

Most real-world linear programming problems are solved on a computer, so we concentrate here on understanding the use of linear programming and the logic on which it is based. The solution procedure in computer codes is some form of the **simplex method**, which is an iterative algebraic procedure for solving linear programming problems.

simplex method
An iterative algebraic procedure for solving linear programming problems.

TABLE E.1	SENSITIVITY ANALYSIS INFORMATION PROVIDED BY LINEAR PROGRAMMING
Key Term	**Definition**
reduced cost	How much the objective function coefficient of a decision variable must improve (increase for maximization or decrease for minimization) before the optimal solution changes and the decision variable "enters" the solution with some positive number
shadow price	The marginal improvement in Z (increase for maximization and decrease for minimization) caused by relaxing the constraint by one unit
range of optimality	The interval (lower and upper bounds) of an objective function coefficient over which the optimal values of the decision variables remain unchanged
range of feasibility	The interval (lower and upper bounds) over which the right-hand-side parameter of a constraint can vary while its shadow price remains valid

Simplex Method

The graphic analysis gives insight into the logic of the simplex method, beginning with the focus on corner points. One corner point will always be the optimum, even when multiple optimal solutions are available. Thus, the simplex method starts with an initial corner point and then systematically evaluates other corner points in such a way that the objective function improves (or, at worst, stays the same) at each iteration. In the Stratton Company problem, an improvement would be an increase in profits. When no more improvements are possible, the optimal solution has been found.[1] The simplex method also helps generate the sensitivity analysis information that we developed graphically.

Each corner point has no more than m variables that are greater than 0, where m is the number of constraints (not counting the nonnegativity constraints). The m variables include slack and surplus variables, not just the original decision variables. Because of this property, we can find a corner point by simultaneously solving m constraints, where all but m variables are set equal to 0. For example, point B in Figure E.6 has three nonzero variables: x_2, the slack variable for packaging, and the slack variable for the additive mix. Their values can be found by simultaneously solving the three constraints, with x_1 and the slack variable for extrusion equal to 0. After finding this corner point, the simplex method applies information similar to the reduced costs to decide which new corner point to find next that gives an even better Z value. It continues in this way until no better corner point is possible. The final corner point evaluated is the optimal one.

Computer Output

Computer programs dramatically reduce the amount of time required to solve linear programming problems. The capabilities and displays of software packages are not uniform. For example, POM for Windows in my**om**lab can handle small- to medium-sized linear programming problems. Inputs are made easily and nonnegativity constraints need not be entered. Microsoft's *Excel* Solver offers a second option for similar problem sizes. See the tutorial in my**om**lab for Supplement E to learn about this second option. More advanced software for bigger problems is available from multiple sources.

Here we show output from POM for Windows when applied to the Stratton Company. Figure E.7 shows the two *data entry* screens. The first screen allows you to enter the problem's name, specify the number of constraints and decision variables, and choose between maximization and minimization. After making these inputs and clicking the OK button, the data table screen is shown. Enter the parameters, give names to each constraint and decision variable (as desired), and specify the type of relationship ($\leq$, $=$, $\geq$) for each constraint. The second screen in Figure E.7 shows the completed data table. The user may customize labels for the decision variables, right-hand-side values, and constraints. Here, the first decision variable is labeled as "X1," the right-hand-side values as "RHS," and the extrusion constraint as "Extrusion." Slack and surplus variables will be added automatically as needed. When all of the inputs are made, click the green arrow labeled "Solve" in the upper-right corner.

Figure E.8 displays the solution with the *Results* screen. All output confirms our earlier calculations and the graphic analysis. Of particular interest is the bottom row that gives the

---

[1] For more information on how to perform the simplex method manually, see Render, Stair, and Hanna, *Quantitative Analysis for Management*, 8th ed., or any other current textbook on management science.

optimal values of the decision variables (X1 = 3 and (X2 = 6), and also the optimal value of the objective function ($342). The shadow prices for each constraint are given in the last column.

▲ FIGURE E.7
Inputs Worksheet

	X1	X2		RHS	Shadow Price
Maximize	34	40			
Extrusion	4	6	<=	48	3
Packaging	2	2	<=	18	11
Additive	2	1	<=	16	0
Solution->	3	6		342	

▲ FIGURE E.8
Results Screen

Click on the Window icon and select the second option in the drop down menu to switch to the *Ranging* screen. It is shown in Fig. E.9. The top half deals with the decision variables. Of particular interest are the reduced costs and the lower and upper bounds. Two tips on interpreting the *reduced cost* information are as follows:

1. It is relevant only for a decision variable that is 0 in the optimal solution. If the decision variable is greater than 0, ignore the reduced cost number. Thus, for the Stratton Company problem the reduced cost numbers provide no new insight because they are always 0 when decision variables have positive values in the optimal solution. Look instead at the lower and upper bounds on the objective function coefficients.

2. It tells how much the objective function coefficient of a decision variable that is 0 in the optimal solution must *improve* (increase for maximization problems or decrease for minimization problems) before the optimal solution would change. At that point, the decision variable associated with the coefficient enters the optimal solution at some positive level. To learn the new solution, apply POM for Windows again with a coefficient improved by slightly more than the reduced cost number.

The top half of this screen also gives the *range of optimality*, or the lower and upper bound over which the objective function coefficients can range without affecting the optimal values of the decision variables. Note that the objective function coefficient for x_1, which currently has a value of $34, has a range of optimality from $26.6667 to $40. While the objection function's Z value would change with coefficient changes over this range, the optimal values of the decision variables remain the same.

The bottom half of Figure E.9 deals with the constraints, including the slack or surplus variables and the original right-hand-side values. Of particular interest are the shadow prices. Two tips on interpreting a *shadow price* follow:

1. The number is relevant only for a binding constraint, where the slack or surplus variable is 0 in the optimal solution. For a nonbinding constraint, the shadow price is 0.

2. The sign of the shadow price can be a positive or negative. The sign depends on whether the objective function is being maximized or minimized, and whether it is a $\leq$ constraint or $\geq$ constraint. If you simply ignore the sign, interpret the shadow price as the benefit of increasing the right-hand side by one unit for a $\leq$ constraint and reducing it by one unit for a $\geq$ constraint. The benefit is a reduction in the objective function value for minimization problems, and an increase for maximization problems. The shadow price can also be interpreted as the marginal loss (or penalty) in Z caused by making the constraint more restrictive by one unit.

Thus, the Stratton Company problem has 4 pounds of the additive mix slack, so the shadow price is $0. Packaging, on the other hand, is a binding constraint because it has no slack. The shadow price of one more packaging hour is $11.

Finally, Figure E.9 reports the lower and upper bounds for the *range of feasibility*, over which the right-hand-side parameters can range without changing the shadow prices. For example, the $11 shadow price for packaging is valid over the range from 16 to 20 hours.

degeneracy
A condition that occurs when the number of nonzero variables in the optimal solution is less than the number of constraints.

The number of variables in the optimal solution (counting the decision variables, slack variables, and surplus variables) that are greater than 0 never exceeds the number of constraints. Such is the case for the Stratton Company problem, with its three constraints (not counting the implicit nonnegativity constraints) and three nonzero variables in the optimal solution (X1, X2, and the additive mix slack variable). On some rare occasions, the number of nonzero variables in the optimal solution can be less than the number of constraints—a condition called **degeneracy**. When degeneracy occurs, the sensitivity analysis information is suspect. If you want more "what-if" information, simply run your software package again using the new parameter values that you want to investigate.

Variable	Value	Reduced Cost	Original Val	Lower Bound	Upper Bound
X1	3	0	34	26.6667	40
X2	6	0	40	34	51
Constraint	Shadow Price	Slack/Surplus	Original Val	Lower Bound	Upper Bound
Extrusion	3	0	48	40	54
Packaging	11	0	18	16	20
Additive	0	4	16	12	Infinity

FIGURE E.9 ▲
Ranging Screen

| EXAMPLE E.5 | **Using Shadow Prices for Decision Making** |

The Stratton Company needs answers to three important questions: Would increasing capacities in the extrusion or packaging area pay if it cost an extra $8 per hour over and above the normal costs already reflected in the objective function coefficients? Would increasing packaging capacity pay if it cost an additional $6 per hour? Would buying more raw materials pay?

SOLUTION

Expanding extrusion capacity would cost a premium of $8 per hour, but the shadow price for that capacity is only $3 per hour. However, expanding packaging hours would cost only $6 per hour more than the price reflected in the objective function, and the shadow price is $11 per hour. Finally, buying more raw materials would not pay because a surplus of 4 pounds already exists; the shadow price is $0 for that resource.

DECISION POINT

Management decided to increase its packaging hours capacity but did not decide to expand extrusion capacity or buy more raw materials.

THE TRANSPORTATION METHOD

A special case of linear programming is the **transportation problem**, which can be represented as a standard table, sometimes called a *tableau*. Figure E.10 is an example. Typically the rows of the table are linear constraints that impose capacity limitations, and the columns are linear constraints that require certain demand levels to be met. Each cell in the tableau is a decision variable, and a per-unit cost is shown in the upper-right corner of each cell. Figure E.10 implies six decision variables (2 rows × 3 columns) and five constraints (2 rows + 3 columns).

Transportation problems can be formulated as a conventional linear programming problem and solved as usual. The **transportation method** simplifies data input and is a more efficient solution technique, but does not provide sensitivity analysis as in Figure E.9. Here we show how location problems and production planning problems can be formulated as transportation problems. We focus on the setup and interpretation of the problem, leaving the rest of the solution process to a computer software package.

transportation problem
A special case of linear programming that has linear constraints for capacity limitations and demand requirements.

transportation method
A more efficient solution technique than the simplex method for solving transportation problems.

Transportation Method for Location

The *transportation method for location* can help solve multiple-facility location problems. We use it here to determine the allocation pattern that minimizes the cost of shipping products from two or more plants, or *sources of supply,* to two or more warehouses, or *destinations.* The rows in Figure E.10 represent the sources of supply, and the columns represent the destinations.

The transportation method does not solve *all* facets of the multiple-facility location problem. It only finds the *best* shipping pattern between plants and warehouses for a particular set of plant locations, each with a given capacity. The analyst must try a variety of location-capacity combinations and use the transportation method to find the optimal distribution for each one. Distribution costs (variable shipping and possibly variable production costs) are but one important input in evaluating a particular location-allocation combination. Investment costs and other fixed costs also must be considered, along with various qualitative factors. This complete analysis must be made for each reasonable location-capacity combination. Because of the importance of making a good decision, this extra effort is well worth its cost.

Plant	Warehouse			Capacity
	San Antonio, TX (1)	Hot Springs, AR (2)	Sioux Falls, SD (3)	
Phoenix	5.00	6.00	5.40	400
Atlanta	7.00	4.60	6.60	500
Requirements	200	400	300	900 / 900

◀ FIGURE E.10
Initial Tableau

Setting up the Initial Tableau   The first step in solving a transportation problem is to formulate its tableau. The basic steps in setting up an initial tableau are as follows:

1. Create a row for each plant (existing or new) being considered and a column for each warehouse.

2. Add a column for plant capacities and a row for warehouse demands and insert their specific numerical values.

3. Each cell not in the requirements row or capacity column represents a shipping route from a plant to a warehouse. Insert the unit costs in the upper right-hand corner of each cell.

For example, Figure E.10 represents the Sunbelt Pool Company that is considering building a new 500-unit plant because business is booming. One possible location is Atlanta. The tableau shows the plant capacities, warehouse requirements, and shipping costs. It shows, for example, that shipping one unit from the existing Phoenix plant to warehouse 1 in San Antonio, Texas, costs $5.00. Costs are assumed to increase linearly with the size of the shipment; that is, the cost is the same *per unit* regardless of the size of the total shipment.

In the transportation method, the sum of the shipments in a row must equal the corresponding plant's capacity. For example, in Figure E.10, the total shipments from the Atlanta plant to warehouses 1, 2, and 3 located in San Antonio, Texas; Hot Springs, Arkansas; and Sioux Falls, South Dakota, respectively, must add up to 500. Similarly, the sum of shipments to a column must equal the corresponding warehouse's demand requirements. Thus, shipments to warehouse 1 in San Antonio, Texas, from Phoenix and Atlanta must total 200 units.

Dummy Plants or Warehouses   The transportation method also requires that the sum of capacities equal the sum of demands, which happens to be the case at 900 units (see Figure E.10). In many real problems, total capacity exceeds requirements, or vice versa. If capacity exceeds requirements by *r* units, we add an extra column (a *dummy warehouse*) with a demand of *r* units and make the shipping costs in the newly created cells $0. Shipments are not actually made, so they represent unused plant capacity. Similarly, if requirements exceed capacity by *r* units, we add an extra row (a *dummy plant*) with a capacity of *r* units. We assign shipping costs equal to the stockout costs of the new cells. If stockout costs are unknown or are the same for all warehouses, we simply assign shipping costs of $0 per unit to each cell in the dummy row. The optimal solution will not be affected because the shortage of *r* units is required in all cases. Adding a dummy warehouse or dummy plant ensures that the sum of capacities equals the sum of demands. Some software packages (such as POM for Windows) automatically add them when the user inputs the data.

Finding a Solution   After the initial tableau has been set up, the goal is to find the least-cost allocation pattern that satisfies all demands and exhausts all capacities. This pattern can be found by using the transportation method, which guarantees the optimal solution. The initial tableau is filled in with a feasible solution that satisfies all warehouse demands and exhausts all plant capacities. Then a new tableau is created, defining a new solution that has a lower total cost. This iterative process continues until no improvements can be made in the current solution, signaling that the optimal solution has been found. When using a computer package, all that you have to input is the information for the initial tableau.

The number of nonzero shipments in the optimal solution will never exceed the sum of the numbers of plants and warehouses minus 1. The Sunbelt Pool Company has two plants and three warehouses, so not more than four (or $2 + 3 - 1$) shipments are needed in the optimal solution.

EXAMPLE E.6	Interpreting the Optimal Solution

The optimal solution for the Sunbelt Pool Company, found with POM for Windows, is shown in Figure E.11. Figure E.11(a) displays the data inputs, with the cells showing the unit costs, the bottom row showing the demands, and the last column showing the supply capacities.

(a) Input Data

	San Antonio	Hot Springs	Sioux Falls	SUPPLY
Phoenix	5	6	5.4	400
Atlanta	7	4.6	6.6	500
DEMAND	200	400	300	

◀ **FIGURE E.11**
POM for Windows Screens for
Sunbelt Pool Company

(b) Optimal Shipping Pattern

Optimal cost = $4580	San Antonio	Hot Springs	Sioux Falls
Phoenix	200		200
Atlanta		400	100

(c) Cost Breakdown

	San Antonio	Hot Springs	Sioux Falls
Phoenix	200/$1000		200/$1080
Atlanta		400/$1840	100/$660

SOLUTION

Figure E.11(b) shows how the existing network of plants supplies the three warehouses to minimize costs for a total of $4,580. Verify that each plant's capacity is exhausted and that each warehouse's demand is filled. Phoenix ships 200 units to warehouse 1 in San Antonio, Texas, and 200 units to warehouse 3 in Sioux Falls, South Dakota, exhausting its 400-unit capacity. Atlanta ships 400 units of its 500-unit capacity to warehouse 2 in Hot Springs, Arkansas, and the remaining 100 units to warehouse 3 in Sioux Falls. All warehouse demand is satisfied: Warehouse 1 in San Antonio is fully supplied by Phoenix and warehouse 2 in Hot Springs is fully supplied by Atlanta. Warehouse 3 in Sioux Falls receives 200 units from Phoenix and 100 units from Atlanta, satisfying its 300-unit demand.

Figure E.11(c) shows the total cost of each shipment. The total optimal cost reported in the upper-left corner of Figure E.11(b) is $4,580, or 200($5.00) + 200($5.40) + 400($4.60) + 100($6.60) = $4,580.

DECISION POINT

Management must evaluate other plant locations before deciding on the best one. The optimal solution does not necessarily mean that the best choice is to open an Atlanta plant. It just means that the best allocation pattern for the current choices on the other two dimensions of this multiple-facility location problem (that is, a capacity of 400 units at Phoenix and the new plant's location at Atlanta) results in total transportation costs of $4,580. Other costs and various qualitative factors also must be considered as additional parts of a complete evaluation. For example, the annual profits earned from the expansion must be balanced against the land and construction costs of a new plant in Atlanta. Thus, management might use the preference matrix approach (see Appendix A, "Decision Making") to account for the full set of location factors.

Transportation Method for Production Planning

Making sure that demand and supply are in balance is central to sales and operations planning (SOP), so it is no surprise that the transportation method can be applied to it. The *transportation method for production planning* is particularly helpful in determining anticipation inventories. Thus, it relates more to manufacturers' production plans than to service providers' staffing plans. In fact, the workforce levels for each period are inputs to the transportation method rather than outputs from it. Different workforce adjustment plans should be evaluated. Thus, several transportation method solutions may be obtained before a final plan is selected.

Using the transportation method for production planning is based on the assumption that a demand forecast is available for each period, along with a possible workforce adjustment plan. Capacity limits on overtime and the use of subcontractors also are needed for each period. Another assumption is that all costs are linearly related to the amount of goods produced; that is, a change in the amount of goods produced creates a proportionate change in costs.

To develop a sales and operations plan for a manufacturer, we do the following:

1. Obtain the demand forecasts for each period to be covered by the sales and operations plan and identify the initial inventory level currently available that can be used to meet future demand.

2. Select a candidate workforce adjustment plan, using a chase strategy, level strategy, or a mixed strategy. Specify the capacity limits of each production alternative (regular time, overtime, and subcontracting) for each period covered by the plan.

3. Estimate the cost of holding inventory and the cost of possible production alternatives (regular-time production, overtime production, and subcontracting). Identify the cost of undertime, if idle regular-time capacity is paid.

4. Input the information gathered in steps 1-3 into a computer routine that solves the transportation problem. After getting the solution, calculate the anticipation inventory levels and identify high-cost elements of the plan.

5. Repeat the process with other plans for regular-time, overtime, and subcontracting capacities until you find the solution that best balances cost and qualitative considerations. Even though this process involves trial and error, the transportation method yields the best mix of regular time, overtime, and subcontracting for each capacity plan.

Example E.7 demonstrates this approach using the *Transportation Method (Production Planning)* module in the POM for Windows package.

EXAMPLE E.7	Preparing a Production Plan with the Transportation Method

The Tru-Rainbow Company produces a variety of paint products for both commercial and private use. The demand for paint is highly seasonal, peaking in the third quarter. Initial inventory is 250,000 gallons, and ending inventory should be 300,000 gallons.

Tru-Rainbow's manufacturing manager wants to determine the best production plan using the following demand requirements and capacity plan. Demands and capacities here are expressed in thousands of gallons (rather than employee-period equivalents). The manager knows that the regular-time cost is $1.00 per unit, overtime cost is $1.50 per unit, subcontracting cost is $1.90 per unit, and inventory holding cost is $0.30 per unit per quarter. Undertime is paid and the cost is $0.50 per unit. It is less than the regular-time cost because only labor costs are involved, not materials and variable overhead going into paint production.

	Demand	Regular-time Capacity	Overtime Capacity	Subcontractor Capacity
Quarter 1	300	450	90	200
Quarter 2	850	450	90	200
Quarter 3	1,500	750	150	200
Quarter 4	350	450	90	200
Totals	3,000	2,100	420	800

The following constraints apply:

a. The maximum allowable overtime in any quarter is 20 percent of the regular-time capacity in that quarter.

b. The subcontractor can supply a maximum of 200,000 gallons in any quarter. Production can be subcontracted in one period and the excess held in inventory for a future period to avoid a stockout.

c. No backorders or stockouts are permitted.

(a) Input Data for Prospective Production Plan

Period	Demand	Regular tm Capacity	Overtime Capacity	Subcontract Capacity		Unit costs	Value
Quarter 1	300	450	90	200		Regular time	1
Quarter 2	850	450	90	200		Overtime	1.5
Quarter 3	1500	750	150	200		Subcontracting	1.9
Quarter 4	650	450	90	200		Holding cost	.3
						Shortage cost	Not allowed
						Idle RT Capacity cost	.5
						Initial Inventory	250

(b) Transportation Tableau

	Quarter 1	Quarter 2	Quarter 3	Quarter 4	Excess Capacity	Capacity
Init Inventory	0	.3	.6	.9	0	250
Quarter 1 RegTime	1	1.3	1.6	1.9	.5	450
Quarter 1 Overtime	1.5	1.8	2.1	2.4	0	90
Quarter 1 Subcontract	1.9	2.2	2.5	2.8	0	200
Quarter 2 RegTime	9999	1	1.3	1.6	.5	450
Quarter 2 Overtime	9999	1.5	1.8	2.1	0	90
Quarter 2 Subcontract	9999	1.9	2.2	2.5	0	200
Quarter 3 RegTime	9999	9999	1	1.3	.5	750
Quarter 3 Overtime	9999	9999	1.5	1.8	0	150
Quarter 3 Subcontract	9999	9999	1.9	2.2	0	200
Quarter 4 RegTime	9999	9999	9999	1	.5	450
Quarter 4 Overtime	9999	9999	9999	1.5	0	90
Quarter 4 Subcontract	9999	9999	9999	1.9	0	200
Demand	300	850	1500	650	270	

▲ FIGURE E.12
POM for Windows Screens for Tru-Rainbow Company

SOLUTION

Figure E.12(a) shows the POM for Windows screen for data input. It looks much like the table shown previously, but with one exception. The demand for quarter 4 is shown to be 650,000 gallons rather than the demand forecast of only 350,000. The larger number reflects the desire of the manager to have an ending inventory in quarter 4 of 300,000 gallons.

Figure E.12(b) shows a second screen regarding how the input data gets translated into the transportation tableau. Some points to note include the following:

1. There is a row for each supply alternative (instead of the "sources" or plants in Figure E.11) on a quarter-by-quarter basis. The last column in each row indicates the maximum amount that can be used to meet demand. The first row is the initial inventory available, and the rows that follow are for regular-time, overtime, and subcontracting production in each of the four quarters. The initial inventory can be used to satisfy demand in any of the four quarters. The second row (regular-time production in period 1) can also be used to satisfy demand in any of the four periods the plan will cover, and so on. The numbers in the last column give the maximum capacity made available for the supply alternatives. For example, the regular-time capacity for quarter 3 increases from the usual 450,000 gallons to 750,000 gallons, to help with the peak demand forecasted to be 1,500,000 gallons.

2. A column indicates each future quarter of demand (instead of "destinations" or warehouses in Figure E.11), and the last row gives its demand forecast. The demand for the fourth quarter is shown to be 650 units, because it includes the desired amount of ending inventory. The Excess Capacity column shows the cost of unused capacity, and the number in the last row (270 units) is the amount by which total capacity exceeds total demand. The unit costs for unused capacity are 0, except for the $0.50 unit cost of unused regular-time capacity.

3. The numbers in the other cells (excluding the cells in the last row or last column) show the cost of producing a unit in one period and, in some cases, carrying the unit in inventory for sale in a future period. These

numbers correspond to the costs in the upper-right corners of the cells in Figure E.10. For example, the cost per unit of regular-time production in quarter 1 is $1.00 per gallon if it is used to meet the demand in quarter 1. This cost is found in row 2 and column 1 of the tableau. However, if it produced to meet demand in quarter 2, the cost increases to $1.30 (or $1.00 + $0.30) because we must hold the unit in inventory for one quarter. Satisfying a unit of demand in quarter 3 by producing in quarter 1 on regular time and carrying the unit for two quarters costs $1.60, or [$1.00 + (2 x $0.30)], and so on. A similar approach is used for the costs of overtime and subcontracting.

4. The cells in the bottom left portion of the tableau with a cost of $9,999 are associated with backorders (or producing in a period to satisfy demand in a period after it was needed). Here we disallow backorders by making the backorder cost an arbitrarily large number, in this case $9,999 per unit. If backorder costs are so large, the transportation method will try to avoid backorders because it seeks a solution that minimizes total cost. If that is not possible, we increase the staffing plan and the overtime and subcontracting capacities.

5. The least expensive alternatives are those in which the output is produced and sold in the same period. For example, the cost for quarter 2 overtime production is only $1.50 per gallon if it is designated to meet demand in quarter 2 (row 6, column 2). The cost increases to $2.10 if it is designated for quarter 4 demand. However, we may not always be able to avoid alternatives that create inventory because of capacity restrictions.

6. Finally, the per-unit holding cost for the beginning inventory in period 1 is 0 because it is a function of previous production-planning decisions.

Figure E.13 shows the POM for Windows screen that displays the optimal solution for this particular workforce adjustment plan. The first row shows that 230 units of the initial inventory are used to help satisfy the demand in quarter 1. The remaining 20 units in the first row are earmarked for helping supply the demand in quarter 3. The sum of the allocations across row 1 for the four quarters (230 + 0 + 20 + 0) does not exceed the maximum capacity of 250, given in the right column. With the transportation method, this result must occur with each row. Any shortfalls are unused capacity, given in the "Excess Capacity"" column. In this case, the undertime cost of $0.50 per unit was sufficiently large that no regular time capacity went unused.

Optimal cost = $4,010	Quarter 1	Quarter 2	Quarter 3	Quarter 4	Excess Capacity	Capacity
Init Inventory	230		20			250
Quarter 1 RegTime	50	400				450
Quarter 1 Overtime			90			90
Quarter 1 Subcontract	20				180	200
Quarter 2 RegTime		450				450
Quarter 2 Overtime			90			90
Quarter 2 Subcontract			200			200
Quarter 3 RegTime			750			750
Quarter 3 Overtime			150			150
Quarter 3 Subcontract			200			200
Quarter 4 RegTime				450		450
Quarter 4 Overtime				90		90
Quarter 4 Subcontract				110	90	200
Demand	300	850	1500	650	270	

FIGURE E.13 ▲
Solution Screen for Prospective
Tru-Rainbow Company
Production Plan

Similarly, the sum of the allocations down each column must equal the total demand for the quarter. For example, the demand for quarter 1 is supplied from 230 units of the initial inventory, 50 units of quarter 1 regular-time production, and 20 units of quarter 1 subcontracting production. Summed together, they equal the forecasted demand of 300 units.

To further interpret the solution, we can convert Figure E.13 into the following table. For example, the total regular-time production in quarter 1 is 450,000 gallons (50,000 gallons to help meet demand in quarter 1 and 400,000 gallons to help satisfy demand in quarter 2).

The anticipation inventory held at the end of each quarter is obtained in the last column. For any quarter, it is the quarter's beginning inventory plus total supply (regular-time and overtime production, plus subcontracting) minus demand. For example, for quarter 1 the beginning inventory (250,000) plus the total from production and subcontracting (560,000) minus quarter 1 demand (300,000) results in an ending inventory of 510,000, which also is the beginning inventory for quarter 2.

Quarter	Regular-time Production	Overtime Production	Subcontracting	Total Supply	Anticipation Inventory
1	450	90	20	560	250 + 560 − 300 = 510
2	450	90	200	740	510 + 740 − 850 = 400
3	750	150	200	1,100	400 + 1,100 − 1,500 = 0
4	450	90	110	650	0 + 650 − 350 = 300
Totals	2,100	420	530	3,050	

Note: Anticipation inventory is the amount at the end of each quarter, where Beginning inventory + Total production − Actual Demand = Ending inventory.

The breakdown of costs can be found by multiplying the allocation in each cell of Figure E.13 by the cost per unit in that cell in Figure E.12 (b). Computing the cost column by column (it can also be down on a row-by-row basis) yields a total cost of $4,010,000, or $4,010 × 1,000.

Cost Calculations by Column		
Quarter 1	230($0) + 50($1.00) + 20($1.90)	= $ 88
Quarter 2	400($1.30) + 450($1.00)	= 970
Quarter 3	20($0.60) + 90($2.10) + 90($1.80) + 200($2.20) + 750($1.00) + 150($1.50) + 200($1.90)	= 2,158
Quarter 4	450($1.00) + 90($1.50) + 110($1.90)	= 794
		Total = $4,010

DECISION POINT

This plan requires too much overtime and subcontracting, and the anticipation inventory cost is substantial. The manager decided to search for a better capacity plan—with increases in the workforce to boost regular-time production capacity—that could lower production costs, perhaps even low enough to offset the added capacity costs.

APPLICATIONS

Many problems in operations and supply chain management, and in other functional areas, lend themselves to linear programming and the transportation method. In addition to the examples already introduced, applications also exist in process management, constraint management, shipping assignments, inventory control, and shift scheduling. The review problems at the end of this supplement and at the end of previous chapters illustrate many of these types of problems. Once the decision maker knows how to formulate a problem generally, he or she can then adapt it to the situation at hand.

INTERNET RESOURCES

my**om**lab and the Companion Website at **www.pearsonglobaleditions.com/krajewski** contain many tools, activities, and resources designed for this supplement.

SOLVED PROBLEM 1

Tutor E.4 in my**om**lab provides a practice example for finding the graphic and algebraic solution.

O'Connel Airlines is considering air service from its hub of operations in Cicely, Alaska, to Rome, Wisconsin, and Seattle, Washington. O'Connel has one gate at the Cicely Airport, which operates 12 hours per day. Each flight requires 1 hour of gate time. Each flight to Rome consumes 15 hours of pilot crew time and is expected to produce a profit of $2,500. Serving Seattle uses 10 hours of pilot crew time per flight and will result in a profit of $2,000 per flight. Pilot crew labor is limited to 150 hours per day. The market for service to Rome is limited to nine flights per day.

a. Use the graphic method of linear programming to maximize profits for O'Connel Airlines.

b. Identify positive slack and surplus variables, if any.

SOLUTION

a. The objective function is to maximize profits, Z:

$$\text{Maximize: } \$2,500x_1 + \$2,000x_2 = Z$$

where

x_1 = number of flights per day to Rome, Wisconsin
x_2 = number of flights per day to Seattle, Washington

The constraints are

$$x_1 + x_2 \leq 12 \text{ (gate capacity)}$$
$$15x_1 + 10x_2 \leq 150 \text{ (labor)}$$
$$x_1 \leq 9 \text{ (market)}$$
$$x_1 \geq 0 \text{ and } x_1 \geq 0$$

A careful drawing of iso-profit lines parallel to the one shown in Figure E.14 will indicate that point D is the optimal solution. It is at the intersection of the labor and gate capacity constraints. Solving algebraically, we get

$$15x_1 + 10x_2 = 150 \text{ (labor)}$$
$$-10x_1 - 10x_2 = -120 \text{ (gate} \times -10)$$
$$5x_1 + 0x_2 = 30$$
$$x_1 = 6$$
$$6 + x_2 = 12 \text{ (gate)}$$
$$x_2 = 6$$

The maximum profit results from making six flights to Rome and six flights to Seattle:

$$\$2,500(6) + \$2,000(6) = \$27,000$$

b. The market constraint has three units of slack, so the demand for flights to Rome is not fully met:

$$x_1 \leq 9$$
$$x_1 + s_3 = 9$$
$$6 + s_3 = 9$$
$$s_3 = 3$$

FIGURE E.14 ▼
Graphic Solution for O'Connel Airlines

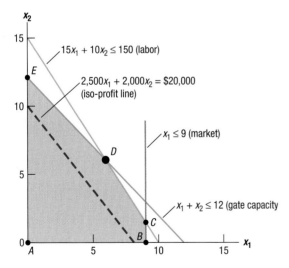

SOLVED PROBLEM 2

The Arctic Air Company produces residential air conditioners. The manufacturing manager wants to develop a sales and operations plan for the next year based on the following demand and capacity data (in hundreds of product units):

	Demand	Regular-time Capacity	Overtime Capacity	Subcontractor Capacity
Jan-Feb (1)	50	65	13	10
Mar-Apr (2)	60	65	13	10
May-Jun (3)	90	65	13	10
Jul-Aug (4)	120	80	16	10
Sep-Oct (5)	70	80	16	10
Nov-Dec (6)	40	65	13	10
Totals	430	420	84	60

Undertime is unpaid, and no cost is associated with unused overtime or subcontractor capacity. Producing one air conditioning unit on regular time costs $1,000, including $300 for labor. Producing a unit on overtime costs $1,150. A subcontractor can produce a unit to Arctic Air specifications for $1,250. Holding an air conditioner in stock costs $60 for each 2-month period, and 200 air conditioners are currently in stock. The plan calls for 400 units to be in stock at the end of period 6. No backorders are allowed. Use the transportation method to develop a plan that minimizes costs.

SOLUTION

The following tables identify the optimal production and inventory plans. Figure E.16 shows the tableau that corresponds to this solution. An arbitrarily large cost ($99,999 per period) was used for backorders, which effectively ruled them out. Again, all production quantities are in hundreds of units. Note that demand in period 6 is 4,400. That amount is the period 6 demand plus the desired ending inventory of 400. The anticipation inventory is measured as the amount at the end of each period. Cost calculations are based on the assumption that workers are not paid for undertime or are productively put to work elsewhere in the organization whenever they are not needed for this work.

One initially puzzling aspect of this solution is that it allocates the initial inventory of 200 units to meet demand in period 4 rather than in period 1. The explanation is that multiple optimal solutions exist and this solution is only one of them. However, all solutions result in the same production and anticipation inventory plans derived as follows:

	Production Plan			
Period	**Regular-time Production**	**Overtime Production**	**Subcontracting**	**Total**
1	6,500	—	—	6,500
2	6,500	400	—	6,900
3	6,500	1,300	—	7,800
4	8,000	1,600	1,000	10,600
5	7,000	—	—	7,000
6	4,400	—	—	4,400

Anticipation Inventory		
Period	Beginning Inventory Plus Total Production Minus Demand	Anticipation (Ending) Inventory
1	200 + 6,500 − 5,000	1,700
2	1,700 + 6,900 − 6,000	2,600
3	2,600 + 7,800 − 9,000	1,400
4	1,400 + 10,600 − 12,000	0
5	0 + 7,000 − 7,000	0
6	0 + 4,400 − 4,000	400

Alternatives		Time Period						Unused Capacity	Total Capacity
		1	2	3	4	5	6		
Period	Initial Inventory	0	60	120	180 [2]	240	300	0	2
1	Regular time	1,000 [50]	1,060 [15]	1,120	1,180	1,240	1,300	0	65
1	Overtime	1,150	1,210	1,270	1,330	1,390	1,450	13	13
1	Subcontract	1,250	1,310	1,370	1,430	1,490	1,550	10	10
2	Regular time	99,999	1,000 [41]	1,060 [12]	1,120 [12]	1,180	1,240	0	65
2	Overtime	99,999	1,150 [4]	1,210	1,270	1,330	1,390	9	13
2	Subcontract	99,999	1,250	1,310	1,370	1,430	1,490	10	10
3	Regular time	99,999	99,999	1,000 [65]	1,060	1,120	1,180	0	65
3	Overtime	99,999	99,999	1,150 [13]	1,210	1,270	1,330	0	13
3	Subcontract	99,999	99,999	1,250	1,310	1,370	1,430	10	10
4	Regular time	99,999	99,999	99,999	1,000 [80]	1,060	1,120	0	80
4	Overtime	99,999	99,999	99,999	1,150 [16]	1,210	1,270	0	16
4	Subcontract	99,999	99,999	99,999	1,250 [10]	1,310	1,370	0	10
5	Regular time	99,999	99,999	99,999	99,999	1,000 [70]	1,060	10	80
5	Overtime	99,999	99,999	99,999	99,999	1,150	1,210	16	16
5	Subcontract	99,999	99,999	99,999	99,999	1,250	1,310	10	10
6	Regular time	99,999	99,999	99,999	99,999	99,999	1,000 [44]	21	65
6	Overtime	99,999	99,999	99,999	99,999	99,999	1,150	13	13
6	Subcontract	99,999	99,999	99,999	99,999	99,999	1,250	10	10
	Demand	50	60	90	120	70	44	132	566

FIGURE E.16 ▲
Tableau for Optimal Production and Inventory Plans

SOLVED PROBLEM 3

The Arid Company makes canoe paddles to serve distribution centers in Worchester, Rochester, and Dorchester from existing plants in Battle Creek and Cherry Creek. Annual demand is expected to increase as projected in the bottom row of the tableau shown in Figure E.15. Arid is considering locating a plant near the headwaters of Dee Creek. Annual capacity for each plant is shown in the right-hand column of the tableau. Transportation costs per paddle are shown in the tableau in the small boxes. For example, the cost to ship one paddle from Battle Creak to Worchester is $4.37. The optimal allocations are also shown. For example, Battle Creek ships 12,000 units to Rochester. What are the estimated transportation costs associated with this allocation pattern?

Source	Destination			Capacity
	Worchester	Rochester	Dorchester	
Battle Creek	$4.37	$4.25	$4.89	12,000
		12,000		
Cherry Creek	$4.00	$5.00	$5.27	10,000
	6,000	4,000		
Dee Creek	$4.13	$4.50	$3.75	18,000
		6,000	12,000	
Demand	6,000	22,000	12,000	40,000

◀ FIGURE E.15
Optimal Solution for Arid Company

SOLUTION

Transportation Costs for Allocation Pattern	
The total cost is $167,000.	
Ship 12,000 units from Battle Creek to Rochester @ $4.25.	Cost = $51,000
Ship 6,000 units from Cherry Creek to Worchester @ $4.00.	Cost = $24,000
Ship 4,000 units from Cherry Creek to Rochester @ $5.00.	Cost = $20,000
Ship 6,000 units from Dee Creek to Rochester @ $4.50.	Cost = $27,000
Ship 12,000 units from Dee Creek to Dorchester @ $3.75.	Cost = $45,000
Total	$167,000

DISCUSSION QUESTIONS

1. A particular linear programming maximization problem has the following less-than-or-equal-to constraints: (1) raw materials, (2) labor hours, and (3) storage space. The optimal solution occurs at the intersection of the raw materials and labor hours constraints, so those constraints are binding. Management is considering whether to authorize overtime. What useful information could the linear programming solution provide to management in making this decision? Suppose a warehouse becomes available for rent at bargain rates. What would management need to know in order to decide whether to rent the warehouse? How could the linear programming model be helpful?

2. Linear programming and the transportation method promise optimal solutions. However, wise managers sometimes, after seeing the optimal results such as in Figures E.8, E.11, and E.13 might decide to implement different plans. How do you explain such decision making?

PROBLEMS

Software, such as OM Explorer, Active Models, and POM for Windows, is available in my**om**lab. Check with your instructor on how best to use it. For linear programming problems with more than two variables, and for transportation problems, use computer software to solve your model formulations. The emphasis in these cases is on modeling problems and interpreting computer output.

1. A business student at Nowledge College must complete a total of 65 courses to graduate. The number of business courses must be greater than or equal to 23. The number of nonbusiness courses must be greater than or equal to 20. The average business course requires a textbook costing $60 and 120 hours of study. Nonbusiness courses require a textbook costing $24 and 200 hours of study. The student has $3,000 to spend on books.

   a. Create a set of linear equations to describe the objective function and the constraints.

   b. Use graphic analysis to find the visual solution.

   c. What combination of business and nonbusiness courses minimizes total hours of study?

   d. Identify the slack or surplus variables.

2. In Problem 1, suppose that the objective is to minimize the cost of books and that the student's total study time is limited to 12,600 hours.

   a. Use graphic analysis to determine the combination of courses that minimizes the total cost of books.

   b. Identify the slack or surplus variables.

3. The Sports Shoe Company is a manufacturer of basketball and football shoes. The manager of marketing must decide the best way to spend advertising resources. Each football team sponsored requires 120 pairs of shoes. Each basketball team requires 32 pairs of shoes. Football coaches receive $300,000 for shoe sponsorship, and basketball coaches receive $1,000,000. The manager's promotional budget is $30,000,000. The company has a limited supply (4 liters or 4,000 cubic centimeters) of flubber, a rare and costly compound used in promotional athletic shoes. Each pair of basketball shoes requires 3 cc of flubber, and each pair of football shoes requires 1 cc. The manager wants to sponsor as many basketball and football teams as resources will allow.

   a. Create a set of linear equations to describe the objective function and the constraints.

   b. Use graphic analysis to find the visual solution.

   c. What is the maximum number of each type of team that the company can sponsor?

4. Mile-High Microbrewery makes a light beer and a dark beer. Mile-High has a limited supply of barley, limited bottling capacity, and a limited market for light beer. Profits are $0.20 per bottle of light beer and $0.50 per bottle of dark beer.

   a. The following table shows resource availability of products at the Mile-High Microbrewery. Use the graphic method of linear programming to maximize profits. How many bottles of each product should be produced per month?

Product			
Resource	Light Beer (X_1)	Dark Beer (X_2)	Resource Availability (per month)
Barley	0.1 gram	0.6 gram	2,000 grams
Bottling	1 bottle	1 bottle	6,000 bottles
Market	1 bottle	—	4,000 bottles

   b. Identify any constraints with slack or surplus.

5. A manufacturer of textile dyes can use two different processing routings for a particular type of dye. Routing 1 uses drying press A, and routing 2 uses drying press B. Both routings require the same mixing vat to blend chemicals for the dye before drying. The following table shows the time requirements and capacities of these processes:

Time Requirements (hr/100 ft)			
Process	Routing 1	Routing 2	Capacity (hr)
Melting	1	1	45
Extruder A	3	0	90
Extruder B	0	1	160

Each kilogram of dye processed on routing 1 uses 20 liters of chemicals, whereas each kilogram of dye processed on routing 2 uses only 15 liters. The difference results from differing yield rates of the drying presses. Consequently, the profit per kilogram processed on routing 1 is $50 and on routing 2 is $65. A total of 450 liters of input chemicals is available.

   a. Write the constraints and objective function to maximize profits.

   b. Use the graphic method of linear programming to find the optimal solution.

   c. Identify any constraints with slack or surplus.

6. The plant manager of a plastic pipe manufacturer has the opportunity to use two different routings for a particular type of plastic pipe. Routing 1 uses extruder A, and routing 2 uses extruder B. Both routings require the same melting process. The following table shows the time requirements and capacities of these processes:

Time Requirements (hr/kg)			
Process	Routing 1	Routing 2	Capacity (hr)
Mixing	2	2	54
Dryer A	6	0	120
Dryer B	0	8	180

Each 100 feet of pipe processed on routing 1 uses 5 pounds of raw material, whereas each 100 feet of pipe processed on routing 2 used only 4 pounds. This difference results from differing scrap rates of the extruding machines. Consequently, the profit per 100 feet of pipe processed on routing 1 is $60 and on routing 2 is $80. A total of 200 pounds of raw material is available.

a. Create a set of linear equations to describe the objective function and the constraints.

b. Use graphic analysis to find the visual solution.

c. What is the maximum profit?

7. The Trim-Look Company makes several lines of skirts, dresses, and sport coats. Recently, a consultant suggested that the company reevaluate its South Islander line and allocate its resources to products that would maximize contribution to profits and to overhead. Each product requires the same polyester fabric and must pass through the cutting and sewing departments. The following data were collected for the study:

Processing Time (hr)			
Product	Cutting	Sewing	Material (yd)
Skirt	1	1	1
Dress	3	4	1
Sport coat	4	6	4

The cutting department has 100 hours of capacity, sewing has 180 hours of capacity, and 60 yards of material are available. Each skirt contributes $5 to profits and overhead; each dress, $17; and each sport coat, $30.

a. Specify the objective function and constraints for this problem.

b. Use a computer package to solve the problem.

8. Consider Problem 7 further.

a. How much would you be willing to pay for an extra hour of cutting time? For an extra hour of sewing time? For an extra yard of material? Explain your response to each question.

b. Determine the range of right-hand-side values over which the shadow price would be valid for the cutting constraint and for the material constraint.

9. The Butterfield Company makes a variety of knives. Each knife is processed on four machines. The processing times required are as follows. Machine capacities (in

hours) are 1,500 for machine 1; 1,400 for machine 2; 1,600 for machine 3; and 1,500 for machine 4.

Processing Time (hr)				
Knife	Machine 1	Machine 2	Machine 3	Machine 4
A	0.05	0.10	0.15	0.05
B	0.15	0.10	0.05	0.05
C	0.20	0.05	0.10	0.20
D	0.15	0.10	0.10	0.10
E	0.05	0.10	0.10	0.05

Each product contains a different amount of two basic raw materials. Raw material 1 costs $0.50 per ounce, and raw material 2 costs $1.50 per ounce. There are 75,000 ounces of raw material 1 and 100,000 ounces of raw material 2 available.

Requirements (oz/unit)			
Knife	Raw Material 1	Raw Material 2	Selling Price ($/unit)
A	4	2	15.00
B	6	8	25.50
C	1	3	14.00
D	2	5	19.50
E	6	10	27.00

a. If the objective is to maximize profit, specify the objective function and constraints for the problem. Assume that labor costs are negligible.

b. Solve the problem with a computer package.

10. Polly Astaire makes fine clothing for big and tall men. A few years ago Astaire entered the sportswear market with the Sunset line of shorts, pants, and shirts. Management wants to make the amount of each product that will maximize profits. Each type of clothing is routed through two departments, A and B. The relevant data for each product are as follows:

Processing Time (hr)			
Product	Department A	Department B	Material (yd)
Shirts	2	1	2
Shorts	2	3	1
Pants	3	4	4

Department A has 120 hours of capacity, department B has 160 hours of capacity, and 90 yards of material are available. Each shirt contributes $10 to profits and overhead; each pair of shorts, $10; and each pair of pants, $23.

a. Specify the objective function and constraints for this problem.

b. Use a computer package to solve the problem.

c. How much should Astaire be willing to pay for an extra hour of department A capacity? How much for an extra hour of department B capacity? For what range of right-hand values are these shadow prices valid?

11. The Nutmeg Corporation produces four different products, each in a 1-pound can: Almond Pack, Walnut Pack, Gourmet Pack, and Thrifty Pack. Three types of nuts are used in Nutmeg's products: almonds, walnuts, and peanuts. Nutmeg currently has 100 pounds of almonds available, as well as 250 pounds of walnuts and 500 pounds of peanuts. Each of Nutmeg's four products must contain a certain percentage of each type of nut, as shown in the following table. The table also shows the revenue per can for each product. Use a computer package to answer the following questions.

   a. Given Nutmeg's current stock of nuts, how many cans of each product should be produced to maximize revenue?

Product	Requirements (%)			Revenue (per can)
	Almonds	Walnuts	Peanuts	
Almond Pack	100	—	—	$4.00
Walnut Pack	—	100	—	$3.00
Gourmet Pack	50	35	15	$2.40
Thrifty Pack	20	20	60	$1.75

   b. If only 80 pounds of almonds were available, how would the revenue-maximizing mix change from part a? Would revenues increase or decrease?

   c. If the Thrifty Pack was switched to 30% almonds, 30% walnuts, and 40% peanuts, how would the revenue-maximizing mix change from part (a)? Would revenues increase or decrease?

12. A small fabrication firm makes three basic types of components for use by other companies. Each component is processed on three machines. The processing times follow. Total capacities (in hours) are 1,600 for machine 1; 1,400 for machine 2; and 1,500 for machine 3.

	Processing Time (hr)		
Component	Machine 1	Machine 2	Machine 3
A	0.25	0.10	0.05
B	0.20	0.15	0.10
C	0.10	0.05	0.15

Each component contains a different amount of two basic raw materials. Raw material 1 costs $0.20 per ounce, and raw material 2 costs $0.35 per ounce. At present, 200,000 ounces of raw material 1 and 85,000 ounces of raw material 2 are available.

	Requirement (oz/unit)		
Component	Raw Material 1	Raw Material 2	Selling Price ($/unit)
A	32	12	40
B	26	16	28
C	19	9	24

   a. Assume that the company must make at least 1,200 units of component B, that labor costs are negligible, and that the objective is to maximize profits. Specify the objective function and constraints for the problem.

   b. Use a computer package to solve the problem.

13. A problem often of concern to managers in processing industries is blending. Consider the task facing Lisa Rankin, procurement manager of a company that manufactures special additives. She must determine the proper amount of each raw material to purchase for the production of a certain product. Each gallon of the finished product must have a combustion point of at least 220°F. In addition, the product's gamma content (which causes hydrocarbon pollution) cannot exceed 6 percent of volume, and the product's zeta content (which cleans the internal moving parts of engines) must be at least 12 percent by volume. Three raw materials are available. Each raw material has a different rating on these characteristics.

	Raw Material		
Characteristic	A	B	C
Combustion point (°F)	200	180	280
Gamma content (%)	4	3	10
Zeta content (%)	20	10	8

Raw material A costs $0.60 per gallon; raw materials B and C cost $0.40 and $0.50 per gallon, respectively. The procurement manager wants to minimize the cost of raw materials per gallon of product. Use linear programming to find the optimal proportion of each raw material for a gallon of finished product. (*Hint:* Express the decision variables in terms of fractions of a gallon; the sum of the fractions must equal 1.00.)

14. The following is a linear programming model for analyzing the product mix of Maxine's Hat Company, which produces three hat styles:

Maximize: $7x_1 + \$8x_2 + \$6x_3 = Z$

Subject to: $2x_1 + 4x_2 + 2x_3 \leq 120$ (machine A time)

$5x_1 + 3x_2 + 2x_3 \leq 400$ (machine B time)

$2x_1 + 2x_2 + 4x_3 \leq 110$ (machine C time)

$x_1 \geq 0 x_2 \geq 0$, and $x_3 \geq 0$

The POM for Windows printout in Figure E.17 shows the optimal solution to the problem. Consider each of the

(a) Results Screen

	X1	X2	X3		RHS	Shadow Price
Maximize	7	8	6			
Machine A	2	4	2	<=	120	.5
Machine B	5	3	2	<=	400	0
Machine C	2	2	4	<=	110	3
Solution->	50	5	0		390	

(b) Ranging Screen

Variable	Value	Reduced Cost	Original Val	Lower Bound	Upper Bound
X1	50	0	7	4.6667	8
X2	5	0	8	7	14
X3	0	7	6	-Infinity	13
Constraint	Shadow Price	Slack/Surplus	Original Val	Lower Bound	Upper Bound
Machine A	.5	0	120	110	220
Machine B	0	135	400	265	Infinity
Machine C	3	0	110	60	120

▲ **FIGURE E.17**
Solution Screens for Maxine's Hat Company

following statements independently, and state whether it is true or false. Explain each answer.

a. If the price of hat 3 were increased to $11.50, it would be part of the optimal product mix. *Hint*: Hat 3 is represented by x_3 and its optimal value currently is 0, which means that it is not to be produced (and not part of the optimal product mix).

b. The capacity of machine B can be reduced to 280 hours without affecting profits.

c. If machine C had a capacity of 115 hours, the production output would remain unchanged.

15. The Washington Chemical Company produces chemicals and solvents for the glue industry. The production process is divided into several "focused factories," each producing a specific set of products. The time has come to prepare the production plan for one of the focused factories. This particular factory produces five products, which must pass through both the reactor and the separator. Each

product also requires a certain combination of raw materials. Production data are shown in Table E.2.

The Washington Chemical Company has a long-term contract with a major glue manufacturer that requires annual production of 3,000 pounds of both products 3 and 4. More of these products could be produced because demand currently exceeds production capacity.

a. Determine the annual production quantity of each product that maximizes contribution to profits. Assume the company can sell all it can produce.

b. Specify the lot size for each product.

16. The Warwick Manufacturing Company produces shovels for industrial and home use. Sales of the shovels are seasonal, and Warwick's customers refuse to stockpile them during slack periods. In other words, the customers want to minimize inventory, insist on shipments according to their schedules, and will not accept backorders.

TABLE E.2	PRODUCTION DATA FOR WASHINGTON CHEMICAL					
	Product					
Resource	1	2	3	4	5	Total Resources Available
Reactor (hr/lb)	0.05	0.10	0.80	0.57	0.15	7,500 hr*
Separator (hr/lb)	0.20	0.02	0.20	0.09	0.30	7,500 hr*
Raw material 1 (lb)	0.20	0.50	0.10	0.40	0.18	10,000 lb
Raw material 2 (lb)	—	0.70	—	0.50	—	6,000 lb
Raw material 3 (lb)	0.10	0.20	0.40	—	—	7,000 lb
Profit contribution ($/lb)	4.00	7.00	3.50	4.00	5.70	

*The total time available has been adjusted to account for setups. The five products have a prescribed sequence owing to the cost of changeovers between products. The company has a 35-day cycle (or 10 changeovers per year per product). Consequently, the time for these changeovers has been deducted from the total time available for these machines.

Warwick employs manual, unskilled laborers who require only basic training. Producing 1,000 shovels costs $3,500 on regular time and $3,700 on overtime. These amounts include materials, which account for more than 85 percent of the cost. Overtime is limited to production of 15,000 shovels per quarter. In addition, subcontractors can be hired at $4,200 per thousand shovels, but Warwick's labor contract restricts this type of production to 5,000 shovels per quarter.

The current level of inventory is 30,000 shovels, and management wants to end the year at that level. Holding 1,000 shovels in inventory costs $280 per quarter. The latest annual demand forecast is as follows:

Quarter	Demand
1	70,000
2	150,000
3	320,000
4	100,000
Totals	640,000

Build a linear programming model to determine the *best* regular-time capacity plan. Assume the following:

- The firm has 30 workers now, and management wants to have the same number in quarter 4.

- Each worker can produce 4,000 shovels per quarter.

- Hiring a worker costs $1,000, and laying off a worker costs $600.

17. JPMorgan Chase has a scheduling problem. Operators work eight-hour shifts and can begin work at midnight, 4 A.M., 8 A.M., noon, 4 P.M., or 8 P.M. Operators are needed to satisfy the following demand pattern. Formulate a linear programming model to cover the demand requirements with the minimum number of operators.

Time Period	Operators Needed
Midnight to 4 A.M.	4
4 A.M. to 8 A.M.	6
8 A.M. to noon	90
Noon to 4 P.M.	85
4 P.M. to 8 P.M.	55
8 P.M. to 12 midnight	20

18. Insight Traders, Inc., invests in various types of securities. The firm has $5 million for immediate investment and wants to maximize the interest earned over the next year. Four investment possibilities are presented in the following table. To further structure the portfolio, the board of directors has

specified that at least 40 percent of the investment must be in corporate bonds and common stock. Furthermore, no more than 20 percent of the investment may be in real estate.

Investment	Expected Interest Earned (%)
Corporate bonds	8.5
Common stock	9.0
Gold certificates	10.0
Real estate	13.0

Write the objective function and constraints for this portfolio investment problem after fully defining the decision variables.

19. The Bull Grin Company produces a feed supplement for animal foods produced by a number of companies. Sales are seasonal, and Bull Grin's customers refuse to stockpile the supplement during slack sales periods. In other words, the customers want to minimize inventory, insist on shipments according to their schedules, and will not accept backorders.

Bull Grin employs manual, unskilled laborers who require little or no training. Producing 1,000 pounds of supplement costs $810 on regular time and $900 on overtime. These amounts include materials, which account for more than 80 percent of the cost. Overtime is limited to production of 30,000 pounds per quarter. In addition, subcontractors can be hired at $1,100 per thousand pounds, but only 10,000 pounds per quarter can be produced this way. Undertime is unpaid.

The current level of inventory is 40,000 pounds, and management wants to end the year at that level. Holding 1,000 pounds of feed supplement in inventory costs $110 per quarter. The latest annual forecast follows:

Quarter	Demand (lb)
1	100,000
2	410,000
3	770,000
4	440,000
Total	1,720,000

The firm currently has 180 workers, a number of whom management wants to keep in quarter 4. Each worker can produce 2,000 pounds per quarter, so regular-time production costs $1,620 per worker. Idle workers must be paid at that same rate. Hiring one worker costs $1,000, and laying off a worker costs $600.

Write the objective function and constraints describing this production planning problem after fully defining the decision variables.

20. The management of Warwick Manufacturing Company is willing to give price breaks to its customers as an incentive to purchase shovels in advance of the traditional seasons. Warwick's sales and marketing staff estimates that the demand for shovels resulting from the price breaks would be as follows:

Quarter	Demand	Original Demand
1	120,000	70,000
2	180,000	150,000
3	180,000	320,000
4	160,000	100,000
Totals	640,000	640,000

Calculate the optimal production plan (including the workforce staffing plan) under the new demand schedule. Compare it to the optimal production plan under the original demand schedule. Evaluate the potential effects of demand management.

21. The Pelican Company has four distribution centers (A, B, C, and D) that require 40,000, 60,000, 30,000, and 50,000 gallons of diesel fuel, respectively, per month for their long-haul trucks. Three fuel wholesalers (1, 2, and 3) indicated their willingness to supply as many as 50,000, 70,000, and 60,000 gallons of fuel, respectively. The total cost (shipping plus price) of delivering 1,000 gallons of fuel from each wholesaler to each distribution center is shown in the following table:

	Distribution Center			
Wholesaler	A	B	C	D
1	$1.30	$1.40	$1.80	$1.60
2	$1.30	$1.50	$1.80	$1.60
3	$1.60	$1.40	$1.70	$1.50

a. Determine the optimal solution. Show that all capacities have been exhausted and that all demands can be met with this solution.

b. What is the total cost of the solution?

22. Fire Brand makes picante sauce in El Paso and New York City. Distribution centers are located in Atlanta, Omaha, and Seattle. For the capacities, locations, and shipment costs per case shown in Figure E.18, determine the shipping pattern that will minimize transportation costs. What are the estimated transportation costs associated with this optimal allocation pattern?

Source	Destination			Capacity
	Atlanta	Omaha	Seattle	
El Paso	$4	$5	$6	12,000
New York City	$3	$7	$9	10,000
Demand	8,000	10,000	4,000	22,000

▲ **FIGURE E.18**
Transportation Tableau for Fire Brand

23. The Acme Company operates four factories that ship products to five warehouses. The shipping costs, requirements capacities, and optimal allocations are shown in Figure E.19. What is the total cost of the optimal solution?

Factory	Shipping Cost per Case to Warehouse					Capacity
	W1	W2	W3	W4	W5	
F1	$1 / 60,000	$3 / 20,000	$4	$5	$6	80,000
F2	$2	$2	$1 / 50,000	$4 / 10,000	$5	60,000
F3	$1	$5	$1	$3 / 20,000	$1 / 40,000	60,000
F4	$5	$2 / 50,000	$4	$5	$4	50,000
Demand	60,000	70,000	50,000	30,000	40,000	250,000

▲ **FIGURE E.19**
Optimal Solution for Acme Company

24. The Giant Farmer Company processes food for sale in discount food stores. It has two plants: one in Chicago and one in Houston. The company also operates warehouses in Miami, Florida; Denver, Colorado; Lincoln, Nebraska; and Jackson, Mississippi. Forecasts indicate that demand soon will exceed supply and that a new plant with a capacity of 8,000 cases per week is needed. The question is where to locate the new plant. Two potential sites are Buffalo, New York, and Atlanta. The two tables at the bottom of this page give data on capacities, forecasted demand, and shipping costs have been gathered.

For each alternative new plant location, determine the shipping pattern that will minimize total transportation costs. Where should the new plant be located?

Plant	Capacity (cases per week)	Warehouse	Demand (cases per week)
Chicago	10,000	Miami	7,000
Houston	7,500	Denver	9,000
New plant	8,000	Lincoln	4,500
Total	25,500	Jackson	5,000
		Total	25,500

	Shipping Cost to Warehouse (per case)			
Plant	**Miami**	**Denver**	**Lincoln**	**Jackson**
Chicago	$7.00	$2.00	$4.00	$5.00
Houston	$3.00	$1.00	$5.00	$2.00
Buffalo (alternative 1)	$6.00	$9.00	$7.00	$4.00
Atlanta (alternative 2)	$2.00	$10.00	$8.00	$3.00

25. The Ajax International Company operates four factories that ship products to five warehouses. The shipping costs, requirements, and capacities are shown in Figure E.20. Use the transportation method to find the shipping schedule that minimizes shipping cost.

26. Consider the facility location problem at the Giant Farmer Company described in Problem 24. Management is considering a third site, at Memphis. The shipping costs per case from Memphis are $3 to Miami, $11 to Denver, $6 to Lincoln, and $5 to Jackson. Find the minimum cost plan for an alternative plant in Memphis. Would this result change the decision in Problem 24?

27. Consider further the Ajax International Company situation described in Problem 25. Ajax decides to close F3 because of high operating costs. In addition, the company decides to add 50,000 units of capacity to F4. The logistics manager is worried about the effect of this move on transportation costs. Currently, F3 is shipping 30,000 units to W4 and 50,000 units to W5 at a cost of $140,000 [or 30,000(3) + 50,000(1)]. If these warehouses were to be served by F4, the cost would increase to $350,000 [or 30,000(5) + 50,000(4)]. As a result, the Ajax logistics manager requests a budget increase of $210,000 (or $350,000 – $140,000).

    a. Should the logistics manager get the budget increase?

    b. If not, how much would you budget for the increase in shipping costs?

28. The Chambers Corporation produces and markets an automotive theft-deterrent product, which it stocks in various warehouses throughout the country. Recently, its market research group compiled a forecast indicating that a significant increase in demand will occur in the near future, after which demand will level off for the foreseeable future. The company decides to satisfy this demand by constructing new plant capacity. Chambers already has plants in Baltimore and Milwaukee and has no desire to relocate those facilities. Each plant is capable of producing 600,000 units per year.

    After a thorough search, the company developed three site and capacity alternatives. Alternative 1 is to build a 600,000-unit plant in Portland. Alternative 2 is to build a 600,000-unit plant in San Antonio. Alternative 3 is to build a 300,000-unit plant in Portland and a 300,000-unit plant in San Antonio. The company's four warehouses distribute the product to retailers. The market research study provided the following data.

Factory	Shipping Cost per Case to Warehouse						Capacity
	W1	**W2**	**W3**	**W4**	**W5**	**Dummy**	
F1	$1	$3	$3	$5	$6	$0	50,000
F2	$2	$2	$1	$4	$5	$0	80,000
F3	$1	$5	$1	$3	$1	$0	80,000
F4	$5	$2	$4	$5	$4	$0	40,000
Demand	45,000	30,000	30,000	35,000	50,000	60,000	250,000

▲ FIGURE E.20
Transportation Tableau for Ajax International

Warehouse	Expected Annual Demand
Atlanta (AT)	500,000
Columbus (CO)	300,000
Los Angeles (LA)	600,000
Seattle (SE)	400,000

The logistics department compiled the following cost table specifying the cost per unit to ship the product from each plant to each warehouse in the most economical manner, subject to the reliability of the various carriers involved.

	Warehouse			
Plant	AT	CO	LA	SE
Baltimore	$0.35	$0.20	$0.85	$0.75
Milwaukee	$0.55	$0.15	$0.70	$0.65
Portland	$0.85	$0.60	$0.30	$0.10
San Antonio	$0.55	$0.40	$0.40	$0.55

As one part of the location decision, management wants an estimate of the total distribution cost for each alternative. Use the transportation method to calculate these estimates.

29. Revisit Problem 18 on the Bull Grin Company. Some cost and demand parameters have changed. Producing 1,000 pounds of supplement now costs $830 on regular time and $910 on overtime. No additional cost is incurred for unused regular time, overtime, or subcontractor capacity. Overtime is limited to production of a total of 20,000 pounds per quarter. In addition, subcontractors can be hired at $1,000 per thousand pounds, but only 30,000 pounds per quarter can be produced this way.

The current level of inventory is 40,000 pounds, and management wants to end the year at that level. Holding 1,000 pounds of feed supplement in inventory per quarter costs $100. The latest annual forecast is shown in Table E.3.

Use the transportation method of production planning to find the optimal production plan and calculate its cost, or use the spreadsheet approach to find a good production plan and calculate its cost.

30. The Holloway Calendar Company produces a variety of printed calendars for both commercial and private use. The demand for calendars is highly seasonal, peaking in the third quarter. Current inventory is 165,000 calendars, and ending inventory should be 200,000 calendars.

Ann Ritter, Holloway's manufacturing manager, wants to determine the best production plan for the demand requirements and capacity plan shown in the following table. (Here, demand and capacities are expressed as thousands of calendars rather than as employee-period equivalents.) Ritter knows that the regular-time cost is $0.50 per unit, overtime cost is $0.75 per unit, subcontracting cost is $0.90 per unit, and inventory holding cost is $0.10 per calendar per quarter. Unused regular-time capacity is not paid.

	Quarter				
	1	2	3	4	Total
Demand	250	515	1,200	325	2,290
Capacities					
Regular time	300	300	600	300	1,500
Overtime	75	75	150	75	375
Subcontracting	150	150	150	150	600

a. Recommend a production plan to Ritter, using the Transportation Method (Production Planning) module of POM for Windows. (Do not allow any stockouts or backorders to occur.)

b. Interpret and explain your recommendation.

c. Calculate the total cost of your recommended production plan.

31. The Cut Rite Company is a major producer of industrial lawn mowers. The cost to Cut Rite for hiring a semiskilled worker for its assembly plant is $3,000, and the cost for

TABLE E.3	FORECASTS AND CAPACITIES				
	Period				
	Quarter 1	Quarter 2	Quarter 3	Quarter 4	Total
Demand (pounds)	130,000	400,000	800,000	470,000	1,800,000
Capacities (pounds)					
Regular time	390,000	400,000	460,000	380,000	1,630,000
Overtime	20,000	20,000	20,000	20,000	80,000
Subcontract	30,000	30,000	30,000	30,000	30,000

laying off one is $2,000. The plant averages an output of 36,000 mowers per quarter with its current workforce of 720 employees. Regular-time capacity is directly proportional to the number of employees. Overtime is limited to a maximum of 3,000 mowers per quarter, and subcontracting is limited to 1,000 mowers per quarter. The costs to produce one mower are $2,430 on regular time (including materials), $2,700 on overtime, and $3,300 via subcontracting. Unused regular-time capacity costs $270 per mower. No additional cost is incurred for unused overtime or subcontractor capacity. The current level of inventory is 4,000 mowers, and management wants to end the year at that level. Customers do not tolerate backorders, and holding a mower in inventory per quarter costs $300. The demand for mowers this coming year is as follows:

Quarter	1	2	3	4
Demand	10,000	41,000	77,000	44,000

Two workforce plans have been proposed, and management is uncertain as to which one to use. The following table shows the number of employees per quarter under each plan:

Quarter	1	2	3	4
Plan 1	720	780	920	720
Plan 2	860	860	860	860

a. Which plan would you recommend to management? Explain, supporting your recommendation with an analysis using the transportation method of production planning.

b. If management used creative pricing to get customers to buy mowers in nontraditional time periods, the following demand schedule would result:

Quarter	1	2	3	4
Demand	20,000	54,000	54,000	44,000

Which workforce plan would you recommend now?

CASE   R.U. Reddie for Location

The R.U. Reddie Corporation, located in Chicago, manufactures clothing specially designed for stuffed cartoon animals such as Snoopy and Wile E. Coyote. Among the popular products are a wedding tuxedo for Snoopy and a flak jacket for Wile E. Coyote. The latter is capable of stopping an Acme rocket at close range . . . sometimes.

For many sales, the company relies upon the help of spoiled children who refuse to leave the toy store until their parents purchase a wardrobe for their stuffed toys. Rhonda Ulysses Reddie, owner of the company, is concerned over the market projections that indicate demand for the product is substantially greater than current plant capacity. The "most likely" projections indicate that the company will be short by 400,000 units next year, and thereafter 700,000 units annually. As such, Rhonda is considering opening a new plant to produce additional units.

Background

The R.U. Reddie Corporation currently has three plants located in Boston, Cleveland, and Chicago, respectively. The company's first plant was the Chicago plant, but as sales grew in the Midwest and Northeast, the Cleveland and Boston plants were built in short order. As the demand for wardrobes for stuffed animals moved west, warehouse centers were opened in St. Louis and Denver. The capacities of the three plants were increased to accommodate the demand. Each plant has its own warehouse to satisfy demands in its own area. Extra capacity was used to ship the product to St. Louis or Denver.

The new long-term forecasts provided by the sales department contain both good news and bad news. The added revenues will certainly help Rhonda's profitability, but the company would have to buy another plant to realize the added profits. Space is not available at the existing plants, and the benefits of the new technology for manufacturing stuffed animal wardrobes are tantalizing. These factors motivate the search for the best location for a new plant. Rhonda identifies Denver and St. Louis as possible locations for the new plant.

Rhonda's Concerns

A plant addition is a big decision. Rhonda has started to think about the accuracy of the data she was able to obtain. She has market, financial, and operations concerns.

Market

The projected demands for years 2 through 10 show an annual increase of 700,000 units to a total of 2,000,000 units for each year. Rhonda has two concerns here. First, what if the projections for each city are off plus or minus 10 percent equally across the board? That is, total annual demands could be as low as 1,800,000 or as high as 2,200,000, with each city being affected the same as the others. Second, the marketing manager has expressed a concern over a possible market shift from the Midwest and Northeast to the West. Under this scenario, additional demand would reach 50,000 units in St. Louis and 150,000 units in Denver, with the other cities staying at the "most likely" demand projections.

Financial

Rhonda has realized that the net present value (NPV) of each alternative is an important input to the final decision. However, the accuracy of the estimates for the various costs is critical to determining good estimates of cash flows. She wonders whether her decision will change if the COGS (variable production plus transportation costs) for each option are off by ±10 percent. That is, what if the variable production costs and transportation costs of St. Louis are 10 percent higher than estimated while the variable production costs and transportation costs for Denver are 10 percent lower than estimated? Or vice versa? Furthermore, what if the estimate for fixed costs are off by ±10 percent? For example, suppose St. Louis is 10 percent higher while

Denver is 10 percent lower, or vice versa. Would the recommendation change under any of these situations?

Operations

The ultimate location of the new plant will determine the distribution assignments and the level of utilization of each plant in the network. Cutting back production in any of the plants will change the distribution assignments of all plants. Because the "most likely" demand projections with a new plant will mean excess capacity in the system, the capacity of the Cleveland plant could be cut in year 2 and beyond. Suppose Cleveland cuts back production by 50(000) units a year from year 2 and beyond. Will this action affect the choice between Denver and St. Louis? What is the impact on the distribution assignments of the plant? Some nonquantifiable concerns also need consideration. First, the availability of a good workforce is much better in Denver than St. Louis because of the recent shutdown of a Beanie Baby factory. The labor market is much tighter in St. Louis and the prognosis is for continued short supply in the foreseeable future. Second, the Denver metropolitan area just instituted strict environmental regulations. Rhonda's new plant would adhere to existing laws, but the area is highly environmentally conscious and more regulations may be coming in the future. It is costly to modify a plant once operations begin. Finally, Denver has a number of good suppliers with the capability to assist in production design (new wardrobe fashions). St. Louis also has suppliers, but they cannot help with product development. Proximity to suppliers with product development capability is a "plus" for this industry.

Data

The following data have been gathered for Rhonda:

1. The per-unit shipping cost based on the average tonmile rates for the most efficient carriers is $0.0005 per mile. The average revenue per outfit is $8.00.
2. The company currently has the following capacity (in thousands) constraints:

	Capacity
Boston	400
Cleveland	400
Chicago	500

3. Data concerning the various locations are found in Table E.4.
4. New plant information:

Alternative	Building and Equipment[1]	Annual Fixed Costs (SGA)[1,3]	Variable Production Costs/Unit	Land[1]
Denver	$12,100	$550	$3.15	$1,200
St. Louis	10,800	750	3.05	800

[1] Figures are given in thousands.
[2] Net book value of plant and equipment with remaining depreciable life of 10 years.
[3] Annual fixed costs do not include depreciation on plant and equipment.

5. The road mileage between the cities is as follows:

	Boston	Cleveland	Chicago	St. Louis	Denver
Boston	—	650	1,000	1,200	2,000
Cleveland		—	350	600	1,400
Chicago			—	300	1,000
St. Louis				—	850
Denver					—

6. Basic assumptions you should follow:

- Terminal value (in 10 years) of the new investment is 50 percent of plant, equipment, and land cost.
- The tax rate is 40 percent.
- Straight-line depreciation is used for all assets over a 10-year life.
- R.U. Reddie is a 100 percent equity company with all equity financing and a weighted average cost of capital (WACC) of 11 percent.
- Capacity of the new plant production for the first year will be 500 (000) units.
- Capacity of the new plant production thereafter will be 900 (000) units.
- Cost of goods sold (COGS) equals variable costs of production plus total transportation costs.
- Costs to ship from a plant to its own warehouse are zero; however, production costs are applicable.

TABLE E.4	LOCATION DATA FOR R.U. REDDIE					
City	Most Likely Demand First Year[1]	Most Likely Demand After Years 2–10[1]	Current Costs, Building and Equipment[1,2]	Annual Fixed Costs (SGA)[1,3]	Variable Production Costs/Unit	Land[1]
Boston	80	140	$9,500	$600	$3.80	$500
Cleveland	200	260	7,700	300	3.00	400
Chicago	370	430	8,600	400	3.25	600
St. Louis	440	500				
Denver	610	670				

[1] Figures are given in thousands.

[2] Net book value of plant and equipment with remaining depreciable life of 10 years.

[3] Annual fixed costs do not include depreciation on plant and equipment.

7. R. U. Reddie operations and logistics managers determined the shipping plan and cost of goods sold for the option of *not* building a new plant and simply using the existing capacities to their fullest extent (status quo solution).

Year 1	COGS = $4,692,000
Boston to Boston	80
Boston to St. Louis	320
Cleveland to Chicago	80
Cleveland to Cleveland	200
Cleveland to St. Louis	120
Chicago to Chicago	290
Chicago to Denver	210
Years 2-10	**COGS = $4,554,000**
Boston to Boston	140
Boston to St. Louis	260
Cleveland to Cleveland	260
Cleveland to St. Louis	140
Chicago to Chicago	430
Chicago to St. Louis	70

QUESTIONS

Your team has been asked to determine whether R.U. Reddie should build a new plant and, if so, where it should be located. Your report should consist of six parts.

1. Write a memo from your team to R.U. Reddie indicating your recommendation and a brief overview of the supporting evidence.

2. Model the location decision as a linear programming problem. The objective function should be to minimize the total variable costs (production plus transportation costs). The variables should be the quantity to ship from each of the plants (including one of the alternative new plants) to each of the warehouses. You should have 20 variables (four plants

and five warehouses). You should also have nine constraints (four plant capacity constraints and five warehouse demand constraints). See the addendum for hints. You will need two models—one for Denver and one for St. Louis.

3. Use a software package for linear programming, such as with POM for Windows, to solve for the optimal distribution plan for each alternative (i.e., Denver and St. Louis). A linear programming model is preferable for this case because of the sensitivity analysis information that it provides.

4. Compute the NPV of each alternative. Use the results from the linear models for the COGS for each alternative. (*Hint:* Your analysis will be simplified if you think in terms of incremental cash flows.) Create an easy-to-read spreadsheet for each alternative.

5. Do a sensitivity analysis of the quantitative factors mentioned in the case: Forecast errors (across the board and market shift), errors in COGS estimate, and errors in fixed cost estimates. Do each factor independent of the others and use the "most likely" projections as the base case. Summarize the results in one table.

6. Use the analysis in question 5 to identify the key quantitative variables that determine the superiority of one alternative over another. Rationalize your final recommendation in light of all the considerations R.U. Reddie must make.

ADDENDUM

Here are some hints for your model.

1. The capacity constraint for Boston would look like this:

   1B-B + 1B-CL + 1B-CH + 1B-D + 1B-SL ≤ 400

   The variable B-CH means Boston to Chicago in this example. You will need a total of four capacity constraints, one for each of the existing sites and one for the alternative site you are evaluating. Remember that the new site will have a capacity limit of 500 in the first year, and 900 in the second year.

2. The demand constraint for Boston would look like this:

   1B-B + 1CL-B + 1CH-B + 1D-B = 140

   The Denver location alternative is depicted in this example (D-B represents the number of units produced in Denver and shipped to Boston). You will need a total of five demand constraints, one for each warehouse location. Notice that the demand constraints have equal signs to indicate that exactly that quantity must be received at each warehouse.

3. Define your variables to be "thousands of units shipped," and omit the three zeros after each demand and capacity value. Then remember to multiply your final decisions and total variable costs by a thousand after you get your solution from the model.

4. Because the capacity and demand changes from year 1 to year 2, you need to run your model twice for each location to get the necessary data. You will also run the model and spread-sheets multiple times for question 5 of the report.

SELECTED REFERENCES

Anderson, D.R., D.J. Sweeney, and T.A. Williams. *An Introduction to Management Science*, 10th ed. Cincinnati: South-Western, 2000.

Asim, R., E. De Falomir, and L. Lasdon. "An Optimization-Based Decision Support System for a Product-Mix Problem." *Interfaces*, vol. 12, no. 2 (1982), pp. 26–33.

Bonini, Charles P., Warren H. Hausman, and Harold Bierman, Jr. *Quantitative Analysis for Management*, 9th ed. Chicago: Irwin, 1997.

Eppen, G. D., F. J. Gould, C. P. Schmidt, Jeffrey H. Moore, and Larry R. Weatherford. *Introductory Management Science: Decision Modeling with Spreadsheets*, 5th ed. Upper Saddle River, NJ: Prentice Hall, 1998.

Fourer, Robert. "Software Survey: Linear Programming." *OR/MS Today* (April 1997), pp. 54–63.

Greenberg, H. J. "How to Analyze the Results of Linear Programs—Part 2: Price Interpretation." *Interfaces*, vol. 23, no. 5 (1993), pp. 97–114.

Hillier, Fredrick, S., Mark S. Hillier, and Gerald Lieberman. *Introduction to Management Science*. Burr Ridge, IL: Irwin/McGraw-Hill, 2000.

Hess, Rick. *Managerial Spreadsheet Modeling and Analysis*. Chicago: Irwin, 1997.

Jayaraman, V., R. Srivastava, and W. C. Benton. "Supplier Selection and Order Quantity Allocation." *Journal of Supply Chain Management*, vol. 35, no. 2 (1999), pp. 50–58.

Love, Robert F., James G. Morris, and George O. Weslowsky. *Facilities Location: Models and Methods*. New York: North-Holland, 1988.

Perry, C., and K. C. Crellin. "The Precise Management Meaning of a Shadow Price." *Interfaces*, vol. 12, no. 2 (1982), pp. 61–63.

Ragsdale, Cliff T., and Rick Hess. *Spreadsheet Modeling and Decision Analysis; A Practical Introduction to Management Science*, 2d ed. Cincinnati, OH: South-Western, 1998.

Render, B., R.M. Stair, and Michael Hanna. *Quantitative Analysis for Management*, 8th ed. Upper Saddle River, NJ: Prentice Hall, 2003.

Verma, Rohit. "My Operations Management Students Love Linear Programming." *Decision Line* (July 1997), pp. 9–12.

Winston, Wayne L., S. Christian Albright, and Mark Broadie. *Practical Management Science*. 3rd ed., Belmont, CA: Duxbury Press, 1996.

APPENDIX 1 NORMAL DISTRIBUTION

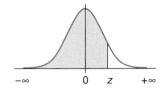

	.00	.01	.02	.03	.04	.05	.06	.07	.08	.09
.0	.5000	.5040	.5080	.5120	.5160	.5199	.5239	.5279	.5319	.5359
.1	.5398	.5438	.5478	.5517	.5557	.5596	.5636	.5675	.5714	.5753
.2	.5793	.5832	.5871	.5910	.5948	.5987	.6026	.6064	.6103	.6141
.3	.6179	.6217	.6255	.6293	.6331	.6368	.6406	.6443	.6480	.6517
.4	.6554	.6591	.6628	.6664	.6700	.6736	.6772	.6808	.6844	.6879
.5	.6915	.6950	.6985	.7019	.7054	.7088	.7123	.7157	.7190	.7224
.6	.7257	.7291	.7324	.7357	.7389	.7422	.7454	.7486	.7517	.7549
.7	.7580	.7611	.7642	.7673	.7704	.7734	.7764	.7794	.7823	.7852
.8	.7881	.7910	.7939	.7967	.7995	.8023	.8051	.8078	.8106	.8133
.9	.8159	.8186	.8212	.8238	.8264	.8289	.8315	.8340	.8365	.8389
1.0	.8413	.8438	.8461	.8485	.8508	.8531	.8554	.8577	.8599	.8621
1.1	.8643	.8665	.8686	.8708	.8729	.8749	.8770	.8790	.8810	.8830
1.2	.8849	.8869	.8888	.8907	.8925	.8944	.8962	.8980	.8997	.9015
1.3	.9032	.9049	.9066	.9082	.9099	.9115	.9131	.9147	.9162	.9177
1.4	.9192	.9207	.9222	.9236	.9251	.9265	.9279	.9292	.9306	.9319
1.5	.9332	.9345	.9357	.9370	.9382	.9394	.9406	.9418	.9429	.9441
1.6	.9452	.9463	.9474	.9484	.9495	.9505	.9515	.9525	.9535	.9545
1.7	.9554	.9564	.9573	.9582	.9591	.9599	.9608	.9616	.9625	.9633
1.8	.9641	.9649	.9656	.9664	.9671	.9678	.9686	.9693	.9699	.9706
1.9	.9713	.9719	.9726	.9732	.9738	.9744	.9750	.9756	.9761	.9767
2.0	.9772	.9778	.9783	.9788	.9793	.9798	.9803	.9808	.9812	.9817
2.1	.9821	.9826	.9830	.9834	.9838	.9842	.9846	.9850	.9854	.9857
2.2	.9861	.9864	.9868	.9871	.9875	.9878	.9881	.9884	.9887	.9890
2.3	.9893	.9896	.9898	.9901	.9904	.9906	.9909	.9911	.9913	.9916
2.4	.9918	.9920	.9922	.9925	.9927	.9929	.9931	.9932	.9934	.9936
2.5	.9938	.9940	.9941	.9943	.9945	.9946	.9948	.9949	.9951	.9952
2.6	.9953	.9955	.9956	.9957	.9959	.9960	.9961	.9962	.9963	.9964
2.7	.9965	.9966	.9967	.9968	.9969	.9970	.9971	.9972	.9973	.9974
2.8	.9974	.9975	.9976	.9977	.9977	.9978	.9979	.9979	.9980	.9981
2.9	.9981	.9982	.9982	.9983	.9984	.9984	.9985	.9985	.9986	.9986
3.0	.9987	.9987	.9987	.9988	.9988	.9989	.9989	.9989	.9990	.9990
3.1	.9990	.9991	.9991	.9991	.9992	.9992	.9992	.9992	.9993	.9993
3.2	.9993	.9993	.9994	.9994	.9994	.9994	.9994	.9995	.9995	.9995
3.3	.9995	.9995	.9995	.9996	.9996	.9996	.9996	.9996	.9996	.9997
3.4	.9997	.9997	.9997	.9997	.9997	.9997	.9997	.9997	.9997	.9998

APPENDIX 2 TABLE OF RANDOM NUMBERS

71509	68310	48213	99928	64650	13229	36921	58732	13459	93487
21949	30920	23287	89514	58502	46185	00368	82613	02668	37444
50639	54968	11409	36148	82090	87298	41396	71111	00076	60029
47837	76716	09653	54466	87987	82362	17933	52793	17641	19502
31735	36901	92295	19293	57582	86043	69502	12601	00535	82697
04174	32342	66532	07875	54445	08795	63563	42295	74646	73120
96980	68728	21154	56181	71843	66134	52396	89723	96435	17871
21823	04027	76402	04655	87276	32593	17097	06913	05136	05115
25922	07122	31485	52166	07645	85122	20945	06369	70254	22806
32530	98882	19105	01769	20276	59401	60426	03316	41438	22012
00159	08461	51810	14650	45119	97920	08063	70819	01832	53295
66574	21384	75357	55888	83429	96916	73977	87883	13249	28870
00995	28829	15048	49573	65277	61493	44031	88719	73057	66010
55114	79226	27929	23392	06432	50200	39054	15528	53483	33972
10614	25190	52647	62580	51183	31338	60008	66595	64357	14985
31359	77469	58126	59192	23371	25190	37841	44386	92420	42965
09736	51873	94595	61367	82091	63835	86858	10677	58209	59820
24709	23224	45788	21426	63353	29874	51058	29958	61220	61199
79957	67598	74102	49824	39305	15069	56327	26905	34453	53964
66616	22137	72805	64420	58711	68435	60301	28620	91919	96080
01413	27281	19397	36231	05010	42003	99865	20924	76151	54089
88238	80731	20777	45725	41480	48277	45704	96457	13918	52375
57457	87883	64273	26236	61095	01309	48632	00431	63730	18917
21614	06412	71007	20255	39890	75336	89451	88091	61011	38072
26466	03735	39891	26361	86816	48193	33492	70484	77322	01016
97314	03944	04509	46143	88908	55261	73433	62538	63187	57352
91207	33555	75942	41668	64650	38741	86189	38197	99112	59694
46791	78974	01999	78891	16177	95746	78076	75001	51309	18791
34161	32258	05345	79267	75607	29916	37005	09213	10991	50451
02376	40372	45077	73705	56076	01853	83512	81567	55951	27156
33994	56809	58377	45976	01581	78389	18268	90057	93382	28494
92588	92024	15048	87841	38008	80689	73098	39201	10907	88092
73767	61534	66197	47147	22994	38197	60844	86962	27595	49907
51517	39870	94094	77092	94595	37904	27553	02229	44993	10468
33910	05156	60844	89012	21154	68937	96477	05867	95809	72827
09444	93069	61764	99301	55826	78849	26131	28201	91417	98172
96896	43769	72890	78682	78243	24061	55449	53587	77574	51580
97523	54633	99656	08503	52563	12099	52479	74374	79581	57143
42568	30794	32613	21802	73809	60237	70087	36650	54487	43718
45453	33136	90246	61953	17724	42421	87611	95369	42108	95369
52814	26445	73516	24897	90622	35018	70087	60112	09025	05324
87318	33345	14546	15445	81588	75461	12246	47858	08983	18205
08063	83575	26294	93027	09988	04487	88364	31087	22200	91019
53400	82078	52103	25650	75315	18916	06809	88217	12245	33053
90789	60614	20862	34475	11744	24437	55198	55219	74730	59820
73684	25859	86858	48946	30941	79017	53776	72534	83638	44680
82007	12183	89326	53713	77782	50368	01748	39033	47042	65758
80208	30920	97774	41417	79038	60531	32990	57770	53441	58732
62434	96122	63019	58439	89702	38657	60049	88761	22785	66093
04718	83199	65863	58857	49886	70275	27511	99426	53985	84077

GLOSSARY

ABC analysis The process of dividing SKUs into three classes, according to their dollar usage, so that managers can focus on items that have the highest dollar value.

acceptable quality level (AQL) The quality level desired by the consumer.

acceptance sampling The application of statistical techniques to determine whether a quantity of material should be accepted or rejected based on the inspection or test of a sample.

action notice A computer-generated memo alerting planners about releasing new orders and adjusting the due dates of scheduled receipts.

activity The smallest unit of work effort consuming both time and resources that the project manager can schedule and control.

activity-on-node (AON) network An approach used to create a network diagram, in which nodes represent activities and arcs represent the precedence relationships between them.

activity slack The maximum length of time that an activity can be delayed without delaying the entire project, calculated as $S = LS - ES$ or $S = LF - EF$.

additive seasonal method A method in which seasonal forecasts are generated by adding a constant to the estimate of average demand per season.

advanced planning and scheduling (APS) systems Computer software systems that seek to optimize resources across the supply chain and align daily operations with strategic goals.

aggregation The act of clustering several similar services or products so that forecasts and plans can be made for whole families.

allowance time The time added to the normal time to adjust for certain factors.

annual plan or financial plan A plan for financial assessment used by a nonprofit service organization.

annuity A series of payments on a fixed amount for a specified number of years.

anticipation inventory Inventory used to absorb uneven rates of demand or supply.

appraisal costs Costs incurred when the firm assess the performance level of its processes.

assemble-to-order strategy A strategy for producing a wide variety of products from relatively few subassemblies and components after the customer orders are received.

assignable causes of variation Any variation-causing factors that can be identified and eliminated.

attributes Service or product characteristics that can be quickly counted for acceptable performance.

auction A marketplace where firms place competitive bids to buy something.

automation A system, process, or piece of equipment that is self-acting and self-regulating.

available-to-promise (ATP) inventory The quantity of end items that marketing can promise to deliver on specified dates.

average aggregate inventory value The total average value of all items held in inventory for a firm.

average outgoing quality (AOQ) The expressed proportion of defects that the plan will allow to pass.

average outgoing quality limit (AOQL) The maximum value of the average outgoing quality over all possible values of the proportion defective.

back office A process with low customer contact and little service customization.

backlog An accumulation of customer orders that a manufacturer has promised for delivery at some future date.

backorder A customer order that cannot be filled when promised or demanded but is filled later.

backward integration A firm's movement upstream toward the sources of raw materials, parts, and services through acquisitions.

balance delay The amount by which efficiency falls short of 100 percent.

bar chart A series of bars representing the frequency of occurrence of data characteristics measured on a yes-or-no basis.

base case The act of doing nothing and losing orders from any demand that exceeds current capacity, or incur costs because capacity is too large.

base-stock system An inventory control system that issues a replenishment order, Q, each time a withdrawal is made, for the same amount of the withdrawal.

batch process A process that differs from the job process with respect to volume, variety, and quantity.

benchmarking A systematic procedure that measures a firm's processes, services, and products against those of industry leaders.

bill of materials (BOM) A record of all the components of an item, the parent–component relationships, and the usage quantities derived from engineering and process designs.

bill of resources (BOR) A record of a service firm's parent–component relationships and all of the materials, equipment time, staff, and other resources associated with them, including usage quantities.

binding constraint A constraint that helps form the optimal corner point; it limits the ability to improve the objective function.

Black Belt An employee who reached the highest level of training in a Six Sigma program and spends all of his or her time teaching and leading teams involved in Six Sigma projects.

block plan A plan that allocates space and indicates placement of each operation.

bottleneck A capacity constraint resource (CCR) whose available capacity limits the organization's ability to meet the product volume, product mix, or demand fluctuation required by the marketplace.

brainstorming Letting a group of people, knowledgeable about the process, propose ideas for change by saying whatever comes to mind.

break-even analysis The use of the break-even quantity; it can be used to compare processes by finding the volume at which two different processes have equal total costs.

break-even quantity The volume at which total revenues equal total costs.

bullwhip effect The phenomenon in supply chains whereby ordering patterns experience increasing variance as you proceed upstream in the chain.

business plan A projected statement of income, costs, and profits.

c-chart A chart used for controlling the number of defects when more than one defect can be present in a service or product.

capacity The maximum rate of output of a process or a system.

capacity cushion The amount of reserve capacity a process uses to handle sudden increases in demand or temporary losses of production capacity; it measures the amount by which the average utilization (in terms of total capacity) falls below 100 percent.

capacity gap Positive or negative difference between projected demand and current capacity.

capacity requirement What a process's capacity should be for some future time period to meet the demand of customers (external or internal), given the firm's desired capacity cushion.

capacity requirements planning (CRP) A technique used for projecting time-phased capacity requirements for workstations; its purpose is to match the material requirements plan with the capacity of key processes.

capital intensity The mix of equipment and human skills in a process.

cash flow The difference between the flows of funds into and out of an organization over a period of time, including revenues, costs, and changes in assets and liabilities.

catalog hubs A system whereby suppliers post their catalog of items on the Internet and buyers select what they need and purchase them electronically.

causal methods A quantitative forecasting method that uses historical data on independent variables, such as promotional campaigns, economic conditions, and competitors' actions, to predict demand.

cause-and-effect diagram A diagram that relates a key performance problem to its potential causes.

center of gravity A good starting point to evaluate locations in the target area using the load–distance model.

centralized placement Keeping all the inventory of a product at a single location such as a firm's manufacturing plant or a warehouse and shipping directly to each of its customers.

certainty The word that is used to describe that a fact is known without doubt.

channel One or more facilities required to perform a given service.

channel assembly The process of using members of the distribution channel as if they were assembly stations in the factory.

chase strategy A strategy that involves hiring and laying off employees to match the demand forecast.

checklist A form used to record the frequency of occurrence of certain process failures.

close out An activity that includes writing final reports, completing remaining deliverables, and compiling the team's recommendations for improving the project process.

closeness matrix A table that gives a measure of the relative importance of each pair of operations being located close together.

collaborative planning, forecasting, and replenishment (CPFR) A nine-step process for supply chain integration that allows a supplier and its customers to collaborate on making the forecast by using the Internet.

combination forecasts Forecasts that are produced by averaging independent forecasts based on different methods or different data or both.

common causes of variation The purely random, unidentifiable sources of variation that are unavoidable with the current process.

competitive capabilities The cost, quality, time, and flexibility dimensions that a process or supply chain actually possesses and is able to deliver.

competitive orientation A supplier relation that views negotiations between buyer and seller as a zero-sum game: Whatever one side loses, the other side gains, and short-term advantages are prized over long-term commitments.

competitive priorities The critical dimensions that a process or supply chain must possess to satisfy its internal or external customers, both now and in the future.

complementary products Services or products that have similar resource requirements but different demand cycles.

component An item that goes through one or more operations to be transformed into or become part of one or more parents.

compounding interest The process by which interest on an investment accumulates and then earns interest itself for the remainder of the investment period.

concurrent engineering A concept that brings product engineers, process engineers, marketers, buyers, information specialists, quality specialists, and suppliers together to design a product and the processes that will meet customer expectations.

constraint Any factor that limits the performance of a system and restricts its output. In linear programming, a limitation that restricts the permissible choices for the decision variables.

consumer's risk (β) The probability of accepting a lot *with* LTPD quality (a type II error).

continuous-flow process The extreme end of high-volume standardized production and rigid line flows, with production not starting and stopping for long time intervals.

continuous improvement The philosophy of continually seeking ways to improve processes based on a Japanese concept called *kaizen*.

continuous review (Q) system A system designed to track the remaining inventory of a SKU each time a withdrawal is made to determine whether it is time to reorder.

control chart A time-ordered diagram that is used to determine whether observed variations are abnormal.

cooperative orientation A supplier relation in which the buyer and seller are partners, each helping the other as much as possible.

core competencies The unique resources and strengths that an organization's management considers when formulating strategy.

core process A set of activities that delivers value to external customers.

corner point A point that lies at the intersection of two (or possibly more) constraint lines on the boundary of the feasible region.

crash cost (CC) The activity cost associated with the crash time.

crash time (CT) The shortest possible time to complete an activity.

critical mass A situation whereby several competing firms clustered in one location attract more customers than the total number who would shop at the same stores at scattered locations.

critical path The sequence of activities between a project's start and finish that takes the longest time to complete.

critical path method (CPM) A network planning method developed in the 1950s as a means of scheduling maintenance shutdowns at chemical-processing plants.

critical ratio (CR) A ratio that is calculated by dividing the time remaining until a job's due date by the total shop time remaining for the job, which is defined as the setup, processing, move, and expected waiting times of all remaining operations, including the operation being scheduled.

cross-docking The packing of products on incoming shipments so that they can be easily sorted at intermediate warehouses for outgoing shipments based on their final destinations; the items are carried from the incoming-vehicle docking point to the outgoing-vehicle docking point without being stored in inventory at the warehouse.

cumulative sum of forecast errors (CFE) A measurement of the total forecast error that assesses the bias in a forecast.

customer contact The extent to which the customer is present, is actively involved, and receives personal attention during the service process.

customer involvement The ways in which customers become part of the process and the extent of their participation.

customer population An input that generates potential customers.

customer relationship process A process that identifies, attracts, and builds relationships with external customers, and facilitates the placement of orders by customers, sometimes referred to as *customer relationship management*.

cycle counting An inventory control method, whereby storeroom personnel physically count a small percentage of the total number of items each day, correcting errors that they find.

cycle inventory The portion of total inventory that varies directly with lot size.

cycle-service level See service level.

cycle time The maximum time allowed for work on a unit at each station.

decision theory A general approach to decision making when the outcomes associated with alternatives are often in doubt.

decision tree A schematic model of alternatives available to the decision maker, along with their possible consequences.

decision variables Variables that are controlled by the decision maker. In simulations, they will change from one run to the next as different events are simulated. In linear programming, they represent choices the decision maker can control.

defect Any instance when a process fails to satisfy its customer.

degeneracy A condition that occurs when the number of nonzero variables in the optimal solution is less than the number of constraints.

Delphi method A process of gaining consensus from a group of experts while maintaining their anonymity.

demand management The process of changing demand patterns using one or more demand options.

dependent demand The demand for an item that occurs because the quantity required varies with the production plans for other items held in the firm's inventory.

dependent variable The variable that one wants to forecast.

design team A group of knowledgeable, team-oriented individuals who work at one or more steps in the process, do the process analysis, and make the necessary changes.

discount rate The interest rate used in discounting the future value to its present value.

discounting The process of finding the present value of an investment when the future value and the interest rate are known.

diseconomies of scale Occurs when the average cost per unit increases as the facility's size increases.

double-sampling plan A plan in which management specifies two sample sizes and two acceptance numbers; if the quality of the lot is very good or very bad, the consumer can make a decision to accept or reject the lot on the basis of the first sample, which is smaller than in the single-sampling plan.

drum-buffer-rope (DBR) A planning and control system that regulates the flow of work-in-process materials at the bottleneck or the capacity constrained resource (CCR) in a productive system.

earliest due date (EDD) A priority sequencing rule that specifies that the job or customer with the earliest due date is the next job to be processed.

earliest finish time (EF) An activity's earliest start time plus its estimated duration, t, or $EF = ES + t$.

earliest start time (ES) The earliest finish time of the immediately preceding activity.

early supplier involvement A program that includes suppliers in the design phase of a service or product.

economic order quantity (EOQ) The lot size that minimizes total annual inventory holding and ordering costs.

economic production lot size (ELS) The optimal lot size in a situation in which replenishment is not instantaneous.

economies of scale A concept that states that the average unit cost of a service or good can be reduced by increasing its output rate.

economies of scope Economies that reflect the ability to produce multiple products more cheaply in combination than separately.

electronic commerce (e-commerce) The application of information and communication technology anywhere along the supply chain of business processes.

electronic data interchange (EDI) A technology that enables the transmission of routine business documents having a standard format from computer to computer over telephone or direct leased lines.

elemental standard data A database of standards compiled by a firm's analysts for basic elements that they can draw on later to estimate the time required for a particular job, which is most appropriate when products or services are highly customized, job processes prevail, and process divergence is great.

employee empowerment An approach to teamwork that moves responsibility for decisions further down the organizational chart—to the level of the employee actually doing the job.

end item The final product sold to a customer.

enterprise process A companywide process that cuts across functional areas, business units, geographical regions, and product lines.

enterprise resource planning (ERP) systems Large, integrated information systems that support many enterprise processes and data storage needs.

Euclidean distance The straight-line distance, or shortest possible path, between two points.

exchange An electronic marketplace where buying firms and selling firms come together to do business.

executive opinion A forecasting method in which the opinions, experience, and technical knowledge of one or more managers are summarized to arrive at a single forecast.

expediting The process of completing a job or finishing with a customer sooner than would otherwise be done.

exponential smoothing method A weighted moving average method that calculates the average of a time series by giving recent demands more weight than earlier demands.

external customers A customer who is either an end user or an intermediary (e.g., manufacturers, financial institutions, or retailers) buying the firm's finished services or products.

external failure costs Costs that arise when a defect is discovered after the customer receives the service or product.

external suppliers The businesses or individuals who provide the resources, services, products, and materials for the firm's short-term and long-term needs.

facility location The process of determining geographic sites for a firm's operations.

feasible region A region that represents all permissible combinations of the decision variables in a linear programming model.

finished goods (FG) The items in manufacturing plants, warehouses, and retail outlets that are sold to the firm's customers.

first-come, first served (FCFS) A priority sequencing rule that specifies that the job or customer arriving at the workstation first has the highest priority.

five S (5S) A methodology consisting of five workplace practices—sorting, straightening, shining, standardizing, and sustaining—that are conducive to visual controls and lean production.

fixed automation A manufacturing process that produces one type of part or product in a fixed sequence of simple operations.

fixed cost The portion of the total cost that remains constant regardless of changes in levels of output.

fixed order quantity (FOQ) A rule that maintains the same order quantity each time an order is issued.

fixed schedule A schedule that calls for each employee to work the same days and hours each week.

flexible (or programmable) automation A manufacturing process that can be changed easily to handle various products.

flexible flow The customers, materials, or information move in diverse ways, with the path of one customer or job often crisscrossing the path that the next one takes.

flexible workforce A workforce whose members are capable of doing many tasks, either at their own workstations or as they move from one workstation to another.

flow shop A manufacturer's operation that specializes in medium- to high-volume production and utilizes line or continuous flow processes.

flow time The amount of time a job spends in the service or manufacturing system.

flowchart A diagram that traces the flow of information, customers, equipment, or materials through the various steps of a process.

focus forecasting A method of forecasting that selects the best forecast from a group of forecasts generated by individual techniques.

focused factories The result of a firm's splitting large plants that produced all the company's products into several specialized smaller plants.

forecast A prediction of future events used for planning purposes.

forecast error The difference found by subtracting the forecast from actual demand for a given period.

forward integration Acquiring more channels of distribution, such as distribution centers (warehouses) and retail stores, or even business customers.

forward placement Locating stock closer to customers at a warehouse, DC, wholesaler, or retailer.

front office A process with high customer contact where the service provider interacts directly with the internal or external customer.

future value of an investment The value of an investment at the end of the period over which interest is compounded.

Gantt chart A project schedule, usually created by the project manager using computer software, that superimposes project activities, with their precedence relationships and estimated duration times, on a time line.

geographical information system (GIS) A system of computer software, hardware, and data that the firm's personnel can use to manipulate, analyze, and present information relevant to a location decision.

graphic method of linear programming A type of graphic analysis that involves the following five steps: plotting the constraints, identifying the feasible region, plotting an objective function line, finding a visual solution, and finding the algebraic solution.

graphs Representations of data in a variety of pictorial forms, such as line charts and pie charts.

Green Belt An employee who achieved the first level of training in a Six Sigma program and spends part of his or her time teaching and helping teams with their projects.

green purchasing The process of identifying, assessing, and managing the flow of environmental waste and finding ways to reduce it and minimize its impact on the environment.

gross requirements The total demand derived from *all* parent production plans.

group technology (GT) An option for achieving line-flow layouts with low volume processes; this technique creates cells not limited to just one worker and has a unique way of selecting work to be done by the cell.

heijunka The leveling of production load by both volume and product mix.

heuristics Solution guidelines, or rules of thumb, that find feasible—but not necessarily the best—solutions to problems.

histogram A summarization of data measured on a continuous scale, showing the frequency distribution of some quality characteristic (in statistical terms, the central tendency and dispersion of the data).

holdout set Actual demands from the more recent time periods in the time series that are set aside to test different models developed from the earlier time periods.

hurdle rate The interest rate that is the lowest desired return on an investment; the hurdle over which the investment must pass.

hybrid office A process with moderate levels of customer contact and standard services with some options available.

immediate predecessors Work elements that must be done before the next element can begin.

independent demand items Items for which demand is influenced by market conditions and is not related to the inventory decisions for any other item held in stock or produced.

independent variables Variables that are assumed to affect the dependent variable and thereby "cause" the results observed in the past.

industrial robot Versatile, computer-controlled machine programmed to perform various tasks.

interarrival times The time between customer arrivals.

intermediate item An item that has at least one parent and at least one component.

internal customers One or more employees or processes that rely on inputs from other employees or processes in order to perform their work.

internal failure costs Costs resulting from defects that are discovered during the production of a service or product.

internal rate of return (IRR) The discount rate that makes the NPV of a project zero.

internal suppliers The employees or processes that supply important information or materials to a firm's processes.

interoperability The ability of one piece of software to interact with others.

inventory A stock of materials used to satisfy customer demand or to support the production of services or goods.

inventory holding cost The sum of the cost of capital and the variable costs of keeping items on hand, such as storage and handling, taxes, insurance, and shrinkage.

inventory management The planning and controlling of inventories in order to meet the competitive priorities of the organization.

inventory pooling A reduction in inventory and safety stock because of the merging of variable demands from customers.

inventory position (IP) The measurement of a SKU's ability to satisfy future demand.

inventory record A record that shows an item's lot-size policy, lead time, and various time-phased data.

inventory turnover An inventory measure obtained by dividing annual sales at cost by the average aggregate inventory value maintained during the year.

ISO 9000:2000 A set of standards governing documentation of a quality program.

ISO 14000:2004 Documentation standards that require participating companies to keep track of their raw materials use and their generation, treatment, and disposal of hazardous wastes.

jidoka Automatically stopping the process when something is wrong and then fixing the problems on the line itself as they occur.

JIT system A system that organizes the resources, information flows, and decision rules that enable a firm to realize the benefits of JIT principles.

job process A process with the flexibility needed to produce a wide variety of products in significant quantities, with considerable divergence in the steps performed.

job shop A manufacturer's operation that specializes in low- to medium-volume production and utilizes job or batch processes.

Johnson's rule A procedure that minimizes makespan when scheduling a group of jobs on two workstations.

judgment methods A forecasting method that translates the opinions of managers, expert opinions, consumer surveys, and salesforce estimates into quantitative estimates.

just-in-time (JIT) philosophy The belief that waste can be eliminated by cutting unnecessary capacity or inventory and removing non-value-added activities in operations.

kanban A Japanese word meaning "card" or "visible record" that refers to cards used to control the flow of production through a factory.

labor-limited environment An environment in which the resource constraint is the amount of labor available, not the number of machines or workstations.

latest finish time (LF) The latest start time of the activity that immediately follows.

latest start time (LS) The latest finish time minus its estimated duration, t, or $LS = LF - t$.

layout The physical arrangement of operations created by the various processes.

lead time The elapsed time between the receipt of a customer order and filling it.

lean systems Operations systems that maximize the value added by each of a company's activities by removing waste and delays from them.

learning curve A line that displays the relationship between processing time and the cumulative quantity of a product or service produced.

learning curve analysis A time estimation technique that takes into account the learning that takes place on an ongoing basis, such as where new products or services are introduced.

level strategy A strategy that keeps the workforce constant, but varies its utilization via overtime, undertime, and vacation planning to match the demand forecast.

line balancing The assignment of work to stations in a line so as to achieve the desired output rate with the smallest number of workstations.

line flow The customers, materials, or information move linearly from one operation to the next, according to a fixed sequence.

line process A process that lies between the batch and continuous processes on the continuum; volumes are high and products are standardized, which allows resources to be organized around particular products.

linear programming A technique that is useful for allocating scarce resources among competing demands.

linear regression A causal method in which one variable (the dependent variable) is related to one or more independent variables by a linear equation.

linearity A characteristic of linear programming models that implies proportionality and additivity—there can be no products or powers of decision variables.

Little's law A fundamental law that relates the number of customers in a waiting-line system to the arrival rate and waiting time of customers.

load–distance method A mathematical model used to evaluate locations based on proximity factors.

lot A quantity of items that are processed together.

lot-for-lot (L4L) rule A rule under which the lot size ordered covers the gross requirements of a single week.

lot size The quantity of an inventory item management either buys from a supplier or manufactures using internal processes.

lot sizing The determination of how frequently and in what quantity to order inventory.

lot tolerance proportion defective (LTPD) The worst level of quality that the consumer can tolerate.

make-or-buy decision A managerial choice between whether to outsource a process or do it in-house.

make-to-order strategy A strategy used by manufacturers that make products to customer specifications in low volumes.

make-to-stock strategy A strategy that involves holding items in stock for immediate delivery, thereby minimizing customer delivery times.

makespan The total amount of time required to complete a *group* of jobs.

Malcolm Baldrige National Quality Award An award named for the late secretary of commerce, who was a strong proponent of enhancing quality as a means of reducing the trade deficit; the award promotes, recognizes, and publicizes quality strategies and achievements.

manufacturing resource planning (MRP II) A system that ties the basic MRP system to the company's financial system and to other core and supporting processes.

market research A systematic approach to determine external consumer interest in a service or product by creating and testing hypotheses through data-gathering surveys.

mass customization The strategy that uses highly divergent processes to generate a wide variety of customized products at reasonably low costs.

mass production A term sometimes used in the popular press for a line process that uses the make-to-stock strategy.

Master Black Belt Full-time teachers and mentors to several Black Belts.

master production schedule (MPS) A part of the material requirements plan that details how many end items will be produced within specified periods of time.

material requirements planning (MRP) A computerized information system developed specifically to help manufacturers manage dependent demand inventory and schedule replenishment orders.

mean absolute deviation (MAD) A measurement of the dispersion of forecast errors.

mean absolute percent error (MAPE) A measurement that relates the forecast error to the level of demand and is useful for putting forecast performance in the proper perspective.

mean squared error (MSE) A measurement of the dispersion of forecast errors.

methods time measurement (MTM) A commonly used predetermined data system.

metrics Performance measures that are established for a process and the steps within it.

minimum-cost schedule A schedule determined by starting with the normal time schedule and crashing activities along the critical path, in such a way that the costs of crashing do not exceed the savings in indirect and penalty costs.

mixed-model assembly A type of assembly that produces a mix of models in smaller lots.

mixed-model line A production line that produces several items belonging to the same family.

mixed strategy A strategy that considers the full range of supply options.

Modified Accelerated Cost Recovery System (MACRS) The only acceptable depreciation method for tax purposes that shortens the lives of investments, giving firms larger early tax deductions.

Monte Carlo simulation A simulation process that uses random numbers to generate simulation events.

most likely time (_m_) The probable time required to perform an activity.

MRP explosion A process that converts the requirements of various final products into a _material requirements plan_ that specifies the replenishment schedules of all the subassemblies, components, and raw materials needed to produce final products.

multiple-dimension rules A set of rules that apply to more than one aspect of a job.

multiplicative seasonal method A method whereby seasonal factors are multiplied by an estimate of average demand to arrive at a seasonal forecast.

naive forecast A time-series method whereby the forecast for the next period equals the demand for the current period, or Forecast = D_t.

nested process The concept of a process within a process.

net present value (NPV) method The method that evaluates an investment by calculating the present values of all after-tax total cash flows and then subtracting the initial investment amount for their total.

network diagram A network planning method, designed to depict the relationships between activities, that consists of nodes (circles) and arcs (arrows).

new service/product development process A process that designs and develops new services or products from inputs received from external customer specifications or from the market in general through the customer relationship process.

nominal value A target for design specifications.

nonnegativity An assumption that the decision variables must be positive or zero.

normal cost (NC) The activity cost associated with the normal time.

normal time (NT) In the context of project management, the time necessary to complete an activity under normal conditions.

normal time (NT) In the context of time study, a measurement found by multiplying the select time ($\bar{t}$), the frequency (F) of the work element per cycle, and the rating factor (RF).

normal time for the cycle (NTC) A measurement found by summing the normal time for each element.

objective function An expression in linear programming models that states mathematically what is being maximized (e.g., profit or present value) or minimized (e.g., cost or scrap).

offshoring A supply chain strategy that involves moving processes to another country.

one-worker, multiple-machines (OWMM) cell A one-person cell in which a worker operates several different machines simultaneously to achieve a line flow.

open orders See scheduled receipts (SR).

operating characteristic (OC) curve A graph that describes how well a sampling plan discriminates between good and bad lots.

operation A group of resources performing all or part of one or more processes.

operations management The systematic design, direction, and control of processes that transform inputs into services and products for internal, as well as external, customers

operations planning and scheduling The process of balancing supply with demand, from the aggregate level down to the short-term scheduling level.

operations scheduling A type of scheduling in which jobs are assigned to workstations or employees are assigned to jobs for specified time periods.

operations strategy The means by which operations implements the firm's corporate strategy and helps to build a customer-driven firm.

optimistic time (_a_) The shortest time in which an activity can be completed, if all goes exceptionally well.

optimization A procedure used to determine the "best" solution; generally utilizes simplified and less realistic views of a problem.

optional replenishment system A system used to review the inventory position at fixed time intervals and, if the position has dropped to (or below) a predetermined level, to place a variable-sized order to cover expected needs.

order fulfillment process A process that includes the activities required to produce and deliver the service or product to the external customer.

order qualifier A demonstrated level of performance of an order winner that is required for a firm to do business in a particular market segment.

order winner A criterion customers use to differentiate the services or products of one firm from those of another.

ordering cost The cost of preparing a purchase order for a supplier or a production order for manufacturing.

organizational learning The process of gaining experience with products and processes, achieving greater efficiency through automation and other capital investments, and making other improvements in administrative methods or personnel.

outsourcing Paying suppliers and distributors to perform processes and provide needed services and materials.

overtime The time that employees work that is longer than the regular workday or workweek for which they receive additional pay.

_p_-chart A chart used for controlling the proportion of defective services or products generated by the process.

pacing The movement of product from one station to the next as soon as the cycle time has elapsed.

parameter A value that the decision maker cannot control and that does not change when the solution is implemented.

parent Any product that is manufactured from one or more components.

Pareto chart A bar chart on which factors are plotted in decreasing order of frequency along the horizontal axis.

part commonality The degree to which a component has more than one immediate parent.

past due The amount of time by which a job missed its due date.

path The sequence of activities between a project's start and finish.

payback method A method for evaluating projects that determines how much time will elapse before the total of after-tax flows will equal, or pay back, the initial investment.

payoff table A table that shows the amount for each alternative if each possible event occurs.

performance rating factor (RF) An assessment that describes *how much* above or below average the worker's performance is on each work element.

periodic order quantity (POQ) A rule that allows a different order quantity for each order issued but issues the order for predetermined time intervals.

periodic review (P) sytem A system in which an item's inventory position is reviewed periodically rather than continuously.

perpetual inventory system A system of inventory control in which the inventory records are always current.

pessimistic time (b) The longest estimated time required to perform an activity.

phase A single step in providing a service.

pipeline inventory Inventory that is created when an order for an item is issued but not yet placed in inventory.

plan-do-study-act cycle A cycle, also called the Deming Wheel, used by firms actively engaged in continuous improvement to train their work teams in problem solving.

planned order release An indication of when an order for a specified quantity of an item is to be issued.

planned receipts Orders that are not yet released to the shop or the supplier.

planning horizon The set of consecutive time periods considered for planning purposes.

plants within plants (PWPs) Different operations within a facility with individualized competitive priorities, processes, and workforces under the same roof.

poka-yoke Mistake-proofing methods aimed at designing fail-safe systems that minimize human error.

postponement The strategy of delaying final activities in the provision of a product until the orders are received.

precedence diagram A diagram that allows one to visualize immediate predecessors better; work elements are denoted by circles, with the time required to perform the work shown below each circle.

precedence relationship A relationship that determines a sequence for undertaking activities; it specifies that one activity cannot start until a preceding activity has been completed.

predetermined data approach A database approach that divides each work element into a series of micromotions that make up the element. The analyst then consults a published database that contains the normal times for the full array of possible micromotions.

preemptive discipline A rule that allows a customer of higher priority to interrupt the service of another customer.

preference matrix A table that allows the manager to rate an alternative according to several performance criteria.

present value of an investment The amount that must be invested now to accumulate to a certain amount in the future at a specific interest rate.

presourcing A level of supplier involvement in which suppliers are selected early in a product's concept development stage and are given significant, if not total, responsibility for the design of certain components or systems of the product.

prevention costs Costs associated with preventing defects before they happen.

priority rule A rule that selects the next customer to be served by the service facility.

priority sequencing rule A rule that specifies the job or customer processing sequence when several jobs are waiting in line at a workstation.

process Any activity or group of activities that takes one or more inputs, transforms them, and provides one or more outputs for its customers.

process analysis The documentation and detailed understanding of how work is performed and how it can be redesigned.

process capability The ability of the process to meet the design specifications for a service or product.

process capability index, C_{pk} An index that measures the potential for a process to generate defective outputs relative to either upper or lower specifications.

process capability ratio, C_p The tolerance width divided by 6 standard deviations.

process chart An organized way of documenting all the activities performed by a person or group of people, at a workstation, with a customer, or on materials.

process choice A way of structuring the process by organizing resources around the process or organizing them around the products.

process divergence The extent to which the process is highly customized with considerable latitude as to how its tasks are performed.

process failure Any performance shortfall, such as error, delay, environmental waste, rework, and the like.

process improvement The systematic study of the activities and flows of each process to improve it.

process simulation The act of reproducing the behavior of a process, using a model that describes each step.

process strategy The pattern of decisions made in managing processes so that they will achieve their competitive priorities.

process structure A process decision that determines the process type relative to the kinds of resources needed, how resources are partitioned between them, and their key characteristics.

producer's risk (α) The risk that the sampling plan will fail to verify an acceptable lot's quality and, thus, reject it (a type I error).

product family A group of customers, services, or products that have similar demand requirements and common process, labor, and materials requirements.

product-mix problem A one-period type of planning problem, the solution of which yields optimal output quantities (or product mix) of a group of services or products subject to resource capacity and market demand constraints.

productivity The value of outputs (services and products) produced divided by the values of input resources (wages, costs of equipment, etc.).

program An interdependent set of projects that have a common strategic purpose.

program evaluation and review technique (PERT) A network planning method created for the U.S. Navy's Polaris missile project in the 1950s, which involved 3,000 separate contractors and suppliers.

project An interrelated set of activities with a definite starting and ending point, which results in a unique outcome for a specific allocation of resources.

project management A systemized, phased approach to defining, organizing, planning, monitoring, and controlling projects.

projected on-hand inventory An estimate of the amount of inventory available each week after gross requirements have been satisfied.

protection interval The period over which safety stock must protect the user from running out of stock.

pull method A method in which customer demand activates production of the service or item.

purchased item An item that has one or more parents but no components because it comes from a supplier.

purchasing The activity that decides which suppliers to use, negotiates contracts, and determines whether to buy locally.

push method A method in which production of the item begins in advance of customer needs.

quality A term used by customers to describe their general satisfaction with a service or product.

quality at the source A philosophy whereby defects are caught and corrected where they were created.

quality circles Another name for problem-solving teams; small groups of supervisors and employees who meet to identify, analyze, and solve process and quality problems.

quality engineering An approach originated by Genichi Taguchi that involves combining engineering and statistical methods to reduce costs and improve quality by optimizing product design and manufacturing processes.

quality loss function The rationale that a service or product that barely conforms to the specifications is more like a defective service or product than a perfect one.

quality of life A factor that considers the availability of good schools, recreational facilities, cultural events, and an attractive lifestyle.

quantity discount A drop in the price per unit when an order is sufficiently large.

R-chart A chart used to monitor process variability.

radio frequency identification (RFID) A method for identifying items through the use of radio signals from a tag attached to an item.

random number A number that has the same probability of being selected as any other number.

range of feasibility The interval (lower and upper bounds) over which the right-hand-side parameter of a constraint can vary while its shadow price remains valid.

range of optimality The interval (lower and upper bounds) of an objective function coefficient over which the optimal values of the decision variables remain unchanged.

raw materials (RM) The inventories needed for the production of services or goods.

rectified inspection The assumption that all defective items in the lot will be replaced with good items if the lot is rejected and that any defective items in the sample will be replaced if the lot is accepted.

rectilinear distance The distance between two points with a series of 90-degree turns, as along city blocks.

reduced cost How much the objective function coefficient of a decision variable must improve (increase for maximization or decrease for minimization) before the optimal solution changes and the decision variable "enters" the solution with some positive number.

reengineering The fundamental rethinking and radical redesign of processes to improve performance dramatically in terms of cost, quality, service, and speed.

reorder point (R) The predetermined minimum level that an inventory position must reach before a fixed quantity Q of the SKU is ordered.

reorder point (ROP) system See continuous review (Q) system.

repeatability The degree to which the same work can be done again.

resource flexibility The ease with which employees and equipment can handle a wide variety of products, output levels, duties, and functions.

resource planning A process that takes sales and operations plans; processes information in the way of time standards, routings, and other information on how the firm produces its services or products; and then plans the input requirements.

revenue management Varying price at the right time for different customer segments to maximize revenues yielded by existing supply capacity.

reverse logistics The process of planning, implementing, and controlling the efficient, cost effective flow of products, materials, and information from the point of consumption back to the point of origin for returns, repair, remanufacture, or recycling.

risk-management plan A plan that identifies the key risks to a project's success and prescribes ways to circumvent them.

rotating schedule A schedule that rotates employees through a series of workdays or hours.

safety stock inventory Surplus inventory that a company holds to protect against uncertainties in demand, lead time, and supply changes.

salesforce estimates The forecasts that are compiled from estimates of future demands made periodically by members of a company's salesforce.

salvage value The cash flow from the sale or disposal of plant and equipment at the end of a project's life.

sample size A quantity of randomly selected observations of process outputs.

sampling plan A plan that specifies a sample size, the time between successive samples, and decision rules that determine when action should be taken.

scatter diagram A plot of two variables showing whether they are related.

scheduled receipts (SR) Orders that have been placed but have not yet been received.

SCOR model A framework that focuses on a basic supply chain of plan, source, make, deliver, and return processes, repeated again and again along the supply chain.

select time ($\bar{t}$) The average observed time based only on representative times.

self-managed team A small group of employees who work together to produce a major portion, or sometimes all, of a service or product.

sensitivity analysis A technique for systematically changing parameters in a model to determine the effects of such changes.

sequencing Determining the order in which jobs or customers are processed in the waiting line at a workstation.

sequential-sampling plan A plan in which the consumer randomly selects items from the lot and inspects them one by one.

service blueprint A special flowchart of a service process that shows which steps have high customer contact.

service facility A person (or crew), a machine (or group of machines), or both necessary to perform the service for the customer.

service level The desired probability of not running out of stock in any one ordering cycle, which begins at the time an order is placed and ends when it arrives in stock.

service system The number of lines and the arrangement of the facilities.

setup cost The cost involved in changing over a machine or workspace to produce a different item.

setup time The time required to change a process or an operation from making one service or product to making another.

shadow price The marginal improvement in Z (increase for maximization and decrease for minimization) caused by relaxing the constraint by one unit.

shortest processing time (SPT) A priority sequencing rule that specifies that the job requiring the shortest processing time is the next job to be processed.

simple moving average method A time-series method used to estimate the average of a demand time series by averaging the demand for the n most recent time periods.

simplex method An iterative algebraic procedure for solving linear programming problems.

simulation The act of reproducing the behavior of a system using a model that describes the processes of the system.

single-bin system A system of inventory control in which a maximum level is marked on the storage shelf or bin, and the inventor is brought up to the mark periodically.

single-digit setup The goal of having a setup time of less than 10 minutes.

single-dimension rules A set of rules that bases the priority of a job on a single aspect of the job, such as arrival time at the workstation, the due date, or the processing time.

single-sampling plan A decision to accept or reject a lot based on the results of one random sample from the lot.

Six Sigma A comprehensive and flexible system for achieving, sustaining, and maximizing business success by minimizing defects and variability in processes.

slack The amount by which the left-hand side of a linear programming constraint falls short of the right-hand side.

slack per remaining operations (S/RO) A priority sequencing rule that determines priority by dividing the slack by the number of operations that remain, including the one being scheduled.

sole sourcing The awarding of a contract for a service or item to only one supplier.

special-purpose teams Groups that address issues of paramount concern to management, labor, or both.

standard deviation (σ) A measurement of the dispersion of forecast errors.

standard time (ST) A measurement found by incorporating the normal time and allowances; $ST = NTC(1 + A)$, where A equals the proportion of the normal time added for allowances.

statistical process control (SPC) The application of statistical techniques to determine whether a process is delivering what the customer wants.

steady state The state that occurs when the simulation is repeated over enough time that the average results for performance measures remain constant.

stock-keeping unit (SKU) An individual item or product that has an identifying code and is held in inventory somewhere along the supply chain.

stockout An order that cannot be satisfied, resulting in a loss of the sale.

straight-line method The simplest method of calculating annual depreciation; found by subtracting the estimated salvage value from the amount of investment required at the beginning of the project, and then dividing by the asset's expected economic life.

subassembly An intermediate item that is *assembled* (as opposed to being transformed by other means) from more than one component.

suggestion system A voluntary system by which employees submit their ideas on process improvements.

supplier relationship process A process that selects the suppliers of services, materials, and information and facilitates the timely and efficient flow of these items into the firm.

supply chain An interrelated series of processes within and across firms that produces a service or product to the satisfaction of customers.

supply chain design Designing a firm's supply chain to meet the competitive priorities of the firm's operations strategy.

supply chain integration The effective coordination of supply chain processes through the seamless flow of information up and down the supply chain.

supply chain management The synchronization of a firm's processes with those of its suppliers and customers to match the flow of materials, services, and information with customer demand.

support process A process that provides vital resources and inputs to the core processes and therefore is essential to the management of the business.

surplus The amount by which the left-hand side of a linear programming constraint exceeds the right-hand side.

sustainability A characteristic of processes that are meeting humanity's needs without harming future generations.

takt time Cycle time needed to match the rate of production to the rate of sales or consumption.

tardiness See past due.

teams Small groups of people who have a common purpose, set their own performance goals and approaches, and hold themselves accountable for success.

technological forecasting An application of executive opinion to keep abreast of the latest advances in technology.

theoretical minimum (TM) A benchmark or goal for the smallest number of stations possible, where the total time required to assemble each unit (the sum of all work-element standard times) is divided by the cycle time.

theory of constraints (TOC) A systematic management approach that focuses on actively managing those constraints that impede a firm's progress toward its goal.

throughput time Total elapsed time from the start to the finish of a job or a customer being processed at one or more workcenters.

time-based competition A strategy that focuses on the competitive priorities of delivery speed and development speed.

time between orders (TBO) The average elapsed time between receiving (or placing) replenishment orders of Q units for a particular lot size.

time compression The feature of simulation models that allows them to obtain operating characteristic estimates in much less time than is required to gather the same operating data from a real system.

time series The repeated observations of demand for a service or product in their order of occurrence.

time-series analysis A statistical approach that relies heavily on historical demand data to project the future size of demand and recognizes trends and seasonal patterns.

time study A work measurement method using a trained analyst to perform four basic steps in setting a time standard for a job or process: selecting the work elements (or nested processes) within the process to be studied, timing the elements, determining the sample size, and setting the final standard.

time value of money The concept that a dollar in hand can be invested to earn a return so that more than one dollar will be available in the future.

tolerance An allowance above or below the nominal value.

total inventory The sum of scheduled receipts and on-hand inventories.

total quality management (TQM) A philosophy that stresses three principles for achieving high levels of process performance and quality: customer satisfaction, employee involvement, and continuous improvement in performance.

tracking signal A measure that indicates whether a method of forecasting is accurately predicting actual changes in demand.

transportation method A more efficient solution technique than the simplex method for solving transportation problems.

transportation problem A special case of linear programming that has linear constraints for capacity limitations and demand requirements.

trend-adjusted exponential smoothing method The method for incorporating a trend in an exponentially smoothed forecast.

two-bin system A visual system version of the Q system in which a SKU's inventory is stored at two different locations.

type I error An error that occurs when the employee concludes that the process is out of control based on a sample result that falls outside the control limits, when in fact it was due to pure randomness.

type II error An error that occurs when the employee concludes that the process is in control and only randomness is present, when actually the process is out of statistical control.

uncontrollable variables Random events that the decision maker cannot control.

undertime The situation that occurs when employees do not have enough work for the regular-time workday or workweek.

usage quantity The number of units of a component that are needed to make one unit of its immediate parent.

utilization The degree to which equipment, space, or the workforce is currently being used, and is measured as the ratio of average output rate to maximum capacity (expressed as a percent).

value analysis A systematic effort to reduce the cost or improve the performance of services or products, either purchased or produced.

value stream mapping (VSM) A qualitative lean tool for eliminating waste or *muda* that involves a current state drawing, a future state drawing, and an implementation plan.

variable cost The portion of the total cost that varies directly with volume of output.

variables Service or product characteristics, such as weight, length, volume, or time, that can be measured.

vendor-managed inventories (VMI) A system in which the supplier has access to the customer's inventory data and is responsible for maintaining the inventory on the customer's site.

visual system A system that allows employees to place orders when inventory visibly reaches a certain marker.

waiting line One or more "customers" waiting for service.

warranty A written guarantee that the producer will replace or repair defective parts or perform the service to the customer's satisfaction.

weeks of supply An inventory measure obtained by dividing the average aggregate inventory value by sales per week at cost.

weighted-distance method A mathematical model used to evaluate layouts (of facility locations) based on proximity factors.

weighted moving average method A time-series method in which each historical demand in the average can have its own weight; the sum of the weights equals 1.0.

work breakdown structure (WBS) A statement of all work that has to be completed.

work elements The smallest units of work that can be performed independently.

work-in-process (WIP) Items, such as components or assemblies, needed to produce a final product in manufacturing.

work measurement The process of creating labor standards based on the judgment of skilled observers.

work sampling method A process that estimates the proportion of time spent by people or machines on different activities, based on observations randomized over time.

work standard The time required for a trained worker to perform a task following a prescribed method with normal effort and skill.

workforce scheduling A type of scheduling that determines when employees work.

$\bar{x}$-chart A chart used to see whether the process is generating output, on average, consistent with a target value set by management for the process or whether its current performance, with respect to the average of the performance measure, is consistent with past performance.

PHOTO CREDITS

CHAPTER 1: p. 22: David Young-Wolff/PhotoEdit Inc., p. 23: Bizuayehu Tesfaye/AP Wide World Photos, p. 29: Tony Savino/The Image Works, p. 32: ROMEO GACAD/AFP/Getty Images/Newscom, p. 33: Ben Margot/AP Wide World Photos, p. 35: Dennis MacDonald/PhotoEdit Inc., p. 37: Ted Horowitz/© Bettmann/CORBIS All Rights Reserved, p. 40: PRNewsFoto/Sonoco/AP Wide World Photos, p. 41: Cancan Chu/CanCan Chu/Getty Images, Inc., p. 42: Newscom, p. 50: Courtesy Starwood Hotels and Aspenleaf Productions.

CHAPTER 2: p. 72: Robyn Beck/AFP/Getty Images/Newscom, p. 76: Courtesy Baxter International, Inc., p. 80: Ng Han Guan/AP Wide World Photos, p. 88: © Corbis/Yiorgos Karahalu/Reuters, p. 108: Courtesy Starwood Hotels.

CHAPTER 3: p. 112: Don Ryan/AP Wide World Photos, p. 113: Wendell Franks/iStockPhoto, p. 116: Myrleen Ferguson Cate/PhotoEdit Inc., p. 119: David Zalubowski/AP Wide World Photos, p. 125: ABB, Inc., p. 125: Alex Wong/Getty Images/Newscom, p. 126: ABB, Inc., p. 128: Courtesy of Just Born, Inc., p. 129: © Corbis/Stephanie Kuykendal.

CHAPTER 4: p. 142: Ryan McVay/Getty Images, Inc.-Photodisc., p. 143: Brent Melton/iStockPhoto, p. 147: Jim Richardson/© Jim Richardson/CORBIS All Rights Reserved, p. 148: Frank Herholdt/Getty Images Inc. - Stone Allstock, p. 159: Intermarket.

CHAPTER 5: p. 194: PRNewsFoto/Verizon Wireless/AP Wide World Photos, p. 195: Jakub Semenluk/iStockPhoto, p. 199: © PA Photos/Petr David Josek/AP, p. 202: Corbis Royalty Free, p. 205: Courtesy of Robert Wood Johnson University Hospital/National Institute of Standards and Technology (NIST), p. 210: Archer Daniels Midland Company, p. 218: Reuters NewMedia Inc/Corbis/Bettmann.

CHAPTER 6: p. 238: Katsumi Kasahara/AP Wide World Photos, p. 239: Robertas Pizas/iStockPhoto, p. 240: featurechinepix/Newscom, p. 242: Mark Wagner/Aviation-images.com, p. 245: Andy Kropa/Redux/Redux Pictures, p. 245: zumaphotos/Newscom, p. 259: Justin Sullivan/Justin Sullivan/Getty Images, Inc.

SUPPLEMENT C: p. 264: Islemount Images/Alamy Images, p. 266: Robert Brenner/PhotoEdit Inc., p. 273: Tom Carter/PhotoEdit.

CHAPTER 7: p. 282: © Ingram Publishing, p. 284: Alamy Images, p. 286: Reprinted Courtesy of Bal Seal Engineering, Inc. Copyright © Bal Seal Engineering, Inc. (2010). "Bal Seal" and "canted-coil" (list trademarks) are trademarks of Bal Seal Engineering, Inc. All rights reserved, p. 288: © Ingram Publishing, p. 294: Cpl. Nicholas Tremblay/United States Marine Corps, p. 294: Paulo Santos/AP Wide World Photos, p. 311: Marty Katz/The New York Times/Redux Pictures.

CHAPTER 8: p. 314: Chang-Ran Kim/Reuters/© Chang-Ran Kim/Reuters/CORBIS All Rights Reserved, p. 318: Katsumi Kasahara/AP Wide World Photos, p. 320: Owen Franken/Corbis/Bettmann, p. 321: Izmostock/Alamy Images, p. 322: John C. Hillery/Reuters Limited, p. 323: AP Wide World Photos, p. 324: Hiroyuki Matsumoto/Black Star, p. 327: © Alamy/Vario Images GmbH & Co KG, p. 331: © Corbis/Artiga Photos, p. 334: Cessna Aircraft Company, p. 339: Thomas Broening Photography.

CHAPTER 9: p. 342: Shawano Cleary/AP Wide World Photos, p. 343: Onur Dongel/iStockPhoto, p. 348: Susan E. Benson/Stock Connection, p. 351: Michael Newman/PhotoEdit Inc., p. 356: Roberto Gonzalez/Orlando Sentinel/Newscom, p. 360: Roslan Rahman/Agence France Presse/Getty Images, p. 361: John Froschauer/AP Wide World Photos.

CHAPTER 10: p. 374: David Duprey/AP Wide World Photos, p. 375: Jakub Semeniuk/iStockPhoto, p. 384: BIOTA Brands of America, Inc./PR Newswire/AP Wide World Photos, p. 388: Andrey Yanevich/Alamy Images, p. 394: Sherwin Crasto/© Sherwin Crasto/Reuters/CORBIS.

CHAPTER 11: p. 408: BMW of North America, Inc., p. 410: Claro Cortes IV/Reuters/© Claro Cortes IV/Reuters/CORBIS All Rights Reserved, p. 411: General Electric Corporate Research & Development Center, p. 412: Artur Silva/Photo Courtesy of the Arts Council of Indianapolis; "Unquestionable Doubt" by Arthur Silva, p. 414: Richard Levine/Alamy Images, p. 418: Chad Ehlers/Alamy Images, p. 420: Courtesy FOCUS Brands, Inc.

CHAPTER 12: p. 434: Wal Mart, p. 435: Alex Stobodkin/iStockPhoto, p. 443: Jeff Greenberg/Alamy Images, p. 452: Tom Payne/Alamy Images.

CHAPTER 13: p. 482: Maria Tore Nicolaysen/Atma Global Knowledge Media Inc., p. 483: Aleaimage/iStockPhoto, p. 487: Mark Peterson/© Mark Peterson/CORBIS All Rights Reserved, p. 502: PRNews Foto/Fiskars Garden & Outdoor Living/Newscom, p. 517: Courtesy of Deckers Corporation.

CHAPTER 14: p. 522: Mark Baker/AP Wide World Photos, p. 523: Richard Cano/iStockPhoto, p. 528: © Getty Images/Angela Wyant, p. 530: Michael Springer/Bloomberg News/Landov Media, p. 531: Stephen Chernin/Getty Images, Inc., p. 534: Courtesy of FujiFilm Imaging Colorants, Inc., p. 536: AP Wide World Photos, p. 539: Bill Stormont/CORBIS- NY, p. 542: Sherwin Crasto/Reuters/© Sherwin Crasto/Reuters/CORBIS All Rights Reserved, p. 545: Northpoint/Nissan North America, Inc., p. 556: Starwood Hotels & Resorts Worldwide, Inc.

CHAPTER 15: p. 560: PRNewsFoto/Dow Corning/AP Wide World Photos, p. 561: iStockPhoto, p. 563: VF Corporation, p. 571: © Alamy/Mode Images Ltd, p. 580: Mike Houska/Winnebago Industries, Inc., p. 581: Todd Gipstein/Corbis/Bettmann, p. 581: Jon Feingersh/Jon Feingersh.

NAME INDEX

Page references that contain letters (F.1, G.1, and the like) indicate materials that are in the my**om**lab supplements.

SUBJECT INDEX

Page references that contain letters (F.1, G.1, and the like) indicate materials that are in the my**om**lab supplements. Page numbers followed by f have figures. Page numbers followed by t have tables.